ACCESS TO
EUROPEAN UNION

law, economics, policies

LONDON BOROUGH OF
BARKING & DAGENHAM

The London Borough of
Barking & **Dagenham**
www.barking-dagenham.gov.uk

I
For

REFERENCE

LIBRARIES

2007

16th edition

EUROPEAN STUDY SERVICE

ISBN 978-2-930119-43-4

© European Study Service
Avenue Paola 43 - B-1330 RIXENSART
TEL.: (+32 2) 652 02 84 - FAX: (+32 2) 653 01 80
RCN: 51147 - TVA: BE-659 309 394

SUMMARY

TABLE OF CONTENTS

FOREWORD

The Flemish master Pieter Bruegel the elder has well illustrated the lack of interest of people for a historic event that takes place under their very eyes. In a painting of 1564, entitled "The Procession to Calvary", he has depicted the Messiah as a small figure sinking down under the cross on his way up the Golgotha. No one of the crowd of Roman soldiers and ordinary people around Him pays any attention to His Martyrdom. They are all looking at a couple of peasants struggling with three soldiers in the forefront of the picture. This everyday brawl is the centre of attention of the crowd and not the event that has changed the course of history. One can hardly blame these people who, at the time of the Crucifixion, were going about their business and were attracted by a boisterous albeit banal happening. As demonstrated by Brueguel, they had not the hindsight that we now have about the importance of the event that they were witnessing.

Likewise, the majority of contemporary Europeans have no notion that they are witnessing an experience that will most probably change again the history of mankind. This history is marked by wars and all kinds, of bloody fights between ethnic, religious and other groups, fights for power, for land, for ideals (real or supposed) or just for the survival of a nation or a group attacked by other nations or groups. The extraordinary event that takes place under our eyes is the fifty-year old experience of peaceful and voluntary unification of different and formerly conflicting nations. The European experience is unique by virtue of its objective of establishing the basis for an increasingly closer union between formerly hostile nations. It is also unique because of its institutions, which have no equal in other international organisations. Lastly, it is unique on account of its achievements: never in human history have different nations cooperated so closely with one another, implemented so many common policies or, in such a short space of time, harmonised ways of life and economic situations which differed so greatly at the outset.

Yet this unique experiment is hardly exciting. It is hidden behind tedious negotiations by complicated institutions using a peculiar jargon incomprehensible to ordinary citizens. Curiously enough it is not the lack but the abundance of information that clouds the European horizon. Information about the work of European institutions is abundant and freely available to citizens for the asking, particularly in electronic form. The problem is that the great majority of citizens do not and never will go asking for information about an experiment that they consider as extremely complex and distant from their everyday problems and interests. On their part, many European mass media report on a daily basis new European policies, laws, programmes and internal and external disputes. Yet, these media accounts are for most citizens like the leaves of a tree, which hide the forest that is stretching out behind. Leaves, like the daily news are ephemeral and unexciting, not worthy of particular attention. On the other hand, the dense forest of European institutions, policies and laws, which produces the political and economic oxygen necessary for the blossoming of small and medium European nations, is obscure and terrifying, if there is no roadmap showing the way through it.

Access to European Union attempts to provide the reader with an overall view and the perspective necessary for understanding the complex organisation, which is the European Community/Union (EC/EU). Indeed, it is virtually impossible to understand the functioning of a particular mechanism or of a specific measure of the Union without having a comprehensive view of the organisation and some knowledge of its development over time. The emphasis of the book is placed on the common policies developed by the EC/EU. Indeed, **an approach to multinational integration** is advanced, based on the setting up and development of common policies by the participating states. This approach is based on the empirical evidence of the European Union, but may also be applied *mutatis mutandis* to other multinational integration schemes elsewhere in the world.

This book aspires to being a textbook for **any student of European integration**, whether academic student of the European integration process, lawyer interested in Community law, which is ceaselessly growing and modified, economist wishing to acquire the latest information on European economic policies, historian wanting to understand the recent history of the continent or businessman seeking to understand the mechanisms of the large market in which he operates. In fact, European integration cannot be properly approached with the particular methods and tools of political science, international relations, economics or law. *Access to EU* follows, therefore, an interdisciplinary, pragmatic approach, which is somewhat distinct from the precise precepts of the disciplines that compose it.

This approach, however, is neither dogmatic nor purely theoretical. The empirical or **pragmatic approach** endeavours to present European policies as they are, with a minimum of value judgments as to their performance. In fact, European policies, as all public policies, have both positive and negative aspects and can therefore be approached either in a positive or a negative way according to the viewpoint of the writer. Moreover, European policies are in a state of perpetual evolution. At a certain point of time, one can reasonably extol their achievements or deplore their failures. In this book we follow an empirical approach of European policies as they are in a particular year: what they try to achieve; what they have achieved so far; which are their main shortcomings; and, finally, which are their short-term prospects.

To help the reader find easily the details of any policy or measure he or she is interested in and/or deduce in an unprejudiced way whether a certain policy is good or bad or whether it has achieved the objectives assigned to it, facts and references are presented in a precise, almost scholastic, manner. All statements about past, present and future developments of common policies as well as all references to European law are based on the official texts of Community acts, published in the **Official Journal of the European Union (OJ)** or in Commission publications, such as the monthly **Bulletin of the European Union** and the annual **General Report** on the Activities of the European Union. In addition to their documentary purpose, the references to the OJ are also meant to help researchers find the official texts of their particular interest, as published in the collections of the OJ or in the electronic database EUR-Lex in the Europa server of the Commission.

PART I: Treaties, law and institutions

In this part of the book we review, in an introductory chapter, the various theories that have endeavoured to **explain the phenomenon of European integration**. We ascertain that all these theories have shed some light on various aspects of the integration process, but they have all missed the fundamental aspect of this process: the development and management of common policies. We, therefore, propose a theoretical synthesis based on the common policies of the European Union, which are, indeed, the main subject of this book. The theoretical propositions advanced in section 1.1.2 are empirically verified in the rest of the book. In the second section of the introductory chapter we briefly recall how, after the Second World War, an ever-increasing number of European States have decided to set aside their differences and engage themselves in **the process of European integration**.

The main objective of the second chapter is to emphasise the **role of the treaties and their reforms in setting new common policies** and ever-higher objectives for pre-existing ones. It shows how the success of the common policies based on the Treaty on the European Coal and Steel Community (ECSC), signed in Paris in April 1951, led to the signing in March 1957, in Rome, of the Treaties on the European Atomic Energy Community (EAEC or Euratom) and of the most important European Economic Community (EEC), extending integration in all economic sectors. We will note that in order to attain their expanding goals, the Member States decided, in Maastricht in 1992, to supplement the amended Treaty establishing the European Community (TEC) as well as the Treaties on the ECSC and EAEC with the new Treaty on the European Union (TEU), which set the objective of political integration. We will see that five years later, the Treaty of Maastricht was replaced by the Treaty of Amsterdam, in order to accommodate the objectives of the new policies on home and judicial affairs and on foreign affairs. We will finally note that the **Treaty of Nice, actually in force**, aims at the smooth functioning of EU institutions after the accession of ten more Member States, but that the **Constitutional Treaty**, actually in the process of ratification by the twenty-five Member States which signed it in October 2004, is needed to help Europe advance in the path of its integration.

In chapter three a metaphorical image is used to explain how **the European Union covers under its roof** the main edifice of the European construction, which is the European Community, and the new wings of the common foreign and security policy and of justice and home affairs. The original **decision-making process** of the Community is clarified, a process that leads to the formation of an equally **original legal system**, based on the treaties and taking the form of regulations, directives and decisions. A particular attention is paid to the **unique financing system** of the European Community based on its own resources inscribed in the Community budget, managed by the Commission.

The final chapter of this part examines the structure and the functions of the **main European institutions**, in the order that they appear in the decision-making process: the European Council, the European Commission, the European Parliament, the Council of Ministers and the Court of Justice. This chapter deals also with other important institutions, the European Central Bank and the Court of Auditors, and with the consultative bodies of the EC/EU, the Economic and Social Committee and the Committee of the Regions. The interaction of these institutions and organs, examined in the section on the European decision-making process, is essential for the development of **the common policies that are analysed in this book**.

Chapter 1

INTRODUCTION TO EUROPEAN INTEGRATION

In 1945, just after the Second World War, Winston Churchill described Europe as "a rubble heap, a charnel house, a breeding ground for pestilence and hate". A year later, on 19 September 1946, in his famous Zurich speech, he proposed as a remedy "to recreate the European Family ... and to provide it with a structure under which it can dwell in peace, in safety and in freedom ... a kind of United States of Europe". Half a century later, realising and exceeding Churchill's vision, the western part of the "European Family" had become an island of peace and prosperity in a world ravaged by hatreds, conflicts, civil wars and misery. The successful formula that European nations had invented to overcome their depression was the integration of the formerly antagonistic nation-states into a union of peacefully interacting and competing nations. The multinational integration formula involves the gradual creation of imperceptible albeit innumerable links between the nations taking part in the process. Those links consist of common policies and common laws, which govern the Member States' economic activities and influence the day-to-day lives and occupations of their citizens.

1.1. The theoretical framework

Many theories, stemming mainly from the theoretical frameworks of political science or international relations, have been developed during the second half of the twentieth century about international and, more especially, European integration. Each has focused on a particular aspect of the phenomenon, while neglecting most of the other aspects. Each, therefore, has had its own merits in shedding scientific light on some parts of a very complicated phenomenon, but none has succeeded in explaining the whole, in structuring scientific observations on all its parts and in predicting its future development. After pointing out the main points of prevalent theories, we attempt in section 1.1.2. to present an explanation of the phenomenon of multinational integration based on the evolutionary development of common policies.

1.1.1. A synopsis of prominent integration theories

As early as the 1920s, **federalists** like Coudenhove-Kalergi perceived that European nations, which had just devastated one another in a nonsensical fratricide war, were a natural entity that could become a significant global force, if only they could succeed in having a federal constitution[1]. After the second catastrophic war for supremacy of one European nation over the others, Altiero Spinelli expressed the view that the national states had lost their *raison d'être*, since they could no longer guarantee the political and economic safety of their citizens and should give way to a federation, called by him "the European Union"[2]. Federalists, thus, put the cart (the ultimate state of European integration) before the horse (the creation of solidarity among former bitter enemies). They had a bright vision, but had not found the means to reach it.

Functionalists like Mitrany[3] rightly pointed out that international organisations are not an end in themselves, but rather the means of addressing the priorities dictated by human needs and have, therefore, to be flexible and modify their tasks (functions) according to the needs of the moment. In their over-optimism, however, for the creation of a cobweb of really international (worldwide), task-oriented organisations, they overlooked and even mistrusted the peacekeeping and welfare functions of a regional organisation like the European Economic Community.

Closer to the European reality, the **transactionalist** theory of Karl Deutsch defines international integration as the attainment, within a territory, of a "sense of community" and of institutions and practices strong enough to assure dependable expectations of "peaceful change" among its population[4]. The assertion that the sense of community among states would depend on establishment of a network of mutual transactions[5] is borne out by the experience of the European Communities. However, this experience proves that first comes the formal institutional framework and on it are built the informal transactions and hence the community spirit, necessary for an effective multinational integration.

Relatively close to the Jean Monnet method of "common action which is the core of the European Community"[6], is the **neofunctionalist** theory, developed mainly by Ernst Haas[7]. Both Monnet and neofunctionalist theorists rejected federalist idealism and brought down Mitrany's functionalism from its international high spheres to the concrete level of several neighbouring states. The Monnet inspired famous declaration of Robert Schuman of 9 May 1950 was quite explicit on the road to be followed by European integration: "Europe … will be built through concrete achievements which first create a *de facto* **solidarity**". Integration was viewed as a process where the constructive functions of the main actors, the common institutions, would induce positive reactions of the political and economic elites, influence the behaviour of other societal groups and bring together the citizens of the different nations. Neofunctionalist logic was built on the "spillover" effect. This meant that economic integration would gradually build solidarity among the participating nations and would in turn create the need for further supranational institutionalisation. Leon Lindberg (1963)[8] defined the "spillover effect" as: "a

---

[1] COUDENHOVE-KALERGI Richard N., *Pan-Europe*, Knopf, New York, 1926.
[2] SPINELLI Altiero, "The Growth of the European Movement since the Second World War", in M. Hodges (ed.), *European Integration*, Penguin, Harmondsworth, 1972.
[3] MITRANY David, *A Working Peace System*, Quadrangle Books, Chicago, 1966.
[4] DEUTSCH Karl W., *Nationalism and Social Communication*, 2nd edition, MIT Press, Cambridge, MA, 1966.
[5] DEUTSCH Karl W., *The Analysis of International Relations*, Prentice Hall, Englewood Cliffs NJ, 1968.
[6] Monnet Jean. "A Ferment of Change", *Journal of Common Market Studies*, n. 1, 1962, p. 203-211.
[7] HAAS Ernst B. The Uniting of Europe: Political, Social and Economic Forces 1950-1957, 2nd edn. Stanford: Stanford University Press, 1968.
[8] LINDBERG Leon, The political Dynamics of European Economic Integration, Stanford CA, Stanford University Press.

situation in which a given action, related to a specific goal, creates a situation in which the original goal can be assured only by taking further actions, which in turn create a further condition and a need for more action and so forth".

Many other neofunctionalist assumptions have been proved correct by European experience, notably that: action by interest groups would not be motivated by idealistic pursuit of the common good, but would be self-regarding and goal driven; perceptions by these groups of shifts in the loci of authority and power would increasingly direct their activity towards the developing supranational arena; the supranational scheme of government at the regional level would be the appropriate regional counterpart to the national state, which would no longer feel capable of achieving welfare aims within its own narrow borders. In economic terms, the creation of a customs union would generate pressures for the establishment of a common market and monetary union. The close economic integration brought about would require supranational regulatory capacity. Thus, political integration would follow economic integration[1].

Some neofunctionalist assertions, namely the withering away of the power-based states system, prompted a strong **intergovernmentalist** alternative to neofunctionalism, despite the strong European evidence in favour of the latter. The Treaties of Maastricht and Amsterdam have, indeed, disproved Stanley Hoffmann's prediction that states would not compromise their sovereignty by moving their integration from the areas of "low politics" (read economics) to the sphere of "high politics", i.e. foreign and security policy[2]. **Liberal intergovernmentalist** analysis provided by Andrew Moravcsik (1993)[3] has failed to explain how national interests, voiced by national governments in international negotiations, can merge and allow European integration to prosper.

Although the neofunctionalist theory has come closer to the European integration process, particularly thanks to its emphasis on the spillover effect, some critics rightly point out certain deficiencies in neofunctionalist reasoning. By highlighting the **multilevel governance** (European, national, regional, etc) of the EC/EU and the interaction of political actors across those levels, Gary Marks *et al.* (1996)[4] have shown the theoretical trap of imagining either the withering away of the state or its stubborn resilience. **Neoinstitutionalists**, like March and Olsen (1984)[5], have demonstrated the importance of institutions (not just formally established supranational organs, but also informal interactions) in providing contexts where actors can conduct a great number of positive sum bargains. **In our point of view**, the neofunctionalist theory should be completed with these missing elements and with another most important factor of the multinational integration process: the gradual formulation, development and multiplication of common policies by the actors of the process. In the next section an empirical approach is advanced taking into consideration this important element.

1.1.2. An empirical approach based on the development of common policies

The **multinational integration process** may de defined as the voluntary establishment by treaty, concluded between independent states, of common institutions and the gradual development by them of common policies pursuing common goals and serving common interests. Being "voluntary", a multinational integration process is clearly dis-

---

[1] BALASSA Bela, *The Theory of Economic Integration*, Allen and Unwin, London, 1962.

[2] HOFFMANN Stanley, "The European Process at Atlantic Crosspurposes", *Journal of Common Market Studies*, No 3, 1964.

[3] MORAVCSIK Andrew, "Preferences and Power in the European Community: A Liberal Intergovernmentalist Approach, Journal of Common Market Studies, No 31 (4).

[4] MARKS G., SCHARPF F., SCHMITTER P.C. and STREECK W., Governance in the European Union, London, Sage.

[5] MARCH J.G. and OLSEN J.P., "The New Institutionalism: Organizational Factors in Political Life", American Political Science Review, No 78.

tinguished from any form of coercive governance or coalition of nations or states. A "multinational" integration process between several nations should be distinguished from a Mitranian "international integration", involving all or most nations of the world. It should also be distinguished from "regional integration", a concept frequently used to denote the integration of various states of a region of the world, but which should, in fact, be reserved to the integration of various regions of a state, a process that is going on in most countries of the world. Multinational integration may go on inside one state containing different nationalities, but, in this case, its institutions are based on a federal constitution rather than on a treaty between independent states.

The "gradual development" of common policies implies that multinational integration is a constantly evolving process without a clearly defined end. Since the process is voluntary, it ensues that independent states may join it at any point, following the procedures and criteria laid down by the group, or leave it, if they consider that the common policies developed or envisaged by the group, according to the majority definition of the common interest, do not coincide any more with their national interests.

The primary goal of multinational integration is the **achievement of peace and security** among the member states as well as between them and the rest of the world. But, unlike a military alliance where this goal is pursued by various pledges of a political and military nature, a multinational integration scheme is built gradually **by means of a large number of common policies**, cementing common interests and creating a real solidarity among the member states. In the words of Jean Monnet, the intellectual father of European integration, "union between individuals or communities is not natural; it can only be the result of an intellectual process... having as a starting point the observation of the need for change. Its driving force must be **common interests** between individuals or communities".

In EC/EU usage, "**common policies**" are the ones that take the place of the essential elements of national policies (notably, agriculture, fisheries and foreign trade). The policies that support and supplement national policies are called "**Community policies**". But, in fact, the distinction, between the two categories is not at all clear-cut. Indeed, all common policies, whether called thus by the Treaties or by Community practice, are in a process of development. They start as mere objectives set in general terms by the Treaties or the institutions and are gradually built up by common or "Community" legal acts. The Treaty establishing the European Community (TEC) clearly declares in its Article 2 that "the Community shall have as its task, by establishing a common market and an economic and monetary union and by implementing **common policies or activities** referred to in Articles 3 and 4, to promote throughout the Community a harmonious, balanced and sustainable development of economic activities...". Articles 3 and 4 of the TEC serve, in fact, as legal bases for common policies in a great number of sectors or for common measures in some other fields (the distinction between common policies and common measures being quantitative rather than qualitative). In this book, the terms "common policy" and "Community policy" are used alternatively, as the latter is taken to mean "the common policy of the Member States of the Community" in a certain field.

Common policies, developed gradually by the actors of the process, foster both **political and economic integration** of the participating states. Although multinational integration depends on political decisions, it greatly affects the economies of the member states. Increasingly, through the stages of customs union, common market and economic and monetary union [see part II], it opens up the participating economies to multinational trade and competition. Obviously, the economies of the member states are greatly influenced by common economic and other policies. As these economies are gradually opened up to multinational trade and competition, **all economic parameters change**:

trade increases enormously within the large internal market, both supply and demand conditions are modified drastically, state intervention is seriously curbed and new dynamics are set in motion, notably concerning trade and investment opportunities. The creation and/or extension of multinational companies and the cross investments between them and national companies tend to bind the economies more closely together. The common policies build, in fact, a new concept and context of political economy, which affects the actions of political leaders and the activities of businessmen of the member states.

Indeed, by bringing about tougher conditions of competition than the ones existing inside the previously protected economies, multinational integration brings about **radical changes in business habits** and creates new business opportunities. Not surprisingly, business associations, constituting powerful interest groups, try to influence the integration process in their favour. They intervene by way of demands, suggestions or criticisms addressed to the principal actors - the common institutions and the governments of the Member States - at various stages of the decision-making process concerning particular policies or the advancement of the integration process itself [see section 9.4.].

In the case of the EC/EU it is clear that the political elite were and still are influenced by **open-minded and dynamic economic elite**. In fact, more than by considerations of security or balance of power at world level, over-emphasised by political scientists, the historic decisions of the Member States were motivated by economic factors: revitalising the two most important economic sectors in the post-war period, coal and steel; creating a large market in order to give a new dynamism to their economies stifled by protectionism; completing the single market to further facilitate trade and investment within a large market; strengthening the single market with a single currency to further facilitate internal transactions and allow European businesses to better face global competition. These decisions and the ensuing common policies were supported, if not provoked, by influential economic groups in the Member States.

Although they are of paramount importance, economic pressures alone cannot start the integration process. The necessary condition for setting the multinational integration process in motion is that the political, economic and other elite of neighbouring countries are earnestly seeking to **serve the interests of their nations**, rather than their own interests or those of a particular class or societal category. Under this condition - which implies democratic regimes - economic and political leaders would sooner or later concur that trade liberalisation better serves the supreme national goals of peace and prosperity than existing protectionist economic policies [see sections 5.1. and 6.1.]. They would then have an option: either to pursue mutual trade liberalisation through intergovernmental cooperation or through multinational integration.

Intergovernmental cooperation is a conventional shelter of national interests, entrenched in the solid and familiar bulwark of national sovereignties defended by national governments. It does not need strong central institutions or a great deal of common legislation. Although it is usually based on a treaty, which prescribes governmental action and behaviour for the reduction of trade barriers and sanctions in case of infringement by a participating state, the respect of the agreement depends more on the goodwill of the participating governments than on common legislation enacted and enforced by supranational bodies. By signing an intergovernmental cooperation agreement for trade liberalisation, such as that of the European Free Trade Area (EFTA) or of the World Trade Organisation (WTO), a government pledges to curb its freedom of action in the domain of tariffs and trade, but does not yield sovereign rights in this field. In case of a grave dispute with its partners, it may free its state from its obligations without serious legal or political consequences, other than the concurrent loss of the rights provided by the agreement.

In contrast, **multinational integration** is a dynamic venture of promoting national interests, depending on many unpredictable internal and external parameters and moved forward perpetually by the ever-changing requirements of the partners and by the extra energy provided by the combination of their forces. While safeguarding the interests of big and small countries alike, it requires common institutions and leads progressively to the establishment of a great number of common policies, to the harmonisation of legislations and to the common management of significant parts of national sovereignties. Small and big countries participating in the process have the same rights and obligations. They pledge themselves to pursue common objectives, which go much beyond trade liberalisation. In addition to this goal, the nations participating in an integration process also want to liberalise the movements of persons and capital and to facilitate the establishment and provision of services by companies from the partner countries. The legal acts needed to achieve all these ends create strong and innumerable ties between the economies, societies and administrations of the participating states. Even though governments have the theoretical possibility to break away from the integration process, these ties make the separation increasingly difficult and costly. It ensues that governments are ever more strictly obligated to follow the rules inscribed in the treaty signed and ratified by them, a treaty often amended to allow the progress of the integration process.

Hence, the **fundamental decision** of a number of states to establish a multinational integration process, outlined in a treaty, signed and ratified by willing governments, is the catalyst, which precipitates a sequence of secondary decisions formulating various common policies. If the implementation of these initial common policies gave satisfactory but not optimal economic results, it would reveal the necessity for more common policies and would thus have a multiplicative effect on the process. There is no predictable end to this process, as it depends on all sorts of internal and external factors. Depending on the stimuli exerted on the actors by those factors, the process may temporarily be slowed down or speeded up, but its general trend is progressive. An abrupt end to the multinational integration process is theoretically possible, but becomes increasingly improbable as the process itself continuously strengthens and multiplies the economic, political and cultural links between the participating nations.

Multinational integration is based on common policies, which develop and multiply thanks to the Community decision-making method that characterizes it. Hence, common policies are the basic elements of a multinational integration process. **A common policy**, as far as multinational integration is concerned, is defined as a set of decisions, measures, rules and codes of conduct adopted by the common institutions set up by a group of states [see section 4.1.] and implemented by the common institutions and the member states. A "real" common policy (to be distinguished from a so-called one) has to be implemented by all the participants and, therefore, needs to be monitored by supranational executive and judiciary authorities. Hence, by adopting a common policy, the participants agree to transfer some of their sovereign powers to common supranational institutions. This transfer of sovereign rights in the framework of common policies is the main drawback but also the fundamental characteristic of multinational integration. It explains why common policies are difficult to adopt, but also why, once adopted, they are the binding (or integrating) elements of the whole multinational structure. Common policies, thus, distinguish multinational integration from intergovernmental cooperation and explain nationalistic scepticism towards the former.

There are four main types of common policies: fundamental and secondary, horizontal and sectoral. **Fundamental** are the common policies, whose basic objectives and scope are inscribed in the Treaty itself and are, therefore, agreed by both the governments and the parliaments of all the Member States. **Secondary** common policies are the ones that are defined by the common legislative bodies within the framework of the fundamental common policies and in accordance with the Community decision-making process. Both fundamental and secondary common policies can be divided into **horizontal** (such as social, competition or environment protection), which affect the overall conditions of the economies and societies of the Member States and **sectoral**, which concern certain sectors of the economies of the Member States (namely industry, energy, transports, agriculture and fisheries). All common policies can be classified in a decreasing order of importance, depending on the scope of the area covered by each one.

Multinational integration itself is, in fact, the most important fundamental common policy, since it is initially chosen by a number of states in preference to isolationism or intergovernmental cooperation. Integration is, indeed, the fundamental course of action (the trunk), decided voluntarily, in common, in a treaty from which all other common policies depend or emanate (like the branches of a tree). As the integration process develops in stages, the passage from one stage to the next - from customs union to common market, then to economic and monetary union and finally to political union - is also based on a fundamental common policy decision inscribed in a treaty [see part II]. These common policies, which frame the stages of the integration process, are the most important ones. In figurative language, they are the stronger branches of the tree. From them stem thinner branches concerning less important fundamental policies also framed in the Treaty, for instance on competition, environment protection or agriculture. From such fundamental policies emanate ever finer secondary policies, which are laid down by the common institutions and are implemented by them and the member states. For environment protection, for instance, there needs to be a general policy for the protection of the atmosphere and then specific measures pursuing this objective defined in regulations, directives or decisions. Such measures may be classified as specific common policies.

Common policies materialise when, where and to the extent that the governments, representing the parties to an integration treaty, believe that the individual interests of their states are better served by them than by national policies. To create a sentiment of mutual confidence, the formulation of a common policy by the common institutions must clearly indicate the **common need** that it addresses, the **common goal** that it pursues and the **common interest** that it serves [see section 3.2.]. The essential element in a common policy is the definition of the common interest in the objectives and measures framed by it. This definition has to satisfy all Member States as far as fundamental common policies are concerned and most Member States concerning secondary common policies. It is possible that some common policies better satisfy the national interests of some participants than those of others. It is inadmissible and hence impracticable that all common policies better satisfy the interests of some members of the group to the detriment of the rest. Indeed, no party to a multinational integration scheme should feel that its national interests are being permanently and systematically damaged by the common policies pursued by the majority of its partners; but, on the other hand, no party to such a scheme may systematically obstruct the common policies proposed by claiming that they do not fully satisfy its national interests. Hence, all parties to a multinational integration scheme must be prepared to accept compromise solutions formulated in the various common policies and, sometimes, to give ground in one field, expecting to gain ground in another field. The hundreds of decisions taken every year by the EC/EU institutions demonstrate the fact that its Member States play the game according to this rule. The few exceptions confirm the rule.

A common policy may develop in two senses: in the sense of its legal evolution, which is required in order to keep up with economic and technical progress in the subject matter that it covers; and in the sense of the expansion of its field, which may happen in order to cover peripheral needs not formerly attended to in the formulation of the policy or new needs, either encountered during the implementation of the measures originally adopted or created by the geopolitical environment of the moment. Moreover, a common policy tends to spill over into the areas of other common policies, produce needs, cause reactions and nourish their development. Thus, common policies are closely knit together, support each other, foster their joint evolution and multiplication and, in so doing, promote the progress of the multinational integration process.

This book brings enough empirical evidence to test the hypotheses advanced above. Chapter 4 examines the structure, the functions and the role of the main actors of European integration, which are the common institutions. The second part of the book examines the most fundamental common policies, which concern the **stages of the European integration process**. Part III focuses on policies that are of particular interest to the citizens of the Union. Part IV examines the **common horizontal policies** - such as social, competition or environment protection - which affect the overall conditions of the economies and societies of the Member States. Part V analyses the **common sectoral policies**, which concern certain sectors of the economies of the Member States. Part VI, presents the **common external policies**, which steer the relations of the Member States with third countries. In the final chapter, conclusions are drawn on the effectiveness of the European integration process and on its possible future development.

The governments which opt for the integration process by the "**Community method**" cannot apply it immediately in all economic sectors, let alone in non-economic fields. The integration process being evolutionary, they have to proceed step by step and apply the integration or Community method, firstly, to the abolition of the most important obstacles hindering the economic relations of their states. As they solve this first series of problems they come across a multitude of lesser problems, which also require solution in order to attend to the efficiency of their markets. If the participants play the game according to the rules set by them in the treaty, they would tend to develop and multiply common policies according to their ever-changing needs. This happens because common policies, like all other public policies, are there to answer the needs which arise in a particular community at a particular time. These needs change and multiply over time. Therefore, not only the objectives that the member states set for each common policy, but also the means that they give to the common institutions to attain them and the measures that the latter adopt in order to implement them have to keep pace with the new and changing economic, political and social needs of the states participating in the integration process.

Since the solutions to arising problems have to be agreed by all (concerning fundamental policies) or the majority of participants (concerning secondary policies) and conciliation of the various interests involved requires many years of negotiations, the integration process is necessarily slow. Until an optimal solution to a particular problem is found by the Community method, the actors of the integration process may and often have to resort to **intergovernmental cooperation**, in order to set common objectives, compare best practices to achieve them and, in any case, avoid widening the disparity of their policies on the matter. It ensues that, in the integration process, all economic policies and a growing number of non-economic ones are made up partly of common policy measures and partly of intergovernmental cooperation measures, the main difference between them being that the first have mandatory effects whereas the latter do not. Intergovernmental cooperation measures serve the learning process and usually pave the way for common policies formulated and managed by the Community method. It follows from what precedes that the intergovernmental method and the Community method are complementary, but that the latter tends to replace the former in a growing number of areas as the integration process marches forward. The reverse cannot happen, since intergovernmental cooperation does not have the institutions necessary to manage the Community method.

1.2. Birth and growth of the Community/Union

The march of European unification began with six countries, pioneers starting out on an unknown road. Some European states did not want and some could not participate in the march. Some states advocated another way forward. Others stood by as spectators and joined the march when they ascertained that it was going along the right path. Finally, after half a century of continuous progress, all European nations are following or want to follow the common march, even if some are dragging their feet and trying to check the speed of the vanguard.

World War II had left Europe clearly divided into two very distinct groups of states. In the East, the Soviet Union with Russian land and population supremacy and with a unifying ideology appealing to impoverished people could annex its neighbouring countries and install friendly regimes. Moreover, it could offer them a kind of security (although under totalitarian regimes), a large market for their imports and exports (although under Russian domination) and a certain safeguard for the most basic interests of their populations - food and shelter. In Western Europe, in the 1950s, the welfare of the populations was not much better than in the East. Although in most Western European countries people lived under democratic regimes and could enjoy some basic human rights and some liberty of speech, the economic situation of the vast majority was not much better than that of their Eastern neighbours. Moreover, these fragile democratic regimes were at threat both from outside - the arrogant superpower that was quickly becoming the Soviet Union - and from inside - the political parties friendly to it.

Was this threat the prime stimulus for European unification? It certainly was a reason for cooperation, but not the primary factor of integration. To face the Soviet threat, most Western European nations had placed themselves, already since 1949, inside the North Atlantic Treaty Organisation (NATO) and hence under the American nuclear umbrella. This umbrella could be a much better deterrent from outside menace than a unification of their inadequate armies. But, this umbrella could not safeguard the fragile democratic regimes from the unrest of people living under subsistence levels. To curb this threat, the stagnating economies of these countries would have to be revamped to absorb the jobless and penniless populations. These economies were separated from each other and from the rest of the world by high tariff and other barriers, which allowed some inefficient public and private companies to survive in the protected national market, but effectively excluded foreign trade and competition and, hence, the expansion that they could provide. To stimulate the development of Western European economies, the barriers between them had to be torn down. But, again, the stimulus of trade liberalisation was not enough in itself to start European unification. A political decision was needed to pursue this liberalisation by multinational integration rather than by intergovernmental cooperation.

The simple way to trade liberalisation in Europe was the creation of a free trade area through intergovernmental cooperation. This course was advocated mainly by the United Kingdom and the Scandinavian countries. According to this view, trade liberalisation in Western Europe could accelerate and exceed the work begun in 1947 at international level by the General Agreement on Tariffs and Trade (GATT). It could thus lead to total abolition of tariff barriers, without any concession of national sovereignty. In parallel, an intergovernmental cooperation for economic development, without legal obligations, could be pursued between Western European nations and the United States of America inside the European Organisation for Economic Cooperation. This organisation was set in place in the 1950s in order to manage the Marshall Plan of the USA for the reconstruction of Europe and was later transformed into the actual Organisation for Economic Cooperation and Development (OECD), which includes most European countries, the USA, other Anglo-Saxon countries and Japan.

But some politicians in continental countries, which had been devastated by the wars between themselves, wanted to go beyond trade liberalisation. They wanted to tie their economies so close together as to make a new civil war in Europe impossible. They wanted to try a method which would combine trade liberalisation with economic integration. As the word integration implies, they wanted to unify their separated economies into a whole. Multinational integration was, at the time, a revolutionary and risky enterprise. It was revolutionary, because it clashed with the well established concept of the nation-state and the national sovereignty that emanated from it. It was a risky enterprise, because it required the setting up of supranational institutions that would prevail over national authorities with unknown consequences. However, it promised to transform the former enemies into partners and, moreover, to make their partnership irrevocable. Six States were ready to take the plunge: France, Germany, Italy, the Netherlands, Belgium and Luxembourg. But, they did not want to gamble all their economies. They decided, first, to bet on their coal and steel sectors.

The choice of coal and steel was not fortuitous. These industries were, in the 1950s, the core of the industrial sectors of the original Member States. The combination of coal, the major energy at the time, with steel, the prime industrial product of the Ruhr valley, had built the might of the Third Reich and helped it to conquer almost all of continental Europe. In post-war Europe, these industries were composed of few and large companies, which were often subsidised, protected from international competition by high tariff and other barriers and were allowed to conclude among themselves agreements leading to national cartels. If these industries were put together in a multinational project managed by supranational authorities, Germany could, from a potential enemy, become a partner with its neighbouring countries. By participating in a scheme, which would control its war industries, Germany would pledge not simply by words but by deeds that it had abandoned forever any intentions of expanding its "Lebensraum". Moreover, if economic integration could work in these highly protected industries, it could work in other sectors. Therefore, the sectors of coal and steel were chosen as a model of European integration for both economic and political reasons.

This, in a nutshell, was the brilliant idea of Jean Monnet, inspired by his business and political activities with the Allies during the war. It was proclaimed by the French Minister of Foreign Affairs, Robert Schuman, on 9 May 1950, a historical date for European unification, recognised as such by the Constitutional Treaty. The Schuman declaration was quite explicit on the road to be followed by European integration: "Europe will not be made all at once, or according to a single plan. It will be built through concrete achievements which first create a de facto solidarity." The ECSC was to be the first achievement. The French idea was immediately welcomed by the German Chancellor, Konrad Adenauer, and by the Prime Ministers of Italy, Belgium, the Netherlands and Luxembourg. Less than a year after the Schuman declaration the founding fathers had negotiated the details of this novel project and were able to sign the ECSC Treaty, in Paris, on 18 April 1951. The institutions that they set up at that time - a High Authority (integrated in 1967 into the European Commission), a Council of Ministers, a European Assembly (which developed into the European Parliament) and a Court of Justice - are still there today, with, of course, extended functions. The durability of the institutions demonstrates how well the original project was designed.

In fact, the very first years of the functioning of the customs union of coal and steel showed that the ECSC model worked and could be extended to all economic sectors.

Already in June 1955, the Ministers for Foreign Affairs of the Six discussed the possibility of creating a common market embracing all products and a separate Community for nuclear energy. Speedy negotiations conducted by the Belgian Minister for Foreign Affairs, Paul-Henri Spaak, were concluded in April 1956 and on 25 March 1957, the Six were able to sign, on Capitol Hill in Rome, the Treaties establishing the European Economic Community (EEC) and the European Atomic Energy Community (EAEC).

The United Kingdom proposed then to the Six the creation of a vast European free trade area between the European Economic Community and the other Member States of the OECD, but the discussions were interrupted during the autumn of 1958 owing to intractable differences of opinion between France and the United Kingdom. The separation between states, which wanted to try the Community method and those, which preferred the intergovernmental cooperation for trade liberalisation took shape in 1959 with the creation of the **European Free Trade Association (EFTA)**, to which the United Kingdom, Norway, Sweden, Denmark, Austria, Portugal, Iceland and Switzerland acceded, with Finland joining at a later date.

Having been impressed, however, by the early successes of the European Community, it was not long before the British Government was rethinking its refusal to play an active role in the work of European unification. It was aware that the United Kingdom could not maintain its political influence in Europe and the world through the intergovernmental cooperation of the EFTA. So in August 1961, the United Kingdom submitted an initial official application to become a full member of the European Community. UK candidature of the EEC was followed by two other EFTA member countries, namely Denmark and Norway, and also by Ireland.

Accession of those countries initially met with the opposition of the President of the French Republic, General de Gaulle, who, being very distrustful of the United Kingdom's intentions, declared, right in the middle of the negotiations in 1963, that he wished to discontinue them. The second British application for accession, in 1967, with which Ireland, Denmark and Norway were yet again associated, was not examined for much time owing to France's misgivings. The issue of the accession of those countries could not be resolved until, following General de Gaulle's resignation in April 1969. After laborious negotiations, the Treaties of Accession were finally signed on 22 January 1972. The **accession of the United Kingdom, Ireland and Denmark** took effect on 1 January 1973, following favourable referenda (Ireland and Denmark) and ratification by the national parliaments. Norway's accession was prevented, however, after 53.49% of the Norwegian population opposed accession to the European Community in a referendum. The membership of the EEC was thus increased to nine, while that of the EFTA was reduced to six.

Once democracy was restored in Greece, Portugal and Spain, these countries submitted applications for accession to the European Community, in 1975 in Greece's case and in 1977 in the other two cases. These countries thus chose to join the novel and hence risky experiment of the EEC rather than the secure but limited refuge of the EFTA. They considered that multinational integration could not only better promote their economic development, but would also uphold their frail democratic regimes, since it required the good functioning of democratic institutions in the participating countries. **Greece** acceded to the Community on 1 January 1981, and **Spain and Portugal** on 1 January 1986. Thus, for a brief moment in its history, the EEC was known as "the Twelve".

With the signature of the Single European Act, in June 1987, the Twelve Member States of the EEC decided to complete their internal market on 31 December 1992. One year before that date, in December 1991, they decided in Maastricht to develop within the single market an economic and monetary union, a judicial and home affairs policy and a common foreign and security policy, thus transforming the European Economic Community into a **European Union (EU)**, including a refurbished European Community (EC).

Since the 1st January 1995, the Europe of Twelve became the Europe of Fifteen, with the **accession of Austria, Finland and Sweden**, the people of Norway having again voted against membership of the Union by a majority of 52.8%. These three nations had weighed the economic advantages of European integration against the political disadvantage of a loss of some sovereign rights and had decided to take the train of integration despite the cost of the fare. The remaining countries of the European Free Trade Area (minus Switzerland), i.e., Norway, Iceland and the Liechtenstein signed with the European Community a Treaty on the **European Economic Area (EEA)**, which came into force on 1 January 1994, creating a large free trade area involving several common policies of the EC/EU [see section 25.1.]. The political elite of Switzerland had applied for EEA membership, but ratification of the Treaty was blocked by referendum. They have also flirted with the idea of EC/EU membership, but have been put off by the negative stance of the population, led by isolationist mass media.

After the fall of the iron curtain in 1989, one after the other the countries of Central and Eastern Europe applied for membership to the EU, thus clearly opting for multinational integration rather than for intergovernmental cooperation inside EFTA. Their preference was guided both by expectations of faster economic development and by hopes of increased political stability inside a Union of democratic countries. The EU encouraged their application by political and financial means [see section 25.2.] and started accession negotiations with **Poland, Hungary, the Czech Republic, Slovakia, Slovenia, Estonia, Latvia, Lithuania** plus **Cyprus** and **Malta**. After conclusion of the negotiations, these ten countries signed the Treaty of Accession in Athens on 16 April 2003[1] and have been full members of the EC/EU since 1 May 2004. We, therefore, now speak of the Union of Twenty five.

The enlargement of the EC/EU is still in progress. The accession negotiations with Romania and Bulgaria are quite advanced and these countries are expected to accede in 2007 or 2008. In December 2004, the EU accepted to start accession negotiations with Croatia and Turkey. As soon as their economic and political situation allows, all Balkan countries are expected to seek a safe haven inside the Union, which, in the next decade, could thus number more than thirty members.

1.3. The attractiveness of the Community method

The growing membership of the Community/Union demonstrates the **extraordinary attractiveness of the multinational integration process**, the Community method, compared to its rival, the intergovernmental cooperation method. The countries, which had originally advocated the latter method, have come, one after the other, to solicit their participation in the integration process. The countries of Western Europe, which still shy away from this process, are nevertheless following many of the policies decided by the countries participating in the process, thanks to the European Economic Area agreement (EEA) [see section 25.1.]. The countries of Central and Eastern Europe, which, after their liberation from the iron curtain, had the option of joining the outer circle of the free trade EFTA/EEA or the inner circle of the EC/EU, have unhesitatingly opted for the lat-

---

[1]   OJ L 236 and OJ C 227E, 23.09.2003.

ter. The facts speak for themselves. There could be no better demonstration of the validity of the multinational integration (Community) method than the attraction that it exerts on outsider neighbouring countries.

What is even more extraordinary is that the membership has kept growing together with the tasks assumed by the team, which means that the newcomers accede to an ever closer union and undertake to adopt all the "acquis communautaire", i.e. all the ever-growing legislation enacted by the institutions set up by the elder members. Earlier accessions happened at the time that the Community had just realised its customs union and was struggling to complete its common market in order to make it a single market. The newcomers could well believe that the integration process would stop at this stage and, in fact, some still wish that it had and feel betrayed that it marches on and on. But, later day accessions happened at times that the Community/Union had declared, in revised Treaties, its intention to proceed to the stages of economic and monetary union and even to political union. Hence, when they signed and ratified these Treaties, they were fully aware that European integration is a process without a specified end, but with the declared objective of bringing the European peoples ever closer together. This means that recent newcomers and applicants are attracted by the economic and political advantages of integration, which, for them, outweigh the disadvantage of ceding parts of their national sovereignties to supranational institutions.

The attraction continues and it seems likely that all the countries in the periphery of the Union will someday ask for accession to it. On its side, the Union does not seem disposed to close its door. The project of the **Constitutional Treaty** declares that the Union shall be open to all European States which respect its values and are committed to promoting them together (Art. I-1). These values are: human dignity, freedom, democracy, equality, the rule of law, respect for human rights, including the rights of persons belonging to minorities, pluralism, non-discrimination, tolerance, justice, solidarity and equality between women and men (Art. I-2). However, there is a problem of definition of the concepts "**European States**" and "**respect its values**". These concepts may be defined either in a narrow or a broad sense. Who will define them? The European institutions (Commission, Parliament, Council) or the peoples of the Union through referendums? And, if these last are asked to give their opinion, by whom and how will they be adequately informed in order to enable them to express themselves on such difficult subjects? It is not easy to answer such questions or those that depend on them, such as: are Turkey, Russia or the Ukraine European States and do they respect the values of the Union? And, if yes, should they be admitted to the Union if they ask for their accession? It is up to the political leaders of the Union to answer these questions. They must however listen to their citizens who by referendums and surveys indicate their reserve to the widening without the deepening of European integration.

In fact, the problem is not so much the continuous enlargement of the Union as that **its actual structures and institutions cannot support its expansion** without their reinforcement. The signing of the Constitutional Treaty was an initial endeavour to strengthen the structures and institutions of the Union. But, it seems that the majority of citizens in some of the twenty-seven nations believe that this effort is not sufficient for the further enlargement of the Union, whereas the majorities in other nations believe quite the opposite: that this strengthening should be avoided in order to discourage the progress of the integration process. In other words, some nations would like a stronger Constitutional Treaty, which would not only allow further enlargements but also help the Union to stand up in the international arena and differentiate itself from other existing and developing superpowers, particularly concerning the social protection of citizens. On the contrary, other nations consider that the present Treaty on the European Union goes too far on the way of integration and would probably be satisfied with only the objectives of the treaty on the European Community, thus stopping further integration and the consequent conferral of national sovereignties to supranational institutions. To better understand the argumentation of the two sides, we should know what these various Treaties stand for.

General bibliography on the EU

- BERGLUND, Sten (et al). *The making of the European Union : foundations, institutions and future trends*. Cheltenham: Edward Elgar, 2006.
- BERTING Jan. Europe: a heritage, a challenge, a promise. Delft: Eburon, 2006.
- CINI, Michelle, BOURNE Angela K. (eds.). Palgrave advances in European Union studies. Basingstoke: Palgrave Macmillan, 2006.
- DINAN Desmond. *Origins and evolution of the European Union*. Oxford: Oxford University Press, 2006.
- DOBSON Lynn. "Normative theory and Europe" in *International Affairs*, v. 82, n. 3, May 2006, p. 511-523.
- EUROPEAN COMMISSION. *EU integration seen through statistics: key facts of 18 policy areas*. Luxembourg: EUR-OP*, 2006.
- FISCHER Thomas C. "An American looks at the European Union", *European Law Journal*, v. 12, n. 2, March 2006, p. 226-278
- FOSSUM John Erik. "Conceptualizing the European Union through four strategies of comparison" in *Comparative European politics*, v. 4, n. 1, April 2006, p. 94-123.
- FOUCHER Michel. *L'Union européenne un demi-siècle plus tard: état des lieux et scénarios de relance*. Paris: Fondation Robert Schuman, 2006.
- GATES Andrea M. *Promoting unity, preserving diversity?: Member State institutions and European integration*. Lanham: Lexington Books, 2006.
- HEARDEN Patrick. "Early American views regarding European unification" in *Cambridge review of international affairs*, v. 19, n. 1, March 2006, p. 67-78.
- JOVANOVIC Miroslav. *The economics of European integration: limits and prospects*. Cheltenham; Northampton, MA: Edward Elgar, 2006.
- McGARRY John, KEATING Michael (eds.). *European integration and the nationalities question*. London: Routledge, 2006.
- MONTBRIAL Thierry de, MOREAU DEFARGES Philippe (sous la dir. de). *L'Europe et le monde*. Institut français des relations internationales (IFRI) (Paris). RAMSES 2007. Paris: Dunod, 2006.
- MOUSSIS Nicholas. *Guide to European Policies*, 12th revised edition. Brussels: European Study Service, 2006.
- O'BRENNAN John. *The Eastern enlargement of the European Union*. London: Routledge, 2006.
- ROTHACHER Albrecht. *Uniting Europe: journey between gloom and glory*. London: Imperial College Press, 2005.
- SANGIOVANNI Mette Eilstrup. *Debates on European integration: a reader*. Basingstoke: Palgrave Macmillan, 2006.
- SJURSEN Helene (ed.). *Questioning EU enlargement: Europe in search of identity*. London: Routledge, 2006.
- ZERVOYIANNI Athina, ARGIROS George, AGIOMIRGIANAKIS George. *European integration*. Basingstoke: Palgrave Macmillan, 2006.

*The publications of the Office for Official Publications of the European Communities (EUR-OP) exist usually in all official languages of the EU.

Chapter 2

EUROPEAN TREATIES

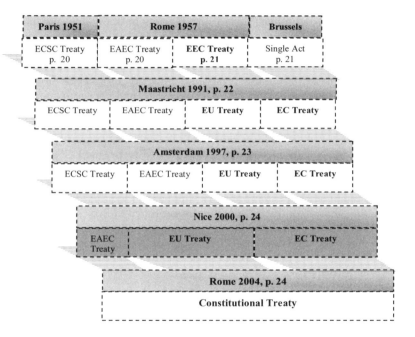

The Treaties are the primary source of European law and hence the legal basis of common policies. The states participating in a multinational integration process set in a treaty the objectives that they wish to attain, the common policies that they wish to implement in order to achieve their goals, the structure and functions of the common institutions that will enact and monitor the common legislation formulated in the framework of the common policies and the fields reserved for the cooperation of their governments. Since common policies need to develop and multiply in order to serve better the ever changing needs and interests of the participating states, the treaty, which outlines them, needs also to be modified, so as to allow these states to attain the higher goals that they set. This is the pattern followed by the European Treaties.

We shall not linger over the basic Treaties of the Communities, because we examine their objectives and main clauses in subsequent chapters in connection with the legal base of the various common policies. The emphasis in this chapter is put on the Treaties as instruments of progress of the European integration. We, therefore, review the main objectives of the original Treaties and those of the Treaties which have replaced them in order to revise some of their provisions and to lay the foundations for more advanced stages of European integration.

2.1. The original Treaties

As we saw above, the first European Treaty, the one establishing the **European Coal and Steel Community (ECSC)**, was signed in Paris on 18 April 1951 by France, Germany, Italy and the Benelux countries and entered into force on 23 July 1952. Its main objective was to eliminate the various barriers to trade and to create a common market in which coal and steel products from the Member States could move freely in order to meet the needs of all Community inhabitants, without discrimination on grounds of nationality. Capital and workers in both sectors should also circulate freely. In order that all this could be achieved, the Treaty laid down certain rules on investment and financial aid, on production and prices, on agreements and concentrations of businesses and on transport. These rules were to be implemented by Community institutions, which would exercise the powers previously held by the states in those sectors: namely a High Authority and a special Council (of Ministers), the decisions of which would be binding on all Member States. Ambitious despite its restricted scope, the ECSC Treaty instituted a European Assembly and a European Court of Justice. The avowed intentions of the founders of the ECSC were, indeed, that it should be an experiment, which could gradually be extended to other economic spheres, culminating in a "European Federation". For this reason, the duration of the ECSC Treaty was limited to fifty years. On 23 July 2002, when it expired, the specific rules concerning the coal and steel sectors were integrated in the Community law and their particular resources, programmes and international obligations were taken over by the European Community[1]. The coal and steel sectors, previously covered by the ECSC Treaty, are dealt with respectively in the chapters on energy and industry.

The Treaty establishing the **European Atomic Energy Community (EAEC**, but more commonly known as **Euratom**) was signed in Rome on 25 March 1957 and came into force on 1 January 1958. Its aim was to create a common market for nuclear materials and equipment, establish common nuclear legislation, introduce a common system for supplies of fissile materials and establish a system for supervising the peaceful use of nuclear energy and common standards for nuclear safety and for the health and safety protection of the population and workers against ionising radiation. The key elements in this Treaty were, however, the coordination of the Member States' research programmes and a joint research programme, implemented in a Joint Research Centre, which was to develop technology and stimulate nuclear production in Europe [see sections 18.2.4. and 18.3.]. Although it was very much in the spotlight at the time of its establishment, Euratom has experienced many ups and downs as a result both of disillusionment as regards nuclear energy's economic prospects and of the ambition of some Member States to develop their own nuclear industry, and not purely for civil purposes. Nevertheless, the

---

[1] Decision 2002/234, OJ L 79, 22.03.2002, Decisions 2002/595 and 2002/596, OJ L 194, 23.07.2002 and Decisions 2003/76 and 2003/77, OJ L 29, 05.02.2003.

EAEC Treaty is still in force and manages quite well the nuclear energy sector of the Community/Union. The subjects concerning it are examined mainly in the chapters on research and energy.

Signed at the same time as the Euratom Treaty on the Capitol Hill in Rome on 25 March 1957, the Treaty establishing the **European Economic Community (EEC)** was likewise brought into force on 1 January 1958. Although the EEC and EAEC treaties are sometimes referred to as the "Treaties of Rome", the "Treaty of Rome" is obviously the EEC Treaty. The essential task, which the Treaty of Rome assigned to the Community institutions, was **the creation of a common market** between the Member States. That involved: (a) the achievement of a customs union entailing, on the one hand, the aboli-tion of customs duties, import quotas and other barriers to trade between Member States and, on the other hand, the introduction of a Common Customs Tariff (CCT) vis-à-vis third countries [see chapter 5]; and (b) the implementation, *inter alia* through common policies, of **four fundamental freedoms**: freedom of movement of goods, of course, but also freedom of movement of salaried workers, freedom of establishment and freedom to provide services by independent persons and companies and, finally, freedom of capital movements [see chapter 6].

Although in the preamble to the EEC Treaty the Member States declared that they were determined to lay the foundations of an ever closer union among the peoples of Europe, the Treaty itself constituted the charter for a common market. It set the objec-tives to be attained so as to arrive at that stage of European integration. However, through its Article 235 (Art. 308 TEC), it gave Member States **the possibility to act in the fields not provided by it** by taking unanimously the measures required to attain one of its objectives. This allowed the Member States to implement a large number of com-mon or, so called, Community policies without amending the Treaty.

Nevertheless, the EEC Treaty had a serious fault: although it had set a timetable for the abolition of customs barriers to trade, it had not done the same for the removal of trade barriers of equivalent effect. This vacuum was covered by **the Single European Act**, which came into force on 1 July 1987. Supplementing the EEC Treaty, the Single Act committed the Community to adopt measures with the aim of progressively estab-lishing the internal market over a period expiring on 31 December 1992. At the same time it consecrated the European Council, European cooperation on foreign policy and social and economic cohesion between Member States. Lastly, it served as a legal base for numerous common policies, notably, social, environmental, research and technology.

The Treaties of Paris and Rome each set up different executive organs. The latter were merged by the Treaty of 8 April 1965 establishing **a single Council and a single Commission** of the European Communities, in order to better manage the expanding common policies. Since 1 July 1967 there has therefore been only a single Council of Ministers and a single Commission, with the latter inheriting the powers of the ECSC High Authority, of the EEC Commission and of the Euratom Commission.

The Treaties establishing the Communities were amended to some extent, notably as regards their provi-sions relating to the functioning of the institutions, by the Treaty concerning the **Accession to the European Economic Community of Denmark, Ireland, the United Kingdom** and Norway. That Treaty was signed in Brussels on 22 January 1972 and brought into force on 1 January 1973, but only for three countries, as a refer-endum in Norway had ruled out that country's accession.

In parallel with the creation of the Community's own resources by the Decision of 21 April 1970 [see section 3.4.], the Member States agreed to amend the Treaties in order to increase the European Parliament's budgetary powers. In fact, a first Budget Treaty was signed on 22 April 1970 and entered into force on 1 Janu-ary 1971, but the European Parliament felt that it did not increase its powers sufficiently. The Commission decided that the Parliament was right and put forward proposals for a further extension of the Parliament's budgetary powers. The **second Budget Treaty**, which governs the Community finances, was the result [see section 3.4.]. That Treaty was signed on 22 July 1975 and entered into force on 1 June 1977. In addition to the creation of a new institution, the Court of Auditors [see section 4.2.2.], it conferred on the European Parliament the exclusive right to give a discharge to the Commission in respect of the implementation of the budget and, "if there are important reasons", to reject the budget as a whole [see section 4.1.3.].

The Treaties establishing the Communities were once again amended as to their institutional clauses, by the Treaty concerning the **Accession of the Hellenic Republic** to the European Economic Community and to the European Atomic Energy Community, signed in Athens on 28 May 1979. By that Treaty the "Nine" became "Ten" from 1 January 1981. They became "Twelve" as from 1 January 1986 by virtue of the Acts of **Accession of Spain and Portugal**, signed in Madrid and Lisbon respectively on 12 June 1985.

2.2. The Treaty of Maastricht

As the abolition of customs barriers to trade, in 1968, had highlighted the technical and administrative obstacles to intra-Community trade, so the effort to abolish the latter, by 1992, had made clear that the completion of the common market would not bring about a real single market as long as there were still monetary obstacles in the way. Therefore, the integrationists in the original six Member States were, already before the completion of the single market, pushing their new partners to step into the next integration stage, that of the economic and monetary union, and even to sketch the final stage, that of political union. The defenders of the intergovernmental method were, however, reticent. They had joined the Community in order to reap the benefits of the single market and had accepted the cessions of sovereignty necessary to that end. But they were reticent to make any more concessions to the Community method of integration and its evolutionary properties.

The compromise solution found in Maastricht, in December 1991, was to split the integration venture in half. The original European Economic Community Treaty was renamed Treaty on the European Community to signify that it set new objectives over and above the original economic ones, notably for monetary and social integration. The United Kingdom was allowed to opt out of these new goals and the people of Denmark, consulted by referendum, decided not to join the monetary union. A new Treaty on European Union was signed at the same time to outline the objectives of political union, in particular those of a judicial and home affairs policy and those of a common foreign and security policy. But, by common agreement, it was decided that these goals would be pursued by intergovernmental cooperation. Hence, the so-called Treaty of Maastricht, which was signed on 7 February 1992, was in fact made up of two separate but interrelated Treaties: the **Treaty on the European Union (TEU)**; and the **Treaty establishing the European Community (TEC)**. These two Treaties separated the European construction into three pillars or edifices [see section 3.1.], distinguished mainly on the basis of the decision-making process: the main pillar or edifice, which is the European Community and where the common work of the participants is regulated by the TEC and where the Community method prevails; the pillar or edifice of justice and home affairs; and the pillar or edifice of the common foreign and security policy (CFSP). The method of construction of the two new pillars or edifices was based on intergovernmental cooperation, since the TEU required unanimity for decision-making and, hence, any Member State could veto a common action. A so-called "Social Protocol" excluded the United Kingdom from the social protection objectives of the TEC.

Thus, since the implementation of the Treaty of Maastricht in 1992, the European Union accompanies and complements the European Community; but since the Treaty on the latter governs a far greater number of activities and much more effectively than the Treaty on the European Union, it is more exact to speak of the European Community/Union (EC/EU), in order to keep in mind that they are two different organisations and legal entities. In fact, for the time being, only the European Community has a legal personality, whereas the European Union has no legal personality at all and can therefore not sign treaties or other international legal instruments. The Constitutional Treaty aims at correcting this peculiar situation by conferring legal personality to the European Union.

The essentially economic character of the Communities was surpassed, in order to allow the establishment of **an entity with global character**. According to Article B of the EU Treaty (Maastricht version), the Union set itself **the following objectives**:

- to promote economic and social progress which is balanced and sustainable, in particular through the creation of an **area without internal frontiers** [see section 6.1.], through the strengthening of economic and social cohesion [see section 12.1.2.] and through the establishment of economic and monetary union, including ultimately a single currency [see chapter 7];

- to assert its identity on the international stage, in particular through the implementation of **a common foreign and security policy** including the eventual framing of a common defence policy, which might in time lead to a common defence [see section 8.2.];

- to strengthen the protection of the rights and interests of the nationals of its Member States through the introduction of **a citizenship of the Union** [see section 9.1.];

- to develop close cooperation on **justice and home affairs** [see section 8.1.];

- to maintain in full the "**acquis communautaire**" [see section 3.3.] and build on it with the aim of ensuring the effectiveness of the mechanisms and the institutions of the Community [see chapter 4].

The European Union was enlarged to fifteen Member States, on 1st January 1995, by way of the Treaties of **Accession of Austria, Sweden and Finland**, signed on 24 June 1994 at the European Council meeting in Corfu[1]. The Accession Treaty of Norway had also been signed at that occasion, but, again, the Norwegian people voted against membership of the Union by a majority of 52.8%.

2.3. The Treaty of Amsterdam

The Treaty signed on 17 June 1997 at Amsterdam, only six years and a half after the signature of the Treaty of Maastricht, did not bring fundamental changes to the integration process, but it marked some progress in several policy areas. The most important development was the transfer, under the European Community's wing, thus entailing the Community decision-making method, of policies related to the free movement of persons, notably concerning visas, asylum and immigration [see section 8.1.]. In particular, it made the Union's **institutional structure** more efficient by extending the co-decision procedure (Parliament/Council) and qualified majority voting in the Council [see section 4.3.]. Another important objective of the Amsterdam Treaty was to place employment and **social protection** at the heart of the Union [see sections 13.3. and 13.5.3.]. While confirming that the Member States bear primary responsibility for employment, the revised Treaty on the European Community engaged them to act together to find solutions to unemployment. The Labour government of the United Kingdom accepted the social objectives of the Treaty and therefore the social policy agreement, exempting the UK from this common policy, was abolished.

Under its European Union wing, the Amsterdam Treaty strengthened the common foreign and security policy by making the European Council (heads of State or government) responsible for defining common strategies to be implemented by the Union and the Member States and by designating a High Representative for the CFSP (the Secretary General of the Council) and a Policy Planning and Early Warning Unit under his responsibility [see section 8.2.].

---

[1] OJ L 1, 01.01.1995.

2.4. The Treaty of Nice

The Treaty that was signed in Nice on 26 February 2001, only three years and a half after the signature of the Treaty of Amsterdam, did not aspire to give a fresh impetus to the European integration process, but only to prepare the institutions of the European Community/Union to function with the representatives of ten *new* Member States. This Treaty, which will stay in force until replaced by the Constitutional Treaty, revised the Treaty of Amsterdam concerning mainly four institutional matters: the replacement of unanimity by qualified majority in decision-making procedures, the enhanced cooperation of some Member States[1], the weighting of votes in the Council and the size and the composition of the Commission.

The Treaty of Nice extended the qualified majority voting to new subjects, thereby boosting the role of the European Parliament in the codecision process with the Council. It reinforced and facilitated the enhanced cooperation of some Member States, in cases where an agreement cannot be reached by normal decision-making procedures. The Protocol on the enlargement of the European Union, adopted at Nice, redefined the weighting of the votes of each Member State in the Council and introduced a population element by specifying that decisions taken by qualified majority on the basis of a Commission proposal should gather at least 72% of the total votes of the members, representing at least 62% of the total population of the Union. As regards the composition of the Commission, the same protocol provides that after the enlargement of the Union each Member State will have one Commissioner until such time as the 27th Member State joins the European Union, but thereafter the number of Commissioners will be smaller than the number of Member States.

The coming into force of the Treaty of Nice was initially held back by the negative result of a referendum of the Irish people, held on 11 June 2001, but the problem was resolved by the positive outcome of a second referendum, held on 19 October 2002. The Treaty of Nice, thus, came into force on 1 February 2003. Under the heading of the city in which it was signed, the Treaty of Nice, as the repealed Treaties of Maastricht and Amsterdam, includes in fact two Treaties: the Treaty on the European Union (**TEU**) and the Treaty establishing the European Community (**TEC**). The existence of two separate Treaties for the Community and the Union, their frequent modifications, the new numbering of their articles and the technocratic language of their texts are daunting and hardly likely to mobilise the public opinion in favour of European integration [see sections 10.1. and 10.4.]. A greater transparency is expected to be achieved with the constitutional Treaty, which, at least, brings the two Treaties into one. **This book follows the numbering of the articles of the TEU and the TEC** adopted in Nice and actually in force, except when referring to past legislation based on previous versions of the Treaties.

2.5. Towards a European Constitution

The Treaty of Nice was conceived by the governments of the Fifteen as a transitory Treaty, allowing the European Community/Union (EC/EU) to function temporarily after the accession of ten new members. They did not want through this provisional Treaty to allow the EC/EU to progress beyond its current state of development. Wanting, however,

---

[1] OJ C 325, 24.12.2002.

to push ahead the process of integration by a substantial reform of the institutional framework of the enlarged Union, the European Council of Nice convened a new inter-governmental Conference (IGC) to propose a new and broader amendment of the Trea-ties. To ensure a good preparation of the upcoming IGC, the European Council of Laeken (14-15 December 2001) decided to convene a Convention on the future of Europe, with the former President of the French Republic, Mr. Giscard d'Estaing as chairman. The Convention brought together representatives of the governments and na-tional parliaments of the Member States as well as representatives of all the European institutions. It is the Convention which decided to call the treaty that it prepared "Treaty establishing a Constitution for Europe". The result of the deliberations of the Convention was presented by its president to the European Council of Thessaloniki (19-20 June 2003) which welcomed the draft constitutional treaty and decided that it was a good starting base for the IGC.

The IGC, which began its work in Rome on October 2003 with the participation of representatives of twenty-five States, broadly took the proposals of the Convention on board and presented the draft of the Constitutional Treaty to the European Council, which adopted it with minor changes on 18 June 2004. The twenty-five heads of state or government of the enlarged Union **signed the new Treaty on 29 October 2004**, in Rome (venue chosen in commemoration of the original Treaty establishing the EEC)[1]. The new Treaty made provision to come into force two years after its signature, antici-pating its ratification by the twenty-five Member States during this time. However, the referendum announced by the British Prime Minister in April 2004 made this coming into force more than doubtful, since all the opinion polls predicted a vast majority for the "no" of the British people. Thus, the negative referendums in France and in the Nether-lands, in 29 May 29 and 1 June 2005, simply confirmed the announced death of the Con-stitutional Treaty. This death cannot certainly rejoice the europhiles, since it prolongs the transitional period of operation of the EC/EU with a treaty that the European Council of Nice, which adopted it, recognized as not being able to satisfy the needs of a Union with twenty-seven members. But, it should not, either, discourage them. It must, on the con-trary, indicate the way to be followed to achieve a viable Constitution, adaptable to the ever-changing internal and external circumstances in which the process of European integration must function [see the European perspectives in the Conclusions].

If it ever came into force, the Constitutional Treaty **would simplify the European construction**. The existing Treaties on the European Union, the European Community and the European Atomic Energy Community would be repealed, thus eliminating the confusion between the Community and the Union. The Union would have a single legal personality under which it would negotiate, sign and implement all its external commit-ments, policies and activities, including trade, aid to development, representation in third countries and in international organisations and foreign and security policy. Both from the interior (its citizens) and from the exterior (third countries) the Union would, thus, be seen as a strong organism rather than as two Siamese frail and precarious (the one named Community and the other Union).

The draft Constitution determines **the symbols which personify the Union**: the flag (a circle of twelve golden stars on a blue background); the anthem (based on the "Ode to Joy" from the Ninth Symphony by Ludwig van Beethoven); the motto ("United in diversity"); the currency (the euro); the Europe day (9 May). Although these emblems of European unification were adopted more or less informally in the past, their consecra-tion in the Constitutional Treaty symbolises the determination of the peoples of Europe

---

[1] OJ C 310, 16.12.2004.

"to transcend their former divisions and, united ever more closely, to forge a common destiny" (Preamble of the Constitution).

Other **important innovations** of this draft Treaty are the attribution of constitutional weight to the Charter for Fundamental Rights, the solemn acknowledgement of the Union's values and objectives, the definition of the conditions for membership of the Union (including conditions for voluntary withdrawal from the Union) and a clearer presentation of the principles determining the distribution of competences between the Union and its constituent parts. The draft Constitution jointly vests the Parliament and the Council of Ministers with legislative and budgetary functions (Art. I-23) [see section 3.3]. Hence, the Parliament would become co-legislator in almost all cases (95% of the legislative areas), with the exception of a dozen areas, where it will only be consulted [see section 4.1.3.]. The codecision procedure would be extended and renamed "ordinary legislative procedure" (Art. I-34) [see section 4.3]. The "European laws" would replace the actual legal instruments of the Union [see section 3.3.], thus simplifying the legal system of the Union and facilitating its understanding by the citizens. The Constitution would establish a permanent President of the European Council, who would take on the work currently assigned to rotating Presidencies [see section 4.1.1.].

The draft Constitution does not extend the Union's competences considerably. The content of most provisions that govern **the Union's policies** would thus remain unchanged, which means that they would continue to develop with the "Community method", which should in the future be called the integration method [see section 1.1.1]. This method, implying qualified majority voting, would be applied also in the field of Justice and Home Affairs, in order to facilitate and improve the establishment of the area of freedom, security and justice.

The integration method would not be extended to the **common foreign and security policy (CFSP)**. The distinction between the CFSP and the other aspects of EU external action of the Union is maintained by the draft Constitution and determines the respective roles of the institutions and the decision-making procedures that they apply. Nevertheless, the creation of the post of Union Minister for Foreign Affairs, who would be a member of the Commission responsible for the representation of the Union on the international scene, would merge the present tasks of the High Representative for the Common Foreign and Security Policy with those of the Commissioner for external relations. Although a member of the Commission and as such in charge of the Commission's responsibilities in the field of external relations, this "European Minister of Foreign Affairs" would chair the External Relations Council and coordinate the other aspects of the Union's external action [see section 4.1.2]. This function could considerably strengthen the Union's role in world affairs, in all areas (foreign policy, security and defence policies, commercial and aid to development policies) [see section 8.2. and Part VI]. Moreover, the enhanced possibilities of Member States to cooperate more closely in the field of defence would underpin the credibility of the Union's foreign policy.

2.6. The treaties as instruments of progress

Few citizens realise that the Nice Treaty, which is in force since the 1st February 2003, is in fact composed of two separate Treaties: the Treaty on the European Union and the Treaty instituting the European Community. Even fewer citizens realise that there is a fundamental difference between the two Treaties. The differentiation originates in the Maastricht Treaty. In this Treaty and in its Amsterdam and Nice amendments, the

EC Treaty was based on the tested "Community method" [see section 4.3.], which had instituted and managed the common policies of the common market. The new policies of the EU were to be governed by a method akin to intergovernmental cooperation, in order to persuade eurosceptic nations to advance towards the stage of political integration without conceding bits of national sovereignty [see section 1.1.2.]. The consequences of this differentiation are explained in the "European Perspectives" in the Conclusions of this book. The experience from the development of the European Community/Union to date indicates, however, that this differentiation is neither inevitable nor eternal.

The frequency and vigour of the amendments of the European treaties show that their authors, i.e. the governments of the Member States, do not consider them as sacred and unalterable, but they use them as perfectible instruments of the multinational integration process. Given that the problems of European states change continually under the pressure of internal and external factors, the common policies must develop regularly in order to face them successfully. This is the reason why the Treaties, which are the primary source of European law and hence the legal basis of common policies, have to be modified frequently. This should also be the case with a constitutional treaty. It should be easily adaptable to the changing internal and external circumstances of the Union.

However, the draft constitutional treaty provides that it must be ratified by all the High Contracting Parties in accordance with their respective constitutional requirements (Art. IV-447), which means that if only one of them does not ratify it, this treaty cannot come into effect. The worst is that the problem of the unanimous ratification, doubled by the difficulty of the referendums in certain countries, would be found in the possible amendments of the project of Constitution. Indeed, its Article IV-443 stipulates that "if, two years after the signature of the treaty amending this Treaty, four fifths of the Member States have ratified it and one or more Member States have encountered difficulties in proceeding with ratification, the matter shall be referred to the European Council". Any pressure coming from the European Council would, however, be ineffective if a government had encountered difficulties with the ratification because of a negative vote of its parliament or the negative results of a referendum and would thus be wedged in a question of principle of a constitutional nature. Consequently, if, against all expectations, the treaty establishing a Constitution for Europe was put into force just as it is, in particular with the clause of its amendment by unanimity, it would doubtless block the subsequent development of the process of the European unification. This great flaw of the current constitutional project must be avoided in the drafting of a viable Constitution [see the conclusions of this book].

Following the declaration by the European Council (16-17 June 2005) on the ratification of the Treaty establishing a Constitution for Europe, which called for a period of reflection in the light of the negative votes in France and the Netherlands on the Constitution, the Commission has presented a **Plan D** for Democracy, Dialogue and Debate[1]. It thus hopes to stimulate a wider debate at European and national levels, in collaboration with future presidencies and the institutions, promote the involvement of citizens and enter into a genuine dialogue on EU policies.

Bibliography on European Treaties

- BREDA Vito. "A European Constitution in a multinational Europe or a multilateral Constitution for Europe?" in European Law Journal 2006, v. 12, n. 3, May, p. 330-344.
- CHATELAIN Jacky. Pourquoi nous sommes européens : défense et illustration du projet de Constitution. Paris: L'Harmattan, 2005.

---

[1] COM (2005) 494, 13 October 20005.

- CLOSA Carlos (et al.). "Symposium: deliberative constitutional politics", *European Law Journal*, v. 11, n. 4, July 2005, p. 379-467.
- CONSTANTINESCO Vlad, GAUTIER Yves, MICHEL Valérie (sous la dir. De). *Le traité établissant une Constitution pour L'Europe: analyses & commentaries*. Strasbourg: Presses universitaires de Strasbourg, 2005.
- DASHWOOD Alan. "The EU Constitution - what will really change?" in Cambridge yearbook of European legal studies 2004-2005, v. 7, 2006, p. 33-56.
- DELOCHE-GAUDEZ Florence. *La Constitution européenne: Que faut-il savoir?* Paris: Presses de Sciences Po, 2005.
- DUTHEIL DE LA ROCHÈRE Jacqueline (et al.). "La Constitution européenne en débat", *Regards sur l'actualité*, n. 307, janvier 2005, p. 3-54.
- DYÈVRE Arthur. "The constitutionalisation of the European Union: discourse, present, future and facts", *European Law Review*, v. 30, n. 2, April 2005, p. 165-189.
- EUROPEAN COMMISSION. *The period of reflection and Plan D*. Luxembourg: EUR-OP*, 2006.
- EUROPEAN PARLIAMENT. *The European Parliament and... the European Constitution*. Luxembourg: EUR-OP*, 2005.
- GIBBS Nathan. "Examining the aesthetic dimensions of the Constitutional Treaty", *European Law Journal,* v. 11, n. 3, May 2005, p. 326-342.
- GOULARD Sylvie. "Union européenne: les racines de la crise. Les leçons de Tocqueville", *Politique internationale*, n. 109, automne 2005, p. 305-325.
- HAENEL Hubert (et al.). "Le Traité constitutionnel et la PESC", *Défense nationale,* année 61, n. 5, mai 2005, p. 9-59.
- JACQUÉ Jean-Paul (et al.). "Le Traité établissant une Constitution pour l'Europe", *Revue trimestrielle de droit européen*, v. 41, n. 2, avril-juin 2005, p. 225-588.
- JOERGES Christian. "La Constitution économique européenne en processus et en procès" in *Revue internationale de droit économique*, v. 20, n. 3, 2006, p. 245-284.
- KÖNIG Thomas, SLAPIN Jonathan B. "From unanimity to consensus : an analysis of the negotiations at the EU's Constitutional Convention" in World Politics 2006, v. 58, n. 3, April p. 413-445.
- LECHEVALIER Arnaud, WASSERMAN Gilbert. *La constitution européenne: dix clés pour comprendre*. Paris: La Découverte, 2005.
- NORMAN Peter. *The accidental Constitution: the making of Europe's constitutional treaty*. Brussels: EuroComment, 2005.
- OTT Andrea, INGLIS Kirstyn. *The constitution of Europe and an enlarging Union: unity in diversity?* Groningen : Europa Law, 2005.
- VIGNES Daniel (et al.). "Les occasions manquées pour l'intégration européenne du fait de la non-entrée en vigueur du traité établissant une constitution pour l'Europe Première partie, l'Union européenne, ses structures et son système juridique" in *Revue du marché commun et de l'Union européenne*, n. 498, mai 2006, p. 325-334.

*The publications of the Office for Official Publications of the European Communities (EUR-OP) exist usually in all official languages of the EU.

Chapter 3

EUROPEAN LAW AND FINANCES

In the previous chapter we explained that, under the generic name of the Treaty of Nice, two different Treaties - the Treaty on the European Union and the Treaty establishing the European Community - actually institute and govern two different organisations. In the first part of this chapter, we analyse these two organisations: the European Union and the European Community. We see when and how the European Union covers the European Community, when each of these organisations should be treated separately and when they should be joined together under the name of **European Community/Union (EC/EU)**.

3.1. European Community and European Union

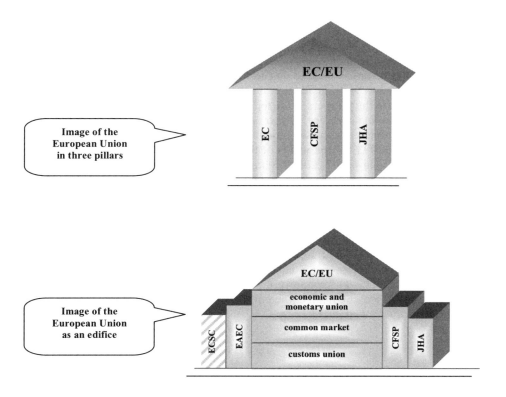

One often hears about **the three "pillars"** of the European Union, the first being the European Community (EC), the second the common foreign and security policy (CFSP) and the third justice and home affairs (JHA). We should say, however, that the image of the EU as three pillars minimises the place of the Community, which is pre-ponderant, since it contains all common policies instituted in the framework of the three original Treaties and all the legislation adopted on their bases since 1952.

The European Union is better visualised **as an on-going construction.** In this im-age, the European Community constitutes the main edifice, solid and functional, thanks to the existence within it of a great number of common policies, which are at various stages of development. Next to it, the CFSP and especially the JHA are still at the stage of foundations, built following the plans drafted under the Treaty on the European Un-ion. Their edifices need to be patiently built with common legal acts. Moreover, the Treaty of Amsterdam has transferred into the Community edifice many subjects, which were originally under the JHA wing. In this wing, intergovernmental cooperation is presently confined to police and judicial cooperation in criminal matters [see section 8.1.2.]. It would be absurd to represent this cooperation as a pillar of the European con-struction.

A closer look at the metaphorical image of the European construction shows that **the main edifice, that of the Community**, is divided horizontally in floors. The floor of the common market is built on the foundations of the customs union. Apart from the four fundamental freedoms (free movement of goods, persons, services and capital), the common market floor consists of numerous horizontal and vertical compartments, which contain the common policies that constitute the bulk of this book. The compartments of coal, steel and nuclear energy, built with the Community method provided by the ECSC and Euratom Treaties, are also found on these first floors of the Community edifice.

The floor of **economic and monetary union (EMU)** was built above the floor of the common market and, therefore, inside the Community edifice [see chapter 7]. The Treaty on European Community has drawn the architectural plans and the "memoran-dum of understanding" that the builders (European institutions and Member States) need to respect in order to succeed in the construction of the EMU. Some of the contractors (Member States), who have advanced faster than others, find themselves already in the "penthouse" of the Community edifice, which shelters the single currency, and have started setting up common policies inside it. The others, including the new Member States will continue to work inside the lower floors, until the time that they are ready and/or willing to join the pioneers in the top floor of the collective edifice.

Apart from the main edifice, which, as we see, is subject to continuous improve-ment, building also started with the putting into effect of the Treaty of Maastricht (TEU), as of November 1, 1993, on **the wings of the CFSP and the JHA** [see chapter 8]. The architects are the same - the heads of States or Governments meeting within the Euro-pean Council. The principal craftsmen are also the same - the Council, the Commission and the European Parliament. The working methods for building these new wings, namely the decision-making process, differed at the outset from those used to build the main edifice, since they were closer to intergovernmental cooperation rather than to the Community decision-making process [see sections 3.3. and 8.2.1.]. The Treaty of Am-sterdam, however, has brought inside the Community edifice the larger part of the JHA wing [see section 8.1.]. Hence, fundamentally only the wing of the CFSP is being built with the very slow method of intergovernmental cooperation. In any case, the new wings under construction, like the main edifice of the Community, find themselves **under the roof of the European Union**.

The "European Community" exists thus and grows under the roof of the "European Union". This is also true for the other two Communities, that of coal and steel and that of atomic energy, which are often mixed with the European Community and indistinctly called "the Community". It is correct to speak about the "**Community**" in respect of everything that happened and that was built up until the 1st November 1993, when the "European Union" came into being. It is even correct to speak about the "Community" for measures taken after that date by following the Community procedure on the basis of the EC Treaty (but also the ECSC and EAEC Treaties). The term "**European Union**" should, however, be used for all measures that concern the new edifices of the construction and, in general, for designating the organisation of European countries, which have decided to create an ever closer union among their peoples, covering relations much broader than the economic relations governed by the original Community. It must be noted, in this context, that the European Community has an international legal personality, which includes the capacity to conclude agreements, whereas the Union does not have such a personality, a defect that the Constitutional Treaty intended to correct.

3.2. The competences of the European Community/Union

When the member states of a multinational integration scheme adopt a fundamental or secondary common policy, they implicitly recognise that it has an added value in relation to their previously independent national policies in a certain field. The very existence of a common policy is due to the fact that it has the potential of better achieving the goals of the member states than the individual national policies pursued in disarray. In other words, common policies exist because the member states appreciate their advantages. The main drawback compared with the expected benefits of the common policies developed by multinational integration is a certain loss of national sovereignty, due to the commitments accepted by the member states. Certainly, the states which opt for the integration process lose some of their independence in terms of goals and means of their national policies, since segments of their national sovereignties are blended into a new concept of "**shared sovereignty**" that is intended to serve better their various national interests. But, this loss of independence is circumscribed by two means: the continuing influence of the member states in the development of the common policies after their inception, through the common institutions in which they participate [see chapter 4]; and the possibility left to the member states to choose the means that suit them best to attain the common goals of the common policies, by virtue of the principles of subsidiarity and proportionality explained below.

The **principle of subsidiarity** means that the Community must not undertake or regulate what can be managed or regulated more efficiently at national or regional levels. This principle, implying multi-level governance [see section 1.1.1.] must be exercised in a spirit of cooperation between the various levels of power. According to the Treaties (Art. 5 TEC and Art. 2 TEU), the European Community/Union must act within the limits of the powers conferred upon it by the Treaties and of the objectives assigned to it therein. In areas which do not fall within its exclusive competence, the Community must take action, in accordance with the principle of subsidiarity, only if and in so far as the objectives of the proposed action cannot be sufficiently achieved by the Member States and can therefore, by reason of the scale or effects of the proposed action, be better achieved by the Community. Any action by the Community must not exceed that which is necessary to achieve the objectives of the Treaties. Article 308 of the EC Treaty enables the Council, by unanimity and after consulting the European Parliament, to introduce the provisions needed to attain a common objective, but does not make it possible to create new powers for the Community. An interinstitutional agreement sets out the procedures for implementing the principle of subsidiarity[1] [see details below].

The **principle of proportionality** implies that, if a Community action proves to be necessary to attain the objectives of the Treaty, the Community institutions must further examine whether legislative action is required or whether other sufficiently effective means can be used (financial support, encouragement of cooperation between Member States by a Recommendation, inducement to take action by a Resolution, etc.) [see details below].

In many areas where common policies have not been agreed, the "**open method of coordination**", established by the Lisbon European Council (23 and 24 March 2000), is used as non-binding means of spreading best practice and achieving greater convergence of national policies. This method involves setting common objectives, translating these objectives into national policy strategies and periodic monitoring on the basis, inter alia, of commonly agreed and defined indicators. The intergovernmental cooperation achieved through this method does not obligate the Member States to follow the objectives set in common, but may through the learning process lead to real common policies.

The **draft Constitutional Treaty** does not depart from current practice on the question of transfer of sovereign rights from the Member States to the Union, but it defines in detail the principles which govern this transfer and guarantees that these principles should not be infringed. According to the Constitution, these principles are: the principle of conferral, under which the Union shall act within the limits of the competences conferred upon it by the Member States in the Constitution (Art. I-11); the clear distinction of the Union's competences into areas of exclusive competence, of shared competence and of support of national policies (Art. I-13 to I-17); and the exercise of these competences in accordance with the principles of subsidiarity and proportionality under the control of national parliaments [see details below].

The powers assigned to the Community by the Treaties are supplementary to those of its Member States. The Community can act in an area only in so far as the competence has been conferred to it by the Member States (principle of conferral). Very few areas come under exclusive European competence. Accordingly, nearly all **common policies have a European dimension and a national dimension**. The appropriate decision-making level - national, European or both simultaneously - depends on the type of each policy measure under consideration. In the case of laws or decisions which must apply uniformly in all Member States, there is little room for national initiative. On the contrary, when the Treaty provides for non-binding coordination of national policies, the scale of European action leaves a wide margin of manoeuvre to the national authorities. As a common policy develops, the European dimension increases at the expense of the national dimension. The Member States accept the decrease of their powers to the extent that their interests are better served by common action than by national action.

The Commission **applies the principles of subsidiarity and proportionality** both to direct its initiatives and to evaluate the need for Community legislation, both future and existing. It conducts wide-ranging consultations and presents whenever necessary reference documents (Green Papers) prior to proposing legislative texts. In the explanatory memorandum accompanying its proposals, the Commission includes a "subsidiarity recital" summarising the objectives of the proposed measure, its effectiveness and why it is necessary. The Council verifies that a proposal of the Commission is in accordance with the provisions of Article 5 (TEC), on the basis of the preamble and the explanatory memorandum of the proposal. The Court of Justice has consistently held that the choice of the legal basis of a Community measure must be based on objective factors, which are amenable to judicial review. Among those factors are included in particular **the purpose and content of the measure**[2]. Difficulties arise if the measure in question pursues several aims for which different

---

[1]   Interinstitutional agreement, OJ C 329, 06.12.1993.
[2]   See Case C-295/90, Parliament v Council, ECR 1992, I-4193.

legal bases can be selected. According to the Court, in that case, the principal aim of the measure should determine the choice of the legal basis[1].

To comply with the principle of proportionality, Community action must be as simple as possible, consistent with satisfactory achievement of its objectives. The Community must therefore legislate only to the extent necessary and give preference to directives rather than regulations and to framework directives rather than detailed measures [see section 3.3.]. Moreover, Community measures must leave as much scope for national decision as possible; and respect well established national arrangements and the working of Member States legal systems. The important thing is to ensure that Community legislation does not impose on national, regional or local authorities or on civil society any constraints which are illogical, superfluous or excessive given the objective.

Under the **principle of conferral**, specified in the draft Constitutional Treaty, the Union shall act within the limits of the competences conferred upon it by the Member States in the Constitution, all other competences remaining with the Member States (Art. I-11). The flexibility of this principle is guaranteed by a clause allowing the Council, by unanimous vote and with the approval of the Parliament, to adopt measures necessary to attain any of the objectives laid down by the Constitution where there is no provision for powers of action to that effect in the Constitution (Art. I-18). This is to say that the Member States - and they alone - may confer to the Union parts of their sovereign powers, if and when they consider that their interests are better served by common action.

The draft Constitution distinguishes between **three categories of Union competences**: exclusive, shared and supportive or coordinating. The areas of exclusive competence of the Union are: customs union and the common commercial policy, competition rules for the functioning of the internal market, monetary policy for the Member States whose currency is the euro and the conservation of marine biological resources (Art. I-13). In those areas, only the Union may legislate and the Member States may implement the Union acts. In the areas of shared competence, which cover most of the common policies examined in this book, both the Union and the Member States may legislate, but the later may exercise their competence to the extent not covered by the Union competence (Art. I-14). The areas where the Union may take action in support or coordination of national policies are notably those of human health protection, industry, culture, tourism and education (Art. I-17). In two areas the Constitution provides specific competences of the Union, which do not fall under one of the three categories above: the coordination of the economic and employment policies of the Member States (Art. I-15); and the definition and implementation of a common foreign and security policy, including the progressive framing of a common defence policy (Art. I-16).

The draft Constitutional Treaty does not change substantially the **principles of subsidiarity and proportionality** (Art. I-11). However, it introduces a major innovation in this regard, requiring that the national parliaments be directly involved in monitoring the proper application of the subsidiarity principle. The Protocol on the application of the principles of subsidiarity and proportionality, annexed to the Constitution, stipulates that the Commission must simultaneously send all its draft legislative acts and its amended drafts to the Union legislator and to the national parliaments of the Member States. Any draft European legislative act must contain a detailed statement making it possible to appraise compliance with the principles of subsidiarity and proportionality. The reasons for concluding that a Union objective can be better achieved at Union level must be substantiated by qualitative and, wherever possible, quantitative indicators. If one third of the parliaments (or only a quarter if the proposal concerns the area of freedom, security and justice) feel that the draft European legislation does not comply with the principle of subsidiarity, the Commission or the institution from which the draft legislative act originates must review its proposal. If the European institutions adopt a measure in spite of the misgivings of some national parliaments, these have the right to bring actions before the Court of Justice, via their Member States, on the grounds of infringement of the principle of subsidiarity.

3.3. The Community legal system

Common policies, which are the essence of multinational integration, are based on **common legislation**. Inherent in the concept of a common policy [see section 1.1.2.] is its **binding force on the member states**. The latter must give the common institutions the legal means to implement common policies and to enforce their decisions on all the parties concerned and on their citizens. Hence, common policies are shaped by legal acts agreed by the common institutions, implemented by the member states and/or the common institutions and controlled by the common institutions [see chapter 4]. The national laws of the member states are harmonised in a great number of fields in the context of

---

[1] See Case C-155/91, Commission v Council, ECR 1993, I-963.

common policies. A special law, based on the treaties and called *acquis communautaire*, is thus built to bring into being common policies, a law that is superimposed and takes **precedence over national law**, even the constitutional law, of the Member States, whether national legislation predates or postdates Community legislation. In fact, according to the Court of Justice, the Member States have definitively transferred sovereign rights to the Community they created, and they cannot subsequently go back on that transfer through unilateral measures[1], unless they decide to break away from the EC/EU. If they do not opt for such a radical measure, they cannot contravene European legislation, to the making of which they have contributed, by invoking their national, even their constitutional law. This is another feature of the multinational integration process, which distinguishes it from intergovernmental cooperation, where decisions may have political consequences but do not carry a legal binding force on the participating states. A multinational integration process, such as that of the EC/EU, could not function, if each Member State could circumvent the common legislation by bringing into play its national - including its constitutional - law.

   The legal acts, which substantiate the common policies, may be undertaken by the competent institutions with legal effect only if they are empowered to do so by the European Treaties (principle of conferral or of attribution of powers). Article 249 of the EC Treaty provides for five forms of legal act, each with a different effect on the Member States' legal systems. Some are directly applicable in place of national legislation, while others permit the progressive adjustment of that legislation to Community provisions.

   The **regulation** has a general scope, is binding in all its elements and is directly applicable in each Member State. Just like a national law, it gives rise to rights and obligations directly applicable to the citizens of the European Union[2]. Regulations enter into force on a date which they lay down or, where they do not set a date, on the twentieth day following their publication in the Official Journal of the European Union. The regulation substitutes European law for national law and is therefore the most effective legal instrument provided for by the EC Treaty. As "European laws", regulations must be complied with fully by those to whom they are addressed (individuals, Member States, European institutions).

   The **directive** binds any Member State to which it is addressed with regard to the result to be achieved, while allowing the national authorities competency as to the form and methods used. It is a sort of Community framework law and lends itself particularly well to the harmonisation of national laws. It defines the objective or objectives to be attained by a common policy and leaves it to the Member States to choose the forms and instruments necessary for complying with it. Since the Member States are only bound by the objectives laid down in directives, they have some discretion, in transposing them into national law, in taking into account of special national circumstances. They must, however, "ensure fulfilment of the obligations arising out of the Treaty or resulting from action taken by the institutions of the Community" (Art. 10 TEC). Although they are generally published in the Official Journal, Directives take effect by virtue of being notified to the Member States to which they are addressed. The latter are obliged to adopt the national measures necessary for implementation of the Directive within time-limits set by it, failing which they are infringing Community legislation.

   The **decision** is binding on the addressees it indicates, who may be one, several, or even all the Member States or one or more natural or legal persons. This variety of po-

---

[1] Judgment of 15 July 1964, case 6/64, Costa/ENEL, ECR 1964, p. 1160.
[2] See on this subject, notably, the judgments of the Court of Justice of 14.12.1971, case 43/71, Politi, ECR 1971, p. 1049 and of 7.2.1973, case 39/72, Commission v Italy, ECR 1973, pp. 114-115.

tential addressees is coupled with a variety in the scope of its contents, which may extend from a quasi regulation or a quasi directive to a specific administrative decision. It takes effect on its communication to the addressees rather than on its publication in the Official Journal. In any case, according to the Court of Justice, a decision can produce direct effects creating for the individuals rights that national jurisdictions must safeguard[1].

The above legal acts are normally used, on the basis of the Treaty and following the Community method [see section 4.3.], for harmonising or approximating national legislations. Their effects are binding on the Member States, the Community institutions and, in many cases, the citizens of the Member States. This is the case of laws or decisions which must apply uniformly in all Member States. However, the objectives of the common policies are also sought by **non-binding concerted action**, taking the form of coordination of national policies, mechanisms for exchanging information, bodies for cooperation, Community programmes and/or financial support.

Therefore, in addition to the above binding acts, which form the Community law, the Council and the Commission can adopt **Recommendations** suggesting a certain line of conduct or outlining the goals of a common policy and **opinions** assessing a current situation or certain facts in the Community or the Member States. Furthermore, the Council and the European Parliament adopt **Resolutions**, which are also not binding, suggesting a political desire to act in a given area. These instruments enable the Community institutions to suggest guidelines for coordination of national legislations or administrative practices in a non-binding manner, i.e. without any legal obligations for the addressees - Member States and/or citizens.

While Resolutions and opinions are published in the "C" series (communications) of the **Official Journal of the European Union (OJ)**, binding acts and recommendations are published in the "L" series (legislation) of the OJ, in order to stress their political importance. The same is true for the **common positions** and **joint actions** of the common foreign and security policy and of justice and home affairs (Art. 12 and 31 of TEU) [see sections 8.1. and 8.2.1.]. They are published in the L series of the OJ, although they do not have a legal binding force on the Member States, since the Court of Justice of the European Communities (CJEC) does not have jurisdiction on their interpretation and implementation. They embody, however, political commitments for joint behaviour and/or action.

The draft **Constitutional Treaty** renames and simplifies the legal instruments of the Union. If it came into force, the institutions would adopt European laws, European framework laws, European regulations, European decisions, recommendations and opinions (Art. I-33). A **European law** would be a legislative act of general application, binding in its entirety and directly applicable in all Member States (like the current regulation). A **European framework law** would be a legislative act binding, as to the result to be achieved, but will leave to the national authorities the choice of form and methods (like the present directive). The European laws and framework laws would be adopted by the European Parliament and the Council in accordance with the ordinary legislative procedure (Art. I-34) [see section 4.3.]. A **European regulation** would be a non-legislative act of general application for the implementation of legislative acts and would have the binding force and applicability of the main act. A **European decision** will be a non-legislative act, either binding in its entirety or binding only those to whom it is addressed. The European Council would adopt decisions, the Council, the Commission and

---

[1] Judgment of 6 October 1970, case 9/70, Grad, ECR 1970, p. 838 and judgment of 12 December 1990, joined cases 100/89 and 101/89, ECR 1990, p. I-4647.

the European Central Bank would adopt regulations and decisions (Art. I-35). **Recommendations** - usually adopted by the Council and in specific cases by the Commission or the European Central Bank - and **opinions** - usually adopted by the advisory Committees - would have no binding force.

The status of the Community law is a unique one, in that its application depends, by and large, on the separate jurisdictions of the Member States. The Community does not seek a total legal harmonisation, which would eliminate the distinctive features of national jurisdictions. However, both the European institutions and the Member States have a duty to ensure that Community law is respected and to take the necessary steps when it is violated. This is a fundamental requirement of any legal system. The European Court of Justice has observed that domestic laws must be reconcilable with the need to apply Community law uniformly so as to avoid unequal treatment of economic operators[1]. The authorities of Member States, including the courts, must ensure compliance with the principle of uniform interpretation of directives, in the light of their wording and purpose[2]. In case of conflict of laws, the national judge must, according to the European Court, not apply any contrary clauses of the national law, whether these are prior or subsequent to Community law[3].

One characteristic common to the Treaties establishing the European Communities is that they are not conventional international treaties which create rights and obligations for the States alone. These Treaties and the **legislation derived from them** engender rights and obligations not only for the Member States but also for their nationals [see section 9.2.]. This **"direct effect"** of Community law means notably that any person may ask his judge to apply the Community law which contradicts the national law[4]. Citizens may thus invoke Community law before national courts and, if necessary, before the Court of Justice of the European Communities [see section 9.3.]. According to the Court, a Member State is obliged to make good damage caused to individuals, even where the national legislature is responsible for a breach of Community law[5]. An individual can apply for the annulment of a decision, a regulation or a directive of a general legislative nature, if he can prove that he is directly and individually affected by its provisions[6]. By virtue of the "Francovich" jurisdiction of the Court, in certain circumstances Community law requires the Member States to compensate for damage sustained by individuals by reason of their failure to transpose a directive into national law where its purpose is to confer rights on them[7]. In the absence of measures transposing a directive within the prescribed period, the directive cannot on its own impose duties on an individual and cannot therefore be relied on in proceedings against him or her (absence of "horizontal" direct effect)[8]. Although a directive cannot of itself impose obligations on an individual, the national court is bound, when applying the provisions of national law enacted for the purpose of transposing obligations laid down by a directive, to consider them, so far as possible, in the light of the wording and purpose of the directive in order to achieve an outcome consistent with the objective pursued by the directive[9].

Community law evolves extremely rapidly. As demonstrated in the footnotes of this book, several hundreds of Community acts are adopted and amended each year. The scope of those acts obviously varies from case to case. Some have a very specific scope or a scope limited in time. Very many regulations, notably in the area of the common agricultural policy, merely implement basic regulations. It is obviously these last regulations, the directives and decisions that form the common policies, which we shall examine in this book. As these acts have been amended several times since first adopted, we often refer in the footnotes, in addition to the Official Journal containing the basic instrument, to the OJ containing the most recent or the most important amendment thereto.

An interinstitutional agreement established an accelerated procedure for the consolidation of Community legislation[10]. The Commission is taking steps to simplify the '*acquis communautaire*', that is, the existing stock of legislation, thus ensuring that all its legislative proposals are consistent with the political priorities of the Community and, where necessary, reviewing the approach followed and identifying the appropriate measures to be taken, such as modification, replacement or withdrawal of pending proposals[11]. In order to secure a reli-

[1] Judgment given on 21 September 1983 on Joined Cases 205/82 to 215/82, Deutsche Milchkontor, ECR 1983, p. 2633.
[2] Judgment of 22 May 2003, Case C-462/99, ECR 2003, p. I-05197.
[3] Judgment of 9 March 1978, case 92/78, Simmenthal v Commission, ECR 1979, p. 777.
[4] Judgment of 5 February 1962, case 26/62, Van Gend & Loos, ECR 1963, p.1.
[5] Judgments of: 5 March 1996, Joined Cases C-46/93 and C-48/93; 23 May 1996, Case C-5/94; and 8 October 1996, Joined Cases C-178/94, C-179/94 et al., ECR 1996.
[6] Judgment of 17 June 1998, Case T-135/96.
[7] Judgment, 19 November 1991, joined Cases C-6/90 and C-9/90, Francovich and Bonifaci, ECR 1991, p. I-5357.
[8] Judgment, 26 February 1986, Case 152/84 Marshall, ECR 1986, p. 723 and Judgment, 14 July 1994, Case C-91/92, Faccini Dori v Recreb, ECR 1994, p. I-3325.
[9] Judgment of 5 October 2004, Joined Cases C-397/01 to C-403/01 *Pfeiffer and others* v *Deutsches Rotes Kreuz*, ECR 2004 p. I-8835.
[10] Interinstitutional agreement, OJ C 102, 04.04.1996.
[11] COM (2005) 462, 27 September 2005.

able, up-to-date and user-friendly body of EU law for the benefit of citizens and businesses, there is a need for repealing obsolete legal texts and rewriting others to make them more coherent and understandable. The **accessibility of Community legislation** could certainly be facilitated, if any amending act incorporated and presented in a single text the original act and all its subsequent amendments.

3.4. The Community finances

The conventional international organisations such as the UN or the OECD are financed by contributions from their member countries. In most instances their financial requirements amount to staff and operational expenditure. If they are entrusted with operational tasks, their financing is generally provided on an "à la carte" basis by those member countries which agreed on those tasks. It is virtually never a question, in such organisations, of financial transfers or even of financial compensation. The European Community, on the other hand, although it is not a federation in the formal sense, pursues many federating common policies, which call for a transfer of resources from the national to the supranational level.

Some common policies of the European Community/Union are clearly in the interest of the stronger and wealthier Member States. This is the case notably of the internal market, competition and taxation policies, because they open the markets of the poorer and less developed Member States to their products and services. Therefore, some other policies are needed to **balance the benefits of the integration process**, by operating capital transfers in favour of the poorer Member States: e.g. agricultural, regional and social policies. These transfers of capital are also in the interest of the wealthier Member States, since they allow their poorer partners to buy more of their products and services. This balance of the benefits of the Member States, which distinguishes, inter alia, a multinational integration scheme from a free trade area one, is organised by the Community budget.

The implementation of many common policies requires, indeed, not only legal but also some financial means. Certainly, not all common policies need common financing. For example, competition and taxation policies are based almost exclusively on legal measures. But the implementation of most common policies is based on a mixture of legal and financial measures. Common regional, education, aid to development policies, e.g., would be seriously restrained without Community financing of their common programmes. There could be no common agricultural or fisheries policies, in the sense that we know them, without common support of prices and/or incomes [see sections 21.4.2, 21.4.3 and 22.3.]. It is a political value judgment whether there should be more or less common financing of this or that common policy and this judgment is subject to a long debate carried out every year among the budgetary authorities of the Community - i.e. politicians from the Member States sitting in the Council and the European Parliament - on the basis of technical reports and proposals provided by the Commission. The result of this multinational political debate is recorded in the **Community budget**.

In the beginning of the European Economic Community, the contribution of the Member States to the Community budget was determined on a scale according to GNP shares or other criteria. Provision had been made in the EEC Treaty for replacing the Member States' initial contributions by **own resources** after establishment of the Common Customs Tariff (CCT) [see section 5.2.1.]. The transfer of customs revenue to the Community budget was a spillover effect [see section 1.1.1.] of the realisation, provided for in the Treaty, of a genuine customs union[1]. In such a union the country of import of

---

[1] Decision 70/243, OJ L 94, 28.04.1970.

goods from a third country is not always the country of final destination of those goods. The revenue from customs duties is therefore often collected in a country other than the country of destination or of consumption. Only the payment of that revenue to the Community, makes it possible to neutralise that effect. This is, moreover, an important integrating element, which again differentiates a customs union from a free trade area [see the introduction to part II].

However, since the realisation of the customs union in 1968, the importance of customs duties was continually diminishing inasmuch as they were being progressively abolished or reduced under the General Agreement on Tariffs and Trade (GATT) and the various tariff concessions granted to the least developed countries [see section 23.4. and chapter 24]. For that reason it was decided, in 1970, to use a proportion of the **value added tax (VAT)** as an additional source of Community financing. That tax, which has a uniform basis of assessment takes fairly accurate account of the economic capacity of the citizens of the Member States, as it is levied at the consumption level [see section 14.2.1.]. The "**uniform base**", which was adopted for calculating the proportions of the VAT yield which countries must pay to the EU, is made up of all taxable supplies of goods and provisions of services in the Union[1].

Since 2001, the system of the European Communities' own resources is based on the following elements[2]:

- the **maximum ceiling** on own resources is fixed at 1.27 % of gross national income (GNI) of the EC/EU;
- **traditional own resources** - essentially customs and agricultural duties - minus 25% retained by the Member States as collection costs;
- 0.5% of the maximum call-in rate from **VAT resources**, aiming at correcting the regressive aspects of the system for the least prosperous Member States;
- **technical adjustments** aiming at the correction of budgetary imbalances in favour of the United Kingdom and originating in the famous battle cry of Margaret Thatcher of 30 November 1979: "I want my money back" [see details below].

However, **Community expenditures** still represent little more than one percent of the cumulative Gross Internal Product of the 25 Member States. More than 90% of the receipts of the European Union are redistributed to the Member States and serve to finance the objectives of the various common policies (redistributive function of the Community budget). Thus, out of a total of EUR 106.3 billion in appropriations for commitments of the 2005 budget, EUR 49.7 billion (46.8%) were allocated to the common agricultural policy, EUR 32.4 billion (30.5%) to structural measures including the Cohesion Fund, EUR 7.9 billion (7.4%) to other internal policies, EUR 5.2 billion (4.9%) to external action of the Union, EUR 6.3 billion (5.9%) to administrative expenditure and the remaining amount to reserves including guarantees[3].

The **management of the Community budget** is entrusted to the Commission (Art. 274 TEC) and is exercised according to a Financial Regulation, which sets the principles and ground rules governing the establishment and implementation of the budget and financial control, ensuring more efficient and effective management and control of European taxpayers' money[4]. Article 280 of the EC Treaty stipulates that the Member States must coordinate their action aimed at protecting the financial interests of the

---

[1] Decision 88/376, OJ L 185, 15.07.1988.
[2] Decision 94/728, OJ L 293, 12.11.1994 and Decision 2000/597, OJ L 253, 07.10.2000, Regulation 1150/2000, OJ L 130, 31.05.2000 and Regulation 2028/2004, OJ L 352, 27.11.2004.
[3] 2005 general budget, OJ L 60, 08.03.2005.
[4] Regulation 1605/2002, OJ L 248, 16.09.2002 and Regulation 2342/2002, OJ L 357, 31.12.2002 last amended by Regulation 1261/2005, OJ L 201, 02.08.2005.

Community against fraud and must take the same measures to counter fraud affecting the financial interests of the Community as they take to counter fraud affecting their own financial interests[1] [see details below].

It is interesting to note that the guarantee of the Community budget covers lenders when the Community floats an issue under one of its financial instruments, such as the balance of payments facility or the financial assistance for certain non-member countries. A **Guarantee Fund for external actions** is designated to reimburse the Community's creditors in the event of default by the recipient of a loan given or guaranteed by the Community in a non-member country[2].

In a report entitled "Financing the European Union - Report on the operation of the own resources system", the Commission concludes that the correction granted to the United Kingdom should be replaced by a "generalised correction mechanism"[3]. It also proposes the introduction of a new system for financing the European Union centred around a main fiscal resource based on the taxation of energy consumption, value added tax (VAT) or corporate income tax by 2014. At the Brussels European Council meeting (15-16 December 2005), the United Kingdom accepted a reduction of the increase in the rebate, from which it has benefited since 1984, to EUR 10.5 billion during the period 2007-13, decoupling the rebate from all enlargement expenditure until 2013.

Like other public funds, the European Union budget runs the risk of having fraudsters enrich themselves at its expense or embezzle the levies which normally should be transferred to the Union. Therefore, the management of **the Community budget is subject to several controls**. As far as anti-fraud is concerned, the Commission has developed an effective information system based on the IRENE database, which stores the cases of fraud and irregularities reported by national authorities in any budgetary area. It has established an anti-fraud strategy and an annual work programme in this field[4]. The Commission has also set up an Advisory Committee for the coordination of fraud prevention, which provides a forum in which the most important cases of fraud can be tracked and horizontal matters relating to prevention and prosecution can be discussed[5] and the European anti-Fraud Office (OLAF)[6], a body independent of the Commission whose members are appointed by decision of the Parliament, the Council and the Commission[7], in order to conduct investigations concerning the Community's financial interests[8]. The Hercule programme promotes activities in the field of the protection of the Communities' financial interests, notably training, technical assistance, development and distribution of know-how and data exchange projects[9]. Finally and most importantly, the Commission adopted Regulations concerning irregularities and the recovery of sums wrongly paid to the Member States in connection with the financing of the structural policies[10], the Cohesion Fund[11] and the common agricultural policy[12]. A Council Regulation lays down general arrangements on inspections carried out by Commission staff in the Member States, providing a legal basis for conducting inspections and on-the-spot checks as part of anti-fraud operations[13].

However, the anti-fraud strategy necessitates an active **cooperation between national and Community administrations**. Indeed, as national customs officers are in reality Community customs officers, since they collect customs revenue on behalf of the Community, so national anti-fraud officers should also be agents of the management of the Community budget. On the basis of this Treaty stipulation, the Regulation on the protection of the Communities' financial interests seeks to protect taxpayers' money more effectively by introducing a common legal framework to combat the waste and misuse of Community resources[14]. It applies to irregularities involving budget expenditure or revenue in all areas covered by common policies and establishes appropriate administrative penalties to be applied uniformly in all Member States in accordance with the same principles and methods. To amplify the Regulation, a **Convention on the protection of the Community's financial interests** drawn up on the basis of Title VI of the TEU requires Member States to establish a specific criminal offence of "fraud against the Community's financial interests" and provides for convergence in respect of penalties[15].

---

[1]   COM (2000) 358, 28 June 2000.
[2]   Regulation 2728/94, OJ L 293, 12.11.1994 and Regulation 2273/2004, OJ L 396, 31.12.2004.
[3]   COM (2004) 505, 14 July 2004.
[4]   COM (94) 92 and COM (95) 23.
[5]   Decision 94/140, OJ L 61, 04.03.1994 and Decision 2005/223, OJ L 71, 17.03.2005.
[6]   Decision 1999/352, OJ L 136, 31.05.1999.
[7]   Decision 1999/352, OJ L 136, 31.05.1999.
[8]   Regulations 1073/1999 and 1074/1999, OJ L 136, 21.05.1999.
[9]   Decision 804/2004, OJ L 143, 30.04.2004.
[10]   Regulation 1681/94, OJ L 178, 12.07.1994 and Regulation 2035/2005, OJ L 328, 15.12.2005.
[11]   Regulation 1831/94, OJ L 191, 27.02.1994 and Regulation 2168/2005, OJ L 345, 28.12.2005.
[12]   Regulation 595/91, OJ L 67, 14.03.1991 and Regulation 1290/2005, OJ L 209, 11.08.2005.
[13]   Regulation 2185/96, OJ L 292, 15.11.1996.
[14]   Regulation 2988/95, OJ L 312, 23.12.1995.
[15]   OJ C 316, 27.11.1995.

Bibliography on European law and finances

- ACKRILL Robert, KAY Adrian. "Historical-institutionalist perspectives on the development of the EU budget system" in *Journal of European Public Policy*, v. 13, n. 1, January 2006, p. 113-133.
- BRAULT Philippe, RENAUDINEAU Guillaume, SICARD François. *Le principe de subsidiarité*. Paris: Documentation française, 2005.
- CAFAGGI Fabrizio (ed.). *The institutional framework of European private law*. European University Institute (EUI) (Florence). Academy of European Law. Oxford: Oxford University Press, 2006.
- CARRUBBA Cliford, MURRAH Lacey. "Legal integration and use of the preliminary ruling process in the European Union", *International Organisation*, v. 59, n. 2, Spring 2005, p. 399-418.
- CHALMERS Damia (et al.). *European Union law: Text and materials*. Cambridge: Cambridge University Press, 2006.
- CURTIS Jan, KLIP André, McCAHERY Joseph. *European integration and Law: four contributions on the interplay between European integration and European and national law to celebrate the 25th Anniversary of Maastricht University's Faculty of Law*. Antwerpen: Intersentia, 2006.
- CUTHBERT Mike. "The impact of 30 years of EU membership on UK law", *European Business Law Review*, v. 16, n. 3, 2005, p. 459-590.
- EUROPEAN COMMISSION. *Deterring fraud by informing the public: Round table on anti-fraud communication*, Luxembourg: EUR-OP*, 2005.
- FAIRHURST John. *Law of the European Union*. Harlow: Pearson/Longman, 2006.
- GARCIA CRESPO Milagros. (ed.). *Public expenditure control in Europe : coordinating audit functions in the European Union*. Cheltenham; Northampton, MA: Edward Elgar, 2005.
- GENEVOIS Bruno, DELPÉRÉE Francis. "Les rapports entre l'ordre juridique interne et l'ordre juridique européen", *Revue française de droit administratif*, 1e partie, v. 21, n. 1, janvier-février 2005, p. 1-68; 2e partie v. 21, n. 2, mars-avril 2005, p. 239-248; 3e partie v. 21, n. 3, mai-juin 2005, p. 465-482.
- HENKE Klaus-Dirk (et al.). "Subsidiarity in the European Union" in *Intereconomics*, v. 41, n. 5, September-October 2006, p. 240-257.
- KALLERMANN Alfred (et al.). *The impact of EU accession on the legal orders of new EU member states and (pre-) candidate countries: hopes and fears*. The Hague: TMC Asser, 2006.
- KERNOHAN David (et al.). *The EU budget process and international trade liberalisation*. Brussels: Centre for European Policy Studies, 2005.
- KOMAREK Jan (et al.). "European contract law: quo vadis?", *Common Market Law Review*, v. 42, n. 1, February 2005, p. 1-177.
- LE MIRE Pierre. *Droit de l'Union européenne et politiques communes*. Paris: Dalloz, 2005.
- LOUIS Jean-Victor. *L'ordre juridique de l'Union européenne*. Bâle: Helbing & Lichtenhahn; Bruxelles: Bruylant; Paris: LGDJ, 2005.
- PRANGE Heiko, KAISER Robert. "The open method of coordination in the European Research Area: a new concept of deepening integration?", *Comparative European Politics*, v. 3, n. 3, September 2005, p. 289-306.
- TOSI Gilbert. "Evolution du service public et principe de subsidiarité" in *Revue française d'économie*, v. 21, n. 1, juillet 2006, p. 3-36.
- TRUBEK David, TRUBEK Louise. "Hard and soft law in the construction of social Europe: the role of the Open Method of Co-ordination", *European Law Journal*, v. 11, n. 3, May 2005, p. 343-364.

*The publications of the Office for Official Publications of the European Communities (EUR-OP) exist usually in all official languages of the EU.

Chapter 4

THE STRUCTURE AND FUNCTIONS OF EUROPEAN INSTITUTIONS

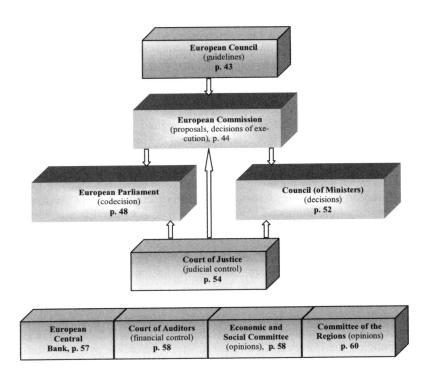

In the first part of this chapter is analysed the structure and the role of the institutions or organs of the European Union. In the second part is examined their interaction which leads to the formation and enforcement of European law, as well as to the development of the common policies that are the main subject of this book. In the third part of the chapter we make some suggestions for a drastic reform of the institutions in view of the enlargement of the EC/EU and its evolution towards a political union.

4.1. The main European Institutions

Common policies, which are the essence of the multinational integration process, are the fruit of intensive negotiations among the parties, which participate in this process. In order to be acceptable to all parties (member states), the conception of a common policy must try to satisfy or, at least, not harm the national interests of the parties and, therefore, the governments of all member states must participate in the decision-making process. Their participation, however, may be direct or indirect. Decisions on fundamental common policies, requiring new transfers of national sovereignties to the shared or supranational sovereignty, are taken by the participating governments (in intergovernmental conferences) and are outlined in treaties, signed by those governments and ratified by them after authorisation by the national parliaments [see chapter 2]. Decisions on secondary common policies, i.e. those needed to attain the goals set in the treaty, including policy guidelines and legal acts based on the treaty, are taken by the **common institutions** set up by the treaty, according to procedures and following the legal forms agreed in this treaty [see sections 3.3. and 4.3.]. In contrast to an organisation based on intergovernmental cooperation, where the governments are the main actors, in a multinational integration process the governments of the member states direct the play from the backstage, but they leave the stage to the actors, that is their representatives, appointed by them and/or by their citizens.

The principal actors of European integration are called "**institutions**" by the European Treaties. However, the qualification of an organ as institutional is changing in various revisions of the Treaties following the development of the European Community/Union. According to the EC Treaty (Nice version) the basic institutional structure of the European Union consists of five institutions: the European Parliament, the Council of Ministers, the Commission, the Court of Justice and the Court of Auditors. According to the draft Constitutional Treaty the institutional framework comprises: the European Parliament, the European Council, the Council of Ministers, the European Commission and the Court of Justice of the European Union. The European Council is therefore recognised by the Constitution as a fully-fledged institution, but the Court of Auditors is not included in the basic institutional framework. It is included in the "other institutions and advisory bodies", as is the European Central Bank (ECB). The constitutional Treaty (like the EC Treaty) recognises the status of "advisory bodies" to the Economic and Social Committee and to the Committee of the Regions.

For analytical purposes, we consider as principal actors of European integration the five organs which intervene principally in the decision-making process and therefore in the governance of the Community/Union: the European Council, which sets the goals of the common policies; the European Commission, which makes the proposals for the decisions to be taken and is mainly responsible for the implementation of the common policies; the European Parliament and the Council of Ministers, which take the decisions; and the Court of Justice, which controls the legality of these decisions.

The **European Administrative School (EAS)** is responsible for designing, organising and evaluating training courses, including management courses for officials of all European institutions, induction courses for new members of staff and compulsory training as part of the process for transferring between functions. Courses are given in both Brussels and Luxembourg[1].

---

[1]   Decisions 2005/118 and 2005/119, OJ L 37, 10.02.2005.

4.1.1. The European Council

The European Council is made up of the **Heads of State** (the President of the French Republic and the Presidents of the Republics of Cyprus, Latvia and Lithuania, responsible for foreign and European affairs) **or of Government** (the Prime Ministers of the other Member States) of the EU and the President of the European Commission. Begun on an informal basis as "Summit meetings" in the early 1960s, the European Council is now explicitly provided for in Article 4 of the Treaty on European Union (Nice). This Article provides that the European Council shall meet at least twice a year, under the chairmanship of the Head of State or Government of the Member State which holds the Presidency of the Council. Departing from the letter of the Treaty, the Seville European Council (21-22 June 2002) has agreed that it shall meet in principle four times a year (twice every six months) and that, in exceptional circumstances, it may hold an extraordinary meeting. European Council meetings are prepared by the General Affairs and External Relations Council, which coordinates all the preparatory work and draws up the agenda. At those meetings the Heads of State or Government and the President of the Commission are assisted by the Ministers of Foreign Affairs and one Member of the Commission.

The European Council is the architect of European construction. It provides the Union with the necessary impetus for its development; it defines the general political guidelines thereof and resolves the most important problems of the construction. The European Council is above all **a forum for free and informal exchanges of views** between the responsible leaders of the Member States. Its strength is its spontaneity and its informality, which bring about a sort of *"esprit de corps"* on the part of Europe's political leaders. Being a venue where package deals can be struck, and thus being free from the rigidity that sometimes paralyses the proceedings of the Council of Ministers, the European Council often acts as an appeal body for politically and economically important business which is deadlocked at ministerial level. It has resolved several issues, which threatened the Community's solidarity and progress, it has provided the impetus for new common policies and it has established the collective responsibility of the leaders of European diplomacy vis-à-vis the major European and world problems.

It should be noted, however, that the Heads of State or Government **do not adopt legal acts formally binding** the Member States [see section 3.3.]. Their deliberations result in the publication of declarations containing guidelines and general directives for future Community action. These declarations have undeniable political value, but no legal binding force. They give the political impetus necessary for common policies, but the latter are constructed with Community provisions adopted subsequently in accordance with the procedures laid down in the Treaties. The situation is quite different in the sphere of the common foreign and security policy where the European Council, in addition to adopting common strategies, can decide upon joint actions or common positions, which bind politically, if not legally, the Member States [see section 8.2.1.].

Apart from considering the European Council as a main institution of the Union, **the draft Constitution** establishes a permanent President of the European Council, who would take on the work currently assigned to rotating Presidencies. He or she would be elected by qualified majority, for a term of two and a half years, renewable once (Art. I-22). This new institutional arrangement was designed to lend a degree of visibility and stability to the Presidency of the European Council. The Permanent President would necessarily have the same nationality as one of the members of the European Council, but would not participate in the voting procedure within this institution. Since he or she would not hold a national office, the President would have the freedom of time and spirit to conduct the necessary discussions and negotiations with the twenty-seven heads of government, usually in their respective capitals, before the meetings of the European Council. Thus, according to the draft Constitution, the President should be able to facilitate cohesion and consensus and drive forward the work of the European Council.

> The draft Constitution does not change much the functions of the European Council. Normally, it would not exercise legislative functions. All European laws or framework laws should be adopted by the Council of Ministers, in most cases jointly with the European Parliament. However, the European Council could also be called upon to debate a legislative act in cases which were clearly defined in the Constitution (so-called "emergency brake" procedure). In addition, the draft Constitution stipulates that certain decisions, of a more constitutional nature, would be taken by the European Council, such as those relating to the composition of the European Parliament (Article I-20), the arrangements for the rotating Presidency of the Council (Article I-24), the system of equal rotation for the composition of the Commission (Article I-26), the suspension of the rights of a Member State in the event of a serious and persistent breach of the values of the Union (Article I-59) and the changeover from a legal basis of unanimous voting to qualified majority voting (Article IV-445). The President of the European Council would ensure the external representation of the Union on issues concerning common foreign and security policy, without prejudice to the responsibilities of the Minister for Foreign Affairs.

4.1.2. The European Commission

From the very beginning of the Community until 2004, the European Commission, usually referred to simply as **the Commission**, was made up of two nationals from each "big" and one national from each "small" Member State. Hence, the Treaty of Nice - adopted at a time when the European Community/Union numbered fifteen Member States, five of which were considered as big (Germany, France, the UK, Italy and Spain) - stated that "the Commission shall consist of 20 Members, who shall be chosen on the grounds of their general competence and whose independence is beyond doubt" (Article 213 TEC). Anticipating the enlargement of the EC/EU, this Treaty provided, however, that the number of members of the Commission could be altered by the Council, acting unanimously. In fact, in the Act of Accession of the ten new Member States (article 45), it was agreed (not without difficulties) that any State acceding to the Union should be entitled to have one of its nationals as a member of the Commission and that a new Commission composed of one national of each Member State should take up its duties on 1 November 2004, after the European elections of June 2004.

Thus, actually, the Commission is composed of 25 members (Commissioners), who are proposed by the government of each Member State and are appointed, for a period of five years, by the Council, acting by a qualified majority and by common accord with the nominee for President. The members of the Commission may not, during their term of office, engage in any other occupation, whether gainful or not. They must not take instructions from any government and all governments must respect this principle and not seek to influence the members of the Commission in the performance of their tasks (Art. 213 TEC). The Heads of State or Government, acting by a qualified majority, nominate the President of the Commission and the nomination must be approved by the European Parliament. The President and the other Members of the Commission are subject as a body to a vote of approval by the European Parliament (Art. 214 TEC). The Parliament examines every Commissioner as to his or her programme and ideas and may put forward objections as to his/her suitability for his/her particular responsibilities inside the Commission, but may not reject his/her appointment. Hence, in case of objections expressed by the Parliament for certain members of the Commission, its President has the option of either assigning other responsibilities to the members in question or of risking the rejection of the body by the Parliament[1].

The **draft Constitutional Treaty provides** that the current composition of the Commission – one Commissioner per Member State – should be maintained until 2014. From then on, the Commission should comprise a number of Commissioners corresponding to two thirds of the number of Member States. The members of the Commission would be chosen according to a system based on equal rotation among the Member States, guaranteeing equal treatment and reflecting the demographic and geographical range of all the Member States (art. I-26). The President of the Commission would be proposed to the European Parliament by the European Council, acting by a qualified majority. The Parliament would elect the candidate, acting by a majority of its component members. If he or she did not obtain the required majority, the European Council, acting by a qualified majority, should within one month propose a new candidate who should be elected by the European Parliament following the same procedure (art. I-27). The European Council, acting by a qualified majority, with the agreement of the President of the Commission, should appoint the Union Minister for Foreign Affairs, who would be a Vice-president of the Commission (art. I-28). The President, the Union Minister for Foreign Affairs and the other members of the Commission would be subject as a body to a vote of consent by the European Parliament (art. I-27).

The Commission is the driving force for European integration. Under the Community decision-making process provided for in the European Community Treaty [see section 4.3.], it alone **has the initiative to make proposals** with a view to Community decision-making. No other body and no individual State can replace the Commission in this task. It alone can amend its proposal, with the sole exception of there being unanimity in the Council to do so. On the basis of the political impetus given by the European Council with declarations and often by the European Parliament with resolutions, it is the task of the Commission to make proposals to the Council and to the Parliament to undertake new activities in the framework of the Treaties. It should be noted that the declarations of the European Council and the resolutions of the Parliament are often prompted by reports of the Commission itself. The **power of initiative**, which is held by the Commission, is particularly important for the development of the common policies and therefore for the progress of the multinational integration process. All common policies, all Community legislation, all Community programmes have been adopted by the legislative bodies with Commission initiatives in the form of explanatory communications and proposals of legal acts.

In its proposals, the Commission is entrusted with the task of defining the common interest in each policy, legal measure or action that it proposes and the representatives of the Member States can only unanimously substitute it in this role. This means that even if only one state believes that the amendment to the proposal of the Commission, promoted by the majority, is contrary to its interests, the proposal cannot be adopted by the Council with qualified majority voting. The proposal must be amended by the Commission itself, which must find a compromise solution that comes closer to the common interest. Of course, if the Commission considers that the minority is exaggerating or filibustering, it can amend its proposal in the sense wanted by the majority, which may thus adopt it. In most cases, however, in the course of the deliberations and negotiations within the Council, the Commission amends its proposal repeatedly in order to encourage concessions here and there and thus reach agreement. The Commission can therefore paralyse the Community's decision-making process, just as it can expedite it, which it

---

[1] See e.g. Decision 2004/642, OJ L 294, 17.09.2004 and Decision 2004/753, OJ L 333, 09.11.2004.

has always done. Year in, year out, it submits some 700 proposals to the Parliament and the Council, which are sooner or later adopted by the decision-making organs.

It should be stressed, however, that the Commission **only proposes legal acts or actions** of the EC/EU. The decisions are taken, usually in tandem, by the European Parliament and the Council with the codecision procedure or, in some cases, by the Council alone, i.e. by the representatives of the Member States. The Commission does not legislate. On the one hand, it proposes legal or administrative measures. On the other hand, it implements the acts and decisions taken by the Member States themselves through their representatives in the Parliament and the Council. The slogan concerning "the laws made by the technocrats of Brussels" is a myth well cultivated by europhobic media. The fault of the Commission and the Member States is that they have not adopted a common policy for the information and education of the citizens, in order to fight this and other myths propagated by the enemies of European unification.

The Commission is also the **guardian of the Treaties** and of the "acquis communautaire" (i.e., all the Community's legislation) [see section 3.3.]. One of its main tasks is to ensure fulfilment of the obligations of the Member States and/or proper application by them of the provisions of the Treaties and of secondary legislation (Art 226 TEC). For that purpose it has investigative power, which it exercises at its own initiative or in response to a request from a government or a complaint from an individual. If, following its investigation, the Commission considers that there is **infringement of Community legislation**, it invites the State concerned to submit its comments within a given period. If the State in question does not comply with the provisions or if the explanations that it provides do not convince the Commission, the latter issues a reasoned opinion to which the Member State is obliged to conform within the prescribed time-limit[1]. If the Member State fails to conform to the reasoned opinion, the Commission refers the matter to the Court of Justice, which arbitrates the dispute and, more often than not, sanctions the irregularity as noted by the Commission and requires the recalcitrant Member State to conform to the Community legal order. There are often differences of opinion between the Member States and the Commission, but the Commission's impartiality in respect of the various Member States has never been called into question.

The Commission is also the **executive body** of the Community and plays, therefore, an **administrative role**. The Treaties confer upon the Commission extensive powers of execution to ensure the attainment of the objectives set out in them: good functioning of the single market, control of the rules of competition, supply of fissile materials, etc. But the Commission's powers are constantly increased by the powers conferred to it by the legislator, i.e. the European Parliament and the Council for the implementation of common policies (Art. 202 TEC)[2]. It is the Commission which implements the decisions of the legislative bodies (the Council and the Parliament) and manages the Community budget [see section 3.4.] and in particular the various Community Funds[3] [see section 12.3.] and the research and technological development programmes [see section 18.2.2.]. The implementation decisions of the Commission usually take the form of the main decisions (regulation, directive or decision).

Finally, the Commission plays a **representative role** by ensuring the representation of the European Union in third countries and in many international organisations. The role of the Commission is particularly important in the conduct of the common commer-

---

[1]   See http://ec.europa.eu/community_law/eulaw/index_en.htm.
[2]   Decision 1999/468, OJ L 184, 17.07.1999 last amended by Decision 2006/512, OJ L 200 22.07.2006 and Regulation 1882/2003, OJ L 284, 31.10.2003.
[3]   Regulation 1105/2003, OJ L 158, 27.06.2003.

cial policy and of the aid to development policy. Acting on behalf of the Community on instructions from the Council, the Commission negotiates tariff agreements, formerly in the context of the General Agreement on Tariffs and Trade (GATT) and now of the World Trade Organisation (WTO) [see section 23.4.], trade and partnership agreements with third countries, association agreements and even, in practice, the agreements on the accession of new member states to the European Union. In order to carry out its representative role, the Commission has its own representations in more than 160 countries with which the EC/EU has diplomatic relations and in international organisations such as the Organisation for Economic Cooperation and Development (OECD), the WTO and the Council of Europe.

The draft **Constitutional Treaty** confirms all the above tasks of the Commission. It asserts that this institution shall ensure the application of the Constitution, and measures adopted by the institutions pursuant to the Constitution. It shall oversee the application of Union law under the control of the Court of Justice. It shall execute the budget and manage programmes. It shall exercise coordinating, executive and management functions, as laid down in the Constitution. With the exception of the common foreign and security policy (CFSP), and other cases provided for in the Constitution, it shall ensure the Union's external representation (Art I-26).

The exception of the CFSP from the external tasks of the Commission is relative, since the **Union Minister for Foreign Affairs** would have the power of proposal and would, thus, have a strong voice in the development of the Union's common foreign and security policy, which should be conducted and carried out as mandated by the Council. The same would apply to the common security and defence policy (Art I-28). Indeed, the Union Minister for Foreign Affairs would play a dual role, one in the Commission, as its Vice-President, and one in the Foreign Affairs Council, as its President. He or she would be responsible within the Commission for tasks incumbent on it in external relations and for coordinating other aspects of the Union's external action. Within the Council, he or she would ensure the consistency of the Union's external action. An ambiguous matter would be the external representation of the Union. The draft Constitution states that the President of the European Council should ensure the external representation of the Union on issues concerning its common foreign and security policy, without prejudice to the powers of the Union Minister for Foreign Affairs (Art. I-22). The question is where the powers of the former would end and those of the latter would begin and if and how the two would be able to ensure the external representation of the Union in tandem.

The Constitution confirms, in particular, the **near monopoly of the legislative initiative** of the Commission (Art. I-26). It can be inferred that the governments of the Member States, which have signed the Constitutional Treaty, have appreciated the work of the Commission to date and agreed to place it as the arbitrator of their national interests. In fact, the Commission can play this role, thanks to two main characteristic elements. Firstly, it is made up of politicians (at its top) and technocrats (at its base) of all nationalities. Secondly, it is controlled by no one national authority, but by multinational organs: the European Council, the European Parliament and the European Court of Justice. Moreover, before making its proposals, it gets advice from scientific, technical, administrative and professional experts from all the Member States.

The **multinational composition** of the college of Commissioners and of the services which work under them means that no one of the officials (often called Eurocrats) or even of the Commissioners can influence a proposal that he or she is working on in the direction of the national interest of one or some Member State(s). If he or she tried to do so, he or she would immediately be called to order by his or her colleagues in the responsible service or in the collegiate body of the Commission. Moreover, the services of the Commission, which are organised in a similar way as national Ministries, do not work in a vacuum. They are advised by specialised committees of experts of all nationalities, established by the Council or the Commission itself. These advisory committees examine a problem from its technical, economic and legal aspects and analyse the pros and cons of all possible solutions, including the inaction of the Community/Union. All these administrative, scientific, technical and national filters through which passes a proposal of the Commission and its eventual amendments ensure that this is the closest possible to the common interest and to the best possible solution at the time of its conception. The Commission listens to all views and arguments expressed in the various committees and usually takes up in its proposal the majority views, believing that upon them can be built a consensus in the decision-making bodies, the European Parliament and the Council. After all, the Commission knows well that, in order for any one of its proposals to have a chance to be adopted by these bodies, it has to fulfil the common interest of all the Member States or of the large majority of them.

Of course, the Commission is not infallible and it may sometimes be mistaken in the evaluation of what is the best solution in the interest of all or most Member States. Therefore, **many subsequent controls** exist, which make it possible to assess and eventually correct a proposal of the Commission. At the same time as it is sent to the decision-making bodies, the proposal of the Commission is, in many cases, sent to the advisory bodies set up by the Treaty: the Economic and Social Committee, consisting of representatives of the various economic and social components of organised civil society, and in particular representatives of producers, farmers, carriers, workers, dealers, craftsmen, professional occupations, consumers and the general interest (Art. 257 TEC); and the Committee of the Regions, consisting of representatives of regional and local bodies who either hold a regional or local authority electoral mandate or are politically accountable to an elected assembly (Art. 263 TEC). These bodies examine the employment, social, environmental, regional and other impacts of a Commission proposal and give their opinion to the decision-making bodies [see sections 4.2.3 and 4.2.4].

All these administrative, scientific, technical and national filters through which passes a proposal of the Commission and its eventual amendments ensure that this is the closest possible to the common interest and to the best possible solution at the time of its conception. In any case, the ultimate judges of the soundness of the Commission's definition of the **best solution in the common interest of the Member States** are the decision-making bodies: the European Parliament and the Council. These bodies have their own multinational committees, which discuss at length all Commission proposals, particularly from the point of view of the various national interests involved in the problem and in its proposed solution. Their opinions weigh heavily in the deliberations of the plenary assembly of the Parliament and of the Ministers sitting in the responsible Council configuration. These discussions often take many months or even years and usually result in many amendments to the original proposal of the Commission. Even if a nationally biased or otherwise discriminatory proposal passed through all the tests of the advisory and decision-making organs, it could be brought before the Court of Justice for annulment by any Member State believing that it violated the word or the spirit of the Treaty.

Inherent in the role of the Commission as guardian of the Community legislation is the administration of the **safeguard clauses** provided for in the Treaties or in the provisions relating to common policies. Here also an independent, objective arbiter is necessary in order to assess whether particular difficulties or special circumstances may authorise a Member State to derogate from the rules of the Treaty or from legislative provisions relating to common policies. In performing this task the Commission obviously takes into consideration the vital interests of the Member State which feels that it is suffering damage in a particular situation, but it surrounds itself with precautions and conditions so that prejudice to the functioning of the single market or to a common policy - and therefore to the common interest - is limited in scope and time.

Approximately 21,000 **permanent officials**, independent of the governments of their respective countries, work under the direction of the members of the Commission. They are divided into more than twenty-four Directorates-General, each of which is responsible for a Community policy, corresponding to the ministries of a national government. And yet the Commission's staff is smaller than that of a good number of national ministries; and furthermore, twenty per cent of the staff is involved in the linguistic work (translation and interpretation), which is absolutely essential to ensure equality of treatment of the 21 official languages of the Union (including Irish, but not including Bulgarian and Romanian)[1]. Under the control and responsibility of the Commission, executive agencies may be entrusted with certain tasks relating to the management of Community programmes[2]. The draft Constitution provides for a **European External Action Service** to be set up to assist the Union Minister for Foreign Affairs in his or her functions and shall work in cooperation with the diplomatic services of the Member States (Article III-296). This service would be composed of officials from relevant departments of the General Secretariat of the Council of Ministers and of the Commission and staff seconded from national diplomatic services.

4.1.3. The European Parliament

The Treaty establishing the **European Coal and Steel Community** in the early 1950s [see section 2.1.] stipulated that the extensive powers it was conferring on the High Authority would be subject to public control by a "Common Assembly" representing "the peoples of the States brought together in the Community". With

---

[1] Regulation 1/1958, OJ 17, 06.10.1958 and Regulation 920/2005, OJ L 156, 18.06.2005.
[2] Regulation 58/2003, OJ L 11, 16.01.2003 and Regulation 1653/2004, OJ L 297, 22.09.2004 amended by Regulation 1821/2005, OJ L 293, 09.11.2005.

the creation, in 1957, of the European Economic Community and the European Atomic Energy Community, the Common Assembly constituted, at its request, an enlarged Assembly, composed of 142 Members, for the three Communities. Holding its inaugural session in Strasbourg on 19 March 1958, the Assembly two days later gave itself the name of "European Parliamentary Assembly". Four years later, on 30 March 1962, it decided (without the blessing of the governments) to take the name **"European Parliament"**, a name sanctioned by the 1987 Single European Act.

During the early years of European construction, the Members of the European Parliament (MEPs) were appointed by the national parliaments and had to be members of them. Although it was provided for by the Treaties of Paris and Rome, election of the European Parliament by **direct universal suffrage** only became a reality in June 1979[1]. Common electoral principles, applicable from 2004, provide for elections to be held by direct universal suffrage, freely and in secret, and for Members of the European Parliament (MEPs) to be elected on the basis of proportional representation using the list system or the single transferable vote, their office being incompatible with that of member of a national parliament[2].

The number of Members of the European Parliament has increased with the successive enlargements of the Community/Union. After the 2004 enlargement, **the number of seats was increased to 732, which were allocated as follows:**

99 to Germany;

78 each to: France, Italy and the United Kingdom;

54 each to: Spain and Poland;

27 to the Netherlands;

24 each to: Belgium, the Czech Republic, Greece, Hungary and Portugal;

19 to Sweden;

18 to Austria;

14 each to: Denmark, Slovakia and Finland;

13 each to: Ireland and Lithuania;

9 to Latvia;

7 to Slovenia;

6 each to: Cyprus, Estonia and Luxembourg; and

5 to Malta.

Thanks to its direct election by the peoples of the Union, the European Parliament is the only real multinational legislative assembly in the world and plays an increasingly important role in the European integration process. Although under the original Treaties the Parliament's role was purely advisory, it has kept growing, particularly in the legislative and budgetary fields, with each amendment of the Treaties. It has to be said, moreover, that the national parliaments rarely exercise their legislative and budgetary powers to the full, subject as they are to the will of the parties which support the governments submitting legislative drafts to them. The European Parliament is not subjected to such constraints. At present **the EP exercises four functions**: legislative, political, supervisory and budgetary.

The European Parliament's first task under the Treaties establishing the original Communities, that of **consultation**, whereby Parliament gives its opinion on Commission proposals, was strengthened by the Single Act of 1987 which introduced a procedure of cooperation with the Council in many Community decisions. The **legislative function** of the Parliament was considerably increased with the Treaties of Amsterdam and Nice. Article 192 (TEC) provides, in fact, for the participation of the European Parliament in the process leading up to the adoption of Community acts through exercise of its powers under the procedures laid down in Articles 251 and 252 (co-decision and cooperation) [see section 4.3.]. Furthermore, the Parliament has the right to give or withhold its **assent** as regards the conclusion of certain international agreements, the acces-

---

[1] Decision 76/787, OJ L 278, 08.10.1976.
[2] Decision 2002/772, OJ L 283, 21.10.2002.

sion of new Member States and the structural and cohesion funds. The assent procedure may be regarded as a joint decision-making power of the Parliament in defining, implementing and monitoring the Community's foreign policy.

The **political function** of the Parliament is also essential. As it represents 456 million citizens (EU-25) and is the European forum par excellence, the Parliament is the virtual contractor for European construction. It often calls upon the other protagonists, the Commission and the Council, to develop or alter existing common policies or to initiate new ones. Indeed, the Treaty gives it the right to request that the Commission submit any appropriate proposals on matters on which it considers a Community act is required (Art. 192 TEC). Should the Commission or the Council fail to act as required for the purpose of implementing the Treaty, the Parliament may initiate proceedings against them before the Court of Justice (Art. 232 TCE) [see section 4.1.5.]. The Commission and the Council have to report to the Parliament for their acts. The Commission must submit to the Parliament each year a "General Report on the Activities of the European Union". The European Council itself reports to the European Parliament on each of its meetings and annually on the progress achieved by the Union.

The **monitoring function** of the Parliament is exercised in particular vis-à-vis the Commission. The President and the other members of the Commission are subject as a body to a vote of approval by the European Parliament (Art. 214 TEC). Therefore, the term of office of the Commission has been increased to five years, to run concurrently with the Parliament's term. The Commission is answerable to the Parliament alone, so as to obviate its bowing before the will of the national governments or of some of their number. The Commission has to account to the European Parliament, defend its position before parliamentary commissions and in plenary sessions. The Parliament may, at the request of a quarter of its members, set up a temporary Committee of Inquiry to investigate alleged contraventions or maladministration in the implementation of Community law (Art. 193 TEC). In case of a serious maladministration, the Parliament may pass a motion of censure against the Commission by a two-thirds majority of its members and thus compel it to resign (Art. 201 TEC), as it has threatened to do in March 1999.

The European Parliament appoints an **Ombudsman** empowered to receive complaints from any citizen of the Union or any natural or legal person residing or having its registered office in a Member State and concerning instances of maladministration in the activities of the Community institutions or bodies, with the exception of the Court of Justice and the Court of First Instance acting in their judicial role[1]. In cases where the Ombudsman establishes that mismanagement has occurred, he refers the matter to the institution concerned, which has three months in which to inform him of its views. The Ombudsman must then forward a report to the European Parliament and the institution concerned and inform the person lodging the complaint of the outcome of such inquiries (Art. 195 TEC). These procedures may help bring the European construction closer to the citizen [see section 9.3.].

As regards **budgetary functions**, the Parliament has to give its agreement to any major decision involving expenditure to be borne by the Community budget. It is effectively the Parliament which, at the end of a conciliation procedure with the Council, adopts or rejects the budget proposed by the Commission. Thus, it exercises a democratic control on the own resources of the Community [see section 3.4.]. It also monitors Community expenditure, since it has the power to give a discharge to the Commission for the management of the Community budget (Art. 272 and 276 TEC).

---

[1] Decision 94/114, OJ L 54, 25.02.1994, Decision 94/262, OJ L 113, 04.05.1994 and Decision 2002/262, OJ L 92, 09.04.2002.

According to the draft **Constitutional Treaty**, the European Parliament should be composed of representatives of the Union's citizens, who should not exceed 750 in number. Representation of citizens should be degressively proportional, with a minimum threshold of 6 deputies per Member State, in order to make sure that, even in the least populous Member States, all the major shades of political opinion would have a chance of being represented in the European Parliament. No Member State should be allocated more than 96 seats. In case of new enlargements of the Union, the European Council should adopt by unanimity, on the initiative of the European Parliament and with its consent, a European decision establishing the composition of the European Parliament, respecting the principles referred to above (Art. I-20). It follows that, since the number of EMPs would never exceed the total of 750 and, since the smaller Member States would always be allocated at least 6 EMPs each, the larger Member States would have to hand down a number of their seats to the acceding Member States.

The draft Constitutional Treaty **enhances significantly the functions** of the European Parliament. If it came into force, the Parliament would, jointly with the Council, exercise legislative and budgetary functions. The draft Constitution extends the codecision procedure, renamed "ordinary legislative procedure", to a large number of articles. The Parliament therefore would become co-legislator in almost all laws and framework laws of the Union, with the exception of a dozen cases, where it would only be consulted. The request for accession of new Member States would be subject to the approval of the European Parliament, which could thus turn down a candidate, even despite the unanimous approval of the governments of the Member States. The President of the Commission would be elected (not approved) by the European Parliament by a majority of its members, acting on a proposal from the European Council. This amendment would clearly establish the responsibility of the President of the Commission vis-à-vis the Parliament [see details below].

Actually, the Parliament's **budgetary powers** differ according to the type of expenditure. For "**compulsory expenditure**" (CE), i.e. expenditure resulting from the Treaties and the decisions adopted pursuant thereto (roughly 50% of appropriations, made up chiefly of those relating to the common agricultural policy), the Parliament may propose modifications provided that they do not increase the total volume of the budget. These modifications are deemed to be accepted if the Council does not reject them by a qualified majority. For "**non-compulsory expenditure**" (NCE), i.e. expenditure which is not the automatic consequence of the various Community provisions (in particular, appropriations allocated to the European Social Fund, research, energy, etc.), the Parliament may not only modify its apportionment but also increase its volume, up to a given limit which depends on the Community's economic situation. That limit may be amended by the Parliament by mutual agreement with the Council.

That demarcation of the budgetary procedure has often been attended by conflicts between the two budgetary authorities, as the Parliament wants to use its budgetary powers to influence Community policies and considers as an unjustified restriction of its powers the, somewhat arbitrary, separation of expenditure into compulsory and non-compulsory. However, the Interinstitutional Agreement of 6 May 1999 on budgetary discipline (adjusted to the financial perspective for enlargement)[1] and the Regulation on budgetary discipline, which limits agricultural expenditure under certain ceilings[2], have recently created the conditions for an institutional budgetary peace. The differentiation of the budgetary powers of the Parliament between compulsory and non-compulsory expenditure is abolished by the draft Constitution. The law determining the annual budget of the Union would be adopted jointly by the EP and the Council, with the Parliament having the final word on the budget as a whole (Art. III-404). The European Parliament would thus have practically the same budgetary functions as a national parliamentary assembly.

The activity of the **European Parliament Committees**, which monitor Community affairs in detail on a continuous basis, has contributed a great deal to developing the European Parliament's influence. These committees produce reports on any subject, which they feel deserves the attention of the Community institutions, and invite the relevant Members of the European Commission to go and state their views or give explanations

[1] OJ C 172, 18.06.1999, p. 1-22 and Decisions 2003/429 and 2003/430, OJ L 147, 14.06.2003.
[2] Regulation 2040/2000, OJ L 244, 29.09.2000.

before them and/or before the plenary session of the European Parliament at the time of the vote. The Opinions, Reports and Resolutions of the Parliament, prepared by the specialist committees, often influence Commission proposals and hence common policies, as they show not only a political desire to make the European integration process progress, but also extensive knowledge of the complicated issues involved in that process.

Every Member of the Parliament may raise any point relating to the activity of the Commission and call it to account by means of **Written or Oral Questions**. Each year the Parliament puts some 3,000 questions, nine-tenths to the Commission and the others to the Council. These questions enable the Parliament not only to keep closely abreast of any new development in Community policy, but also in many instances to initiate such developments. But the EP also monitors the activities (or the inactivity) of the Council and even of the European Council, which gives it an account of its actions, positions and decisions after each of its sessions.

The draft Constitution reinforces the **functions of political control** of the Parliament vis-à-vis the Commission. If it came into force, the President of the Commission would be elected by the European Parliament by a majority of its members, acting on a proposal from the European Council, which should take into account the results of the European elections. The Parliament could turn down the candidate proposed by the European Council and force it to propose another personality for President of the Commission. The President, the Union Minister for Foreign Affairs and the other members of the Commission would be subject as a body to a vote of consent by the European Parliament (Art I-27), which means that the Parliament could reject the composition of the Commission arranged by its President and force him or her to review it. With a motion of censure, carried by a two-thirds majority of the votes cast, representing a majority of its component members, the European Parliament might force the members of the Commission to resign as a body (Art. III-340). These procedures would clearly highlight the responsibility of the Commission vis-à-vis the Parliament. They would also make the functions of the European Parliament resemble those of a national parliament.

4.1.4. The Council

The **Council** is composed of a representative of each Member State at ministerial level, authorised to commit the government of that Member State (Art 203 TEC). While it is usually referred to broadly as "the Council" or "the Council of Ministers", it actually consists of nine specialised **configurations** regrouping several related areas, e.g. general affairs and external relations or economic and financial affairs[1] [see details below]. Each Council configuration is composed of the ministers with responsibility in the matter, but several ministers may participate as full members of the same Council configuration, e.g. the ministers responsible for health and social policy. Although Commission proposals are discussed inside the specialised Council configurations, decisions agreed by all the Member States can be taken without a debate (as "points A" in the agenda) by any Council whatsoever, and this is often the "**General Affairs and External Relations Council**", composed of the Ministers of Foreign Affairs. This is the principal Council configuration and holds separate meetings (with separate agendas and possibly on different dates) dealing, respectively, with: (a) preparation for and follow-up to the European Council, institutional and administrative questions, horizontal dossiers which affect several of the Union's policies; and (b) the whole of the Union's external action, namely common foreign and security policy, foreign trade, development cooperation and humanitarian aid.

The **Council Presidency** changes every six months to another country in alphabetical order, and it is therefore the Minister of the country holding the Presidency who chairs each Council meeting[2]. The rotation of the Presidency has the advantage of giving each country a chance to prove its efficiency in promoting common policies, on the basis of Commission proposals, thus encouraging emulation among the Member States in the advancement of European integration. In order to obviate the problem of differing priorities of twenty-seven presidencies in the enlarged Union, its legislative work is henceforth based on a three-year strategic programme adopted by the European Council. In its

---

[1]   Decision 2004/338, OJ L 106, 15.04.2004 last amended by Decision 2006/34, OJ L 26.01.2006.
[2]   Concerning the order of the exercise of the Presidency see Decision 2/95, OJ L 1, 01.01.1995.

light, an annual operating programme of Council activities is adopted by the General Affairs Council in December each year and is accompanied by six-monthly **indicative agendas** for the various Council configurations.

The Council is assisted by a General Secretariat, consisting of "Eurocrats" of all the nationalities of the Union, separate from their counterparts in the Commission but organised in a similar way. The Council is also assisted by many working parties of national civil servants, which examine the proposals of the Commission and report to the **Permanent Representatives Committee (COREPER)**, which is responsible for preparing the work of the Council and for carrying out the tasks assigned to it by the Council" (Art. 207 TEC). The Coreper sits in two parts. Coreper Part 1, which is composed of the Deputy Permanent Representatives, examines technical questions on the whole. Coreper Part 2, which is composed of the Ambassadors themselves, deals with political questions on the whole. The European Commission participates in all the meetings of the working parties of national experts, of the Coreper and of the Council itself to explain its positions and assist the Presidency in reaching agreement on its proposals. After examining an issue Coreper either submits a report to the Council, preparing the ground for its discussions by drawing attention to the political aspects which deserve particular attention, or, if unanimous agreement has been reached between the Permanent Representatives and the Commission representative, Coreper recommends that the Council adopt the prepared text "as **an 'A' item"**, i.e. without discussion. In both cases the Council's work is facilitated thanks to Coreper's intervention.

On the basis of the original Treaties, the Council was the only legislative authority of the Community and this was the main reason for the then existing democratic deficit of the Community [see section 9.5.]. Subsequent amendments of the Treaties have joined, ever more closely, the European Parliament in the decision-making process, thus making the Council one of the two legislative authorities [see section 4.3.] and reducing, consequently, the democratic deficit. Going a step further, the draft **Constitutional Treaty** specifies that the Council should, jointly with the European Parliament, exercise legislative and budgetary functions (Art. I-23). Hence, the legislative functions of the Council would come close to those of an Upper House or Senate, representing the governments of the Member States, and sharing these functions with the European Parliament, representing directly the peoples of the Union. However, in addition to its legislative and budgetary functions, the Council ensures coordination of the general economic policies of the Member States [see section 7.3.] and plays an important role in defining and implementing the common foreign and security policy (CFSP) [see details below and section 8.2.1.].

The draft **Constitutional Treaty** confirms the existing provisions on the composition of the Council and on its legislative, budgetary, policy-making and coordinating functions (Art. I-23). It stipulates that the Presidency of all Council configurations, other than that of Foreign Affairs, is to be held by Member State representatives on the basis of a system of equal rotation, defined by a European Council decision adopted by a qualified majority (Art. I-24). It separates the responsibilities of the Ministers of Foreign Affairs, who would deal with the external activities of the Union, from those of the Ministers of European Affairs, who would ensure consistency in the work of the different Council configurations.

Despite its composition of representatives of national governments, which are naturally inclined to defend national interests, the Council manages to play well its role as a Community institution seeking and ultimately finding the **common denominator** of problems and policies. Every Council decision is tangible evidence of the Member States' will to develop common policies and measures. That will is not the fruit of chance, but of a good knowledge of each other's problems and interests. That knowledge is gained especially in the Council. At their numerous formal meetings, held usually in Brussels and three months a year in Luxembourg, and during their informal meetings, held at the invitation and in the territory of the country holding the Council Presidency, Ministers form friendships and make alliances for the defence of common interests. Hence, the Ministers participating in a Council formation form a multinational human network, which is very important for the European integration process [see section 9.4].

Those friendships and alliances are formed also in the very numerous specialist **working parties** on the various subjects, composed of members of the national civil services, which discuss the Commission's proposals and prepare Council decisions. The numerous meetings each year of senior officials of the Member States, responsible for agriculture, industry, transport, economic affairs, etc., help to align points of view and facilitate the multinational integration process. An influential human network is thus built among the **civil servants** who attend the work of the committees, which prepare the decisions of the Council. The influence of this network, which is somehow penetrated by the Community spirit, on their colleagues back home is all the more important, since national administrations remain the most ardent defenders of national causes and measures, as each brick added to the communal house removes a little of their own power and authority. Since national, regional and even local interests are not swept away by multinational integration, there is and will always be a need to reconcile common and national interests in order to develop workable common policies. The human networks formed inside the Council at all levels help answer this need.

Actually the nine **Council configurations** are: General Affairs and External Relations (including European security and defence policy and development cooperation); Economic and Financial Affairs (including budget); Justice and Home Affairs (including civil protection); Employment, Social Policy, Health and Consumer Affairs; Competitiveness (Internal Market, Industry and Research, including tourism); Transport, Telecommunications and Energy; Agriculture and Fisheries; Environment; Education, Youth and Culture (including audiovisual affairs)[1].

The draft **Constitutional Treaty** confirms that the Council should meet in different configurations and mentions specifically the two principal ones: the General Affairs Council and the Foreign Affairs Council (Art. I-24). This represents a subject-based splitting of the present General Affairs and External Relations Council. The General Affairs Council would be responsible for ensuring consistency in the work of the various Council configurations and the follow-up to meetings of the European Council. The Foreign Affairs Council, chaired by the Union's Minister for Foreign Affairs, should adopt the European decisions necessary for defining and implementing the common foreign and security policy (CFSP) on the basis of the general guidelines and strategic lines defined by the European Council (Art. III-295). The Council and the Union Minister for Foreign Affairs should ensure that CFSP principles defined by the Constitution are complied with by the Member States (Art. III-294).

4.1.5. The Court of Justice

In a community of states the common rules adopted by the decision-making bodies might be interpreted and applied differently from country to country, if only national courts controlled them. Therefore, the general task assigned to the Court of Justice and to the Court of First Instance is to ensure that Community **law is observed in a uniform manner** in the interpretation and application of the Treaty, of the legal acts and of the decisions adopted by the Council and the Parliament or by the Commission (Art. 220 to 245 TEC). The judgments of the Court of Justice, many important ones of which are referred to in the footnotes of this book, consolidate the European law to which are subject the governments, the national courts, the parliaments and the citizens of the Member States. Although European law is a statute law passed by legislative bodies, it is often amended by them in accordance with the case law of the Court of Justice. The Court plays therefore an important role in the European integration process by clarifying ambiguous legal provisions, adopted sometimes under the pressure of reaching agreement between law-makers of different cultures concerned about various national interests.

The **Court of Justice of the European Communities (CJEC)** consists, in fact, of two bodies, with their seat in Luxembourg: the Court of Justice proper and the Court of First Instance. **The Court of Justice**, often called European Court of Justice (ECJ) consists of one judge per Member State. It sits in chambers or in a Grand Chamber, in ac-

---

[1]   Decision 2004/338, OJ L 106, 15.04.2004 last amended by Decision 2006/34, OJ L 26.01.2006.

cordance with the rules laid down in its Statutes. It is assisted by Advocates-General (Art. 221 TEC). The task of the latter is, acting with complete impartiality and independence, to make, in open court, reasoned submissions on cases which, in accordance with the Statute of the Court of Justice, require his involvement (Art. 222 TEC). The **Court of First Instance** comprises at least one judge per Member State, which means that it may include judges of the same nationality. The number of Judges is determined by the Statute of the Court of Justice, which may provide for the Court of First Instance to be assisted by Advocates-General (Art. 224 TEC).

The **Court of First Instance (CFI)** is the common law judge for all direct actions, i.e. proceedings against a decision (Article 230 TEC), action for failure to act (Article 232 TEC) and action for damages (Article 235 TEC), with the exception of those the statute reserves for the Court of Justice and those which are attributed to a specialised chamber. The CFI has jurisdiction in all actions brought by natural or legal persons and cases relating notably to agriculture, fisheries, the European Funds (regional, social), transport and State aids. The judgments of the CFI may be subject to appeals, confined to points of law, to the Court of Justice (Art. 225 TEC).

Being the supreme court of the Communities, the **Court of Justice** not only gives a coherent and uniform interpretation of European law, but it ensures that all the Member States and their citizens comply with it. Apart from the tendency of governments to interpret European law in the interest of their nations, it is new law and not always well known. The national judges, who are the judges of first instance of the rules and behaviour relative to European law, may turn to the Court of Justice by means of a **referral for a preliminary ruling** to ask it to adopt a position on the interpretation or evaluation of the validity of the provisions of European acts. Although they are normally optional, referrals for a preliminary ruling are obligatory where judicial remedy under national law is no longer possible, i.e. when the court, which has to apply the Community law, is taking its decisions in the final instance. Through its preliminary rulings, the Court plays the role of a legal council whose opinions are binding on the parties concerned. The referral for a preliminary ruling is appreciated by the national courts and stimulates the cooperation between them and the ECJ.

Disputes falling within the unlimited jurisdiction of the Court are made up in particular of cases relating to non-compliance or to the interpretation of the Community's rules of competition. Hearing an appeal by undertakings (firms, businesses) penalised by the Commission for infringing competition law, the Court gives a ruling on the merits of the Commission's decision and on the appropriateness of the penalty imposed on the undertaking. The Court also judges disputes which call into question the Community's civil liability as a result of damage caused by one of its institutions or staff in the exercise of their duties.

According to the draft **Constitutional Treaty**, the Court of Justice of the European Union would include the Court of Justice, the General Court and specialised courts. Hence, the term "Court of Justice of the European Union" would officially designate the two levels of jurisdiction taken together. The supreme body would be called the "Court of Justice" while the Court of First Instance would be renamed "General Court", but their actual composition and tasks would not be changed (Art. I-29). However, the Constitution stipulates that any natural or legal person might institute proceedings against "a regulatory act which would be of direct concern to him or her and would not entail implementing measures" (Article III-365), thus making it easier for citizens to challenge the Union's regulatory acts under which penalties are imposed, even if these acts did not affect them individually.

The Judges and Advocates-General of the Court of Justice and of the Court of First Instance are chosen from persons whose independence is beyond doubt and who possess the qualifications required for appointment to the highest judicial offices in their respective countries or who are jurisconsults of recognised competence. They are appointed by common accord of the governments of the Member States for a term of six years. Every three years there is a partial replacement of the Judges and Advocates-General (Art 223 TEC). Forming an integral part of the Court of Justice of the European Communities, the European Union Civil Service Tribunal rules in cases between the institutions of the European Union and their officials or other servants[1]. The draft **Constitution** provides for the setting up of a panel to give an opinion on candidates' suitability to perform the duties of Judge and Advocate-General, before the governments of the Member States take the decisions regarding their appointment (Art. III-357). European laws, adopted at the initiative of the Commission or of the Court of Justice, might establish **specialised courts** attached to the General Court to hear and determine at first instance certain classes of action or proceeding brought in specific areas (Art. III-359).

In the legal field itself the Court reviews the legality of Community acts. **Proceedings for annulment** may be brought against the decision-making institutions (Council or Council/Parliament and Commission) either by a Member State, or by another institution or even, in certain instances, by an individual[2]. The aim of these proceedings is to annul those acts of the institutions, which are at variance with the provisions of the Treaties or their spirit, which exceed their rights or which do not comply with the procedure laid down. If the action is well founded, the Court declares the act in question to be void. Proceedings for annulment are therefore the means to monitor both the conformity of the acts of the Community legislator with the Treaties and the legality of individual Commission decisions and regulations, as well as to resolve interinstitutional disputes affecting the very exercise of the powers devolving upon each of the institutions from the Treaties. The control of the legality of the acts of the institutions likens the Court to a constitutional jurisdiction.

Proceedings for failure to act, on the other hand, are aimed at securing a ruling where the Council or the Commission has failed to meet its obligation to act, thus infringing the provisions of the Treaties. Such proceedings may also be initiated by a Member State, and possibly by individuals, or another Community institution, but they are admissible only if the institution in question has first been called upon to act. Thus, for example, in September 1982 the European Parliament brought an action for failure to act against the Council for failing to establish the framework for the common transport policy [see section 20.2.1.][3]. In November 1993, the Parliament, on the basis of Article 175 of the EEC Treaty (Art. 232 TEC), brought an action against the Commission for failure to present the proposals necessary for the establishment of the free movement of persons within the internal market[4].

The Court also has jurisdiction to rule on proceedings brought against Member States, which do not meet the obligations imposed on them by the Treaties or secondary legislation. **Proceedings for infringement** may be brought by Community institutions (in practice, the Commission), a Member State or an individual. Referral to the Court by the Commission is the final stage in an action for infringement, taking place following an unsuccessful formal notice to the Member State from the Commission [see section 4.1.2.]. If a State does not comply with an initial judgment, new proceedings may be brought, at the end of which the Court will rule that there has been a violation of the obligations deriving from its initial judgment. Article 228 of the EC Treaty allows the Commission to bring the case of a Member State, which has failed to comply with a ruling of the Court of Justice, again before. If the Court finds that the Member State has indeed failed to comply with its judgment, it may impose a lump sum of penalty payment[5], calculated after a method devised by the Commission[6]. The Court may also order a Member State to pay both a periodic penalty payment and a lump sum fine for a serious and persistent failure to comply with Community law[7]. The efficiency of Community law can nevertheless be guaranteed concurrently by the national courts and through referrals for preliminary rulings if a citizen feels that he or she has been injured by the incriminated act.

4.2. Other institutions and advisory bodies

As mentioned at the beginning of this chapter, the institutions of the EC/EU are evolving along with the evolution of European integration. Of the institutions and advisory bodies that we consider in this section, only the European Economic and Social

---

[1] Decision 2004/752, OJ L 339, 09.11.2004.
[2] See judgment of 1 April 2004, Case C-263/02, ECR 2004, p. I-03425.
[3] OJ C 267, 11.10.1982.
[4] OJ C 1, 04.01.1994.
[5] See e.g., Case C-387/97, Commission v Greece, ECR 2000, p. I-5047 and Case C-304/02, Commission v French Republic, ECR 2005, p. I-06263.
[6] OJ C 63, 28.02.1997.
[7] Judgment of 12 July 2005, Case C-304/02, Commission v French Republic, ECR 2005, p. I-06263.

Committee was provided for in the original Treaties. New institutions and bodies have been created to cover new needs, notably the Committee of the Regions and the European Central Bank. The Court of Auditors is considered as a main institution by the Treaty of Nice, but not by the Constitutional Treaty, probably because it does not participate in the decision-making process. In any case, all these other institutions and advisory bodies are independent of the main institutions.

4.2.1. The European Central Bank

In the framework of the economic and monetary union that it has launched, the Treaty of Maastricht has established a **European system of central banks (ESCB)** and a **European Central Bank (ECB)** [see section 7.2.4.]. The two organs are closely associated. They act within the limits of the powers conferred upon them by the EC Treaty and by the Statute of the ESCB and of the ECB annexed thereto (Art. 8 TEC). The ESCB is composed of the ECB and of the national central banks and is governed by the decision-making bodies of the ECB which are the Governing Council and the Executive Board. (Art 107 TEC). The Governing Council is composed of the Governors of the central banks of all the Member States of the EC/EU, whereas the President, the Vice-President and the other members of the Executive Board of the ECB are appointed by common accord of the governments of the Member States, which have adopted the euro[1] [see section 7.2.3]. Neither the ECB, nor a national central bank, nor any member of their decision-making bodies may seek or take instructions from Community institutions or bodies, from any government of a Member State or from any other body (Art. 108 TEC). The objectives of the ESCB are, primarily, to maintain price stability and, without prejudice to this objective, to support the general economic policies in the Community (Art. 105 TEC). The basic tasks of the ESCB are: to define and implement the monetary policy of the Community, to conduct foreign-exchange operations, to hold and manage the official foreign reserves of the Member States and to promote the smooth operation of payment systems. The ECB, which has legal personality, has the exclusive right to authorise the issue of banknotes within the Community's eurozone (Art. 106 TEC). In order to carry out the tasks entrusted to the ESCB, the ECB may: make regulations to the extent necessary to implement the tasks defined in the Treaty, take decisions necessary for carrying out the tasks entrusted to the ESCB and make recommendations and deliver opinions (Art 110 TEC).

The draft **Constitutional Treaty** gives the European Central Bank the status of an institution, in order to emphasise its independence. It brings together the general provisions on the ECB and the ESCB, without introducing any substantive changes. Accepting the fact that not all the EU Member States need to adopt the euro as their currency, the draft Constitution declares that the European Central Bank, together with the national central banks of the Member States whose currency is the euro, which constitute the Eurosystem, should conduct the monetary policy of the Union, while those Member States whose currency is not the euro, and their central banks, should retain their powers in monetary matters (Art I-30). The Executive Board of the ECB should comprise the President, the Vice-President and four other members, appointed by the European Council, acting by a qualified majority (Art. III-382) and not by unanimity, as is actually the case.

---

[1]   Decision 98/345, OJ L 154, 28.05.1998.

4.2.2. The European Court of Auditors

The second Budget Treaty, signed in July 1975 [see section 2.1.], established the Court of Auditors as the body responsible for the external supervision of the general budget of the Community and the Treaty of Amsterdam recognised it as an institution. It consists of one national from each Member State. The Members of the Court of Auditors are chosen from among persons who belong or have belonged in their respective countries to external audit bodies or who are especially qualified for this office. They are appointed for a term of six years by the Council, acting by a qualified majority after consulting the European Parliament. They are completely independent in the performance of their duties (Art. 247 TEC).

The Court of Auditors examines the accounts of all revenue and expenditure of the Community, particularly the annual budget managed by the Commission, and of all bodies set up by the Community. It examines in particular whether all revenue has been received and all expenditure incurred in a lawful and regular manner and must report on any cases of irregularity. The audit must be based on records and, if necessary, performed on the spot in the other institutions of the Community, on the premises of any body which manages revenue or expenditure on behalf of the Community and in the Member States, including on the premises of any natural or legal person in receipt of payments from the budget (Art. 248 TEC).

The Court of Auditors draws up an annual report after the close of each financial year. This is forwarded to the other institutions of the Community and is published, together with the replies of these institutions to the observations of the Court of Auditors, in the Official Journal of the European Union. The Court must provide the European Parliament and the Council with a statement of assurance as to the reliability of the accounts and the legality and regularity of the underlying transactions. The annual and the specific reports of the Court of Auditors are acknowledged to be a valuable input to Parliament's debates on the discharge to be given to the Commission for its execution of the budget. The growing importance of the Court of Auditors testifies to the will of the European institutions and of the governments of the Member States to extend and improve financial control [see section 3.4.]. This is due to the increasing size of the Community budget, which is a direct consequence of the development of the various common policies that we are examining in this book.

The draft **Constitutional Treaty** does not modify the structure and the functions of the Court of Auditors. It confirms its status as an independent institution, which shall examine the accounts of all Union revenue and expenditure, and shall ensure good financial management (Articles I-31, III-384 and III-385). The only significant change is that it requires the Court to send its annual report to national parliaments, for information, thus increasing the democratic control of the Union's finances.

4.2.3. The Economic and Social Committee

The European Economic and Social Committee (EESC) is the official body which enables the Community institutions to evaluate and take into account in the conception of common policies the **interests of the various economic and social groups**. Its 317 members are proposed by the governments of the Member States (Germany, France, Italy and the United Kingdom proposing 24 each; Spain and Poland 21; Belgium, the Czech Republic, Greece, Hungary, Netherlands, Portugal, Austria and Sweden 12 each; Denmark, Ireland, Lithuania, Slovakia and Finland 9 each; Estonia, Latvia and Slovenia 7 each, Cyprus and Luxembourg 6 each and Malta 5) and are appointed for a term of four years by the Council after consulting the Commission. They must provide a wide representation of the various categories of economic and social life (Art. 257-262 TEC) and divide voluntarily into three groups: the Employers' Group (known as "Group I"), which is made up of representatives of industry, banking or financial institutions, transport operators' federations, etc.; the Workers' Group (known as "Group II"), mainly composed of representatives of trade union organisations; and the Various Interests Group (known as "Group III"), which comprises representatives of agriculture, skilled trades, small and medium-sized enterprises, the professions, consumer associations and organisations representing various interests, such as families or ecological movements. However, the members of the Committee are not elected by the corresponding national groups but are appointed by the governments. This is a flaw that should be corrected in the interest of the democratic legitimacy of the EESC.

The Committee **must be consulted** by the Council or by the Commission in certain areas provided for by the Treaty establishing the European Community. The Committee **may be consulted** by these institutions in all cases where they consider it appropriate. Furthermore, the EESC may issue an **opinion at its own initiative** when it considers such action appropriate (Art. 262 TEC). Whether they are requested by the Commission or the Council or issued at its own initiative, the Committee's Opinions are not binding on the institutions, a shortcoming that weakens their significance. This is a flaw of the role of the Committee that should also be corrected [see section 4.4.]. However, the Committee plays the role of a forum in which the interests of the various socio-professional categories, rather than national arguments, are expressed officially and assessed. The opinions of the EESC on the proposals of the Commission reflect the concerns of economic and societal groups and provide valuable indications of the opposing arguments, of the divergences of interests and of the possibilities of reaching agreement at Community level. Furthermore, the EESC associates in the preparation of Community legislation the economic operators who are ultimately the most directly concerned by the practical effects of the common policies on the European economy. For that reason the Commission often adjusts its proposals to take into account the official positions of the interest groups of the Community. In this limited way the Committee influences decisions and makes its contribution to the formulation of common policies, a contribution that could be greater if better exploited.

The draft **Constitutional Treaty** does not make any fundamental changes to the structure and functions of the Economic and Social Committee, other than lengthening the term of office of its members to five years, so as to coincide with that of the members of the European Parliament. It limits the number of members of the Committee to 350, notwithstanding future enlargements, and specifies that the composition of the Committee would be determined by a European decision adopted unanimously by the Council on a proposal from the Commission (Art. III-389). Before adopting the list of members drawn up in accordance with the proposals made by each Member State, the Council might obtain the opinion of European bodies which are representative of the various economic and social sectors and of civil society to which the Union's activities are of concern (Art. III-390). This would be an improvement to the system of selection of the members of the Committee, but it would certainly be better if the national and European bodies concerned were more involved in the establishment of the list of the members [see section 4.4.].

4.2.4. The Committee of the Regions

The Treaty establishing the European Community officially acknowledges the regional diversity and the role played by regions in the governance of the Community through the Committee of the Regions made up of **representatives of regional and local bodies** (Art. 263-265 TEC). The 317 members of the Committee and an equal number of alternate members (with the same national distribution as the members of the EESC) are proposed by the governments of the Member States and appointed for four years by the Council, acting unanimously. It could be suggested that the mandate of the members of this Committee should be five years, as is that of the other organs, and that their election should be entrusted to the peoples of the regions themselves [see section 4.4.].

The Committee of the Regions **must be consulted** by the Council or the Commission on matters relating notably to employment guidelines, legislation on social matters, environment, education, vocational training, culture, public health, European networks and the Structural Funds. It **may be consulted** in all other cases considered appropriate by one of the two institutions, in particular those which concern cross-border cooperation. It can also issue an **own-initiative opinion** when it considers that specific regional interests are at stake (Art. 265 TEC). The Committee of the Regions thus involves regional and local authorities in the decision-making process and expresses their views on all common policies concerning them. Yet again, these views could have a greater impact on these policies than they now have, if a way was found to make the decision-making organs to take them more seriously into consideration [see section 4.4.].

As in the case of the Economic and Social Committee, the draft **Constitutional Treaty** only lengthens the term of office of the members of the Committee of the Regions to five years, limits their maximum number to 350 and stipulates that the Committee's composition would be determined by the Council acting unanimously on a proposal from the Commission (Art. III-386). However, the draft Constitution does not encourage the Council to obtain the opinion of the regional and local bodies concerned and, therefore, the appointment of the members of the Committee of the Regions would still depend on the proposals of the governments and, consequently, on national rather than on regional political criteria. Moreover, the Constitution does not boost up the importance of the opinions of the Committee of the Regions [see section 4.4.].

4.3. The Community's decision-making process

The Treaties establishing the Communities defined the objectives to be attained, laid down the rules to be implemented, set out timetables to be met and established an institutional framework which provides the Community with an original method of decision-making and legislation. The **Community method implies a decision-making process** entailing: (a) a single and supranational source of the right of initiative; (b) usually co-decision of the European Parliament with the Council, deciding by qualified majority; and (c) control of the decisions by a supranational judicial authority, the European Court of Justice. The Community method is, indeed, an **original combination** of: **technocratic proposals** emanating from the Commission, worked out with the technical advice of experts from all the Member States; **and legislative acts and** political decisions taken by the Council, representing the governments of the Member States, usually in tandem with the European Parliament, representing the peoples of the Union.

The Community method does not imply legislation by the European Commission. The Community Treaties authorise the Commission to propose legislative acts and to execute the legislative and other decisions taken by the legislative bodies. The rhetoric about the "decisions taken by the technocrats of Brussels" (meaning the Commission) is maliciously erroneous. The fact is that the technocrats propose the Community measures; but it is the political institutions representing the democratically elected governments (the Council of Ministers) and the citizens of the Member States (the European Parliament) that take the decisions. Except in a few areas, such as competition, where the Treaties give it full competence, the Commission may only adopt acts implementing the decisions of the legislative bodies.

The Treaties attribute, however, **the initiative for the Community's decision-making procedure** to the Commission [see section 4.1.2.]. It prepares all proposals for Council Regulations, Directives and Decisions. The Commission's role is political in so far as it chooses and prepares the ground on which the construction of the Community is undertaken, but otherwise its role is technocratic as its proposals are based on technical considerations and/or scientific grounds. Using an "impact assessment method", the Commission analyses the direct and indirect implications of a proposed measure (e.g. concerning businesses, trade, employment, the environment and health). The results of each assessment are made public[1]. Moreover, the Commission is responsible for defining in its proposals the common interest or the interest of the Community. To make sure that its proposal is adopted, the Commission must take into consideration the often-divergent interests of the Member States and endeavour to detect and express the common interest. If it does not succeed in this definition or if it does not itself amend its proposal, taking into consideration the positions of the other Community organs, all the Member States together, in total agreement within the Council, must find a different definition of the common interest inherent in a proposal of a common policy or a common measure (Art. 250 TEC); something that happens very rarely.

When adopted by the Commission, a proposal is submitted, depending on the form of the procedure examined below, either to the European Parliament and to the Council for decision or to the first for opinion and to the second for decision and, very often, to the Economic and Social Committee and to the Committee of the Regions for an opinion. **Detailed discussions** begin within the working party of competent national experts, who prepare the Council's decision, the relevant Parliamentary Committee and the groups of experts of the Economic and Social Committee and of the Committee of the Regions. The interest groups at national and Community levels, alerted in good time of this preparatory work, lobby these various technical and political experts and, if the issue is important, public opinion. The Commission has published general principles and **minimum standards for consultation** of interested parties[2]. They enable all those affected by a proposal to express their opinions and, thus, to participate in the legislative process. A database of information on the different bodies consulted gives an overview of the way civil society consultation is organised at European level[3]. The general public has access to the different stages of the legislative process through the Internet-based EUR-Lex service[4].

The interaction of these actors, representing all the Member States and all the interests concerned tends to confirm or redefine the common interest of the proposal formulated by the Commission. As, more often than not, a common policy cannot fully satisfy

---

[1] COM (2002) 276, 5 June 2002.
[2] COM (2002) 277, 5 June 2002.
[3] http://europa.eu.int/comm/civil_society/coneccs/index_en.htm.
[4] http://eur-lex.europa.eu/en/index.htm.

all national interests, negotiations have to take place within and between the main actors in order to find the common denominator that best satisfies most national interests. The text ultimately adopted by the legislative bodies takes into account all national, professional and other interests voiced at various points of the lengthy preparatory work.

It goes without saying that **the Community interest may not harm an "essential interest"** of a Community State, but the definition of an "essential interest" is inevitably subjective. Each Member State has a natural tendency to exaggerate its own problems and minimise those of the others. In other words, the Community decision-making process risks frequently to come to a deadlock, and it has to be emphasised that it is through the joint mediation efforts of the Commission and the Council Presidency that the deadlock can on most occasions be avoided. On the one hand, the majority has to be persuaded to make the necessary concessions to accommodate the minority and, on the other hand, the Member State upholding an extreme or isolated position has to be persuaded that the general advantages of an agreement are more important than its individual interests. Even though they first and foremost assert the interests of their respective governments, the members of the Council usually respect the objectives and needs of the EC as a whole. This is what distinguishes the Council from an intergovernmental conference, where national interests prevail over the common interest [see section 4.1.4.].

The European Parliament is ever more involved in the Community decision-making process under two procedures, co-decision and cooperation with the Council of Ministers. Article 251 (TEC), defines the **co-decision procedure** of the Council with the European Parliament. This procedure was introduced by the EC Treaty at Maastricht and was largely extended by the Amsterdam and Nice amendments of the TEC. It is now applied to practically all important matters covered by this Treaty.

In the co-decision procedure, the Council acting by a qualified majority adopts "common positions", which may be accepted, rejected or amended by the Parliament. If the Council does not agree with the amendments proposed by the Parliament, a **conciliation committee**, composed of equal numbers of representatives of the two institutions, must bring together the different points of view. The Commission can act as an arbitrator between the two decision-making bodies, by accepting in its amended proposal some of the amendments proposed by the Parliament. In the rare cases where a compromise solution is not found, the Parliament may reject the proposed act by absolute majority of expressed votes. Thus, the Parliament has the final word in this legislative procedure. Regulations, Directives and Decisions adopted under the Article 251 procedure are signed both by the President of the European Parliament and the President of the Council. The co-decision procedure has worked well so far. Indeed decisions have been taken fairly quickly as a result of a good working relationship between the institutions, based on the interinstitutional agreement on the Rules of Procedure of the Conciliation Committee, concluded on 21 October 1993.

Article 252 (TCE) defines the **cooperation procedure,** where the Parliament is involved in the legislative process by means of its two readings and the proposal of amendments to the Council's common position. In this procedure, the Commission plays an arbitration role, since it may adopt some or many of the amendments of the Parliament in its own amended proposal; but the Council has the final word, since it may unanimously reject the amended proposal of the Commission. However, this procedure is now limited to a few subject matters.

At present, where the treaties do not provide otherwise, the Council takes decisions by a simple majority of its members. This is rarely the case, however, as in the vast majority of instances the treaties provide that decisions are taken either by unanimity or by qualified majority. Unanimity is undemocratic, because the vote of the smallest country weighs as much as that of the largest and any country can block a decision wished by all its other partners. Therefore, the successive amendments of the Treaties have extended qualified majority voting, notably in the areas where there is participation of the Parliament in the decision-making process. **Qualified majority** is calculated on the basis of votes allocated to each Member State under Article 205 (TEC), as modified by the Accession Act of the ten new Member States. According to the latter, the total number of votes in the Council is 321 and is distributed to the twenty-five Ministers in a weighted manner, so that the influence of a Member State in the decision-making process is more or less related to the size of its population. Actually, **the votes of the Council members are weighted as follows**:

* Germany, France, Italy and the United Kingdom 29 each;
* Spain and Poland 27 each;
* Netherlands 13;
* Belgium, the Czech Republic, Greece, Hungary and Portugal 12 each;
* Austria and Sweden 10 each;
* Denmark, Finland, Ireland, Lithuania and Slovakia 7 each;
* Cyprus, Estonia, Latvia, Luxembourg and Slovenia 4 each; and
* Malta 3.

As a rule, Community decisions taken by qualified majority on the basis of a Commission proposal must gather at least **72% of the total votes of the members, representing at least 62% of the total population** of the Union (on the basis of data supplied by Eurostat)[1]. The same conditions apply to Article 34 of the EU Treaty, but the 232 votes in favour should, in any case, be cast by at least two-thirds of the members. Whilst the qualified-majority voting system of the Treaty of Nice technically opened the door to enlargement, the weighing of the votes in the Council in no way improves the efficiency and transparency of the decision-making process, a fact which gives cause for serious concern as to how it may operate in a Union of 27 or more Member States.

Responding to this concern, **the draft Constitutional Treaty**, firstly, generalises qualified majority voting in the normal legislative process. Secondly, it abandons the weighting of the votes in the Council and, thus, simplifies greatly the system of qualified majority, applicable from November 2009. In effect, Article I-25 of the draft Constitution defines qualified majority as at least **55% of the members** of the Council or the European Council (72%, if the Council is not acting on a proposal of the Commission or of the Union Minister for Foreign Affairs), comprising at least fifteen of them (i.e. 60% of the 25) and representing **at least 65% of the population of the Union**. The constitutional system respects the equality of Member States as each one has one vote in respect of the first criterion, whilst their different population sizes are taken into account in meeting the second criterion. Moreover, the constitutional system, which defines once and for all the criteria of qualified majority, would prevent, during subsequent enlargements, long negotiations on the allocation of votes to Member States and the definition of the qualified majority threshold [see details below].

So as to prevent one or two Member States from blocking further progress of the Union in certain fields, the Treaty of Nice has reinforced and facilitated **enhanced cooperations**, which aim at safeguarding the values and serving the interests of the Union as a whole by asserting its identity as a coherent force on the international scene (Art. 27a to 28 and 40 to 45 (TEU) and 11 (TEC). **In connection with the EC Treaty**, the veto possibility is removed. Member States which intend to establish enhanced cooperation

---

[1] Decision 2004/701, OJ L 319, 20.10.2004.

between themselves must address a request to the Commission, which should submit a proposal to the Council to that effect or inform the Member States concerned of the reasons for not doing so. The assent of the European Parliament is required for an enhanced cooperation in a field coming under the co-decision procedure (Art 11 TEC). **In connection with the common foreign and security policy**, enhanced cooperation is possible for the implementation of a joint action or common position, except in the sphere of the security and defence policy (Art 27b TEU). The Council should act by qualified majority, but the 232 votes in favour of the decision should be cast by at least two-thirds of the members (Art. 23.2 TEU). However, the conditions enabling certain Member States to establish an enhanced cooperation may be difficult to obtain and some are even liable to subjective and hence questionable definitions, in particular the condition that an enhanced cooperation respects the competences, rights and obligations of the Member States which do not participate in it (Art. III-417). It should be said that, until now, enhanced cooperations have either been inscribed in the Treaty (participation in the eurozone) or have been consecrated by it a posteriori (Schengen cooperation agreement) [see section 9.2.]

According to the draft **Constitutional Treaty**, enhanced cooperation should aim to further the objectives of the Union, protect its interests and reinforce its integration process. Such cooperation should be open at any time to all Member States (Articles I-44 and III-416 to III-423). The European decision authorising enhanced cooperation should be adopted by the Council, acting unanimously, as a last resort, if it was established that the objectives of such cooperation could not be attained within a reasonable period by the Union as a whole, and if at least one third of the Member States participated in it..

Where the EC Treaty requires a **co-decision of the Parliament and the Council** on the basis of Article 251, the Commission must submit a proposal to both institutions. The Council, acting by a qualified majority after obtaining the Opinion of the European Parliament, may either adopt the proposal as amended by the Parliament or adopt a common position and communicate it to the European Parliament. Within three months of such communication, the Parliament may approve the common position of the Council, not take a decision (in which case the act in question is deemed to have been adopted in accordance with that common position), reject it (in which case the proposed act is not adopted) or propose amendments to it by an absolute majority of its component members.

Matters obviously become more complicated if the Parliament proposes major amendments to the Council's common position. The latter can naturally, acting by a qualified majority, approve all the amendments, if the Commission agrees with them, or act by unanimity if the Commission has delivered a negative opinion. In this case, it amends its common position in consequence and adopts the act in question. If, however, the Council does not accept all of the amendments tabled by the Parliament, the President of the Council, in agreement with the President of the European Parliament, convenes forthwith a meeting of the **Conciliation Committee**, composed of the members of the Council or their representatives and an equal number of representatives of the European Parliament. The Committee then has the task of reaching agreement on a joint text, by a qualified majority of the members of the Council or their representatives and by a majority of the representatives of the European Parliament. If, within six weeks of its being convened, the Conciliation Committee approves a **joint text**, the European Parliament, acting by an absolute majority of the votes cast, and the Council, acting by a qualified majority, have a period of six weeks from that approval in which to adopt the act in question in accordance with the joint text. If one of the two institutions fails to approve the proposed act, it is deemed not to have been adopted. This is also the case if the Conciliation Committee does not approve a joint text.

In order to understand the **decision-making process within the Council**, it is worth identifying the major stages of a Council meeting. Each Minister arrives in Brussels with a highly technical dossier prepared by his department, which has followed the proceedings in the working party of administrative experts and in the COREPER [see section 4.1.4.]. Each Minister sets out his position, which is normally a starting point for negotiation, in other words extreme. After several rounds of comments the meeting is adjourned to give the Commission and the Presidency the opportunity to draft a compromise. The Commission may amend its proposal to take the compromise into account, and the round of comments resumes. So as not to part empty-handed, Ministers are often obliged to sit until very late at night or to extend the meeting for several days, in which case it becomes a **"marathon session"**.

Each of the three main European institutions, Council, Parliament, Commission, is surrounded by **committees** which contribute to the process of adopting and implementing common policies. The origins of the committees go back to the very early days of the European Community. They developed as a result of the common agricultural policy [see sections 21.3.1 and 21.3.2.], so as to ensure that the duties entrusted to the Commission were carried out in close collaboration with the Member States through the committees [see section 21.3.]. Later on committees were created in the context of practically all common policies. Therefore, a Council Decision of 13 July 1987, called "**commitology Decision**", laid down the procedures to be followed for the different types of committees: management committees, regulatory committees and advisory committees[1]. A large number of these committees work with the European Commission for the management of various common policies, notably the common agricultural policy [see section 21.3.2.]. The Council of Ministers is assisted first and foremost by the Committee of Permanent Representatives (COREPER), by eight specialised committees, including the Special Committee on Agriculture (SCA), and a large number of working parties made of national officials, which prepare Council decisions on common policies [see section 4.1.4.]. The European Parliament is assisted by 19 Parliamentary committees, including the Committee on Agriculture and Rural Development. All these committees constitute multinational human networks, which are very important for advancing the process of European integration [see section 9.4.].

The draft **Constitutional Treaty** would facilitate considerably the system of **qualified majority voting**. Instead of the three criteria required by the Treaty of Nice for a qualified majority (threshold of weighted votes, majority of Member States and 62% of the population of the Union), just two criteria will apply: 55% of the Member States, representing at least 65% of the population of the Union. It should be noted that the third criterion required by the Constitution - 15 Member States in favour of the proposal - is superfluous. In fact, in a Union of 25 Member States, 15 States represent 60% of the total. However, in a Union of more than 25 States, 55% of the total number of States would, mathematically, comprise at least 15 of them and the third criterion would have no sense. A **blocking minority** should include at least four Council members, failing which the qualified majority would be deemed attained. Although clear divisions between "large" and "small" Member States hardly ever occur, this clause would facilitate decision-making in the Council, as it would make more difficult a hypothetical alliance of "big" Member States, three of which could by themselves form a blocking minority, since their populations would represent more than 35% of the Union's population.

4.4. Prospects of European governance

Thanks to the Community method of making and implementing decisions [see section 4.3], the often conflicting national interests are passed through the successive **filters of three institutions**, each defending different but complementary interests: the Commission, the common interest; the Council, the interests of the Member States; the Parliament, the interests of the citizens of the Union. Community policies thus rarely - if ever - can promote the interests of some Member States at the expense of those of some others. In the absence of such filters, an intergovernmental cooperation scheme wishing to serve equally all national interests would have to give equal weight to the positions defended by each one of the participating governments and this would lead to a standstill. If it gave policy leadership to a few Member States, namely the bigger ones, intergovernmental cooperation would lead to conflicts of interests and hence to secessionist tendencies.

"**European governance**" - i.e., the rules, processes and behaviour of the actors that affect the way in which powers are exercised at European level - has worked relatively well up to now, since it has made possible all the achievements of the common policies examined in this book. Therefore, the role of the existing institutions should not be radically changed, nor should new institutions be added, because the rules of the functioning of the protagonists of European integration might be altered, with unknown consequences. However, European governance has already reached its limits of efficiency, even after the improvements brought about by the Treaty of Nice and by the draft Constitutional Treaty. It is doubtful that it could function efficiently in a union of twenty-five

---

[1] Decision 1999/468, OJ L 184, 17.07.1999 last amended by Decision 2006/512, OJ L 200, 22.07.2006.

- and soon more - Member States, which could in addition have the ambition to deepen their political union. In order to enable the Union to better face internal and external challenges, a drastic reform of the institutions is needed.

The structure of the **European Commission**, in particular, should be democratised in parallel with the reinforcement of its role, because its technocratic character, useful as it is, engenders its remoteness from the citizens of the Member States. The Commission is already the executive body of the Community, since it proposes the legislation to the legislative bodies, executes their decisions and controls their implementation by the Member States. It thus plays the role of a "proto-government" of the Union, which has not full democratic legitimacy, since the Commissioners are not elected but are appointed by the governments of the Member States. The solution to this problem would be to entrust the citizens themselves with the election of the members of the Commission at the occasion of European elections. At the same time as they would choose the members of the European Parliament, the voters of each country could elect the Commissioner having the nationality of this country from a short list of candidates prepared by the national parliament. With this system of election in two phases, the national parliaments would play an important role in selecting (by successive votes) two or three personalities capable of assuming European functions, but the Commissioner for each nationality would finally be elected by the citizens of each nation (with the simple majority of the votes cast).

The **president of the Commission** and the **vice-president,** who could also be the Union Minister for Foreign Affairs (according to the constitutional treaty), should be chosen from among these elected personalities by the European Council, acting by qualified majority, and be elected by the European Parliament (as provided for in the draft Constitutional Treaty). The big difference between the system proposed here and the actual system or the one set forth in the draft Constitution is that the president and the vice-president of the Commission would first be elected by their respective countrymen and then would be chosen by the majority of the representatives of the peoples of the Union. They would not come out of the sole inspiration of the heads of State or government and would thus have a double democratic legitimacy, national and European. With such a system of democratic designation of the Commissioners, the citizens would have an important incentive to elect strong personalities as members of the European executive organ, hoping that their compatriot could qualify for a top job, including that of the president and vice-president of the Commission. Moreover, the citizens would feel that they participate in the governance of the Union, since they would elect directly not only the members of one branch of the legislative authority (the European Parliament), but also the members of the executive authority (the European Commission).

The **European Parliament** should play an important role not only in the investiture of the executive authority of the Union, but also in its monitoring. In addition to the legality of the actions of the Commissioners, the Parliament should permanently control their independence in respect of their country of origin and their efficiency in the implementation of their pre-approved work programme. The political role of the European Parliament would thus resemble that of a national parliament, which controls the government of its country. At the same time, the legislative power of the Parliament - through the ordinary legislative procedure - should be extended to all legislative fields, including that of foreign and security policy, which could thus, little by little, become a real common policy and propel the Union on the world scene.

The roles of the **European Economic and Social Committee (EESC) and the Committee of the Regions** [see sections 4.2.3. and 4.2.4.] should be boosted. Actually, these consultative organs suffer from their insufficient representativeness and from their deficient influence on Community decisions. In order to ensure that the members of the EESC are in principle chosen for their competence rather than for their political allegiance, they should be co-opted by the members of the professional and other organisations that they would represent in Brussels without government intervention in their appointment. In order to bring the Committee of the Regions closer to the local and regional populations that it should represent, its members should be chosen directly by them at **European elections**, at the same time as that of European MPs and the Commissioners. To boost the efficiency of opinions of the consultative organs, the competent parliamentary commission(s) should present to the plenary assembly of the European Parliament a report taking up the suggestions and general comments of the EESC and the Committee of the Regions as well as the amendments proposed by them on different points or articles of a European Commission proposal. The assembly should pronounce itself for or against the opinions not only of the parliamentary commission but also of those of the consultative organs. The European Parliament would thus have a central role in the Community legislative process, since its amendments would reflect also the positions of the professional organisations and of the regional authorities.

Bibliography on the European institutions

- BAILEY David J. "Governance or the crisis of governmentality? :Applying critical state theory at the European level" in *Journal of European Public Policy*, v. 13, n. 1, January 2006, p. 16-33.
- BAQUERO CRUZ Julio. "The changing constitutional role of the European Court of Justice", *International Journal of Legal Information*, v. 34, n. 2, Summer 2006, p. 223-245.
- BENZ Arthur, PAPADOPOULOS Yannis (eds.). *Governance and democracy: comparing national, European and international experiences*. Abingdon: Routledge, 2006.
- BERTOLINI Stefano. "Mass politics in Brussels: how benign could it be?" in *Zeitschrift für Staats- und Europawissenschaften*, v. 4, n. 1, 2006, p. 28-56.
- CHARI Raj, KRITZINGER Sylia. *Understanding EU policy making*. London: Pluto press, 2006.
- DEVUYST Youri. *The European Union transformed: Community method and institutional evolution from the Schuman Plan to the Constitution for Europe*. Brussels: PIE - P. Lang, 2006.
- EUROPEAN COMMISSION. *Report from the Commission on the working of committees during 2005*. Luxembourg: EUR-OP*, 2006.
- GIUSTA Paolo. *Ethics matters: practical micro-ethics for civil servants of the European Union*. Luxembourg: EUR-OP*, 2006.
- HAYES-RENSHAW Fiona, WALLACE Helen. *The Council of Ministers*. Basingstoke: Palgrave Macmillan, 2006.
- HOFFMANN Herwig, TÜRK Alexander (eds.). *EU administrative governance*. Cheltenham: Edward Elgar, 2006.
- KREPPEL Amie, GAYE Gungor. *The institutional integration of an expanded EU or how "new" European actors fit into "old" European institutions*. Vienna: Institute for Advanced Studies, 2006.
- LOTH Wilfried (et al.)·*La gouvernance supranationale dans la construction européenne*, Bruxelles: Bruylant, 2005.
- MAES Ivo. "The ascent of the European Commission as an actor in the monetary integration process in the 1960s" in *Scottish Journal of Political Economy*, v. 53, n. 2, May 2006, p. 222-241.
- MÖLLERS Christoph. "European governance: meaning and value of a concept", in *Common Market Law Review*, v. 43, n. 2, April 2006, p. 313-336.
- MOREAU DEFARGES Philippe. *Les institutions européennes*. 7e édition. Paris: Armand Colin, 2005.
- PETERS Anne. "The European Ombudsman and the European Constitution", *Common Market Law Review*, v. 42, n. 3 June 2005, p. 697-743.
- SELCK Torsten. "Explaining the absence of inertia in European Union legislative decision-making", *Journal of Common Market Studies*, v. 43, n. 5, December 2005, p. 1055-1070.
- THOMSON Robert, HOSLI Madeleine. "Who has power in the EU?: The Commission, Council and Parliament in legislative decision-making" in *Journal of Common Market Studies*, v. 44, n. 2, June 2006, p. [391]-417.

- VARSORI Antonio (ed.). *Inside the European Community: actors and policies in the European integration, 1957-1972'*. Baden-Baden : Nomos ; Bruxelles : Bruylant, 2006.
- WALZENBACH G.P.E. (ed.). *European governance: Policy making between politicization and control.* Aldershot; Burlington: Ashgate, 2006.

*The publications of the Office for Official Publications of the European Communities (EUR-OP) exist usually in all official languages of the EU.

Part II: Integration stages

Chapter 5. ***Customs Union***
Chapter 6. ***Common market***
Chapter 7. ***Economic and Monetary Union***
Chapter 8. ***Towards Political Union***

Although the multinational integration process is continuous, four large stages may be distinguished: customs union, common market, economic and monetary union, political union. Such distinction is useful, not only for analytical purposes, but because the passage from one stage to the other necessitates a fundamental decision of the participating member states to transfer new parcels of sovereignty from national to supranational level, sanctioned by treaty agreed by their governments and parliaments [see section 1.1.2.]. The EC/EU is clearly following this evolutionary pattern.

In the isolationist period, usually following a devastating war, like the Second World War, states erect **high protection barriers against foreign trade** and therefore against international competition. These may be customs barriers (tariffs, quotas and measures having equivalent effect), fiscal barriers (higher levels of taxation for goods largely manufactured outside the country), administrative barriers (complicated bureaucratic procedures for imports) or technical barriers (concerning, for example, environment or human health protection) serving in one way or another to discourage or even prohibit imports [see section 6.2.]. This is the zero point in the scale of multinational integration.

Totalitarian regimes apart, such a protectionist system cannot last for long. It leads to **great dissatisfaction on the part of consumers**, whose choice is very restricted, and on the part of the most dynamic and/or less protected businessmen, who find their field of activity limited by the barriers. Dissatisfied citizens, as consumers and voters, and progressive businessmen, as influential interest groups, press the political elite to reduce external protection. Under the sine qua non condition that the latter were susceptible to such pressures and were sincerely seeking the maximisation of national interests - two prerequisites that exclude authoritarian regimes - they would normally start discussing the possibilities of trade liberalisation with like-minded elite in neighbouring countries [see section 1.1.2.]. Indeed, by its very nature, trade liberalisation cannot be decided unilaterally but can only be envisaged in a multinational context. If the economic and political elite of several states were to agree on the desirability of mutual trade liberalisation, they would still have the option to pursue it either within a framework of bilateral or multilateral intergovernmental cooperation, which does not necessitate loss of national sovereignty, or in the framework of a multinational integration process requiring a great number of common policies and, therefore, the transfer of segments of national sovereignty to common institutions.

A **free trade area** is based on intergovernmental cooperation. In such an area, member countries abolish import duties and other customs barriers to the free movement of goods manufactured in the territory of their partners. However, each country retains its own external tariff and its customs policy vis-à-vis third countries. It also retains entirely its national sovereignty. Compared to isolationism, trade liberalisation is a common policy of a group of states, but, since without concessions of sovereignty, there can be no spillover from this unique common policy to other policy areas [see section 1.1.1.], a free trade area should be placed at a low level of multinational integration, before the commencement of the evolutionary process.

By contrast, in a **customs union**, which is the first stage of the evolutionary multinational integration process, free movement concerns not only products manufactured in the territory of the partners, but all products, irrespective of origin, situated in the territory of the member countries. Furthermore, the latter lose their customs autonomy and apply a common external customs tariff to third countries. In order to manage the common customs tariff, the members of a customs union must have a common commercial policy. In addition, trade liberalisation has in this case spillover or multiplicative effects on other common policies, notably, agricultural, taxation and competition. There is therefore, already at this stage - completed by the original six countries of the EEC in July 1968 - some concession of segments of national sovereignty to the common institutions that run the customs union [see chapter 5].

If the implementation of these initial common policies linked with the customs union gave satisfactory but not optimal results, it would reveal the necessity for more common policies inside a **common market** and would consequently have a multiplier effect on the process. In fact, if the members would like to turn a customs union into a real internal market, they would need to ensure not only the free movement of goods and services, but also the free movement of production factors, namely labour and capital. In order to obtain these fundamental freedoms of a common market, the member states had to develop a great number of common policies in pre-established and in new fields, such as social, environment and consumer protection, calling for further sharing of national sovereignties [see chapter 6]. Several amendments of the original Treaties, through the Single European Act, were needed to bring about this evolution [see section 2.1.].

However, even if all the freedoms of a common market were achieved, the single market would still not resemble a genuine internal market, if currency fluctuations and the exchange risk could create new barriers to trade, restrict the interpenetration of the financial markets and impede the establishment of businesses in places where the factors of production would appear to be most propitious for their activities. In order to optimise the conditions of trade, investment and production, the member states of a common market would need, therefore, to move forward to the next stage of economic integration, viz. **economic and monetary union (EMU)**. This would imply a single monetary policy, necessary for the management of a single currency, and the convergence of national economic policies, with a view to achieving economic and social cohesion. A new Treaty, the Treaty of Maastricht, was needed to place the foundations of this new stage of European integration [see section 2.2. and chapter 7].

Even before that integration stage was wholly completed, the member states of a multinational integration scheme would have developed so many economic and political links between themselves that they would feel the need to step forward into the final integration stage, that of political union, by harmonising their justice and home affairs policies, in order to protect efficiently their area of freedom, security and justice, and their foreign policies, so that the economic giant that they had created through economic integration would have a voice commensurate with its size in the international arena [see section 2.3.and chapter 8].

Chapter 5

CUSTOMS UNION

Diagram of the chapter

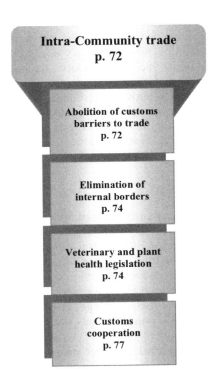

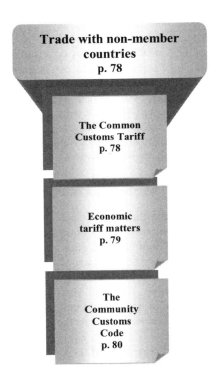

A customs union is a stage of multinational integration, during which the member states agree, by treaty, to refrain from imposing any customs duties, charges having equivalent effect or quantitative restrictions on each other and to adopt an external common customs tariff in their relations with third countries. The common customs tariff implies not only a common customs policy but also a common foreign trade policy [see chapter 23]. Furthermore, the freedom of movement is applicable in a customs union regardless of the origin of goods, thus eliminating customs controls at internal borders.

The founders of the European Economic Community had, from the start, the goal not only of setting up a customs union, but also a common market in which goods, services and capital could be traded freely. In economic integration, they foresaw not only a formula offering economic advantages but also the means to set up the conditions for political union in Europe. In order to achieve this, **a sound foundation** was required. Customs union was, accurately enough, such a foundation; it allowed for unprecedented trade growth in the participating Member States and the construction upon it of the entire European edifice. In fact, all the common policies examined in this book would be unthinkable were they not based on customs union.

5.1. Intra-Community trade

Before the Community treaties came into force, every European country protected its national production with **customs tariffs**, preventing the import of goods at prices lower than those of the national production, and **quantitative restrictions**, preventing the import of certain products in quantities exceeding those which were necessary to satisfy local demand not covered by national production. Thus, a country would import the quantities and qualities not normally supplied by its internal production. As industry was well protected, it saw no need to make large-scale efforts to modernise or reduce production costs. The European consumer, faced with a limited choice and high prices for low quality goods, was the main victim of this **protectionism**. The customs union, limited initially to the coal and steel sectors governed by the ECSC Treaty but rapidly extended to all products and services, thanks to the EEC Treaty [see section 2.1.], aimed at correcting this situation.

5.1.1. The abolition of customs barriers to trade

According to article 23 of the EC Treaty, the Community is based upon a customs union which covers all trade in goods and which involves the prohibition between Member States of customs duties on imports and exports and of all charges having equivalent effect, and the adoption of a common customs tariff in their relations with third countries. The customs union of the EC **covers "all trade in goods"**. This means that products coming from a third country can move freely within the Community if the import formalities have been complied with and any customs duties or charges having equivalent effect, which are payable, have been levied in the importing Member State (Art. 24 TEC).

Articles 13 and 14 of the Treaty of Rome provided that **customs duties and charges having equivalent effect** to customs duties on imports were to be progressively abolished during the twelve-year transitional period from 1 January 1958 to 31 December 1969. Although the Treaty gave the Member States the option of varying the rate of reduction of customs duties according to product (should a sector have difficulties), the reduction was constant and problem-free. The rate of tariff dismantling was even accelerated by two Council decisions, and completed on 1 July 1968, 18 months ahead of schedule. This demonstrates that tariff dismantling caused no major problems to the industries of the Member States, as any country's objection would have prevented the change of schedule provided by the Treaty. The States which acceded to the Community later on had a five-year transitional period to eliminate customs duties in intra-Community trade. This was also problem-free. Certainly, many of the previously protected industries were obliged to renovate or shut down, but many new industries were created or expanded on sound premises.

The accelerated completion of the tariff union meant that, as of 1 July 1968, intra-Community trade was freed of customs duties and quantitative restrictions on imports and exports. However, **other trade obstacles,** such as charges having equivalent effect to customs duties and measures having equivalent effect to quantitative restrictions, were far from gone. The proper functioning of the tariff union required the removal of these obstacles too by the end of the transitional period. Indeed, the Treaty of Rome expressly noted the necessity of "reducing formalities imposed on trade as much as possible" (Art 10 EEC). In reality, as soon as tariff disarmament was accomplished, the "formalities war" was stepped up between Member State administrations anxious to protect national production and at the same time prevent the decrease of their own functions and powers. Of course, every form, every stamp required for cross-border trade had a reason: tax collection, statistics, and customs checks aimed at preventing the import of products not conforming to national regulations, etc. But each stamp meant time and money to the Community's businesses.

A great number of those **trade barriers were hidden in regulations**, such as consumer or environment protection standards, which varied from one State to another [see section 6.1.]. Their restrictive effects were often more damaging than customs duties and quantitative restrictions. Indeed, while customs barriers raised the price of imports or quantitatively limited them, various regulations could completely block the import of a product. Fortunately, such extreme cases were rather limited. However, as seen in the chapter on the common market, the elimination of non-customs barriers to trade proved to be much more difficult and took three times as long as did the elimination of customs barriers.

Despite the non-completion of the customs union by 1968, **the economic results of the free circulation of goods** achieved by it were indisputable. From 1958 to 1972, while trade between the six founding Member States and the rest of the world had tripled, intra-Community trade had been multiplied by nine. Such exceptional trade growth was a key factor in economic development and the raising of the standard of living in all member countries of the original EEC. The stimulating effect of the wider market created a feeling of business confidence, which resulted in investment growth. Consumers emerged as the overall winners; supply was much more diverse and products cheaper than before tariff dismantling. The welfare objective of European integration was undoubtedly well pursued through the customs union. The task of the common institutions was, therefore, to eliminate the remaining problems and increase the benefits of the customs union.

In the eventuality of a **grievance for trade restrictions**, the Commission examines its validity and, pursuant to article 226 of the EC Treaty, calls upon the concerned State to amend or suppress a rule or practice contrary to Community law. If the government concerned does not comply with this request, the Commission brings the matter before the Court of Justice, whose opinion is binding as much for the Member State as it is for Community institutions. It must be said that the majority of these cases are settled after notice the Commission serves notice to the Member State in question. An Advisory **Committee on Customs Matters and Indirect Taxation**. made up of representatives of professional organisations or of consumers concerned by customs and fiscal problems, strengthens the dialogue between the various parties to customs union[1].

---

[1] Decision 91/453, OJ L 241, 30.08.1991.

5.1.2. Elimination of internal borders

The good results of the customs union **spurred the completion of the common market**, examined in the next chapter, itself needed for the completion of the customs union. Indeed, the customs union and the common market, which were the goals of the Treaty of Rome, both suffered from the same problems and finally benefited from the same remedies. Heartened by the evident benefits of the customs union, the Community institutions under the leadership of the Commission waged a "war of attrition on formalities", which, thanks to the Single European Act of 1987 [see section 2.1.], reached a successful conclusion on December 31, 1992.

Since January 1, 1993, no customs formalities are required for trade within the Community. Hence, all checks and all formalities in respect of goods moving within the Community have been eliminated[1]. The Community henceforth forms **one single border-free area** for the purposes of the movement of goods under cover of the TIR (international road transport) and ATA (temporary admission of goods) carnets[2]. This saves a great deal of time for economic operators and thus helps cut the cost of transporting goods within the Community. The absence of duties and formalities bolsters intra-EU trade (dispatches and arrivals) which represents around 65% of the total trade of the Fifteen and up to 80% of the total imports or exports of some countries of the Union.

In order to guarantee the **free movement of persons** provided for by Article 18 of the EC Treaty, controls and formalities appertaining to cabin and hold baggage of persons taking an intra-Community flight and the baggage of persons making an intra-Community sea crossing have been abolished since January 1993[3].

The abandonment of customs formalities, as of 1st January 1993, has necessitated the establishment of a **system for collecting statistical information** on exchanges of goods between Member States directly from undertakings **(INTRASTAT)**. The amendments to customs legislation following the completion of the internal market have also necessitated the updating of the regulations on the completion of statistics on the trading of goods with non-member countries[4]. **EDICOM** is a trans-European network for the collection, production and dissemination of statistics on the intra-Community and extra-Community trading of goods[5].

5.1.3. Veterinary and plant health legislation

Veterinary and plant health legislation is important not only for intra-Community trade, but also for the protection of the environment and of human health. It is in the interest of all Member States to strengthen their common legislation in these fields and, at the same time, not to upset intra-Community trade of foodstuffs.

The **plant health arrangements,** which came into force on 1 June 1993, have made it possible to remove all physical obstacles to trade of plants and plant products[6]. These arrangements include the rules applicable to the intra-Community trade of plants and plant products imported from third countries, the standards for the protection of the environment and human health against harmful or undesirable organisms and the protective measures against the introduction into the Community of organisms harmful to plants or plant products and against their spread within the Community[7]. The Community Plant Variety Office supervises the protection of plant varieties in the Community[8].

---

[1] Regulation 2913/92, OJ L 302, 19.10.1992 and Regulation 648/2005, OJ L 117, 04.05.2005.
[2] Regulation 719/91, OJ L 78, 26.03.1991 repealed by Regulation 2913/92, OJ L 302, 19.10.1992.
[3] Regulation 3925/91, OJ L 374, 31.12.1991 and Regulation 2454/93, OJ L 253, 11.10.1993.
[4] Regulation 1172/95, OJ L 118, 25.05.1995 and Regulation 374/98, OJ L 48, 19.02.1998.
[5] Decision 507/2001, OJ L 76, 16.03.2001 and Decision 787/2004, OJ L 138, 30.04.2004.
[6] Directive 2000/29, OJ L 169, 10.07.2000 last amended by Directive 2006/35, OJ L 88, 25.03.2006.
[7] Directive 2000/29, OJ L 169, 10.07.2000 and Directive 2005/15, OJ L 56, 02.03.2005.
[8] Regulation 2100/94, OJ L 227, 01.09.1994 last amended by Regulation 873/2004, OJ L 162, 30.04.2004.

In the **veterinary field**, the efforts of the Community are mainly geared towards **protecting the health of animals and consequently human health**, while allowing the smooth operation of the internal market. Since January 1, 1992, veterinary checks at intra-Community frontiers have been abolished and are instead carried out at the point of departure[1], while measures were taken to monitor zoonoses and zoonotic agents and thus prevent outbreaks of food-borne infections and intoxications[2]. At the same time, the Community has switched from a system characterised by a policy of systematic preventive vaccination against foot and mouth disease, which could act as an obstacle to the free movement of animals and products, to a policy of non-vaccination and slaughter in the event of an infection source appearing.

Although the elimination of controls at internal frontiers was necessary for the free circulation of animals and animal products in the internal market, it brought about other problems. The epizootic disease of bovine spongiform encephalopathy (BSE - "**mad cow disease**"), which first appeared in the United Kingdom in 1996 and then spread to several other countries, is indicative of the importance of veterinary questions for the customs union. Despite the prohibition of exports of bovine animals over the age of 6 months, of meat and specified meat products from the United Kingdom, the certification of animals and animal products in tandem with increased veterinary checks in the consigning Member State[3], the consumers' concerns spread in all the Member States and the beef market collapsed in the whole Community [see details below, as well as sections 11.2. and 21.4.2.].

Similar problems were created after the detection, in Belgium in June 1999, of **contamination by dioxins** of certain animal products intended for human or animal consumption. The protective measures, taken under the safeguard clause, obliged all Member States to ensure the withdrawal from the market and destruction of any poultry or egg products or food products containing poultry-related products which had come from suspect farms[4]. These cases demonstrate the fact that in a customs union the market problems of a single Member State are **in reality problems of the single market**. Therefore, the measures taken in order to face the problems of a country concern all the members of the Union.

The **Food and Veterinary Office (FVO)**, established in Ireland, is responsible for consumer protection and particularly for the monitoring of all slaughterhouses approved in the Member States for intra-Community trade, as well as of all establishments manufacturing meat products. Veterinary checks on animal products entering the territory of a Member State from third countries are organised at Community level[5]. Veterinary import procedures for animals and animal products from third countries have been computerised (Shift System), thus ensuring smooth operation of the internal market[6].

Intra-Community trade in fresh meat is linked to Community measures on the **struggle against animal diseases**, such as classical swine fever[7], African swine fever[8] and foot-and-mouth disease[9]. A Directive on health problems affecting intra-Community trade in bovine animals and swine lays down conditions for the production and marketing of fresh meat[10]. A Regulation aims at the **protection of animals during transport**[11]. It lays down journey-time limits, rest times, and watering and feeding intervals. A supplementary Directive sets additional animal protection standards applicable to road vehicles used for the carriage of livestock on

---

[1] Directive 89/662, OJ L 395, 30.12.1989 and Directive 2004/41, OJ L 157, 30.04.2004.
[2] Directive 2003/99, OJ L 325, 12.12.2003.
[3] Directives 96/90 and 96/91, OJ L 13, 16.01.1997.
[4] Decision 1999/449, OJ L 175, 10.07.1999 and Decision 1999/601, OJ L 232, 02.09.1999
[5] Directives 97/78 and 97/79, OJ L 24, 30.01.1998.
[6] Decision 92/438, OJ L 243, 25.08.1992 and Regulation 806/2003, OJ L 122, 16.05.2003.
[7] Directive 2001/89, OJ L 316, 01.12.2001.
[8] Directives 85/320 and 85/321, OJ L 168, 28.06.1985.
[9] Directive 2003/85, OJ L 306, 22.11.2003.
[10] Directive 64/432, OJ L 121, 29.07.1964 and Regulation 1/2005, OJ L 3, 05.01.2005.
[11] Regulation 1/2005, OJ L 3, 05.01.2005.

journeys exceeding eight hours[1]. A European Convention for the protection of animals during international transport contains elements inspired by Community legislation, such as the need for transporters to be registered and authorised, and for their personnel to receive proper training[2].

The Community also covers various veterinary activities with a view to ensuring the **rational development of the livestock** production sector and the raising of productivity. Thus, Community rules apply to requirements for feed hygiene[3], additives in feedingstuffs[4], veterinary medicinal products[5], undesirable substances and products in animal feed[6], maximum residue limits of veterinary medicinal products in foodstuffs[7] and the organisation of official inspections, both at external frontiers and inside the Community, in the field of animal nutrition[8]. Community rules prohibit the use in stockfarming of certain substances having a hormonal or thyrostatic action and of beta-agonists having an anabolic effect[9]. They also prevent meat imports from third countries, which do not prohibit the fattening of livestock with hormones, causing loud complaints of these countries, notably the United States.

The acknowledgment by the British Government, in March 1996, that there was a possible link between the disease of bovine animals (BSE) fed on meal made from contaminated meat or slaughter by-products and the Creutzfeldt-Jakob disease of human beings has spurred **many changes to the Community veterinary legislation**. In the field of the customs union, the Council adapted to the new situation pre-existing directives concerning veterinary inspections and checks[10], the movement of feed materials and the marketing of compound feedingstuffs[11]. The measures taken include: a system for the identification and registration of bovine animals and the labelling of beef and beef products[12]; publicity measures to inform consumers of the guarantees offered by the labelling system for beef and veal[13]; measures concerning intra-Community trade in bovine animals and swine[14]; and measures for protection against specified zoonoses in order to prevent outbreaks of food-borne infections and intoxications posing a threat to human health[15]. All the Member States agreed to follow common rules for the prevention, control and eradication of certain transmissible spongiform encephalopathies[16]. All slaughterhouses, cutting plants and animal waste processing plants throughout the European Union are required to apply new standardised rules and imports from third countries are subject to comparable requirements[17].

By setting the permitted levels for certain harmful organisms, a Directive aims to **protect the plants and forests of Europe** from disease and also removes the need for plant health checks in intra-Community trade[18]. By prohibiting the marketing and use of certain substances, another Directive protects human health and, in certain cases, the environment[19]. Another directive regulates the placing of plant protection products (pesticides) on the market[20]. The Community rules on the marketing and use of **pesticides** containing dangerous substances is becoming more and more strict, by overhauling and streamlining the legislation on pesticides to ensure a consistent level of protection for products which are intended for human consumption and animal nutrition[21]. The marketing of compound feedingstuffs[22] and of agricultural and vegetable seeds and propagating material are also regulated[23].

---

[1]   Directive 95/29, OJ L 148, 30.06.1995 and Regulation 411/98, OJ L 52, 21.02.1998.
[2]   Decision 2004/544, OJ L 241, 13.07.2004.
[3]   Regulation 183/2005, OJ L 35, 08.02.2005.
[4]   Regulation 1831/2003, OJ L 268, 18.10.2003 and Regulation 378/2005, OJ L 59, 05.03.2005.
[5]   Directive 2001/82, OJ L 311, 28.11.2001 and Regulation 726/2004, OJ L 136, 30.04.2004.
[6]   Directive 2002/32, OJ L 140, 30.05.2002 and Directive 2006/13, OJ L 32, 04.02.2006.
[7]   Regulation 2377/90, OJ L 224, 18.08.1990 and Regulation 205/2006, OJ L 34, 07.02.2006.
[8]   Regulation 882/2004, OJ L 165, 30.04.2004 and Regulation 776/2006, OJ L 136, 24.05.2006.
[9]   Directive 96/22, OJ L 125, 23.05.1996 and Directive 2003/74, OJ L 262, 14.10.2003.
[10] Directive 96/43, OJ L 162, 01.07.1996.
[11] Directive 96/25, OJ L 125, 23.05.1996 and Directive 2001/46, OJ L 234, 01.09.2001.
[12] Regulation 1760/2000, OJ L 204, 11.08.2000.
[13] Regulation 2071/98, OJ L 265, 30.09.1998 and Regulation 2826/2000, OJ L 328, 23.12.2000.
[14] Directive 97/12, OJ L 109, 25.04.1997 and Directive 98/99, OJ L 358, 31.12.1998.
[15] Directive 2003/99, OJ L 325, 12.12.2003.
[16] Regulation 999/2001, OJ L 147, 31.05.2001 and Regulation 932/2005, OJ L 163, 23.06.2005.
[17] Decision 2000/418, OJ L 158, 30.06.2000 repealed by Regulation 1326/2001, OJ L 177, 30.06.2001.
[18] Directive 2000/29, OJ L 169, 10.07.2000, last amended by Directive 2006/35, OJ L 88, 25.03.2006.
[19] Directive 79/117, OJ L 33, 08.02.1979 and Regulation 850/2004, OJ L 158, 30.04.2004.
[20] Directive 91/414, OJ L 230, 19.08.1991 and Directive 2006/45, OJ L 130, 18.05.2006.
[21] Regulation 396/2005, OJ L 70, 16.03.2005 and Regulation 178/2006, OJ L 29, 02.02.2006.
[22] Directive 79/373, OJ L 86, 06.04.1979 and Directive 2002/2, OJ L 63, 06.03.2002.
[23] Directives 2002/54, 2002/55, 2002/57, OJ L 193, 20.07.2002 and Directive 2004/117, OJ L 14, 18.01.2005.

5.1.4. Customs cooperation

The abolition of administrative procedures on crossing the internal frontiers of the Community heightens the **risk of fraud**, if all the Member States do not apply equivalent control measures. Administrative cooperation must encourage a comparative level of checks, thus ensuring the uniform application of Community law at every point of the EU external borders and guaranteeing mutual trust and equal conditions of competition. The efficiency of a customs union depends, indeed, as much on homogeneous rules as on the quality of its operational structures.

Customs officials make up an important **human network** of the EU. Since they collect customs duties, which must be transferred to the Community budget [see section 3.4.], and guard the external frontiers against illicit trading, the customs officers of the Member States **act in fact in the name of the Community** and must apply the Community law. They must be open to cooperation both among themselves and with the Commission in the spirit of Article 10 of the EC Treaty.

Article 29 of the EU Treaty urges the Council to take measures in order to strengthen cooperation between customs authorities and police forces, both directly and through the European Police Office (Europol). In fact, such measures are taken both in the context of the customs union and of justice and home affairs cooperation [see section 8.1.]. Thus, the Council Regulation on the **mutual assistance** between the Member States' administrations and on their collaboration with the Commission aims to step up fraud prevention, ensure the proper application of customs and agricultural regulations, providing *inter alia* for the administration of a computerised "customs information system" (CIS)[1]. The **Naples II Convention** on Mutual Assistance and Cooperation between Customs Administrations aims to crack down on the proliferation of illicit trafficking in breach of national and Community provisions by making customs cooperation faster and more effective[2].

Modern administrative management increasingly uses **computerised methods**. Therefore, the Council decided the coordination of computerised administrative procedures (CD project)[3]. In this context, several computerised links have been developed. The computerised customs information system (CIS), mentioned above, purports to step up the fight against fraud at the Community's external frontiers. It is set up and maintained by the Member States' customs administrations to help prevent, detect and prosecute serious offences against national and Community laws. A customs files identification database (FIDE) aims to enable the competent authorities of one Member State, when opening a file on or investigating one or more persons or enterprises, to identify the competent authorities of other Member States which are or have been involved in investigating the same parties[4]. The electronic mail system, known as **Scent** (system for a customs enforcement network), is designed to pass urgent messages concerning cases of fraud. Updatings of the Community's integrated tariff multilingual database (Taric), which is managed centrally by the Commission [see section 5.2.1.], are transmitted daily to the Member States by electronic data transfer **(TARIC interface)** and to traders via the Internet. A centralised system for automatic tariff quota management communicates electronically with national administrative departments **(Quotas).**

The Commission conducts in partnership with the Member States, an action programme entitled "Customs 2007" aimed at modernising the national customs administrations, integrating the new States into the "single customs administration" and improving the protection offered by customs to the consumer and the financial interests of the Community through the reform of transit and checks linked with combating fraud, and computerising customs[5]. The Council has decided to frame a **strategy for customs cooperation** under the third pillar as part of the establishment of an area of freedom, security and justice [see sections 3.1 and 8.1.], which

---

[1] Regulation 515/97, OJ L 82, 22.03.1997.
[2] Convention and Council Act, OJ C 24, 23.01.1998.
[3] Decision 86/23, OJ L 33, 08.02.1986.
[4] Protocol, OJ C 139, 13.06.2003.
[5] Decision 253/2003, OJ L 36, 12.02.2003 and Decision 787/2004, OJ L 138, 30.04.2004.

would serve to protect society and the economy more effectively against smuggling and fraud, cross-border organised crime and money-laundering, threats to the environment and cultural heritage[1].

5.2. Trade with non-member countries

Apart from removing obstacles to intra-Community trade, a customs union includes the harmonisation of customs regulations on trade with non-member countries. The efforts aimed at implementing such regulations in the European Union take two solid forms. On the one hand, the Community has established, and manages, a **Common Customs Tariff (CCT)**; on the other hand, Community rules fit into an international context, whose evolution they must follow. Thus, arrangements agreed previously in the context of GATT and, henceforth, of the World Trade Organisation must be transposed into Community law [see section 23.4.].

Customs union requires more than just having a common customs tariff. This tariff must also be applied according to identical rules throughout all Member States. Failure to do this could result in different values attributed to goods for customs purposes or different rules on the release of goods for circulation according to the importing Member State. The **Community Customs Code (CCC)**, which groups together all the provisions of the Community's customs legislation, aims precisely at removing the risk of different interpretations of EU rules in trade between the Member States and third countries [see section 5.2.3.][2]. The common customs legislation grouped together in the customs code is an attribute of the customs union.

5.2.1. The Common Customs Tariff

A customs union is characterised by the existence of **a single external tariff** applied by all Member States to imports coming from third countries. Such imports only have to clear customs once and can then move freely within the common customs area. Reaching an agreement among the original Member States on a single external tariff required a complex striking of balances and compromises, given the different national interests, stemming from the different products that each country wished to protect. The common customs tariff adopted by the European institutions in 1968 is, therefore, a major achievement of European integration.

For the member countries, the CCT meant both the loss of **customs revenue**, which, since 1975, has been a resource of the Community budget, and the option of carrying out an independent customs or trade policy [see sections 3.4. and 23.1.]. No member country can unilaterally decide on or negotiate tariff matters; **all changes to the CCT are decided by the Council** following negotiation (if necessary) and proposal by the Commission. All bilateral (between the EU and non-member countries) and multilateral (in the past inside GATT and now inside WTO) negotiations are carried out by the Commission.

As of 1968, **the Member States are not entitled to unilaterally carry out customs policy**, i.e. suspend customs duties or change CCT. Only the Council can waive the normal application of CCT by means of regulations adopting various tariff measures. Such measures, whether required under agreements or introduced unilaterally, involve reductions in customs duties or zero-rating in respect of some or all imports of a given

---

[1] Council Resolution, OJ C 247, 15.10.2003.
[2] Regulation 2913/92, OJ L 302, 19.10.1992 and Regulation 648/2005, OJ L 117, 04.05.2005.

product in the territory of the Community. They take the form of Community tariff quotas, tariff ceilings or total or partial suspension of duties.

The most important tariff concessions were granted by the Community in the context of the **General Agreement on Tariffs and Trade (GATT)**. In the course of several international negotiations, namely: the "Dillon Round" (1960-62), the "Kennedy Round" (1964-67) and the "Tokyo Round" (1973-79), substantial reductions of customs duties were made on most industrial products. The "Uruguay Round", which was launched on 20 September 1986 and was concluded on 15 December 1993, has achieved major tariff reductions on the part of the 117 participating countries in the sectors of industry, agriculture and services. It has also imposed new rules and disciplines to international trade, rules that the EU has incorporated into Community law [see section 23.4.].

Since 1995, the customs tariff of the European Union takes account of the outcome of the **GATT Uruguay Round of negotiations** [see section 23.2.]. In principle, for each item and sub-item of the tariff nomenclature, both the autonomous rates and the conventional rates resulting from the GATT negotiations are indicated. Several technical annexes to the CCT set out the specific import regimes, such as the import regime for certain agricultural products or the regime for pharmaceutical substances which may benefit from exoneration on duties.

Before effecting any customs operation, it is first necessary to proceed to the "**customs classification**" of the goods concerned. Classification has a determining effect on the proper functioning of agreements between the Community and certain exporting countries. The level of detail of the combined nomenclature has resulted, principally for those SMEs without computerised systems, in a complexity and multiplication of the lines to be declared. Therefore, businesses can request binding tariff information from the authorities in the Member States with responsibility for the classification of goods under the customs nomenclature[1]. This information indicates the tariff heading to be used for specific goods in all of the Member States. It therefore makes a vital contribution to the legal security of businesses and greatly facilitates imports and exports.

The Commission and the Member States cooperate to ensure the proper and uniform application of the **CCT's nomenclature**. This customs instrument is very important, not only for the collection of customs duties, but also for a number of Community activities, such as the preparation of foreign trade statistics and the proper application of various measures regarding commercial, agricultural, fiscal or monetary policies[2]. This activity takes the form of the adoption of Commission regulations, the finalisation of explanatory notes or classification slips in the customs nomenclature. The Community uses the same nomenclature as its main trading partners, thus facilitating trade negotiations. It is called the **Combined Nomenclature (CN)** because it meets the Community's tariff and statistical requirements simultaneously[3].

In parallel with the introduction of the CN, the **Integrated Community Tariff database (Taric)** was established, in order to indicate, in relation to each CN code, the Community clauses applicable to the goods of this code. It incorporates import provisions not included by the CN, such as tariff quotas and preferences, the temporary suspension of autonomous CCT duties, anti-dumping duties and countervailing duties[4] [see section 23.3.2.]. Thus, Taric spans all the Community measures applicable to trade and provides national administrations with information on all Community measures relating to internal and external trade. It is published annually in the Official Journal of the EU, but any modification is immediately transmitted by electronic way to competent administrations[5].

5.2.2. Economic tariff matters

Several **tariff quotas and ceilings** are opened every year, under bilateral agreements with non-member countries or on a unilateral basis in order to secure the Community supply situation for certain products[6]. For the same reason, and also in many cases with the aim of encouraging Community industry to use or introduce new technology, the Council **temporarily suspends**, every year, duties on about 1800 products or groups of

---

[1]   Ibid.
[2]   Regulation 2658/87, OJ L 256, 07.09.1987 and Regulation 996/2006, OJ L 179, 01.07.2006.
[3]   Regulation 2913/92, OJ L 302, 19.10.1992 and Regulation 648/2005, OJ L 117, 04.05.2005.
[4]   Regulation 2658/87, OJ L 256, 07.09.1987 and Regulation 996/2006, OJ L 179, 01.07.2006.
[5]   See OJ C 103, 30.04.2003.
[6]   Regulation 2505/96, OJ L 345, 31.12.1996 last amended by Regulation 151/2006, OJ L 25, 28.01.2006.

products, mainly chemicals and products of the electronics or aircraft industries[1]. Tariffs are also suspended on a number of agricultural and fishery products, to improve the supply of certain types of food and to honour preferential commitments entered into with certain non-member countries.

The legislation on **preferential tariff measures** resulting from agreements concluded between the EU and States or groups of States, with which contractual relations are maintained, has been consolidated in a few main multiannual Regulations. For the sake of simplification and efficiency, the publication of tariff suspensions in separate regulations with a specified date of validity has been replaced by publication in a comprehensive multiannual form[2]. Community exporters operating from one or more Member States may request a single authorisation to export under the provisions governing preferential trade between the European Community and certain countries[3].

As part of its development aid policy, the European Union applies **generalised tariff preferences** to imports from developing countries[4] [see section 24.5.]. To the African, Caribbean and Pacific States (ACP), signatories of the Cotonou Agreement, the EU grants free access to the near-totality of their exports, with the exception of textile products and of the agricultural products that are subject to common market organisations of the common agricultural policy[5] [see section 24.2.].

Following the accession to the EEC of the UK and Denmark, both former **European Free Trade Association (EFTA)** members, free trade agreements were concluded between the Community and the EFTA countries in order to avoid the erection of new obstacles to trade. These bilateral agreements have been replaced, since 1st January 1994, by the **Treaty on the European Economic Area (EEA)**, which, after the accession of Austria, Sweden and Finland to the EU, brings together the Member States of the EC/EU with Norway, Iceland and the Liechtenstein in a vast economic zone guaranteeing, not only free trade, but also the fundamental freedoms of a common market [see section 25.1.].

The **full application of CCT** is thus limited to trade with the United States of America, Canada, Japan, Australia and a few other developed countries [see section 5.2.3.]. Although CCT has become less important, customs union, supported by the instruments of trade policy, which accompany it, ensures sufficient protection for efficient industrial producers in all Member States. As mentioned above, however, **close cooperation between national administrations**, organised by the Commission, is needed to prevent infringements of customs rules and other conditions for access to the Union market [see section 5.1.4.]. Priority areas include fraud prevention, protection of intellectual property rights - particularly trade marks, designs and copyright - and measures to combat counterfeiting [see section 23.2.2.].

5.2.3. The Community Customs Code

A customs union, without borders, presupposes that the customs relations of the Member States with the rest of the world be regulated in the same way. The common customs legislation is, in fact, applicable to the jurisdictions of all Member States as internal law. For this purpose, the **Community Customs Code (CCC)** groups together and presents all of the provisions of customs legislation governing the Community's trade with third countries in the light of its undertakings within the World Trade Organisation [see section 23.4.][6]. It aims to guarantee the clarity of Community customs regulations and remove the risk of divergent interpretations or legal vagueness.

The Code contains, first of all, **the basic rules of common customs legislation**: customs territory of the European Union, customs value, goods origin, etc. The definition of the **customs territory** of the Community includes inter alia the coastal Member States' territorial sea, a matter of particular importance to the fishing and offshore activities of Member States. **Value for customs purposes** can sometimes have a greater impact on trade than customs duties. The Community Customs Code specifies the method by which such value is determined, the customs clearance criteria for goods finished or processed out of their country of origin, and the conditions under which goods are temporarily exempt of import duties. The **rules of origin** determine to what extent products

---

[1] Regulation 1255/96, OJ L 158, 29.06.1996 last amended by Regulation 300/2006, OJ L 56, 25.02.2006.
[2] Regulation 1255/96, OJ L 158, 29, 06.1996 and Regulation 963/2006, OJ L 176, 30.06.2006.
[3] Regulation 1207/2001, OJ L 165, 21.06.2001.
[4] Regulation 980/2005, OJ L 169, 30.06.2005.
[5] Regulation 2286/2002, OJ L 348, 21.12.2002.
[6] Regulation 2913/92, OJ L 302, 19.10.1992 and Regulation 648/2005, OJ L 117, 04.05.2005.

coming from third countries may be exempt of duty by determining the degree of processing or transformation they have undergone. These rules are important for the proper application of preference systems and several provisions of the commercial policy of the European Union [see sections 5.2.2., 23.2.1. and 24.5.].

Common customs regulations, uniformly applicable in the Community's trade relations with other countries, involve setting up **various customs procedures** with economic impact. The Community Customs Code harmonised the legislative, regulatory and administrative provisions relative to customs warehouses procedures, free zones procedures, and usual forms of handling, which can be undertaken in customs warehouses and free zones[1]. Thus, it includes provisions on: the customs treatment of goods entering the Community's customs territory and on the temporary storage of these goods; goods brought into the customs territory of the Community until such goods have received a destination for customs purposes[2]; returned goods in the customs territory of the Community; and admission to free circulation of goods[3]. **Transit systems** (Community transit, common transit and TIR) are at the heart of the customs union and the common commercial policy, but these systems are subject to fraud [see details below]. A common transit procedure exists between the EC countries and the EFTA countries[4]. The EU implements the principles of the revised Kyoto Convention on the simplification and harmonisation of customs procedures[5].

The CCC governs also the **export procedures** of Community goods, the deferred payment of customs duties on imports or exports, the refund or remittance of these duties and the post-clearance collection of export duties not imposed on goods entered for a customs procedure. For Community exports, the Commission has adapted the model certificate of origin to the overall frame recommended by the UN[6]. A Community system of relief from customs duties exists[7].

A Regulation on **checks for conformity** of products imported from third countries with the rules of the Community Directive on product safety aims to ensure an efficient and coherent management of the common external frontier and to equalise the conditions of competition between Community products and imports[8]. It enables the customs authorities of the Member States to temporarily suspend the customs clearance procedure in cases where imported products present characteristics which may constitute a direct health or safety hazard. Agreements on mutual recognition in the field of conformity assessment signed between the European Community and Australia[9], New Zealand,[10] Canada[11], the United States[12] and Japan[13] provide market access throughout the territories of the parties, since they authorise product testing and certification in the exporting countries and no longer only in the countries of destination [see section 6.2.3.]. However, as the United States had failed to respect the procedures for recognition of conformity assessment bodies designated by the Community, the Council decided to suspend the Community's obligations stemming from the mutual recognition agreements binding them[14].

The CCC also governs the **processing of goods under customs control** before their release for free circulation in order to avoid, by use of tariff measures, the processing operations of certain imports, such as certain petroleum products, taking place in third countries rather than in the Community. To facilitate the use of containers in, for example, combined road/rail carriage, a regulatory system for the temporary admission of

---

[1] Ibid.
[2] OJ L 367, 31.12.1988.
[3] Regulation 2913/92, OJ L 302, 19.10.1992 and Regulation 1427/97, OJ L 196, 24.07.1997.
[4] Convention and Decision 87/415, OJ L 226, 13.08.1987, OJ L 226, 13.08.1987.
[5] Decision 2003/231, OJ L 86, 03.04.2003 and Decision 2004/485, OJ L 162, 30.04.2004.
[6] Regulation 2454/93, OJ L 253, 11.10.1993 and Regulation 402/2006, OJ L 70, 09.03.2006.
[7] Regulation 918/83, OJ L 105, 23.04.1983 and Regulation 355/94, OJ L 46, 18.02.1994.
[8] Regulation 339/93, OJ L 40, 10.02.1993.
[9] Decision 98/508, OJ L 229, 17.08.1998 and Decision 2002/800, OJ L 278, 16.10.2002.
[10] Decision 98/509, OJ L 229, 17.08.1998 and Decision 2002/801, OJ L 278, 16.10.2002.
[11] Decision 98/566, OJ L 280, 16.10.1998 and Decision 2002/802, OJ L 278, 16.10.2002.
[12] Decision 1999/78, OJ L 31, 04.02.1999 and Decision 2002/803, OJ L 278, 16.10.2002.
[13] Decision 2001/747, OJ L 284, 29.10.2001 and Decision 2002/804, OJ L 278, 16.10.2002.
[14] Decision 2003/57, OJ L 23, 28.01.2003.

containers is defined[1]. Bearing the mark of their Member State, the containers are deemed to meet the conditions of free circulation provided by articles 23 and 24 (TEC).

Of particular interest are **inward processing arrangements** allowing for the temporary release for free circulation of products coming from third countries processed in a member State and re-exported to a third country. The Member States must properly apply these procedures especially when the inward processing deals with agricultural products and when compensating products are released for free circulation in a Member State other than where the processing took place. In an attempt to lighten the formalities for those involved, specific provisions are applicable to certain inward processing arrangements or processing under customs control carried out in a customs warehouse, free warehouse or free zone[2].

The reverse mechanism, **outward processing arrangements**, is of interest to many European enterprises which, in the context of the international division of labour, export goods with a view to re-importing them following processing, working or repairs. This alleviates the enterprise's production costs and thus favours production in the EU. Established in 1982 as part of the multifibre arrangement for textile and clothing products [see sections 17.3.3. and 23.5.][3], outward processing relief arrangements were expanded, in 1986, to **standard exchange** arrangements and, in 1988, to **triangular traffic** concerning two Member States. The Member States can check the relevant documents in order to ensure that the compensating products have been manufactured using goods temporarily exported.

Customs legislation is **susceptible to fraud**. In order to prevent fraud arising from irregularities of origin, it is necessary to determine uniformly the origin of goods obtained entirely in a certain country, as well as the origin of goods obtained in a country after substantial transformation of raw materials and semi-products originating in other countries. Thus, goods admitted under preference agreements must come entirely from the exporting country or, if imported from a third country, have undergone substantial processing or finishing. The action to combat fraud in the field of rules of origin is mainly concerned with textile products imported from developing countries[4]. The rules on origin are now incorporated in the agreement establishing the World Trade Organisation[5] [see section 23.4.].

The **action to combat fraud** in trade with non-member countries is organised by a Council Regulation on the mutual assistance of the administrative authorities of the Member States and on their collaboration with the Commission to ensure the proper application of customs or agricultural rules[6]. The Community has signed agreements on customs cooperation and mutual administrative assistance in customs matters, including fraud prevention, with the Republic of Korea[7], China[8], Canada[9], Norway[10], the United States[11] and India[12]. It is negotiating similar agreements with the ASEAN member countries [see section 25.6.]. The Community, however, lacks uniform penal provisions to prevent the infraction of customs legislation.

In order to improve the recovery of the Community's own resources **in the event of fraud**, a Regulation raises to 100% the level of the comprehensive guarantee covering Community transit operations for all goods, but provides for substantial reductions of this amount for certain particularly reliable operators[13].

5.3. Appraisal and outlook

The first ten years of the European Economic Community were the years of glory for customs union. The removal of customs duties and quantitative restrictions on imports and exports and the introduction of a common customs tariff, in July 1968, were important achievements of the young Community. They ruled out any "national preference" and gave rise to the "Community preference" for the products of the Member States. They provided formidable stimulus to intra-Community trade and, as expected by

---

[1]   Regulation 2454/93, OJ L 253, 11.10.1993 and Regulation 837/2005, OJ L 139, 02.06.2005.
[2]   Ibid.
[3]   Regulation 3036/94, OJ L 322, 15.12.1994.
[4]   Regulation 1541/98, OJ L 202, 18.07.1998.
[5]   OJ L 336, 23.12.1994.
[6]   Regulation 515/97, OJ L 82, 22.03.1997.
[7]   Agreement and Decision 97/291, OJ L 121, 13.05.1997.
[8]   Agreement and Decision 2004/889, OJ L 375, 23.12.2004.
[9]   Agreement and Decision 98/18, OJ L 7, 13.01.1998.
[10] Agreement and Decision 97/269, OJ L 105, 23.04.1997.
[11] Agreement and Decision 97/541, OJ L 222, 12.08.1997 and Agreement and Decision 2004/634, OJ L 304, 30.09.2004.
[12] Agreement and Decision 2004/633, OJ L 354, 30.11.2004.
[13] Council Regulation 2153/96, OJ L 289, 12.11.1996.

the EEC Treaty, were the foundation for the common market and all the common policies examined in this book.

The realisation of the customs union has also had important effects for the consumers of the member countries. It **contributed to the material wellbeing of the Member States' citizens**, through a remarkable increase of better quality goods at lower prices. Tangible manifestations of the customs union are the products from all over the continent, which are available at affordable prices in local stores in all the Member States. The customs union has also greatly facilitated the travel of the citizens inside the countries of the EC/EU.

What the Treaty had not foreseen was the perseverance of the national administrations, which quickly found obstacles other than those of customs to hinder trade between Member States, protect national production in an arbitrary way and, at the same time, defend their own functions and very existence (as in the case of the restructuring of customs administrations brought about by the abolition of customs controls).

As will be explained in the next chapter, the customs union was finally completed, together with the completion of the single market in 1992. The most striking manifestation of the customs union was the disappearance of customs checks at the borders between Member States. The abolition of customs checks at internal borders was achieved thanks to the abolition of customs administrative documents, which burdened intra-Community trade every year, a far-ranging reform of indirect taxation, examined in the chapter on taxation [see section 14.2.2.] and the entry into force of a series of provisions reorganising fiscal, veterinary, phytosanitary, sanitary and safety checks and the collection of statistical data. The most meaningful aspect of this process is the lightening of the administrative burden of companies carrying out intra-Community sales and purchases and, therefore, the encouragement of intra-Community transactions.

In addition to the internal environment of the Union, **the international environment of customs and commerce** has been profoundly modified in the 1990s. The opening up of free international trade to the Central and Eastern European countries as well as those of the former Soviet Union and the entry into force of the new GATT agreements have been powerful catalysts in the globalisation of trade. At the same time, however, there has been a growing globalisation of illicit traffic in all areas, such as drugs, arms, nuclear material and protected animal species. From a customs viewpoint, this requires strengthened cooperation and mutual assistance between the customs' administrations of Community countries and those of third countries, notably those of other European countries.

Therefore, the abolition of customs formalities at internal borders must be counterbalanced by the **reinforcement of measures at external frontiers.** Customs checks at the Community's external frontiers have to be strengthened for illegal imports from third countries and customs cooperation must ensure that differences in regulations do not give rise to fraud or problems for consumers. National security problems (crime, drugs, terrorism, firearms traffic) will have to be settled jointly and by a detailed exchange of information between the police and security forces of the Member States in the context of police and judicial cooperation in criminal matters [see section 8.1.2.]. Common policies are necessary regarding citizens of non-member countries circulating freely within the Member States, once they have crossed the borders of one of them [see section 8.1.4.]. It is obvious that the customs union has had and continues having important spillover or multiplicative effects [see section 1.1.1.] on a great number of common policies in other economic and even political fields.

The strategy for the Union's customs activities needs to take account of **major changes under way**: EU enlargement, changing role of customs in the collection of revenue, increased involvement in the regulation of external trade, growing new trade patterns, support for economic operators in their efforts to compete fairly, increasing emphasis on the fight against fraud and the involvement of organised crime in fraudulent activities and, last but not least, ensuring the safety of citizens. The big challenge of the Member States customs officers, who are in fact customs officers of the Union, is to ensure a high quality of control at the external borders, applied in an effective, efficient and homogeneous manner. A delicate balance needs to be struck by the customs' officers between ensuring minimum disruption to legitimate trade and free circulation of persons, on the one hand, and the need to detect and deter fraud and illegal activities, on the other.

Bibliography on Customs Union

- AUGIER Patricia, GASIOREK Michael, LAI-TONG Charles. "The impact of rules of origin on trade flows", *Economic Policy*, n. 43, July 2005, p. 567-624.
- CADOT Olivier (et al.). *The origin of goods: rules of origin in regional trade agreements.* Centre for Economic Policy Research. Oxford: Oxford University Press, 2006.
- EGGER Hartmut, EGGER Peter. "The determinants of EU processing trade", *The World Economy*, v. 28, n. 2, February 2005, p. 147-168.
- EUROPEAN COMMISSION. *The contribution of Taxation and Customs Policies to the Lisbon Strategy.* Luxembourg: EUR-OP*, 2005.

  - *Community Programmes Customs 2013 and Fiscalis 2013.* Luxembourg: EUR-OP*, 2006.

  - *Green Paper on detection technologies in the work of law enforcement, customs and other security authorities.* Luxembourg: EUR-OP*, 2006.
- FRANCOIS Joseph, McQUEEN Matthew, WIGNARAJA Ganeshan. "European Union-developing country FTAs: overview and analysis", *World Development*, v. 33, n. 10, October 2005, p. 1545-1565.
- JOERGES Christian, GODT Christine. "Free trade: the erosion of national, and the birth of transnational governance", *European Review: Interdisciplinary Journal of the Academia Europaea*, v. 13, suppl. 1, May 2005, p. 93-117.
- JOVANOVIC Miroslav. *The economics of international integration.* Cheltenham:Edward Elgar, 2006.
- KANAVOS Panos, COSTA-FONT Joan. "Pharmaceutical parallel trade in Europe : stakeholder and competition effects", *Economic Policy,* n. 44, October 2005, p. 751-798.
- KEPPENE Jean-Paul. "La libre circulation des merchandises", *Journal des tribunaux. Droit européen.* v. 13, n. 123, novembre 2005, p.261-266.
- KRAMER Florence (et al.). "La libre circulation des produits", *L'Observateur de Bruxelles*, n. 60, mars 2005, p. I-XI.
- LANGHAMMER Rolf· "The EU offer of service trade liberalization in the Doha Round: evidence of a not-yet-perfect customs union", *Journal of Common market Studies*, v. 43, n. 2, June 2005, p. 311-325.
- MILNER Chris. "Protection by tariff barriers and international transaction costs", *Scottish Journal of Political Economy*, v. 52, n. 1, February 2005, p. 105-121.
- ORGANISATION FOR ECONOMIC CO-OPERATION AND DEVELOPMENT. *Preferential trading arrangements in agricultural and food markets: the case of the European Union and the United States.* Paris: OECD, 2005.
- SAMUELSON Paul Anthony (et al.). "Libre-échange et délocalisations: le débat rebondit", *Problèmes économiques*, n. 2876, 25 mai 2005, p. 2-34·
- SCHWANEN Daniel. "A NAFTA customs union: necessary step or distraction?", *International Journal*, v. 60, n. 2, Spring 2005, p. 399-406.
- SHAFFER Gregory, APEA Yvonne. "Institutional choice in the generalized system of preferences case: who decides the conditions for trade preferences? The law and politics of rights", *Journal of World Trade*, v. 39, n. 6, December 2005, p. 977-1008.
- SOULARD Christophe (et al.). "Les douanes" in *Revue des affaires européennes*, v. 14, n. 4, 2005, p. 549-646.
- VRINS Olivier, SCHNEIDER Marius. *Enforcement of intellectual property rights through border measures: law and practice in the EU.* Oxford:Oxford University Press, 2006.

---

* The publications of the Office for Official Publications of the European Communities (EUR-OP) exist usually in all official languages of the EU.

Chapter 6

COMMON MARKET

Diagram of the chapter

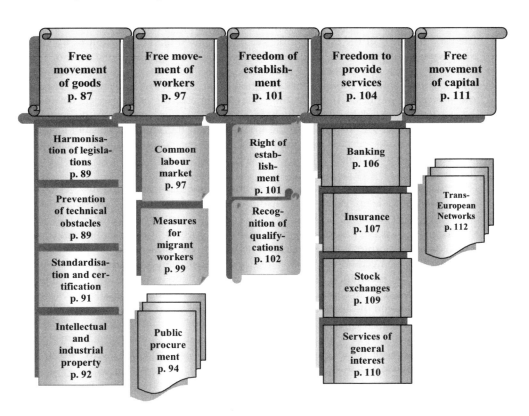

The creation of a single European economic area based on a common market was **the fundamental objective of the Treaty of Rome** [see section 2.1.]. Article 2 of that Treaty set out that objective as follows: "The Community shall have as its task, by establishing a common market and progressively approximating the economic policies of Member States, to promote throughout the Community a harmonious development of economic activities, a continuous and balanced expansion, an increase in stability, an accelerated raising of the standard of living and closer relations between the

States belonging to it". It is obvious that the common market was not an end in itself, but a means to achieve economic and political goals.

It is useful to define here the concepts of "common market", "single market" and "internal market" which are used almost synonymously but which have significant nuances of meaning. The **common market** is a stage in the multinational integration process, which, in the words of a Court of Justice ruling, aims to remove all the barriers to intra-Community trade with a view to the merger of national markets into a **single market** giving rise to conditions as close as possible to a genuine **internal market**[1]. It is worth noting that the Treaty establishing the European Community ignores the concept of the "single market". It refers generally to the stage of the "common market" and to the end result of it, the "internal market", which according to its Article 14 comprises "an area without internal frontiers in which the free movement of goods, persons, services and capital is ensured in accordance with the provisions of this Treaty". The following pages give an illustration of the obstacles which the Community had to clear during the common market stage in order to reach the goal of a single market by the end of 1992, a goal set, in 1985, by the then President of the Commission, Jacques Delors.

The establishment of the common market first required the **elimination of all import and export duties** existing between Member States before the foundation of the Community. We saw in the previous chapter how the Member States effectively removed the customs barriers even before expiration of the period laid down by the Treaty and how immediately after tariff dismantling, they began erecting other barriers between them, in particular technical barriers which, in some cases, were even more difficult to overcome [see sections 5.1. and 6.1.]. In the first section of this chapter, we shall look at how the Member States decided to complete the common market and what measures they decided to take to eliminate technical obstacles to trade and to open up public procurement.

The creation of a common market resembling an internal market implies not only the liberalisation of trade among the participating member states but also necessitates the **free movement of production factors**: labour, capital and services. It further entails the free establishment of persons and companies in all the territory of the member states, in order to exercise their professional or business activities. Hence, in order to speak about a common market, we need to have between the constituent member states the existence of **four fundamental freedoms**: freedom of movement of goods, thanks to the elimination of all trade barriers; freedom of movement of salaried and non salaried workers, thanks to the elimination of all restrictions to their entrance and residence in other Member States; freedom of establishment of persons and companies in the territory of any Member State and of the provision of services by them in the host country; and freedom of capital movements for business or personal purposes. It appears that the **keyword of the common market is freedom**.

6.1. Completion of the internal market

During the first decade of its existence the Community negotiated two very important hurdles towards its economic integration: the achievement of customs union, in July 1968, involving the abolition of customs duties and quantitative restrictions between Member States, the establishment of a common customs tariff and the definition of a common agricultural policy necessary for the free movement of agricultural goods between Member States [see chapter 5 and section 21.1.]. These vital achievements were decided upon by the six origi-

---

[1]   Judgment of May 5 Gaston Schul, , case 15/81, ECR 1982, p. 1409

nal Member States in a favourable economic climate and **a stable monetary environment** guaranteed by the Bretton Woods system.

In August 1971, however, the United States had decided to dismantle the international monetary system, based on **the Bretton Woods agreements**, which had ensured, until then, the monetary stability indispensable to the functioning of the European common market. Unrestrained, the international speculation had, then, thwarted the first attempt to create an economic and monetary union in Europe [see section 7.2.1.]. Moreover, the oil crises of 1973 and 1979 had shaken the European economies [see section 19.1.1.]. Thus, Europe in the early 1980s had sunk into "**Euro-slump**" and "**Euro-pessimism**". Many advocates of intergovernmental free trade arrangements thought at the time that the experiment of European integration was going to fail. They were underestimating the strength of the Community method and the links that it had already created among the Member States.

In January 1985, the President of the Commission, **Jacques Delors**, forcefully declared that in order to achieve the main objective of the EEC Treaty, the creation of a single market, all internal European borders should be eliminated by the end of 1992. Therefore, in June 1985 the Commission forwarded to the European Council a **"white paper" on completing the internal market**[1]. The Milan European Council (28-June 1985) welcomed the programme established in the white paper and decided, by a majority of its members, to call an intergovernmental conference with the brief of drawing up a draft Treaty covering, on the one hand, political cooperation and, on the other, the amendments to the EEC Treaty required for the completion of the internal market. The Commission's proposals for a "single framework" for the amendment of the EEC Treaty and for political cooperation were finalised in the form of a "**Single European Act**" by the Ministers for Foreign Affairs meeting in Intergovernmental Conference on 27 January 1986 [see section 2.1.]. By making significant changes to the Community decision-making process (qualified majority voting in the Council acting in cooperation with the European Parliament) [see section 4.3.], the Single Act not only succeeded in removing the technical barriers to trade, thus creating the Single Market, but has had important spillover effects [see section 1.1.1.] on many common policies, such as transport, taxation and environment protection.

6.2. Free movement of goods

Tariff disarmament completed thanks to the customs union, in July 1968, had eliminated customs barriers to intra-Community trade. But there still remained technical obstacles to trade and the EEC Treaty had not fixed a timetable for their elimination. **Technical barriers to trade result from national regulations** obliging the producers of industrial products and foodstuffs to satisfy certain criteria or to meet certain standards and technical specifications. This legislation is necessary for various reasons: standardising industrial production, guaranteeing the safety of workers, protecting the health of consumers and preventing or reducing environmental pollution, etc. The problem for the common market was not the existence of national regulations, but the differences between them and also the fact that those regulations could be used to protect the national market from products from other Member States which were subject to different standards [see details below]. The impetus given by the Single European Act to the efforts of the Commission helped to eliminate this problem and thus establish the single market.

The free movement of goods within the Community established by Articles 25 to 28 (TEC) is in actual fact safeguarded by the **infringement procedure** provided in Article 226 of the EC Treaty [see section 4.1.2.]. The Commission invokes those procedures

---

[1] COM(85)310 final.

whenever it records an infringement of Community provisions attributable to any authority whatsoever of a Member State (including judicial authorities[1]). It may consider a case as a matter of routine in the light of information provided by Members of the European Parliament or published in the press or in the official journal of a Member State. Usually, however, a **complaint** is brought before it by a company, an association or even another Member State in respect of draft standards or technical rules of a Member State. Article 30 (TEC) allows some restrictions on imports on grounds of public morality, public policy or public security, but specifies that they must not constitute disguised restrictions on trade between Member States[2]. According to the Court of Justice, willing to ensure the survival of a company cannot be a justification founded on this Article[3].

The adoption of the directives establishing the single market solved the major problem in the free movement of goods. A supplementary problem is the not complete or correct **transposition of the directives** relating to the realisation of the single market[4]. A Council Regulation reiterates the obligations of the Member States to take all necessary measures to facilitate the free movement of goods in the Community and establishes an early warning mechanism in the event of an obstacle or the risk of an obstacle to the free movement of goods, as well as a specific mechanism enabling the Commission to request a Member State to take the measures necessary to remove such an obstacle[5]. The Member States have all agreed on the principle that penalties be applicable for breaches of the internal market law[6].

Technical barriers to trade resulted from **disparities in the technical standards** for the production and marketing of goods. The disparity that existed between countries in terms of technical requirements stemmed from historical and economic considerations. A country in which a product was imported rather than manufactured tended to impose stringent requirements on it and checks prior to its being placed on the market, without concerning itself greatly about the economic cost, which that represented. On the other hand a producer country of an industrial product tended to be more tolerant taking into consideration the economic implications of requirements and controls, an excessive stringency of which would penalise its industry. In any case, the various technical regulations could hinder trade even more than customs duties (eliminated thanks to the customs union) [see section 5.1.2.]. Indeed, even a high customs tariff could be paid and a product originating in one country could enter the market of another, if its consumers preferred it. On the other hand, if a product did not comply with the different technical standards, its entry to that country's market was completely blocked.

The result was that the industrialist who wished to export to the other EEC member countries was obliged to bear additional research, development and production costs in order **to comply with all the national standards** which his products had to satisfy. Thus the disparity of the legislation within the Community compelled producers to manufacture different components, increase their production lines, diversify their stocks according to country of destination and have specialised distribution and after-sales services for each country.

All the above **made production on the Community scale more costly** than it should have been and favoured large undertakings (firms, companies) rather than small and medium-sized enterprises (SMEs). Large undertakings, in particular multinationals, had the structure, experience and personnel required to meet the specific requirements of the markets in several countries and could spread the additional costs over long runs in such a way that they represented a negligible fraction of the unit cost of the product. For small companies, however, the additional costs represented a substantial fraction of the production unit cost and could be prohibitive to any exports. The abolition of technical barriers to trade eliminated this disadvantage of SMEs.

Cooperation between the Commission departments and the national administrations has proved to be the most reliable way of ensuring that Community law is observed. A Council resolution calls for developing such cooperation in the areas where it is insufficient and particularly in the area of industrial products[7]. The **Robert Schuman action programme** seeks, by encouraging training and information projects, to improve knowledge

---

[1]   See Judgment of 30 September 2003, case C-224/01 Gerhard Köbler v Republic of Austria; ECR 2003.
[2]   See in this context the Judgment of the Court on German beer, case 178/84, ECR 1987, p. 1227.
[3]   Judgment of 28 March 1995, case C-324/93, ECR 1995, p. 1-0563.
[4]   COM (95) 500, 07.06.1995.
[5]   Regulation 2679/98, OJ L 337, 12.12.1998 and COM (2001) 160, 22 March 2001.
[6]   OJ C 188, 22.07.1995, p. 1-3.
[7]   OJ C 224, 01.08.1996, p. 3-4.

of Community law among the legal professions (judges, prosecutors and lawyers) so as to ensure the good application of the rules of the single market[1].

6.2.1. Harmonisation of legislations

The removal of technical obstacles to trade in **industrial products** is normally based on Article 94 of the EC Treaty (Art. 100 EEC), which provides for the **approximation of** such **provisions** laid down by law, regulation or administrative action that directly affect the functioning of the common market. On this legal basis, the Commission has for many years been trying to align national regulations with Community standards agreed upon in Council directives. Such alignment is not, however, as easy as it seems at first sight. As technical regulations relate to production systems and consequently investments already made, and as their harmonisation sometimes entails the need for industrialists in some Member States to change their production systems by means of new investment expenditure, the removal of technical obstacles to trade used to be the subject of interminable discussions. Each member country tried to persuade its partners that its own technical regulations were the best and should be adopted by the Community.

The **harmonisation directives** have harmonised the national regulations in fields as diverse as motor vehicle equipment, foodstuffs and proprietary medicinal products. Thus, considerable progress has been made in the motor vehicle sector, in particular as a result of the entry into force of the EC type-approval for motor vehicles and their trailers[2]. In the foodstuffs sector a body of Community inspectors is responsible for evaluating and checking the control systems in the Member States[3]. Directives have been adopted in the particularly sensitive areas of food additives, colourings and sweeteners[4]. The harmonisation work relating to pharmaceutical products has culminated in the creation of the single market in medicinal products and in the establishment of a European Agency for the Evaluation of Medicinal Products[5] [see section 17.3.7.].

The laborious procedures involved in the approximation of laws leads to results which are **very useful for economic integration**. Indeed, once the standards are the same in all member countries, type approval of a product granted in any member country is recognised by all the others. The manufacturers need only guarantee that all examples of a product will conform to the prototype that has been approved in the directive. Items which do not conform may not be sold anywhere in the common market, including the producer's home market. Conversely, no Member State may apply more stringent national rules to oppose the import or use of products which meet Community requirements. But, the harmonisation of legislations is also very useful for consumers, since it guarantees them the quality and safety of products circulating in the large market.

6.2.2. Prevention of new technical obstacles

However, whilst some problems were being resolved through the harmonisation of legislations, the Member States, tempted by protectionism, in particular during the gloomy economic climate of the 1970s, were adopting new legislation and **creating further technical obstacles to trade**. The Community institutions' laborious work to re-

---

[1] Decision 1496/98, OJ L 196, 14.07.1998.
[2] Directive 92/53, OJ L 225, 10.08.1992.
[3] Regulation 882/2004, OJ L 165, 30.04.2004.
[4] Directives 94/34, 94/35 and 94/36, OJ L 237, 10.09.1994.
[5] Regulation 726/2004, OJ L 136, 30.04.2004.

move those obstacles therefore resembled the endless tasks of the Danaides, punished by Greek gods to carry water eternally in leaky jars. For that reason, the Commission considered a fresh approach to the problem. For that it relied upon the case law of the Court of Justice. In its judgment of 20 February 1979 in the **"Cassis de Dijon" case** (concerning the sale in Germany of blackcurrant liqueur produced in France), the Court of Justice gave a very broad definition of the obstacles to free trade which were prohibited under Article 30 et seq. of the EEC Treaty (Art. 28 to 31 TEC)[1]. It stated that any product lawfully manufactured and marketed in a Member State should in principle be admitted to the market of any other Member State.

Even if they are applicable without distinction to domestic and imported products, national regulations may not create obstacles unless they are necessary to satisfy mandatory requirements and are directed towards an objective of general interest which is such as to take precedence over the requirements of the free movement of goods, that is one of the basic rules of the Community. In plain language, a country must not bar the way to competing products from another Member State solely because they are slightly different from domestic products. If it does so, the Commission will take proceedings against it as far as the Court of Justice, where it stands every chance of being condemned on the basis of existing case law. According to another Court judgment, **national provisions must not discriminate** against the traders to whom they apply or have the effect of discriminating between the marketing of national products and that of products from other Member States[2].

In parallel with the application of the "Cassis de Dijon" principle, the Commission secured, in 1983, the adoption by the Council of a **procedure for the provision of information** by the Member States on any new technical standards and regulations that they envisage. This procedure was codified in 1998[3], while its field of application was extended to information society services in the new Member States[4]. Thanks to the information procedure, the Commission is notified by the competent authorities of any new technical standards or regulations that they envisage and can thus notify the other Member States and request amendments before their entry into force. This is an example of shared sovereignty: the Member States have agreed to lose their independence of action in the field of standardisation, but have gained in exchange the right of surveying the actions of their neighbours [see section 1.1.2.].

The Court of Justice has ruled that technical regulations which have been adopted in violation of the procedure for the provision of information, i.e. without notification, are inapplicable, have no legal effect for individuals and national courts must decline to apply them[5]. When in exceptional and urgent cases the Member States adopt national measures derogating from the principle of the free movement of goods, they must inform the Commission and through it their partners, allowing the latter to take any appropriate steps[6]. A similar information procedure exists in the framework of the EEA agreement [see section 25.1.]. Transparency is thus ensured throughout the European Economic Area. The information procedure has proved to be a vital instrument for preventing the emergence of new obstacles to trade which can result from technical standards or rules. Furthermore, it is a good instrument for the establishment of a technical environment common to all undertakings.

---

[1] Judgment of 20 February 1979, Case 120/78, ECR 1979, p. 649.
[2] Judgment given on 24 November 1993, Joined Cases C-267/91 and C-268/91, Keck and Mithouard, ECR 1993, p. I-6097.
[3] Directive 98/34, OJ L 204, 21.07.1998 amended by Directive 98/48, OJ L 217, 05.08.1998.
[4] Decision 2004/299, OJ L 98, 02.04.2004 and Decision 2004/330, OJ L 117, 22.04.2004.
[5] Judgment of 30 April 1996, Case C-194/94, CIA Security International v Signalson and Securitel, ECR 1996, p. I-2201.
[6] Decision 3052/95, OJ L 321, 30.12.1995.

6.2.3. Common standardisation and certification policy

As regards the existing rules and standards, at the instigation of the Commission, the Council adopted, in 1985, a **new approach to technical harmonisation and standards**[1]. In cases where full harmonisation of technical standards cannot be applied, because divergences are too great between the essential aims of different national laws, legislative harmonisation is confined to the adoption of the **essential safety requirements** (or other requirements in the general interest) with which products must conform, in order to enjoy free movement throughout the EU. Member States must notify the Commission of any measure that they may take for some reason, which may obstruct the free movement of a model or type of product that is lawfully manufactured or marketed in another Member State[2].

The key to the implementation of the new approach to technical harmonisation is the **common standardisation policy**, i.e. the establishment of standards that determine the specifications for industrial production. The standards are adopted by European bodies, which have the task of elaborating technical specifications that meet the essential requirements laid down by the technical harmonisation Directives, while ensuring that those standards are the result of agreement of all parties concerned: producers, users, consumers, administrations, etc. These bodies are: the European Committee for Standardisation (CEN), the European Committee for Electrotechnical Standardisation (CENELEC) and the European Telecommunication Standards Institute (ETSI). No mandatory nature is attributed to these technical specifications, which have the status of voluntary standards. Industrialists are not obliged but have an interest, if they want to market their products in all the common market, to manufacture them in accordance with the Community directives and hence with Community standards. On the other hand, the national authorities are obliged to recognise that products manufactured in conformity with harmonised standards are presumed to conform to the essential requirements laid down in that Directive.

In order to be able to exercise their positive effects, European standards must, however, also be **certified and recognised by the relevant national bodies**. Reciprocal recognition of certificates of conformity with rules and standards is therefore essential to the free movement of goods. Hence, the Community laid down the guiding principles for the European policy on the mutual recognition of tests and certificates[3], provided for the setting up of the European Organisation for Testing and Certification (EOTC) and adopted conformity assessment procedures and the rules for the affixing and use of the CE conformity marking, intended for use in the technical harmonisation Directives for the marketing of industrial products [see also sections 17.3.6 and 19.2.1.][4]. In order to control the respect of these procedures and rules, the Community set out rules on the inspection and verification of good laboratory practice (GLP)[5]. The **principle of mutual recognition** enables, especially in sectors which have not been harmonised at Community level, the competent authorities of importing Member States to recognise technical specifications, standards and rules applicable in other Member States and the validity of tests carried out by approved laboratories in other Member States offering adequate guarantees of reliability and efficiency.

---

[1] OJ C 136, 04.06.1985, p. 1-9.
[2] Decision 3052/95, OJ L 321, 30.12.1995.
[3] OJ C 10, 16.01.1990, p. 1-2.
[4] Decision 93/465, OJ L 220, 30.08.1993.
[5] Directive 2004/9, OJ L 50, 20.02.2004.

A **single "CE" marking** is used in order to facilitate controls on the Community market by inspectors and to clarify the obligations of economic operators in respect of marking under the various Community regulations[1]. The aim of the CE marking is to symbolize the conformity of a product with the levels of protection of collective interests imposed by the total harmonization directives and to indicate that the economic operator has undergone all the evaluation procedures laid down by Community law in respect of his product. Consumers who see the **Community marking CE** (Communitas Europaea) on a product thus have an indication (not necessarily the proof) that it has been manufactured in conformity with Community standards.

Mutual recognition is intended to ensure the free movement of goods and products of all kinds, thereby avoiding unnecessary recourse to harmonisation by specific legislative measures. It guarantees the preservation of national diversity and of the various traditions and customs, and contributes towards increasing the range of products available to European consumers. On the external level, this mutual recognition of the methods and structures of conformity within the Community facilitates access to the European market for products from third countries. In return, the Community negotiates similar recognition with the latter. It should be noted, however, that businesses often prefer to mutual recognition a formal and complete harmonisation at Community level, because it offers increased legal security.

According to the Court of Justice, it is acceptable for only a minimum degree of harmonisation to be brought about by a Directive based on Article 100a EEC (Art. 95 TEC)[2]. In other words, the use of Article 95 as a legal basis **does not necessarily entail full harmonisation** of the conditions of competition. The Court, thus, acknowledges that the degree of harmonisation sought at Community level may give rise to less favourable treatment of domestic products, compared to imported products which meet only the minimum requirements laid down by a Community Directive.

The new approach to technical harmonisation has given rise to fresh dynamism in the removal of technical barriers to intra-Community trade. Many directives were adopted under it, relating, for example, to the safety of machines[3], appliances burning gaseous fuels[4] and footwear[5].

6.2.4. Protection of intellectual and industrial property

The internal market has become the appropriate environment for achieving economies of scale in the analogue or digital exploitation of intellectual property, which accounts for more than 5% of the Community's gross domestic product (GDP). Community-wide protection of **intellectual and industrial property** helps to ensure the maintenance and development of creativity in the interests of authors, performers, producers, consumers, culture, industry and the public at large. Hence, intellectual property has been recognised as an integral part of property and one of the keys to added value and competitiveness [see also sections 10.3. and 23.4.].

Therefore, a Directive concerns the **legal protection of copyright and related rights** in the framework of the internal market, with particular emphasis on the information society[6]. It provides a secure environment for cross-border trade in copyright-protected goods and services and facilitates the development of electronic commerce in the field of new and multimedia products and services [see details below]. Another directive establishes measures and procedures to ensure the **enforcement of intellectual property rights**, including industrial property rights[7]. It requires the Member States to apply effective, dissuasive and proportionate remedies and penalties against anyone engaging in counterfeiting and piracy so as to create a level playing field for rightholders in

[1] Decision 93/465, OJ L 220, 30.08.1993.
[2] Judgment given on 22 June 1993, Case C-11/92, The Queen v Secretary of State, ex parte Gallaher, ECR 1993, p. I-3545.
[3] Directive 2006/42, OJ L 157, 09.06.2006.
[4] Directive 90/396, OJ L 196, 26.07.1990 and Directive 93/68, OJ L 220, 30.08.1993.
[5] Directive 94/11, OJ L 100, 19.04.1994.
[6] Directive 2001/29, OJ L 167, 22.06.2001.
[7] Directive 2004/48, OJ L 157, 30.04.2004.

the EU. It includes procedures covering evidence, the protection of evidence and provisional measures such as injunctions and seizure. Remedies available to rightholders include the destruction, recall or permanent removal from the market of illegal goods, as well as financial compensation, injunctions and damages.

Directive 89/104 **protects on the territory of the Community every trade mark** in respect of goods or services which is the subject of registration or of an application in a Member State for registration as an individual trade mark, a collective mark or a guarantee or certification mark, or which is the subject of a registration or an application for registration in the Benelux Trade Mark Office or of an international registration having effect in a Member State[1]. Member States remain free to fix the provisions of procedure concerning the registration, the revocation and the invalidity of trade marks acquired by registration.

Companies that wish to adapt their activities to the scale of the Community have at their disposal the legal instrument of the **Community trade mark**, enabling their products or services to be distinguished by identical means throughout the entire Community[2]. A Community trade mark may consist of any signs capable of being represented graphically, particularly words, including personal names, designs, letters, numerals, the shape of goods or of their packaging, provided that such signs are capable of distinguishing the goods produced by one firm from those produced by other firms. The Community trade mark provides uniform protection throughout the Community, which can be obtained by means of a single procedure. This protection enables the proprietor to prevent any other person from using the mark for the same products or services or for similar products if there is a danger of confusion. The Community trade mark is granted (registered) for a period of 10 years, which is renewable, by the Office for Harmonisation in the Internal Market (OHIM) based in Alicante. Its protection on all the territory of the Union is reinforced by the existence of quasi-judicial bodies - the Boards of Appeal of the Office for Harmonisation in the Internal Market - whose decisions may be challenged before the Court of Justice.

As regards industrial property, a Directive seeks to guarantee effective legal protection for **industrial designs** (in machinery, tools, electronic equipment, etc.), by defining a "design", by establishing the conditions governing its protection and the scope of protection including the exclusive right to use the design[3]. The **Community Design** provides uniform protection throughout the Community for registered designs managed by the Office for Harmonisation in the Internal Market (Trademarks and Designs) in Alicante[4].

The directive on the **legal protection of copyright and related rights** harmonises the rights of reproduction, distribution, communication to the public, the legal protection of anti-copying devices and rights management systems. Member States must, in particular, provide for the exclusive right to authorise or prohibit direct or indirect, temporary or permanent reproduction by any means and in any form, in whole or in part: (a) for authors, of their works; (b) for performers, of fixations of their performances; (c) for phonogram producers, of their phonograms; (d) for the producers of the first fixations of films, in respect of the original and copies of their films; and (e) for broadcasting organisations, of fixations of their broadcasts, whether those broadcasts are transmitted by wire or over the air, including by cable or satellite. This Directive also serves to implement a number of international obligations, notably the World Intellectual Property Organisation (WIPO) "Copyright Treaty" and the "Performances and Phonograms Treaty", which improve the means to fight piracy world-wide.

The Court of Justice has established the principle that copyright, like other industrial and commercial property rights, falls within the scope of the Treaty and that, consequently, any discrimination on grounds of

---

[1] Directive 89/104, OJ L 40, 11.02.1989 and Decision 92/10, OJ L 106, 11.01.1992.
[2] Regulation 40/94, OJ L 11, 14.01.1994 and Regulation 422/2004, OJ L 70, 09.03.2004.
[3] Directive 98/71, OJ L 289, 28.10.1998.
[4] Regulation 6/2002, OJ L 3, 05.01.2002.

nationality in the national laws governing the extent or exercise of such rights is prohibited[1]. The Court has also interpreted Directive 89/104 [see above] as protecting the proprietors against imports into the Community, without their consent, of products bearing their trade mark, which have been put on the market of a third country[2].

Under the Protocol relating to the Madrid Agreement concerning the **international registration of marks**, intergovernmental organisations, such as the EC, which have their own regional trade mark registration system may take part in the international registration system. Hence, the Community's accession to the Protocol enables firms to obtain, by submitting a single application, protection of their trade mark not only throughout the Community, as a Community trade mark, but also in countries that are a party to the Madrid Protocol[3] Conversely, holders of international registrations under the Madrid Protocol may apply for protection of their trade marks under the Community trade mark system.

An EC Directive provides a stable legislative framework for the protection of **biotechnological inventions** allowing the use of research results while taking account of the ethical aspects, relating, in particular, to the protection of the human body[4]. A Regulation created a supplementary protection certificate for **plant protection products**, allowing a further five years' protection for inventions in the plant protection field after the basic patent has expired[5].

6.3. Public procurement

In a genuine single market, the public sector must also be open to intra-Community trade and competition. Indeed, **the requirements of the official authorities for works and supplies** of all sorts for the central civil service, regional and local authorities and for public undertakings (companies) and bodies accounts for 15% of the economic activity in the Community. At the end of the 1980s only 2% of the needs of the official authorities were covered by businesses from a Member State other than that of the official authorities concerned, notwithstanding the price, quality and service advantages that they could offer.

In some sectors, such as the aeronautical, energy, transport and telecommunications, procurement by public bodies constituted the largest, if not the sole, part of the market, virtually excluding it from the common market. Thus, the protected high technology industries, of particular interest to the public sector, were treated unfavourably in comparison to traditional industries, as the latter had benefited from the liberalisation of trade. These protected industries were **a paradise for inefficient suppliers of goods and services** who had connections with the civil administration, but public administrations were thus jeopardising their own efficiency. Moreover, the isolation of the markets of high technology industries held back their development, as those industries were the very ones most in need of a large market and the economies of scale that it could offer. It was evident that a common interest existed to open up public procurement to all Community businesses, but the vested interests in each Member State slowed down the adoption of the necessary common measures.

In the context of the single market the award of contracts concluded in the Member States on behalf of the State, regional or local authorities and other bodies governed by public law entities is subject to the respect of the principles of the Treaty and in particular to the principles of freedom of movement of goods, of freedom of establishment and of freedom to provide services and to the principles deriving therefrom, such as the principles of equal treatment, of non-discrimination, of mutual recognition, of proportionality and of transparency. The application of these principles to public procurement was established in the early 1970s[6]. Nevertheless, the opening up of the public sector to Community competition was achieved only in the 1990s through Directives 92/50 relating to the coordination of procedures for the award of public service contracts, 93/36 coordinating procedures for the award of public supply contracts and 93/37 concerning the coordination of procedures for the award of public works contracts.

---

[1] Judgment given on 20 October 1993, Joined Cases C-92/92 and C-326/92, Phil Collins v Imtrat and Patricia v EMI Electrola, ECR 1993, p. I-5145.
[2] Judgment of 16 July 1998, Case C-355/96, ECR 1998 I-4799.
[3] Prtotocol and Council Decision 2003/793, OJ L 296, 14.11.2003.
[4] Directive 98/44, OJ L 213, 30.07.1998.
[5] Regulation 1610/96, OJ L 198, 08.08.1996.
[6] Directive 71/304, OJ L 185, 16.08.1971 and OJ L 1, 03.01.1994.

These Directives were replaced in 2004 by a single Directive on the coordination of procedures for the award of **public works contracts, public supply contracts and public service contracts**, which have a value exclusive of VAT equal to or greater than certain thresholds (generally, EUR 162,000 for public supply and service contracts and EUR 6,242,000 for public works contracts)[1]. Directive 2004/18 draws up provisions of Community coordination of national procedures for the award of such contracts so as to guarantee the opening-up of public procurement to competition. To ensure development of effective competition in the field of public contracts, contract notices drawn up by the contracting authorities of Member States must be advertised throughout the Community. Verification of the suitability of tenderers, in open procedures, and of candidates, in restricted and negotiated procedures with publication of a contract notice must be carried out in transparent conditions. For this purpose, non-discriminatory criteria must be indicated which the contracting authorities may use when selecting competitors and the means which economic operators may use to prove they have satisfied those criteria. Contracts must be awarded on the basis of objective criteria which ensure compliance with the principles of transparency, non-discrimination and equal treatment and which guarantee that tenders are assessed in conditions of effective competition. Consequently, the directive allows the application of two award criteria only: "the lowest price" and "the most economically advantageous tender". In order to guarantee equal treatment, the criteria for the award of the contract should enable tenders to be compared and assessed objectively [see details below].

Similar principles and rules apply to the procurement procedures of entities operating in the **water, energy, transport and postal services sectors (public utility sectors)**, which were originally covered by Directive 93/38 and now by Directive 2004/17[2]. Specific rules guaranteeing the opening up to competition of public procurement contracts above a certain value (EUR 499,000 in the case of supply and service contracts and EUR 6,242,000 in the case of works contracts), awarded by entities operating in these sectors, were necessary because of: (a) the variety of ways in which national authorities can influence the behaviour of these entities, including participation in their capital and representation in the entities' administrative, managerial or supervisory bodies; and (b) the closed nature of the markets in which they operate, due to the existence of special or exclusive rights granted by the Member States concerning the supply to, provision or operation of networks for providing the service concerned. The contracting entities in these sectors, which, by virtue of the existence of exclusive government-regulated networks or concession rights, could formerly not resist political pressure to "buy national", are now obliged to call for tenders throughout the Community. Since particular competition rules apply to telecommunications, shipping and air transport [see sections 17.3.6, 20.3.4 and 20.3.5.], the public procurement contracts in these sectors are not included in the scope of Directive 2004/17.

In view of the rapid expansion of **electronic purchasing systems**, Directives 2004/17 and 2004/18 lay down specific rules for setting up and operating such systems in order to ensure the fair treatment of any economic operator who wishes to take part therein. Electronic auctions can deal only with contracts for works, supplies or services for which the specifications can be determined with precision. Directives 2004/17 and 2004/18 clarify also how the contracting authorities may contribute to the protection of the environment and the promotion of sustainable development. In appropriate cases, in which the nature of the works and/or services justifies applying environmental management measures or schemes during the performance of a public contract, the application of such measures or schemes may be required by the contracting authorities.

---

[1]   Directive 2004/18, OJ 134, 30.04.2004 and Directive 2005/75, OJ L 323, 09.12.2005.
[2]   Directive 2004/17, OJ L 134, 30.04.2004.

In order to **monitor compliance** with Community legislation, the Commission instituted an information system for public procurement (SIMAP) and a system for checking that the execution of projects or programmes financed from the Structural Funds and the other Community financial instruments is carried out in compliance with the Community rules on public procurement[1]. It also strengthened its measures against infringements of the rules governing public procurement on the basis of the proceedings for failure to act, as provided for in Article 226 (TEC) [see section 4.1.2.]. A **common procurement vocabulary (CPV)** is meant to simplify and modernise the process of publishing contract notices[2]. The **Advisory Committee** on the opening-up of public procurement monitors the functioning of the Community Directives, ensures that they are applied uniformly in the Member States and examines complaints from businesses claiming injury at the hands of an irregular procedure for awarding a contract[3]. A **public procurement observatory** is responsible for monitoring the liberalisation of this sector within the Community and the effects of the process on third countries.

A Council Directive concerns the application of **review procedures** to the award of public supply and public works contracts[4]. It provides that contractors and suppliers shall have effective remedies whereby alleged infringements by a contracting authority of Community law in the field of public procurement can be sanctioned at any stage whatsoever in the procedure for the award of a contract. It defines a conciliation procedure to which parties can have recourse to find an amicable settlement to any disputes regarding the application of rules governing public contracts and introduces a mechanism for the rapid correction of clear and evident offences. **Legal recourse in the public utility sectors** is provided by a special Directive, which seeks to ensure that effective and rapid means of recourse exist both at national and Community level as regards procedures for the award of contracts in the sectors of water, energy, transport and telecommunications[5].

The Community legislation on liberalisation of public procurement incorporates certain provisions of the **Government Procurement Agreement** concluded in 1994 in the context of the World Trade Organisation [see section 23.4.] so as to prevent different rules applying at Community and international levels and to exclude reverse discrimination against Community enterprises, i.e. more favourable treatment being given to third-country tenderers[6]. The European Union opens up its public contracts to third states that take similar action. Thus the Community and the USA reached, an Agreement, in 1995, on government procurement. This Agreement gives effect in the area of government procurement to the commitments made in the Uruguay Round of multilateral negotiations and to the results of the bilateral negotiations conducted in this area between the Community and the United States [see section 25.7.][7]. Nevertheless, there exist some restrictions of access to certain public contracts from tenderers from the US[8].

6.4. Free movement of workers

The freedom of movement of salaried and non-salaried workers allows EU citizens to seek, within the Union, **better living and working conditions** than are available to them in their region of origin. It therefore boosts greatly the chances of improving the standards of living of the individual. At the same time, freedom of movement reduces social pressure in the poorest regions of the European Union and allows the living conditions of those remaining to improve. In the EU in general it facilitates the adjustment of the labour supply to the variations in the demand of undertakings and opens the way for more coherent and more effective economic policies at a European level. Thus, freedom of movement of workers contributes to the attainment of the objectives of the common market as well as to the flexibility and efficiency of the labour market.

Free movement is not restricted to workers. Article 18 of the EC Treaty, which has direct effect [see section 3.3.], gives every citizen of the Union the **right to move and reside freely** within the territory of the Member States. A citizen of the European Union who no longer enjoys a right of residence as a migrant worker in the host Member State

---

[1] COM (98) 143, 11 March 1998.
[2] Regulation 2195/2002, OJ L 340, 16.12.2002.
[3] Decision 87/305, OJ L 152, 12.06.1987 and Decision 87/560, OJ L 338, 28.11.1987.
[4] Directive 89/665, OJ L 395, 30.12.1989 amended by Directive 92/50, OJ L 209, 24.07.1992.
[5] Directive 92/13, OJ L 76, 23.03.1992.
[6] Agreement and Decision 94/800, OJ L 336, 23.12.1994 and Directive 98/4, OJ L 101, 01.04.1998.
[7] Decision 95/215, OJ L 134, 20.06.1995.
[8] Regulation 1836/95, OJ L 183, 02.08.1995.

can, as a citizen of the Union, enjoy a right of residence there by direct application of Article 18(1) EC[1]. The same right is enjoyed by his spouse, their descendants under the age of 21 and their dependent relatives in the ascending line. This right contributes to a concrete and practical expression of European citizenship [see sections 9.1 and 9.2]. Freedom of movement may contribute to the attainment of the objectives of the common market, while giving more flexibility and thus greater efficiency to the labour market. The challenge to the Union now is, however, to create a real European mobility area, in which freedom of movement becomes not only a legal entitlement but also a daily reality for people across Europe. This calls for a complex interaction of common policies, some of which are explained below and some in the chapter on social progress [see sections 13.3, 13.4.2. and 13.5.].

Although the **free movement of workers has advantages, it also has disadvantages** such as, the impoverishment of regions of emigration in terms of their most dynamic human capital and an overloading of the social services in the areas of immigration. The free movement of labour within the European Union is therefore no panacea. It has to be channelled and supported by social measures in favour of migrant workers and their families. It has above all to be coupled with an efficient regional policy capable of creating jobs in the less favoured regions of the Union to provide employment for the labour available *in situ*. Under these conditions, freedom of movement is an acquired right of EU workers.

6.4.1. The common labour market

The **EEC Treaty** had the objective, as regards workers, of creating a common labour market, which meant the free movement of labour within the Community and the abolition of any discrimination based on nationality between workers of the Member States as regards employment, remuneration and other conditions of work and employment. Under Article 39 of the EC Treaty (Art. 48 EEC), freedom of movement of workers entails the right, subject to limitations justified on grounds of public policy, public security or public health to accept offers of employment actually made, **to move freely** within the territory of Member States for this purpose, **to stay** in a Member State for the purpose of employment and **to remain** in the territory of that Member State after having been employed in it. The Community legislation that materialised those principles was completed in 1968 and, thus, freedom of movement of workers was achieved, from the legal point of view, at the same time as customs union. This freedom was extended to all the workers in the European Economic Area in 1994 [see section 25.1.].

Nowadays, **all persons residing legally in a Member State** have equal rights of movement and residence in the other States of the Union [see sections 6.5.1 and 9.2.]. Therefore, a directive replaced a range of complex legislation relating to different categories of beneficiaries, including salaried and non salaried workers[2]. For periods of residence of longer than three months, Member States may only require Union citizens to register with the competent authorities in the place of residence. The worker can continue to reside, in the country in which he or she has settled after the termination of his or her employment. In fact, the worker and his or her family members who have resided in a host Member State during a continuous period of five years have a right of permanent residence in that State. The members of the family enjoy the right of residence even after the worker's death.

A directive implementing the **principle of equal treatment** between persons irrespective of racial or ethnic origin, provided in Article 13 of the EC Treaty, seeks to pro-

---

[1] Judgment of 17 September 2002, Case C-413/99, Baumbast and R v Secretary of State for the Home Department, ECR 2002, p. I-07091.
[2] Regulation 1612/68, OJ L 257, 19.10.1968 and Directive 2004/38, OJ L 158, 30.04.2004

hibit discrimination throughout the Community in different areas such as employment, education, social security, health care and access to goods and services[1]. It defines the concepts of direct and indirect discrimination, gives right of redress to victims of discrimination, imposes an obligation on the employer to prove that the principle of equal treatment has not been breached, and offers protection against harassment and victimisation in all the Member States.

The Community has set up a general framework for **combating discrimination** on grounds of religion or belief, disability, age or sexual orientation as regards employment and occupation[2]. A Community action programme to combat discrimination (2001-06) aims to promote measures to combat all forms of discrimination except that based on sex, which is the subject of specific Community action[3] [see section 13.5.5.]. The objective is to change practices and attitudes by mobilising the players involved and fostering the exchange of information and good practice. In particular, the programme seeks to set up databases and promote the networking of those involved. With a Green Paper, the Commission invited interested parties to participate in an extensive debate on the future approach to combating discrimination in the enlarged Union[4].

The Court of Justice has consistently held that the rules on equal treatment prohibit not only overt discrimination but also **any form of concealed discrimination**, which is based on various distinction criteria but has the same effect[5]. However, discrimination exists only where different rules are applied to comparable situations or the same rule is applied to different situations. For instance, where direct taxes are concerned, the Court has ruled that the provisions of the free movement of workers do not in principle preclude the application of national rules under which a non-resident working as an employed person in a Member State is taxed more heavily on his income than a resident in the same employment[6].

The principle of the free movement of workers applies equally to **nationals of third countries**, who stay lawfully in a Member State. Indeed, according to a Judgment of the Court of Justice, a firm established in a member country, which employs lawfully and habitually non-member country nationals, may detach them in another Member State in order to provide services[7]. The principle of free movement applies also to all cases of posting of workers taking place in the framework of a transnational provision of services. Thus, workers posted to another Member State by their employers enjoy at least the terms and conditions compulsory in the host Member State[8].

Article 39(4) of the EC Treaty excludes employment in the **national public service** from the principle of the free movement of workers. However, according to the Commission and the Court of Justice, this exception from the general principle of free movement does not concern jobs, which, even if they are funded by the State, are not public service as such, e.g. bodies responsible for administering commercial services, public health care services, teaching in State educational establishments and research for non-military purposes in public establishments[9]. Moreover, according to the Court of Justice, given the fundamental character of the principles of free movement and of equal treatment, the derogations based on Article 39.4 (ex article 48.4) should not exceed the aims of this exception to the rule[10] and should not contravene the principle of non-discrimination[11].

The principle of free movement of workers cannot be hindered by the **rules of sports associations**. In the **Bosman judgment**, which revolutionised European sport customs, the Court of Justice held, indeed, that Article 48 EEC (Art. 39 TEC) applied to the collective rules adopted by private sports associations since the exercise of sport as an economic activity was covered by Community law[12]. In particular, the Court held that by preventing or deterring nationals of a Member State from leaving their country of origin the transfer rules constituted an obstacle to the free movement of workers. According to the Court, the rules in question are not likely to provide encouragement and financing for small clubs training young players, since there was no guar-

---

[1]   Directive 2000/43, OJ L 180, 19.07.2000.
[2]   Directive 2000/78, OJ L 303, 02.12.2000.
[3]   Decision 2000/750, OJ L 303, 02.12.2000.
[4]   COM (2004) 379, 28 May 2004.
[5]   See, e.g., case 65/81, ECR 1982, p. 33 and case 137/84, ECR 1985, p. 2681.
[6]   Judgment of 14 February 1995, case C-279/93, Finanzamt Köln-Altstadt v R. Schumacker, ECR 1995, p. I-0225.
[7]   Judgment given on 9 August 1994 in Case C-43/93, Vander Elst v OMI, ECR 1994, p. I-3803.
[8]   Directive 96/71, OJ L 18, 21.01.1997.
[9]   See Judgment of 12 March 1998, Commission v Hellenic Republic, Case C-187/96, ECR 1998 p. I-1095.
[10]   Judgment of 12 February 1974, case 152/73, Sotgiu, ECR 1974, p. 153.
[11]   Judgment of 12 March 1998, Case C-187/96, ECR 1998, I-1095.
[12]   Judgment of 15 December 1995, case c-415/93, Jean-Marc Bosman, ECR 1995, p. I-4921.

antee that they would collect such fees and since the amount of the fees bore no relation to the costs actually incurred for the training. The Court also held that under Article 48 (EEC) no rules could require clubs to field, for a given match, only a limited number of professional players who were nationals of other Member States, but it admitted that the nationality requirement was justified in the case of matches between the national teams of different countries.

However, the Court judgment did not definitely solve the question of the **free movement of football and other players** [see section 13.4.1.]. In fact, following complaints by European football associations, the Commission had initiated proceedings in 1999 on the grounds that the International Federation of Football Associations (FIFA) rules were illegal because they denied players the right to negotiate the termination of their contract. The Commission's aim was to strike a balance between the players' fundamental right to free movement and the equally legitimate objective of the integrity of the sport and the stability of the championships. Following discussions between FIFA and the Commission, FIFA's Executive Committee drew up satisfactory rules and application regulations, which were adopted in Buenos Aires on 5 July 2001.

6.4.2. Social security and other measures for migrant workers

Adequate protection by European **provisions in the field of social security** is necessary for the effective use of the right of the citizens of one Member State to stay and work in another State of the Union. Without such protection, persons moving across borders to work or to look for a job, would risk losing all or part of their rights acquired or in the process of being acquired under national legislation (concerning, for example pensions, health insurance, unemployment benefits or family benefits). Article 42 of the EC Treaty (Art. 51 EEC) provides for the adoption of the measures necessary for that purpose through arrangements to secure for migrant workers and their dependents: (a) aggregation, for the purpose of acquiring and retaining the right to benefit, of all periods taken into account under the laws of several countries, and (b) payment of benefits to persons resident in the territories of Member States. The system required by the Treaty was in fact adopted in 1958, but it has undergone many changes and improvements since then.

On the basis of Regulations 1408/71 and 574/72, **pensions of similar nature** acquired in the various Member States may be aggregated, but the person concerned may not obtain total benefits in excess of the highest pension he or she would have obtained if he or she had spent his or her whole insurance career under the legislation of any one of the States in which he or she had been employed[1]. This legislation covers also students moving within the Community, taking account of their specific situation and of the special features of the schemes under which they are insured. Civil servants and persons treated as such have equal treatment as regards general statutory pension rights and special schemes for civil servants prevailing in the Member States[2]. The supplementary pension rights of employed and self-employed persons moving within the European Union are equally guaranteed[3]. Rights and obligations comparable to those applying to EU citizens are granted to nationals of third countries who are legally resident in the Community and who satisfy the other conditions laid down in Regulations 1408/71 and 574/72[4].

The **unemployed person** who leaves for another Member State to seek employment receives, for a maximum period of three months from the date of departure, the benefits of the country in which he or she was last employed, to be paid for by that country. Repayments in respect of health care provided for members of the family resident in a Member State other than that in which the worker is employed and insured are made

---

[1] Regulation 1408/71, OJ L 149, 05.07.1971 and Regulation 574/72, OJ L 74, 27.03.1972, last amended by Regulation 629/2006, OJ L 114, 27.04.2006.
[2] Regulation 1606/98, OJ L 209, 25.07.1998.
[3] Regulation 1223/98, OJ L 168, 13.06.1998.
[4] Regulation 859/2003, OJ L 124, 20.05.2003.

entirely to the institutions of the country of residence. Family allowances are granted under the legislation of, and at the rate laid down in, the country of employment. According to the Court of Justice, such allowances are not subject to requirements as to minimum period of residence[1].

Similar arrangements cover **self-employed persons** and their families[2] as well as employed persons or self-employed persons pursuing activities in the territories of two or more Member States[3]. Concerning health insurance, any insured person staying temporarily in a Member State other than the one in which he or she is insured, for tourist or employment purposes, may be admitted to hospital or receive refunds in respect of urgent medical care in the host State on presentation of the **European health insurance card** ("European card")[4]. This card replaced all paper forms needed for health treatment in another Member State provided for by Regulations 1408/71 and 574/72 giving entitlement to reimbursement of health care costs during a temporary stay in a Member State other than the competent State or the State of residence. The European card simplified access to care in the country visited, while providing a guarantee for the bodies financing the health system in that country that the patient is fully insured in his or her country of origin and that they can therefore rely on reimbursement by their counterparts.

For the effective functioning of a common labour market, it is also necessary that potential migrant workers have at their disposal adequate information regarding the number and nature of jobs available in the Community and the qualifications required. This is the task of the **European Employment Service (EURES)**, a network of some 400 "Euroadvisers" from the national employment services, employer organisations, trade unions, regional administrations and universities, specially trained to deal with the needs of transnational job-seekers and job-providers[5].

The core of the **EURES network** is a computerised databank providing information on transnational job and recruitment opportunities, as well as information on living and working conditions in the countries of the Union, from accommodation to contract law and taxation. The European Commission ensures the coordination of the network. EURES serves both as an employment service at the scale of Europe, having as task to inform, counsel and place job seekers on the territory of the European Economic Area, and as a forum for the examination, at operational level, of all questions relating to employment in Europe. By encouraging trans-border recruitment and acquisition of qualifications, this network makes a real contribution to the creation of a European labour market. More than half a million people seek the EURES services every year. An Internet site on the Europa server is a key source of information for job-seekers and employers as regards living and working conditions in the different Member States, providing access to the EURES database of job vacancies (around 10 000) and links to all the Internet sites of the participating public employment services (http://europa.eu.int/eures/home.jsp?lang=en).

To facilitate the mobility of workers within the Community it was also necessary to ensure and encourage the **education of the children** of migrant workers. That was achieved in a Council Directive, which obliges the Member States to treat the children of migrant workers in the same way as the children of national workers, including as regards the aid granted by the public authorities to school pupils and to students[6]. Two Council Resolutions on school provision for gypsy and traveller children and on school provision for children of occupational travellers respectively, provide for measures to be taken by the Community and the Member States to resolve the specific problems of those poorly educated people[7].

Concerning **sickness insurance** covered by Regulation 1408/71, the Court of Justice has established that, when an insured person has been authorised by the competent institution to go to another Member State for treatment, the institution of the place where the treatment is provided is required to provide him with benefits in kind in accordance with the rules on assumption of the costs of health care which the latter administers,

[1] Judgment given on 10 March 1993, Case C-111/91, Commission v Luxembourg, ECR 1993, I-840.
[2] Regulation 1390/81, OJ L 143, 29.05.1981 and Regulation 1408/71, OJ L 149, 05.07.1971 last amended by Regulation 629/2006, OJ L 114, 27.04.2006.
[3] Regulation 3811/86, OJ L 355, 16.12.1986.
[4] Decisions 2003/751, 2003/752 and 2003/753, OJ L 276, 27.10.2003.
[5] Decision2003/8, OJ L 5, 10.01.2003.
[6] Directive 77/486, OJ L 199, 06.08.1977.
[7] OJ C 153, 21.06.1989.

as if the person concerned were registered with it[1]. An authorisation can be refused on the ground of lack of medical necessity, only if the same or equally effective treatment can be obtained without undue delay at an establishment having a contractual arrangement with the insured person's sickness insurance fund[2].

6.5. Freedom of establishment and recognition of qualifications

Freedom of establishment means the free movement of self-employed persons. For them, as for salaried workers, the basic principle is equality of treatment of all Community citizens, i.e. the abolition of discriminations based on nationality. **Freedom of establishment includes** the right to take up and pursue activities as self-employed persons and to set up and manage undertakings, in particular companies or firms within the meaning of the second paragraph of Article 48 (TEC), i.e., companies established under the conditions laid down for its own nationals by the law of the country where such establishment is effected. The freedom of establishment of companies extends to what is known as freedom of secondary establishment, i.e. the setting up of agencies, branches or subsidiaries (Art. 43 TEC).

6.5.1. Right of establishment

Whereas freedom to provide services chiefly concerns the pursuit of an economic activity by a person in another Member State without having the principal or secondary place of business in that State, **right of establishment entails permanent installation** in a Member State in order to pursue an economic activity in that State. In fact, the situation of the person who establishes himself is characterised by the fact that he creates a permanent link with the country of establishment, unlike somebody who provides services in a country other then that of his permanent establishment. Through its judgment of 21 June 1974 in the Reyners case (Dutch legal practitioner wishing to pursue his profession in Belgium), the Court established the **direct effect** [see section 3.3.] of Treaty provisions concerning the freedom of establishment. It held that any individual may, on the basis of Article 52 of the EEC Treaty (43 TEC), demand directly the same treatment as is applied to nationals[3]. Therefore, no special Community legislation is required.

The right for citizens of EU Member States to work or pursue activities as self-employed persons in the Member States means the **right to enter and to reside** in the member country in which they wish to work or pursue those activities. This right is extended to their spouses, children and other members of their families, including the registered partner if the legislation of the host Member State treats registered partnership as equivalent to marriage[4]. For periods of residence of longer than three months, Member States may only require Union citizens to register with the competent authorities in the place of residence. The self-employed person can continue to reside, in the country in which he or she has settled after the termination of his or her employment. In fact, the self-employed person and his or her family members who have resided in a host Member State during a continuous period of five years have a right of permanent residence in that State. The members of the family enjoy the right of residence even after the self-employed person's death. A residence requirement can be justified only if it is based on

---

[1] Judgment of 12 July 2001, Case C-368/98 Vanbraekel, ECR 2001, p. I-05363.
[2] Judgment of 12 July 2001, Case C-157/99, Geraets-Smits, ECR 2001, p. I-05473.
[3] Judgment of 21 June 1974, Case 2/74, ECR 1974, p. 631.
[4] Directive 2004/38, OJ L 158, 30.04.2004.

objective considerations independent of the nationality of the persons concerned and proportionate to the legitimate aim of the national provisions[1].

Under Article 46 (TEC), the principle of freedom of establishment does not concern national provisions providing for special treatment for foreign nationals on **grounds of public policy, public security or public health**. The Directive on the right of citizens of the Union and their family members to move and reside freely within the territory of the Member States contains an enumeration of the circumstances, which cannot be invoked as grounds for refusal of entry or expulsion and a series of rules concerning the procedure, which must be followed where nationals of Member States may be refused entry or expelled[2]. According to the Court of Justice, Community law precludes the automatic expulsion without right of appeal of the national of a Member State following a criminal conviction which takes account neither of the personal conduct of the person convicted nor of the risk he represents to public order[3].

6.5.2. Recognition of professional qualifications

The abolition, between Member States, of obstacles to the free movement of persons and services is one of the objectives of the Community (Art. 3 TEC). For nationals of the Member States, this includes, in particular, the right to pursue a profession, in a self-employed or employed capacity, in a Member State other than the one in which they have obtained their professional qualifications. After the elimination of apparent discriminations, in accordance with the letter and the spirit of the Treaty, there could remain other obstacles to the freedom of establishment, i.e. the numerous requirements of the Member States with regard to the training of employed and self-employed persons, and the detailed arrangements for pursuing industrial and commercial activities. Even though these requirements were not in themselves discriminatory, they could impede the free establishment, if they differed from country to country and obliged the interested person to **take a new examination** for the recognition of his or her professional competence. That is why Article 47 of the EC Treaty empowers the Council and the Parliament to issue directives for the mutual recognition of diplomas, certificates and other evidence of formal qualifications and for the coordination of national provisions concerning the taking up and pursuit of activities as self-employed persons. Such directives have in fact been adopted for certain professions, notably those of nurses, doctors, architects and lawyers; but they have been abolished by the general directive on the recognition of professional qualifications examined below.

Indeed, in the context of the Lisbon strategy for economic and social renewal [see section 13.3.2.] the internal market strategy for services is aimed in particular at making the free provision of services within the Community as simple as within an individual Member State. This is the objective of the Directive on the **recognition of professional qualifications**[4]. Directive 2005/36 applies to all nationals of a Member State, including those belonging to the liberal professions, wishing to pursue a regulated profession in a Member State other than that in which they obtained their professional qualifications, on either a self-employed or employed basis. It establishes rules according to which a Member State which makes access to or pursuit of a regulated profession in its territory contingent upon possession of specific professional qualifications (the host Member State) should recognise professional qualifications obtained in one or more other Mem-

---

[1]   Judgement of 23 March 2004, Case C-138/02 *Brian Francis Collins v Secretary of State for Work and Pensions*, ECR 2004.
[2]   Directive 2004/38, OJ L 158, 30.04.2004.
[3]   Judgment of 29 April 2004, Joined Cases C-482/01 and C-493/01, Orfanopoulos and others, ECR 2004.
[4]   Directive 2005/36, OJ L 255, 30.09.2005.

ber States (the home Member State) and which allow the holder of the said qualifications to pursue the same profession there, for access to and pursuit of that profession. It also specifies that the provisions of Article 45 of the EC Treaty apply to professions linked to the exercise of public authority, particularly public notaries.

According to this directive, "**regulated profession**" is a professional activity or group of professional activities, access to which or the pursuit of which is subject to the possession of specific professional qualifications; in particular, the use of a professional title. "**Professional qualifications**" are qualifications attested by evidence of formal qualifications, an attestation of competence and/or professional experience. "Evidence of formal qualifications" means diplomas, certificates and other evidence issued by an authority in a Member State. "Aptitude test" is a test limited to the professional knowledge of the applicant, made by the competent authorities of the host Member State with the aim of assessing the ability of the applicant to pursue a regulated profession in that Member State. The aptitude test must take account of the fact that the applicant is a qualified professional in the home Member State or the Member State from which he comes and should cover subjects the knowledge of which is essential in order to be able to pursue the profession in the host Member State.

The recognition of professional qualifications by the host Member State allows the beneficiary to gain access in that Member State to the same profession as that for which he is qualified in the home Member State and to pursue it in the host Member State under the same conditions as its nationals. It also allows the free provision of services in case the service provider moves to the territory of the host Member State to pursue, **on a temporary and occasional basis**, the regulated profession. In this case, the host Member State should exempt service providers established in another Member State from the requirements which it places on professionals established in its territory relating to authorisation by, registration with or membership of a professional organisation or body. However, the exercise of a regulated profession is subject to the professional and disciplinary rules of the host Member State relating to professional qualifications. In order to define the mechanism of recognition under the general system, the various national education and training schemes are grouped into five levels, ranging from a training course not forming part of a certificate or diploma to a diploma certifying that the holder has successfully completed a post-secondary course of at least four years' duration.

Any host Member State in which a profession is regulated must take account of the qualifications obtained in another Member State and assess whether they correspond to those which it requires. The general system for recognition, however, does not prevent a Member State from making any person pursuing a profession on its territory subject to specific requirements due to the application of **professional rules justified by the general public interest**. Rules of this kind relate, for example, to organisation of the profession, professional standards, including those concerning ethics, and supervision and liability. However, directive 2005/36 contains a provision aimed at preventing the circumvention of national requirements by having qualifications recognised in another Member State and then asking the country of origin to recognise them in turn.

In order to promote the free movement of professionals, while ensuring an adequate level of qualification, various professional associations and organisations or Member States are able to propose **common platforms** at European level. A common platform is a set of criteria which make it possible to compensate for the widest range of substantial differences which have been identified between the training requirements in at least two thirds of the Member States including all the Member States which regulate that profession. These criteria may, for example, include requirements such as additional training, an adaptation period under supervised practice, an aptitude test, or a prescribed minimum level of professional practice, or combinations thereof.

Freedom of movement and the mutual recognition of the evidence of formal qualifications of doctors, nurses responsible for general care, dental practitioners, veterinary surgeons, midwives, pharmacists and architects is based on the fundamental principle of automatic recognition of the evidence of formal qualifications on the basis of coordinated minimum conditions for training. In addition, access in the Member States to the professions of **doctor, nurse responsible for general care, dental practitioner, veterinary surgeon, midwife and pharmacist** should be made conditional upon the possession of a given qualification ensuring that the person concerned has undergone training which meets the minimum conditions laid down. Directive 2005/36 adopts the principle of automatic recognition for medical and dental specialisations common to at least two Member States, but restricts new medical specialisations eligible for automatic recognition to those that are common to at least two fifths of the Member States.

The recognition of professional qualifications for **lawyers** for the purpose of immediate establishment under the professional title of the host Member State is covered by Directive 2005/36. This Directive does not affect, however, the operation of Directive 77/249 tending to facilitate the effective exercise by lawyers of freedom to provide services[1], or of Directive 98/5 aiming to facilitate practice of the profession of lawyer on a permanent basis in a Member State other than that in which the qualification was obtained[2]. To the extent that they are regulated, Directive 2005/36 includes also **liberal professions**, which are, according to this Directive, those practised on the basis of relevant professional qualifications in a personal, responsible and professionally independent capacity by those providing intellectual and conceptual services to clients and/or the public.

6.6. Freedom to provide services

Article 49 (TEC) provides that restrictions on "freedom to provide services" within the Community shall be "abolished in respect of nationals of Member States who are established in a State of the Community other than that of the person for whom the services are intended". Any discrimination concerning the provision of services on the basis of nationality is prohibited directly by this Article (without the need of specific Community legislation). Under Article 50 (TEC), **services shall be considered as such** where they are normally provided for remuneration, in so far as they are not governed by the provisions relating to freedom of movement for goods, capital and persons. This Article specifies, however, that the provisions on the free movement of services **cover all activities of an industrial or commercial character** or of craftsmen and the activities of the professions.

The activity must be limited in time, must normally be pursued against payment and must involve some form of foreign aspect, unless the border is physically crossed. The person providing a service may, in order to do so, temporarily pursue his activity in the State where the service is provided, under the same conditions as are imposed by that State on its own nationals (third paragraph of Article 50 TEC). Services provided under a contract outside the country of establishment may be of a long duration. There is nothing, moreover, to preclude an activity for the provision of services from being of a magnitude such as to necessitate the acquisition of real estate in the country of provision of services. However, to constitute a provision of services rather than a permanent establishment, the person providing the service must remain established in his own country and his services must cross borders [see section 6.5.]. The rules of the Treaty nevertheless cover situations where it is the person receiving the services who crosses the border, such as a tourist, and situations where both the person receiving and the person providing the service remain in their respective countries, such as consultation by correspondence. It appears that the freedom of establishment and the freedom to provide services cannot be clearly distinguished in all situations and that they often go together, since a person or company seeks establishment in another Member State in order to provide services in that state. This is why the two freedoms are usually considered as **one: the freedom of establishment and provision of services**.

Services represent almost 60% of the value added of the Community economy and cover a vast spread of economic activities, from banks and insurance to transport and tourism, not to mention data processing and management consultancy. They therefore

---

[1] Directive 77/249, OJ L 78, 26.03.1977.
[2] Directive 98/5, OJ L 77, 14.03.1998.

play an increasingly large part in the economy and employment and are a linchpin for smooth operation of the EU's internal market. Their liberalisation is based on **the principle of mutual recognition**, according to which, if a service is lawfully authorised in one Member State it must be open to users in the other Member States without having to comply with every detail of the legislation of the host country, except those concerning consumer protection. Control has to be exercised by the Government in the territory of which the company providing the services is established, with the authorities of the country in which the service is performed merely ensuring that certain basic rules relating to commercial conduct are observed. This system applies both to the traditional fields of transport, insurance and banking and to the new fields of services, such as information technology, marketing and audio-visual services.

Financial services - banks, insurance companies and stock exchanges - which are closely monitored by the official authorities, are particularly important, as they constitute a vast market and are indispensable for the proper functioning of the other economic sectors. Efficient and transparent financial markets foster growth and employment by better allocation of capital and reducing its cost. They therefore play an essential role in supporting entrepreneurial culture and promoting access to and use of new technologies. The freedoms of establishment and provision of services in the common market required that those services be liberalised from the protectionist measures applied by most Member States. This liberalisation, however, should reconcile two contradictory requirements, viz. the need to maintain very stringent criteria for control and financial security and the need to leave the branch concerned enough flexibility for it to be able to meet the new and ever-more complex requirements of its customers throughout the European market, particularly since the introduction of the euro. The Financial Services Committee helps define the medium- and long-term Community strategy for financial services issues examined below[1].

The distinction between freedom of establishment and freedom to provide services is not always obvious. However, that no longer has any practical relevance since a judgment of the Court of Justice of 3 December 1974 in the Van Binsbergen case established **the direct applicability** of the prohibition on discrimination in respect of the provision of services[2] [see section 3.3.], just as the Reyners case had done for freedom of establishment [see section 6.5.1.]. No individual liberalisation Directives are therefore necessary. Indeed, according to Court case-law, Article 59 EEC (Art. 49 TEC) in itself grants operators properly established in their country of origin the right to supply services in another Member State without the latter being able to prevent the exercise of that right on the grounds that the conditions of supply are different there[3]. Only overriding reasons relating to the public interest may justify an exception to that principle, provided that it is proportionate to the aim in view.

Harmonisation of legislation is henceforth necessary only in very specific instances, to facilitate the exchange of services, notably electronic pay services. Thus, a Directive seeks to harmonise the legislation of Member States concerning measures to **combat illicit devices** which allow unauthorised access to protected services, such as pay television, video or sound recordings on demand, whose remuneration -and often viability - relies on "conditional access" techniques such as encryption or electronic locking[4].

A Commission communication announces a strategy designed to create an environment conducive to the **development of electronic commerce in the context of financial services** and to restore consumer confidence[5]. It explores three policy areas linked to the electronic commerce directive [see section 17.3.5.]: to bring about convergence in consumer and investor protection rules for both contractual and non-contractual obligations; to develop measures to provide secure payment systems and out-of-court redress on a cross-border basis; and to achieve enhanced supervisory cooperation that can meet the new cross-border challenges.

---

[1] Decision 2003/165, OJ L 67, 12.03.2003.
[2] Judgment of 3 December 1974, Case 33/74, ECR 1974, 1299.
[3] Judgments of 25 July 1991, cases C-288/89, ECR 1991, p. I-4007 and C-353/89, ECR 1991, p. I-4069.
[4] Directive 98/84, OJ L 320, 28.11.1998.
[5] COM (2001) 66, 7 February 2001.

6.6.1. Banking

All restrictions on freedom of establishment and freedom to provide services in respect of self-employed activities of **banks and other financial institutions** have been abolished since the 1970s. The laws, regulations and administrative provisions of the Member States relating to the taking up and pursuit of the business of credit institutions have been coordinated within a single regulatory framework[1]. The right of access is based on the mutual recognition of supervision systems, i.e. application of the principle of supervision of a credit institution by the Member State in which it has its head office, and the issue of a "**single bank licence**" which is valid throughout the Community. The single licence authorises a bank established in a Member State to open branches without any other formalities or to propose its services in the partner countries. The principle of reciprocity governs the opening in the Community of subsidiaries of banks from non-member countries. Directive 2006/48 gives a definition of the **own funds** of credit institutions, a definition which is vital to the harmonisation necessary for mutual recognition. It also establishes a minimum level for the **solvency ratio** for credit institutions and the method of calculating the ratio to be observed between own funds and risk assets and off-balance-sheet items.

In the European internal market, the transparency, performance and stability of cross-border payment systems should match the properties of the best domestic payment systems. To this effect, a Directive requires banks to execute **cross-border credit transfers** within reasonable time-limits (five banking business days for the originator's institution and one banking business day for the beneficiary's institution), makes double-charging illegal, requires the reimbursement of the full amount (up to a ceiling of EUR 12 500) in the event of non-execution of transfers and enhances transparency concerning the conditions applying to transfers[2]. A Commission notice supplementing this Directive provides a framework allowing banks to set in place cooperation arrangements aimed at making cross-border credit transfers more efficient without unduly restricting competition, particularly concerning market access and price competition[3].

A Directive on **deposit-guarantee schemes** is designed to protect depositors in the event of an authorised credit institution failing[4]. It stipulates that there must be a guarantee scheme in all Member States, financed by the banking sector and covering all deposits up to EUR 20 000 per depositor (EUR 15 000 in Spain, Portugal, Greece and Luxembourg). The scheme covers depositors not only in institutions in the Member State which authorise them, but also those in branches of such institutions set up in other Member States.

A clear regulatory framework for **electronic money** in the single market aims to enhance business and consumer confidence in this new form of payment, while ensuring that equal competitive conditions prevail for traditional credit institutions and other companies which issue electronic money[5]. Electronic money institutions are included within the general scope of the provisions of the banking coordination directives. Companies which issue electronic money but which do not wish to provide the whole range of banking services have nonetheless the opportunity to operate throughout the single market on the basis of a single licence issued by a single Member State, which places them on an equal footing with credit institutions [see also sections 14.2.1. and 17.3.5.].

---

[1] Directive 2006/48, OJ L 177, 30.06.2006.
[2] Directive 97/5, OJ L 43, 14.02.1997.
[3] OJ C 251, 27.09.1995.
[4] Directive 94/19, OJ L 135, 31.05.1994 and Directive 2005/1, OJ L 79, 24.03.2005.
[5] Directive 2000/46, OJ L 275, 27.10.2000.

Directive 2006/48 permits the **supervision of credit institutions** on a consolidated basis[1]. It defines the object of supervision, consolidation methods and the sharing of responsibilities between Member States for the monitoring of multinational groups, particularly financial companies whose main activity is the holding of interests in credit establishments or other financial establishments. The object of supervision is solvency, the match between own funds and risks and non-financial interests.

On the other hand, Directive 2006/48 seeks to ensure that the Member States **control excessive concentrations of exposures** to a single client, thus avoiding losses that might threaten the solvency of a credit institution and have repercussions on the entire financial system. In particular it stipulates that the large exposures of credit institutions should not exceed 40% of equity capital during a transitional phase, subsequently reduced to 25%, that credit institutions must notify the authorities when they fall to 10% of equity capital and that their aggregate total should not exceed 800% of equity capital.

Other vital factors for the European banking system are: the Directive on **annual accounts and consolidated accounts** of banks and other credit institutions[2]; and the Directive on the obligations of branches established in a Member State of credit institutions and financial institutions having their head offices outside that Member State regarding the publication of **annual accounting documents**[3] [see also section 17.2.1.].

The completion of the internal market for banking, the liberalisation of financial services through the privatisation of a number of State-owned banks and the creation of the euro have led to a consolidation of credit institutions in Europe in recent years. One in six banks in Europe disappeared between 1994 and 1999. While the number of local units fell slightly (- 1.4%) between 1997 and 1999 in the EU, the number of automatic cash dispensers rose by 16.5%. Indeed, **payment cards** are increasingly used in the Member States for obtaining cash from automatic cash dispensers or for paying for products or services directly and electronically at sales-point terminals or even at home. So as to encourage the interconnection of the networks, the Commission issued Recommendations: on consumer protection in the field of the new payment systems, and in particular the relationship between cardholder and card issuer[4]; on the transparency of bank charges relating to cross-border transactions[5]; and on transactions by electronic payment instruments, including electronic money products, and in particular the relationship between issuer and holder[6].

6.6.2. Insurance

The laws, regulations and administrative provisions relating to the taking-up and pursuit of the business of **direct insurance other than life insurance** have been coordinated[7] and the effective exercise of freedom to provide insurance services in the Community is a reality[8]. Community arrangements cover major industrial and commercial risks and provide adequate protection for minor consumers. Also coordinated are the legislations of the Member States concerning **credit insurance** and **suretyship insurance**, on the one hand,[9] and **legal expenses insurance**[10], on the other.

The coordination of the provisions of the Member States and the freedom to provide services **in the field of life assurance** offer policy-holders the choice between all the different types of contract available in the Community, while guaranteeing them adequate protection. The freedoms of establishment and provision of services are implemented through the mutual recognition of authorisations and prudential control systems, thereby making it possible to grant a single authorisation valid throughout the Community[11]. The coordination of the basic rules of prudential and financial supervision provides for single authorisation valid throughout the Community, along with the checking of all of a broker's activities by the Member State of origin.

---

[1] Directive 2006/48, OJ L 177, 30.06.2006.
[2] Directive 86/635, OJ L 372, 31.12.1986 and Directive 2006/46, OJ L 224, 16.08.2006.
[3] Directive 89/117, OJ L 44, 16.02.1989 and OJ L 1, 03.01.1994.
[4] Recommendation 88/590, OJ L 317, 24.11.1988.
[5] Recommendation 90/109, OJ L 67, 15.03.1990.
[6] COM (97) 353.
[7] First Council Directive 73/239, OJ L 228, 16.08.1973 and Directive 2005/68, OJ L 323, 09.12.2005.
[8] Directive 88/357, OJ L 172, 04.07.1988 and Directive 2005/14, OJ L 149, 11.06.2005.
[9] Directive 87/343, OJ L 185, 04.07.1987.
[10] Directive 87/344, OJ L 185, 04.07.1987.
[11] Directive 2002/83, OJ L 345, 19.12.2002 and directive 2005/68, OJ L 323, 09.12.2005.

A **single authorisation system** enables an insurance company with its registered office in a Community Member State to open branches and operate services in all the Member States without the need for authorisation procedures in each country[1]. This system is designed to ensure the free movement of insurance products within the Community and give European citizens the opportunity to take out insurance with any Community insurer, thus finding the coverage best suited to their needs at the lowest cost, while enjoying an adequate level of protection. An Insurance Committee helps the Commission exercise the implementation powers conferred on it by the Council in the field of direct insurance[2].

The approximation of the laws of the Member States relating to insurance against **civil liability in respect of the use of motor vehicles**, and to the enforcement of the obligation to insure against such liability affords adequate protection for the victims of road accidents, irrespective of the Member State in which the accident occurred[3]. The Community legislation imposes compulsory cover for all passengers of the vehicle, covering the entire territory of the Community, including cases where the passenger is the owner, the holder of the vehicle or the insured person himself[4]. Thanks to this legislation and to the Multilateral Guarantee Agreement between national insurers' bureaux signed in Madrid on March 1991, Member States do not need to make any checks on insurance against civil liability in respect of vehicles which are normally based in a Member State or in certain third countries[5].

Harmonised rules concerning **insurance companies,** establish transparency and comparability of their annual and consolidated accounts[6]. While providing for mutual recognition of the existing procedures in the Member States for reorganising and winding up insurance companies and for the appropriate protection of insurance creditors (insured persons, policy-holders, etc.), a directive recognises the exclusive competence of the Member State of origin in adopting such measures in accordance with its own legislation[7]. A regulatory framework for **insurance mediation**, comprising a single system of registration of insurance and reinsurance intermediaries in their home Member State, aims at ensuring a high level of professionalism and competence among them, in order to facilitate the cross-border exercise of their activities and a high level of protection of policy-holders' interests[8].

The Commission may grant derogations, under certain conditions, to certain types of agreements, decisions and concerted practices in the insurance field, under application of Article 81, paragraph 1 of the EC Treaty[9] [see section 15.3.3.]. In fact, the Commission block exemption regulation for the insurance sector exempts, on certain conditions, agreements that relate to: the joint calculation of existing risks and studies on future risks; the joint establishment of non-binding standard policy conditions; the setting-up and operation of groups of insurance undertakings; and the examination and recognition of security devices[10]. Thanks to a Community Directive, however, the insurance supervisory authorities are given more effective means of assessing the actual solvency of an insurance firm belonging to a group, thereby increasing protection for policy-holders[11].

---

[1]   Directive 92/49, OJ L 228, 11.08.1992 and Directive 2005/68, OJ L 323, 09.12.2005.
[2]   Directive 91/675, OJ L 374, 31.12.1991 and Directive 2005/1, OJ L 79, 24.03.2005.
[3]   Directive 2000/26, OJ L 181, 20.07.2000 and Directive 2005/14, OJ L 149, 11.06.2005.
[4]   Directive 90/232, OJ L 129, 19.05.1990 and Directive 2005/14, OJ L 149, 11.06.2005.
[5]   Commission Decision 2003/564, OJ L 192, 31.07.2003.
[6]   Directive 91/674, OJ L 374, 31.12.1991 and Directive 2006/46, OJ L 224, 16.08.2006.
[7]   Directive 2001/17, OJ L 110, 20.04.2001.
[8]   Directive 2002/92, OJ L 9, 15.01.2003.
[9]   Regulation 1534/91, OJ L 143, 07.06.1991 and Regulation 1/2003, OJ L 1, 04.01.2003.
[10] Regulation 358/2003, OJ L 53, 28.02.2003 and Regulation 886/2004, OJ L 168, 01.05.2004.
[11] Directive 98/78, OJ L 330, 05.12.1998 and Directive 2005/68, 09.12.2005.

6.6.3. Stock exchanges and financial services

Community law on stock exchanges and other securities markets is directed towards widening the range of investments at Community level while protecting investors. The conditions for the admission of securities to official stock exchange listing are coordinated and the **single market in securities** is a reality[1] [see details below]. Investment services in the securities field can be freely conducted, although monitored throughout the EU financial area by the Directive on markets in financial instruments[2]. This directive establishes a comprehensive regulatory framework governing the organised execution of investor transactions by exchanges, other trading systems and investment firms and makes sure investors enjoy a high level of protection when employing investment firms, wherever they are located in the EU. An investment firm in any Member State can carry out its activities anywhere in the European Union on the basis of a single authorisation (called a "European passport) issued by the Member State of origin. The conditions governing authorisation and business activity have been harmonised for this purpose. Prudential supervision, based on uniform rules, is carried out by the authorities of the home Member State, but in cooperation with the authorities of the host Member State. Investment firms have right of access to all the regulated markets in the EU. Common standards pertain to the prudential supervision of financial conglomerates (credit institutions, insurance undertakings and investment firms) in order to create a level playing field and legal certainty for the financial establishments concerned.

The equity capital of investment firms and credit institutions must be adequate to safeguard market stability, guarantee an identical level of **protection against bankruptcy** to investors throughout the European Union and to ensure fair competition between banks, which are subject to specific prudential provisions, and investment societies on the securities market. In order to fulfil these objectives, a Directive lays down minimum initial capital requirements and sets the equity capital, which must permanently be held in order to cover position, settlement, exchange and interest rate risks[3]. All Member States must provide for minimum compensation for investors in the event of the failure of an investment firm, authorised to provide services throughout the Union[4]. In cases of insolvency, the collateral security provided in connection with participation in payment and securities settlement systems must be realised first and foremost in order to satisfy the rights of these systems vis-à-vis the insolvent party[5]. The directive setting up common rules for collateral pledged to payment and securities settlement systems aims to limit credit risk and improve the functioning and stability of the European financial markets[6].

In order to combat fraudulent use of privileged stock exchange information, ensure the integrity of European financial markets and enhance investor confidence in those markets a directive prohibits **insider dealing and market manipulation (market abuse)**[7]. Member States must prohibit any person who possesses inside information (as defined in the directive) from using that information by acquiring or disposing of for his own account or for the account of a third party, either directly or indirectly, financial instruments to which that information relates. "Market manipulation" means notably transactions or dissemination of information, which give false or misleading signals as to

---

[1] Directive 2001/34, OJ L 184, 06.07.2001 and Directive 2005/1, OJ L 79, 24.03.2005.
[2] Directive 2004/39, OJ L 145, 30.04.2004 and Directive 2006/31, OJ L 114, 27.04.2006.
[3] Directive 2006/49, OJ L 177, 30.06.2006.
[4] Directive 97/9, OJ L 84, 26.03.1997.
[5] Directive 98/26, OJ L 166, 11.06.1998.
[6] Directive 2002/47, OJ L 168, 27.06.2002.
[7] Directive 2003/6, OJ L 96, 12.04.2003.

the supply of, demand for or price of financial instruments or which employ fictitious devices or any other form of deception or contrivance.

The coordination of the conditions for the **admission of securities to official listing on stock exchanges** situated or operating in the Member States is aimed at providing equivalent protection for investors at Community level, because of the more uniform guarantees offered to investors in the various Member States[1]. It facilitates both the admission to official stock exchange listing, in each such State, of securities from other Member States and the listing of any given security on a number of stock exchanges in the Community. It may accordingly make for greater interpenetration of national securities markets by removing those obstacles that may prudently be removed and therefore contribute to the prospect of establishing a European capital market. The "single passport" for issuers harmonises the requirements for the drawing up, approval and distribution of the **prospectus to be published when securities are offered to the public** or admitted to trading[2]. It aims to ensure that adequate and equivalent disclosure standards are in place in all Member States, so as to afford investors throughout the European Union a uniform degree of protection. Minimum guidelines and common principles are established for the conduct of takeover bids (OPA) for the securities of companies governed by the laws of Member States, where all or some of those securities are admitted to trading on a regulated market[3].

A central factor for the proper functioning of the internal market in transferable securities is the Directive relating to **undertakings for collective investment in transferable securities (UCITS)**[4]. It coordinates the rules governing such undertakings in the Member States with a view, on the one hand, to approximating the investment policies and the conditions of competition between these UCITS at Community level and, on the other hand, to achieving effective and more uniform protection of shareholders in such undertakings. This coordination allows a "European passport" regime, whereby financial undertakings authorised to offer services in one Member State may offer their services throughout the internal market without additional authorisation.

6.6.4. Services of general interest

The **services of general interest** indicate "market" and "non-market" activities, considered to be of general interest by the public authorities, and subjected for this reason to specific public service obligations. Article 86 of the EC Treaty specifies that undertakings entrusted with the operation of (market) services of general economic interest are subject to the rules contained in the Treaty, in particular to the rules on competition, in so far as the application of such rules does not obstruct the performance of the particular tasks assigned to them (postal, telecommunications, transport, electricity, broadcasting, etc.). However, advantages granted to operators of these services must not enable them to compete unfairly at the expense of other companies[5]. The evolutionary concept of "**universal service**", developed by the Community institutions, refers to a set of general interest requirements, which should be satisfied by the operators of such services to make sure that all citizens have access to certain essential services of high quality at prices they can afford[6]. It is sensitive to national diversity and takes into consideration the special features of the European model of society [see section 13.1.].

Article 16 of the EC Treaty specifies that, without prejudice to Articles 73, 86 and 87 (TEC), and given the place occupied by services of general economic interest in the **shared values of the Union**, the Community and the Member States must take care that such services operate on the basis of principles and conditions which enable them to fulfil their missions. A Protocol to the EC Treaty inserted at Amsterdam asserts that **public service broadcasting** is directly related to the democratic, social and cultural needs of each society and to the need to preserve media pluralism. Therefore, the provi-

---

[1] Directive 2001/34, OJ L 184, 06.07.2001 and Directive 2005/1, OJ L 79, 24.03.2005.
[2] Directive 2003/71, OJ L 345, 31.12.2003.
[3] Directive 2004/25, OJ L 142, 30.04.2004.
[4] Directive 85/611, OJ L 375, 31.12.1985 and Directive 2005/1, OJ L 79, 24.03.2005.
[5] COM (2002) 636, 27 November 2002.
[6] COM (2000) 580 and COM (2001) 598, 17 October 2001.

sions of the Treaty are without prejudice to the competence of Member States to provide for the funding of public service broadcasting, provided that certain conditions are met, notably that such funding does not affect trading conditions and competition in the Community [see section 10.2.].

General interest services are **a key element of the single market and of European competitiveness**. They have to contend with significant changes in terms of the economy, technology and consumer requirements. To respond to these changes, Community action is designed to modernise these services to ensure that essential needs continue to be met and that performance is improved. Based on Article 86 of the EC Treaty, Community action takes account of the subsidiarity principle and tries to maintain a balance between market play and general interest in the form of universal service or public service obligations. In a May 2004 the Commission identified a number of guidelines in the field of general-interest services with the aim of formulating a coherent policy in this area[1].

A Directive on common rules for the proper functioning of the internal market, the gradual liberalisation and the improvement of quality of **postal services** set up a Community regulatory framework for these services[2]. It defines the universal postal service which must be guaranteed throughout the Union, sets limits to the postal monopoly and provides a timetable for the controlled opening of the postal market to competition. In order to guarantee the financial viability of the national providers of universal service, the Directive sets out the harmonised criteria for the services which are to be reserved for universal service providers.

6.7. Free movement of capital

Freedom of capital movement is another essential element for the proper functioning of the large European internal market. The liberalisation of payment transactions is a vital **complement to the free movement of goods, persons and services**. Borrowers - individuals and companies notably SMEs - must be able to obtain capital where it is cheapest and best tailored to their needs, while investors and suppliers of capital must be able to offer their resources on the market where there is the greatest interest. That is why it is important that the member states of a common market free capital movements and allow payments to be made in the currency of the member state in which the creditor or beneficiary is established. Obviously, all these conditions must pre-exist before the passage to the stage of an economic and monetary union, involving the circulation of a single currency.

To this end, a 1988 Directive ensures the **full liberalisation of capital movements**[3]. Under this Directive, all restrictions on capital movements between persons (natural or legal) resident in Member States were removed in the beginning of the nineties. Monetary and quasi-monetary operations (financial loans and credits, operations in current and deposit accounts and operations in securities and other instruments normally dealt in on the money market) in particular were liberalised.

However, the EC Treaty, which replaced the EEC Treaty in 1992, went even further than the 1988 Directive in the liberalisation of capital movements. The principle of the free movement of capital and payments is now expressly laid down in the Treaty. Article 56 (TEC) declares, in fact, that all restrictions on the movement of capital between Member States and between Member States and third countries are prohibited. It thus extends the **liberalisation of capital movements to and from third countries**. Article 59, however, authorises temporary safeguard measures to be taken where they are justified on serious political grounds or where capital movements to and from third countries cause serious difficulties for the functioning of economic and monetary union. In addi-

---

[1] COM (2004) 374, 12 May 2004.
[2] Directive 97/67, OJ L 15, 21.01.1998 and Directive 2002/39, OJ L 176, 05.07.2002.
[3] Directive 88/361, OJ L 178, 08.07.1988 and OJ L 1, 03.01.1994.

tion, Article 58 authorises Member States to take all requisite measures to prevent infringements of national law and regulations, in particular in the field of taxation and the prudential supervision of financial institutions.

On the basis of these provisions and of those liberalising banking, stock-exchange and insurance services [see sections 6.6.1. to 6.6.3.], the Community **financial market has been completely liberalised** since January 1, 1993. European businesses and individuals have access to the full range of options available in the Member States as regards banking services, mortgage loans, securities and insurance. They are able to choose what is best suited to their specific needs or requirements for their daily lives and for their professional activities in the large market. The Member States must, however, dissuade the exploitation of the financial market for illegal purposes, notably laundering money generated by criminal or terrorist activities[1] [see details below].

In a 1997 communication the Commission expressed the view that the special powers reserved to Member States in the **management of privatised undertakings,** such as prior authorisations and rights of veto, could constitute an obstacle to the exercise of the fundamental freedoms enshrined in the Treaty, in particular the free movement of capital, although it accepted that they could be justified under exceptional circumstances and on strict conditions[2]. In three rulings on actions brought by the Commission against Member States for failure to fulfil their obligations, the Court of Justice fully upheld the communication of the Commission[3]:

According to the Court of Justice, the free movement of capital is a fundamental principle of the Treaty, which may be restricted only by national rules which are justified by overriding public-interest grounds and that national rules guarantee the attainment of the objective pursued and satisfy the criterion of proportionality[4]. Therefore, the free movement of capital and loans should not be restrained by national provisions that are likely to deter the parties concerned from approaching banks established in another Member State[5]. However, the export of important amounts of money may be subjected to a prior declaration, so that the national authorities may exercise effective supervision in order to prevent infringements of their laws and regulations[6].

The European financial area must not, however, be exploited for the purposes of laundering money generated by criminal activities. This is the aim of a Directive on prevention of the use of the financial system for the purpose of **money laundering and terrorist financing**[7]. Taking stock of the events of 11 September 2001 [see section 8.1.3.], this directive establishes a new international standard on combating serious crime, organised crime and the financing of terrorism. It requires Member States to combat the laundering of the proceeds of serious crime, as defined in Framework Decision 2001/500 on money laundering, the identification, tracing, freezing, seizing and confiscation of instrumentalities and the proceeds of crime [see section 8.1.4]. Consequently, the requirements in terms of identifying clients, retaining documents and declaring suspect transactions also apply to external auditors, real estate agents, notaries, lawyers, dealers in high-value goods such as precious stones or metals or works of art, auctioneers, money transporters and casinos. The Member States must take measures such as identification of customers and economic beneficiaries, the conservation of supporting documents and registrations of the transactions, the informing of the relevant authorities of suspected laundering operations and the determination of applicable sanctions [see also section 8.1.2.].

6.8. Trans-European Networks

A common policy on infrastructure trans-European networks (TENs) is needed for the good functioning of the common market. Indeed, the integration of national markets through the completion of the internal market can only have full economic and social impact, if businesses and citizens enjoy trans-European **transport, telecommunica-**

---

[1] Directive 2005/60, OJ L 309, 25.11.2005.
[2] Communication of the Commission, OJ C 220, 19.07.1997.
[3] Judgments of 4 June 2002, Case C-367/98 *Commission* v *Portugal*, Case C-483/99 *Commission* v *France* and Case C-503/99 *Commission* v *Belgium,* ECR 2002, pp. I-4731, 4781 and 4809.
[4] Judgement of 2 June 2005, Case C-174/04, Commission v Italian Republic, ECR 2005, p. I-04933.
[5] Judgment of 14 November 1995, case C-484/93, Peter Svenson, ECR 1995, p. I-3955.
[6] Joined cases C-358/93 and C-416/93, Bordessa, ECR 1995, p. I-0361 and Joined Cases C-163/94, C-195/94 and C-250/94, Sanz de Lera, ECR 1995, p. I-4821.
[7] Directive 2005/60, OJ L 309, 25.11.2005.

tions and energy networks, which optimise the use of the various legal instruments governing the operation of this market. With a view to enabling citizens, economic operators and regional and local authorities to derive full benefit from the setting up of an area without internal frontiers, the Community strives to promote the interconnection and inter-operability of national networks and access to these networks. It takes account in particular of the need to link island, landlocked and peripheral regions with the central regions of the Community (Art. 154 TEC). To speed up the implementation of networks, and to encourage public-private partnerships, the complex national rules and procedures are streamlined in the case of TENs, by having one approval procedure instead of requiring a series of different approvals for each element of the project.

Article 155 (TEC) provides that, in order to foster the **completion of trans-European networks**, the Community:

- establishes a series of guidelines identifying projects of common interest and providing the objectives, the priorities, the general lines of Community action and coordination with national decisions. These guidelines are adopted in accordance with the procedure contained in Article 251 (co-decision Council-Parliament) and require the approval of the Member State in question:
- adopts measures designed to harmonise technical standards;
- supports the financial efforts made by the Member States for projects of common interest, by carrying out feasibility studies and granting loan guarantees or interest rate subsidies. These decisions are taken by the Council and the European Parliament pursuant to the procedure of Article 251 (TEC);
- contributes to the financing of specific projects in the area of transport infrastructure through the Cohesion Fund.

The **financial instruments**, which facilitate the realisation of these networks, are notably the Cohesion Fund [see section 12.1.2], certain actions provided for under the Structural Funds Regulations, the loans of the European Investment Bank and the loan guarantees of the European Investment Fund [see section 12.3.]. A Council Regulation lays down the legal rules for the granting of Community financial assistance in the field of trans-European networks[1]. It defines the types of aid, the project selection criteria and the procedures for examining, assessing and monitoring applications for funding. It encourages public-private partnerships and risk-capital participation. The Community support to TENs can take the form of contributions to feasibility studies, interest-rate subsidies, loan guarantees and, in duly justified cases, direct grants to investments.

For **transport networks (TEN-T)**, the emphasis is placed on creating high-level service or utility networks alleviating congestion, namely motorways, high speed trains, the organisation of air space and combined forms of transport [see section 20.2.3.]. New or better designed infrastructures should permit: better, safer travel at lower cost in order to improve competitiveness; effective regional planning in order to avoid a concentration of wealth and population; and bridge-building towards Eastern Europe. Community guidelines for the development of the trans-European transport network provide a general framework setting out objectives and indicating the development planned up to the year 2010, and the measures to be taken to achieve this[2]. According to the Commission, it is important developing public/private partnerships for the implementation of TEN transport projects[3].

As regards **telecommunications networks (eTEN)**, the priority objectives are the development of Community wideband networks - called "information highways" - and the creation of telematic networks between government departments - vital for the advancement of information society and for the running of the internal market - particularly in the fields of customs, indirect taxation, statistics and border checks. The Parliament and Council guidelines for trans-European telecommunication networks set up a mechanism by which

---

[1]   Regulation 2236/95, OJ L 228, 23.09.1995 and Regulation 1159/2005, OJ L 191, 22.07.2005.
[2]   Decision 1692/96, OJ L 228, 09.09.1996 and Decision 884/2004, OJ L 167, 30.04.2004.
[3]   COM (97) 654, 4 December 1997.

the Commission, on the basis of a list of common interest projects, establishes a work programme and calls for proposals for individual projects, notably in the context of the *e*Europe initiative[1] [see section 17.3.5.]. The Edicom (Electronic Data Interchange on Commerce) programme facilitates the interoperability at European level of inter-administration telematics networks for statistics on intra-Community trade[2]. The Parliament and Council have established a series of guidelines, including the identification of projects of common interest, for trans-European networks for the electronic interchange of data between administrations (IDA)[3]. They have also adopted a series of actions and measures in order to ensure a secure communications infrastructure, which links the intranets of the EU's national governments, institutions and agencies by means of trans-European networks for electronic IDA[4] [see also section 17.3.6.].

For trans-European energy networks (TEN-E), the chief aim is the gradual integration of natural gas and electricity networks, heightening energy supply security of all regions of the Union and ensuring international competitiveness of European firms, which are big consumers of energy [see section 19.2.1.]. Community guidelines are designed to promote the development of trans-European energy networks and set out the broad lines of action by the Community in this area[5]. A Commission communication examines the problems of interconnecting natural gas and electricity networks with third countries of the European continent, the Mediterranean Basin, Central Asia and the Middle East[6].

Joint **environmental projects** consist of joint action by Member States to devise projects of common interest for protecting or improving the environment, including waste management and water policy.

6.9. Appraisal and outlook

It took nearly a quarter of a century after the removal of customs duties and quantitative restrictions between Member States to complete *in tandem* customs union and common market. However delayed, the **achievement of a single market** is a great step forward in the process of European integration. Free movement reduces the manufacturing and transport costs of goods, facilitates exports and the realisation of important economies. The reduction of administrative and financial costs of intra-Community trade and the realisation of economies of scale tend to liberate the dynamism and the creativity of European businesses and to give them a solid base from which to tackle international competitiveness. In a global economy characterised by fierce competition, particularly between multinational companies, the economies and the companies of small and medium European countries would certainly be much worse off than they are today, if it was not for the large internal market, which is their safe haven and springboard for external markets. This is why, business interest groups back the multinational integration process [see section 1.1.2 and 9.4.]. On its part, the Community helps businesses and particularly SMEs striving to adapt to the conditions of the single market [see section 17.2.].

The common market has also boosted the welfare of the citizens of the Member States. European consumers, previously confined to their respective national markets, now enjoy a huge choice of high quality goods and services at prices dictated by free competition. The free movement of workers, freedom to provide services and freedom of establishment for self-employed persons constitute **fundamental rights**, guaranteeing the citizens of the Community the right to pursue an occupation in any Member State. The citizen of a Member State, be he or she worker, businessman or tourist, can no longer be regarded as an alien in another Member State, but as an EU citizen, and no discrimination against him or her is permitted [see section 9.1.].

---

[1]   Decision 1336/97, OJ L 183, 11.07.1997 and Decision 1376/2002, OJ L 200, 30.07.2002.
[2]   Decision 96/715, OJ L 327, 18.12.1996.
[3]   Decision 1719/1999, OJ L 203, 03.08.1999 and Regulation 885/2004, OJ L 168, 01.05.2004.
[4]   Decision 1720/1999, OJ L 203, 03.08.1999 and Regulation 885/2004, OJ L 168, 01.05.2004.
[5]   Decision 1229/2003, OJ L 176, 15.07.2003.
[6]   COM (97) 125, 26 March 1997.

The implementation of the fundamental freedoms of the common market allows the **production factors of work and capital to operate** without hindrance. Businesses can manufacture and sell their products in accordance with a system of free competition in the Member State in which conditions are most advantageous to them. They can set themselves up wherever they wish in the common market and can call on a multitude of services and sources of capital, which exist in all the Member States. The liberalisation of capital movements contributes to a better allocation of resources within the Union. Public procurement in all Member States is open to tenders from all Community companies. In banking and insurance sectors, where obstacles to cross-border trade were particularly pronounced, the increase in cross-border competition is reflected in a growing number of branches and outlets in other Member States of the Union. The common market has, thus, demonstrated the benefits of multinational integration both concerning economic efficiency and the welfare of the citizens of the Member States.

All this **does not mean that all is well in the best possible single market**. The priority is now to make it work efficiently. This implies, in particular, adequate implementation of the measures taken for the completion of the internal market in every Member State, effective opening-up of public contracts, further mutual recognition of standards, more transparent rules for the internal market and simplification of the taxation system. These requirements for the proper functioning of the common market are not met uniformly and constantly in all Member States. Therefore, penalties for failure to comply with the obligations arising out of the Community law in the internal market field must be reinforced and enforced. Hence, the common market is not yet a completely integrated internal market and this fact handicaps European companies competing in the global market with companies which have as a base a large internal market.

Moreover, although the common market provides a basis for common policies, it cannot by itself solve the structural problems weighing on European economies. Strong common economic, industrial and research policies are needed to hasten the modernisation of European economies and to enhance the competitiveness of European companies in the global market. These policies can and should also boost employment, while safeguarding the European social model. It is an illusion to think that European citizens may be satisfied with a common market that promotes the interests of businesses and not their own interests as workers and consumers. They rightly see the common market not as an end in itself but as a means to their own welfare. If it is not successful to this end, the common market is an incomplete tool and European leaders should perfect it. They should, in particular, develop strategies that will make it possible to safeguard European values inside the global economy and to give effect to those values in the shaping of policies harnessing the globalisation process.

The completion of the single market has furthermore speeded up the process of European integration. Indeed, the "acquis communautaire" on the single market had undeniable **spillover effects** [see sections 1.1.1. and 3.3.] **on practically all common policies**. It prompted a high degree of fiscal harmonisation, thereby removing fiscal frontiers [see section 14.2.2.]. It created a need for strengthened economic and social cohesion and therefore prompted a major step forward for the Community's regional and social policies [see sections 12.1.2. and 13.2.]. It spurred progress on opening up European markets in electricity and gas, transport and telecommunications [see sections 19.2.1, 20.2.1. and 17.3.6.]. It reinforced the legal foundations of consumer and environmental protection policies and those of research and development policies [see sections 11.2, 11.3, 16.2.1 and 18.2.1.]. Lastly and perhaps most importantly, consolidation of the single market was the driving force behind the Maastricht agreements, designed to build economic and monetary union. On the one hand, the single market provides underlying economic support for monetary union and, on the other, the euro provides added value and efficiency to the single market [see section 7.1.].

Bibliography on the Common Market

- BRUIJN Roland de (et al.). *The trade-induced effects of the Services Directive and the country of origin principle*. The Hague: Centraal Planbureau (CPB), 2006.
- BURGESS Michael, VOLLAARD Hans (eds.). *State territoriality and European integration*. Abingdon: Routledge, 2006.
- CLIFTON Judith (et al.). "Privatizing public enterprises in the European Union 1960-2002: ideological, pragmatic, inevitable?" in *Journal of European Public Policy*, v. 13, n. 5, August 2006, p. 736-756.
- DIMITRAKOPOULOS Dionyssis. "More than a market?: The regulation of sport in the European Union" in *Government and Opposition*, v. 41, n. 4, Autumn 2006, p. 561-580.
- DRIJBER Berend-Jan. "The country of origin principle in the proposed directive on services in the internal market", *Revue européenne de droit de consommation*, n. 1, 2005, p. 14-22.
- EUROPEAN COMMISSION. *Deuxième rapport sur la mise en oeuvre de la stratégie pour le marché intérieur 2003-2006*. Luxembourg: EUR-OP*, 2005.
- GKOUTZINIS Apostolos. *Internet banking and the law in Europe: regulation, financial integration and electronic commerce*. Cambridge: Cambridge University Press, 2006.
- GRAHL John, TEAGUE Paul. "Problems of financial integration in the EU", *Journal of European Public policy*, v. 12, n. 6, December 2005, p. 1005-1021.
- HATZOPOULOS Vassilis, DO Thien Uyen. "The case law of the ECJ concerning the free provision of services : 2000-2005" in *Common Market Law Review*, v. 43, n. 4, August 2006, p. 923-991.
- KASTORIS PADOA-SCHIOPPA Fiorella (ed.). *The principles of mutual recognition in the European integration process*. Basingstoke: Palgrave Macmillan, 2005.
- MORIJN John. "Balancing fundamental rights and common market freedoms in Union law: 'Schmidberger' and 'Omega' in the light of the European Constitution" in *European Law Journal*, v. 12, n. 1, January 2006, p. [15]-40.
- MÜGGE Daniel. "Reordering the marketplace: competition politics in European finance" in Journal of Common Market Studies, v. 44, n. 5, December 2006, p. 991-1022.
- PAVELIN Stephen, BARRY Frank. "The single market and the geographical diversification of leading firms in the EU", *The Economic and Social Review*, v. 36, n. 1, Spring 2005, p. 1-17.
- PELKMANS Jacques. *European integration: methods and economic analysis*. 3rd ed. Harlow: Prentice Hall, 2006.
- PFISTER Servane (et al.). "Fonctionnement des systèmes bancaires et financiers", *Revue d'économie financière*, n. 81, 2005, p. 9-235.
- RÜHL Giesela. "Common law, civil law, and the single European market for insurances" in *International and Comparative Law Quarterly*, v. 55, n. 4, October 2006, p. 879-910.
- SKOURIS Vassilios. "Fundamental rights and fundamental freedoms: the challenge of striking a delicate balance" in *European Business Law Review*, v. 17, n. 2, 2006, p. 225-239.
- SHUIBHNE Niamh Nic (ed.). *Regulating the internal market*. Cheltenham: Edward Elgar, 2006.
- VRIES S. A. de. *Tensions within the internal market: the functioning of the internal market and the development of horizontal and flanking policies*. Groningen: Europa Law, 2006.
- WALKNER Christoph, RAES Jean-Pierre. *Integration and consolidation in EU banking: an unfinished business*. Brussels: European Commission, 2005.

The publications of the Office for Official Publications of the European Communities (EUR-OP) exist usually in all official languages of the EU.

Chapter 7

ECONOMIC
AND MONETARY UNION

<u>Diagram of the chapter</u>

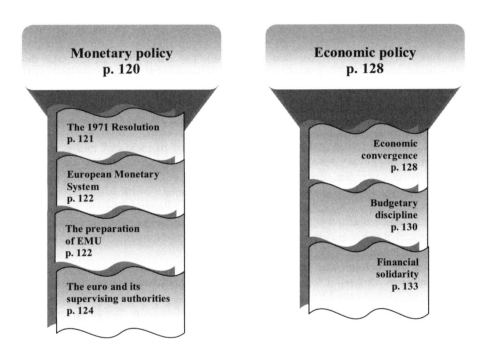

Economic and monetary union (EMU) is **an advanced stage of multinational integration** involving a common monetary policy and closely coordinated economic policies of the member states. EMU has to be based on a common market in goods and services but is itself necessary for the proper functioning of the common market, as exchange rate variations between Member States' currencies hinder trade and investments.

In the early 1970s, the original six members of the European Economic Community tried already to establish an EMU and failed. The reasons were both external - the collapse of the international monetary system - and internal - the non-completion of the stage of the common market. This failure served, however, as a learning experience. The Member States of the European Community understood that they could not rush the multinational integration process, that they should complete the common market stage, adopt many accompanying common policies and commit themselves by treaty to the goal of EMU. The economic and monetary union initiated by the Maastricht Treaty [see section 2.2.] and completed for most Member States with the circulation of the euro is an evidence of the continuity of the multinational integration process [see section 1.1.2.].

7.1. The need for EMU

During the stage of the customs union, exchange rate variations are still possible and, to a certain extent, desirable, because the member states conserve the autonomy of their economic policies and can, by means of those variations, adjust their economies to the new conditions of competition prevailing between themselves and with the rest of the world. During the stage of the common market, however, the **exchange rate variations become more and more inconvenient** for the partners. While equal conditions of competition should prevail in a common market, the devaluation of the currency of a Member State could provide a competitive advantage to its industries, whereas the revaluation of the currency of another Member State could handicap its exports. In fact, **the devaluation** of the currency of a country which is a member of a common market could have an equivalent effect to imposing customs tariffs on all imported products and subsidising that country's exports. Conversely, **the revaluation** of a member country's currency would mean restricting its exports and encouraging its imports, factors which could get in the way of business expansion in countries with strong currencies.

A single market without a single currency is exposed to monetary and economic problems. On the **monetary level**, because of the possibility of upward or downward change in the value of certain currencies of the member states, there is an exchange risk in the event of credit sales to a business in a partner country, and this greatly restricts credit exports in member states. Indeed, an exchange rate adjustment, even a moderate one, may substantially alter the contractual obligations of firms operating in the different member states and at the same time affect the relative wealth of citizens and the purchasing power of consumers.

Currency fluctuations can penalise both investors who have financed their **foreign investments** by exporting capital from their countries and those who have had recourse to the resources of the host country. In the first case, devaluation of the currency of the country in which the investment took place or revaluation of the currency of the investor's country erodes the repatriated capital and profits. In the second case, devaluation in the investor's country or revaluation in the host country means higher amortisation and therefore a greater investment cost than expected. These risks could hinder businesses from investing in partner countries or from borrowing in them capital needed for their investments. Exchange risks, thus, would limit interpenetration of financial markets and therefore economic growth in a single market without a single currency.

From the **economic point of view**, if the common market were divided into autonomous markets as a result of divergent economic policies followed by the member states, the anticipated advantages, in particular economic growth and economic stability, would be greatly reduced. In reality, the interdependence of the economies of members of a common market accelerates the **transmission of cyclical fluctuations** and of the effects of measures intended to deal with them. Attainment of the economic objectives of a member state depends to a large extent on economic conditions in the other member states. An unfavourable economic situation in one member state leads to a reduction in its imports from the other members of the common market, which are affected in turn. On the other hand, a favourable economic situation in one member country has positive effects on the economies of the others and feedback effects on the former. If there were no coordination of economic policies, the differences in economic development - which would take the form of high interest rates in some member states and low rates in others and, conversely, of low exchange rates in the former and high exchange rates in the latter - could result in undesirable capital movements, that is to say from the poorest to the richest countries.

Negative effects can also ensue from **divergences in national short-term economic policies**. If, for example, a member state wished to pursue a deflationary policy by raising interest rates, whilst another member state followed an expansionist policy with low interest rates, capital would emigrate, for short-term investments, from the second country to the first and prevent the attainment of the objectives of both. Even if they pursued the same objectives, but by different means, two member states of a common market without a single currency could bring about undesirable movements of capital. If, for example, in order to pursue a deflationary policy, a state imposed quantitative restrictions on credit, whilst another raised interest rates, capital from the first might go to short-term investment in the second, causing balance of payments problems in the first and inflationary pressures in the second.

The semi-integration, or imperfect integration, which characterises a common market, generates situations that are unstable and in the long term intolerable for member states' economic policies. Those policies are no longer sufficient for regulating short-term economic situations because, firstly, some of their causes lie abroad and, secondly, some economic policy instruments are already beyond the control of the national authorities, including customs duties, import restrictions and export incentives [see sections 5.2. and 23.1.].It can be seen that the increasing interpenetration of the economies in a common market leads to a **dwindling of the independence of national short-term economic policies.** This means that the economies of the member states of a common market cannot be managed effectively by national authorities, i.e. the appropriate ministries and the central banks of those states. It becomes manifest that the loss of autonomy of the national economic and monetary policies of the member states of a common market needs to be counterbalanced by the establishment of a common economic and a single monetary policy. Hence, the member states of a common market that want to complete it need to pass to the next stage of multinational integration, which is that of economic and monetary union.

If economic conditions in the common market are to resemble those in an internal market, it is first and foremost necessary to eliminate exchange rate adjustments, which disrupt trade and investment by affecting in an unpredictable way their profitability. To this end, the member states of a common market must agree the full and **irreversible conversion of their currencies** at fixed parities or, better, **adopt a single currency**. In either case, they need to establish a monetary union within which transaction costs (the costs of foreign-exchange transactions or the costs of exchange rate cover) would disappear altogether. The second possibility, however, which was rightly preferred by the EU, has some additional advantages. The single currency permits a genuine comparison of prices of goods and services within the single market. It is one of the main exchange and reserve currencies in the world and it allows Europeans to pay for their imports from third countries in their own currency, without the intermediation of the dollar.

In other words, the single currency is a necessary attribute of a genuine single market. This is the reason why, in view of the completion of the single market, the Member States of the Community decided, in December 1991, in Maastricht to pursue the path of economic and monetary union. By greatly facilitating the functioning of the single market, the single currency should provide a stable macroeconomic environment, which would be of considerable benefit to businesses. Under *ceteris paribus* conditions, this environment should normally foster trade, improve the allocation of resources, encourage savings and investments, thus enhancing economic growth.

Certainly, all these benefits would be derived from the economic and monetary union under **certain conditions**, notably the engagement of all participating states to scrupulously observe certain criteria ensuring monetary stability, price stability, sound public finances and, thus, sustainable growth. The single currency would thus mean **the loss of monetary independence** of the countries participating in the final stage of the EMU and even some loss of their economic independence, notably because the exchange rate instrument could not be used anymore by one of these countries experiencing particular difficulties [see section 1.1.2.]. However, due to the integration already attained in the common market, the manipulation of the exchange rate could provide only a temporary relief to this country and would create problems to the other members of the common market. Indeed, in order to create the conditions of a single market, the partners would already have adopted a great number of common policies and, thus, would have lost a good deal of the possibility of autonomous management of their economies. The loss of national autonomy inside a common market would have to be compensated by the development of collective disciplines in the economic and monetary fields. This is the objective of economic and monetary union.

Furthermore, the convergence of economic policies of the member states is necessary not only for the good functioning of the single market, but also in order to face the **problems of globalisation**. In fact, in a context of globalisation of the markets, of interdependent economies, of freedom of goods and capital movements, a totally autonomous economic policy is no longer possible. The member states of a common market, even if they had no legal obligation, would have anyway an interest in coordinating their economic policies, in order to face the problems of globalisation. Hence, the countries participating in an EMU lose prerogatives, which in practice they can no longer use. On the other hand, thanks to the EMU, they have a **collective responsibility** with regard to economic and monetary policies of the union and may better use their collective economic and monetary force in order to further their interests in the global market.

7.2. The single monetary policy

The Treaty of Rome did not provide for the monetary organisation of the Community because that Treaty aimed at the realisation of the first two stages of European integration: the customs union and the common. Moreover, at the time of drafting the EEC Treaty an international monetary organisation existed, namely the Bretton Woods system, which ensured the convertibility of all the currencies of the Western World at fixed parities. This system warranted monetary stability, which is indispensable in a common market.

It was just at the time when the Bretton Woods system collapsed, **in early 1971**, that the Member States of the Community **began their effort to organise their monetary affairs** in an economic and monetary union. Acting on a proposal from the Commission based on the "Werner Report", the Council and the Representatives of the Governments of the Member States expressed their political will to establish economic and monetary union in accordance with a phased plan beginning retroactively on 1 January 1971[1]. At the conclusion of that process the Community was to have constituted a single currency area within the international system, possessing such powers and responsibilities in economic and monetary matters as would enable its institutions to administer the union.

---

[1]   OJ C 28, 27.03.1971, p. 1-4.

With hindsight, that initial effort looks like a headlong rush without sound foundations, as it was not based on a real common market. However, that initial effort enabled the Members States to acquire precious experience and devise instruments and mechanisms that were, in 1979, transferred to the European Monetary System (which tried with variable success to stabilise the exchange rates of the common market countries), have been improved over time and were used for the second effort at establishing an economic and monetary union in the 1990s. This second effort had a better foothold than the first. The common market stage had been completed, the Member States had developed closer links through common policies and had engaged themselves in the Maastricht Treaty to advance to the stage of economic and monetary union [see section 2.2.].

7.2.1. The 1971 Resolution

In view of the enlargement of the Community [see section 1.2.], the six original Member States felt the need to tighten the monetary links between them. To that end the "Barre Plan" (of the Commission) of 4 March 1970 and the "**Werner Report**" (of the Council) of 8 October 1970 proposed the attainment by stages of economic and monetary union within the Community. As mentioned above, this was decided by a Resolution of the Council and the Representatives of the Governments of the Member States expressed of 27 March 1971. But Europe had not foreseen **the reaction of the rest of the world** to its intentions. In the two weeks following the Resolution of the EEC countries to put their monetary affairs in order, some of those countries were faced with an influx of short-term capital, creating inflationary pressures. To face this situation, they were obliged to take emergency measures that were at variance with the intentions expressed in their Resolution, especially as regards the narrowing of the margins of exchange rate fluctuations between the currencies of the Community.

The most serious blow to the monetary union of the EEC was to come five months after the March 1971 Resolution. On 15 August 1971 - an historic date for the international monetary system - the United States Administration announced its decision **to suspend the convertibility of the dollar into gold**, to allow its exchange rate to fluctuate and to protect the US market against imports from the rest of the developed world. The United States thus delivered the coup de grace to the Bretton Woods system. Simultaneously they were delivering such a severe blow to the economic and monetary union of the EEC that this union had to be postponed for thirty years, even though the Member States were loath to admit it.

In accordance with the invitation from the Council of 21 March 1971, the Governors of the Central Banks of the Member States decided, in fact, to reduce, as from 24 April 1972, the margins of fluctuation between the Community currencies to 2.25%. This was how the Community's **monetary snake** was born, that is to say the narrow band of fluctuation of participating currencies, with its intervention and short-term support mechanisms. The snake was to operate in a tunnel represented by the fluctuation margins of 4.5% between Community currencies and the dollar. But the snake did not stay in the tunnel for long. On 12 March 1973 the Council, noting the difficulties in complying with the fluctuation margins of Community currencies against the dollar, decided to leave the central banks free not to intervene when the exchange rates for their currencies reached the margins of fluctuation against the dollar. One would then speak of a "**snake without a tunnel**".

The international monetary crisis increased the structural differences and imbalances within the newly enlarged Community. **Speculators were the masters of the game**. It only needed a large number of them to be sellers, at a given moment, of a currency deemed to be the weakest in the snake for that currency to reach its floor. It was for the monetary authorities of the country under fire from speculation to stop the fall in their currency by buying it in against their cash holdings in foreign currency. The fate of the currency under attack then depended on the volume of the foreign exchange reserves, which its central bank had at its disposal and could sacrifice. Thus, most European currencies joined the floating exchange rate system one after the other. Initially that arrangement brought a degree of relief by alleviating the central banks of the impossible task of supporting their weak currencies. In due course, however, there being no mechanism obliging the Member States to pursue stringent, convergent monetary and economic policies, those States sooner or later resorted to the currency creation anticipated by the speculators and became more and more engulfed in inflation, social pressure, economic stagnation and unemployment [see also section 6.1.].

Thus the objectives, which had been set for the first stage of economic and monetary union, could not be attained, and the transition to a genuine second stage, envisaged for early 1974, never took place. Although the first attempt to create an economic and monetary union failed, **the experience acquired in that attempt was valuable** to the Community. The instruments introduced in 1972, viz. the monetary snake, the European Monetary Cooperation Fund (EMCF) and the European unit of account were tried out successfully, improved and passed on to the European Monetary System (EMS).

7.2.2. European Monetary System

Convinced of the advantages of a monetary organisation of the Community, the European Council, in July 1978, laid the groundwork for the introduction of an improved monetary system. Following its guidelines, the Council adopted, in December 1978, a Regulation relating to the **European monetary system (EMS)**[1]. Whereas at world level, since 1971, a country's monetary authorities were no longer obliged to intervene to influence the exchange rate of their currency, the EMS exchange rate mechanism introduced, for member currencies, an obligation to limit fluctuations between the latter to certain fluctuation margins.

In its initial stage the EMS was in reality **an improved, more flexible and sounder "snake"**. The maximum margin tolerated between two currencies in the system remained 2.25%, just as in the snake (6% for the weaker currencies), but a currency's exchange rate fluctuations were no longer calculated, as in the snake, in relation to each of the other currencies in the system, but in relation to the European currency unit. The **ecu** (English initials of the **European Currency Unit**, calling to mind, in French, the old gold coin used for centuries) was based on an assortment, or "basket", of different national currencies, the initial composition of which was determined on the basis of objective criteria relating to the economic importance of each Member State, in particular its gross national product, its intra-Community trade and its contribution to the short-term financial assistance mechanism.

In addition to its general functions as a unit of account, in particular for expressing the amounts in the general budget of the Communities and the common prices for agricultural products, **the ecu was the central element of the European Monetary System**. Thus, the ecu was used as the common denominator in the exchange rate grid for Community currencies, as the basis for establishing the indicator of divergence between Community currencies, as the denominator for intervention operations and as a means of settling credit or debit balances between the central banks.

In general the EMS confirmed the importance of the **collective discipline framework** which it helped to establish. By obliging the countries, which were party to it, to comply with an explicit exchange rate discipline, it made a decisive contribution in the fight against inflation. Over the years, however, the EMS became a genuine mark zone, in which discipline was notably guaranteed by the German Central Bank, the famous Bundesbank. This discipline gave good results until the end of the '80s, but, since 1990, two important phenomena started eroding this discipline within the EMS: the complete liberalisation of capital movements within the Community, which reinforced the speculative capacity of financial intermediaries; and the cost of German reunification, which had resulted in an increasing budgetary deficit in Germany. No system of monetary cooperation can function, however, when the State, which issues the reference currency, cannot guarantee its stability. Just as the inflation drift in the United States put an end to the Bretton Woods system, so the German interest rate drift caused the rupture of the EMS. The lesson gained by the EMS was that monetary organisation was useful, but needed better mechanisms. These were outlined in the Maastricht Treaty.

7.2.3. The preparation of EMU

The Treaty on European Union, signed at Maastricht in 1991 [see section 2.2.], provided for the introduction of a single monetary policy based upon **a single currency managed by a single and independent central bank**. According to the Treaty, the primary objective of the single monetary policy and exchange rate policy should be to maintain price stability and, without prejudice to this objective, to support the general economic policies in the Community, in accordance with the principle of an open market economy with free competition. These activities of the Member States and the Community should entail compliance with the following guiding principles: stable prices, sound public finances and monetary conditions and a sustainable balance of payments (Art. 4 TEC).

The 1971 experience served the EU to prepare successfully the changeover to the single currency. Although economic and monetary union was envisaged as a single process, there were, in fact, **three stages involved**. The **first stage**, marking the beginning of the whole process, came with the entry into force of the Directive on the complete liberalisation of capital movements in July 1990 [see section 6.7.]. The central objectives of this stage were greater convergence of economic policies and closer coopera-

---

[1] Regulation 3181/78, OJ L 379, 30.12.1978 repealed by Regulation 640/2006, OJ L 115, 28.04.2006.

tion between central banks, incorporating greater consistency between monetary practices in the framework of the European Monetary System[1].

As provided for in Article 118 of the EC Treaty, the **composition of the basket of the ecu** was "frozen" on 1 November 1993, the date of the entry into force of the Maastricht Treaty, on the basis of the composition of the basket (in amounts of each national currency) defined on 21st September 1989 at the occasion of the entry into the basket of the peseta and the escudo. The European Council, meeting in Madrid on 15 and 16 December 1995, decided that, as of the start of stage three, **the name given to the European currency should be the euro**, a name that symbolises Europe and should be the same in all the official languages of the European Union, taking into account the existence of different alphabets, i.e. the Latin and the Greek.

The **second stage** of economic and monetary union began on 1st January 1994 and ended on 31 December 1998. During that stage, the Treaty on the European Community compelled each Member State to endeavour to avoid excessive public deficits and initiate steps leading to independence of its central bank, so that the future monetary union encompassed only countries which were well managed economically. Regulation 3605/93 laid down detailed rules and definitions for the application of the excessive deficit procedure (EDP), including the definition of public debt, as well as rules for the reporting of data by the Member States to the Commission, which fulfils the role of statistical authority in the context of the EDP[2]. In the process leading to the **independence of central banks**, the Treaty prohibited them from granting governments overdraft facilities or any other type of credit facility and from purchasing public sector debt instruments directly from them (Art. 101 TEC). Regulation 3605/93 clarified certain implications of this prohibition[3].

Together with the prohibition on the direct monetary financing of public deficits and in order to submit public borrowings to market discipline, the Treaty provided that public authorities should not have privileged access to financial institutions, unless this was based on prudential considerations (Article 102 TEC). The Treaty sought, thus, to institutionalise a sort of **market-induced budgetary control**. To this effect, Council Regulation 3604/93 defined the terms "privileged access", "financial institutions", "prudential considerations" and "public undertakings"[4].

In **preparation for the move to the third stage**, the Treaty required a high degree of convergence assessed by reference to **four specific criteria** [see also section 7.3.1.]: (a) a rate of inflation which is close to that of the three best performing Member States in terms of price stability; (b) a government budgetary position without a deficit that is excessive, meaning a government deficit not exceeding 3% of GNP and total government debt not greater than 60% of GNP (subject to an appraisement by the Council deciding by qualified majority); (c) the durability of convergence achieved by the Member State being reflected in the long-term interest rate levels; and (d) the observance of the normal fluctuation margins provided for by the Exchange Rate Mechanism of the European Monetary System for at least two years (Art. 121 TEC and Protocol on the excessive deficit procedure).

Following the procedure and the timetable set out in the EC Treaty, the Council meeting at the level of Heads of State or Government on 3 May 1998, decided that 11 Member States **satisfied the necessary conditions for the adoption of the single currency** on 1 January 1999: Belgium, Germany, Spain, France, Ireland, Italy, Luxem-

---

[1] Decision 64/300, OJ L 77, 21.05.1964 and Decision 90/142, OJ L 78, 24.03.1990.
[2] Regulation 3605/93, OJ L 332, 31.12.1993 and Regulation 2103/2005, OJ L 337, 22.12.2005.
[3] Ibid.
[4] Regulation 3604/93, OJ L 332, 31.12.1993.

bourg, the Netherlands, Austria, Portugal and Finland. In July 2000, the Council agreed that Greece also fulfilled the convergence criteria and could therefore adopt the single currency. The Council had previously stated that Sweden did not at that stage fulfil the necessary conditions for the adoption of the single currency, because it did not participate in the mechanism of the European Monetary System. It did not examine whether the United Kingdom and Denmark fulfilled the conditions, because, in accordance with the relevant Treaty provisions, the United Kingdom notified the Council that it did not intend to move to the third stage of EMU on 1 January 1999 and Denmark notified the Council that it would not participate in the third stage of EMU. Member States benefiting from an "opt-out" and those which do not meet the criteria from the outset participate nevertheless in all the procedures (multilateral surveillance, excessive deficit...) designed to facilitate their future participation. The Governors of their central banks are members of the ECB General Council.

7.2.4. The euro and its supervising authorities

Stage three of EMU began on 1 January 1999 with the irrevocable fixing of conversion rates between the currencies of the participating countries and against the euro[1]. The ecu was replaced by the euro, and this became a currency in its own right, the currency of those Member States which participate fully in the single monetary policy (Art. 123 TEC). Since that date, monetary policy and the foreign exchange rate policy have been conducted in euros, the use of the euro has been encouraged in foreign exchange markets and new tradeable public debt had to be issued in euros by the participating Member States. The participating Member States have a single monetary policy and a single currency - the euro[2]. They are monitored by the **European Central Bank (ECB)**, which replaced the European monetary Institute (provisional institution of the second stage) and formed together with the central banks of the Member States, the **European System of Central Banks (ESCB).** Neither the ECB nor national central banks may seek or take instructions from governments or Community institutions (Art. 108 TEC). The president, the vice-president and the other members of the Executive Board of the ECB were appointed by decision taken by common accord of the governments of the Member States, which adopted the single currency, after their appointments were endorsed by the European Parliament[3].

All central banks, including those not participating in the single monetary policy, are members of the ESCB from the start of the third stage. The **primary objective of the ESCB** is to maintain price stability. In addition, the ESCB must support the general economic policies in the Community with a view to contributing to the achievement of the objectives of the common policies referred to in Article 2 (TEC). The **basic tasks to be carried out through the ESCB** are: to define and implement the monetary policy of the Community; to conduct foreign exchange operations consistent with the provisions of Article 111 (TEC); to hold and manage the official foreign reserves of the Member States; and to promote the smooth operation of payment systems (Art. 105 TEC). However, exchange policy with regard to the currencies of third countries (US dollar, Japanese yen, etc.) is determined by the Council after consultation of the ECB (Article 111 TEC).

---

[1]   Regulation 2866/98, OJ L 359, 31.12.1998 and Regulation 1478/2000, OJ L 167, 07.07.2000.
[2]   Regulation 974/98, OJ L 139, 11.05.1998 and Regulation 2169/2005, OJ L 346, 29.12.2005.
[3]   Recommendation 98/318, OJ L 139, 11.05.1998 and Decision 98/345, OJ L 154, 28.05.1998.

The **ECB** can adopt regulations and take decisions necessary for carrying out the tasks entrusted to the ESCB (Art. 110 TEC). National authorities must consult the ECB regarding draft legislation within its field of competence[1]. The ECB has powers to: apply minimum reserves and specify the remuneration of such reserves; impose fines and periodic penalty payments on firms for infringing its regulations or decisions[2]; and collect statistical information in order to carry out its tasks[3]. The ECB has the **exclusive right to authorise the issue of euro bank notes** within the Community. The ECB and the national central banks may issue such notes[4]. Member States may issue euro coins subject to approval by the ECB of the volume of the issue (Art. 106 TEC). The ECB must be consulted on any proposed Community act and may submit opinions to Community institutions or to national authorities on matters within its field of competence (Art. 105 TEC). A Council decision defines the scope and conditions of consultation of the Bank by national authorities concerning draft legislation within its field of competence[5].

The Amsterdam European Council of 16 and 17 June 1997 adopted a Resolution laying down the firm commitments of the Member States, the Commission and the Council regarding the implementation of the **Stability and Growth Pact** [see section 7.3.2.]. In this Pact Member States are committed to: respecting the medium term budgetary objective of "close to balance or in surplus" set out in their stability or convergence programmes; correcting excessive deficits as quickly as possible after their emergence; to make public, on their own initiative, recommendations made in accordance with Article 104 (TEC); and not seeking an exemption from the excessive deficit procedure unless they are in severe recession characterised by a fall in real GDP of at least 0,75%.

The Amsterdam European Council also agreed two Regulations that form part of the Stability and Growth Pact for ensuring budgetary discipline in the third stage of EMU. These Regulations set out a framework for **effective multilateral surveillance** and give precision to the excessive deficit procedure. The first concerns the continuity of contracts, the replacement of references to the ecu in legal instruments by references to the euro at a rate of one for one, the conversion rates and rounding rules[6]. In addition to this Regulation, the Directive on consumer protection in the indication of prices of products offered to consumers [see section 11.3.] sets down requirements concerning conversion rates, rounding rules, and the clarity and legibility of price displays[7]. The second Regulation provided for the conditions in which the currencies of the participating Member States would be replaced by the euro from 1 January 1999[8].

A Regulation on denominations and technical specifications of euro coins intended for circulation provided that the first series of euro currency would consist of eight coins (1 cent, 2 cent, 5 cent, 10 cent, 20 cent, 50 cent, 1 euro and 2 euro)[9]. In parallel with the introduction of the euro on 1 January 2002, bank charges for cross-border payments in euro were brought into line with those applying at national level for euro transactions[10]. A Council Framework Decision aims at increasing protection against counterfeiting in connection with the introduction of the euro[11], while two Regulations lay down the

---

[1] Decision 98/415, OJ L 189, 03.07.1998.
[2] Regulation 2531/98, OJ L 318, 27.11.1998 and regulation 134/2002, OJ L 24, 26.01.2002.
[3] Regulation 2533/98, OJ L 318, 27.11.1998.
[4] Decision ECB/1998/6, OJ L 8, 14.01.1999.
[5] Decision 98/415, OJ L 189, 03.07.1998.
[6] Regulation 1103/97, OJ L 162, 19.06.1997 and Regulation 2595/2000, OJ L 300, 29.11.2000.
[7] Directive 98/6, OJ L 80, 18.03.1998.
[8] Regulation 974/98, OJ L 139, 11.05.1998 and Regulation 2169/2005, OJ L 346, 29.12.2005.
[9] Regulation 975/98, OJ L 139, 11.05.1998 and Regulation 423/1999, OJ L 52, 27.02.1999.
[10] Regulation 2560/2001, OJ L 344, 28.12.2001.
[11] Framework Decision 2000/383/JHA, OJ L 140, 14.06.2000 and Framework Decision 2001/888, OJ L 329, 14.12.2001.

measures necessary to this effect[1]. Europol centralises and processes all information designed to facilitate the investigation, prevention and combating of euro counterfeiting[2]. The Pericles exchange, assistance and training programme concentrates on promoting convergence of national measures so as to guarantee equivalent levels of protection of the euro against counterfeiting, on the basis of consideration of best practice[3].

At the starting date of the third stage, on 1 January 1999, the **exchange rate mechanism (ERM)** has replaced the European Monetary System, in order to link currencies of Member States outside the euro area to the euro and help to ensure that they orient their policies to stability, foster convergence and thereby help them in their efforts to adopt the euro. However, the voting rights of these Member States in the Council are suspended for all questions relating to the single currency. A central rate against the euro is defined for the currency of each Member State outside the euro area participating in the exchange rate mechanism. Accordingly, central rates are set for the "pre-in" currencies with a standard fluctuation band against the euro of 15% in either direction. Intervention at the margins will in principle be automatic and unlimited, with very short-term financing available, but the European Central Bank and the central banks of the other participants could suspend intervention if this were to conflict with their primary objective. On the other hand, formally agreed fluctuation bands narrower then the standard one and backed up in principle by automatic intervention and financing may be set at the request of the non-euro area Member State concerned[4].

At 00.00 on 1 January 2002, the national currencies of the twelve Euro-zone States ceased to exist. National notes and coins could be used in most countries for a further eight weeks at the most, but it was no longer possible to make payments in the old national currency units by card, cheque or transfer. After this short period of dual circulation, during which the old notes and coins were exchanged for the new ones, old banknotes can be exchanged for a period of ten years only at central banks. The European institutions and the governments of the participating Member States had carefully planned and therefore succeeded the tremendous enterprise of the changeover to the euro [see details below]. What these authorities had not foreseen and hence neglected was the attempt by many providers of goods and services to profit from the rounding possibilities offered by the new currency. This uncontrolled profiteering has increased inflationary pressures in economies already depressed from the unstable international environment. Most vulnerable were the consumers accustomed to banknotes with a large number of zeros, like the Italians and the Greeks, who did not immediately perceive the price increases in euro. The responsible authorities should now do their best to keep prices down. They should also ensure the practical preparation of the new Member States for the future enlargement of the euro area[5]. In the long-term, however, it is probable that heightened competition will stabilise prices inside the single market.

The capital of the ECB (initially 5 billion euro) is held by the national central banks in proportion to the individual countries' demographic and economic weight[6]. The **external foreign reserves of the national central banks are pooled** at the ECB within certain limits set in Article 30(1) of the Statute of the European System of Central Banks and of the European Central Bank; but the ECB, in case of need, may effect further calls of foreign reserve assets from the national central banks equivalent to an additional EUR 50 billion[7]. The decision-making bodies of the ECB are the Governing Council and the Executive Board. The policy of the ECB

---

[1]   Regulations 1338/2001 and 1339/2001, OJ L 181, 04.07.2001.
[2]   Decision 2005/511, OJ L 185, 16.07.2005.
[3]   Decisions 2001/923 and 2001/924, OJ L 334, 21.12.2001 and Decision 2006/75, OJ L 36, 08.02.2006.
[4]   Resolution of the European Council, OJ C 236, 02.08.1997, p. 5-6.
[5]   COM/2005/0545, 4 November 2005.
[6]   Decision 98/382, OJ L 171, 17.06.1998 and Decision 2003/517, OJ L 181, 19.07.2003.
[7]   Regulation 1010/2000, OJ L 115, 16.05.2000.

aiming at ensuring price stability will be formulated by the Governing Council, which is composed of the fifteen Governors of the central banks of the Member States and of the members of the executive Board. However, as from the date on which the number of members of the Governing Council of the ECB exceeds 21, each member of the Executive Board will have one vote and the number of governors with a voting right will be 15. Voting rights are assigned to the governors under a rotation system[1]. The executive Board, consisting of the President of the ECB, the Vice-President and four other members, appointed by decision taken by common agreement of the governments of the Member States, which have adopted the single currency, implement the ECB monetary policy and give the necessary instructions to the national central banks..

The total **independence of the European Central Bank** is the cornerstone of the Community's new monetary policy. According to the German concept, which has shown its worth through the independence of the Bundesbank, currency is something much too serious to let in the hands of politicians who, legitimately worried about unemployment, are tempted to manipulate the exchange rate or the interest rates to kick-start the economy without drawing on the lessons of the past. Democratic control can and must be exercised *a posteriori* by the dismissal of the governors of national central banks, members of the ECB board, who are judged by their governments to have failed in their task.

At the start of the third stage of EMU, on 1 January 1999, the **Economic and Financial Committee (EFC)** replaced the Monetary Committee. The Member States, the Commission and the ECB may each appoint two members to the Committee, which therefore has a total of 34 members[2]. This has the following tasks: to deliver opinions at the request of the Council or of the Commission, or on its own initiative for submission to those institutions; to keep under review the economic and financial situation of the Member States and of the Community and to report regularly thereon to the Council and to the Commission, in particular on financial relations with third countries and international institutions; to contribute to the preparation of the work of the Council on EMU; to examine, at least once a year, the situation regarding the movement of capital and the freedom of payments and to report to the Commission and to the Council on the outcome of this examination (Art. 114 TEC). According to its statutes, the EFC prepares the Council's reviews of the development of the exchange rate of the euro and provides the framework for the dialogue between the Council and the European Central Bank[3].

It is quite remarkable that the transition to the third stage of economic and monetary union was achieved smoothly in spite of turbulence on the world financial markets and the unprecedented logistical challenge [see section 7.4.]. This was the result of prudent economic policies in the context of EMU. It was also the result of **careful technical and legislative preparation**. As seen in the preceding paragraphs, all Community legislation necessary for the introduction of the euro was adopted before 1 January 1999 and everything happened according to the plans laid down by the common institutions. Thanks to the considerable efforts of all parties involved in this changeover (national administrations, central banks, financial institutions, the retail sector and the security transport sector), as well as the enthusiastic way in which citizens greeted the arrival of the notes and coins, the euro changeover was an unqualified success. Euro payments accounted for most of the cash payments made by the end of the first week in January 2002. By the end of the second week, very little national currency remained in circulation.

The **introduction of the euro is a major event for the international monetary system**, whose cornerstone is the International Monetary Fund (IMF). The EU sought pragmatic solutions for introducing a major international currency into the system which did not require a change in the Articles of the IMF. Thus, the IMF Executive Board agreed to grant the ECB an observer position at that board. The views of the EU/EMU are presented at the IMF Board by the relevant member of the Executive Director's office of the Member State holding the Euro-zone Presidency, assisted by a representative from the Commission. The President of the ECB attends meetings of the G7 Finance Ministers' and Governors' Group for the discussions which relate to EMU, e.g. multilateral surveillance or exchange rate issues. At those meetings a Commission representative is a member of the Community delegation in the capacity of providing assistance to the President of Ecofin/Euro group.

---

[1] Decision 2003/223, OJ L 83, 01.04.2003.
[2] Decision 98/743, OJ L 358, 31.12.1998.
[3] Decision 1999/8, OJ L 5, 09.01.1999 and Decision 2003/476, OJ L 158, 27.06.2003.

7.3. The common economic policy

The Treaty of Rome had considered it desirable that the Member States **regard their economic policies as a matter of common concern**. Article 103 stipulated that they should consult each other and the Commission on the measures to be taken in the light of the prevailing circumstances. Pursuant to that provision of the Treaty, the Council set up an **Economic Policy Committee** for Short-term Economic and Financial Policies[1]. That Committee, which consists of one representative for each Member State and a Commission representative, has the task of preparing the meetings of the **Economic and Financial Affairs (ECOFIN) Council**. It is also responsible for the exchange, on a reciprocal and continuing basis, of information on decisions or measures envisaged by the Member States which could have a considerable effect on the economies of the other Member States or on the internal or external equilibrium of the Member State concerned or which could give rise to a considerable gap between the development of the economy of a country and the jointly defined medium-term objectives.

The Member States signatories to the Treaty of Rome were **not prepared to abandon their sovereign powers** in economic or monetary matters in favour of the Community. Accordingly, the Treaty was confined to defining the objectives to be pursued in national economic policies, including full employment, a stable level of prices and currency and equilibrium of the balance of payments. Elaboration and implementation of economic policy as such, however, remained exclusively within the jurisdiction of the Member States.

The Community's economic policy did not really get off the ground until the Member States decided to undertake the realisation of economic and monetary union. More than other common policies, the economic policy is indispensable to attainment of such union, as it constitutes one of its two wings. The task assigned to it by the Resolution of the Council and of the Representatives of the Governments of the Member States of 22 March 1971 on the realisation by stages of economic and monetary union was the **convergence of the economies** of the Member States, which was an extremely difficult task in view of the structural disparities between the economies which were to participate in that major undertaking before the completion of the single market. Nevertheless the lessons learned during this failed experience were useful for the formulation of an effective common economic policy.

7.3.1. Economic convergence in the European Union

In contrast to monetary policy, Member States **retain ultimate responsibility for economic policy** within the economic and monetary union. They are, however, required to act in such a way as to respect the principle of an open market economy where competition reigns, to regard their economic policies as a matter of common concern and to conduct them with a view to contributing to the achievement of the objectives of the Community (Art. 98 and 99 TEC). Thus, the common economic policy complements the single monetary policy.

Since the second stage of EMU, i.e. since the 1st January 1994, economic policies of the Member States are coordinated at Community level. A Council Decision of 1990 is directed towards the attainment of progressive convergence of economic performance of the Member States[2]. To this effect the **Economic and Financial Affairs Council (ECOFIN)**, acting by a qualified majority on a recommendation from the Commission, formulates, each year in the spring, a draft for the **broad economic policy guidelines (BEPGs)** of the Member States and of the Community, and reports its findings to the European Council. This discusses a conclusion on the broad guidelines of the economic policies of the Member States and of the Community. On this basis, the Commission recommends and the Council, acting on a qualified majority endorses the BEPGs, which

---

[1]   Decision 2000/604, OJ L 257, 11.10.2000.
[2]   Decision 90/141, OJ L 78, 24.03.1990.

lay down the common objectives in terms of inflation, public finance, exchange rate stability and employment (Art. 99 TEC)[1]. The BEPGs are at the centre of economic policy coordination in the European Union. They must be concise, concentrate on the main challenges facing the Union, with particular focus on the euro area, where coordination is most needed, and help to ensure that measures adopted in all Community economic coordination processes are consistent.

The Council, on the basis of reports submitted by the Commission[2], monitors economic developments in each of the Member States and in the Community as well as the consistency of economic policies with the broad guidelines (Art 121 TEC). This **multilateral monitoring** is based on convergence programmes presented by each Member State which specifically aim at addressing the main sources of difficulty in terms of convergence (Art. 99,3 TEC). It also involves a review of budgetary policies, with particular reference to the size and financing of deficits, if possible prior to the drafting of national budgets [see section 7.3.2.]. Multilateral monitoring aims at obtaining from the Member States reciprocal engagements for an autonomous coordination of their policies.

Where it is established that the economic policies of a Member State are not consistent with these guidelines, the Council may, acting by a qualified majority, make the necessary recommendations to the Member State concerned. It may decide to make its recommendations public (Art. 99,4 TEC). The Council may, acting unanimously on a proposal from the Commission, decide upon the measures appropriate to the economic situation, in particular if severe difficulties arise in the supply of certain products. **Where a Member State is in difficulties** or is seriously threatened with severe difficulties caused by exceptional occurrences beyond its control, the Council may, acting unanimously on a proposal from the Commission, grant, under certain conditions, Community financial assistance to the Member State concerned (Art. 100 TEC).

The move to the third stage of economic and monetary union has brought the economies of the Member States adopting the euro closer together. They share a single monetary policy and a single exchange rate. Economic policies and wage determination, however, remain a national responsibility, subject to the provisions of Article 104 (TEC) and of the Stability and Growth Pact. Since national economic developments have an impact on inflation prospects in the euro zone, they influence monetary conditions in that zone. It is for this reason that the introduction of the single currency requires closer Community surveillance and coordination of economic policies among euro zone Member States. Close coordination should, in addition, contribute to the achievement of the Community objectives set out in Article 2 of the EC Treaty. In order to ensure further convergence and the smooth functioning of the single market, non-participating Member States must be included in the coordination of economic policies. This is particularly true for those Member States which participate in the exchange rate mechanism (ERM 2) [see section 7.2.4.].

The **Lisbon strategy for growth and employment** [see section 13.3.2.] calls for synergy and complementarity between the Member States' own programmes and the Community programmes. The Community contributes to the overall economic and employment policy agenda by completing the internal market and by implementing common policies and activities that support and complement national policies, with particular emphasis on a number of key actions with high added value, including: support for knowledge and innovation in Europe; reform of State aid policy; completion of the in-

---

[1] See for example the Recommendation of the Commission for 2003, COM (2003) 170, 8 April 2003 and Council Recommendation OJ L 195, 01.08.2003.
[2] See e.g., COM/2004/0020.

ternal market for services; and support for efforts to deal with the social consequences of economic restructuring[1].

The Resolution of the Amsterdam European Council of 16 June 1997 on **Growth and Employment** aims to strengthen the links between a successful and sustainable EMU, a well-functioning internal market and employment. It asserts that social protection systems should be modernised so as to contribute to competitiveness, employment and growth, establishing a durable basis for social cohesion. To this end, the close coordination of the Member States' economic policies referred to in Articles 4, 98 and 99 (TEC) should be focused in particular on policies for employment[2].

The Luxembourg European Council of 12 and 13 December 1997 adopted a Resolution on **economic policy coordination** in stage three of EMU in which it defined the arrangements for enhanced economic policy coordination, both between Member States participating in the euro and between those Member States and the ones not yet able to participate. It pointed out in particular that the ECOFIN Council was the central decision-making body for such coordination, adding that the ministers of the Member States participating in the euro area would be able to meet informally to discuss issues connected with their shared specific responsibilities for the single currency. This "Euro Group" takes account of the special needs of coordination for Member States participating in the euro area [see also section 7.2.4.].

On the basis of the Treaty and specially agreed instruments, economic policy coordination concentrates on those national policies which have the potential to influence monetary and financial conditions throughout the euro area, the exchange rate of the euro, the smooth functioning of the single market, as well as investment, employment and growth conditions in the Community. Thus, **economic policy coordination includes**:

- the close monitoring of macroeconomic developments in Member States to ensure sustained convergence;
- the close monitoring of exchange rate developments of the euro and other EU currencies, seen as the outcome of all other economic policies;
- the strengthened surveillance of budgetary positions and policies in accordance with the Treaty and the Stability and Growth Pact [see section 7.3.2.];
- the monitoring of nominal and real wage developments with reference to the broad economic policy guidelines;
- the close examination of national employment action plans (NAPs), dealing in particular with active labour market policy in accordance with the employment policy guidelines [see section 13.3.2.];
- the monitoring of Member States' structural policies in labour, product and services markets, particularly insofar as they affect the chances of achieving sustained non-inflationary growth and job-creation.

In view of the 2004 **enlargement**, the Commission reviewed the economic policy strategy and highlighted those general guidelines or policy areas where the specific circumstances of most acceding countries are such that a longer adjustment period could be warranted[3].

7.3.2. Budgetary discipline and the single currency

Budgetary policy is perhaps the area in which differences between Member States are still at their strongest. This stems from the fact that the budget is the most characteristic manifestation of national sovereignty in economic terms. The budget is in fact the main instrument of orientation of the economy in general and of individual government policies, such as regional, social, industrial policies, etc. Through its expenditure side the budget has a direct influence on public investment and an indirect influence, through aids of all sorts, on private investment. Through its revenue side the budget acts on savings and on the circulation of currency. A state's budgetary policy may pursue short-term economic objectives (avoidance of a recession or stemming of inflation) or structural improvement objectives pertaining to the national economy and implemented through productive investments. Clearly, although it is difficult, coordination of budgetary policies is extremely important for economic convergence sought by the Treaty on European Union and for participation of a Member State in the third stage of EMU.

---

[1] COM/2005/330, 20 July 2005.
[2] OJ C 236, 02.08.1997, p. 3-4.
[3] COM (2004) 238, 7 April 2004.

From the third stage of EMU, which began on 1 January 1999, the budgetary policies of the Member States are constrained by three rules: overdraft facilities or any other type of credit facility from the ECB or national central banks to public authorities (Community, national or regional) are prohibited (Art. 101 TEC); any privileged access of public authorities to the financial institutions are banned (Art. 102 TEC)[1]; neither the Community nor any Member State is liable for the commitments of public authorities, bodies or undertakings of a Member State (Art. 103 TEC). Implementing the new arrangements for economic policy coordination, the Council looks closely into actual and prospective developments in Member States' budgetary policies.

The Commission should monitor the development of the budgetary situation and the level of government debt in the Member States with a view to identifying gross errors. In particular it should examine compliance with **budgetary discipline** on the basis of the following two criteria [see also section 7.2.3.]: a) whether the ratio of the planned or actual government deficit to Gross Domestic Product exceeds a reference value (3% of GDP), unless either the ratio has declined substantially and continuously and reached a level that comes close to the reference value or, alternatively, the excess over the reference value is exceptional and temporary and the ratio remains close to the reference value; b) whether the ratio of government debt to gross domestic product exceeds a reference value (60% of GDP), unless the ratio is sufficiently diminishing and approaching the reference value at a satisfactory pace (Art. 104 TEC and Protocol on the excessive deficit procedure).

If a Member State does not fulfil the requirements under one or both of these criteria, the Commission shall prepare a report, taking into account all relevant factors, including the medium term economic and budgetary position of the Member State. The Council shall, acting by a qualified majority on a recommendation from the Commission, and having considered any observations which the Member State concerned may wish to make, decide after an overall assessment whether an **excessive deficit** exists. Where the existence of an excessive deficit is decided, the Council shall make recommendations to the Member State concerned with a view to bringing that situation to an end within a given period. If there is no effective action in response to its recommendations within the period laid down, the Council may, first, make its recommendations public and, then, decide by qualified majority certain measures to be taken by the recalcitrant Member State (Art. 104 TEC).

In view of the difficulties encountered by many Member States in respecting the criteria of the **Stability and Growth Pact (SGP)**, mentioned above [see section 7.2.4 and details below], the European Council meeting in Brussels (22-23 March 2005) agreed on the revision of the Regulations which provide for prevention and correction of excessive deficits. Regulation 1466/97 on the strengthening of the surveillance of budgetary positions requires Member States to submit stability programmes (or convergence programmes in the case of the countries not participating in the single currency) presenting the medium-term objective of a government budgetary position that is close to balance or surplus. In June 2005 three principal changes were introduced to the **preventive arm of the SGP**[2]: (a) the medium-term budgetary objectives will take into account the diversity of economic and budgetary positions and their sustainability, ranging from a deficit of 1% of GDP to a position of balance or in surplus for euro area and the exchange rate mechanism (ERM-II) countries; (b) those countries that have not yet reached their medium-term budgetary objective should pursue an annual improvement of 0.5% of

---

[1] Regulations 3603/93, 3604/93 and 3605/93, OJ L 332, 31.12.1993.
[2] Regulation 1466/97, OJ L 209, 02.08.1997 and Regulation 1055/2005, OJ L 174, 07.07.2005.

GDP in cyclically adjusted terms (with an extra effort being made in economic good times); (c) Member States that have implemented major structural reforms with a verifiable impact on the long-term sustainability of public finances will be allowed to deviate temporarily from the medium-term budgetary objective or the adjustment path towards it.

The purpose of Regulation 1467/97 (**corrective arm of the SGP**) is to speed up and clarify the implementation of the excessive deficit procedure, in particular as regards the sanctions to be imposed on Member States which fail to take appropriate measures to correct an excessive deficit, and it lays down the deadlines which must be observed for the different stages of the procedure[1]. The reference values of 3% and 60% of GDP for the deficit and debt ratios are the anchors of the system. The amendments introduced in June 2005 entail: a new definition of "severe economic downturn"; clarification of "other relevant factors", under the condition that the general government deficit remains close to the 3% ceiling and that the excess is temporary; extension of the deadlines for correcting any excessive deficit, in order to give a country more time to take effective and more permanent action rather than resort to one-off measures; asking Member States in an excessive deficit situation to achieve a minimum annual budgetary effort of at least 0.5% of GDP in structural terms. The economic policy strategy based on growth and stability-oriented macroeconomic policies and continuous progress in economic reform, allows a flexible response to changing economic conditions in the short run whilst safeguarding and strengthening the productive capacity of the economy over the medium term. Member States are required to compile and transmit to the Commission data on their quarterly government debt[2].

According to the Court of Justice, the **excessive deficit procedure** is a stage-by-stage procedure with strict deadlines where the Treaty (Art. 104 TEC), the implementing regulation (1467/97) and the Stability Pact specify the manner in which it is carried out and the respective roles and powers of the institutions. The procedure may result in the imposition of sanctions on Member States. In fact, if a Member State persists in failing to put into practice the recommendations of the Council, the Council may decide to give it notice to take, within a specified time limit, measures for the deficit reduction which is judged necessary in order to remedy the situation. If the Member State fails to comply with the decision of the Council, the latter may decide to apply or intensify one or more of the following measures: to require that the Member State concerned publish additional information, to be specified by the Council, before issuing bonds and securities; to invite the European Investment Bank to reconsider its lending policy towards the Member State concerned; to require that the Member State concerned make a non-interest-bearing deposit of an appropriate size with the Community until the excessive deficit has, in the view of the Council, been corrected; to impose fines of an appropriate size (Art. 104 TEC).

For the first time, in November 2002, the Council noted the existence of an excessive deficit in Portugal (4.1 % of GDP) and asked the Portuguese authorities to implement with resolve their budgetary plans for 2002, aimed at reducing the deficit to 2.8 % of GDP[3]. In January 2003, the Council noted the existence of an excessive deficit in Germany and recommended that the German Government put an end to the excessive deficit situation as quickly as possible[4] It also gave an early warning to France in order to prevent the occurrence of an excessive deficit[5]. On 3 June 2003, the Council, assessing the situation on the basis of Article 104(6) of the EC Treaty, concluded that an excessive deficit existed in France[6]. On 5 July 2004 the Council decided that an excessive deficit existed in Greece and issued a recommendation to the Greek authorities, urging them to take various measures to correct it[7]. In December 2004, the Commission decided to launch an infringement procedure for the continued failure of the Greek authorities to provide the Commission with reliable budgetary data and to strengthen the data monitoring mechanisms so as to ensure that Eurostat, as the statistical authority, can

---

[1] Regulation 1467/97, OJ L 209, 02.08.1997 and Regulation 1056/2005, OJ L 174, 07.07.2005.
[2] Regulation 1222/2004, OJ L 233, 02.07.2004.
[3] Decision 2002/923, OJ L 322, 27.11.2002.
[4] Decision 2003/89, OJ L 34, 11.02.2003.
[5] Recommendation 2003/90, OJ L 34, 11.02.2003.
[6] Decision 2003/487, OJ L 165, 03.07.2003.
[7] Decision 2004/917, OJ L 389, 30.12.2004.

carry out effective checks on the data notified by the Member States[1]. In February 2005 the Council gave notice to Greece, in accordance with Article 104(9) of the EC Treaty, to take measures for the deficit reduction judged necessary in order to remedy the situation of excessive deficit[2]. In March 2006 it also gave the similar notice to Germany[3]. In January 2006, the Council recommended to the United Kingdom to bring an end to the situation of an excessive government deficit[4].

7.3.3. Financial solidarity

In the context of the plan to attain economic and monetary union by stages [see section 7.2.1.], the Council decided, in 1971, to set up machinery for medium-term financial assistance for Member States experiencing balance of payments difficulties. Since 1 January 1999 the Member States participating in the single currency are no longer eligible for Community medium-term financial assistance for their balance of payments. A new regulation aims to establish a medium-term financial assistance facility for Member States' balances of payments[5]. This facility, limited to EUR 12 billion, may enable loans to be granted to one or more Member States which have not adopted the euro, when it is established that they are experiencing, or are seriously threatened with, difficulties in their balance of current payments or capital movements. Until the end of 2005, the facility had not been used by any Member State.

The main Community instrument of financial solidarity is the **European Investment Bank** (EIB). According to Article 267 (TEC) the task of the EIB is to contribute, by having recourse to the capital market and utilising its own resources, to the balanced and steady development of the Community and the implementation of its policies. Thanks to its high credit rating, the Bank borrows on the best terms on the capital markets world-wide and on-lends to the Member States and their financial institutions - which distribute these global loans to SMEs. Since the EIB is a bank, it does not grant interest-rate reductions, but the financial institutions in the Member States and notably those whose vocation is regional development can borrow from the Bank and on-lend at more favourable terms. Some of the loans do have interest-rate subsidies attached, funded by the Community budget [see section 3.4.].

The EIB is a major source of finance for new industrial activities and advanced technology in sectors such as the motor vehicle industry, chemicals, pharmaceuticals, aeronautical engineering and information technologies. It also contributes to the establishment of trans-European telecommunications, transport and energy networks [see section 6.8.], reinforcement of industrial competitiveness [see sections 17.1. and 17.2.3.], environmental protection and cooperation in the development of third countries [see section 23.1.]. However, the main priority of the EIB is to contribute to the development of the least favoured regions of the European Union [see sections 12.1.1. and 12.3.]. These contributions account for around 70% of its financings in the Community.

Established in 1994, the **European Investment Fund (EIF)** is the specialist venture capital arm of the EIB Group. The EIF's tripartite share ownership structure - European Investment Bank (60%), European Commission (30%) and members of the banking sector (28 financial institutions) - facilitates the development of synergies between Community organs and the financial community, enhancing the catalytic effects of the EIB Group's action in support of small and medium enterprises (SMEs). The EIF's main objective is the financing of innovative and jobs creating SMEs through venture capital, in the Union and in the12 applicant countries [see section 17.2.3.]. Acting as a "fund of funds", it acquires stakes in public or private sector venture capital funds with a view of

[1] COM (2004) 784, 1 December 2004.
[2] Decision 2005/441, OJ L 153, 16.06.2005.
[3] Decision 2006/344, OJ L 126, 13.05.2006.
[4] Decision 2006/125, OJ L 51, 22.02.2006
[5] Regulation 332/2002, OJ L 53, 23.02.2002.

strengthening the ability of European financial institutions to inject equity capital into SMEs, especially those in the growth phase.

7.4. Appraisal and outlook

As happened with the first attempt at establishing an economic and monetary union in Europe, in 1971, the launch of the euro coincided with a highly adverse international economic and monetary situation: the terrorist attacks in New York and Madrid, the sizeable devaluation of the dollar, wars in Afghanistan and Iraq on Europe' doorstep and high energy prices, probably related to these wars. In this global situation, the economies of the eurozone have run into unexpected difficulties, largely due to outside factors: the strong competition in world markets from companies working with undervalued currencies; the equally strong competition from countries practicing social dumping, i.e. countries with no social protection and therefore extremely cheap labour force; high prices of imported oil; and last but not least, the precarious situation in the Middle East. In this adverse global situation, the euro has shielded the economies of the eurozone from competitive devaluations, galloping inflation and an increase in the prices of imports, more than 60% of which come from other euro countries. It is highly probable that if European economies had not the shield of the euro, they would have been in a much worse situation than the one in which they found themselves when the euro became the strongest currency in the world.

Despite the adverse global situation, the second effort at creating a European economic and monetary union was an unquestionable success, particularly in view of the great challenge of the changeover to the single currency. Not only was the physical introduction of the euro a historic event, it also represented an unprecedented strategic, logistical and practical challenge. From one day to the next, automatic cash dispensers (ATMs), instead of national currency, had to supply euro banknotes. Several million coin-operated machines and several hundred thousand ATMs had to be recalibrated. Some 15 billion euro banknotes and 50 billion euro coins replaced, in the space of a few weeks, a broadly equivalent quantity of national notes and coins in twelve countries with a combined population of some 310 million.

Citizens and businesses were certainly faced with formidable problems in adapting their habits to the new currency. For the former the problems were mainly psychological. They had to forsake their sentimental attachment to a national currency, in some cases very prestigious, as the Deutsche Mark and in some cases very old, like the Greek Drachma born more than 26 centuries ago. Consumers had to familiarise themselves with the euro and make the necessary effort to construct for themselves a new scale of values. Traders had to display prices and give change in euros. Businesses had to adapt their equipment, prepare to use a new currency and make the most of the increased competition within the single market resulting from greater price transparency. Despite these difficulties and the Cassandras' catastrophic prophesies, the euro was circulated successfully, thanks to an exemplary planning and cooperation of national and European authorities.

Moreover, in spite of the great advance of multinational integration brought about by the EMU, national sovereignties have not suffered unduly. The Member States, which have moved to the third stage of EMU, have undoubtedly **lost the autonomy of their monetary policy**, since they are no longer at liberty to use the two main levers of this policy - exchange rates and interest rates (a freedom which they had already lost to a large extent, due to the interdependence of the European economies). At the same time, however, they lost responsibility for the parity of their currency and the equilibrium of their balance of payments, while enjoying shared responsibility for the parity of the euro against the currencies of third countries and the equilibrium of the collective balance of payments of the euro-zone countries. However, balance of current payments constraints exist for the zone as a whole. Therein lies the importance of the close coordination of economic policies.

Price stability, which is a vital prerequisite for EMU, is also favourable to growth and the efficient use of the pricing mechanism for the allocation of resources. National budgetary policies and consequently government finances are subject to certain constraints anchored in the stability and growth pact, notably respect of the medium-term budgetary objective of close to balance or in surplus by 2004. The most direct "static gain" of the EMU is the ending, within the unified market, of all transaction costs inherent in the use of several currencies, costs representing between 0.3 and 0.4% of the GDP of the Union. Travellers, who previously lost important amounts in the exchange of their currency for those of the countries they visited, should particularly welcome these gains. "Dynamic gains", which cannot be measured directly, could take two forms: those resulting from heightened productivity and those generated by the elimination of the uncertainties concerning the long-term evolution of exchange rates.

Supported by progress achieved by the Member States in economic convergence (sound public finances, very low inflation, exchange rate stability) and the mechanisms for closer coordination of economic policies put in place as part of the introduction of the euro, economic and monetary union has already made the European Union a pole of stability in a world tormented by constant financial crises. In addition, the euro allows a **better balance of the international monetary system**, dominated for half a century by the dollar, which serves as a reference currency for almost 60% of world trade, whereas American exports represent around 12% of world exports. Its economic and commercial weight (16% of world exports) entitles the Union to play an important role in the necessary review of the international monetary and financial system. This review should focus on methods of crisis prevention and management, improved governance of the international monetary and financial system, development assistance and debt relief for developing countries.

As a matter of fact, the economic and monetary union is still in a trial phase. It has not consolidated itself. It suffers, in particular, from a disequilibrium between its strong monetary wing and its feeble economic one. The euro area is a monetary union working under a single monetary policy and **coordinated but decentralised economic policies**. While monetary policy management is the exclusive responsibility of the European Central Bank, economic and budgetary policies are a national prerogative. However, in an integrated monetary and economic zone, overspending and deficient restraint of inflation rates in some countries inflict a collective cost borne by all the countries sharing the same currency. There is a need, therefore, to reinforce existing economic, in particular fiscal, policy coordination mechanisms within the euro area and improve monitoring and evaluation of euro-area economic trends, including inflation, wage increases, investments and euro exchange rates. The strategy should be built upon further reductions of public debt, increases in employment rates and reforms of pension systems. In general, the pace of reform at Member State level needs to be significantly stepped up if the 2010 targets set by the Lisbon European Council are to be achieved [see section 13.3.2.].

European economies suffered dearly from the 11 September 2001 terrorist attacks on the United States, the Iraq invasion and occupation, the rising price of oil and the hindrance of European exports from the fall of the value of the dollar in relation to the euro. As a result of these external and unpredictable circumstances, **most economies of the eurozone were hit by stagnation and rising levels of unemployment**. In these circumstances, the Stability and Growth Pact, agreed in a state of euphoria, began looking like a straitjacket to some countries among the most important of the Eurozone. Since the Community always proceeds by trial and error, it seems likely that the Stability and Growth Pact will be adapted to the new circumstances without, however, abandoning the objective of the convergence of the Member States' economic policies.

Bibliography on the EMU

- AMTENBRINK Fabian, HAAN Jakob de. "Reforming the Stability and Growth Pact" in *European Law Review*, v. 31, n. 3, June 2006, p. 402-413.
- ANGELONI Ignazio (et al.). "The euro and prices: did EMU affect price setting and inflation persistence?" in *Economic Policy*, n. 46, April 2006, p. 353-387.
- ARDY Brian (et al.). *Adjusting to EMU*. Basingstoke: Palgrave Macmillan, 2006.
- ARESTIS Philip, SAWYER Malcolm (eds.). *Alternative perspectives on economic policies in the European Union*. Basingstoke: Palgrave Macmillan, 2006.
- BABIC Borka. "The Stability and Growth Pact: status 2006" in *Monetary Review*, v. 45, 2nd quarter 2006, p. 61-73.
- BALDWIN Richard. *In or out: does it matter?: An evidence-based analysis of the Euro's trade effects*. London: CEPR, 2006.
- BALDWIN Richard, WYPLOSZ Charles. *The economics of European integration*. 2nd ed. Maidenhead: McGraw-Hill Education, 2006.
- BIELER Andreas. *The struggle for a social Europe: trade unions and EMU in times of global restructuring*. Manchester: Manchester University Press, 2006.
- BREUSS Fritz, HOCHREITER Eduard. *Challenges for Central Banks in an enlarged EMU*. Wien; New York: Springer, 2005.
- BUTI Marco, FRANCO Daniele. *Fiscal policy in economic and monetary union: theory, evidence and institutions*. Cheltenham: Edward Elgar, 2005.
- CICCARELLI Matteo, REBUCCI Alessandro. "Has the transmission mechanism of European monetary policy changed in the run-up to EMU?" in *European Economic Review*, v. 50, n. 3, April 2006, p. 737-776.
- DULLIEN Sebastian, SCHWARZER Daniela. "A question of survival?: Curbing regional differences in the eurozone" in *Review of Economic Conditions in Italy*, n. 1, January-April 2006, p. 65-85.
- GIKAS A. (et al.). "EMU and European stock market integration" in *The Journal of Business*, v. 79, n. 1, 2006, p. 365-392.
- GRAUWE Paul de. *Economics of monetary union*. 6th ed. Oxford: Oxford University Press, 2005.
- HAAN Jakob de, EIJFFINGER Sylvester, WALLER Sandra. *The European Central Bank: credibility, transparency, and centralization*. Cambridge, MA ; London : MIT Press, 2005.
- JOVANOVIC Miroslav. *The economics of European integration: limits and prospects*. Cheltenham ; Northampton, MA : Edward Elgar, 2005.
- KORKMAN Sixten. *Economic policy in the European Union*. Basingstoke: Palgrave Macmillan, 2005.
- MATHÄ Thomas. "The euro and regional price differences of individual products in an integrated cross-border area" in *Journal of Common Market Studies*, v. 44, n. 3, September 2006, p. 536-580.
- MOLLE Willem T.M. *The economics of European integration: theory, practice, policy*. Aldershot: Ashgate, 2006.
- SAVAGE James. *Making the EMU: the politics of budgetary surveillance and the enforcement of Maastricht*. Oxford : Oxford University Press, 2005.

Chapter 8

TOWARDS A POLITICAL UNION

Diagram of the chapter

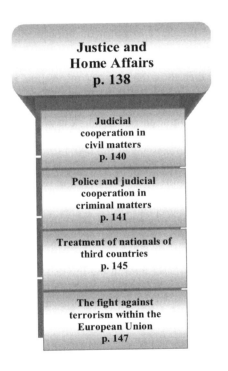

Justice and
Home Affairs
p. 138

Judicial
cooperation in
civil matters
p. 140

Police and judicial
cooperation in
criminal matters
p. 141

Treatment of nationals of
third countries
p. 145

The fight against
terrorism within the
European Union
p. 147

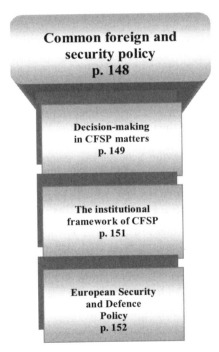

Common foreign and
security policy
p. 148

Decision-making
in CFSP matters
p. 149

The institutional
framework of CFSP
p. 151

European Security
and Defence
Policy
p. 152

Political union is the last stage of the multinational integration process. It involves **common home and judicial policies and a common foreign and security policy**. According to the definition given above [see section 1.1.2.], a common policy entails a set of rules, decisions, measures and codes of conduct adopted by the common institutions set up by a group of states and implemented by the common institutions and the member states. A common policy does not exclude national policies, which continue to exist in all areas not covered by the decisions and rules agreed by the common institutions. Its development, however, requires the implementation by all the participating states of the common home and foreign policies agreed by the common institutions and the monitoring of this implementation by the common institutions. As long as these requirements are not met in certain sectors, political union, even though provided in a Treaty, is deficient or inexistent. In its place there may only exist intergovernmental political cooperation, leaving practically all freedom of action to the participants.

At the same time as they were preparing the economic and monetary union stage, **at Maastricht in 1991**, europhilic nations were also projecting their political union. They, of course, encountered the opposition of their eurosceptic partners. The compromise solution that was found there and then was the division of the European Union into **two Treaties** (that of the European Community and that of the European Union) and into **three construction pillars**: the European Community - the first and main pillar; common foreign and security policy (CFSP); and justice and home affairs (JHA). The first and by far the more important Treaty (although coming second under the general heading of the Maastricht and now the Nice Treaties) and the first pillar were to direct and regulate the first three stages of European integration: the customs union, the common market and the projected economic and monetary union using the Community method of decision-making by the common institutions. The second Treaty and the second and third pillars were intended to direct and manage the stage of political union using the intergovernmental cooperation method.

It was soon apparent that this method was leading nowhere towards the construction of the second and third pillars of the Union and, therefore, the progress of political integration. The disappointment was most felt in the area of the third pillar, where there were matters of common interest to be regulated urgently: the free circulation of citizens and residents of the Member States, a common immigration policy and a common protection of the external borders of the Union from all sorts of illegal trafficking. Concerning the first of these matters, europhilic nations had already taken the lead by signing, in June 1990, the Schengen agreement for the abolition of border checks between themselves. But, the need was felt by all Member States, first, to generalise the experience gained by the pioneers to all the partners and, second, to extend it to other matters of common interest. This need led to the revision of the European Union Treaty, at Amsterdam in 1997. Most of the justice and home affairs pillar (notably questions relating to the free movement of persons, asylum, immigration, the crossing of external borders and judicial cooperation in civil matters) was placed under the Community orbit, i.e. under the Community decision-making procedure. For this reason and in the interest of a systematic analysis, we examine first the so-called "third pillar" and last the "second pillar", both of which should rather be seen as the sites of construction of two wings attached to the main edifice of the European Community [see section 3.1.].

8.1. Justice and home affairs

The common values underlining the objective of **an area of freedom, security and justice** are long-standing principles of the modern democracies of the European Union. The declared objective of the Union is to provide citizens with a high level of safety within an area of freedom, security and justice by developing **common action** among the Member States in the fields of police and judicial cooperation in criminal matters and by preventing and combating racism and xenophobia. The means that disposes the Union to this effect are: closer cooperation between police forces, customs authorities and other competent authorities in the Member States; closer cooperation between judicial and other competent authorities of the Member States; and approximation, where necessary, of rules on criminal matters in the Member States (Art. 29 TEU).

The step-by-step approach of European integration [see section 1.1.2.] is quite evident in the field of **justice and home affairs (JHA)**. Whereas questions relating to the free movement of persons, asylum, immigration, the crossing of external borders and judicial cooperation depended on intergovernmental cooperation in the Maastricht version of the TEU [see section 2.2.], the Amsterdam revision of the TEU has integrated them into the Community framework [see section 2.3.]. This fact has important implications concerning notably the decision-making process [see section 4.3.] and the competence of the Court of Justice in both litigation and interpretation [see section 4.1.5.]. The Community institutions are given a role in police and criminal justice cooperation. The integration of the Schengen *acquis* into the framework of the European Community rewards the efforts of the Member States which embarked on this cooperation and gives the citizens of the Member States, who are crossing internal borders without police controls, the sentiment of belonging to a union[1] [see section 9.2.]. Only **police cooperation and judicial cooperation in criminal matters** are now governed by an **intergovernmental framework**, improved by the creation of the new instrument of "framework decisions" (Title VI TEU) [see section 8.1.2.].

The European Council, meeting in Tampere (15-16 October 1999) agreed on a number of **common policy guidelines** and priorities to develop the Union as an area of freedom and justice, notably: the creation of a genuine European area of justice by improving access of all citizens to justice in all Member States; a Union-wide fight against crime through the cooperation of the competent authorities of the Member States; and the setting up of a common policy on asylum and migration. The European Agency for the Management of Operational Cooperation at the External Borders, established in Warsaw, strives to improve the integrated management of the external borders of the Member States of the European Union[2].

Building on the achievements of the Tampere programme, the European Council of Brussels (4-5 November 2004) adopted the so-called **Hague five-year programme** for strengthening freedom, security and justice in the EU. Its objective is to improve the common capability of the Union and its Member States to guarantee fundamental rights, minimum procedural safeguards and access to justice, to provide protection in accordance with the Geneva Convention on Refugees and other international treaties to persons in need, to regulate migration flows and to control the external borders of the Union, to fight organised cross-border crime and repress the threat of terrorism, to carry further the mutual recognition of judicial decisions and certificates both in civil and in criminal matters, and to eliminate legal and judicial obstacles in litigation in civil and family matters with cross-border implications. This objective is to be achieved by the development of a common asylum system and by improving access to the courts, practical police and judicial cooperation, the approximation of laws and the development of common policies. The programme is to be implemented by the passage to qualified majority voting and co-decision as foreseen by Article 67(2) of the EC Treaty, by appropriate European legal instruments and by operational cooperation between relevant national agencies.

---

[1] Decisions 1999/435 and 1999/436, OJ L 176, 10.07.1999.
[2] Regulation 2007/2004, OJ L 349, 25.11.2004 and Decision 2005/358, OJ L 114, 04.05.2005.

The draft **Constitutional Treaty** proposed to go a step further in the field of JHA, by extending the community method to virtually all aspects of the field of justice and home affairs, thus eliminating the so-called third pillar of the Union [see section 3.1.]. All measures would be adopted in the form of laws or framework laws through the normal legislative procedure, thus abolishing the current panoply of acts such as common positions and framework decisions. The principle of mutual recognition of judicial and extrajudicial decisions would guide judicial cooperation in criminal as in civil matters. Operational cooperation between the competent authorities of the Member States would be extended to the police, customs and other services specialising in the prevention and detection of criminal offences (Art. I-42). As far as the procedures are concerned, the Commission would have sole right of legislative initiative, except in the field of police and judicial cooperation in criminal matters, where the Member States would also have a right of initiative. The Court of Justice would have competence in all JHA matters. Common policies would be developed in the fields of border controls, visas, asylum and immigration (Art III-265). A uniform status of asylum for nationals of third countries would be valid throughout the Union (Art. III-266). The common immigration policy would ensure the efficient management of migration flows, fair treatment of third-country nationals residing legally in Member States, and the prevention of illegal immigration and trafficking in human beings (Art. III-267).

8.1.1. Judicial cooperation in civil matters

Judicial cooperation in civil matters is important since in a genuine European area of justice, individuals and businesses should not be prevented or discouraged from exercising their rights by the incompatibility or complexity of legal and administrative systems in the Member States. The main objective in this area is legal certainty and equal access to justice for all EU citizens, implying easy identification of the competent jurisdiction, clear designation of the applicable law, availability of speedy and fair proceedings and effective enforcement procedures. Procedural rules should respond to broadly the same guarantees, ensuring that people will not be treated unevenly according to the jurisdiction dealing with their case. The rules may be different provided that they are equivalent. The European Council of Tampere (15 and 16 October 1999), therefore, endorsed the principle of **mutual recognition of judicial decisions and judgments**, which is the cornerstone of judicial cooperation in both civil and criminal matters. This principle is already implemented by several Community instruments, which replaced pre-existing Conventions.

A Regulation on **jurisdiction and the recognition and enforcement of judgments** in civil and commercial matters, which replaced the 1968 Brussels Convention, lays down provisions concerning general jurisdiction and special jurisdiction in matters relating to insurance, consumer contracts, individual contracts of employment and some exclusive jurisdictions[1]. It also contains rules on prorogation, examination, admissibility, enforcement of judgments, authentic instruments and court settlements. Another Regulation established a general framework for activities aiming to **facilitate the implementation of judicial cooperation** in civil matters[2]. It has the following objectives: encourage such cooperation; improve mutual knowledge of the Member States' legal and judicial systems in civil matters; facilitate the correct application of Community instruments in

---

[1] Regulation 44/2001, OJ L 12, 16.01.2001 and Regulation 2245/2004, OJ L 381, 28.12.2004.
[2] Regulation 743/2002, OJ L 115, 01.05.2002.

this area; and improve public information on access to justice, judicial cooperation and the legal systems of the Member States.

Specific Regulations concern: the jurisdiction and the recognition and enforcement of **judgments in matrimonial matters** and in matters of parental responsibility for joint children[1]; the **service** in the Member States of judicial and extrajudicial documents[2]; and cross-border **insolvency proceedings** regarding an insolvent debtor's assets[3]. A directive improved access to justice in cross-border disputes by establishing minimum common rules relating to legal aid and other financial aspects of civil proceedings[4]. A **European enforcement order** for uncontested claims allows creditors who have obtained an enforceable decision with regard to a claim that has never been contested by the debtor to proceed directly to its enforcement in another Member State (abolition of exequatur)[5].

The **European judicial network** in civil and commercial matters seeks to facilitate judicial cooperation between the Member States both in areas in which existing instruments apply and in those where no instrument is currently applicable. It also aims to devise, progressively establish and update an information system which is accessible to the public. The network is composed of contact points designated by the Member States, and includes central authorities provided for in Community instruments, in instruments of international law to which the Member States are party or in rules of domestic law in the area of judicial cooperation[6]. A uniform procedure administers the request and direct transmission of evidence and proof between the courts of the Member States in civil or commercial matters[7].

8.1.2. Police and judicial cooperation in criminal matters

Police and judicial cooperation in criminal matters (PJCCM) means that criminal behaviours should be approached in the same way throughout the Union. Article 29 of the TEU declares that the Union's objective is to provide citizens with **a high level of safety** within an area of freedom, security and justice. The Union is set to achieve this objective by preventing and combating crime, organised or otherwise, in particular terrorism, trafficking in persons and offences against children, illicit drug or arms trafficking, corruption and fraud. In the areas of PJCCM, Member States must inform and consult one another within the Council with a view to coordinating their action. To that end, they must establish collaboration between the relevant departments of their administrations (Art. 34 TEU). A Coordinating Committee consisting of senior officials has a coordinating role in the field of PJCCM. It may give opinions for the attention of the Council and contribute to the preparation of the Council's discussions (Art. 36 TEU).

In police and judicial cooperation in criminal matters the Council may, acting unanimously on the initiative of any Member State or of the Commission: (a) adopt **common positions** defining the approach of the Union to a particular matter; (b) adopt **framework decisions** for the purpose of approximation of the laws and regulations of the Member States, which are binding on the latter as to the result to be achieved but leave to the national authorities the choice of form and methods; (c) adopt **decisions** for any other purpose, which are binding but do not entail direct effect and must be implemented by the necessary measures adopted by the Council acting by a qualified majority; and (d) establish **conventions**, which, once adopted by at least half of the Member States, enter into force for those Member States, and may be implemented by measures adopted within the Council by a majority of two-thirds of the Contracting Parties (Art. 34 TEU).

---

[1] Regulation 2201/2003, OJ L 338, 23.12.2003 and Regulation 2116/2004, OJ L 367, 14.12.2004.
[2] Regulation 1348/2000, OJ L 160, 30.06.2000.
[3] Regulation 1346/2000, OJ L 160, 30.06.2000 and Regulation 694/2006, OJ L 121, 06.05.2006.
[4] Directive 2003/8, OJ L 26, 31.01.2003.
[5] Regulation 805/2004, OJ L 143, 30.04.2004 and Regulation 1869/2005, OJ L 300, 17.11.2005.
[6] Decision 2001/470, OJ L 174, 27.06.2001.
[7] Regulation 1206/2001, OJ L 174, 27.06.2001.

The Council must consult the **European Parliament** before adopting any of the above measures and must give it adequate time to deliver its opinion, but is free to take or not take account of this opinion (Art. 39 TEU). Hence, the Parliament has a consultative role, but no co-decision or cooperation role in the field of PJCCM [see section 4.3.]. Another departure from the Community decision-making process is that the initiative for any PJCCM action can be taken not only by the Commission but also by any Member State (Art. 34 TEU). The competence of the **Court of Justice** of the European Communities is limited in giving preliminary rulings on the validity and interpretation of framework decisions and decisions, as well as on the interpretation of conventions in the field of PJCCM and on the validity and interpretation of the measures implementing them. However, the Court has upheld the principle that national criminal law must be interpreted in a manner compatible with Union law[1].

Judicial cooperation in criminal matters includes: cooperation between the competent ministries and judicial authorities of the Member States in relation to proceedings and the enforcement of decisions; facilitation of the extradition between Member States; compatibility of rules applicable in the Member States; prevention of conflicts of jurisdiction between Member States; and the progressive establishment of common rules relating to the constituent elements of criminal acts and to penalties in the fields of organised crime, terrorism and illicit drug trafficking (Art. 31 TEU).

Police cooperation is organised both directly and through the **European Police Office (Europol)**. It covers in particular: operational cooperation between the competent police, customs and other authorities; the collection, storage, processing, analysis and exchange of relevant information; joint initiatives in training and the exchange of liaison officers; and the common evaluation of particular investigative techniques. The Council should notably: enable Europol to coordinate specific investigative actions by the competent authorities of the Member States and assist them in investigating cases of organised crime; promote liaison arrangements between prosecuting/investigating officials; and establish a research, documentation and statistical network on cross-border crime (Art 30 TEU).

The **Europol Convention** was signed on 26 June 1995[2]. Europol's remit includes the fight against terrorism[3] and against serious forms of international crime[4]. The tasks of Europol include also the exchange and analysis of information and intelligence relating to illicit drug trafficking, trafficking in nuclear substances, clandestine immigration networks, traffic in human beings and illicit vehicle trafficking[5]. The Court of Justice has jurisdiction, under certain conditions, to give preliminary rulings on the interpretation of the Europol Convention. The Community finances cooperation activities in the fields of JHA, a major element for the functioning of Europol[6]. The Director of Europol is authorised to enter into negotiations on agreements with third States and non-EU related bodies[7].

Member States which intend to **establish enhanced cooperation** between themselves in the field of PJCCM may be authorised to make use of the institutions, procedures and mechanisms laid down by the Treaties (including the Community decision-making process and Court competence) provided that the cooperation proposed respects the powers of the European Community and aims at developing more rapidly an area of freedom, security and justice (Art. 40 TEU). The authorisation for an enhanced coopera-

---

[1]   Judgement of 16 June 2005, Case C-105/03, Pupino, ECR 2005, p. I-05285.
[2]   Council Act OJ C 316, 27.11.1995 and Decision, OJ C 362, 18.12.2001.
[3]   Decision, OJ C 26, 30.01.1999, p. 22.
[4]   Decision, OJ C 362, 18.12.2001, p. 41.
[5]   Joint Action 96/748/JHA, OJ L 342, 31.12.1996.
[6]   Joint Action 95/401/JHA, OJ L 238, 06.10.1995.
[7]   Decision of 27 March 2000, OJ C 106, 13.04.2000 and Decision 2005/169, OJ L 56, 02.03.2005.

tion is granted by the Council, acting by a qualified majority, on a proposal from the Commission or on the initiative of at least eight Member States, and after consulting the European Parliament (Art. 40a TEU).

Police and judicial cooperation in criminal matters has made much progress, since the inception of this policy in 1991, concerning in particular mutual assistance in criminal matters, criminal proceedings and the fight against drugs, against organised crime and against corruption [see details below].

A European crime prevention network (EUCPN) aims to **organise cooperation** between the Member States in the areas mentioned at Tampere (juvenile, urban and drug-related crime), to collect and analyse information and good practice, and to advise the Council and the Commission[1]. Mechanisms were created for the exchange of information between criminal records of the Member States[2]. A Provisional Judicial Cooperation Unit is intended to improve cooperation between the competent national authorities with regard to investigations and prosecutions in relation to serious crime[3]. Multinational teams were created to evaluate the application at national level of international acts and instruments in the fight against organised crime[4]. Joint investigation teams between the competent authorities of two or more Member States can be created for a limited period in order to carry out criminal investigations[5]. A secretariat was set up for the joint supervisory data-protection bodies established by the Europol and Schengen conventions[6]. Various instruments have been adopted with a view to intensifying the fight against all forms of crime, notably: the exchange of DNA analysis results[7]; a Directory of specialised competencies, skills and expertise to facilitate cooperation between the Member States[8] and a similar Directory for the purposes of counter-terrorist cooperation[9]. Cooperation between liaison officers posted by the law enforcement agencies of the Member States to third countries and international organisations is intended to make the best possible use of Member States' resources[10].

A framework programme on police and judicial cooperation in criminal matters (AGIS) finances cooperation activities in areas falling within Title VI of the Treaty on European Union: judicial cooperation in general and criminal matters, including training; cooperation between law-enforcement authorities or other public or private organisations in the Member States involved in preventing and fighting crime, organised or otherwise; and cooperation between Member States to achieve effective protection of the interests of victims in criminal proceedings[11]. The European Police College (CEPOL) helps train the senior police officers of the Member States, notably concerning knowledge of the national police systems and structures of other Member States, of Europol and of cross-border police cooperation within the European Union[12].

The **European arrest warrant** and harmonised surrender procedures replaced the system of extradition between Member States[13]. When the judicial authority of a Member State issues a decision requesting the surrender of a person, this decision should henceforth be recognised by the judicial authorities of the other Member States *ipso facto* and with a limited number of grounds for refusal. Victims in criminal proceedings are assisted when the crime has been committed in a different Member State from the one in which the victim lives[14]. A Member State should recognise and execute in its territory orders freezing property or evidence issued by a judicial authority of another Member State in connection with criminal proceedings[15]. An intergovernmental cooperation aims at preventing and combating cross-border vehicle crime, paying particular attention to the links between vehicle theft and the illegal car trade and forms of organised crime such as trafficking in drugs, firearms and human beings[16].

The common policy concerning **drug trafficking** deals with: the prevention and detection of illicit cultivation and production of drugs within the EU[17]; sentencing for serious illicit drug-trafficking[18]; the manufac-

---

[1] Decision 2001/427/JHA, OJ L 153, 08.06.2001.
[2] Decision 2005/876, OJ L 322, 09.12.2005.
[3] Decision 2000/799/JHA, OJ L 324, 21.12.2000.
[4] Joint Action 97/827/JHA, OJ L 344, 15.12.1997.
[5] Framework Decision 2002/465, OJ L 162, 20.06.2002.
[6] Decision 2000/641/JHA, OJ L 271, 24.10.2000.
[7] Resolution, OJ C 193, 24.06.1997, p. 2-3.
[8] Joint Action 96/747/JHA, OJ L 342, 31.12.1996.
[9] Joint Action 96/610/JHA, OJ L 273, 25.10.1996.
[10] Decision 2003/170, OJ L 67, 12.03.2003.
[11] Decision 2002/630/JHA, OJ L 203, 01.08.2002.
[12] Decision 2005/681, OJ L 256, 01.10.2005.
[13] Framework Decision 2002/584, OJ L 190, 18.07.2002.
[14] Framework Decision 2001/220/JHA, OJ L 82, 22.03.2001.
[15] Framework Decision 2003/577/JHA, OJ L 196, 02.08.2003.
[16] Decision 2004/919, OJ L 389, 30.12.2004.
[17] Council Resolution, OJ C 389, 23.12.1996, p. 1.
[18] Council Resolution, OJ C 10, 11.01.1997, p. 3-4.

ture and the placing on the market of certain substances used as drug precursors[1]; and the monitoring of trade between the Community and third countries in drug precursors[2]. The European Drug Monitoring Centre and the European Information Network on Drugs and Drug Addiction (Reitox) assist national authorities in the fight against drugs[3]. Legislation on the fight against drug trafficking is harmonised, by establishing minimum common provisions relating to the constituent elements of criminal acts and to penalties[4]. Intergovernmental joint actions for combating drugs concern: the approximation of the laws and practices of the Member States to combat drug addiction and drug trafficking[5]; the exchange of information on the chemical profiling of drugs; cooperation between the customs authorities and business organisations[6]; the collection of customs and police information in the fight against drug trafficking[7]; and information exchange, risk assessment and control of new psychoactive substances[8].

Police cooperation and mutual judicial assistance in **combating organised crime** entails a common definition of a criminal organisation and a common approach to making participation in such an organisation a criminal offence[9]; the creation of a European Judicial Network[10]; the exchange of liaison magistrates[11]; and the surveillance in the territory of another Member State as a necessary part of a criminal investigation in the context of the Schengen agreement[12]. A Joint Action aims at combating the sexual exploitation of children and child pornography[13]. A framework decision defines offences concerning trafficking in human beings for purposes of labour exploitation or sexual exploitation and lays down penalties applicable to persons committing such offences[14]. Another framework decision aims to ensure that all Member States have effective rules governing the confiscation of proceeds from crime[15]. The control of the acquisition and possession of weapons is part of the common policy on the fight against crime[16]. A joint action aims at strengthening the practical application of the 1990 Council of Europe Convention on money-laundering, search, seizure and confiscation of the proceeds from crime[17], while a Framework Decision aims to abolish certain reservations in respect of the "1990 Convention" in order to increase penalties and to improve the processing of requests for mutual assistance between the Member States[18] [see also section 6.7.]. The principle of mutual recognition applies to financial penalties[19]. A system for State compensation to the victims of serious crimes committed on the territory of any Member State facilitates access to compensation for such victims (notably victims of terrorism) regardless of their nationality[20].

A framework decision aims to ensure that both active and passive **corruption in the private sector** are criminal offences in all Member States, that legal persons may also be held responsible for such offences, and that the offences incur effective, proportionate and dissuasive penalties[21]. All **fraud involving non-cash means of payment** (payment instruments, computers and specifically adapted devices) is recognised as a criminal offence and mechanisms are put in place for cooperation between the Member States to prosecute such offences efficiently[22]. A framework decision aims to approximate the criminal law of the Member States in respect of attacks against information systems and ensure that such attacks are punishable in all Member States by effective, proportionate and dissuasive penalties[23].

Intergovernmental cooperation measures include: guidelines for preventing and restraining **disorder connected with football matches**[24]; the establishment of contact points in the Member States for gathering and exchanging information of a police nature, with a view to preventing and combating football-related violence[25];

---

[1]   Regulation 273/2004, OJ L 47, 18.02.2004.
[2]   Regulation 111/2005, OJ L 22, 26.01.2005.
[3]   Regulation 302/93, OJ L 36, 12.02.1993 and Regulation 1651/2003, OJ L 245, 29.09.2003.
[4]   Framework Decision 2004/757, OJ L 335, 11.11.2004.
[5]   Joint Action 96/750/JHA, OJ L 342, 31.12.1996.
[6]   Joint Action 96/699/JHA, OJ L 322, 12.12.1996.
[7]   Joint Action 97/372/JHA, OJ L 159, 17.06.1997.
[8]   Decision 2005/387, OJ L 127, 20.05.2005.
[9]   Joint Action 98/733/JHA, OJ L 351, 29.12.1998.
[10]   Joint Action 98/428/JHA, OJ L 191, 07.07.1998.
[11]   Joint Action 96/277/JHA, OJ L 105, 27.04.1996.
[12]   Decision 2003/725/JHA, OJ L 260, 11.10.2003.
[13]   Framework Decision 2004/68, OJ L 13, 20.01.2004.
[14]   Framework Decision 2002/629/JHA, OJ L 203, 01.08.2002.
[15]   Framework Decision 2005/212/JHA, OJ L 68, 15.03.2005.
[16]   Directive 91/477, OJ L 256, 13.09.1991.
[17]   Joint Action 98/699/JHA, OJ L 333, 09.112.1998 and Framework Decision 2001/500, OJ L 182, 05.07.2001.
[18]   Framework Decision 2001/500/JHA, OJ L 182, 05.07.2001.
[19]   Framework Decision 2005/214/JHA, OJ L 76, 22.03.2005.
[20]   Directive 2004/80, OJ L 261, 06.08.2004.
[21]   Framework Decision 2003/568/JHA, OJ L 192, 31.07.2003.
[22]   Framework Decision 2001/413/JHA, OJ L 149, 02.06.2001.
[23]   Framework Decision 2005/222/JHA, OJ L 69, 16.03.2005.
[24]   Recommendation, OJ C 131, 03.05.1996, p. 1-11.
[25]   Decision 2002/348/JHA, OJ L 121, 08.05.2002.

cooperation on law and order and security at meetings attended by large numbers of people, such as sporting events, rock concerts, demonstrations and road-blocking protest campaigns[1].

The EU supports the drawing-up of the proposed United Nations convention against organised crime[2] and the effective functioning of the **International Criminal Court (ICC)**[3]. The EU and ICC have signed an agreement on cooperation and assistance[4]. A European network of contact points provides on request any available information that may be relevant in the context of investigations into genocide, crimes against humanity and war crimes[5]. Member States cooperate in the investigation and prosecution of persons accused of having committed or participated in genocide, crimes against humanity or war crimes as defined in the Statute of the International Criminal Court[6]. The EU regrets the American decision not to ratify the convention and to give US personnel exemption from the jurisdiction of the ICC.

8.1.3. Common treatment of nationals of third countries

The Member States of the EU are all subject to **migration pressures** from many - and often new - sources to which they have to respond by finding the balance between economic and humanitarian considerations in line with Community legislation and key international agreements. The abolition of internal border controls and the notion of a common external border reinforces the desirability for the Union to develop more common approaches and closer cooperation in the immigration policy area. These are new concerns for the Community which emerged with the completion of the single market and which are taken into account by the Treaty on European Union. Hence, the common policy on the treatment of nationals of third countries is a spillover effect of the single market legislation [see section 1.1.2.].

In fact, the **abolition of checks at internal borders** of the Community is effective both for the citizens of the Member States and for third country nationals, once they have crossed the external frontiers of a Member State. In other words, freedom of movement applies to all those within the territory of the Community. This is why the Member States must have common rules for the crossing of their borders by foreigners and for the treatment of foreigners within their territory. This common need has led to the adoption of common policies in the fields of visas, immigration, the right of asylum, the status of refugees and extradition [see details below]. Thus, the Member States have established a Community Code on the rules governing the movement of persons across borders (Schengen Borders Code)[7]. A Directive determines: (a) the terms for conferring and withdrawing long-term resident status granted by a Member State in relation to third-country nationals legally residing in its territory, and the rights pertaining thereto; and (b) the terms of residence in Member States other than the one which conferred long-term status on them for third-country nationals enjoying that status[8]. The ARGO programme (2002-2006) is designed to help promote administrative cooperation in the fields of external borders, visas, asylum and immigration, particularly from the point of view of implementing and properly applying the relevant Community rules[9].

Visa policy is now under Community competence. A Council regulation established a uniform format for visas for nationals of third countries[10]. This single, clearly identifiable visa is issued by the Member States and includes all the necessary information. It meets the highest technical standards, notably as regards safe-

---

[1] Joint Action 97/339/JHA, OJ L 147, 05.06.1997.
[2] Joint Position 1999/235/JHA, OJ L 87, 31.03. 1999.
[3] Common Position 2003/444, OJ L 150, 18.06.2003.
[4] Decision 2006/313, OJ L 115, 28.04.2006.
[5] Decision 2002/494, OJ L 167, 26.06.2002.
[6] Decision 2003/335, OJ L 118, 14.05.2003.
[7] Regulation 562/2006, OJ L 105, 13.04.2006.
[8] Directive 2003/109, OJ L 16, 23.01.2004.
[9] Decision 2002/463, OJ L 161, 19.06.2002 and Decision 2004/867, OJ L 371, 18.12.2004.
[10] Regulation 1683/95, OJ L 164, 14.07.1995 and Regulation 334/2002, OJ L 53, 23.02.2002.

guards against counterfeiting and falsification. It guarantees, however, protection of the personal data involved. Another regulation determined the third countries whose nationals are subject to the visa requirement for crossing the external borders of the European Union, and those whose nationals are exempt from that requirement[1]. A regulation facilitates the free movement within the EU territory of holders of long-stay visas pending the issue of their residence permit[2]. An EC Directive harmonised financial penalties imposed on carriers transporting into the territory of the Member States third-country nationals lacking the documents necessary for admission[3]. Another directive lays down rules governing the admission of students into the European Union for a period exceeding three months and sets out the elements to be taken into consideration by the Member States for authorising such admissions[4]. Several measures were adopted in the context of cooperation in the field of JHA, notably: a joint action on airport transit arrangements[5]; consular cooperation regarding visas[6]; the organisation of pre-frontier assistance and training assignments to airports outside the Union[7]; and a system for exchanging information with a view to facilitating the detection of false and stolen documents[8]. The visa information system (VIS) enables authorised national authorities to enter and update visa data, and consult them electronically[9].

Immigration policy has entered the Community arena through the prior consultation procedure on migratory policies towards third countries, in place since 1988[10]. The European Monitoring Centre on Racism and Xenophobia in Vienna was set up in order to provide objective, reliable and comparable data and improve the exchange of information and experience in these fields[11]. A directive determines the conditions under which third-country nationals residing lawfully in the territory of a Member State may exercise the right to family reunification[12]. A regulation laid down a uniform format for residence permits for third-country nationals with high technology specifications, including enhanced anti-forgery, counterfeiting and falsification standards[13]. A joint action aims to combat racism and xenophobia in the field of judicial cooperation[14]. With a Green Paper, the Commission launched a process of in-depth discussion on the most appropriate form of Community rules concerning the conditions of entry and residence of third-country nationals for economic reasons[15]. Another Green Paper concerns the European migration network (EMN), which was set up in 2002 as a pilot action in response to the need to improve the exchange of information concerning all aspects of migration and asylum[16]. In a communication, the Commission set out the measures to be taken in order to create a European framework for the integration of immigrants in accordance with the common basic principles of policy on immigration[17].

A directive provides a definition of the facilitation of **illegal immigration** and approximates legal provisions concerning precise definition of the infringement in question and exemptions[18]. A framework decision aims at strengthening of the penal framework to prevent the facilitation of unauthorised entry, transit and residence by defining minimum rules for penalties, liability of legal persons and jurisdiction[19]. An immigration liaison officers' network enables contacts to be established and maintained with the authorities of third countries and facilitates the collection and exchange of information aimed at combating illegal immigration, promoting the return of illegal immigrants and assisting the management of legal migration[20]. A secure web-based information and coordination network for Member States' migration management services serves for exchanging information on illegal migratory flows[21]. Moreover, a Community programme for financial and technical assistance in the areas of migration and asylum (AENEAS) aims at helping third countries to manage their migration flows, combat illegal immigration and govern the return of illegal immigrants to the country of ori-

[1] Regulation 539/2001, OJ L 81, 21.03.2001 and Regulation 851/2005, OJ L 141, 04.06.2005.
[2] Regulation 1091/2001, OJ L 150, 06.06.2001.
[3] Directive 2001/51, OJ L 187, 10.07.2001.
[4] Directive 2004/114, OJ L 375, 23.12.2004.
[5] Joint Action 96/197/JHA, OJ L 63, 13.03.1996.
[6] OJ C 80, 18.03.1996, p. 1.
[7] Joint Position 96/622/JHA, OJ L 281, 31.10.1996.
[8] Decision 2000/261/JHA, OJ L 81, 01.04.2000.
[9] Decision 2004/512, OJ L 213, 15.06.2004.
[10] Decision 88/384, OJ L 183, 14.07.1988.
[11] Regulation 1035/97, OJ L 151, 10.06.1997 and Regulation 1652/2003, OJ L 245, 29.09.2003.
[12] Directive 2003/86, OJ L 251, 03.10.2003.
[13] Regulation 1030/2002, OJ L 157, 15.06.2002.
[14] Joint Action 96/443/JHA, OJ L 185, 24.07.1996.
[15] COM (2004) 811, 11 January 2005.
[16] COM/2005/606, 28 November 2005.
[17] COM (2005) 389, 1 September 2005.
[18] Directive 2002/90, OJ L 328, 05.12.2002.
[19] Decision 2002/946, OJ L 328, 05.12.2002.
[20] Regulation 377/2004, OJ L 64, 02.03.2004.
[21] Decision 2005/267, OJ L 83, 01.04.2005.

gin[1]. Agreements on the readmission of persons residing without authorisation have been signed with Albania[2] and Sri Lanka[3].

Directive 2005/85 has put in place a system of minimum standards necessary for the granting and withdrawing of **refugee status** in the Member States, concerning notably access to legal assistance, personal interviews and the right of appeal[4]. Another directive lays down rules for determining which applicants for international protection qualify for refugee status and for subsidiary protection status, offered to persons who do not qualify as refugees but who would face a real risk of suffering serious harm, if returned to their country of origin[5].

Several **means of the asylum policy** were adopted in the Community context. A directive aims to give the European Union the means to act in the event of a mass influx of displaced persons by means of a mechanism for immediate protection, establishing minimum standards for giving this protection and for ensuring a balance of efforts between the Member States in receiving refugees and displaced persons[6]. The range of instruments available on EU asylum policy include: the exchange of information concerning assistance for the voluntary repatriation of third-country nationals[7]; the monitoring of the implementation by the Member States of measures adopted concerning asylum[8]; minimum standards on information, documentation, health, accommodation, clothing and money on the reception of applicants for asylum[9]; and criteria and mechanisms for determining the Member State responsible for examining an application for asylum lodged in one of the Member States by a third-country national, incorporating the related Dublin Convention into the Community framework[10]. The resources of the European Refugee Fund are divided among the Member States in proportion to the number of asylum-seekers they receive and the number of refugees they accommodate on their territory[11]. A centralised system, "Eurodac", was set up for processing, comparing and transmitting in digital format fingerprints of asylum seekers and certain other third-country nationals[12]. The principle of mutual recognition covers an **expulsion** decision issued by a competent authority in one Member State against a third-country national[13].

8.1.4. The fight against terrorism inside the European Union

The **common policy for the fight against terrorism** has two wings: one in the realm of justice and home affairs policy; and one attached to the European security and defence policy [see section 8.2.3]. In the light of the attacks in the United States on 11 September and following on from the decisions taken since the Tampere European Council, the Justice and Home Affairs Council met on 20 September 2001 to take the necessary measures to maintain the highest level of security and any other measure needed to combat terrorism. It decided to set up within Europol a team of counter-terrorist specialists for which the Member States appoint liaison officers from police and intelligence services specialising in the fight against terrorism, whose remit includes the following tasks: to collect in a timely manner all relevant information and intelligence concerning the current threat; to analyse the collected information and undertake the necessary operational and strategic analysis; to draft a threat assessment document listing targets, damage, potential *modi operandi* and consequences for the security of the Member States.

A framework decision aims to approximate the **definition of terrorist offences** in all Member States, including those offences relating to terrorist groups, and to provide for penalties and sanctions for natural and legal persons who have committed or are re-

---

[1] Regulation 491/2004, OJ L 80, 18.03.2004.
[2] Agreement and Decision 2005/371, OJ L 124, 17.05.2005 and Decision 2005/809, OJ L 304, 23 November 2005.
[3] Agreement and Decision 2005/372, OJ L 124, 17.05.2005.
[4] Directive 2005/85, OJ L 326, 13.12.2005.
[5] Directive 2004/83, OJ L 304, 30.09.2004.
[6] Directive 2001/55, OJ L 212, 07.08.2001.
[7] Decision 97/340/CFSP, OJ L 147, 05.06.1997.
[8] Decision 97/420/CFSP, OJ L 178, 07.07.1997.
[9] Directive 2003/9, OJ L 31, 06.02.2003.
[10] Regulation 343/2003, OJ L 50, 25.02.2003 and Decision 2006/188, OJ L 66, 08.03.2006.
[11] Decision 2004/904, OJ L 381, 28.12.2004.
[12] Regulation 2725/2000, OJ L 316, 15.12.2000 and Decision 2006/188, OJ L 66, 08.03.2006.
[13] Directive 2001/40, OJ L 149, 02.06.2001 and Decision 2004/191, OJ L 60, 27.02.2004.

sponsible for such offences[1]. A Directive aims at the prevention of the use of the financial system for the purpose of money laundering and terrorist financing[2] [see section 6.7]. On the other hand, a regulation obliges the Member States to incorporate in **new passports** a digital photograph and fingerprints of the holder. It also harmonises security standards for the production of passports and other travel documents issued by the Member States[3]. The **Judicial Cooperation Unit, Eurojust**, brings together Member States' magistrates (prosecutors, judges or police officers) specialising in counter-terrorism in order to examine any measure whereby current investigations into terrorism can be properly coordinated[4].

The Police Chiefs Task Force brings together the heads of **EU counter-terrorist units** in order to discuss further: improved operational cooperation between Member States and third countries; coordination of measures implemented in the Member States to guarantee a high level of security, including in the field of air safety; the missions to be entrusted to the team of counter-terrorist specialists within Europol. A Counter-Terrorism Task Force within Europol and an EU counter-terrorism coordinator within the Council aim to improve coordination and visibility of the EU's actions in this field. A European network for the protection of public figures, consisting of national police services and other competent services, aims at developing common approaches and promoting the exchange of information, the selection and the training of appropriate staff[5].

The Council invited Member States to ratify the United Nations Convention for the **Suppression of the Financing of Terrorism**, and to take the implementing measures necessary. The European Union and the Member States review the relevant EC and EU instruments in order to achieve greater coherence and effectiveness as well as ensuring that banking systems do not facilitate the generation and transfer of terrorist funds, including those resulting from drugs-related criminal activities [see section 6.7.]. The Schengen information system (SIS) is used by Europol and Eurojust in the fight against terrorism[6] [see sections 8.1.2 and 9.2]. The Member States have agreed to enlarge the scope of information exchanges to include all terrorist offences without limiting them to an exhaustive list of individuals and entities, while also making this information available to Europol and Eurojust[7].

8.2. Common foreign and security policy

Common foreign policy has taken its first steps thanks, notably, to the institution by the Single European Act [see section 2.1.] of **European political cooperation**, which provided for reciprocal information procedures and regular contacts in order to harmonise the viewpoints of the Member States in the field of international policy. The Treaty on European Union took a further step forward on the Single Act. Whereas under the latter, the Member States undertook to "strive to draw up" and implement in common a European foreign policy, in Title V of the EU Treaty they "undertake to define" and implement a **common foreign and security policy (CFSP)**. This policy, called the second pillar of the European Union [see section 3.1.], remains, however, an intergovernmental process distinct from the institutional framework of the Community and removed from the jurisdiction of the Court of Justice (Art. 28,1 TEU). The Member States are advancing with caution into this new ground which, in the long term, will imply major transfers of national sovereignty [see section 1.1.2 and the European perspectives in the conclusions].

According to the European Union Treaty, the **objectives of CFSP** are: to safeguard the common values, fundamental interests, independence and integrity of the Union; to strengthen the security of the Union in all ways; to preserve peace and strengthen international security, in accordance with the principles of the UN Charter, the Helsinki Final Act and the Paris Charter; to promote international cooperation; to develop and consolidate democracy and the rule of law, as well as respect for human rights and fundamental

---

[1] Decision 2002/475, OJ L 164, 22.06.2002.
[2] Directive 2005/60, OJ L 309, 25.11.2005.
[3] Regulation 2252/2004, OJ L 385, 29.12.2004.
[4] Decision 2002/187, OJ L 63, 06.03.2002 and Decision 2003/659, OJ L 245, 29.09.2003.
[5] Decision 2002/956, OJ L 333, 10.12.2002.
[6] Regulation 871/2004, OJ L 162, 30.04.2004 and Decision 2005/451, OJ L 158, 21.06.2005.
[7] Decision 2005/671, OJ L 253, 29.09.2005.

freedoms (Art. 11 TEU). However, in order to pursue these ambitious objectives, the TEU gives the common institutions some means dependent on an **intergovernmental cooperation method**: defining the principles of and general guidelines for the common foreign and security policy; deciding on common strategies; adopting joint actions; adopting common positions; and strengthening systematic cooperation between the Member States in the conduct of policy (Art. 12 TEU).

In the framework of their **systematic cooperation** the Member States must inform and consult one another within the Council on any matter of foreign and security policy of general interest in order to ensure that their combined influence is exerted as effectively as possible (Art. 16 TEU). The diplomatic and consular missions of the Member States and the Commission delegations in third countries and their representations in international organisations must step up cooperation by exchanging information, carrying out joint assessments and contributing to the implementation of the CFSP (Art. 20 TEU).

Member States must **coordinate their action in international organisations** and at international conferences. All the Member States or those participating in such fora must uphold the common positions and keep each other informed of any matter of common interest. Member States which are permanent or temporary members of the United Nations Security Council must keep the other Member States fully informed and ensure the defence of the positions and the interests of the Union (Art. 19 TEU).

According to the draft **Constitutional Treaty**, the Union would have competence in matters of common foreign and security policy and the Member States should actively and unreservedly support this common policy (Art. I-16). But this so-called "common policy" would still be conducted by intergovernmental cooperation [see the European perspectives in the conclusions].

8.2.1. Decision-making in CFSP matters

There are several departures from the Community method [see section 4.3.] concerning decision-making in CFSP matters. Whereas in Community decision-making only the Commission has the right to propose and hence the responsibility to define the common interest and ensure the coherence of action, in CFSP all the Member States and the Commission have the power to propose. The risks are inconsistency of the proposed action with the other policies of the EC/EU and disregard of the interests of the Member States in the minority, which cannot block the proposal. There are also two independent executive organs of the policy, since the Commission entrusts one of its members with the responsibility of the external relations of the Community and the Council appoints its Secretary General as High Representative for CFSP. Here again there is a risk of incoherence in the management of policy instruments and resources. Finally and most importantly, instead of the classical forms of Community acts [see section 3.3.], CFSP decisions take special forms, are usually taken by the Council acting unanimously and are not subjected to the control of the Court of Justice.

It transpires that the CFSP method is an improved intergovernmental cooperation method, but not much more than that. Probably, the most useful improvement is the definition by the European Council of **common strategies** in areas where the Member States have important interests in common. Since the definition of common strategies depends on the identification of common interests by the majority of the Member States, common strategies are a useful framework to find strategic answers to international crises and to increase the Union's efficiency by permitting decisions to be taken **by major-**

ity voting (subject to the remark above). Common strategies set out their objectives, duration and the means to be made available by the Union and the Member States. On the basis of the general guidelines defined by the European Council, the Council takes the decisions necessary for defining and implementing the CFSP, usually by unanimous voting [see details below]. It recommends common strategies to the European Council and implements them (Art. 13 TEU).

Common positions adopted by the Council define the approach of the Union to a particular matter of a geographical or thematic nature. Member States must ensure that their national policies conform to the common positions (Art 15 TEU). Article 3 of the Union Treaty contains an obligation to ensure the consistency of the Union's activities. Therefore, a common position adopted on the basis of Article 12 (TEU), while respecting the division of responsibilities set out in the Treaty, has to be compatible with the guidelines governing the EU's economic relations with a third country and with the objectives and priorities of its external policies, although it is the European Community that is responsible for adopting practical measures [see introduction to Part VI].

Joint actions adopted by the Council address specific situations where operational action by the Union is deemed to be required. They lay down their objectives, scope, the means to be made available to the Union, if necessary their duration, and the conditions for their implementation. Joint actions commit the Member States to the positions they adopt and in the conduct of their activity. Whenever a Member State plans to adopt a national position or take national action pursuant to a joint action, it must provide information in time to allow, if necessary, for prior consultations within the Council. Member States may take the necessary measures as a matter of urgency having regard to the general objectives of the joint action, and inform the Council immediately of any such measures (Art. 14 TEU).

Decisions on CFSP matters are taken by the **Council acting unanimously** but any member of the Council may abstain in order to allow a decision to be taken. In such a case, although it will not be obliged to apply the decision, it will accept that the decision commits the Union and will refrain from any action likely to conflict with or impede Union action based on that decision. If the abstaining members represent more than one third of the votes in the Council, the decision shall not be taken. The "**constructive abstention**" allows some Member States not to participate in a joint action, thus making it easier to adopt initiatives which have a broad measure of support (two thirds of the weighted majority).

On matters not having military or defence implications, the Council **may act by qualified majority**, when adopting a decision on the basis of a common strategy defined by the European Council, and when adopting any decision implementing a joint action or a common position. However, if a member of the Council declares that, for important and stated reasons of national policy, it intends to oppose the adoption of a decision to be taken by qualified majority, the Council may, acting by qualified majority, request that the matter be referred to the European Council for decision by unanimity (Art. 23 TEU). The possibility of a blocking veto remains, even for a common position or action to be taken in the framework of a common strategy, even though a Member State has to offer some explanations to use it. Such explanations are not a deterrent of veto, if one Member State is determined to defend its interests, which diverge from those of the majority. It transpires that the CFSP method is an improved intergovernmental cooperation method, but not much more than that. Even if the improvements brought by the Constitutional Treaty were implemented, the foreign and security policy could not become a "common policy" by the means put at its disposal.

A European Union Institute for Security Studies based in Paris and a European Union Satellite Centre with its headquarters at Torrejón de Ardoz in Spain support the decision-making process of the Union in the context of the CFSP, in particular of the ESDP, and contribute to its development, notably by conducting research and analysis in relevant fields[1]. **Administrative expenditure** concerning the CFSP is charged to the Community budget (Art. 28 TEU). On 13 June 1994, the Council defined the categories of expenditure regarded as administrative, to be financed from the "Council" section of the general budget. Concerning **operational expenditure** to be financed by the Member States, the Council agreed on sharing out on the basis of the gross national product.

---

[1]   Joint Actions 2001/554/CFSP and 2001/555/CFSP, OJ L 200, 25.07.2001.

8.2.2. The institutional framework of CFSP

Subject to the requirement laid down in Article 3 of the EU Treaty for the Council and the Commission **to ensure consistency in external relations**, and in accordance with their respective responsibilities under the Treaties, the Presidency, the Secretary-General/High Representative and the Commissioner for external relations, must cooperate closely in order to ensure overall continuity and coherence of action by the Union in external relations [see introduction to Part VI].

The Secretary-General of the Council, who is the **High Representative for the CFSP**, assists the Council in the matters coming within the scope of the CFSP, by contributing, in particular, to the formulation, preparation and implementation of policy decisions and, at the request of the Presidency, by conducting political dialogue with third parties (Art. 26 TEU). More specifically, according to the Helsinki European Council (10-11 December 1999), the High Representative of the Union **has the following tasks**:

*   assist the Presidency in coordinating work in the Council to ensure coherence on the various aspects of the Union's external relations;
*   contribute to preparing policy decisions and formulating options for the Council on foreign and security policy matters, so that it constantly focuses on the major political issues requiring an operational decision or political guidance;
*   contribute to the implementation of foreign and security policy decisions in close coordination with the Commission, Member States and other authorities responsible for effective application on the ground.

The Presidency represents the Union in all matters falling within the CFSP. It is responsible for the implementation of common measures and expresses the position of the Union in international organisations and conferences. The Commission is closely involved in those tasks of the Presidency. The latter is assisted by the High Representative for the CFSP and may be assisted by the next Member State to hold the Presidency (Art. 18 TEU). Thus, after Amsterdam, the so-called "**EU Troika**" on foreign policy consists of the Presidency, the High Representative for the CFSP and the Commission (the Commissioner for external relations), but may be enlarged to the next Presidency and/or a special representative appointed by the Council with a mandate in relation to particular policy issues. The Presidency must consult the European Parliament on the main aspects and the basic choices of the CFSP and must ensure that its views are duly taken into consideration (Art. 21 TEU).

The draft Constitution's principal amendment to the provisions of the Treaty on European Union was the institution of a **Union Minister for Foreign Affairs**, who would wear two hats, being both one of the Commission's Vice-Presidents and the President of the Foreign Affairs Council. This association of the Commission and the Council in the person of the Foreign Affairs Minister could be beneficial for the common foreign and security policy. Exercising the right of initiative of the Commission, the Union Minister for Foreign Affairs would contribute to the development of the CFSP, which he or she would carry out as mandated by the Council. The same would apply to the common security and defence policy (Art I-28). He or she would have responsibilities incumbent on the Commission in external relations and for coordinating the CFSP with other aspects of the Union's external action. By presiding over the Foreign Affairs Council, the Foreign Affairs Minister would contribute by his proposals to the preparation of common foreign and security policy and ensure implementation of European decisions adopted by the European Council and the Council of Ministers. The Foreign Affairs Minister would represent the EU in matters concerning the common foreign and security policy, conduct political dialogue on the Union's behalf and express the Union's position in international organisations and at international conferences and forums (Article III-305).

Although it is fully associated in the work carried out in the common foreign and security policy field, the European Commission [see section 4.1.2] does not have exclusive **right of initiative**. Both it and any Member State can refer to the Council any question relating to the common foreign and security policy and can submit proposals to the Council (Art. 22 TEU). A **Political Committee** consisting of Political Directors of the Member States monitors the international situation in the areas covered by common foreign and security policy and contributes to the definition of policies by delivering opinions to the Council at the latter's request or on its own initiative. It also monitors the implementation of agreed policies, without prejudice to the responsibilities of the Presidency, Commission and COREPER (Art. 25 TEU) [see section 4.1.4.].

A **Policy Planning and Early Warning Unit**, under the responsibility of the Secretary-General of the Council and consisting of personnel drawn from the General Secretariat of the Council, the Commission, the Member States and the WEU, has the following tasks: monitoring and analysing developments in areas relevant to the CFSP; providing assessments of the Union's foreign and security policy interests; providing early warning of events or situations which may have significant repercussions for the CFSP; producing policy option papers to be presented under the responsibility of the Presidency as a contribution to policy formulation in the Council.

According to the Constitutional Treaty, the Minister for Foreign Affairs would be in charge of a **European External Action Service** set up to assist the Minister in his or her functions (Article III-296). This service would be composed of officials from relevant departments of the General Secretariat of the Council of Ministers and of the Commission and staff seconded from national diplomatic services. This multinational service could develop into a real European diplomatic corps; a development which could enhance the image of the Union in the world and bring home the views of third countries on the EU as such rather than on its individual Member States.

However, the draft Constitution marked **no real progress in terms of decision-making** in the area of the CFSP. The use of legislative instruments such as European laws and framework laws would be excluded. The Council of Ministers would continue to decide by unanimity in most cases and, therefore, Member States would still have the right of veto. By way of derogation from the unanimity rule, the Council would act by qualified majority: when adopting European decisions defining a Union action or position on the basis of a European decision of the European Council relating to the Union's strategic interests and objectives; when adopting a European decision defining a Union action or position, on a proposal which the Union Minister for Foreign Affairs has presented following a specific request to him or her from the European Council; and when adopting a European decision implementing a European decision defining a Union action or position (Art. III-300). This "switchover" from unanimity to qualified majority would not apply to decisions with military implications or in the area of defence. Moreover, any Member State could declare its intention to oppose the adoption of a decision by qualified majority, the only difference with the actual situation being that it would have to cite "vital" rather than merely "important" reasons of national policy. But, of course, the definition of "vital" reasons could be as subjective as that of "important".

8.2.3. European security and defence policy

Common foreign and security policy covers all questions related to the security of the European Union, including the **progressive framing of a European security and defence policy (ESDP)**, which might in time lead to a common defence, should the European Council so decide. It shall in that case recommend to the Member States the adoption of such a decision in accordance with their respective constitutional requirements. The progressive framing of a common defence policy will be supported, when considered appropriate, by cooperation between the Member States in the field of armaments (Art. 17 TEU). The language used here gives an indication of the Member States' extreme caution in venturing into the field of common defence involving, in the long term, the integration of their Armed Forces. According to the Brussels European Council (October 1993) this policy must be aimed in particular at reducing risks and uncertainties which could impair the territorial integrity and political independence of the Union and of its Member States, their democratic nature, their economic stability and the stability of the neighbouring regions.

In this field, a diminishing role is played by the **Western European Union (WEU)**, the political and military alliance set up in May 6, 1955 and binding its member countries by a clause of automatic military engagement in the event of aggression against one of its signatories. The institutions of the WEU (Council, General Secretariat and Parliamentary Assembly) remain separate from those of the European Union, but must work in close cooperation with the latter and harmonise their work methods [see details below]. Not disposing an operational structure, the WEU plays essentially the role of a forum for political consultation. The EU Treaty stipulates that the WEU is an integral part of the development of the Union supporting it in framing the defence aspects of the CFSP and providing it with an operational capability. The EU shall foster closer institutional relations with the WEU with a view to the possibility of its integration into the Union (Art. 17 TEU).

To assume their responsibilities across the full range of conflict prevention and crisis management tasks defined in the EU Treaty, the so-called **Petersberg tasks**, the Member States, at the Helsinki European Council (10-11 December 1999), have decided to **develop more effective military capabilities** and establish new political and military structures for these tasks. In this connection, the objective is for the Union to have an autonomous capacity to take decisions and, where NATO as a whole is not engaged, to launch and then to conduct EU-led military operations in response to international crises. For this purpose, a "common European **headline goal**" was set: to deploy 60 000 men in less than 60 days and to sustain them for at least one year, for the purpose of EU-led conflict prevention and crisis management tasks (Petersberg tasks). Although the goal was attained in 2003, the capability development mechanism (CDM) presents several problems, such as command and control arrangements for operational headquarters, the principles and framework for capability requirements and coordination and synergy with NATO. The "2010 headline goal" is the capability to deploy forces on the ground no later than 10 days after the decision to launch the operation.

To pursue the headline goal of the European Security and Defence policy (ESDP), the following permanent **political and military bodies** have been established within the Council:

(a) a standing **Political and Security Committee (PSC)** in Brussels, composed of national representatives of senior/ambassadorial level, deals with all aspects of the CFSP, including the common European security and defence policy. In the case of a military crisis management operation, the PSC will exercise, under the authority of the Council, the political control and strategic direction of the operation[1];

(b) the **Military Committee (MC)**, composed of the chiefs of defence or their military delegates and a Chair appointed by the Council on the Committee's recommendation, gives military advice, makes recommendations to the PSC and provides military direction to the Military Staff[2];

(c) the **Military Staff (MS)**, composed of military personnel seconded from Member States to the General Secretariat of the Council, provides military expertise and support to the ESDP, including the conduct of early warning, situation assessment and

---

[1] Decision 2001/78, OJ L 27, 30.01.2001.
[2] Decision 2001/79, OJ L 27, 30.01.2001.

strategic planning for Petersberg tasks including identification of European national and multinational forces[1].

According to the Helsinki European Council, all Member States (defence ministers) are entitled to participate fully and on an equal footing in all decisions and deliberations of the Council and Council bodies on EU-led operations, but the commitment of national assets by Member States to such operations will be **based on their sovereign decision**. Russia, Ukraine and other European States engaged in political dialogue with the Union and other interested States may be invited to take part in the EU-led operations. A "European capability action plan", agreed by the Council on 19 November 2001, should incorporate all the efforts and investments, developments and coordination measures executed or planned at both national and multinational level with a view to improving existing resources and gradually developing the capabilities necessary for the Union's activities. The Council established a mechanism, called "Athena" having the necessary legal capacity for the financing of EU operations with military or defence implications[2].

Article 17 of the EU Treaty does not rule out the development of **closer cooperation between two or more Member States** on a bilateral level, in the framework of the WEU and the Atlantic Alliance, provided such cooperation does not run counter to or impede multilateral cooperation. Thus, on 5 November 1993, France, Germany and Belgium took the important initiative of placing under common command certain units of their armies. The **Eurocorps**, which is placed under the authority of a "Joint Committee" made up of the Heads of Staff and political directors of the three countries, could be used autonomously by these three countries, or else placed at the disposal of NATO and the WEU.

The same Article 17 (TEU) underlines that the policy of the Union does not prejudice the specific character of the security and defence policy of certain Member States, respects the obligations of certain Member States under the **North Atlantic Treaty Organisation (NATO)** and is compatible with the common security and defence policy established within that framework. For the Member States concerned, this means that the actions and decisions they undertake within the framework of EU military crisis management will respect at all times all their Treaty obligations as NATO allies. The Member States of the EU have agreed to have permanent and continuing consultations with the non-EU European allies, covering the full range of security, defence and crisis management issues. In the case of an EU-led operation using NATO assets and capabilities, non-EU European allies will, if they wish, participate in the operation, and will be involved in its planning and preparation in accordance with the procedures laid down within NATO. In the case of any EU-led operation not requiring recourse to NATO assets and capabilities, non-EU European allies will be invited, upon a decision of the Council, to participate. In taking decisions on participation, the Council will take account of the security concerns of the non-EU European allies.

The European Council met in extraordinary session on 21 September 2001 in order to analyse the international situation following the terrorist attacks in the United States and to impart the necessary impetus to the actions of the European Union. Stating that terrorism is a real challenge to the world and to Europe, the European Council has decided that **the fight against terrorism** will, more than ever, be a priority objective of the European Union, which should play a greater part in the efforts of the international community to prevent and stabilise regional conflicts.

---

[1]   Decision 2001/80, OJ L 27, 30.01.2001 and Decision 2005/395, OJ L 132, 26.05.2005.
[2]   Decision 2004/197, OJ L 63, 28.02.2004 and Decision 2005/68, OJ L 27, 29.01.2005.

In the light of the **terrorist attacks in Madrid** on 11 March 2004, the Brussels European Council (25-26 March 2004) decided to revise the EU's action plan to combat terrorism, setting the following objectives: deepen the international consensus and enhance international efforts to combat terrorism; reduce the access of terrorists to financial and other economic resources; maximise capacity within EU bodies and Member States to detect, investigate and prosecute terrorists and prevent terrorist attacks; protect the security of international transport and ensure effective systems of border control; enhance the capability of the European Union and of Member States to deal with the consequences of a terrorist attack; address the factors which contribute to support for, and recruitment into, terrorism. Moreover, the European Council declared that in the spirit of the solidarity clause laid down in Article I-43 of the draft Treaty establishing a Constitution for Europe, the Member States and the acceding States shall act jointly in a spirit of solidarity mobilise all the instruments at their disposal, including military resources, if one of them is the victim of a terrorist attack.

The draft **Constitutional Treaty** would strengthen the ESDP. More missions were added to the so-called Petersberg tasks, such as joint disarmament operations, military advice and assistance tasks, conflict prevention and post-conflict stabilisation. The draft Constitution also states that all these tasks may contribute to the fight against terrorism (Article III-309). A solidarity clause was introduced whereby the other Member States would provide assistance if a Member State was the victim of a terrorist attack or a natural or man-made disaster. In this case, the Union would mobilise all the instruments at its disposal, including the military resources made available by the Member States, in order to assist the Member State concerned (Article I-43). More important is the **mutual defence clause** of the draft Constitution asserting that, if a Member State was the victim of armed aggression on its territory, the other Member States would have towards it an obligation of aid and assistance by all the means in their power, in accordance with Article 51 of the United Nations Charter (Article I-41(7)).

The **European Defence Agency (EDA)** was set up in 2004 in order to develop projects and programmes aimed at supporting the development of European security and defence policy[1]. Subject to the Council's authority and open to participation by all willing Member States, the Agency aims at developing defence capabilities in the field of crisis management, promoting and enhancing European armaments cooperation, strengthening the European defence industrial and technological base (DTIB), creating a competitive European defence equipment market and promoting research aimed at leadership in strategic technologies for future defence and security capabilities. A Green Paper of the Commission aims at the gradual creation of a European defence equipment market (EDEM) which is more transparent and open between Member States[2].

The **European Security and Defence College (ESDC)** is a network dealing with security and defence policy issues in the European Union[3]. This college aims to provide training in the field of ESDP and to promote a common understanding of European security and defence policy among civilian and military personnel.

Eleven EU States are members of the **Western European Union (WEU)**, whereas Ireland, Denmark, Sweden and Finland have opted for the "observer" status. The other European members of NATO, Norway, Turkey and Iceland are considered as "associate members", while Hungary, Poland, the Czech Republic, Slovakia, Romania, Bulgaria, Lithuania, Latvia and Estonia are considered as "associate partners". With a view to strengthening the European pillar of the Atlantic Alliance, the Member States of the WEU state their readiness to develop further the close working links between the WEU and the Alliance and to strengthen the role, responsibilities and contributions of the WEU Member States in the Alliance. The WEU should act in conformity with the positions adopted in the Atlantic Alliance. However, WEU Member States may intensify their coordination on Alliance issues which represent an important common interest, with the aim of introducing joint positions agreed in the WEU into the process of consultation in the Alliance. A Council Decision concerns the arrangements for enhanced cooperation between the EU and the WEU, notably close coordination of consulta-

---

[1] Joint action 2004/551/CFSP, OJ L 245, 17.07.2004 and Decision 2004/658/CFSP, OJ L 300, 25.09.2004.
[2] COM (2004) 608, 23 September 2004.
[3] Joint Action 2005/575/CFSP, OJ L 194, 26.07.2005.

tion and decision-making processes in each organisation[1]. All EU Member States participate fully on an equal footing in planning and decision-making in the WEU[2]. On its part, the WEU has undertaken to contribute to the gradual formulation of a common EU defence policy, monitor its implementation by developing its operational role and draw up, in conjunction with the EU, arrangements designed to strengthen cooperation between the two organisations.

The **Organisation for Security and Cooperation in Europe (OSCE)** is also called upon to play a key role in pan-European security and cooperation. 52 States participate in the OSCE: all the EU Member States, the countries of Central and Eastern Europe, the members of the Commonwealth of Independent States (CIS), the United States and Canada. The OSCE charter, known as Helsinki II, includes provisions for conflict prevention and crisis management. It also provides for the establishment of a security forum. The European Commission takes part in the OSCE's activities, contributing to its work on the economic and human dimension of the security model.

The **Stability Pact in Europe**, signed the 21 March 1995 in Paris, is a European Union initiative launched by the Brussels European Council of October 1993[3]. This Pact is designed to foster peace and stability in Europe, by resolving the problem of minorities, reinforcing the inviolability of frontiers, strengthening the development of democracy and regional cooperation in Central and Eastern Europe. The OSCE was entrusted with the follow-up and the implementation of the Pact. The stabilisation effort is currently centred on south-eastern Europe [see section 25.3.].

In the framework of the implementation of the EU strategy **against proliferation of weapons of mass destruction**, the EU supports the aims of the Organisation for the Prohibition of Chemical Weapons (OPCW)[4]. The EU has pledged compliance with the international non-proliferation system enacted by the Convention on the prohibition of the development, production and stockpiling of bacteriological (biological) and toxic weapons and on their destruction[5]. The EU promotes the strengthening of the Biological and Toxin Weapons Convention (BTWC)[6]. It is actively promoting the early entry into force of the Comprehensive Nuclear Test-Ban Treaty[7] and is supporting the draft international code of conduct against ballistic missile proliferation[8]. A joint action of the Council is intended to contribute to the strengthening of the international nuclear non-proliferation system, by promoting transparency in nuclear-related export controls[9]. A Community regime exists for the control of exports of dual-use military/civilian items and technology[10]. Joint actions concerning anti-personnel mines include a moratorium on the production and on the export of such mines and a major Union contribution to international mine clearance under the Ottawa Convention[11]. The Community has undertaken action in mine-clearing operations[12] and against anti-personnel mines in developing countries[13].

In conclusions adopted on 18 March 2003, the Council recognised the importance of the defence industry as a substantial regional, national and transnational employer requiring a national, regional and EU-wide perspective on its working methods. Since standardisation was an important pre-condition to fulfil the building of a strong **European defence industry**, the Council considered that the gradual setting-up of a European defence equipment market and the consolidation of a European industrial base should call for an effort to rationalise the relevant standards[14].

In conclusions on **international terrorism** adopted on 8 October 2001, the Council welcomed the adoption of Resolution 1373 (2001) by the United Nations Security Council and reiterated the Union's determination to attack the sources which fund terrorism, in close cooperation with the United States. In fact the EU imposed certain specific restrictive measures directed against certain persons and entities associated with Usama bin Laden, the Al-Qaida network and the Taliban[15]. The Council affirmed that the provision or collection of funds to be used for terrorist acts should be criminalised, and that consequently, these financial assets or economic resources should be frozen[16]. A Regulation created a Community legal instrument for combating the

---

[1]   Decision 1999/404/CFSP, OJ L 153, 19.06.1999.
[2]   Council Decision 1999/321, OJ L 123, 13.05.1999.
[3]   Decision 93/728/CFSP, OJ L 339, 31.12.1993 and Decision 94/367/CFSP, OJ L 165, 01.07.1994.
[4]   Joint Action 2004/797/CFSP, OJ L 349, 25.11.2004 and Joint Action 2005/913/CFSP, OJ L 331, 17.12.2005.
[5]   Common Position 96/408/CFSP, OJ L 168, 06.07.1996.
[6]   Common Position 1999/346/CFSP, OJ L 133, 28.05.1999 and Joint Action 2006/184, OJ L 65, 07.03.2006.
[7]   Common Position 1999/533/CFSP, OJ L 204, 04.08.1999 and Decision 2003/567, OJ L 192, 31.07.2003.
[8]   Common position 2001/567/CFSP, OJ L 202, 27.07.2001 and Joint Action 2002/406, OJ L 140, 30.05.2002.
[9]   Joint Action 97/288/CFSP, OJ L 120, 12.05.1997.
[10] Regulation 1334/2000 and Decision 2000/402/CFSP, OJ L 159, 30.06.2000 and Regulation 394/2006, OJ L 74, 13.03.2006.
[11] Joint Action 97/817/CFSP, OJ L 338, 09.12.1997.
[12] Regulation 1725/2001, OJ L 234, 01.09.2001.
[13] Regulation 1724/2001, OJ L 234, 01.09.2001 and Regulation 2110/2005, OJ L 344, 27.12.2005.
[14] COM (2003) 113, 11 March 2003.
[15] Common position 2002/402/CFSP and Regulation 881/2002, OJ L 139 29.05.2002 last amended by Regulation 357/2006, OJ L 59, 01.03.2006.
[16] Common positions 2001/930/CFSP, 2001/931/CFSP, OJ L 344, 28.12.2001 and Common Position 2006/380, OJ L 144, 31.05.2006.

funding of terrorism[1]. The EU concluded an agreement with NATO on the security of information[2]. The fight against terrorism is progressively incorporated into all aspects of the Union's external relations policy.

The European Union Police Mission in Bosnia and Herzegovina is one example of the European Union's commitment to stabilise post-conflict regions, and to help establish the rule of law. By promoting stability, including by strengthening local law enforcement capabilities, norms and standards, the European Union helps to deny terrorist organisations the opportunity to take root. In March 2003, an EU military operation was launched in the Former Yugoslav Republic of Macedonia using NATO assets and capabilities on the basis of the UN Security Council resolution 1371[3].

8.3. Appraisal and outlook

The two wings of the last storey of the European edifice are built at uneven pace. The wing of internal affairs has much advanced, while the wing of external affairs is far behind. This is due to the different methods used for the construction of each one. The perception of the need for a **common policy in internal affairs** has led to the effective disbanding of the so-called third pillar of the Union and to the placement of most subjects concerning it inside the principal edifice of the Community managed by the Community decision-making procedure. As in all areas where common policies exist, much progress was made since the entry into force of the Treaty of Amsterdam and particularly since the programme set by the Tampere European Council for the creation of an **area of freedom, security and justice**. The achievements of the common policy include: reinforcement of the rights of citizens and their families to move and reside freely in the territory of the Union; foundations of a common immigration and asylum policy; consolidation of the integrated management of external borders; better access to justice, notably through application of the principle of mutual recognition in the civil and commercial spheres; introduction of a European arrest warrant; and cooperation through legislation to combat cross-border crime and terrorism. In the aftermath of the terrorist attacks of 11 September 2001, Member States reinforced their **counter-terrorism** machinery in addition to enhancing international cooperation. They also assessed their counter-terrorism capacity, adopting new laws and allocating additional financial or personnel resources to strengthen their machinery. They placed special emphasis on the exchange of information, coordination and cooperation at both national and international levels, protection of critical infrastructure, including the identification and protection of vulnerabilities, and crisis and management of their consequences. Nowadays, the greatest challenge of the Union in this area is tackling the root causes of **illegal migration** by its aid to development policy, notably through the promotion of economic growth, good governance and the protection of human rights in countries of origin [see section 24.1].

To safeguard its area of freedom, security and justice, the Union must also develop a capacity to act and be regarded as a significant partner on the international scene. This is the objective of the foreign policy of the Union. The Treaty on the EU invites the Union to "assert its identity on the international scene", but it does not give it the instruments to pursue this goal effectively. Certainly, some progress has been made. The **common foreign and security policy** (CFSP) has been given in Amsterdam more coherent instruments and a more effective decision-making procedure. Common strategies and "constructive abstention" give the possibility to the European Council and the Council to act by qualified majority, even if some Member States do not agree with a common

---

[1] Regulation 2580/2001, OJ L 344, 28.12.2001 and Decision 2006/379, OJ L 144, 31.05.2006.
[2] Decision 2003/211, OJ L 80, 27.03.2003.
[3] Joint Action 2003/92, OJ L 34, 11.02.2003, Decision 2003/202, OJ L 76, 22.03.2003 and Decision 2003/222, OJ L 82, 29.03.2003.

policy. Through the recent development of the European security and defence policy (ESDP) and the strengthening of its capabilities, both civil and military, the Union has established crisis-management structures and procedures which enable it to analyse and plan, to take decisions and, where NATO as such is not involved, to launch and carry out military crisis-management operations. These are signs that the common foreign and security policy of the Union is slowly gaining momentum.

But there is still much confusion in the external activities of the Union and its Member States are **still not speaking with a single voice** in the scene of world affairs. It is no wonder, therefore, that the Member States of the Union were radically divided when their supposedly common foreign and security policy was tested for the first time: the March 2003 war and occupation of Iraq under American aegis, without the consent of the Security Council of the United Nations. The prevailing intergovernmental cooperation, even if improved by the Constitutional Treaty, cannot lead to a really common policy. The very term "common foreign and security policy" is misleading. The citizens hear "common policy" and do not see anything resembling that. If the Treaty called for a cooperation in foreign and security policy, the citizens would at least understand better what is meant by it. Now, they rightly believe that they are derided when their political leaders speak about a common policy and at the first test of such a policy hide behind their national interests (real or imaginary), in order to undermine it. The truth is that a common policy cannot be achieved with intergovernmental cooperation.

In fact, the external activities of the Union are conducted through two parallel channels: the Community method in the fields of foreign trade and of aid to development; and the loose mechanisms of the common foreign and security policy, which do not allow the Union to exert all its potential influence on world affairs [see Part VI and section 8.2.1.]. The Union thus resembles an imposing edifice sheltering internal economic and other common policies, an edifice without any outlet to the outside, other than the small windows possibly opened in case of need by the foreign policies of the Member States, provided these are not contradictory. So as to start becoming a common policy, the CFSP should **be provided with the means of such a policy**, i.e. basically decision-making by an enhanced majority of the Member States and the population of the Union with full participation of the Commission, the Parliament, the European Court of Justice and specific organs in the taking and the execution of the common decisions [see section 4.3.].

To assume its responsibilities as a global power, the EU should **rule out the use of unanimity** and hence of the veto in the common foreign and security policy. This policy should be given the necessary resources (budget, efficient procedures, network of external delegations, etc.). The actual functions of the High Representative for the CFSP and of the Commissioner for External Relations should be merged into the tasks of the Minister for Foreign Affairs (envisaged by the Constitutional Treaty), ensuring coherent single representation of collective EU external interests, a leading role in crisis management and consistency with other common policies such as trade and aid to development. The Commissioner/High Representative for External Relations should be proposed by the European Council and named by the European Parliament [see section 4.4.]. Finally, the two wings of the foreign and security policy should back each other and make a coherent whole, because a foreign policy that cannot be enforced cannot be respected.

The same considerations apply to the common defence policy. The Community decision-making method should be applied to the European security and defence policy (ESDP), thus making it really common and truly European. The ESDP should be based on a common armament policy, which could rationalise, boost and make more competitive the armaments industries of the Member States. This could mean, inter alia, that the single market and common commercial policy could be applied to the defence industries. This integration could alleviate the current deficiencies of European military capabilities in the field of intelligence, logistics, communications and air transport systems. Effective public procurement and standardisation of armaments industries could help restructure, rationalise and strengthen European defence. When Europe realised its full defence potential, it would be ready to assume its role as a global player.

The European Union does not have to wait until it has built up its feeble military forces in order to have an independent international policy and world influence capable to rival those of the United States. The world today is not one in which military forces are automatically the most effective means of power. NATO is a relic of the Cold War. It no longer serves to protect Europe from any threat. On the other hand, for the United States, NATO has to exist because it provides the indispensable material and strategic infrastructure for American military and strategic deployments throughout Europe, Eurasia, the Middle East and Africa. NATO procures, indeed, to the United States a military presence, usually with extraterritorial privileges in most EU countries. If NATO is, as it claims, an alliance of independent and politically equal countries, the EU countries, which have an overwhelming majority in it, should have the democratic right to direct its political decisions towards their own national interests, which may but do not necessarily coincide with those of the USA.

An important element of both JHA and CFSP is the **protection of the external borders** of the Union. The single market and the Schengen agreement have de facto rendered common the external borders of the EU. Even the innermost countries of the Union are exposed to illegal actions and threats occurring at the borders of the outermost countries. There is a clear common interest for the development of a common policy for the management of the external borders of the Union, in order to protect them against illegal immigration, trafficking of goods and human beings and, of course, passage of terrorists. This policy should entail common legislation, integrated risk analysis, burden sharing, cooperation mechanisms and coordinated staff. Moreover, major external challenges confront Europe's area of freedom, security and justice, namely terrorism, organised crime and illegal immigration. The EU should therefore promote the rule of law, security and stability outside its borders by means of all its external policies, including the CFSP. Citizens would certainly appreciate such a policy, which would be "common" not just in name.

Bibliography on JHA and CFSP

- BONO Giovanna. "EU security policy after 9/11" in *Studia diplomatica*, v. 59, n. 1, 2006, p. 5-116.
- BRETHERTON Charlotte, VOGLER John. *The European Union as a global actor.* London: Routledge, 2006.
- CRUM Ben. "Parliamentarization of the CFSP through informal institution-making?: The fifth European Parliament and the EU High Representative" in *Journal of European Public Policy*, v. 13, n. 3, April 2006, p. 383-401.
- DUKE Simon, VANHOONACKER Sophie. "Administrative governance in the CFSP: development and practice" in *European Foreign Affairs Review*, v. 11, n. 2, Summer 2006, p. 163-182.
- DÜVELL Franck. *Illegal immigration in Europe: beyond control?* Basingstoke:Palgrave Macmillan, 2006.
- ELGSTRÖM Ole, SMITH Michael (eds.). *The European Union's roles in international politics: concepts and analysis.* Abingdon: Routledge, 2006.
- ENDERLEIN Henrik. "The euro and political union: do economic spillovers from monetary integration affect the legitimacy of EMU?" in *Journal of European Public Policy*, v. 13, n. 7, 2006, p. 1133-1146.
- GARCIA-JOURDAN Sophie. *L'émergence d'un espace européen de liberté, de sécurité et de justice.* Bruxelles: Bruylant, 2005.
- GARBAGNATI KETVEL Maria Gisella. "The jurisdiction of the European Court of Justice in respect of the Common Foreign and Security Policy" in *International and Comparative Law Quarterly*, v. 55, n. 1, January 2006, p. 77-120.
- GOSALBO BONO Ricardo. "Some reflections on the CFSP legal order" in *Common Market Law Review*, v. 43, n. 2, April 2006, p. 337-394.

- MÜLLER-BRANDECK-BOCQUET Gisela (ed.). *The future of the European foreign, security and defence policy after enlargement.* Baden Baden: Nomos, 2006.
- HOUBEN Marc. *International crisis management: the approach of European states.* London : Routledge, 2005.
- OJANEN Hanna. "The EU and NATO: two competing models for a common defence policy" in *Journal of Common Market Studies*, v. 44, n. 1, March 2006, p. 57-76.
- PEERS Steve. *EU justice and home affairs law.* 2nd ed. Oxford: Oxford University Press, 2006.
- PEERS Steve, ROGERS Nicola (eds.). *EU immigration and asylum law: text and commentary.* Leiden: M. Nijhoff, 2006.
- ROHAN Sally. *Western European Union: International Politics Between Alliance and Integration.* London: Routledge, 2006.
- SCHIERUP Carl-Ulrik (et al.). *Migration, citizenship, and the European welfare state: a European dilemma.* Oxford: Oxford University Press, 2006.
- SCHMITT Burkard. *Defence procurement in the European Union: the current debate.* Paris: Institute for Security Studies, 2005.
- STEFANOU Constantin, XANTHAKI Helen (eds.). *Financial crime in the EU: criminal records as effective tools or missed oppurtunities?* The Hague: Kluwer Law International, 2005.
- WALSH James I. "Intelligence-sharing in the European Union: institutions are not enough" in *Journal of Common Market Studies*, v. 44, n. 3, September 2006, p. 625-643.

Part III: Policies concerning the citizens

Chapter 9.   Citizens' rights and participation
Chapter 10. Information, audiovisual policy and culture
Chapter 11. Consumer protection policy

European citizens are present at and are taking part both wittingly and unwittingly in, an experience that will leave its mark on the history of the planet for a long time: the gradual and free unification of nations, which until very recently were hostile to each other. The **keyword of the multinational integration experience is freedom**: freedom of movement of persons, of goods, of services and of capital [see chapter 6]; freedom based on human rights, democratic institutions and the rule of law [see section 8.1.], but, also and above all freedom of States and their people to belong or not to the Union [see section 1.1.2]. Economic and political freedom is the water of the mortar for the construction of the European edifice. The citizens who love these freedoms should normally be conscious or unconscious supporters of European integration, if only they realised the effects of this integration on their professional and everyday lives. As we will see in the next chapter, however, most citizens of the Union are unaware of the benefits of European integration.

The fact is that **all Europeans take part** in one way or another in the construction of Europe: the housewife filling her basket with products from the four corners of the European Union; the motorist choosing the car which suits him without regard to its origin; the worker employed by a Community firm in his country or the firm's country; the businessman rushing across borders to conclude deals with foreign partners; the student studying in a partner country; the young person participating in an exchange programme; the pensioner from a northern country who takes his vacations or his residence in a country of Southern Europe; the citizen of one of those countries who aspires to come into contact with the lifestyle and culture of his neighbours. They all participate in the construction of the large European edifice without realising it. Why? Because all these activities, which were difficult or unthinkable at the time of economic protectionism and which now appear so natural, bring the citizens of the Member States close to each other and to the process of European integration.

Each time the citizens choose a product or service from a partner country, they unknowingly contribute their grain of sand to the mortar necessary to cement the European edifice [see section 3.1.]. The citizens are not aware of the importance of these acts because they find them as natural as the air they breathe. In fact, they have become as essential to their daily lives as that air. They should, however, realise that their lives would be very different if they did not enjoy the freedom of choice made possible by European integration.

The title of this part of the book is misleading, since it limits the policies concerning the citizens to only three fields. In reality, measures of great importance to the individual in areas such as employment, social protection, the fight against poverty and health care

are part of social policy and are dealt with in the Chapter on social progress. That Chapter also tackles the major issues of education and training, security at work and public health. Other measures of concern for the citizens are covered by the common policies on justice and home affairs, environment protection, etc. Thus, the following pages look at measures of interest to the individual not touched upon in other parts of this book, notably the rights of citizens, information, audiovisual and cultural activities and protection of consumers' interests.

Chapter 9

CITIZENS' RIGHTS AND PARTICIPATION

<u>Diagram of the chapter</u>

In their great majority citizens ignore the many rights that they have acquired thanks to European integration, some of which are founded directly on the EC and EU Treaties, but most are based on the policies and the legislation derived from them. This ignorance is due to deficient information of the general public, which the European institutions are trying unsuccessfully to develop, but which should be boosted by a common policy of the Community and the Member States [see chapter 10]. A good cooperation between Community and national information sources is also necessary for an efficient protection of the health, safety and economic interests of European consumers [see chapter 11].

9.1. Citizenship of the Union and its attributes

The Treaty of Nice (following the Treaty of Amsterdam) establishes the **citizenship of the Union**, which is complementary to national citizenship. Every person holding the nationality of a Member State is a citizen of the Union. Citizens of the Union, thus defined, enjoy the rights conferred by the Treaty and are subject to the duties imposed thereby (Art. 17 TEC). Every citizen of the Union is, in the territory of a third country in which the Member State of which he or she is a national is not represented, entitled to protection by the diplomatic or consular authorities of any Member State, on the same conditions as the nationals of that State (Art. 20 TEC). Two Decisions specify the **right to diplomatic protection**[1]. This right is not negligible, as there are many cases where one Member State is not represented in a third country. It includes assistance in the event of death, illness or serious accident, arrest, detention or assault as well as help and repatriation in the event of difficulty. In practical terms, EU nationals whose passport or travel document is lost, stolen or temporarily unavailable in a country where their own Member State has no representation, may obtain an **emergency travel document**, from the diplomatic or consular representation of another Member State[2].

In addition, every citizen of the Union residing in a Member State of which he or she is not a national has the **right to vote and to stand as a candidate** at European and municipal elections in the Member State in which he resides, under the same conditions as nationals of that State (Art. 19 TEC). A Community directive lays down arrangements for the exercise of the right to vote and to stand as a candidate **in elections to the European Parliament** in the Member State of residence[3]. While including provisions to ensure freedom of choice and to prevent individuals from voting or standing for election in two constituencies at once, the Directive is based on the principles of equality and non-discrimination and is designed to facilitate the exercise by the citizens of the Union of their right to vote and to stand for election in the Member State where they reside.

The Directive laying down detailed arrangements for the exercise of the right to vote and stand as candidates in **municipal elections** ensures the same rights to Union citizens in elections by direct universal suffrage at local government level[4]. Member States may, however, reserve for their own nationals the posts of mayor and deputy mayor, which involve participation in an official authority or in the election of a parliamentary assembly. The Directive also allows Member States where the proportion of nationals of other Union countries exceeds 20% to restrict the right to vote and stand as candidate to those who meet certain criteria regarding length of residence.

Article 6 of the TEU states that the Union is founded on the principles of liberty, democracy, respect for **human rights and fundamental freedoms**, and the rule of law. While respecting the national identities of its Member States, the Union must respect fundamental rights, as they result from the constitutional traditions common to the Member States, as general principle of Community law. The EC Treaty explicitly acknowledges that human rights include economic and social rights, and lays down the principle of equal rights for citizens without discrimination based on sex, racial or ethnic origin, religion or belief, disability, age or sexual orientation (Art. 13 TEC). Upon a proposal from one-third of the Member States, the Parliament or the Commission, the Council, acting by a four-fifths majority of its members and with the assent of Parliament, can declare that a clear danger exists of a Member State committing a serious breach of fundamental rights and address to that Member State appropriate recommendations.

The average citizen may think that fundamental freedoms are a normal attribute of any democratic State; not particularly of the European Union. This is certainly right, but the EU guarantees that **a State that does not respect the fundamental freedoms of its citizens cannot become a member** and that the government of a Member State cannot injure its citizens' rights, if it does not want to exclude its country from the Union. Indeed, Article 49 of the TEU makes membership of the Union conditional upon the respect of the principles set

[1]   Decision 95/553/EC, OJ L 314, 28.12.1995.
[2]   Decision 96/409/CFSP, OJ L 168, 06.07.1996.
[3]   Directive 93/109, OJ L 329, 30.12.1993.
[4]   Directive 94/80, OJ L 368, 31.12.1994 and Directive 96/30, OJ L 122, 22.05.1996.

out in Article 6 and Article 7 (TEU) provides action in the event of a breach by a Member State of the principles on which the Union is founded. The Council, in the composition of the Heads of State or Government, acting by unanimity, but without taking into account the vote of the representative of the Member State concerned, may determine the existence of a serious and persistent breach by a Member State of those principles. Where such a determination has been made, the Council, acting by a qualified majority, may decide to suspend certain of the rights deriving from the application of the Treaty to the State in question, including its voting rights in the Council. The Commission has outlined the criteria for assessment of a "clear risk" and a "serious and persistent" breach, making it clear that the procedure is geared to tackling risk or actual breach through a comprehensive political approach[1].

With a view to bringing citizens closer to the European Union and its institutions, and intensifying links between citizens from different Member States, particularly by way of town-twinning arrangements, a Community action programme gives financial support to bodies working in the field of **active European citizenship** and promoting civic participation[2]. This is a drop in the ocean of citizen's ignorance and indifference that we expose in the next chapter [see section 10.1.].

9.2. Citizens' rights

Protection of fundamental rights is a founding principle of the Union and an indispensable prerequisite for its legitimacy. Article 6 of the EU Treaty states that "the Union shall respect fundamental rights, as guaranteed by the European Convention for the Protection of Human Rights and Fundamental Freedoms signed in Rome on 4 November 1950 and as they result from the constitutional traditions common to the Member States, as general principles of Community law". Moreover, the **Charter of fundamental rights of European citizens** was officially proclaimed at the Nice European Council (7-9 December 2000) by the European Parliament, the Council and the Commission[3]. It is divided into chapters dealing with the universal values of human dignity, freedom, equality, solidarity, citizenship and justice. It is designed to make more visible and explicit to the European Union's citizens the fundamental rights, which are already derived from a variety of international and Community sources, such as the European Convention on Human Rights, the Community Treaties and the case-law of the Court of Justice. Alongside the standard civil and political rights and the rights of citizens deriving from the Community Treaties, the charter incorporates fundamental social and economic rights, such as the rights of workers to collective bargaining, to take strike action and to be informed and consulted. The charter is likely to become mandatory through the Court of Justice's interpretation of it as belonging to the general principles of Community law[4].

With the emergence of information systems spanning the entire internal market, the European Union has increasingly to concentrate on the **protection of the personal data** of its citizens [see also sections 17.3.5. and 17.3.6.]. Thus a Directive aims at the development of the information society and the service sector in the EU, while guaranteeing individuals a high level of protection with regard to the processing of personal data (safe harbour privacy principles)[5]. Accordingly, it imposes obligations on data controllers such as public authorities, companies and associations, and establishes rights for data subjects, such as the right to be informed of processing carried out, the right of access to data and the right to ask for data to be corrected. In any event, the Directive prohibits the processing of sensitive data, such as data revealing racial or ethnic origin, political opinions, religious or philosophical beliefs, or state of health, except in certain circumstances that are exhaustively listed, in particular when the data subject has given his explicit

---

[1] Communication of the Commission, COM (2003) 606, 15 October 2003.
[2] Decision 2004/100, OJ L 30, 04.02.2004.
[3] Solemn proclamation, OJ C 364, 18.12.2000.
[4] COM(2000) 644, 11 October 2000.
[5] Directive 95/46, OJ L 281, 23.11.1995.

consent or where a substantial public interest requires such processing (e.g. medical or scientific research). Community institutions and bodies must also protect the fundamental rights and freedoms of individuals, and in particular their right to privacy with respect to the processing of personal data [1]. An independent supervisory body, the European Data Protection Supervisor, monitors the application of the relevant rules[2].

In addition to the fundamental rights, as defined in the Charter of the Union and in the European Convention for the Protection of Human Rights and Fundamental Freedoms signed in Rome on 4 November 1950, the citizens of the European Union have many rights, some of which they are not even aware of because they appear obvious. Their self-evident nature is a consequence of the existence of the Union and the membership of their State of origin to it. The Court of Justice has established that Community law, independent from the legislation of the Member States, can create obligations and rights for individuals[3]. These rights are so numerous that it would be tedious to list them all here. Almost all **the provisions of Community law examined in this book create rights** and obligations for the citizens of the EU's Member States, particularly as regards professional activities. The weight of this law is growing as European integration marches forward. It is superimposed on national law and in many cases simply replaces it [see section 3.3.]. It therefore has growing influence over the professional and day-to-day lives of European citizens.

Some examples may illustrate the importance of Community law **for the professional activities** of citizens. Traders have the right to consider the entire European Union as a potential market and therefore to purchase in any of the Member States and sell anywhere in the Union without any import duties or quantitative restrictions [see sections 5.1. and 6.2.]. Workers have the right to seek employment anywhere they wish in the Union, set up home with their family in the country where they are working and remain there even after they have lost their job [see section 6.4.1.]; they have the right to exactly the same social benefits as the citizens of the Member State in which they are residing [see section 6.4.2.]. Industrialists have the right to set up subsidiaries or branches anywhere in the EU where they feel that favourable growth conditions for their company exist and to transfer capital to and from these subsidiaries without restriction [see section 6.7.]. They have the right to borrow investment capital from a financial institution established in another country of the Union under the conditions prevalent in that country [see section 6.6.1.]. Farmers have the right to guaranteed prices for their produce and therefore to a certain guarantee of income [see sections 21.4.2. and 21.4.3.]; sea fishermen also enjoy this right [see section 22.3.]. Members of the professions - lawyers, architects, doctors and so on - have the right to set up a practice and to work in any Member State [see section 6.5.].

Some Community policies influence not only the professional life, but also the **everyday life of citizens**. Thus, important measures for the citizens in the fields of employment, vocational training, security at work and public health have their origin in the Community social policy. Furthermore, obligations imposed on industrialists by the Community policies of environment and consumers' protection have important effects on the quality of life of citizens. The citizens have the right to purchase goods in any one country of the Union at the conditions prevailing in that country and to take them to their country of origin without paying customs duties or any tax supplements [see section 5.1.2.]. They have the right to use any banking, insurance, telecommunications and

---

[1]   Regulation 45/2001, OJ L 8, 12.01.2001.
[2]   Decision 1247/2002, OJ L 183, 12.07.2002.
[3]   Judgment of 5 February 1963, case 26/62, van Gend en Loos, ECR 1963, p. 1.

audiovisual service offered in the large European market. They have the right to be treated by the administrative or judicial authorities of a country of the Union in the same way as the nationals of that country, i.e. without any discrimination on grounds of nationality (Art 12 TEC). This right covers a wide range of situations and human relations such as financial, contractual, family or student, which fall within the scope of Community law[1].

The Nice Treaty confers on every citizen of the Union a primary and individual **right to move and reside freely** within the territory of the Member States, subject to the limitations and conditions laid down in the Treaty and to the measures adopted to give it effect (Art. 2 TEU and Art. 18 TEC). Therefore, Directive 2004/38 replaced various instruments of Community law concerning freedom of movement and residence with a single text, aimed at reinforcing this fundamental entitlement of EU citizens by means of more flexible conditions and formalities and better protection against expulsion[2]. By virtue of this Directive, EU citizens enjoy right of residence provided that they satisfy certain conditions, notably if they themselves and the members of their families have sickness insurance covering all the risks in the host Member State. The directive facilitates considerably the freedom of movement and right of residence of family members of EU citizens, including the registered partner if the legislation of the host Member State treats registered partnership as equivalent to marriage. In addition, family members enjoy enhanced legal protection, notably in the event of the death of the EU citizen on whom they depend or the dissolution of the marriage, subject to certain conditions. The right of residence in any Member State has been teamed up with a number of practical measures such as the mutual recognition of driving licences[3].

Many EU countries signed, on June 19, 1990, the **Schengen Convention** for the abolition of border checks at the frontiers between them, the reinforcement of controls at external borders and the cooperation among their administrations[4]. To this end, they developed various cooperation tools, notably the Schengen Information System (SIS), a computerised data bank containing all search warrants issued by the Member States in the system and all supplementary information necessary in connection with the entry of alerts[5]. A Protocol annexed to the Treaty of Amsterdam integrates the Schengen "acquis" - i.e., the existing legislation - into the framework of the European Union[6] and allows the signatories to the Schengen Convention (the Member States of the Union minus the United Kingdom and Ireland plus Norway and Iceland[7]) to initiate between them, within the legal and institutional framework of the Union, cooperation in the areas covered by the Convention. Ireland participates in all aspects of the Schengen *acquis* with the exception of those elements linked to border controls, notably cross-border surveillance and hot pursuit[8]. The United Kingdom participates in cooperation in police, judicial and criminal matters, drug trafficking and the Schengen information system[9]. A Community Code establishes rules governing the movement of persons across borders as well as rules governing border control of persons crossing the external borders of the Member States of the European Union (**Schengen Borders Code**)[10]. Some new functions were

---

[1] Judgment of 12 May 1998, Case C-85/96, ECR 1998, p. I-2691.
[2] Directive 2004/38, OJ L 158, 30.04.2004.
[3] Directive 91/439, OJ L 237, 24.08.1991 and Directive 2003/59, OJ L 226, 10.09.2003.
[4] Schengen Convention, OJ L 239, 22.09.2000.
[5] Regulation 2424/2001 and Decision 2001/886, OJ L 328, 13.12.2001 and Regulation 871/2004, OJ L 162, 30.04.2004.
[6] Decisions 1999/435 and 1999/436, OJ L 176, 10.07.1999.
[7] Agreement, OJ L 149, 23.06.2000.
[8] Decision 2002/192, OJ L 64, 07.03.2002.
[9] Decision 2000/365, OJ L 131, 01.06.2000 and Decision 2004/926, OJ L 395, 31.12.2004.
[10] Regulation 562/2006, OJ L 105, 13.04.2006.

introduced in the SIS II, including in the fight against terrorism[1] [see details below and section 8.1.4.].

The services in the Member States which are responsible for issuing registration certificates for vehicles have the right of access to data entered into the **Schengen information system (SIS)**, for the sole purpose of checking whether the vehicles presented to them have been stolen, misappropriated or lost[2]. The services concerned are thus able to use those data for the administrative purpose of properly issuing registration certificates for vehicles.

Tourism or business travel in the EU is much facilitated by European law. Travellers can buy goods without any limits in the Member State visited at the same conditions as the nationals of that State. Checks on the car insurance green card were abolished, as were the disembarkment cards upon arrival in a partner country. Citizens of the Member States can carry a near limitless sum of currency on their intra-Community trips, whereas, before the liberalisation of capital movements they could take only limited tourist allowance. On package tours, they have won protection against the unfair practices of tour operators under Community legislation[3] [see section 11.3.]. On air trips, they are also protected against the over-reservation practices of airlines[4] [see section 20.3.5.]. In the event of illness or accident in a Member State other than that of residence they are covered by the social security system on presentation of the European Health Insurance Card (EHIC), which proves their entitlement to social security cover in the country of residence [see section 6.4.2.]. The euro has much facilitated travel inside the euro zone countries [see section 7.2.4.]. In the ports and airports of the Member States, special channels exist for citizens of the European Union who possess a uniform passport[5]. Persons passing internal frontiers in the Schengen area have not to go through a passport control[6]. The movement of owners of pet animals within the EU is greatly facilitated[7].

EU citizens must feel at home in all the Member States of the Union. As a consequence, the right to travel freely throughout the Union is backed up by the **right to reside** where they choose in the EU[8]. This basic right is made tangible by a number of Community Regulations abolishing work permits and guaranteeing migrant workers and members of their families entitlement to social security and trade union rights, vocational training, free education for their children and, in general, the same treatment as national workers [see section 6.4.2.]. According to the Court of Justice, a student who is lawfully resident and has received a substantial part of his secondary education in another Member State, and has consequently established a genuine link with the society of that State, should be able to pursue his studies under the same conditions as a national of that Member State[9].

US anti-terrorism legislation establishes that air carriers operating passenger flights to or from the United States must make **passenger name record (PNR)** information available to the US Customs Service upon request. PNR is a data record of each passenger's travel requirements which contains all information necessary to enable reservations to be processed and controlled by the booking and participating airlines. Although the US measures potentially conflict with Community and Member States' legislation on data protection, and in particular with Directive 95/46 [see section 17.3.6.], the EU and the USA reached an agreement providing a legislative framework enabling air carriers to transfer passenger data to the US authorities and allowing the latter access to data held by the European authorities on Community territory, while respecting the principles laid down in the data-protection directive. However, the Council decision implementing this agreement was annulled by the Court of Justice upon application of the European Parliament[10].

9.3. The defence of citizens' rights

Citizens should be conscious of their rights, some of which were mentioned above, to be able to defend them when they think that a Member State is not respecting them. They should also know that they are entitled to **defend their rights** acquired through

---

[1] Decision 2005/211, OJ L 68, 15.03.2005, Decisions 2005/727 and 2005/728, OJ L 273, 19.10.2005 and Decisions 2006/228 and 2006/229, OJ L 81, 18.03.2006.
[2] Regulation 1160/2005, OJ L 191, 22.07.2005.
[3] Directive 90/314, OJ L 158, 23.06.1990.
[4] Regulation 261/2004, OJ L 46, 17.02.2004.
[5] Resolutions, OJ C 241, 19.09.1981, p. 1-7, OJ C 185, 24.07.1986, p. 1 and OJ C 200, 04.08.1995, p. 1.
[6] Decision 2000/586, OJ L 248, 03.10.2000.
[7] Regulation 998/2003, OJ L 146, 13.06.2003 last amended by Regulation 590/2006, OJ L 104, 13.04.2006.
[8] Directive 2004/38, OJ L 158, 30.04.2004.
[9] Judgement of 15 March 2005, Dany Bidar, Case C-209/03, ECR 2005, p. I-2119.
[10] Decision 2004/496, OJ L 183, 20.05.2004 and Judgement of 3 May 2006, Joined Cases C-317/04 and C-318/04, ECR 2006.

Community law. They can do so by taking their case to the national courts, which can either issue a ruling or turn to the Court of Justice for a preliminary ruling[1], or by simply and inexpensively lodging a complaint with the Commission or a petition with the European Parliament (Art. 21 and 194 TEC). The Parliament has a Committee on Petitions which examines the complaints of citizens, mainly relating to social security, the recognition of professional qualifications or environment protection[2]. If the complaint concerns instances of mismanagement in the activities of the Community institutions or bodies, the citizen may address himself or herself to the **Ombudsman** appointed by the European Parliament (Art. 21 and 195 TEC) [see section 4.1.3.][3].

Regardless of whether they are lodged with it or with the Parliament, the Commission is obliged to examine the **grievances of citizens**, which number around one thousand per year. Sometimes they are not justified and the Commission must explain to the citizen why this is the case. Not infrequently, however, they are justified and the Commission must address the Member State in question and ask it for explanations. If it does not get a good answer it must formally ask the Member State to correct its legislation or administrative practices which are causing injury to one or several citizens either of the State in question or of another Member State. If the Member State does not come into step with Community law as requested by the Commission, the latter must take the State to the Court of Justice, which will give a final ruling on the obligations of the Member State. According to the Court, the Member States are obliged to compensate for damage caused to individuals by violations of Community law attributable to them[4]. The citizens of the European Union therefore have powerful means at their disposal to obtain justice under Community law. They are sometimes more favoured than if they were just citizens of an individual State, for they can go beyond national judicial bodies to international ones in order to defend their rights and interests.

It goes without saying that if they are to defend these rights, they must be aware of them. The fact is that the vast majority of the citizens of the Member States are not **aware of their rights as citizens** of the European Union. The task of informing them therefore falls both to national and Community authorities, which are not very active in this area. The **information deficit**, examined in the following chapter [see section 10.1.2.], weakens the defence of citizens' rights. On the contrary, the multinational human networks, which are growing in number and influence in the Union, may, among other things, defend the rights of citizens of different Member States.

9.4. Human networks and multinational integration

In chapter 4 we examined the major role played by the common institutions in the European integration process. What needs to be brought out here is the secondary - albeit important - role played by transnational human networks, i.e. various economic, professional, administrative and other interest groups. The success of the European integration process is largely founded on the interaction of the secondary and main actors. The former expose the various national, professional or societal interests concerned by common

---

[1]   Judgment of 25 July 2002, Case C-50/00 P, Unión de Pequeños Agricultores v Council, ECR 2002, p. I-6677.
[2]   Resolution, OJ C 175, 16.07.1990, p. 214.
[3]   Decision 94/114, OJ L 54, 25.02.1994, Decision 94/262, OJ L 113, 04.05.1994 and Decision 2002/262, OJ L 92, 09.04.2002.
[4]   Judgment of November 19, 1991 in the joint cases C-6/90 and C-9/90, Francovich, ECR 1991, p. I-5357.

policies. The latter filter those interests in order to arrive to generally accepted decisions [see section 4.3.]. If those decisions do not satisfy the common interests of certain groups, these may continue their pressures on the main actors, with more chances of success the more transnational they are.

A vast number of multinational networks bring together **representatives of various economic interests and professions**, employers' or employees' associations, non-governmental organisations, scientists and other experts of all nationalities. They take part in various formal or informal committees, which counsel, inform or lobby the Commission and the other main actors, or in ad hoc groups set up by programmes or projects of the various policies (e.g., education, research and environment). The members of these networks tend to convey to their fellows back home the "European spirit" or the logic of multinational integration. The influence of trade unions or associations for consumer or environment protection at European level should not be underestimated. It is certain that the positive or negative attitude of such a group may influence the position of the governments of one or more Member States and thus have an effect on or even block a common policy decision.

An influential network is made up of the various **officials of the Member States**, called "national experts" in EU jargon, who take part in the numerous working parties and committees at Commission or Council level and prepare the decisions of the ministers [see section 4.1.4.]. During their frequent meetings they come to know each other, understand the positions of their partners and discern the common interest in a proposed common policy. An important function of this network is to render more intelligible the Community logic and mechanisms to national administrations back home, which keep national reflexes and are generally reluctant to shed a fraction of their power to the common administration in "Brussels". Through national experts, the national positions, which are at the outset very rigid, are progressively softened so as to allow finally a compromise decision by the ministers. When the decision is taken, the initiated in the Community spirit may prepare the ground for its implementation at national level, an equally difficult and essential task.

The most influential among secondary human networks is made up of **business leaders**. It is natural that they are concerned mostly by economic integration. By bringing about tougher conditions of competition inside the single market than the ones existing previously inside the protected national markets, multinational integration, on the one hand, threatens vested interests and, on the other, creates new business opportunities through market expansion and innovation. It ensues, that economic operators - big national businesses, state controlled companies, multinational companies and associations of enterprises, including the small and medium ones - cannot be apathetic onlookers in the integration process. They constitute powerful interest groups, which intervene by way of demands, suggestions or criticisms addressed to the managers - the governments of the member states - or to the principal actors - the common institutions - at various stages of the decision-making process, concerning particular policies or the advancement of the integration process itself. Economic integration may, indeed, begin and advance only if progressive and competitive elements have the upper hand within economic interest groups [see section 1.1.2.]. Conversely, if these groups are dominated by conservative, protectionist elements, which have sufficient influence on the political elite at national or multinational level, they may stall the integration process or put off decisions on common policies. The EC/EU experience proves that business groups at national and European levels are dominated by dynamic elements, which support and influence the multinational integration process.

Last but not least, many thousand **students and other young people** participate every year in Community exchange programmes, create friendships and come close to the lifestyles and behavioural patterns of their neighbours [see section 13.4.2.]. They thus create vast and strong links among the nations of the Union, which increase and firm up every year.

9.5. The so-called democratic deficit

Numerous critics of European integration point out at the "democratic deficit" as cause of the indifference of the citizens of the Union, insinuating that the citizens do not participate in the Community decision-making process, which is therefore undemocratic and causes the estrangement of the citizens from European institutions. They overlook the fact that the alienation of citizens from politics is not peculiar to the EC/EU, but characterises practically all representative democracies, where a great proportion - in some countries the majority - of citizens abstain from national elections. They also forget the fact that European **citizens already have almost the same influence** on the shaping of European law as they have on the shaping of national law. They indirectly influence it through the choice of the political parties, which make up the national governments and which therefore are involved in all European decisions adopted by the Council of Ministers. In addition, citizens have a direct say in the election of the members of the European Parliament, which has an important participation in the legislative process, thanks to improvements brought by successive European Treaties [see section 4.1.3].

It is true that the Parliament does not participate fully in all sectors of the European integration and that this situation should get better with a subsequent amendment of the Treaty, constitutional or not [see sections 2.5 and 4.4.]. But already the power and control of the European Parliament has greatly increased since the early days when it had a purely consultative role in the legislative process and when, as a consequence, the democratic deficit at European level was substantially greater than that at the national level. Now, most decisions are taken jointly by the Council, representing the democratically elected governments of the Union, and by the European Parliament, representing directly the citizens of the Union [see section 4.3.]. It follows that **the "democratic deficit" is another myth** propagated by eurosceptic circles. Paradoxically, these same circles are among the most vehement detractors of the extension of the codecision procedure to the common foreign and security policy, which would practically eliminate the remnants of the democratic deficit.

Furthermore, the viewpoints of European citizens concerning various common policies are also expressed by the **national parliaments**, which manifest a growing interest in European integration. Indeed, the Conference of European Affairs Committees (COSAC) of the national parliaments may examine any legislative proposal or initiative which might have a direct bearing on the rights and freedoms of individuals and may address to the European institutions any contributions which it deems appropriate on the legislative activities of the Union.

Article 191 of the EC Treaty states that **political parties at European level** are important as a factor for integration within the Union and that they contribute to forming a European awareness and to expressing the political will of the citizens of the Union. A regulation aims to establish a long-term framework for European political parties and their financing from the Community budget, while also laying down minimum standards of democratic conduct for such parties[1]. In accordance with this regulation, a political party at European level must satisfy certain conditions, notably: it must be represented, in at least one quarter of Member States, by Members of the European Parliament or it must have received, in at least one quarter of the Member States, at least three per cent of the votes cast in each of those Member States at the most recent European Parliament elections; and it must observe in its programme and in its activities, the principles on which the European Union is founded, namely the principles of liberty, democracy, respect for human rights and fundamental freedoms, and the rule of law.

Far from being detached from the European integration process, national parliaments and the political parties, which dominate them, **are instrumental in** its launching, development and monitoring. Since the advancement of common policies means less liberty of action for national policies, some parties may refuse this loss of independence of action and may, therefore, block or try to block further common action. They may

---

[1]   Regulation 2004/2003, OJ L 297, 15.11.2003.

even, when in government, remove their state from the integration process. The latter option becomes more difficult at more advanced stages of integration, when economic actors and the citizens in general would, in case of isolation, lose the facilities and free-doms of action to which they have been accustomed inside the integrated market [see section 1.1.2.]. The experience to date proves that practically all major parties in the great majority of the Member States are in favour of the general objectives of European integration. This is demonstrated by the fact that there is little or no change of national behaviour towards European policies when there is a change of a parliamentary majority and, therefore, of a government in a Member State. Instead of showing public misgivings about the democratic legitimacy of European integration, the overall evidence brings out **an extraordinary political consensus** on the main elements of the common policies that determine it.

The draft **Constitutional Treaty** defines, for the first time, the democratic founda-tions of the Union, which are based on three principles: those of democratic equality, representative democracy and participatory democracy. The principle of **democratic equality** means that all citizens of the Union must receive equal attention from its insti-tutions, bodies, offices and agencies (Art. I-45). The principle of **representative democ-racy** means that citizens are directly represented at Union level in the European Parlia-ment, while Member States are represented in the European Council by their Heads of State or Government and in the Council by their governments, themselves democrati-cally accountable either to their national Parliaments, or to their citizens (Art. I-46). The principle of **participatory democracy** means that the institutions must give citizens and representative associations the opportunity to make known and publicly exchange their views in all areas of Union action (Art I-47). The main innovation in this area is that one million citizens who are nationals of a significant number of Member States could take the initiative of inviting the Commission to submit any appropriate proposal on matters where citizens consider that a legal act of the Union is required. This right of initiative would give those European citizens who complain about the "democratic deficit in Europe" a means of directly making their voices heard.

As strange as this may seem, **the way referendums were organised in the past** for the ratification of European Treaties was undemocratic on several accounts. First of all, it is highly unusual that a treaty, be it called constitutional, be subject to a referendum for its ratification. Treaties are negotiated and signed by gov-ernments and they are ratified by them after the assent of their parliaments. This is the case because treaties are very complicated legal instruments that cannot be well understood by ordinary citizens. European treaties are even more complicated than average international treaties. They contain not only new elements, necessary for bringing the integration process forward, but also all the previous provisions on which the construction of the existing stages of the integration process was based, notably customs union, the common market and economic and monetary union. It is absurd to ask citizens to approve or reject a new instrument that contains some new measures promoting the integration process and all the pre-existing measures on which this process has been based since half a century.

The referendum on a new treaty should either concern exclusively the new provisions of this treaty com-pared to those in effect or, if it also concerned the provisions in force, should allow the citizens of a Member State to opt for the secession of their country from the Union, if they are not satisfied with its ends or results. If the subject of the referendum is not made that clear, it would give the opportunity to demagogues at both ex-tremes of the political spectrum to deprecate not just the new elements of the integration process, but also elements of the acquis communautaire, like the European social model or the common agricultural policy, which function satisfactorily in the opinion of the majority of the Member States. With the information deficit that prevails, demagogues are free to disseminate all sorts of lies on the European Union and to exert a nega-tive influence on public opinion. It is contrary to the concept of democracy to have the citizens decide on the basis of lies, which thanks to propaganda, they have accepted as truths. Hence, a referendum may estrange rather than bring the citizens closer to the integration process.

Moreover, it is highly undemocratic to ask only the citizens of some Member States to express them-selves directly by referendum, whereas the citizens from the other Member States should be contented with the normal procedure of the ratification approved by the representatives of their national parliaments. This is discrimination between citizens of the Member States, condemned in principal by the Treaty itself. Democratic considerations and the principle of the equality of the citizens of the Union require that they all express themselves on the ratification of a new treaty in the same way: either indirectly through their representatives or directly through referenda held the same day in all countries, so that the results in one country do not influence the citizens of the others. If the second alternative was preferred, the governments and the common institutions should make a greater effort at informing the citizens about the issues at stake.

Instead of submitting a complex legal instrument to the approval or disapproval of the citizens, it would be more logical to separate the new elements of the treaty, describe them in a non legalistic language, explain why the responsible governments have agreed to them by signing the treaty and ask the citizens if they want this new treaty to be ratified and be brought into force or if they want to leave things as they are with the existing treaty. All the governments concerned should agree to such a straightforward paper at the same time as they sign the Treaty, so that the citizens of all Member States have the same explanations and reasons for the new elements of the common enterprise and are asked the same questions about its progress or standstill. It would, indeed, be hypocritical and improper for a government to put its signature on a draft treaty (which is in fact a draft contract with its partners) and present it in a different way from its partners, knowing or hoping that its citizens will reject it [see the European perspectives in the conclusions].

9.6. Appraisal and outlook

Given that the economic activities of the Member States are guided by European law, the **activities of individual citizens are influenced** and governed to a large extent by the common policies which dictate that law. Regulations on the right of entry and residence in the Member States, freedom of movement of workers, freedom of establishment of and provision of services by individuals and businesses, vocational training, protection of the environment and of the consumer, to mention but a few, are all the outcome of the various common policies. It is true that because of the complexity of the Community law and the inertia of public administrations, certain categories of citizens still have difficulties in the exercise of their rights of free movement and residence, but these exceptions, which should be rapidly corrected, do not invalidate the rules of the free movement of persons and of non-discrimination.

The Union also contributes to the elevation of the standard of living of its citizens. There are certainly still important differences in prosperity between the various regions of the Union, which this endeavours to iron out [see chapter 12]. However, a **European social model** exists already and guarantees, not only fundamental human rights and the democratic and pluralistic principles, but also fundamental rights of workers: training adapted to the technical progress, fair pay allowing decent living conditions and social protection covering the hazards of life, illness, unemployment and old age [see section 13.5.]. This social model, which is defended by the majority of political parties in the Member States, places the European Union in the vanguard of social progress in the world.

Citizens are aware that the multinational integration process provides **a guarantee of peace and prosperity** in Western Europe and therefore support the idea of the Community in principle. But this Community - integrated since 1993 into the overall organisation of the European Union - is perceived as something distant, formless, cumbersome and incomprehensible. Citizens are largely unaware of the extent to which they are surrounded by the workings of the Union in their daily and professional lives. They hardly understand the rights that emanate from the citizenship of the Union and they ignore the rights that derive from European legislation.

Ignorance brings indifference and indifference is more dangerous for the European construction than the so-called democratic deficit, which is shrinking while indifference is expanding. The citizens need to know the rights that they are entitled to from European integration and to understand that they are respected by the Member States. Otherwise, the citizenship of the Union and the Union itself seem vague concepts, generating doubts, confusion or even rejection of the EU. The European institutions and the Member States should, therefore, permanently strive to ensure an easy access of the citizens to **simple and factual information about their rights** and generally about the common policies that establish those rights. As we will see in the next chapter, citizens' information is deficient or even non existent in many Member States, including those where it is needed most.

Bibliography on citizens' rights

- BACHE Ian, GEORGE Stephen. *Politics in the European Union*. 2nd ed. Oxford: Oxford University Press, 2006.
- BACHE Ian, JORDAN Andrew (eds.). *The europeanization of British politics*. Basingstoke: Palgrave Macmillan, 2006.
- BELOT Céline, CAUTRÈS Bruno (sous la dir. de). "Vers une européanisation des partis politiques ?", *Politique européenne*, n. 16, printemps 2005, p. 5-213.
- BINZER HOBOLT Sara. "Direct democracy and European integration" in *Journal of European Public Policy*, v. 13, n. 1, January 2006, p. 153-166.
- BROSIG Malte (ed.). *Human rights in Europe: a fragmented regime?* Frankfurt am Main: P. Lang, 2006.
- BRUTER Michael. *Citizens of Europe? : The emergence of a mass European identity*. Basingstoke: Palgrave Macmillan, 2005.
- DOMM Rory. Public Support for European integration. London:Routledge, 2006.
- EUROPEAN COMMISSION. *Better off in Europe: how the EU's single market benefits you*. Luxembourg: EUR-OP*, 2006.
- EUROPEAN FOUNDATION FOR THE IMPROVEMENT OF LIVING AND WORKING CONDITIONS. *First European quality of life survey: Life satisfaction, happiness and sense of belonging*. Luxembourg: EUR-OP*, 2005.
- EGEBERG Morten (ed.). Multilevel Union administration: the transformation of executive politics in Europe.
- GLASIUS Marlies, KALDOR Mary (eds.). *A human security doctrine for Europe: project, principles, practicalities*. London: Routledge, 2006.
- GIORGI Liana (et al. eds.). *Democracy in the European Union: towards the emergence of a public sphere*. Abingdon: Routledge, 2006.
- JACOBY Edmond (et. Al.). "Les familles sans frontières en Europe : mythe ou réalité ? 101e Congrès des notaires de France", *Les Petites affiches*, v. 394, n. 74, 14 avril 2005, p. 1-59.
- KLIVER Philipp. *The national parliaments in the European Union: a critical view on EU constitution-building*. The Hague: Kluwer Law International, 2006.
- LEVEAU Rémy, MOHSEN-FINAN Khadija (sous la dir. de). *Musulmans de France et d'Europe*. Paris: CNRS, 2005.
- MAHER Imelda (et al.). "Critical perspectives on governance, legitimacy and democracy in the European Union: a symposium." in *European Law Journal*, v. 12, n. 6, November 2006, p. 707-763.
- MOINY Yves. *Protection of personal data and citizens' rights of privacy in the fight against the financing of terrorism*. Brussels: Centre for European Policy Studies, 2005.
- RITTBERGER Berthold, SCHIMMELFENNIG Frank. *The constitutionalization of the European Union: explaining the parliamentarization and institutionalization of human rights*. Vienna: Institute for Advanced Studies, 2005.
- SMITH Karen Elizabeth. "Speaking with one voice?: European Union co-ordination on human rights issues at the United Nations" in *Journal of Common Market Studies*, v. 44, n. 1, March 2006, p. 113-137.
- VINK Maarten. *Limits of European citizenship: European integration and domestic immigration policies*. Basingstoke: Palgrave Macmillan, 2005.

The publications of the Office for Official Publications of the European Communities (EUR-OP) exist usually in all official languages of the EU.

Chapter 10

INFORMATION, AUDIOVISUAL AND CULTURAL POLICIES

Diagram of the chapter

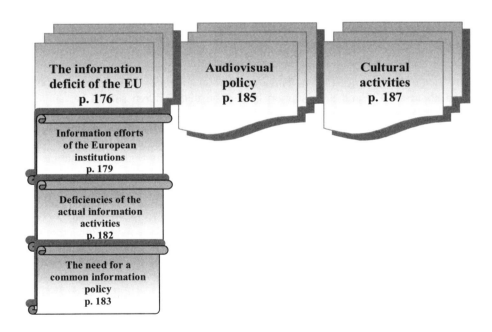

The point was made in the previous chapter that the citizens are silent, but indispensable, actors in the construction of Europe. The EC/EU could not have been built by the political elite, without the implicit consent of the citizens involved in the process. In fact, European citizens are generally in favour and consider as evident the fundamental principles and ideals the Union stands for, notably peace among their previously antagonistic nations, respect for human rights and the rule of law, economic development and social protection. The **public opinion survey known as "Eurobarome-**

ter", which is conducted each spring and autumn under the auspices of the Commission, shows that, at the end of 2004, the EU citizens (from the 25 Member States) were largely convinced that EU membership was a "good" rather than a "bad thing" (56% vs. 13%). 53% of European citizens interviewed consider that their country has on balance benefited from being a member of the European Union, versus 34% who believe the opposite. 50% of the citizens had a positive image of the EU, compared to 15% who had a bad image. Almost one out of two respondents (47%) declared that the Union gives them a feeling of hope. 52% of the respondents in the 25 countries had confidence in the European Commission and 57% had confidence in the European Parliament. The European public is even largely in favour of projects which are subject to controversy among the EU institutions and the governments of the Member States, such as a European constitution (63% vs. 10%), the EMU with a single currency (66% vs. 27% and 75% vs. 19% in EU 12), the common defence (74% vs. 15%) or the foreign policy (67% vs. 19%).

10.1. The information deficit of the Union

Although they are well disposed towards European integration, most citizens either ignore its achievements or take them for granted. In the Eurobarometer surveys, three fourths of the citizens say that they are not well informed about the institutions and policies of the European Union. It is interesting to note that good information greatly enhances the positive attitude of the public towards European integration. Indeed, two out of three citizens who claim to be well informed have a positive image of the EU as against one out of three who admit to being ill informed. However, the latter are the vast majority in the 25 countries (55%). Three out of four citizens would like to be better informed about the EU and 85% support the notion that children should be taught in school about the way European Union institutions work. Civic education on EU institutions is even the first priority theme for the very large majority of Europeans. Apparently, the citizens are aware that something important is happening in Europe, in which they cannot participate for lack of general knowledge and day-to-day information and they call for better access to European affairs for themselves and their children.

The information deficit, acknowledged by the citizens themselves, means that they are ill informed about the reasons, the goals and the achievements of European policies, laws and measures. Ignorance brings disregard for the obscure phenomenon. At best, citizens take for granted or fail to see that the EC/EU is behind the many rights that they have acquired thanks to European integration, some of which we examined in the previous chapter [see section 9.2.], particularly the right to a peaceful, liberal and law secured existence. For uninformed Europeans, the peaceful coexistence and emulation of different European nations is self-evident and not to be attributed to unfamiliar Treaties, policies or common legislation. Uninterested citizens tend to forget the tariffs and other barriers hindering trade and therefore limiting their choice of goods and services from other European countries, in the pre-integration years [see section 5.1.1]. They do not recall the erstwhile controls at borders, the restrictions on movement, establishment and work in neighbouring countries, the limited amounts at their disposal when travelling abroad, the general restrictions on capital movements, the snags of dealing in several currencies, etc. Young Europeans tend even to disregard the bloody wars fought by their forefathers with nations that they themselves now consider friendly and allied to their own nation.

Many explanations have been advanced for the negative vote of the French and Dutch citizens at the referendums of 29 May and 1 June 2005 on the **ratification of the**

Constitutional Treaty: national rather than European concerns, social protection versus free competition, fear of actual and future enlargements of the Union, etc. They all have their grain of truth; but to our mind, the main cause of the negative stance of two nations that were among the original builders of the European edifice is the ignorance of most citizens of the objectives and the achievements of European integration to date.

Instead of a democratic deficit, which as we explained in the previous chapter is largely overstated [see section 9.5.], we should rather speak about **an information deficit** in European affairs. The information deficit originates from the early days of the customs union and the common market, when the issues of European unification were too technical to really interest the public and the threat of the communist block was considered a sufficient justification of this unification. Now that the communist threat has disappeared and the evolutionary integration process generates, every day, new common policies and laws affecting all sectors of the economy and society of the Member States, the citizens are bewildered about their impact on their lives. Furthermore, in order to judge the common enterprise on its real advantages and disadvantages, they need to have matter-of-fact information on the benefits and drawbacks already drawn and those expected from it, as well as on the real management difficulties that it is facing. Responsible for the information deficit are the European institutions, which shy away from the development of a common information and communication policy, the governments of the Member States, which prefer to present the accomplishments of the Union as their own, and the media, which find more interesting to criticise the problems of the Union than present its achievements. Let us examine one by one these various factors of the information deficit of the Union.

The information deficit is partly due to the European institutions, notably the Commission, the Council and the Parliament, which do not join their forces to build a common communication policy. In their defence, it may be said that they are not encouraged - if they are not discouraged - by the governments of the Member States, which do not feel that they have a common interest in setting up a common information policy. In order to assume the political credit of modernisation, governments, when proposing innovating laws to national parliaments, transposing in effect Community directives, or when changing their administrative practices to comply with European law, rarely take the trouble to explain to the general public that they are thus fulfilling their Community obligations.

Paradoxically, however, the providers of information themselves, the mass communication media, have their share of responsibility in the information deficit of the Union. In fact, the **media** can play an important role in the multinational integration process by shaping public opinion and by exerting pressure on the political decision makers for or against common policies. They may also ignore or report incorrectly important issues of the integration process and, thus, leave the public ignorant or lead it astray as to the advantages and disadvantages of particular common policies or the integration process in general. If the majority of the media adopt attitudes different from the majority of the political elite of a nation, concerning the issue of integration or particular aspects of it, this may lead to a different stance of the majority of the public from that of the majority of the political elite of the nation. We may thus have the following antidemocratic phenomenon: the popular media transforming the political consensus existing among the democratically elected leaders of a nation, concerning the major political issues discussed at European level [see section 9.5.], into a public opinion dissent on those issues, orchestrated by non-elected opinion leaders (media tycoons, trendy journalists, popular television speakers, etc.) and/or a vociferous minority (party, movement or union)[1].

In contrast to eurosceptic media, which systematically provide disinformation rather than information, unbiased mass media **rarely report the decisions of the EC/EU;** probably because they are too technical, too detailed and often quite difficult to understand for the general public and sometimes for the journalists themselves. Instead of bringing forward the need and/or the common interest of measures in discussion, the media (particularly the popular ones) tend to highlight the usual and comprehensible disagreements in the deliberations of the Council, stemming from different socioeconomic structures, cultural traditions and vested interests. Moreover, the media of a country tend to present as right the national points of view and as wrong those of the other Member States. When a compromise solution is found within the framework of the co-decision procedure of the Council and the Parliament (as happens with 95% of the technocratic proposals of the Commission, after thorough deliberation and many amendments introduced by the political bodies), and a Community measure (regulation, directive or decision) is adopted, the same media tend either to ignore it or to summarise its content in small print and in a language difficult to understand for the average citizen. Furthermore, as a compromise solution is halfway between the best possible solution and no solution at all, even an unprejudiced journalist can easily disregard or belittle the achievement that it represents and emphasize its shortcomings. The resulting information in such a case is half-right or half-wrong, according to one's standpoint. But, again, it should be said, in the journalists' discharge, that they need clear, simple and interesting press releases on which to work; and these can only be provided by the European institutions. We thus have a vicious circle: the governments do not mandate the European institutions to set up a common information and communication policy; hence the institutions do not provide interesting factual information to the media; and these, on their turn, do not report to the public the activities of the institutions worthy of note.

In spite of the 900 journalists from more than 60 countries accredited to the Commission, the European public is still **ignorant or ill informed about European integration**. Few and far between are the European topics, which make the headlines in the printed press and radio and television transmissions. Worse still, it is the crises, the temporary set-backs, which make the headlines, because they are more sensational than the unexciting decisions, secured on an almost daily basis after patient negotiations, which become European laws and affect the day-to-day lives of citizens, on occasion much more than the laws adopted by the national parliaments.

On the other hand, the lack of interest of the media in most member countries for European affairs is a sure sign of the **lack of major dissensions** in those countries for the progress of the European integration process. Characteristically, it is only the media in the countries with strong eurosceptic sentiments that deal at length and usually negatively with proposals for new steps in the process, whereas the media in most other countries tend to ignore them or relate them succinctly, albeit factually.

Governments, often use European measures as instruments of internal politics. If the Community measure is popular, governments will tend to present as their own initiative the national law or decree implementing the Community decision, hardly mentioning the common framework of the action. On the contrary, if the measure is unpopular, "Brussels" is often made responsible by the governments of the Member States for an action that they have themselves adopted (in the Council) or even encouraged (in the European Council). Of course, not all governments behave the same way and at all times. Some are more open than others about their involvement in European affairs. The latter are probably the ones, whose citizens need more clear and objective information concerning common policies and the implication of their own institutions in them.

---

[1] The best example is the bitter opposition of the media tycoon Rupert Murdoch to the will of the Labour government of the UK to adopt the euro.

10.1.1. Information efforts of the European institutions

At present each of the three main European institutions has its own means and instruments to carry out its information policy. While preserving full autonomy, the Parliament and the Commission have established an Inter-Institutional Group on Information to coordinate their policies. They carry out jointly some priority information campaigns on subjects of topical interest, such as the euro (before its circulation), the new enlargement of the Union or the debate on the future of Europe. The Commission Representations and the European Parliament External Offices in the Member States are co-operating locally on an ad-hoc basis. Although it shares some means of communication with the Commission and the Parliament, such as the Europa server and the Europe by Satellite (EBS) - a television news instrument offering live coverage of the institutions' work and news summaries - the Council has a separate information and communication policy from the other institutions. As it has few budgetary resources for this purpose, it operates its own relations with the press and media. In general, except for a limited co-operation between the Commission and the Parliament, the three main European institutions have independent and heterogeneous information activities.

Although the Helsinki European Council in December 1999 called on the European Parliament, the Council and the Commission to pool their efforts to put out co-ordinated general information on the Union and to optimise the use of resources, the Commission did not seize the opportunity of this invitation to propose a common information policy. Instead, it publishes, almost every year, a new paper on how to improve its own information and communication policy. Although in its White Paper on a **"European communication policy"**[1] it acknowledges that the success of this much needed policy depends on the involvement of all the key players – the other EU institutions and bodies, the national, regional and local authorities in the Member States, European political parties and the civil society – it does not explain how these players would get involved in the communication partnership. Instead of proposing a European Parliament and Council decision or regulation, which would engage all European institutions and Member States to participate in the communication effort, it advocates a "European Charter or Code of Conduct on Communication" which would define common principles to be followed by the players on a voluntary basis. Instead of proposing a common civic education for young Europeans, it invites the Member States to explore the best ways to bring together European teachers in this field with a view to exchanging ideas on innovative approaches to civic education. Instead of proposing that each important new Community measure (directive, regulation, decision) be accompanied by an explanatory press release in all official languages, it encourages EU institutions to explore with a wide range of media players how to better provide the media (pan-European, national and local) with material which is relevant for them, with a view to adapting the information to the needs of different countries and segments of the population. Instead of asking each Minister participating in a Council session, which would have adopted an important measure, to comment in his or her own words the common press release, it calls for a partnership with the Member States to publicize public and parliamentary discussion on the Commission's annual strategic priorities and discussions between national ministers and European Commissioners or other such matters, which might be of interest for the Commission but of no interest at all for the general public.

The information and communication strategy for the European Union implemented by the Commission with the hypothetical voluntary synergy of the Member States,

---

[1]   COM/2006/35.

which should improve perception of the European Union and institutions and of their legitimacy[1], is clearly inadequate, as demonstrated by the indifference of citizens at the European elections of June 2004. Expressing its concern at the low voter turnout in those elections, the Brussels European Council (18-19 June 2004) recognised the need to strengthen a sense among the citizens of the importance of the work of the Union and its relevance to their daily lives. It would be up to the Commission to propose that the Union faces this need with a common communication policy.

As a matter of fact, **the Commission is the main provider of information on the EC/EU.** Major European affairs and problems, which occasionally attract television attention, are presented and commented in the press room of the Commission by its President, the competent Commissioner or a spokesperson. Rarely is press attention focussed on the European Parliament and almost never on the Council of Ministers. Although it practically monopolises Community information, the Commission is not a secretive organisation and is even a good provider of information, as far as its activities are concerned. Its Representations in the capitals and other major cities of the Member States are open to the interested public. Its Office of Official Publications (EUR-OP) publishes hundreds of documents every year on all common policies. Its Europa server on the Internet gives free and user-friendly access to more than 60 databases, each of which contains several hundred thousand documents in the 21 official languages of the European Union[2]. All the documents listed in the footnotes of this book are accessible at the Eur-lex database. The addresses of the general and of some of the most interesting free sites of Europa are the following:

- **(Europa gateway)** http://europa.eu.int/index_en.htm
- **(general information)** http://europa.eu/abc/index_en.htm
- **(European legislation)** http://eur-lex.europa.eu/RECH_menu.do?
- **(common policies)** http://europa.eu.int/scadplus/scad_en.htm
- **(official publications)** http://bookshop.europa.eu/eGetRecords?Template=
- Test_EUB/en_index&indLang=EN
- **(Bulletin of the EU)** http://europa.eu/bulletin/en/welcome.htm
- **(Who's Who in the institutions)** http://europa.eu.int/idea/en/index.htm
- **(calls for tenders)** http://ted.eur-op.eu.int/Exec?DataFlow=
- ShowPage.dfl&Template=TED/sitemap

Moreover, the Commission does not make any secret of its intentions concerning legislation in preparation. All its proposals are communicated directly to the press the day of their adoption and are published in the very informative monthly *Bulletin of the European Union*, available in paper and electronic form. In case of preparation of new policies or changes in existing policies, the Commission publishes **Green Papers** (reflection documents inviting a debate on the options of a policy before the preparation of proposals) and **White Papers** (general documents announcing a programme of actions)[3]. A White Paper usually presents the points of view of interested parties (organisations, associations, institutions…) at national and Community level on a Green Paper, along with the conclusions and intentions of the Commission. This step by step approach is meant to promote an exchange of views between the Commission and the interested parties on legislation in preparation.

---

[1]   COM (2002) 350, 2 July 2002.
[2]   Regulation 1/1958, OJ 17, 06.10.1958 and Regulation 920/2005, OJ L 156, 18.06.2005.
[3]   The index provides references to several Green and White Papers.

Article 1 of the Treaty on European Union stipulates that decisions are taken as openly and as closely as possible to the citizen. Article 255 of the Treaty establishing the European Community specifies that any citizen of the Union and any natural or legal person residing or having its registered office in a Member State has a right of access to documents of the Parliament, the Council and the Commission, subject to the principles and conditions defined by these institutions. In December 1993 the Council and the Commission approved a code of conduct laying down general rules on such right of access[1]. On the basis of this code the Commission introduced practical procedures, which enable the public to have simple, rapid and decentralised access to its documents[2]. The Council has also made available to the public certain categories of its documents (almost 60% of all its documents)[3]. A regulation defines the principles, conditions and limits (on grounds of public or private interest) governing the right of access to Parliament, Council and Commission documents provided for in Article 255 of the EC Treaty in such a way as to ensure the widest possible access to documents[4]. The Parliament, the Council[5] and the Commission[6] have amended their rules of procedure accordingly. However, the Council still meets behind closed doors when acting as legislator, a fact that hinders the transparency of the legislative process.

Transparency must go hand in hand with the **quality of drafting of Community legislation**. A declaration to the Final Act attached to the Amsterdam Treaty noted that the quality of drafting of Community legislation is crucial if it is to be properly implemented by the competent national authorities and better understood by the public and the business world. It urged the three institutions involved in the procedure for adopting Community legislation [see section 4.3.] to lay down guidelines on the quality of the drafting of the said legislation, which they did[7]. The Commission has pledged itself to codify and render readable the Community legislation[8] and it presents an annual report giving a factual account of how the principles of subsidiarity and proportionality are applied and explaining the Union's policy-making process[9] [see section 3.2.] .

The **information policy** of the Commission is designed to contribute to the objectives of transparency and accessibility of Community legislation. The aim is to inform citizens of the nature and the scale of the challenges facing the European Union, to demonstrate the comparative benefits of European integration and to show people in concrete terms, at local level, the effect of European policies on their daily lives. To attain these objectives the Commission uses several instruments, such as: the **Commission Representations** in the Member States, which act as discussion and information fora and as centres for coordinating national relays to reach both the public at large and specialised audiences in the Member States; and the **Europe Direct** site, which provides a dialogue in all the languages of the Union through a free number, e-mail, letter or fax, enabling citizens and businesses find out about their rights and get advice about all sorts of opportunities in the EU, e.g., Community programmes that can help implement projects [10]. Various other activities of the Commission are designed to improve the dissemination of available information. They include the activities of the Office for Official Publications and of the Statistical Office, the management of the historical archives of the Communities and the provision of information to universities.

The Union's **Office for Official Publications (OPOCE or EUR-OP)** publishes and distributes, on behalf of all the institutions, the Official Journal of the European Union (OJ) and other publications. The Official Journal is published every day in 21 languages and every year contains more than a million pages, giving a measure of the work volume of the Office for Official Publications and its importance for citizens who want to keep abreast of European affairs. The distribution network of EUR-OP is built on an increasing number of bookshops in the Member States and in several third countries.

In addition, all the legislation of the EU/EC (Treaties, secondary legislation in force, legislation in preparation and Court of Justice decisions) is stored in the interinstitutional computerised documentation system on Community law (http://europa.eu.int/eur-lex/en/index.html). Responding to the enlargement of the EU and the European Parliament's call, in a resolution of 19 December 2002, for free access to CELEX, the new EUR-Lex site is merged with CELEX to provide free access to the vast corpus of existing documentation on the law of the European Union in 21 languages. For example, this system can supply without supplementary research the text of a basic regulation and all its subsequent amendments. We should emphasise once again, however, that this excellent and free information source is useless, unless one knows the exact references of the legislative act, Court ruling or Commission proposal, as mentioned in the footnotes of this book.

Comparable, reliable and relevant statistics throughout the Community are a source of growing interest to the general public. Article 285 of the Treaty establishing the European Community stipulates that the pro-

[1] Code 93/730, OJ L 340, 31.12.1993 and Decision 2001/840, OJ L 313, 30.11.2001.
[2] Decision 2001/937, OJ L 345, 29.12.2001.
[3] Decision 2001/840, Annex III, OJ L 313, 30.11.2001.
[4] Regulation 1049/2001, OJ L 145, 31.05.2001.
[5] Decision 2001/840, OJ L 313, 30.11.2001.
[6] Decision 2001/844, OJ L 317, 03.12.2001 and Decision 2006/548, OJ L 215, 05.08.2006.
[7] Interinstitutional agreement, OJ C 73, 17.03.1999.
[8] COM (2001) 645, 21 November 2001.
[9] COM (2001) 728, COM (2002) 275 and COM (2003) 71.
[10] Tel: 0080067891011, electronic address: http://europa.eu.int/europedirect.

duction of **Community statistics** shall conform to impartiality, reliability, objectivity, scientific independence, cost-effectiveness and statistical confidentiality. A Regulation establishes a legislative framework for the systematic and programmed production of Community statistics on the basis of uniform standards or, in specific cases, of harmonised methods with a view to the formulation, application, monitoring and assessment of the policies of the Community[1]. Indices of consumer prices and of household consumption expenditure are harmonised[2] as are short-term economic statistics[3] and labour force sample surveys intended to provide comparable statistics on the level and structure of employment and unemployment[4]. A Regulation established a common framework for the production, transmission and evaluation of comparable labour cost indices in the Community[5]. Other Regulations concern: the trading of goods between Member States[6]; national and regional accounts in the Community (SEC 95)[7]; quarterly financial accounts for general government[8]; the harmonisation of gross national income at market prices (GNI Regulation)[9]; and Community statistics on income and living conditions (EU-SILC)[10].

The **Statistical Office of the European Union (Eurostat)**, which works alongside national statistical offices, aims at developing a "Community statistical space" based on a set of standards, methods and organisational structures that make it possible to produce comparable, reliable and relevant statistics throughout the Community. It draws up statistics that attempt to meet the needs of the general public arising from the various Community policies: economic, industrial, agricultural, social, regional and so on. The **general statistical classification** of economic activities within the European Communities (NACE), adopted in 1990, is one of the cornerstones of the Community's statistical system and is often adopted by the countries of the EFTA and of Central and Eastern Europe for their own statistical purposes[11]. The Member States have agreed to pass on data subject to statistical confidentiality to the Statistical Office, on condition that all the necessary steps are taken to ensure confidentiality[12]. The Eurostat database provides electronic versions of all publications free of charge.

Researchers into European integration now enjoy access to the **European Community's historical archives**. Under the 30-year rule, the archives of the ECSC have been open to public consultation since 1952 and those of the EEC and Euratom since 1958[13]. The Archis data base lists the files stored in the archives of the Florence European University Institute. In addition, the Council has recommended to the Member States to increase cooperation in the field of archives in Europe[14].

The Commission also promotes teaching on European integration at university level, notably by granting financial support for the setting-up of "**Jean Monnet chairs**", a symbolic term for full-time teaching posts devoted to European integration. The Jean Monnet Project "European Integration in University Studies" is designed to encourage the development of centres of excellence on European issues at universities and support academic initiatives related to the teaching of European integration (theory, history, economic, legal, social and political aspects). Actually, the Jean Monnet network consists of more than 1600 professors specialising in European integration studies in Europe and many non-European countries. The European Community Studies Association network ("ECSA-Net") on the Internet, coordinated by the Commission, provides up-to-date information for the Euristote database on research into European integration, Jean Monnet chairs and courses, postgraduate research and degrees, European documentation centres and a worldwide directory of specialised teachers and researchers.

10.1.2. The deficiencies of the actual information activities

A cursory view of the information activities of European institutions gives the impression of a flood of documentation - coming mainly from the Commission - rather than of an information drought. But floods can be more harmful than droughts, if the soil is not prepared to receive the overflow. In this case, the soil is totally unprepared, because

---

[1]   Regulation 322/97, OJ L 52, 22.02.1997.
[2]   Regulation 2494/95, OJ L 257, 27.10.1995 and Regulation 701/2006, OJ L 122, 09.05.2006.
[3]   Regulation 1165/98, OJ L 162, 05.06.1998 and Regulation 1158/2005, OJ L 191, 22.07.2005.
[4]   Regulation 577/98, OJ L 77, 14.03.1998 and Regulation 2257/2003, OJ L 336, 23.12.2003.
[5]   Regulation 450/2003, OJ L 69, 13.03.2003.
[6]   Regulation 638/2004, OJ L 104, 07.04.2004.
[7]   Regulation 2223/96, OJ L 310, 30.11.1996 and Regulation 1267/2003, OJ L 180, 18.07.2003.
[8]   Regulation 501/2004, OJ L 81, 19.03.2004.
[9]   Regulation 1287/2003, OJ L 181, 19.07.2003.
[10] Regulation 1177/2003, OJ L 165, 03.07.2003 and Regulation 1553/2005, OJ L 255, 30.09.2005.
[11] Regulation 3037/90, OJ L 293, 24.10.1990.
[12] Regulation 1588/90, OJ L 151, 15.06.1990 and Regulation 322/97, OJ L 52, 22.02.1997.
[13] Regulation 354/83, OJ L 43, 15.02.1983 and Regulation 1700/2003, OJ L 243, 27.09.2003.
[14] Recommendation 2005/835, OJ L 312, 29.11.2005.

the citizens do not and never will make an effort to get the existing information, but rightly expect that they will be automatically informed, through their familiar media, about European affairs and decisions that are of interest to them. When they say in Euro-barometer surveys that they want to be informed about the institutions and policies of the EU, they mean that this information should come to them, not that they should go after it. Useful as they are to interested persons (researchers, interest groups and other special-ists), the Commission publications and Internet sites are ignored and are therefore use-less for the large majority of citizens.

Indeed, information by the Commission suffers from two inherent defects. Firstly, it is addressed to a few initiated persons rather than to the average citizen, who does not read sophisticated publications or surf in the Europa server of the Commission. Sec-ondly, information by the Commission reflects mainly its own proposals rather than the policies decided upon by the governments of the Member States and the Parliament of the peoples of the Union. Therefore, journalists and through them the public get the - partly right - impression that, through its information activities, the Commission defends its own policies rather than the common policies of the Member States.

The result of information deficiency, combined with disinformation on the part of eurosceptic media, is **the indifference or, worse, the dissatisfaction of citizens**, who quite sincerely believe that, instead of progressing in the field of European unification, the European Union is a theatre of infighting among European politicians; that it is to-tally unable to monitor global phenomena - such as globalisation, climate change and international conflicts - and that it is even responsible for some of their national prob-lems, such as unemployment and the cost of living. It is this mismatch between high expectations and totally or partly false perceptions of the public that endangers European unification. The indifference and/or dissatisfaction of citizens, demonstrated in European elections, opinion polls and referendums, must be recognised as a major failure of the integration process and a grave danger for its future.

10.1.3. The need for a common communication policy

The signed but not ratified Constitutional Treaty of the Union provides for the in-formation of workers and consumers, but not for that of the citizens. Whereas a Constitu-tion should be based on the respect of its citizens, its authors have willingly or unwill-ingly disregarded the danger of disrespect brought about by the deficient information and civic education of the citizens of the Union. It is strange that, whereas the citizens them-selves recognize their problem of understanding the European institutions and decisions, the political leaders ignore it or underrate it. If they ever examine seriously the Euro-barometers or other opinion surveys in their countries, they will understand that the citi-zens do not ask for a direct participation in the decision making process of the Union, but for a clear information as to how and why decisions are taken and as to what bearing they have on their lives. If this demand of the citizens was taken seriously into consid-eration, a common information and communication policy, covering all other common policies, could easily be conceived and implemented.

By **common information and communication policy** we mean a policy with a common set of guidelines, decisions, rules, measures and codes of conduct adopted by the European institutions and implemented by the European institutions and the govern-ments of the Member States [see section 1.1.2]. Although the Treaties do not explicitly call for such a policy, the Commission could, on the basis of the abovementioned Hel-sinki mandate of the European Council, take the initiative to propose it to the other institutions, as it usually does concerning all policies and measures. The Commission is the appropriate institution to consult, through a GreenPaper, national and professional experts, formulate and propose, in a White Paper [see section 10.1.1], a common information and communication policy with common goals, common means and multi-level implementation: European, national, regional and local. Thereafter, the Council and the European Parliament, with their own committees and experts, could work on the proposals of the Commission to make them acceptable to all parties concerned. The ensuing common communication policy should entail two basic elements: a common information and communication strategy of the European institutions and the governments of the Member States and a structure to carry it out, with at its head a European Press Agency.

The common strategy should encourage and give guidelines to the European institutions and the governments of the Member States to participate, together with regional and local authorities, in the common information tasks, in respect of the specific national and regional information needs. Coordination between the information services of the European institutions and the governments of the Member States should be assigned to a European Press Agency, i.e. an inter-institutional body, based in Brussels, depending from and representing all the European institutions: not only the three decision-making institutions of the Union, the Commission, the Council and the European Parliament, but also the European Ombudsman, the European Court of Justice, the Economic and Social Committee and the Committee of the Regions. The European Press Agency should, indeed, attract the attention of specific publics - i.e. professional and other non-governmental organisations and regional and local administrations - interested in the activities of the Ombudsman, the decisions of the Court of Justice and the opinions of the Committees.

But, of course, the attention of ordinary citizens should be attracted primarily to the activities and decisions of the main institutions, which have an effect on their professional and everyday lives. Press-conferences should present both the important proposals of the Commission and the major decisions of the Council and the Parliament. In the latter case, apart from the spokesmen of the institutions, it would be interesting to have the president of the Council and the chairman of the relevant parliamentary committee present a fresh decision to the press. Such a presentation should explain the problem addressed, the consequences of inaction, the reasons calling for common action in preference to individual action by the Member States, the main objectives aimed at by the decision and the most important means provided for attaining them. But, this common presentation should only be the basis of the information campaign on important decisions. On this basis should be built nationally oriented information by the ministers and the members of the competent parliamentary committee involved in a decision, addressed to the national media both in Brussels and at home.

It would, indeed, be quite reasonable that, upon adopting an important European law or measure, the responsible ministers give an accurate account to the journalists of their countries of the reasons of this law or measure, its goals and its effects on the professional or daily lives of the citizens of their states. Thus, each minister participating in the Council, which would have taken an important decision, would present in his or her own words and language the decision taken and/or circulate a press-release to national and regional media, based on the common press-release prepared by the European Press Agency. If he or she had voted against the measure taken, he or she should explain his or her disagreement, but also the reasoning having prevailed among his or her colleagues in the Council. The same information function should be performed by the members of the European Parliament, who should explain, through the media, why they have voted for or against a measure, along with the objectives and means agreed by the Assembly. Disapproval of a decision should not prevent the authorities and politicians of a Member State from participating in factual information about it. As a matter of fact, the concept of a common information and communication policy and respect for the democratic functioning of the institutions implementing it would call for the dissenting minority to join the majority in implementing a measure agreed by the latter.

Journalists, commentators and politicians of the opposition could, of course, criticise the measure taken and eventually blame the responsible minister for not having well defended national interests. In this way, citizens would have the double benefit of having a first-hand account of the reasons and objectives of a European measure, together with the arguments for and against it. They would thus be incited to think about the measure and take a stand on it, as they do about national measures and options. They would also come to know who and how represent them in Brussels. Eurosceptic media would, then, hopefully, avoid spreading false information about European decisions. In any case, they would not be able to claim that decisions are taken in secret by the "Eurocrats of Brussels", pointing at the Commission, when the citizens would be able to see for themselves that their own representatives, Ministers and European MPs, take part in the decision-making process in Brussels and can be appraised for their negotiating skills or called to account for any harm to national interests, actually or supposedly brought about by a common measure co-authored by them.

10.2. Audiovisual Policy

The audiovisual sector, which covers programme production and distribution ("software") and equipment manufacturing ("hardware"), has a great potential for growth and job creation in Europe. The European film and television programme industry, which plays a strategic role in the development of the audiovisual sector, is, in addition, **a prime vector of European culture** and a living testimony to the traditions and identity of each country. It must, therefore, illustrate the creative genius and the personality of the peoples of Europe; but, to do this, it must be competitive in an open, worldwide market[1].

In contrast to the information policy, the Member States of the Union have felt the need for a common audiovisual policy. A Protocol, annexed to the TEC in Amsterdam, asserts that **public broadcasting** in the Member States is directly related to the democratic, social and cultural needs of each society and to the need to preserve media pluralism [see also section 6.6.4.]. Member States may therefore provide for the funding of public service broadcasting in so far as such funding is granted to broadcasting organisations for the fulfilment of the public service remit as conferred, defined and organised by each Member State, and such funding does not affect trading conditions and competition in the Community.

The audiovisual sector in Europe took on a totally new face at the end of the 1980s, with the rapid growth in broadcasting by cable and telecommunications satellites and the emergence of the first European direct broadcasting satellites. However, **national markets in the Member States were too narrow** to be able to offer at competitive rates the equipment and programmes required by the new technologies and the proliferation of channels. This was a handicap for the European audiovisual sector, which was expected to be one of the principal service sectors in the 21st century.

---

[1] COM (94) 96, 6 April 1994.

Scattered and confined in their smallish national markets, European producers found themselves in conditions of uneven competition in the international arena as far as the costs were concerned. Europe should unify its audiovisual market to enable European producers to participate profitably in this technological revolution. Otherwise, it had to rely on powerful American and Japanese audiovisual industry, capable of covering cheaply international markets. American movies and serials and Japanese cartoons can defy world competition, because their cost is amortised on the large national market. European producers were doomed to disappear or be confined in their national markets.

At the same time a "technological revolution" was underway with the introduction of **high definition television (HDTV)** that gives to the image an almost perfect quality and makes it possible for the image to be accompanied by four sound channels, thus permitting, for example, a stereophonic sound and the simultaneous transmission of dialogues in two languages at the choice of the spectator. To prepare this revolution, the **Community's strategy on new technologies in the audiovisual sector** sought the cooperation between the Member States for the promotion of the European standard for HDTV, the aid for technological development and the aid to audiovisual operators for launching services using the new technology[1]. A single regulatory framework now covers the converging telecommunications, information technology and audiovisual sectors, including digital television[2] [see section 17.3.6.].

A particular regulatory framework was also necessary to permit the free provision of audiovisual services in the European space. To this end, a Directive concerning the exercise of television broadcasting activities (**"television without frontiers"**) aimed at the free movement of television programmes within the Community through the freedom to pick up and re-transmit programmes from another Member State. It consequently lays down the principle that compliance with the rules is to be enforced by the broadcasting State, without interference from the country of retransmission of the programme. The Directive introduced minimum harmonisation of advertising (breaks, duration, advertising for certain products, ethical rules), sponsorship, protection of minors and right of reply, while promoting the production and distribution of European audiovisual works. It stipulates that the Member States must ensure, "where practicable" and by appropriate means, that broadcasters reserve a majority proportion of their transmission time, excluding certain types of programme, for European works. The Directive also specifies that at least 10% of airtime or of the programming budgets should be earmarked for European works by independent producers. The 1989 Directive was amended in 1997 in order to clarify certain definitions of terms such as "television advertising" and "European works", to introduce rules on teleshopping and broadcasting for self-promotional purposes and to strengthen the protection of minors, in particular by making it compulsory for unencoded programmes likely to be unsuitable for minors to be preceded by a sound or visual warning[3].

The **"MEDIA 2007"** programme of support for the European audiovisual sector (2007-2013) aspires to strengthen the audiovisual sector economically to enable it to play its cultural roles more effectively[4]. It aims, in particular, to (a) preserve and enhance European cultural and linguistic diversity and its cinematographic and audiovisual heritage; (b) increase the circulation and viewership of European audiovisual works inside and outside the European Union; (c) strengthen the competitiveness of the European audiovisual sector in the framework of an open and competitive European market fa-

[1]   Decision 89/337, OJ L 142, 25.05.1989 and Decision 89/630, OJ L 363, 13.12.1989.
[2]   Directive 2002/21, OJ L 108, 24.04.2002.
[3]   Directive 89/552, OJ L 298, 17.10.1989 and Directive 97/36, OJ L 202, 30.07.1997.
[4]   Decision 1718/2006, OJ L 327, 24.11.2006.

vourable to employment. Upstream of audiovisual production it helps the acquisition and improvement of skills in the audiovisual field and the development of European audiovisual works. Downstream of audiovisual production it supports the distribution and promotion of European audiovisual works. In general it aspires to strengthen the structure of the European audiovisual sector, particularly SMEs and to reduce the imbalances in the European audiovisual market between high audiovisual production capacity countries and countries or regions with low audiovisual production capacity and/or a restricted geographic and linguistic area. The Community participates in the **European Audiovisual Observatory** aimed at boosting the competitiveness of European audiovisual industry[1].

The aims of the directive "television without frontiers" have broadly been met, with a substantial increase in the number of television channels in Europe, and especially in the United Kingdom, as well as in the broadcasting of European works and independent productions[2]. Member States have given themselves the means to achieve the overriding objectives of public interest that the Directive aims to safeguard[3]. According to the Court of Justice, the "Television without frontiers Directive" does not allow a Member State to apply to television broadcasts from other Member States a provision of domestic law, which prohibits the broadcasting of advertisements on television that are designed to attract the attention of children under 12 years of age[4]. The Court has also ruled that the transmission and broadcasting of television signals comes within the rules of the Treaty relating to the provision of services and that there cannot be any discrimination in the application of legal rulings or taxing in respect of satellite dishes[5]. According to the Directive coordinating certain rules concerning copyright and rights related to copyright applicable to satellite broadcasting and cable retransmission, broadcasting right Member States must provide an exclusive right for the author to authorize the communication to the public by satellite of copyright works[6].

Emphasising that national aid to the film and audiovisual industries is one of the chief means of **ensuring cultural diversity** and may contribute to the emergence of a European audiovisual market, the Council has confirmed that the Member States are justified in conducting national policies to support the creation of film and audiovisual products[7]. A Council recommendation proposes the development of the competitiveness of the European audiovisual and information services industry by promoting national frameworks aimed at achieving a comparable and effective level of protection of minors and human dignity[8]. Another recommendation aims to improve conditions of conservation, restoration and exploitation of the European film heritage and remove obstacles to the development and competitiveness of related industrial activities[9].

10.3. Cultural activities

Although the Treaty of Rome had not provided for any action in the cultural field, some measures in this field were taken already in the 1980s, in particular: the annual naming of a European "**cultural capital**"[10]; the agreement on special entry conditions to museums and cultural events for young people[11]; and the creation of transnational cultural routes[12]. A Community action lays down the procedure for designating the European Capitals of culture for the period 2005 to 2019[13].

Since the late 1980s, the Community is **promoting books and reading**[14]. Other permanent cultural activities of the European Commission concern: encouragement of the cooperation between foundations promoting art and culture (patronage); support for a growing number of **training grants** and for cultural and artistic

[1]   Decision 1999/784, OJ L 307, 02.12.1999 and Decision 2004/2239, OJ L 390, 31.12.2004.
[2]   COM (2000) 442, 17 July 2000.
[3]   COM (2002) 778, 6 January 2003.
[4]   Judgment of 9 July 1997, Joined cases C-34/95 and C-36/95, ECR 1997, p. I-3843.
[5]   Judgment of 18 June 1991, Case C-260/89 ERT, ECR I-2925 and Judgment of 29 November 2001, Case C-17/00, ECR 2001, I-09445.
[6]   Directive 93/83, OJ L 248, 06.10.1993.
[7]   Resolution, OJ C 73, 06.03.2001.
[8]   Recommendation 98/560, OJ L 270, 07.10.1998.
[9]   Recommendation 2005/865, OJ L 323, 09.12.2005.
[10] OJ C 153, 22.06.1985, p. 2.
[11] OJ C 348, 31.12.1985, p. 2-3.
[12] OJ C 44, 26.02.1986, p. 2.
[13] Decision 1419/1999, OJ L 166, 01.07.1999 and Decision 649/2005, OJ L 117, 04.05.2005.
[14] OJ C 183, 20.07.1989, p. 1-2.

projects throughout the European Union; an annual operation under which financial aid is granted to projects for the preservation and promotion of Europe's **architectural heritage** selected by a European jury. The Athens Parthenon, the cathedral of Aix-la-Chapelle and the Forum Romanum in Rome are among those already granted aid. The Community encourages European artistic and cultural creation, cultural events, cultural exchanges and other projects involving all artistic disciplines. It also supports a number of high-profile activities of which the best known are the Youth Orchestra and the Baroque Orchestra of the European Community.

Culture was brought fully into the action scope of the Community through the Treaty of Maastricht [see section 2.2.]. The common cultural policy **does not aim at any harmonisation of the cultural identities** of the Member States, but, on the contrary, at the conservation of their diversity. Article 151 (TEC) states, in fact, that the Community should contribute to the flowering of the cultures of the Member States, while respecting their national and regional diversity and at the same time bringing the common cultural heritage to the fore. Its action aims at encouraging cooperation between Member States and, if necessary, supporting and supplementing their action in the following areas: improvement of the knowledge and dissemination of the culture and history of the European peoples; conservation and safeguarding of cultural heritage of European significance; non-commercial cultural exchanges; artistic and literary creation, including in the audiovisual sector.

In order to achieve these objectives, **four means are employed**: cooperation between Member States; consideration for cultural aspects under other Community policies, including competition policy, concerning in particular aid to promote culture and heritage conservation (Art. 87 TEC); cooperation between the Community and its Member States with third countries and the competent international organisations; specific measures to support action taken by Member States which may take two forms: incentive measures, excluding any harmonisation of the laws and regulations of the Member States [see section 6.2.1.], adopted unanimously by the Council acting under the co-decision procedure after consultation of the Committee of the Regions; and recommendations unanimously adopted by the Council. The departure from the normal co-decision procedure [see section 4.3.] denotes that a Member State may not be forced by a qualified majority in the Council to take an action that it considers to be harmful to its cultural identity.

The European Union must strike a balance between the objectives arising from the completion of the internal market and those relating to the **protection of the national heritage**. In fact, a Council Regulation subjects the **export outside the Community of cultural goods** of artistic, historical or archaeological value to an export licence issued by the Member State on whose territory it is lawfully located[1]. In the same vein, a Directive provides for the return of cultural objects unlawfully removed from the territory of a Member State unlawfully removed from the on or after 1 January 1993[2]. It notably establishes a judicial procedure for the return of cultural objects and cooperation between the competent authorities of the Member States.

A rigorous, effective system for the **protection of copyright and related rights** is one of the main ways of ensuring that European cultural creativity and production receive the necessary resources and of safeguarding the independence and dignity of artistic creators and performers [see also sections 6.2.4 and 23.4.]. Therefore, **copyright** is protected at European Union level by a Directive that harmonises the term of copyright at 70 years after the death of the author in the case of literary, artistic, cinematographic or audiovisual works[3]. For the last two categories, calculation of the term of protection

---

[1]   Regulation 3911/92, OJ L 395, 31.12.1992 and Regulation 974/2001, OJ L 137, 19.05.2001.
[2]   Directive 93/7, OJ L 74, 27.03.1993 and Directive 2001/38, OJ L 187, 10.07.2001.
[3]   Directive 93/98, OJ L 290, 24.11.1993 and Directive 2001/29, OJ L 167, 22.06.2001.

begins after the death of the last of the persons to survive from among the principal director, the author of the screenplay, the author of the dialogue and the composer of the music. The same Directive harmonises at 50 years the term of protection of the main **related rights** (those of performers, producers of phonograms or of films and broadcasting organisations). It also provides collective and obligatory management of the rights for cable retransmission through collective societies representing the various categories of rightholders.

A Directive recognises the "resale right" as an intellectual property right of the author of an original work of art and enables the author and her or his heirs to receive a royalty based on the sale price obtained for any resale of the work by auction houses, art galleries or any other art dealer[1]. Another Directive provides protection for both paper-based and electronic databases for a period of 15 years from their completion, so as to create an attractive environment for investment in them while preserving the interests of users[2]. The Community is a contracting party in the World Intellectual Property Organisation (WIPO) Copyright Treaty and in the Performances and Phonograms Treaty[3]. These Treaties help to guarantee a high level of protection of works while permitting public access to contents which might be transmitted via the Internet, for example [see also section 6.2.4.]. The rental and lending of copyright works, notably phonograms and films, and the subject matter of related rights are also protected[4]. A directive engages Member States to protect **computer programs**, by copyright, as literary works within the meaning of the Berne Convention for the Protection of Literary and Artistic Works[5].

Emphasising that **conservation of cinema heritage** can play a decisive role in consolidating the cultural identity of European countries, the Council has called on the Member States to cooperate in the following areas: participation in a transnational study on the situation regarding European cinema archives; stepping up the exchange of experience, knowledge and good practice; encouraging the progressive networking of European archival databases; and the possible use of these collections for educational and scientific purposes and for purposes specific to archives[6]. On its part, the Commission has clarified certain legal aspects relating to cinematographic and other audiovisual works and in particular the specific compatibility criteria for national aid to film and television production[7].

The "Culture 2000" programme is designed to rationalise and reinforce the effectiveness of activities in the field of cultural cooperation within the framework of a single financing and programming instrument[8]. It contributes to the promotion of a common European cultural area, by fostering cooperation between creative artists, cultural operators, private and public promoters, those responsible for the activities of cultural networks and other partners, as well as between the cultural institutions of the Member States. Another programme of Community action provides financial support to organisations active at European level in the field of culture[9].

10.4. Appraisal and outlook

Information is a key instrument of any policy making, let alone multinational policy-making. Citizens rightly distrust the common policies, which they do not understand for lack of proper information. The role of information has been underestimated and largely neglected in the EC/EU, with the result of a growing estrangement of the European public from European policies, which become ever more complicated as they advance and, hence, increasingly difficult to understand. As we saw above, three fourths of European citizens believe that they are ill informed about European affairs. This information deficit is endangering European unification. The more ignorant the citizens are about the institutions, the goals and the mechanisms of the integration process, the more

---

[1]   Directive 2001/84, OJ L 272, 13.10.2001.
[2]   Directive 96/9, OJ L 77, 27.03.1996.
[3]   Decision 2000/278, OJ L 89, 11.04.2000.
[4]   Directive 92/100, OJ L 346, 27.11.1992 and Directive 2001/29, OJ L 167, 22.06.2001.
[5]   Directive 91/250, OJ L 122, 17.05.1991 and Directive 93/98, OJ L 290, 24.11.1993.
[6]   Resolution, OJ C 193, 11.07.2000.
[7]   COM (2001) 534 and COM (2004) 171, 16 March 2004.
[8]   Decision 508/2000, OJ L 63, 10.03.2000 and Regulation 885/2004, OJ L 168, 01.05.2004.
[9]   Decision 792/2004, OJ L 138, 30.04.2004.

easily **public opinion may be misled** about particular issues or the general thrust of the process.

The lack of generalised information combined with a sharp disinformation on the part of eurosceptic media is an explosive mixture placed under the foundations of European unification, because it separates citizens in two categories: the apathetics and the dogmatics. The vast silent majority is indifferent, because it finds living and working conditions generally acceptable in Europe, compared with other parts of the world, but does not credit the EC/EU with a significant role in shaping those conditions. On the other hand, a minority, which is systematically irritated against the deeds or supposed misdeeds of the European institutions (notably that of usurping national sovereignty), underestimates or even denies all the achievements of the Union in terms of peace, relative prosperity and unobstructed movement of goods, services, labour and capital. This situation is harmful, not only to the progress of European integration, but also to the good functioning of its democratic institutions [see section 4.3.] that are debased in the eyes of the citizens by some activists with dubious motives.

The states which participate in the integration process have, consequently, a common interest in developing **a common information and communication policy about this process.** This means using simple language, which can be used by the mass media, to put forward the reasons for European policies, the consequences of inertia and the benefits of common action in the interests of all participants. This would not be propaganda, but information necessary in a democratic community concerned with encouraging participation of all its members in communal life. This factual information is necessary in order to bring the citizens closer to the institutions of the Union and thus bridge the information and the democratic gaps. Priority should be given to information on issues close to the daily lives of citizens, such as price stability and employment as well as on issues of major political interest, such as the future of Europe and the place of the Union in the world. The Commission should take the initiative to propose a common communication policy with common goals, common means and multi-level implementation: European, national, regional and local.

Likewise, the European institutions - the Commission, the Council and the Parliament - should encourage the Member States to introduce the **teaching of the history, the institutions and the goals of European integration** in the high schools. This, again, would not be indoctrination dangerous for the democracy, but rather a civic education, necessary for the correct functioning of the democratic institutions at European level. The proper functioning of democratic institutions depends on well-informed and educated citizens. As revealed by public opinion surveys, practically all the citizens in all the Member States demand with insistence better information for themselves and better education for their children. They are right, because the two go together. The civic education of the young about the basic facts of European unification should, indeed, be the trunk on which would grow and be constantly developed, by the institutions and the Member States, the branches and leaves of the European information tree relating to all common policies and activities.

The cultural activities of the Union rightly emphasise the **cultural diversity of the nations that make it up** rather than trying to promote a common culture; but the national cultural identities should not overshadow the common cultural heritage of European peoples. Consciousness of a common cultural heritage is part of the process of an ever closer union among the peoples of Europe. The proper historical dimension, in particular, could contribute to a better mutual understanding of the cultures of European peoples. History lessons taught from the national angle, accentuate the divisions, the wars and the hatreds among European nations rather than their common cultural heritage. The Ministers of Education should one day agree on a textbook of European history and culture, which could make young Europeans understand that the national cultural particularities, which make up Europe's cultural wealth, are all parts of the same European civilisation of Greek-Roman origin.

In this respect, an effective **European audiovisual policy**, which is still in its inception phase, can enhance not only the common European cultural identity, but also the various national identities that enrich it. Certain Community measures could improve the industry's competitiveness, such as support systems for the distribution of non-domestic European works, the encouragement of private investment in European audiovisual production on foreign markets, the organisation of a pan-European prize-giving ceremony by the audiovisual profession and, last but not least, the launching of digital television in a competitive environment. Digital cinema, facilitating the circulation of European audiovisual works, could promote European cinema, which is in constant decline in recent years.

Information, audiovisual and cultural policies are important for the European integration process, because once the citizens understand better the significance of this process for their wellbeing and their liberties, they may become active supporters (rather than apathetic onlookers) of **the unification of Europe**. They may, thus tend to participate more eagerly at European elections and oppose extremist anti-European parties at national elections. They may also lodge more complaints with the Commission when they regard a measure taken by a national, regional or local authority as contravening Community law [see section 9.3.]. They may thus make them comply more fully with that law and be more prepared to provide their bricks for the further construction of the European edifice.

Bibliography on information, audiovisual and cultural policies

- BEAT GRABER Christoph. "The new UNESCO Convention on Cultural Diversity: a counterbalance to the WTO?" in *Journal of International Economic Law*, v. 9, n. 3, September 2006, p. 553-574.
- CAUTRÈS Bruno. "Les opinions publiques et la construction européenne", *Questions internationales*, n. 13, mai-juin 2005, p. 89-96.
- EUROPEAN COMMISSION. *Mobile broadcasting: technological developments, market opportunities regulations and policy*. Luxembourg: EUR-OP*, 2006.
  - Follow-up to the White Paper on a New Impetus for European Youth: Implementing the common objectives for participation by and information for young people in view of promoting their active European citizenship. Luxembourg: EUR-OP*, 2006.
- GIFFORD Chris. "The rise of post-imperial populism : the case of right-wing euroscepticism in Britain", *European Journal of Political Research*, v. 45, n. 5, August 2006, p. 851-869.
- HERBILLON Michel (sous la dir. de). La fracture européenne : Après le référendum du 29 mai : 40 propositions concrètes pour mieux informer les Français sur l'Europe. Rapport au Premier ministre. Paris : Documentation française, 2005.
- IFFLY Catherine, MARTIN Éric. "Le projet de Convention internationale sur la diversité culturelle comme réponse au marché mondial de la culture". *Etudes internationales*, v. 36, n. 2, juin 2005, p. 201-217.
- JUND Sarah (et al.). "Culture et marché", *ERA-Forum: scripta iuris europaei*, n. 1, 2005, p. 3-130.
- KEA EUROPEAN AFFAIRS. *The economy of culture in Europe: a study prepared for the European Commission*. Brussels:EC: KEA European Affairs, 2006.
- McLAREN Lauren M. *Identity, interests and attitudes to European integration*. Basingstoke: Palgrave Macmillan, 2006.
- MEYER Christoph. *The europeanization of media discourse: a study of quality press coverage of economic policy co-ordination since Amsterdam*. Journal of Common Market Studies, v. 43, n. 1, March 2005, p. 121-148.
- MOUSSIS Nicolas. "Pour rapprocher les citoyens de l'Union: une politique commune de la communication", *Revue du marché commun et de l'Union européenne*, n. 481, septembre 2004, p. 500-508.

- NANZ Patrizia. *Europolis: Constitutional patriotism beyond the nation state*. Manchester: Manchester University Press, 2006.
- ROBERT Jacques. "Un gâchis référendaire", *Revue du droit public et de la science politique en France et à l'étranger*, v. 121, n. 4, juillet-août 2005, p. 839-847.
- ROHRSCHNEIDER Robert, WHITEFIELD Stephen (eds.). *Public opinion, party competition and the European Union in post-communist Europe*. Basingstoke: Palgrave Macmillan, 2006.
- SAMPOL Célia. "Les médias d'Europe centrale et l'intégration européenne" in *Courrier des pays de l'Est*, n. 1055, mai-juin 2006, p. 40-51.
- TAYLOR NELSON SOFRES, EOS GALLUP EUROPE. *Eurobarometer 62*. Brussels: European Commission, May 2005.
- THEILER Tobias. *Political symbolism and European integration*. Manchester: Manchester University Press, 2005.
- UPSON Richard, *Connecting with citizens: does the EU have the will to tackle its information deficit?* Bruxelles: European Citizen Action Service (ECAS), 2006.
- VREESE Claes de, BOOMGAARDEN Hajo. "Media effects on public opinion about the enlargement of the European Union" in *Journal of Common Market Studies*, v. 44, n. 2, June 2006, p. 419-436.

---

*The publications of the Office for Official Publications of the European Communities (EUR-OP) exist usually in all official languages of the EU.

Chapter 11

CONSUMER POLICY

Diagram of the chapter

Consumer information p. 194	**Protection of health and physical safety** p. 195	**Protection of economic and legal interests** p. 199

A common policy to protect consumers and users of products and services is essential for the functioning of the single market in the interest of the citizens. The aim of the common consumer policy is to ensure that the European Union's consumers draw maximum benefit from the existence of the internal market and play an active role in it. The single market must serve their maximum wellbeing and give them **a free choice of goods and services** of the best possible quality and at the best possible price, without consideration for their origin or for the nationality of their supplier [see section 6.1.]. Furthermore, within the single market consumers must enjoy a similar level of protection to that provided within a national market. For these reasons, the goods and services offered in the single market should be safe and the consumers should dispose of the necessary information so as to make the good choices.

Article 153 (TEC), gives the Community the task of contributing to the **protection of health, safety and economic interests** of consumers, as well to the promotion of their right to information, education and to organise themselves in order to safeguard their interests. The attainment of those objectives should be pursued through: (a) measures adopted pursuant to Article 95 (harmonisation of legislations) in the context of the completion of the internal market [see section 6.2.1.]; and (b) measures which support, supplement and monitor the policy pursued by the Member States. In order to help achieve the objectives of consumer protection, a Council Resolution demands that allowance be made for consumers' interests in **other Community policies**[1]. Obviously, the common consumer policy should interact with other common policies, notably in the fields of agriculture, fisheries, environment protection and the harmonisation of legislations necessary for the internal market.

Following a public consultation, based on a Green Paper[2], the Commission set out its **consumer policy strategy** at European level for the years 2002 to 2006[3]. It defined three mid-term objectives: ensuring a high common level of consumer protection; guaranteeing effective enforcement of consumer protection rules; and guaranteeing the proper involvement of consumer organisations in EU policies. The Council called on the Commission to implement the strategy in line with the stated objectives, with particular emphasis on incorporating consumer protection into other Community policies and activities, and paying particular attention to specific areas such as services of general interest, the general safety of products and services[4].

These three objectives are designed to make it easier to integrate consumer concerns into all other common policies, to maximise the benefits of the single market for consumers and to prepare for enlargement of the European Union. A short-term programme, which is regularly reviewed, provides for the actions necessary to achieve these objectives, including: action on the safety of services; the development of an administrative cooperation framework between Member States and of redress mechanisms for consumers; the review of mechanisms for participation of consumer organisations in EU policy-making; and the setting-up of education and capacity-building projects.

The competent authorities in the Member States designated as responsible for the enforcement of the laws that protect consumers' interests must cooperate with each other and with the Commission in order to ensure compliance with those laws and the smooth functioning of the internal market and in order to enhance the protection of consumers' economic interests[5]. The Commission is advised in the field of consumer protection by a **European Consumer Consultative Group** composed of: (a) one member representing national consumer organisations from each Member State; and (b) one member from each European consumer organisation[6]. Its main task is to ensure that the requirements of consumers are taken into account in the formulation of Community policies.

11.1. Consumer information

Consumer information seeks to ensure that consumers are able to **compare the prices** for the same product within a country and are as well informed as possible on price differences between the Member States. The **indication of the prices** of the products represents an important means of information and protection of consumers. A Community Directive imposes the indication of the price per unit of measurement of all products sold in the shops, thereby giving the consumer a clear idea of the unit cost of the product in question and enabling him or her to compare different products and to make the best choice[7]. The selling price and the unit price must be unambiguous, easily identifiable and clearly legible. They must relate to the final price of the product and must refer to the quantity declared in accordance with national and Community provisions.

Labelling of products is also an important way of achieving better information and transparency for the consumer and ensuring the smooth operation of the internal market[8].

---

[1]   OJ C 3, 07.01.1987, p. 1-2.
[2]   COM (2001) 531, 2 October 2001.
[3]   COM (2002) 208, 7 May 2002.
[4]   Council Resolution, OJ C 11, 17.01.2003.
[5]   Regulation 2006/2004, OJ L 364, 09.12.2004 and Directive 2005/29, OJ L 149, 11.06.2005.
[6]   Decision 2003/709, OJ L 258, 10.10.2003.
[7]   Directive 98/6, OJ L 80, 18.03.1998.
[8]   Council resolution, OJ C 110, 20.04.1993, p. 1-2.

Two communications of the Commission are designed to encourage multilingual information and to improve cooperation between producers, distributors and consumers on the subject of labelling of products in the internal market[1]. The language requirements, the trade name, the stated quantity of the ingredients and other provisions are specified in the Directive on the labelling, presentation and advertising of foodstuffs[2].

The Commission encourages the creation and operation of consumer information centres for consumers by covering a part of the costs of organisations, which are willing to assume this information task and appear capable of doing so efficiently. In addition, the Commission gives financial aid to radio and TV stations to encourage them to give a European dimension to broadcasts on consumer problems. It publishes the "European consumer guide to the single market" and organises the "European Young Consumer Competition" to encourage young people to become aware of consumer issues.

11.2. Protection of health and physical safety

The Community turned its attention to the physical safety of consumers in the 1970s. But for many years, efforts in this field were **overshadowed by other common policies**, notably the agricultural one and that of removing technical barriers to trade. This was particularly true of the Directive on the alignment of legislation on cosmetics[3] and that on the classification, packaging and labelling of dangerous preparations[4]. These directives, however, adapted over the years to technical progress, have gradually become more protective of human health. Other directives aim directly at this objective, notably the Directive concerning food additives authorised for use in foodstuffs intended for human consumption[5] and the Directive on measures to monitor certain substances and residues thereof in live animals and animal products[6].
The accident at the Chernobyl nuclear power plant in April 1986 gave the Community an opportunity to complete its legislation on **radioactive contamination**. In addition to ad hoc measures adopted in order to coordinate national measures covering agricultural produce[7] and definition of conditions under which agricultural produce originating in third countries could be imported[8], the Council adopted in December 1987 a Regulation setting maximum permitted levels of radioactive contamination of foodstuffs and of feeding stuffs following a nuclear accident or any other case of radiological emergency[9].

The effort to complete the internal market proved the effective trigger of a genuine policy to protect the health and physical safety of consumers. In the 1980s the Community placed the wellbeing of its citizens high on its list of priorities by adopting **general legislation guaranteeing the safety of individuals** in their capacity as users of products, regardless of the origin of the latter. This is the aim of a Directive on the approximation of the laws of the Member States concerning products which, appearing to be other than they are, endanger the health or safety of consumers[10]. This Directive prohibits the marketing, import and either manufacture or export of **dangerous imitations of foodstuffs**. Such products can be withdrawn from the market by a Member State and the Commission and the other Member States are informed of their existence.

A major Directive in the context of the single market was adopted in 1988 dealing with **toy safety**[11]. It sets the basic safety requirements that must be met by all toys manufactured in the Community or imported from third countries. The European standardisation committees then adopt harmonised standards and manufacturers respecting these are

---

[1] COM (93) 456 and Council resolution, OJ C 128, 09.05.1994.
[2] Directive 2000/13, OJ L 109, 06.05.2000 and Directive 2003/89, OJ L 308, 25.11.2003.
[3] Directive 76/768, OJ L 262, 27.09.1976 and Directive 2006/65, OJ L 198, 20.07.2006.
[4] Directive 1999/45, OJ L 200, 30.07.1999 and Directive 2004/66, OJ L 168, 01.05.2004.
[5] Directive 89/107, OJ L 40, 11.02.1989 and Directive 94/34, OJ L 237, 10.09.1994.
[6] Directive 96/23, OJ L 125, 23.05.1996 and Regulation 882/2004, OJ L 165, 30.04.2004.
[7] Recommendation 86/156, OJ L 118, 07.05.1986.
[8] Regulation 3955/87, OJ L 371, 30.12.1987.
[9] Regulation 3954/87, OJ L 371, 30.12.1987 and Regulation 2218/89, OJ L 211, 22.07.1989.
[10] Directive 87/357, OJ L 192, 11.07.1987.
[11] Directive 88/378, OJ L 187, 16.07.1988 and Directive 93/68, OJ L 220, 30.08.1993.

covered by a presumption that their toys meet the basic safety requirements defined in the Directive [see section 6.2.3.]. This Directive consequently promotes the free movement of goods while encouraging the manufacture of high-quality danger-free toys for the Union's children.

Since it is difficult to adopt Community legislation for every product, it is necessary to establish at Community level a general safety requirement. This general legal instrument is provided by a Directive on **general product safety**[1]. The purpose of this Directive is to ensure that products placed on the market, which are intended for consumers or likely, under reasonably foreseeable conditions, to be used by consumers even if not intended for them, are safe. Producers are obliged to place only safe products on the market, conforming to the specific rules of national law of the Member State in whose territory the product is marketed drawn up in conformity with the Treaty and in accordance with Directive 98/34 laying down a procedure for the provision of information in the field of technical standards and regulations [see section 6.2.2.]. Distributors are required to act with due care to help to ensure compliance with the applicable safety requirements, in particular by not supplying products which they know or should have presumed, on the basis of the information in their possession and as professionals, do not comply with those requirements. Where producers and distributors know or ought to know that a product that they have placed on the market poses risks to the consumer they must immediately inform the competent authorities of the Member States thereof. Member States must ensure that producers and distributors comply with their obligations, establish or nominate authorities competent to monitor the compliance of products with the general safety requirements and lay down the rules on penalties applicable to infringements of the national provisions adopted. The Commission must promote and take part in the operation in a European network of the authorities of the Member States competent for product safety. This network must be coordinated with other Community procedures, in particular the **Community Rapid Information System (RAPEX)**, which is described in Annex II of the directive and is essentially aimed at a rapid exchange of information in the event of a serious risk [see details below].

Regulation 178/2002 lays down the general principles and procedures in matters of **food law and food safety** and establishes the European Food Safety Authority[2]. Whilst ensuring the effective functioning of the internal market, it aims at ensuring a high level of protection of human health and consumers' interest in relation to food, taking into account in particular the diversity in the supply of food including traditional products. It establishes common principles and responsibilities, the means to provide a strong science base, efficient organisational arrangements and procedures to underpin decision-making in matters of food and feed safety. The **European Food Safety Authority** must provide scientific advice, independent information and scientific and technical support for the Community's legislation and policies in all fields which have a direct or indirect impact on food and feed safety.

The Community legislation governing **food hygiene**[3], health issues related to the marketing of **products of animal origin**[4] and the organisation of **official controls** on such products[5] has been recast in 2004. Henceforth, a distinction is made between aspects of food hygiene and matters to do with animal health and official controls, thus providing scope for defining clearly the responsibilities of food business operators and

---

[1]   Directive 2001/95, OJ L 11, 15.01.2002, repealing Directive 92/59, OJ L 228, 11.08.1992 from 15 January 2004.
[2]   Regulation 178/2002, OJ L 31, 01.02.2002 and Regulation 1642/2003, OJ L 245, 29.09.2003.
[3]   Regulation 852/2004, OJ L 157, 30.04.2004.
[4]   Directive 41/2004, OJ L 157, 30.04.2004.
[5]   Regulation 854/2004, OJ L 157, 30.04.2004 and Regulation 882/2004, OJ L 165, 30.04.2004.

the competent authorities in the Member States. A key point of the new legislation is that every operator involved in the food chain will bear primary responsibility for food safety, with a single, transparent hygiene policy being applicable to all foodstuffs and all operators (from the farm to the table), together with effective instruments to guarantee food safety and manage any future crisis in the sector. Administrative measures with criminal sanctions and financial penalties may be imposed on any Member State which fails to comply with Community feed and food law[1]. In 2005, rigorous Community measures were taken for the control of **avian influenza**, including provision of contingency plans in the event of human contamination[2].

The food safety policy of the Community is based on the **precautionary principle**. This principle is an integral part of a structured approach to risk analysis based on assessment, management and communication of risk. In specific circumstances where, following an assessment of available information, the possibility of harmful effects on health is identified but scientific uncertainty persists, provisional risk management measures necessary to ensure the high level of health protection chosen in the Community may be adopted, pending further scientific information for a more comprehensive risk assessment [see details below]. Indeed, according to the Court of Justice, when there is uncertainty regarding the risk to human health or safety, the Community institutions are empowered to take protective measures without having to wait until the reality and seriousness of those risks becomes fully apparent[3].

In accordance with the precautionary principle, a Directive aims at monitoring the deliberate release into the environment and on the placing on the market of **genetically modified organisms (GMOs)** as or in products[4]. Products containing GMOs must be clearly labelled and the public must be informed and consulted prior to the release and placing on the market of GMOs and products containing GMOs. Member States must establish public registers of all locations where GMOs are grown and have agreed deadlines for phasing out antibiotic resistance markers in GMOs which could have adverse effects on human health and the environment. Genetically modified micro-organisms may be used solely under conditions of contained use[5]. A Regulation provides a framework for the **traceability of products** consisting of or containing GMOs, and food and feed produced from GMOs, with the objectives of facilitating accurate labelling, monitoring the effects on the environment and, where appropriate, on health, and the implementation of the appropriate risk management measures including, if necessary, withdrawal of products[6]. Another Regulation lays down Community procedures for the authorisation and supervision of genetically modified food and feed and lays down provisions for the **labelling** of genetically modified food and feed[7].

According to the Court of First Instance the precautionary principle could be applied only where there was a risk, notably for human health, which had not yet been conclusively demonstrated, but it could not be based on unverified conjecture[8]. Before any preventive measures were taken, the competent public authority had to conduct a **risk assessment** with two complementary components: a scientific component (as thorough a scientific risk assessment as possible taking account notably of the urgency of the situation) and a political

---

[1] Regulation 882/2004, OJ L 165, 30.04.2004.
[2] Directive 2005/94, OJ L 10, 14.01.2006.
[3] Judgments of 5 May 1998, Cases C-180/96 and C-157/96, ECR 1998 I-2265.
[4] Directive 2001/18, OJ L 106, 17.04.2001 last amended by Regulation 1830/2003, OJ L 268, 18.10.2003 and Decisions 2002/811, 2002/812 and 2002/813, OJ L 280, 18.10.2002.
[5] Directive 90/219, OJ L 117, 08.05.1990, Directive 98/81, OJ L 330, 05.12.1998 and Decision 2001/204, OJ L 73, 15.03.2001.
[6] Regulation 1830/2003, OJ L 268, 18.10.2003.
[7] Regulation 1829/2003, OJ L 268, 18.10.2003.
[8] Judgments of 11 September 2002, Case T-13/99 (ECR 1999, p. II-1961) *Pfizer Animal Health SA* v *Council* and Case T-70/99 *Alpharma Inc.* v *Council*, ECR 2002, p. II-3495.

component (risk management), with the public authority determining the desired level of protection and consequently deciding on an appropriate measure given the level of risk it had determined. "Risk" thus constituted a function of the probability that use of a product or a procedure would adversely affect human health. "Hazard" ("danger") was, in this context, commonly used in a broader sense and described any product or procedure capable of having an adverse effect on human health.

Taking account of the bovine spongiform encephalopathy (BSE) experience [see sections 5.1.3 and 21.4.2.], **animal-health rules** govern the placing on the market and importation from third countries of products of animal origin, with a view to preventing the spread of animal diseases[1]. Other rules are applicable to the collection, transport, storing, handling, processing and use or disposal of **animal by-products** in order to prevent them from presenting a risk to animal or public health[2]. They prohibit the recycling of dead animals and condemned animal material into the feed chain. The only raw material allowed to be used for the production of animal feed is material derived from animals declared fit for human consumption. More generally, a regulation lays down requirements for feed hygiene, so as to ensure a high level of consumer protection with regard to food and feed safety[3].

A directive aims to approximate the laws of the Member States with a view to maintaining both a high level of public health protection and the free circulation of products marketed in the Community as **foods containing concentrated sources of nutrients** (vitamins and minerals) and presented for supplementing the intake of those nutrients from the normal diet[4]. It establishes specific rules on labelling and criteria for fixing the maximum quantities of vitamins and minerals in these products. Foods and food ingredients treated with ionising radiation [see sections 13.5.7 and 19.2.3.] are also subjected to Community checks[5].

After the BSE or **"mad-cow" crisis** of 1996, the Commission set up a **Scientific Steering Committee**, made up of distinguished scientific experts, to provide sound scientific advice and coordinate the work of the various sector-specific scientific committees in the field of consumer health[6]. Eight scientific sector-specific committees are required to draw the Commission's attention to any specific or emerging problem falling within their remit and to provide scientific advice on the basis of trends in existing scientific data. The Community "Food and Veterinary Office", has responsibility for monitoring the observance of veterinary and plant-health legislation and food hygiene rules both within the European Union and in countries which provide it with foodstuffs. However, recommendations issued by the scientific committees are not always taken into consideration by the Member States[7]. On February 2006, the Commission established interim protection measures in relation to suspected cases of highly pathogenic **avian influenza** in wild birds in the Community[8].

Thanks to the Community system of **rapid information exchange** on dangers arising from the use of consumer products **(RAPEX)**, the Member States and the Commission can take the necessary urgent steps when it becomes known that a particular consumer product is a source of immediate and serious danger to consumer health and physical safety. Managed by the Commission, the system has permitted the withdrawal from the market of several dangerous products, particularly foodstuffs. Early-warning systems cannot work properly, however, if the Member States do not apply the appropriate measures fully and in good time when a risk arises, as was the case of Belgium which infringed Community procedures by not informing the Commission and the other Member States immediately that dioxin had been found in foodstuffs and in animal feed in June 1999 [see section 5.1.3.].

Another information network, the Community system of information and monitoring of **accidents in the home and during leisure (EHLASS)**, included in the programme of Community action on injury prevention (1999 to 2003), is geared to the collection of data from the casualty departments of 65 hospitals in the fifteen Member States and from household surveys covering the nature and origin of home and leisure accidents[9]. Analysis of the data enables Member States to take appropriate measures to reduce the number of accidents and victims by means of information campaigns, negotiation with industry and introduction of standards of regulations.

Physical safety and health of consumers is integrated in **other common policies**, particularly: the agricultural policy (definition of dairy products and imitation dairy products, regulation of organic products, veterinary problems, promotion of high quality products and, in general, food policy) [see sections 5.1.3. and 21.4.2.]; research policy (food quality and safety) [see section 18.4.1.]; the process of completing the internal market (machinery, foodstuffs, construction materials) [see section 6.2.]; and public health policy (measures to combat smoking, etc.) [see section 13.5.8.].

---

[1] Directive 2002/99, OJ L 18, 23.01.2003.
[2] Regulation 1774/2002, OJ L 273, 10.10.2002 last amended by Regulation 208/2006, OJ L 36, 08.02.2006.
[3] Regulation 183/2005, OJ L 35, 08.02.2005.
[4] Directive 2002/46, OJ L 183, 12.07.2002 and Directive 2006/37, OJ L 94, 01.04.2006.
[5] Directive 1999/2, OJ L 66, 13.03.1999.
[6] Decision 2004/210, OJ L 66, 04.03.2004.
[7] COM (1998) 598, 18 November 1998.
[8] Decision 2006/115, OJ L 48, 18.02.2006 and Decision 2006/135, OJ L 52, 23.02.2006.
[9] Decision 1786/2002, OJ L 271, 09.10.2002.

11.3. Protection of economic and legal interests

With the opening up of the markets, the economic interests of the consumers had to be protected uniformly in the single market. Thus, the Directive on **liability for defective products** seeks to ensure a high level of consumer protection against damage caused to health or property by a defective product and at the same time to reduce the disparities between national liability laws which distort competition and restrict the free movement of goods[1]. It establishes the principle of objective liability or liability without fault of the producer in cases of damage caused by a defective product. In the aftermath of the "mad cow" crisis, its scope was extended to primary agricultural products (such as meat, cereals, fruit and vegetables) and game products. "Producer" is taken to mean: any participant in the production process; the importer of the defective product; any person supplying a product whose producer cannot be identified. The injured person does not need to prove the negligence or fault of the producer, but only the actual damage; the defect in the product; and the causal relationship between damage and defect. The producer's liability is not altered when the damage is caused both by a defect in the product and by the act or omission of a third party. However, when the injured person is at fault, the producer's liability may be reduced. "Damage" means: damage caused by death or by personal injuries; damage to an item of property intended for private use or consumption other than the defective product, with a lower threshold of 500 euros. The injured person has three years within which to seek compensation.

Going a step further, the Directive on certain aspects of the sale of consumer goods and associated guarantees introduced the **principle of the conformity of the product with the contract**[2]. The Directive is concerned both with commercial guarantees and with the legal guarantee, which includes all legal protection of the purchaser in respect of defects in the goods acquired, resulting directly from the law, as a collateral effect of the contract of sale. The seller is liable to the consumer for any lack of conformity which exists when the goods are delivered to the consumer and which becomes apparent within a period of two years unless, at the moment of conclusion of the contract of sale, the consumer knew or could not reasonably be unaware of the lack of conformity. When a lack of conformity is notified to the seller, the consumer is entitled to ask (in a logical sequence) for the goods to be repaired or replaced free of charge or for an appropriate reduction to be made to the price or to have the contract rescinded. On top of the legal guarantee, the commercial guarantee offered by a seller or producer should be legally binding under the conditions laid down in the guarantee document and the associated advertising.

Directive 84/450 seeks to protect consumers, traders and the public in general against **misleading advertising** and its unfair consequences[3]. It has the merit of defining a Community concept of "misleading advertising", namely advertising which in some way misleads the people to whom it is addressed, a concept which is very useful at a time when evolution in communications techniques, particularly television and Internet, means that advertising has become a transnational phenomenon. When a user considers that an advertising text or presentation has misled him or her, he or she can launch proceedings against the manufacturer. As amended in 1997, the Directive on misleading advertising introduced a uniform regulatory framework on **comparative advertising**, defined as the advertising that explicitly or by implication identifies a competitor or

---

[1] Directive 85/374, OJ L 210, 07.08.1985 and Directive 1999/34, OJ L 141, 04.06.1999.
[2] Directive 1999/44, OJ L 171, 07.07.1999.
[3] Directive 84/450, OJ L 250, 19.09.1984 and Directive 2005/29, OJ L 149, 11.06.2005.

goods or services offered by a competitor. Such advertising is allowed under certain conditions, namely: it must not be misleading within the meaning of the Directive; it must objectively compare material, relevant, verifiable and representative features of goods and services, including prices; and it must neither create confusion in the market place between trade marks or trade names nor discredit or denigrate a competitor's marks, goods, services or activities.

Directive 2005/29 approximates the laws of the Member States on **unfair commercial practices**, including unfair advertising, which directly harm consumers' economic interests and thereby indirectly harm the economic interests of legitimate competitors[1]. It covers those practices (actions or omissions) which by deceiving the consumer prevent him from making an informed and thus efficient choice. Aggressive commercial practices, which are also prohibited by this Directive, cover those practices - such as harassment, coercion, the use of physical force and undue influence - which significantly impair the consumer's freedom of choice.

A number of Directives concern **contractual relations**. The Community is concerned in particular with the protection of consumers in respect of contracts negotiated away from business premises (**door-to-door sales**). A Directive grants consumers seven days in which to reconsider and renounce any agreement on a door-to-door sale[2]. The trader must inform the consumer in writing of the right of renunciation at his or her disposal.

In the same spirit, a Directive lays down minimum consumer protection rules concerning **distance contracts** regardless of the technology used (e.g. mail-order, telephone, fax, computer, television, etc.) and regardless of the product or service marketed, with the exception of financial services[3]. The underlying purpose of the Directive is to provide consumers with information in advance and to ensure that transactions are transparent. When any offer of goods or services is made, and when a sales contract is drawn up, the identity of the supplier and the commercial nature of the proposal must be clearly stated (at the beginning of the call in the case of a telephone communication). Other details, which must be made clear, include the price of the proposed product or service, the technical characteristics, the arrangements for payment and the conditions governing withdrawal from the contract. The consumer's agreement must be obtained before any goods or services, for which payment is required, are supplied. The consumer is entitled to a period of seven working days in which to withdraw from the contract without penalty. A supplier who fails to fulfil his or her obligations must reimburse any sums paid.

A special directive concerning the **distance marketing of consumer financial services** provides for common rules for selling contracts by phone, fax or Internet. It is designed to offer consumers much-needed protection and rights and to increase their confidence in e-commerce, both within individual Member States and across borders[4]. Its main features are: the prohibition of abusive marketing practices seeking to oblige consumers to buy a service they have not solicited ("inertia selling"); rules to restrict other practices such as unsolicited phone calls and e-mails ("cold calling" and "spamming"); an obligation to provide consumers with comprehensive information before a contract is concluded; and a consumer right to withdraw from the contract during a cool-off period, except in cases where there is a risk of speculation.

---

[1] Directive 2005/29, OJ L 149, 11.06.2005.
[2] Directive 85/577, OJ L 372, 31.12.1985 and OJ L 1, 03.01.1994.
[3] Directive 97/7, OJ L 144, 04.06.1997 and Directive 2005/29, OJ L 149, 11.06.2005.
[4] Directive 2002/65, OJ L 271, 09.10.2002 and Directive 2005/29, OJ L 149, 11.06.2005.

Another Directive concerns **unfair terms in contracts** concluded between a consumer and a professional[1]. It establishes, in particular, a distinction between contractual terms negotiated among the parties and terms which the consumer has not negotiated expressly. A non-negotiated clause is to be regarded as unfair where it creates a significant imbalance, to the detriment of the consumer, between the rights and obligations of the parties to the contract. The Directive establishes the principle that consumers are not bound by unfair terms in contracts, and makes Member States responsible for implementing appropriate and effective means of ensuring that professionals cease to use such terms.

Uniform protection in the European Union is provided to all consumers who use credit to finance their purchases. The Directive on **consumer credit** obliges the Member States to apply common rules to all forms of credit, thus avoiding the distortion of competition among suppliers and protecting consumers without regard to their nationality. This is done by certain prescribed guarantees, notably the calculation of the effective annual rate of interest and all the cost factors which the consumer must pay in order to obtain the credit. As amended in 1998, the Directive provides for the application of a single Community formula for calculating the annual percentage rate of charge for consumer credit[2].

A Council Directive on **package travel, including package holidays and package tours**, protects millions of tourists against possible corrupt practices by the organisers of these popular holidays[3]. Contract clauses must be recorded in writing and the consumer must receive a copy of them. The information supplied cannot be misleading: brochures placed at the disposal of the consumer must contain clear and precise information on prices, means of transport, type of accommodation, its situation, category and so on. In principle, prices cannot be revised, unless express provision is made for this in the contract. Even when surcharges are possible, they are subject to certain conditions. If the organiser cancels the package, the consumer has the right either to another package of equivalent or higher quality, or to reimbursement of all sums already paid, without prejudice to any compensation. The consumer also has the right to compensation if the organiser does not supply a large part of the service agreed upon. Finally, the organiser or the travel agency must give proof of sufficient guarantees to ensure repayment of the sums paid or the repatriation of the consumer in the event of insolvency or bankruptcy.

Still in the field of tourism and of cross-border vacations, a Directive protects purchasers of **timeshare rights** to one or more immovable properties[4]. The purchaser must be provided with a description relating, in particular, to the property itself, its situation, details of any communal services to which the purchaser will have access and the conditions governing such access, the period of enjoyment, the price and an estimate of the charges payable. The contract and the document describing the property covered by the contract must be drawn up in the official language (or one of the languages) of the Member State in which the purchaser resides or, if he or she so wishes, in the language (or one of the languages) of the Member State of which he or she is a citizen. In addition, the vendor must provide the purchaser with a certified translation of the contract in the official Community language (or one of the languages) of the Member State in which the property is situated. In any case, the purchaser is entitled to withdraw within 10 days without giving any reason. Any advance payment by the purchaser before the end of that cooling-off period is prohibited.

---

[1]   Directive 93/13, OJ L 95, 21.04.1993.
[2]   Directive 87/102, OJ L 42, 12.02.1987 and Directive 98/7, OJ L 101, 01.04.1998.
[3]   Directive 90/314, OJ L 158, 23.06.1990.
[4]   Directive 94/47, OJ L 280, 29.10.1994.

The Commission has encouraged the inter-operability of all **payment cards** throughout the Community through the harmonisation of electronic payment systems. It has also monitored the relationship between card holders and issuers, with a view to establishing uniform contract terms, notably as regards who is liable in the event of loss, theft, poor operation or counterfeiting, as part of the process of obtaining the inter-operability of payment cards throughout the Community[1].

Many Directives protect consumers while also **helping remove obstacles to trade** in goods and services [see section 6.2.1.]. This is true notably of the Directives on the making-up by volume of certain prepackaged liquids[2]; on the ranges of nominal quantities and nominal capacities permitted for certain prepackaged products[3]; on the indication of alcoholic strength by volume in the labelling of alcoholic beverages for sale to the end consumer[4]; and on the organic production of agricultural products and indications referring thereto on agricultural products and foodstuffs[5].

All this offers a clear demonstration that citizens' interests are increasingly taken into consideration in the single market. However, consumers must also have the **means to exercise and defend their rights** in the Community legal context, where traditional - and often costly - legal proceedings are ill-adapted to transfrontier conflicts and put off would be complainants. This is why the Council invited the Commission to assist the Member States with the networking of the national contact points, forming a Community-wide extra-judicial network geared to facilitating the out-of-court settlement of cross-border disputes[6]. A Directive on injunctions for the consumers' interests encourages consumer representatives to bring injunctions against unlawful commercial practices where Community law as it stands is infringed in one Member State to the detriment of consumers in another Member State[7]. Such unlawful practices may arise, in particular, from misleading advertising, distance selling or consumer credit.

11.4. Appraisal and outlook

The European Union shows a growing interest in the protection of the physical safety and of the economic interests of its citizens. This is a natural evolution since the single market has increased not only the choice of goods and services from the partners, but also the risks to consumers of all the Member States from defective products, notably foodstuffs, produced in one of them. Those risks were amply demonstrated during the mad cow crisis, which originated in the United Kingdom in 1996, and the scandal of dioxin-contaminated foodstuffs of Belgian origin, in 1999 [see section 5.1.3.]. While on these occasions, the Community consumer protection legislation proved its usefulness at preventing the spread of diseases and contaminations, it also revealed its limits, concerning its implementation by the Member States. With the increasing number of economic transactions between individuals and businesses from different Member States, there is also a growing need for their protection from dishonest business practices through uniform measures, supplementing the different national measures. Moreover, consumer representatives should be given the support they need to be effective in increasingly complex and technical debates, and the consumer's voice should be heard more systematically in the decision-making process.

Consumer protection is not only a necessary complement of other common policies, such as agriculture and fisheries, but also an important factor contributing to the affection or disaffection of European citizens towards the Union. Human nature tends, indeed, to disregard all the good attributes of a socio-political organisation, such as the European Union, when a serious, albeit temporary, problem shows the defects of this organisation. This is why, the European institutions should be very careful, not only to enact Commu-

---

[1]   Recommendation 87/598, OJ L 365, 24.12.1987 and Recommendation 88/590, OJ L 317, 24.11.1988.
[2]   Directive 75/106, OJ L 42, 15.02.1975 and Directive 89/676, OJ L 398, 30.12.1989.
[3]   Directive 80/232, OJ L 51, 25.02.1980 and Directive 87/356, OJ L 192, 11.07.1987.
[4]   Directive 87/250, OJ L 113, 30.04.1987 and OJ L 1, 03.01.1994.
[5]   Regulation 2092/91, OJ L 198, 22.07.1991 and Regulation 780/2006, OJ L 137, 25.05.2006.
[6]   Commission Recommendation,98/257 OJ L 115, 17.04.1998 and Commission Recommendation 2001/310, OJ L 109, 19.04.2001.
[7]   Directive 98/27, OJ L 166, 11.06.1998 and Directive 2005/29, OJ L 149, 11.06.2005.

nity legislation, which safeguards the health and the economic interests of all European citizens, but also to impose on the Member States to strictly implement this legislation by adequate national measures.

Consumer protection is currently faced with a fragmented set of regulations and a fragmented system of enforcement. The lack of clarity and security concerning consumer rights seriously dents their confidence and trust to the Community legislation. But fragmentation is also harmful for companies, particularly SMEs, as the differing treatment of identical commercial practices in each Member State is a strong deterrent to developing cross-border sales and exploiting the internal market. Moreover, existing Community rules are not satisfactory, as they concern only a limited number of commercial practices and are often obsolete, behind market developments or intended to solve a specific problem facing consumers. A greater degree of harmonisation of the rules regulating business-consumer commercial practices is needed for the development of a fully functioning consumer internal market.

Bibliography on consumer protection policy

- BUTTIGIEG Eugene. "Consumer interests under the EC's competition rules on collusive practices", *European Business Law Review,* v. 16, n. 3, 2005, p. 643-718.
- DICKIE John. *Producers and consumers in EU e-commerce law.* Oxford; Portland, Or.: Hart, 2005.
- EUROPEAN COMMISSION. *Healthier, safer, more confident citizens: a Health and Consumer protection Strategy*; COM/2005/115. Luxembourg: EUR-OP*, 2005.
  - *Protection of Consumers in respect of Distance Contracts.* COM/2006/514. Luxembourg: EUR-OP*, 2006.
  - *The unfair commercial practices Directive: new laws to stop unfair behaviour towards consumers.* Luxembourg: EUR-OP*, 2006.
- FAIRGRIEVE Duncan. *Product liability in comparative perspective.* Cambridge: Cambridge University Press, 2005.
- FAIRGRIEVE Duncan, HOWELLS Geraint. "General product safety: a revolution through reform?" in *The Modern Law Review,* v. 69, n. 1, January 2006, p. 59-69.
- GILIKER Paula. "Unifying European contract law: identifying a European pre-contractual obligation to inform" in *Cambridge yearbook of European legal studies 2004-2005,* v. 7, 2006, p. 135-159.
- GORMLEY Laurence (ed.). "Special issue on competition law and the consumer in the EU", *European Business Law Review,* v. 17, n. 1, 2006, p. 1-104.
- GRUNDMAN Stefan, SCHAUER Martin (eds.). *The architecture of European codes and contract law.* Alphen aan den Rijn: Kluwer Law International, 2006.
- HOEK Aukje van (et al. eds.). *Multilevel governance in enforcement and adjudication.* Antwerpen: Intersentia, 2006.
- JAHN Gabriele, SCHRAMM Matthias, SPILLER Achim. "The reliability of certification : quality labels as a consumer policy tool", *Journal of Consumer Policy,* v. 28, n. 1, March 2005, p. 53-73.
- LANDO Ole." Liberal, social and 'ethical' justice in European contract law" in *Common Market Law Review,* v. 43, n. 3, June 2006, p. 817-833.
- NAZZINI Renato. "The wood began to move: an essay on consumer welfare, evidence and burden of proof in Article 82 EC cases" in European Law Review 2006, v. 31, n. 4, August, p. 518-539.
- NEBBIA Paolisa. "Standard form contracts between unfair terms control and competition law" in *European Law Review,* v. 31, n. 1, February 2006, p. 102-113.
- SADELEER Nicolas de. "The precautionary principle in EC health and environmental law" in *European Law Journal,* v. 12, n. 2, March 2006, p. 139-172.
- SNYDER Francis (et al.). "Food safety in European Union law", *European Law Journal,* v. 10, n. 5, September 2004, p. 495-648.
- STUYCK Jules, TERRYN Evelyne, VAN DYCK Tom. "Confidence through fairness? Unfair business-to-consumer comercial practices in the internal market" in *Common Market Law Review,* v. 43, n. 1, February 2006, p. 107-152.
- TUEDA Isabelle. "L'adaptation du droit des contrats d'origine internationale et communautaire à la dématérialisation des échanges" in *Revue internationale de droit comparé,* v. 58, n. 3, juillet-septembre 2006, p.925-949.
- UGLAND Trygve, VEGGELAND Frode. "Experiments in food safety policy integration in the European Union" in *Journal of Common Market Studies,* v. 44, n. 3, September 2006, p. 607-624.

*The publications of the Office for Official Publications of the European Communities (EUR-OP) exist usually in all official languages of the EU.

Part IV: Horizontal policies

Chapter 12. Regional policy
Chapter 13. Social policy
Chapter 14. Taxation policy
Chapter 15. Competition policy
Chapter 16. Environment policy

In **Part IV we examine the horizontal policies of the Union**, that is to say the objectives set, the means employed and the measures taken in common by the Member States of the Union in order to support and supplement their policies in five broad areas of their economic and socio-political activities: regional development, social progress, taxation, competition and environmental protection. All these common policies were launched during the stages of the customs union and the common market and are being continuously developed in order to further the higher goals set for the stages of economic and monetary union and political integration.

The **common regional policy** by means of the Structural Funds aims to help the poorer regions of the Community to face the increased trade and competition from the more developed regions imposed by the single market and the economic and monetary union. Such a union, implying abandonment of the use of exchange rate adjustment as a means of balance of the national economy, would be to the detriment of the poorer Member States without an efficient common regional policy revolving around sufficient capital transfers from the richer to the poorer regions of the EU. The common regional policy aims, therefore, at the economic and social cohesion of the Union.

The acceleration in the process of European integration since the middle of the 1980s has resulted in major progress in the **common social policy**, spanning fields such as vocational training, social protection and worker health and safety. This process is stepped up in the economic and monetary union, which takes out of governments' hands many economic and monetary instruments and hence their ability to tackle their social problems alone. Therefore, the Amsterdam Treaty identified the promotion of a high level of employment as a Community objective and introduced a coordinated strategy for employment.

The **common taxation policy** has gone beyond the Treaty requirements of fiscal neutrality. The Member States succeeded in replacing their various cumulative multi-stage turnover taxes with a uniform value added tax, the structures of which have been closely harmonised. The abolition of tax frontiers, made possible by the approximation of VAT rates and excise duties, made a vital contribution to the final completion of the single market. As economic and monetary union advances, approximation is also required for company and savings taxes.

The **common competition policy** plays the role of economic regulator in the common market. It prevents market compartmentalisation, abolished in the single market, from being restored by means of agreements between large companies. It also prevents multinational companies from exploiting their dominant position or monopolising a market by acquisition of independent firms. As regards State interventionism, the role of the common competition policy is to confine it to aid which fits in with the common objective of adjusting the structures of the European Union's production mechanism to internal and external changes.

The **common environment policy** is vital for the quality of life of the citizens of the Union. In a European economy, which faces strong international competition, the challenge of policy-makers is to take measures that make it possible to painlessly achieve the objective of growth, which is compatible with the essential requirements of the environment. The EU follows, indeed, a coherent programme for sustainable growth. However, the EU cannot work alone for the protection of the environment of the globe. Using its economic power, it should lead the way to a better international coordination in this area.

Chapter 12

REGIONAL DEVELOPMENT POLICY

Diagram of the chapter

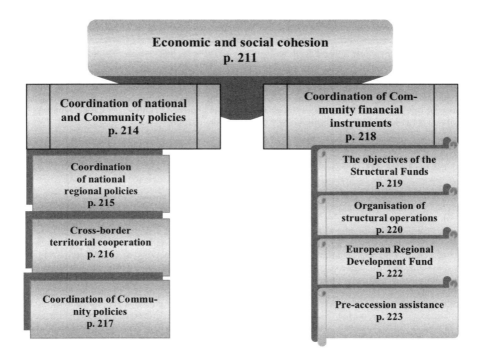

The main objective of the common regional policy is the reduction of existing regional disparities and the prevention of further regional imbalances in the EU by transferring Community resources to problem regions using the financial instruments of the Community known as the Structural Funds. The common regional policy of the EU does not seek to supersede national regional policies. In accordance with the principle of subsidiarity [see section 3.2.], the Member States, through their own regional policies, are the first ones who must solve the problems in their regions by promoting infrastructures and financially supporting job-creation investments. However, the common regional policy coordinates national regional policies by formulating guidelines and establishing certain principles in order to **avoid competition for regional aid between Member States**. It coordinates also the various policies and financial instruments of the EU to give them a "regional dimension" and thus more impact on regions most in need of care.

The **Committee of the Regions** set up by the Treaty of Maastricht in order to enhance the role of regional authorities in the institutional system of the Union [see section 4.2.4.], plays an important role in the forecasting of regional tendencies and in the management of structural interventions of the EU. In the enlarged Union, where the unequal distribution of wealth among regions would be greatly increased, the democratic legitimacy and the role of the Committee of the Regions should also be increased [see section 4.4.].

The common regional policy keeps step with the overall multinational integration process. Although a stated objective of the **Treaty of Rome** was to reduce the development gap between the different regions of the Community, it did not endow the common institutions with any instruments to this end, other than the loans of the European Investment Bank and the assessment by the Commission of regional aid granted by the Member States, with the aim notably of preventing the States outbidding one another in an attempt to attract foreign investment. With the prospect of completion of the Single Market by 1992, the **Single European Act** [see section 2.1.] acknowledged the major contribution that a common regional policy could make to improve the economic and social cohesion of the Community. This was the starting point for the Community's new regional policy based notably on the coordination of its financial instruments and the coordination of national and Community policies to help regions which need an extra push towards economic prosperity. The 1988 reform of the Structural Funds, in the context of a package of measures including the reform of the common agricultural policy and the equilibrium of the Community budget, known as "Delors package I" [see section 3.4.], has led to better integration of the various actions conducted under the banner of structural policies and contributed to the concept of an all-round, consistent strategy for economic and social cohesion in the Community. The Structural Funds have been reformed again in 1999 and once more in 2006.

12.1. The need for a common regional policy

Throughout history, the economic map of Europe was shaped by **localisation factors** such as the nature and topography of land, climate, waterways and natural protection from invaders. Having remained basically unchanged for centuries, these factors attracted people living primarily off the land to certain regions rather than others. The industrial revolution profoundly changed the economic geography of Europe; industry was attracted to certain regions by the existence of energy sources (coal), raw materials (metals), waterways, harbour sites and cities. The other factors still played a role of course, but it was progressively reduced.

People followed businessmen to the industrialised areas; so too did the State. It brought with it the infrastructure, public utilities and administrative fabric absolutely necessary for industrial growth. **Infrastructure**, in the broad sense of the word, includes means of transport, communication and telecommunication, housing, and any facilities allowing for the creation or extension of towns. Public utilities that are related to them range from such classical services as the distribution of water and electricity, to universities, research and training centres, as well as various elements related to the quality of life such as park maintenance, cultural and leisure facilities, etc.

All these economic, administrative, cultural and social factors create "**external economies**", i.e. advantages resulting from a combination of factors without imposing specific costs on undertakings (businesses, firms, companies). Other conditions being equal, it is not surprising to see businessmen going wherever they can find external economies and large markets, made up of large population concentrations. In fact, modern firms tend to seek a combination of favourable features, including infrastructure and human resource endowments, when taking their decisions about where to locate. The problem is that uneven patterns of development have historically resulted in widely different endowments in infrastructures (transport, energy, telecommunications, etc.) and in human capital (the knowledge and skills accumulated in the workforce).

More recently, innovation has evolved into a continuous process requiring the rapid introduction of new technological advances and therefore a constant interaction between research laboratories and businesses either developing or using new technology. Hence, the economic success of a region depends to a large extent on the possibilities available for securing **access to research and technological development (R & D)** on an ongoing basis. The problem for weaker regions is that their productive base consists largely of small and medium-sized enterprises (SMEs), usually working in traditional sectors and lacking an outward-looking perspective [see section 17.1.4.]. In many regions, highly qualified people are in short supply and ancillary services, such as banking, are inadequate, thus inhibiting innovation. In fact, most factors which favour R & D and innovation (organisation, management, commercial, financial and technical skills required introducing a new or improved product or process onto the market) are almost always found in developed regions.

These factors and trends of the **concentration of economic activities** are so compelling that opposing them would be in vain were it not for the fact that they have certain limits. At a certain point, external economies can thus become diseconomies when pollution and communications congestion lead to costs and discomfort for businesses and people employed by them. Moreover, factors affecting location of economic activities are not immutable. The establishment requirements of the post-industrial "information society" are not those of the industrial society. Indeed, the **information technologies (CITs)** have brought together industries traditionally not so closely linked (telecommunications, information technology and the media), reducing the effects of distance and encouraging the decentralisation of business activities [see section 17.3.5.]. Through its powerful networking effects, the information society can contribute to the geographical and economic opening up of the poor regions of the Union.

In addition, the phenomenon of **globalisation of economies and markets**, which involves the intensification of international competition through the emergence of a potentially unique world-wide market for an expanding range of goods and services, brings out the importance of regional policy. In this context, international competitiveness is based much less on static comparative advantages of the regions, such as territorial concentration and natural resources endowment, and increasingly more in qualitative dynamic parameters, such as factor mobility, social consensus, pertinent information and the capacity to combine production factors effectively. These qualitative parameters offer the possibility of decentralised economic growth, if they are systematically put together by an adequate policy. The Member States and the European Union can profit from these trends and changes to **balance the development of their regions better**. This time, they must precede businessmen and people in order to make sure that necessary movements are not carried out in a disorderly fashion, as were the preceding ones.

By assisting the problem regions build up their infrastructure networks, the Member States and the Union can help them to both develop their markets for the benefit of all and better balance the European economy in the light of future changes. Of course, each Member State carries out its own regional policy, which generally aims at favouring the development of the national territory's less prosperous regions by means of **transferring resources from wealthier regions**. The means normally used by Member States to remedy regional problems are of two types: firstly, improving the infrastructure and the social and cultural development of backward regions, and secondly, various premiums, subsidies and tax incentives for attracting private investment in these regions. The general objective of these measures is to create or re-establish a better distribution of economic activities and population over the national territory. To do this, certain governments also try to discourage investments in highly developed regions. The advantages of such measures are twofold: favouring the transfer of resources towards poor regions while halting the disproportionate expansion of congested regions.

Certainly, it is primarily up to the national authorities to solve the problems of their regions, namely by promoting infrastructures or giving incentives to businesses to attract their investments in disadvantaged regions. The scale of the effort required to stimulate economic activity in the least advanced regions means that public funds must be used in conjunction with private investment. **Regional aid**, when judiciously applied, is a vital instrument to regional development and to continued and balanced expansion within the European Union. But given the possibility of competition inside a single market between the various regions in order to attract Community and foreign investments (including those from partner countries), the advantages granted can go beyond compensation for material difficulties faced by investors in the areas to be promoted. Thus, part of the aid granted would merely serve a reciprocal neutralisation. The national regional actions would simply be more expensive and grant unwarranted profits to benefiting undertakings [see also section 15.5.]. Therefore, the prime objective of EU regional policy is to **coordinate national regional policies** by formulating guidelines and setting priorities at European level, which effectively help close the gap between regions.

In addition, the EU has a common interest in regional development through structural change. The very essence of economic integration is **the optimisation of the market mechanism** at a European scale. But a market policy based on some sort of spontaneous balance between the various economic parameters essentially benefits rich regions. Indeed, prior to the creation of the common market, economic activities had developed in a national context; certain activities usually grouped in certain regions were protected from international competition by customs barriers. With the opening of borders, European and foreign (American, Japanese...) companies wanting to set up business in the EU market are normally attracted in European regions where infrastructure is most developed, where labour is most qualified, and where the economic environment is most adapted to their activities. Economic concentration invites more concentration. The common regional policy strives to make up for this tendency in order to achieve **a better-balanced growth within the common market**. Its goals and mechanisms are coordinated and interact with those of other common policies, notably social, enterprise, environment, agricultural and fisheries policies.

12.1.1. The classification of EU regions

Economic, social and territorial disparities at both regional and national level have **increased in the enlarged European Union**. At the dawn of the 21st century, gross domestic product (GDP) per head in the lagging regions of the Union averaged 66% of the EU15 average, which stood at EUR 20,213 per head. The enlargement to ten new countries in 2004 and to two more in 2007 reduced the EU average GDP per head to EUR 16,500. The population living in regions with GDP per head of less than 75% of the present EU average was increased from 71 million to 174 million, or from 19% of the EU15 total to 36% of the EU27 total. Three groups of countries can be distinguished in the EU of 27 in terms of GDP per head. The first group with GDP per head 20% above the new average was formed by the EU15 Member States, apart from Greece, Portugal and Spain. These three cohesion countries plus Cyprus, the Czech Republic, Slovenia and Malta formed the second group, with GDP per head between 68% (the Czech Republic) and 95% (Spain) of the EU 27 average. The remaining 8 countries formed the third group, with GDP per head only 40% of the EU27 average.

The identification of the priority regions and areas at Community level are based on the **common classification of territorial units for statistics (NUTS)**[1]. On this basis, Regulation 1083/2006, laying down general provisions on the Structural Funds, identifies three categories of regions covered by priority objectives: (a) the Convergence objective; (b) the Regional competitiveness and employment objective; and (c) the European territorial cooperation objective[2] [see section 12.3.1].

The regions eligible for funding from the Structural Funds under the **Convergence objective** are regions corresponding to level 2 of the common classification of territorial units for statistics (NUTS level 2) whose gross domestic product (GDP) per capita, measured in purchasing power parities and calculated on the basis of Community figures for the period 2000 to 2002, is less than 75% of the average GDP of the EU-25 for the same reference period. These regions are to be found both in the new and the old Mem-

---

[1] Regulation 1059/2003, OJ L 154, 21.06.2003 and Regulation 1888/2005, OJ L 309, 25.11.2005.
[2] Regulation 1083/2006, OJ L 210, 31.07.2006.

ber States. The latter are the regions suffering from the statistical effect linked to the reduction in the Community average following the enlargement of the European Union. These regions would have been eligible for Convergence objective status had the eligibility threshold remained at 75% of the average GDP of the EU-15. They benefit for that reason from substantial **transitional aid** in order to complete their convergence process. This aid is to end in 2013 and is not to be followed by a further transitional period. In addition, the Member States eligible for funding from the Cohesion Fund under the convergence objective are those whose gross national income (GNI) per capita, measured in purchasing power parities and calculated on the basis of Community figures for the period 2001 to 2003, is less than 90 % of the average GNI of the EU-25 and which have a programme for meeting the economic convergence conditions referred to in Article 104 of the EC Treaty. In reality the Convergence objective for 2007-2013 applies to 100 regions, including 16 granted transitional "phasing-out" status – accounting for just over 35% of the EU27 population[1].

The regions eligible for funding from the Structural Funds under the **Regional competitiveness and employment (RCE) objective** are those not eligible under the convergence objective or the transitional support objective. The NUTS level 2 regions totally covered by Objective 1 in 2006 under Article 3 of Regulation 1260/1999 whose nominal GDP level per capita will exceed 75% of the average GDP of the EU15 are eligible, on a transitional and specific basis, for financing by the Structural Funds under the Regional competitiveness and employment objective. Hence the RCE objective applies in principle to the rest of the Union, or to 155 regions with 61% of EU27 population, while another 13 regions are classified as "phasing-in" (almost 4% of the EU population).

A **European territorial cooperation** objective covers regions having land or sea frontiers, the areas for transnational cooperation being defined with regard to actions promoting integrated territorial development and support for interregional cooperation and exchange of experience. These are NUTS level 3 regions of the Community along all internal and certain external land borders and all NUTS level 3 regions of the Community along maritime borders separated, as a general rule, by a maximum of 150 kilometres. For the purpose of interregional cooperation, cooperation networks and exchange of experience, the entire territory of the Community shall be eligible.

Moreover, certain regions or areas benefit from specific measures and/or additional funding, notably: areas with an extremely low population density in Finland and Sweden, as referred to in Protocol 6 to the 1994 Act of Accession; the outermost regions mentioned in Article 299 of the EC Treaty, and areas with a natural handicap, i.e. certain islands, mountainous areas and areas with a low population density, as well as for certain border areas of the Community following enlargement.

12.1.2. Economic and social cohesion of the Union

The wider European market reinforces the polarisation of pre-existing economic activities and thus **accelerates the agglomeration and concentration process**. If measures were not taken at national and European level, the completion of the internal market would tend further to widen existing inequalities in the distribution of economic activities throughout the territory of the EU. That is why, the objective of economic and social cohesion, implying the desire to reduce disparities between the various regions of the Community, was introduced by the Single European Act [see section 2.1.]. On top of the single market, **the achievement of economic and monetary union** promises enhanced

---

[1] COM/2006/281.

prospects for the developed and the less favoured regions alike. The reduction of trans-frontier transaction costs and the elimination of exchange rate risk may promote regional specialisation and intra-Community trade in goods and services. The weaker regions can benefit from this specialisation by exploiting more fully their comparative advantages. Furthermore, increased capital mobility in EMU, supported by the single currency and the tendency towards quasi-uniform inflation rates, tends to equalise interest rates for any given level of risk, which should favour the less developed regions where capital is often relatively scarce and capital costs, therefore, relatively high.

At the same time, however, Member States participating in the euro-zone **lose certain fiscal and monetary policy options** as well as the ability to adjust the exchange rate. Exchange rate flexibility is important in that, in principle, it enables a country, through devaluation, to offset a loss in international competitiveness in a relatively painless manner. As such, it facilitates short-term adjustment to general or country-specific economic shocks. The removal of the possibility of exchange rate adjustment, therefore, represents a more important loss to the least developed countries of the euro-zone, which are the ones that must carry out the most important structural changes. Those countries must invest most, while spending least so as to conform to the Maastricht criteria and to the requirements of the Stability Pact [see section 7.2.4. and 7.3.2.].

In addition, those countries could **lose the advantage of lower labour costs.** As long as markets were protected by customs and other barriers, salaries in certain countries were much lower than in others, compensating for the lower productivity of a labour force that was not very qualified. But in a common market, and even more in an economic and monetary union, freedom of movement for workers, better information on respective situations and trade union demands tend to align revenues towards the levels already attained in the more prosperous regions. This may be a positive outcome from a social point of view but it is one which engenders inflationist tendencies and creates difficulties for businesses in areas where productivity is low. If these businesses have to shut down, the workers lose their jobs and their revenue increase is merely an illusion.

From both an economic and social point of view, neither the weakest member countries nor the European Union can tolerate a substantial part of their patrimony being left to underdevelopment because of economic integration. The prosperity of certain areas of the union cannot be paid for by the decline or stagnation of other areas. Wide **disparities are intolerable in a community**, if the term is to have any meaning at all. Furthermore, disparities do not just imply a poorer quality of life for the disadvantaged regions, but indicate a failure to take advantage of economic opportunities that could benefit the Union as a whole.

For all these reasons, the Treaty on the European Union states in its Article 2 that the strengthening of **economic and social cohesion is a fundamental objective of the Union**. Article 158 of the EC Treaty provides that, in order to strengthen its economic and social cohesion, the Community is to aim at reducing disparities between the levels of development of the various regions and the backwardness of the least favoured regions or islands, including rural areas. Article 159 of the Treaty requires this action to be supported by the Structural Funds, the European Investment Bank (EIB) and the other existing Financial Instruments. Although all Community policies can contribute to reinforcing economic and social cohesion, as is stated in Article 159 (TEC), a major role is, certainly, played by the Structural Funds (Art. 161 TEC).

Initially the "**Structural Funds**" included the European Regional Development Fund (ERDF), the European Social Fund (ESF), the European Agricultural Guidance and Guarantee Fund (EAGGF) - Guidance Section, and the Financial Instrument for Fisheries Guidance (FIFG). After the reforms of the common agricultural and the common fisheries policies, in 2005, the instrument providing aid for rural development, namely the European Agricultural Fund for Rural Development (EAFRD) [see section 21.5.1], and that of the fisheries sector, namely the European Fisheries Fund (EFF) [see section 22.4] have been integrated into the instruments under the common agricultural policy and the common fisheries policy. They must be coordinated with the instruments under the cohesion policy, but are not included in those instruments. The Structural Funds should take complementary action over and above that of the EAFRD and of the EFF to promote the economic diversification of rural areas and of areas dependent on fisheries. However, the exclusion of the agricultural and fisheries instruments means that the Funds providing assistance under the cohesion policy are nowadays limited to the European Regional Development Fund (ERDF), the European Social Fund (ESF) and the Cohesion Fund. Hence, the Cohesion Fund is now fully integrated into the programming of structural assistance, a fact that should increase the coherence in the intervention of the various Funds.

The greater regional diversity of the Union [see section 12.1.1] and the expansion of its land and sea borders after the enlargements of 2004 and 2007 have increased the importance of transnational and interregional cooperation in the Community. Therefore, the cohesion policy of the Community was completely revised in 2006. Regulation 1083/2006, repealing Regulation 1260/1999, lays down the **general rules** governing the European Regional Development Fund (ERDF), the European Social Fund (ESF) and the Cohesion Fund[1]. It defines the objectives to which the Structural Funds and the Cohesion Fund are to contribute, the criteria for Member States and regions to be eligible under those Funds, the financial resources available and the criteria for their allocation. It determines that the resources available for commitment from the Funds for the period 2007 to 2013 shall be EUR 308,041,000,000 at 2004 prices, indexed at 2% per year. It also defines the context for cohesion policy, including the method for establishing the Community strategic guidelines on cohesion, the national strategic reference framework and the process for examination at Community level. To this end, Regulation 1083/2006 lays down the principles and rules on partnership, programming, evaluation, management, including financial management, monitoring and control on the basis of responsibilities shared between the Member States and the Commission.

According to Regulation 1083/2006, cohesion policy should contribute to increasing growth, competitiveness and employment by incorporating the Community's priorities for sustainable development as defined at the Lisbon European Council of 23 and 24 March 2000 [see section 13.3.2.] and at the Göteborg European Council of 15 and 16 June 2001 [see section 16.2]. On the other hand, the improvement and simplification of cooperation along the external borders of the Community entail the use of the instruments of the Community's external assistance, in particular a European Neighbourhood and Partnership Instrument and the Instrument for Pre-Accession Assistance established by Regulation 1085/2006[2]. Therefore, these actions are closely aligned to Structural Fund and Rural Development practices.

Article 161 (TEC) and a Protocol annexed to the Treaty of Maastricht [see section 2.2.] have provided for the creation of the **Cohesion Fund** in order to strengthen the economic and social cohesion of the Community. According to Regulation 1084/2006, repealing Regulation 1164/94, assistance from the Cohesion Fund shall be given to actions in the following areas, according to the investment and infrastructure needs specific

---

[1] Regulation 1083/2006, OJ L 210, 31.07.2006.
[2] Regulation 1085/2006, OJ L 210, 31.07.2006.

to each Member State receiving assistance[1]: (a) trans-European transport networks, in particular priority projects of common interest as identified by Decision 1692/96[2]; and (b) the environment within the priorities assigned to the Community environmental protection policy under the policy and action programme on the environment [see section 16.2]. Assistance from the Fund may be suspended if the Council has decided in accordance with Article 104(6) of the Treaty that excessive government deficit exists in a beneficiary Member State, and has established that the Member State concerned has not taken effective action in response to a Council recommendation.

It should be stressed that the objective of economic and social cohesion means a great deal more than the mere redistribution of funds to the poorest Member States and regions. It requires coherent action through a coordination of national and common economic policies. Therefore, the common regional policy has two wings. Firstly, it seeks to **coordinate national regional policies** by formulating guidelines and establishing certain principles in order to avoid distortion of competition between Member States through their regional aid schemes. Secondly, it **coordinates the various policies and financial instruments of the EU** to give them a "regional dimension" and thus more impact on regions most in need of care. These two wings of the Community regional policy are examined in the rest of this chapter.

With growing European integration, the Union increasingly shares responsibility with the Member States for **the maintenance of the European model of society**. This model reflects the values of the social market economy, which seeks to combine a system of economic organisation based on market forces, freedom of opportunity and enterprise with a commitment to the values of solidarity and access for all members of society to social protection and services of general interest. Therefore, the policies of economic and social cohesion, which are linked with the objectives of the European model of society, are considered to be a factor in strengthening the productivity of European society and contributing to economic and social wellbeing [see also section 13.2.].

12.2. Coordination of national and Community policies

The first part of Community regional policy is the coordination and monitoring of the **regional policies of the Member States**. Article 87 (TEC) states that any aid which distorts or threatens to distort competition by favouring certain undertakings or the production of certain goods shall, in so far as it affects trade between Member States, be incompatible with the common market. But in the very same article 87, paragraphs 3(a) and (c) specify that the following may be considered to be compatible with the common market: "aid to promote the economic development of areas where the standard of living is abnormally low or where there is serious underemployment" and, more generally, "aid to facilitate the development of certain economic activities or of certain economic areas, where such aid does not adversely affect trading conditions to an extent contrary to the common interest". In monitoring regional aid, the Commission should seek on the basis of economic criteria to determine which are the least-favoured regions of the EU and establish for each of them the level of aid intensity so that the aid be targeted at those areas of the Union which are really experiencing difficulties. The monitoring of State aid thus makes a considerable contribution to the economic and social cohesion of the Union.

---

[1]   Regulation 1084/2006, OJ L 210, 31.07.2006.
[2]   Decision 1692/96, OJ L 228, 09.09.1996, last amended by Decision 884/2004, OJ L 167, 30.04.2004.

12.2.1. Coordination of national regional policies

On the basis of Article 87(3)(a) and (c) of the EC Treaty, State aid granted to promote the economic development of certain disadvantaged areas within the European Union may be considered to be compatible with the common market by the Commission. It ensues that the European Commission determines the compatibility or incompatibility of a given national regional aid with the common market. Article 88 (TEC) states that the Commission shall, in cooperation with the Member States, keep **under constant review all systems of aid** existing in those States. It must be informed, in sufficient time to enable it to submit its comments, of any plans to grant or alter aid. The Member States notify the Commission of proposed levels of regional aid and the latter either approves or amends them, often to lower levels. The Member State concerned must not put its proposed measures into effect until the procedure initiated by the Commission has resulted in a final decision. If the State concerned does not comply with this decision within the prescribed time, the Commission or any other interested State may refer the matter to the Court of Justice directly, which happens quite often.

The successive enlargements of the Community have boosted its regional diversity and accentuated the need for new instruments to control regional aid. This is why article 158 (TEC) gave fresh impetus to the aim of stronger economic and social cohesion and stipulated that the Community should attempt to close the gap between its regions and help the less-favoured regions to catch up. In fact, by addressing the handicaps of the disadvantaged regions, national regional aid promotes the economic, social and territorial cohesion of Member States and the European Union as a whole. However, the important political and economic developments in the beginning of the 21st century, notably the accelerated process of integration following the introduction of the single currency, the enlargement of the European Union on 1 May 2004 and the anticipated accession of Bulgaria and Romania have created the need for a comprehensive review of the **criteria applied by the Commission** when examining the compatibility of national regional aid with the common market under Article 87(3a) and (3c) of the EC Treaty.

These criteria are codified in the **Guidelines on national regional aid** for 2007-2013[1]. According to these guidelines, regional aid should, in general, be granted under a multi-sectoral aid scheme which forms an integral part of a regional development strategy with clearly defined objectives. Such a scheme may also enable the competent authorities to prioritise investment projects according to their interest for the region concerned. Also as a general rule, aid promoting the economic development of areas where the standard of living is abnormally low (Art. 87, 3a) is considered as threatening to distort competition less than aid facilitating the development of certain economic activities which may adversely affect trading conditions within the common market (Art. 87.3c). Where, exceptionally, it is envisaged to grant individual ad hoc aid to a single firm, or aid confined to one area of activity, it is the responsibility of the Member State to demonstrate that the project contributes towards a coherent regional development strategy and that, having regard to the nature and size of the project, it will not result in unacceptable distortions of competition.

Regional **aid for large investment projects**, while covered by the regional aid guidelines, is also subject to specific rules, because it might be granted to large firms which are little affected by region-specific problems, but which possess considerable

---

[1] OJ C 54, 04.03.2006, p. 13-44.

bargaining power vis-à-vis the authorities granting aid and may cause unjustified distortions in competition[1] [see details below].

For sectors included in the list of sectors with serious structural problems drawn up by the Commission, all regional investment aid to **large investment projects** (involving eligible expenditure above EUR 25 million) must be individually notified to the Commission for scrutiny. The Commission may authorise investment aid if the Member State can demonstrate that the market for the product concerned is growing fast, even though the sector is deemed to be in decline. The list includes the motor industry and the synthetic fibres industry, but not the steel industry, because all investment aid in this sector is prohibited due to its over-capacity. For investments above EUR 50 million, Member States must notify the Commission a priori of their draft aid programmes. Ex-post, they must inform it on: the aid granted (the scheme, legal basis, net grant equivalent), the beneficiary firm and the investment project (nature, place of implementation, total cost and eligible cost).

Member States do not have to notify national regional aid schemes which fulfil all the conditions laid down in the group exemption Regulations adopted by the Commission pursuant to Regulation 994/98 concerning certain categories of **horizontal State aid** [see section 15.5.1]. However, the regional aid guidelines for 2007-2013 limit regional aid to that which is necessary to allow coverage of the most disadvantaged regions and a limited number of regions which are disadvantaged in relation to the national average in the Member State concerned. Accordingly, the guidelines fix the limit for the overall population coverage by regional aid schemes to 42% of the population of the EU-27.

In applying rules on State aids for regional purposes, **the Commission's objectives are two-fold**: ensuring that aid is concentrated in the most disadvantaged regions and maintaining a differential in aid intensity between regions, to enable the poorest ones to compensate for their structural weaknesses. Under Article 87,3(a) of the EC Treaty as interpreted by Community legislation, aid for investments in the least developed regions of the Union may be up to 75% of the cost and, under certain conditions, temporary operating aids may also be granted. In practice, however, the 75% ceiling is rarely reached as the countries concerned lack the necessary financial resources.

12.2.2. Cross-border territorial cooperation

In view of the difficulties encountered by the Member States in carrying out and managing cross-border, transnational and interregional cooperation, the new legislative framework [see section 12.1.2], provides for the creation of a Community-level cooperation instrument allowing the creation of cooperative groupings with their own legal personality, called "**European groupings of territorial cooperation**" (**EGTC**)[2]. An EGTC is an optional cooperation instrument at Community level. The objective of an EGTC should be to facilitate and promote cross-border, transnational and/or interregional cooperation, with the exclusive aim of strengthening economic and social cohesion. An EGTC may be made up of members belonging to one or more of the following categories: (a) Member States; (b) regional authorities; (c) local authorities; and (d) bodies governed by public law. The decision to establish an EGTC should be taken at the initiative of its prospective members. An EGTC may act on behalf of its members, and notably the regional and local authorities of which it is composed.

An EGTC should carry out the tasks given to it by its members in accordance with Regulation 1082/2006. Its tasks are defined by the convention agreed by its members, but should be limited to the facilitation and promotion of **territorial cooperation** to strengthen economic and social cohesion. Specifically, the tasks of an EGTC should be limited primarily to the implementation of territorial cooperation programmes or projects co-financed by the Community through the European Regional Development Fund, the European Social Fund and/or the Cohesion Fund. However, an EGTC may carry out actions of territorial cooperation which are at the sole initiative of the Member States and their regional and local authorities with or without a financial contribution from the Community.

---

[1]   Communication from the Commission OJ C 70, 19.03.2002, p. 8-20.
[2]   Regulation 1082/2006, OJ L 210, 31.07.2006.

One of the **tasks of the European Regional Development Fund** is the promotion of European territorial cooperation by assisting notably[1]:

1. the development of cross-border economic, social and environmental activities through joint strategies for sustainable territorial development;
2. the establishment and development of transnational cooperation, including bilateral cooperation between maritime regions not covered under point 1, through the financing of networks and of actions conducive to integrated territorial development, and,
3. the reinforcement of the effectiveness of regional policy by promoting: (a) interregional cooperation focusing on innovation and the knowledge economy and environment and risk prevention; (b) exchanges of experience concerning the identification, transfer and dissemination of best practice including on sustainable urban development; and (c) actions involving studies, data collection, and the observation and analysis of development trends in the Community.

12.2.3. Coordination of Community policies

The general Regulation on the Structural Funds specifies that the Commission and the Member States must ensure that the operations of the Funds are consistent with other Community policies and operations[2]. Indeed, several **common policies favour by their nature the process of integration and cohesion**. Thus, the common social policy has an important impact on labour law, health and security at work, free movement of workers and equal opportunities for men and women in the poor regions of the Union. Community research programmes develop research capabilities in weaker Member States strengthening their scientific and technological base and accelerating innovation and economic development. The common agricultural policy has also a positive cohesion effect, with the cohesion countries receiving net transfers through it.

Since any economic activity is of necessity localised in one area, the majority of the Community's measures, be it in agriculture, industry, transport or research, have an impact at regional level. The Community's regional policy consequently attempts to ensure consistency between regional objectives and those of other common policies by the European Spatial Development Perspective (ESDP)[3]. The purpose of assessing Community measures from a regional viewpoint is to correct any negative regional effects, which they may have, or to enhance any positive ones. A Community framework for cooperation supports awareness-raising on sustainable urban development and urban environment, through development and transfer of good practices and cooperation between actors involved in sustainable development[4].

The possibilities for coordinating the objectives and means of **enterprise policy** with those of regional policy are utilised in the creation and management of **Business and Innovation Centres (BICs)** in towns and cities of the Community [see section 17.2.3.]. The BICs are public or private professional structures which offer a multiservice assistance to innovative SMEs. Their integrated range of business services includes: basic assistance with management, technical approval, innovation, marketing strategy, raising of capital, development of business skills; SME access to venture capital; and provision of premises for SMEs. The BICs are linked in a European Business and Innovation Centre Network (EBN) which helps them with their management and promotes cooperation. Around two thirds of the Centres are cofinanced by the ERDF.

In the operations of the Structural Funds, particular attention is devoted to compliance with rules governing the protection of the environment, competition (Art. 87 and 88 TEC) and public procurement. The role of the common regional policy in the process of multinational integration deserves to be emphasised by an adequate **information policy**. To this effect, the Commission encourages the Member States to improve the transparency of information for beneficiaries under the Structural Funds and to enhance public awareness of the role the Union plays in the development of their regions[5].

---

[1] Regulation 1080/2006, OJ L 210, 31.07.2006.
[2] Regulation 1083/2006, OJ L 210, 31.07.2006.
[3] OJ C 36, 09.02.1979, p. 10-11.
[4] Decision 1411/2001, OJ L 91, 13.07.2001 and Decision 786/2004, OJ L 138, 30.04.2004.
[5] Regulation 1159/2000, OJ L 130, 31.05.2000.

A Commission communication promotes Structural Fund **assistance in the cultural sphere** in order to improve the contribution of culture to regional development, particularly through the media, the information society, historical heritage and regional identity[1]. Another Commission communication seeks to facilitate the **development of the information society** in the poorest regions of the Union, through an integrated approach of telecommunications infrastructure, information technologies and training programmes for businessmen and public administrators[2].

12.3. Coordination of Community financial instruments

The coordination of the financial instruments of the Community is ensured by the Regulation laying down general provisions on the European Regional Development Fund, the European Social Fund and the Cohesion Fund[3]. According to article 9.4 of this Regulation, the Commission and the Member States shall ensure the coordination between the assistance from these Funds, the European Agricultural Fund for Rural Development (EAFRD), the European Fisheries Fund (EFF) and the interventions of the EIB and of other existing financial instruments, notably the European Investment Fund (EIF). Such coordination should also cover the preparation of complex financial schemes and public-private partnerships. The Commission is assisted by a Coordination Committee of the Funds set up by Article 103 of the Regulation. In addition, the national strategic reference framework may also contain, the procedure for coordination between Community cohesion policy and the relevant national, sectoral and regional policies of the Member State concerned.

In order to maximise the stimulus provided by the budget resources deployed, making use of appropriate financial instruments, the Community assistance provided in the form of grants may be combined in an appropriate way with loans and guarantees of the **European Investment Bank (EIB)** [see section 7.3.3.]. The latter is the longest standing regional development instrument, for the Treaty of Rome called upon it to ensure a balanced and smooth development of the common market in the interests of the Community (Art. 267 TEC). Almost 75% of EIB financing in the Community contribute to regional development, although they pursue other objectives such as those of promoting SMEs and trans-European networks [see section 6.8.]. The EIB notably supplies long-term capital for the financing of infrastructure projects in the fields of transport, energy and telecommunications.

Article 267 of the EC Treaty confirms that the loans and guarantees of the EIB will **facilitate projects for developing less-developed regions**, for modernising or converting undertakings or for developing fresh activities as well as for projects of common interest to several Member States. This Article makes specific reference to the desired interaction between EIB operations and Structural Funds measures, stating that "in carrying out its task, the Bank shall facilitate the financing of investment programmes in conjunction with assistance from the Structural Funds and other Community financial instruments", which concern regions whose development is lagging behind and declining industrial areas. The Bank also plays an active role in the financing of trans-European networks and thus in the implementation of the support instruments financed by the Community budget: interest rate subsidies on its own loans, co-financing of feasibility studies and co-financing of guarantee funds.

---

[1] COM (96) 512, 20 November 1996.
[2] COM (97) 7, 22 January 1997.
[3] Regulation 1083/2006, OJ L 210, 31.07.2006.

12.3.1. The objectives and methods of the Structural Funds

The action taken by the Community under Article 158 of the EC Treaty is designed to strengthen the economic and social cohesion of the enlarged European Union in order to promote its **harmonious, balanced and sustainable development**. This action is taken with the aid of the Structural Funds, the European Investment Bank (EIB) and other existing financial instruments. It is aimed at reducing the economic, social and territorial disparities which have arisen in the enlarged Union, particularly in countries and regions whose development is lagging behind and in connection with economic and social restructuring and the ageing of the population. According to the Regulation laying down general provisions on the European Regional Development Fund, the European Social Fund and the Cohesion Fund, the action taken under the Funds shall incorporate, at national and regional level, the Community's priorities in favour of sustainable development by strengthening growth, competitiveness, employment and social inclusion and by protecting and improving the quality of the environment[1]. To that end, the ERDF, the ESF, the Cohesion Fund, the EIB and the other existing Community financial instruments should each contribute towards achieving the **following three objectives**:

(a) **the Convergence objective**, which is aimed at speeding up the convergence of the least-developed Member States and regions by improving conditions for growth and employment through the increasing and improvement of the quality of investment in physical and human capital, the development of innovation and of the knowledge society, adaptability to economic and social changes, the protection and improvement of the environment, and administrative efficiency. This objective constitutes the priority of the Funds. The ERDF, the ESF and the Cohesion Fund contribute, each in accordance with the specific provisions governing it, towards achieving this objective. Overall resources for the Convergence objective – including transitional and specific support [see section 12.1.1] - amount to 251,2 billion EUR, i.e. 81.54 % of the resources available for commitment from the Funds for the period 2007 to 2013 (EUR 308 billion).

(b) the **Regional competitiveness and employment objective**, which is aimed at strengthening the competitiveness and attractiveness of regions, as well as employment by anticipating economic and social changes, including those linked to the opening of trade. The means employed towards those aims are: the increasing and improvement of the quality of investment in human capital, innovation and the promotion of the knowledge society, entrepreneurship, the protection and improvement of the environment, and the improvement of accessibility, adaptability of workers and businesses as well as the development of inclusive job markets. The least-developed regions, which are eligible under the Convergence objective, are not eligible under this objective. The ERDF and the ESF contribute, each in accordance with the specific provisions governing it, towards achieving the regional competitiveness and employment objective. The Cohesion Fund may also intervene, under certain conditions, in Member States eligible for its support. Overall resources for the Regional competitiveness and employment objective – including transitional and specific support [see section 12.1.1] – amount to 49.1 billion EUR, i.e. 15.95% of the resources available for commitment from the Funds for the period 2007 to 2013.

(c) the **European territorial cooperation objective**, which is aimed at strengthening cross-border cooperation through joint local and regional initiatives, strengthening transnational cooperation by means of actions conducive to integrated territorial development linked to the Community priorities, and strengthening interregional cooperation

---

[1]   Regulation 1083/2006, OJ L 210, 31.07.2006.

and exchange of experience at the appropriate territorial level. Only the ERDF contributes towards achieving this objective, but the Cohesion Fund may also intervene, under certain conditions, in Member States eligible for its support. Overall resources for the European territorial cooperation objective shall amount to 7.8 billion EUR, i.e. to 2.52% of the resources available for commitment from the Funds for the period 2007 to 2013 (EUR 308 billion).

Under the three objectives above, assistance from the Funds should, according to their nature, take into account specific economic and social features, on the one hand, and specific territorial features, on the other. The assistance should, in an appropriate manner, support sustainable urban development particularly as part of regional development and the renewal of rural areas and of areas dependent on fisheries through economic diversification. The assistance should also support areas affected by geographical or natural handicaps which aggravate the problems of development, particularly in the outermost regions as referred to in Article 299(2) of the Treaty as well as the northern areas with very low population density, certain islands and island Member States, and mountainous areas.

A **PEACE programme** in support of the peace process in Northern Ireland for the period 2007 to 2013 is implemented under the European territorial cooperation objective, in order to promote social and economic stability in the regions concerned. It includes, notably, actions to promote cohesion between communities. The eligible area is the whole of Northern Ireland and the border counties of Ireland.

12.3.2. The organisation of structural operations

The objectives of the Funds are pursued in the framework of a **multiannual programming system** organised in several stages comprising the identification of the priorities, the financing, and a system of management and control[1]. The Council establishes at Community level concise **strategic guidelines** on economic, social and territorial cohesion defining an indicative framework for the intervention of the Funds, taking account of other relevant Community policies. For each of the objectives of the Funds, those guidelines give effect to the priorities of the Community with a view to promoting its harmonious, balanced and sustainable development. The Member States present a **national strategic reference framework** which ensures that assistance from the Funds is consistent with the Community strategic guidelines on cohesion. Each national strategic reference framework constitutes a reference instrument for preparing the programming of the Funds for the period 1 January 2007 to 31 December 2013. A Member State may present at the same time the national strategic reference framework and the operational programmes.

A national strategic reference framework is prepared by each Member State in **partnership** (i.e. close cooperation) with the Commission and appropriate authorities and bodies such as: (a) the competent regional, local, urban and other public authorities; (b) the economic and social partners; (c) any other appropriate body representing civil society and non-governmental organisations. The partnership covers the preparation, implementation, monitoring and evaluation of operational programmes. The implementation of operational programmes is the responsibility of Member States at the appropriate territorial level, in accordance with the institutional system specific to each Member State. However, the budget of the European Union allocated to the Funds is implemented within the framework of shared management between the Member States and the Commission in accordance with the Regulation applicable to the general budget of the European Communities[2]. In accordance with their respective responsibilities, the Commission and the Member States ensure the coordination between the assistance from the Funds,

---

[1]   Regulation 1083/2006, OJ L 210, 31.07.2006.
[2]   Regulation 1605/2002, OJ L 248, 16.09.2002.

the EAFRD, the EFF and the interventions of the EIB and of other existing financial instruments.

According to the **principle of additionality**, the contributions from the Structural Funds must not replace public or equivalent structural expenditure by a Member State. This principle means that the Funds provide assistance which complements national actions, including actions at the regional and local levels, integrating into them the priorities of the Community. In particular, the assistance co-financed by the Funds must target the European Union priorities of promoting competitiveness and creating jobs, including meeting the objectives of the Integrated Guidelines for Growth and Jobs (2005 to 2008)[1]. To this end, the Commission and the Member States must ensure that 60% of expenditure for the Convergence objective and 75% of expenditure for the Regional competitiveness and employment objective for all the Member States of the European Union as constituted before 1 May 2004 is set for the abovementioned priorities. At their own initiative, Member States that acceded to the European Union on or after 1 May 2004 may decide to apply these provisions.

The activities of the Funds in the Member States take the form of **operational programmes** within the national strategic reference framework. An operational programme is a document submitted by a Member State and adopted by the Commission setting out a development strategy with a coherent set of priorities to be carried out with the aid of a Fund, or, in the case of the Convergence objective, with the aid of the Cohesion Fund and the ERDF. Each operational programme must cover a period between 1 January 2007 and 31 December 2013 and only one of the three objectives referred to above, save as otherwise agreed between the Commission and the Member State. The Commission should appraise the proposed operational programme to determine whether it contributes to the goals and priorities of the national strategic reference framework and the Community strategic guidelines on cohesion.

Operational programmes submitted under the Convergence objective must be drawn up at the **appropriate geographical level** and at least at NUTS level 2 [see section 12.1.1], but where there is a contribution from the Cohesion Fund, they must be drawn up at national level. Operational programmes submitted under the Regional competitiveness and employment objective must be drawn up at NUTS level 1 or NUTS level 2, in accordance with the institutional system specific to the Member State, for regions benefiting from financing by the ERDF. They must be drawn up by the Member State at the appropriate level if they are financed by the ESF. Operational programmes submitted under the European territorial cooperation objective for cross-border cooperation must be drawn up, as a general rule, for each border or group of borders by an appropriate grouping at NUTS level 3, including enclaves. However, interregional cooperation and exchange of experience programmes must relate to the whole territory of the Community.

As part of an operational programme, the Structural Funds may finance expenditure in respect of an operation comprising contributions to support **financial engineering instruments** for enterprises, primarily small and medium-sized ones, such as venture capital funds, guarantee funds and loan funds, and for urban development funds, that is, funds investing in public-private partnerships and other projects included in an integrated plan for sustainable urban development. The Member State or the managing authority may entrust the management and implementation of a part of an operational programme, as a **global grant**, to one or more intermediate bodies, designated by the Member State or the managing authority, including local authorities, regional development bodies or non-governmental organisations.

A **major project** is an operation comprising a series of works, activities or services intended in itself to accomplish an indivisible task of a precise economic or technical nature, which has clearly identified goals and whose total cost exceeds EUR 25 million in the case of the environment and EUR 50 million in other fields. **Operation** is a project or group of projects selected by the managing authority of the operational programme concerned or under its responsibility according to criteria laid down by the monitoring committee and implemented by one or more beneficiaries. The **beneficiary** is an operator, body or firm, whether public or private, responsible for initiating or initiating and implementing operations. **Intermediate body** is any public or private body or service which acts under the responsibility of a managing or certifying authority, or which carries out

---

[1] Decision 2005/600, OJ L 205, 06.08.2005.

duties on behalf of such an authority vis-à-vis beneficiaries implementing operations. **Public expenditure** is any public contribution to the financing of operations whose origin is either the budget of the State, of regional and local authorities or the budget of the European Communities. **Irregularity** is any infringement of a provision of Community law resulting from an act or omission by an economic operator which has, or would have, the effect of prejudicing the general budget of the European Union by charging an unjustified item of expenditure to the general budget.

12.3.3. European Regional Development Fund

Article 160 of the EC Treaty provides that the **European Regional Development Fund (ERDF)** is intended to help to redress the main regional imbalances in the Community. The ERDF has been reformed five times since its creation in 1975, demonstrating both the Community's growing commitment to regional development and its increased experience on this matter. Nowadays, the **ERDF is governed** by the general Regulation 1083/2006[1] and by the special Regulation 1080/2006[2], which establishes its tasks, the scope of its assistance with regard to the Convergence, Regional competitiveness and employment and European territorial cooperation objectives as defined in Regulation 1083/2006, and the rules on eligibility for assistance. Pursuant to these Regulations, the ERDF contributes to the financing of assistance which aims to reinforce economic and social cohesion by redressing the main regional imbalances through support for the development and structural adjustment of regional economies, including the conversion of declining industrial regions and regions lagging behind, and support for cross-border, transnational and interregional cooperation. In so doing, the ERDF must give effect to the priorities of the Community, and in particular the need to strengthen competitiveness and innovation, create and safeguard sustainable jobs, and ensure sustainable development.

The ERDF **contributes towards the financing of**:

(a) **productive investment** which contributes to creating and safeguarding sustainable jobs, primarily through direct aid to investment in small and medium-sized enterprises (SMEs);

(b) investment in **infrastructure**;

(c) development of **endogenous potential** by measures which support regional and local development, including support for and services to enterprises, in particular SMEs, creation and development of financing instruments such as venture capital, loan and guarantee funds, local development funds, interest subsidies, networking, cooperation and exchange of experience between regions, towns, and relevant social, economic and environmental actors;

(d) **technical assistance** which, either at the initiative of the Commission or at the initiative of the Member State, may finance the preparatory, management, monitoring, evaluation, information and control activities of operational programmes together with activities to reinforce the administrative capacity for implementing the Funds.

The ERDF focuses its assistance on **thematic priorities**. The type and range of actions financed within each priority reflect the different nature of the Convergence, Regional competitiveness and employment and European territorial cooperation objectives [see section 12.3.1].

Under the **Convergence objective**, the ERDF focuses its assistance on supporting sustainable integrated regional and local economic development and employment by mobilising and strengthening endogenous ca-

---

[1] Regulation 1083/2006, OJ L 210, 31.07.2006.
[2] Regulation 1080/2006, OJ L 210, 31.07.2006.

pacity through operational programmes aimed at the modernisation and diversification of economic structures and at the creation and safeguarding of sustainable jobs.

Under the **Regional competitiveness and employment objective**, the ERDF focuses its assistance in the context of sustainable development strategies, while promoting employment, primarily on the following three priorities: (1) innovation and the knowledge economy; (2) environment and risk prevention; and (3) access to transport and telecommunication services of general economic interest.

Under the **European territorial cooperation objective**, the ERDF focuses its assistance on the following priorities: (1) the development of cross-border economic, social and environmental activities through joint strategies for sustainable territorial development; (2) the establishment and development of transnational cooperation, including bilateral cooperation between maritime regions not covered under point 1, through the financing of networks and of actions conducive to integrated territorial development; and (3) reinforcement of the effectiveness of regional policy.

In the assistance of the ERDF particular attention is paid to ensuring complementarity and **consistency with other Community policies**, and in particular with the Seventh Framework Programme for research, technological development and demonstration activities and the Competitiveness and Innovation Framework Programme. Actions supported by the ERDF in favour of small and medium-sized enterprises must take into account and support the implementation of the European Charter for Small Enterprises [see section 17.2]. Furthermore, a synergy is pursued between support granted, on the one hand, from the ERDF and, on the other hand, that granted from the European Social Fund [see section 13.3.3], the Cohesion Fund [see section 12.1.2], the European Agricultural Fund for Rural Development (EAFRD) [see section 21.5.1] and the European Fisheries Fund [see section 22.4].

Within the operational programmes co-financed by the ERDF the arrangements for interregional cooperation take account of the special features of **areas with natural handicaps**. Moreover, building on the experience and strengths of the URBAN Community initiative provided in the previous general framework of the Structural Funds, **sustainable urban development** is supported by fully integrating measures in that field into the operational programmes co-financed by the ERDF, paying particular attention to local development and employment initiatives and their potential for innovation.

12.3.4. Pre-accession assistance

In order to improve the efficiency of the Community's External Aid, a new framework for programming and delivery of assistance was adopted at the same time as the 2006 reform of the Structural Funds. The Regulation establishing an **Instrument for Pre-Accession Assistance (IPA)** constitutes one of the general instruments directly supporting European External Aid policies[1]. In the interests of coherence and consistency of Community assistance, assistance for candidate countries as well as for potential candidate countries is granted in the context of a coherent framework, taking advantage of the lessons learned from earlier pre-accession instruments, but this assistance is also **consistent with the development policy** of the Community in accordance with Article 181a of the EC Treaty.

The Community assists candidate countries and potential candidate countries in their progressive alignment with the standards and policies of the European Union, including where appropriate the acquis communautaire, with a view to membership. A distinction is however made between **candidate countries** (Croatia, Turkey, The former Yugoslav Republic of Macedonia) and **potential candidate countries** (Albania, Bosnia, Montenegro, Serbia, including Kosovo). In general, assistance for candidate countries as well as for potential candidate countries supports a wide range of institution-building measures. On the one hand it supports them in their efforts to strengthen democratic institutions and the rule of law, reform public administration, carry out economic reforms, respect human as well as minority rights, promote gender equality, support the development of civil society and advance regional cooperation as well as reconciliation and reconstruction. On the other hand, Community assistance contributes to sustainable development and poverty reduction in all these countries. Assistance for candidate countries

---

[1] Regulation 1085/2006, OJ L 210, 31.07.2006.

additionally focuses on the adoption and implementation of the full acquis communautaire and prepares candidate countries for the implementation of the Community's agricultural and cohesion policy. Assistance for potential candidate countries may include
some alignment with the acquis communautaire, but is centred on support for investment
projects, aiming in particular at building management capacity in the areas of regional,
human resources and rural development.

Assistance is programmed and implemented according to **the following components**: (a) Transition Assistance and Institution Building; (b) Cross-Border Cooperation;
(c) Regional Development; (d) Human Resources Development; (e) Rural Development.
The Transition Assistance and Institution Building, and Cross-Border Cooperation
Components are accessible to all beneficiary countries, in order to assist them in the
process of transition and approximation to the EU, as well as to encourage regional cooperation between them. The Regional Development Component, the Human Resources
Development Component, and the Rural Development Component are accessible only to
candidate countries accredited to manage funds in a decentralised manner, in order to
help them prepare for the time after accession, in particular for the implementation of the
Community's cohesion and rural development policies. Potential candidate countries and
candidate countries that have not been accredited to manage funds in a decentralised
manner may however be eligible, under the Transition Assistance and Institution Building Component, for measures and actions of a similar nature to those which are available
under the Regional Development Component, the Human Resources Development
Component and the Rural Development Component.

Assistance is provided on the basis of a comprehensive **multi-annual strategy** that
reflects the priorities of the Stabilisation and Association Process, as well as the strategic
priorities of the pre-accession process. In order to assist with the financial part of this
strategy, the Commission presents a multi-annual indicative financial framework, as an
integral part of its annual enlargement package. Multi-annual indicative planning documents are established by country in close consultation with the national authorities, so as
to support national strategies and ensure the engagement and involvement of the country
concerned. Assistance is provided through multi-annual or annual programmes, established by country and by component, or, as appropriate, by group of countries or by
theme in accordance with the priorities defined in the multi-annual indicative planning
documents. Programmes specify the objectives pursued, the fields of intervention, the
expected results, the management procedures and total amount of financing planned.
Assistance is managed in accordance with the rules for External Aid contained in the
Financial Regulation applicable to the general budget of the European Communities[1].

The **Cross-Border Cooperation Component** supports both candidate countries and potential candidate
countries in cross-border, and, where appropriate, transnational and interregional cooperation among themselves and between them and the Member States. The **Regional Development Component** supports countries
only candidate countries in policy development as well as preparation for the implementation and management
of the Community's cohesion policy, in particular in their preparation for the European Regional Development
Fund and the Cohesion Fund. The **Human Resources Development Component** supports the candidate countries in policy development as well as preparation for the implementation and management of the Community's
cohesion policy, in particular in their preparation for the European Social Fund. The **Rural Development
Component** supports candidate countries in policy development as well as preparation for the implementation
and management of the Community's common agricultural policy.

Assistance under Regulation 1085/2006 may, inter alia, finance investments, procurement contracts,
grants including interest rate subsidies, special loans, loan guarantees and financial assistance, budgetary support, and other specific forms of budgetary aid, and the contribution to the capital of international financial
institutions or the regional development banks to the extent that the financial risk of the Community is limited

---

[1]   Regulation 1605/2002, OJ L 248, 16.09.2002.

to the amount of these funds. Assistance may also be used to cover the costs of actions linked to preparation, follow-up, control, audit and evaluation directly necessary for the administration of the programme and the attainment of its objectives, in particular studies, meetings, information and publicity, expenses linked to informatics networks aiming at information exchange, as well as any other expenses for administrative and technical assistance of which the Commission can avail itself for the administration of the programme.

12.4. Appraisal and outlook

The common regional policy has grown in importance since the Treaty made it an **essential instrument of economic and social cohesion**, itself necessary for the progress of economic and monetary union, implying the convergence of the Member States' economies. Indeed, the regional policy of the Union promotes the concept of European solidarity by completing and guiding the action of the Member States in view of a balanced European integration, profitable not only to the poor regions, but also to the rest of the Union.

In view of the new objective of economic and monetary union that it set, **the Treaty of Maastricht** provided both a frame of reference and support for the common regional policy, notably by establishing economic and social cohesion as a fundamental objective of the Union, creating the Cohesion Fund, setting up the Committee of the Regions and promoting trans-European infrastructure networks. By signing and ratifying this Treaty, the Member States acknowledged that the objectives of the EMU and of economic and social cohesion should be pursued in parallel. As seen in the Chapter on economic and monetary union, such union, implying the abandonment of the use of exchange rate adjustment as a means of rebalancing the national economy, would not be feasible without an efficient regional policy revolving around sufficient capital transfers from the richer to the poorer regions of the EU [see sections 7.2.3. and 7.4.]. The problem for the least-favoured regions is, in particular, to ensure that the effort to stabilise the budget does not choke off the investment in basic infrastructure, education and training which those regions require.

The efforts of the Union to develop its poorest regions are proving to be successful. The gross domestic product (GDP) per head of poorer regions is converging towards the Community average. Between 1986 and 1996, GDP per head in the 10 poorest regions increased from 41% of the EU average to 50%, and in the 25 poorest regions it rose from 52% to 59%. GDP per head in the four Cohesion countries went up from 65% of the EU average to 77% in 1999. The Cohesion Fund enabled the beneficiary countries (Spain, Greece, Ireland and Portugal) to sustain a substantial level of public investment in the areas of the environment and transport, while complying with the goals of reducing expected budget deficits through the convergence programmes drawn up in the context of economic and monetary union. The structural and cohesion policies have largely contributed to these results. But it is not only the poorest Member States which have benefited. Indeed, the capital transfers carried out in the framework of an efficient regional policy are not just an offering to the less fortunate in the Union. They are also in the economic interest of the more prosperous States, since they develop markets for their products and help to stimulate growth in all the territory of the Union. Estimates show that almost 40% of all funding that flows into the poorest Member States returns to the richer ones in the form of purchase of know-how or capital equipment.

The big question is how the Structural Funds of the Union will cope with the **accession of 12 Member States**, most of which have a per capita GDP far below that of the EU15. The Convergence regions (including those in phasing-out) are characterised by low levels of GDP and employment, as well as high unemployment. Their total share in EU27 GDP in 2002 was only 12.5% compared to a 35% population share. Therefore, since 2006, the complete overhaul of the Structural Funds and of the Cohesion Fund is geared more to the structural problems of the poorest regions of old and new Member States. It remains to be seen if the new common regional policy will substantially reduce the regional diversity of the Union. The fact is that real needs persist throughout the EU requiring continued investment, in order to raise growth potential in line with the Lisbon objectives [see section 13.3.2.].

Bibliography on regional policy

- ALTROCK Uwe (et al. eds.). *Spatial planning and urban development in the new EU Member States: from adjustment to reinvention.* Aldershot: Ashgate, 2006.
- ASHEIM Bjørn (et al. eds.). *Clusters and regional development: critical reflection and explorations.* London: Routledge, 2006.
- BRADLEY John (ed.). *Integration, growth and cohesion in an enlarged European Union.* New York : Springer, 2005.
- BUCK Nick (et al.). *Changing cities: rethinking urban competitiveness, cohesion and governance.* Basingstoke: Palgrave Macmillan in association with the ESRC Cities Programme, 2005.
- CAPELLO Roberta (ed.). Knowledge and accessibility for regional cohesion in the enlarged Europe. Special issue of: *Scienze Regionali,* v. 5, n. 2. 2006.
- COMMITTEE OF THE REGIONS. *Procedures for local and regional authority participation in European policy making in the Member States.* Luxembourg: EUR-OP*, 2005.

    - *Open days: European week of Regions and Cities: Investing in Europe's Regions and Cities: public and private partners for growth and jobs.* Luxembourg: EUR-OP*, 2006.
- DUDEK Carolyn Marie. *EU accession and Spanish regional development: winners and losers.* Bruxelles: PIE - P. Lang, 2005.
- DULLIEN Sebastian, SCHWARZER Daniela. "A question of survival?: Curbing regional differences in the eurozone" in *Review of Economic Conditions in Italy,* n. 1, January-April 2006, p. 65-85.
- ERIKSSON Jonas (ed.). *From policy takers to policy makers: adapting EU cohesion policy to the needs of the new member states.* Stockholm: Swedish Institute for European Policy Studies (SIEPS), 2005.
- EVANS Andrew. *EU regional policy.* Richmond: Richmond Law & Tax, 2005.
- EUROPEAN COMMISSION. *The Impact of European Integration and Enlargement on Regional Structural Change and Cohesion : EURECO: final report.* Luxembourg: EUR-OP*, 2006.

    - *Information society and the regions: linking European policies.* Luxembourg: EUR-OP*, 2006.

    - *Cohesion policy in support of growth and jobs: Community strategic guidelines 2007-13.* Luxembourg: EUR-OP*, 2006.
- JAZRA BANDARRA Nelly. "La politique de cohésion dans l'Union européenne et l'élargissement: nouvelles orientations pour la période 2007-2013" in *Revue du Marché commun et de l'Union européenne,* n. 496, mars 2006, p. 177-188.
- LEONARDI Robert. *Cohesion policy in the European Union: the building of Europe.* Basingstoke: Palgrave Macmillan, 2005.
- MATTILA Mikko. "Fiscal transfers and redistribution in the European Union: do smaller Member States get more than their share?" in *Journal of European Public Policy,* v. 13, n. 1, January 2006, p. 34-51.
- MÉNDEZ Carlos, WISHLADE Fiona, YUILL Douglas. "Conditioning and fine-tuning europeanization: negotiating regional policy maps under the EU's competition and cohesion policies" in *Journal of Common Market Studies,* v. 44, n. 3, September 2006, p. 581-605.
- STIFTEL Bruce, WATSON Vanessa (eds.). *Dialogues in urban and regional planning.* London: Routledge, 2005.
- WEATHERILL Stephen, BERNITZ Ulf (eds.). *The role of regions and sub-national actors in Europe.* Oxford; Portland, Or. : Hart, 2005.

*The publications of the Office for Official Publications of the European Communities (EUR-OP) exist usually in all official languages of the EU.

Chapter 13

SOCIAL PROGRESS POLICIES

<u>Diagram of the chapter</u>

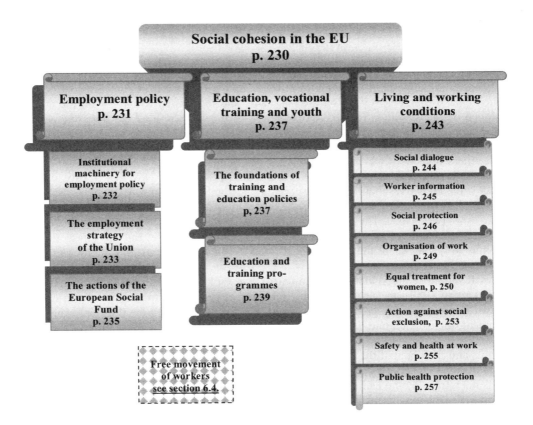

Social cohesion in the EU
p. 230

Employment policy
p. 231

Education, vocational
training and youth
p. 237

Living and working
conditions
p. 243

Institutional
machinery for
employment policy
p. 232

The employment
strategy
of the Union
p. 233

The actions of the
European Social
Fund
p. 235

The foundations of
training and
education policies
p, 237

Education and
training pro-
grammes
p. 239

Social dialogue
p. 244

Worker information
p. 245

Social protection
p. 246

Organisation of work
p. 249

Equal treatment for
women, p. 250

Action against social
exclusion, p. 253

Safety and health at work
p. 255

Public health protection
p. 257

Free movement
of workers
see section 6.4.

Given the varied economic structures of the Community Member States, their social problems were at the launch of the European integration process - and still are to some extent - quite different. It would not have been possible at the start - and that still holds true - to entrust the common social policy with the task of solving all the Member States' social problems. Such a solution depends to a great extent upon economic policy, which is still to a large degree in the hands of the individual governments. But as European integration advances and the Member States delegate significant economic and monetary policy instruments to the European Union, the latter **commits itself increasingly to the advancement of social progress** for all the peoples who make it up.

As we will see below, the Treaty of Rome aimed mainly at the free movement of workers [see section 6.4.] and relied above all on the functioning of the common market to improve living and working conditions in all Member States [see section 6.1.]. In line with the reform of the Structural Funds, which constituted the financial side of economic and social cohesion, the European Council, despite the opposition of Mrs. Thatcher, who was then Prime Minister of the United Kingdom, agreed in December 1989 on the **Community Charter of the fundamental rights of workers**, which represented the legal side of social cohesion and stressed particularly the alignment of social standards in the Member States: social protection; freedom of association and of collective bargaining; equal treatment for men and women; information, consultation and participation of workers; the protection of health and safety at the workplace; and the protection of children and adolescents, the elderly and the disabled. The Commission, which had proposed the Charter, proposed immediately after its adoption by the majority of heads of State of Government, a series of Community laws in order to implement it. But due to the unanimity rule required and the negative position of the United Kingdom, very few social measures were adopted before the completion of the internal market, which they should in principle follow in step. In order to get out of the impasse, eleven (out of the then twelve Member States), on the one hand, and the United Kingdom, on the other, signed at Maastricht a Social Protocol allowing the former to adopt alone the social measures that they deemed useful.

However, the anomaly of a common policy where one Member State did not share the others' objectives was corrected at Amsterdam, in June 1997, when **the Labour British Government decided to accede** to the social provisions of the new Treaty and to accept the Directives that had already been agreed under the Social Agreement. Protocol N° 14 on social policy annexed to the TEC and the Agreement on social policy attached thereto were repealed. The new Chapter 4 on Social Policy of the TEC incorporates most of the provisions of the Maastricht Social Agreement, notably: the objectives of the Community Charter of the Fundamental Social Rights of Workers and the measures to achieve those objectives.

It should be noted that the Community Charter of the Fundamental Social Rights of Workers of 1989 was surpassed by the **Charter of Fundamental Rights of the European Union** solemnly proclaimed in Nice, on 7 December 2000, by the European Parliament, the Council and the Commission[1] [see section 9.2.]. The 2000 Charter exceeds the 1989 Charter, on the one hand, because it guarantees not only social rights but all rights and freedoms of the citizens of the Union and, on the other, because it is an official document agreed by all Member States whereas, as seen above, the Social Charter was not agreed by the United Kingdom. The proposed incorporation of the Charter of fundamental rights of citizens into the Constitutional Treaty would place the institutions of the Union under a legal obligation to ensure that in all its areas of activity, fundamental rights would not only be respected but also actively promoted.

---

[1]   Solemn Declaration, OJ C 364, 18.12.2000.

13.1. The need for a common social policy

The objectives of the common social policy are very close to those of the common regional policy. The latter is directed towards improving the lot of the least-favoured regions of the European Union, the social policy that of its poorest citizens. Both seek to **even out the economic and social imbalances** in the Union and to ensure that the advantages ensuing from the functioning of the common market are shared amongst all the countries and all the citizens. Several of their measures are complementary, and their financial instruments are closely coordinated in order to put them into effect.

A Community social policy, which was necessary for the social cohesion of the Community as early as the stage of the progressive implementation of the common market, was provided for in vague terms in the EEC Treaty. Although its signatories stated that they were resolved to ensure social progress by common action and affirmed as the essential objective the improvement of the living and working conditions of their peoples, they remained entirely independent in the field of social policies. They placed their faith above all in the automatic improvement of social conditions, relying on the **knock-on effect that economic integration would produce**. They were not wrong in that, but they were not completely right either.

It is certain that the progressive integration of the economies in itself promotes the convergence of the social conditions of the States of the Community. The most characteristic social features of the Community during the first forty years of its existence have been the moderate growth of the population, increased life expectancy and shorter working life, the widespread extension of compulsory education and the mass entry of women into economic activities. In addition to those general phenomena there have been structural changes within sectors and sectoral movements from agriculture to industry and from the latter to the service industries. Thus, it is not by chance that the problems of employment, social security and the vocational training of certain categories of workers (the young, the old and women) are priorities in every Member State. It is, therefore, true that the closer the economic conditions become in a multinational integration scheme, the more the **social problems of the member states become similar** and more similar, not to say common, solutions become necessary. Likewise, the free movement of workers and transnational trade union contacts have promoted a degree of **upward levelling** of wages, social benefits and social protection.

Increased prosperity brought about largely by European integration, did not, however, resolve all the Community's social problems. It even made some of them more acute or gave rise to new ones, viz. problems of disadvantaged regions and categories of persons who do not participate fully in the general progress; problems of structural unemployment; problems relating to the distribution of income and wealth; contradictions between economic and social values and, on occasion, dramatic changes in lifestyle with negative consequences for the behaviour of young people. Since the Treaty on the European Community actually calls for a social model based on the market economy, democracy and pluralism, respect of individual rights, free collective bargaining, equality of opportunity for all, social welfare and solidarity, it instructs the common institutions to strive to attain those objectives.

A dynamic social policy is essential for an efficient **industrial policy**. Adequate vocational training for workers and the improvement of the occupational and geographical mobility of labour are prerequisites for the efficiency of European industry. **Technological progress** and improved training lead to the strengthening of the requirements as regards social protection, to worker participation and to the improvement of the quality of life and of work. At the same time, however, technological progress gives rise to numerous structural changes accompanied by tension on the labour market. A common approach must be taken to these phenomena so as not to give rise to distortions of competition within the common market. In fact, given the increasing economic interdependence of the member countries, any one of their number which decided to carry out a social reform on its own might handicap some of its industrial sectors or even its economy in general.

At the dawn of the 21st century, the European societies are faced with **new common challenges**. The globalisation of trade and production, the impact of new technologies on work, society and individuals, the high level of unemployment of some categories and the ageing of the population are all combining to put severe strains on the social fabric of all the Member States. While the basic responsibility in these areas lies with the Member States, full cooperation between them, within the Union, plays an important role in ensuring that the **national systems of social protection** do not develop in ways which conflict with overall Union employment objectives or standards, distort conditions of competition, or inhibit the free movement of people within the Union.

13.2. Social cohesion in the European Union

Economic and social cohesion is an objective of the Community (Art. 2 and 3 TEC). Whereas the common regional policy deals mainly with economic cohesion, the common social policy tries to strengthen social cohesion. Article 136 of the EC Treaty declares that the Community and the Member States, having in mind fundamental social rights such as those set out in the European Social Charter signed at Turin on 18 October 1961 and in the 1989 Community Charter of the Fundamental Social Rights of Workers, have as their objectives the promotion of employment, improved living and working conditions, so as to make possible their harmonisation while the improvement is being maintained, proper social protection, dialogue between management and labour and the development of human resources. This last goal entails effectual education and training policies. Article 136 states also that the objectives of social progress and cohesion that it sets should ensue not only from the functioning of the common market, which will favour the harmonisation of social systems, but also from the procedures provided for in the Treaty and from the approximation of provisions laid down by law, regulation or administrative action (particularly in the context of the single market). However, the measures taken by the Community and the Member States to attain the objectives of Article 136 must take account of the diverse forms of national practices, in particular in the field of contractual relations, and the need to maintain the competitiveness of the Community economy.

To attain social cohesion in the Union **minimum social standards are needed**, having regard to differing national systems and needs, and to the relative economic strengths of the Member States. The establishment of a framework of basic minimum standards guarantees acceptable social and physical security conditions to all the workers in the Union. At the same time, it provides a bulwark against reducing social standards to increase the competitiveness of the businesses of one Member State and, hence, against using low social standards as an instrument of unfair economic competition. These basic standards should not over-stretch the economically weaker Member States, but they should not prevent the more developed Member States from implementing higher standards.

The **effort to complete the single market** at the end of the 1980s was to mean a fresh start for the Community's social policy and its financial instrument, the European Social Fund (ESF) [see section 13.3.3]. The Single European Act and, later on, the Maastricht Treaty stated that "in order to promote its overall harmonious development, the Community shall develop and pursue its actions leading to the strengthening of its economic and social cohesion" (Art. 158 TEC). The Structural Funds, and especially the **European Social Fund** (ESF), represent the main instruments for promoting social cohesion within the Union [see section 12.1.2.]. As we saw under the heading of coordination of financial instruments in the chapter on regional development, the ESF contributes to the attainment of the Objectives set out set out in the context of the Community structural policy [see section 12.3.1.].

The **social policy agenda,** proposed by the Commission and approved by the Nice European Council in December 2000, provides the roadmap for employment and social policy, translating the policy objectives of the Lisbon strategy for economic and social renewal into concrete measures[1] [see section 13.3.2.]. A high level of social cohesion is central to the Lisbon agenda. Strategies which strive for gender equality, for the eradication of poverty and social exclusion and for the modernisation of social protection systems, in particular pension and healthcare systems, play a key role in this agenda. In short, the Union aims at social progress and cohesion through the specific policies for employment, education and professional training, as well as through the promotion and improvement of living and working conditions, including social protection and social inclusion. These are the subjects examined in the following parts of this chapter.

13.3. Common employment policy

Unemployment became a matter of serious concern for all the countries of the Community around the mid-1970s. Until then employment problems in the Community merely consisted of structural and regional imbalances in a general context of full employment. A series of very variable economic factors led to the **rapid deterioration of the employment situation** in the Community, viz.: the inflation and economic recession of the late 1970s and early 1980s, resulting from monetary and energy crises [see sections 7.2.1. and 19.1.1.], lively competition from recently industrialised countries in Asia with cheap labour, a degree of saturation of demand in Europe for industrial goods and the evolution of the economy and of European companies towards a post-industrial stage. Many jobs thus became superfluous and disappeared. Others were created, but required new qualifications which most of the unemployed did not possess. At the same time, women, most of who had previously stayed at home, joined the labour market in force [see section 13.5.5.].

Averaging more than 10% of the active population of the Member States (with important differences between them), in the beginning of the 21st century, the unemployment rate of the European Union is seen as **its gravest social problem**. The economic and social costs of this unemployment are enormous. They include not only the direct expenditure on providing social security support for the unemployed, but also: the loss of tax revenue which the unemployed would pay out of their income if they were working; the increased burden on social services; rising poverty, crime and ill-health. Special concern focuses on the lack of prospects for new entrants to the labour market, especially young people and women and for people excluded from regular work [see section 13.5.6.]. Under the pressure of these problems was endorsed the employment strategy of the Union.

---

[1] COM (2000) 379 and COM (2003) 312, 2 June 2003.

13.3.1. Institutional machinery for employment policy

Thanks to a **levy system** on the production of the industries concerned, the European Coal and Steel Community (ECSC) was better placed than the European Economic Community (EEC) to cope with the employment problems. Article 56 of the **ECSC Treaty** contained provisions on employment in the coal and steel industries. Useful lessons can probably be learned from experience gained with the ECSC, which has operated in exceptionally close association with the social partners and with co-financing redeployment aid for the workers losing their jobs from the industries concerned. This system has cushioned the social impact of tremendous job losses in these industries in the 1970's and the 1980's. After the expiry of the ECSC Treaty in July 2002 [see section 2.1.], the ownership, management and destination of funds from the ECSC were transferred to the European Community, represented by the Commission[1].

Unlike the ECSC Treaty, the EEC Treaty did not prepare the Community Institutions sufficiently to cope with the employment problems which started plaguing the Community since the mid-1970s. Of course Article 118 of that Treaty gave the Commission the task of promoting close cooperation between States in the social field with regard to employment *inter alia*. To do so, however, it could act, in accordance with that Article, only by making studies, delivering opinions and arranging consultations. The Commission has used and is still using those means, which were supplemented by the new means developed thanks to the EC Treaty [see sections 12.3.2 and 12.3.3.].

In view of mutual information and coordination, the Commission set up a programme of employment statistics, and publishes reports on employment forecasts for each sector, based on national work and containing homogeneous quantitative data[2]. It keeps a continuous inventory of the measures taken in the countries of the Community to tackle the employment problems.

In collaboration with the national administrations, the European Commission has prepared an information system on employment policies - the **European Employment Observatory** - whose main task is to run a network between Member States and the Commission with a view to pooling information. The Observatory provides services to the public in the form of periodic publications and regularly updated databases. It also prepares comparative political analyses and tenders advice. In its current form the Observatory relies on three information networks.

- **MISEP** (Mutual Information System on Employment Policies) is a network of representatives of the national administrations responsible for employment in the Member States and the Commission. MISEP's chief task is to exchange and disseminate information in the field of employment policies;
- **SYSDEM** (System of Documentation, Evaluation and Monitoring of Employment Policies) is a network of independent labour market experts (one per Member State) which produces comparative and thematic studies of employment policies and labour market policies throughout the EU;
- **RESEARCH** is a high-level group that tenders advice on employment policy and labour market policy issues and produces assessment reports on the employment situation and on employability.

The Commission examines the information thus obtained, studies the trends which affect employment in the Member States and publishes reports and bulletins assessing the rapid changes currently taking place in the Union's labour market[3]. It communicates this information to the **Standing Committee on Employment** (made up of representatives of the Commission, the Council and the social partners at European level) to provide them with an opportunity of discussing the employment situation, the measures taken in each country and the coordination of employment strategy at Community level[4]. The main task of this Committee is to ensure that there is continuous dialogue, concertation and consultation between the Council, the Commission and the social partners in order to enable the social partners to contribute to the coordinated employment strategy and to facilitate coordination by the Member States of their policies in this field reflected in both the Employment Guidelines and the Broad Economic Policy Guidelines (BEPGs) [see sections 13.3.2 and 7.3.1.].

The Standing Committee on Employment should not be confused with the **Employment Committee**, made up of representatives of the Member States, whose main tasks are to monitor the employment situation and employment policies in the Member States and the Community; and to formulate opinions at the request of either the Council or the Commission or on its own initiative, and to contribute to the preparation of the Council proceedings referred to in Article 128 of the EC Treaty[5].

---

[1]   Decisions 2003/76 and 2003/77, OJ L 29, 05.02.2003.
[2]   Regulation 577/98, OJ L 77, 14.03.1998 and Regulation 2257/2003, OJ L 336, 23.12.2003.
[3]   See, e.g., COM (2005) 120.
[4]   Decision 2003/174, OJ L 70, 14.03.2003.
[5]   Decision 2000/98, OJ L 29, 04.02.2000.

13.3.2. The employment strategy of the Union

On the basis of Article 118 EEC, which enjoined it to promote a close cooperation among the Member States in the field of employment without having recourse to formal legislation, the Commission, in the 1980s, led the Council adopt guidelines for a Community labour market policy[1] and a series of Community **Resolutions and programmes in the field of employment**. These Council Resolutions aimed at:

- a Community action to combat unemployment[2];
- the promotion of employment for young people[3];
- combating unemployment amongst women[4];
- the contribution of local employment initiatives to combating unemployment[5];
- action to combat long-term unemployment[6];
- promoting the integration or reintegration of women into working life[7]; and
- assisting the long-term unemployed[8].

Despite their non-compulsory character, these Resolutions have had some practical effects. Thus, the Resolution on the promotion of employment for young people gave rise to many initiatives of the European Social Fund, whether measures in favour of young people establishing undertakings (companies, businesses), innovative practices on the part of undertakings or aid for the integration of disadvantaged young people. The Resolution on long-term unemployment led to a job creation programme being adopted for specific groups of long-term unemployed (**ERGO**). Likewise, local job-creation schemes formed the subject of an important action programme for the local development of employment (**LEDA**) aimed at pinpointing and removing the obstacles to those schemes. The Commission also set up a system for exchanges of information for local employment initiatives (**ELISE**) and a support programme for innovative local or regional job creation schemes (**SPEC**).

On the basis of these last experiences, the Commission presented in a communication the elements of a European strategy for encouraging **local development and employment initiatives (LDEI)**[9]. These are viewed in terms of local projects calling for a legal and financial partnership between the public and private sectors and geared to meeting new needs such as, home-help services, child care, assistance for young people facing difficulties, cultural heritage, crafts and tourism, waste management, protection and conservation of natural areas. The proliferation of LDEIs has created a major dynamic impetus affecting the entire territory of the European Union and combining entrepreneurial spirit, employment and local diversity.

These first experiences of the Community could not, of course, by themselves combat unemployment on a large scale. In the 1990s it has become clear that reducing unemployment necessarily requires **pro-active labour market policies**. A radical new look is needed at the whole range of available instruments, which can influence the employment environment, whether these be regulatory, fiscal or social security incentives. The educational system, labour laws, work contracts, contractual negotiation systems, the social security system and business management form the pillars of the "employment environment" in each Member State and combine to give each of them a distinctive appearance. According to the subsidiarity principle [see section 3.2.], the vast bulk of these measures should be for individual Member States to decide upon in responding to their diverse national situations. However, the Union can and must play an important role by: firstly, providing a forum where a common broad framework strategy can be agreed; and secondly, by underpinning national measures with complementary financial support through the European Social Fund.

The EU Treaty sets among the objectives of the Union, mentioned in Article 2 (TEU), that of promoting economic and social progress and a "high level of employment". The new **Title on Employment** of the EC Treaty urges the Member States and the Community to work towards developing a coordinated strategy for employment and particularly for promoting a skilled, trained and adaptable workforce and labour markets responsive to economic change (Art. 125 TEC). To this end, Member States must regard promoting employment as a matter of common concern and must coordinate their action in this respect within the Council (Art. 126 TEC). The Community must encourage co-

---

[1] OJ C 168, 08.07.1980.
[2] Resolution, OJ C 186, 21.07.1982, p. 1-2.
[3] Resolution, OJ C 29, 04.02.1984, p. 1-3.
[4] Resolution, OJ C 161, 21.06.1984 p. 4-6.
[5] Resolution, OJ C 161, 21.06.1984 p. 1-3.
[6] Resolution, OJ C 2, 01.01.1985, p. 3-5.
[7] Resolution, OJ C 333, 28.12.1988, p. 1-2.
[8] Resolution, OJ C 157, 27.06.1990, p. 4-6.
[9] COM (95) 273, 13 June 1995.

operation between the Member States, support and, if necessary, complement their action (Art. 127 TEC). The European Council should each year consider the employment situation of the Community and adopt conclusions thereon, on the basis of which the Council should draw up employment guidelines, consistent with the broad guidelines of economic policies [see section 7.3.1.], which the Member States should take into account in their employment policies (Art 128 TEC). The Council, under the co-decision procedure with the Parliament [see section 4.3.], may adopt incentive measures designed to encourage cooperation between Member States and to support their action in the field of employment through initiatives aimed at developing exchanges of information and best practices (Art 129 TEC). Indeed, a Council decision aimed at: fostering cooperation in the field of employment as regards analysis, research and monitoring; identifying good practices and promoting exchanges and transfers of information and experience; and developing an active information policy[1].

An extraordinary European Council on employment took place in Luxembourg on 20 and 21 November 1997. It enacted the definition, as from 1998, of **guidelines for employment** and placed emphasis on harnessing systematically the common policies of the Community in support of employment. In adopting the 1999 employment guidelines, the Council set out the subsequent procedures for monitoring the application of the guidelines by the Member States[2]. These guidelines help the Member States to devise their own strategies, while preserving the four-pillar structure established in 1998[3]: improving employability, i.e. giving unemployed people and workers in general better opportunities to find work, with the emphasis on suitable training; developing entrepreneurship; encouraging adaptability; and strengthening equal opportunities policies for women and men. By mid-June, each Member State must submit to the Council and the Commission a report concerning the implementation of the previous national action plan and describing the adjustments made to this plan in the light of the changes introduced by the current employment guidelines. By the end of the year, the Council adopts guidelines for the Member States' employment policies for the next year and publishes a recommendation on the implementation of employment policies in the Member States[4]. The Commission monitors the employment strategy pursued by the Member States and publishes an annual report on employment rates considering how each Member State could help to achieve the goal of raising employment rates as an objective of economic policy. The Council has provided a legal basis for Commission activities forming part of the European employment strategy, concerning analysis, research, cooperation and action in the field of employment[5].

Going a step further in the coordination of employment policies, the Cologne European Council (3 and 4 June 1999) adopted a **European Employment Pact** aimed at a sustainable reduction of unemployment. The European Employment Pact embodies a comprehensive overall approach bringing together all the Union's employment policy measures, which support and mutually reinforce one another. In the broad economic policy guidelines (BEPGs), the Member States and the Community agree annually on the main elements of their economic policy [see section 7.3.1.]; in the employment guidelines the Member States and the Community agree annually on the main elements of the coordinated employment strategy; in the macroeconomic dialogue (within the framework of the ECOFIN Council), information and opinions of the relevant Commu-

[1]   Decision 98/171, OJ L 63, 04.03.1998.
[2]   Resolution, OJ C 69, 12.03.1999, p. 2-8.
[3]   Resolution, OJ C 30, 28.01.1998, p. 1-5.
[4]   See, e.g. Decision 2005/600 and Recommendation 2005/601, OJ L 205, 06.08.2005.
[5]   Decision 98/171, OJ L 63, 04.03.1998.

nity institutions and the social partners are exchanged in an appropriate manner concerning the question of how to design macroeconomic policy in order to increase and make full use of the potential for growth and employment [see section 7.3.1].

The Lisbon European Council (23 and 24 March 2000) agreed to a **strategic goal** to be pursued over the first decade of the 21st century, with the aim of boosting employment, economic reform and social cohesion within the framework of a knowledge-based economy. The three key elements of this strategy are geared to: preparing the transition to a knowledge-based economy and society by means of policies tailored more to the needs of the information society and research and development, stepping up the process of structural reform to boost competitiveness and innovation, while completing the internal market; modernising the European social model, investing in people and combating social exclusion; and sustaining a healthy economic outlook and favourable growth prospects by applying an appropriate macroeconomic policy mix. Implementation of the Lisbon strategic goal involves: fixing guidelines for the Union combined with specific timetables for achieving the goals in the short, medium and long terms; translating these European guidelines into national and regional policies; and periodic monitoring, evaluation and peer review.

Drawing on lessons learnt from five years of implementing the **Lisbon strategy**, the European Council in March 2005 decided on a fundamental relaunch. It agreed to refocus priorities on jobs and growth coherent with the sustainable development strategy, by mobilising to a greater degree all appropriate national and Community resources. With the European **Employment Strategy** being seen as a key component of the Lisbon agenda, the Commission promotes a new generation of employment guidelines entailing three overall objectives (full employment, quality and productivity at work, cohesion and an inclusive labour market) focusing on the following priorities: active and preventive measures for the unemployed and the inactive; making work more worthwhile; fostering entrepreneurship to create more and better jobs; transforming undeclared work into regular employment; promoting active ageing; developing and reinforcing immigration policy; promoting adaptability in the labour market; investing in human capital and strategies for lifelong learning; fostering gender equality; supporting integration and combating discrimination in the labour market for people who are at a disadvantage; and addressing regional employment disparities[1]. Responding to the invitation of the European Council, the Commission made proposals for the application of the open coordination method in the field of social protection in the framework of the Lisbon strategy[2].

13.3.3. The actions of the European Social Fund

According to Article 146 (TEC) the **European Social Fund (ESF)** aims to: (a) render the employment of workers easier and to increase their geographical and occupational mobility within the Community; and (b) facilitate their adaptation to industrial changes and to changes in production systems, in particular through vocational training and retraining. The ESF is administered by the Commission, which is assisted in this task by a Committee composed of representatives of the governments, trade unions and employers' organisations (Art. 147 TEC).

Regulation 1083/2006 establishes the framework for action by the Structural Funds and the Cohesion Fund for the period 2007 to 2013 and lays down, in particular, their objectives, principles and rules concerning partnership, programming, evaluation and management[3] [see section 12.1.2]. **The ESF is therefore governed** by Regulation 1083/2006 and by Regulation 1081/2006, which establishes its tasks, the scope of its assistance, specific provisions and the types of expenditure eligible for assistance[4]. The

---

[1]   COM (2003) 6, 14 January 2003.
[2]   COM (2003) 261, 27 May 2003.
[3]   Regulation 1083/2006, OJ L 210, 31.07.2006.
[4]   Regulation 1081/2006, OJ L 210, 31.07.2006.

tasks of the ESF are all the more important in consideration of the importance of the European social model and its modernisation in view of the challenges arising from the enlargement of the Union and the phenomenon of economic globalisation.

The main task of the ESF is to contribute to the priorities of the Community as regards strengthening economic and social cohesion by improving employment and job opportunities, encouraging a high level of employment and more and better jobs. In order to better contribute to the implementation of the objectives and targets agreed at the Lisbon and Göteborg European Councils [see sections 13.3.2 and 16.2], the ESF must support actions in line with measures taken by Member States on the basis of the guidelines adopted under the European Employment Strategy, as incorporated into the Integrated Guidelines for Growth and Jobs, and the accompanying recommendations [see section 13.3.2]. In so doing, the ESF must take into account the relevant priorities and objectives of the Community in the fields of education and training, increasing the participation of economically inactive people in the labour market, combating social exclusion - especially that of disadvantaged groups such as people with disabilities - and promoting equality between women and men and non-discrimination. The ESF must also act to tackle the relevant dimensions and consequences of demographic changes in the active population of the Community, in particular through lifelong vocational training.

With a view to better anticipating and managing change and increasing economic growth, employment opportunities for both women and men, and quality and productivity at work under the **Convergence and Regional competitiveness and employment objectives** [see section 12.3.1], assistance from the ESF focuses, in particular, on improving the adaptability of workers and enterprises, enhancing human capital and access to employment and participation in the labour market, reinforcing the social inclusion of disadvantaged people, combating discrimination, encouraging economically inactive persons to enter the labour market and promoting partnerships for reform. In addition to these priorities, in the least developed regions and Member States, under **the Convergence objective** and with a view to increasing economic growth, employment opportunities for both women and men, and quality and productivity at work, the ESF helps to expand and improve investment in human capital and to improve institutional, administrative and judicial capacity, so as to prepare and implement reforms and enforce the acquis.

Within the framework of the **Convergence and Regional competitiveness and employment objectives**, the ESF supports actions in Member States under the following priorities:
(a) increasing adaptability of workers, enterprises and entrepreneurs with a view to improving the anticipation and positive management of economic change;
(b) enhancing access to employment and the sustainable inclusion in the labour market of job seekers and inactive people, preventing unemployment, in particular long-term and youth unemployment, encouraging active ageing and longer working lives, and increasing participation in the labour market;
(c) reinforcing the social inclusion of disadvantaged people with a view to their sustainable integration in employment and combating all forms of discrimination in the labour market;
d) enhancing human capital, in particular by promoting the design and introduction of reforms in education and training systems; and
(e) promoting partnerships, pacts and initiatives through networking of relevant stakeholders, such as the social partners and non-governmental organisations;
Within the framework of the **Convergence objective**, the ESF supports actions in Member States under the following priorities:
(a) expanding and improving investment in human capital; and
(b) strengthening institutional capacity and the efficiency of public administrations and public services at national, regional and local level and, where relevant, of the social partners and non-governmental organisations, with a view to reforms, better regulation and good governance especially in the economic, employment, education, social, environmental and judicial fields.

The Member States must ensure that operational programmes include a description of how gender equality and equal opportunities are promoted in the preparation, implementation, monitoring and evaluation of operational programmes. Member States shall promote a balanced participation of women and men in the management and implementation of operational programmes at local, regional and national level, as appropriate. Particular attention should also be paid to the participation of target groups, the integration of migrants, including those seeking asylum, the identification of policy issues and their subsequent mainstreaming, innovation and experimentation techniques.

13.4. Education, vocational training and youth policies

The problems of employment and vocational training are related, as very often the jobs offered require qualifications, which those seeking employment lack. That is why **employment and vocational training policies are also linked**. In fact, training is an instrument of active labour market policy. At the same time, measures promoting vocational training or retraining promote the employment or re-employment of workers in sectors where qualified labour is needed. Many workers cannot secure employment without becoming specialised, but they cannot acquire specialisation through experience until they have found a job. Breaking this vicious circle through vocational training is vital as workers should be able to change more frequently jobs throughout their working lives in the future.

Vocational training is not only a basic human right, enabling workers to realise their full potential, but also a **prerequisite for technological progress** and regional development. Indeed, a skilled, adaptable and mobile workforce is an essential component in the competitiveness, productivity and quality of companies, since it allows industries and regions to adapt rapidly to the requirements of technology and market trends and thus to become or remain competitive. Unemployment is in fact rife especially in the traditional industries in decline (steel, shipbuilding, textiles...), whilst the new industries (information technology, telecommunications, aerospace...) are badly in need of qualified labour. Tomorrow's trades will require the autonomy, the independence of spirit, the analytical ability and the capacity to make diagnoses, qualities which depend on knowledge. The new qualifications can help the European economy to effect the necessary structural changes in the information society and enable it better to face competition from the newly industrialised countries. The EU's education and training policies aim therefore to develop human resources throughout people's working lives, starting with basic education and working through initial training to continuing training.

13.4.1. The foundations of education and training policies

Underlying the common education policy is the collection and dissemination of information on the programmes and projects of the various higher education establishments in the Member States. An **Education Information Network** in the European Community, under the name of EURYDICE, is available to users with responsibilities in the field of education, such as the Community institutions, national authorities and officials responsible for higher education in the Member States[1]. The Eurydice network is the chief instrument for providing information on national and Community structures, systems and developments in the field of education. The network assists the drawing up of comparative analyses, reports and surveys on common priority topics determined inter

---

[1] Resolution, OJ C 329, 31.12.1990, p. 23-24 and Council Conclusions, OJ C 336, 19.12.1992, p. 7.

alia in the Education Committee and in the Advisory Committee on Vocational Training[1]. A Community action programme supports bodies and their activities which seek to extend and deepen knowledge of the building of Europe, or to contribute to the achievement of the common policy objectives in the field of education and training[2]. Another Community action programme provides financial support to organisations active at European level in the field of youth[3].

An organ of the common policy on professional training is the **European Centre for the Development of Vocational Training (CEDEFOP)**, located in Thessaloniki[4]. Cedefop's programme of work focuses on two priority areas, namely qualifications and vocational training systems. The former is essentially concerned with the transparency of qualifications and new occupations at European level and the impact of new forms of work organisation and qualifications on training systems. The latter is concerned with strategies for the optimum combination of types and phases of training with a view to achieving a lifelong learning process and with improved teacher training.

The **European Training Foundation (ETF)**, established in Turin, supports the reform of vocational education and training and management training in over 40 partner countries and territories, divided into four main geographical blocs (Mediterranean region, western Balkans, eastern Europe and central Asia, candidate/acceding countries), and provides technical assistance to the Commission for the Tempus programme[5] [see section 13.4.2.].

As agreed at the Lisbon European Council (23 and 24 March 2000) [see section 13.3.2.], the *e*Learning initiative is designed to make good the shortcomings in Europe in the use of new information and communications technologies, thereby accelerating the pace of change in education and training systems and helping Europe to move towards a knowledge-based society[6]. The key objectives are focused on: improving infrastructure, notably equipping all schools in the Union; training the population at all levels by making schools, training centres and other places of learning accessible to all; development of high-quality multimedia services and content; and networking of schools (European Schoolnet). Moreover, a Council Resolution invited the Commission to promote the **involvement of young people** in the development, execution and evaluation of Community youth activities and programmes[7]. The Commission mobilises Community programmes and instruments to achieve these objectives.

A Council decision seeks to promote mobility and flexibility in Europe's labour market, by improving transparency and facilitating the mutual recognition of diplomas, qualifications and competences within a single EU-level framework known as "**Europass**", taking the form of a structured, personalised portfolio incorporating a set of pre-existing documents with separate characteristics: "Europass-CV", "Europass-Mobility" (for periods of learning in other countries), "Europass-Diploma supplement" (for higher education), "Europass-Certificate supplement" (for vocational training), "Europass-Language portfolio" (for linguistic skills)[8].

Sporting activities are covered in a declaration to the final act of the Amsterdam Treaty, which contains two essential principles: that sport has a role in forging identity, which amounts to saying that national identities in this field should be respected; and

---

[1]   Decision 2004/223, OJ L 68, 06.03.2004.
[2]   Decision 791/2004, OJ L 138, 30.04.2004.
[3]   Decision 790/2004, OJ L 138, 30.04.2004.
[4]   Regulation 337/75, OJ L 39, 13.02.1975 and Regulation 2051/2004, OJ L 355, 01.12.2004.
[5]   Regulation 1360/90, OJ L 131, 23.05.1990 and Regulation 1648/2003, OJ L 245, 29.09.2003.
[6]   COM (2000) 318, 24 May 2000.
[7]   Resolution, OJ C 42, 17.02.1999, p. 1-2.
[8]   Decision 2241/2004, OJ L 390, 31.12.2004.

that sports associations should be listened to by the bodies of the European Union when important questions affecting sport are at issue, which gives them a consultative function in these matters [see section 6.4.1.]. A Council Resolution invited the Commission to devise, in cooperation with the Member States, a coherent approach with a view to exploiting the non-formal educational potential of sporting activities[1].

Amongst European actions in the university field one must include the Convention setting up the **European University Institute in Florence**[2]. The Institute specialises in research in four areas, viz.: history and civilisation, economics, law and political and social sciences. The task of the Institute is to contribute to the development of the cultural and scientific heritage of Europe, as a whole and in its constituent parts. The Institute runs interdisciplinary research programmes on the main issues European society has to address, especially those involving European integration. Its research work has to cover the great movements and institutions, which characterise the history and development of Europe. The Commission contributes financially towards the Institute's scientific and research activities, namely the research library and European library (Eurolib programme). In addition, the Commission covers the cost concerning the historical archives of the European Communities, which are managed by the Institute.

The Community has concluded agreements for cooperation in the fields of higher education and vocational training with the United States[3] and Canada[4]. These cooperation programmes seek to encourage, on the one hand, exchanges of knowledge, students and staff and, on the other, interaction between higher education establishments, training providers and undertakings in the EU, the USA and Canada.

A Council Resolution advocated that Community languages be taught at an early stage in order to **promote European multilingualism** while preserving cultural diversity[5]. A Council Recommendation urged the Member States to establish transparent systems of **quality assessment and quality assurance in higher education** based on a series of essential features, including evaluation of programmes or institutions through internal assessment, external review, and involving the participation of students, publication of results and international participation. [6]. Following this Recommendation, the European Association for Quality Assurance in Higher Education (ENQA) was established in 2000 and has a growing membership of quality assurance or accreditation agencies in all Member States. Another recommendation calls on the Member States to encourage all higher education institutions active within their territory to introduce or develop rigorous internal quality assurance systems and to give them freedom to choose one agency among any of the agencies registered in a "European Register of Quality Assurance Agencies" (European Register)[7].

13.4.2. Education and training programmes

The Maastricht Treaty [see section 2.2.] has consecrated Community action in the fields of education, vocational training and youth. Article 149 (TEC) specifies that the Community contributes to the development of **quality education** by encouraging cooperation between Member States and, if necessary, by supporting and supplementing their action in the fields of: developing the European dimension in education, particularly through the teaching and dissemination of languages; mobility of students and teachers; cooperation between educational establishments; exchanges of information and experience; exchanges of young people and socio-educational instructors; and the development of distance education. Incentive measures, excluding any harmonisation of the laws and regulations of the Member States, are adopted by the Council acting in accordance with the procedure referred to in Article 251 (co-decision with the European Parliament). Community action must, however, fully respect the responsibility of the Member States for the content of teaching, the organisation of education systems and vocational training and their cultural and linguistic diversity. An Internet portal brings together the measures taken by the European Union to promote language learning and linguistic diversity[8]. The

[1] Resolution 2000/C 8, JO C8, 12.01.2000.
[2] Convention, OJ C 29, 09.02.1976, p.1-10.
[3] Decision 95/487 and Agreement, OJ L 279, 22.11.1995, p. 11-17 and Decision 2001/196, OJ L 71, 13.03.2001.
[4] Decision 95/523 and Agreement, OJ L 300, 13.12.1995, p. 18-22 and Decision 2001/197, OJ L 71, 13.03.2001.
[5] OJ C 1, 03.01.1998.
[6] Recommendation 98/561, OJ L 270, 07.10.1998.
[7] Recommendation 2006/143, OJ L 64, 04.03.2006.
[8] http://europa.eu/languages/en/home.

Commission promotes a framework strategy for multilingualism[1]. It is evident that the EU not only **respects the cultural diversity** of its Member States but also encourages it [see section 10.3.].

According to Article 150 of the EC Treaty, the Community implements a **vocational training policy**, which supports and supplements the action of the Member States and which aims to: facilitate adaptation to industrial changes, in particular through vocational training and retraining; improve initial and continuing vocational training in order to facilitate vocational integration and reintegration into the labour market; facilitate access to vocational training and encourage mobility of instructors and trainees; stimulate cooperation between educational or training establishments and firms; and develop exchanges of information and experience on issues common to the training systems of the Member States. This Article is the foundation of the common training policy.

The Union's new generation of education and training programmes is designed to develop a European dimension of education from the primary school to the university and to establish a genuine European market in skills and training. Indeed, the three five-year programmes (1 January 2000 to 31 December 2004) in the fields of education (Socrates), vocational training (Leonardo da Vinci) and youth are interlinked by means of a **common framework encompassing six broad elements**: physical mobility for people; different forms of virtual mobility (use of new information and communications technologies); development of cooperation networks; promotion of linguistic and cultural skills; development of innovation through pilot projects based on transnational partnerships; and ongoing improvement of Community references (databases, exchanges of good practice) for the systems and policies relating to education, training and youth in the Member States. During the years 2000-2004, the three programmes *gave* the opportunity to 2.5 million young Europeans to participate in an exchange programme, a very important fact for multination integration [see section 9.4.].

The **SOCRATES programme in the field of education** pursues four primary objectives: to strengthen the European dimension in education at all levels; to promote improvement of knowledge of the languages of the Union; to promote mobility in the field of education and remove obstacles in this connection, in particular by improving the recognition of diplomas and periods of study; and to encourage innovation in the development of educational practices. It comprises measures and projects intended to promote transnational cooperation in the field of education, centred around three themes: cooperation in higher education through the promotion of student and teaching staff mobility, the establishment of university networks and the incorporation of the European dimension into all levels of study (Erasmus and Lingua strands); cooperation in secondary school education through the promotion of partnerships between schools in different Member States and networks of schools for the joint pursuit of educational projects, with special reference to languages, the new information technologies, cultural heritage and environmental protection (Comenius strand); and measures applicable to all levels of education, concerning the promotion of language skills, open and distance education, and exchange of information and experience[2]. The projects funded by Socrates include joint syllabus development, masters' programmes, European modules, an Internet-based European schools network, integrated language courses and the development of the European dimension in a given academic discipline [see details below].

The **LEONARDO da Vinci programme in the field of vocational training** (2000-2004), which is endowed with EUR 1 150 million, aims at boosting quality, inno-

---

[1]   COM/2005/596, 22 November 2005.
[2]   Decision 253/2000, OJ L 28, 03.02.2000 and Regulation 885/2004, OJ L 168, 01.05.2004.

vation and the European dimension in vocational systems and practices, through transnational cooperation[1]. The three objectives pursued by the action programme are social and occupational integration of young people, development of access to high-quality continuing training, and helping those in difficult circumstances to integrate better on the labour market. The Community measures implemented under the programme fall into five categories: mobility projects; pilot projects; linguistic competence; transnational networks; and reference material [see details below].

The action **programme in the youth field** (2000-2004) incorporates the pre-existing "**Youth for Europe**" programme, which seeks to help young people in their education outside the formal school system and the new "European voluntary service for young people"[2]. Both strands of the programme for youth focus on four aspects: individual mobility within the framework of European voluntary service; group mobility entailing transnational exchanges; initiatives giving young people an opportunity to play an active role in society; and activities tying in with other areas of Community action. The programme aims to help young people acquire the knowledge and skills to help them in their future development. It seeks also to foster a spirit of initiative, enterprise and creativity, promote respect for human rights and combat racism and xenophobia [see details below].

The **Trans-European Mobility programme for University Studies (TEMPUS III)** (2000-2006) is designed to promote, in line with the general guidelines and objectives of the Phare and Tacis programmes [see sections 25.2. and 25.4.], the development of higher education systems in the eligible countries (independent States of the former Soviet Union, non-associated countries of Central Europe, Mongolia and Mediterranean countries) through cooperation with partners in the EU Member States[3]. Joint European projects (JEPs), involving at least one Member State University, a partner in another Member State and a university in a beneficiary country, are the main instruments of the programme. In addition, Tempus III supports the provision of individual grants to teachers, trainers, university administrators, senior ministerial officials, education planners and other experts in the higher education field from the eligible countries or from the Community, with a view to promoting, through courses, seminars and visits, the development and restructuring of higher education systems in the eligible countries [see details below].

Over the five years 2000-2004, the three programmes - Socrates, Leonardo, Youth - should enable 2.5 million Europeans to benefit from a mobility programme: 1.2 million students and 200 000 teachers under the Socrates programme, 400 000 young people undergoing training under the Leonardo programme and 660 000 young people under the youth-oriented programme.

The **Socrates programme** encompasses six main actions:

Action 1, "COMENIUS" on school education, seeks to enhance the quality and reinforce the European dimension of school education, in particular by encouraging transnational cooperation between schools and contributing to improved professional development of staff directly involved in the school education sector, and to promote the learning of languages and intercultural awareness.

Action 2, "ERASMUS" on higher education, seeks to enhance the quality and reinforce the European dimension of higher education, to encourage transnational cooperation between universities, to boost European mobility in the higher education sector and to improve transparency and academic recognition of studies and qualifications throughout the Community. Participating universities conclude "institutional contracts" with the Commission covering all the Erasmus activities approved. Such contracts will normally be of three years' duration and will be renewable.

Action 3, "GRUNDTVIG" on adult education and other educational pathways, seeks to encourage the European dimension of life-long learning, to contribute - through enhanced transnational cooperation - to

---

[1] Decision 1999/382, OJ L 146, 11.06.1999 and Regulation 885/2004, OJ L 168, 01.05.2004.
[2] Decision 1031/2000, OJ L 117, 18.05.2000 and Regulation 885/2004, OJ L 168, 01.05.2004.
[3] Decision 1999/311, OJ L 120, 08.05.1999 and Decision 2002/601, OJ L 195, 24.07.2002.

innovation and improved availability, accessibility and quality of other educational pathways, and to promote the learning of languages.

Action 4, "LINGUA" on teaching and learning of languages aims to support transversal measures relating to the learning of languages, with a view to helping to promote and maintain linguistic diversity within the Community, to improve the quality of language teaching and learning and to facilitate access to life-long language learning opportunities tailored to individual requirements. Lingua both complements and enriches measures related to the promotion of language-learning under other actions of the Socrates programme, in particular Actions 1, 2 and 3.

Action 5: "MINERVA" on open and distance learning, information and communication technologies in the field of education, supports transversal measures relating to open and distance learning (ODL) and the use of information and communication technologies (ICT), including multimedia, in the field of education. In so doing, it complements and enriches the corresponding measures provided for within the other actions of the Socrates programme.

Action 6 on observation and innovation, contributes to improving the quality and transparency of education systems and furthering the process of educational innovation in Europe through the exchange of information and experience, the identification of good practice, the comparative analysis of systems and policies in this field, and the discussion and analysis of matters of common educational policy interest to be determined by the Council.

The Leonardo programme supports the following measures:

- **transnational mobility projects** for people undergoing vocational training, especially young people, and for trainers, notably: preparation and implementation of transnational placement projects for people undergoing initial vocational training, students, young workers and recent graduates; transnational projects of exchanges between undertakings, on the one hand, and vocational training organisations or universities, on the other; study visits for those responsible for vocational training;
- **transnational pilot projects** to develop and transfer innovation and quality in vocational training, including actions aiming at the use of information and communication technologies (ICT) in vocational training;
- **projects to develop language competencies** in a vocational training context, notably projects on less widely used and taught languages;
- **vocational training networks**, bringing together in the Member States, at the regional or sectoral level, the public and private players concerned;
- **actions undertaken on a transnational basis** on priority themes of common interest, notably those establishing comparable data on vocational training systems and arrangements, practices and various approaches to qualifications and competencies in the Member States;
- **joint actions with other Community actions** promoting a Europe of knowledge, particularly the Community programmes in the fields of education and youth;
- **accompanying measures** such as: management, coordination, monitoring and evaluation activities by the Member States.

The **youth programme comprises** five categories of action:

Action 1 "Youth for Europe", which has two facets: intra-Community exchanges for young people; and exchanges of young people (Community residents) with third countries;

Action 2 "European voluntary service" (EVS), which supports transnational projects with various Member States or with third countries that involve young people, actively and personally, in activities designed to help meet the needs of society in a wide range of fields (social, sociocultural, environmental, cultural, etc.), activities constituting at the same time an experience of informal education with a view to acquiring social and cultural skills[1];

Action 3, "Youth initiatives", involving projects in which young people actively and directly participate in innovative and creative schemes and in schemes which focus on the social commitment of young people at local, regional, national or European level;

Action 4, "Joint actions" undertaken with other Community schemes relating to the Europe of knowledge, in particular Community programmes in the field of education and vocational training;

Action 5, "Support measures", notably: training and cooperation in relation to those involved in youth policy; information for young people and youth studies.

Responding to a Commission White Paper suggesting a new framework for European cooperation in youth matters[2], the Council called on the Member States and the Commission to ensure that those policies and initiatives affecting young people at national and European level take account of issues such as the needs, situation, living conditions and expectations of young people[3]. The Council supported the Commission pro-

---

[1]   Decision 1686/98, OJ L 214, 31.07.1998.
[2]   COM (2001) 681.
[3]   Council resolution, OJ C 168, 13.07.2002.

posal aiming to include the youth dimension in other policies and programmes, at both national and European level.

In association with the **TEMPUS programme** the European Community provides support for **joint European projects (JEPs)** associating at least one university in an eligible country, one university from a Member State and a partner establishment (university, company or institution) in another Member State. Support for JEPs can be provided for activities according to the specific needs of the establishments concerned and in line with the priorities established, including:

- joint education and training actions, particularly with a view to curriculum development and updating,
- measures for the reform and development of higher education and its capacity, particularly by restructuring the management of higher education establishments and systems;
- the promotion of cooperation between universities, industry and institutions;
- the development of mobility for teachers, administrative staff of universities and students;
- activities to ensure the success of a JEP involving two or more eligible countries.

13.5. Common measures for the improvement of living and working conditions

The concern of the European Union for the living and working conditions of its citizens is not new, but its commitment in this respect has grown apace with economic integration. In article 117 of the EEC Treaty the States of the Community agreed on "the need to **promote improved working conditions and an improved standard of living for workers**, so as to make possible their harmonisation while the improvement is being maintained". They expected such a development to ensue, in the first place, from the functioning of the common market, which would favour the harmonisation of social systems and, to the extent necessary, from the approximation of provisions laid down by law, regulation or administrative action.

In Article 136 of the EC Treaty the Member States declare having as **their objectives** the promotion of employment, improved living and working conditions, proper social protection, dialogue between management and labour, the development of human resources with a view to lasting employment and the combating of social exclusion. Under Article 137 of the EC Treaty, the Community **supports and complements the activities of the Member States** tending to improve, in particular: the working environment so as to protect workers health and safety, the working conditions, the information and consultation of workers, the integration of persons excluded from the labour market and the equality of opportunities between men and women. The Council and the Parliament adopt, by means of Directives, minimal requirements for the gradual implementation of these objectives. These subjects are examined below.

The determination of wages is the sole responsibility of the Member States. Wages are, in fact, usually determined within the framework of collective bargaining or by reference to such bargaining by various practices in the Member States. The notion of a **guaranteed minimum wage** depends on different criteria in the Member States of the EU and its definition is left to them. However, the Social Charter of 1989 called on the Member States to ensure that workers secure an **equitable remuneration** (which is a different notion from the minimum wage), meaning a reward for work done which is fair and sufficient to enable them to have a decent standard of living[1].

The **European Foundation for the Improvement of Living and Working Conditions**, which is located in Dublin, has the task to develop and to pursue ideas on the medium and long-term improvement of living and working conditions in the light of practical experience and to identify factors leading to change[2].

---

[1] Commission opinion, COM/93/388.
[2] Regulation 1365/75, OJ L 139, 30.05.1975 and Regulation 1111/2005, OJ L 184, 15.07.2005.

13.5.1. The social dialogue in the EU

The legal process has difficulty in keeping pace with progress in European integration, technological change and the organisation of work. These changes require new mechanisms of social organisation parallel to legislation and State regulation. The social and cultural traditions of the Member States make it possible to build a European model of consensus, reconciling economic effectiveness and social solidarity. The **social partners** can play a crucial role in this process, both through cooperation between the state, employers and the trade unions on economic and social policies, and through the establishment of relations based on agreement between employers and the trade unions. The **Economic and Social Committee** [see section 4.2.3.], which is composed of employers' representatives, workers' representatives and other interest groups, is the oldest and most institutional provider of the opinions of the social partners to the decision-making bodies [see sections 4.2 and 4.4.].

The social dialogue which was under way from the beginning of the Community, was consecrated first by the Single European Act and then by the Treaty on European Union, which commits the Commission to develop the **dialogue between management and labour at European level** by submitting to them its guidelines for proposals in the social field (Art. 138 TEC). Social dialogue at European level covers the negotiations between European social partners themselves and between them and the organs of the European Union. This dialogue contributes to the improvement of mutual understanding between the social partners and to the stimulation and/or acceptance of economic and social policies implemented at European level.

At general European level the social partners are represented by the European Trade Union Confederation (ETUC), the Union of Industries of the European Community (UNICE) and the European Centre of Public Enterprises (CEEP). The **Tripartite Social Summit for Growth and Employment** is intended to ensure that there is continuous consultation between the Council, the Commission and the social partners on economic, social and employment matters[1]. The summit consists of representatives, at the highest level, of the Council Presidency, the two subsequent Presidencies, the Commission and the social partners.

At sectoral level, the social dialogue is promoted through the Sectoral Dialogue Committees, which are established in those sectors where the social partners make a joint request to take part in a dialogue at European level, and where the organisations representing both sides of industry fulfil certain criteria[2]. Since 1995, the Commission and the social partners have set up, in Florence, the European Centre for Industrial Relations (ECIR)[3].

The dialogue between social partners may lead to common opinions and/or, should the partners so desire, to **contractual relations, including agreements**. Such agreements may be implemented either in accordance with the procedures and practices specific to management and labour in each Member State or, in matters concerning working conditions, at the joint request of the signatory parties, by a Council decision on a proposal from the Commission (Art. 139 TEC). Thus, the social partners negotiated and signed, on 14 December 1995, a collective agreement, that entitles both male and female workers to unpaid **parental leave** of at least three months' duration and to time off work in the event of an unforeseen family emergency. At the request of the social partners, a 1996 Directive, which originally excluded the United Kingdom but in 1998 was extended to it, lays down minimum requirements concerning parental leave and absence by dint of "force majeure"[4].

---

[1]   Decision 2003/174, OJ L 70, 14.03.2003.
[2]   Decision 98/500, OJ L 225, 12.08.1998, p. 27-28.
[3]   COM (95) 445, 25 December 1995.
[4]   Directive 96/34, OJ L 145, 19.06.1996 and Directive 97/75, OJ L 10, 16.01.1998.

13.5.2. Worker information, consultation and participation

In addition to the social dialogue, the 1989 Social Charter, now incorporated in the EC Treaty (Art. 136 and 137), stipulates that information, consultation and participation for workers must be **developed along appropriate lines**, taking account of the practices in the various Member States. Such information, consultation and participation must be implemented in due time, particularly in the following cases:

- when technological changes which, from the point of view of working conditions and work organisation, have major implications for the work-force, are introduced into undertakings;
- in connection with restructuring operations in undertakings or in cases of mergers having an impact on the employment of workers;
- in cases of collective redundancy procedures; and
- when workers, especially transboundary ones, are affected by the employment policies of the company where they are employed.

A general framework for minimum requirements relating to the right of employees to be informed and consulted is applicable to undertakings and establishments operating **within a single Member State** and with at least 50 or 20 employees respectively[1]. The emphasis is on fostering social dialogue and ways of ensuring information for employees and effective consultation of their representatives at the earliest possible stage of the company decision-making process. Employers must inform employees about: the recent and foreseeable development of the company's activities and its economic and financial situation; the situation, structure and reasonably foreseeable developments of employment within the company; decisions which may lead to substantial changes in work organisation or in contractual relations (consultation between the employer and employees entails dialogue and exchange of views, including efforts to reach prior agreement on the decision in question).

The information and consultation of workers **in multinational companies** is pursued by Directive 94/45 - extended in 1998 to the United Kingdom - providing for the establishment of a **European Works Council** or a procedure for the purposes of informing and consulting employees in European-scale undertakings[2]. The companies or groups of companies concerned are those with more than 1000 employees in total in the Community and with at least two establishments in different Member States, each employing at least 150 people. The Directive also covers undertakings or groups of undertakings with headquarters outside the territory of the Member States, in so far as they meet the above criteria. The Directive provides for the establishment, at the initiative of the company or group management or at the written request of at least 100 employees or their representatives in at least two Member States, of a "special negotiating body" with the task of concluding an agreement between the management and the employees' representatives, on the scope, composition, powers and term of office of the European committee to be set up in the undertaking or group, or the practical arrangements for an alternative procedure for the information and consultation of employees.

In parallel with the regulation on the statute for a European company, with the Latin designation *Societas Europaea* **(SE)** [see section 17.2.1.], the Council adopted a directive supplementing this statute with regard to the involvement of employees[3]. The rules relating to **employee involvement in the SE** seek to ensure that the creation of an SE

---

[1] Directive 2002/14, OJ L 80, 23.03.2002.
[2] Directive 94/45, OJ L 254, 30.09.1994 and Directive 97/74, OJ L 10, 16.01.1998.
[3] Regulation 2157/2001 and directive 2001/86, OJ L 294, 10.11.2001 and Regulation 885/2004, OJ L 168, 01.05.2004.

does not entail the disappearance or reduction of practices of employee involvement existing within the companies participating in the establishment of an SE. Therefore, when the management or administrative organs of the participating companies draw up a plan for the establishment of an SE, they must as soon as possible after publishing the draft terms of merger or creating a holding company or after agreeing a plan to form a subsidiary or to transform into an SE, take the necessary steps (including providing information about the identity of the participating companies, concerned subsidiaries or establishments, and the number of their employees) to start negotiations with the representatives of the companies' employees on arrangements for the involvement of employees in the SE. For this purpose, a **special negotiating body** representative of the employees of the participating companies and concerned subsidiaries or establishments must be created in accordance with the provisions laid down in the directive. The special negotiating body and the competent organs of the participating companies must determine, by written agreement, arrangements for the involvement of employees within the SE. Member States must lay down standard rules on employee involvement which must satisfy the provisions of the directive.

The directives above concern the information of workers in European-size companies. The Directives discussed below concerning **large-scale redundancies** and the maintenance of workers' rights in the event of **company take-overs** stipulate that the workers must be informed and consulted in good time, so that they can make constructive proposals [see section 13.5.3.]. By the same token, the 1989 Directive on the improvement of the health and safety of workers in the workplace, also makes worker participation compulsory [see section 13.5.7.].

Another issue is **worker participation in the company's capital and profits**. Some see this as relinquishing management control, diminishing the shareholders' authority and "forfeiting dividend income". Others believe that allowing employees to share in the profits makes for greater flexibility in their earned income, has a stabilising effect in macro economic terms and is a motivating force resulting in greater productivity and consequently in an improved financial performance. Siding with the latter point of view, the Council has adopted a Recommendation concerning the promotion of employee participation in a company's capital and profits[1]. The Recommendation, which has not a binding character, encourages the Member States to: ensure that they have the appropriate legal structures for implementing various forms of financial participation effectively; consider the possibility of offering tax or other incentives for doing this; encourage the distribution of information about participation and about the experiences of other countries in the Community; and make sure that the social partners have a wide enough range of formulae to choose from based on consultations between employers and employees or their representatives. In any event, companies and employees alike must be able to decide freely whether or not to participate. From a Commission report on the implementation of the Council Recommendation by the Member States, it emerges that participation in profits goes hand in hand with better productivity, and that participation schemes have positive effects on wage flexibility, employment and worker involvement[2]. The Commission provided guidance for the development of employee financial participation in Europe by outlining the transnational obstacles hampering the introduction of Europe-wide financial participation schemes and by proposing concrete measures to overcome them[3].

13.5.3. Social protection

The **European Social Protection Committee (ESPC)**, composed of two representatives from each Member State and two representatives of the Commission, is an advisory body responsible for assisting the Council and the Commission[4]. Its main tasks are to monitor social protection policies in the Member States and the Community, to foster exchanges of information, experience and good practice between the Member States and with the Commission, and to prepare an annual report. In 1990, the Commission set up a system for mutual information on social protection (the MISSOC programme), which is run by a network of national correspondents and coordinated by the European Institute of Social Security.

---

[1]   Recommendation 92/443, OJ L 245, 26.08.1992.
[2]   COM (96) 697, 8 January 1997.
[3]   COM (2002) 364, 5 July 2002.
[4]   Decision 2004/689, OJ L 314, 13.10.2004.

As part of the implementation of the Charter of workers' fundamental social rights, the Council adopted, in 1992, two important Recommendations. The first is aimed at helping the most disadvantaged by inviting the Member States to recognise **a general right to guaranteed resources** and benefits for anyone living in a Member State who has insufficient means[1]. The second is aimed at promoting **a harmonisation of social protection objectives and policies**, so that the free movement of people is not impeded by the different levels of social protection in the Member States and social protection is not adversely affected by competition between the various national systems[2]. This last Recommendation is particularly important because the Member States acknowledge in it that comparable trends lead to common problems and challenges (unemployment, ageing, changing family structures) and that a single market can be created while maintaining the diversity of social protection systems in the Member States, mainly as regards the arrangements for financing and organising them, but that the long-term objective of the Union is the convergence of social protection systems. In view of this objective and the changes made necessary by the deteriorating relationship between the size of the labour force and the number of pensioners, the Commission launched a debate on the future of social protection, particularly concerning its financing and the way to make it more employment-friendly[3].

Article 136 (TEC) names proper social protection and improved living and working conditions among the objectives of the Community and the Member States. **Social protection in the strict sense** usually means social security, while **social protection in a broad sense** includes social security among other social rights of the citizens. In fact, under the heading "solidarity", the Charter of Fundamental Rights of the European Union[4] [see section 9.2.] mentions several rights, such as: the workers' right to information and consultation within the undertaking; the protection in the event of unjustified dismissal; fair and just working conditions; protection of young people at work; and, of course, social security and social assistance.

Concerning this last subject, namely social protection in the strict sense, the Charter of Fundamental Rights declares that the Union recognises and respects the entitlement to social security benefits and social services providing protection in cases such as maternity, illness, industrial accidents, dependency or old age, and in the case of loss of employment, in accordance with the rules laid down by Community law and national laws and practices. The Charter acknowledges that everyone residing and moving legally within the European Union is entitled to social security benefits and social advantages in accordance with Community law and national laws and practices. According to the subsidiarity principle, however, the Member States must apply Community law if and where it exists. Concerning social security, Community provisions concern only the implementation of the principle of equal treatment for certain categories of workers, i.e. immigrants [see section 6.4.2.] and women [see section 13.5.5.]. For the rest, social security is covered by the national law of each Member State. Actually, social protection expenditure represented 27.5% of gross domestic product (GDP) in the EU in 2001, with marked disparities from one Member State to another, ranging from 31.3% in Sweden to 14.6% in Ireland.

In fact, the Member States have preferred coordination rather than harmonisation of social protection and particularly social security legislation. On these subjects the Council decides alone (without the Parliament) and by unanimity, which means that any Member State may veto the adoption of Community legislation (Art 137 TEC). It is true that as systems of social protection reflect the traditions and existing social benefits of each individual State, it is not easy to change them. However, in an internal market and even more in an economic and monetary union, differences between the various social security systems can constitute distortions of competition, hinder the free movement of labour and exacerbate regional imbalances. Therefore, a regulation aims to coordinate

---

[1]   Recommendation 92/441, OJ L 245, 26.08.1992, p. 46–48.
[2]   Recommendation 92/442, OJ L 245, 26.08.1992, p. 49–52.
[3]   COM (95) 466, 31 October 1995.
[4]   Solemn declaration, OJ C 364, 18.12.2000.

national social security systems so as to eliminate obstacles to freedom of movement, thereby allowing EU citizens to move freely within the Community, whether for purposes of study, leisure or work, without losing any social security rights or protection to which they are entitled[1].

The Community has already made headway when the term "social protection" is taken in its broadest sense to cover social security and the right to work. An important Community measure for the social protection of employees, particularly those of multinational companies, is the Directive on the approximation of the laws of the Member States relating to **collective redundancies**[2]. Employers who envisage such redundancies have to hold consultations with workers' representatives on the possibilities of avoiding or reducing such redundancies. Moreover, the employer has to notify any proposed collective redundancy to the competent official authority and may not implement it before the expiry of a period of 30 days which the authority uses to try to find solutions to the problems that have arisen and/or to lessen the impact of the redundancies. This Directive is particularly important for workers employed by multinational companies which operate in one or more EU countries, as, by laying down provisions common to all Member States, it prevents multinational companies from taking advantage of differences between national laws.

In the same vein, a Directive on the approximation of the laws of the Member States aims at safeguarding employees' rights in the event of **transfers of undertakings**, businesses or parts of businesses[3]. Before any such amalgamation, the workers' representatives have to be informed of the reasons for it and of its consequences for the employees and of the measures envisaged in their favour. In principle, the workers' rights and obligations are transferred to the new employer for at least a year and agreement on the conditions of the take-over has to be reached in consultation with the work force. Failing agreement between the employer or employers and the workers, an arbitration body gives a final ruling on the steps to be taken in favour of the workers. A representation scheme not dependent on the employer's will is necessary for compliance with the Directive[4].

But the workers' interests also need to be protected **in the event of the insolvency** of their employer, especially where assets are not sufficient to cover outstanding claims resulting from contracts of employment or employment relationships, even where the latter are privileged. To prevent such situations, a Council Directive obliges Member States to set up guarantee institutions independent of the employers' operating capital so that their assets are inaccessible to proceedings for insolvency[5]. In such an eventuality, those institutions must settle the claims of employees arising prior to the insolvency of the employer, including contributions under social security schemes.

A Directive on the **protection of young people at work** prohibits work by children (less than 15 years of age or still subject to compulsory full-time schooling), with the exception of certain cultural, artistic or sporting activities. Children of at least 14 years of age may take up combined work/ training schemes, in-plant work-experience schemes and certain light work[6]. The Directive asks Member States to strictly regulate work done by adolescents of more than 18 years of age, by imposing specific rules in respect of

---

[1]   Regulation 883/2004, OJ L 166, 30.04.2004.
[2]   Directive 98/59, OJ L 225, 12.08.1998.
[3]   Directive 2001/23, OJ L 82, 28.03.2001.
[4]   Judgments given on 8 June 1994, Cases C-382/92 and C-383/92, Commission v United Kingdom, ECR 1994, p. I-2435.
[5]   Directive 80/987, OJ L 283, 20.10.1980 and Directive 2002/74, OJ L 270, 08.10.2002.
[6]   Directive 94/33, OJ L 216, 20.08.1994.

working time, daily rest periods, weekly rest periods and night work, and laying down technical, health and safety standards.

A clear link exists nowadays between social protection systems and the European employment strategy [see section 13.3.2.][1]. Noting with satisfaction the views expressed by the Commission in its communication on a concerted **strategy for modernising social protection**[2], the Council, on 29 November 1999, underlined the need for cooperation between the Member States and at European level, entailing a structured and ongoing dialogue, follow-up and exchange of information, experience and good practice. The Commission proposes to make use of the "open method of coordination" for modernising social protection, calling on the Member States to draw up preliminary reports taking stock of their respective systems, for analysis by the Commission, with a view to identifying common reform objectives. The Commission refers to three principles which could serve as a basis for reform: accessibility of care, taking into account the needs and difficulties of all groups and individuals; high-quality care keeping up with medical advances and the emerging needs associated with an ageing population; the long-term financial sustainability of this care, aiming to make the system as efficient as possible[3].

With the progressive ageing of Europe's population, the problems of retirement and post-retirement become increasingly acute and require cooperation between Member States. In a Resolution on **flexible retirement arrangements** the Council wants older people to continue to play an active part in society and maintain a link with the labour market[4]. It emphasises that a flexible retirement policy could constitute a rational response to changing demographic patterns and to labour-market changes, but that flexible retirement arrangements are a matter for each Member State, bearing in mind the principle of subsidiarity [see section 3.2.]. However, it calls on the Commission to promote exchanges of information and to examine whether measures taken by the Member States need to be completed.

In a communication entitled "The future evolution of social protection from a long-term point of view: safe and sustainable pensions", the Commission proposed formalising and strengthening cooperation between the Member States by using the "**open method of coordination**"[5]. This involves setting common objectives, translating these objectives into national policy strategies and, finally, as part of a mutual learning process, periodic monitoring on the basis, *inter alia*, of commonly agreed and defined indicators. The overall strategy proposed by the Commission covers the three pillars of the pension systems, i.e. statutory social security schemes, occupational schemes and personal pension schemes. On the basis of the national strategy reports submitted in September 2002, the Commission noted that all the Member States had, to varying degrees, launched reforms aimed at safeguarding the adequacy of pensions in the future without undermining public finances or overburdening future generations. However, it concluded that most of the Member States would have to make further reforms to guarantee adequate and sustainable pensions in an ageing society. Extending working life was one possible solution proposed, with older workers being encouraged to stay longer in the labour market and given incentives through pension schemes[6].

13.5.4. The organisation of work

Social protection in the EU covers also **atypical work**, i.e. other forms of work than that for an indefinite period, such as work for a specific duration, interim work, temporary work and seasonal work. These different forms of work enable companies to organise their work and their production in such a way as to improve productivity and thus become more competitive. Similarly, they enable workers to adapt the hours they work to suit their personal and family circumstances. But in a single market, certain essential conditions must be determined both to avoid distortions of competition and to protect the workers who opt for or accept (for want of something better) these new forms of work. These two objectives are contained in the Directives on atypical work. Thus a Directive guarantees satisfactory health and safety conditions of workers with a fixed-duration employment relationship (whose duration is fixed by objective criteria) or a temporary employment relationship (between the employer - a temporary employment agency - and

---

[1] COM (1998) 243, 23 April 1998.
[2] COM (1999) 347, 14 July 1999.
[3] COM (2004) 304, 20 April 2004.
[4] OJ C 188, 10.07.1993, p. 1-2.
[5] COM (2001) 362, 3 July 2001.
[6] COM (2002) 737, 17 December 2002.

the employee)[1]. Another Directive, based on a framework agreement on fixed-term work concluded between the social partners, ensures compliance with the principle of non-discrimination *vis-à-vis* employment of indefinite duration[2].

Contract duration is but one of the areas where there have been changes in the organisation of work in Europe. Alongside traditional work practices of indefinite time, recent years have seen the growth of **new forms of work**: homeworking (out-workers), part-time work, job sharing, job splitting, being "on call", distance working, etc. These new work forms have arisen as a result of new technologies, to accommodate companies' needs for flexibility and to meet the personal and family demands of many workers. However, they can obscure the situation of these workers if there is no written proof of the essential points of the employment relationship. Therefore, a Directive provides for the drawing up of a written declaration **regarding an employment relationship**[3]. It stipulates that an employer shall notify an employee of the essential aspects of the contract or employment relationship by written declaration not later than two months after the commencement of employment. Essential aspects are considered to be: the place of work, the nature of the work and the category of employment, the duration of the employment relationship, the number of hours worked and paid holidays, pay and social rights. The Commission meanwhile recommended that the Member States ratify the International Labour Organisation's Convention on home work[4].

A Directive concerning certain aspects of the **organisation of working time** lays down a basic set of minimum provisions covering more particularly: the maximum weekly working time (48 hours), the minimum daily rest period (11 uninterrupted hours), the minimum period of paid leave (4 weeks), conditions relating to night work and the maximum period of such work (8 hours), and breaks in the event of prolonged periods of work[5]. Although, in theory, most workers in the European Union enjoy better organisation of working time than is embodied in the European Directive, this is intended to exercise a pressure on the Governments of the Member States to better enforce the relative legislations. Another Directive aims to prevent part-time workers from being treated less favourably than full-time workers, concerning particularly employment conditions and continuing training[6].

A special directive aims at the enforcement of seafarers' hours of work on board ships using Community ports[7]. Special directives concern also the organisation of working time and hence the improvement of health and safety protection regarding: **mobile workers** (flying personnel) in civil aviation[8]; those performing road transport activities and self-employed drivers[9].

13.5.5. Equal treatment for men and women

Article 141 of the EC Treaty (ex-Art. 119 EEC) stipulates that each Member State shall ensure the application of the principle that men and women should receive **equal pay for equal work.** This principle means: (a) that pay for the same work at piece rates shall be calculated on the basis of the same unit of measurement; and (b) that pay for work at time rates shall be the same for the same job. The original Community's concern

[1]   Directive 91/383, OJ L 206, 29.07.1991.
[2]   Directive 1999/70, OJ L 175, 10.07.1999.
[3]   Directive, 91/533, OJ L 288, 18.10.1991.
[4]   Recommendation 98/370, OJ L 165, 10.06.1998, p. 32.
[5]   Directive 2003/88, OJ L 299, 18.11.2003.
[6]   Directive 97/81, OJ L 14, 20.01.1998 and Directive 98/23, OJ L 131, 05.05.1998.
[7]   Directive 1999/95, OJ L 14, 20.01.2000.
[8]   Directive 2000/79, OJ L 302, 01.12.2000.
[9]   Directive 2002/15, OJ L 80, 23.03.2002 and Directive 2006/22, OJ L 102, 11.04.2006.

for equality of the sexes - compared to its non-commitment in other important issues - stemmed from the fact that competition between Community countries could be distorted by the employment in some of them of women who were paid less than men for the same job. Moreover, unequal conditions of employment and remuneration between the sexes could be eliminated only through Community action, as no country could go it alone with a reform, which would be likely to alter conditions of competition to its detriment, in particular in industries employing large numbers of women. In any case, the EC Treaty places the achievement of equal treatment between men and women among the tasks of the Community (Art. 2 TEC).

The original Member States did not hasten to take the legislative and administrative measures necessary in order to implement the principle of non-discrimination based on the sex, as they were invited to do by Article 119 (EEC). However, the Court of Justice in three famous judgments bearing the name of Gabrielle Defrenne, air hostess of Sabena, established that, although Article 119 had a horizontal direct effect and could be evoked in national courts, it needed **interpretation by the Community legislative authority**, particularly concerning indirect or disguised discriminations and equal working conditions other than payment[1].

The opinion of the Court was followed by the Commission in its proposals and finally by the Council, which adopted a Directive on the approximation of the laws of the Member States relating to the **application of the principle of equal pay** for men and women[2]. The purpose of that Directive was to eliminate any discrimination on grounds of sex as regards all aspects and conditions of pay. It called on the Member States to "cleanse" their legal provisions of all discriminatory aspects and to repeal all collective or contractual provisions that were at variance with the principle of equal pay. Thus, for instance, the Court of Justice has established that the employers' contributions in favour of a pension scheme should be considered as part of gross payment and that, in this context, the burden of proof of non-discrimination based on sex should be borne by the employer[3]. A Commission code of practice on the implementation of equal pay for work of equal value for women and men, drawn up in close collaboration with the social partners, aims to provide concrete advice for employers and collective bargaining partners at business level to ensure that the principle of equality is applied to all aspects of pay[4].

Equal pay was only one battle won in the war against discrimination against women, which was based on historical and cultural causes and was reinforced in practice by the education system, inadequate vocational guidance and the demanding role imposed on women as wives and mothers. Therefore, a Directive on the **implementation of the principle of equal treatment** of men and women in matters of employment and occupation prohibits any indirect discrimination, i.e. the ways in which women are disadvantaged in relation to men in spite of apparently equal treatment, viz.: individual or collective contracts concerning employment and working conditions[5]. For example, according to the ECJ, a discriminatory recruitment system is contrary to Directive 76/207[6], as is a general exclusion of women from military posts involving the use of arms[7]. A specific Directive provides for the equal treatment between men and women engaged in

---

[1] Judgments of: 25 May 1971, Case 80/70, ECR 1971, p. 445; 8 April 1976, Case 43/75, ECR 1976, p. 455; and 15 June 1978, Case 149/77, ECR 1978, p. 1365.
[2] Directive 2006/54, OJ L 204, 26.07.2006.
[3] Judgment of 11 March 1981, Case 69/80, Worringham, ECR 1981 and judgment of 17 October 1989, Case 109/88, ECR 1989.
[4] COM (96) 336, 17 July 1996.
[5] Directive 2006/54, OJ L 204, 26.07.2006.
[6] Judgment of 30 June 1988, Case 318/86, ECR 1988, p. 3559.
[7] Judgment of 11 January 2000, Case C-285/98 Kreil v Germany, OJ C 63, 04.03.2000.

an activity, including agriculture, in a self-employed capacity, and on the protection of self-employed women during pregnancy and motherhood[1]. It should be noted that the Directives on the equal treatment of men and women complete Directive 2000/78 laying down a general framework for combating discrimination on the grounds of religion or belief, disability, age or sexual orientation as regards employment and occupation [see section 6.4.1].

The principle of equal opportunity means, among other things, that there should be no discrimination based on sex especially as regards: the scope and the conditions governing the right to any work regime; the calculation of contributions; the calculation of benefits and the conditions governing the duration and preservation of pension rights. Two Directives concern, indeed, the implementation of the principle of equal treatment for men and women in matters of social security[2] and in occupational social security schemes[3]. According to the ECJ, the provisions concerning social security do not apply to women who have never been employed, those who do not look for a job and those who have voluntarily stopped working[4].

On the contrary, again according to the Court, the principle of non-discrimination applies indifferently to both men and women. Indeed, in its "Barber" judgment the Court of Justice held that any sex discrimination in the granting or calculation of an occupational pension, notably the differentiation of the age of pension according to the sex, is prohibited by Article 119 (EEC)[5]. As the Barber judgment had important financial implications for the professional schemes of social security, the Council amended the 1986 Directive in order to bring it into line with Article 119 of the EEC Treaty as interpreted by the Court in this judgment[6]. According to the Court, however, different treatment of **stable relationships between two persons of the same sex** and marriages or stable relationships outside marriage between persons of opposite sex in matters of social security, does not constitute discrimination directly based on sex[7].

Measures must be taken in all Member States to improve the **health and safety protection of women workers** who are pregnant, have just given birth or are breast-feeding[8] [see also section 13.5.7.]. These measures on the one hand prohibit the dismissing of the women workers in question and their exposure to specific agents or working conditions which could endanger their health and safety, and on the other ensure the preservation of the rights derived from the employment contract and of maternity leave of at least fourteen consecutive weeks. In addition, according to the ECJ, the non-recruitment of pregnant women or the laying off of women who have a bad health condition after having given birth are discriminatory and cannot be tolerated[9]. The dismissal would be illegal even if the worker was recruited for a fixed period and because of her pregnancy was unable to work during a substantial part of the term of the contract[10]. A Declaration to the Final Act of the Amsterdam European Council of June 1997 urges the Member States, when adopting measures referred to in Article 141 (TEC) to aim at improving the situation of women in working life.

---

[1]   Directive 86/613, OJ L 359, 19.12.1986.
[2]   Directive 79/7, OJ L 6, 10.01.1979.
[3]   Directive 86/378, OJ L 225, OJ L 225, 12.08.1986 repealed by Directive 2006/54, OJ L 204, 26.07.2006.
[4]   Judgment of 27 June 1989, Joined cases 48/88, 106/88 and 107/88, ECR 1989, p. 1963.
[5]   Judgment given on 17 May 1990, Case C-262/88, Barber v Guardian Royal Exchange, ECR 1990, p.1889.
[6]   Directive 96/97, OJ L 46, 17.02.1997.
[7]   Judgment of 17 February 1998, Case C-249/96, ECR 1998 I-621.
[8]   Directive 92/85, OJ L 348, 28.11.1992.
[9]   Judgments of 8 November 1990, Cases C-177/88 and C-179/88, ECR 1990, I-3941 and I-3979.
[10] Judgment of 4 October 2001, Case C-109/2000, ECR 2001, p. I-06993.

Under the Community legislation and the case law of the Court of Justice, any woman who feels that she is the subject of discrimination on grounds of sex or her matrimonial or family situation **may bring proceedings before the national courts** and enjoy, in so doing, legal protection against any attempt at reprisals on the part of her employer. She can directly, or through the Commission, bring the matter before the Court of Justice of the European Communities. According to the case-law of the Court of Justice, national courts must be consistent in ensuring the full effect of Community rules, where necessary disregarding any national provisions to the contrary[1]. Following the "Bilka" judgment, the national court must determine if a discriminatory practice is objectively justifiable on reasons other than the sex and if it is proportionate[2]. Consolidating the relevant case law of the Court of Justice, notably the Worringham case mentioned above, the Community law places the burden of proof in cases of discrimination based on sex on the defendant (employer) rather than on the plaintiff (employee)[3].

However, in the "Kalanke" case the Court held that national rules giving absolute and unconditional priority to women holding the same qualifications as their male counterparts would also entail sex-based discrimination[4]. In this case, the Court has not condemned the implementation of positive action measures in general, but only a rigid quota system under which there is no possibility of taking particular individual circumstances into account. Thus, in another case the Court has held that a candidate belonging to the underrepresented sex may be granted preference over a competitor of the opposite sex, provided that the candidates possess equivalent or substantially equivalent merits[5].

But equal treatment for men and women would lead to a high level of female unemployment as long as the **occupational qualifications** of the sexes were not the same. For that reason, the equal opportunities dimension is increasingly taken into consideration in other common policies, notably on employment and on vocational training [see sections 13.3.2. and 13.4.2.]. The common employment strategy provides a good example of the positive consequences of incorporating the gender dimension into a broadly coordinated economic process.

The gender balance of sexes in economic activities is affected by **structural economic change**, in particular the growing role of services, the new technologies and the new flexibilities of work contracts that public and private enterprises are seeking. This is especially relevant to homeworking and teleworking, which offer significant opportunities for women, but under certain conditions. Positive and sustained action is needed to maximise the opportunities and reduce the dangers. A Resolution of the Council and of the representatives of the Member States on equal participation by women in an employment-intensive economic growth strategy aims at improving the flexibility of working hours, promoting a high level of skills among women and encouraging self-employment and the creation of businesses by women[6]. A Council Recommendation aims to promote the balanced participation of women and men at all levels of the decision-making process in the political, economic, social and cultural life[7]. A Community programme coordinates, supports and finances the implementation of horizontal activities in the fields covered by the Community framework strategy on gender equality, whilst also complementing the Community action programme on combating discrimination in general [see section 6.4.1.][8]. Another Community action programme assists organisations working to promote equality between men and women, notably the European women's lobby[9].

Responding to a Council Resolution, the Commission adopted, on November 27, 1991, a Recommendation combined with a Code of Good Practice on the protection of the dignity of women and men at work in which it invites the Member States to take steps with a view to improving the prevention of and fight against all forms of **sexual harassment**[10]. A Resolution of the Council and the representatives of the governments of the Member States calls on the latter to take action aimed at promoting and disseminating a diversified and realistic image of men and women in advertising and the media[11].

13.5.6. Action to combat social exclusion

Social exclusion represents one of the major challenges facing the European Union. The challenge cannot be addressed merely by offering better assistance to those who are excluded or at risk of exclusion from work, but also requires active measures to tackle

---

[1]   Judgment given on 25 July 1991, Case C-345/89, Stoeckel, ECR 1991, I-4047.
[2]   Judgment of 13 May 1986, Case 170/84, Bilka-Kaufhaus, ECR 1986, p. 1607.
[3]   Directive 2006/54, OJ L 204, 26.07.2006.
[4]   Judgment of 17 October 1995, case C-450/93, Kalanke, ECR 1995, p. I-3051.
[5]   Case C-407/98, Abrahamsson and Anderson, ECR 2000, p. I-5539.
[6]   OJ C 368, 23.12.1994, p. 3-6.
[7]   Recommendation 96/694, OJ L 319, 10.12.1996.
[8]   Decision 2001/51, OJ L 17, 19.01.2001 and Decision 1554/2005, OJ L255, 30.09.2005.
[9]   Decision 2004/848, OJ L 157, 30.04.2004 and Decision 1554/2005, OJ L255, 30.09.2005.
[10]   Resolution, OJ C 157, 27.06.1990, p. 3-4 and Recommendation 92/131, OJ L 49, 24.02.1992.
[11]   OJ C 296, 10.11.1995, p. 15-16.

the obstacles to social inclusion. Article 137 (TEC) gives the Community a specific role in **supporting and complementing the activities of the Member States** as regards the integration of persons excluded from the labour market. In compliance with the principle of subsidiarity however, initiatives to combat poverty and social exclusion are primarily the preserve of the Member States' local, regional and national authorities. The European Union can only complete and stimulate the work of the Member States in these fields by promoting the exchange of information, the comparison of experiences, the transfer of know-how and the demonstration of the validity of the projects based on partnerships. Thus, the Community action against social exclusion is mainly centred on vocational training [see section 13.4.2.].

A Community action programme, covering the period from 1 January 2002 to 31 December 2006, encourages cooperation between Member States to combat poverty and social exclusion[1]. The objectives of the **social exclusion action programme** are, in particular, to improve understanding of social exclusion and poverty, to organise discussions on policies pursued and mutual lessons, and to develop the capacity of actors to address social exclusion and poverty effectively, by promoting innovative approaches and supporting networks of all those involved at EU, national and regional levels.

The **European Year for all (2007)**[2] aimed at: (a) raising awareness of the right to equality and non-discrimination; (b) stimulating debate on ways to increase the participation in society of groups that are victims of discrimination and a balanced participation of men and women; (c) facilitating and celebrating diversity and equality, irrespective of sex, racial or ethnic origin, religion or belief, disability, age or sexual orientation; and (d) promoting good relations between all in society.

Various initiatives of the Community help combat poverty and social exclusion. Food surpluses from the common agricultural policy are distributed in the framework of winter aid campaigns for the most needy organised by non-governmental organisations (NGOs). The Commission supports the work of the European Anti-Poverty Network and has established a permanent dialogue with this group.

The **European Year of People with Disabilities 2003** aimed at raising public awareness on the rights of people with disabilities and the positive contribution they can make to society, as well as consideration of the problems they face as a result of their disability and the many forms of discrimination to which they are exposed[3]. In fact, the Council adopted resolutions inviting the Member States to promote employment and social integration, the accessibility of cultural infrastructure and cultural activities for people with disabilities as well as their integration into society through education and training systems adapted to their needs[4]. It has called on the Member States and the Commission to: promote greater cooperation and exchanges of experience at national and European level, especially with bodies and organisations operating in the disability arena; devise new ways of promoting the employment and social integration of people with disabilities; and incorporate the disability dimension into all relevant policies[5].

Concerning the improvement of **access for people with disabilities**, particular emphasis is placed on interlinking of related issues in the fields of employment, education and vocational training, transport, the internal market, the information society, the new technologies and consumer policy[6]. Lack of mobility is a factor restricting the participatory rights of people with disabilities, to the detriment of all. Advances must be made consistently on all fronts, in order to get the best results out of enhanced access for people with disabilities[7].

In a resolution on an **information society for all**, the Council affirmed that the information society should not be the source of new exclusions[8]. It called upon the Member States to tap the potential of "e-inclusion" for disadvantaged people (the unemployed and inactive people, and people at risk of exclusion such

---

[1]   Decision 50/2002, OJ L 10, 12.01.2002 and Decision 786/2004, OJ L 138, 30.04.2004.
[2]   Decision 771/2006, OJ L 146, 31.05.2006.
[3]   Decision 2001/903, OJ L 335, 19.12.2001.
[4]   Council resolution, OJ C 134, 07.06.2003.
[5]   Council resolution, OJ C 175, 24.07.2003.
[6]   Resolution, OJ C 186, 02.07.1999.
[7]   COM(2000) 284, 12 May 2000.
[8]   Council resolution, OJ C 292, 18.10.2001.

as older workers and disabled persons), to remove the barriers which exist in the information society, and to encourage partnerships of all stakeholders, with an emphasis on regional and local dimensions.

In a resolution on **transforming undeclared work into regular employment**, the Council set out guidelines advocating preventive actions and sanctions aimed at eliminating undeclared work, encompassing simplified administrative procedures, reduced costs and constraints affecting the creation and development of small businesses, removal of disincentives to declare work, and increased surveillance, with the active support of the social partners[1].

13.5.7. Safety and health at work

The **European Agency for Health and Safety at Work**, based in Bilbao has as main tasks: the collection and dissemination of technical, scientific and economic information on health and safety at work; the promotion of and support for exchanges of information and experience between Member States; the provision of information necessary for the Commission in the preparation and evaluation of legislation; and the operation of a network linking Member States' national networks[2]. The Commission is assisted by an Advisory Committee on Safety and Health at Work[3].

The Community has for a long time been involved in the area of workers' safety. The ECSC and Euratom Treaties assigned more tasks to these Communities in this field than the EEC Treaty to the European Economic Community [see section 2.1.]. Article 46 of the **ECSC Treaty** called upon the High Authority (Commission) to "obtain the information it requires to assess the possibilities for improving working conditions and living standards for workers in the industries within its province and the threats to those standards". Article 55 called upon it to "promote technical and economic research relating" inter alia "to occupational safety" in those industries. ECSC "social research" has developed from multiannual programmes decided upon by the Commission in the fields of hygiene and safety in mines, the effort to combat pollution at the workplace and ergonomics[4]. A safety and Health Commission for the Mining and Other Extractive Industries prepares opinions and makes proposals to the Governments in those fields[5].

By virtue of the powers conferred on it by the **Euratom Treaty**, the Community has been able to implement an efficient policy for the protection of workers and the general public against the **risks linked with radioactivity**. The Council Directive of 1 June 1976 laying down the revised basic standards for the health protection of the general public and workers against the dangers of ionising radiation strengthened and improved the practical organisation of radiation protection in the Community[6] [see section 19.2.3.]. That was highly appropriate at a time when public opinion was beginning to worry about the consequences of radioactivity for the environment and human health. In the health field, the Directive lays down basic measures for the radiation protection of persons undergoing medical examination or treatment.

Despite the limited competences that assigned the EEC Treaty to the European Community, Directives were adopted concerning the protection of workers, notably from the major accident hazards of certain industrial activities[7] [see section 16.3.5.] and exposure to asbestos[8]. After the 1987 Single Act [see section 2.1.] had increased the Community's authority as regards the health and safety of the work force, the Commission set up a mutual information system for legislative and administrative acts of the Member States concerning health and security of workers at the place of work[9]. At the instigation of the Commission, the Council adopted, in 1989, a **Framework Directive** on the introduction of measures to encourage improvements in the safety and health of workers at the workplace[10]. This Directive lays down three main principles: the employer's general obligation to guarantee the workers' health and safety in all work-related aspects, in particular by preventing professional risks, by keeping the work force informed and by training; the obligation of every worker to contribute to his own health and safety and that of oth-

---

[1]   Council Resolution, OJ C 260, 29.10.2003.
[2]   Regulation 2062/94, OJ L 216, 20.08.1994 and Regulation 1112/2005, OJ L 184, 15.07.2005.
[3]   Council decision, OJ C 218, 13.09.2003.
[4]   Resolution OJ C 257, 14.10.1986.
[5]   OJ 28, 31.08.1957.
[6]   Directive 96/29/Euratom, OJ L 159, 29.06.1996.
[7]   Directive 96/82, OJ L 10, 14.1.1997 and Directive 2003/105, OJ L 345, 31.12.2003.
[8]   Directive 83/477, OJ L 263, 24.09.1983 and Directive 2003/18, OJ L 97, 15.04.2003.
[9]   Decision 88/383, OJ L 183, 14.07.1988.
[10] Directive 89/391, OJ L 183, 29.06.1989.

ers by using the work facilities correctly and respecting the safety instructions; the absence or limited liability for employers for things caused by abnormal unforeseen circumstances or exceptional events. By laying down the main principles concerning health and safety at work in the Community, the framework Directive is the foundation on which all other directives aiming at the improvement of the working environment to protect workers' health and safety (Art. 137 TEC) are superimposed.

This is particularly the case as regards the specific Directives laying down **minimum requirements on**:

- workplaces[1];
- work equipment and machinery[2];
- personal protective equipment[3];
- the manual handling of loads involving some kind of risk - notably of dorsal/lumbar damage for workers[4];
- work using display screens[5];
- exposure at work to carcinogenic agents[6];
- exposure at work to biological agents[7]
- minimum health and safety requirements on temporary and mobile sites[8];
- safety and/or health signs in the workplace[9];
- the protection of workers in the mineral-extracting industries by drilling[10];
- the protection of workers in surface and underground mineral-extracting industries[11];
- the protection of workers from the risks related to hazardous chemical agents at the workplace[12];
- the protection of workers potentially at risk from explosive atmospheres (e.g. flammable and/or combustible gases, vapours, mists or dusts)[13];
- exposure of workers to the risks arising from physical agents (mechanical vibrations)[14];
- exposure to the risks arising from physical agents (noise)[15]; and
- exposure to the risks arising from physical agents (artificial optical radiation)[16].

These Directives guarantee the right to safety at work for the workers in all Member States, including those which previously had not high safety standards. Workers having an interim or specific duration work relation must enjoy the same health and safety conditions as the other workers of an undertaking[17]. As seen above, a directive aims at improving the health and safety of pregnant workers and workers who have recently given birth or are breastfeeding[18] [see section 13.5.5.]. The Council recommends that the

---

[1]   Directive 89/654, OJ L 393, 30.12.1989.
[2]   Directive 89/655, OJ L 393, 30.12.1989 and Directive 2001/45, OJ L 195, 19.07.2001.
[3]   Directive 89/656, OJ L 393, 30.12.1989.
[4]   Directive 90/269, OJ L 156, 21.06.1990.
[5]   Directive 90/270, OJ L 156, 21.06.1990.
[6]   Directive 2004/37, OJ L 158, 30.04.2004.
[7]   Directive 2000/54, OJ L 262, 17.10.2000.
[8]   Directive 92/57, OJ L 245, 26.08.1992.
[9]   Directive 92/58, OJ L 245, 26.08.1992.
[10] Directive 92/91, OJ L 348, 28.11.1992.
[11] Directive 92/104, OJ L 404, 31.12.1992.
[12] Directive 98/24, OJ L 131, 05.05.1998.
[13] Directive 1999/92, OJ L 23, 28.01.2000.
[14] Directive 2002/44, OJ L 177, 06.07.2002.
[15] Directive 2003/10, OJ L 42, 15.02.2003.
[16] Directive 2006/25, OJ L 114, 27.04.2006.
[17] Directive 91/383, OJ L 206, 29.07.1991.
[18] Directive 92/85, OJ L 348, 28.11.1992.

Member States recognise, in the context of their policy on preventing occupational hazards and accidents, the right of self-employed workers to health and safety protection, and their duties in this area[1].

The **new Community strategy on health and safety at work** aims at a global approach to well-being at work, taking account of changes in the world of work and the emergence of new risks, especially of a psycho-social nature. According to the Commission, the strategy should be based on: consolidating a culture of risk prevention, including psychological and social risks such as stress, harassment, depression and alcoholism; combining a variety of political instruments, such as social dialogue and corporate social responsibility; and building partnerships between all players in the field of health and safety[2].

13.5.8. Public health protection

Public health was brought fully into the action scope of the European Union by a special title of the Maastricht Treaty, which, as amended at Amsterdam to heed the "mad cow" and dioxin lessons [see sections 5.1.3. and 11.2.], states that a **high level of human health protection** shall be ensured in the definition and implementation of all Community policies and activities. Article 152 (TEC) invites the Community to contribute towards ensuring a high level of human health protection by encouraging cooperation between the Member States and by fostering cooperation with third countries and the competent international organisations.

The **programme of Community action** in the field of public health (2003-2008) complements national policies aiming to protect human health and improve public health[3]. The general objectives of the programme are: (a) to improve information and knowledge for the development of public health; (b) to enhance the capability of responding rapidly and in a coordinated fashion to threats to health; (c) to promote health and prevent disease through addressing health determinants across all policies and activities. The programme should thereby contribute to: ensuring a high level of human health protection in the definition and implementation of all Community policies and activities; tackling inequalities in health; and encouraging cooperation between Member States.

The measures under the programme underpin the **health strategy of the Community** and should yield Community added value by responding to needs arising out of conditions and structures established through Community action in other fields, by addressing new developments, new threats and new problems for which the Community would be in a better position to act to protect its people, by bringing together activities undertaken in relative isolation and with limited impact at national level and by complementing them in order to achieve positive results for the people of the Community. The programme can provide a significant added value to health promotion by facilitating the exchange of experience and best practices and by providing a basis for a common analysis of the factors affecting public health. Also, the programme may have added value in the event of threats to public health of a cross-border nature, such as infectious diseases, environmental pollution or food contamination.

A Community **health-monitoring system** aims to facilitate the planning, monitoring and evaluation of Community programmes, provide the Member States with appropriate health information to make comparisons and to support their national health poli-

---

[1]   Recommendation 2003/134, OJ L 53, 28.02.2003.
[2]   Commission communication, COM (2002) 118, 11 March 2002.
[3]   Decision 1786/2002, OJ L 271, 09.10.2002 and Decision 786/2004, OJ L 138, 30.04.2004.

cies. It entails action aimed at establishing Community health indicators, developing a Community-wide network for sharing health data and facilitating analyses and reporting in the health sphere. Actually, the Community leads actions against AIDS, cancer, particularly by combating smoking, and drug dependence.

As regards the acquired immune deficiency syndrome (**AIDS**), the Member States decided, first, to introduce a procedure for the periodical and rapid exchange of epidemiological data at Community level and machinery for the exchange of information on national measures taken[1]. The Community **network for the epidemiological surveillance** and control of communicable diseases ensures continuous surveillance and provides an early warning and response system to deal with the appearance or recurrence of these diseases in the Member States[2]. The Community participates in a research and development programme aimed at developing new clinical interventions to combat HIV/AIDS, malaria and tuberculosis through a long-term partnership between Europe and developing countries, undertaken by several Member States[3]. The EC is part to the World Health Organisation Framework Convention on Tobacco Control, which is concerned mainly with labelling, advertising, tax measures, manufacturers' civil and criminal liability, financing of national tobacco control programmes and action to combat illicit trade in tobacco products[4].

In the framework of the **action plans to combat cancer**, the Community has adopted several measures against smoking, notably a Directive concerning the manufacture, presentation and sale of tobacco products[5] and a Directive concerning the maximum tar content of cigarettes[6]. A Resolution on banning smoking in places open to the public, which provided guidelines to the Member States for the protection of non-smokers from environmental tobacco smoke[7], was reinforced by a recommendation on the prevention of smoking and on initiatives to improve tobacco control[8]. A milestone Directive prohibits all forms of advertising and sponsorship of tobacco products in the media other than television, i.e. in the press and other printed publications, in radio broadcasting and in information society services[9]. Another Directive prohibits all forms of television advertising for cigarettes and other tobacco products and provides that television programmes may not be sponsored by undertakings whose principal activity is the manufacture or sale of cigarettes and other tobacco products[10].

For the **prevention of drug dependence,** the Community has set up a customs cooperation and has taken a number of measures in the framework of its justice and home affairs policy [see sections 5.1.4. and 8.1.2.]. The European Monitoring Centre for Drugs and Drug Addiction (EMCDDA), established in Lisbon, has at its disposal, as a key instrument in its fight against drugs, a European Information Network on Drugs and Drug Addiction[11]. In connection with the European Union Drugs Strategy, the Council made a number of recommendations concerning information and counselling, emergency services, networking between agencies, appropriate integration of health and social services, and training and qualification for professionals, in order to reduce substantially the incidence of drug-related health damage and the number of deaths[12].

The activities carried out inside the thematic priority area "life sciences, genomics and biotechnology for health" of the **common research policy** [see section 18.4.1.] may have numerous applications in various health-related sectors, and notably in the development of new diagnostic tools and new treatments capable of helping to combat diseases that are not at present under control[13].

13.6. Appraisal and outlook

The common social policy makes an important contribution to European integration, notably in helping achieve the **social cohesion** necessary among the Member States. It is interesting to note in the following paragraphs that each of the four wings of this policy makes a different contribution to the integration process. They, nevertheless,

---

[1] OJ C 197, 27.07.1988, p. 8 and OJ C 329, 31.12.1990, p. 21-22.
[2] Decision 2119/98, OJ L 268, 03.10.1998 last amended by Regulation 1882/2003, OJ L 284, 31.10.2003.
[3] Decision 1209/2003, OJ L 169, 08.07.2003.
[4] Decision 2004/513, OJ L 213, 15.06.2004.
[5] Directive 2001/37, OJ L 194, 18.07.2001.
[6] Directive 90/239, OJ L 137, 30.05.1990.
[7] OJ C 189, 26.07.1989, p. 1-2.
[8] Recommendation 2003/54, OJ L 22, 25.01.2003.
[9] Directive 2003/33, OJ L 152, 20.06.2003.
[10] Directive 89/552, OJ L 298, 17.10.1989 and Directive 97/36, OJ L 202, 30.07.1997.
[11] Regulation 302/93, OJ L 36, 12.02.1993 and Regulation 1651/2003, OJ L 245, 29.09.2003.
[12] Recommendation 2003/488, OJ L 165, 03.07.2003.
[13] Decision 2002/834, OJ L 294, 29.10.2002.

reinforce each other and interact with other common policies, notably the economic and monetary, industrial, research and development ones, in fostering the social cohesion necessary in an economic and monetary union.

The **freedom of movement of workers** was essential for the completion of the common market and, therefore, was examined under that heading [see section 6.4.]. By virtue of the Community regulations adopted in their favour, migrant workers and self-employed persons from any Member State enjoy fair conditions compared with nationals of the host country with regard to access to employment, social security, the education and vocational training of their children, living and working conditions and the right to exercise union rights. The common labour market is handicapped, however, by the existence of different languages, customs and working methods and, although the EU is taking measures to overcome these hurdles to the free movement of workers, it will certainly need much time before it encompasses a really homogeneous labour market.

The **common employment policy** is striving to ensure that the national employment policies and the common policies of the EU, notably in the economic and monetary field, work together in a consistent manner so as to boost economic reforms and employment while maintaining price stability. The coordinated employment strategy aims to harness structural reforms and modernisation to improve the efficiency of the labour market, while maintaining a non-inflationary growth dynamic. The employment guidelines, agreed by the Council, help the Member States to devise their own employment strategies, while pursuing common goals, such as: improving employability, with the emphasis on suitable training; developing entrepreneurship; encouraging the adaptability of the work force; and strengthening equal opportunities policies for women and men. The Lisbon agenda has shifted the focus of the European employment strategy from the fight against unemployment towards the wider priority of more and better jobs in an inclusive society and has helped employment creation in the EU [see section 13.3.2.]. However, performance varies considerably among the Member States and reforms are not pursued in a sufficiently comprehensive way by all of them, whether in terms of creating and maintaining employment or improving vocational skills and the quality of jobs.

The **common education and training policies** complement the common employment policy by encouraging the adaptation of the work force to the new conditions of the industrial and service sectors in Europe and in the rest of the world. The cooperation and exchange of experiences through the Community programmes helps the Member States develop the European dimension in education, the teaching of languages, the vocational training and retraining needed in the information society and in the global economy. At the same time, these programmes build networks of teachers, instructors and young people who participate actively in the European integration process [see section 9.4.].

The **common policy for the improvement of living and working conditions** is aimed at the convergence of social protection systems and through it at the social cohesion of the Union. Community directives fixing common minimum standards guarantee the rights, the physical safety and health of workers, particularly the women and the young, in all Member States. The establishment of a framework of basic minimum standards provides a bulwark against using low social standards as an instrument of unfair economic competition. The social bedrock, which is thus being built, is indispensable for the good functioning of economic and monetary union where the competition between the various regions of the Union is enhanced. However, economic and social developments in European countries make it necessary to modernise social protection systems in order to attain four main objectives: creating more incentives to work and provide a secure income; safeguarding pensions with sustainable pension schemes; promoting social inclusion; and ensuring the high quality and sustainability of health protection.

At present, the Community has to **address major industrial change** both of a quantitative and qualitative nature: the globalisation of production and markets, the acceleration of technological change and the changes to production systems [see section 17.1.]. These factors as a whole are having a profound effect on the Community's industrial scene and a significant impact on employment and the dynamics of human resources in the Community. EU labour markets must become more inclusive, with employment opportunities extended to all, at the same time as they become more adaptable to economic conditions. The Community's social policy must anticipate future changes in employment and in qualifications requirements. Workers' qualifications must be adapted to meet future changes and to minimise the economic and social cost of changes already occurring.

The joint Council and Commission reports on employment, drawn up in accordance with Article 128 of the EC Treaty, note the progress made in the employment field throughout the Union (increase in labour productivity, job creation, reduction in unemployment, etc.) in line with the objectives set at the Lisbon European Council. Significant persistent weaknesses nevertheless indicate the need for continuing structural reform, particularly in the face of a less favourable economic outlook. Key issues for the future include: measures to boost employment rates, improve the quality of work and promote equal opportunities and active ageing, investment in human resources, a more effective strategy geared to social inclusion and greater emphasis on regional disparities. The challenge of the European employment strategy consists in raising the employment rate by promoting employability and by removing obstacles and disincentives to take up or remain in a job, while preserving high protection standards of the European social model.

While wealth creation is essential for social progress, this progress cannot be founded simply on the basis of the competitiveness of economies, but also on the **efficiency of European society** as a whole. This efficiency can itself be founded on a well-educated, highly motivated and adaptable working population. Economic and social progress must, therefore, go hand in hand to preserve the shared values, which form the basis of the European social model. These include the market economy, democracy and pluralism, respect of individual rights, free collective bargaining equality of opportunity for all, social welfare and solidarity. Modernisation of the European **social model** is essential in the face of the ageing of the population, which threatens the financial sustainability of social systems, and as a response to globalisation, which challenges Europe's competitiveness; it is also vital from the point of view of maintaining high levels of prosperity, social cohesion, environmental protection and quality of life in Europe.

The European Union should promote the principles of the European social model in **the rest of the world**, which suffers from poverty, inequalities and exploitation. It is important that the respect of the fundamental human rights, in particular the right to association and collective bargaining as well as the protection against compulsory work and work of children, be enforced at international level in the framework of the United Nations Organisation. The EU could and should contribute to the globalisation of solidarity and respect of human rights in the world.

Bibliography on social policy

- ALBERS Detley, HASELER Stephen, MEYER Henning (eds.). *Social Europe: a continent's answer to market fundamentalism.* London: London Metropolitan University, 2006.
- BACH Maurizio (et al. eds.). *Europe in motion: social dynamics and political institutions in an enlarging Europe.* Berlin: Sigma, 2006.
- BARRETT Gavin. "Light acquired on acquired rights: examining developments in employment rights on transfers of undertakings", *Common Market Law Review,* v. 42, n. 4, August 2005, p. 1053-1105.
- BLANCHARD Olivier. "European unemployment: the evolution of facts and ideas" in *Economic Policy,* n. 45, January 2006, p. 5-59.
- BLANPAIN Roger (et al. eds.). *The European social model.* Antwerpen: Intersentia, 2006.
- CANTILLON Bea, MARX Ive (eds.). *International cooperation in social security: how to cope with globalisation?* Antwerpen: Intersentia, 2005.
- CRAIG John, LYNK Michael (eds.). *Globalization and the future of labour law.* Cambridge: Cambridge University Press, 2006.
- DE BURCA Grainne. *EU law and the welfare state: in search of solidarity.* Oxford: Oxford University Press, 2005.
- DELANTY Gerard, RUMFORD Chris. *Rethinking Europe: social theory and the implications of Europeanization.* London: Routledge, 2005.
- EUROPEAN COMMISSION. *Communication from the Commission on the Social Agenda,* COM/05/33. Luxembourg: EUR-OP*, 2005.
  - *Global Europe: Competing in the world : A contribution to the EU's Growth and Jobs Strategy.* COM/2006/567. Luxembourg: EUR-OP*, 2006.

- EUROPEAN FOUNDATION FOR THE IMPROVEMENT OF LIVING AND WORKING CONDITIONS. European Works Councils and transnational restructuring. Luxembourg: EUR-OP*, 2006.
- FALKNER Gerda. "Forms of governance in European Union social policy: continuity and/or change" in *International Social Security Review*, v. 59, n. 2, April-June 2006, p. 77-103.
- JACOBI Otto, KIRTON-DARLING Judith (eds.). "Sectoral social dialogue", *Transfer*, v. 11, n. 3, Autumn 2005, p. 309-464.
- McDONALD Linda. *Wellness at work: protecting and promoting employee health and wellbeing.* London: Chartered Institute of Personnel and Development (CIPD), 2005.
- McGAURAN Anne-Marie, McNAMARA Tony (eds.). "Gender equality phase 3: the theory and practice of gender mainstreaming", *Administration*, v. 53, n. 2, 2005, p. 1-135.
- MORTENSEN Jörgen. *Ageing, health and retirement in Europe: the AGIR Project.* Brussels: Centre for European Policy Studies, 2005.
- PÉPIN Luce. *The history of European cooperation in education and training: Europe in the making: an example.* Luxembourg: EUR-OP*, 2006.
- REGALIA Ida (ed.). *Regulating new forms of employment: local experiments and social innovation in Europe.* London: Routledge, 2006.
- ROMANO Frank. "La politique sociale européenne et le Royaume-Uni: la fin de la polémique?" in *Humanisme et entreprise: Cahiers du Centre d'études et de recherches*, nouvelle série, n. 276, avril 2006, p. 73-99.

*The publications of the Office for Official Publications of the European Communities (EUR-OP) exist usually in all official languages of the EU.

Chapter 14

TAXATION POLICY

Diagram of the chapter

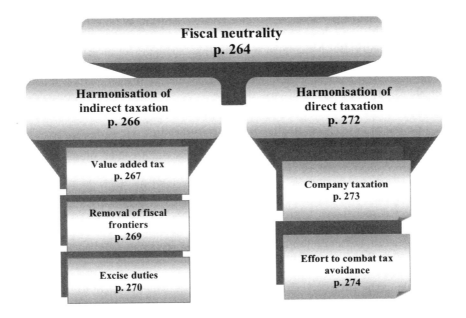

The EEC Treaty was very cautious as regards tax harmonisation. What it wanted above all was the introduction and observance of **the rule of fiscal neutrality in Community trade**, i.e. equal tax treatment for domestic production and imports from other member countries. Beyond that, the Treaty merely invited the Commission to examine how turnover taxes could be harmonised. The Treaty did not call for any harmonisation or other Community action with regard to direct taxes.

The fiscal objectives of the Treaty were attained rapidly. Cumulative multi-stage taxes, which did not guarantee fiscal neutrality, were replaced by **a new turnover tax, the value added tax**, and the structures of that tax were harmonised in all Community Member States, old and new. The principle of fiscal neutrality was thus guaranteed, but at the price of maintaining tax barriers, which were necessary for the collection of VAT and excise duties in the country of destination of goods.

However, in the single market goods must be able to move completely freely, and to achieve this, tax has to be imposed on them either in the country of origin or in that of destination. This led, at the end of the 1980s, to the **alignment of VAT and excise duties**. At the same time the harmonisation of direct taxes has begun, especially concerning those on companies and savings, in order to make the growth of companies and capital movement independent of tax considerations. Inside the economic and monetary union, tax harmonisation should progress at the same pace as economic integration.

14.1. The need for a common tax policy

Having economic and social structures which differed in many ways, the States which were to form the European Economic Community also had rather **dissimilar tax systems**, both as regards financial policy, that is to say in particular the composition of the tax burden as between direct and indirect taxes, and the technical organisation of taxation. In the short term there was no question of making a single fiscal territory of the European Community. But pending such unification, some urgent measures in the taxation field were needed for the common market to work properly. These measures were centred on achieving fiscal neutrality and equal conditions of competition among the Member States, the two subjects discussed below.

14.1.1. The fiscal neutrality in the common market

If the member states of a common market had absolute freedom in the fiscal field, they could very quickly **replace the customs barriers to trade by tax barriers**. They could in fact, while lowering their customs duties in accordance with the timetable laid down by the Treaty, raise their domestic taxes in such a way that the total burden on imports remained unchanged. It was therefore necessary that indirect taxes, in particular turnover tax, have no influence on intra-Community trade flows. In other words, **fiscal neutrality** between domestic production and imports from the partner countries was needed. To secure fiscal neutrality in a common market the turnover tax of the country of origin or of the country of destination would have to be imposed on all goods.

If the rule of **the tax of the country of origin** were adopted, there would be a danger of creating trade flows based artificially on the difference in the taxes rather than on the difference in comparative costs, but there would be pressure on the Member States to approximate the rates of their taxes, and fiscal frontiers could be removed, as imported goods would already have paid taxes at the rate of the country of origin. If, on the other hand, the system of the **tax of the country of destination** were applied, production could be concentrated where the comparative economic advantages were greatest rather than where taxation would be lower, as all products in competition on a market, whether of domestic origin or imported, would be uniformly subject to the tax on consumption in force on that market. However, under that system the tax barriers would have to be maintained in order to levy the taxes of the country of destination on imported goods and the Member States would not be encouraged to approximate the rates of their taxes. This was the price, which the founding Member States, in light of the low level of integration of their economies, paid in opting for the system of taxation in the country of destination.

Even if the system of the tax of the country of destination were imposed uniformly, fiscal neutrality could still not be ensured if some countries in the common market applied a system of **cumulative multi-stage turnover tax**, which was the case in five of the original six Community countries. Under that system tax was levied on the product for each transaction and therefore its total size was not only a function of its rate but also of the number of transactions which had been carried out up to the stage of final distribution. A product was therefore taxed less heavily if it was manufactured by a vertically integrated undertaking (firm, business) than where it was manufactured and distributed by various small firms. It is immediately evident that such a system would distort competition in the common market by favouring integrated large companies originating in certain member countries or third countries. In addition, such a system would not make possible genuine fiscal neutrality in intra-Community trade, as it would be very difficult to monitor each product at every stage of manufacture and distribution in order to ascertain the exact amount of the tax it had borne.

Recognising this difficulty, Article 97 (now repealed) of the EEC Treaty allowed Member States which levied a turnover tax calculated on a **cumulative multi-stage tax system** to establish average rates for products or groups of products in the case of internal taxation imposed by them on imported products or of repayments allowed by them on exported products. But the Treaty did not provide any rule for establishing average rates. It merely prohibited taxation of products of other Member States in excess of that imposed on similar domestic products (Art. 95 EEC, present Art 90 TEC) and repayment of internal taxation on products exported to Member States at a rate that exceeds the taxation actually imposed (Art. 96 EEC, present Art. 91 TEC). Those were ceilings inside which the Member States were at liberty to establish the average rates of their multi-stage taxes.

In addition, there existed important **specific taxes on consumption, known as excise duties**, whose structures and levels varied greatly in the countries of the Community. Those differences stemmed not only from historic reasons, but also from economic and social ones. Given that the main reason of existence of excise duties was their yield, States had a tendency to impose higher levels on certain products of major consumption, and those products were not necessarily the same in every State. Some goods were regarded as luxury products in some States but not in others. Moreover, if a Member State of the Single Market taxed heavily certain products which are dangerous to health, such as alcoholic drinks, in order to restrain their consumption, whereas another country preferred to attack other products, such as tobacco products, illegal traffics might develop between the two countries frustrating the objectives of both. Be that as it may, the differences between Member States in excise duty structures could give rise to significant disturbances in conditions of competition, especially where products heavily taxed in one State mainly came from the others. In such instance consumption naturally moved towards lower-taxed alternative products, as is the case of wine and beer. In the interest of the proper functioning of the common market and the attainment of the Community agricultural, energy and transport objectives, the structures of those taxes needed to be harmonised.

14.1.2. Taxation and conditions of competition

Just behind the harmonisation of the structures of all indirect taxes came, of course, the harmonisation of their rates. It is obvious that in order to create completely impartial conditions of competition in the common market **a common system of taxes on consumption is needed**, comprising not only the same structures, but also very approximate rates or, indeed, the same rates wherever possible. In effect, the different rates of taxes could have a different influence on the consumption of various products in the common market and could distort the conditions of competition between the undertakings of the Member States. Where the tax burden on a product is lower in one country than in another, if the other conditions of competition are equal in both countries, the undertakings which manufacture the product in the first country are in a much more **favourable competitive position** than their counterparts in the second country, as they can have increased demand and high profits in their principal market.

Moreover, there are grounds for questioning whether, in spite of the harmonisation of tax structures and the alignment of indirect taxation, fiscal neutrality exists, when some states have much more recourse than others to **direct taxation**. It is true that such states tax the products of their partners less than do those which have more recourse to indirect taxes, but the terms of trade and productivity offset to a large extent the fiscal disparities of member states' companies. Moreover, states clearly apply certain categories of tax on the basis of historic habit, sociological structure and economic conditions. Some mainly apply indirect taxes, which are easily collected, whilst others have greater recourse to direct taxation, which is fairer from the social viewpoint. The member states of a common market need to have sufficient autonomy in the tax field so as to have enough room for manoeuvre to act in the light of their economic situations.

In fact, the requirements for tax harmonisation increase together with progress in economic integration. Whilst fiscal neutrality in a customs union is ensured by the harmonisation of the structures of turnover tax and excise duties, in a common market and even more so **in an economic and monetary union** gradual harmonisation of the levels of those taxes and even of direct taxation are also necessary, to ensure fair competition throughout the single market. The long-term goal is to reach a taxation framework conducive to enterprise, job creation and environment protection in the Union[1]. Tax harmonisation may have spillover effects [see section 1.1.1.] on the development of the common enterprise, employment and environment policies.

Disparities in direct taxes work to the advantage of **multinational companies**, as they are able to concentrate their profits in the State which taxes them least. For that purpose they use holding companies, transfer prices within the group and international debenture loans. The holding companies are established in countries with low taxation, known as tax havens. They group, by various means, a large proportion of the profits of their subsidiaries established in countries with normal taxation and reinvest them in the same or other companies. One means of concentrating profits in low-taxation countries is the practice of transfer prices between units within the same group, which can vary greatly from actual market prices.

However, in a single market, production costs and the profitability of invested capital must not be influenced too differently from country to country by taxation. In fact, lower company taxation in one state than in the others is tantamount to a subsidy, which is incompatible with the definition of a common market. Moreover, countries which have high taxes on company revenue or which do not give favourable treatment to reinvested profits may, in an EMU, where there is no exchange rate adjustment, lose capital to countries in which company taxation is more favourable. Such capital movements are undesirable, as they do not lead to optimum use of financial resources and production factors in an EMU. Therefore, the **gradual harmonisation of direct taxation is necessary** to ensure that conditions of competition are not distorted in the EMU.

14.2. Harmonisation of indirect taxation

Indirect taxes are **those on turnover, production or consumption of goods and services** - regarded as components of cost prices and selling prices - which are collected without regard to the realisation of profits, or indeed income, but which are deductible when determining profits. Customs duties are a form of indirect taxation. That is why, following the removal of customs barriers in a common market, Member States could be tempted to replace them with fiscal barriers, i.e. with internal taxes. That danger was foreseen in the EEC Treaty, Articles 95 to 98 of which contained provisions to obviate it, together with Article 99, which called upon the Commission to consider how the legislation of the various Member States concerning turnover taxes, excise duties and other forms of indirect taxation could be harmonised in the interest of the common market. Indeed, the Commission, assisted by two committees of experts, examined the harmonisation of indirect taxation and proposed the adoption by all Member States of a system of turnover taxes which did not distort conditions of competition either within a country or between Member States. Such a system was the tax on value added.

The **cumulative multi-stage taxes**, which were practised by five of the six countries of the original Community, had the specific characteristic of levying turnover tax on raw materials, semi-processed products, component parts and finished products each time they were sold by one firm to another. The result was that the taxes on the various stages of production of a product burdened its consumer price all the more inasmuch as it had taken numerous transactions to manufacture and distribute it and, consequently, the system burdened more

---

[1]   COM (96) 546, 22 October 1996.

the production of small and medium sized enterprises (SMEs). Moreover, given the inherent complexity of cumulative taxes, the fixing of average levels for compensation measures at frontiers in respect of such taxes did not rule out the unfavourable treatment of imports and the favourable treatment of exports. Hence, the Commission was convinced, at the beginning of the 1960s, that the only radical solution to the problems arising from cumulative multi-stage taxes was to replace them by the value added tax.

14.2.1. Value added tax

When it was **adopted for the first time, in France in 1954, value added tax (VAT)** was regarded as merely another tax on turnover or on consumption and did not attract the attention of other countries. It was only since 1962, with the publication of two reports ordered by the Commission recommending its adoption by all Member States, that its interest for the Community was understood. Acting on the basis of Commission proposals, the Council adopted on 11 April 1967 two Directives on the harmonisation of the legislation of Member States concerning turnover taxes[1]. Those two Directives laid the groundwork for the common value added tax system and a third one, adopted in 1969, introduced it in the tax systems of the Member States[2].

According to Article 2 of the first Directive of 1967, **VAT is a general tax on consumption**, i.e. a tax on all expenditure on goods and services. The tax is levied at each stage of an economic activity on the value added at that stage. It is paid by all those involved in the production and distribution of a product or service, but it is not an element in the costs of those intermediaries and does not appear as an item of expenditure in their accounts, as it is not they who bear the tax, but the end consumer.

The tax is proportional to the price of the products and services irrespective of the number of transactions, which have taken place at the stages preceding that to which it is applied. At the time of each transaction, the amount of VAT, calculated on the price of the good or service, is reduced by the amount of the taxes previously paid on the cost of the various components of the cost price. The total sum which changes hands at each stage in the production or distribution includes the VAT paid up to that point, but the amount of the tax is recovered at each sale, except for the final sale to the **final consumer**, who purchases the product or service for his private use. The tax is paid to the State by the vendor in each transaction. However, the latter does not bear the burden of the VAT, as his purchaser has advanced the full amount of the VAT to him. Tax paid at previous stages, on deliveries made or services rendered to the taxable person, and the tax paid on imports, is deductible from the turnover tax of that taxable person. Given this **deductibility of taxes already paid**, VAT is neutral from the point of view of domestic competition, i.e. it does not favour vertically integrated undertakings, as did the cumulative multi-stage taxes. But VAT is also neutral from the point of view of international competition, since it cannot favour domestic products. Calculation of the tax paid is easy, as it appears on all invoices and documents accompanying the product.

The **sixth directive** on the harmonisation of turnover taxes established a package of common rules making it possible to define the scope of the tax and the method of determining tax liability, i.e. the territorial application of the tax, the taxable persons, the taxable transactions, the place of applicability of such transactions, the chargeable event, the taxable amount, the detailed procedures for applying rates of taxation, the exemptions and the special schemes[3]. In Community jargon all these rules are known as "**the uniform basis of assessment of VAT**", and that basis is particularly important in that

---

[1] Directives 67/227 and 67/228, OJ 71, 14.04.1967 and Directive 77/388, OJ L 145, 13.06.1977.
[2] Directive 69/463, OJ L 320, 20.12.1969.
[3] Directive 77/388, OJ L 145, 13.06.1977 last amended by Directive 2006/69, OJ L 221, 12.08.2006.

VAT is a basic source of revenue for the Community [see section 3.4.]. Moreover, Directive 77/388 harmonised the laws on turnover tax structures of the Member States in the fields of the **provision of services**, agricultural production, small undertakings and exempt activities and operations linked with importation, exportation and international trade in goods. Subject to Council approval, a Member State may introduce into its legislation special measures for derogation from the common system of value-added tax, either in order to simplify the procedure for charging the tax or to prevent certain types of tax evasion or avoidance, or in the form of an agreement with a non-member country or an international organisation. Regulation 1777/2005 lays down implementing measures for Directive 77/388[1] [see details below].

A directive amending the sixth directive put in place uniform taxation rules for radio and television broadcasting services and for certain electronically supplied services, making it as easy and straightforward as possible to comply with these rules, particularly in the fields of supply, electronic networks, services linked to software and computers in general, and of information, cultural, arts, sports, science, education and leisure services[2]. These rules allow Member States to subject to VAT services provided electronically and radio and television broadcasting services supplied on subscription or pay-per-view basis in the European Union and to exempt these services from VAT if they are provided for consumption outside the Union [see also sections 6.6.1. and 17.3.5.]. Another directive amended the rules for the application of VAT and harmonised the rules on the place of **taxation of natural gas and electricity**[3]. Supplies to dealers are taxable at the place of their business or fixed establishment for which the goods are supplied, whereas supplies to end consumers are taxable at the place of consumption of gas and electricity, which is usually the place where the customer's meter is located.

The sixth Directive had laid down the principle that any taxpayer was entitled to the deduction or refund of VAT in whichever country he incurred expenditure subject to tax. An eighth Directive on the matter, adopted by the Council in 1979, lays down the common arrangements for the refund to **taxable persons not established in the territory of the country** of VAT borne by them on imports or purchases of goods or services in a Member State[4]. The thirteenth Directive, adopted in 1986, does likewise for refunds to **taxable persons not established in Community territory**[5]. The tenth Directive applies VAT to the **hiring out of moveable tangible property**[6]. An amendment to the sixth Directive allows Member States wishing to do so to apply on an experimental basis, until the end of 2010, a reduced rate of VAT on two or, in exceptional cases, three categories of labour-intensive services, such as minor repair services, repairs to private dwellings, cleaning and hairdressing[7].

Since some non-Member countries do not impose VAT on **telecommunications services**, these services are subject to VAT in the Community at the place of establishment of the recipient of the services, while services rendered by Community operators to consumers in non-Member countries are not subject to VAT in the Community[8].

With the aim of more **uniform application** of the current VAT system and improved functioning of the internal market guidelines, Regulation 1777/2005 sets out important aspects of the basic VAT directive, such as the definition of the taxable person, the place of supply of goods and services, and the special scheme for electronically supplied services.

---

[1]   Regulation 1777/2005, OJ L 288, 29.10.2005.
[2]   Directive 2002/38, OJ L 128, 15.05.2002 and Directive 2006/58, OJ L 174, 28.06.2006.
[3]   Directive 2003/96, OJ L 283, 31.10.2003 and Directive 2004/74, OJ L 157, 30.04.2004.
[4]   Directive 79/1072, OJ L 331, 27.09.1979.
[5]   Directive 86/560, OJ L 326, 21.11.1986.
[6]   Directive 84/386, OJ L 208, 03.08.1984.
[7]   Directive 2006/18, OJ L 51, 22.02.2006.
[8]   Directive 1999/59, OJ L 162, 26.06.1999.

14.2.2. Removal of fiscal frontiers

One of the main challenges to the **completion of the single market** was in the tax field [see section 6.1.]. Prior to 1992, goods and services moving within a Member State were taxed differently from those that were exported. On exportation, the product benefited from full tax remission and was in return subject to the VAT of the country of import at the crossing of borders. The tax was paid to the country in which the goods arrived at the final consumption stage. The protection, which that system afforded against tax evasion, depended on **controls at borders**. Without a check at the border to ensure that the goods which were the subject of an application for the reimbursement of tax had actually been exported, it would be all too easy for dishonest operators to invoice goods at the zero rate for exportation and subsequently resell them on the internal market, either free of tax, thus placing their competitors in a disadvantageous position with regard to price, or by including the tax component in the price, but keeping its amount for themselves. That would not only have constituted a loss of tax revenue for the exporting State, but also a source of serious trade distortion. For the authorities of the importing State, on the other hand, frontier controls were used to tax imported goods at the rates prevalent in the country in question, so as to collect the revenue due to them and, at the same time, make sure that these products did not unduly compete with national products.

The export refunds and import taxes, which accompanied intra-Community trade, and the resultant controls, constituted the so-called "**fiscal frontiers**". To remove those barriers to trade, it was vital that cross-border trade be treated in the same way as purchases and sales within a State. The Commission actually proposed that as from 1 January 1993 all sales of goods and services should be taxed at the rate of the country of origin[1]. But the Council did not follow the Commission's lead. In conclusions of 9 October 1989, adopted unanimously (necessary condition in order to counter the proposal of the Commission) [see section 4.3.], it considered that conditions could not be fulfilled for a system of taxation in the country of origin and that it was therefore necessary to continue, for a limited period, to levy VAT and excise duty in the State of consumption.

The Directive on the **approximation of VAT rates** supplemented Directive 77/388 and completed the common VAT system[2]. It stipulates that, during the operational period of the transitional VAT arrangements (where the VAT rate is that of the country of destination and not that of the country of origin), the Member States shall apply **a standard VAT rate of at least 15%**. However, the standard VAT rate varies between 15 and 25% in the twenty-five Member States. In fact, in September 2004 the standard VAT rate was:
- **15,** in Luxembourg and Cyprus;
- **16,** in Germany and Spain;
- **17.5,** in the United Kingdom;
- **18,** in Greece, Estonia, Latvia, Lithuania and Malta;
- **19,** in the Netherlands, Portugal, the Czech Republic and Slovakia
- **19.6,** in France;
- **20,** in Italy, Austria and Slovenia;
- **21,** in Belgium and Ireland;
- **22,** in Poland and Finland; and
- **25,** in Denmark, Sweden and Hungary.

All the higher VAT rates existing in several Member States have been abolished, leading to a significant fall in consumer prices in some sectors, such as automobiles. The Member States however enjoy the option of applying, alongside the normal rate, one (or two) **reduced rates**, equal to or higher than 5%, applicable only to certain goods and services of a social or cultural nature. Examples include foodstuffs, pharmaceuticals,

---

[1] Commission proposal, OJ C 250, 19.09.1987, p. 2.
[2] Directive 77.388, OJ L 145, 13.06.1977, Directive 92/77, OJ L 316, 31.10.1992 and Directive 2004/66, OJ L 168, 01.05.2004.

passenger transport services, books, newspapers and periodicals, entrance to shows, museums and the like, publications and copyright, subsidised housing, hotel accommodation, social activities and medical care in hospitals. The preservation of the zero and extra-low rates (below 5%) is authorised on a transitional basis, along with reduced rates on housing other than subsidised housing, catering and children's clothes and shoes.

The common system of VAT dispensed with customs procedures[1]. Intra-Community trade in goods between taxable bodies is subject to taxation in the country of destination. In the case of sales between companies subject to VAT, i.e. the vast majority, the vendor exempts the deliveries made to clients in other Member States. In his VAT return, he indicates, in a separate box, the total of his exempted intra-Community sales. In another return (usually quarterly), he lists the VAT number of his customers in the other Member States and the total amount of his sales to each of them during the period in question. The purchaser applies VAT to his purchase in another Member State, termed an "acquisition". He must declare the total amount of these acquisitions in a separate box in his normal VAT return and can request the deductibility of this VAT in the same return.

Individuals travelling from one Member State to another pay VAT there where they purchase the goods and are no longer subject to any VAT-related taxation or any border formality when they cross from one Member State to another. In return, the system of travellers' allowances (tax free sales in ports, airports, etc.) was abolished in intra-Community travelling[2].

In the framework of the transitional system, the seventh VAT Directive has introduced certain special systems. For **remote sales** (mail order) of an undertaking to individuals and other non-taxable bodies, VAT is counted at the rate in force in its Member State, except when its sales in the Member State of destination are above a certain limit (generally, EUR 100,000 per year) or if it prefers taxation in that State. **New vehicles** (cars, boats, aircraft) which form part of the operating stock of the vendor and which do not have a mileage of more than 3,000 kilometres are taxed in the country of registration, i.e. in the purchaser's country of origin, whereas second-hand vehicles are subject to the VAT rates practised in the country of the vendor. **Institutional non-taxable bodies** (government authorities) and **exempted taxable bodies** (banks, insurance companies...) are able to purchase goods in other countries, paying the VAT applicable in the country of origin, provided that their purchases do not overstep a certain threshold to be set by each Member State. For **second-hand goods, works of art, collectors' items and antiques**, sales between individuals are free of VAT and those realised by second-hand dealers and tradesmen are taxed in the Member State of destination on the dealer's profit margin and not on the total value of the goods[3].

The abolition of frontier controls and the resultant **fraud risk** require cooperation between government authorities in the area of indirect taxation to combat tax evasion. This cooperation is based primarily on regular exchanges of data between the relevant authorities of the Member States on intra-Community trade[4]. The backbone of the system is an on-line network linking the relevant administrations of the Member States ("SCENT- taxation"), enabling rapid and efficient information exchange designed to combat fraud in the VAT and excise-duties fields. The **Fiscalis programme** seeks to improve the operation of taxation systems in the internal market through effective initial and continuous training of the officials in charge of this area[5].

14.2.3. Excise duties

In a fiscally integrated Community a number of major **special taxes on consumption (excise duties)**, i.e. taxes on the consumption of certain products, yielding substantial revenue to the States, must be maintained alongside VAT. Excise duties make it possible to impose a much larger tax burden on a small number of products than that borne

---

[1]   Directive 91/680, OJ L 376, 31.12.1991 and Directive 92/111, OJ L 384, 30.12.1992.
[2]   Directive 94/4, OJ L 60, 03.03.1994 and Directive 98/94, OJ L 358, 31.12.1998.
[3]   Directive 94/5, OJ L 60, 03.03.1994.
[4]   Regulation 1798/2003, OJ L 264, 15.10.2003 and Regulation 885/2004, OJ L 168, 01.05.2004.
[5]   Decision 2235/2002, OJ L 341, 17.12.2002 and Regulation 885/2004, OJ L 168, 01.05.2004.

by the vast majority of goods that are only subject to VAT, which has very few, and fairly low, rates. If the various excise duties in the Community States were abolished, the resultant losses of revenue would have to be offset by increasing VAT rates, which would be certain to have an inflationary effect on their economies. Thus, for example, manufactured tobacco products and mineral oils bear, without major drawbacks, very high taxes, which on average yield more than 10% of the tax revenue of the EU States. Moreover, within the overall context of a tax scheme, excise duties constitute **flexible components**, which can easily be manoeuvred if further tax revenue is needed. As they are separate taxes, excise duties can easily be adapted to the various economic, social and structural requirements. Lastly, they can be levied specifically in order to reduce consumption of certain products, such as tobacco products and alcoholic drinks, for public health reasons, and petroleum products for reasons of environment linked energy savings and reduction of energy dependence.

But if some excise duties had to be maintained in the Community two conditions had to be met so as **not to disturb the common market**: their structures had to be harmonised, so as to remove taxation indirectly protecting national production; and their rates had to be harmonised so as to eliminate, in trade between Member States, taxation and tax refunds as well as frontier controls, which disturbed the free movement of goods within the common market.

Taking account of these conditions, a Directive defines the **general arrangements** for the holding and movement of products subject to excise duty[1]. In contrast to the harmonised VAT system, the general arrangements for excise duties are definitive. The taxable event takes place at the stage of manufacture in the Community or of import into the Community from a third country. The tax is payable when the product is put up for consumption and must be acquitted in the country of actual consumption. The Member States have the option of introducing or maintaining taxation on other products and services, provided however that this taxation does not give rise to border crossing formalities in trade between the Member States.

Excise duties are paid by the consignee in the country of destination and the appropriate provisions are taken to this effect. For commercial operations, the Community system is similar to that applied within a state. The movement of products subject to suspended excise duty is run through interconnected bonded warehouses and is covered by an accompanying document, which has been harmonised at Community level. The payment of the excise due in the Member State of destination can be assumed by a fiscal representative established in this State and designated by the consignor. The appropriate provisions are taken to enable the exchange of information between all the Member States concerned by the movement of goods subject to excise with a view to ensuring effective fraud control[2]. Individuals can purchase the products of their choice in other Member States, inclusive of tax, for their personal use. Denmark, Finland and Sweden are, however, authorised by the Council to continue restricting the quantities of certain alcoholic drinks and tobacco products which individuals purchase in other Member States and import for their own consumption. Following these general guidelines, seven specific directives harmonise the structures and minimum excise duty rates on manufactured tobaccos, mineral oils, spirits and alcoholic beverages.

The Directive on taxes which affect the consumption of **manufactured tobacco** was consolidated in 1995[3]. It lays down general principles for the harmonisation of the structure of the excise duty on manufactured

---

[1] Directive 92/12, OJ L 76, 23.03.1992 and Directive 2004/106, OJ L 359, 04.12.2004.
[2] Decision 1152/2003, OJ L 162, 01.07.2003.
[3] Directive 95/59, OJ L 291, 06.12.1995 and Directive 2002/10, OJ L 46, 16.02.2002.

tobacco. Directive 92/79, on the approximation of excise-duty rates on cigarettes, stipulates that total excise duty (specific duty plus proportional duty calculated on the basis of the maximum retail sales price, before VAT) must constitute at least 57% of the retail selling price (inclusive of all taxes) and which shall not be less than EUR 60 per 1000 cigarettes for cigarettes of the price category most in demand. Directive 92/80, on the approximation of taxes on manufactured tobaccos other than cigarettes (cigars, cigarillos, tobacco for rolling cigarettes and other tobaccos for smoking), sets minimum total excise duties for these products, but grants the Member States the option of applying them either as specific excise duty per unit, or proportional excise duty calculated on the basis of the maximum retail sales price, or a combination of the two[1].

Directive 2003/96 has restructured the Community framework for the **taxation of energy products and electricity**, establishing minimum rates of taxation of mineral oils, coal, natural gas and electricity when used as motor fuel or heating fuel[2].

Directive 92/83 covers the harmonisation of excise-duty structures on **spirits and alcoholic beverages**[3]. Directive 92/84 sets minimum excise duties on spirits and alcoholic beverages at the following levels: EUR 550 per hectolitre of pure alcohol; EUR 45 per hectolitre for intermediary products; EUR 0 for wine; EUR 1.87 per hectolitre per degree of alcohol in the finished product for beer[4]. However, the Commission rightly believes that greater convergence is needed between the rates of excise duty applied in different Member States, so as to reduce distortions of competition and fraud, induced by different rates for the various categories of alcoholic drinks[5].

14.2.4. Other indirect taxation

Various other indirect taxes whose harmonisation is important for European integration also exist in addition to value added tax and special taxes on consumption. Examples of these are taxes on insurance policies and taxes on motor vehicles intended for the carriage of passengers, which vary greatly between Member States. The Commission proposes a number of policy measures and initiatives in the area of **passenger car taxation**, in order to provide definitive solutions for the problems faced by citizens and the car industry, and thus improve the functioning of the internal market. It explores the possibilities of modernising and simplifying the existing vehicle taxation systems, and in particular of including new parameters in the tax bases of passenger-car related taxes, in order to make them partially or totally CO_2-based[6]. Since registration tax appears to be the source of most problems encountered in this area, the Commission suggests, as a valid option for future action, a gradual reduction in this tax and preferably complete abolition over a transitional period matched with the gradual transfer of registration tax to annual circulation tax and fuel tax.

Also important from the point of view of competition are capital duty and stamp duty levied on shares in registered capital (shares and securities), as their diversity can give rise to double taxation and distortions of competition and constitute obstacles to the free movement of capital. In order to prevent such problems, a 1969 Directive concerning indirect taxes on the **raising of capital** provided for the harmonisation of capital duties and the abolition of stamp duties, which were deemed to be undesirable from the economic point of view[7]. However, when that Directive was applied it became clear that capital duties could be set at too high a level, especially in certain company-restructuring operations. For that reason it was amended to facilitate the contribution of risk capital to undertakings by reducing their fiscal burden[8].

14.3. Harmonisation of direct taxation

Taxes on the revenue of undertakings (firms, companies, businesses) and private individuals, which are not incorporated in cost prices or selling prices and the rate of which is often progressive, may be regarded as direct taxes. The two important categories of direct taxes are **income tax and capital gains tax**. Article 92 of the EC Treaty prohibits, as regards such taxes, countervailing charges at frontiers, i.e. the application of

---

[1]   Directives 92/78, 92/79 and 92/80, OJ L 316, 31.10.1992 and Directive 2002/10, OJ L 46, 16.02.2002.
[2]   Directive 2003/96, OJ L 283, 31.10.2003 and Directive 2004/74, OJ L 157, 30.04.2004.
[3]   Directive 92/83, OJ L 316, 31.10.1992.
[4]   Directive 92/84, OJ L 316, 31.12.1992.
[5]   COM (2004) 223, 26 May 2004.
[6]   COM (2002) 431, 6 September 2002.
[7]   Directive 69/335, OJ L 249, 03.10.1969.
[8]   Directive 85/303, OJ L 156, 15.06.1985.

remissions and repayments in respect of exports to other Member States. Derogations may not be granted unless the measures contemplated have been previously approved for a limited period by the Council. Apart from that provision, the EC Treaty does not deal with direct taxes and does not call for them to be harmonised.

Whilst the harmonisation of indirect taxes was necessary from the outset to avoid obstacles to trade and to free competition and later to make the removal of fiscal frontiers possible, the harmonisation of direct taxes was not considered indispensable at the common market stage. It gradually became clear, however, that the free movement of capital and the rational distribution of production factors in the Community required a **minimum degree of harmonisation of direct taxes**. In effect, the convergence of Member States' economic policies [see section 7.3.1.] necessitates a coordination of the fiscal instruments used by them. Likewise, the global competitiveness of European businesses requires that the taxation of companies operating in several Member States does not place them at a disadvantage in relation to their competitors restricting their activities to the purely national level. The Commission had tabled proposals to this end in 1969, right after the realisation of the customs union. The Council needed 21 years of debate (!) before it could approve these proposals, vital for transnational cooperation and company mergers in the single market.

14.3.1. Company taxation

The first Directive concerning business taxation, adopted by the Council in July 1990 relates to the taxation system applicable to the **capital gains generated upon the merger**, division, transfer of assets, contribution of assets or exchange of shares between two companies operating in different Member States[1]. National regulations consider this type of operation as a total or partial liquidation of the company making the contribution and subject it to capital gains tax. This is usually set in an artificial manner, since it compares the market value of the good in question (the company itself, a building, land or a share package) to the value entered in the balance sheet, traditionally underestimated. Such a calculation is unjust, insofar as no liquidation is taking place in effect, but two companies from different Member States are forming closer links. The Community solution consists of not taxing the capital gain at the time when the merger or contribution of assets takes place but rather when it is collected. This solution encourages the formation of "European companies", which usually result from the merger of companies originally established in different Member States.

The second Council Directive of July 1990 relates to the common fiscal system applicable to **parent companies and subsidiaries** situated in different Member States[2]. There can be little doubt that the decision by a company to set up a subsidiary in another Member State of the Community would be adversely affected by the fact that the dividends of the latter would be subject, on the one hand, to corporation tax in the country where it had its domicile and, on the other, to a non-recoverable withholding tax, in the Member State where the subsidiary would be domiciled. The Directive abolishes withholding taxes on dividends distributed by a subsidiary to its parent company established in another Member State.

A **code of conduct on business taxation** engages the Member States not to bring in any tax rules which constitute harmful tax competition and to phase out existing rules including withholding taxes on interest and royalty payments between companies form-

---

[1]   Directive 90/434, OJ L 225, 20.08.1990 and Directive 2005/19, OJ L 58, 04.03.2005.
[2]   Directive 90/435, OJ L 225, 20.08.1990 last amended by Directive 2003/123, OJ L 7, 13.01.2004.

ing part of a group[1]. A group within the framework of the Council has the task to assess the tax measures that may fall within the scope of the code and to oversee the provision by the Member States of information on those measures[2]. A Commission notice clarifies the application of the State aid rules to measures relating to direct business taxation[3].

A common system of taxation is applicable to interest and royalty payments made between **associated companies in different Member States[4]**. Therefore, interest or royalty payments arising in a Member State are exempted from any taxes imposed on those payments in that State, whether by deduction at source or by assessment. For budgetary reasons, Greece, Spain and Portugal may apply transitional measures in introducing the new system.

The Commission has proposed a strategy for providing companies with a **consolidated corporate tax base (CCCTB)** for their EU-wide activities as a fundamental part of the strategy for achieving the Lisbon goals[5], but it acknowledges the existence of many problems in its implementation[6].

In July 1990, representatives of the Member States also signed a Convention providing for the introduction of an **arbitration procedure** in the event of disagreement between the tax authorities of the Member States relating to a cross-border operation[7]. This ensures the avoidance of double taxation arising when an adjustment to the profits of a company carried out by the tax authority of one Member State is not matched by a similar adjustment in the Member State of the partner company. Such double taxation would penalise European transnational cooperation. A time limit has been placed on the procedure, so that lengthy delays lasting for several years and generating additional costs cannot develop. The company concerned by the measures in question becomes rapidly a party to the procedure and consequently has an opportunity to put its viewpoint forward.

In the "Schumacker" case, the Court of Justice found that, although direct taxation does not as such fall within the competence of the Community, the powers retained by the Member States must nevertheless be **exercised consistently with Community law**, and in particular with the rules governing the free movement of workers, which require the abolition of any discrimination based on nationality[8]. Thus, tax benefits granted only to residents of a Member State can constitute indirect taxation by reason of nationality, but only where different rules were applied to comparable situations or the same rule was applied to different situations. Where direct taxes are concerned, however, the Court found that the situations of residents and non-residents are not, as a rule comparable and, therefore, a non-resident can be taxed by a Member State more heavily on his income than a resident in the same employment.

14.3.2. Effort to combat tax avoidance

The most important and urgent problems for the Community in the area of direct taxation were posed by **international tax avoidance**. In addition to the substantial budgetary losses for States and the fiscal injustice, international tax avoidance generates abnormal capital movements and distortions of conditions of competition. Therefore, a 1977 Directive instituted a **mutual assistance by the competent authorities** of the Member States in the field of direct taxation (income tax, company tax and capital gains tax) and certain excise duties and taxation of insurance premiums[9]. That Directive introduced a procedure for the systematic exchange of information directed towards enabling them to effect a correct assessment of direct taxes in the Community. It permits the Member States to coordinate their investigative action against cross-border tax fraud and to carry out more procedures on behalf of each other. A regulation lays down a set of

---

[1]   Resolution, OJ C 2, 06.01.1998, p. 2-5.
[2]   Council conclusions, OJ C 99, 01.04.1998, p. 1-2.
[3]   Commission notice, OJ C 384, 10.12.1998.
[4]   Directive 2003/49, OJ L 157, 26.06.2003 and directive 2004/66, OJ L 168, 01.05.2004.
[5]   COM/2001/582, 23.10.2001.
[6]   COM/2006/157, 05.04.2006.
[7]   Convention 90/436, OJ L 225, 20.08.1990, p. 10-24.
[8]   Judgment of 14 February 1995, case C-279/93, Finanzamt Köln-Altstadt/R. Schumacker, ECR 1995, p. I-0225.
[9]   Directive 77/799, OJ L 336, 27.12.1977, Directive 2003/93, OJ L 264, 15.10.2003 and Directive 2004/106, OJ L 359, 04.12.2004.

conditions and procedures to assist administrative authorities in preventing fraud and distortions of competition in movements of excisable products[1].

However, the liberalisation of capital movements as from 1 July 1990 [see section 6.7.], has **increased the risk of tax evasion**. In fact, Community residents can nowadays freely transfer their savings to bank accounts in any Member State without the corresponding income necessarily being declared to the tax authorities of the State of residence. Since, in several Member States, there is no "withholding tax" on bank interest paid to non-residents, investments would flow towards those States, thus avoiding any taxation. Such capital movements, motivated purely by tax considerations, would be contrary to the optimum allocation of resources, which is the objective of establishing a common financial area [see section 6.6.].

In order to lessen the risk of tax distortion, evasion and avoidance, it was necessary to intensify the exchange of information between tax authorities and to remove the encouragement to invest in a Member State, which applies a more favourable tax scheme than the Member State of the investor, by introducing in all the Member States a relatively low withholding tax. These objectives are aimed at by the Directive ensuring a minimum of effective **taxation of savings income** in the form of interest payments within the Community[2]. Under the terms of the Directive, each Member State should automatically provide the other Member States with information on savings income of their residents. However, Belgium, Luxembourg and Austria may, for a transitional period (until the end of 2009), instead apply a non-final withholding tax to the interest on savings of non-residents. This should be applied at a rate of 15% for the first three years, after which it should rise to 20%, and the percentage of revenue transferred to the Member State of residence of the saver by the Member State of the paying agent should be 75%. In order to preserve the competitiveness of European financial markets, the European institutions entered into discussions with key third countries, such as the USA, Switzerland, Liechtenstein, Monaco, Andorra and San Marino, to promote the adoption of equivalent measures in those countries, notably effective exchange of information. Agreements have been reached with the European countries, notably Switzerland[3], Liechtenstein[4], Andorra[5] and San Marino[6].

Since **in the global economy** capital has become very mobile, the states have a tendency to displace the tax burden towards less mobile bases, such as work, thus driving economic activity towards the black market and/or aggravating the effects on the costs of labour and employment. The most important aspects from the international point of view are: the concealment by some taxpayers of their taxable activities beyond the borders of their states in countries in which the level of taxation is low or the risk of discovery small; the possibilities of avoidance open to multinational companies, especially through the manipulation of transfer prices between undertakings in the same group; and the tax arrangements for holding companies, which is a problem outside the European Union's remit, as a large number of those companies are established in tax havens outside the Union.

---

[1] Regulation 2073/2004, OJ L 359, 04.12.2004.
[2] Directive 2003/48, OJ L 157, 26.06.2003 and decision 2004/587, OJ L 257, 04.08.2004.
[3] Decisions 2004/911 and 2004/912, OJ L 385, 29.12.2004.
[4] Decision 2004/897, OJ L 379, 24.12.2004.
[5] Decision 2005/356, OJ L 114, 04.05.2005.
[6] Decision 2005/357, OJ L 114, 04.05.2005.

14.4. Appraisal and outlook

The aim of creating a unified fiscal area in the European Union is ambitious, even if unification means the harmonisation of national tax laws rather than the creation of a federal tax system. Fiscal unification could only be achieved progressively, in line with the convergence of the national economies. It was, however, urgent for the common market to harmonise turnover tax structures and consequently to **achieve fiscal neutrality**, i.e. equal tax treatment of domestic products and products imported from the Member States. That was to a large extent achieved with the adoption of the VAT system by all the original Member States at the beginning of the 1970s and by the new Member States after their accession. Such a close harmonisation of turnover taxes as that resulting from the adoption by all Member States of the value added tax with a uniform basis of assessment was not called for by the Treaty of Rome. The Member States therefore went beyond what was required of them by the Treaty.

Twenty years later, under pressure from the completion of the single market which required the abolition of fiscal frontiers, the Member States also agreed to harmonise their excise duties, thus proving that when the political will exists, the technical problems of multinational integration can always be overcome. Indeed, the harmonisation of VAT rates and of excise-duty structures and rates, achieved in 1992, meant a great deal of **upheaval in the tax revenue of the Member States** that rely heavily on revenue from indirect taxation. However, despite the reservations and the predictions of impending disaster among some fiscal experts, they have been able to carry out this harmonisation without major upset. This fact tends to demonstrate that the multinational integration process brings about dynamic effects that are sometimes overlooked by conservative considerations [see section 1.1.2.].

The harmonisation of indirect taxation is very important, not just for the smooth operation of the internal market but also for the **convergence of economic conditions in the Member States** [see section 7.3.1.]. The VAT and excise duties arrangements enable companies to sell, purchase and invest in all the Member States without being subject to controls or formalities arising from the crossing of borders. Individuals can purchase goods in all the Community countries and, without restriction, bring them back for their personal consumption without any checks or taxation on border crossing. The trans-European computerised networks ensure the imposition of goods and services in all the Member States in accordance with Community tax legislation.

Some very important areas of direct taxation, such as personal income tax, are not directly targeted by the harmonisation process, and the propensity to align the rates and the progressivity effect is markedly less. **As EMU advances**, however, a procedure for the coordination of national fiscal policies will have to be introduced to enable these policies to converge progressively in parallel with the convergence of economic policies. Such coordination should not necessarily aim at uniform tax rates, but should strive to reduce the continuing distortions in the single market, to get tax structures to develop in more employment and environment-friendly way and to prevent losses of tax revenue. Indeed, all Member States have common problems, notably that of capital evasion to fiscal paradises and even that of competition among themselves in order to attract capital while penalising their work forces. If they would put together part of their sovereignty in the fiscal field so as to take common measures, Member States could better face international competition and avoid seeing the money market forces obstruct their common goals.

The definitive VAT system should be as simple as possible for enterprises, particularly SMEs, in order to make Community firms more competitive both within the internal market and in other markets by cutting costs of transactions. Moreover, the definitive system should preserve the neutral effect of VAT on competition as regards the origin of goods and services. It should prevent fraud mechanisms known as "carousel fraud", whereby goods can move within the Community without being taxed. It should also satisfy Member States' justified budgetary interests by avoiding falls in tax revenue throughout the Community and shifts in tax revenue between Member States. Last but not least, the definitive system should be simple and transparent, thus promoting voluntary compliance with the law and allowing a better utilisation of resources assigned to the detection and combating of fraud.

As regards **direct taxation**, the harmonisation process will of necessity be longer, because it is more difficult. However, differences in corporate taxation between the Member States influence investment location and lead to distortions of competition. Given that companies in the EU need to comply with twenty-seven different sets of rules, tax obstacles hamper cross-border economic activity and restructuring operations. These obstacles can be removed only by a combination of targeted measures and a comprehensive solution (creation of one consolidated corporate tax base) enabling companies to view their investments in the different Member States as investments in a domestic market. Moreover, in order to tackle harmful tax competition between Member States, the Community must reverse the trend towards higher taxation of labour as a means of compensating for loss of tax income form the mobile production factor that is capital and devise a code of conduct on company taxation inside the single market. Harmonisation of company taxation should preserve and strengthen economic efficiency in the internal market, while boosting the competitiveness of European companies in the world arena.

Bibliography on taxation policy

- AGUNDEZ-GARCIA Ana. *The delineation and apportionment of an EU consolidated tax base for multijurisdictional corporate income taxation: a review of issues and options.* Luxembourg: EUR-OP*, 2006.
- AMATUCCI Andrea (et al. eds.). *International tax law.* Alphen aan den Rijn: Kluwer Law International, 2006.
- ANDERSSON Krister. "An economist's view on source versus residence taxation: the Lisbon objectives and taxation in the European Union" in *Bulletin for International Taxation*, v. 60, n. 10, October 2006, p. 395-401.
- BÉNASSY-QUÉRÉ Agnès (et al.). *Tax competition and public input.* Paris: CEPII, 2005.
- BONTE Christophe. "La fiscalité de l'épargne dans l'UE: un droit de veto accordé à un pays tiers" in *Revue du Marché commun et de l'Union européenne*, n. 494, janvier 2006, p. 35-41.
- CADOSCH Roger (et al.). "The 2006 Leiden Alumni Forum on taxation of cross-border dividends in Europe and the relation with third countries: the cases pending before the European Court of Justice" in *Intertax*, v. 34, n. 12, December 2006, p. 622-635.
- CERIONI Luca. "Commission communication and general developments regarding home state taxation" in *European Taxation*, v. 46, n. 8, August 2006, p. 375-382.
    - "The possible introduction of common consolidated base taxation via enhanced cooperation: some open issues" in *European Taxation*, v. 46, n. 5, May 2006, p. 187-196.
- COURJON Odile. "Nouveau projet de directive TVA sur les services: mode d'emploi", *Les Petites affiches*, v. 394, n. 222, 8 novembre 2005, p. 9-15.
- DE WOLF Michel. *Souveraineté fiscale et principe de non-discrimination dans la jurisprudence de la Cour de justice des Communautés européennes et de la Cour suprême des État-Unis.* Bruxelles: Bruylant; Paris: LGDJ, 2005.
- DOUMA Sjoerd. "The three Ds of direct tax jurisdiction: disparity, discrimination and double taxation" in *European Taxation*, v. 46, n. 11, November 2006, p. 522-533.
- EURA-AUDIT INTERNATIONAL. *Les impôts en Europe = Taxes in Europe: 2006.* Paris: Delmas, 2006.
- GORMLEY Laurence. *EU taxation law.* Richmond: Richmond Law & Tax, 2006.
- MAITROT DE LA MOTTE Alexandre. *Souveraineté fiscale et construction communautaire: recherche sur les impôts directs.* Paris: LGDJ, 2005.
- MARTINEZ-MONGAY Carlos, SEKKAT Khalid. *Progressive Taxation, Macroeconomic Stabilization and efficiency in Europe.* Brussels: European Commission, 2005.
- MÖSSNER Manfred. "Source versus residence: an EU perspective" in *Bulletin for International Taxation*, v. 60, n. 12, December 2006, p. 501-506.
- ORGANISATION FOR ECONOMIC COOPERATION AND DEVELOPMENT. *Recent tax policy: trends and reforms in OECD countries.* Paris: OECD, 2005.

- ROHATGI Roy. *Basic international taxation. Volume one, Principles of international taxation.* Richmond: Richmond Law & Tax, 2005.
- SERLOOTEN Patrick. *Droit fiscal des affaires.* Paris: Dalloz, 2005.
- UHL Susanne. "Time for a tea party? Why tax regimes beyond the nation state matter, and why citizens should care" in *European review: interdisciplinary journal of the Academia Europaea*, v. 14, n. 4, October 2006, p. 565-585.

Chapter 15

COMPETITION POLICY

Diagram of the chapter

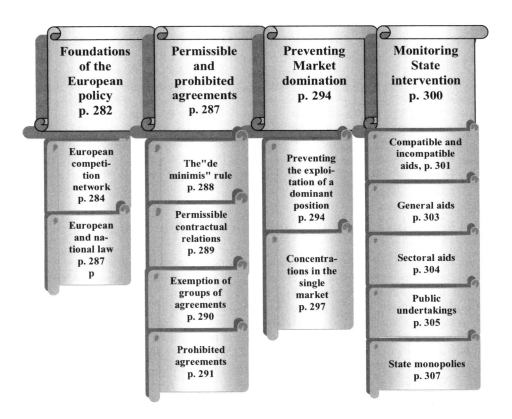

The essence of the single market is the possibility of undertakings to compete on equal terms on the markets of all the Member States. Therefore, the common competition policy is **essential to the achievement and maintenance of the single market** [see section 6.1.]. It ensures the competitive conduct of undertakings (firms, companies, businesses) and protects the interests of consumers by enabling them to procure goods and services on the best terms. It promotes economic efficiency by creating a climate favourable to innovation and technical progress [see section 17.1.]. It prevents anti-competitive practices on the part of companies, which might choke off the competitive dynamics generated by the completion of the single market.

Common competition rules, necessary for preserving a level playing field for all undertakings in the internal market, may go against national interests and have to be complied with by all governments, which accounts for the **need for a neutral and respected referee placed above the clash of national interests**. The EC Treaty allocates that role to the European Commission. This is indeed one of the few areas in which the Commission has autonomous, supranational power and, in addition to its initiative role, it has the responsibility of taking primary decisions [see section 4.1.2.]. Under the control of the Court of Justice, the Commission establishes Community law on competition, which provides a framework for and orientates national laws [see section 3.3.]. In effect, the national competition authorities put into effect their own national competition law which, in many respects, takes its cue from Community competition law. This means that in many areas the implementation of Community rules can be assigned to Member States' authorities and courts, thus relieving the Commission from routine work.

The common competition policy affects virtually all the **other common policies**, which must comply with its rules [see section 1.1.2]. This is true in particular of industrial policy, as regards structural and sectoral measures, regional policy, as regards State aid for the poor regions, energy and transport policies, as regards the major public and multinational undertakings in those sectors, and agricultural and fisheries policies, as regards common market organisations. A proactive competition policy facilitates business activity, wide dissemination of knowledge, a better deal for consumers and efficient economic restructuring throughout the internal market[1]. Since competition policy is impacting upon the economic performance of Europe, it is a key element of a coherent and integrated policy to foster the competitiveness of Europe's industries and to attain the goals of the Lisbon strategy.

15.1. The need for a common competition policy

Before the opening up of borders to intra-Community trade and competition, prices in some sectors in most countries were artificially maintained at a level that allowed marginal undertakings to survive. **The consumer bore the cost of protecting non-profitable businesses**. In other sectors, unprofitable businesses were supported by aids of all kinds, and it was therefore the taxpayer that kept them alive. Hence, both consumers and taxpayers had a great interest in seeing the unprofitable undertakings disappear from the market thanks to the fair play of competition. This common interest of the citizens of the Member States is a major driving force of the multinational integration process [see section 1.1.2.].

National rules alone cannot ensure competition in a common market. They must be completed by Community rules to cover the cases, which affect trade between the Member States and where, therefore, there is Community competence. In contrast to national competition policies, the common competition policy has **a market integration objective**. It must ensure the unity of the common market by preventing undertakings from dividing it up amongst themselves by means of protective agreements. It must obviate the monopolisation of certain markets by preventing major companies from abusing their dominant position to impose their conditions or to buy out their competitors. Lastly, it

---

[1]   COM (2004) 293, 20 April 2004.

must prevent governments from distorting the rules of the game by means of aids to private sector undertakings or discrimination in favour of public undertakings.

15.1.1. Buoyancy of competition in the large market

The very essence of the large market of the European Union is the liveliness of competition. The large market actually enables undertakings to produce on a large scale, to put in hand modern methods of production and to reduce their costs, to the **benefit of consumers**. Thanks to the common market, consumers have a choice between domestic products and products from partner countries, imported free of quantitative restrictions and customs duties [see section 5.1.]. Their choice naturally turns towards better-quality products, taking into account their price, irrespective of their origin. Consumers are therefore the judges of the performance of businesses in the large market. The least viable firms are obliged to modernise or shut down.

However, in spite of the disappearance of unprofitable firms in the common market, the number of undertakings actually in competition with one another in a specific market increases and the **possibilities for market domination decrease**, as partners' products compete with domestic products on equal terms. In the enlarged market, national monopolies become oligopolies and the number of firms in oligopoly-type markets increases. This results in a tendency towards a drop in the economic clout of national monopolies and oligopolies. Competitive pressures spur firms to greater efficiencies and reduce the prices in high price Member States to levels nearer those in lower priced Member States.

The increase of competition as a result of the creation of the common market involves the upheaval of supply conditions, the **renunciation of traditional habits and behaviour** and, in some instances, the loss of monopoly profits. Such developments cannot leave businessmen indifferent. Their attitude may be positive or negative. In most cases, they will endeavour to preserve or even increase their share of the market by reducing their cost prices through restructuring, investment outlay and rationalising production and distribution methods [see section 17.1.]. Such an approach is in the interest both of consumers, who benefit from plentiful supply on the best possible conditions, and of the businessmen themselves, as they learn to live with the common market and to cope better with international competition. Vertical agreements between producers and local distributors can be used pro-competitively to promote market integration.

15.1.2. Negative reactions to intensified competition

Some businesses might **react negatively to the competitive pressure** imposed by the common market. To counter intensified competition, they might try to strengthen existing national agreements or to establish new horizontal agreements (between producers) and vertical restraints (within distribution chains) at European level. Other companies, having a dominant position in a specific market, might attempt to establish a monopoly in it by buying-out their competitors. Monopolisation of a market can be achieved in two ways: by agreement or by concentration. **An agreement** is defined as an understanding between undertakings which remain autonomous, for the purpose of specific behaviour on the market, in particular the restriction of competitive practices. **Concentrations** eliminate the autonomy of participating undertakings by grouping them under a single economic administration, notably by integrating capital and management. It can be seen that agreements have the effect of imposing a specific behaviour, whilst concentrations entail changing the structure of undertakings.

Some agreements are conservative in nature, as they are generally intended to protect established interests, including less competitive firms. By artificially limiting competition between participating companies, such agreements isolate them from the pressures, which would normally push them to conceive new products or more efficient production methods. On the other hand, concentrations mostly contribute to eliminating (through mergers) the least viable and least efficient undertakings. Agreements may be in the interest of the consumer and may be permitted if they are directed towards research, specialisation and cooperation to improve production and distribution methods. **Concentrations are in principle acceptable**, as the market, extended by economic integration, calls for larger undertakings and because, through the improvement of structures, rationalisation of production and the securing of internal economies, they reduce production costs to the advantage of the consumer. However, where concentrations exceed certain limits, they begin to present dangers, as the very large company can exploit its dominant market position to remove all competition. For that reason, European institutions must monitor not only agreements, but also concentrations.

In order to ensure that undertakings operating in the internal market enjoy the same conditions of competition everywhere, efforts have to be made to combat not only unfair practices on the part of undertakings, but also **discriminatory measures on the part of States**. Economic integration and the increasing liberalisation of international trade greatly weaken the classical methods of commercial protection, viz. high customs duties and quantitative restrictions on imports as well as technical barriers to trade. For that reason, States have more frequent recourse to **aids as an instrument of economic policy**, especially given that increased competition and more rapid technological change reveal structural weaknesses in several sectors and regions. Some aids are doubtless justified on the grounds of social policy or regional policy, while others are necessary to direct businesses towards the requisite adjustments at an acceptable social cost. But the Member States' aid policies are often aimed at artificially ensuring the survival of sectors undergoing structural difficulties. Such aid measures run counter to the changes to the production structures inherent in technological progress and their social cost is often greater than the sums allocated to them, as they block production factors which could be better employed elsewhere. In addition, such uncoordinated measures at European level lead to spiralling aid, as each country finds itself obliged to follow in its neighbour's footsteps whenever the latter supports an economic activity. All these reasons necessitate European control of national aids.

One of the most intricate problems in the field of competition is posed by **public undertakings** and undertakings controlled by the public authorities. Member States use them as instruments for attaining various economic, political and social objectives such as directing investment towards certain sectors or regions, administering certain unprofitable public services, handling certain economic activities regarded as strategic, acting as the nation's standard bearer in the arena of international competition and employ persons who do not find jobs in the private sector. In return for the manifold services they render to governments, the latter tend to discriminate in favour of public undertakings. The various privileges, which are granted to them, can distort conditions of competition vis-à-vis undertakings in the private sector of their own nationality and those of their partners in the common market. It is this latter aspect of relations between Member States and their public undertakings that is of particular concern for the European institutions.

15.2. Foundations of the European policy

Protectionist agreements, concentrations, national aids and discrimination in favour of public undertakings are incompatible with the common market. They **must be controlled by the European institutions** on the basis of European criteria, because the Member States' competition policies, even when they are stringent, are not efficacious at European level. Therefore, Article 3 of the EEC Treaty, given over to the principles of the Community, provided for the institution "of a system ensuring that competition in the internal market is not distorted", and the whole chapter on competition allocated to the

Community the task of organising intra-Community trade, free from tariff barriers, on the basis of the law of supply and demand.

The competition rules of the Treaty are interpreted and applied through Council regulations and Commission regulations as well as through general communications and individual decisions of the Commission. Regulation N° 17 of 1972, first Regulation implementing Articles 85 and 86 of the EEC Treaty[1], was replaced by Regulation 1/2003 on the implementation of the rules on competition laid down in Articles 81 and 82 of the EC Treaty (which have the same content as Articles 85 and 86 EEC)[2]. Whereas Regulation 17/62 was based on prior notification and centralised Commission authorisation of agreements, Regulation 1/2003 is based on ex post control and on a **decentralised application of the competition rules** of Articles 81(1), 81(3) and 82 by the national authorities and courts, thus relieving the Commission of the examination of trivial cases and the industry of the costs connected with notification. On the basis of this regulation, agreements, decisions and concerted practices caught by Article 81(1) of the Treaty, which do not satisfy the conditions of Article 81(3), are prohibited, no prior decision to that effect being required. This is also the case concerning an abuse of a dominant position referred to in Article 82 of the Treaty. On the contrary, agreements, decisions and concerted practices, which satisfy the conditions of Article 81(3) of the Treaty [see section 15.3.2.], are not prohibited, no prior decision to that effect being required.

The basic principle of Regulation 1/2003 is the application by all decision-making bodies of a single set of rules whenever there is an effect on trade between Member States. The administrative constraints on cooperating companies are reduced thanks to the removal of the prior notification requirement. Where their transactions affect trade between Member States, they have to deal only with Community law instead of 25 legislative systems, which helps ensure homogeneous conditions of competition. Eliminating the notification requirement also helps the Commission to focus on combating the most serious restrictions and abuses, all the more so since the regulation increases the means at its disposal for detecting and punishing cartels and other infringements. The national competition authorities and the Commission cooperate within a network in order to monitor business agreements and punish infringements of the Community competition rules. National courts are enabled to protect the individual rights of citizens under Community law by granting damages and interest or by ruling on the performance of contracts. The decentralisation ensures, by way of information-exchange and cooperation mechanisms, equal treatment for economic players throughout the EU and consistent application of the rules.

A series of documents, known as the "**modernisation package**" and designed to modernise antitrust procedures, supplements Regulation 1/2003. The package comprises a regulation relating to the conduct of proceedings by the Commission pursuant to Articles 81 and 82[3] and six Commission notices outlining key aspects of the new system for implementing Articles 81 and 82, including the functioning of the network of competition authorities, the new platform for cooperation between the Commission and the national competition authorities. The other documents cover the application of Article 81(3) under the new system, the concept of the effect on trade between Member States, cooperation between the Commission and the courts of the Member States, informal guidance given by the Commission to companies and the handling of complaints by the Commission.

Since 1 January 1994, the competition rules of the European Union have been extended to the whole **European Economic Area (EEA)**. Articles 81 and 82 (TEC), which ban agreements and abuse of dominant position respectively, are therefore now applicable in Norway, Iceland and Liechtenstein in accordance with Articles 53 and 54 of the EEA Agreement [see section 25.1.]. Less strict rules of competition are contained in the association and cooperation agreements concluded with the independent States of the former Soviet Union.

An Agreement between the European Communities and the Government of the **United States of America** is intended to promote cooperation and coordination between the competition authorities of the two parties aimed at combating anticompetitive practices with a global dimension[4]. Cases of common interest are notified between the parties and may give rise to detailed exchanges of information with a view to ensuring consistency between the procedures followed and the remedies applied within the two judicial systems. A supplementary

---

[1] Regulation 17, OJ 13, 21.02.1962 and Regulation 3385/94, OJ L 377, 31.12.1994.
[2] Regulation 1/2003, OJ L 1, 04.01.2003 and Regulation 1419/2006, OJ L 269, 28.09.2006.
[3] Regulation 773/2004, OJ L 123, 27.04.2004.
[4] Decision 95/145 and Agreement, OJ L 95, 27.04.1995, p. 45-52.

Agreement between the EC and the US aims at the application of positive comity principles in the enforcement of their competition laws[1]. It allows either party to request the other to investigate and take action on anti-competitive behaviour occurring in the territory of the latter. Mergers are not covered by this agreement. Similar agreements on cooperation on anti-competitive activities exist also between the European Community and the Governments of **Canada**[2] and **Japan**[3]. Such cooperation benefits competition authorities and companies alike, by finding solutions that are compatible with each party's rules.

Following the expiry on 23 July 2002 of the Treaty establishing the **European Coal and Steel Community** [see section 2.1.], the sectors previously covered by that Treaty and the procedural rules and secondary legislation derived from it are subject to the rules of the EC Treaty. According to the Commission, the transition and the accompanying modifications and the substantive and procedural differences between the two regimes (ECSC and EC) do not pose any major problems[4].

15.2.1. European competition network

Council Regulation No 17 of 1962 laid down a system of supervision requiring restrictive practices affecting trade between Member States to be notified to the Commission in order for them to qualify for an exemption[5]. The Commission thus had the exclusive power to authorise restrictive practices meeting the conditions of Article 81 (3) (formerly Article 85(3)) of the EC Treaty. This system of centralised authorisation was necessary and proved very effective in establishing **a "competition culture" in Europe** at a time when the interpretation of Article 81 (restrictive practices) and Article 82 (abuse of a dominant position) was still uncertain and when the Commission was making an effort to integrate national markets which were still very heterogeneous. During the forty years of the existence of Regulation 17/62, however, a great number of individual decisions were made by the Commission applying the exemption criteria of Article 81(3) of the Treaty. National competition authorities and national courts are therefore nowadays well aware of the conditions under which the benefit of Article 81.3 can be granted. Individual exemption decisions taken by the Commission are thus no longer indispensable to ensure a uniform application of Article 81(3) of the Treaty. Moreover, a system of notifications, entailing a great scrutiny workload for the Commission, is no longer workable in a Union of 27 Member States.

Therefore, at the proposal of the Commission, Regulation 1/2003 replaced its absolute powers in the field of competition by a network of competition authorities, called the **European Competition Network (ECN)**, which is a key plank of the new enforcement system. Formed by the Commission and the competition authorities of the Member States, this network of public authorities applies the Community competition rules in close cooperation, providing for an allocation of cases according to the principle of the best-placed authority, the objective being that each case should be handled by a single authority. In addition, the Commission consults an Advisory Committee on Restrictive Practices and Dominant Positions, composed of representatives of the competition authorities of the Member States.

The Commission may continue to adopt so called "block" exemption regulations by which it declares Article 81(1) of the Treaty inapplicable to categories of agreements, decisions and concerted practices. It may still adopt individual decisions prohibiting serious cartels affecting trade between the Member States and having the effect of restricting competition. Where the Commission, acting on a complaint or on its own initiative, finds that there is an infringement of Article 81 or of Article 82 of the Treaty, it may by

---

[1] Decision 98/386 and Agreement, OJ L 173, 18.06.1998, p. 26-31.
[2] Decision 1999/445 and Agreement, OJ L 175, 10.07.1999.
[3] Decision 2003/520 and Agreement, OJ L 183, 22.07.2003.
[4] Commission communication, OJ C 152, 26.06.2002.
[5] Regulation 17/62, OJ 13, 21.02.1962 and Regulation 1/2003, OJ L 1, 04.01.2003.

decision require the undertakings and associations of undertakings concerned to bring such infringement to an end. For this purpose, it may impose on them any behavioural or structural remedies which are proportionate to the infringement committed and necessary to bring the infringement effectively to an end.

On their side, **national competition authorities and courts** are empowered to apply Community law. They have the power to apply not only Article 81(1) and Article 82 of the Treaty, which have direct applicability by virtue of the case-law of the Court of Justice, but also Article 81(3) of the Treaty. This means that national competition authorities are empowered to withdraw the benefit of a Community block exemption regulation [see section 15.3.3.]. National competition authorities may take the following decisions: requiring that an infringement be brought to an end, ordering interim measures, accepting commitments, imposing fines, periodic penalty payments or any other penalty provided for in their national law. National courts may apply Community competition rules in lawsuits between private parties, acting as public enforcers or as review courts. They can apply Article 81 of the EC Treaty in three types of proceedings: contractual liability proceedings (disputes between parties to an agreement); non-contractual liability proceedings (disputes between a third party and one or more parties to the agreement); and applications for injunctions. In any case, national courts may ask the Commission for information or for its opinion on points concerning the application of Community competition law.

Compliance with Articles 81 and 82 of the Treaty and the fulfilment of the obligations imposed on undertakings and associations of undertakings under Regulation 1/2003 is enforceable by means of fines and periodic penalty payments. The rules on periods of limitation for the imposition of fines and periodic penalty payments were laid down in Regulation 2988/74[1], which also concerns penalties in the field of transport. The imposition or non-imposition of a fine, and the amount thereof, depend in particular on the gravity of the infringement, its duration and the size of the undertakings involved. An intentional infringement usually leads to a heavier fine than when undertakings are simply guilty of negligence. Practices that have already in the past been frequently punished by the Commission also carry heavier fines, as the earlier decisions of the Commission and of the Court of Justice should have alerted undertakings to the unlawful nature of such behaviour. The Commission may also impose on undertakings and associations of undertakings fines where, intentionally or negligently, they supply incorrect or misleading information, do not supply information within the required time-limit or refuse to submit to inspections.

Commission action in the area of competition is controlled, from the legal standpoint, by the **Court of Justice**, which can rescind or amend any formal Commission decision, i.e. negative clearances, decisions granting or refusing an exemption, orders to put an end to infringements, etc. [see section 4.1.5.]. The Court may also confirm, reduce, repeal or increase the fines and penalty payments imposed by the Commission. Any natural or legal person in respect of whom a decision has been taken may institute proceedings before the Court, as may any other person directly and individually concerned by a decision of which he is not the addressee. The Commission's competition policy is controlled, from the political standpoint, by the **European Parliament** [see section 4.1.3], which adopts positions on its guidelines and scrutinises its annual report on competition.

---

[1] Regulation 2988/74, OJ L 319, 29.11.1974.

In practical terms, the competition authorities of each Member State are required to work closely with the Commission and the competition authorities of the other Member States so as to guarantee the maintenance of a system which ensures that competition is not distorted and promote **uniform application of the competition rules**. The competition authorities of the Member States must, when acting under Article 81 or Article 82 of the Treaty, inform the Commission in writing before or without delay after commencing the first formal investigative measure. This information may also be made available to the competition authorities of the other Member States. The information of the Commission is also mandatory in case of a decision requiring that an infringement be brought to an end, accepting commitments or withdrawing the benefit of a block exemption Regulation. National competition authorities may also exchange between themselves information, including any confidential information, necessary for the assessment of a case that they are dealing with under Article 81 or Article 82 of the Treaty.

The Commission is empowered throughout the Community to **require such information to be supplied as is necessary** to detect any agreement, decision or concerted practice prohibited by Article 81 of the Treaty or any abuse of a dominant position prohibited by Article 82 of the Treaty. Undertakings are obliged to answer factual questions and to provide documents, even if this information may be used to establish against them or against another undertaking the existence of an infringement. The Commission is also empowered to undertake such inspections as are necessary to detect any agreement, decision or concerted practice prohibited by Article 81 of the Treaty or any abuse of a dominant position prohibited by Article 82 of the Treaty. It is in particular empowered to interview any persons who may be in possession of useful information and to record the statements made. Officials and other persons authorised by the Commission are empowered to enter any premises where business records may be kept, including private homes. The competition authorities of the Member States must cooperate actively in the exercise of these powers.

Where the Commission, acting on a complaint or on its own initiative, finds that there is an infringement of Article 81 or of Article 82 of the Treaty, it may by decision require the undertakings and associations of undertakings concerned to bring such infringement to an end. For this purpose, it may impose on them any **behavioural or structural remedies**, which are proportionate to the infringement committed and necessary to bring the infringement effectively to an end. The initiation by the Commission of proceedings for the adoption of a decision relieves the competition authorities of the Member States of their competence to apply Articles 81 and 82 of the Treaty. If a competition authority of a Member State is already acting on a case, the Commission must only initiate proceedings after consulting with that national competition authority.

In order to ensure the effective enforcement of the Community competition rules and the proper functioning of the cooperation mechanisms contained in Regulation 1/2003, the competition authorities and courts of the Member States must apply Articles 81 and 82 of the Treaty where they apply national competition law to agreements and practices which may affect trade between Member States. In order to create a level playing field for businesses, the application of **national competition laws** may not lead to the prohibition of such agreements, decisions and concerted practices, if they are not also prohibited under Community competition law. The notions of agreements, decisions and concerted practices are autonomous concepts of Community competition law covering the coordination of behaviour of undertakings on the market as interpreted by the Community Courts. However, Regulation 1/2003 does not preclude Member States from implementing on their territory national legislation, which protects other legitimate interests provided that such legislation is compatible with general principles and other provisions of Community law. This is particularly the case of legislation which prohibits undertakings from imposing on their trading partners, obtaining or attempting to obtain from them terms and conditions that are unjustified, disproportionate or without consideration.

In any national or Community proceedings for the application of Articles 81 and 82 of the Treaty, the burden of proving an infringement of Article 81(1) or of Article 82 of the Treaty (**burden of proof**) rests on the party or the authority alleging the infringement. The undertaking or association of undertakings claiming the benefit of Article 81(3) of the Treaty must bear the burden of proving that the conditions of that paragraph are fulfilled.

In accordance with Articles 53 and 54 of the **Agreement on the European Economic Area** [see section 25.1.], the European Commission must verify whether the cases referred to it come under these articles. It must act in cases likely to affect inter-State trade within the EEA, and also when the practices in question threaten to upset trade between one of the EU States and one or several of the EFTA States, on condition that the companies in question achieve over 67% of their combined turnover for the EEA on the territory of the EU. On the other hand, the EFTA Surveillance Authority decides in cases involving firms whose turnover on EFTA territory is equal or above 33% of turnover on EEA territory, except when trade within the EU is affected. Responsibility is shared out in the same way for negative clearance applications concerning a dominant position. Community-scale concentrations naturally remain under the responsibility of the Commission. The latter has laid out in a Regulation the details of the implementation of the competition rules established in the EEA Agreement[1].

---

[1]   Regulation 3666/93, OJ L 336, 31.12.1993.

15.2.2. European law and national competition law

In the field of competition, national competence and Community competence are autonomous and parallel, the latter being defined by the criterion of the effect of trade among Member States. In a concrete case there may be juxtaposition of the validity of European law and national law. In any case, **European law takes precedence over national law** [see section 3.3.]. National authorities may take action against an agreement, pursuant to national law, even where the position of that agreement with regard to Community rules is pending before the Commission. They can also apply the Community competition law. However, the decision resulting from **a national procedure may not run counter to the Commission's decision**. Where the latter precedes the national decision, the competent authorities of the Member State are obliged to observe its effects. Where, on the other hand, the Commission's decision post-dates the national decision and is at variance with its effects, it is for the national authorities to take appropriate measures in conformity with it.

The **Member States cannot oppose Commission decisions**, whereas the Commission can request the competent authorities of the States concerned to proceed with any verification it deems necessary or to collect fines or penalty payments it has imposed. National courts can apply the Community law or refer matters of Community law to the Court of Justice of the European Communities for a preliminary ruling. Appeal courts are obliged to request a preliminary ruling where a decision on the point at issue is necessary to enable them to deliver their judgment.

The Court of Justice has consistently held that **government measures could be regarded as contrary to the competition rules** laid down in the EC Treaty, if they were to impose or encourage the conclusion of agreements contrary to Article 81 (ex Art. 85), to heighten the effects of an agreement (e.g. by guaranteeing provisions of an existing agreement in a given market) or to delegate to private operators the power to take concerned decisions on economic action. On the other hand, national legislation could not be regarded as contrary to the Community rules merely because it had restrictive effects on competition similar to those resulting from measures prohibited by Article 81[1].

As regards **national aids** and discrimination in favour of **public undertakings**, on which the Member States are responsible for infringements of the free-competition arrangements, the precedence of Community law on competition is even more clear-cut. Likewise, it is quite evident that law must be applied by supranational bodies with the power to compel national authorities to comply with their decisions. According to the Court of justice, if a government measure has not been notified to the Commission under Article 92 of the EEC Treaty (Art. 87 TEC) or the Commission has not yet decided whether the measure in question is compatible, the national court must refer any disputes to the Commission for clarification or to the Court for a preliminary ruling[2].

15.3. Permissible cooperations and prohibited agreements

Article 81 of the EC Treaty declares that all agreements between undertakings, decisions by associations of undertakings and concerted practices which may affect trade between Member States and which have as their object or effect the prevention, restriction or distortion of competition within the common market shall be **prohibited as incompatible with the common market**. In particular, this article prohibits agreements which: (a) directly or indirectly fix purchase or selling prices or any other trading conditions; (b) limit or control production, markets, technical development, or investment; (c)

---

[1] Judgments of 17 November 1993, cases C-2/91, C-185/91 and C-245/91, ECR 1993, I-5751, I-5801 and I-5851.
[2] Judgment of 11 July 1996, Case C-39/94, ECR 1996, p. I-3547.

share markets or sources of supply; (d) apply dissimilar conditions to equivalent transactions with other trading parties, thereby placing them at a competitive disadvantage; (e) make the conclusion of contracts subject to acceptance by the other parties of supplementary obligations which, by their nature or according to commercial usage, have no connection with the subject of such contracts. Prohibited agreements shall be automatically void.

However, under **paragraph 3 of Article 81,** the Commission may declare the provisions of paragraph 1 of that Article inapplicable in the case of any agreement or category of agreements between undertakings, any decisions by associations of undertakings and any concerted practice or category of concerted practices, on the following conditions: that they contribute to improving the production or distribution of goods or to promoting technical or economic progress, while allowing consumers a fair share of the resulting benefit, and that they do not afford such undertakings the possibility of eliminating competition in respect of a substantial part of the products in question. On the basis of Regulation 1/2003, agreements, decisions and concerted practices, caught by Article 81(1) of the Treaty, which satisfy the conditions of Article 81(3) of the Treaty, are not prohibited, no prior decision to that effect being required. These conditions can, however, be controlled at any time by the European competition network [see section 15.2.1.].

It ensues that not all agreements between Community undertakings are prohibited - far from it. Most are even desirable with a view to improving the structures of European industry, as we see in the relevant chapter [see section 17.2.4.]. In parallel with the elimination of situations incompatible with the system of competition and market unity, the Commission has in fact always pursued a policy of encouraging cooperation between undertakings where, in its opinion, such cooperation is compatible with the common market and can produce favourable economic effects.

Over the years, the Commission has endeavoured to specify, in a double series of measures, some of which were individual and some general or sectoral (e.g., air transport or telecommunications) [see sections 17.3.6. and 20.3.5.], those agreements **not covered by the prohibition** in Article 85 paragraph 1 (present Art. 81 TEC) [see section 15.3.2.] and those which, although covered by the prohibition, were **likely to be exempted from it** [see sections 15.3.1. and 15.3.3.]. Individual exemption decisions do not lend themselves to ill-considered generalisation, as the conditions for exemption can only be specific on a case-by-case basis. However, some types of clearly defined agreements are covered by group exemptions.

15.3.1. The "de minimis" rule

In a notice on **agreements of minor importance (de minimis)**, the Commission quantifies, with the help of market share thresholds, what is not an appreciable restriction of competition under Article 81 of the EC Treaty[1]. The Commission holds the view that an agreement between undertakings, even if it affects trade between Member States, does not appreciably restrict competition within the meaning of Article 81(1) of the EC Treaty if :(a) the aggregate market share held by the parties to the agreement does not exceed 10% on any of the relevant markets affected by the agreement, where the agreement is made between undertakings **which are actual or potential competitors** on any of these markets; or (b) the market share held by each of the parties to the agreement does not exceed 15% on any of the relevant markets affected by the agreement, where

---

[1]   Commission notice, OJ C 368, 22.12.2001, p. 13.

the agreement is made between undertakings which **are not actual or potential competitors** on any of these markets. In these cases the Commission will not institute proceedings either upon application or on its own initiative.

Agreements entered into by SMEs whose annual turnover and balance-sheet total do not exceed EUR 40 million and 27 million respectively and which have a maximum of 250 employees are rarely capable of appreciably affecting trade between Member States and are not, in principle, investigated by the Commission. However, there exists a "blacklist of hardcore restrictions" - such as price-fixing, market-sharing or territorial protection - which, because of their nature are regarded as typically incompatible with Article 81(1) of the EC Treaty and hence liable to be caught by the ban on agreements, even if the parties' market shares are below the above-mentioned thresholds.

15.3.2. Permissible contractual relations

Agreements between undertakings are not regarded as restricting competition and, therefore, do not need to be notified to the Commission where their purpose is a **form of authorised cooperation,** such as: the joint carrying out of comparative studies, the joint preparation of statistics and models, the joint study of markets, cooperation on accounting, joint financial guarantees, the joint execution of research and development contracts, the joint use of means of production, storage and transport and, under certain conditions, the joint performance of orders, joint selling, joint after-sales and repair service and joint advertising[1].

In order to lift any doubts the Commission specified in two communications the characteristics of very common contractual relations concerning exclusive representation and subcontracting, which do not fall under the prohibition of Article 81, paragraph 1, provided that they do not establish absolute territorial protection. Thus, the Commission considers that an **exclusive representation** contract concluded between a "commercial agent", who does not accept any liability for the financial risks involved in the transactions and he in fact acts only as a simple middleman for a "principal", is not covered by Article 81 paragraph 1[2] [see details below]. **Subcontracts** are also allowed according to the Commission[3] [see also section 17.2.4.]. Subcontracting usually involves, for a small undertaking, known as the "subcontractor", performance of an order for a large undertaking, known as the "principal", in accordance with the directives of the latter. The Commission considers that the obligation to supply only to the latter manufactured objects or work executed does not restrict competition within the meaning of Article 81 of the EC Treaty (former Article 85).

In the case of exclusive representation, it must be ascertained whether or not there is economic integration between the agent and the principal, and to judge that the Commission attaches greater importance to economic reality than to the legal form of relations between undertakings. Thus, the distributor who holds, as owner, a considerable stock of the product covered by the contract or who, at his own expense, provides a significant service to his clientele free of payment or who himself determines the selling prices or the other conditions of the transaction, is regarded as a self-employed trader, in which case Article 81 paragraph 1 (TEC) applies. However, Article 85 paragraph 1 does not apply in relations between a parent company and its subsidiary, where the latter is not free to determine its action on the market.

---

[1] OJ C 75, 29.07.1968, p. 3-6.
[2] OJ 139, 24.12.1962.
[3] Communication of the Commission, OJ C 1, 03.01.1979, p. 2-3.

15.3.3. Exemption of categories of agreements

Whereas the contractual relations mentioned above are not prohibited by Article 81, paragraph 1, the contractual relations mentioned below are in principle prohibited but can be exempted from the prohibition. Indeed, under paragraph 3 of Article 81, the Commission may declare the **provisions of paragraph 1 inapplicable** in the case of certain agreements or categories of agreements which contribute to improving the production or distribution of goods or to promoting technical or economic progress, while allowing consumers a fair share of the resulting benefit. A Council Regulation empowers the Commission to apply Article 81(3) of the Treaty by regulation to certain categories of agreements, decisions and concerted practices falling within the scope of Article 81(1)[1]. Another Council Regulation lays down the conditions under which the Commission may declare by way of regulation that the provisions of Article 81(1) do not apply to certain categories of agreements and concerted practices[2].

The instrument of the **"block-exemption" regulation** is used by the Commission to discharge a class of similar agreements whose pro-competitive benefits outweigh their anti-competitive effects. These Commission Regulations identify clearly-defined categories of agreements which automatically benefit from the exemption provision of Article 81, paragraph 3, provided that they do not seal off markets by preventing access and parallel trade. These block exemption Regulations are particularly useful for SMEs and were in many respects specifically designed for their benefit.

Following a 1997 Green Paper[3] and a communication of the Commission on the application of the Community competition rules to vertical restraints, Regulation No 17/62 and Regulation 19/65 have been amended with the aim of creating a single block exemption covering all vertical agreements or restraints[4]. Indeed, the general **exemption for certain vertical agreements** has replaced three regulations, one on exclusive distribution, one on exclusive purchasing and one on franchise agreements. Such agreements are concluded between firms operating at different (vertical) levels of the production or distribution chain - in practice all industrial distribution and supply agreements between firms whose market shares do not exceed 30% - and govern the conditions under which distribution firms may acquire from producers, sell or re-sell final or intermediate goods or services. Above the 30% threshold, agreements are not presumed to be unlawful but may require an individual examination. The Commission has issued guidelines intended, first, to clarify how the provisions of the block exemption should be interpreted and, second, to explain the general criteria applicable when examining agreements not covered by the block exemption or when withdrawing the benefit of the exemption regulation[5].

The Commission is favourable to **joint ventures of a cooperative character**, particularly when they can introduce more quickly into Europe a new technology, the development costs of which are very high. Under certain conditions cooperative joint ventures concerning specialisation agreements, research and development agreements, patent licensing agreements and know-how licensing agreements enjoy a block exemption[6] [see details below].

---

[1]   Regulation 2821/71, OJ L 285, 29.12.1971 last amended by Regulation 1/2003, OJ L 1, 04.01.2003.
[2]   Regulation 19/65, OJ 36, 06.03.1965 last amended by Regulation 1/2003, OJ L 1, 04.01.2003.
[3]   COM (96) 721, 22 January 1997.
[4]   Regulations1215/1999 and 1216/1999, OJ L 148, 15.06.1999.
[5]   Commission notice, OJ C 291, 13.10.2000.
[6]   Regulation 151/93, OJ L 21 of 29.01.1993 and OJ C 43, 16.02.1993.

Thus, a block exemption concerns the **specialisation agreements,** i.e. agreements under which the parties mutually undertake not to manufacture certain products themselves in order to specialise in the manufacture of other products[1]. Agreements on specialisation in production generally contribute to improving the production or distribution of goods, because the undertakings concerned can concentrate on the manufacture of certain products and thus operate more efficiently and supply the products more cheaply. Agreements on specialisation in the provision of services can also be said to generally give rise to similar improvements. On condition that the combined market share of the participating undertakings does not exceed 20% of the relevant market, the exemption covers unilateral or reciprocal specialisation agreements as well as joint production agreements, by virtue of which two or more parties agree to produce certain products jointly.

Consumers can generally be expected to benefit from the increased volume and effectiveness of **research and development** through the introduction of new or improved products or services or the reduction of prices brought about by new or improved processes. Therefore a block exemption is granted, under certain conditions and a market share limitation of 25%, to agreements entered into between two or more undertakings, which pursue joint research and development of products or processes and/or joint exploitation of the results of that research and development [2]. An exemption is also granted to **technology transfer agreements** (licences, patents, know-how and software copyright) entered into between two undertakings permitting the production of contract products[3]. Such agreements are usually considered to improve economic efficiency and be pro-competitive as they can reduce duplication of research and development, strengthen the incentive for the initial research and development, spur incremental innovation, facilitate diffusion and generate product market competition.

The regulations cited above, and regulations on exemption by category dealt with in the sections on insurance (in the chapter on the common market) and air transport (in the chapter on transport), authorise, under certain conditions, the forms of cooperation between undertakings which are the most commonplace and which do not restrict competition in a manner which is incompatible with the rules of competition of the Treaty. They thus govern the vast majority of agreements existing in the Community, providing them with basic legal certainty. The Commission can therefore give its undivided attention to the **prohibited agreements examined below, which are usually secret** and which really impede free competition and trade in the common market.

15.3.4. Prohibited agreements

We shall not attempt, here, to describe all the forms of horizontal agreements which are prohibited by the rules of competition of the Treaties. Each case differs depending on the product concerned, the market involved and the imagination of the executives of the participant undertakings. We shall confine ourselves to **a few characteristic cases** of agreements incompatible with the common market, as emerging from Commission decisions. The Commission judges the advantages and disadvantages of an agreement or category of agreements not on the basis of purely legal criteria, but also using the criterion of the general interest of the producers and consumers in a sector. In addition, it applies the "de minimis" rule, discussed above, to agreements that infringe the rules of competition but the economic impact of which is insignificant.

The sharing of markets is particularly restrictive of competition and at variance with the objectives of the common market, as agreements based on the principle of reciprocal respect of national markets for the benefit of the participants established there have the effect of obstructing intra-Community trade in the products concerned. Through the system of fixing supply quotas on the basis of the total sales of members of the agreement, those members waive the freedom to apply an independent sales policy, but have, on the other hand, the possibility of applying a prices policy shielded from the competition of their partners. The following are celebrated cases of penalised market-sharing agreements: the case of the Community quinine producers, who had decided amongst themselves, by gentleman's agreements, on price regulation and quotas covering all their sales on the internal market and abroad[4]; and the case of the major sugar

---

[1] Regulation 2658/2000, OJ L 304, 05.12.2000.
[2] Regulation 2659/2000, OJ L 304, 05.12.2000.
[3] Regulation 772/2004, OJ L 123, 27.04.2004.
[4] Decision 69/240, OJ L 192, 05.08.1969.

undertakings, which controlled intra-Community trade in sugar for human consumption[1]. Other important cases of prohibited and penalised market sharing agreements are:,that concluded under the aegis of Cembureau, the European Cement Federation covering 9 associations of undertakings and 33 European cement producers [2]; that of the Japanese video games maker Nintendo and seven of its official European distributors[3]; the cartel of the plasterboard producers[4], and the minimum fees determined by the Belgian Architects Association[5]

Agreements on the fixing of prices or of other conditions of transactions seriously limit competition, because they prevent purchasers from benefiting from the competitive behaviour that producers would have shown had the agreement not existed. As they are coupled with reciprocal respect for national markets, they are also likely to have an adverse effect on intra-Community trade. The Commission has therefore prohibited: concerted practices for the purpose of the application by the participating undertakings, on the same dates and in respect of the same categories of product (colorants), identical rates of price increases[6]; horizontal price fixing agreements and horizontal exclusive dealing agreements[7]; the publishing by trade associations of tariff schedules or recommended charges without regard to any differences in firms' cost structures[8]; and concerted methods for calculating a price supplement, as was the case of a price cartel in the stainless steel sector[9]. It should be noted that many cases of prohibited cartels combine **market sharing and fixing of prices**, notably: the one concerning the world market for graphite electrodes[10], the cartel of industrial tube producers[11], and the cartel of the main producers of copper plumbing tubes[12].

Restrictions on access to the market by new entrants are also prohibited. Access to the market can be impeded where a large number of retailers on this market are tied by an obligation to sell only the products of the manufacturer with whom they have a contract or vertical arrangements having a similar exclusionary effect on third parties. This is why, the Commission condemned the exclusivity conditions imposed by Unilever as part of its terms for supplying freezer cabinets to its Irish retailers[13]. In other cases, new competitors can be prevented from entering the market through a horizontal agreement or concerted practice, as in the aforementioned case of the Dutch crane-hire market[14].

The most complicated cases are those of **exclusive distribution agreements,** which are covered by a category exemption, but not where they provide for absolute territorial protection **which prevents parallel imports**. This is the case of agreements, which stand in the way of the distributor re-exporting the products in question to other Member States or of such products being imported from other Member States in the concessionaire's area and being distributed there by persons other than the concessionaire. Commission policy on the matter was clearly set out in its decision of 23 September 1964 in the

---

[1] Decision 73/109, OJ L 140, 26.05.1973.
[2] Decision 94/815, OJ L 343, 30.12.1994.
[3] Decision 2003/675, OJ L 255, 08.10.2003.
[4] Decision 2005/471, OJ L 166, 28.06.2005.
[5] Decision 2005/8, OJ L 4, 06.01.2005.
[6] Decision 69/243, OJ L 195, 07.08.1969.
[7] Decision 95/551, OJ L 312, 23.12.1995.
[8] Decision 96/438, OJ L 181, 20.07.1996.
[9] Decision 98/247/ECSC, OJ L 100, 01.04.1998.
[10] Decision 2002/271, OJ L 100, 16.04.2002.
[11] Decision 2004/421, OJ L 125, 28.04.2004.
[12] Decision 2006/485, OJ L 192, 13.07.2006.
[13] Decision 98/531, OJ L 246, 04.09.1998.
[14] Decision 95/551, OJ L 312, 23.12.1995.

"Grundig-Consten" case[1], essentially upheld by the Court of Justice in its judgment of 13 July 1966[2]. The Commission continues to fight against distribution systems which impede parallel trade, such as that of Volkswagen, which prohibited its Italian dealers from selling Volkswagen and Audi cars to foreign buyers, thereby restricting intra-Community trade[3] or DaimlerChrysler, which instructed the members of its German distribution network for Mercedes passenger cars not to sell cars outside their respective territories and to oblige foreign consumers to pay a deposit of 15% to DaimlerChrysler when ordering a car in Germany[4].

Isolation of a market within the Community can also occur, without exclusive business relations being agreed upon as in the previous case, through agreements concluded between producers from a Member State in order to grant habitual customers **rebates whose levels are fixed collectively** on the basis of total purchases from those producers during the reference period. This was the case of the agreement of German manufacturers of ceramic tiles[5]. The aggregation of the discount bases induced customers not to consider offers, even if more favourable, from producers in the other Member States, so as to group their purchases with producers participating in the agreement and thus secure the highest possible levels of rebate.

Joint selling is, as a general rule, permitted by the Commission in the context of association agreements, as referred to above. The same is not true, however, of **joint sales agreements** through which the participating undertakings share amongst themselves, in accordance with a specific scale, the total quantity of products on offer through a sales point at uniform prices and on uniform sales terms. The three factors together - the action of the joint body, the apportionment of supply quotas and price-fixing - prevent any competition between the participants on the markets concerned and deprive purchasers of any choice between different offers. For that reason, the Commission penalised the three main French fertiliser producers, the purpose of whose cooperation was to ensure the distribution of their complex fertilisers in Germany solely through the intermediary of a joint commercial company called "Floral"[6].

Joint purchasing agreements may also result in a restriction of competition where the large purchasing capacity of the participating undertakings enables them to abuse their strength vis-à-vis the suppliers. That was the case with the wholesalers participating in the Dutch cooperative VBA, the world's largest flower auction, who had undertaken not to market any products other than those supplied through the VBA[7]. On the other hand, the Commission authorised the Eurovision system of joint purchasing of broadcasting rights for international sporting events. Although the system restricts competition, because of the combined purchasing power enjoyed by the European Broadcasting Union, the Commission accepted it, because it contributes to the development of a genuine European broadcasting market and facilitates cross-border broadcasting, particularly important for the members of the EBU from smaller countries[8].

There are, of course, several other types of unauthorised horizontal agreements, such as those which fix discriminatory conditions in transactions with third parties competing with each party in the agreement, or those aimed at ousting a current competitor from the market or closing it to a potential competitor. Other types of agreements which are normally exempt are liable to come within the scope of Article 81 paragraph 1 (TEC) if they restrict competition and are not covered by the "de minimis" rule, e.g. joint advertising agreements, if they prevent the participants from also promoting their products independently; agreements for the use of a common quality label, if that label may not be used by all manufacturers whose products meet the quality standards in question, and even agreements on the exchange strategy of the participants. In the event of doubt as to the legitimacy of an agreement, undertakings concerned that wish to avoid fines would be **well advised to notify the agreement to the Commission** and ask for a negative clearance.

The Commission acts cautiously with regard to agreements that it considers incompatible with the Treaty. It tries to gather indisputable evidence of the infringement of Article 81 paragraph 1 (TEC), which can, on occasion, take several years, as nowadays restrictions of competition rarely take the form of written agreements obliging contractors to carry out unlawful acts on pain of penalty. They usually take the form of concerted practices based on "gentlemen's agreements", material evidence of which is difficult to find. The Commission's cautious approach on the matter [see section 15.2.1.] has the disadvantage of being slow, but it adds weight to its decisions which are usually upheld by the Court of Justice in the event of the undertakings charged bringing proceedings before it. Those decisions therefore make clear the Community's policy on major

---

[1] Decision 64/566, OJ 161, 20.10.1964, p. 2545.
[2] Joined cases 56 and 58/64, ECR 1966, p. 299.
[3] Decision 98/273, OJ L 124, 25.04.1998.
[4] Decision 2003/792, OJ L 300, 18.11.2003.
[5] Decision 71/23, OJ L 10, 13.01.1971.
[6] Decision 80/182, OJ L 39, 15.02.1980.
[7] Decision 88/491, OJ L 262 of 22.09.1988.
[8] Decision 93/403, OJ L 179, 22.07.1993.

types of prohibited agreements. It should be noted that, according to the Court, actions taken by several under-takings may be the expression of a single complex infringement covered partly by the concept of "agreement between undertakings" and partly by the concept of "concerted practice" both of which are prohibited by Article 81 (TEC)[1].

15.4. Preventing market domination

We shall see in the relevant chapter that, from the point of view of the Community's industrial and enterprise policies, concentrations of small and medium-sized undertakings into larger units are in principle desirable and should be encouraged, as they lead to economies of scale, the rationalisation of the production and distribution of products in the common market and promote technical progress [see section 17.2.1.]. But **if the concentration exceeds certain limits**, which vary from sector to sector, it may result in the formation of monopolies or, more often, oligopolies and the consequent restrictions of competition and intra-Community trade. This occurs in particular where an undertaking, which dominates a sector by virtue of its size and economic strength, acquires the smaller undertakings in competition with it one by one.

15.4.1. Preventing the exploitation of a dominant position

Article 82 of the EC Treaty (ex Art. 86 EEC) stipulates that "**any abuse by one or more undertakings of a dominant position** within the common market or in a substantial part of it shall be prohibited as incompatible with the common market in so far as it may affect trade between Member States". Apart from the fact that this Article does not prohibit the obtaining of a dominant position, but only abuse thereof, it leaves several issues obscure, although they are now clarified by various standard Commission decisions and judgments of the Court of Justice.

First, **domination of a given market** cannot be defined solely on the basis of the market share held by an undertaking or of other quantitative elements, but must also be looked at in the light of its ability to exercise an appreciable influence on the functioning of the market and on the behaviour of other firms. In its judgment of 14 February 1978 in the case of "United Brands Company v. Commission"[2] the Court upheld and enlarged the definition of the dominant position adopted by the Commission as early as its decision of 9 December 1971[3] in the "Continental Can Company" case[4]. It thus stated that the dominant position referred to in Article 86 (EEC)"relates to a position of economic strength enjoyed by an undertaking which enables it to prevent effective competition being maintained on the relevant market by giving it the power to behave to an appreciable extent independently of its competitors, customers and ultimately of its consumers".

The definition of **the relevant market** or of the market in question is also of great importance, as the more strictly that market is defined in time and space, the greater the likelihood that a dominant position can be identified in the common market. In its judgment of 13 February 1979 in the "Hoffman-La Roche v. Commission" case, the Court of Justice felt, in common with the Commission[5], that each group of vitamins constitutes a separate market and that one product can belong to two separate markets if it can be used

[1]   Judgments of 8 July 1999, Cases C-49/92P, C-199/92P and C-235/92P.
[2]   Judgment of 14 February 1978, Case 27/76, United Brands Company v Commission, ECR 1978, p. 207.
[3]   Decision 72/21, OJ L 7, 08.01.1972.
[4]   Judgment of 21 February 1973, Case 6/72, Europemballage Corporation et Continental Can Company, ECR 1973, p. 215.
[5]   Decision 76/642, OJ L 223, 16.08.1976.

for several purposes[1]. The Court held that actual competition must be able to exist between products that belong to the relevant market, which presupposes an adequate degree of interchangeability or substitutability between such products. For the Commission, the assessment of demand substitution entails a determination of the range of products, which are viewed as substitutes by the consumer and their competition can thus affect the pricing of the parties' products. The Commission's notice on the relevant market is an analytical tool which makes it possible to calculate firm's market shares[2].

As regards the concept of the **distortion of trade between Member States,** which is the same for Articles 81 and 82 (TEC), the Commission and the Court of Justice agree that a concentration in which an undertaking occupies a dominant position in the common market or in a substantial part of it will always be of importance for trade between Member States. In its judgment of 13 July 1966 in the "Grundig-Consten" case the Court opined that the concept of damage to trade between Member States should be seen as a question of "whether the agreement is capable of constituting a threat... to freedom of trade between Member States in a manner which might harm the attainment of the objectives of a single market between States"[3]. It goes without saying that abuse of a dominant position is judged all the more harshly because it tends to compartmentalise the relevant market and make economic interpenetration more difficult. That was the case with British Leyland, which refused to issue type-approval certificates for left-hand-drive "Metro" vehicles in order to prevent the re-importation of such vehicles from other Member States[4].

Lastly, as regards the concept of **abuse of a dominant position,** Article 82 is more explicit, as it stipulates that "abuse may in particular, consist in: (a) ... imposing unfair purchase or selling prices or other unfair trading conditions; (b) limiting production, markets or technical development ...; (c) applying dissimilar conditions to equivalent transactions with other trading parties ..." and "(d) making the conclusion of contracts subject to acceptance by the other parties of supplementary obligations" which have no connection with such contracts. We note that the concept of abuse of a dominant position is similar to the concept of restriction or distortion of competition given by article 81 TEC [see section 15.3.].

Generally speaking, an undertaking in a dominant position **may abuse its power on the market in one of the following ways**:

- by setting the prices on the dominated market, (as in the case of Deutsche Telekom AG (DT) concerning the prices for access to its fixed telecommunications network[5]);
- by imposing discriminatory commercial fees on service providers (as in the case of the Aéroports de Paris concerning groundhandling, catering, cleaning and freight handling services[6];
- by "tying" the products or services of the dominated market to other products or services (as in the case of Microsoft Corporation concerning the position of Windows on the market for PC operating systems[7]);

---

[1] Judgment of 13 February 1979, case 85/76, ECR 1979, p. 461.
[2] OJ C 372, 09.12.1997, p. 5-13.
[3] Joined Cases 56 and 58/64, Consten-Grundig v Commission, ECR 1966, p. 299.
[4] OJ L 207, 02.08.1984 and case 226/84, British Leyland PLC v Commission, ECR 1986, p. 3263.
[5] Decision 2003/707, OJ L 263, 14.10.2003.
[6] Decision 98/513, OJ L 230, 18.08.1998.
[7] Case COMP/C-3/37.792, 24.03.2004.

- by imposing on its customers agreements for the exclusive purchase of products (such as the vitamins in the Hoffmann-La Roche case[1]) or services (as in the case of the company operating Frankfurt airport[2]);
- by restricting competition from imports (as in the case of Irish Sugar plc[3]); or
- by attempting to eliminate competition by "predatory pricing", i.e. by selling below cost for a short period of time until the competitors are driven out of the market (as in the case of Deutsche Post AG concerning the market for business parcel services[4]) and in the case of Wanadoo Interactive, a subsidiary of France Télécom, concerning access to the Internet by the general public[5].

It is certain that the Commission and the Court regard it as an abuse where an undertaking in a dominant position strengthens that position by means of a concentration or of **the elimination of competitors**, with the result that competition, which continued in spite of the existence of the dominant position, is virtually eliminated as regards the products concerned in a substantial part of the common market. The Commission accordingly imposed heavy fines on: AKZO Chemie, which is the chemical division of the Dutch multinational group AKZO, for having abused its dominant position on the organic peroxides market by trying to eliminate a small competitor from the market by applying prolonged, selective price-cuts designed to damage its business[6]; and British Sugar plc for implementing a series of abuses designed to eliminate a smaller competitor from the retail sugar market[7]. On July 24, 1991, the Commission imposed a record fine on Tetra Pak for having deliberately attempted to eliminate its actual or potential competitors, in breach of Article 86 of the EEC Treaty (Art. 82 TEC). On 24 March 2004, the Commission fined Microsoft Corporation EUR 497 million, because it used the near-monopoly position enjoyed by its Windows product on the market for PC operating systems to restrict competition on other software markets: work group server operating systems; and the market in media players[8].

In its aforementioned judgment in the "Hoffmann-La Roche" case the Court of Justice for the first time gave a **general definition of abuse** by stating that it is an "objective concept relating to the behaviour of an undertaking in a dominant position which is such as to influence the structure of a market where, as a result of the very presence of the undertaking in question, the degree of competition is weakened and which, through recourse to methods different from those which condition normal competition in products or services on the basis of the transactions of commercial operators, has the effect of hindering the maintenance of the degree of competition still existing in the market or the growth of that competition". In the British Midland/Aer Lingus case, the Commission showed its determination to proceed against any airline or any other holder of a dominant position which tries to stand in the way of the development or maintenance of competition[9].

The "United Brands Company" judgment defines the scope of the concept of abuse by confirming the obligation for an undertaking in a dominant position to respect the principle of proportionality when it imposes restrictions on its resellers, even if in so doing it is pursuing legitimate objectives such as maintaining the quality of its products or protecting its commercial interests[10]. Such objectives cannot, a fortiori, be invoked when in reality their purpose is to eliminate competitors. Hence Tetra Pak, the largest Community producer in the milk carton industry, was censured for having obtained an exclusive licence concerning technology for a method of sterilising cartons for long shelf-life milk[11]. Technological prominence may even entail certain

---

[1]   Decision 76/142, OJ L 223, 16.08.1976.
[2]   Decision 98/190, OJ L 72, 11.03.1998.
[3]   Decision 97/624, OJ L 258, 22.09.1997..
[4]   Decision 2001/354, OJ L 125, 05.05.2001.
[5]   Case COMP/38.233, 16.07.2003.
[6]   Decision 85/609, OJ L 374, 31.12.1985 and judgment of 3 July 1991, case C-62/86, Akzo Chemie v Commission, ECR 1986, p. 1503.
[7]   Decision 88/518, OJ L 284, 19.10.1988.
[8]   Case COMP/C-3/37.792, 24.03.2004.
[9]   Decision 92/213, OJ L 96, 10.04.1992.
[10] Judgment of 14 February 1978, case 27/76, ECR 1978, p. 207.
[11] Decision 88/501, OJ L 272, 04.10.1988 and case T-51/89, ECR 1990, II-309.

obligations for undertakings in a dominant position vis-à-vis their competitors. In 1984 the Commission obliged IBM to communicate systematically in good time to its competitors in the Community appropriate information on its interfaces in order to enable them to connect their products to its large medium-sized data-processing systems and to its network or systems interconnection system. On 3 July 2001, the Commission ordered IMS Health, the world leader in data collection on pharmaceutical sales and prescriptions, to license its "brick structure", which segmented Germany into sales zones or "bricks" and had become a national standard in the German pharmaceutical industry, because refusal to grant a licence constituted a prima facie abuse of a dominant position[1]. On 5 December 2001, the Commission decided that the Belgian postal service operator De Post/La Poste abused its dominant position by making a preferential tariff for its general letter mail service subject to acceptance of a supplementary contract covering a new business-to-business ('B2B') mail service[2].

In the aforementioned judgment in the Hoffmann-La Roche case, the Court of Justice felt that the prohibitions listed in Article 86 (EEC), in spite of that Article's necessarily vague wording, did not show the indeterminate and unforeseeable nature alleged by Roche. According to the Court an undertaking which dominates a market must take that fact into account and itself seek legal security under the European law. As the Court stressed in its judgment of 19 June 1978 in the BP v. ABG case, such a clearance would not, however, free the Commission from its obligations peculiar to the market, where the competitive position of operators is particularly threatened, to comply scrupulously with Article 86 of the EEC Treaty[3]. The Court thus confirmed that the purpose of Article 86 (Art. 82 TEC) is to preserve an effective competition structure in the common market, especially where it is jeopardised by the elimination of independent economic operators by an undertaking in a dominant position.

15.4.2. Controlling concentrations in the single market

Concentrations are arrangements whereby one or more companies acquire control of other companies and thus change the structure of the companies involved and of the market they operate in. The most **important forms of concentrations** of undertakings are the holding of a company in the authorised capital of another company or of other companies, the total or partial acquisitions by a company of the assets of other companies and, lastly, the merger of two or more companies which are legally independent into a new company. Concentrations allow economies of scale to be obtained, production and distribution costs to be reduced, profitability to be improved and technical progress to be speeded up. All of that facilitates the international competitiveness of Community undertakings and may provide consumers with part of the benefits of economic integration. It is, however, obvious that where the concentration in an industry exceeds certain limits it can lead to monopoly or oligopoly structures, which restrict competition and jeopardise consumers' interests.

Cross-border mergers of limited liability companies, involving the takeover of one by the other or the founding of a new company, encounter many legislative and administrative difficulties in the Community, due to various types of limited liability company governed by the laws of different Member States. Therefore, Directive 2005/56 facilitates the **cross-border merger of limited liability companies** as defined therein, notably a company with share capital and having legal personality, possessing separate assets which alone serve to cover its debts[4]. The laws of the Member States are to allow the cross-border merger of a national limited liability company with a limited liability company from another Member State if the national law of the relevant Member States permits mergers between such types of company. In order to facilitate cross-border merger operations, each company taking part in a cross-border merger, and each third party concerned, remains subject to the provisions and formalities of the national law which would be applicable in the case of a national merger. The directive includes provisions

[1] Decision 2002/165, OJ L 59, 28.02.2002.
[2] Decision 2002/180, OJ L 61, 02.03.2002.
[3] Judgment of 29 June 1978, Case 77/77, ECR 1978, p. 1513.
[4] Directive 2005/56, OJ L 310, 25.11.2005.

aimed at preserving workers' participation rights in the event of cross-border mergers [see sections 13.5.2 and 17.2.1].

Directive 2005/56 is without prejudice to the application of the legislation on the control of concentrations between undertakings. As mentioned above, Article 86 of the EEC Treaty **prohibited abuse of a dominant position, but not its existence or creation**. This means that the EEC Treaty did not request authorisation by the Commission for a concentration operation, which could lead to a dominant position. The EC Treaty has not altered this situation. However, the Commission undertook to **fill the legislative vacuum in the EEC Treaty** on the basis of Article 3 thereof. In the Commission's view, since that Treaty had the objective of ensuring the functioning of an undistorted system of competition, the exploitation of a dominant position should be regarded as abusive if it in practice prevented the functioning of undistorted competition. A concentration of undertakings that results in the **monopolisation of a market** should therefore be dealt with as abuse of a dominant position within the meaning of Article 86 of the EEC Treaty. For the first time in 1971 the Commission translated that interpretation into fact by adopting a Decision applying Article 86 (EEC) in the case of the concentration of an undertaking occupying a dominant position, namely Continental Can Cy, with a competing undertaking[1]. The Commission considered that Continental Can Cy had abused its dominant position by **taking control of one of its potential main competitors**, thus strengthening the said dominant position in such a way that competition in a substantial part of the common market was virtually eliminated with regard to the products concerned. The judgment delivered by the Court of Justice on 21 February 1973 confirmed the correctness of the Commission's approach to the application of Article 86 (Art. 82 TEC) to abuse of the dominant position by the concentration[2]. More recently, the Court has ruled that any merger, which created or strengthened a **collective dominant position** enjoyed by the parties concerned, was likely to prove incompatible with the system of undistorted competition envisaged in the Treaty[3].

Thus, with the support of the Court of Justice, the Commission could exercise an *a posteriori* **control of concentrations** of undertakings, one of which had already achieved a dominant position. However, knowing that "prevention is better than cure", the Commission wanted a preventive policy in the field of concentrations. Already in 1973, it had submitted to the Council a proposal for a regulation on the control of mergers. It took sixteen years of discussions in the Council for the **Regulation on the control of concentrations between undertakings** finally to be adopted in December 1989. Still, this Regulation provided a high threshold for obligatory notification of concentrations and the Commission, after some new discussions, succeeded, in June 1997, to persuade the Council to reduce it[4].

According to this Regulation, compulsory notification covers mergers involving undertakings whose aggregate world-wide **turnover** exceeds 2.5 billion euro (general threshold), and the turnover in each of at least three Member States exceeds 100 million euro. The system whereby a merger is referred to the national authorities by the Commission or vice versa is simplified, with the aim of ensuring both that the authority best placed to examine the situation is given charge of the file, in accordance with the subsidiarity principle [see section 3.2.], and that multiple notifications are avoided. Thus, the Commission only takes action on mergers if they have a Community dimension and on restrictive practices only if they affect trade between Member States. In these cases

---

[1] Decision 72/21, OJ L 7, 08.01.1972.
[2] Case 6/72, Europemballage Corporation v Commission, ECR 1973, p. 215.
[3] Judgment of 31 March 1998, Joined Cases C-68/94 and C-30/95, ECR 1998 I-1375.
[4] Regulation 4064/89, OJ L 395, 30.12.1989 repealed by Regulation 139/2004, OJ L 24, 2901.2004.

its position, its experience and its powers of inquiry place it at the best level to assess the factors involved. Moreover, the Commission can authorise a national anti-cartel office to investigate a concentration, which may have significant effects on a local market. The Commission has to base its decision principally on criteria of competition, but may also **take into consideration other factors**, such as economic and technical progress.

To ensure the effective application of the principle of compulsory notification, the Commission has adopted a Regulation covering, among other points, time limits and hearings, the form, content and other **provisions relating to notifications**[1]. According to this Regulation, notifications relating to Regulation 139/2004 on the control of concentrations between undertakings and to Article 57 of the EEA Agreement must be submitted in the manner prescribed by "Form CO" or, under certain conditions in "Short Form", while reasoned submissions for a pre-notification referral must take the "form RS". The three forms are set out in the Annexes of the Regulation of the Commission.

The procedures established for dealing with notifications enable the Commission to make effective use of its powers in this area. The Commission grants authorisation, within the space of a month, to the vast majority of operations which do not create or reinforce a dominant position in the common market or a substantial part of it[2]. In a large number of cases the authorisation of the Commission is granted subject to compliance with conditions and obligations[3]. Only when serious doubts exist as to the operations' compatibility with the common market does it decide to open a detailed investigation as provided for in the second part of the procedure.

According to Commission **guidelines on the assessment of mergers** between competitors (horizontal guidelines) mergers and acquisitions are called into question only where they increase the market power of the companies concerned to an extent likely to have adverse consequences for consumers, in particular in the form of price increases, poorer-quality goods or reduced choice[4]. Any merger or acquisition which would significantly impede competition should be prohibited. A merger's anti-competitive effects result from the creation or strengthening of a single firm's dominant position or from a situation of oligopoly. A merger may impede competition, either because it involves the loss of a competitor on the market, thereby eliminating an important competitive constraint, or because it makes coordination between the remaining companies on the market more likely.

Few concentration operations have actually been **prohibited by the Commission, notably**: the take-over of de Havilland by Aérospatiale and Alenia, justified by very high market shares in a global market, high barriers to entry and the maturity of the market[5]; the joint venture, Holland Media Groep (HMG), because it would be uniquely able to offer advertisers coordinated scheduling on the Dutch television market[6]; the creation of the joint venture Nordic Satellite Distribution (NSD), because it would reinforce the anti-competitive effects foreclosing the Nordic satellite television market[7]; the merger of Bertelsmann/Kirch/Premiere and Deutsche Telekom/BetaResearch, which would have created a monopoly position for Premiere in digital pay-television in Germany and a dominant position for technical services for pay-television by BetaDigital and Deutsche Telekom[8]; the acquisition by Volvo of its main Swedish competitor Scania, which would have changed the market structure of trucks, buses and coaches, to the detriment of customers[9]; and the acquisition of control of Legrand by Schneider Electric, because the merger between the two main French manufacturers of electrical equipment would have considerably weakened the functioning of the market in a number of countries, particularly in France[10].

In many cases of projected concentration the Commission invites the parties concerned to **propose appropriate amendments to their projects** rendering them compatible with the common market. Thus, the Regulation on mergers does not prevent undertakings from entering into strategic alliances; it allows them to

[1] Regulation 802/2004, OJ L 133, 30.04.2004.
[2] See, for example, Commission Decision 95/404, OJ L 239, 07.10.1995, (Swissair/Sabena).
[3] See, for example, Commission Decision 97/816, OJ L 336, 08.12.1997 (Boeing/McDonnell Douglas).
[4] SEC (2003) 1441, 16 December 2003.
[5] Case IV/M.53, 02.10.1991.
[6] Case IV/M.553, 20.09.1995.
[7] Case IV/M/490, OJ L 53, 02.03.1996.
[8] Case IV/M/1027, 27.05.1998.
[9] Case COMP/M.1672, 14.03.2000.
[10] Decision 2004/275, OJ L 101, 06.04.2004, annulled for irregularities, Case T-310/01.

seek complementarities, acquire an international dimension, penetrate new markets and take advantage of the single market, without jeopardising competition within it. Thus, the Commission authorised Pfizer Inc., subject to compliance with the undertakings given by the parties, to acquire Pharmacia Corporation, thereby creating the largest pharmaceutical company in the world[1].

It is interesting to note that under the cooperation agreement concluded between the European Union and the **United States** on the application of their competition rules, the Commission investigates mergers of American companies in parallel with the US Department of Justice [see section 15.2.]. This cooperation led to the 29 September 1999 authorisation, subject to conditions, of the merger between the two US companies Exxon and Mobil[2]. However, on 28 June 2000, the Commission decided to prohibit the merger between the US telecommunications firms MCI WorldCom Inc. and Sprint Corp., because the transaction would have led to the creation of a dominant position on the market for top-level universal Internet connectivity to the detriment of consumers worldwide and especially in the Member States of the European Union[3]. On 3 July 2001, the Commission decided to prohibit General Electric's proposed acquisition of Honeywell Inc., because that merger would create or strengthen dominant positions on several markets in aero-engines, avionics and other aircraft components and systems in the Member States of the EU[4].

15.5. Monitoring State intervention

Competition in the common market can be distorted not only by the behaviour of undertakings, but also by State intervention. The **arguments adduced by governments for intervening** in economic activities are numerous, but they all have a socio-political ring: to prevent the closure of undertakings which might give rise to collective redundancies, which are unacceptable in social and regional terms. At national level, undertakings experiencing difficulties make public opinion and the official authorities aware of their predicament, especially when they are big companies, regarded as "flagship undertakings" and/or they occupy a large number of workers whose jobs are endangered.

The social and regional consequences of structural changes should indeed be attenuated, but the changes themselves should **not be opposed by artificially ensuring the survival** of obsolete industries or sectors in decline. The question should be asked, on a case-by-case basis, whether aid is really needed, rather than a radical change in production structures and methods, and whether aid for an industry in difficulty in one Member State of the EU might not harm the interests of the same industries established in the other Member States. It is, indeed, obvious that State intervention may involve a conflict of interests between the economic operators benefiting from such intervention and their competitors in the other Member States, which will be placed in a less favourable position and will press their governments to redress the situation. Unilaterally conceived State initiatives cannot, therefore, but trigger reciprocation from partner countries and lead to costly operations for everyone. In order to avoid retaliation from partner countries and squandered resources, therefore, a "code of good conduct" is needed for the Member States in this area.

In fact, as other forms of protectionism recede, the importance of State aids as an anti-competitive mechanism tends to grow. Beyond their negative effect on competition, State aids can also have **serious implications for economic cohesion** within the EU [see section 12.1.2.]. Large and well developed Member States are able to outbid less developed Member States on the periphery of the Union in the aid race. Indeed, the four largest Member States account for 88% of all aid granted in the Union.

---

[1]   Case No COMP/M.2922, OJ C 110, 08.05.2003, p. 24.
[2]   Case COMP/M.1822, 02.02.2000.
[3]   Case COMP/M.1741, 28.06.2000.
[4]   Case COMP/M.2220, 03.07.2001.

Aid of a regional character was examined in the chapter on regional development [see section 12.2.1.]. The following paragraphs look at other State operations: general aid, sectoral aid, national monopolies and public undertakings.

The Commission processes more than one thousand aid applications every year. The annual total amount of aid in the EU-15 stands at around EUR 50 billion, around 70% of which concerns horizontal objectives of common interest, such as strengthening economic and social cohesion, protection of the environment, promotion of research and development, and small and medium-sized enterprises. **All the Member States grant aid to their companies**, but the percentage of GNP absorbed by this aid varies from 2% to 4%, with the highest percentage granted by the wealthiest countries. National aids, useful or otherwise, may distort competition between undertakings, some of which enjoy subsidies or tax reductions while others do not. It is this harmful impact on competition which prompts the Commission to take action on behalf of the Community, particularly when the aid granted runs counter to the cohesion objective because it is to the detriment of the poorer regions of the Community [see section 12.1.2.]. In order to instigate a reduction of the overall level of State aid as a percentage of gross domestic product, the Commission has taken steps on a number of fronts, such as: devising indicators of the effectiveness and efficiency of State aid; intensifying the assessment of the impact of aid on competition on the basis of economic criteria; and encouraging exchanges of experience and concerted evaluation exercises[1].

15.5.1. Compatible and incompatible aids

Article 87 of the EC Treaty (ex Art. 92 EEC) stipulates that "any aid granted... which distorts or threatens to distort competition by favouring certain undertakings or the production of certain goods shall, in so far as it affects trade between Member States, **be incompatible with the common market"**. Given the high degree of integration of the Community's economy, most national subsidies are likely to be considered trade-distorting, even for products which are not exported to other Member States, if they compete on their home market with imports from other Member States. The Commission has devised a mechanism for fixing and revising the reference rates used to calculate the grant equivalent of aid[2]. The form of the aid is irrelevant: for example outright grants, soft loans, tax concessions, guarantees, the supply of goods or services at less than cost are all subject to Community State aid control. However, under the **"de minimis" rule**, aid of less than EUR 100 000 over three years is judged not to affect trade between Member States and thus need not be notified to the Commission[3].

Paragraph 2 of Article 87 considers that the following shall be **compatible with the common market**, provided that aid is granted without discrimination related to the origin of the products concerned: aid having a social character granted to individual consumers, aid to make good the damage caused by natural disasters or exceptional occurrences and aid granted to certain areas of Germany affected by the division of that country (before 1991).

Paragraph 3 of Article 87, for its part, stipulates that the following **may be considered to be compatible** with the common market: aid to promote the economic development of areas with economic or social problems; aid to promote the execution of an important project of common European interest or to remedy a serious disturbance in the economy of a Member State; aid to facilitate the development of certain economic activities or of certain economic areas, where such aid does not adversely affect trading conditions; aid to promote culture and heritage conservation[4]; and such other categories of aid as may be specified by decision of the Council.

---

[1] COM (2002) 555, 16 October 2002.
[2] OJ C 31, 03.02.1979.
[3] Regulation 69/2001, OJ L 10, 13.01.2001.
[4] Point inserted at Maastricht.

The Council has empowered the Commission to adopt block exemption regulations for certain **categories of horizontal aid** (in favour of SMEs, research and development, environment protection, employment and training) and for aid below a given threshold[1]. A Commission decision of 22 July 1998 clarifies the circumstances in which public funding for training may be caught by the competition rules on State aid and sets the criteria which it applies in ascertaining whether such aid is compatible with the common market. A Commission notice of 11 November 1998 sets out the criteria it applies when examining or reviewing Member States' measures relating to direct business taxation[2].

So that the Commission may adopt a position on the possible application of one of the above derogations from the incompatibility of aid, the Member States are obliged, under Article 88 paragraph 3 of the EC Treaty (ex Art. 93) to **inform it in sufficient time**, through a detailed questionnaire, of any plans to grant new aid or alter existing aid. Such aid may not be granted by Member States until the Commission has taken a final decision on it. In case the Member States fail to fulfil their obligation to notify proposals to grant aid, the Commission reserves the right to take a provisional decision requiring them to recover, with interest, any aid paid illegally pending a final decision by it on the compatibility of the aid with the common market[3]. In order to increase legal certainty and transparency in the Commission's decision-making process, a Council Regulation lays down detailed rules for the application of Article 88 of the EC Treaty[4].

Under the procedure of monitoring national aids, the Commission gives notice to the Member State proposing to grant aid to submit its comments within a given time limit, normally set at one month. The other Member States are also invited to submit their comments on the proposed aid in question, as are other interested parties, which are apprised through **publication in the Official Journal of the European Union.** In the light of those comments, the Commission may decide either not to object to the proposed aid or to require that it be abolished or to call for certain alterations to be made to it. If the Member State concerned is not in agreement with the Commission's decision it may, within two months, refer the matter to the Court of Justice. According to the Court, however, the only defence available to a Member State in such a case is to plead that proper fulfilment of its obligations under Article 87.2 (TEC) was absolutely impossible[5].

A Court of Justice ruling of February 14, 1990 provided some highly useful clarifications to the State aids vetting system and more specifically: to **the procedural rules** of Article 93, paragraph 3 (EEC), which oblige the Member States to inform the Commission of planned State aids so that it can take a decision on their compatibility prior to implementation; and to the obligation for the Member States to demand repayment of aid not eligible for one of the dispensations provided for under Article 92 EEC (Art. 87 TEC) and which is consequently incompatible with the common market[6]. In another judgment the Court specified that only benefits granted directly or indirectly out of State resources are to be regarded as aid within the meaning of Article 92(EEC)[7]. According to the Court, if a firm in receipt of State aid has not brought direct annulment proceedings under the second paragraph of Article 173 of the EEC Treaty (Art. 230 TEC) against a Commission decision declaring the aid to be unlawful (even though it was fully informed of the decision) within the periods prescribed, that firm cannot plead that the Commission decision is unlawful[8]. The Council has no power to declare a measure of State aid compatible where the Commission has already declared the aid in question incompatible with the common market[9].

In order to enhance transparency in the field of State aid policy, the Commission opened, in 2001, a State aid register and a State aid scoreboard[10]. The latter instrument, which is a source of information on the State aid situation in the European Union and the Commission's activities in the State aid monitoring field, is available on the Europa server[11].

---

[1]   Regulation 994/98, OJ L 142, 14.05.1998.
[2]   OJ C 384, 10.12.1998, p.3.
[3]   OJ C 156, 27.06.1995, p. 5.
[4]   Regulation 659/1999, OJ L 83, 27.03.1999.
[5]   Judgment of 29 January 1998, Case C-280/95, ECR 1998 I-259.
[6]   Judgment of 14 February 1990, Case C-301/87, France v Commission, ECR 1990, p. I-0307.
[7]   Judgment of 24 January 1978, Case 82/77, Van Tiggele, ECR 1978, p. 25.
[8]   Judgment of 9 March 1994, Case C-188/92, ECR 1994, I-833.
[9]   Judgment of 29 June 2004, Case C-110/02, Commission v Council, ECR 2004.
[10] COM (2001) 412, 18 July 2001 and COM (2001) 782, 20 December 2001.
[11] (http://europa.eu.int/comm/competition/state_aid/scoreboard).

15.5.2. General aids

Aid from which any undertaking whatsoever can benefit, without regard to its geographical location or to the sector to which it belongs, is regarded as general aid. Owing to this lack of a specific character, such aid cannot lay claim to an exemption provision provided for in the Treaty. The Commission has to be able to verify, prior to their being granted, that general aids are in **response to genuine economic or social needs**, that they lead to an improvement in the structures of beneficiary undertakings and that they do not give rise to problems at Community level. The Commission tries to prevent aid that does not pursue clearly defined objectives. For that reason, it requires Member States, when applying general aid arrangements, either to notify it in advance of the relevant regional or sectoral programmes or, if there are no such programmes, to inform it of significant individual cases.

The Commission systematically prohibits **State export aid** within the Community and normally prohibits aid, which does not have a **counterpart in the Community interest**. Aid on which no time limit is placed and which is required to support current activities ("**operating aid**") is just as unacceptable as aid for intra-Community exports. According to the Court of Justice, State **participation in the capital of undertakings** is likely to be considered State aid coming within the scope of Article 92 *et seq.* of the EEC Treaty (Art. 87 *et seq.* TEC).

However, certain general aids are granted to achieve **legitimate objectives** and may be approved by the Commission under certain conditions, specified in its communications. In addition to regional development aids [see section 12.2.1.], this is generally the case for research and development aids[1], aids in favour of small and medium-sized enterprises[2], environmental protection aids[3], aids for rescuing and restructuring firms in difficulty[4], vocational training aids[5] and aids for employment[6] [see details below].

Thus, the Commission established since 1986 a Community framework for State **aids for research and development**. Under the new framework for this type of aids, preference is given to projects in favour of SMEs, to undertakings investing in the less developed regions of the Union or which fit into the framework programme for research and technological development with its specific priorities [see section 18.2.2.]. In order to reduce red tape, prior notification is required only for individual research projects costing more than EUR 25 million and benefiting of more than EUR 5 million in aid.

The framework for aid to **small and medium-sized enterprises** differentiates between small enterprises, for which the ceiling of aid intensity is 15%, and medium-sized enterprises for which gross aid intensity should not exceed 7.5%. Consistency between policy in favour of SMEs and the principle of economic and social cohesion is provided by variations in the proportion of aid permitted. Thus, in regions eligible for regional aid, the permissible aid ceiling stands at 10% or 15%, depending on the seriousness of the problems faced by the areas in question. The ceilings of aid intensity are calculated either as a percentage of the investment's eligible costs or as a percentage of the wage costs of employment created or a combination thereof. Aid for consultancy and other services to SMEs can reach proportions of 50%.

The Commission authorises subsidies helping companies adapt to **environmental protection** standards and notably those encouraging them to make efforts in relation to the requirements of the Community programme on the environment and environmentally sustainable development [see section 16.2.]. The Community framework is designed to ensure that State aid granted for environmental purposes complies with the "polluter pays" principle and is consistent with the internal market and the Community's competition policy.

Aids granted to assist companies facing a particularly difficult market situation, such as structural overcapacity, are accepted only in exceptional circumstances as part of a wider plan to reduce the overcapacity. The Community guidelines on State aid for **rescuing and restructuring firms** in difficulty set out the Commis-

---

[1] OJ C 45, 17.02.1996, p. 5-14 and OJ C 111, 08.05.2002, p. 3.
[2] Regulation 70/2001, OJ L 10, 13.01.2001 and Regulation 1040/2006, OJ L 187, 08.07.2006.
[3] Commission decision, OJ C 37, 03.02.2001, p. 3-15.
[4] OJ C 244, 01.10.2004, p. 2.
[5] Regulation 68/2001, OJ L 10, 13.01.2001 and Regulation 1040/2006, OJ L 187, 08.07.2006.
[6] Regulation 2204/2002, OJ L 337, 13.12.2002 and Regulation 1040/2006, OJ L 187, 08.07.2006.

sion's approach to examining aid of this type, in particular: there must be a restructuring plan capable of ensuring the viability of the firm; aid must be limited to the strict minimum needed for implementing the plan; criteria ensuring that the distortion of competition will be strictly limited must be met. Aid to finance **social measures** exclusively for the benefit of employees who are displaced by restructuring are not taken into consideration in determining the size of any capacity reduction required.

Vocational training aid is exempt from the notification requirement, provided that the aid intensity does not exceed a certain percentage of the project's overall cost. So, for a project involving: specific training, in which case the aid intensity may not exceed 25% for large firms and 35% for small or medium-sized enterprises (SMEs); general training, in which case the aid intensity may not exceed 50% for large firms and 70% for SMEs; both specific and general training, in which case the aid intensity may not exceed 25% for large firms and 35% for SMEs.

The Commission regulation on the application of Articles 87 and 88 of the EC Treaty to State **aid for employment** allows Member States to grant aid for job creation and the recruitment of disadvantaged or disabled workers without having to apply for prior authorisation from the Commission. Other types of employment aid are not prohibited but require prior notification. At the same time, the regulation enables Member States to reduce individual grants to companies, which involve a greater risk of distorting competition. In force until 2006, the regulation introduces a block exemption system for both types of State aid mentioned above, up to certain ceilings so as to avoid any "perverse" distortional effects. It covers selective measures for certain sectors or regions, and not general employment-policy measures, which do not constitute State aid.

15.5.3. Sectoral aids

The Commission's policy on sectoral aids involves examining whether the problems facing certain industries may justify the granting of State aid while ensuring that such aid does not unduly delay the necessary changes, does not distort competition to an extent counter to the common interest and is in line with the attainment of the Community's objectives, or at least will not hinder that goal.

The symbiosis of national economies in the common market is reflected by very similar economic developments in the Member States, even though their economic structures are not homogeneous. The difficulties justifying intervention by a Member State are often to be found in some or all of its partners. A **"Community framework"** encompassing national measures may therefore be elaborated when the conditions in a sector so dictate. Such a framework should include guidelines for the objectives to be attained at Community level and a description of how to achieve that. The framework for aids to sectors in crisis could generally be based on the criterion of "overcapacity", for which the definition and implementing provisions should take account of the features of the specific market in question such as progress in production technologies and the degree of globalisation. Community frameworks have existed in the past for aids to shipbuilding[1], maritime transport[2], the steel industry[3], the synthetic fibres industry[4] and the motor vehicle industry[5].

In February 2002 the Commission considered that the specific sectoral frameworks should be integrated into a multisectoral framework[6]. It has therefore approved the recasting of the rules applicable to regional aid to **large investment projects**, including in steel, the motor vehicle and synthetic fibres sectors[7] [see section 12.2.1.]. Under this framework no advance notification of aid below certain thresholds for large investment projects is required, provided that aid is granted in accordance with a regional aid scheme approved by the Commission. The framework is aimed at setting up a quicker,

---

[1]   Regulation 1540/98, OJ L 202, 18.07.1998.
[2]   COM (96) 81 and OJ C 205, 05.07.1997.
[3]   Decision 2496/96, OJ L 338, 28.12.1996.
[4]   OJ C 96, 30.03.1996, p. 11-14 and OJ C 368, 22.12.2001, p.10.
[5]   OJ C 279, 15.09.1997, p. 1-8 and OJ C 368, 22.12.2001, p. 10.
[6]   Communication from the Commission, OJ C 70, 19.03.2002, p. 8-20.
[7]   Communication from the Commission OJ C 70, 19.03.2002.

simpler and more transparent system of controlling public authority support for major investment projects in the European Union. The new system enhances Member States' responsibility as regards implementation of the State aid rules and guarantees proper control of State aid levels in an enlarged and more heterogeneous Community.

In the field of **aid to shipbuilding** a Council Regulation implements the provisions of the OECD Agreement on respecting normal competitive conditions in the commercial shipbuilding and repair industry[1] [see section 17.3.2.]. The purpose of the Regulation is to make shipbuilding subject to the same rules as any other industry as regards State aid by prohibiting contract-related aid (operating aid). Only aid for innovation, R & D, environmental protection, total or partial closures and restructuring, and regional aid is nowadays authorised in this sector, subject to certain conditions.

In keeping with its communication on a new maritime strategy, the Commission adopted new guidelines for State aid in the **maritime transport sector** [see section 20.3.4.]. Recognising that vessels registered in the European Union are at a competitive disadvantage compared with non-EU vessels as regards fiscal costs, the Commission authorises Member States to exempt shipping from fiscal and social charges, or to reimburse these charges. The guidelines also take a positive approach to training aid and to compensation for public service obligations.

The **Steel Aid Code** applies to steel firms the Community rules applicable to aid for research and development and for environmental protection with a view to ensuring fair competition in this particularly sensitive industry. After the expiry of the ECSC Treaty [see section 2.1.], State aid for the closure of steel firms is allowed in accordance with the tight conditions laid down in the steel aid code.

15.5.4. Public undertakings

The public sector, made up of public undertakings, joint ventures and undertakings controlled by the public authorities by means of holdings, varies in size from one EU country to another. The larger the public sector, the more difficult it is for the public authorities to resist the temptation to make the companies controlled by them the instrument of their economic policy, giving them, in return, a privileged position in various respects. Although the interpenetration of the Member States' economies reduces the effectiveness of that instrument, an exceptional situation for public undertakings would constitute a serious danger for the free competition in the single market.

While remaining neutral with regard to the legal position on ownership in the Member States, the EC Treaty stipulates, in **Article 86**, that "in the case of public undertakings and undertakings to which Member States grant special or exclusive rights, Member States shall neither enact nor maintain in force any measures contrary to the rules contained in this Treaty ...". Such undertakings therefore **have the same obligations as private firms,** including those laid down in Article 12 (prohibition of discrimination on grounds of nationality) and 81 to 89 inclusive (rules of competition). Still, the distinction is difficult to draw between an operation to salvage and replenish capital used up by losses, which is permitted under Article 295, which declares that the EC Treaty does in no way prejudice the rules in Member States governing the system of property ownership, and an aid operation, disguised, for example, as non-remunerated acquisitions of holdings or as other advantages, prohibited by Article 87 paragraph 1. Article 86, paragraph 3 (TEC) confers on the Commission the task of ensuring the application of these provisions and the power to address directives or decisions to Member States where necessary.

However, Article 86(2) allows exceptions to the rules of competition of the Treaty **in favour of public utility undertakings**, entrusted with the operation of services of general economic interest (water, energy, transport and telecommunications) or having the character of a revenue-producing monopoly, so as not to obstruct the performance, in law or in fact, of the particular tasks assigned to them. Nevertheless, the development of

---

[1] Regulation 1540/98, OJ L 202, 18.07.1998.

Community trade must not be affected by aid to these undertakings to such an extent as would be contrary to the interests of the Community.

Indeed, governments grant certain public enterprises **statutory monopoly protection**. Such exclusive monopoly rights are awarded for various public policy reasons, such as ensuring security of supply, providing a basic service to the whole population or avoiding the costs of duplicating an expensive distribution network. Such practices are common, notably for utilities (energy and water), postal services, telecommunications and to some extent in broadcasting, transport (air and maritime), banking and insurance. These exclusive rights could prevent, however, the creation of a real internal market in the sectors in question, if Member States could protect from competition their monopolistic enterprises. Member States must, therefore, not take measures, which could lead their public enterprises enjoying monopoly rights to infringe Community rules on competition or the free movement of goods and services.

In any case, greater **transparency of the financial relations** between States and their public undertakings is needed, in order to enable the Commission to decide whether transfer of public funds to those undertakings are compatible with the rules laid down in the Treaty. That is precisely the aim of a Commission Directive, which obliges Member States to supply the Commission, at the latter's request, with information on public funds made available directly or indirectly to public undertakings, thus covering not only "active transfer" of public funds, such as the provision of capital and the covering of losses, but also "passive transfers", such as the forgoing by the State of income of profits or of a normal return on the funds used[1].

The Commission recognises that the operation of **services of general economic interest** - in the sense of Article 86(2) of the EC Treaty - must not be prejudiced. However, it is examining on a sector-by-sector basis whether less restrictive practices are possible, how to limit statutory monopoly rights to the essential activities and whether competing services could use existing networks or new technologies would permit the construction of alternative networks.

Commission directives have paved the way for liberalisation in the **satellite telecommunications** sector, thus helping the development of trans-European networks in this sector and facilitating the European information society. The Commission Directive on free competition on the Community markets in **telecommunications terminal equipment** (modems, telex and telefax terminals, private satellite stations, etc.) prohibits any exclusive rights to import, market, connect, bring into service and maintain such equipment[2] [see section 17.3.6.]. Similarly, the Commission Directive on competition in the markets for **electronic communications networks and services** aims at: the abolition of existing exclusive and special rights; the prohibition of the granting of new rights in the electronic communications sector; and the guarantee of the right of firms to benefit from freedom of establishment and freedom to supply services within an undistorted competitive framework[3]. In any case, according to the Court, the regulatory prerogatives enjoyed by national telecommunications organisations must be dissociated from their commercial activities[4].

A judgment of the Court of justice clarified the **concept of State aid in relation to public undertakings**[5]. The Court found that the provision of logistical or commercial assistance by a public undertaking to its private-sector subsidiaries can be regarded as aid within the meaning of Article 92 of the EEC Treaty (Art 86

---

[1] Directive 80/723, OJ L 195, 29.07.1980 and Directive 2005/81, OJ L 312, 29.11.2005.
[2] Directive 88/301, OJ L 131, 27.05.1988 and Directive 94/46, OJ L 268, 19.10.1994.
[3] Directive 2002/77, OJ L 249, 17.09.2002.
[4] Judgment given on 27 October 1993, Joined Cases C-46/90 and C-93/91, Lagauche and Others, ECR 1993, p. I-5267.
[5] Judgment of 11 July 1996, Case C-39/94, SFEI v La Poste and Others, ECR 1996, p. I-3547.

TEC) if the remuneration received in return is less than that which would have been demanded under normal market conditions. In another judgment the Court, after observing that, in the context of competition law, the **concept of "undertaking"** encompasses any body engaged in an economic activity, regardless of its legal status or the way in which it is financed, held that social security schemes cannot be considered to be undertakings, because they do not exercise an economic activity but fulfil an exclusively social function. They are therefore not subject to the competition rules of the Treaty[1].

The Court of Justice acknowledges that public utility undertakings, unlike others, **have to subsidise their less viable activities from their more profitable business** if they are to provide their services in balanced economic conditions. On the other hand, the exclusion of competition is not justified, according to the Court, in the case of specific services, which are dissociable from the service operated in the general interest and meet the special needs of economic operators[2]. The Court recognises also the public service mission of electricity distribution companies, even if they operate regionally and have no exclusive rights, but holds that account must be taken of the economic conditions in which the undertaking operates[3].

15.5.5. State monopolies of a commercial character

Article 37 of the EEC Treaty (Art. 31 TEC) added to the general provisions of Article 90 (Art. 86 TEC) on `public undertakings the provision that the Member States would progressively adjust any State monopolies "of a commercial character so as to ensure that when the transitional period has ended no discrimination regarding the conditions under which goods are procured and marketed exists between nationals of Member States". That rule allowed exceptions in order to dispose of agricultural products or obtain for them the best return and in order to enable Member States to comply with their obligations under international agreements.

At the outset virtually all commercial monopolies in the Community presented problems with regard to Article 37 (EEC). The Commission accordingly, as from 1962, initiated a series of proceedings against Member States, which refused or neglected to carry out the progressive adjustment of their monopolies. For a long time those Commission efforts came up against the unwillingness of Member States which administered **lucrative monopolies**, such as the tobacco and alcohol monopolies, or monopolies regarded as important for national security, like the French oil monopoly. In 1980, some ten years later than the timetable envisaged in Article 37 (EEC), the final stage of the adjustment of State monopolies of a commercial character was reached, but some Member States are still fighting a rearguard action to protect some of the privileges of their monopolies, such as the exclusive import and export rights for gas and electricity[4].

15.6. Appraisal and outlook

Competition policy has traditionally been seen as a prerogative of the nation-state. The EC/EU is the first group of states to practice a policy, which tries to deal with the impact that distortions of competition have on trade. The basic objective of the common competition policy is to prevent the unity of the common market from being called into question by measures that have the effect of giving preference to certain economic operators (businesses, companies) and of restoring the partitioning of domestic markets. In fact, whatever means are used to **correct the rigours of competition**, the usual effect consists in raising prices to restore business profitability, at the expense of the consumer or the taxpayer.

From the beginnings of the Community, an administrative practice developed gradually by the Commission and confirmed by the case-law of the Court of Justice has made it possible to interpret and improve the rules of the Treaty in order to establish a range **of principles of fair behaviour** which, while not hindering free enterprise, indicates to economic operators the rules to be complied with to ensure that free trade and equal opportunity are guaranteed within the common market. The practices of businesses

---

[1] Judgment given on 17 February 1993, Joined Cases C-159/91 and C-160/91, ECR 1993, I-664.
[2] Judgment given on 19 May 1993, Case C-320/91, ECR 1993, p. I-2563.
[3] Judgment given on 27 April 1994, Case C-393/92, ECR 1994, p. 1477.
[4] See e.g. Commission Recommendations 83/403, OJ L 233, 24.08.1983, 87/390, OJ L 203, 24.07.1987 and 88/90, OJ L 56, 02.03.1988.

directed towards impeding imports or exports, fixing production or sales quotas and generally sharing the market are accordingly actively proceeded against. Agreements, which have the effect of concentrating demand on specific producers, and exclusive distribution agreements which prevent traders and consumers from purchasing products in any Member State under the customary conditions there, are also prohibited. Companies which practice the prohibited restrictions of competition, thus jeopardising the unity of the common market, have to expect to have heavy fines imposed on them.

Legal proceedings are also brought against undertakings which **abuse a dominant position** by refusing to supply a long-standing customer, by applying discriminatory prices, unlawful practices which cause or could cause damage to customers or consumers or, lastly, by absorbing one another thus eliminating competition in a market. It would be absurd to take legal action against horizontal agreements between undertakings whilst at the same time permit the monopolisation of certain markets through uncontrolled vertical integration of undertakings in a dominant position. That is why, the Regulation on the control of major concentration transactions filled a legal vacuum which had been causing problems for a long time. The **control of concentrations** does not mean the prohibition of concentrations. Just as concentrations are dangerous when they strengthen the dominant position of major undertakings, so are they desirable when they strengthen the competitive position of small and medium-sized enterprises. Refraining from a strictly legal approach to problems of competition, the Commission conducts in fact two parallel policies: a policy for the elimination of abuse by major companies and a policy of encouragement of cooperation and concentration between SMEs [see section 17.1.4.]. Even in regard to large companies, the Commission follows a double policy. On the one hand, it vigorously pursues all forms of corporate conduct that cause serious restrictions of competition and deprive other firms and consumers of the benefits of an open market economy. On the other, it authorises certain forms of cooperation (strategic alliances) between firms, taking the view that, provided certain guarantees are given that competition should not be distorted, such cooperation between undertakings can help them adjust to the new European and global economic environment [see section 17.2.4.].

As regards State aids, the role of the Community competition policy is not only to prevent national initiatives that are harmful to intra-Community trade or to the economic activity of the other Member States, but also to limit state intervention to aid which fits in with the prospect of adjusting the structures of the Community's production mechanism to changes in demand and to the international division of labour. The Commission tries to ensure that aid to undertakings does not constitute the resurgence of protectionist measures in a new form. The common competition policy is thus not only pivotal to the good functioning of the single market, but also a complement to Community sectoral policies - in particular in the industrial, energy, agriculture and transport sectors - aimed at improving production structures. Through its effect on the structure of markets, competition policy influences the competitiveness of the European economy and hence helps to orient the Union's macroeconomic framework towards better employment conditions.

It is no exaggeration to state that the Commission's competition policy has **an influence on "industrial morality"** in the Community. A very large majority of businesses respect the Community competition rules and the observations of the Commission. There are just a few companies that yield only after lengthy discussions with the Commission or even following the judgment of the Court of Justice, which always has the last word in problems relating to competition. For its part, the Commission is adopting a pragmatic approach towards increased competition resulting from a number of factors, including rapid technological change, the completion of the single market, the globalisation of markets and economic difficulties in several sectors. It is modernising its rules and practices in the areas of restrictive practices, abuses of dominant positions, mergers and State aid, focussing on opening up markets where a competitive environment is not yet fully established, while at the same time guaranteeing a level playing field for all and safeguarding the provision of services in the general interest.

Bibliography on competition policy

- AKMAN Pinar. "Article 82 reformed?: the EC discussion paper on exclusionary abuses" in *The Journal of Business Law*, December 2006, p. 816-829.
- ALLAN Bill (et al.), "The antitrust treatment of unilateral effects: an EC perspective" in *Competition policy international*, v. 2, n. 1, Spring 2006, p. 43-154.
- ANDERMAN Steven. Interface between intellectual property rights and competition policy. Cambridge: Cambridge University Press, 2006.
- ANDERMAN Steven, KALLAUGHER John. *Technology transfer and the new EU competition rules: intellectual property licensing after modernisation.* Oxford: Oxford University Press, 2006.
- ANDREANGELI Arianna. "The impact of the modernisation regulation on the guarantees of due process in competition proceedings" in *European Law Review*, v. 31, n. 3, June 2006, p. 342-363.
- BAXTER Simon, DETHMERS Frances. "Collective dominance under EC merger control: after Airtours and the introduction of unilateral effects is there still a future for collective dominance?" in *European Competition Law Review*, v. 27, n. 3, March 2006, p. 148-160.
- BELLIS Jean-François. "Review of the Commission's decisions on fines by the Community Courts" in *ERA-Forum: scripta iuris europaei*, n. 1, 2006, p. 27-39.
- BERGH Roger van den, CAMESASCA Peter. *European competition law and economics: a comparative perspective.* 2nd ed. London: Sweet & Maxwell, 2006.
- BISHOP Simon, WALKER Mike. *The economics of EC competition law: concepts, application and measurement.* London: Sweet & Maxwell, 2006.
- COMBE Emmanuel. *Économie et politique de la concurrence.* Paris: Dalloz, 2005.
- CROCIONI Pietro. "Can state aid policy become more economic friendly?" in *World Competition*, v. 29, n. 1, March 2006, p. 89-108.
- DAMRO Chad. "Transatlantic competition policy: domestic and international sources of EU-US cooperation" in *European journal of international relations*, v. 12, n. 2, June 2006, p. 171-196.
- EUROPEAN COMMISSION. *State aid action plan:* The Economics of Horizontal Mergers : Unilateral and Coordinated Effects. Luxembourg: EUR-OP*, 2006.
- HILDEBRAND Doris. *Economic analyses of vertical agreements; a self-assessment.* The Hague: Kluwer Law International, 2005.
- LEE Darin (ed.). *Competition policy and antitrust.* Oxford: Elsevier, 2006.
- LESGUILLONS Henry. "Les clauses de non-concurrence en droit européen de la concurrence = Non-compete clauses in European competition law" in *Revue de droit des affaires internationales = International Business Law Journal*, n. 4, juin 2006, p. 495-533.
- PERRIN Benjamin. "Challenges facing the EU network of competition authorities: insights from a comparative criminal law perspective" in *European Law Review*, v. 31, n. 4, August 2006, p. 540-564.
- VÖLCKER Sven. "Developments in EC competition law in 2005: an overview" in *Common Market Law Review*, v. 43, n. 5, October 2006, p. 1409-1446.
- WIJCKMANS Franck, TUYTSCHAEVER Filip, VANDERELST Alain. *Vertical agreements in EC competition law.* Oxford: Oxford University Press, 2006.
- ZHU Shiley. "Converge? Diverge?: A comparison of horizontal merger laws in the United States and European Union" in *World competition: law and economics review*, v. 29, n. 4, December 2006, p. 635-651.

*The publications of the Office for Official Publications of the European Communities (EUR-OP) exist usually in all official languages of the EU.

Chapter 16

ENVIRONMENT POLICY

Diagram of the chapter

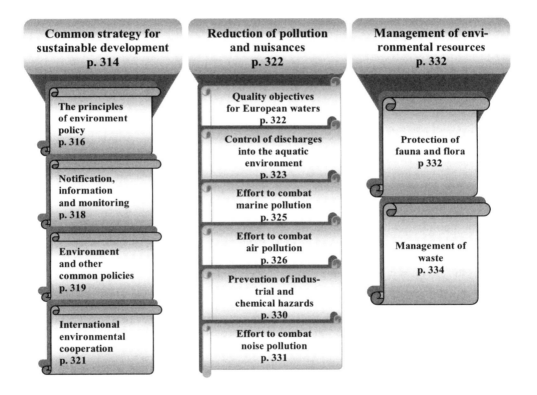

Common strategy for sustainable development p. 314	Reduction of pollution and nuisances p. 322	Management of environmental resources p. 332
The principles of environment policy p. 316	Quality objectives for European waters p. 322	Protection of fauna and flora p 332
Notification, information and monitoring p. 318	Control of discharges into the aquatic environment p. 323	Management of waste p. 334
Environment and other common policies p. 319	Effort to combat marine pollution p. 325	
International environmental cooperation p. 321	Effort to combat air pollution p. 326	
	Prevention of industrial and chemical hazards p. 330	
	Effort to combat noise pollution p. 331	

Up to the end of the 1960s no European country had a clearly defined environment policy. Student unrest in France and Germany in May 1968, the United Nations Conference on the Human Environment, held in Stockholm in June 1972, and the publication in the same period of the report by the Club of Rome on "the limits of growth" alerted European public opinion to the **ecological problems of economic development** and questioned the hierarchy of the values extolled by the consumer society.

The Governments of the Community States were obliged hastily to design measures against pollution and nuisances so as to **open a safety valve to an ecological movement** likely to swing the pendulum to the other extreme, to impose "zero growth", to block technological progress and with it, perhaps, economic and social progress. But all the Member States had to act together, as any country which took measures on its own against pollution or nuisances, or measures more stringent than its neighbours, would be likely to penalise its industry, which would have to bear the cost. Having done so, it would be forced to block the placing on its market of more pollutant, noisy or dangerous products from its more lax partners, which would bring the risk of technical barriers to trade [see section 6.2.].

The Summit Conference of Heads of State and Government held in Paris in 1972 opened the way to the implementation of a common policy on environmental protection. The Commission went to work and prepared wide-ranging action programmes for the reduction of pollution and nuisances and for the management of environmental resources. In record time by Community standards the Community provided itself with many concrete measures, a fact proving that, when there is pressure from public opinion, political will and the absence of deep-rooted national policies, the European institutions are capable of **legislative work comparable to that of an individual State**.

16.1. The need for a common environment policy

European industrial society developed apace for a century (1860-1960) without a second thought for the ecological consequences of its growth. As we saw in the chapter on regional development, economic activities centred on certain places, for geographical and economic reasons, with no regard to the environment [see section 12.1.]. But, virtually **every human activity and industrial process affects the natural environment**, either through atmospheric or water pollution, noise pollution or even by the destruction of the countryside. Although environmental damage had been going on for a century, it was not until the 1960s and 1970s that it took on alarming proportions, for three main reasons: increased town-dwelling, very rapid economic expansion and the ill-considered use of new production techniques and of new products, chiefly derived from oil.

In the mosaic of States called Europe the **common market in terms of pollution** was established before the common market in goods. Polluted air and water moved freely across borders well before the idea emerged to open them to foreign goods. Each European State was thus immediately concerned by what was happening in its neighbouring countries with regard to the environment. It must not be forgotten that virtually every large lake and large watercourse in Europe is shared by two or more States, that the Mediterranean and the North Sea represent a common heritage for several European States and that those seas, lakes and rivers are used as common dumping grounds for the industrial waste of several countries. In the field of nature conservation and the protection of wildlife, too, a country that protected migratory birds or endangered species would be wasting its time if its neighbours killed them. If the mess was to be stopped, action therefore had to be taken together.

Not only neighbourliness, but also the comparable socio-economic development of the European countries, argued in favour of Community action to protect the environment. The **phenomena common to all European States** of the expansion of industrial activities, the increase in the urban population within megalopoles and the drift away from increasingly large tracts of territory originally used and maintained by agriculture required comparable measures and means to be utilised in the Member States to cope with them.

Common environmental problems **needed common solutions**. Short of seriously affecting the competitive capacity of its economy, no European State could hope to resolve its environmental problems by acting on its own. The fight against pollution in fact imposes certain expenditure on industrialists to adapt their products or their manufacturing processes. Such expenditure is all the greater, the more stringent are the standards laid down by the public authorities. If a State of the Union imposed stringent and **costly anti-pollution measures** on its industry, it might penalise it vis-à-vis its competitors from other States which were less attentive to the damage caused by pollution or which had different ideas as to how to apportion expenditure for the fight against pollution. Competition would therefore be distorted in the common market. It was therefore necessary for the same rules to be imposed on all European producers.

The free **movement of goods** within the common market would also be affected if each Member State laid down different standards for products put on sale on its market [see section 6.2.]. The country, which laid down more stringent standards than its neighbours, for example, on restrictions on the noise of certain engines or on the exhaust emissions of motor vehicles, would impede imports of related products from other countries. Protection against pollution and noise could thus quickly deteriorate into protection against foreign products. In other words, national environment policy could be used to thwart the internal market in a very subtle manner. On the other hand, environmental policy can make a huge contribution to growth, jobs and quality of life, with environmental measures having a positive impact on job creation, public health and healthcare costs, energy security and energy efficiency.

Lastly, it has to be said that the **European institutions are better placed than governments** to have a long-term view of environmental problems and requirements. Even when they are certain of remaining in office for fairly long time, national governments, being preoccupied with short-term problems, are rarely in a position to plan long-term strategies in this non-profit-making sector. Its relative detachment from the day-to-day problems peculiar to each Member State and its right of initiative with regard to the harmonisation of legislation make it possible for the European Commission to conceive a long-term programme against pollution [see section 4.1.2.]. Let us not forget, however, that in the case of the common environment policy, as in any other common policy, the "Eurocrats" of Brussels (the Commission), assisted by national technocrats (scientific and administrative committees), only propose the measures considered scientifically and technically necessary to protect the environment. It is the politicians in the European Parliament and the Council who take the final decisions [see section 4.3.], taking into consideration the industrial and political cost of precautionary measures proposed. These decisions, however, are taken collectively and concern all Member States.

The cost of the overexploitation of natural resources is far greater than the current clean-up activities such as waste and waste-water treatment. Moreover, the new environmental technologies, called **"clean-technologies"** present a dual advantage for European countries, since, on the one hand, they generate less waste and reduce emissions and, on the other, they minimise the use of natural resources. By improving the production process in terms of energy and natural resources efficiency, new technologies can reduce the dependence of the European Union on costly oil imports. By increasing product lifetime and by facilitating reuse and recycling, clean technologies can make more attractive the labour-intensive activities of control, repair and recycling.

To ensure better use of public resources while avoiding duplication on the part of European laboratories, very costly environmental research needs to be coordinated in a Community research and technological development programme [see section 18.2.2.]. Likewise, the control of jointly established standards requires the elaboration and implementation of efficient measurement methods recognised by all, the preparation of type-approved apparatus and, on occasion, the setting up of trans-European monitoring networks or even joint supervision bodies. Therefore, the objectives of the common environment policy can be linked to the objectives of the common industrial, energy, transport and employment policies.

One of the most urgent problems calling for a common approach was the elimination of industrial and urban waste. Even if the damaging effect of waste did not go beyond the confines of a region, European action would be necessary if **the elimination or re-use of waste** entailed substantial cost and led to differences between the conditions of production and distribution of certain goods in the common market. The most important waste for the EU is obviously waste whose disposal, owing to its toxicity, non-biodegradability, bulk or whatever reason, requires a solution that goes beyond a region or even a State.

16.2. Common strategy for sustainable development

Sustainable development is a key objective set out in the Treaty, for all European Community policies (Art. 3 TEC). It aims at the continuous improvement of the quality of life on Earth of both current and future generations, by combating the abusive exploitation of natural resources and of human beings. Consequently, it is based on the principles of democracy, solidarity, the rule of law and respect for fundamental rights including freedom and equal opportunities for all. It seeks to promote a dynamic economy respecting the environment, human values, cultural diversity, full employment, a high level of education, health protection, social and territorial cohesion in a peaceful and secure world. Concerning the environment, in particular, sustainable development seeks to prevent and reduce environmental pollution and promote sustainable production and consumption, respecting the limits of the planet's natural resources, in order to break the link between economic growth and environmental degradation.

The European Union's environment programme now aims at a development, which takes into account the present economic and social needs without jeopardising, through resource misuse, the **development possibilities of future generations**[1]. To be sustainable, growth must be decoupled from negative environmental impacts and be based on sustainable consumption and production patterns. This means that short term economic gains at the expense of the environment should be replaced by a more sustainable model of economic and social development, which may constitute the basis for greater efficiency and competitiveness, both at a Union level and internationally.

The Göteborg European Council (15-16 June 2001) approved a **European Union strategy for sustainable development**, proposed by the Commission[2], based on: coordinated development of common policies addressing the economic, environmental and social dimensions of sustainability and having sustainable development as their core objective; a set of headline objectives to limit climate change and increase use of clean energy, address threats to public health, manage natural resources more responsibly; and the steps to implement the strategy and review its progress at every spring meeting of the European Council (Cardiff process launched in 1998).

The **sixth Community environment action programme** sets out environmental objectives for the years 2001 to 2010 and outlines the action that needs to be taken to achieve them[3]. The programme focuses on four priority issues:

1. **tackling climate change** by reducing greenhouse gases according to the objectives of the Kyoto Protocol [see section 16.3.4.], i.e. achieving the Community's target of reducing emissions by 8% by 2008 to 2012 (compared to 1990 levels) and by 20 to 40% by 2020, through structural changes and stronger efforts on energy-saving, especially in the transport and energy sectors, the establishment of an EU-wide emissions trading scheme, further research and technological development;

---

[1] COM (2001) 31, 24 January 2001.
[2] COM (2001) 264, 15 May 2001.
[3] Decision 1600/2002, OJ L 242, 10.09.2002.

2. **nature and biodiversity**, i.e. protecting and restoring the structure and functioning of natural systems and halting the loss of biodiversity notably through: the implementation of environmental legislation; protection, conservation and restoration of landscapes; completion of the Natura 2000 network to avert the threats to the survival of many species and their habitats in Europe, through a set of sectoral biodiversity action plans; new initiatives for protecting the marine environment; and a thematic strategy for protecting soils[1];

3. **environment and health**, i.e. achieving a quality of the environment which does not endanger human health, necessitating *inter alia:* a fundamental overhaul of the Community's risk-management system for chemicals[2], a strategy for reducing risks from pesticides, protection of water quality in the Union, noise abatement and a thematic strategy for air quality;

4. **sustainable management of natural resources** by decoupling resource use from economic growth, in particular through: improved resource efficiency; taxation of resource use; increased recycling and waste prevention with the aid of an integrated product policy.

The **global monitoring for environment and security (GMES)** initiative aims at coordinating European activities in the field of satellite observation and remote sensing so as to provide support for government policies (in particular concerning the environment, agriculture, regional development, fisheries, transport and common foreign and security policy) by developing a global independent European monitoring capacity to be operational by 2008[3] [see also sections 18.2.4 and 18.4.1] .

16.2.1. The foundations of the common environment policy

Although the Community had enough economic and political arguments for dealing with environmental problems [see section 16.1.], **it did not initially have a solid legal basis** for so doing. In order to set Community objectives for the reduction of pollution and nuisances, reference could only be made to Article 2 of the EEC Treaty, which assigned to the Community the task, *inter alia*, of promoting "an accelerated raising of the standard of living" of the populations belonging to it. In order to undertake urgent measures to stop the process of deterioration of the environment, the Community provisions had to be based on Article 235 of that Treaty (Art. 308 TEC), which specifically permitted action in areas in which the Treaty had not provided the necessary powers, but which required unanimity of the Member States, with the slowness that it involved.

The legal basis of environment policy was considerably enlarged by the Single Act of 1987 [see section 2.1.] and **firmly established by the Maastricht Treaty** [see section 2.2.]. As revised at Amsterdam, Article 2 of that the EU Treaty sets the achievement of balanced and sustainable development among the objectives of the Union. The common environment policy has now the **following objectives**: preserving, protecting and improving the quality of the environment; protecting human health; rationalising the utilisation of natural resources; promoting measures at international level to deal with regional or world-wide environmental problems (Art. 174 TEC).

According to Article 175 (TEC), the Council acting under the **co-decision procedure** with the European Parliament [see section 4.3.] and after consultation of the Economic and Social Committee and of the Committee of the Regions takes the measures necessary for the implementation of the objectives of Article 174. Still, **the unanimity of the Council** acting after consultation of the European Parliament and the ESC is needed for: provisions primarily of a fiscal nature; measures concerning town and country planning; and measures significantly affecting a Member State's energy supply.

---

[1] COM(2001) 162, 27 March 2001.
[2] See Commission White Paper, COM (2001) 88, 13 February 2001.
[3] COM/2004/65, 3 February 2004.

The Member States finance and implement environment policy. However, without prejudice to the principle that the polluter pays, if a measure involves costs deemed disproportionate for the public authorities of a Member State, notably a cohesion State [see section 12.1.2.], the Council, in the act adopting that measure, lays down appropriate provisions in the form of temporary derogations and/or financial support from the Cohesion Fund (Art. 175 TEC).

Indeed, the activities, which the Community undertakes or wishes to undertake to protect the environment and conserve nature in Europe and in the rest of the world, are becoming increasingly costly and must be planned over the long term. Awareness of this provided the impetus for the creation of a **financial instrument for the environment, LIFE**, which seeks to promote the development and implementation of the Community's environment policy and legislation by financing priority projects in the Community, such as the "Natura 2000" network, and by providing technical assistance to the associated countries of Central and Eastern Europe as well as countries in the Mediterranean region or in Baltic coastal areas[1]. It provides financial assistance for preparatory measures, demonstration schemes, awareness campaigns, incentives, technical assistance and measures necessary for the maintenance or restoration of biotopes, natural habitats and species [see section 16.4.]. In addition to LIFE, Community support through the Structural Funds and the Cohesion Fund facilitates the realisation of joint environmental projects (Jeeps) in the poorest Member States. Furthermore, the Community grants financial support to non-governmental organisations active in the field of environmental protection, in order to help them contribute, to the development and implementation of Community environmental policy and legislation in different regions of Europe[2].

The protective measures adopted under Article 175 (TEC) do not prevent any Member State from maintaining or introducing more stringent national measures (Art. 176 TEC). However, environmental protection can no longer be used as a pretext for technical barriers to trade. Internal market policy and environment policy must therefore march forward side by side. To this end, the Commission adopted on March 26, 1991, the guidelines for a legislative model seeking to reconcile the demands of the environment with those of the market. This model sets **two stages for the definition of environmental standards**. The first consists of the setting by the Commission of a high-level standard, in accordance with Article 95, paragraph 3 of the EC Treaty. This standard should be based on the technology available within a specific time span and should be applied by all the Member States as rapidly as possible. During the second stage, the Council sets a "target" standard, corresponding to the highest level of protection which can be reasonably envisaged in light of the latest scientific and technological developments.

16.2.2. The principles of the common environment policy

The common environment policy is based on the **precautionary and preventive action** principles, on the principle that environmental damage should to the extent possible be **rectified at source** and on the principle that **the polluter should pay** (Art. 174 TEC).

Indeed, the European Union's work on the environment is marked more and more by an integrated, **preventive approach** taking account of human activities and their consequences for the environment as a whole. The pro-active policy of voluntary prevention is manifested in the Directive on **the assessment of the effects of certain public and private projects** on the environment and on natural resources, which takes into account the commitments entered into under the international "Espoo" Convention on Environmental Impact Assessment in a Transboundary Context, particularly concerning the

[1] Regulation 1655/2000, OJ L 192, 28.07.2000 and Regulation 1682/2004, OJ L 308, 05.10.2004.
[2] Decision 466/2002, OJ L 75, 16.03.2002 and Decision 786/2004, OJ L 138, 30.04.2004.

types of project for which impact assessment is compulsory[1]. According to this Directive, the promoter of the project, whether it be industrial, agricultural or relating to infrastructure, has to supply detailed information on its possible consequences for air, water, soil, noise, wild animals and their habitats, etc. The decision of the public authority as to whether to authorise the project must weigh the economic, social or other advantages of the project against its environmental consequences. In accordance with the UN Convention on Access to Information, Public Participation in Decision-Making and Access to Justice in Environmental Matters (the Århus Convention), the public (one or more natural or legal persons) may participate in the drawing-up of environmental standards concerning waste, air quality and the protection of water. Member States should ensure that members of the public concerned have access to a review procedure before a court of law or another independent and impartial body established by law to challenge the substantive or procedural legality of decisions, acts or omissions subject to the public participation provisions of the Directive[2]. Another Directive imposes an assessment, including the preparing of an environmental report, during the preparation of a plan or programme and before its adoption or submission to the legislative procedure[3]. The authorities and the public affected or likely to be affected by or having an interest in the decision-making process have the opportunity to express their opinion on the environmental effects of a draft plan or programme.

The **"polluter pays" principle**, which is mentioned in Article174, paragraph 2, of the EC Treaty, means that the cost incurred in combating pollution and nuisances in the first instance falls to the polluter, i.e. the polluting industry. Given, however, that the polluting industry can pass the cost of the prevention or elimination of pollution on to the consumer, the principle amounts to saying that **polluting production should bear**: **the expenditure** corresponding to the measures necessary to combat pollution (investment in apparatus and equipment for combating pollution, implementation of new processes, operating expenditure for anti-pollution plant, etc.); **and the charges** whose purpose is to encourage the polluter himself to take, as cheaply as possible, the measures necessary to reduce the pollution caused by him (incentive function) or to make him bear his share of the costs of collective purification measures (redistribution function). The Community guidelines on State aid for environmental protection, which we have seen in the chapter on competition [see section 15.5.2.], are designed to ensure that aid granted for environmental purposes complies with the "polluter pays" principle.

Based on the "polluter pays" principle, an important directive establishes a framework of **environmental liability** with regard to the prevention and remedying of environmental damage, including transboundary damage, but excluding damage caused by *force majeure* or expressly authorised activities[4]. It aims at preventing environmental damage to water resources, soil, fauna, flora and natural habitats and at making the polluters pay whenever damage cannot be avoided. Risky or potentially risky activities include activities releasing heavy metals into water or the air, installations producing dangerous chemicals, landfill sites and incineration plants. Member States are required to ensure that all environmental damage is restored, which entails assessing the gravity and extent of the damage and determining the most appropriate restoration measures to be taken. If the costs of implementing the prevention and restoration measures were not borne directly by the operator who caused the pollution, the competent authority must make sure that they are recovered from the operator. Member States are also required to

---

[1]   Directive 85/337, OJ L 175, 05.07.1985 and Directive 2003/35, OJ L 156, 25.06.2003.
[2]   Directive 2003/35, OJ L 156, 25.06.2003.
[3]   Directive 2001/42, OJ L 197, 21.07.2001.
[4]   Directive 2004/35, OJ L 143, 30.04.2004 and Directive 2006/21, OJ L 102, 11.04.2006.

promote the development of financial security products and encourage operators to take out financial security cover. Non-governmental environmental protection organisations and persons who have a sufficient interest, i.e. who have suffered damage, can request the competent authority to take action and challenge any action or inaction by the competent authorities.

Another means for the prevention of pollutions is the "**eco-label**", which guides the consumers towards "clean" products [see section 11.1.] and incites the industrialists to produce them, thus contributing to the efficient use of resources planned and to a high level of environmental protection[1]. The scheme functions on a voluntary basis and may be applied to a product belonging to product groups for which ecological criteria have been set by the Commission in accordance with the regulation.

A competent body in the Member State, in which the product is manufactured, placed on the market for the first time or imported is responsible for deciding whether or not to **grant the eco-label**, after assessment of the ecological performance of the product in accordance with the general principles given in the Regulation and the specific criteria set by the Commission, assisted by a committee of representatives of the Member States. In this way, the Commission established the ecological criteria for several categories of manufactured products, including laundry detergents[2], dishwater detergents[3], indoor paints and varnishes[4] and refrigerators[5].

Prevention is also the objective of the Regulation on the "**eco-audit**" scheme, which allows voluntary participation by companies in the industrial sector in a Community eco-management and audit scheme (EMAS)[6]. This scheme is based on three elements: the establishment and implementation by the companies in question of environmental policies, programmes and management systems for their production sites; systematic, objective and periodical evaluation of the efficiency of these programmes and systems by independent verifiers; and annual information for the general public in the form of "environmental declarations" by companies participating in the system. A Community logo is meant to raise the profile of businesses determined to improve their environmental performance by participating in the scheme.

16.2.3. Notification, information and monitoring

The **European Environment Agency**, which is established near Copenhagen, provides the Commission and the national authorities with the technical, scientific and economic information necessary for the framing and implementation of measures and legislation relating to the environment[7]. Being a Community body open to third countries because of the multinational character of problems and work concerning the environment, the Agency acts as a European network for monitoring and obtaining information on the environment. The **European pollutant release and transfer register** ("the European PRTR") aims to contribute to the prevention and reduction of pollution by providing data for policy-makers as well as facilitating public participation in decision-making[8].

In any event, the Commission receives information on the legislative or administrative intentions of the Member States. It verifies the transposition by the Member States of Community legislation into national law and initiates proceedings against States which either fail to implement Community provisions on the environment in full or correctly or do not give notification of domestic measures on the environment. The Commission has an important ally in the matter, namely **the citizens in the Member States**, who are concerned at environmental damage and make a growing number of complaints

[1] Regulation 1980/2000, OJ L 237, 21.09.2000.
[2] Decision 95/365, OJ L 217, 13.09.1995.
[3] Decision 1999/427, OJ L 167, 02.07.1999 last amended by Decision 2003/31, OJ L 9, 15.01.2003.
[4] Decision 96/13, OJ L 4, 06.01.1996.
[5] Decision 96/703, OJ L 323, 13.12.1996.
[6] Regulation 761/2001, OJ L 114, 24.04.2001 last amended by Regulation 196/2006, OJ L 32, 04.02.2006.
[7] Regulation 1210/90, OJ L 120, 11.05.1990 and Regulation 1641/2003, OJ L 245, 29.09.2003.
[8] Regulation 166/2006, OJ L 33, 04.02.2006.

to it each year [see section 9.3.]. When it receives a complaint from an individual citizen or association, the Commission carries out an inquiry to verify the facts, and if it considers that Community law has been infringed it initiates the procedure provided for in Article 226 of the EC Treaty [see section 4.1.2.]. A Directive, implementing the UN Aarhus Convention, guarantees freedom of access to and dissemination of information on the environment held by public authorities and sets the basic conditions under which information on the environment should be made available to the public[1]. The latter, through pressure that it can exercise on national authorities can contribute a great deal to improving the respect of Community legislation.

In 1973 the Representatives of the Governments of the Member States meeting in Council adopted an Agreement on information for the Commission and for the Member States with a view to possible harmonisation throughout the Community of urgent measures concerning the protection of the environment and intervention if the draft rules did not comply with Community policy[2]. However, since the end of the 1980s national drafts were increasingly notified under the Directive laying down a procedure for **the provision of information in the field of technical standards and regulations**, discussed under the heading of technical barriers to trade in the chapter on the common market[3] [see section 6.2.]. As the Court of Justice noted in its judgment of 20 September 1988 on the "Danish bottles" case[4], national environmental measures are likely to affect completion of the internal market and therefore need to be notified under the general notification procedure.

For their own information, the national and Community authorities dispose of a common procedure for the setting up and constant updating of an **inventory of sources of information on the environment** in the Community[5]. A Council Directive standardised and rationalised the environment reports produced by the Member States[6]. The Member States have established a reciprocal exchange of information and data from networks and individual stations measuring ambient air pollution[7]. Common monitoring mechanisms such as the Parliament and Council recommendation providing for minimum criteria for environmental inspections in the Member States[8], seek to integrate the environmental objectives of the Union into national policies.

The Community action programme promoting non-governmental organisations (NGOs) primarily active in the field of environmental protection supports the systematic involvement of NGOs at all stages of the Community environmental policy-making process and contributes to the strengthening of small regional or local associations working to apply the acquis communautaire in relation to the environment and sustainable development in their local area[9].

16.2.4. Environment and other common policies

Article 6 of the EC Treaty, stipulates that environmental protection requirements must be integrated into the **definition and implementation of other Community policies**. This is meant to ensure environmental protection in all its forms by means of prior analysis of the potential problems in this sector and of the adoption of measures which integrate environmental requirements into the planning and performance of economic and social activities. In fact, many environmental issues such as climate change, acidification and waste management can only be tackled by an interplay between the main economic public and private actors, not only by legislative means, but also by an extended and integrated mix of other instruments, such as standards, certification systems, voluntary schemes or economic instruments. Therefore, the sustainable protection of the environment depends to a large extent on the common policies pursued in the fields of indus-

---

[1] Directive 2003/4, OJ L 41, 14.02.2003.
[2] OJ C 9, 15.03.1973 and OJ C 86, 20.07.1974, p. 2.
[3] Directive 98/34, OJ L 204, 21.07.1998 last amended by Directive 98/48, OJ L 217, 05.08.1998.
[4] Case 302/86, ECR 1988, p. 4607.
[5] Decision 76/161, OJ L 31, 05.02.1976.
[6] Directive 91/692, OJ L 377, 31.12.1991 and Decision 97/622, OJ L 256, 19.09.1997.
[7] Decision 97/101, OJ L 35, 05.02.1997 last amended by Decision 2001/752, OJ L 282, 26.10.2001.
[8] Recommendation 2001/331, OJ L 118, 27.04.2001.
[9] Decision 466/2002, OJ L 75, 16.03.2002 last amended by Decision 786/2004, OJ L 138, 30.04.2004.

try, energy, transport, agriculture and tourism, which are in turn dependent on the capacity of the environment to sustain them.

In a communication, drawn up in response to a request by the Cologne European Council in June 1999, the Commission set out a long-term Community strategy for the progressive **integration of environmental issues with economic policy**[1]. The essential elements of this strategy are as follows: a transparent approach to environmental integration, based on efficient target setting derived from a comprehensive analysis of the available scientific and technical data; consistency of the economic policy with the strategy for sustainable development; integration of the examination of the environmental impact of economic activity and regulation into the process of multilateral surveillance of structural reform and into the economic reform process; incorporation of the objectives of environmental integration into the broad economic policy guidelines (BEPGs) [see section 7.3.1.]; contribution of taxation policies to environmental integration; use of an appropriate mix of market-based instruments and regulations, including the removal of subsidies which are harmful to the environment.

In the related field of **civil protection**, a Solidarity Fund is destined to provide rapid financial assistance to the population of the regions hit mainly by major natural disasters[2]. A Community action programme aims at organising the levels of preparedness in each Member State and at achieving closer Community cooperation for the protection of the population, the environment and property in the event of a natural or technological disaster[3]. A Council Resolution aims at strengthening the capabilities of the European Union in the field of civil protection, notably by the use of advanced information and telecommunications systems, of developing information campaigns and education aimed at the public and of pooling experience and exchanges of persons between Member States[4]. The Community encourages cooperation between schools and national training centres active in the field of civil protection by supporting the creation of a network between such establishments[5].

Enterprise policy can contribute to sustainable development through sustainable use of natural resources, waste management, innovation and standardisation. The industrial sector has to take ecological requirements increasingly into account in the choice of products and manufacturing processes. Thus, henceforth the environment is one of the factors making a difference to the competitive position of companies or industries. Below we shall examine the constraints imposed on heavily polluting sectors like the chemicals, steel and detergents sectors. On the other hand, the so-called "Eco-industry" is a rapidly expanding market with increasing importance for Europe. It covers not only the supply of goods and services to firms for pollution control and abatement but also the expenditures made for improving production methods, using energy more efficiently and developing less polluting products. In addition, the harmonisation of laws on quality standards for industrial products is in reality targeted on a twofold objective: the uniform protection of man and the Community environment, and the removal of barriers to trade resulting from differences in the standards or technical specifications in Community countries. These two objectives are pursued by environmental control of products and the granting of a Community eco-label[6] [see section 16.2.2.].

Environment policy has close ties with **energy policy**, as the production and use of energy are amongst the principal sources of air pollution (burning of fossil fuels) and water pollution (through the discharge of cooling-waters and polluting substances by refineries and nuclear power stations). It is obvious that the policy for the rational use of energy and encouragement of soft (non-polluting) energy is first and foremost in the interests of the environment. It should also be noted that, with the exception of the management of radioactive waste, the bulk of Community work on nuclear safety is carried out in the framework of the Euratom Treaty and therefore under energy policy rather than environment policy [see sections 18.3.1. and 19.2.3.].

---

[1] COM (2000) 576, 20 September 2000.
[2] Regulation 2012/2002, OJ L 311, 14.11.2002 and Decision 2002/1010, OJ L 358, 31.12.2002.
[3] Decision 1999/847, OJ L 327, 21.12.1999 and Decision 2005/12, OJ L 6, 08.01.2005.
[4] Resolution, OJ C 82, 13.03.2001.
[5] Resolution, OJ C 43, 16.02.2002.
[6] Regulation 1980/2000, OJ L 237, 21.09.2000.

The various **means of transport**, particularly in urban areas, are another source of pollution and many environmental measures are designed to reduce it. With the aim of defining a common strategy on transport and environment policies, the Commission adopted a Green Paper in February 1992 on the impact of transport on the environment[1]. After taking stock of the adverse effects of transport on the environment and reviewing trends and forecasts relating to transport demand and traffic volume, the Commission outlined a common strategy for developing transport in an environmentally compatible way.

The Community action programme on the environment is underpinned by a multiannual programme of **research in the field of the environment** and the climate covering the study of the natural environment, global change, environmental technologies, space technologies for environmental monitoring and the human dimension of environmental change [see section 18.4.1.]. The development of clean products and processes in the European Union does not only prevent rapidly increasing clean-up costs but also stimulates the diffusion of Community research to the rest of the world who needs it badly.

The **common agricultural policy** developed during the 1970s without any consideration whatsoever for the environment. Thus, it resulted in the ill-considered use of pesticides and fertilisers, which are very harmful to the environment. Fortunately, such excesses seem to have been curbed since the mid-1980s, and agricultural and environmental policies now have a common goal, which is to improve the Union's rural area [see section 21.5.3.]. In this framework, the Council adopted: a Regulation on organic production of agricultural products and its presentation on agricultural products and foodstuffs[2]; a Directive on the placing of plant protection products on the market[3]; and a Directive on the protection of waters against pollution caused by nitrates from agricultural sources[4].

The sustainable development of resources is fully integrated into the **common fisheries policy** by means of measures taken to conserve resources, preserve marine biodiversity and rationalise fishing. The environmental impact of fisheries is taken into account, in particular, by the systematic consultation of scientific experts when legislative measures on the exploitation of resources are drafted. Improved measures for sustainable fishing are also developed by scientific research [see section 22.2.]

Community **regional policy** and environment policy are complementary, as regional aid can help to reverse inordinate urbanisation, which gives rise to ecological problems, whilst measures to combat pollution can have a dissuasive effect on the establishment of industries in congested regions of the European Union. This is why, the Community framework on State aids for environmental protection takes account of the environmental programme and encourages the application of the "polluter pays" principle [see section 15.5.2.]. The Cohesion Fund, the Structural Funds [see sections 12.1.2. and 12.3.], the rural development policy of the common agricultural policy and the conservation of fishery resources policy [see sections 21.5.2. and 22.2.2.] take increasingly account of the sustainable development objective of the common environment policy.

16.2.5. International environmental cooperation

Some forms of pollution are threatening not only the European ecological systems but also the **natural balance of the entire planet**, e.g. climate change, ozone layer, bio-diversity). These problems have to be tackled on an international basis. Participation by the Community as such in the work of specialist international bodies geared to preserving the world's natural wealth and preventing barriers to international trade forestalls differences of opinion amongst the Member States and highlights their common interests. Furthermore, active participation by the Community in the work on the environment of other international organisations, such as the OECD, the Council of Europe and the United Nations, enables Community law to follow international thinking in that area. As we shall see in the following sections, the Community as such has signed several international conventions for the protection of the environment.

The Community as a body participated in the **United Nations Conference on the environment and development (UNCED)**, the so-called "Earth Summit", held in Rio de Janeiro from June 3 to 14, 1992. This conference culminated in the adoption of the Rio Declaration and the "Agenda 21", which is the international community's action programme for the environment and development in the twenty-first century and contains a number of innovative features, namely acknowledgement of the need for sustainable development; shared but differentiated responsibility of States; and world partnership. The environmentally sustainable development strategy is now incorporated in the Community programme on the environment. The European Community is a contracting party to the UN Convention on Climate Change, the Kyoto Protocol of this Convention [see section 16.3.4.] and several Conventions for the protection of the atmosphere, the sea and inland waters. It is actively involved in the international work to follow up the UNCED, particularly in the meetings of the Commission on

---

[1] COM (92) 46.
[2] Regulation 2092/91, OJ L 198, 22.07.1991 and Regulation 780/2006, OJ L 137, 25.05.2006.
[3] Directive 91/414, OJ L 230, 19.08.1991 and Directive 2005/25, OJ L 90, 08.04.2005.
[4] Directive 91/676, OJ L 375, 30.12.1991.

Sustainable Development which concern forest conservation, the protection of biodiversity, urban and rural environment, land management and coastal resource management of developing countries.

The agreement on the **European Economic Area** (EEA) between the EU and the EFTA countries institutes, among other things, a close environmental cooperation [see section 25.1.]. Relations between the countries of Western Europe and the European countries **candidates for accession** have an environmental component, so as to redress the ecological situation at the same time as the economic situation of those countries [see section 25.2.]. One of the aims pursued by projects supported in the framework of the PHARE programme is directly to improve the environmental situation in the countries aided and even to lay the foundations of a coherent policy in this area.

16.3. Reduction of pollution and nuisances

The efforts of the Community environment policy to combat pollution and nuisances are more specifically directed towards: the fixing of quality objectives for European waters, the control of discharges into the aquatic environment of the European Union, efforts to combat sea and air pollution, the prevention of industrial accidents and efforts to combat noise pollution. These various groups of activity are examined in succession below.

16.3.1. Quality objectives for European waters

Water is an element indispensable not only to human life, but also to many of man's activities, from fishing to industry, by way of agriculture. **Water plays an essential role in the natural ecological balance** by procuring a substantial proportion of the oxygen necessary for life. In addition, seas, lakes and rivers are of great value for recreational activities and leisure, which are indispensable for town-dwellers. The Commission considers that appropriate water pricing has a key role to play in the development of sustainable water policies given that the sustainability of water resources is at stake in many river basins in Europe, from both a quantitative and a qualitative point of view[1].

The physical interdependence of the various surroundings that make up the aquatic ecosystem, such as surface fresh water, groundwater and seawater, **necessitates the coherent management of these resources**. The fact that watercourses often cross several countries and that lakeshores also extend across the territories of several countries dictates the common management of these resources. Comparable, and sometimes common, management of water is indispensable, *inter alia*, to prevent distortions of competition between major water-using undertakings. Therefore, Directive 2000/60 establishing a framework for Community action in the field of water policy lays down a basis for coordinating the Member States' policies and measures to protect inland surface waters, transitional waters, coastal waters and groundwater[2]. The **principal objectives of this policy** are to:

- prevent further deterioration and protect and enhance the state of aquatic ecosystems;
- promote sustainable use of water based on the long-term protection of available water resources;
- ensure the progressive reduction of pollution of groundwater and prevent further pollution thereof;

---

[1] COM (2000) 477, 26 July 2000.
[2] Directive 2000/60, OJ L 327, 22.12.2000.

- provide a sufficient supply of good quality surface water and groundwater as needed for sustainable, balanced and equitable water use; and
- protect territorial and marine waters.

To achieve these objectives, the EU States lay down quality objectives or quality standards so as to manage water rationally and limit water pollution. Supplementing Directive 2000/60 on water policy, a decision establishes a list of 33 substances or groups of substances, some of which are identified as "priority hazardous substances", discharges of which must be halted, and others as "priority substances under review"[1]. Quality objectives, which vary according to the intended use of the water (drinking water, bathing water or water suitable for fish-breeding), lay down the **pollution or nuisance levels not to be exceeded** in a given surrounding or part thereof. European directives fix certain mandatory values, which must not be exceeded, and some guide values, which Member States endeavour to comply with [see details below].

Concerning the quality of **water intended for human consumption** and water used in the food-manufacturing industries, a Directive lays down "mandatory" values and "guide" values i.e. maximum admissible concentrations of numerous undesirable elements for all water supplied for human consumption or used in the food industries[2], with the exception of natural mineral waters, which are governed by another Directive[3].

As regards **bathing water**, Directive 2006/7 lays down quality standards for running or still fresh water and sea water in regions in which bathing is authorised or tolerated[4]. The Directive lays down a sampling procedure and fixes the frequency of the checks to be carried out and the methods of analysis to be applied to areas where the number of bathers is highest, and in particular at peak bathing times. The Member States have to forward to the Commission each year a summary report concerning the most significant properties of their bathing waters. The Commission publishes an annual summary report on bathing water quality in the Community, including bathing water classifications, conformity with this Directive and significant management measures undertaken. Thus, this Directive represents an impressive undertaking for cleaning up Europe's coastlines, requiring substantial investment in wastewater purifiers and diffusers, an undertaking that has proved to be well worth the effort. Indeed, thanks to the Community directive there has been a big improvement in the quality of bathing waters in recent years.

A Directive aims to protect or improve the quality of those running or standing **fresh waters** which support, or which, if pollution were reduced or eliminated, would become capable of supporting fish life[5]. A Directive of 1979, on the quality required of shellfish waters, is directed towards protecting and improving such waters in order to permit the development of molluscs in favourable conditions and to contribute to the good quality of edible shellfish[6].

16.3.2. Control of discharges into the aquatic environment

To attain and maintain the water-quality objectives described above, strict methods must be used to **reduce pollution caused by certain dangerous substances** discharged into the European aquatic environment, i.e. inland surface water, groundwater, internal coastal waters and territorial sea waters. Some toxic substances discharged into the water are, of course, chemically or biologically diluted and decomposed until their toxicity disappears, but others are persistent, i.e. they retain their chemical composition, and therefore their danger to the environment and to man, for a lengthy period, which can, in some cases, be several years.

For this reason a Community Directive contains provisions on the collection, processing and discharge of **urban waste water** and biodegradable water from some indus-

---

[1] Decision 2455/2001, OJ L 331, 15.12.2001.
[2] Directive 98/83, OJ L 330, 05.12.1998.
[3] Directive 80/777, OJ L 229, 30.08.1980.
[4] Directive 2006/7, OJ L 64, 04.03.2006.
[5] Directive 2006/44, OJ L 264, 25.09.2006.
[6] Directive 79/923, OJ L 281, 10.11.1979 repealed by Directive 2000/60, OJ L 327, 22.12.2000.

trial sectors, and on the disposal of sludges[1]. In particular, the Directive stipulates that as a general rule, waste water which enters into collection systems must, before disposal, be subjected to secondary treatment in accordance with a timetable adjusted to the size of the population covered and the type and situation of the collection water. Another Directive concerns the protection of waters against pollution caused by nitrates from agricultural sources[2].

A Directive on pollution caused by certain dangerous substances discharged into the aquatic environment of the Community is directed towards curbing the process of the deterioration of that environment by **prohibiting or restricting the discharge of toxic substances**[3]. The latter are divided into two lists: a "black list" grouping particularly toxic, persistent and bioaccumulable substances, and a "grey list" which mainly concerns substances whose harmful effects are limited to one locality and depend on the properties of the receiving waters. The "black list" is constantly amended in the light of the development of scientific and technical knowledge of the toxicity of the various substances[4]. Whether substances from the first list or the second list are involved, the Directive provides for authorisations granted for all discharges into Community waters, issued by the competent authority of the Member State concerned for a limited period [see details below].

The elaboration of Community standards is a lengthy and complicated process. The Commission has to propose, for each substance from the two lists, the **maximum values not to be exceeded in a surrounding**, taking into account both the toxicity of the substance, its persistence and its bioaccumulation properties, as well as the best technical means available for disposing of them. Acting on Commission proposals, in the context of implementing Directive 2006/11, the Council adopted Directives on: **mercury**[5], **cadmium**[6], **hexachlorocyclohexane**[7] and **other dangerous substances** on the "black list" in Directive 2006/11, such as carbon tetrachloride, DDT and pentachlorophenol[8]. All these lists of dangerous substances and the measures necessary for controlling their discharge into the aquatic environment appear fastidious at first sight, but they are costly for polluting undertakings and very useful for consumers, who would otherwise be deprived of drinkable water in Europe if they did not exist.

The **growing use of chemical compounds** in industry, agriculture and in products of household use poses ever-more serious dangers to the environment and human health. Hence, **detergents** are a significant cause of pollution of the Community's aquatic ecosystem. The formation of foam in waters into which detergents are discharged in large quantities limits the contact between water and air, makes oxygenation difficult, jeopardises the photosynthesis necessary for the life of aquatic flora, has an adverse effect on waste water purifying processes and constitutes a risk of the transmission of bacteria and viruses. For those reasons and in order to prevent technical barriers to trade the Community has harmonised the laws of the Member States relating to the placing on the market and the use of detergents[9].

One very dangerous industrial sector for the aquatic environment is that of the manufacture of **titanium dioxide**, which is a pigment used for the manufacture of paints, varnishes, plastics, inks, etc. Untreated waste from factories which produce titanium dioxide is known as "red sludge". The alteration of the colour and transparency of water which it causes leads to the reduction of photosynthesis and phytoplankton and, in the most serious cases, to the disappearance of all life from estuary waters and the waters of the receiving sea. Hence, a Directive on waste from the titanium dioxide industry, provides for the control by the Member States of the operations for treating such waste[10] and another Directive sets procedures for harmonising the programmes for the reduction and eventual elimination of pollution caused by waste from the titanium dioxide industry[11].

---

[1] Directive 91/271, OJ L 135, 30.05.1991 and Directive 98/15, OJ L 67, 07.03.1998.
[2] Directive 91/676, OJ L 375, 31.12.1991.
[3] Directive 2006/11, OJ L 64, 04.03.2006.
[4] Directive 86/280, OJ L 181, 04.07.1986 and Directive 91/692, OJ L 377, 31.12.1991.
[5] Directive 82/176, OJ L 81 of 27.03.1982 and Directive 91/692, OJ L 377, 31.12.1991.
[6] Directive 83/513, OJ L 291, 24.10.1983 and Directive 91/692, OJ L 377, 31.12.1991.
[7] Directive 84/491, OJ L 274, 17.10.1984 and Directive 91/692, OJ L 377, 31.12.1991.
[8] Directive 86/280, OJ L 181, 04.07.1986 and Directive 91/692, OJ L 377, 31.12.1991.
[9] Regulation 648/2004, OJ L 104, 08.04.2004 last amended by Regulation 907/2006, OJ L 168, 21.06.2006.
[10] Directive 78/176, OJ L 54, 25.02.1978 and Directive 91/692, OJ L 377, 31.12.1991.
[11] Directive 92/112, OJ L 409, 31.12.1992.

In addition to its own work to combat the pollution of the aquatic environment, the Community participates in the work carried out in the **framework of international cooperation**, including: the Convention on the Protection of the Rhine[1]; the Convention for the protection of the marine environment of the north-east Atlantic[2]; the Convention on the protection and use of transboundary watercourses and international lakes[3]; and the Convention on cooperation for the protection and sustainable use of the Danube[4].

16.3.3. Effort to combat marine pollution

The marine environment is a precious asset, since oceans and seas cover 70% of the Earth's surface and contain 90% of its biosphere. Of all forms of pollution, sea pollution is one of the most dangerous because of its consequences for fundamental biological and ecological balances, the degree of degradation already reached, the diversity of sources of pollution and the difficulty of monitoring compliance with measures adopted. Apart from the accidental spillage of hydrocarbons in the sea, the **main sources of sea pollution are land-based ones**, i.e. the discharge of effluent from land and discharges of waste at sea. Therefore, the measures taken to control discharges into the aquatic environment, examined above, combat marine pollution.

The danger of serious pollution from **massive discharges of hydrocarbons** for the coasts of the EU States and for the seas surrounding them became a matter of common concern, in 1978, after the shipwreck of the giant oil tanker "Amoco-Cadiz" and the serious pollution of the coasts of Brittany that ensued. In June 1978 the Council set up an action programme of the European Communities on the control and reduction of pollution caused by hydrocarbons discharged at sea[5]. In order to implement this action programme the Commission set up under its aegis an Advisory Committee on the Control and Reduction of Pollution Caused by Hydrocarbons Discharged at Sea[6]. International standards for ship-source pollution are incorporated into Community law and ensure that persons responsible for environmental disasters resulting both from the pollution caused by accidents involving ships carrying substances harmful to the marine environment and from deliberate discharges by ships, including tank-cleaning and waste oil disposal at sea, are subject to **adequate penalties**[7].

It should be noted that the Community effort to combat marine pollution is based on voluntary measures and cooperation between the Member States. Thus, a **Community framework for cooperation** in the field of accidental marine pollution from harmful substances, whatever their origin, aims at the prevention of the risks and at efficient mutual assistance between Member States in this field, including compensation for damage in accordance with the polluter-pays principle[8] [see also section 20.3.4.].

In a Resolution, the Council underlines that Community measures on maritime safety and pollution control **must apply to all vessels operating in the European Union waters** irrespective of their flag. In its view, further EU action in this field should have the following objectives: to tighten up ship inspection and withdraw sub-standard vessels; to improve shipping safety; to identify environmentally sensitive areas, on the basis of current legislation and international guidelines, and to propose specific measures for those areas to the International Maritime Organisation (IMO)[9].

In fact, the effort to combat pollution of the seas requires action not only at Community, but at international level too. The Community accordingly participates as such in the **international agreements** against the

---

[1] Protocol of signature and Decision 2000/706, OJ L 289, 16.11.2000.
[2] Convention, OJ L 104, 03.04.1998 and Annex V, OJ L 118, 19.05.2000.
[3] Convention and Decision 95/308, OJ L 186, 05.08.1995.
[4] Convention and Decision 97/825, OJ L 342, 12.12.1997.
[5] Resolution, OJ C 162, 08.07.1978, p. 1-4.
[6] Decision 80/686, OJ L 188, 22.07.1980 and Decision 87/144, OJ L 57, 27.02.1987.
[7] Directive 2005/35, OJ L 255, 30.09.2005.
[8] Decision 2850/2000, OJ L 332, 28.12.2000 and decision 787/2004, OJ L 138, 30.04.2004.
[9] Resolution, OJ C 271, 07.10.1993, p. 1-3.

pollution of the North Sea and the Mediterranean, including: the Bonn Agreement for cooperation in dealing with pollution of the North Sea by oil and other dangerous substances[1]; the Helsinki Convention on the protection of the Baltic Sea[2]; the Convention for the protection of the marine environment of the North-East Atlantic (OSPAR Convention)[3]; the Barcelona Convention on the Protection of the Mediterranean Sea against Pollution[4]; the Protocol concerning cooperation in combating pollution of the Mediterranean Sea by oil and other harmful substances in cases of emergency[5]; and the Protocol for the Protection of the Mediterranean Sea against Pollution from Land-based Sources[6]. The revision of the Barcelona Convention and its Protocols, signed in June 1995, extended its scope to cover coastal zones and introduced sustainable development objectives and principles such as prevention and the "polluter pays" [see section 16.2.2.], use of the best available technologies and use of impact assessments[7]. The Council has authorised the Member States to sign, ratify or accede to, in the interest of the European Community, the Protocol of 2003 to the International Convention on the Establishment of an International Fund for Compensation for Oil Pollution Damage[8].

16.3.4. Effort to combat air pollution

Industrial and household activities depend much on the **burning of fossil fuels**. Such burning causes the emission into the air of sulphur dioxide (SO_2), due to the presence of certain quantities of sulphur in the fuel and of very fine particles of partly burned carbon and hydrocarbons which are highly pollutant for the air and highly toxic for human health. Since several of the most industrialised regions of the European Union are situated in frontier areas, **sulphur dioxide and suspended particulate matter** are carried from one European region to another according to wind direction. The European States therefore have to act in unison to prevent air pollution and at the same time to prevent the effects on the functioning of the common market resulting from barriers to trade in fuels and on the conditions of competition between industries using such fuels.

The framework Directive 96/62 defines the basic principles of a **common strategy on air quality objectives for ambient air**[9]. These are: the establishment of air quality objectives based on limit values and alert thresholds for the principal harmful substances; the assessment of air quality in the Member States on the basis of common methods and criteria; the maintenance and improvement of air quality; and the measures to be taken where there is a risk of the limit values being exceeded. The most polluting substances that the EU endeavours to reduce are: ozone in ambient air (tropospheric ozone), sulphur dioxide, carbon dioxide, carbon monoxide, lead and its compounds.

In order to attain and maintain air quality standards, a whole gamut of measures to limit the **emission of sulphur dioxide and other pollutants** is, of course, required. Therefore, a Directive set limit values not to be exceeded and guide values to be used as reference points for air quality with regard to sulphur dioxide and suspended particulates[10]. Community Directives limit the sulphur content of certain liquid fuels[11], the emissions of sulphur and other pollutants from industrial plants[12], from large combustion plants[13] and from internal combustion engines installed in non-road mobile machinery[14].

---

[1]   Agreement and Decision 84/358, OJ L 188, 16.07.1984 and Decision 93/540, OJ L 263, 22.10.1993.
[2]   Convention and Decisions 94/156 and 94/157, OJ L 73, 16.03.1994.
[3]   Convention and Decision 98/249, OJ L 104, 03.04.1998 and Annex V to the Convention, OJ L 118, 19.05.2000.
[4]   Convention and Decision 77/585, OJ L 240, 19.09.1977.
[5]   Protocol and Decision 81/420, OJ L 162, 19.06.1981.
[6]   Protocol and Decision 83/101, OJ L 67, 12.03.1983.
[7]   COM (95) 202.
[8]   Decision 2004/246, OJ L 78, 16.03.2004 and Decision 2004/664, OJ L 303, 30.09.2004.
[9]   Directive 96/62, OJ L 296, 21.11.1996.
[10] Directive 1999/30, OJ L 163, 29.06.1999 and Decision 2001/744, OJ L 278. 23.10.2001.
[11] Directive 93/12, OJ L 74, 27.03.1993, Directive 1999/32, OJ L 121, 11.05.1999 and Directive 2005/33, OJ L 22.07.2005.
[12] Directive 84/360, OJ L 188, 16.07.1984 and Directive 91/692, OJ L 377, 31.12.1991.
[13] Directive 2001/80, OJ L 309, 27.11.2001.
[14] Directive 97/68, OJ L 59, 27.02.1998 and Directive 2004/26, OJ L 146, 30.04.2004.

A major source of air pollution addressed by the Community is pollution by emissions from motor vehicles. **Carbon monoxide** resulting from the incomplete combustion of organic substances used in fuel was tackled first owing to its adverse consequences for human health and the environment. A 1970 Directive concerning the harmonisation of legislation on measures against air pollution by motor vehicle emissions obliged Member States to introduce three types of test to control gas emissions from positive-ignition engines of motor vehicles[1]. The technical controls of vehicles laid down by that Directive led to a significant reduction in emissions of carbon monoxide and unburned hydrocarbons by each vehicle. However, that effect was to a large extent neutralised by the increase in the number of vehicles in circulation in the Community States. For that reason the 1970 Directive was adapted to technical progress on several occasions in order to reduce the permissible levels of carbon monoxide emissions [see details below].

Another first-category air pollutant is **lead** and its compounds. A large proportion of the total quantity of this element in the air comes from emissions from petrol-engine vehicles. A 1982 Directive fixed a limit value for lead in the air[2]. Compliance with that limit required very costly measures for the Member States motor-vehicle industry. In order to prevent barriers to trade and the upheaval of conditions of competition, it was necessary to proceed in stages with the approximation of the laws of the Member States concerning the lead content of petrol, allowing the European motor vehicle industry and the petrol production and distribution industry time to adapt to the new conditions. That was done in a 1985 Directive and **lead-free petrol** won little by little and without problems the markets of the Member States. New Directives, repealing the former ones, concern the quality of petrol and diesel fuels[3] and limit values for sulphur dioxide, nitrogen dioxide and oxides of nitrogen, particulate matter and lead in ambient air[4].

Whereas it is a pollutant in the lower atmosphere (troposphere), with adverse effects on vegetation, ecosystems and the environment as a whole, **ozone** is a natural element in the upper atmosphere (stratosphere), produced by photochemical reaction. The **stratospheric ozone layer** is vital to mankind, as it filters a large proportion of the sun's ultraviolet rays. A reduction in that layer could lead to a large increase in the number of skin cancers or considerable damage to agriculture on the planet. Emissions of **carbon dioxide (CO_2)** and of chemicals such as chlorofluorocarbons (CFCs) and halons contribute to the "**greenhouse effect**" and hence to global warming. Effective combating of this phenomenon requires concerted action at international level. Therefore, the European Union is signatory of the Framework **Convention on Climate Change of the United Nations**, the objective of which is to stabilise greenhouse gas concentrations in the air at a level avoiding dangerous climate change[5]. Particular reference should be made to the Protocol on Substances that Deplete the Ozone Layer and therefore on the control of greenhouse gas emissions, signed at Montreal in 1987 and amended several times[6]. An EC regulation is intended to implement the commitment agreed by the parties to the Montreal Protocol, and provides for measures are designed to help to speed up the process of regeneration of the ozone layer[7].

The Conference of the Parties to the UN Framework Convention on Climate Change, held in Marrakech (Morocco) from 7 to 9 November 2001, paved the way for

---

[1] Directive 70/220, OJ L 76, 06.04.1970 and Directive 2003/76, OJ L 206, 15.08.2003.
[2] Directive 82/884, OJ L 378, 31.12.1982 repealed by Directive 1999/30, OJ L 163, 29.06.1999.
[3] Directive 98/70, OJ L 350, 28.12.1998 and Directive 2003/17, OJ L 76, 22.03.2003.
[4] Directive 1999/30, OJ L 163, 29.06.1999.
[5] Vienna Convention, Montreal Protocol and Decision 88/540, OJ L 297, 31.10.1988.
[6] UN Convention, amendment to the Montreal Protocol and Decisions 94/68 and 94/69, OJ L 33, 07.02.1994, amendment to Montreal Protocol and Decision 2002/215, OJ L 72, 14.03.2002.
[7] Regulation 2037/2000, OJ L 244, 29.09.2000 last amended by Regulation 1366/2006, OJ L 264, 25.09.2006.

ratification of the Kyoto protocol, thus imposing an obligation on 38 industrialised countries (excluding the USA, which rejected their previous engagement) to cut their total greenhouse gas emissions by 5.2% and 8% (compared with 1990 levels) between 2008 and 2012[1]. The EU played a leading role, particularly in finding a compromise solution among industrialised countries for "flexibility mechanisms", such as the exchange of emission allowances with less polluting countries. Under the Kyoto Protocol, the European Union has committed to reduce its overall emissions of the six greenhouse gases controlled by the protocol to 8% below the 1990 level by 2012. Each EU-15 Member State has an individual target set under a burden-sharing agreement. The rest of the Member States each have reduction targets of 6% or 8%, except Cyprus and Malta which have no targets. A mechanism for monitoring CO_2 emissions and other greenhouse gas emissions provides for the Member States to compile inventories of CO_2 emissions and national abatement programmes evaluated by the Commission[2].

In the framework of Directive 96/62 on ambient management, a 2002 directive (replacing the 1992 one) aims to bring about a significant improvement in management of the ozone problem by establishing long-term objectives, target values for 2010, an alert threshold and an information threshold for **concentrations of ozone in ambient air** in the Community, designed to avoid, prevent or reduce harmful effects on human health and the environment as a whole[3]. A directive on national emission ceilings for certain atmospheric pollutants and relating to ozone in ambient air set the limit values to be met by each Member State by 2010 and provided for measures to reduce pollution due to acidification and ozone[4]. A parallel directive in the energy sector fixed the target for renewable and environment-friendly energy sources to cover 12% of gross energy consumption by 2010[5] [see section 19.3.5.]. These targets are assisted by Community research on "sustainable development, global change and ecosystems" [see section 18.4.1.].

The Community approach is based on **emissions trading**, one of the flexible mechanisms recommended in the protocol to attain the reduction target. Under this system, companies are allocated greenhouse gas emission allowances, in line with their government's environmental objectives, and can then trade them with each other to achieve the best cost-effectiveness[6]. The "Clean air for Europe" (CAFE) programme, proposed by the Commission and endorsed by the Council, aims to establish a coherent, long-term thematic strategy and integrated policy to combat air pollution through cost-effective measures[7].

The Community strategy is based mainly on a Directive on **energy end-use efficiency and energy services**[8] [see also section 19.3.1.]. The purpose of this Directive is to enhance the cost-effective improvement of energy end-use efficiency in the Member States by: (a) providing the necessary indicative targets (9% for the ninth year of its application) as well as mechanisms, incentives and institutional, financial and legal frameworks to remove existing market barriers and imperfections that impede the efficient end use of energy; and (b) creating the conditions for the development and promotion of a market for energy services and for the delivery of other energy efficiency improvement measures to final consumers. To achieve the objectives of the Directive, Member States

[1] Decision 2002/358, OJ L 130, 15.05.2002.
[2] Decision 280/2004, OJ L 49, 19.02.2004.
[3] Directive 2002/3, OJ L 67, 09.03.2002.
[4] Directive 2001/81, OJ L 309, 27.11.2001.
[5] Directive 2001/77, OJ L 283, 27.10.2001.
[6] COM (2000) 87, 8 March 2000.
[7] COM (2001) 245 and Council conclusions adopted on 29 October 2001.
[8] Directive 2006/32, OJ L 114, 27.04.2006.

have to prepare three national energy efficiency action plans and to ensure that the public sector fulfils an exemplary role regarding investments, maintenance and other expenditures on energy-using equipment and energy services.

A Community procedure established a reciprocal exchange of information and data from networks and individual stations measuring air pollution within the Member States in order to monitor the formation in the air of sulphur dioxide and black smoke and to create a database to make it possible to study the phenomenon of transboundary air pollution[1]. The Community information system is also important for the implementation of the **Geneva Convention on long-range transboundary air pollution**[2], particularly concerning the programme for monitoring and evaluation of the long-range transmission of air pollutants in Europe (EMEP)[3].

A 1989 Directive was directed towards reducing by more than half the **air pollution caused by cars** below 1.4 litres[4]. Another Directive made the emission standards applicable to light commercial vehicles as stringent as those in force for private cars[5]. The limit values, which are compulsory from 1 January 1996 for new type approvals, should normally bring about a 50% reduction in pollutant emissions[6]. A new directive set EU-wide air quality standards for benzene and carbon monoxide (CO_2) in ambient air to be met by 1 January 2010, thus reducing emissions of benzene by 70 % and peak levels of CO_2 by a third[7]. To implement this strategy, the Commission has obtained commitments from the European Automobile Manufacturers' Association (ACEA) and its Japanese and Korean counterparts for reducing progressively CO_2 emissions to 140 g/km by 2009 through technological developments and market changes[8]. A Community scheme monitors the average specific emissions of carbon dioxide from new passenger cars[9]. The Commission considers that satisfactory progress is being made, notably by the ACEA, with implementation of the Community strategy aiming to reduce average specific CO_2 emissions from new passenger cars to 120 g CO_2 /km by 2010[10].

Directive 2005/55 entails the measures to be taken against the emission of gaseous and particulate pollutants from compression ignition (**diesel**) engines for use in vehicles, and the emission of gaseous pollutants from positive ignition engines fuelled with natural gas or liquefied petroleum gas for use in vehicles[11]. Another Directive monitors the emission of pollutants from diesel engines for use in wheeled agricultural or forestry tractors[12]. Other Directives relate to air quality standards for **nitrogen dioxide**[13] the reduction of environmental pollution by **asbestos**[14], by fluorinated greenhouse gases covered by the Kyoto Protocol[15] and the control of **volatile organic compound** (VOC) emissions resulting from the storage of petrol and its distribution to service stations[16] or from the use of organic solvents in certain activities and installations[17].

Wanting to **go further**, the Commission stresses the need to: reduce energy intensity, by improving energy management and reducing consumption; reduce carbon intensity, by making greater use of renewable energy sources; combine legislative and voluntary policies and instruments; and promote an integrated approach bringing together the European Union, the Member States, the regional authorities and industry[18]. Integrating environmental issues and sustainable development into the definition and implementation of policies is a central factor in fulfilling the Community's commitments under the Kyoto Protocol. The strategies for integrating the environmental dimension into the agriculture, transport and energy sectors have been agreed.

---

[1] Decision 97/101, OJ L 35, 05.02.1997.
[2] Convention and Decision 81/462, OJ L 171, 27.06.1981 and 1998 Protocol, OJ L 81, 19.03.2004.
[3] Protocol and Decision 86/277, OJ L 181, 04.07.1986.
[4] Directive 89/458, OJ L 226, 03.08.1989.
[5] Directive 93/59, OJ L 186, 28.07.1993.
[6] Directive 94/12, OJ L 100, 19.04.1994.
[7] Directive 2000/69, OJ L 313, 13.12.2000.
[8] COM (1998) 495, 29 July 1998, COM (1999) 446, 14 September 1999 and Recommendations, OJ L 100, 20.04.2000.
[9] Decision 1753/2000, OJ L 202, 10.08.2000.
[10] COM (2002) 693, 9 December 2002.
[11] Directive 2005/55, OJ L 275, 20.10.2005 last amended by Directive 2006/51, OJ L 152, 07.06.2006.
[12] Directive 77/537, OJ L 220, 29.08.1977 and Directive 97/54, OJ L 277, 10.10.1997.
[13] Directive 1999/30, OJ L 163, 29.06.1999 last amended by Decision 2001/744, OJ L 278, 23.10.2001.
[14] Directive 87/217, OJ L 85, 28.03.1987 and Regulation 807/2003, OJ L 122, 16.05.2003.
[15] Regulation 842/2006, OJ L 161, 14.06.2006.
[16] Directive 94/63, OJ L 365, 31.12.1994.
[17] Directive 1999/13, OJ L 85, 29.03.1999 and Directive 2004/42, OJ L 143, 30.04.2004.
[18] COM (97) 196, 14 May 1997.

16.3.5. Prevention of industrial and chemical hazards

National and Community rules against pollution cannot in themselves prevent serious industrial accidents which are catastrophic for the environment, like those in Seveso in Italy in 1976 and Bhopal in India in 1984. For that reason, rules should be taken concerning controls on land-use planning when new installations are authorized and when urban development takes place around existing installations. Therefore, Directive 96/82 aims at the **prevention of major accidents which involve dangerous substances** and the limitation of their consequences for man and the environment, with a view to ensuring high levels of protection throughout the Community in a consistent and effective manner[1]. It provides for: definition, by each establishment covered, of a major-accident prevention policy; submission, by each establishment where dangerous substances are present in large quantities, of safety reports demonstrating that the major accident hazards have been identified, that the design, construction, operation and maintenance of the installation are sufficiently safe and that the emergency plans have been drawn up; taking account, in land-use policies, of the objectives of preventing major accidents, limiting the consequences and improving the procedures for consulting and informing the public.

Independently of accident hazards control, the framework Directive 96/61 aims at an **integrated pollution prevention and control (IPPC)**[2]. Its across-the-board approach involves the various media (air, water, soil) by applying the principle of the best environmental option, in particular in order to avoid transferring pollution from one medium to another. It provides that the operators of certain polluting plants submit requests for operating permits to the competent authority in the Member States, with the issuing of a permit being conditional on compliance with basic obligations such as not to exceed emission limit values set by the Directive. The Community has established a scheme for greenhouse gas **emission allowance trading** within its territory ("Community scheme")[3]. The scheme aims both to achieve a pre-determined emission reduction and to decrease the resulting costs. It is based on granting authorised emissions allowances, purchasing emissions permits from companies which have not used up their full allowance and imposing fines in the event of misuse of this scheme.

A European **pollutant emission register (EPER)**, introduced in 2003, contains data concerning emissions of 50 pollutants from some 20 000 industrial facilities across the EU. Both the public and industry may use EPER data to compare the environmental performance of individual facilities or industrial sectors in different countries and to monitor the progress made in meeting environment targets set in national and international agreements and protocols[4].

Major pollution of water, air and soil is caused by **chemical products discharged in the form of by-products or industrial waste**. The problems here are identifying the dangerous substances and monitoring their utilisation and disposal. This is why, under the Directive on the approximation of the laws relating to the classification, packaging and **labelling of dangerous substances** each Member State undertook to act as a representative of its European Community partners when authorising the introduction of a new chemical product into the whole Community market[5]. For that purpose, the producer or importer has to provide the State into whose market the product is first intro-

---

[1] Directive 96/82, OJ L 10, 14.01.1997 and Directive 2003/105, OJ L 345, 31.12.2003.
[2] Directive 96/61, OJ L 257, 10.10.1996 and Regulation 166/2006, OJ L 33, 04.02.2006.
[3] Directive 2003/87, OJ L275, 25.10.2003 and Directive 2004/101, OJ L 338, 13.11.2004.
[4] Decision 2000/479, OJ L 192, 28.07.2000.
[5] Directive 67/548, OJ L 196, 16.08.1967 and Directive 2004/73, OJ L 152, 30.04.2004.

duced with a "**base set**". That dossier is composed of a whole range of information on the physico-chemical properties of the new product concerned, its possible effects on health and the environment, the uses for which it is intended, the quantities produced, the proposed classification and labelling and a general evaluation of the dangers. That information is forwarded to the Commission, which sends it to each Member State and to the advisory Scientific Committee on Health and Environmental Risks (SCHER), which examines the toxicity and ecotoxicity of chemical compounds[1]. Businesses are authorised to place on the market only "EC" labelled and, accordingly controlled, dangerous substances[2] [see section 6.2.3.].

A Regulation seeks to ensure systematic evaluation of the risks arising from substances in the **European Inventory of existing commercial substances (EINECS)** on the basis of information supplied by the manufacturers or importers and covering around 10,000 substances present on the market, with variable degrees of requirements depending on the quantities involved[3]. It provides, notably for systematic data collection, the establishment of lists of substances to be evaluated as a priority and the evaluation of risks, and sets up for this purpose close cooperation between the Member States, the Commission and industry.

The **placing on the Community market** for use in the Member States of certain dangerous substances and preparations are restricted by a Directive, which is constantly adapted to technical progress[4]. Export from and import into the Community of certain dangerous chemicals are governed by a Council Regulation based on the principle of "prior informed consent", compatible with the procedure established by the United Nations Environment Programme, which consists of granting the authorities of an importing country discretionary power as to whether to accept or refuse import of a substance which is prohibited or strictly regulated by the Community[5].

The classification of a chemical substance as dangerous or harmless obviously necessitates sound laboratory tests. Accordingly, a Directive organises the implementation by the Member States of the principles of **good laboratory practice** and the verification of their applications for tests on chemical substances[6].

16.3.6. Effort to combat noise pollution

Noise has intensified considerably with the development of industrialisation and urbanisation, in particular through the use of increasingly numerous and noisy machines in road transport and air transport. Noise has been the subject of studies which have shown that, depending on its intensity and nature, it gives rise to certain consequences for the person exposed to it, from discomfort to psychological, or even pathological, effects. Action needed to be taken at Community level, as measures taken nationally to reduce noise nuisances could effect the functioning of the common market by creating **technical barriers to trade** in products subject to anti-noise specifications [see section 6.2.] or distortions of competition between noisy plants, on which different investment or operating costs would be imposed. Although based first and foremost on commercial and economic considerations, the harmonisation of national rules constitutes an instrument for combating noise nuisances in the Community.

Thus, a Directive concerning the **exhaust system of motor vehicles** lays down the permissible sound levels for the various categories of motor vehicles intended for use on the road and having at least four wheels. It has been adapted to technical progress several times[7]. Another Directive on components and characteristics of **two or three-wheel motor vehicles** is aimed at reducing the level of pollutant emissions, while limiting the sound output of these particularly noisy vehicles[8].

A significant source of noise is aircraft, the number of which increases each year. Sound pollution in this area needed to be limited, but without giving rise to distortions of competition between aircraft manufacturers and between users (airlines). Therefore, Community Directives limit **noise emissions from subsonic aircraft**, which land in the territory of the Community[9], and from subsonic **civil jet aircraft**[10], while they provide for

---

[1] Decision 2004/210, OJ L 66, 04.03.2004.
[2] Directive 96/56, OJ L 236, 18.09.1996.
[3] Regulation 793/93, OJ L 84, 05.04.1993.
[4] Directive 76/769, OJ L 262, 27.09.1976 and Directive 2005/90, OJ L 33, 04.02.2006.
[5] Regulation 304/2003, OJ L 63, 06.03.2003 last amended by Regulation 777/2006, OJ L 136, 24.05.2006.
[6] Directive 2004/10, OJ L 50, 20.02.2004.
[7] Directive 70/157, OJ L 42, 23.02.1970 and Directive 1999/101, OJ L 334, 28.12.1999.
[8] Directive 97/24 OJ L 226, 18.08.1997 last amended by Directive 2006/72, OJ L 227, 19.08.2006.
[9] Directive 80/51, OJ L 18, 24.01.1980 repealed by Regulation 1592/2002, OJ L 240, 07.09.2002.
[10] Directive 89/629, OJ L 363, 13.12.1989 and OJ L 1, 03.01.1994.

the phasing out of the noisiest of these aeroplanes[1] [see section 20.3.5.]. Since 2002, the Community applies the "balanced approach" to noise management, recommended by the International Civil Aviation Organisation (ICAO), concerning the introduction of noise-related operating restrictions at Community airports[2] [see section 20.3.5.].

Another major source of noise pollution is that of the various **equipment for use outdoors**, such as compressors, tower cranes, welding and power generators, concrete-breakers and lawnmowers. To protect the health and well-being of citizens, permissible noise levels for such equipment had to be reduced; but their noise emission had to be harmonised in order to prevent obstacles to the free movement of such equipment[3]. Thus, Member States should not prohibit, restrict or impede the placing on the market or putting into service in their territory of equipment which complies with Community requirements, bears the CE marking and the indication of the guaranteed sound power level and is accompanied by an EC declaration of conformity.

A directive relating to the **assessment and management of environmental noise** defines a common approach intended to avoid, prevent or reduce on a prioritised basis the harmful effects, including annoyance, due to exposure to environmental noise[4]. It also aims at providing a framework for developing Community measures to reduce noise emitted by the major sources, in particular road and rail vehicles and infrastructure, aircraft, outdoor and industrial equipment and mobile machinery.

16.4. Management of environmental resources

The Community environment programme is not confined to the effort to combat pollution and nuisances, but also seeks to make an active contribution to improving the environment and the quality of life through the rational management of space, the environment and natural resources. The measures provided for in that section of the Community environment programme can be grouped under the headings of the **protection of flora and fauna** in Europe and the **management of waste** in the Community. The financial instrument LIFE can finance projects in these areas, such as the conservation of biotopes of particular importance for the Community, projects for the conservation of endangered species and the location and restoration of areas contaminated by waste and/or dangerous substances[5]. LIFE III (2000-04) consists of "LIFE-Nature", "LIFE-Environment" and "LIFE-Third countries" and allows participation by the applicant countries [see section 16.2.1.].

16.4.1. Protection of flora and fauna

Species of wild flowers and the animal populations form **part of European heritage**. Apart from the fact that they represent non-renewable genetic assets, they participate in many natural functions which ensure overall ecological balances, such as the regulation of the development of undesirable organisms, the protection of the soil against erosion and the regulation of aquatic ecosystems. The genetic assets represented by all present-day animal and plant species constitute a resource of ecological, scientific and economic interest of inestimable value for the future of mankind. However, industrialisation, urbanisation and pollution are threatening a growing number of wild species and undermining the natural balances resulting from several million years of evolution.

A Community Directive aims to **protect natural and semi-natural habitats** and wild fauna and flora[6]. It provides for the establishment of a European ecological network of special conservation areas, "Natura 2000", made up of sites which are home to types

[1]   Directive 92/14 OJ L 76, 23.03.1992 last amended by Regulation 991/2001, OJ L 138, 22.05.2001.
[2]   Directive 2002/30, OJ L 85, 28.03.2002.
[3]   Directive 2000/14, OJ L 162, 03.07.2000 and Directive 2005/88, OJ L 344, 27.12.2005.
[4]   Directive 2002/49, OJ L 189, 18.07.2002.
[5]   Regulation 1655/2000, OJ L 192, 28.07.2000 and Regulation 1682/2004, OJ L 308, 05.10.2004.
[6]   Directive 92/43, OJ L 206, 22.07.1992 and Directive 97/62, OJ L 305, 08.11.1997.

of natural habitats of species of interest to the Community. The Member States must take appropriate steps to avoid their deterioration or any other disturbances affecting the species.

A significant means of protecting wildlife threatened with extinction is to restrict and **control rigorously international trade in plants and animals** belonging to such species and products made from them. Therefore, the Community implements the Convention on International Trade in Endangered Species of Wild Fauna and Flora (CITES), which aims at protecting 2.000 species through the stringent control of international trade. However, the relevant Community Regulation covers a wider field than the Convention, dividing the species into four classes to be given protection, ranging from statistical monitoring of trade to a total trading ban, depending on the degree of the threat of extinction[1]. Special attention is given to re-exportation, control of commercial activities involving such specimens and definition of the infringements, which Member States are required to penalise.

For the protection of wildlife, the Community depends on the **work of international bodies**, in particular the Council of Europe, directed towards ensuring the protection of wildlife and the conservation of the characteristic biotopes or ecosystems, in particular in wetlands, which are essential to such life. It has signed as such all the European conventions for the conservation of migratory species and wild animals. Most important in that context is the Ramsar Convention on Wetlands of International Importance Especially as Waterfowl Habitat[2]. In 1982, the Community as such signed the Convention on the Conservation of Migratory Species of Wild Animals, known as the "Bonn Convention"[3], and the Convention on the Conservation of European Wildlife and Natural Habitats, called the "Berne Convention"[4]. Those three Conventions, together with the Conventions for the Conservation of Salmon in the North Atlantic Ocean[5] and for the Conservation of Atlantic Tuna[6], which concern the conservation of fishery resources, were to provide the framework for Community action in the field of the protection of flora and fauna. The European Community's accession to the International Plant Protection Convention is intended to secure common and effective action to prevent the spread and introduction of pests of plants and plant products, and to provide appropriate measures for their control[7].

To implement the international Conventions, the Community has taken specific measures relating to **certain particularly endangered species**. These measures include: a Directive on the conservation of wild birds, which establishes the list of species which may be hunted, the list of species which may be marketed and the list of prohibited methods of hunting and trapping[8]; a Regulation prohibiting the importation of certain products derived from cetaceans (whales, etc.), in order to contribute to the conservation of such endangered species[9]; a Directive prohibiting imports into the Community of skins of harp seal pups and of hooded seal pups, the hunt for which had shocked public opinion[10]; a Regulation prohibiting the use of leghold traps in the Community and the introduction into the Community of pelts and manufactured goods of certain wild animal species originating in countries which catch them by means of leghold traps[11] and an agreement between the Community and Canada and Russia on international humane trapping standards[12]. The Community prohibits the issue of import permits for ivory derived from the African elephant, with a view to contributing in that way to putting a stop to the slaughter thereof. The Community as such is signatory to the European Convention for the Protection of Vertebrate Animals used for Experimental and other Scientific Purposes, which establishes the conditions under which experiments on vertebrate animals may be authorised[13].

The situation of several plant species in Europe and elsewhere in the world is no less worrying, owing to the encroachment on the countryside by towns, soil erosion and soil destruction and the abandonment of rural life by an ever-increasing number of citizens. Thousands of hectares of forests are destroyed in Europe each year by fires and pollution. To curb this problem, two Regulations aim at the **protection of the Community's**

---

[1] Regulation 338/97, OJ L 61, 03.03.1997 and Regulation 1332/2005, OJ L 215, 19.08.2005.
[2] Recommendation 75/66, OJ L 21, 28.01.1975.
[3] Convention, Decision 82/461, OJ L 210, 19.07.1982 and Decision 98/145, OJ L 46, 17.02.1998.
[4] Convention and Decision 82/72, OJ L 38, 10.02.1982.
[5] Convention Decision 82/886, OJ L 378, 31.12.1982.
[6] Convention and Decision 86/238, OJ L 162, 18.06.1986.
[7] Convention and Decision 2004/597, OJ L 267, 14.08.2004.
[8] Directive 79/409, OJ L 103, 25.04.1979, last amended by Directive 2006/105, OJ L 363, 20.12.2006.
[9] Regulation 348/81, OJ L 39, 12.02.1981.
[10] Directive 89/370, OJ L 91, 09.04.1983 and Directive 89/370, OJ L 163, 14.06.1989.
[11] Regulation 3254/91, OJ L 308, 09.11.1991.
[12] Agreement and Decision 98/142, OJ L 42, 14.02.1998.
[13] Convention and Decision 1999/575, OJ L 222, 24.08.1999.

forests: one against atmospheric pollution[1]; and the other against fire[2]. On the basis of the first Regulation, the Commission has set up a system for coordinating and evaluating the intensive and continuous monitoring of European forest ecosystems. The Community and its Member States are parties to the United Nations Convention to combat desertification in countries seriously hit, particularly in Africa[3]. The Community has signed together with the Alpine countries the Convention on the protection of the Alps, which aims at safeguarding the Alpine ecosystem and securing environmentally sustainable development for the populations[4].

The European Union is a party in the Convention on the **Conservation of Biological Diversity**, which was drafted under the auspices of the United Nations Environment Programme (UNEP)[5]. The objectives of this Convention are: the conservation of biological diversity; the sustainable use of its components; and the fair and equitable sharing of the benefits arising from genetic resources. Under this Convention, the Community undertook to define its own strategy to promote biodiversity. The Commission and the Council agree that this strategy should aim at preventing and attacking the causes of reduction and loss of biological diversity and should be built around four major themes: conservation and sustainable use of biological diversity; sharing of benefits arising out of the utilisation of genetic resources; research, identification, monitoring and exchange of information; and education, training and awareness[6].

16.4.2. Management of waste

As the penalty paid for economic development and urbanisation, the accumulation of **waste destroys the environment** and is at the same time proof of regrettable profligacy. Waste of all kinds, i.e. household waste, industrial waste, sewage sludge from waste water, agricultural waste and waste from the extractive industries, accounts for some 3 billion tons each year in the EU.

Included amongst "waste" are **toxic substances** and substances which are hazardous for man and the environment, as they can pollute the water table by percolation, contaminate micro-organisms and appear in the food chain through complex and little-known means. But "waste" also includes scrap metal, paper, plastics and waste oils, which can be recycled, which is important in a Europe becoming increasingly poor in raw materials.

In view of the close interdependence of waste management and many industrial and commercial activities, the lack of a Community design for waste management is likely to affect not only environmental protection, but also the completion of the internal market by creating distortions of competition and unjustified movements of investment, or even the partitioning of the market. The objectives of a **Community strategy on waste management** are: (a) prevention, by encouraging the use of products which create less waste; (b) increasing its value, through the optimisation of collection and sorting systems; (c) the laying down of stringent standards for final disposal, as contained in the Council Directives on new municipal waste-incineration plants and on existing municipal waste-incineration plants[7]; and (d) rules governing the carriage of dangerous substances, so as to ensure safe and economic carriage and the restoration of contaminated areas, taking into account the civil liability of the polluter. The principle of producer responsibility is a key component in future Community legislation on waste management[8].

The **"framework Directive" for Community waste policy** obliges the Member States to take measures to ensure that waste is eliminated without endangering human health and without damaging the environment, and in particular without giving rise to risk to water, air or soil, fauna or flora, without causing discomfort through noise or

---

[1] Regulation 3528/86, OJ L 326, 31.11.1986 and Regulation 804/2002, OJ L 132, 17.05.2002.
[2] Regulation 2158/92, OJ L 217, 31.07.1992 and Regulation 805/2002, OJ L 132, 17.05.2002.
[3] Convention and Decision 98/216, OJ L 83, 19.03.1998.
[4] Convention and Decision 96/191, OJ L 61, 12.03.1996 and Decision 2005/923, OJ L 337, 22.12.2005.
[5] Convention and Decision 93/626, OJ L 309, 13.12.1993.
[6] COM (1998) 42, 4 February 1998 and Council conclusions of 16 October 2001.
[7] Directive 2000/76, OJ L 332, 28.12.2000.
[8] COM (96) 399, 30 July 1996 and resolution, OJ C 76, 11.03.1997, p. 1-4.

smell and without affecting areas or landscapes[1]. It also aims to set up an integrated and appropriate network of waste disposal plants, to encourage disposal as close as possible to the waste production site, thus reducing the dangers inherent in waste transport, and to promote clean technologies and products which can be recycled and reused.

A directive aims at preventing or reducing as far as possible the adverse **effects of landfills** on the environment, particularly pollution of surface water, groundwater, soil and air, and on the global environment, including the greenhouse effect, and the resulting risks to human health during the whole lifecycle of the landfill[2]. An accompanying decision on the acceptance of waste at landfills lays down the procedures for characterising waste, for checking that it complies with the acceptance criteria and for on-site verification that it is identical to the waste described in the accompanying documents[3].

A Regulation on the monitoring and control of **waste transfers** within, on entrance to and exit from the Community seeks to put an end to what has been termed "waste tourism" within the Community and the unrestricted export of waste to the developing countries[4]. In cases of waste transfers between the Member States, a distinction is made between wastes for disposal and those for value addition. For the first category, the principles of proximity, priority to value addition and self-sufficiency apply. For the second, a notification system applies with a follow-up document and the compulsory existence of a contract between the notifying party and the consignee. Although there are exceptions under certain conditions, normally exports of waste to third countries and imports into the Community of waste from third countries are prohibited.

A Directive on **toxic and dangerous waste** contains a list of substances the collection, disposal and reuse of which necessitate special precautions[5]. The list includes mercury and cadmium, certain solvents and pharmaceutical preparations, ethers, tar and asbestos. The Directive provides for standard authorisation arrangements for plants, establishments or undertakings which store, treat or discharge waste containing such substances. It gives priority to the promotion of clean technologies and of products generating little or less waste and to the establishment of an information system on the Community situation as regards waste management. Another Directive aims to prevent or reduce as far as possible adverse effects on the environment and risks to human health, brought about as a result of the management of waste from the **extractive industries**[6]. The Community is a party to the Basle Convention on the control of cross-border movements of dangerous wastes and their disposal[7].

The Community wants to prevent or reduce as far as possible the negative effects on the environment, in particular the pollution of air, soil, surface water and groundwater and the resulting risks to human health, from the incineration and co-incineration of waste. To that end, a Directive lays down stringent operating conditions and technical requirements and sets emission limit values for **waste incineration** and co-incineration plants[8]. Concerning the disposal of waste oils, which are very polluting for the water and the soil, a Directive prohibits the discharge into the environment of any semi-liquid or liquid composed wholly or in part of mineral oil or synthetic oil[9]. Another Directive does likewise with regard to polychlorinated biphenyls (PCBs) and polychlorinated terphenyls (PCTs)[10].

Recycling plays an increasingly important role in Community waste management policy. That is especially true of waste paper, which represents between 40 and 50% of the volume and 15 and 20% of the tonnage of urban waste. The recycling of a ton of waste paper, which is less polluting than the manufacturing cycle for pulp, replaces the equivalent of 2 or 3 cubic meters of wood, viz. approximately 15 to 20 small trees. Moreover, it replaces imports in this sector, which is, after the oil sector, is the resource most in deficit in the Community's trade balance. The Council accordingly recommended to the Member States that every effort be made to re-use waste paper and to use recycled paper[11]. A Directive on packaging and packaging waste aims at preventing the producing of packaging waste, reusing packaging and recycling packaging[12].

---

[1] Directive 2006/12, OJ L 114, 27.04.2006.
[2] Directive 1999/31, OJ L 182, 16.07.1999.
[3] Decision 2003/33, OJ L 11, 16.01.2003.
[4] Regulation 259/93, OJ L 30, 06.02.1993 last amended by Regulation 2557/2001, OJ L 349, 31.12.2001.
[5] Directive 91/689, OJ L 377, 31.12.1991 and Regulation 166/2006, OJ L 33, 04.02.2006..
[6] Directive 2006/21, OJ L 102, 11.04.2006.
[7] Convention and Decision 93/98, OJ L 39, 16.02.1993.
[8] Directive 2000/76, OJ L 332, 28.12.2000.
[9] Directive 75/439, OJ L 194, 25.07.1975 2000/76, OJ L 332, 28.12.2000.
[10] Directive 96/59, OJ L 243, 24.09.1996 and Regulation 850/2004, OJ L 158, 30.04.2004.
[11] Recommendation 81/972, OJ L 355, 10.12.1981.
[12] Directive 94/62, OJ L 365, 31.12.1994 and Directive 2005/20, OJ L 70, 16.03.2005.

Waste electrical and electronic equipment (WEEE) is one of the target areas regulated by the Community. A Directive aims at the prevention of WEEE, and in addition, the reuse, recycling and other forms of recovery of such wastes so as to reduce the disposal of waste[1]. It also seeks to improve the environmental performance of all operators involved in the life cycle of electrical and electronic equipment, e.g. producers, distributors and consumers. Another directive restricts the use of certain hazardous substances in new electrical and electronic equipment[2].

16.5. Appraisal and outlook

Thanks to the Treaty of Maastricht environment protection has graduated to the status of a common policy and falls into the **priority objectives of the Union**. Environmental constraints must be integrated into the definition and implementation of other common policies. The uniform application in all Member States of environmental standards is, in fact, indispensable not only for the preservation of Europe's environment, but also for the good functioning of the internal market and for economic and social cohesion [see section 12.1.2].

It is very difficult to evaluate the specific results of the European measures in this area, first because the quality of the environment is a highly subjective notion and therefore difficult to define, and secondly because the policy to combat pollution is a **Sisyphean task**. The quality objectives that it lays down are incessantly thrust aside by economic development and urbanisation. It is true that the annual reports of the Commission to the Parliament and the Council on the implementation of the European Community's environment programme show that significant progress has been achieved on phasing out ozone-depleting substances, reducing emissions of certain pollutants into the atmosphere and surface waters, improving water quality and reducing acidification. But, the state of the environment overall remains a cause for concern, particularly in respect to growing consumption of natural resources, chemical risks, soil degradation, global warming and biodiversity losses.

Moreover, serious problems and excessive delays in the enforcement and implementation of the environment directives exist in many Member States, which also have a bad record on producing the necessary reports and information in general. To make the Union a highly eco-efficient economy, the environmental dimension of the Lisbon Process [see section 13.3.2.] should be strengthened, so as to give equal attention to economic, social and environmental considerations in policy-making and decision-taking processes. In any case, a permanent vigilance is required of citizens, who can lodge complaints with the Commission whenever they observe that European standards are not being complied with by an undertaking or by public or private works in their country or a neighbouring country. Likewise, mechanisms are needed for handling complaints and carrying out environmental investigations outside the courts [see section 9.3.].

However, the European Union cannot work in isolation in this field. Even if it were to succeed in significantly reducing and preventing pollution in its territory, it would still be open to water and air pollution from the other countries of Europe and the other regions of the world. For that reason the Union must play a leading role in international negotiations and take more visible action in the framework of **international organisations** such as the Council of Europe and the United Nations. Thus, the accession to the Union of **Central and Eastern European countries** must go hand-in-hand with increased consideration of environmental constraints, which have been tragically neglected

---

[1]   Directive 2002/96, OJ L 37, 13.02.2003.
[2]   Directives 2002/95 and 2002/96, OJ L 37, 13.02.2003.

in the past. The European Environment Agency, which is open to the other countries of Europe, plays an important part in this area.

The environmental interdependence of all the countries in the world is particularly marked with regard to the **greenhouse effect** and its climatic consequences for the globe. The Union is on target to meet the objectives set for 2008-2012 concerning greenhouse gas emissions. Projections show that the EU-25 and the EU-15 could reduce their emissions by 11.3% and 9.3% respectively by 2010, compared to base year level; but the attainment of these objectives requires significant efforts from the Member States. Therefore, the EU should promote the use and competitiveness of renewable energy sources, the reduction of greenhouse gas emissions from motor vehicles with the aid of fuels with low pollutant content and energy efficiency in buildings, equipment and industrial processes. It may encourage the best available technologies and research and development and provide, within the framework of the guidelines on State aid, flexibility at national level to ensure the effectiveness of policies and measures to tackle climate change. Common action is needed to progressively reduce or remove fossil fuel and other subsidies, tax schemes and regulations which militate against efficient use of energy. Conversely, economic measures, such as tax incentives or reduced VAT rates, are needed to encourage good practice by consumers and promote clean and renewable energy sources.

However, the European Union cannot curb the greenhouse phenomenon alone. It should summon other industrialised countries and, particularly, the United States, as the biggest emitter of greenhouse gases, to comply with standards agreed in international fora. In November 2001 at Marrakech, the EU - taking along Russia, Australia, Canada and Japan - saved the Kyoto protocol from sinking under the pressure of the United States abandonment of its responsibilities. This example shows that, when the EU wants, it can take the lead effectively in environment-friendly actions. It should take the initiative to call for international **environmental governance**, based on coherent international, regional, sub-regional and national institutional environmental architecture topped by a World Environment Organisation, capable of responding to current challenges.

In a European economy that undergoes structural change, the challenge facing those with responsibility for environment policy is to develop instruments which will make it possible painlessly to achieve the objective of **growth which is compatible with the essential requirements of the environment**. Strong economic performance must go hand in hand with sustainable use of natural resources and levels of waste, maintaining biodiversity, preserving ecosystems and avoiding desertification. This involves foreseeing the ecological problems of technological development and limiting them from the outset, for example by encouraging the selection of new chemical products before they are launched on the market and the systematic evaluation of the likely impact on the environment of any new economic activity. Yet, there is no major conflict between economic growth and a healthy and clean environment. The inflationary effect of environment policies is negligible. On the other hand, the "**environment industry**" is probably in a position to help the European economies to restructure themselves on new bases by directing them towards new activities that employ advanced technology and a skilled workforce. Environmental technologies (new and innovative, environment friendly technologies) have the potential to contribute to growth and competitiveness, by reducing the costs of environmental protection, while at the same time improving the environment and protecting natural resources. However, a series of market and institutional obstacles obstruct the use of these technologies. Energy market prices, in particular, lead to systematic under-investment in innovative technologies. These obstacles could be overcome by internalising environmental costs to provide incentives for further research in this field.

Promoting a sustainable economic growth in Europe entails the combination of more competitive industrial production with less environmental degradation, more efficient use of energy and raw materials resources and higher employment rates. Indeed, there can be a **synergy between environmental policy and employment policy** so as to rectify the overuse of environmental resources and the underuse of human resources [see section 13.3.2.]. However, this synergy is not automatic, but has to be induced by certain measures, first and foremost being the restructuring of tax systems by reducing non-wage labour costs and by incorporating environmental and resource costs into the market prices of goods and services. In addition, environmental education and training coupled with financial incentives should encourage public authorities, private and public companies and consumers to move towards cleaner, more environment friendly and more labour intensive production methods and products.

At the international level, the EU should aim at promoting sustainable development and the effective participation of all players, ensuring greater consistency, better implementation of environmental standards and greater integration of environmental concerns into states' internal policies, improving the coordination of international environmental institutions and giving the international environmental architecture an appropriate financial foundation for the challenges it has to face. In view of the 2004 conclusions of the United Nations Intergovernmental Panel on Climate Change (IPCC) regarding the risks of global warming of more than 2° C and the need to stabilise greenhouse gas emissions below this limit, it is obviously necessary to stabilise these emissions during the next two decades and then reduce them by at least 15% or even 50% by 2050 compared to 1990 levels. The EU is aware of the need to start promptly the consideration of the post-2012 framework and to get a commitment by all parties to the climate convention.

Bibliography on environment policy

- AGRA EUROPE. *European environment & packaging law.* London : Tunbridge Wells: Agra Europe, 2006.
- BAKER Susan. *Sustainable development.* London: Routledge, 2006.
- BARRETT Scott (et al.). "Kyoto and beyond: alternative approaches to global warming" in *The American economic review*, v. 96, n. 2, May 2006, p. 22-38.
- BARRY John, ECKERSLEY Robyn. *The state and the global ecological crisis.* Cambridge, MA; London: MIT Press, 2005.
- BETLEM Gerrit, BRANS Edward (eds.). *Environmental liability in the EU: the 2004 directive compared with US and Member State law.* London: Cameron May, 2006.
- BOHNE Eberhard. *The quest for environmental regulatory integration in the European Union: integrated pollution prevention and control, environmental impact assessment and major accident prevention.* Alphen aan den Rijn: Kluwer Law International, 2006
- EUROPEAN COMMISSION. *Europe's sustainable development strategy: research for a better future.* Luxembourg: EUR-OP*, 2006.
  - *Soil protection: the story behind the strategy.* Luxembourg: EUR-OP*, 2006.
  - *LIFE and European forest.* Luxembourg: EUR-OP*, 2006.
- EUROPEAN ENVIRONMENT AGENCY. *European Environment outlook.* Luxembourg: EUR-OP*, 2005.
- HANSJÜRGENS Bernd. *Emissions trading for climate policy: US and European perspectives.* Cambridge: Cambridge University Press, 2005.
- HELM Dieter. *Climate-change policy.* Oxford: Oxford University Press, 2005.
- JACOBS Francis. "The role of the European Court of Justice in the protection of the environment" in *Journal of Environmental Law*, v. 18, n. 2, 2006, p. 185-205.
- MEGA Voula. *Sustainable development, energy and the city: A civilisation of concepts and actions.* New York; London: Springer, 2005.
- MUNIER Nolberto. *Introduction to sustainability: road to a better future.* Dordrecht: Springer, 2005.
- ORGANISATION FOR ECONOMIC COOPERATION AND DEVELOPMENT. *Cost-Benefit Analysis and the Environment: Recent Developments.* Paris: OECD, 2006.
- SULLIVAN Rory. *Rethinking voluntary approaches in environmental policy.* Cheltenham, UK; Northampton, MA: Edward Elgar, 2005.
- TANAKA Yoshifumi. "Regulation of land-based marine pollution in international law: a comparative analysis between global and regional frameworks" in *Zeitschrift für ausländisches öffentliches Recht und Völkerrecht*, v. 66, n. 3, 2006, p. 535-574.
- TORRE-SCHAUB Marta. "Marché unique et environnement: quelle intégration?" in *Revue internationale de droit économique*, v. 20, n. 3, 2006, p. 317-338.
- WATSON Michael. "The use of criminal and civil penalties to protect the environment: a comparative study" in *European environmental law review*, v. 15, n. 4, April 2006, p. 108-113.

The publications of the Office for Official Publications of the European Communities (EUR-OP) exist usually in all official languages of the EU.

Part V. Sectoral Policies

In **Part V we consider the sectoral policies of the Union**, that is to say, the policies concerning big sectors of the economies of the Member States, industry, research, energy, transports, agriculture and fisheries. We will see that in the last three sectors the Treaties required explicitly the development of common policies, whereas for industry they asked for no policy as such, but the whole multinational integration process was geared towards the restructuring and competitiveness of European industry. Common research and energy policies were partially defined in the sectoral Treaties, notably that on Euratom. The various legal foundations of the main sectoral policies certainly account for their dissimilar development; but so do as well the different requirements that the Member States set for those policies during the stages of the customs union, the common market and more recently the economic and monetary union.

Whilst, the EEC Treaty made no call for a common or Community **industrial policy**, it chiefly regulated the common market in industrial products (free trade, rules of competition, approximation of laws, tax provisions...). It assumed that the abolition of protectionist measures and the opening-up of the markets, thanks to the common market would provide sufficient impetus for the restructuring of sectors and undertakings. We saw that this assumption was partly invalidated because of national protectionism, which persisted until the early 1990s by means of technical barriers to trade [see section 6.1.]. Now that the single market has become a reality, small and medium-sized enterprises (SMEs) must adjust to the new conditions of heightened competition. The new **enterprise policy** of the Community shores up their efforts. The common enterprise policy, however, aims to help SMEs in both the industrial and service sectors adjust to the new conditions of the large internal market. This is also the goal of common sub-sectoral policies, notably in declining or fast growing industrial sectors, which need to be freed from old protectionist practices so as to better face the new conditions of competition in Europe and the world.

A common **research policy** is also a vital rung on the ladder of the European Union's industrial development. It is essential for the definition of industrial strategy, for technical progress in high-technology sectors, for the mastery of the Community's energy problems and, finally, for the adaptation of businesses to the post-industrial information society.

Research is a key feature of the common **energy policy**, the aim of which is to reduce Europe's dependence on imported energy and raise the competitiveness of European industry through the development of cheap, safe and clean energies. Due to its foundation on the ECSC and Euratom sectoral Treaties [see section 2.1.], the common policy is well advanced in the sectors of coal and nuclear energy and very little in the oil and gas sectors.

Unlike most other Community policies, **transport policy** was specifically mentioned in the EEC Treaty, even with the specification that it should be a common policy. We will note that diverging national interests have impeded progress of the transport policy during the first thirty years of the Community's existence; but the completion of the single market, which has resulted in strong growth in demand for transport services for both goods and persons, went in step with a large-scale liberalisation in the areas of road haulage, sea and air transport.

By contrast, the **common agricultural policy** (CAP) covered a great deal of ground during the first years of the Community. However, of all the policies examined in this book, the CAP has been the most controversial and the most versatile, since it is reformed every five years or so to respond both to internal and external requirements. The CAP presents, indeed, a good example of the constant adaptation of a common policy to new societal needs and to the changing European and international competition and trade requirements.

The **fisheries policy**, initially a part of the common agricultural policy, gives a good illustration of how a common policy can develop. It starts out with a few isolated measures addressing a particular situation or shared problems in a sector and, little by little there is a realisation that if the common achievements are to be safeguarded, other measures are required leading to a full-grown common policy. Thanks to this policy and despite the growing depletion of fishing resources in the waters of the Union and worldwide, there is a single market for fisheries products.

Chapter 17

INDUSTRIAL AND ENTERPRISE POLICIES

Diagram of the chapter

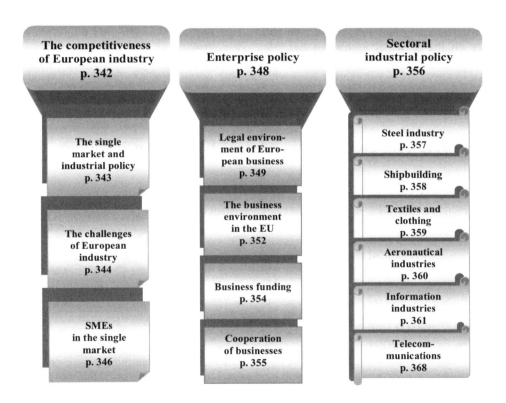

The competitiveness of European industry p. 342	Enterprise policy p. 348	Sectoral industrial policy p. 356
The single market and industrial policy p. 343	Legal environment of European business p. 349	Steel industry p. 357
The challenges of European industry p. 344	The business environment in the EU p. 352	Shipbuilding p. 358
SMEs in the single market p. 346	Business funding p. 354	Textiles and clothing p. 359
	Cooperation of businesses p. 355	Aeronautical industries p. 360
		Information industries p. 361
		Telecommunications p. 368

The Treaty establishing the European Economic Community organised the achievement of customs union in great detail with regard to the industrial products of the Member States, but **made no call for an industrial policy as such**. In fact the founding fathers of the EEC had hoped that the liberalisation of trade and increased competition inside the common market could, on their own, bring about the structural

changes that Community industry needed. As was explained in the chapter on the common market, this hope was tardily realised because of the tardy completion of the single
market [see section 6.1.]. However, an important part of the common industrial policy,
concerning the harmonisation of legislations, standardisation and public procurement,
was dealt with in the chapter on the common market [see section 6.2.].

In the absence of a specific structural policy for the industrial sector, a large part of
the present chapter is devoted to **enterprise policy**. In the run-up to the completion of
the single market, in the early 1990s, the Community has, in fact, paid close attention to
small and medium-sized enterprises (SMEs), which account for almost 99% of the industrial fabric of the Community and for 70% of total employment in the private sector
of the Member States and which face problems of integration in the single market. The
enterprise policy, however, covers not only industrial firms but also firms in other economic sectors, in particular craft, tourism and the distributive trade. Concerning the
tourism sector, in particular, it should be noted that, despite the common interest in developing a common policy for the promotion of European tourism, the Council, has done
nothing more, until now, than invite the Member States to help implement the cooperation approach between tourism stakeholders through the open method of coordination,
i.e. without using Community legal instruments[1]. However, a Commission communication introduces a renewed EU tourism policy, outlining the Commission's future initiatives on the principal aspects of European policy-making and the ways partnerships
amongst concerned stakeholders should evolve[2].

The last part of this chapter deals with sectoral industrial policy, that is, Community
policy for industries in decline in Europe, such as steel and shipbuilding, and "infant" or
fast growing industries, such as information and telecommunications technologies.

17.1. The competitiveness of European industry

Whilst the European Treaties did not make provision for a Community industrial
policy, they **dealt primarily with the industrial sector** of the Member States. In fact,
the Treaties establishing the European Coal and Steel Community (ECSC) and the European Atomic Energy Community (EAEC) constituted sectoral policies in the relevant
industrial sectors, while the Treaty establishing the European Economic Community
(EEC) chiefly regulated the common market in industrial products [see section 2.1.]. But
the ECSC and EAEC (Euratom) Treaties were more precise than the EEC Treaty or even
the EC Treaty. They included provisions both on the attainment of the common market
and on the structural policy of the sectors to which they related, and they gave powers to
the Community institutions to formulate such policies [see details below].

Certainly, the customs union enhanced the ability of European industry to compete
both on its own market and globally. As from 1968, with the introduction of the **Common Customs Tariff** and by virtue of its uniform duties, the Community had available
to it a valuable instrument for conducting an effective commercial policy and for press-
ing on towards the liberalisation of international trade [see section 5.2.1.]. That instrument has been used successfully by the Commission, which has negotiated, on behalf of
the Community, the reduction of the customs protection of the major commercial powers
within the framework of the General Agreement on Tariffs and Trade (GATT) [see section 23.4.].

---

[1] COM (2001) 665 and Council resolution, OJ C 135, 06.06.2002.
[2] COM (2006) 134, 17.03.2006.

However, the easing of international protectionism did not suffice to redress the competitive situation of Community industry. To be able to measure up to the American and Japanese multinational companies, European industries had to find the **dimension most appropriate to the new conditions of competition** and improve their productivity by seeking new products and new production methods. Only the large European market could offer them those conditions of competitiveness.

17.1.1. The single market and industrial policy

Since the common market was not fully operational, until 1993, it **could not have as significant an impact** on industrial structures as the founding fathers of the EEC had hoped. The industrial sector certainly benefited from customs union, without which the development of the Member States' industries would probably not have been the same. But the impact of the common market was principally felt in sectors producing major consumer goods, such as the motor vehicle and domestic electrical appliances sectors, and very little on high technology industries, like information technologies and telecommunications, which were dominated by protected public enterprises.

In the absence of a legal basis for a real industrial policy, Community institutions limited themselves to **examine industrial developments** without being able to influence them. They thus set in place coordinated statistical instruments to measure investment in industry, the business cycle in industry and small craft industries and industrial activity[1]. Later on, those industrial statistical instruments were completed with annual surveys of industrial production[2], of the labour costs in industry and the services sector[3], with structural business statistics[4] and with short-term statistics[5].

The completion of the single European market, topped by the single currency, presents businesses with an opportunity to **benefit from economies of scale**, to cut their administrative and financial costs, to gain easier access to public procurement in other Member States and to cooperate more closely with each other across borders. Thus, the single market represents an essential base for business to look, think and act strategically beyond national borders. Certainly, the tendency of multinational enterprises to acquire a dominant position in the single market under the guise of achieving a sufficient critical size must be monitored by the competition authorities, [see section 15.4.2.], allowing, however, European companies to pursue business strategies, which may safeguard their competitiveness at world level,.

Several objectives of the Community industrial policy were attained through the completion of the single market. Thus, since the beginning of the1990s, **European standardisation** provides manufacturers with technical specifications recognised as giving a presumption of conformity to the essential requirements of Community directives [see section 6.2.3.]. European standards are not only required for the purpose of removing technical barriers to trade; increasingly they are also becoming a key element for the promotion of industrial competitiveness by lowering costs for producers and enabling the emergence of new markets, particularly for developing new technologies. At the same time, greater standardisation of products places a premium on product innovation, manufacturing excellence, design and reliability rather than on the more traditional factors of competitiveness like proximity to markets, distribution systems and customer loyalty.

Very important for European industrial competitiveness is also **public procurement**, which is now opened up thanks to the legislation of the single market [see section 6.3.]. Its importance for industry is threefold. Firstly, the vast size of public procurement

---

[1] Directive 72/221, OJ L 133, 10.06.1972 and EEA Agreement, OJ L 1, 03.01.1994.
[2] Regulation 3924/91, OJ L 374, 31.12.1991.
[3] Regulation 3949/92, OJ L 404, 31.12.1992.
[4] Regulation 58/97, OJ L 14, 17.01.1997 and Regulation 2056/2002, OJ L 317, 21.11.2002.
[5] Regulation 1165/98, OJ L 162, 05.06.1998.

- 16% of GDP - means that access to the public markets is very important for all firms. Secondly, public procurement may enhance technological capability by increasing the marketable demand of high technology products. Thirdly, public procurement being concentrated on a relatively small group of industries, these industries need a competitive market for public procurement in order to develop the necessary products and skills to be successful internationally.

17.1.2. The challenges of European industry

Although European industry now benefits from the advantages of a single large market, it is faced with new challenges. **Globalisation of economies and markets**, which enables greater economies of scale to be reaped and better specialisation for distinctive market segments, entails the intensification of international competition. In the context of this globalisation, European businesses must be able to face international competition. Although it has not deteriorated, apparent labour productivity in Community manufacturing still lags a good way behind that of the US and Japanese industry. Economic operators and public authorities in Europe must therefore pay more attention to the factors influencing productivity: technological development, investment in R&D, the rate of capacity utilisation, the cost and skill of the labour force, management skills and the organisation of production [see details below].

Apart from globalisation of markets and competition, European industry must prepare to face the challenge of the **new industrial revolution**, the one resulting from the development of information and communications technologies. These reduce the traditional distinctions between electronics, information technology, telecommunications and the audiovisual sectors [see sections 17.3.5 and 17.3.6.]. This revolution has far-reaching effects on production structures and methods. It spells changes in the way companies are organised, in managerial responsibilities and relations with workers, particularly concerning the organisation of work. There is therefore a need for structural adjustment and the steady shifting of resources towards the most productive outlets. In general, business competitiveness depends increasingly on the **ability to innovate**, notably by the development of new products and services.

In the information technology sector, for example, almost 80% of income is derived from products that have been on the market for two years or less. It is therefore essential to promote **innovative activities**, including the creation of innovative businesses, and to facilitate the dissemination and exploitation of research results and support technology transfer. Innovation is a complex phenomenon involving many players (firms, universities, research centres and financial operators, etc.). Europe needs to exploit more effectively its research activities and its high level of creativity in terms of knowledge and know-how by ambitious innovation policies at Community, national and regional levels in all sectors [see section 18.4.1.].

In a market economy, such as that of the EU, the main initiative and responsibility for **structural adjustment** lies with business. The role of public authorities is above all as a catalyst and pathfinder for innovation. This means that public authorities may take accompanying measures to assist and speed up the process of adjustment, particularly in the area of infrastructure provision (for example, education, energy, telecommunications and research), but can never substitute for the decisions to be made by business. The Commission recommends taking action in three areas to support structural change: improving the regulatory environment for business (by taking better account of the competitiveness dimension and providing a better assessment of the cumulative impact of regulation on specific industries); better mobilising the different Community policies which can work together to strengthen the take-up and use of knowledge, boost productivity and help companies to innovate; extending the sectoral dimension of European industrial policy to new sectors, such as the automotive sector or other areas of manufacturing[1].

To compare the productivity levels, employment rates and export market shares of the European Union with those of its major competitors, the United States and Japan, the Community uses the tool of **benchmark-**

---

[1]   COM (2004) 274, 21 April 2004.

ing, which makes it possible to monitor progress on an ongoing basis and assess the situation against continuously improving best practice worldwide[1]. Key areas for improvement are the functioning of markets, innovation and intangible investment and the priorities within these areas, which are suitable for benchmarking, such as price, quality of service and the number of innovatory services provided. To disseminate the benchmarking technique, the Commission set up a High-level Group on Benchmarking consisting of industrialists and having as its task the selection of pilot projects, and the setting up of a network of experts to carry out the pilot projects in the Member States[2]. A medium-term work programme aims at the organisation of an ongoing debate with industry on competitiveness, in order to ensure that all aspects of this question are taken into consideration.

17.1.3. The foundations of industrial policy

With the entry into force, in November 1993, of the Treaty of Maastricht [see section 2.2.], industrial competitiveness became one of the stated objectives of European integration. Article 3 of the EC Treaty states, in fact, that the action of the Community includes, *inter alia*, the **strengthening of the competitiveness of Community industry**. The Title on Industry of the TEC announces that the Community and the Member States must ensure the existence of the conditions necessary for the competitiveness of the Community's industry. For this purpose, in accordance with a system of open and competitive markets, **their action aims at**: speeding up the adjustment of industry to structural changes; encouraging an environment favourable to initiative and to the development of undertakings throughout the Community, particularly small and medium-sized undertakings; encouraging an environment favourable to cooperation between undertakings; and fostering better exploitation of the industrial potential of innovation and research and technological development policies (Art. 157 TEC).

This article forms the legal basis for Community action in the fields of industry and business. It specifies however that it does not provide a basis for the introduction by the Community of any measures that could lead to a distortion of competition. The objectives set out above may be **pursued by the following means**: the mutual consultation of the Member States and, where necessary, the coordination of their action, in liaison with and upon initiative of the Commission; the coordination with other Community policies and activities; and specific measures in support of action taken in the Member States decided by the Council acting unanimously on a proposal from the Commission after consultation of the European Parliament and the Economic and Social Committee. The unanimity rule required for specific measures in the industrial sector denotes the reluctance of the Member States to weaken national policies in favour of a common industrial policy. Hence, most industrial policy is carried out not at EU level but under the competence of the Member States.

Yet, industrial competitiveness depends on policies such as competition, the internal market, research and development, education, trade and sustainable development. Therefore, the common industrial policy must ensure that other common policies contribute to the competitiveness of Europe's industry. It therefore covers a very wide field, while many of its instruments are the instruments of other policy fields[3]. The **common industrial strategy is based on three principles**: consistent recourse to all common policies with a bearing on industrial activity, in particular that of protection of the environment[4]; improved access of Community businesses to non-Community markets and to measures against unfair trading practices and in favour of international industrial coop-

---

[1] COM (96) 463, 9 October 1996.
[2] COM (97) 153, 16 April 1997.
[3] COM (2002) 714, 11 December 2002.
[4] Resolution, OJ C 331, 16.12.1992, p. 5-7.

eration [see sections 23.2.2. and 23.4.][1]; and the positive adjustment to industrial changes through a consistent approach[2]. On these principles is based the **Community action programme to strengthen the competitiveness** of European industry[3]. Its broad action lines are: promoting intangible investment, e.g. by exploiting the competitive advantages associated with better protection of the environment; developing industrial cooperation; ensuring fair competition; and modernising the role of the public authorities, thus relieving businesses of unnecessary bureaucratic burdens. They have also agreed on a common policy framework in the **business services sector**, as a factor for the competitiveness of European industry and for the creation of employment[4].

17.1.4. SMEs in the single market

During the 1960s and the 1970s, economists extolled the **advantages of multinational undertakings**: scale economies, new production and distribution technologies, modern personnel management, production and distribution planning at European scale. Politicians offered all sorts of advantages to multinational undertakings to incite them to invest in their country or region and thus assist in its development and in the absorption of the redundant manpower of the primary sector. In fact, multinationals - practically all American - mainly exploited the over-valued dollar to buy at a good price European firms and/or eliminate from the markets that interested them the large and medium-sized national companies.

During the 1980s the rise of the multinationals had slowed. The European Commission defended more and more vigorously the tendencies of large firms to monopolise certain markets [see section 15.4] and the tendencies of national and regional authorities to give them large incentives in the form of aids [see section 12.2.1]. Trade unions claimed more and more rights and social benefits for European workers. Monetary and monopolistic super-profits started diminishing for the multinationals. Thus, they stopped investing in Europe and started practising the so-called "social dumping", that is setting up plants in countries with low labour costs. Now, it is clear that, because of the technological development and the globalisation of the markets several traditional industries and "national champions" are in decline, while **new industries and operators are emerging**, often offering products and services with a higher value-added content. These new operators are quite often small businesses. Although it is clear that economies of scale exist and are very important in certain types of production, such as the production in very large numbers of standard products, it is also clear that the management structures of small enterprises are simpler and more flexible than those of big firms and that this, other things being equal, can be a serious advantage. Social relations are also better in smaller as compared to bigger firms. Moreover, small enterprises absorb the most vulnerable categories in the labour market, i.e., women and young persons. Last but not least, small businesses are present in new expanding markets and "market niches", less vulnerable to international competition.

As was seen above, Article 157 (TEC) states, among other things, that the Community and the Member States shall encourage "an environment favourable to initiative and to the development of undertakings throughout the Community, particularly small and medium-sized undertakings". This is the base of the common enterprise policy, a policy in favour of small businesses, known in Community jargon as **small and medium-sized enterprises (SMEs)**. But what are the SMEs?

Until the mid-1990s, different definitions of SMEs were used in Community policies (competition, Structural Funds, R&D, tendering for public procurement, etc.). This diversity could give rise to doubts among public authorities and even to confusion among the businessmen concerned. Therefore, the Commission adopted a recommendation concerning the **definition of micro, small and medium-sized enterprises** used in Community policies[5]. An enterprise is considered to be any entity engaged in an economic activity, irrespective of its legal form. The category of micro, small and medium-sized enterprises (SMEs) is made up of enterprises which employ fewer than 250 per-

---

[1]   Resolution, OJ C 178, 15.07.1992, p. 1-3.
[2]   COM (92) 2000.
[3]   Decision 96/413, OJ L 167, 06.07.1996.
[4]   COM (1998) 534, 21 September 1998.
[5]   Recommendation 2003/361, OJ L 124, 20.05.2003.

sons and which have an annual turnover not exceeding EUR 50 million, and/or an annual balance sheet total not exceeding EUR 43 million. Within the SME category, a small enterprise is defined as an enterprise which employs fewer than 50 persons and whose annual turnover and/or annual balance sheet total does not exceed EUR 10 million. A microenterprise is defined as an enterprise which employs fewer than 10 persons and whose annual turnover and/or annual balance sheet total does not exceed EUR 2 million. However, the Commission recommends to remove from the SMEs category non-autonomous enterprises, i.e. those which have holdings entailing a controlling position (partner enterprises) or those that are linked to other enterprises.

This definition serves as a reference for Community programmes, policy and legislation concerning SMEs and thus provides an overall framework, which can increase the coherence, effectiveness and visibility of all measures to assist these enterprises. It should be noted that with this definition, the Union (Fifteen) numbers some 17 million SMEs, providing over 75% of its employment, accounting for 50% of investment and representing 60% of its wealth.

In addition to quantitative and easily verifiable criteria, SMEs are often also identified by **qualitative criteria**, focusing chiefly on the ownership of their capital, their management and their methods of financing. A SME is often a family business, whose management and ownership are in the hands of the same person(s). Day-to-day running of a SME falls upon the company head, enabling flexibility and rapidity in the decision-making process and a personalised relationship with staff, suppliers and customers. Finally, a SME is heavily dependent on self-financing due to difficult access to the financial markets and it often suffers from limited availability of financial resources. These qualitative identification criteria merge with a small undertaking's main characteristics, characteristics which can occasionally prove a handicap, but which can also be to their advantage.

Of course, SMEs have **their weak points, which are notably**: (a) the difficulty to face the complicated administrative and legal environment created by the completion of the internal market and the globalisation of production; (b) lack in management training for many businessmen and/or lack of willingness to delegate part of the management to qualified associates; and (c) funding difficulties, despite the increase and the differentiation of sources of financing in the large market. It is clearly more difficult and relatively more costly for SMEs than for large firms to have access to world technological capital, to avail themselves of the most sophisticated management techniques and business services and to find their proper place in the global economy and even in the EU's single market.

Small and, above all, medium-sized businesses, must, first and foremost, **rely on their own efforts to achieve success** in the single market. In order to succeed they must make the effort to adapt to their new environment by abandoning some of their family-style management habits and/or their production and marketing methods and cooperate with each other in order to overcome some of the handicaps which are attributable to their size, in particular with regard to supply and the distribution of their products over a number of Member States. In so doing SMEs must, however, **be assisted** by their trade organisations, their governments and the European institutions. That is why a common enterprise policy is needed to provide a framework for and coordinate the efforts deployed by the Member States to assist their SMEs, without distorting competition by favouring certain undertakings or the production of certain goods within the meaning of Article 87 of the EC Treaty [see section 15.5.1.].

17.2. Enterprise policy

The **European Charter for Small Enterprises,** endorsed by the Feira European Council (19 and 20 June 2000), states that the situation of small business in the European Union can be improved by action to stimulate entrepreneurship, to evaluate existing measures, and when necessary, to make them small-business-friendly, and to ensure that policy-makers take due consideration of small business needs. In this Charter the Member States pledged themselves to: strengthen the spirit of innovation and entrepreneurship; achieve a regulatory, fiscal and administrative framework conducive to entrepreneurial activity; ensure access to markets on the basis of the least burdensome requirements that are consistent with overriding public policy objectives; facilitate access to the best research and technology; improve access to finance and performance continuously, so that the EU will offer the best environment for small business in the world; listen to the voice of small business; and promote top-class small business support. The Charter commits the Member States to work along ten lines of action in order to achieve these objectives. The Charter has political rather than legal value, since it cannot be called upon in courts, but small business organisations in the member countries may exercise pressures on their governments to honour their commitments.

The multiannual **programme for enterprise and entrepreneurship** (2001-2005) provides for an enterprise policy to be implemented via a new coordination procedure with the Member States (the BEST procedure) [see section 17.2.2.] and aims in particular at the needs of SMEs in more than 30 countries (European Union, EEA and applicant countries)[1]. The programme is intended to enhance the growth and competitiveness of business in a knowledge-driven globalised economy, to promote entrepreneurship, to simplify and improve the administrative and regulatory framework for business so that research, innovation and business creation in particular can flourish, to improve the financial environment for business (in the form of loan guarantees and support for risk capital provision) and to give business easier access to Community support services, programmes and networks.

Following the conclusions of the Lisbon European Council (23 and 24 March 2000) on a new strategic goal [see section 13.3.2.], the Commission put forward the guidelines of an enterprise policy designed to meet the challenges of **globalisation and the knowledge-driven economy** and a proposal on a multiannual programme of action to achieve these objectives[2]. The policy guidelines include: encouraging all businesses to adopt successful business models incorporating electronic commerce between firms; facilitating risk-taking and a spirit of enterprise thus helping build a dynamic enterprise environment for the creation, growth and innovation of enterprises, supported by risk capital and an effective research and development policy; and ensuring that enterprises have effective access to internal and global markets. Concerning **innovation policy** in a knowledge-driven economy, the Commission proposes five objectives: coherent national innovation policies; a regulatory framework conducive to innovation; encouragement for the creation and growth of innovative enterprises; improvements to key interfaces in the innovation system; a society open to innovation[3].

In a 2005 communication the Commission highlights the major challenges SMEs face daily, proposes new actions to strengthen their capacity to sustain in the market, to grow and to create jobs and new ways to enhance dialogue and consultation with SME stakeholders[4]. Aiming ta the implementation of the Lisbon Integrated Guidelines and the Community Lisbon Programme, the Communication provides a coherent framework for the various enterprise policy instruments and aims at making the "**Think Small First**" principle effective across all EU policies. On 13 March 2006, the Council welcomed the Commission's aim to promote a coherent and single approach for SMEs.

---

[1]   Decision 2000/819, OJ L 333, 29.12.2000 and decision 1776/2005, OJ L 289, 03.11.2005.
[2]   COM (2000) 256, 26 April 2000.
[3]   COM (2000) 567, 20 September 2000.
[4]   COM/2005/551, 10 November 2005.

In a communication on the implementation of the Lisbon programme, the Commission draws attention to the huge untapped potential of SMEs to create growth and employment and proposes ways to simplify rules and regulations, promote entrepreneurial culture, and assist SMEs to access innovation, finance, training and the European and international markets[1].

Although for practical reasons we are examining enterprise policy in the chapter for industry, it should be stressed that this policy concerns not just industry but practically every economic sector, in particular craft business and distribution. Indeed, the new policy dovetails with common policies that predate it, viz. those concerning the operation of the single market, economic and social cohesion, research and technological development and environmental protection. Thus, given that it supplements and is itself supplemented by other common policies, the **common enterprise policy has three broad objectives**, which we shall examine below: to create a legal framework which lends itself to the setting up and development of enterprises in the Community; to create an economic environment which will help enterprises reach their full development in the single market; and to promote cooperation between enterprises situated in different regions of the Community.

17.2.1. The legal environment of European business

The objectives pursued by the Community through its efforts at harmonisation in the area of **company law and accounting** are: the mobility of firms in order to allow them to benefit from the advantages of a unified market; the equality of the conditions of competition between firms established in different Member States; the promotion of commercial links between the Member States; the stimulation of cooperation between firms across borders and the facilitation of cross-border mergers and acquisitions. Appropriate Community measures are needed to provide for legal structures which facilitate cross-border establishment and investment, and to smooth discrepancies between national systems of company law which discourage or penalise these activities.

By virtue of the freedom of establishment laid down by the EC Treaty, undertakings formed in accordance with the law of one Member State do not encounter administrative problems in establishing themselves in the territory of another Member State [see section 6.5.1.]. The same cannot be said of **the real economic and legal problems of establishment**, which cannot disappear by the sole virtue of the provisions of the Treaty. Indeed, as the common market develops, companies see a constant increase in the transnational dimension of their relations with third parties, be they shareholders, employees, creditors or others. That development multiplies the danger of conflict between the various national measures, which guarantee the rights of those people. It is accordingly understandable that the Community's first effort of structural policy concerned **the coordination of the company law** of the Member States by means of Council Directives, based on Article 54.3.g. of the EEC Treaty (Art.44.2.g TEC), which provides for coordination of the safeguards which are required by Member States of Community companies for the protection of the interests of members and others. On the basis of this article, a number of directives harmonised several aspects of the company law of the Member States.

The first Directive lays down a **system of disclosure** applicable to all companies in order to coordinate safeguards for the protection of the interests of members and others and to facilitate public access to information on companies[2]. It obliges Member States to keep a register of companies, which anyone may examine, and to ensure that certain information is published in a national gazette. Also to protect the interests of members and others, the second Directive provides for the harmonisation of the standards and procedures relating to the **formation of public limited liability companies** and the maintenance and alteration of their capital. An amendment to this Directive aims to ensure that this type of company does not make use of a subsidiary for the acquisition of its

---

[1] COM/2005/551, 10 November 2005.
[2] Directive 68/151, OJ L 65, 14.03.1968 and Directive 2003/58, OJ L 221, 04.09.2003.

own shares[1]. The third Directive introduces into the legal systems of all member countries the procedure for **the merger of public limited liability companies**, with the transfer of the assets and liabilities of the acquired company to the acquiring company[2]. The sixth Directive regulates **the hiving-off process**, i.e. the division of an existing company into several entities[3]. The eleventh Directive imposes measures in respect of disclosure in the Member State in which a branch is situated, in order to ensure the protection of persons who through **the intermediary of the branch** deal with a company who is governed by the law of another Member State[4]. The twelfth Directive deals with **single-member private companies** and allows, under certain conditions, the limitation of liability of the individual entrepreneur throughout the Community[5].

The fourth, seventh and eighth Directives create **a code of European accounting legislation** which is harmonised to a great extent, even though it is still far from being complete. The fourth concerns the **annual accounts of certain types of companies**[6]. It notably authorises the Member States to simplify accounting requirements for small and medium-sized enterprises, defined according to their balance sheet, their turnover and the number of employees (maximum of 50 for small enterprises and 250 for medium-sized). The seventh Directive concerns the **consolidated accounts of companies** which form part of a "group" of undertakings, i.e. parent companies and their subsidiaries[7]. The consolidated accounts must give a true reflection of a company's assets and liabilities, its financial situation and the results of the various undertakings making up the group. The eighth Directive defines the qualifications of persons responsible for carrying out the **statutory audits of accounting documents**[8]. These individuals must have received high-level theoretical and practical training, have passed an examination of professional competence and have been approved by the relevant authority in the Member State where they are performing their duties.

It should be noted, however, that accounts prepared in accordance with the accounting Directives and the national laws which implement them do not meet the more demanding standards drawn up by the International Accounting Standards Committee (IASC) in collaboration with the International Organisation of Securities Commissions (IOSCO). Therefore, a regulation requires companies, including banks and insurance companies, to draw up their consolidated accounts in accordance with international accounting standards (IAS) from 2005[9] [see also sections 6.6.1. and 6.6.2.]. By improving the reliability, transparency and comparability of company accounts throughout the European Union, this regulation aims to remove barriers to cross-border trade in transferable securities, reduce the cost of capital for companies and ultimately strengthen their competitiveness.

Specific Directives, mentioned in the chapter on the common market, deal with the annual accounts and consolidated **accounts of banks and insurance undertakings** [see sections 6.6.1. and 6.6.2.]. Other Directives, examined in the chapter on taxation, concern the **taxation system** applicable to mergers, divisions, transfers of assets and exchanges of shares concerning companies of different Member States and the Community system of taxation applicable in the case of parent companies and subsidiaries of different Member States [see section 14.3.1.][10]. These Directives remove the main tax obstacles to cooperation and restructuring of enterprises within the European Union.

More than 31 years after the Commission proposal for the creation of the **European company** (a record in Community legislation), the Council finally adopted the two legislative instruments necessary for its creation, the regulation on the statute for a European company and a directive supplementing this statute with regard to the involvement of employees[11]. These legal provisions, which will enter into force together on 8 October 2004, will make it possible for a company to be set up within the territory of the Community in the form of a public limited-liability company, with the Latin name *Societas*

---

1   Directive 77/91, OJ L 26, 30.01.1977 and Directive 2006/68, OJ L 264, 25.09.2006.
2   Directive 78/855, OJ L 295, 20.10.1978 and OJ L 1, 03.01.1994.
3   Directive 82/891, OJ L 378, 31.12.1982 and OJ L 1, 03.01.1994.
4   Directive 89/666, OJ L 395, 30.12.1989 and OJ L 1, 03.01.1994.
5   Directive 89/667, OJ L 395, 30.12.1989 and OJ L 1, 03.01.1994.
6   Directive 78/660, OJ L 222, 14.08.1978 and Directive 2006/46, OJ L 224, 16.08.2006.
7   Directive 83/349, OJ L 193, 18.07.1983 and Directive 2006/46, OJ L 224, 16.08.2006.
8   Directive 2006/43, OJ L 157, 09.06.2006.
9   Regulation 1606/2002, OJ L 243, 11.09.2002.
10 Directives 90/434 and 90/435, OJ L 225, 20.08.1990 and Directive 2005/19, OJ L 58, 04.03.2005.
11 Regulation 2157/2001 and directive 2001/86, OJ L 294, 10.11.2001 and Regulation 885/2004, OJ L 168, 01.05.2004.

Europaea (**SE**). An SE is entered in a register in the Member State where its registered office is situated. Every registered SE is publicised in the Official Journal of the European Union. An SE must take the form of a company with share capital of at least EUR 120 000. The rules relating to **employee involvement in the SE** seek to ensure that the creation of an SE does not entail the disappearance or reduction of practices of employee involvement existing within the companies participating in the establishment of an SE [see section 13.5.2.].

The **Statute for the European company** provides enterprises with an optional new instrument, which makes cross-border enterprise management more flexible and less bureaucratic and may help improve the competitiveness of European enterprises. The SE makes it possible to operate Community-wide while being subject to Community legislation directly applicable in all Member States. Several options are available to enterprises from at least two Member States wishing to form an SE: a merger, a holding company, the creation of a subsidiary, or transformation into an SE. The statute allows a public limited-liability company, which has its registered office and head office within the Community, to transform itself into an SE without going into liquidation. An SE may itself set up one or more subsidiaries in the form of SEs. The registered office of an SE may be transferred to another Member State under certain conditions, but without winding up of the SE or creating a new legal person. Subject to the Regulation on the statute of SEs, an SE should be treated in every Member State as if it were a public limited-liability company formed in accordance with the law of the Member State in which it has its registered office.

The statute for a **European cooperative society (SCE)** is modelled on that of the European company, with the changes required by the specific characteristics of cooperative societies[1]. It allows the creation of a new legal entity for the organisation of economic operations in two or more Member States in the form of a cooperative society. It is supplemented by a Directive providing arrangements for the involvement of employees in a SCE[2] [see details below].

The harmonisation of company law and the creation of European companies facilitate the interpenetration of markets and the concentration of companies at European level. But it is also necessary for Community undertakings to be able **to cooperate easily amongst themselves**, which is by no means straightforward. The various forms provided for by national laws for cooperation between domestic undertakings are not adapted to cooperation at common market level, owing specifically to their attachment to a national legal system, which means that cooperation between undertakings from several countries must be subject to the national law governing one of the participating undertakings. Economic operators, however, do not readily accept attachment to a foreign legal system, both for psychological reasons and owing to ignorance of foreign laws. Such legal barriers to international cooperation are particularly important where the parties involved are SMEs.

It was therefore necessary to introduce a legal instrument covered by Community law, which would make adequate cooperation between undertakings from different Member States possible. This is the purpose of the **"European Economic Interest Grouping" (EEIG)**, an instrument for cooperation on a contractual basis created by a Council Regulation in 1985[3]. The EEIG is not an economic entity separate from and independent of its members, behaving autonomously and trying to make profits for itself.

---

[1] Regulation 1435/2003, OJ L 207, 18.08.2003.
[2] Directive 2003/72, OJ L 207, 18.08.2003.
[3] Regulation 2137/85, OJ L 199, 31.07.1985 and OJ L 1, 03.01.1994.

It is a hybrid legal instrument offering the flexibility of a contract and some of the advantages of company status, including notably legal capacity. It serves as an economic staging post for the economic activity of its members. It enables them, by virtue of pooled functions, to develop their own activity and thus increase their own profits. Each member of the Grouping remains entirely autonomous both in economic and legal terms. That is a pre-condition for the existence of the European Economic Interest Grouping and distinguishes it from any other form or stage of merger. The Grouping ensures the equality of its members. None of them could give the others or the Grouping itself binding directives. Lastly, the Grouping may not seek profit for itself, may provide services only to its members and must invoice them at the cost price. These services can consist of marketing, the grouped purchase of raw materials or the representation of its members' interests.

Natural persons, companies and all other "legal entities" falling under public or private law can form part of an EEIG. **Groupings can be created in all sectors of the economy**, from agriculture to industry, trade, the craft sector or services. The grouping must incorporate at least two bodies: the board of members and the manager or managers. The board of members is the supreme body. It can take any decision for the purposes of attaining the grouping's objective. The members of the EEIG have considerable liberty to organise its management in line with the needs of the cooperation venture. An EEIG can be constituted without capital; it can even have no assets. Members enjoy a great deal of flexibility regarding how they decide to finance the grouping's activities. An EEIG can, in all the Member States, be a holder of rights and obligations, conclude contracts, be a party to legal proceedings and have its own assets in accordance with the objectives set by its members. Due to its full legal capacity, it is obliged to assume responsibility for its commitments on its own assets. Nevertheless, in the event of default by the grouping, its members are jointly and severally liable with regard to third parties for the debts of the grouping.

The Commission supports the effective **promotion and development of cooperatives** in the European Union, noting that they are an integral element in achieving the Lisbon objectives and that they are playing an increasingly important and positive role as vehicles for the implementation of many Community objectives in fields such as employment policy, social integration, regional and rural development and agriculture. According to the Commission the statute for a European cooperative society is already an effective instrument for cross-border and pan-European cooperation between cooperatives[1].

17.2.2. The business environment in the EU

In the run-up to the completion of the single market the Community has endeavoured in particular to remove any obstacles to cross-border business activity, so as to help companies take advantage of new commercial opportunities on partner countries markets and, in general, to improve the environment in which Union business operates. Nevertheless, because of the complex nature of certain European provisions and **inadequate knowledge of the European legislation** concerned [see section 3.3.], businessmen often regard that legislation as an impediment to the entrepreneurial spirit. The European Union should therefore ensure that the impact of its legislation on enterprises, in particular SMEs, is not in conflict with the common objective of seeing enterprises reach their full development in the single market.

The European institutions try, indeed, to take into account the problems and conditions which are specific to SMEs when drawing up and implementing common policies (regional, social, research, environment, etc.). All proposals presented by the Commission to the Council and the Parliament are accompanied by an **impact assessment describing their likely effects on businesses**, in particular small and medium-sized enterprises, and on job creation. Through the "impact assessment method", the Commission analyses the direct and indirect implications of a proposed measure (e.g. concerning

---

[1]   COM (2004) 18, 23 January 2004.

businesses, trade, employment, the environment and health). The results of each assessment are made public[1]. The impact assessment also gives details of the consultations that have taken place with the trade organisations concerned by the proposal[2]. The Community's legislative authorities are thus kept fully informed of the implications of a proposal on business and employment [see section 4.3.].

It is advisable, however, to ensure that Member States do not complicate matters when transposing Community legislation into national law. Therefore, the Council recommended to the Member States to implement programmes of **administrative simplification** covering both new legislative proposals and existing legislation and to examine the impact of all proposed legislation or rules on the administrative burden on enterprises[3]. In a resolution on realising the full potential of SMEs, the Council called on the Member States and the Commission to examine how the business environment for SMEs could be improved by removing the structural impediments resulting from the legal, financial and administrative framework[4]. At the invitation of the Amsterdam European Council, the Commission set up in July 1997 a **Business Environment Simplification Task Force (BEST)**, consisting of independent experts, which has the job of proposing concrete measures to improve the quality of legislation and reduce the constraints on SME development.

In order to improve the European business environment, a directive aims at combating **late payment in commercial transactions** in the public as well as the private sector[5]. This directive obliged the Member States to limit the deadline for payment at thirty days from the invoice date, unless otherwise specified in the contract and it harmonised the interest on late payments at seven percentage points above the European Central Bank rate. It also provided for retention of title by the seller until the time of payment of the purchase price and accelerated recovery procedures for undisputed debts with a maximum 90 days between the lodging of the creditor's action and the time when the writ of execution becomes enforceable.

It is also necessary to improve the quality and flow of information on the internal market and other fields of Community policy directed towards enterprises, in particular SMEs. The **Euro-Info-Centre (EIC) network** is designed to respond to SMEs' requests for information covering in particular the internal market (legal, technical and social aspects of Community trade) and the possibility of benefiting from Community funding. The EICs have three major objectives: to provide information about all single market issues and opportunities of interest to enterprises; to assist and advise businesses on participation in European activities; and to act as a channel of communication between enterprises and the Commission.

Some 260 EICs are disseminated throughout the regions of the Member States, the EFTA countries, the countries of Central and Eastern Europe and Mediterranean countries. They are integrated in host organisations which have experience in providing information and advice to firms and which are well established in their local environment, e.g. chambers of commerce, local development agencies, trade organisations and business consultants. They constitute a network which can exchange information on Community, national and regional legislation and the procedures which are of direct concern to businesses in their respective regions.

By their nature it is generally more difficult for smaller enterprises to participate in **research and development programmes** (R & D). Firstly, the administrative costs of applying to participate and organising the required cooperation are relatively high for SMEs and, secondly, they do not have the same facility of access to long-term finance as larger companies. On the other hand, small businesses often have greater flexibility, crea-

---

[1] COM (2002) 276, 5 June 2002.
[2] Resolution, OJ C 331, 16.12.1992, p. 3-4.
[3] Recommendation, OJ L 141, 02.06.1990, p. 55-56 and resolution, OJ C 331, 16.12.1992, p. 3-4.
[4] Resolution, OJ C 18, 17.01.1997, p. 1-5.
[5] Directive 2000/35, OJ L 200, 08.08.2000.

tivity and dynamism, characteristics which qualify them well to contribute to the innovative process. Therefore the **sixth Community R & D programme** encourages research activities involving SMEs[1] [see section 18.4.]. Specific schemes for SMEs exist in the form of actions on collective and cooperative research. In addition, SMEs participate, for the most part, in the activities implemented under the priority thematic areas of research within networks of excellence, integrated projects and specific targeted research projects. Joint actions for innovation and SMEs aim notably: at the rationalisation and coordination of networks providing information and assistance on the Community's research and innovation activities such as the CORDIS information service; provision of information and advice; access to private finance; the creation of innovative start-ups, principally via European organisations and funds (European Investment Fund, European Investment Bank, and the Eurotech Capital scheme).

Several **recommendations of the Commission**, addressed to the Member States, aim at improving the business environment for European SMEs. In order to make it easier for non-incorporated SMEs to finance themselves the Commission recommended to the Member States to set the **tax burden** on reinvested earnings, in the case of sole proprietorships, at the same level as that applied to non-distributed corporate income[2]. Taking account of the fact that 10% of business closures in the European Union have their origin in a badly administered inheritance, the Commission, in a Recommendation on the **transfer of enterprises**, advocated changes in the law of succession and easing the taxation burden, in order to facilitate the continuity of enterprises and the jobs which go with them[3]. In order to improve and simplify the environment for **starting up business**, a Commission Recommendation invited the Member States to reduce the fiscal, social, environmental and statistical burdens imposed on business start-ups[4]. The Committee for improving and simplifying the environment for enterprises, consisting of representatives of the Member States and representatives of SMEs at European level is charged with carrying out consultations on legislative and administrative provisions which hamper the creation, growth and transfer of enterprises, e.g. in the fields of financial instruments, capital markets, internationalisation of activities and statistical reporting obligations[5].

17.2.3. Business funding

Many European SMEs experience financing problems. They have less equity capital than their counterparts in the United States or Japan and they are more dependent than large firms on direct institutional finance (bank overdrafts, short and long-term loans), which is more expensive. The Commission noted that the situation could be improved easily by providing them with effective advice regarding both their management methods and their relations with their financial backers[6]. It also suggested improving coordination and communication between the various European, national, regional and local programmes aimed at strengthening the financial position of SMEs. The risk capital action plan (RCAP), adopted by the Cardiff European Council in June 1998, encourages venture capital investments by the structural funds and other capital markets, particularly in the seed and start-up phases, which have traditionally been the weakest links of the financing cycle in Europe[7].

The **European Investment Bank (EIB)** through its Global Loans and the **European Investment Fund (EIF)** are the financial institutions of the Community in support of SMEs [see section 7.3.3.]. The EIF's activity is centred upon two areas, venture capital and guarantees. EIF's venture capital instruments consist of equity investments in venture capital funds and business incubators that support SMEs, particularly those that are early stage and technology-oriented. EIF's guarantee instruments consist of providing guarantees to financial institutions that cover credits to SMEs. Both instruments implemented by the EIF for SMEs are complementary to the Global Loans provided by the European Investment Bank to financial intermediaries in support of SME financing [see

---

[1] Decision 2002/834, OJ L 294, 29.10.2002.
[2] Recommendation 94/390, OJ L 177, 09.07.1994, p. 1-19.
[3] Recommendation 94/1069, OJ L 385, 31.12.1994, p. 14-17.
[4] Recommendation 97/344, OJ L 145, 05.06.1997, p. 29-51 and COM/2006/117, 14.03.2006.
[5] Resolution, OJ C 294, 22.10.1994, p. 6-8.
[6] COM (93) 528.
[7] COM (2001) 605, 25 October 2001 and COM (2002) 563, 16 October 2002.

details below]. EIF's instruments are implemented in the context of the multiannual programme for enterprise and entrepreneurship (2001-05) [see section 17.2.].

SMEs are particularly interested in the possibility of Community funding under the common regional policy. The Regulation on the **European Regional Development Fund**[1] provides for a series of measures to support local development initiatives and the activities of SMEs [see sections 12.3.1. and 12.3.3.]. It supports notably:

- productive investment which contributes to creating and safeguarding sustainable jobs, primarily through direct aid to investment primarily in small and medium-sized enterprises (SMEs);
- measures which support regional and local development, including support for and services to enterprises, in particular SMEs;
- aid to R&TD, notably in SMEs, and to technology transfer, improvement of links between SMEs, support for the provision of business and technology services to groups of SMEs and fostering of entrepreneurship and innovation funding for SMEs through financial engineering instruments;
- aid and services to SMEs to adopt and effectively use information and communication technologies (ICTs) or to exploit new ideas;
- aid to SMEs to promote sustainable production patterns through the introduction of cost-effective environmental management systems and the adoption and use of pollution-prevention technologies;
- tourism, including promotion of natural assets as potential for the development of sustainable tourism.

The Business and Innovation Centres (BICs), set up by the Commission and public and private regional partners are designed to promote business creation and expansion by providing a comprehensive programme of services (training, finance, marketing, technology transfer, etc.) to SMEs which are developing innovative technology-based projects [see section 12.2.3.][2].

Through the leverage effect of its venture capital and guarantee instruments, the **European Investment Fund** is able to contribute to the development of SMEs in the EU Member States and the candidate countries in the framework of the Lisbon strategy [see section 13.3.2.]. The EIF does not invest in SMEs directly, but instead always works through financial intermediaries. These intermediaries are given full delegation of activity. The EIF is not involved in individual investment/credit decisions. SMEs in search of finance are requested to contact an EIF intermediary in their country/region for information on eligibility criteria and application procedures. The EIF's engagement plays a catalytic role in the creation of investment funds, because it has the effect of attracting other investors and bestows to these funds the critical size allowing them to launch their investment activities.

17.2.4. Cooperation between businesses

The opening up of markets as a result of economic integration in the Community is bringing with it faster structural change and greater competitive pressures on businesses. In many situations, cooperation or partnership between small businesses in different regions or countries of the Community can **help to meet the challenge of the wider market** and to compete with larger ones, especially if the arrangements concerned are based on complementarity resulting in mutual benefits. Moreover, cooperation can foster the modernisation and diversification of SMEs. There are different forms of cooperation, e.g. joint ventures, syndicates, agreements covering non-financial links (the grant-

---

[1]   Regulation 1083, 2006, OJ L 210, 31.07.2006.
[2]   Special report No 5/93, OJ C 13, 17.01.1994, p. 1-11.

ing/purchasing of licences, the transfer of know-how, marketing, etc.) or the acquisition of holdings. It may be formal, i.e. based on a contract, e.g. via a European economic interest grouping [see section 17.2.1.], or informal. Before taking part in any form of cooperation, firms must of course consider whether that cooperation is legal, since cooperation agreements sometimes give rise to problems in connection with the provisions of the Treaties concerning competition [see section 15.3.]. Such cases are, however, rare. As stated in the chapter on competition, the Commission is in favour of cooperation between SMEs and agreements of minor importance [see section 15.3.1.][1].

While cooperation between Community firms is regarded as desirable and is generally authorised, it still has to overcome problems of a technical and psychological nature. SMEs investing in other Member States prefer to create subsidiaries rather than joint ventures, or to enter into looser cooperation agreements without the obligation to create a new legal entity. The **Business to Europe (B2Europe)** initiative of the Commission is a means of strengthening the links between the various Community networks and providing businesses with a range of services which answer their needs, including cooperation between them in various countries of the Union.

17.3. Sectoral industrial policy

Sectoral industrial policy is largely linked with commercial policy. The **commercial policy measures** that have the greatest consequences for industrial sectors are manipulations of the customs tariff, anti-dumping measures, trade agreements and various export incentives. By virtue of customs union, most of those measures are already in the hands of the European institutions [see sections 23.3. and 23.5.]. Other sectoral policy measures are the **incentives used by governments** to modernise and guide national industries, such as grants to certain research bodies, to documentation centres and centres for the dissemination of knowledge, to productivity centres and to vocational training centres. Some such measures are already centralised at European level. The others **require Community coordination**, inasmuch as they may disturb conditions of competition on the single market.

Also still in the hands of governments are the most direct and best-known sectoral measures, i.e. **aids of every kind**: grants, loans, interest rate subsidies, etc. Aids for the improvement of certain sectors and aids to "infant industries" are characteristic examples of sectoral measures. The main grounds for them are employment promotion, regional development or even national prestige where important undertakings, regarded as "flagship companies", are involved [see section 15.5.3.]. Since sectoral aids and the conditions under which they are granted vary greatly from one EU State to another, they may affect trade between Member States and distort or threaten to distort competition. Therefore, the objective of industrial policy should be to create the conditions that allow better control of such aids. Moreover, the effectiveness of the Community's policies to promote greater cohesion could be improved by a progressive reduction in aid intensities in the central and more prosperous regions.

It is for that reason that Articles 87 and 88 of the EC Treaty provide for Commission control of the aids which States grant directly or indirectly to certain undertakings or the production of certain goods. Such **aids must be notified to the Commission**, which has the power to authorise them or prohibit them in accordance with the criteria laid down in the Treaty or under secondary legislation [see section 15.5.]. Thus, although

---

[1]	OJ C 231, 12.09.1986, p. 2-4.

the most powerful instrument of sectoral industrial policy is still in the hands of the governments, the Commission may prevent such national aids from distorting conditions of competition or running counter to the objectives of the EU's industrial policy.

The best way to prevent individual sectoral measures by governments that are harmful to the common interest and at the same time to restructure European industry is the **common sectoral policy**. This has developed in the most vulnerable sectors at international level, either because the markets are saturated (steel, shipbuilding, textiles) or because they are not yet well developed at European level (aeronautics, information industries, telecommunications). We shall examine Community policy in those sectors below.

17.3.1. Steel industry

The steel industry was one of the two strategic sectors **governed by the European Coal and Steel Community (ECSC)**. Those strategic sectors were subjected to common rules and a common authority. Intra-Community trade was liberalised and increased by almost 130% during the first five years of the ECSC's existence. In 1974, Community steel represented approximately 7% of the total industrial production in the original Member States. The turning point for that industry, as for many others, was the 1973 energy crisis and the 1975 economic recession that ensued. As the crisis developed, the Community assumed ever-increasing responsibilities, enabling it, on the one hand, to stabilise the market in order to remedy the constant deterioration of the financial situation of undertakings and, on the other hand, to encourage the adjustment of industrial structures to the new market conditions. For that reason, in October 1980, with the agreement of the Council of Ministers, the Commission declared a state of "**manifest crisis**" in the steel sector[1]. That situation - which was provided for in the ECSC Treaty - allowed the Commission to lay down compulsory restrictions on steel production and deliveries to the Community. Those restrictions took the form of the quarterly fixing of production quotas, only part of which could be delivered to the Community market.

At the same time (1980) the Commission introduced a Community system for framing national aids to the steel industry. That system was strengthened in 1981 with the entry into force of a stricter "**code of aids**", covering all public financial assistance. The restructuring plan for the Community steel industry thus constituted a coherent package that disciplined steel production and prices as well as the granting of national sectoral and social aids. By allowing the European steel industry to sell its products at more profitable prices, those direct intervention measures facilitated the adjustment of undertakings to the new market conditions. Thus, with a view to completion of the single market, the Commission took the opportunity offered it to abolish as from 1988, following eight years of containment of the steel sector, the quota system and certain accompanying measures.

The **Community rules for State aid** to the steel industry provide a framework for reasonable intervention without distortion of the competition conditions in the common steel market[2].Nowadays, the **steel market is closely monitored**, on the one hand, by way of information that steel companies must communicate to the Commission concerning their investments[3] and, on the other, in the framework of the Strategic Research Agenda (SRA) of the European Steel Technology Platform (ESTEP). The "external aspect of steel", entails a few tariff quotas and the prior statistical monitoring of imports from Central and Eastern European countries to ensure that they do not harm the Community steel industry [see section 23.5.]. Since the ECSC Treaty expired in July 2002, the regulatory framework on steel products came into line with the European policy applied to the whole of manufacturing[4].

In a resolution adopted on 14 March 2002, the European Parliament deplored the **American protectionist decision** to impose extraordinary tariffs of up to 30% on steel imports in violation of World Trade Organisation (WTO) rules and backed the Commis-

---

[1] Decisions 2794/80, 2795/80 and 2796/80, OJ L 291, 31.10.1980.
[2] Decision 2496/96, OJ L 338, 28.12.1996.
[3] Decision 3010/91, OJ L 286, 16.10.1991.
[4] COM (1999) 453, 5 October 1999.

sion in its decision to take a case immediately to the WTO and take all necessary measures to safeguard the EU steel industry in line with WTO rules [see section 25.7.]. As the severe American restrictions threatened to deflect a large amount of steel products away from the United States and on to the Community market and thus to cause serious harm to Community producers, the Commission introduced prior Community surveillance to all the products concerned by the above US measures[1]. Following the conditions laid down by the WTO safeguard agreement, the Commission imposed indeed provisional safeguard measures against imports of seven American steel products[2]. The Council established additional customs duties on imports of certain products originating in the USA and applied concession suspensions not only to steel products but also to other products with a view to offsetting the effects of the safeguard measures taken by the United States in March 2002[3]. The WTO ruled the American safeguard action incompatible with its rules and the US government repealed it on 5 December 2003. The EU countermeasures were lifted as of the following day[4].

Prior Community surveillance continues for imports of certain iron and steel products originating in certain third countries[5]. The Community has concluded an agreement with the Russian Federation on trade in certain steel products[6], while imposing certain restrictions on imports of certain steel products from this country[7].

17.3.2. Shipbuilding and maritime industries

The shipbuilding industry - another problem sector - **has been losing momentum in Europe** since the early 1960s. In 1960 the shipyards of the Community countries accounted for half the world production of ships. In 1975 their share of the world market in shipbuilding had fallen to 22%. As early as that year, half the world production of vessels came from Japanese yards, whilst the shipyards of certain developing countries, such as South Korea, were becoming seriously competitive. The 1973 oil crisis [see section 19.1.1.] and the ensuing economic recession led fleets to a massive amount of laying-up and of cancelled orders. Shipyards then found themselves with a large **excess production capacity**, especially with regard to tankers. At present, the world market for merchant vessels is still in crisis and weak prices are persisting because of the extremely low prices offered by Korean shipyards[8]. In the EU, in 2002, orders were down by almost 80 % compared with 2000; demand had decreased in almost all market segments (container ships, cruise ships, tankers and LNG carriers); prices for new ships had declined further and were at their lowest for more than a decade. Consequently, shipyards were going bankrupt, with large-scale lay-offs as a result[9].

In the absence of a legal basis provided by the EEC Treaty, the Council could not or would not take the socio-economic measures necessary for the restructuring of the European shipbuilding industry. Thus, the only means available to Community policy in the shipbuilding sector remained the coordination of national aids. Seven successive Directives covered the Community framework for aid to shipbuilding during the 1980s and 1990s. By avoiding spiralling aids and by contributing to the restructuring of undertakings, the **Community framework for aid to shipbuilding** made it possible for the European industry to become more competitive and direct State aid towards the building of types of vessels for which Community yards were more competitive[10].

The multilateral negotiations launched in 1989 under the auspices of the OECD between the main producing countries (European Union, Japan, South Korea, Norway, United States), which together account for more than 70% of world shipyard output, led to an agreement in July 1994 on the elimination of all obstacles to normal conditions of

---

[1] Regulation 76/2002, OJ L 16, 18.01.2002 and Regulation 1337/2002, OJ L 195, 24.07.2002.
[2] Regulation 560/2002, OJ L 85, 28.03.2002 and Regulation 2142/2003, OJ L 321, 06.12.2003.
[3] Regulation 1031/2002, OJ L 157, 15.06.2002 repealed by Regulation 2168/2003, OJ L 326, 13.12.2003.
[4] Regulation 2168/2003, OJ L 326, 13.12.2003.
[5] Regulation 469/2005, OJ L 78, 24.03.2005.
[6] Decision 2005/803, OJ L 303, 22.11.2005.
[7] Regulation 1899/2005, OJ L 303, 22.11.2005.
[8] COM (2000) 263, 3 May 2000.
[9] COM (2002) 622, 13 November 2002.
[10] OJ C 317, 30.12.2003, p. 11-14.

competition in the sector as from 1 January 1998. Consequently, a Council Regulation on aid to shipbuilding implements the provisions of the **OECD Agreement on respecting normal competitive conditions** in the commercial shipbuilding and repair industry, although this agreement, pending its ratification by the USA, has still not entered into force [see section 23.5.][1]. Hence, problems continue. Community inquiries reveal that South Korea is distorting competition on the world market in shipbuilding through dumping practices. The Council has authorised the Commission to initiate WTO proceedings against South Korea in May 2001 and introduced a temporary defence mechanism for the Community shipbuilding industry to counter unfair trade practices by the Republic of Korea in world shipbuilding markets until the conclusion of dispute settlement proceedings at the WTO[2] [see section 23.5.]. In any case, the Community Regulation prohibits contract-related aid (operating aid) as from 31 December 2000 [see section 15.5.3.][3]. The Commission concentrates its efforts on defending European industry against unfair trade practices by shipbuilders in third countries and on improving its competitiveness by encouraging research and supporting closer industrial cooperation[4].

17.3.3. Textiles and clothing industries

The textiles and clothing industries experienced difficulties from as early as the late 1960s, as a result in particular of the slow growth of domestic demand and the rapid development of **exports from the developing countries**. In fact those industries, in common with all industries which need neither high technology nor capitalist concentration, lose their competitive advantage in Europe to industries from countries which have a relatively cheap workforce. In addition, the European textile industry with some 2.3 million employees in the late 1990s was facing unfair trade conditions due to fraudulent imports and insurmountable tariff and non-tariff barriers in some third countries. The European Social Fund was able to help those who lost their jobs in the textiles and clothing sectors, but such assistance was no more than temporary relief pending a genuine Community textile policy. Set in motion in the early 1990s this policy has two defensive wings: an internal wing and an external wing.

On the internal level, the Commission **monitors national aids** and applies a policy aiming at preventing such aids from giving rise to distortions of competition within the Community or having the effect of transferring labour problems and structural difficulties from one country to another[5] [see section 15.5.3].

The **external aspect** of the common textiles policy aims at organising international trade in textiles in order to provide breathing space for the Community industry without frustrating the industrialisation hopes of the developing countries. Such organisation was sought within the framework of the General Agreement on Tariffs and Trade (GATT) through the arrangement on international trade in textiles, commonly known as the "Multifibre Arrangement" (MFA). However, the **agreement on textiles and clothing**, concluded within the framework of the Uruguay Round aims at the progressive liberalisation of textile and clothing products within the World Trade Organisation [see section 23.5.]. In this context, the Commission proposes to strengthen the protection of intellectual property rights and measures to tackle fraud and counterfeiting in the fields of the internal market and commercial policy [see section 23.2.2.], to promote the harmonisation of customs duties under the WTO's Doha Development Agenda, and to remove non-tariff barriers to trade in order to boost access to markets[6].

---

[1] Regulation 3094/95, OJ L 332, 30.12.1995 and Regulation 2600/97, OJ L 351, 23.12.1997.
[2] Regulation 1177/2002, OJ L 172, 02.07.2002 last amended by Regulation 502/2004, OJ L 81, 19.03.2004.
[3] Regulation 1540/98, OJ L 202, 18.07.1998.
[4] COM (97) 470 and COM (1999) 474.
[5] Communication from the Commission OJ C 70, 19.03.2002.
[6] COM (2003) 649, 29 October 2003.

In view of the elimination of import quotas on 1 January 2005, **the Commission put forward a series of initiatives** to stimulate research and innovation, guarantee lifelong education and vocational training, reserve a Structural Fund annual contribution to cover unforeseen local or sectoral crises linked to economic and social restructuring, provide appropriate tools to combat counterfeiting and piracy, improve access to markets outside the EU, encourage agreements between all pan-Euro-Mediterranean partners, and strengthen cooperation with China[1].

17.3.4. Aeronautical and aerospace industries

The aeronautical and aerospace industry consists of two technologically and economically separate sectors, which, however, are closely associated on account of their industrial and political implications and the stakeholders involved and they are examples of where Europe has a tradition of success, and economic and commercial potential. Both sectors could build a strong technological and industrial base in support of the European Security and Defence Policy [see section 8.2.3.]. However, United States investment in aerospace is three to six times higher, depending on the sector. In an increasingly demanding competitive environment, foreseeable aviation requirements worldwide correspond to some 14000 new aircraft over the first 15 years of the 21st century, representing a market worth EUR 1000 billion. However, whilst the European market constitutes 20% of the world market in civil aircraft and aviation, the share of the European industry in the world market is less than 10%. The American industry is by far the leading world exporter of both civil and military aircraft. In the aerospace field, American supremacy is even more pronounced.

During the 1970s the aeronautical industry pushed intra-European collaboration further than any other industrial sector, but on a bilateral rather than Community level (Concorde and Airbus projects). Such bilateral or multilateral projects suffered from contradictions between national policies, the non-existence of a common commercial strategy and the lack of joint financing. Whilst the Concorde and Airbus programmes were both remarkable technical successes, only the Airbus programme was an immediate commercial success. The **success of the "Airbus industries" consortium** troubles the United States, which sees its commercial supremacy threatened in the domain of civil aircraft. Although the Community is not directly involved in Airbus, it brings its full weight to bear in the negotiations with the Americans in international fora, such as the World Trade Organisation.

The Community **policy in the aeronautical industry** is based on non-compulsory legislation, on concerted action and consultation between the Member States, particularly concerning external aspects[2]. In addition to genuine liberalisation of the aeronautics market, the sector's competitiveness hinges first and foremost on research and development. Since 1989, the Community has been co-financing a research programme in the aeronautical sector. As we will see in the next chapter, a thematic priority area of the **Sixth Community R & D programme** aims to help the Community consolidate its position in aeronautics and space by developing its mastery of the most advanced technologies in this area[3] [see section 18.4.1.]. Research covers as a matter of priority the development of advanced technologies for integrated design and production, and for reduction of energy consumption, emissions and noise for various aircraft concepts, as well as the development of technologies improving operational safety and efficiency.

The European Space Agency (ESA) began work in 1975. At present ESA has 17 Member States. I Its membership coincides with that of the EU-15 plus Switzerland and Norway. The EU and ESA have no formal relationship, but they have a cooperation agreement. During its first 25 years, ESA raised Europe's status from a minor to a major player, with a high degree of self-sufficiency in most aspects of space technology and a capacity for innovations of world class. Ariane rockets developed by ESA have captured a large part of the market in commercial launches of satellites, although the US space industry benefits from large public funding and technological stimulation from the military space sector, which is relatively small in Europe.

In a communication entitled " Europe and space: Turning to a new chapter", which was adopted in agreement with the **European Space Agency (ESA)**, the Commission defined the objectives of a Community strategy for space: strengthening the foundation for space activities so that Europe preserves independent and affordable access to space; enhancing scientific knowledge; and exploiting the benefits of space-based tools for markets and society[4]. This strategy aims to establish the right political and regulatory

---

[1]   COM (2004) 668, 13 October 2004.
[2]   Resolution, OJ C 59, 13.03.1975, p. 1-2 and Council statement, OJ C 69, 13.03.1977, p. 6.
[3]   Decision 2002/834, OJ L 294, 29.10.2002.
[4]   COM(2000) 597, 27 September 2000.

conditions for space activities, to catalyse joint R & D efforts and to bring together all the players around common political objectives in projects of Europe-wide interest.

A Framework Agreement between the European Community and the European Space Agency aims at the coherent and progressive development of an **overall European Space Policy**[1]. In particular, this policy seeks to: link demand for services and applications using space systems in support of the Community policies with the supply of space systems and infrastructure necessary to meet that demand; and secure Europe's independent and cost-effective access to space and the development of other fields of strategic interest necessary for the independent use and application of space technologies in Europe.

A key element of the European space policy is the development of a **global navigation satellite systems (GNSS)** at European level offering a service meeting the needs of civilian users[2] [see also section 18.4.1.]. The European satellite radio-navigation policy is presently implemented through the Galileo and EGNOS programmes. **Galileo** is the first European space programme to be financed and managed by the European Union in association with the European Space Agency. It is expected to contribute to the development of numerous applications in areas that are associated, directly or indirectly, with Community policies, such as transport (positioning and measurement of the speed of moving bodies), insurance, motorway tolls and law enforcement (surveillance of suspects, measures to combat crime). **EGNOS** is a tripartite programme between the European Community, the ESA and Eurocontrol aiming at augmenting the American GPS and Russian GLONASS signals for reliability purposes on a broad geographical area. It is independent from and complementary to Galileo.

In view of the fact that substantial private sector participation is a fundamental element for the success of Galileo in its deployment and operational phases and the need to ensure that essential public interests related to the strategic nature of the European satellite radio-navigation programmes are adequately defended and represented, a Regulation set up a Community agency, called the **European GNSS Supervisory Authority**, to manage the public interests relating to the European GNSS programs[3]. This is the licensing authority vis-à-vis the private concession holder responsible for implementing and managing the Galileo deployment and operating phases. It is entrusted with the responsibility of managing the agreement with the economic operator charged with operating EGNOS. It should coordinate Member States' actions in respect of the frequencies necessary to ensure the operation of the system and hold the right to use all these frequencies wherever the system is located. The Council, acting unanimously, may give the necessary **instructions to the European GNSS Supervisory Authority** and the concession holder of the system in the event of a threat to the security of the European Union or of a Member State arising from the operation or use of the system, or in the event of a threat to the operation of the system, in particular as a result of an international crisis[4].

17.3.5. Information industries

The economic and social development of nations depends, increasingly, on the use of information and knowledge, with the aid of the enormous progress made in **information and communications technologies (ICTs)**. Harnessing the opportunities opened up by the digitalisation of information in all its forms, these technologies are transform-

---

[1] Framework Agreement and Decision 2004/578, OJ L 261, 06.08.2004.
[2] COM (1998) 29, 21 January 1998.
[3] Regulation 1321/2004, OJ L 246, 20.07.2004
[4] Joint Action 2004/552, OJ L 246, 20.07.2004.

ing dramatically many aspects of economic and social life, such as working methods and relations, the organisation of businesses, the focus of education and training, and the way people communicate with each other. The **information society** is the dawning of a multimedia world (sound - text - image) representing a radical change comparable with the first industrial revolution. It goes hand in hand with the "non-physical" economy, based on the creation, circulation and exploitation of knowledge. The conditions of access to information, to the networks carrying it (broad band networks called "information highways") and to the services facilitating the use of the data (including high value-added services, databases, etc.) are vital components of the Union's future competitiveness. ICTs are also the vehicle for a growing number of societal services such as health, education, transport, entertainment and culture. Since they are amongst the highest growth activities, and they are also highly skilled activities, these technologies have a high potential for employment creation.

The problem is that, although there is a strong demand for information in Europe, the suppliers could be anywhere in the world since the delivery is instantaneous. Indeed, **the United States and Japan have a head-start** as suppliers of information, because they each have a single system of standards and a single national language. Europe, thus, has to overcome large handicaps in this field. It should be noted that under the Information Technology Agreement, concluded in March 1997 under the auspices of the World Trade Organisation, tariffs on information technology products of countries accounting for 92% of world trade were eliminated as of January 2000, a fact which intensifies further investment competition[1] [see section 23.4.].

A multiannual Community programme aims to stimulate the development and use of **European digital content (eContentplus programme)** on the global networks and to promote linguistic diversity in the information society[2]. It proposes action over a period of four years (2005-2008) aimed at making digital content in Europe more accessible, usable and exploitable, by facilitating the creation and diffusion of information, in areas of public interest, at Community level. This action is intended to create an environment favourable to business initiatives where European creativity, cultural diversity and technological strengths can be commercially exploited. The sixth Framework Research and Development programme seeks, inter alia, to boost hardware and software technologies and applications at the heart of the creation of the information society and to harness the knowledge-based society for the benefit of the citizens[3] [see section 18.4.1.].

By guaranteeing recognition of **electronic signatures** throughout the European Union, a Directive on a common framework for electronic signatures was the first step towards establishing a European framework for development of electronic commerce [see also section 6.6.1.][4]. This framework is provided by the so-called **electronic commerce directive**[5]. This Directive harmonises certain legal aspects, such as determining the place of establishment of service providers, the transparency obligations for providers and for commercial communications, the validity of electronic contracts and the transparency of the contractual process, the responsibility of Internet intermediaries, on-line dispute settlements and the role of national governments. It clarifies the application of key internal market principles (freedom of establishment of service providers and free movement of services) to information society services, affirming the country-of-origin

---

[1] Decision 97/359, OJ L 155, 12.06.1997 and Regulation 2216/97, OJ L 305, 08.11.1997.
[2] Decision 2005/456, OJ L 160, 23.06.2005.
[3] Decision 2002/834, OJ L 294, 29.10.2002.
[4] Directive 1999/93, OJ L 13, 19.01.2000.
[5] Directive 2000/31, OJ L 178, 17.07.2000.

principle by which service providers must comply with the legislation of the Member State of origin.

The action plan "*e*Europe" of the Commission, which was endorsed by the Feira European Council (19-20 June 2000), seeks to remove the key barriers to the uptake of the Internet in Europe, aiming in particular at: providing a cheaper, faster and more secure Internet; investing in skills; giving the public access to the Internet and encouraging its use[1]. A new programme called "Safer Internet plus" (2005-2008) aims to promote safer use of the Internet and new online technologies, in particular for children, and to combat illegal and unwanted content[2].

In the framework of the "*e*Europe" action plan, a regulation lays down the conditions for designating the registry responsible for the organisation, administration and management of the **Internet ".eu" country code top-level domain (ccTLD)** and establishes the general policy framework within which the Registry functions[3]. Domain names and the related addresses are essential elements of the global interoperability of the World Wide Web (www), since they allow users to locate computers and websites on the Web. TLDs are also an integral part of every Internet e-mail address. The ".eu" TLD should promote the use of, and access to, the Internet networks and the virtual market (electronic commerce) place based on the Internet, by providing a complementary registration domain to existing country code TLDs and should in consequence increase choice and competition. The establishment of the ".eu" TLD registry, which is the entity charged with the organisation, administration and management of the ".eu" TLD, should contribute to the promotion of the European Union image on the global information networks and bring an added value to the Internet naming system in addition to the national ccTLDs. A Commission Regulation laid down public policy rules concerning the implementation and functions of the .eu top level domain and the principles governing registration[4].

There is a close correlation between the development prospects of individual **technologies and products** (telephones, interactive disk readers and combinations thereof), of the programs (computer software, databases, audiovisual programmes, etc.) and of the associated services and networks. The European Union is in a strong competitive position in several of these fields and has every means of retaining or winning a substantial share of the market. It should, however, remove various administrative obstacles to an optimal exploitation of ICTs, create an appropriate regulatory and political environment and encourage the implementation of trans-European telecommunication services. The Directive laying down a procedure for the information in the field of technical standards and regulations covers national regulations on information-society services, in order to ensure a clear and predictable legal framework for their development within the internal market[5]. A Council Decision provides a common approval procedure for connection to the analogue public switched telephone networks (PSTNs) of terminal equipment such as modems and telephone answering machines[6].

Data interchange, particularly important for industrial competitiveness, focuses on telecommunications, legal aspects, security, provision of information for the public, as well as existing or new multisectoral projects. A **European Network and Information Security Agency** has the task of assisting the Commission and the Member States to help them meet the requirement of network and information security, and to prevent, address and respond to related problems[7].

In order to promote the implementation of the eEurope 2005 action plan which aims, in particular, to ensure e-inclusion of Europe's citizens, the Commission gave the Member States, whose situations in this area vary greatly, various options for the transition **from analogue to digital broadcasting[8]**. In the context of the expiry of the eEurope action plan at the end of 2005, the Commission launched a wide policy debate on EU

---

[1]   Decision 2256/2003, OJ L 336, 23.12.2003 and Decision 2113/2005, OJ L 344, 27.12.2005.
[2]   Decision 854/2005, OJ L 149, 11.06.2005.
[3]   Regulation 733/2002, OJ L 113, 30.04.2002.
[4]   Regulation 874/2004, OJ L 162, 30.04.2004 and Regulation 1654/2005, OJ L 266, 11.10.2005.
[5]   Directive 98/34, OJ L 204, 21.07.1998 and Directive 98/48, OJ L 217, 05.08.1998.
[6]   Decision 98/482, OJ L 216, 04.08.1998.
[7]   Regulation 460/2004, OJ L 77, 13.03.2004.
[8]   COM (2003) 541, 17 September 2003.

strategy beyond 2005 on the information society[1]. Pointing out the ambitious nature of the objectives set in the context of the Lisbon strategy and the vital role of information and communication technologies (ICTs), it stresses the need for continuity in terms of information society policy.

As part of the moves to set up a European information area, where **processing of personal data** is expected to develop significantly, a Directive aims at the protection of individuals with regard to the processing of personal data[2] [see section 9.2.] and another Directive sets specific rules for the processing of personal data and the **protection of privacy** in the electronic communications sector[3] [see section 17.3.6.].

17.3.6. Telecommunications

Digital technologies, developed by the information industry, allow the integrated transmission of sound, text and image in one communication system and project Europe into the information era, radically changing the modes of consumption, production and organisation of work. On the other hand, advanced **communications technologies and services** are a vital link between industry, the services sector and market as well as between peripheral areas and economic centres. These services are therefore crucial for consolidation of the internal market, for Europe's industrial competitiveness and for economic and social cohesion in Europe. They can also contribute to social progress and to cultural development. The common policy on telecommunications is developing since the 1990s around four axes: the creation of a single market of telecommunications equipment and services; the liberalisation of telecommunication services; the technological development of the sector with the assistance of Community research; and the balanced development of the regions of the Union by means of trans-European telecommunication networks.

The **regulatory framework for telecommunications terminal equipment** follows and affects the new approach to standardisation, testing and certification that we have examined in the chapter on the common market [see section 6.2.3.]. A Council Decision and a Resolution on standardisation in the field of information technology and telecommunications pursue the objective of creating a **European market in telecommunications equipment**[4]. Such standardisation of information technology and telecommunications prevents distortions of competition and ensures exchanges of information, the convergence of industrial strategies and, ultimately, the creation and exploitation of a vast European information technologies and telecommunications (IT&T) market. European standards are used in many Community policies, above all those connected with the single market, *e*Europe [see section 17.3.5.], general product safety and environment protection. A Directive establishes a single market for radio equipment and telecommunications terminal equipment and prescribes the mutual recognition of their conformity based on the principle of the manufacturer's declaration[5].

European institutions and standardisation bodies endeavour to ensure the coherence with the regulatory framework applicable to information equipment in order to meet the challenge of interoperability. The Commission collates requirements with regard to standardisation on the part of users and establishes the priorities of a work programme, which is entrusted to the CEN (European Committee for Standardisation) and the CENELEC (European Committee for Electrotechnical Standardisation), with the participation of the CEPT (European Conference of Postal and Telecommunications Administrations). In addition to the European Telecommunication Standards Institute (ETSI),

---

[1] COM (2004) 757, 19 November 2004.
[2] Directive 95/46, OJ L 281, 23.11.1995.
[3] Directive 2002/58, OJ L 201, 31.07.2002 and Directive 2006/24, OJ L 105, 13.04.2006.
[4] Decision 87/95, OJ L 36, 07.02.1987 and resolution, OJ C 117, 11.05.1989, p. 1.
[5] Directive 1999/5, OJ L 91, 07.04.1999.

private organisations representing industry and consumers are involved in the pre-standardisation process and in the effective application of harmonised standards in the Member States, including for public contracts.

The creation of a single market in telecommunications services necessitated the progressive **liberalisation of telecommunications markets**, which were traditionally State monopolies. Telecommunications services had to be liberated and conditions of free provision of services by the networks had to be defined. To pursue this objective, which represents the second axis of the Community policy in this sector, the Commission adopted a Directive based on Article 90 of the EEC Treaty (Art. 86 TEC), requiring Member States to introduce arrangements ensuring free competition on the Community market in telecommunications terminal equipment (modems, telex terminals, receive-only satellite stations, etc.)[1] [see section 15.5.4.]. This Directive gives users the possibility of connecting terminal equipment, which they are able to procure freely without being obliged to apply to a single national telecommunications authority. Through its successive amendments, the Directive entitles suppliers of telecommunications services to use capacity on cable television networks for all telecommunications services, primarily data communications, "closed" corporate networks and multimedia services. It also requires Member States to abolish the exclusive and special rights remaining in telecommunications, the restrictions on the installations used for mobile networks and the obstacles to direct interconnection between such networks. Last but not least, the Commission Directive provided for the complete liberalisation of voice telephony and telecommunications infrastructures on 1 January 1998.

Liberalisation of telecommunications services cleared the way for the **creation of the single telecommunications market**. This is the aim of the "telecoms package", adopted in 2002. The package constitutes a single regulatory framework covering the converging telecommunications, media and information technology sectors. It is made up of a framework Directive and four specific Directives concerning access, authorisation, universal service and protection of privacy. National regulatory authorities must contribute to the development of the internal market by cooperating with each other and with the Commission to ensure the consistent application, in all Member States, of the provisions of those Directives.

Directive 2002/21 established a harmonised **regulatory framework** for electronic communications networks and services across the EU[2]. This Directive covers all electronic communications networks and services within its scope, namely: transmission systems and, where applicable, switching or routing equipment and other resources which permit the conveyance of signals by wire, by radio, by optical or by other electromagnetic means, including satellite networks, fixed (including Internet) and mobile terrestrial networks, electricity cable systems, networks used for radio and television broadcasting, and cable television networks. It sets out a number of principles and objectives for regulators to follow, as well as a series of tasks in respect of management of scarce resources such as radio spectra and numbering.

The aim of **the "access directive"** is to lay down a framework of rules that are technologically neutral, but which may be applied to specific product or service markets in particular geographical areas, to address identified market problems between access and interconnection suppliers[3]. It covers, in particular, access to fixed and mobile networks, as well as access to digital broadcasting networks, including access to conditional

---

[1] Directive 2002/77, OJ L 249, 17.09.2002.
[2] Directive 2002/21, OJ L 108, 24.04.2002.
[3] Directive 2002/19, OJ L 108, 24.04.2002.

systems and other associated facilities such as electronic programme guides and application programme interfaces. The directive provides legal certainty for market players by establishing clear criteria on their rights and obligations and for regulatory intervention [see details below]. It indicates clearly what obligations concerning access and interconnection can be imposed in which circumstances, whilst at the same time allowing for sufficient flexibility to allow regulatory authorities to deal effectively with new market problems that hinder effective competition.

The aim of the "**authorisation directive**" is to implement an internal market in electronic communications networks and services through the harmonisation and simplification of authorisation rules and conditions in order to facilitate their provision throughout the Community[1]. According to the Directive, "general authorisation" means a legal framework established by the Member State ensuring rights for the provision of electronic communications networks or services and laying down sector specific obligations that may apply to all or to specific types of electronic communications networks and services. The general authorisation system should apply to all such services and networks regardless of their technological characteristics and should limit administrative barriers to entry into the market to a minimum.

The aim of the "**universal users**" directive is to ensure universal service provision for public telephony services in an environment of greater overall competitiveness, with provisions for financing the cost of providing a universal service in the most competitively neutral manner and for ensuring a maximum of information transparency[2]. It also establishes the rights of users and consumers of electronic communications services, with corresponding obligations on undertakings. It aims to ensure the interoperability of digital consumer television equipment and the provision of certain mandatory services, such as leased lines. Finally, it lays down harmonised rules for the imposition of "must carry" obligations by Member States on network operators.

The **protection of privacy** directive translates the principles set out in Directive 95/46 [see section 9.2.] into specific rules for the telecommunications sector[3]. In fact, publicly available electronic communications services over the Internet open new possibilities for users but also new risks for their personal data and privacy, in particular with regard to the increasing capacity for automated storage and processing of data relating to subscribers and users. Therefore, the Directive on privacy and electronic communications harmonises the provisions of the Member States required to ensure an equivalent level of protection of fundamental rights and freedoms, and in particular the right to privacy, with respect to the processing of personal data in the electronic communication sector and to ensure the free movement of such data and of electronic communication equipment and services in the Community. However, another Directive harmonises Member States' provisions concerning the obligations of the providers of publicly available electronic communications services or of public communications networks with respect to the **retention of certain data** which are generated or processed by them, in order to ensure that the data are available for the purpose of the investigation, detection and prosecution of serious crime, as defined by each Member State in its national law[4].

The EU has promoted the coordinated introduction of a third-generation **mobile and wireless communications system (UMTS)** networks and services (mobile telephones, messaging, wireless Internet access, multimedia applications) throughout the Community by harmonising frequencies and standards needed to

---

[1] Directive 2002/20, OJ L 108, 24.04.2002.
[2] Directive 2002/22, OJ L 108, 24.04.2002.
[3] Directive 2002/58, OJ L 201, 31.07.2002 and Directive 2006/24, OJ L 105, 13.04.2006.
[4] Directive 2006/24, OJ L 105, 13.04.2006

launch the system[1]. The Commission has clarified the assessment criteria for national schemes for the **costing and financing of universal service**[2]. It has also issued recommendations on interconnection charges[3], on accounting separation and on cost accounting[4]. Incumbent telephone operators, who own cable TV networks, might have no incentive to upgrade them to be able to supply telecommunications services which might compete with those offered by their telecommunications networks. In order to reduce this conflict of interest, a Commission Directive requires a legal separation of the two networks. Telecommunications operators are, thus, required to hive their cable television operations off in a structurally separate company[5].

The Commission has also set out the **competition rules to access agreements**, which are central in enabling market participants, including new economic agents, to reap the benefits of liberalisation in the telecommunications sector[6]. In order to stimulate competition and technological innovation and hence promote the availability of a complete range of telecommunications services, including broad-band multimedia and high-speed Internet services, newcomers should have access to "local loops", i.e. the physical circuits between the subscribers' premises and the telecommunications operator's local switch or equivalent facility in the local access network[7]. Therefore, a regulation aims at introducing fair competition on the local access market[8].

As required by Directive 2002/21, the Commission has adopted guidelines on market analysis and the assessment of significant market power (SMP) for **electronic communications networks and services**[9]. As the framework directive gives a definition of a company with SMP, based on the concept of "dominant position" within the meaning of Article 82 of the EC Treaty [see section 15.4.1.], the guidelines set out the principles that national regulatory authorities will apply in defining the relevant markets and assessing the existence of a dominant position on those markets. As a result of the deployment of interactive digital services using the "Multimedia home platform" standard, the only open standard for application programming interfaces (APIs) adopted by EU standards bodies, European citizens should have at their disposal an increasingly wide range of interactive television services[10].

A policy and legal framework decision ensures the coordination of policy approaches and, where appropriate, harmonised conditions with regard to the availability and efficient use of the **radio spectrum** necessary for the establishment and functioning of the internal market in several sectors[11]. The frequency spectrum serves a wide range of activities in sectors such as telecommunications, broadcasting, transport, research and public services. The range is so wide that congestion is almost inevitable, since the demand for frequencies exceeds the supply. The "radio spectrum" framework decision concerns the use of electromagnetic waves propagated in space without artificial guide in certain frequencies, taking into consideration inter alia economic, safety, health, public interest, freedom of expression, cultural, scientific, social and technical aspects of Community policies as well as the various interests of radio spectrum user communities. Activities pursued under this Decision take due account of the work of international organisations related to radio spectrum management, e.g. the International Telecommunication Union (ITU) and the European Conference of Postal and Telecommunications Administrations (CEPT). As mandated[12], the CEPT produced a frequency plan and a channel arrangement allowing six types of preferred applications to share the band in order to meet several Community policy needs. The **pan-European land-based public radio paging service (ERMES)** enables pan-European public radio paging services, including assistance for people with disabilities[13].

Technological development in telecommunications - third axis of the Community policy in this sector - is pursued by research in advanced communication technologies and services. A key action of the fifth R & D framework programme (1988-2002) aimed at promoting excellence in the technologies and networks, including broadband ones, which are crucial to the information society, at speeding up their introduction and broadening their field of application[14].

The fourth axis of Community telecommunications policy turns round **trans-European telecommunications networks** [see section 6.8.], which are, in reality, national digital networks interconnected, managed in a coherent fashion and using different vectors (cables, terrestrial and satellite radio transmission). With the aid of these networks, it is possible to transmit a multitude of texts, images and sound transmissions, stored and combined in databases, for use in the most diverse applications (manufacturing activity, education, medical care, leisure, tourism, etc.). These networks irrigate all economic activities and transform the ways of life and work

---

[1] Decision 128/1999, OJ L 17, 22.01.1999.
[2] COM (96) 608 and COM (1998) 494, 3 September 1998.
[3] Recommendation 98/195, OJ L 73, 12.03.1998 and Recommendation 98/511, OJ L 228, 15.08.1998.
[4] Recommendation 98/322, OJ L 141, 13.05.1998.
[5] Directive 1999/64, OJ L 175, 10.07.1999.
[6] COM (96) 649, 10 December 1996.
[7] COM (2000) 237, 26 April 2000 and Recommendation 2000/417, OJ L 156, 29.06.2000.
[8] Regulation 2887/2000, OJ L 336, 30.12.2000.
[9] Commission guidelines, OJ C 165, 11.07.2002.
[10] COM (2004) 541, 30 July 2004.
[11] Decision 676/2002, OJ L 108, 24.04.2002.
[12] Decision 710/97, OJ L 105, 23.04.1997 and OJ L 139, 10.06.2000.
[13] Directive 2005/82 and Decision 2005/928, OJ L 344, 27.12.2005.
[14] Decision 182/1999, OJ L 26, 01.02.1999.

of European citizens. The guidelines for the development of these networks cover all telecommunications networks, including satellites, mobile networks and integrated services digital networks (ISDN). They aim at optimising the use of Community instruments and financial resources, facilitating the transition to the information society, making European firms more competitive and improving economic and social cohesion [see section 12.1.2.].[1]. Euro-ISDN already offers a wide range of services, designed mainly for enterprises: videosound, videoconference, computerised exchange of data, texts and images, bank transactions at a distance.

Telematics applications play a central role in the development of trans-European networks. Therefore, the Community has adopted a series of guidelines, actions and measures in order to create and operate a telematic network for the electronic interchange of data between administrations (IDA), particularly those needed for the operation of the internal market and the implementation of common policies [see section 6.8.].[2]. Telematics applications also promote: the interconnection of networks in universities and national research institutes; the interconnection of library services, notably those of national libraries; networks for cooperation between local authorities in tele-working and tele-services; cooperation among staff specialising in public health and tele-medicine; access of handicapped and elderly people to communications and information technologies (TIDE); language-learning and telematics translation services (Euramis); the use of telematics tools in the road transport sector[3]; and the operation of satellite navigation services[4]. The programme of interoperable delivery of **pan-European e-government services (IDABC)** includes horizontal measures in support of interoperability, which are intended to favour the exchange of data and services, in order to permit public administrations, businesses and citizens to interact electronically with administrations across national borders[5].

17.3.7. Other industrial sectors

In addition to the sectors we have just examined, the European Union is incidentally interested in certain sectors such as the motor vehicle industry or the chemicals industry, in particular as regards the functioning of the internal market, the encouragement of intangible investment in research and development and the **coordinated approach of their problems vis-à-vis the outside**.

Thus, in the **automobile industry**, the European type-approval system for vehicles is designed to help to lower makers' costs, while maintaining identical technical specifications and a high level of protection of motorists and pedestrians throughout the European Union[6]. The approximation of the laws of the Member States aims to increase the safety of motor-vehicles, concerning in particular, safety belts, seats, their anchorages and head restraints[7]. The Regulation on the application of Article 81(3) of the Treaty to categories of vertical agreements and concerted practices [see section 15.3.3.] in the motor vehicle sector is meant to increase competition and bring tangible benefits to European consumers as regards vehicle sales and after-sales servicing[8].

In the **pharmaceutical industry**, the free movement of its products in the common market has long been pursued by the harmonisation of legislations and regulations monitoring their marketing. Nowadays this is done by the Community authorisation system for medicinal products for human and veterinary use[9]. The authorisation can be given either by a centralised or a decentralised procedure[10]. Under the centralised procedure, applications for marketing authorisations are submitted to the European Agency for the Evaluation of Medicinal Products, which conducts the scientific evaluation of the application and gives its opinion to the Commission, which adopts a decision, subject to endorsement by a committee of representatives of the Member States. The marketing authorisation obtained at the end of this procedure is valid throughout the Community. Under the decentralised procedure, the pharmaceuticals company concerned asks one or more Member States to recognise the marketing authorisation issued by another Member State.

Biotechnology, i.e. genetic engineering, which makes it possible to obtain new chemical, pharmaceutical or food products and highly competitive processes in a large number of industrial and agricultural activities, is mainly developed in the pharmaceutical industry. Indeed, two thirds of the new medicines undergoing clinical trials are derived from modern biotechnology. Also preponderant in enzyme production, biotechnology can provide important energy (fuel) and industrial outlets for agricultural raw materials. It should be noted that, while reinforcing European competitiveness, Community legislation endeavours to ensure the protection of

---

[1]   Decision 1336/97, OJ L 183, 11.07.1997 and Decision 1376/2002, OJ L 200, 30.07.2002.
[2]   Decisions 1719/1999 and 1720/1999, OJ L 203, 03.08.1999 and Regulation 885/2004, OJ L 168, 01.05.2004.
[3]   Resolution, OJ C 264, 11.10.1995, p. 1-3.
[4]   COM (94) 248.
[5]   Decision 2004/387, OJ L 181, 18.05.2004.
[6]   Directive 70/156, OJ L 42, 23.02.1970 and Directive 2006/40, OJ L 161, 14.06.2006.
[7]   Directive 74/408, OJ L 221, 12.08.1974, Directive 76/115, OJ L 24, 30.01.1976, and Directives 2005/39, 2005/40 and 2005/41, OJ L 255, 30.09.2005.
[8]   Regulation 1400/2002, OJ L 203, 01.08.2002.
[9]   Directive 2001/83, OJ L 311, 28.11.2001 last amended by Directive 2004/27, OJ L 136, 30.04.2004 and Regulation 726/2004, OJ L 136, 30.04.2004.
[10] Regulation 726/2004, OJ L 136, 30.04.2004.

both human health by a contained use of genetically modified micro-organisms[1] and the environment by a deliberate release of genetically modified organisms [see section 11.2.]. The Community has concluded the Cartagena Protocol on Biosafety to the Convention on Biological Diversity[2].

Stressing the strategic importance of the life sciences and biotechnology sector, as well as the ethical issues involved, and pointing out its potential in many fields such as healthcare, agriculture, food, industry and the environment, the Commission is proposing a strategy aimed at helping Europe to master the frontier technologies. This strategy, supplemented by an action plan with recommendations to the Member States, local authorities, industry and all interested parties, is based on several lines of action; notably: harvesting the potential of this sector, in particular by reinforcing the scientific resource base; and a responsible policy with regard to life sciences and biotechnology, the preparation, implementation and monitoring of which should be based on a regular dialogue with the general public and all the stakeholders, as well as scientific data, and should respect the fundamental values and regulatory principles of the EU (e.g. the precautionary principle, safeguarding the internal market and providing consumer information)[3]. In conclusions adopted on 6 June 2002, the Council considered that the Commission's communication constituted a useful basis for a balanced, coherent and effective framework necessary to enable the EU to exploit the full potential of biotechnology, while taking account of societal values and concerns.

17.4. Appraisal and outlook

Generally speaking, the EU intervenes in the industrial sector only to create an environment conducive either to the expansion of undertakings throughout the internal market (enterprise policy) or to the activity of certain industrial branches which present common problems, to enable them to cope better with increased competition at European and world levels (sectoral policy).

Although disparities remain between Member States' industrial structures, we are nonetheless in the presence of a parallel development of the various parameters in the secondary sector. **The completion of the single market**, in 1992, provided a fillip to the restructuring of European industry. The removal of the physical, technical and fiscal barriers to intra-Community trade gave rise to strengthened trade and therefore bolstered competition within the Community. Thanks to the removal of border controls and technical trade barriers, businesses can now supply a single product for the whole of the single market. Manufacturers no longer have to produce for fifteen separate markets. This situation increases competition enormously in the internal market. Greater competition results in the alignment of national suppliers' prices on those of foreign suppliers, who penetrate markets that had previously been protected. In the short term that squeezes the profit margins of undertakings which had been protected and/or enjoyed monopoly situations. Some of them are even forced to leave the market.

The elimination of the least competitive producers enables, however, those firms which survive to **expand on the market**. They are thus able to: better exploit and maximise their production capabilities, or even increase them (economies of scale); strengthen their domestic efficiency by restructuring and concentrating their activities and by improving allocation of human, technical and financial resources; improve their organisation and the quality and variety of their products, and innovate both as regards the production process and the products offered. This competitive pressure has already caused the wind of change to sweep the Union's industrial fabric.

Entrepreneurship and a well-functioning internal market are vital to growth and job creation. The regulatory environment should encourage entrepreneurial activity and make it as simple as possible to set up new businesses. Creation of a favourable business environment implies the **elimination of superfluous and niggling regulation**. The in-

---

[1] Resolution, OJ C 136, 08.05.1996, p. 4-7.
[2] Protocol and Decision 2002/628, OJ L 201, 31.07.2002.
[3] COM (2002) 27, 24 January 2002.

ternal market must be made as unbureaucratic as possible. Both the Union and the Member States must therefore facilitate market entry and exit for businesses of all sizes, improve access to finance and know-how, improve regulation and reduce administrative burdens. The regulatory framework should be clear and predictable, while regulation should be limited to what is strictly necessary for achieving clearly-defined objectives. The common enterprise policy aims at this end, but it is not certain that the national policies follow suit. Member States should transpose faster Community legislation on the internal market and related subjects into national legal and administrative practice. On the other hand, company law and corporate governance practices need to be modernised in the wake of corporate governance scandals and in view of the growing trend for European companies to operate cross-border in the internal market, the continued integration of European capital markets, the rapid development of new information and communication technology and the enlargement of the EU to new Member States, most of which have not a long-established business culture.

The Treaty on European Union emphasises the need for competitiveness, making it a priority for the European Union. In fact, there has been a substantial improvement in industrial competitiveness in recent years, due to the combined effect of the completion of the internal market and of the efforts made on restructuring, investment and productivity. But, **European companies have yet to overcome the handicaps** with which they contend as a result of their previous isolation inside closed markets. In order to overcome these handicaps, the EU must promote services to industry, develop transnational industrial cooperation, reinforce competition and modernise the role of the public authorities. Common legislation and institutions must improve corporate financing by eliminating institutional and regulatory barriers to the development of venture capital so as to facilitate risk-taking.

Generally speaking, the Community policy for the improvement of the business environment is based on the **open method of coordination** and on voluntary tools, such as the exchange of best practices in order to enable the Member States to learn more efficiently from each other. In fact, Member States have made significant progress in implementing the recommendations of the European Charter for Small Enterprises and are increasingly acting as sources of mutual inspiration and good practice. One may ask, however, if the intergovernmental cooperation may by itself face the new challenges of European industry.

Globalisation, geared to the opening-up of world markets, the mastery of technology, speed of action, innovation and intangible investment, is an opportunity for Europe to seize, and one to which it must adjust without delay. European industries must adapt their structures, production and marketing methods to the conditions and opportunities existing worldwide. On their side, European institutions could better promote access by European companies to the world market. An open but vigilant policy, based on the rigorous enforcement of international rules agreed in the **framework of the World Trade Organisation**, is a necessary complement to internal market opening [see sections 6.2. and 23.4.]. Identification of precise problems and specific action to remove them can make a significant contribution to improving the outlets for the European industries [see section 23.3.].

Last but not least, the European Union **must move faster towards the "information society"** by creating a common information area. This consists of several indivisible elements: trans-European infrastructure (terrestrial cable infrastructure, radio communications networks and satellites); the basic telecommunications services, interactive access to databases and training of the users, that is of the general public, to optimal use of information and communication technologies. If the e-economy is not rapidly developed by the Community and the Member States, the European Union risks not to attain the strategic goal for the decade, set by the Lisbon Summit in 2000, to become the world's most dynamic and competitive knowledge-based economy. To promote e-business skills in Europe, the EU and the Member States should aim at narrowing gaps and addressing mismatches in e-skills, explore the most effective means of assisting the cross-border mobility of ICT and e-business professionals and encourage learning and training for e-skills.

In the telecommunications sector, the exposing of former monopoly operators to competition and the introduction of new entrants to this market has led to an increase in productivity and to lower charges for users. The Community measures for telecommunications mean that the same rules apply to all converging technologies, creating more competition and a level playing field in Europe. Thanks to the opening up of the telecommunications markets, the coordinated measures in the field of mobile and wireless communications systems, Europe is a prime mover in digital multimedia and the management of optical communications networks and services and mobile communications. Technological convergence affords all business and citizens new opportunities for access to the information society. The common information area that is created through telecom liberalisation is not only an indispensable requirement of the productivity and competitiveness of European industry, but is also an important factor for economic and social cohesion [see section 12.1.2.].

Bibliography on industrial and enterprise policies

- BELESSIOTIS Tassos (et al.). *EU competitiveness and industrial location.* Luxembourg: EUR-OP*, 2006.
- BIANCHI Patrizio, LABORY Sandrin (eds.). *International handbook of industrial policy* Cheltenham: Edward Elgar, 2006.
- BISHOP Simon (et al.). *The efficiency-enhancing effects of non-horizontal mergers.* Luxembourg: EUR-OP, 2005.
- BUZELAY Alain. "La politique industrielle européenne: quelle signification?" in *Revue du Marché commun et de l'Union européenne,* n. 494, janvier 2006, p. 10-15.
- EUROPEAN COMMISSION. *Implementing the Community Lisbon Programme: a policy framework to strengthen EU manufacturing - towards a more integrated approach for industrial policy.* Luxembourg: EUR-OP*, 2005.
    - *European space policy: preliminary elements.* Luxembourg: EUR-OP*, 2005.
    - *Communication from the Commission to the European Council: An innovation-friendly, modern Europe.* Luxembourg: EUR-OP*, 2006.
    - *Report on the implementation of the European Charter for Small Enterprises in Moldova and the countries in the western Balkans.* Luxembourg: EUR-OP*, 2006.
    - *The acquis of the European Union under the management of DG Enterprise and Industry: list of measures (The "Pink Book).* Luxembourg: EUR-OP*, 2006.
- HIRSCH-KREINSEN Hartmut (et al.). *Low-tech innovation in the knowledge economy.* Frankfurt am Main: P. Lang, 2005.
- HUMPHREYS Peter, SIMPSON Seamus. *Globalisation, convergence and European telecommunications regulation.* Cheltenham: Edward Elgar, 2005.
- JOHNSON Debra, TURNER Colin. *European business.* London: Routledge, 2006.
- KIRCHESCH Kai. *The influence of financial risks on the investment decision of enterprises.* Baden-Baden: Nomos, 2005.
- MALERBA Franco. *Sectoral systems in Europe: innovation, competitiveness & growth: ESSY: final report.* Luxembourg: EUR-OP, 2005.
- MATTEUCCI Nicola (et al.). "Productivity, workplace performance and ICT: industry and firm-level evidence for Europe and the US", *Scottish Journal of Political Economy,* v. 52, n. 3, July 2005, p. 359-386.
- NONES Michele, DARNIS Jean-Pierre. "Control of foreign investments in Aerospace and Defence", *The International Spectator,* v. 40, n. 3, July-September 2005, p. 83-90.
- PEERSMAN Gert, SMETS Frank. "The industry effects of monetary policy in the euro area", *Economic Journal,* v. 115, n. 503, April 2005, p. 319-342.
- PIGGOTT Judith, COOK Mark (eds.). *International business economics: a European perspective.* Basingstoke: Palgrave Macmillan, 2006.
- RENDA Andrea (ed.). *Last call for Lisbon?: suggestions for the future regulation of e-communications in Europe : final report of a CEPS Task Force.* Brussels: Centre for European Policy Studies, 2006.
- STROHM Andreas (et al.). An industrial policy for Europe?: from concepts to action. Luxembourg: European Union. European Investment Bank, 2006.

---

*The publications of the Office for Official Publications of the European Communities (EUR-OP) exist usually in all official languages of the EU.

Chapter 18

RESEARCH AND
TECHNOLOGY POLICY

Diagram of the chapter

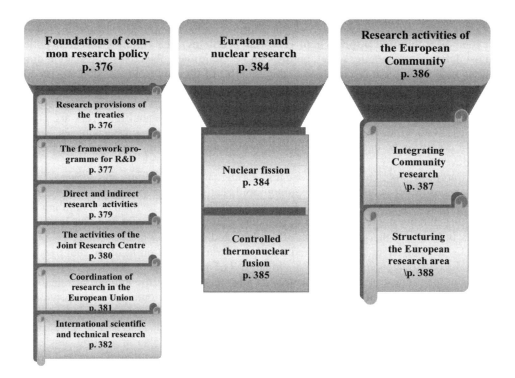

Foundations of common research policy p. 376	Euratom and nuclear research p. 384	Research activities of the European Community p. 386
Research provisions of the treaties p. 376		
The framework programme for R&D p. 377	Nuclear fission p. 384	Integrating Community research \p. 387
Direct and indirect research activities p. 379		
The activities of the Joint Research Centre p. 380	Controlled thermonuclear fusion p. 385	Structuring the European research area \p. 388
Coordination of research in the European Union p. 381		
International scientific and technical research p. 382		

conomic and social progress and the competitiveness of European States at world level come about through efficacious scientific research and technological development. European research, however, is handicapped in the international arena as a result of the **fragmentation of research policies pursued in the Member States** of the Union and the resulting dispersion of efforts. The common research and development policy is therefore essential for European integration. The aim of that policy is to coordinate national research policies and to define and implement research programmes of European interest, i.e. programmes geared to the large market, of interest to all Member States and necessitating technical and human resources which Member States cannot put together individually. At world level, only the coordinated research of the Member States can allow the European Union to play a leading role in vast international programmes such as the one on global change.

Common research policy is closely **linked to the common industrial policy**, which we have just examined, and to the common energy policy, which we shall examine in the next chapter. Indeed, research is essential for the definition of industrial strategy, especially in high-technology sectors, by offering a common reference basis for technology forecasting and development. It is also necessary for the promotion of **reliable energy sources**, which reduce Europe's dependence on imported oil, particularly for the development of thermonuclear fusion.

18.1. The need for a common research policy

Although the challenges facing the European nations change over time, and with them the scientific and technical research priorities, certain immutable reasons militate in favour of a **common approach to research problems**. The common research policy must define the economic, social, political and even military objectives of research, draw up an inventory of the resources available in terms of human resources, laboratories and funds, set the priorities and apportion the work among the laboratories of the Member States. In this way it can be ensured that no important sector is neglected, that duplication is avoided and that the Union's human, material and financial resources are put to best use. Labour distribution can also ensure that Europe's smallest countries, which would otherwise be excluded owing to a lack of resources, can participate in research and development.

Europe is experiencing a massive transformation of its economy and society. Traditional industrial structures are undergoing rapid change. The problems that are observed in the structures of the traditional European industries, like textiles, shipbuilding and steel, are notably the results of the movement of production to countries with low wage levels induced by the globalisation of markets and economies [see sections 17.1. and 17.3.]. The transfer of European traditional industrial production to other countries can be offset only by new industries with a high level of technology.

Europe's industrial competitiveness, its jobs, its quality of life and the sustainability of growth depend on it being at the leading edge of the development and utilisation of **information society technologies**. Advances in information processing and communications are opening up exciting new possibilities [see sections 17.3.5. and 17.3.6.]. However, the increasing diversity and complexity of systems is also presenting new challenges for their development and use. Continuous efforts are required, in research, technological development and demonstration to tackle the universal issues such as access, ease of use, cost-effectiveness and interoperability and standardisation. They should also address the social changes brought about by the introduction and more widespread use of new information and communications technologies.

Innovation requires constant and organised interdependence between the upstream phases linked to technology, and the downstream phases linked to the market, such as the development of new business concepts, new means of distribution, marketing or design. This means that, in order to have **industrially efficient innovation**, the needs of the market should be taken into account, particularly by modernising the approaches and practices of marketing, and synergies in research and technological development (R & D) should be facilitated by trans-European cooperation. These considerations are particularly pertinent for SMEs, which are innovative by their nature, but which do not exploit efficiently their R & D potential because of their structural and financial handicaps [see section 17.1.4.].

Society is making increasing demands for better living conditions, better safety, and better use of scarce resources including secure and economic energy supplies and services. Availability of a sufficient and economic energy supply must be assured to promote industrial competitiveness and to maintain the quality of life for Europe's citizens [see section 19.1.]. At the same time, the environmental impact of energy production and use must be reduced. Indeed, rising population and per-capita use of resources, globalisation of economic markets and natural variability in earth systems are causing or exacerbating major environmental problems [see section 16.3.]. R & D in the fields of **energy, environment and sustainable development** is essential for the social well-being of Europe's citizens and the implementation of policies formulated at Community level or deriving from international environmental commitments - in particular, the implementation of the Kyoto Protocol [see section 16.3.4.].

The promotion of scientific and technological excellence is an essential prerequisite for Europe to succeed in the competitive environment of international research and scientific development. Access to **major research infrastructures**, in particular, is indispensable for researchers working at the forefront of science. The ability of European research teams to remain competitive with teams elsewhere in the world depends on their being supported by state-of-the-art infrastructures. As most of the major research infrastructures in Europe are operated by national authorities, principally for the benefit of their national researchers, access to these infrastructures is often restricted largely or even entirely to national research teams. The result is that researchers do not always have the opportunity to access the infrastructures most appropriate for their work. European R & D should therefore make available major research infrastructures in all Member States to competent multinational teams of researchers.

European research would be poorly exploited without coordination and without common measures for the **dissemination of the knowledge** acquired. A wealth of accumulated knowledge in documents and prototypes and an industry capable of exploiting it are not, in fact, sufficient to ensure that such knowledge makes the transition to the industrial production stages. First, there needs to be a wide dissemination of that knowledge throughout the Member States to those capable of exploiting it. Moreover, with the inflow of knowledge, recourse to the traditional methods of collating and classifying scientific information is no longer sufficient; ever-greater use of information processing and international networks and databanks are needed. In fact, knowledge obtained from European R & D is disseminated and optimised both in the framework of the specific R & D programmes and by centralised action of the horizontal programme on promotion of innovation and encouragement of SME participation[1].

In a period of increasing social challenges, such as unacceptable levels of unemployment, an ageing population, the globalisation of economies, an increase in inequalities and social exclusion, Europe has set as an objective its **economic and social cohesion** [see section 12.1.2.]. The common research policy has to pursue this objective as well. Furthermore, the process of European integration itself has given rise to a new object of study, European society, which is different from the sum of its components, although clearly dependent on them. Social sciences must therefore be in a position to respond to these challenges, overcome national boundaries, through reinforcing cooperation between them and enhancing their analytical capacity and thereby supporting policy-making. European R & D may build-up European strengths in fields associated with further economic growth and quality of life.

---

[1] Decision 1999/172, OJ L 64, 12.03.1999.

18.2. The foundations of the common research policy

Whilst we now see clearly the need for and objectives of Community research policy, that was probably not the case when the **EEC Treaty** was framed [see section 2.1.]. That is why the Treaty, apart from a rather vague reference to the coordination of research and the dissemination of agricultural knowledge in its Article 41 (Art. 35 TEC), did not give the Community Institutions any powers to finance or even coordinate Member States' research in the other sectors of the economy. This is now changed with the new provisions of the EC Treaty [see section 2.2.], the new concepts of the framework programme [see section 18.2.2.] and of direct and indirect actions [see section 18.2.3.] and, above all, the new missions of the Joint Research Centre [see section 18.2.4.]. These are the main subjects of this part of the chapter.

18.2.1. Research provisions of the Community Treaties

The Maastricht Treaty improved the position enjoyed by research in the process of European construction. Article 163 of the EC Treaty **consecrated research and technological development as a policy of the Community**, stating that the latter shall aim to strengthen the scientific and technological foundations of Community industry and boost its competitiveness at international level and shall promote the research activities deemed necessary by virtue of other Community policies. To this end, it adds, the Community shall in all the Member States encourage undertakings, including small and medium-sized enterprises, research centres and universities, in their research and technological development activities of high quality. Through its support for their cooperation efforts, the Community aims to enable undertakings to draw full benefit from the potential of the internal market, in particular through the opening up of national public contracts, the definition of common standards and the removal of legal and fiscal obstacles to cooperation.

The Community and the Member States coordinate their research and technological development activities (Art. 165 TEC). In pursuit of the objectives detailed in Article 163 (TEC), the Community conducts the following **priority activities**, complementing the R & D activities in the Member States (Art. 164 TEC):

(a) implementation of research, technological development and demonstration programmes, by promoting cooperation with and between undertakings, research centres and universities;
(b) promotion of cooperation in the field of Community research, technological development and demonstration with third countries and international organisations;
(c) dissemination and optimisation of the results of activities in Community research, technological development and demonstration; and
(d) stimulation of the training and mobility of researchers in the Community.

The **Euratom Treaty** gives an even more important place to the development of (nuclear) research, devoting its first Chapter to it [see section 2.1.]. Article 4 makes the Commission responsible for promoting and facilitating nuclear research in the Member States and for complementing it by carrying out a European Atomic Energy Community research and training programme. For purposes of coordinating and complementing research undertaken in Member States, the Commission calls upon Member States, persons or undertakings to communicate to it their programmes relating to the research which it specifies in the request. By its opinions the Commission should discourage unnecessary duplication and should direct research towards sectors which are insufficiently explored, of which it should publish at regular intervals a list. (Art. 5 EAEC).

Euratom research and training programmes are determined by the Council, acting unanimously on a proposal from the Commission, which consults the Scientific and Technical Committee. The funds required for carrying out these programmes are included each year in the research and investment budget of the European Atomic Energy Community (Art. 7 EAEC). After consulting the Scientific and Technical Committee, the Commission establishes a joint Nuclear Research Centre (Art. 8 EAEC), which is now called **Joint Research Centre** [see section 18.2.4.]. The Commission may, by contract, entrust the carrying out of certain parts of the Community research programme to Member States, persons or undertakings, or to third countries, international organisations or nationals of third countries (Art. 10 EAEC). To **encourage the carrying out of research programmes** communicated to it the Commission may: provide financial assistance within the framework of research contracts; supply, either free of charge or against payment source materials or special fissile materials; place installations, equipment or expert assistance at the disposal of Member States, persons or undertakings, either free of charge or against payment; promote joint financing by the Member States, persons or undertakings concerned (Art. 6 EAEC).

The second Chapter of the Euratom Treaty is given over to the **dissemination of information.** As regards information which is owned by the Community, Member States, persons or undertakings shall have the right, on application to the Commission, subject to suitable remuneration, to obtain non-exclusive licences under patents, rights, etc., which belong to the Community (Art. 12 EAEC). The Commission must communicate free of charge to the Member States, persons and undertakings any non-patentable information acquired by the Community (Art. 13 EAEC). As regards information, which the Community does not own, the Commission must endeavour, by amicable agreement, to secure both the communication of information, which is of use to the Community in the attainment of its objectives and the granting of licences under patents, rights etc., covering such information (Art. 14 EAEC).

18.2.2. The framework programme for R & D

A two-phased **decision-making process** exists for Community research programmes. Every five years, the Council acting under the co-decision procedure with the European Parliament [see section 4.3.], after consulting the Economic and Social Committee, adopts a multiannual research and technological development **framework programme**. By laying down the objectives, the priorities and the overall funds for Community action and their apportionment in broad terms, the framework-programme constitutes a "guide" for decisions on specific programmes to be taken during the five years covered. In addition, the framework programme has the desired characteristic of making visible, for scientific establishments, undertakings or Member States, the medium-term research possibilities afforded by the Community. By providing clear indications of the specific measures that the Community intends to undertake, it allows the various European research operators better to programme their efforts and Community research to take its proper place in the concert of European cooperation actions.

The framework programmes are implemented through **specific programmes** [see sections 18.3. and 18.4.] adopted by the Council, acting by a qualified majority, after consultation of the European Parliament and the Economic and Social Committee (Art. 166 TEC). The **sixth framework programme** (2002-2006) takes account of the priority activities ascribed to Community R & D by the EC Treaty[1].With a budget of EUR 16.27 billion, this programme is intended to make a reality of the European research area by strengthening its foundations, by integrating research capacities in Europe more effectively, and by structuring and simplifying their implementation. This objective is based on two main principles: firstly, introducing instruments with integrating effects (networks of excellence, integrated projects, EU participation in jointly-implemented na-

---

[1]   Decision 1513/2002, OJ L 232, 29.08.2002 and Decision 786/2004, OJ L 138, 30.04.2004.

tional programmes) and structuring effects (measures to promote closer links between research and innovation, human resources and mobility, development of infrastructures); secondly, greater concentration on certain priority areas where Community action can bring about the greatest value added (in particular genomics, information society technologies, food safety, sustainable development and the role of citizens and governance in the European knowledge-based society). In addition, the new framework programme fully integrates the accession candidate countries into all its activities and makes significant international cooperation possible, particularly as a result of the opportunity for third-country researchers and bodies to have access to a substantial part of the activities. The European Community framework programme is implemented through three specific programmes concerning the structuring, integration and strengthening of the European research area, as well as direct actions by the Joint Research Centre.

The parallel Euratom framework programme, with a budget of EUR 1.23 billion, covers all activities relating to research, technological development, international cooperation, dissemination and utilisation of results, as well as training in the following areas: waste treatment and storage, controlled thermonuclear fusion, the nuclear activities of the Joint Research Centre; as well as other activities relating to nuclear safety and safeguards (radiation protection, new processes for harnessing nuclear energy). The Euratom framework programme is implemented through two specific programmes concerning nuclear energy and direct actions by the Joint Research Centre.

Recognising the big gap between the EU and its competitors as regards investment in research and technological development, and at the request of the European Council, the Commission set out an action plan aimed at giving Europe a stronger public research base and to make it more attractive to private investment in research and innovation[1]. The action plan comprises four main sets of actions aimed at:

- coordinating the efforts of the Member States by creating "European technology platforms" designed to devise and implement common strategies for the development, deployment and use of technologies in Europe;
- improving the effectiveness of public support through actions to promote the career of researchers, to bring public research and industry closer together, and to develop and exploit fully the potential of European and national public financial instruments;
- increasing the level of public funding for research by encouraging and monitoring the redirection of public budgets; and
- improving the research and technological innovation environment in Europe, in particular with regard to the fiscal environment and the treatment of research in companies' management and reporting practices.

The research programme of the **Research Fund for Coal and Steel** follows the lines of the earlier ECSC programmes [see section 19.2.2.] and supplements the framework programme[2]. It contains guidelines which set out the criteria for participation in the programmes, eligibility criteria for projects applying for funding and operational arrangements for the programme, particularly as regards the procedures to be followed, the evaluation and selection of projects, provisions on contracts, and the monitoring and dissemination of results.

The Council has called upon the Commission, in close cooperation with the Member States and in the context of the "eEurope" action plan [see section 17.3.5.], to present costed initiatives for setting up a very high-speed trans-European research network and for mapping centres of excellence in all Member States[3]. In addition, the Council invited the Member States and the Commission to cooperate in order to identify and take action to remove current obstacles to the mobility of researchers in order to facilitate the creation of a genuine European scientific community[4].

The Commission proposes that the **seventh framework programme** of the European Community for research, technological development and demonstration activities (2007-13) be organised in four specific programmes, corresponding to four major objectives of European research policy[5]. Under the "Cooperation" programme, support would be given to the whole range of research activities carried out in transnational cooperation, including international cooperation between the European Union and third countries. The "Ideas" pro-

[1]   COM (2003) 226, 30 April 2003.
[2]   Decision 2003/78, OJ L 29, 05.02.2003.
[3]   Resolution, OJ C 205, 19.07.2000.
[4]   Resolution, OJ C 367, 21.12.2001.
[5]   COM (2005) 119, 6 April 2005.

gramme would provide for the creation of a European Research Council, which would support investigator-driven frontier research carried out by individual teams competing at European level, in all scientific and technological fields. The "People" programme would strengthen activities supporting training and career development of researchers, referred to as 'Marie Curie' actions. The "Capacities" programme would support research infrastructures, research for the benefit of small and medium-sized enterprises and regional research-driven clusters. The Euratom framework programme would be organised in two specific programmes. The first programme would consist of fusion energy research, aimed at developing the technology for a safe, sustainable, environmentally responsible and economically viable energy source. It would also include nuclear fission and radiation protection. The second programme would cover the activities of the Joint Research Centre in the field of nuclear energy, providing scientific and technical support to the policy-making process.

18.2.3. Direct and indirect research activities

Community research policy does not necessarily mean the "communitarisation" of all programmes or the joint financing of all research and technological development (R & D) activities in the Member States. In application of the subsidiarity principle [see section 3.2.], a distinction has to be made between various forms of research. With regard to **fundamental research and basic research**, which necessitate very large investment and highly specialised researchers and whose results can be expected only in the fairly distant future, it is in the interest of the EU countries to pool their efforts in **direct actions** financed entirely by the European Union and bringing together researchers of several nationalities.

For the **development of leading-edge technology** (nuclear, information, aeronautical and aerospace technologies, etc), on the other hand, **indirect actions** promoting the coordination of research carried out in the Member States is better suited to ensure industrial success, the transnational restructuring of undertakings, the opening up of public contracts, and even the grouping of purchases by public electricity, telecommunications and transport services. European R & D is therefore distinguished into direct actions and indirect actions.

Direct actions are research activities proper pursued by the Commission in the research establishments of the **Joint Research Centre (JRC)** and paid for entirely from the Community budget [see sections 3.4. and 18.2.4.]. The European dimension of its research is one of the fundamental strengths of the JRC. Its activities are characterised by a multidisciplinary approach based on the broad span of its capabilities. This multidisciplinarity is reflected in the diversity of subjects covered by its institutes and helps it meet Europe's scientific challenges as they rise. The JRC, however, must carry out its activities in close cooperation with the scientific community and enterprises in Europe.

The second form taken by Community R & D, **indirect research**, which absorbs more than 80% of the financial resources of Community R & D, is conducted in research centres, universities or undertakings, with financial assistance from the Commission and on conditions laid down by the rules governing participation in the various programmes, notably the participation of at least two partners from different Member States. Community financial assistance covers, as a general rule, 50% of the total cost of research work.

The Commission, with the assistance of the Advisory Committees on Management and Coordination (ACMC)[1], prepares the research programmes on indirect action which are adopted by the Council. The Commission then publishes in the Official Journal of the European Union calls for tenders for researchers from the Member States, specifying the research objectives written into the European programme. The tenders are appraised by the Commission and the Committees on the basis of criteria determined in advance and aimed at ensuring the best possible results. There are no national quotas for research

---

[1] Decision 84/338, OJ L 177, 04.07.1984.

assistance. The main criteria for selecting projects are, firstly, their scientific and technical quality and, secondly, their effects on growth and competitiveness. The rules for the participation of undertakings (companies, firms), research centres and universities from Member States and from associated candidate countries in the implementation of the sixth EC and Euratom framework programmes aim at flexible operating conditions, at a large degree of autonomy in project implementation and at a broad dissemination of research results[1].

The indirect R & D actions are of various kinds: shared-cost actions, which are the principal mechanism for implementing the specific programmes, as well as training fellowships, support for networks, concerted actions and accompanying measures.
(a) **Shared-cost actions** are:

- research and technological development projects, i.e. projects designed to obtain new knowledge likely to be useful either to develop new or significantly to improve existing products, processes and/or services and/or to meet the needs of Community policies,

- demonstration projects, i.e. projects designed to prove the viability of new technologies which offer a potential economic advantage but which cannot be commercialised directly,

- combined R & D/demonstration projects, i.e. projects with both a research and technological development component and a demonstration component,

- access to research infrastructures, by covering the additional costs of receiving Community researchers and making facilities available.

- cooperative research projects, i.e. projects enabling at least three mutually independent SMEs from at least two Member States to entrust the resolution of their common technological problems to third legal entities with appropriate research capacities jointly.

(b) **Training fellowships** are defined in the context of the fourth activity (Marie Curie fellowships)[2];
(c) **Support for research training networks** exists in the context of the fourth activity and thematic networks bringing together, for instance, manufacturers, users, universities, research centres, organisations and research infrastructures around a given scientific and technological objective (Marie Curie Research Training Networks)[3];
(d) **Concerted actions**, are the actions designed to coordinate R & D projects already in receipt of funding, in order to exchange experience acquired, to expand the research efforts of the various players so as to reach a critical mass, to disseminate results and to inform users;
(e) **Accompanying measures** contribute to the implementation of the specific programmes or the preparation of future activities, with a view to enabling them to achieve their strategic objectives.

18.2.4. The activities of the Joint Research Centre

The JRC is an autonomous Directorate General of the Commission and acts as **a science and technology and reference centre** for the Union. It has at its disposal a unique combination of facilities and skills which transcend national borders. Close to the policy formulation process while remaining independent of vested commercial or national interests, it serves the common interest of the Member States. The largest establishments of the JRC are situated at Ispra (Italy), while specialised institutes are located at Geel (Belgium), Petten (Netherlands), Karlsruhe (Germany) and Seville (Spain)[4].

The mission of JRC is to provide customer-driven scientific and technical support for the conception, development, implementation and monitoring of Community policies. In implementing its mission, the JRC endeavours to coordinate R & D activities carried out in the Member States. Its work depends on intensive networking with public and private institutions in the Member States through, for example, research networks,

[1] Regulations 2321/2002 and 2322/2002, OJ L 355, 30.12.2002.
[2] Decision 2002/835, OJ L 294, 29.10.2002.
[3] Ibid.
[4] Decision 96/282, OJ L 107, 30.04.1996.

joint projects or staff exchanges[1]. This is important because the JRC's mission is complementary to the indirect action part of the framework programme. While the indirect actions are the main mechanism for developing and testing new ideas, the JRC's role is to help apply them in the service of the policy-maker. The two selection criteria for JRC activities are: relevance to Community policies and subsidiarity [see section 3.2.] implying that JRC research must be in an area where Community involvement is appropriate. The JRC provides notably support where it has special or even unique expertise and facilities in the Community or where it is entrusted with activities necessary for the framing and implementation of Community policies and tasks incumbent on the Commission pursuant to the Treaty which require impartiality, notably standardisation activities [see section 6.2.3.]. Thus, JRC operates in areas where its unique pan-European identity provides an added value to Community R & D. The JRC carries out two research programmes: one for the European Community and the other for the European Atomic Energy Community (Euratom).

JRC's **specific programme of direct actions for the European Community** (2002-2006) is clearly focused on the safety of citizens in its different aspects, e.g. health, environment and combating fraud[2]. Activities carried out in accordance with the JRC mission are concentrated on two priority thematic areas [see section 18.4.1.]: (a) food, chemical products and health, with particular attention to: food safety and quality; genetically modified organisms; chemical products; and biomedical applications; and (b) environment and sustainability, with particular attention to: climate change and technologies for sustainable development; improvement of air quality, protection of the European environment; development of reference measurements and networks; technical support for the objectives of global monitoring for environment and security (GMES) [see sections 16.2 and 18.4.1]. Horizontal activities in domains for which the JRC has specific competence are: technological and economic foresight work based on the activities of European networks; reference materials and measurements; and the safety of citizens and control technologies.

The JRC's **specific programme for Euratom** is focused on direct actions which have a high European added-value or which correspond to tasks entrusted to the Commission by the Euratom Treaty[3]. Even if nuclear fission is today considered a mature technology, both the safety of nuclear installations and the management of the fuel cycle, notably the management of waste, require continued efforts as they are matters of public concern. Public authorities maintain vigilance and push for continuous safety improvement and industry maintain a strong interest in new technologies and further improvements. The JRC supports these efforts which are at the core of its mission. Thus, activities on fission safety take advantage of the JRC's unique facilities and focus on areas where the JRC is considered a reference centre for the Community such as actinides and areas of public concern such as severe accidents and the handling of waste. Work on ageing of reactor materials reflects the increasing importance of this issue for safety authorities and industry.

18.2.5. Coordination of research in the European Union

Several scientific bodies assist the Commission in its tasks of conceiving and managing the Community policy of research and technological development. The **Scientific and Technical Research Committee (CREST)** is an advisory body which assists the Commission and the Council in the R & D field by identifying strategic priorities, establishing mutual consistency between national and Community policies, and helping to formulate Community strategy with regard to international cooperation[4]. The European Group on Ethics in Science and New Technologies (EGE) advises the Commission on ethical subjects related to research and new technologies, such as the legal protection of biotechnological inventions or the cloning of human beings[5].

---

[1] COM/2001/215.
[2] Decision 2002/836, OJ L 294, 29.10.2002.
[3] Decision 2002/838, OJ L 294, 29.10.2002.
[4] Resolution, OJ C 264, 11.10.1995, p. 4-5.
[5] Directive 98/44, OJ L 213, 30.07.1998.

In fact, in order to implement Article 165 of the EC Treaty, which requires the Community and the Member States to coordinate their research and technological development activities, the coordination of national and Community policies is based as far as possible on **European scientific networks**, notably CREST. One of the main purposes of this coordination is to help determine the priorities for future Community R & D activities bringing Community added-value in compliance with subsidiarity, and help improve the use made of the resources available in the European Union. These scientific networks help knit the scientific fabric of the European Union.

By a decision founded on the Euratom Treaty, the Commission set up a consultative committee referred to as the **European Research Advisory Board**[1]. The task of this Committee is to advise the Commission on design and implementation of Community policy in research and technological development and in particular on the realisation of the European research area and the use of policy instruments such as the Community research and technological development framework programmes. It provides advice on various aspects of Community research policy or developments in science and technology in Europe and worldwide. The Committee is composed of 45 members, appointed by the Commission in a personal capacity. 20 members with an academic focus are nominated by the Commission on the basis of a proposal from the European Science Foundation (ESF). 20 members with a business and industrial focus are nominated on the basis of a proposal from the Union of Industrial and Employers' Confederations of Europe (UNICE). 5 members are identified by the Commission.

18.2.6. International scientific and technical cooperation

International cooperation represents an important dimension of the sixth Framework Programme. Under the specific programme "integrating and strengthening the European Research Area"[2] [see section 18.4.1.], international activities are carried out in the **two forms** of:

- participation of researchers, teams and institutions from third countries in projects within the different thematic priority fields, related to issues arising at world level and being subjects of international efforts;
- specific international cooperation activities with some groups of countries, as a support to Community external relations and development aid policies [see details below].

European research is also **coordinated on a broader level than that of the Fifteen**. In fact, the specific research programmes of the Community are open to the participation of EFTA countries (Switzerland, Norway, Iceland, Liechtenstein) and of the countries of Central and Eastern Europe and the new independent States of the former Soviet Union [see sections 25.1, 25.2 and 25.4.]. **Scientific and technical cooperation (Cost)** covers the countries of the EFTA and of Central and Eastern Europe. It is managed by a Committee of Senior Officials and by specialised committees. It takes the form of memoranda of understanding by the Cost States on the execution of Cost activities in the most varied fields, such as medicine, transport or materials. The Council concludes coordination agreements between the Community and the Cost countries relating to concerted actions forming part of the Community research programme[3].

In 1988 the EAEC (Euratom) concluded a quadripartite Agreement (Community, Soviet Union, United States and Japan) for the execution of a conceptual design project for an **International Thermonuclear Experimental Reactor (ITER)**, with the four parties providing equal contributions on an equal footing. In 1992, the four parties - Rus-

---

[1]   Decision 2001/531, OJ L 192, 14.07.2001.
[2]   Decision 2002/834, OJ L 294, 29.10.2002.
[3]   See e.g., Decision 88/615, OJ L 344, 13.12.1988 and Decision 92/181, OJ L 85, 31.03.1992.

sia having replaced the Soviet Union - signed a Cooperation Agreement for the detailed study of ITER which it is hoped will demonstrate the scientific and technological feasibility of using fusion energy for peaceful purposes[1]. ITER should lead to a demonstration electricity generating power plant (DEMO). Euratom participation in the ITER initiative requires the implementation of an accompanying programme adapted to it, including the operation of the JET machine and the continuation of research into fusion physics and technology [see section 18.3.2.][2].

The general objective of the international cooperation activities carried out under the Framework Programme is to help open up the activities of the seven thematic priorities [see section 18.4.1.] to participation by third-country researchers and institutions. Carried out in support of the Community's foreign policy and development aid policy, these specific activities will concern three groups of countries: the Mediterranean third countries including the Western Balkans, Russia and other Newly Independent States (NIS), and the developing countries. The activities in question have the following **particular objectives**:

- to help European researchers, businesses and research organisations in the EU and the countries associated with the Framework Programme to have access to knowledge and expertise existing elsewhere in the world;
- to help ensure Europe's strong and coherent participation in the research initiatives conducted at international level in order to push back the boundaries of knowledge or help to resolve the major global issues, for example as regards health and environment;
- to lend support, in the scientific and technological field, to the implementation of the Community's foreign policy and development aid policy.

The Community participates in the financing and in the research activities of the International Association for the Promotion of Cooperation with Scientists from the New Independent States (INTAS)[3]. In 1992, the Community, the United States of America, Japan and Russia concluded an Agreement setting up an **International Science and Technology Centre (ISTC)**[4]. Established in Moscow, the ISTC channels the know-how of military research scientists and technicians of the former Soviet Union into non-military projects. A similar Agreement between the European Communities, the United States, Canada, Sweden and Ukraine strives to redirect the talents of Ukrainian weapons scientists and engineers towards peaceful activities[5]. Moreover, the Commission finances an International Association for the promotion of cooperation with scientists from the independent States of the former Soviet Union.

The EU's scientific cooperation with the **countries of the Third World** forms part of the R & D framework programme. The research programme in the field of sciences and technologies for development covers the areas of tropical agriculture (improving food plant production using systems suited to local conditions, restoring the environment, etc.) and medicine, health and nutrition (new methods for diagnosing and treating diseases, improving the nutrition of the population)[6].

However, the Community has also for a number of years been developing its cooperation with non-European **industrialised countries**, such as the United States, Canada and Australia, notably in the fields of energy, biotechnology and the environment. In 1995, the EAEC (Euratom) and the United States signed an R & D cooperation agreement on the monitoring of nuclear safety and a general Nuclear Energy Cooperation Agreement. Euratom signed, also in 1995, a memorandum of understanding for cooperation in the field of controlled thermonuclear fusion[7]. Euratom has also concluded agreements for cooperation in the peaceful uses of nuclear energy with the Republics of Uzbekistan[8] and Kazakhstan[9]. On its part, the European Community concluded Agreements on scientific and technical cooperation with Canada[10], Israel[11], South Africa[12], the United States[13], the Republic of India[14], the Ukraine[15], the Kingdom of Morocco[16], the Tunisian Republic[1],

---

[1] Agreement and Decision 92/439, OJ L 244, 26.08.1992, Protcol 2 and Decision 94/267, OJ L 114, 05.05.1994.
[2] Decision 2002/837, OJ L 294, 29.10.2002.
[3] Decision 94/807, OJ L 334, 22.12.1994 amended by Decision 96/392, OJ L 163, 02.07.1996.
[4] Regulation 3955/92 and Regulation 3956/92, OJ L 409, 31.12.1992 and Regulation 501/94, OJ L 64, 08.03.1994.
[5] Regulation 1766/98, OJ L 225, 12.08.1998 and Regulation 2387/98, OJ L 297, 06.11.1998.
[6] COM (96) 344, 19 July 1996.
[7] Decision 95/355, OJ L 211, 06.09.1995.
[8] Draft agreement, OJ L 269, 21.10.2003.
[9] Decision 2004/282, OJ L 89, 26.03.2004.
[10] Agreement and Decision 96/219, OJ L 74, 22.03.1996.
[11] Agreement and Decision 2003/457, OJ L 154, 21.06.2003.
[12] Agreement and Decision 97/763, OJ L 313, 15.11.1997.
[13] Agreement and Decision 2004/756, OJ L 335, 11,11,2004.
[14] Decision 2002/648, OJ L 213, 09.08.2002.
[15] Agreement and Decision 2003/737, OJ L 267, 17.10.2003.
[16] Agreement and Decision 2004/126, OJ L 37, 10.02.2004.

Egypt[2], Chile[3], Brazil[4] and Mexico[5]. By setting out the areas and the forms of cooperative activities (such as joint research projects, visits and exchanges of scientists), these agreements seek to encourage, develop and facilitate cooperation activities in areas of common interest in which the parties carry out research and scientific and technological development.

18.3. Euratom and nuclear research

Nuclear energy has the potential to provide Europe with a secure and sustainable electricity supply at a competitive price. Efforts to develop the safety and security of nuclear energy systems can strengthen the Community's industrial competitiveness, through exploiting the European technological advance and enhance the public acceptance of nuclear energy. Minimising radiation exposure from all sources, including medical exposures and natural radiation, may improve the quality of life and may help in addressing health and environmental problems. The Commission has specific Treaty obligations in nuclear energy and it has always relied on the JRC to provide a technical support that can keep up with technological developments and face new challenges. However, both the focus of the Euratom Treaty and the missions of the JRC have undergone radical changes since the early days, the most important being that Euratom research is now mainly concerned with nuclear fission safety, on the one hand, and with thermonuclear fusion, on the other.

18.3.1. Nuclear fission

The sixth framework programme of the European Atomic Energy Community (Euratom) for nuclear research and training activities (2002 to 2006) comprises the following headings[6]:

- controlled thermonuclear fusion [see section 18.3.2.];
- management of radioactive waste;
- radiation protection;
- other activities in the field of nuclear technologies and safety;
- nuclear activities of the Joint Research Centre.

Nuclear fission energy supplies 35% of electricity in the Community. It constitutes an element in combating climate change and reducing Europe's dependence on imported energy. Some of the power plants of the current generation will continue to be operated for at least 20 years. For these reasons, the main objectives of the nuclear fission programme of Euratom are to help ensure the safety of Europe's nuclear installations, to improve the competitiveness of Europe's industry, to ensure the protection of workers and the public and the safe and effective management and final disposal of radioactive waste and to explore more innovative concepts that are sustainable and have potential longer-term economic, safety, health and environmental benefits. A further objective is to contribute, through education and training, towards maintaining within the Union a high level of expertise and competence in nuclear fission.

Research on the safety of nuclear fission has several aspects:

---

[1]   Agreement and Decision 2004/127, OJ L 37, 10.02.2004.
[2]   Agreement and Decision 2005/492, OJ L 182, 13.07.2005.
[3]   Decision 2003/589, OJ L 199, 07.08.2003.
[4]   Decision 2005/781, OJ L295, 11.11.2005.
[5]   Decision 2005/766, OJ L 290, 04.11.2005.
[6]   Decision 2002/668, OJ L232, 29.08.2002 and Decision 2004/444, OJ L 127, 29.04.2004.

(a) **management of radioactive waste**, including research into processes for long-term storage in deep geological strata and research aimed at reducing the hazards associated with waste;

(a) **radiation protection**, with research aimed at helping operators and regulatory authorities to protect workers and the public during operations in the nuclear fuel cycle, to manage nuclear accidents and radiological emergencies and to restore contaminated environments.

(b) operational **safety of existing installations**, with research focusing on measures to maintain and improve the safety of existing installations, including the safety aspects of prolonging the lifespan of reactors;

(b) **safety of the fuel cycle**. Here research is directed towards the development of improved methods for assessing, managing and enhancing the safety of the entire cycle, including existing reactors, to provide a better basis for policy choices, to promote the adoption of best safety practice that is both cost-effective and acceptable in a broader context, and to enhance public confidence. Particular issues concern the prevention and management of accidents and the management and disposal of radioactive waste.

18.3.2. Controlled thermonuclear fusion

Euratom is also actively engaged in the development of controlled thermonuclear fusion, which is safe for the environment. **Thermonuclear fusion** is a process which occurs on the surface of the Sun, releasing prodigious energy. In the Sun's core at temperatures of 10 to 15 million degrees Celsius, hydrogen is converted to helium providing enough energy to sustain life on Earth. Man has conceived of reproducing on earth, in a controlled fashion, what happens on the Sun. In fact, by heating gases such as deuterium (abundant in all forms of water) and lithium (plentiful in the Earth's crust) or tritium (manufactured from lithium) to a temperature of 100 million degrees Celsius, their electrons are completely separated from the atomic nuclei, atoms fuse and a fantastic release of energy within that "plasma" ensues. However, one must first obtain that extraordinary temperature, which is feasible, and the plasma must thereafter be confined within a magnetic space known as a "torus", which is more difficult. The objective of Community research is to produce and contain plasma, which has the properties required for the reactors of the future, in a magnetic field known as "tokamak". For reasons bound up with the complexity of fundamental knowledge in physics and the technological problems to be resolved, the developments needed for the possible application of fusion for energy production take the form of a process in several steps, each of which has an impact on the next one.

Thermonuclear fusion research is pursued since 1978 at Culham (United Kingdom) in an establishment which does not form part of the Joint Research Centre, but which is administered by a **joint undertaking**, the Joint European Torus (JET), within the meaning of Article 45 of the Euratom Treaty [see section 19.2.3.][1] and whose Board of Governors is made up of representatives of the participating States and of the Commission, with a budget 80% of which is financed by the Community[2]. The fusion physics and technology activities seek to develop the capacity, especially within an association of JET and the European industry, to construct and operate an experimental reactor. The Community research effort is currently geared towards the launching of the "Next Step" project and the construction of the demonstration machine (DEMO) in the context of the ITER international cooperation project[3] [see section 18.2.6.].

The efforts deployed in the context of the integrated European research programme on controlled thermonuclear fusion have enabled Europe to become a world leader in the field of research into fusion by magnetic confinement. Remarkable results have been achieved on the JET, such as the first-ever production of 2 megawatts of fusion power for one second in November 1991 and 12 megawatts of such power in September

---

[1] Decisions 78/471 and 78/472, OJ L 151, 07.06.1978 and Decision 98/585, OJ L 282, 20.10.1998.
[2] Decision 96/305, OJ L 117, 14.05.1996.
[3] Decision 2002/668, OJ L 232, 29.08.2002.

1997, enabling the European Union to hold a place in the forefront of world research in the field of fusion by magnetic confinement..

The aim of Euratom R & D, in the context of the ITER cooperation project, is to develop the necessary basis for the possible **construction of an experimental reactor** (the "Next step"), with the objective of demonstrating the scientific and technological feasibility of fusion power production as well as its potential safety and environmental benefits. The longer-term aim is the development of a demonstration reactor (DEMO) and then a prototype reactor. The objective of this will be to demonstrate the scientific and technological feasibility of fusion energy production, bearing in mind the socio-economic aspects. The precise arrangements for implementing the project are made in the framework of international cooperation and subsequent developments depend on the decisions taken concerning Europe's contribution to the ITER project and the site where the machine is to be installed.

18.4. Research activities of the European Community

The **sixth framework programme** is carried out to further the objective set out in Article 163(1) of the EC Treaty, "of strengthening the scientific and technological bases of Community industry and encouraging it to become more competitive at international level". In order to achieve this more effectively, and in order to contribute to the creation of the European Research Area and to innovation, this programme is structured around the following **three headings**, under which the priority activities set out in Article 164 of the Treaty [see section 18.2.1.] are undertaken:

- focusing and integrating Community research,
- structuring the European Research Area,
- strengthening the foundations of the European Research Area.

The activities under these three headings should contribute to the integration of research efforts and activities on a European scale as well as to the structuring of the various dimensions of the European Research Area. We examine the activities under the first two headings in more detail below. Activities under the third heading aim to strengthen the coordination and support the coherent development of R & D policies in Europe by providing financial support for measures such as the opening up of national programmes.

Networks of excellence aim to strengthen and develop Community scientific and technological excellence by means of the integration, at European level, of research capacities at national and regional level. A network of excellence is implemented by a joint programme of activities involving some or, where appropriate, all of the research capacities and activities of the participants in the relevant area to attain a critical mass of expertise and European added value. Each network aims at advancing knowledge in a particular area by fostering cooperation between capacities of excellence in universities, research centres, enterprises, including SMEs, and science and technology organisations.

Integrated projects are designed to give increased impetus to the Community's competitiveness or to address major societal needs by mobilising a critical mass of research and technological development resources and competences. Each integrated project should be assigned clearly defined scientific and technological objectives and should be directed at obtaining specific results applicable in terms of, for instance, products, processes or services. Under these objectives integrated projects may include more long-term or "risky" research.

In order to help the **development of SMEs in the knowledge society** and the use of the economic potential of SMEs in an enlarged and better integrated European Union, SMEs, including small and micro enterprises as well as craft enterprises, are encouraged to participate in all areas and all instruments of the sixth framework programme, in particular in the context of the activities carried out in the priority thematic areas. Specific targeted projects and coordination actions are used as a "stairway of excellence" to facilitate the access of smaller research actors of scientific excellence, including SMEs, as well as research actors from associated candidate countries, to the activities of the framework programme.

18.4.1. Integrating Community research

The activities carried out under the **specific programme** on "integrating and strengthening the European research area" (2002-2006)[1] represent the major part of the research efforts deployed under the sixth framework-programme. They are intended to contribute to the general objective of the Treaty of strengthening the scientific and technical bases of Community industry and encouraging it to be more competitive at international level, while promoting all the research activities deemed necessary by other Chapters of the Treaty. The Joint Research Centre (JRC) provides independent customer-driven support for the formulation and implementation of Community policies, including the monitoring of implementation of such policies, within its areas of specific competence.

In order to bring about European added value by assembling a critical mass of resources, the specific programme focuses on seven, clearly defined **thematic priority areas** where Community research efforts should be integrated by pulling them together and making them more coherent, on a European scale. The seven priority thematic areas identified by this programme are:

1. life sciences, genomics and biotechnology for health;
2. information society technologies;
3. nanotechnologies and nanosciences, knowledge-based multifunctional materials, and new production processes and devices;
4. aeronautics and space;
5. food quality and safety;
6. sustainable development, global change and ecosystems;
7. citizens and governance in a knowledge-based society.

The activities carried out under the theme "**life sciences, genomics and biotechnology for health**" are intended to help Europe exploit, by means of an integrated research effort, breakthroughs achieved in decoding the genomes of living organisms, more particularly for the benefit of public health and citizens and to increase the competitiveness of the European biotechnology industry. "Post-genomic" research based on analysis of the human genome and genomes of other organisms, will culminate in numerous applications in various health-related sectors, and notably in the development of new diagnostic tools and new treatments capable of helping to combat diseases that are not at present under control, offering major potential markets. This research may also have implications on research on areas such as environment and agriculture.

The activities of the thematic priority "**Information society technologies**", pursuant to the conclusions of the Lisbon European Council and the objectives of the eEurope initiative [see section 17.3.5.], are intended to stimulate the development in Europe of both hardware and software technologies and applications at the heart of the creation of the information society. The future competitiveness of European industry and the living standards of Europe's citizens depend largely on future efforts in IST research in order to prepare the future generation of products, processes and services. The objective of Community research is to increase the competitiveness of European industry and allow European citizens in all Union regions the possibility of benefiting fully from the development of the knowledge-based society.

Community research carried out in the area of "**nanotechnologies and nanosciences, knowledge-based multifunctional materials** and new production processes and devices" is intended to help Europe achieve a critical mass of capacities needed to develop and exploit, especially for greater eco-efficiency and reduction of discharges of hazardous substances to the environment, leading-edge technologies for the knowledge-based

---

[1]   Decision 2002/834, OJ L 294, 29.10.2002.

extremely small products, services and manufacturing processes. Nanotechnology is the application of microe-
lectronics to the fabrication and manipulation of structures and appliances at the scale of the nanometre (nm),
i.e. a measure of length of one billionth of a metre. Lying at the frontier of quantum engineering, materials
technology and molecular biology, nanotechnology is one of the foreseeable hubs of the next industrial revolution. Where materials are concerned, the aim is to develop intelligent materials, which are expected to add
considerable value in terms of applications in sectors such as transport, energy, electronics and the biomedical
sector.

The aim of activities carried out in the area of "**aeronautics and space**" is two-fold: to strengthen, by integrating its research efforts, the scientific and technological bases of the European aeronautics and space
industry and encouraging it to become more competitive at international level; and to help exploit the potential
of European research in this sector with a view to improving safety and environmental protection. Community
aeronautical research activities aim to increase the competitiveness of the European industry with regard to
civil aircraft, reduce the environmental impact of aviation, increase aircraft safety and safety of the air transport system. Community space activities carried out in close coordination with the European Space Agency
(ESA) address: research on satellite-based information systems and services relevant for the Galileo satellite
navigation project [see section 17.3.4.]; and research on satellite-based systems relevant for the global monitoring for environment and security (GMES) [see sections 16.2 and 18.2.4]..

Research activities carried out under the thematic priority "**food quality and safety**" are intended to help
establish the integrated scientific and technological bases needed to develop an environmentally friendly production and distribution chain of safer, healthier and varied food, including sea-food and to control food-
related risks, relying in particular on biotechnology tools taking into account the results of post-genomic research, as well as to control health risks associated with environmental changes. The food crises, and in particular bovine spongiform encephalopathy (BSE) [see sections 5.1.3. and 21.4.2.], have highlighted both the
complexity of food safety issues and the fact that in most cases they have international and cross-border implications. Given that small enterprises constitute a major part of the food sector, the Community research effort
focuses on the adaptation of knowledge and processes to the specific characteristics of these enterprises.

The activities carried out under the theme of "**Sustainable development, global change and ecosystems**" are intended to strengthen the scientific and technological capacities needed for Europe to be able to
implement sustainable development and to integrate its environmental, economic and social objectives with
particular regard to renewable energy, transport, and sustainable management of Europe's land and marine
resources. Under the 1997 Kyoto Protocol to the 1992 United Nations framework Convention on climate
change, the European Union is required to reduce its greenhouse gas emissions by 8% until 2012, compared
with the 1990 levels [see section 16.3.4.]. Achieving the above objective requires a major effort to deploy
technologies currently under development. Community action is important to ensure coordination of Europe's
contribution to world efforts.

Community research carried out under the thematic priority "**Citizens and governance in a knowledge-
based society**" is intended to mobilise European research capacities in economic, political, social sciences and
humanities that are necessary to develop an understanding of, and to address issues related to, the emergence of
the knowledge-based society and new forms of relationships between its citizens, on the one hand, and between its citizens and institutions, on the other. This research should more particularly help to ensure the harnessing and exploitation of an exponentially increasing quantity of information and knowledge and an understanding of the processes at work in this area. What is at stake is the relationship between citizens and institutions in a complex political and decision-making environment characterised by the coexistence of national,
regional and European decision-making levels and the increasing role of civil society and its representatives in
the political debate.

18.4.2. Structuring the European research area

The activities carried out within the specific programme entitled "structuring the
European research area" are applicable to all fields of research and technology[1]. They
have specific vocations, distinct from, and complementary to, the activities implemented
within other parts of the framework programme, notably those within the "Integrating
and strengthening the European Research Area" programme in the priority thematic areas. This programme has four main headings: research and innovation; human resources
and mobility; research infrastructures; and science and society.

The activities carried out under the heading **research and innovation** are intended
to stimulate technological innovation, utilisation of research results, transfer of knowl-

[1] Decision 2002/835, OJ L 294, 29.10.2002.

edge and technologies and the setting up of technology businesses in the Community and in all its regions. The overall aim is to make a tangible improvement in Europe's innovation performance by stimulating a better integration between research and innovation, and by working towards a more coherent and innovation-friendly policy and regulatory environment across the European Union. To this end, the actions of this heading focus on improving the knowledge, understanding and capabilities of the actors involved - research workers, industrialists, investors, public authorities at European, national and regional levels, and others - by encouraging more intensive and fruitful interactions between them, and by providing strategic information and services, as well developing new methodologies and tools, to assist them in their particular endeavours.

The activities carried out under the heading **"human resources and mobility"** are intended to: support the development of abundant world-class human resources in all the regions of the Community by promoting transnational mobility for training purposes, the development of expertise or the transfer of knowledge, in particular between different sectors; support the development of excellence; and help to make Europe more attractive to third country researchers. Promoting transnational mobility creates opportunities for significantly improving the quality of the training of researchers, promotes the circulation and exploitation of knowledge, and helps to establish world-class centres of excellence that are attractive throughout Europe.

The development of a European approach with regard to **research infrastructures**, and the carrying out of activities in this area at Union level, aim at: ensuring wider access to the infrastructures existing in the different Member States; increasing the complementarity of the facilities in place; and multiplying optimum construction choices in European terms.

Science/society issues need to a large extent to be addressed at European level on account of their strong European dimension. This is bound up with the fact that very often they arise on a European scale (as the example of food safety problems shows). The activities carried out under this heading are intended to encourage the development of harmonious relations between science and society and an informed dialogue between researchers, industrialists, political decision-makers and citizens.

More particularly, the actions undertaken under the heading **research and innovation** focus on:
- networking the players and users and encouraging interaction between them;
- encouraging transregional cooperation;
- experimenting with new tools and approaches;
- putting services in place and consolidating them;
- stepping up economic and technological intelligence; and
- analysing and evaluating innovation in Community research projects.

18.5. Appraisal and outlook

Competitiveness and sustainability are the keys to the long-term future of the Union's economy. They entail the capacity of citizens, enterprises, regions, nations and the Community to generate and use the knowledge, science and technology of tomorrow, in high-quality goods, processes and services, and in new and more efficient organisational forms. By strengthening the innovative capacity of the European industrial system and by fostering the creation of businesses and services built on emerging technologies and new market opportunities, European R & D helps EU countries face the major challenges of society, in particular employment. In parallel, research into sustainable mobility and environmentally and consumer friendly processes, products and services may contribute to improving quality of life and working conditions.

The promotion of sustainable development in Europe is not possible unless economic objectives relating to technological development, competitiveness and growth are reconciled with **societal goals** such as quality of life, employment, security, health and a high quality environment. Moreover, improving the quality of life of European citizens and disconnecting economic growth from environmental degradation contributes to European competitiveness and employment. For instance, the need for energy equipment suppliers and operators to effectively respect the environment is vital both for strengthening their global competitiveness and for creating new jobs, such as in the water industry, renewable energy technologies, rational use of energy and reuse of resources. These are some of the objectives of the sixth framework R & D programme.

The individual and collective expertise of the Community's researchers is a considerable asset. However, scientific research takes place in **a strongly competitive worldwide environment** and compared with its main competitors, the Community has a relative shortage of researchers, a high fragmentation and duplication of research effort and a certain isolation of research teams, particularly in the peripheral and less-favoured regions of the Community. Three Member States (the Federal Republic of Germany, France and the United Kingdom) account for three quarters of total R&D expenditure in the European Union, and regional differences are very marked.

The research and technological development powers vested in the Community, particularly since the 1990s, have provided a basis for raising the **competitiveness of European undertakings**, notably small and medium enterprises. The participation of SMEs in all R & D activities is stimulated and encouraged by the Community framework-programme. Their important potential to contribute to the innovation process is fully recognised. Activities related to innovation and participation of SMEs are given a particular emphasis in all specific programmes to help bridge the gap between research results and their effective exploitation in potential applications by the business and policy-making sectors. However, by comparison with performance elsewhere, the relative weakness of private-sector investment in R & D within the Union is striking. More effort is needed to strengthen the interactions between public research bodies and industry.

Europe has established **a leading R & D role in many areas**, notably nuclear safety, thermonuclear fusion, telecommunications' technologies and biochemistry. The Joint Research Centre, in particular, plays a principal role in various subjects such as climate change, bovine spongiform encephalopathy, genetically-modified organisms, the safety of chemicals, nuclear forensics and cybersecurity. This role must be sustained and remain at the cutting-edge. In other areas improvements are needed for the future benefit of society, as well as the business and industrial sectors. The development of new concepts such as eco-industry, transport intermodality, new generations of aircraft and other means of transport, and innovative approaches to the integration of new technologies will help to generate a strategic vision of research in all industrial sectors throughout Europe and to prepare European industry for the challenges of the 21st century. It is essential to increase knowledge in order to achieve the Lisbon objective. Investing in knowledge is the best way for the European Union to foster economic growth and create more and better jobs, while at the same time ensuring social progress and environmental sustainability. Europe must promote the "knowledge triangle": producing knowledge, diffusing it through education and applying it through innovation.

Innovation is still handicapped in Europe by the dispersion of research efforts and by the difficulty of translating the results of these efforts into new products and services. To promote innovation and, therefore, the competitiveness of European business, the legal and regulatory as well as the tax environment should be improved. Technologies targeted on major industrial priorities reflecting the needs of industry as it endeavours to innovate must be developed alongside the traditional research programmes. At the same time it is important to improve the acceptance of science and research in the business community with the objective of creating a favourable environment for research and technological development, and in particular for participation in activities carried out under Community framework programmes. The right conditions for R & D need to be developed - in particular by businesses - so the EU can move towards its R & D investment target of approaching 3 % of GDP.

Bibliography on research policy

- AHO Esko (et al.). *Creating an innovative Europe: report of the independent expert group on R&D and innovation appointed following the Hampton Court Summit.* Luxembourg: EUR-OP*, 2006.
- BOSSUAT Gérard, SEBESTA Lorenza. Les coopérations européennes pour la recherche scientifique et technique = European cooperations in research and development matters. *Journal of European Integration History*, v. 12, n. 2, 2006.
- CALSTER Geert van. "Regulating nanotechnology in the European Union" in *European environmental law review*, v. 15, n. 8/9, August/September 2006, p. 238-247.
- EUROPEAN COMMISSION. *The state and prospects of European energy research: comparison of Commission, Member and non-Member States' R&D portfolios.* Luxembourg: EUR-OP*, 2006.

  - *Communication from the Commission to the European Council: The European Institute of Technology : further steps towards its creation.* Luxembourg: EUR-OP*, 2006.

  - *CORDIS: the European gateway to research and development.* Luxembourg: EUR-OP*, 2006.

  - *Design measures to promote growth of young research-intensive SMEs and start-ups: Report of the CREST Expert Group : second cycle of the Open Method of Coordination in favour of the 3% objective.* Luxembourg: EUR-OP*, 2006.

  - *Report from the Commission: annual report on research and technological development activities of the European Union in 2005.* Luxembourg: EUR-OP*, 2006.

  - *Social values, science and technology: key conclusions, recommendations and key messages: from the Report of the Science Policy Research Group to the European Commission.* Luxembourg: EUR-OP*, 2006.

  - *Coordination of national and European R&D policies and programmes in ICT: Overview report.* Luxembourg: EUR-OP*, 2006.

- EUROPEAN FOUNDATION CENTRE. *Giving more for research in Europe: strengthening the role of philanthropy in the financing of research: Brussels, 27 & 28 March 2006: conference report.* Luxembourg: EUR-OP*, 2006.
- GLADER Marcus. *Innovation markets and competition analysis: EU competition law and US antitrust law.* Cheltenham: Edward Elgar, 2006.
- HOLZHACKER Ronald, HAVERLAND Markus (eds.). *European research reloaded: cooperation and integration among europeanized States.* Dordrecht:Springer, 2006.
- LINK Albert. Public/private partnerships : innovation strategies and policy alternatives. New York: Springer, 2006.
- MULDUR Ugur. *A new deal for an effective European research policy : the design and impacts of the 7th Framework Programme.* Dordrecht: Springer, 2006.
- ORGANISATION FOR ECONOMIC COOPERATION AND DEVELOPMENT. *Government R&D funding and company behaviour: measuring behavioural additionality.* Paris: OECD, 2006.
- RUBIN DE CERVIN Almoro, ZULEGER Volker. *Large R&D projects: Commission practice under the R&D framework from 1996 to 2006.* Berlin: Lexxion Verlag - NP NewLaw Publishers, 2006.
- STAJANO Attilio. *Research, quality, competitiveness: European Union technology policy for the information society.* Berlin: Springer-Verlag, 2006.
- TAPLIN Ruth (ed.). *Innovation and business partnering in Japan, Europe and the United States.* London: Routledge, 2006.
- WESTKAMP Guido. "Research agreements and joint ownership of intellectual property rights in private international law" in *IIC: international review of industrial property and competition law*, v. 37, n. 6, 2006, p. 637-661.

---

*The publications of the Office for Official Publications of the European Communities (EUR-OP) exist usually in all official languages of the EU.

Chapter 19

ENERGY POLICY

Diagram of the chapter

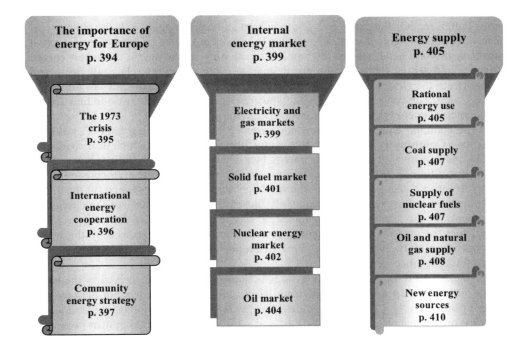

The importance of
energy for Europe
p. 394

The 1973
crisis
p. 395

International
energy
cooperation
p. 396

Community
energy strategy
p. 397

Internal
energy market
p. 399

Electricity and
gas markets
p. 399

Solid fuel market
p. 401

Nuclear energy
market
p. 402

Oil market
p. 404

Energy supply
p. 405

Rational
energy use
p. 405

Coal supply
p. 407

Supply of
nuclear fuels
p. 407

Oil and natural
gas supply
p. 408

New energy
sources
p. 410

Successive oil shocks, their impact on the economic and monetary system at international and EEC level and Community efforts to reduce its dependence on imported oil are the closely interrelated problems which topped the economic agenda in the1970s. The Community was ill prepared to cope with these problems, for when the founding Treaties were signed in the 1950s, it was almost self-sufficient in energy and hoped that a new source - atomic energy - would soon take over from coal, the traditional source. Time proved otherwise and it was oil which made a spectacular entry onto the Community market in the1960s.

In that **two Community Treaties dealt** uniquely with the energy of the past (coal - ECSC) and the perceived one of the future (nuclear - Euratom), the Commission did not have the legal instruments at its disposal to assume responsibilities in the energy sector (oil - EEC) which had since become the dominant player. The Community perceived the risks of its dependence from imported oil during the October 1973 energy crisis. From 1974 onwards, Community objectives began to be defined and steps taken to reduce dependence on imported crude oil and petroleum products. It was from this point that a common energy policy began to take shape at a snail's pace.

19.1. The importance of energy for Europe

Energy policy is important because **energy is at the core of economic and social activity** in industrialised countries. Energy costs affect not only industries with large energy consumption but also industry as a whole and even the cost of living of citizens, notably because of the impact of energy prices on transport cost and heating. While respecting the subsidiarity principle [see section 3.2.] and the environmental requirements for sustainable development [see sections 16.2. and 16.3.4.], European energy policy aims, therefore, at influencing energy production and consumption with the objective of securing economic growth and safeguarding the wellbeing of the citizens of the Union. It must, on the one hand, ensure the smooth functioning of the single market in energy products and services and, on the other, guarantee the supply of relatively cheap and secure (from the strategic and environmental viewpoints) energy resources to the States of the Union. The common energy policy thus revolves around two axes: the functioning of the internal energy market and the security of energy supplies.

The common energy policy was not forgotten by the "founding fathers", who **devoted two Community Treaties to this sector**: the ECSC Treaty, which deals with coal and Euratom, which covers nuclear energy [see section 2.1.]. They failed, however, to give the institutions of the European Economic Community any clear responsibility for the hydrocarbons sector. Although with hindsight this may be questioned, in the 1950s coal was in abundant supply, was relatively inexpensive and met 65% of the energy requirements of the six founding countries. It was therefore seen as the energy, which would fuel the creation of the common market. Furthermore, impressed by the recent demonstration at Hiroshima of the force of atomic energy, experts were predicting a bright future for its peaceful use.

No clear need for a common or even national oil policy was perceived in **the years when oil was cheap and supply certain**, which was the case throughout the post-war years up to the early 1970s. This golden era was anchored in major oil discoveries by Western oil companies in the Middle East and Africa and in the legal system governing the exploitation of oil reserves. The central principle of this system was the granting of a prospecting and working monopoly over a given area by the producer country to one or several foreign companies (licence). The activity spectrum of these companies covered all of the petroleum industry activities (prospecting, production, transport, refining, storage and distribution) and they enjoyed a strong position enabling them, in the vast majority of exporting countries and in relation to most of the importing countries, to regulate petroleum output and marketing terms.

Although the Governments of the then six Member States showed a clear tendency towards an "every man for himself" policy, they nevertheless approved a "Protocol of Agreement on Energy Problems" in April 1964[1]. In this Protocol, they stated their commitment to the development and implementation of a Community energy policy, without considering it necessary to set a time limit for its definition. Time was however running against them, for world oil demand grew more rapidly than supply and around 1970 **the market changed**

---

[1]   Protocol of Agreement, OJ L 69, 30.04.1964, p. 99-100.

from a buyer's to a seller's one. Oil-producing countries became aware of the power which they wielded and changed their attitude towards consumer countries and oil companies. The calm which had reigned in the oil sector during most of the post-war period was suddenly shattered in 1970 and replaced by an incessant stream of demands by producing countries, by agreements concluded and broken and finally by a mad rush for self-survival among consumer countries.

Very few specific measures were adopted in the oil sector until the crisis hit this sector. Among the rare few was one on the obligation of the Member States to maintain minimum stocks of petroleum products as a security measure[1] and one on the notifying of the Commission of investment projects of interest to the Community in the petroleum, natural gas and electricity sectors[2]. Special mention must be made of a Directive adopted by the Council in July 1973, just a few months before the October 1973 crisis, urging the Member States to take measures, appoint bodies and prepare intervention plans to **mitigate the effects of possible supply restrictions**[3].

19.1.1. The 1973 crisis

The first occasion for a showdown between producer countries on the one hand and consumer countries and their oil companies on the other came with **the Kippur war between Israel and the Arab countries** from October 6 to 16, 1973. During this war and in the following months, the Arab countries successfully wielded the weapon represented by their oil resources. They notably placed an embargo, for several months, on exports to countries which were branded "enemies of the Arab cause" - including practically all the countries of Western Europe - while reducing their overall oil output level. They decided to overturn the principle of price setting for crude oil through agreements with the oil companies and hiked up prices on a unilateral basis. Finally, they stepped up their claims to holdings in the companies producing crude oil. Under the combined impact of these measures, oil prices quadrupled in just a few months and uncertainty clouded the quantity and price situation which the world's biggest importer, the European Community, would have to face. A common trade policy for oil could have considerably boosted the negotiating leverage of the EEC Member States, if only it had existed; but even after the bitter lesson of their weakness in the face of a united front of producing countries, the European States were **not ready to shed a bit of their sovereignty** in the oil sector in order to collectively negotiate the terms of their supply.

In the Member States, the **first effect of the crisis was a shortage of oil**, which led to a number of measures to restrict consumption (no use of cars on Sundays, speed limits, heating restrictions and so on). As shortage fears diminished, prices and their financial consequences became the uppermost concern. Although supply difficulties tailed off after December 1973, the **prices for crude oil kept growing** to reach twelve times their pre-crisis level (36 dollars the barrel compared to 3) after the second oil-shock provoked by the Iran-Iraq war of 1979. This abrupt increase in crude oil prices in the space of six years dealt a devastating blow to the economies in several regions of the world, including Europe. The Community Member States, accustomed to trade surpluses, saw these frittered away into a deficit situation. Recession began to bite in nearly all the European countries and gave rise to what was termed "Euro-stagnation" or "Euro- slump" [see section 6.1.].

Aside from these economic consequences, the 1973 crisis created a **sense of insecurity** among the European countries, and rightly so, for it revealed the vulnerability of their economies due to their dependence on available quantities and price levels of the vital fuel, oil. The cartel of producer countries inspired much less confidence than its predecessor, the cartel of the "seven sisters" (Exxon, Shell, B.P., Mobil, Texaco, Chevron and Gulf). The concept of everyone settling their own affairs and entrusting multinational oil companies with the common good took a serious blow when the seven sisters and their poorer relations such as Total, Elf and Agip lost ownership of their crude oil resources and were therefore unable to continue guaranteeing the supply security of Europe. This awareness of the Community's energy vulnerability led to the need for a coherent system of external relations to guarantee supply security.

---

[1] Decision 68/416, OJ L 308, 23.12.1968.
[2] Regulation 1056/72, OJ L 120, 25.05.1972 repealed by Regulation 736/96, OJ L 102, 25.04.1996.
[3] Directive 73/238, OJ L 228, 16.08.1973.

19.1.2. International energy cooperation

After the October 1973 oil crisis, the United States took the initiative of organising an international conference in Washington in February 1974, whose work culminated in the conclusion of the International Energy Agreement and in the creation of the International Energy Agency under the auspices of the Organisation for Economic Cooperation and Development (OECD). The Agreement on an **International Energy Programme**, signed in November, 1974, by the OECD member countries is a wide-ranging cooperation programme which seeks: to ensure, in the event of crisis, a common level of oil supply autonomy and common measures to restrict demand and share out the available oil; to establish an information system on the international oil market; to implement a long-term cooperation programme to reduce dependence on oil imports and to promote cooperation relations with producer countries and with other consumer countries.

The International Energy Agency (IEA) was set up on November 15, 1974 by the OECD's Council. Its main tasks are to: draw up and implement a long-term cooperation programme on the development of resources and energy savings; analyse national programmes for energy conservation and the development of new energy resources; improve the information system on oil and natural gas markets; create a statistics centre for energy; introduce a mechanism to restrict demand and share out oil resources in the event of supply difficulties. The European Commission has observer status within the Agency and coordinates, on the one hand, the positions of the EU Member States and, on the other, the action of the IEA with that of the EU, particularly in the areas where there is Community competence such as that of the commercial policy. The introduction of a contingency scheme by the IEA, on 17 January 1991, together with the commencement of Allied hostilities against Iraq - in compliance with UN Resolutions and under US command - after Kuwait's invasion, was instrumental in calming the oil markets, which remained stable until the end of the conflict.

The 1973 crisis gave rise to several initiatives seeking to establish **"dialogue" between oil producer and consumer countries**. These have not borne much fruit. There are occasional meetings between the European Commission and the secretariats of the Organisation of Petroleum Exporting Countries (OPEC) and the Organisation of Arab Petroleum Exporting Countries (OAPEC), which discuss oil trade, the situation on the international energy market and the interest of all, consumers and producers alike, in avoiding too large price fluctuations. This dialogue is certainly useful, but cannot in itself lay the foundation for cooperation between the European Union and energy producing countries, notably the Gulf countries where the World's most important hydrocarbon reserves are located.

Pan-European cooperation in the energy field is assisted by the Instrument for Pre-Accession Assistance (IPA) and by the European Neighbourhood and Partnership Instrument (ENPI) for candidate and other neighbouring countries [see sections 25.2. and 25.4.]. Technical assistance programmes in the energy field cover the drafting and planning of energy policy in these countries, energy supply and demand, tariff system and pricing, energy savings, the interconnection of East-West networks, training, environmental protection, the reshaping of the energy industry and nuclear safety. Agreements between the European Atomic Energy Community (Euratom) and the Russian Federation in the field of nuclear safety and in the field of controlled nuclear fusion provide for cooperation between the parties concerning reactor safety research, radiation protection, nuclear waste management, decommissioning, decontamination and dismantling of nuclear installations, and research and development on accountancy and control of nuclear material[1]. A multilateral environmental programme and a protocol establish a coherent legal framework for implementing nuclear-related projects in the Russian Federation[2].

The **European Energy Charter** attempts to put some order in energy supply and demand conditions in Europe. It lays down the principles, the objectives and ways of achieving pan-European cooperation in the field of energy. Signed in the Hague on December 17, 1991 by almost all European countries as well as by the Community, Canada, the United States, and Japan, the Charter is in fact a code of good practice. Its interest is to give the first tangible demonstration of a consensus based upon solidarity and complementarity, in particular between the countries of Western Europe - with their know-how and advanced technologies - and those of Central and Eastern Europe, including the countries of the former Soviet Union, which have relatively abundant energy resources.

The **Charter pursues the following operational objectives**: expansion of trade, especially through free market operation, free access to resources and the development

---

[1]   Agreement on nuclear fusion, Agreement on nuclear safety and Decision 2001/761/Euratom, OJ L 287, 31.10.2001.
[2]   Framework Agreement, Protocol and Decision 2003/462, OJ L 155, 24.06.2003.

of infrastructure; cooperation and coordination of energy policies; and the optimal use of energy and protection of the environment. These objectives should be attained through the implementation of joint measures by the signatory countries in six specific priority fields: access to resources; use of resources; investment arrangements; liberalisation of trade; harmonisation of technical specifications and safety rules; research and technological development and innovation.

The implementation of the Charter is provided by the **European Energy Charter Treaty**, signed in Lisbon on 17 December 1994[1]. This Treaty is designed to develop new relations between the main European countries, most of the independent States of the former Soviet Union and Central and Eastern Europe, Canada, the United States and Japan concerning the transit of energy products between east and west, trade, investment and energy cooperation. The European Commission assists the Secretariat of the Conference, which is established in Brussels. The practical implication of the Energy Charter is the diversification of the supplies of European Union countries in oil and natural gas and, hence, their decreasing dependence from Middle Eastern sources.

Russia has signed but not ratified the Energy Charter Treaty and the Partnership and Cooperation Agreement between **the EU and Russia** (signed in 1994 and in force since 1997) has not solved the energy problems between the two parties. Therefore an energy dialogue was deemed necessary to resolve energy questions. Since its launch in 2000, the energy dialogue between the European Union and Russia has resolved a number of difficulties between the two parties. It has contributed to the smooth operation of the internal market, sustainable development with the ratification by the Russian Federation of the Kyoto Protocol, and the security of energy supply. This exchange has also resolved important questions such as the preservation of long-term supply contracts and the abolition of measures which are contrary to Community competition rules. European and Russian companies investing in the energy sector have benefited from this dialogue, which thus helps the creation of a pan-European energy market[2].

On 25 October 2005, the EU and eight partners in south-east Europe (Albania, Bosnia and Herzegovina, Bulgaria, Croatia, Former Yugoslav Republic of Macedonia, Romania, Serbia and Montenegro and UNMIK, on behalf of Kosovo) signed the **Energy Community Treaty** in order to create the legal framework for an integrated energy market[3]. As a result of this treaty, the internal market for energy will be extended into the Balkan peninsula as a whole. This means that the relevant *acquis communautaire* on energy, environment and competition will be implemented there. Market opening, investment guarantees and firm regulatory control of the energy sectors will also be enhanced.

19.1.3. Community energy strategy

A consultative committee, known as the "**European Energy and Transport Forum**", is made up of qualified individuals competent to consider matters relating to energy and transport as well as the interaction between these two policies[4]. It includes representatives of operators, manufacturers and managers of networks and infrastructures, transport users and energy consumers, trade unions, environmental protection and safety associations and the academic world. It acts as monitoring centre for energy and transport policy, particularly on competitiveness and structural adjustments in these sectors, while having due regard for environmental, social and safety concerns. A Commission Green Paper entitled "Towards a **European Strategy for the Security of Energy Supply**" noted that the European Union is becoming increasingly dependent on external energy

---

[1] Final Act of the Conference, Annex 1, Annex 3 and Decision 94/998, OJ L 380, 31.12.1994, Amendment to the Treaty and Decision 98/537, OJ L 252, 12.09.1998 and Decision 2001/595, OJ L 209, 02.08.2001.
[2] COM (2004) 777, 13 December 2004.
[3] Treaty, OJ L 198, 20.07.2006 and Decision 2005/905, OJ L 329, 16.12.2005.
[4] Decision 2001/546, OJ L 195, 19.07.2001.

sources and that its dependence could rise to 70% in 20 to 30 years' time (compared with 50% at present)[1]. It therefore stressed the need to balance supply policy against clear action for a demand policy. The Commission called for a genuine change in consumers' behaviour so as to orientate demand towards better managed, more efficient and more environmentally friendly consumption, particularly in the transport and building sectors, and to give priority to the development of new and renewable sources on the energy supply side in order to respond to the challenge of global warming.

European **energy markets** face a number of problems: the growing threats of climate change, slow progress in energy efficiency and the use of renewables, the need for transparency, further integration and interconnection of national energy markets and the need for large investments in energy infrastructure. Moreover, Europe has to deal with major challenges in **energy supply**: the ongoing difficult situation on the oil and gas markets, the increasing import dependency and limited diversification achieved so far, high and volatile energy prices, growing global energy demand, security risks affecting producing and transit countries as well as transport routes.

Following the ideas of the Commission, a multiannual programme for actions in the field of energy, called **"Intelligent Energy - Europe"** (2003-2006), supports sustainable development in the energy context, making a balanced contribution to the achievement of the following general objectives: security of energy supply, competitiveness, and environmental protection[2]. Four specific areas are covered: rational use of energy and demand management (SAVE), new and renewable energy sources (ALTENER), the energy aspects of transport (STEER) and international promotion in the field of renewable energy sources and energy efficiency (COOPENER). Six types of actions are proposed for each area: implementation of strategy, creation of financial and market structures and instruments, promotion of systems and equipment to facilitate the transition between demonstration and commercialisation, development of information and education structures, and the monitoring and evaluation of the impact of the actions.

In a 2006 Green Paper the Commission defines a European energy policy, which should aim at three major objectives: sustainable development, competitiveness and security of supply[3]. It calls for a debate in six major domains:

- the achievement of an **internal energy market**, with measures concerning, amongst other things, a priority European interconnection plan and a European energy regulator, which could have decision-making powers for common rules and approaches;

- the **security of energy supply**, which should be based on the principle of solidarity between Member States with the creation of a European energy supply observatory and a revision of the existing Community legislation on oil and gas stocks;

- a more sustainable, efficient and diverse **energy mix**, which can be achieved through an analysis of all advantages and drawbacks of different sources of energy;

- an action plan on **energy efficiency and renewable energy** sources which would lay down feasible objectives by 2020 and beyond, in order to establish a climate of stability for investments and improve competitiveness of renewable energy in Europe;

- a plan for strategic **energy technologies** in order to allow European companies to take a place at the forefront of this sector;

- a **common external energy policy** creating a pan-European energy community with a common regulatory space reflecting the interdependence between Europe and its suppliers, including Russia, its principal supplier, and guaranteeing infrastructures necessary for the EU's security of supply.

---

[1] COM (2000) 769.
[2] Decision 1230/2003, OJ L 176, 15.07.2003 and Decision 787/2004, OJ L 138, 30.04.2004.
[3] COM/2006/105, 08.03.2006.

19.2. Internal energy market

The **first wing of the common energy policy** aims to establish a genuine internal market for the products and services of the energy sector. Through the removal of barriers, whether of public or private origin, and the establishment of common rules, the opening up of energy markets should ensure the availability of energy on the most economic conditions for the end-users whether these are high energy consuming industries or just private individuals. The energy sector, a source of high value contracts, finds itself in the front-line of general public procurement policy and should benefit from the openness it provides [see section 6.3.]. Fiscal alignment by the convergence of the real rates of excise taxes, pursued by taxation policy, is crucially important for the completion of the internal market for oil products [see section 14.2.3.]. Last but not least, the introduction of competition in those sectors in which public monopolies persist could play a prime role in the integration of the markets and in the competitiveness of the EU economy [see section 15.5.4.].

The establishment of a real internal market for energy also depends on the development of **energy trans-European networks**, which should "irrigate" the whole territory of the European Union with cheap, diversified - from the supply point of view - and environment-friendly energy [see section 6.8.]. This development is particularly important for the less favoured regions, which previously had no access to the big interconnected networks for gas and electricity, this being a cause but also a consequence of their underdevelopment [see section 12.1.1.]. In the meantime, the Regulation on notifying the Commission of investment projects of interest to the Community in the petroleum, natural gas and electricity sectors aims at a certain coordination of trans-European energy investments[1].

In general, the full **application of Community internal market law** - and in particular of provisions relating to the free movement of goods and services, to monopolies, to undertakings (firms, businesses) and to State aids - is the main path to a better integrated energy market. The integration of this market is fundamental for the competitivity of the economy of the EU and for the wellbeing of its citizens. But the energy sector does not fully benefit from this integration because the Member States still use the security of supply and the diversity of their energy situation as excuse for the preservation of their national monopolies and of their different regulatory frameworks.

19.2.1. Electricity and gas markets

The prime objective in the field of the internal energy market is to **liberalise and integrate the electricity and natural gas markets**. The most important challenge here is to apply the competition rules of the Treaty to the monopolies for transmission and distribution of gas and electricity, even though these are entrusted with the operation of services of general economic interest [see sections 6.6.4. and 15.5.4.]. Another issue is the reconciliation of the objectives of the prevention of trade barriers and of energy efficiency by way of the adoption of European standards established by the European Standardisation Bodies (CEN/CENELEC) [see section 6.2.3.]. A final problem is in the monitoring of the markets and the cooperation on interconnected systems between national regulatory authorities in both the gas and electricity sectors.

---

[1] Regulation 736/96, OJ L 102, 25.04.1996.

In the early 1990s, some concrete steps were taken in the direction of the integration of the electricity and gas markets. Thus, a Directive relating to the **transit of electricity** through the major European networks, aims at contributing to better integration of the internal market in electricity, through removing the obstacles to electricity trade between major networks[1]. Similarly, a Directive on the **transit of natural gas** through major networks aims at facilitating trade in natural gas[2]. Contracts on the transit of electricity and natural gas between major networks are negotiated between the entities with responsibility for these networks and the relevant bodies in the Member States. Transit conditions must be non-discriminatory and impartial as regards all the parties involved, must not contain unfair clauses or unjustified restrictions and must not place in danger either supply security or the quality of the service provided. Should a disagreement arise, parties concerned by transit contracts have the right to take their case to a conciliation body set up and presided by the Commission. A Directive, on the **transparency of gas and electricity prices** charged to industrial end-users, makes it compulsory for gas and electricity distribution concerns to communicate price data twice a year covering all the main categories of gas and electricity consumers[3].

Serious steps towards the **liberalisation of the electricity and gas sectors** were taken in the late 1990s. Community Directives, revised in 2003, set up common rules for the internal market in electricity[4] and gas[5]. They are based on a balanced approach concerning access to the systems, public service obligations and competition rules and on the broad application of the subsidiarity principle [see section 3.2.], in order to take account of the different national electricity and gas systems, thus facilitating their incorporation into national law. The Directives lay down the rules relating to the organisation and functioning of the electricity and gas sectors, access to the market, the criteria and procedures applicable to calls for tenders and the granting of authorisations and the operation of systems. They also set up a European Regulators Group for Electricity and Gas, but they give the regulatory authorities in the Member States, an essential role in the smooth operation of the internal market.

A Regulation set up fair rules for **cross-border exchanges in electricity**, thus enhancing competition within the internal electricity market, taking into account the specificities of national and regional markets[6]. To this end, it established a compensation mechanism for cross border flows of electricity and set up harmonised principles on cross-border transmission charges and the allocation of available capacities of interconnections between national transmission systems.

Directive 2005/89 establishes measures aimed at safeguarding **security of electricity supply** so as to ensure the proper functioning of the internal market for electricity and to ensure: (a) an adequate level of generation capacity; (b) an adequate balance between supply and demand; and (c) an appropriate level of interconnection between Member States for the development of the internal market[7].

Regulation 1775/2005 aims at setting non-discriminatory rules for **access conditions to natural gas transmission systems** taking into account the specificities of national and regional markets with a view to ensuring the proper functioning of the internal gas market[8]. This objective includes the setting of harmonised principles for tariffs, or

---

[1]   Directive 90/547, OJ L 313, 13.11.1990 repealed by Directive 2003/54, OJ L 176, 15.07.2003.
[2]   Directive 91/296, OJ L 147, 12.06.1991 repealed by Directive 2003/55, OJ L 176, 15.07.2003.
[3]   Directive 90/377, OJ L 185, 17.07.1990 and Directive 93/87, OJ L 277, 10.11.1993.
[4]   Directive 2003/54, OJ L 176, 15.07.2003 last amended by Decision 2006/859, OJ L 332, 30.11.2006.
[5]   Directive 2003/55, OJ L 176, 15.07.2003.
[6]   Regulation 1228/2003, OJ L 176, 15.07.2003 last amended by Decision 2006/770, OJ L 312, 11.11.2006.
[7]   Directive 2005/89, OJ L 33, 04.02.2006.
[8]   Regulation 1775/2005, OJ L 289, 03.11.2005.

the methodologies underlying their calculation, for access to the network, the establishment of third party access services and harmonised principles for capacity allocation and congestion management, the determination of transparency requirements, balancing rules and imbalance charges and facilitating capacity trading.

A series of guidelines are designed to create a favourable environment for the development of trans-European energy **networks in the electricity and gas sectors**. [see section 6.8.][1]. They set the following objectives: strengthening the security of the EU's energy supplies by improving the efficiency and reliability of all European electricity and gas systems; ensuring effective operation of the internal market by providing an infrastructure which allows supply to respond to the demand for natural gas and electricity throughout the EU; promoting economic and social cohesion by facilitating the development and reducing the isolation of the less-favoured, peripheral and island regions. They also take account of the rapidly changing market, especially for natural gas, the acceleration towards the extension of the interconnected networks across the European continent and the prospects of Union enlargement. Priority projects must be compatible with sustainable development, have a significant impact on the competitive operation of the internal market and/or contribute to strengthening security of supply in the Community.

In order to attain these objectives, the guidelines envisage, on the one hand, broad lines of action to identify projects of common interest and, on the other, technical, administrative, legal and financial measures, concerning in particular authorisation procedures. Indeed, unlike transport networks, the realisation of trans-European energy networks is not in the first instance a financing problem, because investments in these networks are generally lucrative. The problem in this sector is that **investments are often hampered by administrative constraints**, notably delays and blockages in obtaining the authorisations needed for the construction and operation of oil and gas pipelines, by exclusive import and export rights and by transport monopolies. Moreover, natural gas pipelines have to be built from gas fields, which are often located at great distances from the markets in Western Europe. Since trans-European networks have to be developed on all the countries of Europe and the basin of the Mediterranean, the priority for the European Union in this sector is to remove or bypass these obstacles. Therefore, the Commission recommends increased transparency and coordination of authorisation procedures and collaboration between the Member States and, where appropriate, with the third countries concerned[2].

The Court of Justice has recognised that the **exclusive rights** granted to certain establishments to import and export gas and electricity give rise to discrimination against importers and exporters established in other Member States, contrary to Article 37 (new Art. 31) of the EC Treaty. According to the Court, this type of discrimination can only be justified by Article 90 (new Art. 86 TEC) if the tasks assigned to undertakings entrusted with the operation of services of general interest can be achieved only through the grant of exclusive rights and provided that the development of trade is not affected to an extent contrary to the interests of the Community[3].

19.2.2. Solid fuel market

The single market in the coal sector was **regulated, until July 2002, by the European Coal and Steel Community (ECSC) Treaty** [see section 2.1.]. Thanks to this Treaty, import and export taxes, taxes having equivalent effect, and quantitative restrictions on product movement were abolished. The Paris Treaty laid down rules for agreements, company concentrations and dominant positions, and prohibited unfair competitive practices and discriminatory practices, i.e. the application by a seller of dissimilar conditions to comparable transactions and especially on the grounds of the nationality of the buyer. It thus succeeded to ensure that users have equal access to sources of production and to promote the development of international trade. The "acquis communautaire" in the coal sector is now guaranteed by the EC Treaty.

The ECSC has enabled Europe to maintain a leading position in the field of mining technology and clean coal combustion. Considerable spin off effects have also been seen in other industries. Although the ECSC Treaty succeeded in creating a common coal

---

[1] Decision 1364/2006, OJ L 262, 22.09.2006.
[2] Recommendation 1999/28, OJ L 8, 14.01.1999.
[3] Judgment of 23 October 1997, Cases C-157/94, C-158/94, C-159/94 and C-160/94, ECR 1997, p. I-5699, I-5789, I-5815 and I-5851.

market, it was **not able to prevent coal from being swept aside by oil**, which is a more flexible, easier to handle and a less expensive product. Preservation of coal's supremacy would have required measures much more drastic and expensive, in the form of a coal policy modelled on the Common Agricultural Policy [see sections 21.1.1 and 21.4.]. Europe of the1960's, awash with oil supply, was not prepared to pay the price of its energy independence. Thus, investment in the coal industry of the EU continued to fall during the 1990s in the face of international competition and as a result of the gradual shift in Member States' domestic policies.

The **coal industry has not had luck** on its side. When the common market was taking its first steps, Community coal undertakings only partially benefited from soaring demand because extraction conditions and limited financing possibilities made sizeable short-term production rises impossible. Then, from 1958 onwards, the decisive entry of oil dealt the coal industry a hard blow obliging the closure of most coalmines in Europe. The remaining coalmines were faced with such large cost rises that even after the great surge of oil prices in the 1970s, they only managed to stabilise production.

However, **the common coal market has several achievements**, such as the gradual switch from a regulated management system conditioned by the war to a free market governed by competition; the abolition of agreements, concerted practices, dominant positions and other monopoly structures which were characteristic of this market; the impact of integration on intra-Community trade; and last but not least, the orderly retreat of the coal industry, which has meant that 700,000 workers have been laid off in this sector during the 1970s and the 1980s in the original Member States without social upheaval thanks to Community measures providing aid, and that none of these States gave in to the temptation to pass on its difficulties to its neighbours, which could have been catastrophic.

Practically, only Germany, France, the United Kingdom, Poland, Hungary and the Czech Republic still produce coal. Given that the objective of security of energy supply justifies maintaining subsidised coal production, albeit on acceptable economic terms, the new Regulation on **State aid to the coal industry** allows the maintenance of coal-producing capability supported by State aid, while encouraging restructuring and activity reduction in this industry[1]. The information submitted to the Commission by the Member States is based on common definitions and criteria, so as to ensure comparability of data and enable the Commission to monitor compliance with the conditions for the granting of aid[2].

19.2.3. Nuclear energy market

The economic factors pertaining to the nuclear energy market have also not evolved in the manner predicted at the time of signature of the Euratom Treaty [see section 2.1.]. In the1950's, it was thought that the arrival on the industrial scene of nuclear energy was just around the corner and the drop in energy prices, which caused this event to be postponed, could not have been foreseen. Nuclear energy in fact only attained economic competitiveness after the 1973 crisis and the momentous increase of oil prices. In the period prior to this, the **absence of a genuine nuclear energy market** forced each Member State to create an artificial one through vast government research programmes targeted more at the acquisition of basic knowledge than at the encouragement of industrial projects. This pushed the Member States off the straight and narrow path defined by the EAEC (Euratom) Treaty onto parallel technological roads, such as uranium enrichment systems, and sparked off a serious crisis in Euratom between 1965 and 1972.

Nevertheless, the Euratom Treaty provides for a well-functioning **common nuclear energy market**, characterised by: the abolition of customs duties, charges having equivalent effect and all quantitative restrictions on imports and exports of natural and enriched uranium and other nuclear materials (Art. 93 EAEC); the free movement and free establishment of individuals and companies in the common nuclear energy market (Art. 96 and 97 EAEC); the free movement of capital for the financing of nuclear activi-

---

[1]   Regulation 1407/2002, OJ L 205, 02.08.2002.
[2]   Decision 2002/871, OJ L 300, 05.11.2002.

ties (Art. 99 and 100 EAEC); the free determination of prices as a result of balancing supply and demand within the Supply Agency (Art. 67 EAEC) and the prohibition of discriminatory pricing practices designed to secure a privileged position for certain users (Art. 68 EAEC). Economic operators have to inform the Commission of major investment projects prior to their implementation (Art. 41 EAEC) and thus the Commission can inform governments and economic operators in the Member States of the aims and prospects for nuclear energy production in the Community (Art. 40 EAEC).

One interesting feature of the Euratom Treaty is that it offers special status and certain advantages to **joint undertakings**, which are of primordial importance to the development of the Community's nuclear industry (Art. 45 EAEC). The Council, acting unanimously on a Commission proposal, can grant each joint undertaking all or some of the advantages listed in Annex III to the Euratom Treaty, such as recognition that public interest status applies to the acquisition of immovable property required for the establishment of the joint undertakings or the exemption from all duties and charges when a venture is established (Art. 48 EAEC). In 1978, this status was granted to an undertaking of vital importance for the growth of the Community nuclear industry, namely the joint venture which, as seen in the previous chapter, builds the **Joint European Torus (JET)**, a thermonuclear fusion prototype [see section 18.3.2.][1].

Safety, a major feature of the common nuclear energy market, is perhaps the most important joint achievement in this field. This achievement is, however, of fundamental importance, because it determines the acceptance of the nuclear energy by the public. **Nuclear safety** is moreover approached from various different angles. Chapter VII of the Euratom Treaty provides for "safeguards". The Commission must be informed of the basic technical specifications of any nuclear plant. The Commission also has to approve procedures for the chemical processing of irradiated materials (Art. 78 EAEC). It must check that all ores, source materials and special fissile materials are not diverted from their intended uses as declared by the users (Art. 77 EAEC) and that the latter respect international safeguards and non-proliferation arrangements laid down by an Euratom Regulation[2]. The Commission can send inspectors to the Member States who must be given access at any time to all premises, all information and all individuals to the extent necessary to check the ores, source materials and special fissile materials used by the 750 or so nuclear installations, including some 130 reactors, in the Community (Art. 81 EAEC). The **Euratom Safeguards Office** has the task of ensuring that nuclear material is not diverted from its intended use within the European Union and that the Community's safeguards obligations under agreements with third countries or international organisations are complied with. In fact, during the early 1990's the Euratom Safeguards Office was called several times to take action in relation to cases of trafficking in nuclear materials from Eastern Europe, but in subsequent evaluations (in 1999 and 2000), the Safeguards Office did not find any indication that nuclear material had been diverted from its intended peaceful use[3].

Should individuals or undertakings be found to have infringed their **safety obligations**, the Commission can impose penalties, which can in serious cases take the form of the total or partial removal of source materials or special fissile materials[4]. Member States are obliged to ensure that the penalties are implemented and, if necessary, that the infringements are corrected by those responsible for them (Art. 83 EAEC). An Agreement between Euratom and the International Atomic Energy Agency (IAEA) allows a number of joint inspections of Community installations enabling the IAEA to rationalise its inspection activities and reduce their cost by

[1]   Decision 78/471 and 78/472, OJ L 151, 07.06.1978 and Decision 98/585, OJ L 282, 20.10.1998.
[2]   Regulation 302/2005, OJ L 54, 28.02.2005.
[3]   COM (2003) 764.
[4]   See, e.g., Decision 92/194, OJ L 88, 03.04.1992

relying on the Euratom infrastructure (New Partnership Approach). The aim of the IAEA safeguard system, in which the Euratom Safeguards Office plays an important role, is to develop new techniques and methods for the effective detection of undeclared nuclear activities. The European Atomic Energy Community has signed the International Convention on Nuclear Safety concluded in September 1994 in the context of the IAEA[1]. Its aim is to promote a high level of safety in nuclear power stations worldwide, to prevent accidents and to reduce their consequences by defining statutory obligations. In the framework of its strategy against proliferation of weapons of mass destruction, the EU supports IAEA activities under its nuclear security programme[2]. The EAEC has signed agreements for cooperation in the peaceful uses of nuclear energy with the United States[3] and Argentina[4].

In addition to this, there is a Community programme on **protection against radiation**, namely health protection measures for the population in general and workers in particular against the dangers of ionising radiation (Chapter III, Euratom). Community Directives set basic safety standards for the protection of public health and worker health against the dangers inherent in ionising radiation [see section 13.5.8.][5], particularly in relation to medical exposure to such radiation[6], and organise the monitoring of transfers of radioactive waste between the Member States and on entrance to and exit from the Community[7]. The Community is active in the field of research on reactor safety which, as seen in the previous chapter, is conducted in the Joint Research Centre and in specialised national research centres [see section 18.2.4.]. The harmonisation of safety criteria and practices in the Member States produced significant results, particularly with regard to the seismic re-evaluation of nuclear power stations and to highly-automated safeguards systems.

Indeed, since 1990, the Commission has initiated an **inter-European cooperation** for the exploitation of nuclear installations. The cooperation notably relates to nuclear safeguards in the countries of Central and Eastern Europe and in the Commonwealth of Independent States (CIS). This cooperation has allowed the Euratom Safeguards Office to become better acquainted with specific features of the nuclear capacity of the former Soviet Union, chiefly with regard to the mixed (civil/military) nature of the installations. The Euratom Safeguards Office offers the services of its specialists to assist in training CIS inspectors and thus provide a sufficiently high level of materials safeguards. The Instrument for Pre-Accession Assistance (IPA) and the European Neighbourhood and Partnership Instrument (ENPI) [see sections 25.2. and 25.4.] help candidate countries and other countries on the periphery of the EU improve the safety of their nuclear installations. Moreover, the Commission is empowered to use Euratom borrowings to finance projects which increase the safety of nuclear power stations in many of these countries[8]. The Community contributes to the European Bank for Reconstruction and Development fund set up to assist Ukraine in transforming the Chernobyl sarcophagus into a safe and environmentally stable system[9]. Cooperation agreements between the European Community and Ukraine in the fields of nuclear safety and controlled nuclear fusion are aimed at the definition and application of scientifically warranted and internationally accepted nuclear safety guidelines, including dismantling of nuclear installations, research and development on nuclear material safeguards, and prevention of illicit trafficking of nuclear material[10].

19.2.4. Oil market

Although it is less developed than the nuclear market, a **single market in petroleum products exists** in many respects. On the basis of the EEC (now the EC) Treaty governing the oil market, all quantitative restrictions to trade between Member States and all measures having equivalent effect have been abolished. Tariff obstacles to trade in petroleum products were phased out in July 1968. On the external market, the Common Customs Tariff set a zero rate for oil and very low rates for refined products. The latter were further reduced in the framework of the General Agreement on Tariffs and Trade [see section 23.4.]. All the freedoms written into the Treaty of Rome, such as freedom of establishment and the freedom to provide services, are applicable in the oil sector [see chapter 6].

---

[1] Decision 1999/819, OJ L 318, 11.12.1999.
[2] Joint action 2004/495/CFSP, OJ L 182, 19.05.2004 and Joint Action 2005/574/CFSP, OJ L 193, 23.07.2005.
[3] Agreement 96/314, OJ L 120, 20.05.1996, p. 1-36.
[4] Agreement 97/738, OJ L 296, 30.10.1997, p. 32-40.
[5] Directive 96/29, OJ L 159, 29.06.1996.
[6] Directive 97/43, OJ L 180, 09.07.1997.
[7] Directive 2006/117, OJ L 337, 05.12.2006.
[8] Decision 77/270, OJ L 88, 06.04.1977 and Decision 94/179, OJ L 84, 29.03.1994.
[9] Decision 98/381, OJ L 171, 17.06.1998 and Decision 2001/824, OJ L 308, 27.11.2001.
[10] Decision 2002/924, OJ L 322, 27.11.2002.

Even if the **common oil market is not yet perfect**, petroleum products can move freely from Member State to Member State. The big oil companies have been able to build refineries at certain nerve centres in the common market to supply refined products to networks covering neighbouring regions in two or more Member States. This means that refinery production and distribution activities can be rationalised to meet supply in surrounding regions without regard to national borders. Oil and gas pipelines consequently start their journey from the major ports of the Mediterranean and the North Sea, cut across one or several Member States and supply crude oil to the refineries of different oil companies situated in another Member State. Before the creation of the common market, it would have been unthinkable for a European state to entrust the supply of a product as vital as oil to the good will of one or several neighbouring countries. The European Community has rendered self-evident certain situations, which would have been inconceivable in the protectionist post-war period [see section 1.1.2.].

It must be said, however, that in a single market organised in the same manner as a national market, **price differences** for oil products, other than those due to transport costs, should logically only have been marginal and temporary, as they **should have been corrected by the transfer of products** from low-price to high-price regions in a short period of time. This is not yet the case in the internal market of the European Union where the pre-tax price differences for petroleum products are still important. The specificities of the oil market account in part for these price differences, as, usually, oil products are transferred at prices which do not make allowance for market conditions in the country of destination. This may be due to the **oligopolistic structure of the oil industry** and in particular to the sales policy of the large companies which have a near 80% market share. While the oil multinationals trade petroleum products on a large scale, they do so at subsidiary-to-subsidiary transfer prices, which do not upset the conditions on each specific market.

The levelling out of petroleum product prices in the internal common market has also come to grief on **different price regulations** existing in the Member States. These regulations set the maximum prices at which the main petroleum products can be sold and are powerful economic and energy policy instruments. The problem is that there is no one simple formula for setting petroleum product prices and energy policy priorities vary from Member State to Member State. As a consequence, there is considerable variation in maximum price systems. The system, which exists in a particular country, influences the market policy of large oil companies and particularly the production cut in the refineries. Since the production cut is relatively flexible, it is in the interests of oil companies to produce larger quantities of the products which they can sell at a high price on any market at a given moment, while keeping prices within the ceilings stipulated by regulations.

19.3. Energy supply

Security of energy supply, the second wing of the common energy policy, is defined as the ability to ensure the continued satisfaction of essential energy needs by means of, on the one hand, sufficient internal resources exploited under acceptable economic conditions and, on the other, of accessible, stable and diversified external sources. With this definition, most European countries had a more secure energy supply in the 1950s than they had in the 1970s or even in the 1990s, despite their efforts in those three decades. Indeed, at the beginning of the 1950s, the Community's energy economy revolved around indigenous resources, chiefly coal. In 1955, coal met 64% of gross internal energy consumption in the then Community of Six; but little by little, **demand switched from primary energy to processed energy**, chiefly electricity and petroleum products. Due to strong growth in demand for light petroleum products (chiefly petrol), heavy fuels became residual products, which refiners wanted to get rid of at any price, often below that of crude oil. Unfortunately for coal, its main competitors were these heavy, industrial use fuels. In that oil was almost exclusively imported from third countries, the consequences on the Community's energy independence were plain to see. Energy independence was sacrificed on the altar of rapid industrial growth, stimulated by low energy prices.

Security of supply is closely bound up with energy demand. Steadily growing demand constitutes a major risk where the security of energy supply is concerned. Following a Commission Green Paper, entitled "Towards a European strategy for the **security of energy supply**"[1], a consensus has emerged around some key issues, such as the need to considerably improve energy efficiency, to step up the promotion of renewables, to reduce environmental damage from energy use, to improve the investment climate in supplier and transit countries, and to develop the producer-consumer dialogue[2].

19.3.1. Energy objectives and rational energy use

Few Community measures have aimed directly at **rational energy use**. These were notably: the Directive on summertime arrangements[3], which it was felt could save electricity; and the Directive on crude-oil savings relating to the quality of petrol and diesel fuels[4]. However, the **harmonisation of legislations** in the context of the common market, while ensuring that standards for rational energy use did not become new technical barriers to the free movement of goods and did not distort competition within the common market, encouraged energy savings [see section 6.2.]. Such harmonisation was achieved by Directives, such as those on: setting of ecodesign requirements for energy-using products[5], the alignment of legislation covering the fuel consumption of motor vehicles[6] and the energy performance of buildings[7].

As part of the SAVE programme [see section 19.1.3], the Council has already adopted: a Directive on the standardisation of efficiency requirements for new hot-water boilers fired with liquid or gaseous fuels[8]; a Directive allowing consumers to choose the most energy-efficient domestic appliances, thanks to a label indicating their consumption of energy and other resources[9]; and a Directive on energy efficiency requirements for household electric refrigerators, freezers and combinations thereof[10]. In this context, the Commission has adopted Directives concerning the energy labelling of: refrigerators and freezers[11]; household dishwashers[12]; and household lamps[13].

Energy objectives converge with the environmental objectives pursued by the Directive on **energy end-use efficiency and energy services**[14] [see section 16.3.4], which seeks to enhance the cost-effective improvement of energy end-use efficiency in the Member States by: (a) providing the necessary indicative targets to remove market barriers and imperfections that impede the efficient end use of energy; and (b) creating the conditions for the development of a market for energy services and other energy efficiency improvement measures.

Thanks in part to various measures taken by the Member States at the prompting of Community institutions and in part to the reduction of energy demand and the increase of internal production, notably in the North Sea, the EU, in 2000, imported about half of its total energy needs compared with two-thirds twenty five years earlier. However, despite these improvements, the problems have not gone away. The **European Union still has to cope with a massive oil bill**, vast amounts of investment, and the implications for environmental pollution and energy dependence that cannot be reduced in any significant manner in the medium term.

[1] COM (2000) 769, 29 November 2000.
[2] COM (2002) 321, 26 June 2002.
[3] Directive 97/44, OJ L 206, 01.08.1997.
[4] Directive 98/70, OJ L 350, 28.12.1998 last amended by Directive 2003/17, OJ L 76, 22.03.2003.
[5] Directive 2005/32, OJ L 191, 22.07.2005.
[6] Directive 80/1268, OJ L 375, 31.12.1980 and Directive 2004/3, OJ L 19.02.2004.
[7] Directive 2002/91, OJ L 1, 04.01.2003.
[8] Directive 92/42, OJ L 167, 22.06.1992 and Directive 2005/32, OJ L 191, 22.07.2005.
[9] Directive 92/75, OJ L 297, 13.10.1992.
[10] Directive 96/57, OJ L 236, 18.09.1996 and Directive 2005/32, OJ L 191, 22.07.2005.
[11] Directive 94/2, OJ L 45, 17.02.1994 last amended by Directive 2003/66, OJ L 170, 09.07.2003.
[12] Directive 97/17, OJ L 118, 07.05.1997 and Directive 2006/80, OJ L 362, 20.12.2006.
[13] Directive 98/11, OJ L 71, 10.03.1998.
[14] Directive 2006/32, OJ L 114, 27.04.2006.

This is why, the Commission is proposing more drastic measures, notably **a tax based on the consumption of carbon dioxide**[1]. Such a tax would increase the price of energy, except for renewable sources, and help to save energy. It would thus set in motion dynamic changes, which would have beneficial consequences for the environment and a major impact on the Union's energy sector. This proposal is still under discussion within the Council, because it presents obvious difficulties, particularly due to its effects on the competitiveness of European industries compared to that of their competitors in the world. Other energy consuming countries should be persuaded to follow the Community's policies in this area, a particularly difficult task given the energy consumption habits of some countries.

19.3.2. Coal supply

Coal supply was essential for European reconstruction and economic growth at the time of creation of the European Coal and Steel Community. Regular supply of coal to the common market was the **prime objective of the ECSC Treaty** [see section 2.1.]. Chapter IV of the Treaty outlined measures to be taken in the event of shortage, notably through the sharing out of ECSC resources among the industries covered by its jurisdiction; but such a situation never developed. On the contrary, as mentioned above, Community coal, which played the lead role on the energy stage in the1950s, was relegated by the beginning of the 1960s to a supporting one by the newcomer to the scene, oil, and its demand declined sharply. Despite the great increase in electricity prices since the two oil shocks of the 1970s, the majority of Community mines were still not competitive and demand for coal continued to decline.

Coal is the most abundant non-renewable energy source available and will continue to play a very important role as a regulator of the Union's energy market, particularly in the generation of energy. In any case, **the European Union does not face a problem in coal supply**, both as far as indigenous resources are concerned, which are abundant, and imports from several third countries, which are more competitive. After the expiration of the ECSC Treaty in July 2002, the common commercial policy of the EC covers the coal products [see chapter 23]. Any imported coal released for free movement in a Member State circulates freely in all the Community. However, there is Community surveillance of imports of hard coal originating in third countries[2]. The monitoring system entails the provision by the Member States of information concerning their imports of hard coal, including the prices charged and the breakdown of hard coal imports between electricity production and use in the Community steel industry.

19.3.3. Supply of nuclear fuels

Nuclear energy makes a significant contribution to the policy of diversifying energy supply and reducing overall emissions of CO_2. Supply of nuclear fuels is **a matter dealt with in some depth in the Euratom Treaty** [see section 2.1.]. Article 52 of this Treaty stipulates that supply of ores, source materials and special fissile materials is accomplished with respect of the principle of equal access to resources and through a common supply policy. For this purpose, all practices that seek to provide certain users with a privileged position are forbidden. The Treaty set up a **Supply Agency,** the organisation of which is provided for in Articles 53 and 54 (EAEC). The Agency, which has legal status and is financially independent, is governed by Statutes adopted by the Council on the basis of a Commission proposal. The Euratom Supply Agency is under the control of the Commission, which issues it with policy guidelines, has a right of veto on its deci-

---

[1] COM (92)226, 27.05.1992.
[2] Regulation 405/2003, OJ L 62, 06.03.2003.

sions and appoints its Director General[1]. In contrast with the coal and oil sectors, the nuclear sector is endowed with a strong common supply policy, exercised by the Agency, under the control of the Commission.

Article 52 (EAEC) grants the Agency two fundamental rights: (a) an option right on ores, source material and special fissile materials produced in the Member States and (b) the exclusive right to conclude contracts for the supply of ores, source materials and special fissile materials originating inside or outside the Community. The Agency's main role is to act as an **intermediary between producers and users.** Under Article 60 (EAEC), possible users periodically inform the Agency of their supply needs, specifying quantities, nature, places of origin, uses, price terms and so on, which would form the clauses of a contract which they would like to conclude. Producers inform the Agency of the supplies that they can put on the market, with all their specifications and notably the duration of the contracts. The Agency informs all potential users of supplies and of the demand volume brought to its attention, and invites them to order. Once it has all the orders, it makes known the terms at which they can be satisfied. In fact, the option right of the Agency, described in Article 57 (EAEC), gives it a *"de jure"* **monopoly** on the trade of ores, raw materials and special fissile materials intended for peaceful nuclear use in the Community.

The Agency, acting in the framework of agreements concluded between the Community and a third country or international organisation, has also the **exclusive right to conclude agreements** whose main object is the supply of ores, source materials or special fissile materials, such as uranium, plutonium, thorium and heavy water, originating outside the Community (Article 64 EAEC). In 1962, the Agency set this in motion by concluding a framework contract with the United States Atomic Energy Commission (USAEC) enabling Community undertakings to obtain enriched uranium at good price, regularity and safety terms. Since then the contract has been renewed and simplified as regards administrative formalities for the purchase of special fissile materials and other contracts have been concluded, notably with Canada and Australia, enabling the Community to diversify its supply sources in nuclear materials.

The bulk of Community supply continues to come via multiannual contracts, but due to the fact that the requirements of electricity companies for natural uranium and short- and medium-term enrichment services are now by and large met, very few long-term contracts are now concluded. The Agency rather concludes on spot purchases and swap transactions. The Community's level of dependence on imports of natural uranium is over 70% and its main suppliers are the independent States of the former Soviet Union, and in particular Russia, but there are eight external supplier countries and none accounts for more than 25% of total supplies. Thus, **the supply of the Union in nuclear fuels is quite secure**. Nevertheless, the Euratom Supply Agency encourages electricity companies to diversify their sources of supply in order to avoid excessive dependence on any one particular source. The uranium enrichment market in Europe is in fact very stable, with users in the Union covering most of their needs through long-term contracts with European suppliers.

19.3.4. Oil and natural gas supply

Contrary to the EAEC Treaty's concern for the supply of nuclear fuels, the **EEC Treaty did not show any particular interest** for the supply of oil and natural gas. The general clauses under the title "trade policy" clearly could not form the basis of a supply policy for products as important as oil and natural gas. The EEC Treaty did not even give the Community institutions the possibility of collecting and publishing information of vital importance for the common oil market, such as those covering investments, production or imports, as is done by the ECSC and Euratom Treaties for their respective areas. In light of the growing importance of oil in the 1960s, this vacuum was partly filled by the Council.

The most important measure is the **strategic storage of petroleum products**. A Council Directive obliges the Member States to maintain a minimum stock level of 90

---

[1]   OJ 32 11.05.1960, p. 777-779 and OJ L 193, 25.07.1975, p. 37-38.

days' consumption for crude oil and/or petroleum products, as a buffer against the effects of accidental or deliberate interruption in supplies and against the economic and political leverage enjoyed by suppliers[1]. Another measure is a Council Decision setting a Community target for the reduction of primary energy consumption in the event of supply difficulties of crude oil and petroleum products in order to ensure that these difficulties are spread fairly among all consumers[2].

A directive establishes measures to safeguard an adequate level of **security of gas supply**[3]. It clarifies the general roles and responsibilities of the different market players and implements specific non-discriminatory procedures to safeguard security of gas supply. While contributing to the smooth functioning of the internal gas market, it provides for a common framework within which Member States should define general, transparent and non-discriminatory security of supply policies compatible with the requirements of the competitive internal gas market.

In the context of the completion of the internal market, a Directive on the conditions for granting and using **authorisations for oil and gas prospecting, exploration and extraction** is designed to ensure non-discriminatory access to and pursuit of these activities by Community companies in non-member countries under conditions which encourage greater competition in this sector[4]. However, Member States have sovereign rights over oil and gas resources on their territories. They therefore retain the right to determine the areas within their territory to be made available for oil and gas prospecting, exploration and production.

A Community procedure for information and consultation on **crude-oil supply costs** and the consumer prices of petroleum products was set up in 1976 and simplified in 1999 via the publication of a "weekly bulletin" by the Commission[5]. The Council adopted in 1979 a Regulation introducing the **registration of crude oil imports and petroleum products** in the Community[6]. On the basis of this Regulation and one specifying the rules under which registration of crude oil imports into the Community is carried out[7], the Member States notify the Commission of information revealing the terms at which imports have taken place. This information system was improved in the 1980s in the framework of the International Energy Agency, and it contributes to the transparency of the Community's oil market.

On 30 May 2000, the Council invited the Commission to monitor and analyse on an ongoing basis, in close cooperation with the Member State and the European gas industry, developments in the **security of EU gas supply** in terms of both internal (short-term and operational) and external (longer-term and strategic) security aspects, and to agree together with the Member States (in conformity with the principle of subsidiarity) on the most appropriate ways of ensuring transparency and regular exchange of data and relevant information between the different market players, including the gas industry, and the authorities.

Thanks to the massive exploitation of British oil in the 1980s, to crude oil savings achieved by the quality of petrol and diesel fuels[8] and the **diversification of supply sources**, Community supply of oil and natural gas was undoubtedly better guaranteed at the beginning of the 1990s than at the beginning of the1970s, as demonstrated by the lack of panic in response to the Gulf crisis at the end of 1990, sparked by Iraq's invasion of Kuwait. However, the Community is still vulnerable as regards its oil and natural gas supply and lacks a genuine policy in this field. Although there is a common interest in a common development of strategic relations with external suppliers, the governments of the Member States continue to guard their prerogatives jealously.

---

[1] Directive 98/93, OJ L 358, 31.12.1998.
[2] Decision 77/706, OJ L 292, 16.11.1977.
[3] Directive 2004/67, OJ L 127, 29.04.2004.
[4] Directive 94/22, OJ L 164, 30.06.1994.
[5] Decision 1999/280, OJ L 110, 28.04.1999 and Decision 1999/566, OJ L 216, 14.08.1999.
[6] Regulation 1893/79, OJ L 220, 30.08.1979 and Regulation 4152/88, OJ L 367, 31.12.1988.
[7] Regulation 2592/79, OJ L 297, 24.11.1979 and Regulation 1370/90, OJ L 133, 24.05.1990.
[8] Directive 98/70, OJ L 350, 28.12.1998 last amended by Directive 2003/17, OJ L 76, 22.03.2003.

19.3.5. New technologies and new energy sources

Fortunately for the Union, new energy technologies and new energy sources offer **an alternative route to supply security**. Moreover, **new and renewable energies** (solar, wind, hydroelectric, geothermal, biomass) can generate economic activity, thereby creating added value and employment in Europe. Furthermore, they both improve the quality of the environment and standards of living, and are particularly important for the less developed regions of the EU, which have considerable potential for the development of renewable energy resources. For these reasons, a directive commits the Member States to meeting national targets for their future consumption of **electricity from renewable energy sources** consistent with the indicative overall target of 12% of gross inland energy consumption in 2010[1]. In this context, a directive establishes a framework for the promotion and development of cogeneration, that is, the simultaneous generation in one process of heat and electrical and/mechanical power, as a means of improving security of energy supply[2].

The **ALTENER programme** , which is part of the multiannual programme for action in the field of energy (2003 - 2006)[3] [see section 19.1.3.], aims at the promotion of new and renewable energy sources for centralised and decentralised production of electricity and heat and their integration into the local environment and the energy systems. It focuses among other things on legislation and standardisation to accelerate the maturity of the market for renewable energies such as hydroelectric power, biofuels (deriving from agricultural and forestry products, residues and waste) and biomass (from cereals, oil seeds, pulses and beets).

Under the thematic priority of "sustainable development, global change and ecosystems" [see section 18.4.1.], the **common research policy** tries to encourage the deployment of technologies and to help promote changes in energy demand patterns and consumption behaviour by improving energy efficiency and integrating renewable energy into the energy system[4]. The aim is to bring to the market improved renewable energy technologies and to integrate renewable energy into networks and supply chains. The research effort is focused notably on: energy savings and energy efficiency, including those to be achieved through the use of renewable raw materials; the efficiency of combined production of electricity, heating and cooling services, by using new technologies; and alternative motor fuels, such biofuels, natural gas and hydrogen.

A Directive aims at promoting the use of biofuels or other renewable fuels to replace diesel or petrol for transport purposes in the Member States, with a view to contributing to objectives such as meeting climate change commitments, environmentally friendly security of supply and promoting renewable energy sources[5].

19.4. Appraisal and outlook

There is a general impression that a common energy policy is non-existent or, at best, ineffective. This impression arises chiefly from **confusion between energy policy and oil supply policy**. The latter is clearly of vital importance and is still lacking. But it is only a part of energy policy. It cannot be denied that the common coal, oil and nuclear energy markets have been largely achieved thanks to Community policy. But their exis-

---

[1]   Directive 2001/77, OJ L 283, 27.10.2001.
[2]   Directive 2004/8, OJ L 52, 21.02.2004.
[3]   Decision 1230/2003, OJ L 176, 15.07.2003 last amended by Decision 787/2004, OJ L 138, 30.04.2004.
[4]   Decision 2002/834, OJ L 294, 29.10.2002.
[5]   Directive 2003/30, OJ L 123, 17.05. 2003.

tence tends to be taken for granted and similarly significant achievements are expected in the area of supply, notably oil supply. The fact that the EEC Treaty and now the EC Treaty did not provide for such a policy is often forgotten. The silence of the Treaty means, however, that the Member States do not want to commit themselves in a common policy for oil and gas supply.

Another fact often overlooked is that in the1960s, all the Member States chose to boost industrial growth through low energy prices rather than promoting indigenous energy production by high prices. This preference for the industrial rather than energy sector culminated, at Community level, in a system diametrically opposed to the one existing for agriculture [see section 21.2.]. It was a political decision, the advantages of which cannot be denied, even with hindsight of the post-1973 events. In any case, the Member States, due to their different energy situations and interests, have proven unable to conduct a common supply policy, which would have increased their negotiation power towards their main oil suppliers.

Thanks to the increase of internal production - notably in the North Sea - and to the diversification of fuels and suppliers, the Union is now in a much more comfortable situation than the one the Community has experienced in the mid-1970s. However, despite these improvements, the problems have not gone away. Since international political and economic developments are liable at any time to cause considerable increases in the price of oil and of products indexed to it, **the EU is always at risk** as regards competitiveness, employment and growth. This is why, a policy framework is needed in which Member States would be working towards agreed common objectives, notably balance and diversification in relation to the different sources of supply (by products and by geographical zones), the development of renewable sources and clean technologies, assisted by Community financial and fiscal measures and closely coordinated with other common policies, particularly the environment, transport and enterprise policies. Concerning hydrocarbon supply, in particular, the EU should ideally develop a common policy similar, as far as possible, to the one for the supply of nuclear fuels [see section 19.3.3.]. At least, it should promote greater coherence between national policies and develop a common voice in support of energy policy objectives when addressing third countries, more open relations with the producer countries, notably the OPEC countries, and enhanced cooperation with Central European countries and Russia.

Energy is certainly an important factor determining the economic performance of a country or of a group of countries such as the EU. The absence of a common oil and gas supply policy handicaps the common energy market and renders energy prices higher than they could be if the Union could use its economic weight to negotiate its overall supplies with producing countries as it does concerning its supplies of nuclear fuels. High energy prices mean a serious **competitive disadvantage for the businesses of the European Union** as compared with those of its main trading partners. Furthermore, economic performance is not measured only by industrial competitiveness, but also by the welfare of citizens in terms of the employment situation and the state of the environment. The reduction of greenhouse gas emissions requires common policies, such as a sustained commitment to energy efficiency and energy saving, a commitment to make more systematic use of energy sources with low or no CO_2 emissions and a reduction in the impact of the use of energy sources with high CO_2 emissions.

The best and most efficient way of taking into consideration **environmental concerns** would be the internalisation of external costs and benefits, which still charge the society at large with a large part of the cost of polluting activities. The internalisation of external costs could be achieved through fiscal measures such as the CO_2/energy tax proposed by the Commission, but such a tax would risk to penalise the European industry alone, whereas all polluting industries of developed countries should be equally concerned. The EU should use its international weight to persuade other major industrial competitors to follow suit, an undoubtedly difficult task, given the American attitude on this subject [see section 16.3.4.].

The availability of secure, sustainable and competitive sources of energy is essential to economic growth, prosperity and quality of life in the industrialised world. Economic progress in the developing world will lead to major increases in global energy demand, with possible implications for fuel prices, and could increase the already adverse effects of energy consumption on health and the environment of the planet. These problems can only be mitigated through concerted international effort to develop promising technologies and new energy sources. In view of the expected growth in demand for energy worldwide, in the foreseeable future, increasing use should be made in both developed and developing countries of all potential energy sources and all new technologies. The common energy policy could thus encourage sustainable development both in Europe and in the rest of the world.

Bibliography on energy policy

- BURTEEL Paul. *A competitive electricity market of European dimension: a goal within reach.* Brussels: Eurelectric, 2006.
- CAMERON Peter. "The consumer and the internal market in energy: who benefits?" in *European Law Review*, v. 31, n. 1, February 2006, p. 114-124.
- CRIQUI Patrick (et al.). "Charbon" in *Revue de l'énergie*, v. 57, n. 573, septembre-octobre 2006, p. 293-333.
- DEFFEYES Kenneth. *Beyond oil: the view from Hubbert's peak.* New York: Hill and Wang, 2005.
- EUROPEAN COMMISSION. Green Paper: A European Strategy for Sustainable, Competitive and Secure Energy. COM/2006/105. Luxembourg: EUR-OP*, 2006.

  - *Energy and environment in the European Union: tracking progress towards integration.* Luxembourg: EUR-OP*, 2006.

  - *Energy technologies: knowledge, perception, measures.* Luxembourg: EUR-OP*, 2006.

  - *Energy futures: the role of research and technological development.* Luxembourg: EUR-OP*, 2006.

  - *Transition to a sustainable energy system for Europe: the R&D perspective: a summary report by the Advisory Group on Energy.* Luxembourg: EUR-OP*, 2006.

- FINON Dominique. "L'interdépendance gazière de la Russie et de l'Union européenne: quel équilibre entre le marché et la géopolitique?" in *Revue de l'énergie*, 57e année, n. 574, novembre-décembre 2006, p. 373-394.
- GRESSIER Claude (et al.). "L'énergie et les transports" in *Transports*, année 51, n. 439, septembre-octobre 2006, p. 281-312.
- HELM Dieter (ed.). "The new energy paradigm", *Oxford Review of Economic Policy*, v. 21, n. 1, Spring 2005, p. 1-153.
- JOSKOW Paul (et al.). "Regulation of the electricity market" in *CESifo DICE Report: Journal for Institutional Comparisons*, v. 4, n. 2, Summer 2006, p. 3-38.
- JONES Christopher (et al. eds.). *EU energy law.* 2nd ed. Leuven: Claeys & Casteels,2006.
- KONOPLYANIK A. "Russian gas to Europe: from long-term contracts, on-border trade and destination clauses to ...?", *Journal of Energy & Natural Resources Law*, v. 23, n. 3, August 2005, p. 282-307.
- KUNSTLER James Howard. *La fin du pétrole: le vrai défi du XXIe siècle.* Paris: Plon, 2005.
- LESTRANGE Cédric de. *Géopolitique du pétrole: un nouveau marché, de nouveaux risques, des nouveaux mondes.* Paris: Technip, 2005.
- MARKANDYA Anil (et al.). "Energy intensity in transition economies: is there convergence towards the EU average?" in *Energy economics*, v. 28, n. 1, January 2006, p. 121-145.
- MONS Ludovic. *Les enjeux de l'énergie : pétrole, nucléaire, et après?* Paris: Larousse, 2005.
- ORGANISATION FOR ECONOMIC COOPERATION AND DEVELOPMENT. *Resources to reserves: oil and gas technologies for the energy markets of the future.* Paris: OECD, 2005.

*The publications of the Office for Official Publications of the European Communities (EUR-OP) exist usually in all official languages of the EU.

Chapter 20

TRANSPORT POLICY

Diagram of the chapter

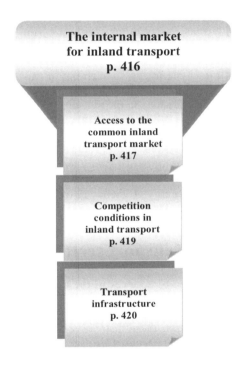

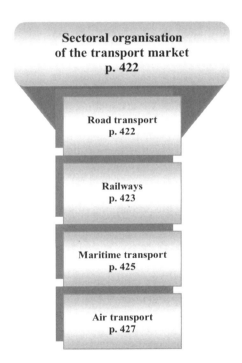

The internal market for inland transport — p. 416

Access to the common inland transport market — p. 417

Competition conditions in inland transport — p. 419

Transport infrastructure — p. 420

Sectoral organisation of the transport market — p. 422

Road transport — p. 422

Railways — p. 423

Maritime transport — p. 425

Air transport — p. 427

The EEC Treaty sought **a common policy for inland transport**, namely roads, rail and inland waterways, but not for maritime and air transport (Art 84 EEC, Art. 80 TEC). The concept of a common transport market was consequently limited at the outset to inland transport and more specifically, in light of the highly specific situation of railway and inland waterway undertakings, to road transport. However road haulage services represent by far the bulk of goods carriage in the European Community. They, therefore, play a principal role in the good functioning of the single market by enabling the free movement of goods and persons. Thus, the common transport market had to be completed together with the single market for goods in 1992.

In addition to the integration of inland transport markets, Community policy in this sector seeks to **organise the various means of transport** in accordance with "Community rules", i.e. measures tending towards the approximation of the economic conditions and the structures of each mode of transport in the Member States. For many years, the Community institutions concentrated upon harmonising road haulage rates, but achievements are thin on the ground. The aim in the railway sector was to improve the financial situation of railway companies, but the many provisions adopted with this aim in mind have, thus far, had little impact. By way of contrast, sea and air transport which only made their entrance onto the Community stage in the middle of the 1970s, have seen spectacular progress recently, not only in the completion of the internal market in these sectors, but also of their Community organisation.

A communication of the Commission entitled "The common transport policy - Sustainable mobility: perspectives for the future" provides an updated **framework for the future development of the transport policy**[1]. The Commission identifies three priority areas for action, for which it lists the main measures designed to: improve the **efficiency and competitiveness** of Community transport by: liberalising market access, establishing integrated transport systems and developing the trans-European network; establishing **fair pricing** on the basis of the marginal social cost and improving working conditions; and improving **transport quality** through targeted action on safety, primarily on air, maritime and road transport, and protection of the environment. Concerning in particular environment protection, the Commission believes that the introduction of a rational policy for achieving a reduction in carbon dioxide emissions in the transport sector (accounting for 26% of total CO_2 emissions in the Union in 1995) would make it possible to halve them by 2010[2] [see also section 16.3.4.]. To this end, the **"STEER"** programme, which is part of the multiannual programme for actions in the field of energy (2003-2006)[3] [see section 19.1.3.], supports initiatives relating to all energy aspects of transport, the diversification of fuels, such as through new developing and renewable energy sources, and the promotion of renewable fuels and energy efficiency in transport, including the preparation of legislative measures and their application.

20.1. The special interest for the transport sector

Article 51 TEC (ex-Art. 61 EEC) makes the provision of services in the transport sector dependent on the special clauses of the title relating to transport. Article 71 TEC (ex-Art. 75 EEC) stipulates that the common policy should take into account the **"distinctive features"** of (inland) transport sector. At the outset, these distinctive features were based on the facts: (a) that transport undertakings were dependent upon infrastructure decided and built by the States; (b) that in general, competition took place between large State controlled railway monopolies and a multitude of small road haulage and inland waterway transport operators; (c) that the State required certain undertakings, notably the railways, to fulfil public service obligations, which distort competition conditions; and (d) that supply and demand were extremely rigid in this sector.

The Treaty of Rome and its successor, the Treaty establishing the European Community, show **special interest in the transport sector for several reasons**. First of all, economic integration was expected to lead to growth in trade and consequently in trans-

---

[1]   COM (1998) 716, 1 December 1998.
[2]   COM (1998) 204, 31 March 1998.
[3]   Decision 1230/2003, OJ L 176, 15.07.2003.

port flows. The EEC Treaty therefore saw the transport sector as one of the major motors of economic integration. On its side, the healthy operation of the transport sector depended to a large extent on healthy trade and business in the Community.

Secondly, transport costs, which put a serious strain on the cost price of certain goods, **could act as a barrier to trade** or a source of discrimination between European businesses of various nationalities. At the outset, the situation was most complex in the road transport sector, which represents 80% of goods carriage between the Member States. Depending on the routes, international road traffic was either restriction free or subject to prior authorisation or to the granting of authorisations in the framework of a quota. Authorisation issuing provisions (length of validity, possibility of return trip loaded, etc.) varied from one route to the next. The conditions governing Community transit differed from one State to the next and provisions relating to combined rail/road transport were practically non-existent. It is obvious that all this had to be changed in order to create a common market for transport.

Infrastructure choices for means of communication, their construction and use have considerable impact on regional development, the environment, town and country planning, traffic safety and energy consumption. Coordination of investment decisions can eliminate the risk of works whose socio-economic profitability is not sufficient and can open the way to the economies of scale offered by the wider internal market. The provisions of the TEC on trans-European networks and economic and social cohesion provide a new basis for the Community to devise a strategy for the development of transport infrastructure. This strategy should allow, amongst other things, the less favoured peripheral regions of the Union to take full advantage of the opportunities which stem from the completion of the internal market.

Nowadays, the priority in the transport sector is moving towards building modern infrastructures and, in particular, **trans-European networks**, which help complete the internal market by reinforcing the links between the Member States [see section 6.8.]. These networks also permit: better, safer travel at lower cost, thus improving both industrial competitiveness and quality of life; effective planning in Europe, thus avoiding a concentration of wealth and population; and bridge-building towards Central and Eastern European countries, which is essential in view of their integration into the Union. Building trans-European transport networks requires Community action to coordinate the various national activities and so complete the internal market and facilitate interconnection and interoperability in the transport sector.

The continuing integration of the economies of the Member States necessarily entails increased transport movements across frontiers and places new challenges for the European transport policy. Thus, in addition to the consolidation of the internal market in transport, the Treaty of Amsterdam set two new objectives for the common transport policy: transport safety and environment protection. Article 71 of the EC Treaty declares that **transport safety** is one of the objectives to be attained by the transport policy. Safety requirements may fall within the area of the Community's exclusive powers, for example, because they affect the free circulation of vehicles or transport services. In other cases, in application of the subsidiarity principle [see section 3.2.], transport safety is a matter which should be addressed by the Community when it is in a position to act usefully.

All power-driven transport means consume energy and cause air, soil, water or marine pollution. Most polluting for the environment is road transport, which consumes over 80% of the total final energy used in the transport sector and contributes over 75% to its total CO_2 emissions. To **reduce pollution caused by the transport sector**, it is essential in this sector, as in that of energy, to: set progressively higher standards for gaseous emissions; incorporate into the transport prices the cost of transport, namely road, infrastructure; and internalise the external costs of pollution by means of financial and fiscal instruments, such as the tax on CO_2. Those measures which, in addition to environmental protection, would facilitate road decongestion and increase transport safety, would, however, have a direct impact on the competitive position of transport systems and operators. For this reason, measures of this kind could best be taken within the Community framework.

It is worth bearing in mind that transport and communications are in themselves **a major economic sector**. Transport is an industry of the future whose main growth factors are: structural changes in the manufacturing industry, which is transferring its production sites from urban areas to new industrial sites; the evolution of production methods, which encourages stock reduction and more flexible, more varied and more rapid delivery systems; the increasing importance of the services sector and the dispersion of its activities to multiple sites, which stimulates professional mobility; the increase in income levels and the evolution of demographic structures, which boosts demand for leisure, tourism and family reunions. The transport sector involves **40% of public investment in the Member States**. Investments, whether they originate from the public sector (construction of transport infrastructure) or from the private one (all kinds of means of transport), indisputably affect employment in the industrial sector. Moreover, the testing of technological innovations in the transport sector (aircraft, high-speed trains, underwater tunnels, etc.) stimulates innovation in industry in general.

20.2. The internal market for inland transport

Title V of the EC Treaty is devoted to transport policy. It states that common policy in the transport sector should be implemented via **common rules applicable to international transport**, through the admission of non-resident carriers to the national transport market and through all other appropriate provisions (Art 71 TEC). According to the Treaty, aids which respond to the need for the coordination of transport services or for the reimbursement for the discharge of certain obligations inherent in the concept of public service are compatible with the common market (Art. 73 TEC). Any discrimination, which takes the form of carriers charging different rates and imposing different conditions for the carriage of the same goods over the same transport links on grounds of the country of origin or destination of the country in question, must be abolished (Art. 75 TEC). The Member States may not impose rates and conditions involving any element of support or protection in the interest of one or more particular undertakings or industries, unless authorised by the Commission (Art. 76 TEC).

The first Community measures adopted in the inland transport sector sought **to integrate national transport markets** together with the creation of the general common market for goods and services. In this sector, it was necessary to create a genuine internal market in which transport operators from all the Member States would have access under the same conditions as those prevalent on their national markets. This implied freedom of establishment, the removal of barriers to freedom of movement and the harmonisation of competition conditions.

No special problems were encountered in the free movement of individuals and the right of establishment in the transport sector. The Regulation of 1968 on the **free movement of workers** within the Community was applied to the inland transport sector in the same way as to other economic sectors [see section 6.4.][1]. The **right of establishment** formed part of the general programme to remove restrictions to the freedom of establishment adopted by the Council in December 1961 [see section 6.5.1.], but was also the subject of a specific Directive on mutual recognition of diplomas and certificates of road carriers[2]. It was the **free movement of services**, meaning free access of all operators in the transport market, that was the source of complex problems, due to restrictive national regulations in the Member States, particularly for road haulage services. This subject merits our particular attention.

---

[1]   Regulation 1612/68, OJ L 257, 19.10.1968 and Directive 2004/38, OJ L 158, 30.04.2004.
[2]   Directive 96/26, OJ L 124, 23.05.1996 and Directive 2004/66, OJ L 168, 01.05.2004.

20.2.1. Access to the common inland transport market

Article 75 of the EEC Treaty (Art. 71 TEC) stipulated that, in order to open up access to the Community transport market, the Council should draw up common rules applying to international transport services from or to a destination in another Member State (intra-Community traffic) or crossing the territory of one or several Member States (Community transit). Considerable legislative harmonisation was necessary for the attainment of the Treaty's objectives in this area, naturally requiring a great deal of time and effort. From the access viewpoint, the **carriage of goods by road** was the hardest nut to crack. International road haulage required the authorisation of the States to be crossed, usually granted on a bilateral basis by the States in question. This authorisation system sought to protect national railways and hauliers and naturally acted as a brake on the opening up of the Community transport market.

Work began fairly early on to break down the defences of this protectionist system by liberalising certain special transport services such as frontier transport, mail carriage and, notably, combined road/rail carriage[1]. However, these specific measures only concerned a minute proportion of carriage by road between the Member States, the bulk of which was subject to **a system of quotas and bilateral authorisations.** Instead of abolishing these bilateral quotas, the Council, in 1968, merely created a small Community quota representing less than 10% of the bilateral quotas.

The clear lack of political commitment to creating a "common" transport policy eventually exasperated the European Parliament. With the support of the European Commission and on the basis of Article 175 of the EEC Treaty (Art. 232 TEC), it adopted a Resolution relating **to proceedings for failure to act** against the Council on September 16, 1982 [see section 4.1.5.]. The Parliament stated, indeed, that only minimum provisions had been adopted in the area of transport policy, falling well short of the objectives set in the Treaty, particularly in Articles 3 and 74. The judgment delivered by the Court of Justice on May 22, 1985 was a partial success for the Parliament and the Commission[2]. The Court established that the Council had, in violation of the Treaty, failed to ensure the free provision of services in the area of international transport and to define conditions for the admission of non-resident transport operators to the national transport market of a Member State. Acting on the Court judgment and on the entry into force of the Single European Act [see section 2.1.], the Council finally established freedom of access to the inland transport market.

The **liberalisation of the internal goods carriage market** was at long last established by a Regulation on access to the market in the carriage of goods by road within the Community and departing from or en route to a Member State, or crossing the territory of one or several Member States[3]. This Regulation replaced the formerly existing quantitative restrictions and bilateral authorisations by qualitative conditions (fiscal, technical and safety) with which a carrier must conform in order to obtain the Community **road haulage operator licence** and which are specified in the directives on access to the transport profession, mentioned below. The licence is valid for six years, but the criteria for holding it have to be controlled every three years. Thanks to a uniform document, the **"driver attestation"**, the regularity of the employment status of a driver of a Community vehicle engaged in international carriage under cover of a Community authorisation can be effectively checked by inspecting officers of all Member States[4]. Should economic crisis hit the road haulage market, the Commission can take measures to prevent any further capacity increases on the market affected[5]. A Regulation laying down the conditions under which non-resident carriers may operate national **road haulage services within a Member State (cabotage)** is the culmination of many years of work towards the liberalisation of the road haulage sector[6]. These Regulations have completed the internal goods carriage market.

The **freedom to provide passenger transport services by road** for hire or reward or on one's own account is also guaranteed by a Council Regulation[7]. It notably provides

---

[1]   Directive 75/130, OJ L 48, 22.02.1975 repealed by Directive 92/106, OJ L 368, 17.12.1992.
[2]   Case 13/83, European Parliament v Council, ECR 1985, p. 1513.
[3]   Regulation 881/92, OJ L 95, 09.04.1992 and Act of Accession OJ C 241, 29.08.1994.
[4]   Regulation 484/2002, OJ L 76, 19.03.2002.
[5]   Regulation 3916/90, OJ L 375, 31.12.1990.
[6]   Regulation 3118/93, OJ L 279, 12.11.1993 and Regulation 484/2002, OJ L 76, 19.03.2002.
[7]   Regulation 684/92, OJ L 74, 20.03.1992 and Regulation 11/98, OJ L 4, 08.01.1998.

for the liberalisation of shuttle services by coach and bus with sleeping accommodation, along with nearly all occasional services, and simplifies authorisation procedures by introducing a Community licence based on a harmonised model. The detailed rules with regard to documentation covering the international carriage of passengers are laid out in a Commission Regulation[1]. Another Council Regulation lays down the conditions under which non-resident carriers may operate **national road passenger transport services (cabotage)** within a Member State[2]. It authorises cabotage, under certain conditions, for regular services performed during a regular international service, excluding purely internal urban and suburban services. Despite cabotage liberalisation, when a bus or coach company wants to gain a permanent foothold in another national market, the simplest way to do so remains to establish itself on that market. Thus, the impact of cabotage on the national markets of the Member States is marginal and insignificant, with cabotage operations carried out mainly in adjacent Member States.

The **admission to the occupation** of road haulage operator and road passenger transport operator and the mutual recognition of diplomas, certificates and other evidence of qualifications intended to facilitate for these operators the right to freedom of establishment in national and international transport operations are guaranteed by a Directive[3]. It stipulates that individuals or undertakings wishing to exercise the occupation of road haulier or road passenger transport operator must satisfy certain conditions relating to good repute (no insolvency), sufficient financial capacity for correct management of the undertaking and professional skills acquired through attendance of a training course or through practical experience.

The **controls carried out by Member States** in relation to means of transport by road or by inland waterway are no longer performed at the Community's internal frontiers but as part of the normal procedures performed throughout Community territory[4]. These controls concern not only the means of transport registered or put into circulation in the Member States but also those registered in third countries.

The ASOR[5] and Interbus[6] agreements on the international occasional carriage of passengers by coach and bus govern traffic not only between the Community and the Central and Eastern European countries concerned but also between the third countries themselves, thus establishing a degree of fiscal, social and technical harmonisation in addition to market access rules. With a view to enlargement, the transitional points system (écopoints) applicable to heavy goods vehicles travelling through Austria[7] and Switzerland[8] was extended to include the acceding countries. An agreement between the EC and the Former Yugoslav Republic of Macedonia (FYROM) provides for unrestricted access for Community transit through this country and for FYROM traffic through the Community to or from a third country[9]. Agreements establish certain conditions for the carriage of goods by road and the promotion of combined transport between the European Community and the Republics of Bulgaria and Romania[10].

A 1995 Directive on the licensing of railway undertakings establishes common conditions of **access to the Community rail market**, in particular by requiring that undertakings applying for a licence meet specified standards of financial capacity and professional competence[11].

International waterway transport has enjoyed freedom of navigation embodied in international treaties, such as that for navigation on the Rhine, since before the creation of the Community. However, a 1976 Directive ensures reciprocal recognition of navigability licences for inland waterway vessels[12] and a 1987 Directive lays down conditions for access to the profession of waterway transport operator[13]. A single boatmas-

[1] Regulation 2121/98, OJ L 268, 03.10.1998 last amended by Regulation 1792/2006, OJ L 362, 20.12.2006.
[2] Regulation 12/98, OJ L 48, 04.01.1998.
[3] Directive 96/26, OJ L 124, 23.05.1996 last amended by Directive 2004/66, OJ L 168, 01.05.2004.
[4] Regulation 3912/92, OJ L 395, 31.12.1992.
[5] Agreement and Decision 82/505, OJ L 230, 05.08.1982 and Regulation 56/83, OJ L 10, 13.01.1983.
[6] Agreement and Decision 2002/917, OJ L 321, 26.11.2002.
[7] Regulation 2327/2003, OJ L 345, 31.12.2003 and Regulation 863/2004, OJ L 161, 30.04.2004.
[8] Regulation 2888/2000, OJ L 336, 30.12.2000 and Regulation 862/2004, OJ L 161, 30.04.2004.
[9] Decision 97/832, OJ L 348, 18.12.1997.
[10] Regulation 685/2001, OJ L 108, 18.04.2001 and Regulation 861/2004, OJ L 161, 30.04.2004.
[11] Directive 95/18, OJ L 143, 27.06.1995 and Directive 2004/49, OJ L 164, 30.04.2004.
[12] Directive 76/135, OJ L 21, 29.01.1976 and Directive 78/1016, OJ L 349, 13.12.1978.
[13] Directive 87/540, OJ L 322, 12.11.1987.

ters' certificate issued by a Member State using a Community-designed model is mutually recognised by the Member States[1]. Any operator can transport goods or passengers by inland waterway between Member States or transit through them, provided he satisfies certain rules set out in a Community Regulation[2].

20.2.2. Competition conditions in inland transport services

For there to be effective freedom to provide services, all transport operators in the Member States had to **be placed on an equal footing** from the viewpoint of competition conditions, a really difficult requirement. In effect, rail transport systems based on the exploitation of single networks constituted monopolies or oligopolies. Service obligations in the public interest tended to involve the granting of correlative special or exclusive rights. Rail transport operators frequently relied on public finance, including subsidies not compatible with the functioning of the common market.

After the achievement of customs union [see section 5.1.2.], a 1968 Regulation sanctioned the **application of competition rules** to the rail, road and inland waterway transport sectors[3]. This Regulation in principle forbids, for all three modes of transport, agreements between companies, decisions of association and concerted practices, along with abuse of a dominant position in the common market. Yet, an exemption is granted to agreements which contribute to productivity, along with certain types of agreements, decisions and concerted practices in the field of transport which have as sole object and impact the application of technical improvements or technical cooperation. A Commission Regulation facilitates the presentation of complaints, applications and notifications by natural or legal persons who claim a legitimate interest[4].

However, competition rules alone do not suffice to guarantee free competition in the transport sector. Competition conditions for different modes of transport and for the undertakings of different Member States running the same type of transport services must also be harmonised. The first step in this direction was taken by the Council Decision of May 13, 1965 on the harmonisation of **certain provisions affecting competition** in transport by rail, road and inland waterway[5]. Under this Decision, the Council agreed to take action in three fields: State intervention, taxation and social regimes in the transport sector. This was a commitment and a clearly defined framework for the common transport policy to eliminate disparities, which could distort competition between modes of transport and between undertakings operating the same mode of transport; but, it needed application provisions in order to work. One of the most important measures was a Regulation providing for separate accounting of public service activities and commercial activities in transport undertakings, abolishing public service obligations and replacing them, when public interest justifies the preservation of transport services of no commercial viability for the operator, by **public service contracts** negotiated between governments and undertakings[6]. Many other measures harmonising the conditions of competition were taken in the fields of State aids, taxation and social legislation [see details below].

A 1970 Regulation provides arrangements on the **granting of aids for combined transport** by rail, road and inland waterways, thus giving Member States the possibility of developing this mode of transport[7]. Although it allows aids for investments in infrastructure, fixed and mobile equipment used in combined trans-

---

[1] Directive 91/672, OJ L 373, 31.12.1991 and Act of Accession OJ C 241, 29.08.1994.
[2] Regulation 1356/96, OJ L 175, 13.07.1996.
[3] Regulation 1017/68, OJ L 175, 23.07.1968 and Regulation 1/2003, OJ L 1, 04.01.2003.
[4] Regulation 773/2004, OJ L 123, 27.04.2003 last amended by Regulation 1792/2006, OJ L 362, 20.12.2006.
[5] Decision 65/271, OJ 88, 24.05.1965.
[6] Regulation 1191/69, OJ L 156, 28.06.1969 and Regulation 1893/91, OJ L 169, 29.06.1991.
[7] Regulation 1107/70, OJ L 130, 15.06.1970 and Regulation 543/97, OJ L 84, 26.03.1997.

ports and for investments relating to the costs of running combined transport services transiting through the territory of certain third countries (Switzerland and the States of former Yugoslavia), it defines rules for the non distortion of competition between the transport operators of different nationalities. Agreements for the promotion of combined transport exist also with Hungary[1] and Bulgaria[2]. Community financial assistance may be granted for actions of an innovative nature to promote combined transport[3].

In the area of **fiscal harmonisation**, a common VAT system was introduced in the transport sector by the two first Directives of April 1967 and by the sixth Directive of May 17, 1977 [see section 14.2.1.]. But the real harmonisation of taxation on road haulage is pursued by means of the Directive on the application by Member States of taxes on certain types of infrastructure requiring heavy goods vehicles to contribute towards the costs they engender through an excise duty on diesel oil, vehicle taxes or tolls and charges for the use of road infrastructure ("Eurovignette")[4]. The system of charging for the use of road infrastructure is based on the "user pays" principle and hence the "polluter pays" principle [see section 16.2.2], through the variation of tolls taking account of the environmental performance of vehicles. Member States may also maintain or introduce tolls or user charges provided they do not discriminate on the basis of carrier nationality or consignment origin or destination.

A Regulation aims to harmonise the conditions of competition between modes of inland transport, especially with regard to the road sector, to improve social conditions for employees who are covered by it, as well as to improve general road safety[5]. It does so mainly by means of the provisions pertaining to **maximum driving times** per day (9 hours), per week (56 hours) and per period of two consecutive weeks (90 hours), the provision which obliges drivers to take a regular weekly rest period of 45 hours at least once per two consecutive weeks and the provisions which prescribe that under no circumstances should a daily rest period be less than an uninterrupted period of nine hours. To prove that they are actually respecting the social and safety provisions, road hauliers must, in accordance with another Regulation, install and regularly use electronic **recording equipment in vehicles** ("tachographs") for passenger or goods carriage which are registered in a Member State[6]. The Member States must organise an adequate and regular inspection system for road transport undertakings[7].

Several Directives relate as much to **road safety** as to competition conditions between transport undertakings in different Member States. Thus, a Directive deals with the approximation of the laws of Member States relating to **roadworthiness tests** for motor vehicles and their trailers[8]. The growing density of road traffic has meant that all the Member States are up against the same safety problems on the same scale. On the other hand, if the frequency and checking methods of those tests were not harmonised, the immobilisation of vehicles for periodic checks and the costs resulting from these could affect competition conditions in the road haulage sector from Member State to Member State, giving rise to a need for harmonisation of their frequency and standardisation of checking methods.

With a view to evening out competition between carriers and improving road safety, a Directive provides for the generalised installation and compulsory use of **speed limiters** on heavy vehicles for the carriage of goods and passengers[9]. For heavy vehicles, speed is limited to 90 km/h and for coaches with a maximum weight in excess of 10 tons, the limit is set at 100 km/h. With regard to the safety of persons, property and the environment, a Directive imposes upon all undertakings the activities of which include the transport and related loading or unloading of dangerous goods by road, rail or inland waterway to appoint safety advisers responsible for helping to prevent the risks inherent in such activities[10].

20.2.3. Transport infrastructure

Infrastructure plays a determinant role in the competition conditions enjoyed by the various modes of transport. Through its choice of means of communication, the State determines the expansion and link up possibilities of the various modes of transport. Transport undertakings are dependent upon the infrastructure, which they use, in as much as decisions on its construction and maintenance are taken by governments. However, transport users are usually **not obliged to pay the full cost of the infrastructures**

---

[1]   Agreement and Decision 2001/266, OJ L 108, 18.04.2001.
[2]   Agreement and Decision 2001/265, OJ L 108, 18.04.2001.
[3]   Regulation 2196/98, OJ L 277, 14.10.1998.
[4]   Directive 1999/62, OJ L 187, 20.07.1999 and Directive 2006/38, OJ L 157, 09.06.2006.
[5]   Regulation 561/2006, OJ L 102, 11.04.2006.
[6]   Regulation 3821/85, OJ L 370, 31.12.1985 and Regulation 561/2006, OJ L 102, 11.04.2006..
[7]   Directive 2006/22, OJ L 102, 11.04.2006.
[8]   Directive 96/96, OJ L 46, 17.02.1997 and Directive 2003/27, OJ L90, 08.04.2003.
[9]   Directive 92/6, OJ L 57, 02.03.1992 and Directive 2002/85, OJ L 327, 04.12.2002.
[10] Directive 96/35, OJ L 145, 19.06.1996.

that they use. This is particularly true of road infrastructures and has contributed to the phenomenal expansion of road transport. In other respects, transport networks having been designed largely from a national point of view, there were in post-war Europe many missing links, bottlenecks and obstacles to inter-operability between national networks. Moreover, whereas the central regions of the Community suffered from a growing congestion and had to bear a disproportionate burden of the costs of cross-frontier traffic, there was an under-investment in peripheral areas contributing to their economic underdevelopment.

The EEC Treaty did not give the Community institutions any powers in this field. However, at the instigation of the Commission, a **consultation procedure** and a Transport Infrastructure Committee were established in the late 1970s and improved over time[1]. This procedure enabled better planning at national level both as regards time scale and geographical aspects. In addition, the European Investment Bank and the Structural Funds have much helped the financing of infrastructures. But the overall infrastructure deficit of the Community has increased with the accession of peripheral States. This is why, the development of transport infrastructures was provided for in the EC Treaty under the heading of trans-European networks.

Indeed, the new Article 155 of the EC Treaty calls for a series of guidelines covering the objectives, priorities and broad lines of measures envisaged in the sphere of **trans-European networks** [see section 6.8.]. These networks are not only necessary in order to complete the internal market, improve the links between the European regions, avoid traffic congestions, reduce environment pollution and improve the competitiveness of European industries, but they can also enliven the European economy through the realisation of very big projects and thus contribute to its growth. Community financial assistance is granted under certain rules to projects of common interest[2]. Concerning trans-European transport networks (TEN-T) the goal is not so much the improvement of transport infrastructure in general but the integration of the Community's transport system through the completion and combination of its networks, taking particular account of its more geographically isolated regions.

A Commission White Paper entitled "**Fair payment for infrastructure use**" recommends the gradual harmonisation of infrastructure charging systems based on the "user pays" principle, according to which all users of transport infrastructure would have to pay for all the costs they generate, including environmental costs[3]. A first measure in this sense is the creation of a European **electronic road toll service**, which aims to secure the interoperability of toll systems in the internal market and to contribute to the elaboration of infrastructure charging policies at European level, making it possible to fund, in part, new infrastructure and to ensure a better traffic flow on the main routes of the trans-European network[4].

The Council has adopted the master plans on the high-speed rail, the combined transport, the road and inland waterway networks. These master plans, which are indicative in nature and do not entail any financial commitments on the part of any Member State or the Community, aim at **supplying the missing links between national networks**, making them technically compatible and opening up the Community's isolated regions. Community guidelines spell out the criteria and specifications applicable to projects of common interest in order to ensure by 2010 optimum and environmentally sound exploitation of all modes of transport[5]. These guidelines set out a precise but flexible framework for action for the national and regional authorities and serve as a reference for Community intervention.

---

[1]   Decision 1692/96, OJ L 228, 09.09.1996, last amended by Decision 884/2004, OJ L 167, 30.04.2004.
[2]   Regulation 2236/95, OJ L 228, 23.09.1995 and Regulation 1159/2005, OJ L 191, 22.07.2005.
[3]   COM (1998) 466, 22 July 1998.
[4]   Directive 2004/52, OJ L 166, 30.04.2004.
[5]   Decision 1692/96, OJ L 228, 09.09.1996, last amended by Decision 884/2004, OJ L 167, 30.04.2004.

20.3. Sectoral organisation of the transport market

In addition to the proper functioning of the internal market for transport, the common transport policy also tackles the sector-by-sector **organisation of the various modes of transport**. This requires the approximation of the economic conditions and the structures of each mode of transport in the Member States. The Treaty of Rome did not call for specific action in this field, but nevertheless stated that there should be common rules applicable to international transport to or from the territory of a Member State, or passing across the territory of one or more Member States (Article 75,1,a EEC). The European institutions slowly put in place common rules, first for road transport rates and for improving the financial situation of the railways and, then in reaction to the Court of Justice ruling of April 4, 1974 on the interpretation of Article 84 of the EEC Treaty[1], on the organisation of activities and the establishment of the internal market for the sea and air transport sectors. For concision's sake, all measures adopted in the last two sectors are examined in this part of the chapter, since they often pursue simultaneously the two objectives of the common transport policy, namely the proper functioning of the internal market and the organisation of the sector.

20.3.1. Road transport

The part of road haulage in the total freight transport of the Community increased from around 50% in 1970 to almost 70% in 1990. This increase was partly due to the choice of the Member States **not to charge the prices of road transport with the cost of infrastructures**. In 1968, the Council, acting on a proposal by the Commission, had introduced bracket tariffs only for the carriage of goods by road between the Member States. This experimental system was replaced, since 1990, by a single system providing a **free price setting** applicable to all carriage of goods by road between the Member States[2]. This new tariff regime allows for the introduction of cost indexes, i.e. indicators of the various cost elements, which a haulier should take into account when drawing up a transport price to be negotiated with the client, but the real cost of infrastructures is not among those indicators. However, the Commission's approach to infrastructure charging based on the "user pays" principle [see section 20.2.3.] could have an important bearing on the harmonisation of road transport costs and prices in the Community[3].

The form and content of **registration certificates** for motor vehicles have been harmonised in order to facilitate road traffic within the Community, simplify procedures for the re-registration of vehicles in another Member State, and step up the fight against illegal vehicle trafficking[4]. Common rules command the recognition in intra-Community traffic of the distinguishing sign of the Member State in which motor vehicles and their trailers are registered[5].

The Community aims not only at the harmonisation of conditions of competition and the protection of the environment but also at **road safety**, which becomes an ever more important problem of the EU. The principal actions taken so far in the area of road safety have been concerned with the harmonisation of rules relating to vehicle construction and vehicle inspection, through the adoption of over 100 Directives, notably on:

---

[1]   Judgment of 4 April 1974, Case 167-73, Commission v French Republic, ECR 1974, p. 359.
[2]   Regulation 4058/89, OJ L 390, 30.12.1989 and EEA Agreement, OJ L 1, 03.01.1994.
[3]   COM (1998) 466, 22 July 1998.
[4]   Directive 1999/37, OJ L 138, 01.06.1999 last amended by Directive 2003/127, OJ L 10, 16.01.2004.
[5]   Regulation 2411/98, OJ L 299, 10.11.1998.

minimum tyre tread depth[1]; the periodic inspection of vehicles[2]; speed limiters for heavy vehicles[3]; the mandatory wearing of seat belts[4]; compulsory installation of digital equipment to monitor the activities, notably the working hours, of lorry drivers (tachographs)[5]; and the general standards for the Community model driving licence in paper or "credit card" format, including harmonised codes for additional or restrictive information[6]. Minimum safety requirements for tunnels have become obligatory in the trans-European road network[7]. How many citizens realise that these life-saving measures are based on the - according to eurosceptic rhetoric - "niggling legislation of Brussels" [see section 10.1.]?

Aiming at road safety, the Member States can carry out unexpected roadside inspections of commercial vehicles used for the carriage of passengers and goods to check the safety and environmental protection systems and equipment fitted to them so as to detect defects[8]. At road safety aims also the directive concerning the organisation of working time for mobile workers performing road transport activities and for self-employed drivers[9]. The Council has approved the creation of a Community database on road accidents (CARE)[10] and adopted a Resolution concerning young drivers of cars and two-wheeled vehicles[11]. Another Council Resolution aims at encouraging the use of telematics in the transport sector and particularly the harmonised deployment of road traffic information and warning services[12].

The authorised **weights and dimensions of road vehicles** intended for the transport of goods and passengers in the Community have been harmonised, in order to remove the barriers to free movement between Member States created by differences in the standards. Thus, a Directive lays down for certain road vehicles, including buses, circulating within the Community the maximum authorised dimensions in national and international traffic and the maximum authorised weights in international traffic[13]. However, to give a reasonable depreciation period for existing vehicles, Member States are allowed to authorise, for national goods services on their territory, vehicles exceeding the maximum lengths and widths set in the Directive until 31 December 2006.

Another Directive harmonises the rules applicable to the national and intra-Community **transport of dangerous goods** so as to ensure, on the one hand, a high level of safety compatible with the European Agreement concerning the international carriage of dangerous goods by road (ADR), and on the other, the creation of a single market for such transport services within the EU[14]. A supplementary Directive establishes uniform procedures for checks on the transport of dangerous goods by road[15].

20.3.2. Railways

Railways, once the dominant means of transport, were **relegated by the car** in the 1960s. In the early 1990s, railway transport represented around 15% of freight transport in the Community, whereas twenty years before it represented practically the double. The bulky organisation of the railways has not given them sufficient flexibility to structure their service to new transport requirements, to the "European dimension" and to competition from other modes of transport. The Member States must shoulder part of the blame for the unfortunate situation in which their railways find themselves. They oblige the railways to bend to the requirements of public service and regional development,

---

[1] Directive 89/459, OJ L 226, 03.08.1989 and EEA Agreement, OJ L 1, 03.01.1994.
[2] Directive 96/96, OJ L 46, 17.02.1997 and Directive 2003/27, OJ L90, 08.04.2003.
[3] Directive 92/24, OJ L 129, 14.05.1992 last amended by Directive 2004/11, OJ L 44, 14.02.2004.
[4] Directive 91/671, OJ L 373, 31.12.1991 and Directive 2003/20, OJ L 115, 09.05.2003.
[5] Regulation 3821/85, OJ L 370, 31.12.1985 last amended by Regulation 561/2006, OJ L 102, 11.04.2006.
[6] Directive 2006/126, OJ L 403, 30.12.2006.
[7] Directive 2004/54, OJ L 167, 30.04.2004.
[8] Directive 2000/30, OJ L 203, 10.08.2000 last amended by Directive 2003/26, OJ L 90, 08.04.2003.
[9] Directive 2002/15, OJ L 80, 23.03.2002.
[10] Decision 93/704, OJ L 329, 30.12.1993.
[11] OJ C 351, 30.12.1993, p. 1.
[12] OJ C 309, 05.11.1994, p. 1-2.
[13] Directive 96/53, OJ L 235, 17.09.1996 and directive 2002/7, OJ L 67, 09.03.2002.
[14] Directive 94/55, OJ L 319, 12.12.1994 last amended by Directive 2006/89, OJ L 305, 04.11.2006.
[15] Directive 95/50, OJ L 249, 17.10.1995 last amended by by Directive 2004/112, OJ L 367, 14.12.2004.

which is not required of their private competitors, the road hauliers, while not raising the capital endowment of railway undertakings in line with this obligation. This forces the railways into the red and hampers their modernisation.

Nowadays, however, there is some light at the end of the tunnel in the shape of the high speed trains, which have given a new lease of life to European railways. The new momentum has led to the **"railway package"** of measures designed to speed up market integration by removing major obstacles to cross-border services, ensure a high standard of operational safety on the railways and help to reduce costs and facilitate operations through greater harmonisation of technical standards in the railway industry.

Thus, a Directive on the **development of the Community's railways** purports to make relations between the railways and the public authorities more transparent and to ensure the financial, administrative, economic and accounting independence of the railway undertakings[1]. It entails the total opening of the rail freight markets. It also allows access to new railway operators into the combined transport market, in order to stimulate a higher quality of service from all concerned. Another Directive establishes the general framework for a uniform, non-discriminatory Community system regarding access to railway infrastructure, so that railway undertakings and their customers can reap the full benefits of the internal market in this sector, while ensuring high standards of safety[2]. However, undertakings applying for a licence to the Community railway market must meet specified standards of financial fitness and professional competence[3]. The licences, granted by the Member State in which a railway undertaking is established, are valid throughout the territory of the Community. Harmonised technical specifications ensure the uninterrupted movement of high-speed trains throughout the European Union[4] as well the interoperability of the trans-European conventional rail system[5], while a uniform set of national safety rules purports to avoid distorting competition between modes for the transport of dangerous goods[6]. **Multimodal transport** is encouraged by granting Community financial assistance to improve the environmental performance of the freight transport system (Marco Polo programme)[7].

The **European Railway Agency** plays a key role in technically aligning the railway systems[8]. Working in close liaison with experts in the field, it provides technical support for the work on interoperability and safety. The Agency's areas of activity are, firstly, the development of common safety standards and the development and management of a system to monitor safety performance and, secondly, the long-term management of the system for establishing, registering and monitoring the technical specifications of interoperability.

Good intentions towards the railways have abounded. Member States have adopted common rules concerning, on the one hand, the obligations inherent in the concept of a public service, which affects first and foremost the railways[9], and, on the other, the standardisation of the accounts of railway undertakings[10], thus-facilitating the allocation of railway infrastructure capacity and the levying of charges for the use of railway infrastructure and safety certification[11]. Member States must ensure that charging and capacity allocation schemes for railway infrastructure follow the principles set down in Directive 2001/14 and thus allow the in-

---

[1]   Directive 91/440, OJ L 237, 24.08.1991 and Directive 2004/51, OJ L 164, 30.04.2004.
[2]   Directive 2001/14, OJ L 75, 15.03.2001 and Directive 2004/49, OJ L 164, 30.04.2004.
[3]   Directive 95/18, OJ L 143, 27.06.1995 and Directive 2004/49, OJ L 164, 30.04.2004.
[4]   Directive 96/48, OJ L 235, 17.09.1996 and Directive 2004/50, OJ L 164, 30.04.2004.
[5]   Directive 2001/16, OJ L110, 20.04.2001 and Directive 2004/50, OJ L 164, 30.04.2004.
[6]   Directive 96/49, OJ L 235, 17.09.1996 and Directive 2000/62, OJ L 279, 01.11.2000.
[7]   Regulation 1692/2006, OJ L 328, 24.11.2006.
[8]   Regulation 881/2004, OJ L 164, 30.04.2004.
[9]   Regulation 1191/69, OJ L 156, 28.06.1969 and Regulation 1839/91, OJ L 169, 29.06.1991.
[10] Regulation 1192/69, OJ L 156, 28.06.1969 and Regulation 3572/90, OJ L 353, 17.12.1990.
[11] Directive 2001/14, OJ L 75, 15.03.2001 last amended by Directive 2004/49, OJ L 164, 30.04.2004.

frastructure manager to market and make optimum effective use of the available infrastructure capacity. These harmonisation measures have not had much impact on the economic situation of railways. Until the early1990s, railways failed to break out of the vicious circle created by the shrinking of their market, rising expenditure, insufficient revenue and greater State intervention. Rail transport statistics help formulate the common policy in this sector[1].

20.3.3. Inland waterway transport

Inland waterways, which accounted for almost 14% of freight transport in the Community, in the early 1970s, represented only 9% of that transport twenty years later. Yet, well-equipped waterways, such as the Rhine and the Rhone, are **particularly efficient for bulk traffic** and are capable of handling much more than the current traffic, provided investment is made in maintenance and works to improve the existing network.

The Community institutions reacted late in the day to the need for structural improvements in inland waterway transport in order to fight over-capacities and, hence, most over-capacity reductions in this sector were carried out at national level. However, since the 1970s, a package of Community measures provided for the gradual abolition by 1 January 2000 of the system of minimum compulsory tariffs and the rotation chartering systems and the implementation until 31 December 1999 of a system of national aid to support investment in waterway terminals or in fixed and mobile trans-shipment facilities[2]. The **"old for new" arrangements** introduced by a 1989 Regulation, under which the owner of a vessel that is to be taken into service for the first time must either scrap old tonnage or make a special contribution to the inland waterways fund, are maintained until 2003, by which time the inland waterway transport market should be fully liberalised[3].

A Community framework for deploying and utilising harmonised **river information services** supports the development of inland waterway transport with a view to strengthening its safety, efficiency and environment-friendliness, and facilitating interfaces with other modes of transport[4].

20.3.4. Maritime transport

Established in the early 1990s, the **internal maritime transport market** is functioning quite well. In 1986, the Council applied the principle of freedom to provide services, (Art. 49 and 50 TEC) to shipping services between the Member States and third countries[5]. In 1992, the freedom to provide services was extended to maritime transport within Member States **(maritime cabotage)** for Community shipowners who have their ships registered in and flying the flag of a Member State, provided that these ships comply with all the conditions for cabotage in that Member State[6]. For vessels carrying out mainland cabotage and for cruise liners, all matters relating to manning are the responsibility of the State in which the vessel is registered. However, for ships smaller than 650 Gt. and for vessels carrying out island cabotage, all matters relating to manning are the responsibility of the host State. The ability to transfer ships from one register to another within the Community may improve the operating conditions and competitiveness of the Community merchant fleet[7]. A Directive concerning the Agreement on the organisation of working time of seafarers, concluded by the European Community Shipowners' Association and the Federation of Transport Workers' Union in the European Union, is important for levelling both working conditions of sailors and competition conditions in this area[8].

Detailed rules were laid down for the application of Articles 81 and 82 of the EC Treaty (ex-Articles 85 and 86) to maritime transport in order to ensure that competition is not unduly distorted within the common market. Community guidelines for **State aid**

---

[1]   Regulation 91/2003, OJ L 14, 21.01.2003 last amended by Regulation 1192/2003, OJ L 167, 04.07.2003.
[2]   Regulation 1107/70, OJ L 130, 15.06.1970 and Regulation 543/97, OJ L 84, 26.03.1997.
[3]   Regulation 718/1999, OJ L 90, 02.04.1999.
[4]   Directive 2005/44, OJ L 255, 30.09.2005.
[5]   Regulation 4055/86, OJ L 378, 31.12.1986 and Regulation 3573/90, OJ L 353, 17.12.1990.
[6]   Regulation 3577/92, OJ L 364, 12.12.1992.
[7]   Regulation 789/2004, OJ L 138, 30.04.2004.
[8]   Directive 1999/63, OJ L 167, 02.07.1999.

in the maritime transport sector are intended to make public assistance transparent and to define what kinds of aid scheme can be introduced to support the Community's maritime interests[1]. Block exemptions [see section 15.3.3.] exist for certain concerted practices between liner shipping companies (**maritime conferences and consortia**), which provide international liner shipping services from or to one or more Community ports[2]. Thanks to these exemptions from the general rules of Articles 81 and 82, shipowners may jointly organise services, thus rationalising their activities as maritime carriers and obtaining economies of scale and cost reductions, while at the same time providing users with a better-quality service. They allow notably the coordination and joint fixing of sailing timetables, the determination of ports of call, the exchange, sale or cross-chartering of space or "slots" on vessels, the pooling of vessels, port installations and operation offices.

International **safety standards for passenger vessels** are applied in the Community. Thus, the International Conventions for the Safety of Life at Sea (SOLAS) and for the prevention of pollution by ships (MARPOL) are applicable to the Member States - and therefore to ships flying their flags[3] [see details below]. The Member States must subject cargo ships and passenger ships to initial and annual surveys to check in particular compliance with the SOLAS Convention[4]. Passenger ships operating on domestic voyages, which are not covered by the SOLAS international Convention, are covered by a Community Directive, which is intended to guarantee maximum safety for passengers and, at the same time, to provide a level playing field based on convergent standards in Community shipping[5]. In order to ensure that the maximum capacity of ships is not exceeded and to provide accurate information to the emergency services in the event of an accident, another Directive obliges shipping companies operating to or from Community ports to count and register the crew members and persons sailing on board passenger ships[6]. The Community implements the International Management Code for the Safe Operation of Ships and for Pollution Prevention adopted by the International Maritime Organisation (ISM Code)[7]. Ships using Community ports and sailing in the waters under the jurisdiction of the Member States must respect the international standards for ship safety, pollution prevention and shipboard living and working conditions (port State control)[8].

The independent **European Maritime Safety Agency** assists the Commission with drafting maritime legislation, monitoring application by the Member States and coordinating inquiries after accidents at sea or after accidental or illicit pollution caused by ships[9]. It is meant to: ensure a level playing field in the sector; provide technical and scientific support and a high level of stable expertise to properly apply the Community legislation in the fields of maritime safety and ship pollution prevention; monitor the implementation of this legislation by the Member States; and evaluate the effectiveness of the measures in place. A Directive sets up common rules and standards for ship inspection and survey organisations in order to ensure a high level of competence and independence of these organisations[10]. To prevent marine pollution (such as that caused by the "Erika" and "Prestige" accidents off the coasts of France in December 2000 and

---

[1]   OJ C 205, 05.07.1997.
[2]   Regulation 823/2000, OJ L 100, 20.04.2000 and Regulation 611/2005, OJ L 101, 21.04.2005.
[3]   Regulation 2158/93, OJ L 194, 03.08.1993.
[4]   Directive 1999/35, OJ L 138, 01.06.1999 and Directive 2002/84, OJ L 324, 29.11.2002.
[5]   Council Directive 98/18, OJ L 144, 15.05.1998 and Directive 2003/75, OJ L 190, 30.07.2003.
[6]   Directive 98/41, OJ L 188, 02.07.1998 and Directive 2003/25, OJ L 123, 17.05.2003.
[7]   Regulation 336/2006, OJ L 64, 04.03.2006.
[8]   Directive 95/21, OJ L 157, 07.07.1995 and Directive 2002/84, OJ L 324, 29.11.2002.
[9]   Regulation 1406/2002, OJ L 208, 05.08.2002 and Regulation 724/2004, OJ L 129, 29.04.2004.
[10] Directive 94/57, OJ L 319, 12.12.1994 and Directive 2002/84, OJ L 324, 29.11.2002.

Spain in December 2002), a Regulation established an accelerated phasing-in scheme for the application of the double-hull or equivalent design requirements of the MARPOL 73/78 Convention to single hull oil tankers[1].

Member States must take all necessary steps to ensure that tankers carrying oil, gas and chemicals and docking in the Community's sea ports be obliged to respect certain **safety conditions**. Member States with a North Sea or Channel coastline must take steps to ensure that ships in these areas are piloted by properly qualified sea pilots[2]. The Community **vessel traffic monitoring** and information system aims at enhancing the safety and efficiency of maritime traffic, improving the response of authorities to incidents, accidents or potentially dangerous situations at sea, including search and rescue operations, and contributing to a better prevention and detection of pollution by ships[3].A Directive strives to improve safety at sea and prevent pollution of the marine environment by improving the safety performance of equipment carried on board and strengthening the powers of the authorised inspection bodies[4]. Directive 2005/65 imposes various measures to be taken by the Member States to enhance port security[5]. The Member States of the EU have agreed to sign, ratify or accede to the International Convention on Civil Liability for Bunker Oil Pollution Damage (the Bunkers Convention)[6]. They have also agreed to ratify or accede to the International Convention on Liability and Compensation for Damage in connection with the Carriage of Hazardous and Noxious Substances by Sea (the HNS Convention), tending to improve protection at international level for victims of marine pollution[7]. A Committee on Safe Seas and the Prevention of Pollution from Ships (COSS) assists and advises the Commission on all matters of maritime safety and prevention or reduction of pollution of the environment by shipping activities[8].

Market monitoring was rendered necessary at the end of the 1970s by the problem of unfair competition from the fleets of certain State-trading countries and certain Far East countries. This competition had to be countered by shared information and possibly by common action. Therefore, an information system was established to keep the Community institutions abreast of the activities of the fleets of third countries[9]. A Council Decision provides for the possibility of counter-measures in the event of unfair competition in international merchant shipping[10]. Member States should take coordinated action when a measure introduced by a third country or by its agents restricts or threatens to restrict the free access of shipping from a Member State to ocean trade[11]. A Community procedure should be followed to counteract unfair pricing practices by certain shipowners who are nationals of third countries and are servicing international cargo shipping routes, when these practices seriously upset the structure of trade on a route to, from or within the Community[12].

International shipping relations are clearly of vital importance in the maritime transport sector. This is why one of the first measures taken in this area was the introduction of a consultation procedure on international links and on action relating to such matters within international organisations[13]. Most of the rules and requirements for seagoing vessels are negotiated in the International Maritime Organisation (IMO), a specialised agency of the United Nations, of which all EU Member States are members. The Community has incorporated in a Directive the rules on quality standards for training programmes and institutes, the issue of certificates, medical standards and rest periods for seafarers contained in the IMO Convention on Standards of Training, Certification and Watchkeeping for Seafarers[14].

20.3.5. Air transport

For air transport, in the same way as for maritime transport, the Court of Justice interpretation of Article 84 of the EEC Treaty[15] [see section 20.3.], heralded the **application of the Treaty's general rules**, notably those relating to competition and right of establishment. This was no simple matter for the air transport sector for, unlike shipping companies, the major airlines were state-owned and had a near monopoly at national level. Each State, anxious to fly the national airline colours around the world and exploit certain advantages arising

---

[1]   Regulation 417/2002, OJ L 64, 07.03.2002 and Regulation 1726/2003, OJ L 249, 01.10.2003.
[2]   Directive 79/115, OJ L 33, 08.02.1979.
[3]   Directive 2002/59, OJ L 208, 05.08.2002.
[4]   Directive 96/98, OJ L 46, 17.02.1997 and Directive 2002/84, OJ L 324, 29.11.2002.
[5]   Directive 2005/65, OJ L 310, 25.11.2005.
[6]   Decision 2002/762, OJ L 256, 25.09.2002.
[7]   Decision 2002/971, OJ L 337, 13.12.2002.
[8]   Regulation 2099/2002, OJ L 324, 29.11.2002 and Regulation 415/2004, OJ L 68, 06.03.2004.
[9]   Decision 167/2006, OJ L 33, 04.02.2006.
[10]   Decision 83/573, OJ L 332, 28.11.1983.
[11]   Regulation 4058/86, OJ L 378, 31.12.1986.
[12]   Regulation 4057/86, OJ L 378, 31.12.1986.
[13]   Decision 77/587, OJ L 239, 17.09.1977.
[14]   Directive 2001/25, OJ L 136, 18.05.2001 and Directive 2005/45, OJ L 255, 30.09.2005.
[15]   Judgment of 4 April 1974, Case 167-73, Commission v French Republic, ECR 1974, p. 359.

for example from its geographical situation or special relationship with certain parts of the world, jealously guarded its airline or airlines. This had practical consequences on flight routes and fares.

At the time of the Court ruling, air services between the Member States were regulated by **bilateral agreements.** These official agreements were often supplemented by confidential memoranda exchanged between aviation authorities which interpreted, filled in or even modified the provisions of the agreements and which occasionally depended upon commercial arrangements between airlines. Fares for scheduled air services were by and large negotiated by airlines on a multilateral basis, but in the final analysis were set by the States. Usually, the States took on board the international fares and carriage conditions set in the framework of the **International Air Transport Association (IATA).** The IATA gave the airline operating a scheduled service the option of filing a set of fares with it. But since each of these fares had to be approved by at least two governments, innovative fares were not possible at a national level. The States were in favour of consultation on fares and did not wish for any far-reaching competition. Covered by the governmental decisions, which they were simply implementing, the airlines escaped Articles 85 and 86 of the EEC Treaty and disposed of a captive market. The need for a common air transport policy and also the difficulties, which it was up against, were manifest.

In this context, it was natural that the first Council measures did not tackle the crux of the problem, namely the lack of competition. Instead, the Council set up in 1979 a **consultation procedure for relations** between Member States and third countries in the field of air transport and on action relating to such matters within international organisations, such as the International Civil Aviation Organisation (ICAO), the European Civil Aviation Conference (ECAC) and Eurocontrol[1].

At the same time, the Member States engaged themselves to check that civil subsonic aircraft registered on their territory had a noise limitation certificate, a measure of interest both from an ecological viewpoint and from that of the harmonisation of structures in the Member States[2]. After trying several measures, without succeeding to stop the deterioration in the noise level around its airports [see section 16.3.6.], the Community adopted the **"balanced approach" to noise management**, recommended by resolution A33/7 of the ICAO[3]. This approach requires careful assessment of all different options to mitigate noise, including reduction of aeroplane noise at source, land-use planning and management measures, noise abatement operational procedures and operating restrictions, without prejudice to relevant legal obligations, existing agreements, current laws and established policies.

The liberalisation of air transport in the Community was achieved progressively, between 1987 and 1992, with three packages of Regulations. The third air transport package, adopted by the Council on 22 June 1992, constituted the final stage in the liberalisation of Community air transport. It has achieved the freedom to provide services within the Community, technical and economic harmonisation and free price setting.

The Regulation on the **licensing of air carriers** defines the technical and economic requirements which airlines must meet in order to obtain national licences authorising them to operate on Community territory without restrictions on the grounds of nationality[4]. The licences in question are: the air operator's certificate (AOC), which affirms the technical quality and competence of the airline concerned; and the operating licence, granted to undertakings which comply with certain conditions regarding nationality and which meet certain economic criteria and are covered by a suitable insurance scheme. This Regulation guarantees, then, that only airlines under Community control, and with adequate technical and economic capacity, are able to take advantage of the opening up of the European market.

The Regulation on **access for air carriers** to intra-Community air routes opens up all airports on the territory of the Community to all those who are registered according to the above-mentioned Regulation[5]. It provides, in particular, for: the abolition of the previously existing sharing of passenger capacity between airlines; the unrestricted exercise of the **'fifth freedom'** (the right to pick up passengers in a Member State other than that in which the airline is registered and to disembark them in a third Member State); and

---

[1]   Decision 80/50, OJ L 18, 24.01.1980.
[2]   Regulation 1592/2002, OJ L 240, 07.09.2002 last amended by Regulation 1701/2003, OJ L 243, 27.09.2003.
[3]   Directive 2002/30, OJ L 85, 28.03.2002.
[4]   Regulation 2407/92, OJ L 240, 24.08.1992.
[5]   Regulation 2408/92, OJ L 240, 24.08.1992 last amended by Regulation 1882/2003, OJ L 284, 31.10.2003.

the authorisation to undertake **cabotage operations** (to pick up passengers in a Member State other than that in which the airline is registered and to disembark them in that same Member State).

Finally, the Regulation on **fares and rates for air services** guarantees the unrestricted setting of new passenger fares and cargo rates for scheduled air services and charter flights under certain conditions safeguarding the interests of both the industry and of consumers[1]. It defines, in particular, the arrangements for the examination of new fares and rates by the Member States and the system of 'double disapproval' (whereby a new fare or rate may not be turned down unless both Member States concerned disapprove of it). If this is not the case, Community air carriers may freely fix passenger fares. Charter fares and air cargo rates are freely fixed by the parties to the air transport contract.

The EU encourages better information for air passengers, greater protection for passengers' rights, improved service and simplified handling of disputes[2]. A Regulation drawing up common rules for the **compensation of passengers refused the right to board** due to over-booking[3] is of particular importance to the ordinary citizen. It stipulates that should a passenger be refused the right to board, he has the right to choose between full reimbursement of the price of the ticket for the part of the journey, which he was unable to carry out, or rescheduling on a later date of his choice. Regardless of the choice made by the passenger, the air carrier must pay, immediately after the boarding refusal, compensation that varies in line with the distance of the flight and the rescheduling delay. The carrier must moreover offer passengers refused the right to board meals, hotel accommodation if necessary and the cost of a telephone call and/or telefax message to the place of destination.

As regards, more particularly, the operation of **air freight services,** a Council Regulation seeks to open up access to the market, liberalise fares and boost the operating flexibility of these services[4]. A Member State approves airfreight carriers whose licence has been issued by another Member State and which has been authorised by the State of registration to exercise third-, fourth- and fifth-freedom traffic rights. Fifth freedom traffic rights are exercised on a service, which is the extension of a service on departure from the State where the carrier is registered or a preliminary to a service whose end destination is this State. The prices applied by Community air carriers for freight transport are set freely by mutual agreement of the parties to the transport contract. Air carriers operating services within the Community must place all their standard freight rates at the disposal of the general public on request.

The establishment of **common rules in the field of civil aviation** aims at guaranteeing European citizens high safety and environmental protection standards and at facilitating activity in the aeronautics industry in Europe[5]. Aeronautical products are henceforth subject to certification to verify that they meet essential airworthiness and environmental protection requirements relating to civil aviation, notably to the design, production, maintenance and operation of aeronautical products, parts and appliances. Appropriate essential requirements cover operations of aircraft and flight crew licensing. They apply to third-country aircraft and other areas in the field of civil aviation safety. In addition, a Community blacklist contains airlines that are banned throughout the Euro-

---

[1] Regulation 2409/92, OJ L 240, 24.08.1992.
[2] Council resolution, OJ C 293, 14.10.2000.
[3] Regulation 261/2004, OJ L 46, 17.02.2004.
[4] Regulation 2408/92, OJ L 240 of 24.08.1992 last amended by Regulation 1882/2003, OJ L 284, 31.10.2003.
[5] Regulation 1592/2002, OJ L 240, 07.09.2002 and Regulation 1701/2003, OJ L 243, 27.09.2003.

pean Union and a series of measures aimed at better informing air passengers about the identity of the airline they are travelling with[1].

In order to respond to increasing concerns over the health and welfare of passengers during flights, the common rules aim, among other things, to develop aircraft designs which better protect the safety and health of passengers. An independent Community body, the **European Aviation Safety Agency** assists the Commission in the preparation of the necessary legislation and the Member States and the industry in its implementation. It is able to issue certification specifications and certificates as required. It is allowed to develop its expertise in all aspects of civil aviation safety and environmental protection [see details below].

A package of common rules on the use of airspace throughout the Community, called the "**single European sky**" package, aims at improving and reinforcing safety, and at restructuring airspace on the basis of traffic flow rather than according to national boundaries, at encouraging cross-border air navigation service provision and at establishing a framework for the modernisation of systems[2] [see details below]. The specific regulatory framework is based on a system of authorisation for the supply of air navigation services that permit enforcement of the rules defined in Community law, conformity assessment mechanisms enabling Member States' authorities to check compliance, and provisions and procedures for payment of air navigation services. The measures concern an integrated, harmonised management of Community airspace, which implies the supply of services by flexible and efficient providers guided by demand from airspace users and therefore they entail a less rigid interpretation by States of national sovereignty over their airspace. Development of these measures requires, in addition to greater involvement of industry and the social partners, recourse to the technical expertise of the European Organisation for the Safety of Air Navigation (Eurocontrol) and the possible creation of a military cooperation framework.

Strong growth rates in air traffic inside and to and from Europe have placed severe strain on some parts of the air transport infrastructure and have worsened air traffic delays. In a 1995 Resolution, the Council invited the Member States and the Commission to coordinate their actions in the framework of the **European Organisation for the Safety of Air Navigation (Eurocontrol)**, the independent organisation responsible for coordinating the Member States' air traffic management systems, in order to combat congestion and better manage crises situations in the European airspace[3]. As a matter of fact, the Regulation, which is designed to achieve the gradual harmonisation and integration of national air-traffic systems, makes mandatory the technical specifications drawn up by Eurocontrol, thus allowing the Commission to adopt Eurocontrol standards[4]. The accession by the European Community to Eurocontrol, aiming at ensuring consistency between the two institutions and improving the regulatory framework for air traffic management, forms part of the overall strategy to build up a single sky over the single market[5]. Accession by the Community was preceded, in 1997, by revision of the 1960 convention setting up Eurocontrol in order to extend Eurocontrol's powers to all aspects of air traffic management and provide the organisation with more efficient decision-making mechanisms, reinforcing discipline on the part of its Member States[6].

---

[1]   Regulation 2111/2005, OJ L 344, 27.12.2005.
[2]   Regulations 549/2004 to 552/2004, OJ L 96, 31.03.2004.
[3]   OJ C 323, 04.12.1995.
[4]   Regulation 552/2004, OJ L 96, 31.03.2004.
[5]   Decision 2004/636, OJ L 304, 30.09.2004.
[6]   COM (2002) 292, 6 June 2002.

As part of the third liberalisation package for air transport, the Council has established a code of conduct guaranteeing the transparent, efficient and non-discriminatory allocation of **slots for civil aviation** at Community airports[1]. The code, which was amended in 2002 to help air carriers adjust to the sharp fall in demand following the terrorist attacks of 11 September 2001 in the USA, is based on the "use it or lose it" principle. It lays down conditions of access for new entrants to the market, for free exchange of slots and for safeguard mechanisms where there is a clear imbalance between air carriers. In the same context, a Directive on access to the groundhandling market at Community airports is designed to enable European airlines to benefit from real choice of providers of groundhandling services so as to better manage their operating costs and adjust their own services to users' needs[2]. Statistical returns in respect of the carriage of passengers, freight and mail by air provide the statistical basis for developing a Community aviation policy[3].

On the international scene, the Community concluded the 1999 **Montreal Convention**[4], which lays down new rules on liability in respect of the international carriage by air of persons, baggage and cargo, which are expected to replace those of the Warsaw Convention of 1929. Both Conventions provide for the possibility of unlimited liability. In this context, a regulation on insurance requirements for air carriers and aircraft operators introduced minimum insurance requirements for all aircraft flying into and out of Community airports or overflying Community territory, applicable also to third-country carriers[5].

The Commission, acting in close and regular contact with the relevant authorities in the Member States, can take measures to ensure the **application of the competition rules** of Articles 81 and 82 of the EC Treaty to transactions between airlines which have an impact on routes between the EU and third countries[6]. It can approve certain **categories of agreements** and concerted practices in the air transport sector[7], notably those concerning joint planning and coordination of schedules, joint operations, consultations on passenger and cargo tariffs on scheduled air services and slot allocation at airports[8]. These exemptions pursue two aims: encourage airlines to cooperate with a view to improving the service on offer to passengers, particularly in the exploitation of new or low density lines, while remaining competitive from the viewpoint of fares and service quality. In addition there exists a block exemption for agreements subject to the code of conduct for computerised reservation systems (CRS), the purpose of which is to ensure that there is fair competition between air carriers and that users are well informed[9]. In order to protect European airlines, which are subject to the competition rules, from the unfair practices of subsidised third-country airlines, a regulation enables the Commission to open an investigation following a complaint from industry or on its own initiative and, if necessary, to take redressive measures in the form of duties levied on third-country carriers receiving State aid or on State-controlled airlines, in proportion to the damage suffered by the European carriers[10].

The **"single European sky" package** contains a framework regulation and three implementing regulations. The "framework regulation" establishes a harmonised regulatory framework for the creation of the single European sky initiative, aiming at enhancing safety standards and overall efficiency for general air traffic in Europe, optimising capacity meeting the requirements of all airspace users and minimising delays[11]. The "services regulation" aims at establishing common requirements to guarantee the safe and efficient provision of air navigation services in a seamless and interoperable manner throughout the Community[12]. The "airspace regulation" establishes common procedures for design, planning and management ensuring the efficient and safe performance of air traffic management[13]. The "interoperability regulation" concerns: interoperability between the different systems, constituents and associated procedures of the European air traffic management network (EATMN); and the introduction of new agreed and validated concepts in air traffic management operation and technology[14]. The issuing of a Community **air traffic controller licence** aims to increase safety standards and to improve the operation of the Community air traffic control system[15].

In the field of **air safety**, a cooperation and mutual assistance procedure governs the investigation of civil aviation accidents and incidents[16]. Moreover, a Directive aims to ensure that relevant information is reported, collected, stored, protected and disseminated on any operational interruption, defect, fault or other irregular circumstance that has or may have influenced flight safety and that has not resulted in an accident or

---

[1] Regulation 95/93, OJ L 14, 22.01.1993 and Regulation 793/2004, OJ L 138, 30.04.2004.
[2] Directive 96/67, OJ L 272, 25.10.1996.
[3] Regulation 437/2003, OJ L 66, 11.03.2003 last amended by Regulation 546/2005, OJ L 91, 09.04.2005.
[4] Convention and Decision 2001/539, OJ L 194, 18.07.2001.
[5] Regulation 785/2004, OJ L 138, 30.04.2004.
[6] Regulation 411/2004, OJ L 68, 06.03.2004.
[7] Regulation 3976/87, OJ L 374, 31.12.1987 and Regulation 411/2004, OJ L 68, 06.03.2004.
[8] Regulation 1617/93, OJ L 155, 26.06.1993 last amended by Regulation 1105/2002, OJ L 167, 26.06.2002.
[9] Regulation 2299/89, OJ L 220, 27.07.1989 and Regulation 323/1999, OJ L 40, 13.02.1999.
[10] Regulation 868/2004, OJ L 162, 30.04.2004.
[11] Regulation 549/2004, OJ L 96, 31.03.2004.
[12] Regulation 550/2004, OJ L 96, 31.03.2004.
[13] Regulation 551/2004, OJ L 96, 31.03.2004.
[14] Regulation 552/2004, OJ L 96, 31.03.2004.
[15] Directive 2006/23, OJ L 114, 27.04.2006.
[16] Directive 94/56, OJ L 319, 12.12.1994.

serious incident[1]. Certain measures concern both air safety and market organisation. This is the case of the Directive on the mutual recognition of crew licences[2] and of the Regulation on the harmonisation of the technical requirements and administrative procedures in the field of civil aviation[3]. A Directive limits the operation in the Community of aircraft from developing countries not complying with the requirements of the Convention on International Civil Aviation[4] [see section 16.3.6.]. Another Directive on the safety of third-country aircraft using Community airports formalises the assessment procedure for non-Community air carriers and requires Member States to ground aircraft found or suspected to be dangerous[5]. A Regulation determines the air-carrier liability in the event of death, wounding or any other bodily injuries suffered by a passenger and provides for rapid payment of a lump sum to the victims or entitled persons in the case of an accident[6]. Following the terrorist attacks of 11 September 2001 in the USA, the EU adopted common rules in the field of civil aviation security, in order to prevent acts of unlawful interference against civil aviation[7]. Each Member State is required to adopt a national civil aviation security programme and to appoint an authority with specific and exclusive powers to coordinate and manage its implementation.

A particularly thorny problem in the field of air transport is that of **Community competence in foreign relations**. Member States have resisted the exercise of this competence and have continued to negotiate agreements with third countries, concerning, for example, access of the Community internal market by third-country operators. The Commission brought infringement proceedings against seven Member States which had concluded what are known as "open skies" agreements with the United States, on the ground that the agreements infringed the Treaty rules on freedom of establishment and the Community's exclusive external competence. On the question of freedom of establishment, the Court agreed with the Commission that there was discrimination contrary to the freedom of establishment guaranteed by the Treaty, because the Member State concluding such an agreement reserved rights for its own airlines[8]. On the question of the infringement of the Community's exclusive external competence, the Court said that Article 80(2) of the EC Treaty merely provided for a power for the Community to take action which was dependent on there being a prior decision of the Council. In the absence of such a decision, there was no express external Community competence. However, according to the Court, international commitments did affect the common rules where they fell within an area which was already largely covered by such rules, or where the Community had included in its internal legislative acts, such as the provisions on the establishment of fares and rates on intra-Community routes, and those relating to computerised reservation systems and the allocation of airport slots. Following the ruling by the Court of Justice, the Commission asked the Council for a mandate to negotiate a new generation of agreements incorporating non-discriminatory traffic rights for national and international flights throughout Union territory, ensuring effective competition and guarantying a high level of safety and environmental protection[9]. On 5 June 2003, the Council accepted the Commission's request to create an "open aviation area" framework for air transport relations between the Member States of the Union and third countries, including the United States. On 30 March 2004, the Council approved the text of the "Declaration of competence" of the Community and authorised the Presidency to deposit the declaration with the International Civil Aviation Organisation (ICAO) in Montreal, together with the instrument for ratification of the Montreal Convention for the Unification of Certain Rules for International Carriage by Air. A regulation is designed to establish a framework consistent with the operation of the international aviation market, within which Member States can continue to negotiate and implement the agreements in question, while complying with the Community law applicable in this "joint competence" area[10].

---

[1]   Directive 2003/42, OJ L 167, 04.07.2003.
[2]   Directive 91/670, OJ L 373, 31.12.1991.
[3]   Regulation 3922/91, OJ L 373, 31.12.1991 and Regulation 1069/1999, OJ L 130, 26.05.1999.
[4]   Directive 2006/93, OJ L 374, 27.12.2006.
[5]   Directive 2004/36, OJ L 143, 30.04.2004 and Regulation 2111/2005, JO L 344, 27.12.2005.
[6]   Regulation 2027/97, OJ L 285, 17.10.1997 and Regulation 889/2002, OJ L 140, 30.05.2002.
[7]   Regulation 2320/2002, OJ L 355, 30.12.2002 and Regulation 849/2004, OJ L 158, 30.04.2004.
[8]   Judgment of 5 November 2002, Cases C-466/98, C-467/98, Case C-468/98, C-469/98, C-471/98, C-472/98, C-475/98, and 476/98, *Commission* v *United Kingdom; Denmark, Sweden,. Finland, Belgium, Luxembourg, Austria and Germany*, ECR 2002.
[9]   COM (2002) 649, 19 November 2002.
[10] Regulation 847/2004, OJ L 157, 30.04.2004.

20.4. Appraisal and outlook

Until the end of the 1980s, the Community achievements in the transport sector did not measure up to the clear need for a policy expressly mentioned in the Treaty of Rome as **a crucial cornerstone of the common market**. In fact, during thirty years the Member States rejected measures of liberalisation proposed by the Commission which, they maintained, would upset competition conditions, both between the various modes of transport and within each one of them. Council deliberations revolved around the sophistic question of whether market liberalisation or harmonisation of competition conditions should come first. The Council's failure to act, forcefully pointed out by the European Parliament in its 1982 resolution, was chiefly due to an **absence of political commitment** to pushing economic integration in this field. As a consequence, national experts, who prepared the Council meetings, played a very important role in examining the Commission's proposals [see section 9.4.]. Since these proposals, by their very nature, were likely to perturb vested interests and the economic policy concepts of the Member States, very often there was exaggerated defence of national interest and sectoral perception of the problems, which did not make sufficient allowance for the requirements of European integration. These requirements finally prevailed, however. Whether under pressure from the European Parliament and public opinion or the need to integrate transport into the post-1992 single market, **transport policy stepped on the accelerator** in the middle of the 1980s, particularly in three fields: road haulage, maritime transport and air transport.

The greatest breakthrough for the common transport policy has undoubtedly been in the area of **liberalising international road haulage services**. All the quotas applicable to cross-border transport within the Community were replaced by a system of Community licences issued on the basis of qualitative criteria. The fact that the liberalisation introduced gradually since the early 1990s has not upset the road haulage market, shows that the fears of some national administrations of the common transport market upsetting their national markets were exaggerated.

In the area of **maritime transport**, which is the carrier for 85% of the EEC's external trade, the Member States undertook to apply the rules of free competition and the principle of free provision of services to this sector. They also agreed to fight unfair tariff practices and unsafe seafaring methods, while guaranteeing free access to ocean trades and even to cabotage. All cabotage services in Europe have been liberalised between January 1999 and December 2002. The market has not been adversely affected. Cargo volumes and the number of passengers transported have remained relatively stable.

As regards **air transport**, the liberalisation measures completed in 1992 have had a major impact on competition between air carriers. Additional routes were opened, new services were introduced, monopolies were put under pressure, inefficient national companies were forced to modernise or close down and new companies were created. Nevertheless, basic fares are still too high if compared to those in other regions of the world, especially the United States. The costs of air transport remain high, largely because of heavy infrastructure charges and airport fees. Access to the market is still too difficult, mainly due to bilateral agreements between the Member States and third countries. Despite the temporary slowdown caused by the terrorist attacks of 11 September 2001, the main concern for the future is the saturation of the Community's airports and air corridors, due to substantial increase in air traffic. To meet this challenge, air safety should be enhanced through the creation of a European aviation safety authority.

Bibliography on transport policy

- BANISTER David. "Transport and urban sprawl: the EU perspective" in *Scienze Regionali*, v. 5, n. 3, 2006. p. 97-105.
- BOVIS Christopher. "State aid and European Union transport: a reflection on law, policy and practice", *Journal of World Trade*, v. 39, n. 4, August 2005, p. 587-636.
- COMBES Michel (et al.). *Transport aérien: gagner ensemble = Air transport: winning together*. Paris: Publisud, 2006.
- CROZET Yves. "L'avenir des transports", *Sociétal*, n. 48, 3ème trimestre 2005, p. 59-100.
- EUROPEAN COMMISSION. *Information society and transport: linking European policies*. Luxembourg: EUR-OP*, 2006.
  - *Keep Europe moving: Sustainable mobility for our continent - Mid-term review of the European Commission's 2001 Transport White Paper*. Luxembourg: EUR-OP*, 2006.
  - *Road transport policy: Open roads across Europe*. Luxembourg: EUR-OP*, 2006.
  - *Maritime transport policy: improving the competitiveness, safety and security of European shipping*. Luxembourg: EUR-OP*, 2006.
  - *Transport and environment facing a dilemma: TERM 2005: indicators tracking transport and environment in the European Union*. Luxembourg: EUR-OP*, 2006.
  - *Freight Transport Logistics in Europe - the key to sustainable mobility*. Luxembourg: EUR-OP*, 2006.
- EUROPEAN CONFERENCE OF MINISTERS OF TRANSPORT. *50 years of transport research: experience gained and major challenges ahead*. Paris: ECMT, 2005.
  - *Improving transport accessibility for all: guide to good practice*. Paris: ECMT, 2006.
- GILLE Alain. "La co-modalité outil du développement durable" in *Transports*, année 51, n. 436, mars-avril 2006, p. 73-82.
- GÓMEZ-IBÁÑEZ José. *Competition in the railway industry: an international comparative analysis*. Cheltenham: Edward Elgar, 2006.
- HISELIUS Lena. *External costs of transports imposed on neighbours and fellow road users*. Lund: Lund University, 2005.
- KERNOHAN David (ed.). *Integrating Europe's transport system: practical proposals for the mid-term review of the transport white paper*. Brussels: Centre for European Policy Studies, 2006.
- RAJ Pravin (et al. eds.). *Connected transportation*. Walmer: Torworth, 2006.
- RICHARDS Martin. *Congestion charging in London: the policy and politics*. Basingstoke: Palgrave Macmillan, 2006.
- TILLING Christina (et al.). "Infrastructure, transport and public services" in *South East Europe Review*, v. 9, n. 1, 2006, p. 7-96.
- VON DEN STEIN Erwin. *National interest and international aviation*. Alphen aan den Rijn: Kluwer Law International, 2006.

The publications of the Office for Official Publications of the European Communities (EUR-OP) exist usually in all official languages of the EU.

Chapter 21

AGRICULTURAL POLICY

Diagram of the chapter

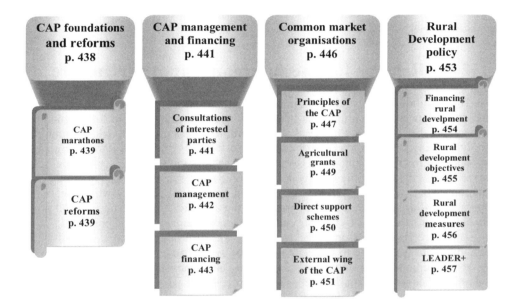

CAP foundations and reforms p. 438	CAP management and financing p. 441	Common market organisations p. 446	Rural Development policy p. 453
CAP marathons p. 439	Consultations of interested parties p. 441	Principles of the CAP p. 447	Financing rural develpment p. 454
CAP reforms p. 439	CAP management p. 442	Agricultural grants p. 449	Rural development objectives p. 455
	CAP financing p. 443	Direct support schemes p. 450	Rural development measures p. 456
		External wing of the CAP p. 451	LEADER+ p. 457

The share of agriculture in the EU-27 gross domestic product (GDP) is just under 3%; but the sector is the principal source of income for around 20% of its population, which live in predominantly rural regions that would be devastated without its contribution. Moreover, the combined agricultural and food sector forms an important part of the EU economy, accounting for 15 million jobs (8.3% of total employment) and 4.4% of GDP. The EU is the world's largest producer of food and beverages, with combined production estimated at EUR 675 billion. Finally and most importantly, the self-sufficiency of the EC/EU in basic agricultural products is vital, not only for the wellbeing of its citizens, but also for the political independence of its Member States. The economic, **social and political importance of agriculture** is, therefore, much greater than its share in the GDP of the Union.

Without a shadow of a doubt, agriculture is the economic sector where **the process of European integration is furthest advanced**. This achievement is all the more significant in that State interventionism and the conflicts of national interests complicated the task of creating a common policy in this sector. Indeed, prior to the common market, the Member States were actively interventionist in agriculture [see section 21.1.]. National interventionism had to be corrected to enable free trade and free play of competition in the agricultural sector. The creation of the **Common Agricultural Policy (CAP)** is therefore an exemplary achievement of the multinational integration process.

Nonetheless, the common agricultural policy is **difficult to manage**, for it implies the use of common prices, common price management instruments, joint financing of support measures and common external protection. All these cumbersome but unavoidable mechanisms form part of the CAP's market organisation. The latter is one of **the CAP's two wings**, the other being rural development policy. Although the common market in agricultural products has ensured supply security of foodstuffs at reasonable prices for consumers, it would not have been sufficient in itself to attain the other objectives of the Treaty, namely increased agricultural productivity and a higher standard of living for farmers. The latter required an active socio-structural policy, interacting with other common policies, such as the regional and social, to guarantee the Community's rural areas a place in the single market.

21.1. Reasons for special treatment of agriculture

The founding fathers of the European Economic Community were well aware of the need to include the agricultural markets of the Member States in the future common market. But they were also aware that the **common agricultural market could not simply be achieved** by abolishing the barriers to free movement and introducing common competition rules, as in the sectors of industry and the services [see section 6.2.]. This is why Article 32 of the EC Treaty (ex Art. 38) states in its first paragraph that the common market includes agriculture and trade in agricultural products, while specifying in paragraph 4 that the operation and growth of the common market in agricultural products must be accompanied by the introduction of a common agricultural policy.

There are several reasons why agriculture was afforded "special treatment". The most important is that due to the **very nature of agriculture**, which is at the mercy of weather conditions, crop and livestock diseases and many other factors which often elude human control and make it very difficult to ensure a perfect balance between agricultural output and the demand for foodstuffs. In addition, demand has very pronounced social and political characteristics. Governments are obliged to ensure that demand for basic commodities is satisfied at all times and at reasonable prices. The original Community was far from self-sufficient in foodstuffs and conditions on the world market provided no justification for the unilateral opening up of markets. Consequently, if food security was to be guaranteed at stable prices, the Community had to organise its own agriculture. This was quite reasonable, since the agricultural output of the different Member States was complementary. Northern Europe could supply cereals, dairy products and meat, whereas Southern Europe could specialise in fruit and vegetables, citrus fruit and wines.

However, the diversity of the agricultural sector of the six founding Member States, which increased with each enlargement of the Community, generated difficulties for the unification of their agricultural markets, providing further justification for an **interventionist agricultural policy**. Different natural, structural, social and trade conditions, the prominence of agriculture in the national economy and different farming traditions led to the use in each European State of agricultural policy instruments which diverged considerably as to their application scope and magnitude. The common policy therefore had to not only align structurally different agricultural systems, but also to iron out tenaciously held privileges resulting from the interplay of national political institutions: State monopolies or similar regulations, price guarantees, farm income aid, export subsidies, direct or indirect import restrictions, customs protection and so on. A new agricultural policy stepping in the shoes of the national ones had to be defined. The complexity of the latter created the need for the blending of national policies into one common agricultural policy.

One could ask **why organise agricultural markets at all?** The answer is that the agricultural markets of the Member States were already organised in various ways at national level. Indeed, almost all states in the world intervene in one way or another to ensure the income of their farmers and stable supply for their consumers. The only difference is that the system of intervention varies from one to the other. They can however be divided into two main categories: direct income aid systems for farmers, which existed in the United Kingdom before its entry to the Community and was called deficiency payments; and the system of price support on the internal market combined with external protection, the system chosen for the bulk of the original EEC's agricultural production[1].

The system of support for agricultural prices was thought, at the time, to be better adapted to the interests of the original Community. In effect, under the alternative **direct income aid** system, agricultural products are imported at world prices, generally low when they are in ample supply, and the income of national farmers topped up by a subsidy from the budget. This system is better adapted to countries, which are almost self-sufficient in agricultural products and/or where farmers are not very numerous. If the original EEC countries, which were not yet self-sufficient in agricultural products and had a large number of farmers, were to begin purchasing openly on the world market, initially lower world prices would drive out of work many European farmers and, then, as soon as demand would exceed supply, world prices would escalate and cause important price increases and even penury of certain foodstuffs for low-income consumers.

Under the **system of price support**, on the other hand, in order to provide national farmers with sufficient income, internal prices which are higher than the world prices for agricultural products are practised and the difference is compensated by import levies or customs duties and by export refunds (subsidies)[2]. The higher prices stimulate agricultural output and productivity. They also tend to guarantee self-sufficiency in basic agricultural products and foodstuffs, which is another point in their favour. If they are set too high they can naturally lead to production surpluses, which is a negative point, but which results more from the manner in which the system is applied than from the system itself. Inasmuch, however, as agricultural prices determine farmer income, it is socio-politically very difficult for Agricultural Ministers within the Council to cut these prices, even if the Commission, in its pricing proposals, provides them with arguments in favour of reducing surplus production through prices [see section 4.3.]. These same Ministers are, however, conscious of their own failings, since they periodically accept to revise the system through a CAP reform [see section 21.2.2.].

As will be seen in the nest section, the CAP was reformed four times in forty years, blending gradually the systems of price and income support. Thus, after its major reforms, in 1999 and 2003, the **European model of agriculture** is based on competitive,

---

[1] OJ 11, 01.08.1958.
[2] Regulation 800/1999, OJ L 102, 17.04.1999 last amended by Regulation 1847/2006, OJ L 355, 15.12.2006.

multifunctional and sustainable farming. This means that European agriculture is broadening its horizons, since farmers also perform a range of additional tasks, notably in the fields of environment and countryside conservation. As a result of their high population density and geographical differentiation, European countries must produce these services in addition to actual farm produce itself. The EU cannot afford to confine nature and the environment to some reserves. Therefore, agriculture must also be maintained in less-favoured areas as well. Since it is not developed in a vacuum, however, the European model of agriculture has to prove its worth, both internally in addressing issues such as market development, rural development, satisfactory farm incomes and environmental protection, and externally, in facing the challenges of an enlarged Union and heightened competition inside the World Trade Organisation [see section 23.4.].

21.2. CAP foundations and reforms

The **objectives** of the common agricultural policy are specified in Article 33 of the EC Treaty (ex-Art. 39): higher agricultural productivity; guarantee of a fair standard of living to farmers; market stabilisation; supply security and reasonable prices for consumers. In order to attain these objectives, Article 40 of the EEC Treaty (actual Art. 34 TEC) called for the **common organisation of agricultural markets** which, depending on the product, could take one of three forms: common coordination rules, compulsory coordination of the various national market organisations or European market organisation. It is interesting to note that it is always this last and most stringent concept that has been applied to the common organisation of agricultural markets.

The market policies were later supplemented by rural development policies to form the second pillar of the CAP. The guiding principles for the CAP, market and rural development policies, were set out by the European Council of Göteborg of June 2001 [see section 16.2]. According to its conclusions, strong economic performance must go hand in hand with the sustainable use of natural resources and levels of waste, maintaining biodiversity, preserving ecosystems and avoiding desertification. To meet these challenges, the CAP should contribute to achieving sustainable development by increasing its emphasis on encouraging healthy, high-quality products, environmentally sustainable production methods, including organic production, renewable raw materials and the protection of biodiversity.

The EEC Treaty was prudent as regards the **applicability of competition rules** to the agricultural sector, a sector where State intervention was rife. According to Article 42 (actual Art. 36 TEC), the applicability of the general Articles on competition was subordinated to specific provisions of the common agricultural policy. As early as 1962, however, the Council decided that the Treaty competition rules applicable to undertakings (Art. 85 to 91 EEC, Art. 81 to 86 TEC) should also be applied to agricultural undertakings [see section 15.3.]. Only cooperatives and farming associations could be granted a special regime. As it turned out, certain common market organisations assigned specific functions to producers' groups, thus involving them in the common policy[1] [see section 21.4.2.].

Competition rules for **State intervention** (Art. 92 to 94 EEC, Art. 87 to 89 TEC) became applicable to agricultural markets as and when common market organisations were established. Many of the market organisations consequently incorporate specific provisions on national or Community aid. The Member States became obliged to notify the Commission of all aid granted to agriculture as early as 1962. Since this date, the Commission has treated aid to agriculture in the same way as all other national aid.

The other Articles of the Treaty devoted to agriculture were chiefly transitional provisions. Article 43 EEC (Art. 37 TEC), however, was of special importance. It stipulated that a conference of the Member States was to be called by the Commission as soon as the Treaty had entered into force to enable the Member States

---

[1] Regulation 1257/1999, OJ L 160, 26.06.1999 and Regulation 1698/2005, OJ L 277, 21.10.2005.

to compare their agricultural policies and consequently come to an agreement on an outline of the common agricultural policy. This conference was called by the Commission in Stresa (Italy) in July 1958. Agricultural officials from the six signatory States, despite their different points of view and different situations as importers or exporters of agricultural produce, succeeded in reaching a general agreement on the protection of the common agricultural market against distorted external competition, on the need for a structural policy and a farm price policy and on the principle that farmers should be paid in a manner comparable to workers in other sectors. The **Stresa Conference clarified the agricultural objectives of the Treaty**, stipulating that for European agriculture to be internationally competitive, its structures should be overhauled, but that the family nature of European farms should be preserved; that for common farm prices to offer a decent standard of living, they should be set above world prices but not at a level encouraging over-production[1].

21.2.1. CAP marathons

The Commission's first proposals for common market organisations in June 1960 fired the starting gun for the hard-hitting negotiations in the Council, which became known as "**agricultural marathons**". Each of these negotiating rounds produced a common market organisation for the various agricultural products: cereals, pigmeat and poultry meat, eggs, beef and veal and dairy products, fruit and vegetables and wine etc. Despite the difficulties encountered in satisfying all the varying interests, it was to the credit of the young Community that by the end of 1963 a common market organisation existed for almost 85% of the agricultural output of the then six Member States.

Three years later, however, the **CAP came upon its first and only serious crisis**, which shook the whole Community. Indeed, the completion of the common agricultural policy required the Community to take control of the Member States' expenditure under the common market organisations. The Commission suggested in March 1965 that the common agricultural market be completed on July 1, 1968, together with the customs union for industrial products. However, the Council failed to meet its deadlines and, as a consequence, the Community lived through the most serious crisis in its history. In order to press its points of view, France under de Gaulle practised for seven months an **"empty chair" policy** in the Council and thus blocked any new Community initiative.

Work on the common agricultural policy only got back on track after **the Luxembourg compromise** of January 28, 1966 [see section 4.3.]. It culminated, in May 1966, in a Council agreement on Commission proposals for the financing of the agricultural policy[2]. This agreement under its belt, the Council was able to make fresh progress on the common market organisation for practically all agricultural products. Thanks to these decisions, the common agricultural market was able to be an integral part of the customs union created on July 1, 1968 [see section 5.1.].

21.2.2. CAP reforms

With most of the major decisions on the common market organisation thus taken, the Commission turned its attention to structures. In December 1968 it submitted to the Council a "Memorandum on the reform of agriculture in the European Economic Community: Agriculture 1980", otherwise known as the **Mansholt Plan** after the Commissioner who had inspired it. On this basis, the Council, after many "marathon sessions", adopted in April 1972 the Directives of the **first reform of the CAP** dealing respectively with: the modernisation of farms; measures to encourage the cessation of farming and the reallocation of utilised agricultural area for the purposes of structural improvement and the provision of socio-economic guidance for and the acquisition of occupational skills by persons engaged in agriculture[3].

The other structural measures which were adopted later on covered mountain and hill farming and farming in certain less-favoured areas, the processing and marketing of agricultural produce and producer groups and associations thereof. But other problems also emerged, such as permanent surpluses of the main agricultural products and continuing imbalances in the Community. To face these problems, the **second CAP reform** recommended by the Commission was approved by the Brussels European Council on February 11-13, 1988, which gave the green light to the "**Delors package I**". This package covered, in addition to reform of the common agricultural policy, the level of agricultural expenditure, budgetary discipline, the system of own resources and the reform of the Structural Funds, including the EAGGF Guidance section [see section 12.3.]. Acting on this European Council agreement, the Council of Ministers adopted the measures necessary for a new reform of the common agricultural policy, in April 1988[4]: market related measures, such as the system of stabilisers (maximum guaranteed quantities) and the co-responsibility levies; and structural measures in favour

---

[1] OJ 11, 01.08.1958.
[2] Regulation 130/66, OJ 165, 21.09.1966 last amended by Regulation 966/71, OJ L 105, 12.05.1971.
[3] Directives 72/159, 72/160 and 72/161, OJ L 96, 23.04.1972 last amended by Regulation 1698/2005, OJ L 277, 21.10.2005.
[4] Regulation 1094/88, OJ L 106, 27.04.1988 and Regulation 1137/88, OJ L 108, 29.04.1988.

of afforestation, the diversification of agriculture and incentives for the set-aside of farmland. But since the impact of this set of measures proved to be too small, because technical progress allowed a large increase of agricultural output despite the restrictions, the Commission, in 1991, proposed a much more radical reform of the market mechanisms.

After several agricultural "marathons", the Council, on May 21, 1992, reached a political agreement on the Commission's proposals for the **third reform** of the CAP. The Council upheld the three guidelines proposed by the Commission: a substantial cut in the target prices of agricultural products in order to make them more competitive on internal and external markets; full and sustained compensation of this drop in farmers' income by compensatory amounts or premiums not linked to the quantities produced; and recourse to measures limiting the use of means of production (set-aside of arable land, withdrawal of part of the land for major crops, limits on livestock numbers per hectare of fodder area). At the same time, the Council decided to increase measures to conserve the environment and landscapes, encourage the early retirement of certain categories of farmers with the transfer of their land to other uses and facilitate the use of farmland for other purposes, such as afforestation or leisure. Through this profound revision of its agricultural legislation, the Community, which is the world's biggest trading entity, has made possible the liberalisation of international trade through the GATT Uruguay Round of negotiations[1] [see section 23.4.].

However, the third reform of the CAP was not the last. In its outlook document of 15 July 1997 called **"Agenda 2000"** [see section 15.1.2.], the Commission considered it necessary to continue the 1992 reform of the CAP and press ahead with the transition to world market prices, particularly through a substantial drop in the common support prices for cereals and beef and veal offset by an increase in income premiums for Community farmers[2]. According to the Commission, this approach was justified for a variety of reasons: the danger of further market imbalances, the prospect of a new round of trade negotiations within the WTO, the desire for a more environment-friendly and quality-oriented agriculture, the prospect of enlargement to the countries of Central and Eastern Europe and, last but not least, the interest of the consumer for lower prices and safer food products.

The political agreement of the Berlin European Council on the Commission's outlook paper "Agenda 2000", resulted in the **fourth reform of the CAP**, in March 1999, taking account of the future enlargement of the EU. The reform package included a set of regulations that aimed to develop a more modern and sustainable European agricultural sector, thus ensuring that agriculture can be maintained over the long term at the heart of a living countryside[3].

Established in July 1966, the CAP was reformed a first time in April 1972, a second time in February 1988, a third time in May 1992, a fourth time in March 1999 and a fifth time in September 2003. Five major reforms of a common policy in less than 40 years may indicate that the Member States that conceived it and those that joined them later on have never considered it as perfect; but may also show that they were willing to learn from their experience and able to **adapt their common policy** to the changing internal and external circumstances.

Successive reforms have contributed to the competitiveness of European agriculture by reducing price support guarantees and encouraging structural adjustment. **The fifth CAP reform**, carried out in September 2003, provides for a single farm payment for European Union farmers, independent from production and subject to compliance with environmental, food safety, animal and plant health and animal welfare standards, and requirements to keep all farmland in good agricultural and environmental condition ("cross-compliance")[4]. The introduction of decoupled direct payments encourages farmers to respond to market signals generated by consumer demand rather than by quantity-related policy incentives. The reform is aimed at enabling the farmers of the twenty-seven Member States to be more competitive and be more market-oriented whilst stabilising their income, and at channelling more resources into programmes on the environ-

---

[1]   Regulation 3290/94, OJ L 349, 31.12.1994 and Regulation 1340/98, OJ L 184, 27.06.1998.
[2]   COM (97) 2000, 15 July 1997.
[3]   Notably, Council Regulation 1257/1999, OJ L 160, 26.06.1999 last amended by Regulation 1698/2005, OJ L 277, 21.10.2005 and Regulation and 1259/1999, OJ L 160, 26.06.1999, repealed by Regulation 1782/2003, OJ L 270, 21.10.2003.
[4]   Regulations 1782/2003 to 1788/2003, OJ L 270, 21.10.2003 and Regulation318/2006, OJ L 58, 28.02.2006.

ment, quality and animal welfare by reducing direct payments to large farms. It is expected also to strengthen the European Union's hand in the trade negotiations in the World Trade Organisation.

After its fourth and fifth reforms, the CAP is targeted not just at agricultural producers but also at the wider rural population, consumers and society as a whole. Thus **the new CAP seeks to promote**:

- a clear connection between public support and the range of services which society as a whole receives from the farming community;
- a competitive agricultural sector which is capable of exploiting the opportunities existing on world markets without excessive subsidy, while at the same time ensuring a fair standard of living for the agricultural community;
- an agricultural sector that is sustainable in environmental terms, contributing to the preservation of natural resources and the natural and cultural heritage of the countryside;
- the maintenance of vibrant rural communities, capable of generating employment opportunities for the rural population [see section 21.5];
- production methods which are safe and capable of supplying quality products that meet consumer demand and reflect the diversified and rich tradition of European food production.

21.3. CAP management and financing

The unity of the European Union's agricultural market requires common prices, common support instruments for these prices, common external protection, joint financing and, in general, **joint management**, for which the European Commission has responsibility. The Commission, as for other areas of Community activity, is also invested with the power of initiative, i.e. the power to make proposals [see section 4.1.2.]. Hence, the genesis of any agricultural policy measure, adopted by politicians in the Parliament and the Council, is a Commission proposal, based on technocratic criteria.

21.3.1. Consultations of interested parties and experts

A **vast number of experts** are involved in drafting and implementing the common agricultural policy. The Commission, acting in accordance with the Treaty, naturally consults the Committee of the Regions and the Economic and Social Committee (ESC) on all its major proposals in the field of the CAP. The ESC is made up of representatives of the various socio-professional categories and farmers are therefore also in its midst [see section 4.2.3.]. In addition, the Commission cooperates closely with **farmers' professional bodies** to ensure that allowance is made for their interests in the drafting of common policy and the management of the common market organisations. This is why a large number of professional farming bodies operate at European level, the most important of which are: the Committee of Agricultural Organisations in the European Community (**COPA**), an umbrella body for farmers; the General Committee for Agricultural Cooperation in the EC (**COGECA**), which represents farm cooperatives; and the Commission of the Agriculture and Food Industries (**CIAA**), representing these industrial sectors. The European Centre for Promotion and Training in Agricultural and Rural Areas (**CEPFAR**) seeks to promote information and the basic and advanced vocational training of agricultural experts. A communication strategy is intended to provide consistent, objective and comprehensive information on the common agricultural policy both inside and outside the Community[1].

However, consultation of these large general organisations tends to be on the mainstream policies of the CAP. The Commission rapidly felt a need to be better informed on specific problems in each agricultural sector. As a consequence, as part of the process of implementing the common market organisations, it has set up an **advisory committee for each product or product group** falling under a common market organisation.

---

[1]   Regulation 814/2000, OJ L 100, 20.04.2000 and Regulation 2208/2002, OJ L 337, 13.12.2002.

The socio-economic interest groups represented in these committees are: agricultural producers, agricultural co-operatives, the agricultural and food-manufacturing industries, the agricultural products and foodstuffs trade, farm workers and workers in the food industry, and consumers. The advisory committees give an opinion on the proposals put before them during the drafting phase within the Commission. No vote is taken for the advisory committee opinion, which is in no way binding for the Commission[1]. However, the advisory committees enable the Commission to learn the views of interested parties on the major sectors of farm policy (arable crops, animal products, etc.) and they are often seen by their members as opportunities for dialogue and participation in decision-making, a highly important factor for building a consensual policy in a sector involving very different interests.

Scientific committees, made up of experts from all Member States, give advice to the Commission on the very important matters of consumer health and food safety. Eight committees meet about ten times a year, and the Commission consults them whenever there is a legal requirement to do so, and whenever a matter of special relevance to one of them arises. A Scientific Steering Committee (SSC) has a multidisciplinary role. One of its tasks is to coordinate the work of the scientific committees to provide an overall view of consumer health matters, and to deliver scientific advice on matters not covered by the mandates of the other scientific committees, e.g. on transmissible spongiform encephalopathies. The operation of the scientific committees and, in particular, of the SSC, is based on the three principles of excellence, independence and transparency.

After all this preparatory work inside the services of the Commission, once a Commission proposal in the area of the common agricultural policy has been put before it, the Council entrusts the preparation of its proceedings to a committee of senior officials known as the **Special Committee on Agriculture** (SCA). In the area of agriculture, the SCA assumes the role normally fulfilled by the Committee of Permanent Representatives (Coreper) [see section 4.1.4.].

21.3.2. CAP Management

After adoption of the basic regulations by the Council comes management of the common organisations. Management is either the joint responsibility of the Commission and Council or that of the Commission alone. For general policy decisions such as the annual setting of farm prices, undertaken in application of the basic regulations, the **full procedure** is used: the Commission after consulting professional organisations submits a proposal to the Council, which takes a decision after consultation with the European Parliament and very often the Economic and Social Committee as well as the Committee of the Regions [see section 4.3.]. For long-application management provisions, such as adjustments of market mechanisms or of basic criteria, a **medium-length procedure** is used: the Commission proposes measures to the Council, which takes a decision without consulting either the European Parliament or the Economic and Social Committee.

The implementation provisions for basic regulations and management measures in the strict sense of the term, which are applicable on average for a few weeks or a few months, are adopted by the Commission using a procedure known as the **"Management Committee" procedure**, whereby the Commission acts after having received the opinion of the relevant management committee[2]. Management committees comprise representatives of the Member States dealing with a specific sector [see section 9.4.]. They give their opinion on the Commission's plans for the management of agricultural markets. There is a management committee for each category of product: cereals, milk products, beef and veal, wine, fruit and vegetables, etc. Very important management commit-

---

[1]   Decision 2004/391, OJ L 120, 24.04.2004.
[2]   Regulation 2602/69, OJ L 324, 27.12.1969.

tees are notably: the Committee of the EAGF, which deals exclusively with matters relating to and the Committee on rural development, which assists the Commission with the management of the common agricultural and rural development policies. **Regulatory committees**, also made up of representatives of all the Member States, play a role similar to that of the management committees for decisions about the regulations that apply in general areas such as food safety legislation, common veterinary or plant health standards, etc.

The **management committees** vote by qualified majority. In cases where the Commission is empowered by the Council to take decisions after consultation of a management committee, it must submit a draft of the measures, which it intends adopting, to the relevant committee in good time. If the committee issues a favourable opinion or no opinion at all, the Commission can proceed with the adoption of the planned measures. Should a negative opinion be given, the Commission can adopt the measures but must notify them to the Council, which has one month to adopt a different decision by a qualified majority[1].

The voting arrangements for **regulatory committees** are the same as for management committees. However, the committee's opinion is binding on the Commission, which cannot adopt the measures unless the committee's opinion is favourable. When the committee delivers an unfavourable opinion on the Commission's proposed measures, or when no opinion is delivered, the Commission cannot take any decision, even a provisional one; it must pass the proposal on to the Council immediately. The Council must act within a period laid down in each instrument to be adopted by it, but this period may in no case exceed three months. It may adopt the proposal by a qualified majority, or amend it by unanimity. If the Council has not acted by the end of the period, the measures initially proposed are adopted by the Commission. If, within the time limit, the Council rejects the proposed measures by a simple majority, the Commission may not take a decision; however, it may consult the committee again, on the same proposal or different measures.

21.3.3. CAP financing

Article 34 of the EC Treaty (Art. 40 EEC) - devoted to the gradual development of the common agricultural policy - declared that one or several agricultural guidance and guarantee funds should be created to enable the common organisation of agricultural markets to fulfil its goals. On January 14, 1962 during the first agricultural marathon, the Council opted for the creation of one single fund to finance all Community market and structural expenditure in the various agricultural sectors: the **European Agricultural Guidance and Guarantee Fund (EAGGF)**. The Fund was set up in 1962, but the arrangements on the financing of the common agricultural policy were finalised in 1970.

The reform of the common agricultural policy in June 2003 and April 2004 [see section 21.2.2] introduced major changes having a significant impact on the economy of rural territories of the Community in terms of agricultural production patterns, land management methods, employment and the wider social and economic conditions in the various rural areas. Consequently, the European Agricultural Guidance and Guarantee Fund (EAGGF) was abolished and two European agricultural funds were created in 2005, namely the **European Agricultural Guarantee Fund (EAGF)**, for the financing of market measures, and the **European Agricultural Fund for Rural Development (EAFRD)**, for the financing of rural development programmes[2].

As of January 2007, **the EAGF finances** in a context of shared management between the Member States and the Community the following expenditure, which is effected in accordance with Community law: (a) refunds for the exportation of agricultural products to third countries; (b) intervention measures to regulate agricultural markets; (c) direct payments to farmers under the common agricultural policy; and (d) the Community's financial contribution to information and promotion measures for agricultural

---

[1] Decision 1999/468, OJ L 184, 17.07.1999 last amended by Decision 2006/512, OJ L 200, 22.07.2006.
[2] Regulation 1290/2005, OJ L 209, 11.08.2005.

products on the internal market of the Community and in third countries, undertaken by Member States on the basis of Community programmes and selected by the Commission. **The EAFRD finance**s in a context of shared management between the Member States and the Community the Community's financial contribution to rural development programmes implemented in accordance with the Community legislation on support for rural development [see section 21.5]. Budget discipline takes account of the reform of the CAP as provided for by Regulation 1782/2003. The Commission and Member States share the costs of payments under the EAFRD and amounts to be recovered following the detection of irregularities and negligence.

The EAGF and the EAFRD may each respectively finance on a centralised basis, on the initiative of the Commission and/or on its behalf, the preparatory, monitoring, administrative and technical support, evaluation, audit and inspection measures required to implement the common agricultural policy, including rural development. **Paying agencies** are the departments or bodies of the Member States which, in respect of payments made by them and as regards communicating and keeping information, provide sufficient guarantees. They are controlled by **certification bodies**, which are designated by each Member State with a view to certifying the truthfulness, completeness and accuracy of the accounts of the accredited paying agency, taking account of the management and control systems set up. Each Member State must adopt all legislative, regulatory and administrative provisions and take any other measures necessary to ensure effective protection of the financial interests of the Community.

21.3.4. Control of agricultural expenditure

Approximately half of the EU budget goes towards financing the CAP, or around 0.6% of Community GDP [see section 3.4.]. Given the size of the agricultural budget, it is essential for the credibility of the CAP that proper systems are in place to ensure that these funds are spent correctly and to prevent fraud. Indeed, European taxpayers have a right to expect that all public money is spent efficiently, whether this is under national or EU budgets. As seen above, **most of this expenditure is managed by the Member States**, who therefore have the main responsibility for administering payments and checks on payments.

However, it is clearly **the Commission's responsibility** to make sure that efficient systems and procedures are set up at national level, that the accounts presented by the Member States are correct and complete and that expenditure complies with specific rules and regulations. In this task, the Commission is assisted by the Management Committee for Direct Payments, consisting of representatives of the Member States and chaired by a representative of the Commission[1]. Commission auditors verify that Member States' payment and audit systems are reliable and that they meet Community standards. If the systems put into place by a Member State prove to be unsatisfactory, the Commission must, under the clearance of accounts procedure, refuse to finance all or part of the expenditure concerned. Recovery can be made for individual cases where irregularities have been found or where systematic failures are revealed. The financial consequences of irregularities are, however, borne by the Community, unless government departments of the Member States are responsible for the irregularities or incorrect payment of sums[2].

Fraud concerning agricultural expenditure often hits the headlines in the Member States and fuels the criticism of the CAP's opponents. In order to protect the financial interests of the Community budget, Regulation 1290/2005 provides that measures should be taken by Member States to satisfy themselves that transactions financed by the

---

[1]   Regulation 1782/2003, OJ L 270, 21.10.2003 and Decision 1999/468, OJ L 184, 17.07.1999.
[2]   Regulation 1258/1999, OJ L 160, 26.06.1999 repealed by Regulation 1290/2005, OJ L 209, 11.08.2005.

Funds are actually carried out and are executed correctly[1]. Member States should also prevent and deal effectively with any irregularities committed by beneficiaries. So that the Commission can fulfil its obligation to check on the existence and proper functioning of management and inspection systems for Community expenditure in the Member States, provision is made, irrespective of the inspection carried out by Member States themselves, for checks by persons delegated by the Commission who are able to request assistance from the Member States in their work.

As regards the EAGF, sums recovered after the detection of irregularities should be paid back to this Fund where the expenditure is not in conformity with Community legislation and no entitlement existed. A procedure permits the Commission to safeguard the interests of the Community budget by deciding on a partial charging to the Member State concerned of sums lost as a result of irregularities and not recovered within reasonable deadlines. Subject to Member States complying with obligations under their internal procedures, the financial burden should be divided fairly between the Community and the Member State. In certain cases of negligence on the part of the Member State, the full sum may be charged to the Member State concerned.

As regards the EAFRD, sums recovered or cancelled following irregularities should remain available to the approved rural development programmes of the Member State concerned as these sums have been allocated to that Member State. In order to protect the financial interests of the Community budget, provision is made for cases where the required measures are not taken by Member States following the detection of irregularities.

In the context of the **integrated administration and control system (IACS)** mentioned below [see section 21.4.3] each Member State must set up a computerised data base, which must record, for each agricultural holding, the data obtained from aid applications. Moreover each Member State must manage, on the basis of maps or land registry documents or other cartographic references, an **identification system for agricultural parcels** as well as a system for the **identification and registration of payment entitlements**, allowing verification of entitlements and cross-checks with the aid applications and the identification system for agricultural parcels.

In the context of the integrated system, the Council has reinforced physical checks at the export of agricultural products having obtained a refund[2]. It has also established a legal framework making it possible to identify unreliable economic operators in the field of export refunds and of sales at reduced prices of products held in public storage ("black list") and to make them known to the national authorities concerned[3]. The Member States, in co-operation with the Commission, have introduced advanced techniques to map land surfaces and verify land use. Once satellite images and aerial photographs are placed on computer file, advanced software can be used to identify and measure individual parcels, to verify the crops grown, and even to count olive trees. Computer analysis of the aerial or satellite photographs can check the information in a beneficiary's claim form, and on-farm inspections can thus focus on land parcels where discrepancies are detected[4]. The knowledge that at any time a "spy in the sky" can check a claimant's fields acts as a powerful disincentive to fraud and irregularity.

In the case of livestock, the identification and registration system also facilitates **veterinary health surveillance**. Bovine animals must be identified with a number shortly after birth or entry into the Community, using tamper-proof ear-tags. Electronic animal identification may contribute greatly to the efficient traceability of animals in the EU, facilitating both sanitary and veterinary checks with a view to protecting consumers and run checks on the correctness of payments made to farmers. It may also make available data which is important for the management of the meat market, the health of the livestock and hence the health of European consumers. After the disastrous experience of the mad cow disease, there is no need to stress the importance of this last point [see sections 5.1.3. and 21.4.2.].

21.3.5. Agrimonetary questions and the euro

As will become clear below, one of the cornerstones of the common agricultural market is the possibility for all producers in the sectors under a common market organisation to be able to sell their products to an intervention body, at a guaranteed price, which is set each year by the Council and is the same for all the Member States. For this to be possible, the common agricultural policy requires a denominator common to the different currencies in which guaranteed prices are expressed. This requirement provided the impetus for the creation in 1962 of the Unit of Account (UA) a fictive currency or rather measuring standard whose value

---

[1] Regulation 1290/2005, OJ L 209, 11.08.2005 last amended by Regulation 320/2006, OJ L 58, 28.02.2006.
[2] Regulation 386/90, OJ L 42, 16.02.1990 and Regulation 2090/2002, OJ L 322, 27.11.2002 last amended by Regulation 1847/2006, OJ L 355, 15.12.2006.
[3] Regulation 1469/95, OJ L 145, 29.06.1995 and Regulation 745/96, OJ L 102, 25.04.1996.
[4] Decision 1445/2000, OJ L 163, 04.07.2000 and Decision 786/2004, OJ L 138, 30.04.2004.

corresponded to the gold parity of the US Dollar registered with the International Monetary Fund (IMF). After the creation of the European Monetary System in 1979, the UA was replaced by the ecu [see sections 7.2.1. and 7.2.2.].

Since the ecu consisted of the weighted value of the Member States' currencies, the revaluation or devaluation of an individual currency used to lead to a change in the value of the ecu and in the relative position of each currency towards it. **"Green rates"**, lying somewhere between the value of the ecu and the official exchange rate for a given national currency, were introduced in 1969 as a compromise between the interests of strong-currency countries, which rejected cuts in their farmers' earnings after revaluations of their currencies, and those of weak-currency countries, which refused to support the revenues of the farmers of the most prosperous countries of the Union. As a consequence, every time there was a change in the central rate of a national currency, the green rates were changed in turn and all the monetary gaps were closed by "Monetary Compensatory Amounts" (MCAs). The application of the MCA regime naturally engendered technical and administrative difficulties complicating the normal process of marketing agricultural produce within and outside the Community and distorting competition.

The **introduction of the euro**, on 1 January 1999, ended the previously existing problems concerning the fixing of common prices and intervention measures. It led to a major reform and simplification of the agrimonetary system. Agricultural conversion rates have been discontinued. Agricultural prices and aid in the participating Member States is paid in euros. Community aid too is paid and collected in euros[1]. In the case of the Member States outside the eurozone, the euro exchange rate is used for the necessary conversions into their national currencies, unless they decide to make payments in euro. For those Member States the value of a payment is determined by the exchange rate on the date of the operative event (a price or an aid) and not on the date of actual payment.

The use of **the euro benefits the CAP**, not only by simplifying its procedures and reducing its budget costs through the abolition of the green rates, but also through the simplification and transparency of aid schemes for farmers, price stability and increased competitiveness in Community agriculture. Like their American counterparts, who can use their national currency (the dollar) for export transactions, European enterprises now have the euro and are able to invoice their products in the currency in which their costs are also denominated, thereby avoiding an exchange risk.

21.4. Common market organisations

The common agricultural market is underpinned by **common market organisations (CMOs)**, which remove obstacles to intra-Community trade and create common protection at the external borders. At present, almost all the Community's agricultural production is regulated by common organisations. Article 32 of the EC Treaty (ex-Art. 38) defines agricultural products as products of the soil, livestock products and fishery products, along with products of first-stage processing which are directly related to these products. Foodstuffs are considered as products of second-stage processing and are therefore not included in agricultural products. To make matters as clear as possible, products covered by the provisions under the heading "agriculture" are listed in Annex II of the Treaty. This is why, in Community terminology, agricultural arrangements are often stated as being applicable to "Annex II products".

The market organisation regulations, which came into force in 2000 as a result of **the fourth reform of the CAP** [see section 21.2.2.], concern the arable crops, beef, milk and wine sectors, the new rural development framework, the horizontal rules for direct support schemes and the financing of the CAP[2]. These regulations introduced gradual

---

[1]   Regulation 2800/98, OJ L 349, 24.12.1998 and Regulation 2813/98, OJ L 349, 24.12.1998.
[2]   Regulations 1251/1999 to 1259/1999, OJ L 160, 26.06.1999 and Regulation 1782/2003, OJ L 270, 21.10.2003.

cuts in institutional prices - compensated by income support - with the objective of bringing Europe's agricultural prices into closer touch with world market prices, thus helping improve the competitiveness of agricultural products on domestic and world markets with positive impacts on both internal demand and export levels [see sections 21.4.2. and 21.4.4.].

The **fifth CAP reform** (September 2003) established common rules for direct support schemes under the common agricultural policy and support schemes for producers of certain crops (durum wheat, protein crops, rice, nuts, energy crops, starch potatoes, milk, seeds, arable crops, sheep meat and goat meat, beef and veal and grain legumes)[1]. The reform takes account of increased consumer concerns over **food quality and safety and environmental protection**. Indeed, the full payment of direct aid is henceforth linked to compliance with rules relating to agricultural land, agricultural production and activity, which should serve to incorporate in the common market organisations basic standards for the environment, food safety, animal health and welfare and good agricultural and environmental condition. The reform includes a reduction in direct payments ("modulation") for bigger farms to finance the rural development policy and introduces a financial discipline mechanism to ensure that the farm budget fixed until 2013 is not exceeded. The reform of the support schemes for farmers concerns also the ten new Member States since May 2004[2].

The market organisation of each agricultural product uses different mechanisms defined by its basic regulation and adopted by the Council using the full-blown procedure [see section 21.3.2.], but all of them are underpinned by, on the one hand, internal market measures, more often than not relating to price setting and support, and, on the other, by a trade regime with third countries, which is in conformity with the Agreement on agriculture concluded in the context of the GATT Uruguay Round [see section 23.4.].

21.4.1. The principles of the CAP

Three basic principles defined in 1962 characterise the common agricultural market and consequently the common market organisations: market unity, Community preference and financial solidarity. Whereas, the introduction of the euro has consolidated market unity [see section 21.3.5.], the third and fourth reforms of the CAP [see section 21.2.2.] have had an important effect on Community preference and financial solidarity.

Market unity means that agricultural products move throughout the European Union under conditions similar to those in an internal market, thanks to the abolition of quantitative restrictions to trade (quotas, import monopolies...) and the removal of duties, taxes and measures having equivalent effect. Market unity supposes common agricultural prices throughout the EU. The Council, acting on a proposal from the Commission, thus, early in each marketing year, sets common agricultural prices expressed formerly in ecu and, since 1999, in euro[3] [see section 21.3.5.]. In principle, the common agricultural prices should be attained through the free play of supply and demand so that the only variations in the prices paid to farmers in all regions of the Union result from natural production conditions and distance from main centres of consumption. But in reality, as will be seen below, the common market organisations incorporate intervention measures, the force of which varies according to product, in order to support the common prices should there be insufficient demand or external supply at lower prices.

---

[1] Regulations 1782/2003 to 1788/2003, OJ L 270, 21.10.2003 and Regulation 1156/2006, OJ L 208, 29.07.2006.
[2] Regulation 583/2004, OJ L 91, 30.03.2004 and Decision 2004/281, OJ L 93, 30.3.2004.
[3] See, e.g., Council Regulations 1400/1999 to 1405/1999, OJ L 164, 30.06.1999 and Council Regulations 1671/1999 to 1680/1999, OJ L 199, 30.07.1999.

Community preference, the second bulwark of the common agricultural market, signifies that products of Community origin are bought in preference to imported products, in order to protect the common market against low-price imports and fluctuations in world prices. This principle, spread throughout the world, is enacted through import and export measures. The European Union tries to bring the prices of imports into the EU at the prices practised on the common market. The price gap between the world market and the minimum guaranteed price in the EU was formerly covered by variable import levies, which after the GATT Uruguay Round have been progressively replaced by fixed customs duties [see section 21.4.4. and 23.5.]. To the extent that external prices taxed with import duties are at the same level as internal prices, it is not to the advantage of European traders to buy supplies from outside the EU and they therefore give preference to Community products. But whereas this was practically always the case with the import levies, it is much less certain with the customs duties.

The third basic principle of the common agricultural market is that of **financial solidarity**. It is implemented through the intermediary of the European Agricultural Guarantee Fund (EAGF) and signifies that the Member States are jointly liable as regards the financial consequences of the common agricultural markets policy. Since the European Union organises agricultural markets and defines and applies the intervention measures on them, it is logical that it is responsible for the financial consequences of these measures. The EAGF therefore covers all the expenditure rendered necessary by the common market organisations. The other side of the coin is that the customs duties, collected at the Union's frontiers on imports from third countries, do not go into the coffers of the Member States but are a source of revenue for the Community budget [see section 3.4.].

The 1992 CAP reform, which made possible the 1993 GATT Agreement [see sections 23.4 and 23.5.], has affected the fundamental principles of the CAP, since it has supplemented the original price support with a direct income aid system. It has, in fact, introduced a **mixed system**: price support was reduced, but the farmers' revenue was maintained at its previous level by subsidies. In other words, the reduction of price support was compensated by the support of the revenue of the farmers. This system was amplified by the 1999 reform. The new policy for rural development seeks to establish a coherent and sustainable framework for the future of Europe's rural areas. It seeks to complement the reforms introduced into the market sectors by promoting a competitive, multi-functional agricultural sector in the context of a comprehensive, integrated strategy for rural development [see section 21.5.3.]. The guiding principles of the new policy are those of decentralisation of responsibilities - thus strengthening subsidiarity and partnership - and flexibility of programming based on a "menu" of actions to be targeted and implemented according to Member States' specific needs.

21.4.2. Agricultural grants and product quality

The **2003 CAP reform** altered the basis of direct aid to producers, paid to farmers or producers' associations, progressively phasing it out and decoupling it from production [see section 21.4.3]. This decoupling, which began on 1 January 2005 for most Common Market Organisations (CMOs), separates grants received from production. The vast majority of subsidies is henceforth paid independently from the volume of production. To avoid abandonment of production, Member States may choose to maintain a limited link between subsidy and production under well defined conditions and within clear limits. These new "single farm payments" are linked to the respect of environmental, food safety and animal welfare standards. Severing the link between subsidies and production is intended to make EU farmers more competitive and market orientated, while providing the necessary income stability. More money will be available to farmers for environmental, quality or animal welfare programmes by reducing direct payments for bigger farms.

The **key elements of the reformed CAP are:**

- the "single farm payment" for EU farmers is independent from production and is linked to the respect of environmental, food safety, animal and plant health and animal welfare standards, as well as the requirement to keep all farmland in good agricultural and environmental condition ("cross-compliance"),
- limited coupled elements are intended to avoid abandonment of production,
- a strengthened rural development policy with new measures is intended to promote the environment, quality and animal welfare and to help farmers to meet EU production standards,
- a reduction in direct payments ("modulation") for bigger farms helps to finance the new rural development policy,
- a mechanism for financial discipline aims to ensure that the farm budget fixed until 2013 is not overshot,

Connected with the question of agricultural grants is the question of the **quality of agricultural products** and foodstuffs. The quality and characteristics of these products are often linked to their geographical origin. Two Council Regulations are designed to raise consumer awareness of the producers' efforts to improve the quality of their products. The first establishes a Community system for the protection of **geographical indications and designations of origin** for agricultural products and foodstuffs[1], supplemented by lists of some 480 names of agricultural and food products drawn up by the Commission[2]. It spells out with what requirements a product or foodstuff should comply in order to qualify for a protected designation of origin (PDO) or for a protected geographical indication (PGI). The other Regulation lays down the rules under which an agricultural product or foodstuff may be recognised and registered as **traditional speciality guaranteed**[3]. It introduces an instrument for registering the names of products, thus enabling producers who so wish to obtain certificates of the 'specific character' of a traditional product (or foodstuff), the specific character being defined as the feature which distinguishes the product or foodstuff clearly from other similar products or foodstuffs belonging to the same category.

Another Regulation concerns **organic production** of agricultural products and indications referring thereto (labelling) on agricultural products and foodstuffs[4]. A European Union symbol (logo), based on the 12 stars symbol of the EU, identifies agricultural products and foodstuffs whose names are registered under the rules on the protection of geographical indications and designations of origin[5]. The Community finances generic, collective information and promotion campaigns (public relations, publicity and dissemination of scientific information) for agricultural products on the internal market[6].

---

[1]   Regulation 510/2006, OJ L 93, 31.03.2006.
[2]   Regulation 1107/96, OJ L 148, 21.06.1996 last amended by Regulation 704/2005, OJ L 118, 05.05.2005.
[3]   Regulation 509/2006, OJ L 93, 31.03.2006.
[4]   Regulation 2092/91, OJ L 198, 22.07.1991 and Regulation 780/2006, OJ L 137, 25.05.2006.
[5]   Regulation 510/2006, OJ L 93, 31.03.2006.
[6]   Regulation 2826/2000, OJ L 328, 23.12.2000 and Regulation 2060/2004, OJ L 357, 02.12.2004.

It also finances measures promoting the conservation, characterisation, collection and utilisation of genetic resources in agriculture[1].

In the context of various **food aid programmes**, large quantities of food from intervention stocks are supplied both to designated organisations for distribution to the most deprived persons in the Community[2] and to the undernourished populations of numerous countries in the world [see section 24.7.][3].

Support measures may be specific to a certain market organisation, in order to face particular problems. Thus, in order to face the consequences of the **mad cow disease** (Bovine spongiform encephalopathy -BSE), in addition to veterinary measures [see section 5.1.3.], measures were taken in order to limit the negative consequences of banning beef exports from the United Kingdom to third countries[4]. To increase consumer protection by improving information on the origin of meat, the Council established a system for the identification and registration of bovine animals, involving, in particular, the provision of a passport for each animal, the creation of a computerised database in each Member State and the labelling of beef and veal and of products derived from them[5]. The EAGGF helped farmers affected by the crisis[6].

A new subject of concern for the common agricultural policy is biotechnology and **genetically modified organisms (GMOs)** [see section 11.2.]. The Community is aware that the new technologies have great potential for reducing the cost of feedingstuffs and even for improving the quality of foodstuffs, but it is also mindful of certain risks that have to be carefully examined. It therefore follows the **precautionary principle** and defends it on the international stage. This policy has already been denounced by external competitors as protectionist and will certainly lead to fierce battles inside the World Trade Organisation. The Community claims that the precautionary policy is not intended to protect the incomes of its farmers but the health of its citizens. Indeed, in recent years the Community has constantly refined its standards in the areas of food safety, quality, and environmental and animal protection. This has led to higher costs for European farmers and harmed their competitiveness. Rather than protecting European farmers' interests, the precautionary principle seems, therefore, to be very demanding on them as well as on their external competitors. After all, consumers have the right to decide whether they should eat uncertain foodstuffs at lower prices or high quality products at higher prices.

21.4.3. Direct support schemes for farmers

In order to promote more market-oriented and sustainable agriculture, the 2003 reform of the CAP completed the shift from production support to producer support by introducing a system of **decoupled income support for each farm**[7]. Regulation 1782/2003 established common rules on direct payments under income support schemes in the framework of the common agricultural policy which are financed by the European Agricultural Guarantee Fund (EAGF)[8]. These schemes are: an income support for farmers (referred to as the "single payment scheme"); and- support schemes for farmers producing durum wheat, protein crops, rice, nuts, energy crops, starch potatoes, milk, seeds, arable crops, sheep meat and goat meat, beef and veal and grain legumes. In order to leave farmers free to choose what to produce on their land, including products which are still under coupled support, the single payment is not conditional on production of any specific product. However, in order to avoid distortions of competition some products are excluded from production on eligible land.

The new system combines a number of pre-existing direct payments received by a farmer from various schemes in a single payment, determined on the basis of previous entitlements, within a reference period, adjusted to take into account the full implementation of measures introduced by the reform of the CAP. While decoupling leaves the actual amounts paid to farmers unchanged, it is aimed to significantly increase the effec-

[1]   Regulation 870/2004, OJ L 162, 30.04.2004.
[2]   Regulation 3149/92 OJ L 313, 30.10.1992 last amended by Regulation 133/2006, OJ L 23, 27.01.2006.
[3]   Regulation 1292/96, OJ L 166, 05.07.1996.
[4]   Regulation 716/96, OJ L 99. 20.04.1996 last amended by Regulation 2109/2005, OJ L 337, 22.12.2005.
[5]   Regulation 1760/2000, OJ L 204, 11.08.2000.
[6]   Regulation 1357/96, OJ L 175, 13.07.1996.
[7]   Regulation 1782/2003, OJ L 270, 21.10.2003 and Regulation 318/2006, OJ L 58, 28.02.2006.
[8]   Regulation 1290/2005, OJ L 209, 11.08.2005.

tiveness of the income aid. The single farm payment is therefore made **conditional upon cross-compliance** with environmental, food safety, animal health and welfare, as well as the maintenance of the farm in good agricultural and environmental condition.

In order to establish the amount to which a farmer should be entitled under the new scheme, the single payment is based on the amounts granted to him during a reference period. This payment is established at farm level. The overall amount to which a farm is entitled is split into parts (**payment entitlements**) and linked to a certain number of eligible hectares. Specific provisions should be laid down for aid not directly linked to an area taking into account the peculiar situation of sheep and goat rearing. To take account of specific situations, a national reserve is established. That reserve may also be used to facilitate the participation of new farmers in the scheme.

All the amounts of direct payments to be granted in a given calendar year to a farmer in a given Member State are reduced progressively for each year until 2012 (**modulation**). The amounts resulting from application of these reductions are made available as additional Community support for measures under rural development programming financed by the European Agricultural Fund for Rural Development (EAFRD)[1] [see sections 21.3.3 and 21.5.1].

In order to improve the effectiveness and usefulness of the administration and control mechanisms, each Member State must establish an **integrated administration and control system (IACS)** for certain Community aid schemes with a view to including the single payment scheme, the various support schemes, specific regional aids as well as controls on the application of the rules on cross compliance, modulation and the farm advisory system[2] [see also section 21.3.4]. The integrated system must comprise: (a) a computerised data base, (b) an identification system for agricultural parcels,(c) a system for the identification and registration of payment entitlements, (d) aid applications, (e) an integrated control system, and (f) a single system to record the identity of each farmer who submits an aid application.

A farmer receiving direct payments must respect the **statutory management requirements**, provided by the competent national authority. Member States must, in particular, ensure that all agricultural land, especially land which is no longer used for production purposes, is maintained in good agricultural and environmental condition. Therefore, Member States must define, at national or regional level, minimum requirements for good agricultural and environmental condition, taking into account the specific characteristics of the areas concerned, including soil and climatic condition, existing farming systems, land use, crop rotation, farming practices, and farm structures.

A Commission Regulation abolished the obligation of prior notification for *de minimis* **aid** in the agriculture and fisheries sectors, because the very low levels of aid granted in the agriculture sector do not fulfil the criteria of Article 87(1) of the Treaty, provided that certain conditions are met[3]. This is the case where both the amount of aid received by individual producers remains small, and the overall level of aid granted to the agriculture sector does not go above a small percentage of the value of production.

21.4.4. External wing of the CAP

The external wing of the common market organisations seeks to protect European agricultural prices against low price imports. In the same way as intervention on the internal market attempts to prevent the market prices falling too far below the intervention prices, intervention at the external borders tries to prevent low priced imports from upsetting the European market. The **threshold price** (cereals, sugar, dairy products, olive

---

[1] Regulation 1698/2005, OJ L 277, 21.10.2005 last amended by Regulation 1944/2006, OJ L 367, 22.12.2006..
[2] Regulation 1782/2003, OJ L 270, 21.10.2003 last amended by Regulation 1156/2006, OJ L 208, 29.07.2006.
[3] Regulation 1860/2004, OJ L 325, 28.10.2004.

oil) or the **sluice-gate price** (pigmeat, eggs and poultry) is a minimum price above which imports from third countries enjoy free access. For products for which a target price or guide price exists, the threshold price is determined in such a manner that the sales price of the imported product, allowance made for transport costs, is on a par with this price. For products for which there is no guide price (fruit and vegetables, table wine), the **reference price** is the minimum price at which a third country product can be imported and a tax is collected if the reference price is not respected.

The gap between the world price and the threshold price was originally bridged by import levies. Following the GATT agreements of December 1993, this gap is now partially closed by **customs duties**. However, for certain product groups such as cereals, rice, wine and fruit and vegetables, certain supplementary mechanisms that do not involve the collection of fixed customs duties are introduced in the basic regulations of the CAP by a Regulation, which lays down the adaptations and transitional measures required in order to implement the agreements concluded in the GATT framework [see sections 23.4. and 23.5.][1].

The across-the-board **tariff concessions** which result from multilateral trade negotiations, such as those of the GATT and now the WTO, are only part of the commitments weighing upon the EU's agricultural relationships. There are in addition preferential bilateral agreements with the ACP countries [see section 24.2.] and the majority of Mediterranean countries [see section 25.5.], in the form of association agreements or cooperation agreements, which provide for concessions in the agricultural sector [see also section 5.2.2.]. In addition, tariff reductions are granted by the Community under the Generalised System of Preferences (GSP) to almost all the developing countries [see section 24.5.], notably in the framework of the United Nations Conference on Trade and Development (UNCTAD) and in the framework of the Europe Agreements with the countries of Central and Eastern Europe [see section 25.2.]. The Community supplies the Russian Federation agricultural products free of charge from intervention stocks or purchased on the EU market[2].

In the past, when internal prices were higher than world prices, exporters received **subsidies, known as "refunds"**, to offset the difference between their purchase price on the European market and their sales price on world markets. As part of the Union's international commitments to the WTO, the subsidised exports of certain groups of agricultural products are limited each year in terms of both volume and value. **Inward processing** arrangements are applicable to certain goods resulting from the processing of agricultural products to enable Community industry to maximise its export potential [see section 5.2.3.][3]. **Export taxes** may be imposed on certain products, in exceptional circumstances, in order to avoid disturbance of the Community market and safeguard supplies at reasonable prices for consumers in the European Union[4].

Aligning Community prices with those on the world market as a result of the 1999 CAP reform, should make it possible to export without subsidies, and therefore without quantitative ceilings. As the second-largest agricultural exporter and by far the largest processed food exporter, the EU certainly takes a keen interest in the smooth functioning of world trade and in fair international competition in agricultural trade. It calls, in particular, for all export credits to be subject to compliance with agreed trade rules, as was already agreed in principle in the Uruguay Round. The EU seeks, however, to ensure that in the **next round of negotiations** greater attention is paid to the justified interests of consumers and that the WTO is not used as a pretext for placing products on the market where there are legitimate concerns about their safety. It also maintains that its new CAP addresses important non-trade issues that cannot be negotiated at world level, in particular the need to strengthen the multifunctional role of agriculture as a means of ensuring the vitality of rural areas, and animal and environmental protection [see sections 12.1.1. and 16.4.1.].

[1]   Regulation 3290/94, OJ L 349, 31.12.1994 and Regulation 1340/98, OJ L 184, 27.06.1998.
[2]   Regulation 2802/98, OJ L 349, 24.12.1998.
[3]   Regulation 3448/93, OJ L 318, 20.12.1993 and Regulation 2580/2000, OJ L 298, 25.11.2000.
[4]   See, e.g., Regulation 865/97, OJ L 123, 15.05.1997.

21.5. Rural development policy

According to the Treaty, in working out the common agricultural policy and the special methods for its application, account is to be taken of the particular nature of agricultural activity which results from the social structure of agriculture and from structural and natural disparities between the various rural areas. Main objectives of the common agricultural policy are: (a) to increase agricultural productivity by promoting technical progress and by ensuring the rational development of agricultural production and the optimum utilisation of the factors of production, in particular labour; and (b) thus to ensure a fair standard of living for the agricultural community, in particular by increasing the individual earnings of persons engaged in agriculture (Art. 33 TEC). Unlike market organisation and pricing policy, which requires uniform provisions and centralised management, socio-structural policy **may remain more in the realm of the Member States** in that it has to be adjusted to the specificities of the different regions. But structural policy blueprinting and supervision is brought under the wing of the Community to promote economic and social cohesion and prevent uneven competition conditions for Community producers [see sections 12.1.2. and 12.2.1.].

Rural areas face particular challenges as regards growth, jobs and sustainability in the enlarged Union. But they offer real opportunities in terms of their potential for growth in new sectors, the provision of rural amenities and tourism, their attractiveness as a place in which to live and work, and their role as a reservoir of natural resources and highly valued landscapes. Therefore, a **rural development policy** accompanies and complements the market and income support policies of the common agricultural policy and thus contributes to the achievement of that policy's objectives as laid down in the Treaty. Rural development policy also takes into account the general objectives for economic and social cohesion policy set out in the Treaty and contributes to their achievement, while integrating other major policy priorities, such as the Lisbon strategy on competitiveness. The rural development policy currently aims at restoring and enhancing the competitiveness of rural areas, thus contributing to the maintenance and creation of employment in those areas. The reformed rural development policy covers, since January 2007, all rural areas in the Community through a single instrument, the European Agricultural Fund for Rural Development (EAFRD) [see sections 21.3.3 and 21.5.1].

The European Union's new policy for rural development - as the second pillar of the CAP - seeks to establish a coherent and sustainable framework for the future of rural areas aiming at restoring and enhancing competitiveness and therefore contributing to the maintenance of employment. Structural intervention favours diversification and widening the economic fabric in rural areas. It aims to exploit the endogenous potential of these areas in order to create new jobs or develop new extra income sources thus contributing to stabilising their population. The four **basic principles** of the new policy are:

1. **subsidiarity and partnership** achieved through the decentralisation of programming arrangements and consultation at regional and local level;
2. **multi-functionality** that rewards farmers for the range of services they provide in meeting the expectations of consumers and wider society, including the preservation of the rural heritage, while emphasising the creation of alternative sources of income;
3. **a multi-sectoral approach** that seeks to develop the rural economy by creating new sources of income and employment, by developing rural services and conserving the countryside and the rural heritage;
4. **efficiency and flexibility** sought through the implementation of strategic, integrated programmes, based on a "menu" of measures implemented according to the needs and circumstances in the Member States and regions.

   Agricultural structural policy requires exact information on farm income and on production parameters of the agricultural economy in the Community. This is the task of the **Farm accountancy data network**

(FADN)[1]. The FADN relies on the services of farm accountancy offices in the Member States and on the participation of specially selected agricultural holdings to produce objective and practical data on the economic situation of the various categories of agricultural holdings, including those upon which a close watch needs to be kept at European level[2]. Thanks to the use of individual data, the FADN can carry out detailed analyses which make allowance for the variety of European agriculture. The FADN's conclusions form part of the prior study to any major Commission proposal. Parallel to the FADN is the European forestry information and communication system (EFICS)[3].

21.5.1. The financing of rural development

Rural development and accompanying measures during the period 2000-06 were financed by the EAGGF Guarantee Section or Guidance Section, depending on their regional context [see section 12.3.2.]. Thus, Community support for early retirement, less-favoured areas and areas with environmental restrictions, agri-environmental measures and afforestation were **financed by the EAGGF Guarantee Section** throughout the Community. Community support for other rural development measures was financed by the **EAGGF Guidance Section** in areas covered by Objective 1 (integrated into the programmes) **and Guarantee Section** in areas outside Objective 1 [see sections 12.1.1. and 12.3.1.].

Through two Regulations adopted in 2005, the EAGGF was split in two different but complementary instruments: the European Agricultural Guarantee Fund (EAGF), for the financing of market measures, and the **European Agricultural Fund for Rural Development (EAFRD)** [see section 21.3.3]. Regulation 1698/2005 established the European Agricultural Fund for Rural Development (EAFRD)[4]. The EAFRD contributes to the promotion of sustainable rural development throughout the Community in a complementary manner to the market and income support policies of the common agricultural policy, to cohesion policy and to the common fisheries policy. Support for rural development should, in particular, contribute to achieving the following objectives: (a) improving the competitiveness of agriculture and forestry by supporting restructuring, development and innovation; (b) improving the environment and the countryside by supporting land management; and (c) improving the quality of life in rural areas and encouraging diversification of economic activity.

In the context of Regulation 1698/2005, the Council, on a proposal from the Commission, should adopt **strategic guidelines** aiming at reinforcing the content of rural development policy in line with the Community's priorities. On the basis of the strategic guidelines, each Member State should prepare its rural development national strategy plan constituting the reference framework for the preparation of the rural development programmes, whose duration should be of seven years. The programming of rural development should comply with Community and national priorities and complement the other Community policies, in particular the agricultural market policy, cohesion policy and common fisheries policy. In accordance with their respective responsibilities, the Commission and the Member States mustl ensure the coordination between the assistance from the different Funds, i.e. the ERDF, the ESF, the Cohesion Fund [see section 12.3], the European Fisheries Fund (EFF) [see section 22.4], and the interventions of the European Investment Bank (EIB), and of other Community financial instruments.

---

[1] Regulation 79/65, OJ L 109, 23.06.1965 and Regulation 660/2004, OJ L 104, 08.04.2004.
[2] Regulation 571/88, OJ L 56, 02.03.1988 and Regulation 204/2006, OJ L 34, 07.02.2006.
[3] Regulation 1615/89, OJ L 165, 15.06.1989 and Regulation 1100/98, OJ L 157, 30.05.1998.
[4] Regulation 1698/2005, OJ L 277, 21.10.2005 last amended by Regulation 1944/2006, OJ L 367, 22.12.2006.

EAFRD assistance is implemented through close consultations (partnership) between the Commission and the Member State and with the authorities and bodies designated by the Member State under national rules and practices. Each Member State must submit a national strategy plan indicating the priorities of the action of the EAFRD and of the Member State concerned taking into account the Community strategic guidelines, their specific objectives, the contribution from the EAFRD and the other financial resources.

21.5.2. Rural development policy objectives and guidelines

According to **Article 33(2,a)** of the EC Treaty, in working out the common agricultural policy and the special methods for its application, account is to be taken of the particular nature of agricultural activity which results from the social structure of agriculture and from structural and natural disparities between the various agricultural regions. A common rural development policy should accompany and complement the other instruments of the common agricultural policy and thus contribute to the achievement of the policy's objectives as laid down in Article 33(1) of the Treaty. This policy should take into account the objectives set out in Articles 158 and 160 (TEC) for the common policy of economic and social cohesion and contribute to their achievement [see section 12.1.2.]. Within the framework of the objectives established in Regulation 1698/2005, the strategic guidelines set out in Decision 2006/144 aim at the integration of **major policy priorities** as spelt out in the conclusions of the Lisbon and Göteborg European Councils[1] [see sections 13.3.2 and 16.2].

Enhancing the competitiveness of Community agriculture and promoting food quality and environment standards, under the fifth CAP reform, entail a drop in institutional prices for agricultural products and a shift from production support to producer support by a system of decoupled income support for each farm. While decoupling should leave the actual amounts paid to farmers unchanged, it should make the single farm payment conditional upon cross-compliance with environmental, food safety, animal health and welfare, as well as the maintenance of the farm in good agricultural and environmental condition. In order to help farmers to meet the standards of modern, high-quality agriculture the Member States should establish a comprehensive system offering advice to commercial farms. Therefore a national farm advisory system should help farmers to become more aware of material flows and on-farm processes relating to the environment, food safety, animal health and welfare.

The new generation of rural development strategies and programmes for the period 2007-2013 is built around four axes, namely:

- axis 1, on **improving the competitiveness** of the agricultural and forestry sector through a range of measures targeting human and physical capital in the agriculture, food and forestry sectors (promoting knowledge transfer and innovation) and quality production;
- axis 2, on **improving the environment and the countryside** by measures protecting and enhancing natural resources, as well as preserving highnature value farming and forestry systems and cultural landscapes in Europe's rural areas;
- axis 3, on **improving the quality of life** in rural areas and diversification of the rural economy by measures helping to develop local infrastructure and human capital in rural areas to improve the conditions for growth and job creation in all sectors and the diversification of economic activities; and

---

[1] Decision 2006/144, OJ L 55, 25.02.2006.

- axis 4, introducing possibilities for innovative governance through locally based, bottom-up **integrated approaches to rural development**, based on the Leader experience.

The resources devoted to **axis 1** should help develop high-quality and value-added products that meet the diverse and growing demand of Europe's consumers and world markets. Therefore, they should contribute to a strong and dynamic European agrifood sector by focusing on the priorities of knowledge transfer, modernisation, innovation and quality in the food chain, and on priority sectors for investment in physical and human capital.

To protect and enhance the EU's natural resources and landscapes in rural areas, the resources devoted to **axis 2** should contribute to three EU-level priority areas: biodiversity and the preservation and development of high nature value farming and forestry systems and traditional agricultural landscapes; water; and climate change.

The resources devoted to the fields of diversification of the rural economy and quality of life in rural areas under **axis 3** should contribute to the overarching priority of the creation of employment opportunities and conditions for growth by promoting capacity building, skills acquisition and organisation for local strategy development and by helping ensure that rural areas remain attractive for future generations. In promoting training, information and entrepreneurship, the particular needs of women, young people and older workers should be considered.

Support under **axis 4 (Leader)** offers the possibility, in the context of a community-led local development strategy building on local needs and strengths, to combine all three objectives: competitiveness, environment and quality of life/diversification. Integrated approaches involving farmers, foresters and other rural actors should safeguard and enhance the local natural and cultural heritage, raise environmental awareness, invest in and promote specialty products, tourism and renewable resources and energy.

Regulation 1782/2003 (fifth CAP reform) [see section 21.2.2.] established: **common conditions for direct payments** under the various income support schemes in the framework of the CAP which are financed by the European Agricultural Guarantee Fund (EAGF), except those provided for under Regulation 1257/1999; an income support for farmers ("single payment scheme"); and special support schemes for farmers producing certain crops[1] [see section 21.4.3]. In order to achieve a better balance between policy tools designed to promote sustainable agriculture and those designed to promote rural development, a system of progressive reduction of direct payments was introduced on a compulsory Community-wide basis for the years 2005 to 2012. All direct payments, beyond certain amounts, should be reduced by a certain percentage each year.

21.5.3. Rural development measures

In order to **improve the competitiveness** of the agricultural and forestry sector (axis 1 of the rural development strategy), Member States are encouraged to focus support on the following key actions:

- restructuring and modernisation of the agriculture sector;
- improving integration in the agrifood chain;
- facilitating innovation and access to research and development (R & D);
- encouraging the take-up and diffusion of information and communications technologies (ICT);
- fostering dynamic entrepreneurship and encouraging the entry of young farmers into the profession;
- developing new outlets for agricultural and forestry products;
- improving the environmental performance of farms and forestry.

So as to **improve the environment and the countryside** (axis 2 of the rural development strategy), Member States are encouraged to focus support on key actions such as:

- promoting environmental services and animal-friendly farming practices;
- preserving the farmed landscape and forests;
- combating climate change by appropriate agricultural and forestry practices;

---

[1] Regulation 1782/2003, OJ L 270, 21.10.2003 and Regulation 318/2006, OJ L 58, 28.02.2006.

- consolidating the contribution of organic farming;
- promoting territorial balance and the attractiveness of rural areas;

In order to **improve the quality of life** in rural areas and **encourage diversification** of the rural economy (axis 3 of the rural development strategy), Member States are encouraged to support the following key actions:

- raising economic activity and employment rates in the wider rural economy;
- encouraging the entry of women into the labour market;
- putting the heart back into villages by integrated initiatives combining diversification and business creation;
- developing micro-business and crafts, which can build on traditional skills or introduce new competencies;
- training young people in skills needed for the diversification of the local economy;
- encouraging the take-up and diffusion of information and communication technologies;
- developing the provision and innovative use of renewable energy sources;
- encouraging the development of tourism;
- upgrading local telecommunications, transport, energy and water infrastructures.

To build **local capacity for employment and diversification** (Leader or axis 4 of the rural development strategy), Member States are encouraged to focus support on key actions such as:

- building local partnership capacity and promoting skills acquisition;
- promoting private-public partnership by encouraging the Leader innovative approaches to rural development;
- promoting cooperation and innovation by local initiatives such as Leader and support for diversification;
- improving local governance by fostering Leader innovative approaches to linking agriculture, forestry and the local economy.

21.5.4. The Community initiative LEADER+

Since its launch in 1991, the LEADER Community initiative has encouraged the active involvement of local rural communities in the development of their local economy. This participative approach to rural development has produced positive results. In particular, the experience gained from LEADER I and II has demonstrated that the territorial development strategy was the appropriate one to restore vitality to the rural territories, to stimulate the creation and maintenance of activities and hence to increase their attractiveness. The Community initiative, **LEADER+** goes a step further. Its objective is to encourage the implementation of high quality, original strategies for integrated sustainable development of rural areas. Leader+ is at the same time an instrument of assistance in the new rural development policy, accompanying and complementing the CAP, and an instrument of assistance in the economic and social cohesion policy aiming to ensure the viability of rural Europe [see section 12.1.2.][1]. Its objective is to encourage, on the basis of local partnerships, the emergence and experimentation of rural territorial development strategies, integrated and in a pilot form.

LEADER+ is applicable in all rural areas of the Community, but the selected territories must have demonstrated their capacity to support the proposed development project in terms both of coherence and sufficient critical mass. The **development strategy**

---

[1] Regulation 1083/2006, OJ L 210, 31.07.2006.

must demonstrate its foundation and coherence with the territory, its economic viability, its sustainable character (in environmental terms), its pilot character and more particularly its specificity and originality in relation to the operations of the mainstream programmes as well as the transferable character of the methods proposed.

The development strategy, according to the circumstances, must be linked to a **development theme** particularly interesting at local and European level: the use of information technology in rural areas; improving the quality of life in rural areas; adding value to local products and making the best use of natural and cultural resources. Strategies focusing on equal opportunities for women, and on young people in rural areas are also given priority.

The beneficiaries of LEADER+ should be a unity of partners defined as **"Local Action Group" (LAG)**. They must constitute a balanced and representative unity of partners from different socio-economic environments of the territory (including the public sector). They must demonstrate their capacity to set out together a development strategy for the territory and to implement it. Cooperations within the same country (interterritorial cooperation) or between several countries (transnational cooperation) are eligible when they are dedicated to a clearly defined theme and consist of the implementation of a common operation. The beneficiaries of the Community initiative are under the obligation to participate actively in the dissemination and transfer of their experiences. A **European Observatory of Rural Territories** guided by the Commission is responsible for the animation of the network of rural areas, information distribution and the spotting of good practices.

21.5.5. Rural development measures for EU candidate countries

The **candidate countries for EU membership must adopt the massive body of EU legislation** - known as the "acquis communautaire" [see section 3.3.] - in order to take part fully in the internal market. In the field of agriculture, this means, for example, harmonising legislation in the areas of veterinary and phytosanitary health, and the free movement of animals and agricultural products. Therefore, EU pre-accession aid supports projects that help the candidates prepare for accession, while familiarising the authorities and other relevant organisations with the methods used to implement Community support measures.

The **Instrument for Pre-Accession Assistance (IPA)** [see section 12.3.4] stipulates that assistance for candidate countries should, inter alia, focus on the adoption and implementation of the full acquis communautaire, and in particular prepare candidate countries for the implementation of the Community's agricultural and cohesion policy[1]. The Rural Development Component of IPA provides support for countries listed in Annex I (Croatia, Turkey, the Former Yugoslav Republic of Macedonia) in policy development as well as preparation for the implementation and management of the Community's common agricultural policy. It contributes to the sustainable adaptation of the agricultural sector and rural areas and to the candidate countries' preparation for the implementation of the acquis communautaire concerning the Common Agricultural Policy and related policies. It may in particular contribute towards the financing of the type of actions provided for under Regulation 1698/2005 on support for rural development by the European Agricultural Fund for Rural Development (EAFRD).

---

[1]   Regulation 1085/2006, OJ L 210, 31.07.2006.

21.6. Appraisal and outlook

The common agricultural policy intrigues those who take an interest in European integration, both because of its advance on other common policies and because of its complexity. The resources in its grasp represent nearly 50% of the Community budget [see section 3.4.]; the instruments that it applies are extremely varied and the terms that it uses to describe them would appear to be chosen precisely to prevent outsiders from understanding what they are. A close look, however, reveals that the complexity of the agricultural policy is due first and foremost to the variety of natural and economic situations which exist, the first relating to production and marketing conditions for different products, the second to the fact that the fifteen Member States have different structures and different climatic conditions.

Despite its complexity, the CAP has more than achieved its objectives. Customs duties, quantitative restrictions and measures having equivalent effect have been relegated to the dustbin of history and trade between the Member States has been fully liberalised. The **single agricultural market** signifies that a good originating in one Member State can be stored in another and marketed in a third. It can also be exported to third countries from any Member State. The merchandise of third countries gains entry to the common market by crossing just one of the Member States' borders. This liberalisation has led to considerable growth in the range of agricultural products and foodstuffs available to consumers.

In addition, the common market organisation has buffered the European agricultural market against major fluctuations on the world market. In normal times, it **has provided market stability** through a policy of staggering supply (storage, monthly increases), of surplus disposal (refunds, denaturing) or of diversifying supply (imports from third countries, export levies). In times of crisis, it has resorted to drastic measures ranging from import or export bans to the withdrawal from the market of part of production or even the reduction of production factors.

Market stabilisation is not an end in itself. It is a path to the other objectives of the common agricultural policy, notably that of food supply security. Thanks to the CAP, **the European Union has been spared any serious food shortages**, which would have jeopardised both the common agricultural policy and European integration itself. Comparison of the abundance of foodstuffs in Western Europe with the shortages in Eastern Europe, before and after the fall of communist regimes, is a sufficient gauge of the CAP's success. An additional and not less important one, is the independence of Western Europe in foodstuffs, which should be compared to its dependence on imported energy, namely oil [see section 19.1.1.]. The price of the Community's independence in foodstuffs has not been too high to pay. It goes without saying that the level of common prices corresponds to Europe's industrial and social development level. These prices are naturally enough not below those of the world market, but they are not much above them either.

The so-called **"European model of agriculture"** aims at a sustainable development of rural areas through a diversified and multifunctional agriculture. The new CAP is based on two elements: lowering institutional prices for key products and offsetting the impact of these cuts on producer incomes by means of direct payments. While improving competitiveness of European agricultural products at world level, the 1999 reform has consolidated the foundations for a diversified and multifunctional agriculture contributing to sustainable development. The production of renewable raw materials and high quality food products, the protection of the environment and the maintenance of the vitality of rural regions and the countryside are considered services to the society, which have to be rewarded to ensure that they continue to be available in future.

Farmers in Europe are a special socio-economic category that other Europeans value, as the roots of their millenary traditions and cultures. The number of farmers in Europe is already so low that a further decrease would be catastrophic for cultivations, rural areas, landscapes and even the European traditions which farmers preserve. The agri-environmental arrangements incorporated into the common market organisations and the aid schemes for rural development open up a new future for farmers alongside their traditional role, as **guardians of the environment and of Europe's rural heritage**. In a Europe where urbanisation is proceeding apace, this new role may be as vital for city-dwellers in need of calm and a breath of fresh air as the food produced by farmers. City-dwellers should acknowledge that rural areas, with their products, their traditions, their landscapes and their calm, are preserving their own standards of living. It is therefore only just that these city-dwellers, as taxpayers, also contribute to the upkeep of the green areas which surround their cities. This approach signifies that farmers are rewarded not only for what they produce but also for their general contribution to society.

On the other hand, agricultural markets are increasingly operating in economic globalisation. The fourth CAP reform should make it easier for European agriculture to participate in this process and guide production towards effective demand, while taking account of consumers' requirements in terms of quality. WTO negotiations are the ideal venue for creating stable conditions and rules for fair international competition in agricultural trade, but a fresh round of agricultural negotiations cannot deal only with the traditional agricultural trade issues. European farmers, food industry and agricultural policy must adjust to a series of new demands from consumers for high quality and for adequate information on the origin and composition of foodstuffs. The **concerns of the European consumers** have an increasingly marked effect on demand. They cannot be ignored in the name of globalisation and free trade. Foreign as well European foodstuffs have to pass the examination of European consumers, which is likely to become stricter as various food scandals come to the fore. Higher quality means higher production costs, but also higher consumer prices. This challenge has to be met, not only by European farmers, but also by their competitors world-wide.

Bibliography on the common agricultural policy

- BLANDFORD David, HILL Brian (eds.). *Policy reform and adjustment in the agricultural sectors of developed countries*. Wallingford; Cambridge, MA.: CABI Publishing, 2006.
- CARDWELL Michael, RODGERS Christopher. "Reforming the WTO legal order for agricultural trade: issues for European rural policy in the Doha Round" in *International and Comparative Law Quarterly*, v. 55, n. 4, October 2006, p. 805-838.
- DAVIDOVA Sophia (et al. eds.). *Integrated development of agriculture and rural areas in Central European contries*. Oxford: Lexington Books, 2006.
- DIAKOSAVVAS Dimitris (ed.). *Coherence of agricultural and rural development policies*. Paris: OECD, 2006.
- DIXON Janine, MATTHEWS Alan. "Impact of the 2003 mid-term review of the Common Agricultural Policy" in *Quarterly Economic Commentary*, Spring 2006, p. 36-52.
- EUROPEAN COMMISSION. *The EU rural development policy 2007-2013*. Luxembourg: EUR-OP*, 2006.
  - *Simplification of the Common Agricultural Policy*. Luxembourg: EUR-OP*, 2006.
  - *Biofuels in the European Union: an agricultural perspective*. Luxembourg: EUR-OP*, 2006.
  - *Special focus: Innovation in Leader +*. Luxembourg: EUR-OP*, 2006.
  - *Development of agri-environmental indicators for monitoring the integration of environmental concerns into the common agricultural policy*. Luxembourg: EUR-OP*, 2006.
- GARZON Isabelle. *Reforming the Common Agricultural Policy: history of a paradigm change*. Basingstoke: Palgrave Macmillan, 2006.
- HOUSE OF LORDS. EUROPEAN UNION COMMITTEE. *The future financing of the Common Agricultural Policy*. London: Stationery Office, 2005.
- JAZRA BANDARRA Neely. "Devenir du monde rural face aux orientations de la politique européenne 2007-2013" in *Revue du Marché commun et de l'Union européenne*, n. 499, juin 2006, p. 391-400.
- LYNGGAARD K. *The Common Agricultural Policy and organic farming: an institutional perspective on continuity and change*. Wallingford: CABI Publishing, 2006.

- MAGNUSSON Andreas. *The EU Common Agriculture Policy and a changing world trade order.* Sindelfingen: Libertas- Europäisches Institut, 2006.
- MILLET Montserrat, GARCIA-DURAN Patricia. "La PAC face aux défis du cycle de Doha" in *Revue du Marché commun et de l'Union européenne*, n. 494, janvier 2006, p. 16-23.
- O'CONNOR Bernard (ed.). *Agriculture in WTO Law.* London: Cameron May, 2005.
- ORGANISATION FOR ECONOMIC COOPERATION AND DEVELOPMENT. *Trade, agriculture and development: policies working together.* Paris : OECD, 2006.
- SHUCKSMITH Mark (et al.). *The CAP and the regions: the territorial impact of the common agricultural policy.* Wallingford; Cambridge, MA. : CABI Publishing, 2005.
- WILSON R. *Law of the common agricultural policy.* Bristol: Jordans, 2006.

*The publications of the Office for Official Publications of the European Communities (EUR-OP) exist usually in all official languages of the EU.

Chapter 22

FISHERIES POLICY

Diagram of the chapter

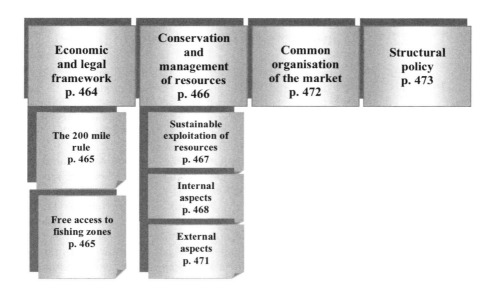

Economic and legal framework p. 464

Conservation and management of resources p. 466

Common organisation of the market p. 472

Structural policy p. 473

The 200 mile rule p. 465

Sustainable exploitation of resources p. 467

Free access to fishing zones p. 465

Internal aspects p. 468

External aspects p. 471

Fisheries policy, which the Treaty of Rome initially made part of the Common Agricultural Policy by placing fishery products, products of the soil and stock-farming products in the same basket, became a fully-fledged common policy in 1983. It no longer has much in common with the CAP, apart from the fact that it makes use of instruments of market organisation comparable to those of the CAP. Although the fishery sector does not carry the same weight in the Gross Domestic Product and does not employ as many people as agriculture, the establishment of a common policy required just as much effort as the Common Agricultural Policy.

The fishery resources policy, which embraces both internal and external policy, was the most troublesome to put into practice. It is the forum for such thorny questions as total allowable catch (TAC), the sharing out of TAC between the Member States (quotas) and access of the vessels from one Member State to the territorial waters of the others. Resources policy also has to cope with difficult negotiations with third countries to settle questions of access for Community vessels to their waters and vice versa. Although this kingpin of the common fisheries policy (CFP) is analysed first, it was the last arrival on the fisheries scene.

The origins of the two other pillars of the CFP date back to 1970. The common organisation of markets has clearly covered a great deal of ground since then and its reform, in 1981, opened the door to the final compromise on fisheries. Structural policy, for its part, has been torn by national differences on the question of resource conservation. For many years it was restricted to interim measures and was only firmly established with the agreement on resources, reached in January 1983.

To facilitate the management and development of the common fisheries policy, the Commission has established a permanent dialogue with professional and non-professional organisations (consumers, environment and development) inside the Advisory Committee on Fisheries and Aquaculture[1]. On its side, the Council has established seven regional advisory councils with a view to improving governance under the common fisheries policy and involving stakeholders more closely in the development of the sector[2].

22.1. Economic and legal framework

The market in fishery products is similar to that in agricultural products. This is why the EC Treaty stipulates that by agricultural products is meant products of the soil, stock-farming products and fishery products and that the operation and establishment of a common market for all of these products must be accompanied by the introduction of a Common Agricultural Policy (Articles 32 and 33). This is therefore the fundamental reason for and legal basis of a common policy in the fisheries sector.

The Treaty consequently placed fisheries policy and the Common Agricultural Policy in the same basket and the two were initially one and the same. More precisely, the organisation of the market and structural policy covering fisheries formed part of the Common Agricultural Policy. There is however a basic difference between products of the soil and stock-farming on the one hand and fisheries products on the other. Whereas the first two remain within the boundaries laid down by man, fish have no respect for frontiers! Migratory fish, such as herring and tuna, do not have to show their passports when they enter the economic zone of a Member State! There are therefore problems relating to fisheries resources, which simply do not exist for products of the soil and stock farming. This is the first reason why a specific common policy was required for fisheries products. This specificity is now acknowledged by the EC Treaty in Article 3, which speaks of a common policy in the fields of agriculture and fisheries.

The second justification for a common fisheries policy is specific to this sector. Between 1956 and 1965, world fish production rose by 50%. Investments over this period of economic growth, vessel modernisation and higher productivity pushed up catches to such a high level that stock replenishment was threatened and the commoner species, such as herring, began to be exhausted. In times of surplus, storage aid, export subsidies and import restrictions were required. In times of shortage, on the other hand, it was necessary to regulate and monitor fishing to ensure that the seas fished by the Member States did not become empty of fish. All of this had to be achieved at Community level, if the aim was a common fisheries market.

---

[1] Decision 1999/478, OJ L 187, 20.07.1999 and Decision 2004/864, OJ L 370, 17.12.2004.
[2] Decision 2004/585, OJ L 256, 03.08.2004.

22.1.1. The 200 mile rule

The development which revolutionised fishing in Community waters and beyond was the adoption of the 200 mile rule. Since the end of the Second World War, certain coastal states had begun to eat into the "mare liberum" to reserve for themselves the riches which they held, particularly fish. National bagging of coastal waters, traditionally held at canon range - taken to be three nautical miles - was unilaterally extended by several States to 12 miles after the failure of the 1958 and 1960 United Nations Conferences to uphold their demands.

But certain Latin American countries were already calling for a reserved fishing zone of 200 miles. They sought thus to protect themselves against the dynamism of North America vessels, 200 miles being the distance from the coasts of Chile to the Humboldt Current, a warm current which stimulates fish spawning and marks the boundary of a zone rich in fishery resources. The North Americans, for their part, were not adverse to the idea of keeping their own waters, also rich in fish, for their own vessels. The vote in the US Congress at the beginning of 1976 in favour of the extension of a fishery conservation zone to 200 miles stepped up the pace of the so-called "creeping jurisdiction" movement. Mexico and Iceland had already adopted similar measures in the North Atlantic. They were to be followed by Canada and Norway.

Over the same period, the Commission became increasingly conscious of the fact that the movement to extend fishery limits to 200 miles would create special problems for the EEC, notably as regards access to the fishing zones of the Member States and the conservation of resources. But at the same time it was aware that the movement in this direction was unstoppable. It proposed negotiating briefs moving with the tide, which were accepted by the Council on July 27, 1976. The Community was therefore ready to accept the 200-mile limit introduced by the United Nations Convention on the Law of the Sea[1].

22.1.2. Free access to fishing zones

The implementation of the rule of the United Nations of a **200 mile fishery conservation zone** provided a striking illustration of the need for a common conservation policy for these new Community resources. The principle of free access to the fishing zones of Member States was incorporated into the Regulation establishing the fisheries structural policy, adopted as far back as 1970, the year in which accession negotiations were opened with four countries - the United Kingdom, Ireland, Denmark and Norway - all major fishing nations, the total catch of which amounted to double that of the six founding Member States.

The principle of equal access to fishing zones therefore formed part of the "acquis communautaire" (existing Community legislation) which applicants had to accept. Although they attempted to abolish the rule of equal access during accession negotiations, they only succeeded in postponing its full application. Articles 100 to 103 of the **Act of Accession** granted a temporary derogation to the 1970 Community Regulation, authorising the Member States to maintain until December 31, 1982 exclusive fishing rights for their vessels in waters up to six nautical miles from their coasts (stretched to twelve miles for certain regions of the acceding States and of France), provided that the historic fishing rights of vessels from other Member States were respected in these waters [see details below]. Despite this temporary derogation, the principle of equal access to economic zones was one of the main causes for the negative votes of the Norwegian people on Community membership, in 1973 as in 1994 [see section 1.2.].

The Commission felt that **the total allowable catch** should be shared out in accordance with the golden rule of the common market, namely freedom from all form of discrimination [see sections 5.1 and 6.1.]. This amounted to equality of access for the vessels of the Member States to Community waters. However, the very uneven spread of fishery resources between the waters of the Member States and the fact that fishermen consider it their exclusive right to fish in the strip of coastal water under the jurisdiction of their State and to continue to fish in areas where they have traditionally fished, even if

---

[1]   Decision 98/392, OJ L 179, 23.06.1998.

these areas are no longer covered by open access but fall into the economic zone of an-other Member State, give a measure of the difficulties faced by a Community policy of fishery resources management and conservation.

The Accession Act further stipulated that at the latest six years after accession, the Community would set fishing conditions in such a manner as to guarantee the protection of fishing grounds and the conservation of the sea's biological resources. But fishing conditions were turned on their head in September 1976 by the adop-tion of the 200-mile limit by the United Nations Conference. In October 1976, the Commission put forward proposals for the establishment of a Community system for the management and conservation of fishery re-sources. This system was based upon three main ideas: **selective conservation measures, catch quotas and fishing licences.** Selective conservation measures include, for example, measures to stop or restrict fishing at certain periods, to define types of fishing vessels, to set norms for the mesh sizes of fishing nets or to define the minimum size and weight for each species fished. Catch quotas represent the sharing out between the Member States of the Total Allowable Catch (TAC). Fishing licences are the manner in which national quotas are shared out at national level, with the registration and the granting of a licence to each fishing vessel and/or skipper.

There could be grounds for viewing these quotas as measures having equivalent effect to quantitative re-strictions, forbidden by Articles 28 *et seq.* of the EC Treaty (ex-Art. 30 *et seq.*). This point was made at the Court of Justice, which rejected this argument, concluding that catch quotas were applicable at production stage, whereas Articles 28 *et seq.* concern distribution. The Court further declared that although the quotas sought to restrict short-term production, their aim was to avoid the depletion of fishery resources which would jeopardise consumer supply in the long term[1]. The main significance, however, of this judgment was that it acted as a forerunner to the Community decision-making process by clarifying the **Community's powers** in the fisheries sector. The Court noted that in the internal framework, the Community had the power to take all measures concerning the conservation of fishery resources and that on the external front, the Community had the power to enter into international stock conservation commitments. The Court ruled that the powers of the Member States in the area of the conservation of fishery resources were of a temporary nature and, in accor-dance with the provisions of Article 102 of the Act of Accession, should cease at the latest from the sixth year after accession.

In another judgment the Court confirmed that, in matters concerning the high seas which fall under its ju-risdiction, the Community has the same legislative powers as are enjoyed under international law by the flag State, namely the power to introduce measures for the conservation of marine stocks applying to vessels flying the flag of a Member State or registered in a Member State[2].

22.2. Conservation and management of resources

The need for a policy to conserve fishery resources became evident towards the middle of the sixties, when, after long years of overfishing, production began to stagnate and the Community's levels of self-supply began to fall for certain popular species, nota-bly herring and tuna. Since a similar situation prevailed in the rest of the world, the con-cept of a **total allowable catch (TAC)** was adopted by the United Nations Conference on the law of the sea, culminating in the extension of fishing zones to 200 miles[3]. Under the TAC rule, each coastal state uses scientific data to set a catch level which enables sufficient reproduction of fishery stocks, then it determines the amount which can be fished by its own vessels and that which can be granted to third countries in exchange for or through sale of catch rights. The central aim of the TAC is to conserve and enhance existing fishing zones in the interests of both the fishing industry and consumers.

In a Resolution of November 3, 1976 made public on May 7, 1981[4], the Council agreed that the Member States would extend, by concerted action, the limits of the fish-ing zones to 200 miles from January 1, 1977 for North Sea and North Atlantic coasts,

---

[1]   Judgment of 14 July 1976, joined cases 3/76, 4/76 and 6/76, Kramer, ECR 1976.
[2]   Judgment of 24 November 1993, Case C-405/92, ECR 1993.
[3]   Decision 98/392, OJ C 155, 23.05.1997.
[4]   OJ C 105, 07.05.1981.

without prejudice to action of a similar nature for other fishing zones under their jurisdiction, notably the Mediterranean. From January 1, 1977, the Community's exclusive economic zone therefore embraced numerous and potentially rich fishing grounds, the conservation and correct management of which was the responsibility of the Community.

While the extension of **the economic zones** to a distance of 200 miles off coasts - or to the median line when the distance between coasts did not permit a limit of 200 miles - extends the rights of coastal States in these zones, it also means greater obligations for them. The most significant of these obligations is that of conserving biological resources which, given the interdependence of fishery stocks, is a matter of some importance to fishermen and consumers both of the coastal state and of neighbouring states.

Article 6 of the EC Treaty imposes the integration of **environmental protection** requirements into the common fisheries policy. The conservation of fisheries resources and the preservation of marine biodiversity are common objectives of the fisheries policy and of the environment policy. The environmental impact of fisheries and the sustainable development of resources are taken into account, in particular, by the systematic consultation of scientific experts when legislative measures on the exploitation of resources are drafted by the Commission. The Commission tries to coordinate the common fisheries policy with the Community's nature conservation policy, in order to achieve sustainable fishing [see section 16.2.4.][1]. But the proposals of the Commission, which are based on scientific opinions, are generally revised upwards by the Ministers responsible for fisheries, who at the annual fixing of TAC often yield to the pressures exercised by the influential fishing lobbies.

Fisheries research is essential for both the decision-making process and the implementation of the common fisheries policy, particularly the conservation and management of resources[2]. The collection and management of the fisheries data needed to conduct the common fisheries policy is coordinated inside a Community framework[3]. The Community contributes financially towards the expenditure incurred by the Member States in collecting data and in financing studies and pilot projects for carrying out the common fisheries policy[4]. Under the thematic priority of "global change and ecosystems" [see section 18.4.1.], the common research policy seeks to preserve the ecosystems and protect biodiversity which would also contribute to the sustainable use of marine resources and environment[5].

Stressing the need to ensure sustainable resources and apply the principles of good governance, the Commission proposed, in May 2002, a **new multiannual framework for the conservation of resources** and management of fisheries[6]. The main elements of this framework are: strengthening of technical measures; specific measures for fisheries management in the Mediterranean Sea; incorporating environmental concerns into fisheries management; the improvement of scientific advice; new rules on fleet policy, to limit capacity through a simple system, financial measures and restriction of aid; a new regulatory framework for control and enforcement, including effective penalties; a joint fisheries inspection structure; and a new strategy for aquaculture.

22.2.1. Sustainable exploitation of resources

The question of equal access conditions and that of the allocation of resources between Member States formed the crux of the design and implementation of the common fisheries policy. In this field as in many others, the diverging interests of the Member States proved to be a formidable obstacle. Many of them, pushed by the 200-mile rule out of the waters in which they had traditionally fished, had to fall back on the North Sea, where overfishing had already frittered away available resources. Since the three Member States, which had acceded to the Community in 1973 (United Kingdom, Ireland, Denmark), had much vaster and richer fishery zones than the founding members,

---

[1] COM (1999) 363, 14 July 1999.
[2] COM (93) 95, 16.03.1993.
[3] Regulation 1543/2000, OJ L 176, 15.07.2000 and Regulation 1639/2001, OJ L 222, 17.08.2001.
[4] Decision 2000/439, OJ L 176, 15.07.2000 and Decision 2005/703, OJ L 267, 12.10.2005.
[5] Decision 2002/834, OJ L 294, 29.10.2002.
[6] COM (2002) 181, 28 May 2002.

the latter jealously coveted their resources. Founding members, to shore up their claims, called upon the Community principle of equal access to and working of fishing grounds in the sea waters under the sovereignty of the Member States by boats flying the flag of one of the Member States. This principle, embodied in the 1970 Regulation establishing the policy of fishery structures, was fiercely fought by applicant States, who succeeded in winning a temporary derogation running to December 31, 1982. Hence, the Community conservation and management of resources policy was first adopted in 1983 and was completely reviewed in 2002[1] [see section 22.2.2.]. This policy covered both internal and external aspects that we examine successively.

Against this backdrop, the Commission put together in October 1976 its first proposals for a Community system to conserve fishery resources, revolving around three main principles: restriction of catches by the setting of an annual total allowable catch (TAC); the allocation of available resources between the vessels of the Member States, allowance made for the interests of coastal fishermen; and technical measures to manage resources and monitor the system. These proposals sparked off six years of "marathon" negotiations, which would not have been out of place in the Common Agricultural Policy. Although the Member States hammered out agreements on many points, such as interim measures and the external aspects of the resource conservation policy, the stumbling blocks were Community regulations on access to fishing grounds and diverging national interests in this area. France and other continental Member States claimed "**historic rights**" in fishing grounds situated in British waters. The United Kingdom, which held nearly 60% of the Community's fishery resources in its waters, called for a preferential system for its fishing industry within a strip of 12 miles off the coast.
Discussions continued as the deadline of 1982, the last year under which the derogation to the principle of equal access granted by Article 100 of the 1972 Act of Accession, drew closer. During this year at the latest, the Council, in accordance with Article 101 of the Act of Accession, had to examine the provisions which could replace the derogations running to December 21, 1982. If it failed to do so, freedom of access would normally have become applicable in the fishery sector, as provided for by the Regulation on fishery structures. Either the risk of this, the Commission's tireless efforts or the pressure of public opinion, which had come to see the negotiations as somewhat of a red herring, pushed France and the United Kingdom in June 1981 into a compromise maintaining the status quo. The system in force was to be extended for ten years, possibly renewable, during which the United Kingdom would keep an exclusive 12-mile zone off its coast, but would respect the historic rights of fishermen from other Community Member States. The Commission took the Franco-British arrangement on board in its proposals and a group of Regulations implementing the Community policy to conserve fishery resources was adopted on January 25, 1983.

22.2.2. Internal aspects

The Council framework regulation on the **conservation and sustainable exploitation of fisheries resources** lays down the basis for ensuring the long-term viability of the fisheries sector[2]. The approach is founded on scientific advice and the precautionary principle on the one hand, and on good governance and consistency with the other Community policies on the other. Among the measures which the Council may adopt are multiannual recovery plans for the most threatened stocks, including measures to reduce fishing effort where necessary, and multiannual management plans for other stocks. Where there is a serious threat to the conservation of resources or the marine ecosystem, the Commission and the Member States may take the necessary emergency measures lasting for six and three months respectively. The Member States may also adopt conservation and management measures applicable to fishing vessels inside their 12 nautical mile zone, provided that they are non-discriminatory and prior consultation between the Commission and the Member States has taken place, and that the Community has not adopted measures specifically for that area. Concerning access to waters and resources, the regulation lays down rules on allocating fishing opportunities and reviewing the ac-

---

[1] Regulation 2371/2002, OJ L 358, 31.12.2002 and Regulation 1242/2004, OJ L 236, 07.07.2004.
[2] Regulation 2371/2002, OJ L 358, 31.12.2002 and Regulation 1242/2004, OJ L 236, 07.07.2004.

cess rules, and extends until 31 December 2012 the existing rules restricting access to resources inside the 12 nautical mile zones of the Member States.

To ensure the **effective implementation of the common fisheries policy** a series of measures are provided for: the establishment of a Community system of fishing licences, administered by the Member States and applicable to all Community fishing vessels, both in its waters as in those of third countries[1]; the issuing and management by the Member States of special fishing permits (authorisation of exploitation of specific fisheries)[2]; the setting of the objectives and detailed rules for restructuring the Community fisheries sector with a view to achieving a balance on a sustainable basis between resources and their exploitation[3] and of multi-annual guidance programmes (MAGPs) designed to implement these objectives and rules[4]; and the establishment of systems for the management of fishing effort and for control of the CFP [see details below].

When, for a particular species or related species, restriction of catch volume is necessary, the total allowable catch (TAC) for certain fish stocks and groups of fish stocks, the share available to the Community, the allocation of this share between Member States, total catch allocated to third countries and the specific conditions under which all this must take place are drawn up every year[5]. The same is true of the setting of guidance prices for fishery products[6]. The **annual allocation of catch quotas** between the Member States is a process almost as difficult as the annual setting of agricultural prices. In both cases, a delicate balance must be struck between the aspirations of the different Member States.

The annual setting of TACs and their allocation between the Member States are, naturally enough, based on certain criteria. **TAC setting** takes into account scientific opinions on the need to protect fishing grounds and fish stocks, balancing them against the interests of Community consumers and fishermen. It was mentioned above that quite often the latter interests weigh more than the scientific opinions. However, TAC setting also takes into consideration the agreements which the Community has with third countries, such as Norway and Canada. The allocation of the TACs between Member States (catch quotas) is also carried out in light of traditional fishing activities, possible loss of fishing potential in the waters of third countries and the specific needs of regions which are particularly dependent on fishing and its related industries. In order to improve the conditions for exploiting resources, **special fishing permits** may be issued to Community fishing vessels and to vessels flying third-country flags operating in the Community fishing area[7], or, inversely, to Community vessels operating in the waters of a third country in the context of a fisheries agreement[8].

A Community framework covers specific measures to conserve and manage **fishery resources in the Mediterranean**[9]. Projects which can be financed by the Community notably include the restructuring of traditional fisheries, the adaptation of specialised fisheries (sponges, coral, sea urchin), the monitoring of fishing activities, the development of a statistical network and the coordination of research and the use of scientific data. A Regulation lays down certain technical measures for the conservation of fishery

---

[1] Regulation 1281/2005, OJ L 203, 04.08.2005.
[2] Regulation 1627/94, OJ L 171, 06.07.1994.
[3] Decision 97/413, OJ L 175, 03.07.1997 and decision 2002/70, OJ L 31, 01.02.2002.
[4] Commission decisions 98/119 to 98/131, OJ L 39, 12.02.1998 and decision 2002/652, OJ L 215, 10.08.2002.
[5] See, for example, Regulation 51/2006, OJ L 16, 20.01.2006.
[6] Regulation 104/2000, OJ L 17, 21.01.2000 and Regulation 1759/2006, OJ L 335, 01.12.2006.
[7] Regulations 1626/94 and 1627/94, OJ L 171, 06.07.1994.
[8] Regulation 3317/94, OJ L 350, 31.12.1994.
[9] Regulation 3499/91, OJ L 331, 03.12.1991.

resources in the Mediterranean[1]. Technical measures exist also for the conservation of fishery resources in the waters of the Baltic Sea, the Belts and the Sound[2].

The policy of resource management, which was traditionally based on quantitative limitation of catches, was complemented in 1995 by a **system for the management of the fishing effort**. It establishes the criteria and procedures for bringing fleet capacities and efforts under control in the Community waters of the Atlantic and aims at a spatial distribution of fishing effort which preserves the existing balances between different areas[3]. It also establishes a system for the management of fishing effort relating to certain Community fishing areas and resources by fixing the annual maximum fishing effort for each Member State and each fishery, defined by the fleet capacity deployed and by the fleet's activity in terms of days at sea. Specific access requirements and associated conditions are applicable to fishing for deep-sea stocks[4].

Technical conservation measures are defined to protect marine biological resources, particularly juveniles[5]. They concern, for example, mesh sizes, levels of by-catches, minimum marketing sizes and catch restrictions in certain zones, during certain periods or with certain gear[6]. The use of drift-nets for fishing certain species in certain waters is banned. The use of explosives, poison, sleep-inducing substances or fire arms for fishing is forbidden. Fish which do not reach the minimum size must be immediately thrown back into the sea. Purse seines may be used only for catching the target species without endangering marine mammals. A specific regulation lays down technical measures for the conservation of certain stocks of highly migratory species, in accordance with the recommendations adopted by regional fisheries organisations and various bilateral agreements of the Community with third countries[7].

All the catches of a stock or group of stocks subject to a quota and landed by fishing vessels of a Member State are counted against the **quota of the Member State** in question. When the quota has been exhausted, the Member State sets a date from which the fishing of this stock is forbidden. The final decision in this matter rests however with the Commission, who informs the Member States of its decision. Quotas can be exchanged between Member States after notification of the Commission. Rules also exist for remedying the injury caused by the halting of certain fishery activities[8].

If resources are to be fished in an optimal manner, there must be **permanent monitoring of fishing** by surveillance ships. Member States authorities are obliged to inspect fishing vessels flying their flag in accordance with certain common rules and methods, including satellite monitoring, to ensure that restrictions on fishing possibilities are respected. A Community Fisheries Control Agency, based in Vigo (Spain) coordinates the fisheries inspection and control activities of the Member States[9]. Fishing vessel captains must keep a log book listing the quantities of each species caught and kept and must submit a declaration listing the quantities unloaded after each trip to the authorities in the place of unloading. A **Community fishing vessel register** establishes rules on the collection by Member States of the data necessary to determine their vessels fishing effort exerted on fish stocks, so as to ensure balanced exploitation of them[10]. The characteristics for fishing vessels are defined by Regulation[11]. Another Regulation establishes a list of types of behaviour which seriously infringe the rules of the common fisheries policy, notably unlawful fishing either without the necessary authorisation or in prohibited areas[12].

The inspectors of the Member States are, however, themselves **monitored by the Commission**[13]. It exercises its power to monitor the observance by Member States of TAC, quotas and technical conservation measures by sending inspectors to fishing ports in the Member States and on board surveillance ships in Community waters and in certain international waters. In this framework, it opens infringement proceedings against Member States, which overstep their catch quotas or fail to respect their obligations in the area of surveillance or fishery resource conservation and management. The Community makes a financial contribution to national expenditure for the modernisation and development of surveillance and monitoring facilities rendered necessary by the implementation of the common fisheries policy[14].

---

[1]   Regulation 1626/94, OJ L 171, 06.07.1994 and Regulation 973/2001, OJ L 137, 19.05.2001.
[2]   Regulation 2187/2005, OJ L 349, 31.12.2005.
[3]   Regulation 1954/2003, OJ L 289, 07.11.2003.
[4]   Regulation 2347/2002, OJ L 351, 28.12.2002 and Regulations 2269/2004 and 2270/2004, OJ L 396, 31.12.2004.
[5]   Regulation 850/98, OJ L 125, 27.04.1998 and Regulation 1568/2005, OJ L 252, 28.09.2005.
[6]   Regulation 894/97, OJ L 132, 23.05.1997 and Regulation 1239/98, OJ L 171, 17.06.1998.
[7]   Regulation 1936/2001, OJ L 263, 03.10.2001 and Regulation 869/2004, OJ L 162, 30.04.2004.
[8]   Regulation 493/87, OJ L 50, 19.02.1987.
[9]   Regulation 2847/93, OJ L 261, 20.10.1993 and Regulation 768/2005, OJ L 128, 21.05.2005.
[10] Regulation 26/2004, OJ L 5, 09.01.2004 last amended by Regulation 1799/2006, OJ L 341, 07.12.2006.
[11] Regulation 894/97, OJ L 132, 23.05.1997 and Regulation 850/98, OJ L 125, 27.04.1998 last amended by Regulation 973/2001, OJ L 137, 19.05.2001.
[12] Regulation 1447/1999, OJ L 167, 02.07.1999.
[13] Regulation 2740/1999, OJ L 328, 22.12.1999.
[14] Decision 2004/465, OJ L 157, 30.04.2004 and Decision 2006/2, OJ L 2, 05.01.2006.

22.2.3. External aspects

The external aspects of the resource policy are governed by the Council Resolution of November 3, 1976, known as **The Hague Agreements** and made public on May 7, 1981[1]. In this Resolution, the Council agreed that from January 1, 1977, fishing by third country vessels within the economic zone of the Community would be governed by agreements between the Community and the third countries in question. It also agreed that there was a need to ensure, through **Community agreements**, that the Community's fishing industry was granted or kept rights in the waters of third countries.

As a consequence, although the Community had not yet settled its internal fishery problems, by the end of 1976 it presented itself to the outside world as a single coastal State, obliging third countries which wished to fish in the fishing zones of the different Member States to conclude an agreement with the Community as such. The framework agreements negotiated by the Commission in the Community's name implied recognition of the Community's jurisdiction over the **Community 200 mile zone**, its right to set TACs within this zone and to give third countries access to the surplus part of TACs while obtaining access for the Member States to the surplus of co-signatory third countries.

Since this date, numerous fishery agreements have been concluded between the Community and countries with rich fishing grounds such as Madagascar, Angola, Mauritania, Morocco, Mozambique, the Seychelles and Senegal. These agreements and their renewal are negotiated by the Commission and concluded after a Council Decision, often in the form of an exchange of letters, defining the fishing rights of the Community and the financial compensation to be paid by it to the government of the country in question[2]. Fisheries agreements cover some 25% of supply of the Community market and are highly important to the sector, creating significant numbers of jobs in both the EU and partner countries[3].

On the multilateral front, the Community is either a member or an observer of several **international fishery organisations**, such as the North-West Atlantic Fisheries Organisation (NAFO)[4], the North East Atlantic Fisheries Commission (NEAFC)[5], the International Council for the Exploration of the Sea (ICES)[6]; the International Baltic Sea Fishery Commission (IBSFC)[7] and the General Fisheries Commission for the Mediterranean[8]. The Community is also a signatory of the Agreement relating to the implementation of Part XI of the United Nations Convention on the Law of the Sea, which concerns the exploitation of the seabed[9]. It had a major influence on the text of the Agreement, concluded in the framework of that Convention, on the conservation and management of straddling stocks and highly migratory species such as tuna and swordfish[10]. It accepted the FAO Agreement whereby the contracting parties undertook to monitor the fishing activities on the high seas of vessels flying their flag with regard to international conservation and management measures[11]. The Community has signed the Convention on the conservation and management of fishery resources in the southeast Atlantic and participates in the regional fisheries organisation striving to ensure the long-term conservation and sustainable use of fishery resources in the Convention area[12].

In order to contribute to responsible fisheries in the mutual interest of the parties concerned, the Commission is proposing that bilateral fisheries relations gradually **move from access agreements to partnership agreements**, which would comply with the Community's international commitments and be based on the prin-

---

[1] OJ C 105, 07.05.1981.
[2] See, for example, Regulation 953/2005, OJ L 164, 24.06.2005 and Decision 2005/669, OJ L 252, 28.09.2005.
[3] COM (96) 488, 30 October 1996.
[4] Convention and Regulation 3179/78, OJ L 378, 30.12.1978.
[5] Convention and Decision 81/608, OJ L 227, 12.08.1981.
[6] Arrangement, OJ L 149, 10.06.1987.
[7] Convention and Decision 83/414, OJ L 237, 26.08.1983.
[8] Decision 98/416, OJ L 190, 04.07.1998 and Decision 2000/487, OJ L 197, 03.08.2000.
[9] Convention and Decision 94/562, OJ L 215, 20.08.1994.
[10] Agreement and Decision 98/414, OJ L 189, 03.07.1998.
[11] Agreement and Decision 96/428, OJ L 177, 16.07.1996.
[12] Decision 2002/738, OJ L 234, 31.08.2002.

ciples underlying the common fisheries policy, i.e. economically, socially and environmentally sustainable fisheries based on the best available scientific data[1].

22.3. Common organisation of the market

Contrasting sharply with the gestation of the policy for the management and conservation of fishery resources, the creation of a **common market for fishery products** did not come up against major difficulties. Such a market organisation was moreover expressly provided for by the Treaty, with Articles 32 and 34 (ex-Art. 38 and 40 TEC) stipulating that the operation and development of the common market for agricultural products (including fishery products) should be accompanied by the establishment of a common (agricultural) policy and that the latter should incorporate common organisation of the market. Common organisation of the market in fishery and aquaculture products was born in October 1970 and amended several times at later stages. The most recent Regulation in this field aims at ensuring that the rules governing the organisation of the market in fishery products contribute positively to better management and utilisation of resources. It provides for consumers to be informed by means of labelling of fishery products when offered for retail sale, strengthens the role of producer organisations and overhauls the intervention mechanisms, the main purpose of which is to act as a safety net[2].

One of the measures necessary to implement the common organisation of markets is the application of **common standards for the marketing** of the products in question, to ensure that products which do not meet a sufficient quality level are not marketed and to stimulate trade on the basis of fair competition. A Regulation sets common marketing standards for certain fresh or chilled fish for human consumption[3]. In accordance with this Regulation, fish freshness plays a determinant role in assessment of its quality. The common marketing standards therefore take the form of a breaking down into freshness grading on the one hand and size grading on the other, the latter due to differences in consumers' buying habits. The application of these standards means that there must be inspection of the products subject to them. Member States must therefore submit products to a **conformity check**, which can take place at all the marketing stages and also during transport. The Member States must also take all appropriate steps to penalise infringements of marketing standards.

A **guide price** is set at the beginning of the fish marketing year for the main fresh or chilled products[4]. This price is based on the average of the prices recorded on wholesale markets or in representative ports during the three previous fish marketing years. It makes allowance for possible evolution in production and demand and for the need to ensure stable market prices and to contribute to supporting the income of producers, without forgetting consumers' interests. A **Community withdrawal price** is set in line with the freshness, size or weight and presentation of the product, which must be equal to at least 70% while not exceeding 90% of the guide price.

Within this range, producers' organisations can **set a withdrawal price** below which they no longer sell the products supplied by their members. Should this situation arise, the organisations must grant compensation to member producers in line with the quantities of the main fresh or chilled products withdrawn from the market. The organi-

---

[1]   COM (2002) 637, 23 December 2002.
[2]   Regulation 104/2000, OJ L 17, 21.02.2000 last amended by Regulation 1759/2006, OJ L 335, 01.12.2006.
[3]   Regulation 2406/96, OJ L 334, 23.12.1996 and Regulation 790/2005, OJ L 132, 26.05.2005.
[4]   See, for example, Regulations 2032/2006 and 2033/2006, OJ L 414, 30.12.2006.

sations set up intervention funds formed by contributions based on the quantities put on sale or run a compensation system to finance these withdrawal measures. A **producers' organisation** is taken as being any recognised organisation or association of such organisations, set up on the initiative of producers in order to take measures ensuring that fishing is carried out in a rational manner, to improve sales conditions for their production and to stabilise prices.

The adjustment of supply to market requirements is left in the hands of producers' organisations, but they must not hold a dominant position on the common market. The Member States officially recognise producers' organisations which so request provided that they meet certain conditions[1]. They can be granted national aid in the three years following their recognition, to help with their operation and with the investments engendered by the application of common rules. The European institutions have established a close dialogue with the fishing industry and groups affected by the common fisheries policy[2]. Moreover, regional fisheries workshops, within the wider framework of the dialogue with the sector, serve as a forum for all those with an interest in the common fisheries policy to exchange views on its implementation, in particular from the standpoint of the features peculiar to the various regions and fishing zones.

As part of their support for the organisations' activities, the Member States grant **financial compensation** to organisations operating in accordance with Community regulations. Financial compensation is only granted for products which, once put up for sale under normal conditions, do not find a buyer at the Community withdrawal price. Products for which financial compensation has been paid must be disposed off for use other than human consumption[3].

The common organisation of the market in fishery products entails a system governing **trade in these products with third countries**[4]. It lays down the criteria and conditions for allocating catches in Community waters to vessels of third countries authorised to fish in those waters. For the main fishery products, a "free-at-frontier price" is set on the basis of the prices recorded by the Member States. Depending on the products, various measures can be taken should the free-at-frontier price remain below the reference price during at least three successive market days and if large quantities of products are imported from third countries. However, the fishing vessels of third countries may land directly and market their catches at Community ports, subject to special conditions concerning health checks, declaration and prices[5]. The Community suspends customs duties on imports of certain fisheries products, which are necessary for its supplies[6]. Inasmuch as is necessary to enable economic export on a large scale of fishery products on the basis of the prices for these products on the world market, the difference between the latter and Community prices can be made up by an **export refund**[7].

22.4. Structural policy

The fishery sector is at least as vulnerable as agriculture. Production depends on several factors that cannot be controlled by producers: weather, water pollution, delimitation of fishing zones. The sea-fishing sector, which makes up the bulk of the fishing industry, has a highly specific social structure and arduous living and working conditions. Fishing is moreover often economically vital in certain coastal regions without other economic resources and it is a major breadwinner for the people living in these regions. This is why the common organisation of the fishery market must be accompanied by a common structural policy. This fact was recognised in 1970, which saw the combined adoption of the Regulation establishing a common structural policy and that of the Regulation creating a common organisation of the market for the fishery products sector.

Despite the structural measures that were thus implemented during the seventies and the eighties, the fisheries sector was confronted in the early nineties by a very seri-

---

[1] Regulation 104/2000, OJ L 17, 21.01.2000 last amended by by Regulation 1759/2006, OJ L 335, 01.12.2006.
[2] Regulation 657/2000, OJ L 80, 31.03.2000.
[3] Regulation 2509/2000, JO L 289, 16.11.2000.
[4] Regulation 2371/2002, OJ L 358, 31.12.2002 and Regulation 1242/2004, OJ L 236, 07.07.2004.
[5] Regulation 1093/94, OJ L 121, 12.05.1994.
[6] Regulation 2803/2000, OJ L 331, 27.12.2000 last amended by Regulation 1771/2003, OJ L 258, 10.10.2003.
[7] Regulation 686/78, OJ L 93, 07.04.1978.

ous structural crisis, characterised notably by: the widespread chronic overcapacity of the fleets; the over-capitalisation and high debt levels of the companies; the restrictions brought to certain fishing techniques in respect of the conservation of resources; the setting of Community standards with regard to hygiene, health, product quality as well as safety on board. Moreover, many coastal regions suffered from a fragile socio-economic fabric, in particular the areas dependent on fishing, for many of which - if one took account of the induced activities - fishing was the principal or even the only activity.

On account of the aggravation of the structural problems of the fisheries sector in the enlarged EU, the former Financial Instrument for Fisheries Guidance (FIFG) was replaced in 2006 by the **European Fisheries Fund (EFF)**[1]. The assistance under the European Fisheries Fund (hereinafter EFF) aims in particular to: (a) support the common fisheries policy so as to ensure exploitation of living aquatic resources and support aquaculturem to ensure durability; (b) promote a sustainable balance between resources and the fishing capacity of the Community fishing fleet; (c) promote a sustainable development of inland fishing; (d) strengthen the competitiveness of the operating structures and the development of economically viable enterprises in the fisheries sector; (e) foster the protection and the enhancement of the environment and natural resources where related to the fisheries sector.

The objectives of the EFF are pursued within the framework of close cooperation ("**partnership**") between the Commission and the Member State. This partnership concerns regional, local and other public authorities, as well as other appropriate bodies, including those responsible for the environment and for the promotion of equality between men and women, the economic and social partners and other competent bodies. The partners concerned should be involved in the preparation, implementation, monitoring and evaluation of assistance. The EFF provides assistance which complements national, regional and local actions, integrating into them the priorities of the Community. The programming system takes the form of one single operational programme per Member State, in accordance with its national structure. Programming should ensure coordination of the EFF with other funds geared to sustainable development and with the Structural Funds and other Community funds. The programming exercise covers the period from 1 January 2007 to 31 December 2013.

22.5. Appraisal and outlook

The Treaty of Rome did not provide for a fully-fledged fisheries policy, for it included fishery products in the products to be covered by the Common Agricultural Policy. Little by little, however, the specific characteristics of the fisheries sector pushed for a separate common policy. Towards the end of the sixties, therefore, the Community began to turn its attention to the need to protect its resources in the Atlantic and the North Sea, under serious threat from overfishing. Its concern was heightened by the creation of exclusive economic zones, decided upon within the United Nations Conference on the law of the sea. A Community policy to conserve fishery resources was necessary to protect the most threatened species in Community waters. Its main manifestations have been the setting of total allowable catches (TACs), the allocation of catch quotas between the Member States and technical management and surveillance measures. Through an external fisheries policy, the Community has sought to guarantee its own fleet access to the waters of countries with surplus resources and to restrict access to

---

[1]   Regulation 1198/2006, OJ L 223, 15.08.2006.

Community waters for foreign vessels, notably Soviet, Polish and Japanese factory ships.

Six years of negotiations were required before, on January 25, 1983, the Community reached one of its "historic compromises". On this date, a Community system of resource conservation, endeavouring to protect the biological resources of the sea under severe threat from modern fishing methods, was added to the common fisheries policy. This system introduced measures to restrict fishing and set conditions under which it could take place, along with measures governing access to the waters of the Member States. Measures to conserve and manage fishery resources thus came to join the "common organisation of the market", which sets common marketing standards for fisheries and aquaculture products, dividing them up into a freshness grading and seeking to ensure that products which do not reach a satisfactory quality level are not marketed. It obliges the Member States to carry out conformity control checks on these products and to apply sanctions to any infringements. This policy therefore helps protect consumer interests. Producers' interests are not neglected either in the common fisheries policy. Structural policy, inaugurated in 1970, makes use of common measures to restructure, modernise and develop the fishery sector, to develop aquaculture, encourage experimental fishing and adapt Community fishing capacities to disposal possibilities.

This does not mean that the Community fisheries sector is riding on the crest of a wave. The CFP currently faces multiple challenges: a number of stocks are in a critical state, the Community fleet is suffering from over-capacity, the fisheries sector is beset by economic fragility and employment is on the decline. The depletion of resources, due notably to the over-fishing of juveniles combined with fleet over-capacity, make the entire European fisheries sector extremely vulnerable from the economic and social viewpoint. The results achieved in the areas of surveillance systems, inspection and surveillance activities, fleet controls and the application of penalties are not satisfactory, because there are many differences in how the Member States are implementing controls at national level and the cooperation and coordination arrangements established by them are not adequate. Some Member States do not fulfil their obligation to notify catches to the Commission and the multi-annual guidance programmes (MAGPs) have not ensured effective control of the real capacity of the fleets. In order to redress this situation, there must be reduction in both fishing and fishing capacity through more stringent regulation of access to resources and closer monitoring of vessel movements in order to respect the general interest. At international level, the EU should coordinate its development cooperation policy and the external aspects of the common fisheries policy, stressing the importance of environmental and socioeconomic factors for promoting sustainable and responsible fisheries.

In light of the lasting nature of restrictions on authorised catches, fishery concerns should seek to raise the qualitative value of their production, an objective that is consistent both with the common fisheries policy and with consumer protection policy. Due to the fall in prices for the majority of species, to the imperatives of freshness and hence of conservation and to operating constraints, many firms in the sector are, however, facing a shortage of financial resources and a lack of profitability. This crisis situation is tending to become entrenched because of the growing share of imports, upon which the Community market is already dependent for over 50% of its supply. To remedy the crisis, actions should be taken to improve resource management and restructure the industry within the framework of the new structural rules. The aim of these actions should be to avoid the collapse of fisheries by achieving a better match between resources and fishing capacities; but account should also be taken of the development of regions dependent on fishing. Outside its waters, the EU should promote rational and responsible exploitation of fishery resources, particularly through partnership with developing countries of the African coast.

Bibliography on the common fisheries policy

- CACAUD Philippe. *Fisheries laws and regulations in the mediterranean: a comparative study*. Rome: FAO, 2005.
- CADRIN Steven, FRIEDLAND Kevin, WALDMAN John (eds.). *Stock identification methods : applications in fishery science*. Burlington, MA: Elsevier Academic Press, 2005.
- COCHRANE Kevern. *Guide du gestionnaire des pêcheries: les mesures d'aménagement et leur application*. Rome: FAO, 2005.
- DA-ROCHA José-Maria, GUTIÉRREZ Maria-José. "The optimality of the Common Fisheries Policy: the northern stock of hake" in *Spanish economic review*, v. 8, n. 1, March 2006, p. 1-21.
- EUROPEAN COMMISSION. *Legal aspects of the enforcement of the rules of the Common Fisheries Policy*. Luxembourg: EUR-OP*, 2005.

  - *Rebuilding our marine ecosystems, protecting our future*. Luxembourg: EUR-OP*, 2005.

  - *Annual Report from the Commission to the Council and the European Parliament on Member States' efforts during 2005 to achieve a sustainable balance between fishing capacity and fishing opportunities*. Luxembourg: EUR-OP*, 2006.

  - *Communication from the Commission to the Council and the European Parliament on improving the economic situation in the fishing industry*. COM/2006/103. Luxembourg: EUR-OP*, 2006.

  - *Reports from Member States on behaviours which seriously infringed the rules of the Common Fisheries Policy in 2004*. Luxembourg: EUR-OP*, 2006.

  - *Communication from the Commission to the Council and the European Parliament on improving the economic situation in the fishing industry*. Luxembourg: EUR-OP*, 2006.

  - *The European Fisheries Fund: 2007-2013*. Luxembourg: EUR-OP*, 2006.

- FOOD AND AGRICULTURE ORGANIZATION OF THE UNITED NATIONS. *Discards in the world's marine fisheries: an update*. Rome: FAO, 2005.
- GABRIEL Otto, BRANDT Andres von. *Fish catching methods of the world*. Oxford, UK; Ames, Iowa: Blackwell Pub., 2005.
- GRAFTON Quentin (et al.). *Economics for fisheries management*. Cheltenham: Ashgate, 2006.
- HONNELAND Geir, HENRIKSEN Tore, SYDNES Are. *Law and politics in ocean governance: the UN Fish Stock Agreement and regional fisheries management regimes*. Leiden: Brill, 2006.
- HOUSE OF LORDS. EUROPEAN UNION COMMITTEE. *European Union fisheries legislation: report with evidence*. London: Stationery Office, 2005.
- ORGANISATION FOR ECONOMIC COOPERATION AND DEVELOPMENT. *Why fish piracy persists: the economics of illegal, unreported and unregulated fishing*. Paris: OECD, 2005.

  - *Using market mechanisms to manage fisheries: smoothing the path*. Paris: OECD, 2006.

  - *Financial support to fisheries: implications for sustainable development*. Paris: OECD, 2006.

- SCHARE Teresa. *Europe and the "tragedy of the commons": a detailed analysis of the European common fisheries policy (CEP)*. Genève: Institut européen de l'Université de Genève, 2006.

The publications of the Office for Official Publications of the European Communities (EUR-OP) exist usually in all official languages of the EU.

Part VI: External policies

Chapter 23. Commercial Policy
Chapter 24. Development Aid Policy
Chapter 25. External relations

The EU Treaty in its first pages (Article 2) declares that **the Union has the objective of asserting its identity on the international scene**, in particular through the implementation of a common foreign and security policy, including the progressive framing of a common defence policy, which might in time lead to a common defence. The **EC/EU is in fact present on the world stage in three roles**, played mainly under its European Community hat: common commercial policy, development aid policy and external relations. The first two are leading roles - as the EC/EU is the world's largest trading entity and the largest provider of funds for the developing countries - while the role of the external relations of the Community, which is for the time being secondary, is completed and often intermingled with the developing role of the Union in a common foreign and security policy (CFSP) [see chapter 8 and the European perspectives in the conclusions]. The three often overlap as development aid is tied in with commercial policy and commercial policy with the Community's external relations or the Union's CFSP. But, whereas the commercial and the development aid policies are managed with the successful Community method and have a global impact, the CFSP is run with the ineffective intergovernmental method and is common only in name. As the three policies should ideally support each other, the ineptness of the CFSP of the Union handicaps the performance of the policies of the Community.

The European Community/Union, through one or other of its international roles, has **diplomatic relations with 162 countries**, which for their part have representations in Brussels. The EC/EU has its own representations, set up by the Commission, in most of these countries and in **international organisations**. In organisations such as the General Agreement on Tariffs and Trade (GATT), the Community speaks in the name of and in place of the Member States, through the mouthpiece of the Commission [see section 4.1.2.]. It participates in the work of the Organisation for Economic Cooperation and Development (OECD) and has observer status in the United Nations and in some of its specialised organisations. It has relations with other international organisations, such as the Council of Europe. It is represented, by the President of the Commission, at the economic summits of the most industrialised countries, called "the G8", which bring together twice a year the Heads of State or Government of four of its Member States - France, Germany, the United Kingdom and Italy - with those of the United States, Canada, Japan and Russia.

The European Community has signed and manages **association or cooperation agreements** with more than 120 countries and is also responsible for numerous multilateral agreements. When these agreements cover an area for which it has exclusive responsibility, such as international trade, agriculture or fisheries, the Community is the sole party to them on behalf of its Member States. In other cases (some agreements on the environment, transport and so on), the Community is a party in addition to its Member States.

If one adds the **international personalities** of the fifteen Member States - with their different and sometimes conflicting interests in the international arena - to the occasionally identical but at times distinct activities of the European Community and the European Union, one understands that the external relations of the former and the foreign policy of the later are bewildering subjects, not only for the partners of the Union, but also for the Member States themselves. Having examined the common foreign and security policy as a component of the future political integration of the Union, we now try to instil some systematic order in the study of the external relations of the Community.

Chapter 23

COMMERCIAL POLICY

Diagram of the chapter

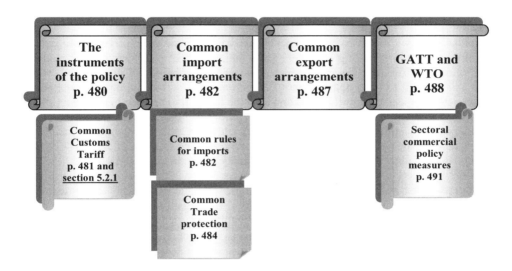

The creation of a **customs union** in the Community in 1968 was implemented internally through the abolition of customs duties, quantitative restrictions and measures having equivalent effect between Member States [see section 5.1.] and, on the external front, through the **introduction of a common customs tariff and a common commercial policy**. In fact, goods imported from third countries had to be treated in the same way by all Member States in order to circulate freely in the customs union [see section 5.2.]. But the customs union itself had to be integrated into the existing international economic order, regulated by the 1948 General Agreement on Tariffs and Trade (GATT).

This is why, in Article 110 of the EEC Treaty (Art. 131 TEC), the Member States declared that in creating a customs union, they intended to contribute, in accordance with the common interest, to the **harmonious development of world trade**, the gradual removal of restrictions to international trade and the lowering of customs barriers. They have kept their word. The creation of the customs union has led to strong growth in intra-Community trade, but the Community has not become introverted. Instead, it has developed into the world's biggest importer and exporter. In addition, the rules of the GATT [see section 23.4.], and the various international agreements drawn up under its aegis, formed the legal basis for the Community's own commercial policy instruments and action, notably in the field of tariffs, the application of safeguard measures, anti-dumping and anti-subsidies actions.

23.1. The instruments of the policy

The common commercial policy was founded on uniform principles, notably as regards tariff charges, the conclusion of tariff and commercial agreements and the harmonisation of liberalisation measures, export policies and trade defence measures, including those to be taken in cases of dumping and subsidies (Art. 133 TEC, ex-Art. 113 EEC). The implementation of the common commercial policy therefore falls **into the Community's sphere of competence**. The European institutions draw up and adapt the common customs tariff, conclude customs and trade agreements, harmonise measures to liberalise trade with third countries, specify export policy and take protective measures, notably to nip unfair trading practices in the bud. If agreements have to be negotiated with third countries, the Commission submits recommendations to the Council, which then authorises it to open negotiations. The Commission is the Community's negotiator and consults a special committee appointed by the Council to assist it in this task (known as "133 Committee"). It works within the framework of guidelines issued by the Council. In exercising the powers granted to it by Article 133 (TEC), including the conclusion of agreements, the Council acts by a qualified majority [see sections 4.1.4. and 4.3.].

In international agreements, **the Community as such, represented by the Commission** [see section 4.1.2.], is more often than not a party alongside the Member States, which means that it takes part in the negotiations, signs the agreements and if necessary participates in their management as a member of the organisation in question. In areas for which the Community has exclusive responsibility (agriculture, fisheries), the Member States are not at the forefront; the Commission negotiates and manages the agreements on the basis of a negotiating brief delivered by the Council (world commodity agreements, traditional trade agreements, preferential agreements, association agreements)[1]. According to Article 307 (TEC), rights and obligations arising from agreements concluded by the Member States before their accession to the Community [see section 1.2.] are not affected by the provisions of the EC Treaty [see sections 2.2. and 2.3.]; but to the extent that such agreements are not compatible with this Treaty, the Member States concerned must take all appropriate steps to eliminate the incompatibilities established[2].

Given the complexity of international relations and of external policy instruments in the broad sense of the term, the **Community powers occasionally spill out of the framework** defined in Article 133 (TEC). In such cases, the Community institutions cannot act alone [see section 4.3.]. They must draw in the Member States, a fact that considerably complicates the negotiating process and the conclusion of international agreements [see details below]. However, the Treaty of Amsterdam provides that the Council will be able, unanimously, to decide to extend the application of Article 133

---

[1] See: judgment of 31 March 1971, case 22/70, AETR, ECR 1971, p.263; and opinion of 26 April 1977, ECR 1977, p. 741.
[2] See judgment of 14 October 1980, case 812/79, Burgoa, ECR 1980, p.2787.

(commercial policy) to international negotiations and agreements on services and intellectual property rights in addition to those already covered by this provision.

The **Common Customs Tariff (CCT)** is the key to the Community's commercial policy [see section 5.2.1.]. As seen in the Chapter on customs union and as will be seen later in this Chapter [see section 23.2.1.], the blueprinting and evolution of the CCT have taken place against the backdrop of the General Agreement on Tariffs and Trade (GATT). CCT tariffs were low at the outset, responding to the central objective of liberalisation of international trade. They have been cut even further in the framework of successive GATT negotiations [see section 23.4.]. It should be borne in mind that the Commission, acting on a negotiating brief issued by the Council, and not the Member States individually, is the Community's negotiator in the GATT/WTO arena.

Instead of becoming a "**Fortress Europe**" when the single market was completed in 1992 [see section 6.1.], as feared by some of its trade partners, the Community made important concessions in order to allow the conclusion of the GATT Uruguay Round in 1993. However, one of the central principles of GATT and WTO is that of balance of mutual advantages (global reciprocity). This means, for the European Union, that it can tie access for third country economic operators to the benefits of the single market with the existence of similar opportunities for European undertakings (businesses, companies) in the country in question, or at the least to the absence of any discrimination. This implies a case-by-case approach for third countries, but a common approach by the Member States. The single market obliges the latter to show a united face to third countries. At the same time, the globalisation of the economy is creating a state of interdependence and a growing realisation that trade problems need to be solved wherever possible in a multilateral framework.

The **concepts of "commercial policy" and "Community competence"** have been enlarged thanks to the opinions of the Court of Justice. Indeed, the Court has stated that Article 113 of the EEC Treaty (Art. 133 TEC) cannot be interpreted in a manner which would have the effect of restricting the common commercial policy to the use of instruments designed to influence only the traditional aspects of external trade, excluding more developed mechanisms[1]. The Court has formulated the limits of the action of the Member States in areas where powers are shared with the Community: measures must be "common", must involve close cooperation "both in the process of negotiation and conclusion and in the fulfilment of the obligations entered into", and must ensure "unity in the international representation of the Community"[2]. On the dispute between the Community and the Member States regarding jurisdiction for concluding the Uruguay Round, the Court ruled in an opinion that the Community has exclusive powers in relation to trade in goods and in the cross-border supply of services. However, with respect to the other issues relating to the agreements on services and intellectual property, the Court ruled that powers are shared between the Community and the Member States[3]. Where, the powers are shared and, therefore, the Community and the Member States are obliged to cooperate on the negotiation, conclusion and implementation of international agreements, as those concluded within the Food and Agriculture Organisation (FAO), there is, according to the Court, a need for single representation of the Community and, therefore, the Member States have not the right to vote[4].

The rare **bilateral agreements** which still exist between the Member States and third countries, notably state-trading nations, are subject to Community vetting. Every year the Council, acting on a Commission proposal, authorises the extension or the tacit renewal for a year of certain trade agreements concluded by the Member States with third countries, insofar as they do not constitute a barrier to the implementation of the common commercial policy[5]. Member States must notify the Commission of all bilateral treaties, agreements or arrangements concerning commercial relations with third countries the extension of which is proposed. The Commission must notify the other Member Statesand start consultations involving such co-ordination as will

---

[1] Opinion 1/78 of the Court of Justice of 14 November 1978, ECR 1978, p. 2871.
[2] Opinion 2/91 of the Court of Justice of 19 March 1993, ECR I-1061.
[3] Opinion 1/94 of the Court of Justice of 15 November 1994, p. 5267.
[4] Judgment of 19 March 1996, Case C-25/94, Commission v Council, ECR 1996, p. I-1469.
[5] Decision 2001/855, OJ L 320, 05.12.2001.

ensure the proper functioning and the strengthening of the common market as well as the establishment of uniform principles of common commercial policy in relation to the country in question[1].

In case of exceptional trade problems, a Member State may have recourse to the **safeguard clause** provided for in Article 134 of the EC Treaty (ex Art. 115). This Article stipulates that in order to ensure that the execution of commercial policy measures taken by any Member State is not obstructed by a deflection of trade, or where disparities between such measures lead to economic difficulties in one or several States, the Commission can recommend ways of bringing about the requisite cooperation between Member States. Failing this, it authorises the Member States to take the necessary protective measures, the conditions and details of which it determines. In urgent cases, however, the Member States can themselves take the necessary steps and notify the other Member States and the Commission of them. The Commission then decides if these measures should be changed or abolished altogether[2].

The systematic production of **Community statistics** on the balance of payments, international trade in services and foreign direct investment is designed to ensure the smooth functioning of the common commercial policy and particularly trade negotiations[3].

23.2. Common import arrangements

The Customs Union is one of the linchpins of the common commercial policy. The other main elements are the **common import arrangements** and the **common protective measures**. Together they contribute to ensuring an even competition playing field for Community undertakings, giving them access to equal prices for imported raw materials and levelling the quantities and prices of competitor products.

23.2.1. Common rules for imports

The common rules for imports were established by Council Regulation of 22 December 1994[4]. **They apply to imports of products originating in third countries**, with the exception, on the one hand, of textiles subject to specific import arrangements, discussed under the heading of sectoral measures of the commercial policy, and, on the other, products originating from certain third countries, including Russia, North Korea and the People's Republic of China, mentioned below. Apart from those exceptions, imports into the Community are free and not subject to any quantitative restrictions. The Regulation strives to establish a balance between a Community market normally open to the world following the conclusion of the Uruguay Round and more rapid and simplified procedures in case of a risk of serious injury caused by imports of a product to Community producers.

The Regulation establishes a **Community information and consultation procedure**. The examination of the trend of imports, of the conditions under which they take place and of serious injury or threat of serious injury to Community producers resulting from such imports covers the following factors in practice: a) the volume of imports; b) the price of imports; and c) the consequent impact on the Community producers of similar or directly competitive products as indicated by trends in certain economic factors such as production, capacity utilisation, stocks, sales, market share, prices and so on [see details below].

Where the trend in imports of a product originating in a third country threatens to cause injury to Community producers, import of that product may be subject, as appropriate, to prior or retrospective **Community surveillance**. Products under prior Commu-

---

[1]   Decision 69/494, OJ L 326, 29.12.1969.
[2]   Decision 87/433, OJ L 238, 21.08.1987.
[3]   Regulation 184/2005, OJ L 35, 08.02.2005 and Regulation 602/2006, OJ L 106, 19.04.2006.
[4]   Regulation 3285/94, OJ L 349, 31.12.1994 and Regulation 2200/2004, OJ L 374, 22.12.2004.

nity surveillance may be put into free circulation only on production of an import document endorsed by the competent authority designated by Member States and valid throughout the EU, regardless of the Member State of issue [see details below]. The surveillance may be confined to imports into one or more regions of the Community (regional surveillance).

Where a product is imported into the Community in such increased quantities and/or on such terms as to cause, or threaten to cause, serious injury to Community producers, the Commission may, acting at the request of a Member State or on its own initiative take **safeguard measures**, i.e.: limit the period of validity of import documents required in compliance with surveillance measures; alter the import rules for the product in question by making its release for free circulation conditional on production of an import authorisation granted under certain provisions and in certain limits laid down by the Commission. As regards Members of the World Trade Organisation (WTO), safeguard measures are taken only when the two conditions indicated above (quantities and terms of imports) are met. No safeguard measure may be applied to a product originating in a developing country Member of the WTO as long as that country's share of Community imports of the product concerned does not exceed 3% and that the import share of all developing countries does not account for more than 9% of such imports.

Following the information and consultation procedure, when trends in imports appear to call for surveillance or protective measures, the Commission must be informed of this fact by the Member States. This information must contain all available evidence, drawn from certain specific criteria. The Commission then passes on forthwith this information to all the Member States. Consultations may be held either at the request of a Member State or on the initiative of the Commission. These consultations must take place within eight working days of the Commission receiving the information. They take place within an advisory committee consisting of representatives of each Member State and chaired by a representative of the Commission (**133 Committee**) [see section 23.1.]. These consultations concern notably: a) the terms and conditions of import, import trends and the various aspects of the economic and commercial situation as regards the product in question; and b) the measures, if any, to be taken.

When, after consultations have taken place, it is apparent to the Commission that there is sufficient evidence, it initiates an **investigation** within one month of receipt of information from a Member State and publishes a notice in the Official Journal of the European Union, giving a summary of the information received and asking for any relevant information, including the views of the interested parties. The Commission seeks all information it deems to be necessary and, where it considers it appropriate, after consulting the Committee, endeavours to check the information with importers, traders, agents, producers, trade associations and organisations. The Member States supply the Commission at its request and following procedures laid down by it with all information at their disposal on developments in the market of the product being investigated.

The decision to impose Community or regional, prior or retrospective **surveillance** is taken by the Commission. In the case of retrospective surveillance, however, any Member State may refer the Commission's decision to the Council, which, acting by a qualified majority, may confirm, amend or revoke it. The imposition of surveillance measures implies a monthly communication by the Member States to the Commission of certain information on the imports in question. Surveillance measures are of limited duration. Failing provisions to the contrary, they cease to be valid at the end of the second half calendar year following that in which they were introduced. In any case, the Community surveillance measures are few and far between, concerning mostly steel products[1].

Any Member State may also refer to the Council the Commission's decision on safeguard measures. The Council, acting by a qualified majority, may confirm, amend or revoke the decision of the Commission. It may also transform the Community surveillance measures into safeguard measures. The duration of safeguard measures must be limited to the period of **time necessary to prevent or remedy serious injury** and to facilitate adjustment on the part of Community producers. The period should not exceed four years. The combination of safeguard measures and anti-dumping or anti-subsidy measures on the same imported product should not result in those measures having an effect greater than that intended by the Community's trade defence policy instruments[2].

---

[1] Regulation 2248/94, OJ L 242, 17.09.1994 last amended by Regulation 1565/95, OJ L 150, 01.07.1995 and Regulation 2385/2002, OJ L 358, 31.12.2002.
[2] Regulation 452/2003, OJ L 69, 13.03.2003.

In addition to the general common rules for imports, there still exist some **specific rules**. The most important of such rules apply to imports from certain third countries, notably Russia and the other countries of the Commonwealth of Independent States, Albania, the People's Republic of China, North Korea and Vietnam[1]. These rules establish the liberalisation of imports, namely the absence of any quantitative restrictions on the part of EU Member States. However, for a limited number of products originating in the People's Republic of China (notably footwear, tableware, kitchenware of porcelain or china and certain toys), owing to the sensitivity of the Community industry, they set out quantitative quotas and special surveillance measures. Apart from these special rules, the Community procedures on information and investigation, as well as the safeguard measures concerning imports from these countries are quite similar to those set out by the general common rules applicable to imports in the EU. Community importers can now use a uniform import licence, valid throughout the EU. Other specific import regimes concern textile products and the agricultural sector and are examined under the heading of "Sectoral commercial policy measures".

23.2.2. Common trade protection

As seen above, the Community can introduce surveillance and safeguard measures in the framework of the common rules for imports when imports at prices viewed as normal are causing or risk causing serious injury to Community producers. In cases where the **export price is lower than the normal value of a like product (dumping)**, the Community can take trade protection measures, notably through the application of **anti-dumping duties**. Community rules being compatible with those of the World Trade Organisation, economic operators must comply with only one set of rules for imports into the EU [see sections 23.2.1. and 23.4.]. These rules apply automatically in the new States acceding to the EU, as of May 2004[2]. On the jurisdictional level, anti-dumping and anti-subsidy cases must be brought before the Court of First Instance[3].

According to the Regulation on **protection against dumped imports** from countries not members of the EC, anti-dumping duty may be applied to any dumped product whose release for free circulation in the Community causes injury[4]. A product is considered as having been dumped if its export price to the Community is less than a comparable price for the like product, in the ordinary course of trade, as established for the exporting country. The term like product means a product that is identical in all respects or has characteristics closely resembling those of the product under consideration. In order to determine the dumping, the normal price and the dumped price must be defined and these two values must then be compared [see details below]. It should be noted that these definitions as well as the anti-dumping procedures are, after the Uruguay Round, similar in the EU and in other WTO countries.

Provisional measures may be taken by the Commission, after consultation with the Member States, no sooner than 60 days but not later than nine months from the initiation of the proceedings. The final conclusions of the investigation must be adopted within a further six months. The amount of the **provisional anti-dumping duty** must not exceed the margin of dumping as provisionally established. Investigation may be terminated without the imposition of provisional or definitive duties upon receipt of satisfactory voluntary undertakings from the exporter to revise his prices or to cease exports to the area in question at dumped prices.

Where a provisional duty has been applied and the facts established show that there is dumping and injury, the Council decides, irrespective of whether a definitive anti-dumping duty is to be imposed, what proportion of the provisional duty is to be definitively collected. If the **definitive anti-dumping** duty is higher than the provisional duty,

---

[1]   Regulation 519/94, OJ L 67, 10.03.1994 and Regulation 427/2003, OJ L 65, 08.03.2003.
[2]   Commission notice, OJ C 91, 15.04.2004 and OJ 231, 16.09.2004.
[3]   Decision 94/149, OJ L 66, 10.03.1994.
[4]   Regulation 384/96, OJ L 56, 06.03.1996 and Regulation 2117/2005, OJ L 340, 23.12.2005.

the difference must not be collected. If the definitive duty is lower than the provisional duty, the duty must be recalculated. Provisional or definitive anti-dumping duties must be imposed by Regulation, and collected by Member States in the form, at the rate specified and according to the other criteria laid down in the Regulation imposing such duties.

The rules on **protection against subsidised imports** from countries not members of the European Community are also established by Regulation[1]. Here again the Community legislation is compatible with WTO rules and, therefore, business must comply with only one set of rules. A **countervailing duty** may be imposed for the purpose of offsetting any subsidy granted, directly or indirectly, for the manufacture, production, export or transport of any product whose release for free circulation in the Community causes injury. A subsidy is deemed to exist if: 1) there is a financial contribution by a government or by a private body entrusted by it (direct transfer of funds, loan guarantees, fiscal incentives, etc.); and 2) a benefit is thereby conferred.

Subsidies, which are not specific to an enterprise or industry or group of enterprises or industries, cannot be subjected to countervailing measures. Even when they are specific, subsidies cannot be subjected to countervailing duties, if they are given: for research activities; pursuant to a general framework of regional development; to promote adaptation of existing facilities to new environmental requirements. The amount of subsidies to be subjected to countervailing duties is calculated in terms of the benefit conferred to the recipient, which is found to exist during the investigation period. Where all conditions are met, a provisional or definitive **countervailing duty** is imposed following procedures similar to the ones described above concerning the imposition of anti-dumping duties.

In December 1994, the Council adopted a Regulation destined to improve Community **procedures on commercial defence** and to ensure the exercise of the Community's rights under international trade rules, in particular those established under the auspices of the World Trade Organisation (WTO)[2]. This Regulation allows the Community to respond to obstacles to trade, i.e. to any trade practice adopted or maintained by a third country in respect of which international trade rules establish a right of action. Thus, following the Community examination procedures and after consultation with the Member States, the Commission may take any commercial policy measures which are compatible with existing international obligations and procedures, notably: (a) suspension or withdrawal of any concession resulting from commercial policy negotiations; (b) the raising of existing customs duties or the introduction of any other charge on imports; (c) the introduction of quantitative restrictions or any other measures modifying import or export conditions or otherwise affecting trade with the third country concerned. The Commission has thus initiated procedures concerning e.g.: the US Anti-dumping Act of 1916 and US practices with regard to cross-border music licensing[3]; trade practices maintained by South Korea affecting trade in commercial vessels[4] and practices followed by India affecting trade in wines and spirits[5].

An important trade defence instrument of the Community is related to customs action against goods suspected of **infringing certain intellectual property rights**, particularly counterfeit and pirated goods[6]. As these breaches have been escalating in recent years, notably as regards the methods used by fraud gangs and the internationalisation of

---

[1] Regulation 2026/97, OJ L 288, 21.01.1997 and Regulation 461/2004, OJ L 77, 13.03.2004.
[2] Regulation 3286/94, OJ L 349, 31.12.1994 and Regulation 356/95, OJ L 41, 23.02.1995.
[3] Commission notices, OJ C 58, 25.02.1997 and OJ C 177, 11.06.1997.
[4] Commission notice, OJ C345, 02.12.2000 and Decision 2002/818, OJ L 281, 19.10.2002.
[5] Commission notice, OJ C 228, 17.09.2005.
[6] Regulation 1383/2003, OJ L 196, 02.08.2003.

traffic, and as other property rights such as geographical indications, designations of origin and new plant varieties are affected, the Community legislation has become more stringent [see sections 6.2.4 and 23.4.]. It gives customs administrations a legal arsenal enabling them, in collaboration with right holders, to better prevent and control intellectual property right infringements. Action by the customs authorities involves, for the period necessary to determine whether suspect goods are indeed counterfeit goods, pirated goods or goods infringing certain intellectual property rights, suspending release for free circulation in the Community, export and re-export. The measures applicable to goods which have been found to be counterfeit, pirated or generally to infringe certain intellectual property rights aim to deprive those responsible for trading in such goods of the economic benefits of the transaction and penalise them so as to constitute an effective deterrent to further transactions of the same kind.

An **investigation** to determine the existence, degree and effect of any alleged dumping is initiated upon a written **complaint** submitted to the Commission or to a Member State by any natural or legal person, or any association acting on behalf of the Community industry. Where, in the absence of any complaint, a Member State is in possession of sufficient evidence of dumping and of injury resulting therefrom for the Community industry, it must immediately communicate such evidence to the Commission. The investigation is conducted by the Commission in cooperation with the Member States[1]. It covers both dumping and injury.

Normal value is generally based on the prices paid or payable, in the ordinary course of trade, by independent customers in the exporting country. Where there are no or insufficient sales of the like product in the ordinary course of trade, or where such sales do not permit a proper comparison, the normal value of the like product is calculated on the basis of the cost of production in the country of origin plus a reasonable amount for selling, general and administrative costs and for profits. In the case of imports from non-market economy countries, normal value is determined on the basis of the price or constructed value in a market economy third country, or the price from such a third country to other countries, including the Community, or where these are not possible, on any other reasonable basis.

The **export price** is the price actually paid or payable for the product sold for export to the Community. Where there is no export price or where it appears that the export price is unreliable because of association or a compensatory arrangement between the exporter and the importer or a third party, the export price may be constructed on the basis of the price at which the imported product is first resold to an independent buyer or on any reasonable basis. In such cases, allowance must be made for all costs incurred between import and resale (transport, insurance, general expenses), including duties and taxes, and for a reasonable profit margin.

A **fair comparison** must then be made between the export price and the normal price. This comparison must be made at the same level of trade and in respect of sales made at as nearly as possible the same time and with due account taken of other differences which affect price comparability. Where the normal value and the export price as established are not taken on such a comparable basis due allowance, in the form of adjustments, must be made in each case for differences in factors which are claimed, and demonstrated to affect prices and, therefore, price comparability, notably: the physical characteristics of the product concerned; import charges and indirect taxes; discounts, rebates and quantities; transport, insurance, handling and ancillary costs; and the cost of any credit granted.

The **dumping margin** is the amount by which the normal value exceeds the export price. Where dumping margins vary, a weighted average margin may be established. The determination of the **serious injury** caused to the Community industry or the threat of such injury must be based on positive evidence and involve an objective examination of both (a) the volume of the dumped imports and the effect of the dumped imports on prices in the Community market for like products, and (b) the consequent impact of these imports on the Community producers of the like products.

Reports on the Community's anti-dumping and anti-subsidy activities supplied by the Commission every year to the Council and Parliament suggest that the European Community makes cautious use of the trade defence instruments. When the instruments are used, they are used with care and self-restraint while ensuring effective protection against unfair trade practices. At the end of 2003, 156 anti-dumping measures and 17 countervailing measures were in force in the Community. Only 0.3% of total imports to the European Union were the subject of anti-dumping and antisubsidy measures. The cases range from anti-dumping and countervailing duties on imports of colour television receivers originating in China, Korea, Malaysia and Thailand[2] to anti-dumping duties on imports of imports of ammonium nitrate from Russia and Ukraine[3]. In some cases,

---

[1]   See, e.g., Regulation 275/2004, OJ L 47, 18.02.2004.
[2]   Regulation 1531/2002, OJ L 231, 29.08.2002 and Regulation 999/2004, OJ L 183, 20.05.2004.
[3]   Regulation 945/2005, OJ L 160, 23.06.2005.

however, the Commission accepts undertakings offered by countries involved in anti-dumping proceedings[1]. As for measures taken by other countries against Community exports, 30% of anti-dumping and countervailing measures affecting the Community or its Member States are habitually taken by the United States[2].

23.3. Common export arrangements

Article 132 of the EC Treaty stipulates that the **aid arrangements applied to exports** by the Member States should be harmonised to ensure that there is a level competition playing field for the Community's exporting undertakings. As regards **export credits**, the Community applies the arrangement concluded in the framework of the Organisation for Economic Cooperation and Development (OECD) and providing guidelines for officially supported export credits ("consensus")[3]. These guidelines confine official support to the interest rates for export credits to certain countries. Concerning **export credit insurance** for transactions with medium- and long-term cover, a Directive aims to harmonise the various public systems for such insurance in order to prevent distortion of competition among EU firms[4]. It lays down the common principles which must be observed by export credit insurers and which concern the constituents of cover (scope of cover, causes of loss and exclusions of liability and indemnification of claims), premiums, country cover policy and notification procedures.

The Commission contributes from the Community Budget [see section 3.4.] to **export promotion** and notably to closer cooperation at Community level and to research for joint action in favour of European exports (international exhibitions, trade forums, conferences, seminars) in coordination with Community programmes and with Member States' export promotion programmes [see details below]. The cooperation with trade federations and with national export promotion organisations pursues two aims: first of all, to ensure that any activities on a particular market strengthen the Community dimension and secondly, to focus activities on a number of target countries, the list of which is topped by China, Japan, the countries of ASEAN (Association of South East Asian Nations) [see section 25.6.] and the countries of Central and Eastern Europe [see section 25.2.].

Community exports to third countries are free or, in other words, are not subject to quantitative restrictions, with the exception of a few products for certain Member States and of petroleum oil and gases for all the Member States[5]. However, when exceptional market trends, which cause scarcity of an essential product, justify protective measures in the opinion of a Member State, it can set in motion the **Community information and consultation procedure**. Consultations take place within an Advisory Committee and cover notably the conditions and terms of exports and, if necessary, the measures which should be adopted.

Should the Community market be in a critical situation due to **a lack of essential products** and should the interests of the Community demand immediate action, the Commission, at the request of a Member State or acting on its own initiative, can make exports subject to the granting of an **export authorisation**, issued if certain provisions and restrictions defined by it, while waiting for a Council Decision, are satisfied. The Council can uphold or invalidate the Commission's Decision, in light of the international commitments of the Community or of all its Member States, notably as regards trade in primary products. **Quantitative export restrictions** can be limited to specific destinations or to the exports of certain regions of the Community. They must

---

[1]   Commission Regulation 588/2005, OJ L 98, 16.04.2005 and Commission Regulation 858/2005, OJ L 143, 07.06.2005.
[2]   COM (2002) 484, 4 September 2002.
[3]   Decision 2001/76, OJ L 32, 02.02.2001 and Decision 2002/634, OJ L 206, 03.08.2002.
[4]   Directive 98/29, OJ L 148, 19.05.1998.
[5]   Regulation 2603/69, OJ L 324, 27.12.1969 and Regulation 3918/91, OJ L 372, 31.12.1991.

give due consideration to the volume of contracts concluded at normal terms, before bringing in a protective measure. Export restrictions may depend on political or security reasons. The objective of Regulation 304/2003 is also to ensure that the provisions of Directive 67/548[1] and of Directive 1999/45[2] regarding the classification, packaging and labelling of chemicals dangerous to man or to the environment when they are placed on the market in the European Community shall also apply to all such chemicals when they are exported from the Member States to other Parties or other countries.

A Community budget heading covers the Commission's **strategy to improve access for Community businesses** to other countries' markets, such as identification and analysis of trade barriers in other countries, the establishment and development of databases and the dissemination of information on trade barriers, studies concerning the implementation by other countries of their obligations under international trade agreements and the production of information packs on the legal and economic aspects of removing these barriers[3]. The Commission, in cooperation with the Member States, finances activities, research studies and pilot projects linked to education and public awareness on bilateral relations between the Union and the industrialised countries in North America, Asia and Australasia, aiming notably at the improvement of the Union's visibility (opening of the EU centres)[4].

Whereas customs tariffs diminish thanks to the Uruguay Round and the rules of the World Trade Organisation impose in principle the freedom of international exchanges, European companies are still faced with **obstacles to trade and investment in a large number of countries**. The European Community has the necessary power to redress these situations; but its Member States must lend a supporting hand in combating trade barriers by joining forces with the European Commission. Having asked Member States and business circles to inform it on the most persistent trade and investment barriers on the main export markets, the Commission established an ongoing inventory of tariff and non-tariff barriers to trade in goods and services and the progress made towards removing them in the form of an interactive electronic database accessible to businessmen via the Europa server on the Internet[5].

23.4. GATT and WTO

The **General Agreement on Tariffs and Trade (GATT)** came into being in 1947. Along with the International Monetary Fund and the World Bank it was one of the institutions set up in the post-war period to help regulate the international economy and prevent a recurrence of the disastrous protectionist policies undertaken between the two World Wars. GATT was charged with overseeing international trade in goods and, in particular, the liberalisation of this trade by means of a negotiated reduction in tariff barriers. The scope of the GATT was, therefore, somewhat limited initially, but the conclusion of the Uruguay Round negotiations enlarged its field of activities and placed them under the auspices of the **World Trade Organisation (WTO)**. The Member States of the EC were the contracting parties to the GATT, but, because of the common commercial policy, they participated as "the Community" in the work of GATT and now participate as such in the WTO, that superseded the GATT since 1995. The Commission is the single negotiator and spokesman of the European Community in WTO [see section 4.1.2.]. The Community as such is signatory to a number of international GATT agreements.

The EC Member States and other industrial countries made major tariff concessions - particularly in favour of the developing countries - during the successive GATT **negotiating rounds** between 1960 and 1979 under the aegis of the General Agreement on Tariffs and Trade [see section 5.2.2.]. Thanks to the Dillon (1960-1962) and Kennedy Rounds (1965-1967), the customs tariffs of the States participating in the General Agreement were slashed by nearly 50%[6]. Following the Tokyo Round (1973-1979), a

---

[1] Directive 67/546, OJ 196, 16.08.1967 last amended by Directive 2006/102, OJ L 363, 20.12.2006.
[2] Directive 1999/45, OJ L 200, 30.07.1999 last amended by Directive 2006/8, OJ L 19, 24.01.2006.
[3] Decision 98/552/EC, OJ L 265, 30.09.1998.
[4] Regulation 382/2001, OJ L 57, 27.02.2001 and Regulation 1900/2005, OJ L 303, 22.11.2005.
[5] Electronic address: http://mkaccdb.eu.int.
[6] Agreement and Decision 68/411, OJ L 305, 19.12.1968.

fresh one-third reduction in customs tariffs was agreed upon, to be implemented in eight stages the last of which was timed for January 1, 1987[1]. These tariff reductions made a considerable contribution to keeping the international trade system open, despite the fact that in the first years of the 1980s, the world economy went through the worst period in its post-war history causing protectionist pressures to flare up. Since 1985, the Community committed itself wholeheartedly to the process of launching a new cycle of multilateral trade negotiations under the GATT. The round got underway at the Punta del Este (Uruguay) Conference in September 1986.

The **Uruguay Round negotiations** encompassed the revision of GATT rules and disciplines, plus the adoption of disciplines for "new" areas: the trade-related aspects of intellectual property rights, trade-related investment measures and international trade in services. Also on the agenda were the sensitive issues of agriculture and textiles, areas in which trade was traditionally subject to special rules and for which the participants were to devise an agreement for their gradual incorporation into the GATT framework. The conclusion of the Uruguay Round, in December 1993, resulted in a strengthening of the rules and disciplines of international trade, thanks to the reform of the provisions on safeguards, subsidies, anti-dumping measures, the balance of payments, the "standards" and "public procurement" codes. All these GATT agreements have been incorporated into Community law [see sections 6.2.4 and 23.2.2.].

Market access for industrial products has been considerably improved by a reduction of one third or more in the customs duties imposed by the industrialised countries and many developing countries on the following sectors: building materials, agricultural machinery, medical equipment, steel, beer, spirits, pharmaceutical products, paper, toys and furniture [see section 5.2.]. The average level of tariffs for industrialised countries fell from 5% to about 3.5%, whereas it stood at 40% or more prior to the various rounds of GATT negotiations. In total, close to 40% of the EU's industrial imports are now duty free. On their part, developing countries apply substantial reductions of their customs duties on these products, whereas prior to the Uruguay Round they had taken very few such commitments. The EU played a major role in pushing through the conclusion, in March 1997, of the **Information Technology** Agreement under which tariffs on information technology products of countries accounting for 92% of world trade were phased out completely on 1 January 2000 [see also section 17.3.5.][2].

A first step was taken towards the liberalisation of world trade in services. It should be noted that trade is not limited to exchange of goods but also increasingly involves services, a sector which contributes nearly half of the EU's GDP. The **General Agreement on Trade in Services (GATS)** includes general rules for trade in this area, specific provisions for certain service sectors and national schedules showing the services and activities which each country agrees to open up to competition, with possible limitations[3] [see details below].

The Uruguay Round negotiations included also the protection of **trade-related intellectual property (TRIPs)**[4]. Intellectual property concerns an ever-increasing part of world trade, be it related to pharmaceuticals, computer software, books or records. As trade has increased so too have cheating, counterfeiting and copying. A further problem has been the appropriation of brand names and, in the case of wines and foodstuffs, certain geographical appellations. The conclusions of the Uruguay Round have reinforced existing international conventions, for example the Bern and Paris Conventions for the

---

[1]   Agreement and Decision 80/271, OJ L 71, 17.03.1980.
[2]   Decision 97/359, OJ L 155, 12.06.1997 and Regulation 2216/97, OJ L 305, 08.11.1997.
[3]   Annex 1, OJ L 336, 23.12.1994, p 191-212 and Fifth Protocol, OJ L 20, 27.01.1999, p. 40-53.
[4]   Annex 1 – Annex 1C, OJ L 336, 23.12.1994, p. 214-233.

protection of literary and artistic works, by bringing them within the ambit of the GATT dispute settlement procedures [see details below].

The Uruguay Round resulted also on an Agreement on **trade-related investment measures (TRIMs)**[1]. An illustrative list of non-permissible measures is included in the agreement, covering such things as local content rules, trade balancing and local sales requirements. Such measures must be phased out over a two- to seven-year period, depending upon whether the country is developed or developing. The TRIMs Agreement is particularly important for the EU, which is responsible for 36% of direct foreign investment in the world and receives 19% of such investments on its territory.

The **World Trade Organisation (WTO)**, established in 1995, has replaced the GATT, taking all the agreements concluded under its auspices, and settling trade disputes on a multilateral basis[2]. In fact, the WTO brings together under a single decision-making and administrative body the three agreements resulting from the Uruguay Round: the General Agreement on Tariffs and Trade (GATT), the General Agreement on Trade in Services (GATS) and the Agreement on trade-related aspects of intellectual property rights (TRIPs). The WTO operates on the basis of a ministerial conference, which must meet at least once every two years, and of a General Council made up of representatives of all the member countries. The European Community as well as all its Member States are members of WTO, a code of conduct defining the participation of the Community and its Member States in areas of shared power.

Thus, **the GATT continues to exist**, while frozen in its pre-Uruguay Round situation, for those countries that are not in a position to accept the entire package of its conclusions. On the contrary, the WTO is open to those who agree to abide by the entire Uruguay Round package of rules. This increases the certainty of the world exchange system, since all the members of the WTO are perfectly aware of their own rights and obligations and of those of their partners. The national law of each contracting party must be in conformity with the rules of the WTO, thus precluding unilateral action.

The **GATS agreement** establishes notably the principles: of the most favoured nation provisions, i.e. the principle that all third countries must be treated equally; of transparency on market access; and of national treatment, meaning that a company from a third country cannot be placed at a competitive disadvantage in relation to a domestic country. The Agreement established for the first time a multilateral framework based on satisfactory rules and comprising sufficient commitments to trigger the liberalisation process. The audiovisual sector was included in the GATS, which means that the rules relating to transparency and of progressive liberalisation apply to it. However, the EU has made no market access commitment nor, as a result, any commitments on national treatment. It also took an exemption from the principle of most favoured nation conditions and is, therefore, not bound to give equal treatment to all third countries. Basic telecommunications services were covered by the fourth protocol to the GATS, in February 1997, in a balanced package of measures respecting the most-favoured nation principle[3]. The fifth protocol to the GATS, based likewise on the most favoured nation principle, provides better market access to financial services covering more than 95% of world trade in the banking, insurance and securities sectors[4].

The **TRIPs agreement** has resulted in a strengthening of intellectual property rights concerning the protection of trade marks, industrial designs, patents and geographical appellations. A clear set of principles has been established for the enforcement through the national courts of intellectual property rights, any breaches being subject to sanctions under the dispute settlement procedure. The Community has amended the Regulation on the Community trade mark [see section 6.2.4.], notably in order to comply with the national treatment obligation established by the TRIPs Agreement[5]. According to the Court of Justice, even though questions relating to the TRIPs Agreement fall largely within the jurisdiction of the Member States, where a provision of the agreement is to be applied to situations covered both by national and by Community law, it is in the Com-

[1]   Annex 1 – Annex 1A, OJ L 336, 23.12.1994, p. 100-102.
[2]   Agreement and Decision 94/800, OJ L 336, 23.12.1994, p. 1-10.
[3]   Fourth Protocol and Decision 97/838, OJ L 347, 18.12.1997.
[4]   Fifth Protocol and Decision 1999/61, OJ L 20, 27.01.1999.
[5]   Regulation 3288/94, OJ L 349, 31.12.1994.

munity interest to avoid any differences of interpretation and national courts should apply the Community trade mark law[1].

The Agreement on **Government Procurement**, of which are part the EU, the United States, Japan and a limited number of other countries on a reciprocal basis, is open to all and is largely based on the Community rules on public procurement concerning, in particular, the procedures, the thresholds which apply and the recourse mechanisms if firms believe that they have been denied equal treatment [see section 6.3.][2]. The Agreement is founded on "national treatment", in accordance with which foreign suppliers of goods and services must be dealt with in the same way as national suppliers. It includes, in principle, water, ports, airports, electricity and urban transport, although not every country has made a commitment in each sector.

The unique structure of the WTO allows an integrated system of **dispute settlement**. The parties must refrain from making rulings themselves regarding violations and must abide completely by the provisions of the dispute settlement procedure in dealing with all matters, including the determination of "cross-retaliation". The Agreement establishes an appeals procedure providing for a review of the conclusions of the "panels" of first instance. A Dispute Settlement Board (DSB) oversees the proceedings. Safeguard measures are authorised, but their scope is limited both in terms of the measures taken and of their duration. A Safeguards Committee monitors all measures taken and ensures that they are in conformity with the agreement. An EC regulation defines the measures that may be taken by the Community following a report adopted by the WTO dispute settlement body concerning anti-dumping and anti-subsidy measures[3]. One of the first procedures initiated by the EU concerned the failure of the USA to repeal their Anti-dumping Act of 1916[4]. On their side, the USA have led battles inside the WTO and succeeded in modifying to their satisfaction the common organisation of the market in bananas[5] and on meat produced with the aid of hormones [see section 25.7.][6].

23.5. Sectoral commercial policy measures

In the framework of the General Agreement on Tariffs and Trade, several agreements or arrangements had been concluded in particularly **sensitive sectors**. The agreements to which the Community and/or its Member States were signatories sought to ensure the orderly growth of international trade in textiles, beef and veal, dairy products and civil aircraft. The most important of these arrangements was that on international trade in textiles, better known as the **Multifibre Arrangement (MFA)**, signed in 1974, in the framework of the GATT and owing its name to the fact that it covers most textile products, spanning artificial and synthetic fibres, cotton and wool. Under the terms of the Arrangement, signatories had undertaken not to introduce new unilateral or bilateral restrictions on trade in textiles and to regulate their trade relations by bilateral agreements The Community had based its textiles policy on this clause of the MFA, concluding with supplier countries bilateral agreements revolving chiefly around the principle of voluntary restraint of export quantities by signatory countries for a limited number of products, with gradual growth of the authorised quantities.

The Multifibre Arrangement was revised in order to progressively liberalise the international trade in textiles as provided in the GATT Agreement of 15 December 1993. In fact, the WTO **Agreement on Textiles and Clothing (ATC)** will govern trade between all Members of the WTO until such time as they have been integrated into normal WTO rules and disciplines[7]. This integration will be phased in three stages and will be completed in January 2005. The Agreement provides in particular for the strengthening of the GATT rules and disciplines, notably as regards market access, dumping, subsidies and counterfeiting. It contains a transitional safeguard clause in order to prevent any serious market disturbance in the importing countries.

A Community Regulation modifying the common rules for **imports of certain textile products** from third countries lays down a clear Community procedure for the selection of products to be integrated and notified to the WTO at each stage[8]. This Regulation also establishes the annual growth rates, which are applied automatically to remaining Community quantitative limits on imports from WTO members at each ATC stage. Another Regulation lays down common rules for imports of textile products from certain third countries not covered by bilateral agreements, protocols or other agreements, notably the countries of the Commonwealth of Independent States and the People's Republic of China[9]. It eliminates the exceptions and derogations resulting from the remaining national commercial policy measures and establishes quantitative restrictions and surveillance measures applicable at Community level for a limited number of products originating from these coun-

[1] Judgment of 16 June 1998, Case C-53/96, ECR 1998, I-3603.
[2] Annex 4, OJ L 336, 23.12.1994, p. 273-289.
[3] Regulation 1515/2001, OJ L 201, 26.07.2001.
[4] Commission notice, OJ C 58, 25.02.1997.
[5] Regulation 404/93, OJ L 47, 25.02.1993 amended by Regulation 2587/2001, OJ L 345, 29.12.2001.
[6] Decision 96/22, OJ L 125, 23.05.1996.
[7] Annex 1 – Annex 1A, OJ L 336, 23.12.1994, 50-85.
[8] Regulation 3289/94, OJ L 349, 31.12.1994.
[9] Regulation 517/94, OJ L 67, 10.03.1994 and Regulation 1791/2006, OJ L 363, 20.12.2006.

tries. Common rules seek to promote, through cooperation between the Contracting Parties, the orderly and equitable development of trade in textiles between the Community and supplier countries and to defuse the real risk that international trade in textile products be disrupted[1]. Such Community agreements on trade in textile products exist with China - which is the European Union's main supplier of textiles and clothing[2], Taiwan[3], Armenia, Azerbaijan, Georgia, Kazakhstan, Kyrgyzstan, Moldova, Tajikistan, Turkmenistan[4], the Socialist Republic of Vietnam[5], Egypt[6], Russia[7], Ukraine[8], Belarus[9] and Serbia[10]. The Community has also concluded market access arrangements with India and Pakistan[11] and Brazil[12],.

The specific nature of ship-purchase transactions makes it impossible to apply to **shipbuilding** the general anti-dumping and anti-subsidy measures in force [see section 23.2.2.]. A Community Regulation, based on the OECD Shipbuilding Agreement, accordingly institutes a procedure specific to this sector [see section 15.5.3. and 17.3.2.][13]. It lays down detailed rules for determining the existence of an injurious pricing and of an injury to Community industry, initiating proceedings, undertaking an investigation, imposing and levying an injurious pricing charge, counter-measures, etc. Since it has not been ratified by the United States, the OECD agreement has still not entered into force. The world market for merchant vessels is still in crisis and weak prices are persisting because of the extremely low prices offered by Korean shipyards. [see section 17.3.2.]. An agreement between the European Community and the Government of the Republic of Korea commits the latter to refrain from any direct or indirect intervention to underwrite loss-making Korean shipyards, to apply internationally accepted financial and accounting principles and to ensure that Korean shipyards set prices that reflect market conditions[14]. Nevertheless, as unfair trading practices by the Republic of Korea continue, the EU introduced a temporary defence mechanism and initiated proceedings against this country at the WTO[15].

Commercial policy measures for **steel products** exist in relation to several Central and Eastern European countries and some Independent States of the former Soviet Union. Agreements between the European Coal and Steel Community and Russia[16] and Ukraine[17] are designed to establish a framework for the gradual liberalisation of trade in steel products and to enable the Russian and Ukrainian steel industries to adapt gradually to normal competitive conditions, including State aid, competition and environmental protection.

In the **automobile sector**, Japanese car imports were a key sectoral problem to be settled. In 1991, the Community has reached an agreement with Japan on trade in motor vehicles in the single market. In accordance with the joint declaration between the Community and Japan, the Community market is progressively harmonised - thus replacing the national reception procedures by a single Community reception - and imports gradually liberalised in the five protected markets (France, Italy, Portugal, Spain and United Kingdom). For its part, Japan undertook to "moderate" exports in line with the market hypotheses on which negotiations were based, namely the evolution of supply and demand, including production within the Community. Japan must also remove technical barriers to imports of Community vehicles. Joint half-yearly monitoring provides a bilateral check on the application of this arrangement. The Commission conducts bilateral dialogues on market access with Japan and a number of other countries such as Brazil, Korea, Poland, Ukraine and Egypt.

Among the various agreements concluded at the Uruguay Round, several concern the **agricultural sector**, notably the Agreement on Agriculture[18]. In order to reduce the trade-restricting effects of national policies, including the common agricultural policy, whilst ensuring that domestic objectives could be pursued, it was agreed to convert the various forms of protection into customs duties. The Agreement on Agriculture requires, in particular, the abolition of variable import levies provided for under the common market organisations and the fixing of customs duties in the Common Customs Tariff. However, for certain product groups, such as cereals, rice, wine and fruit and vegetables, certain supplementary mechanisms not involving the collection of fixed customs duties are inserted into the basic Regulations of the CAP by a Regulation which sets out the adjustments and transitional arrangements required in the agricultural sector in order to implement the agree-

---

[1]   Regulation 3030/93, OJ L 275, 08.11.1993 last amended by Regulation 54/2007, OJ L 18, 25.01.2007.
[2]   Decision 95/155, OJ L 104, 06.05.1995.
[3]   Regulation 3060/95, OJ L 326, 30.12.1995.
[4]   Decision 96/593, OJ L 263, 16.10.1996.
[5]   Agreement and Decision 2003/453, OJ L 152, 20.06.2003.
[6]   Decision 98/355, OJ L 162, 05.06.1998.
[7]   Decision 98/491, OJ L 222, 10.08.1998.
[8]   Agreement and Decision 2005/196, OJ L 65, 11.03.2005.
[9]   Agreement and Decision 2005/228, OJ L 72, 18.03.2005.
[10] Agreement and Decision 2005/272, OJ L 90, 08.04.2005.
[11] Memorandums of understanding and Decision 96/386, OJ L 153, 27.06.1996.
[12] Decision 2002/877, OJ L 305, 07.11.2002.
[13] Regulation 384/96, OJ L 56, 06.03.1996 and Regulation 2117/2005, OJ L 340, 23.12.2005.
[14] Agreed Minutes and Decision 2000/409, OJ L 155, 228.06.2000.
[15] Regulation 1177/2002, OJ L 172, 02.07.2002 and Regulation 502/2004, OJ L 81, 19.03.2004.
[16] Decision 2136/97, OJ L 300, 04.11.1997 and Decision 244/2001, OJ L 35, 06.02.2001.
[17] Decision 97/482, OJ L 210, 04.08.1997 and Decision 2002/1001, OJ L 349, 24.12.2002.
[18] OJ L 336, 23.12.1994, p. 22-39.

ments concluded during the Uruguay Round [see section 21.4.4.][1]. The granting of export subsidies is limited henceforward to certain groups of agricultural products. In addition, such subsidies are limited in terms of quantity and value. Developed countries, including all the Member States of the EU, committed themselves to reduce export subsidies by 36% and the actual volume of subsidised exports by 21% over a six-year period. Moreover, the Community undertook to cut the global level of internal support by 20% over a period of six years, this being in line with the figures agreed in the CAP reform. The result is a better compatibility of the CAP and the GATT but also a Community agriculture more market-oriented and competitive. The access into the Community market is certainly facilitated, but the principle of Community preference is maintained.

23.6. Appraisal and outlook

A little known fact in Europe is that **the Member States of the European Union no longer have an independent foreign trade policy**. More than 60% of their trade is intra-Community and as such depends on the rules of the single market which prohibit any trade protection or trade promotion measures [see section 6.1.]. For the remaining 40% of their trade, the main instruments of commercial policy, the Common Customs Tariff, the common import arrangements and the common protective measures are in the hands of the organs of the EU, the Commission and the Council. Together they contribute to ensuring an even competition playing field for Community businesses, giving them access to equal prices for imported raw materials and other products they need. At the same time, the common commercial policy facilitates the work of Community importers who can use a uniform import licence, valid throughout the EU.

With more than 18% of world exports, compared to less than 16% for the United States and less than 10% for Japan, **the European Union has a stake in the freedom of international trade**. Far from building "Fortress Europe" through trade protection, the Community made very important concessions, particularly in the agricultural sector, to allow the conclusion of the GATT Uruguay Round. It should be noted that one Member State acting alone could not make such concessions without jeopardising its economy and certainly not one single state could obtain from its trading partners the concessions obtained by the Community. Being the world's leading commercial superpower, the Community is certainly respected and heeded in the context of the GATT and of the World Trade Organisation.

One of the central principles of the latter is that of **balancing mutual advantages (global reciprocity)**. This means, for the European Union, that it can tie access for third country economic operators to the benefits of its single market with the existence of similar opportunities for European businesses in the country in question, or at the least to the absence of any discrimination. This implies a case-by-case approach for third countries, but a common approach by the Member States. The single market obliges the latter to show a united face to third countries.

However, whereas customs tariffs are diminishing thanks to the Uruguay Round and the rules of the World Trade Organisation impose in principle the freedom of international exchanges, **European companies are still faced with obstacles to trade and investment** in a large number of countries. Thus, an environment conducive to international exchanges and investments is still lacking in many Asian and South American countries and even the United States resorts to protectionist measures under pressure from its industries in difficulties, such as steel [see section 25.7.]. The European Community has the necessary power to redress these situations through a bilateral approach (action vis-à-vis the countries concerned) and a multilateral approach (actions within the

---

[1] Regulation 3290/94, OJ L 349, 31.12.1994 and Regulation 1340/98, OJ L 184, 27.06.1998.

WTO); but the Member States must lend a supporting hand in combating trade barriers by joining forces with the European Commission. To face the problems arising from the **globalisation of trade**, the EU should not try to block this irreversible phenomenon, as advocated by anti-globalisation groups, but to harness it by strict international rules and strong institutions [see European Perspectives in conclusions].

Bibliography on the common commercial policy

- ADLUNG Rudolph. "Public services and the GATS" in *Journal of International Economic Law*, v. 9, n. 2, June 2006, p. 455-485.
- BEETSAM Roel (et al.). "Trade spill-overs of fiscal policy in the European Union: a panel analysis" in *Economic Policy*, n. 48, October 2006, p. 639-687.
- BERMANN George, MAVROIDIS Petros. *Trade and human health and safety*. Cambridge: Cambridge University Press, 2006.
- BILLIET Stijn. "From GATT to WTO: the internal struggle for external competences in the EU" in *Journal of Common Market Studies*, v. 44, n. 5, December 2006, p. 899-919.
- BLIN Olivier. "La stratégie communautaire dans l'Organisation mondiale du commerce" in *Journal du droit international*, v. 133, n. 1, janvier-février-mars 2006, p. 89-125.
- CARDWELL Michael, RODGERS Christopher. "Reforming the WTO legal order for agricultural trade: issues for European rural policy in the Doha Round" in *International and Comparative Law Quarterly*, v. 55, n. 4, October 2006, p. 805-838.
- CHAISSE Julien. "Adapting the European Community legal structure to the international trade" in *European Business Law Review*, v. 17, n. 6, 2006, p. 1615-1635.
- CHAUDRY Peggy. "Managing intellectual property rights: government tactics to curtail counterfeit trade" in *European Business Law Review*, v. 17, n. 4, 2006, p. 939-958.
- EMCH Adrian. *The Biret cases: what effects do WTO dispute settlement rulings have in EU law?* Madrid: Instituto de Estudios Europeos de la USP-CEU, 2005.
- EUROPEAN COMMISSION. *Global Europe: Europe's trade defence instruments in a changing global economy: a Green Paper for public consultation*. Luxembourg: EUR-OP*, 2006.
- FLANAGAN Robert. *Globalization and labor conditions: working conditions and worker rights in a global economy*. Oxford: Oxford University Press, 2006.
- GRANT Wyn, KELLY Dominic. *The politics of international trade in the twenty-first century: actors, issues and regional dynamics*. Basingstoke: Palgrave Macmillan, 2005.
- HENSON Spencer, WILSON John Sullivan (eds.). *The WTO and technical barriers to trade*. Cheltenham: Edward Elgar, 2005.
- McCORMICK Rachael. "A qualitative analysis of the WTO's role on trade and environment issues" in *Global environmental politics*, v. 6, n. 1, February 2006, p. 102-124.
- ORGANISATION FOR ECONOMIC COOPERATION AND DEVELOPMENT. *Agricultural Policy and Trade Reform: potential effects at global, national and household levels*. Paris: OECD, 2006.
- PALLEMAERTS Marc (ed.). *EU and WTO law: How tight is the legal straitjacket for environmental product regulation?"* Brussels: VUB Brussels University Press, 2006.
- SWINBANK Alan, DAUGBJERG Carsten. "The 2003 CAP reform: accommodating WTO pressures" in *Comparative European politics*, v. 4, n. 1, April 2006, p. 47-64.
- TARASOFSKY Richard, PALMER Alice. "The WTO in crisis: lessons learned from the Doha negotiations on the environment" in *International Affairs*, v. 82, n. 5, September 2006, p. 899-915.
- THARAKAN P.K.M. (et al.). Global trade policy 2006. *Thematic issue of: The World Economy*, v. 29, n. 10, October 2006.
- VAN DIJCK Pitou, FABER Gerrit. "How to save the Doha Round: a European perspective" in *European Foreign Affairs Review*, v. 11, n. 3, Autumn 2006, p. 291-309.

The publications of the Office for Official Publications of the European Communities (EUR-OP) exist usually in all official languages of the EU.

Chapter 24

DEVELOPMENT AID POLICY

Diagram of the chapter

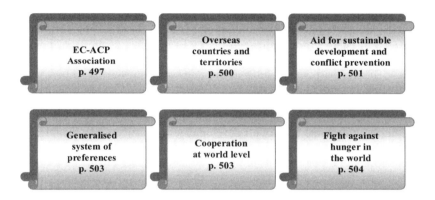

D evelopment aid reflects **both the search for solidarity** between the developed countries of the EU and the disadvantaged countries of the world **and the economic necessity for the Union** of guaranteeing its raw material supply and creating outlets for its products. Aware that advantages granted at world level, notably through the GATT negotiations mentioned in the previous chapter [see section 23.4.], diminished the attractiveness of regional preferences, the EC/EU has been caught up in a process of continually expanding its aid to developing countries. It now views every agreement with developing countries as an instrument in an all-embracing political, social and economic development strategy.

24.1. Objectives and instruments of the policy

Article 177 of the EC Treaty specifies that Community policy in the sphere of development cooperation is **complementary to the policies pursued by the Member States and must foster**: the sustainable economic and social development of the developing countries; the smooth and gradual integration of the developing countries in the world economy; and the campaign against poverty in the developing countries. Article

301 (TEC) allows the Community to apply politically motivated economic sanctions, thus making every cooperation agreement an instrument of a broad political, social and economic approach.

Indeed, within the framework of the Community cooperation policy, the Community provides financial aid for the implementation of both development cooperation operations[1] and other operations which contribute to the general **objective of developing and consolidating democracy** and the rule of law and to that of respecting human rights and fundamental freedoms in third countries[2]. In addition, the Community provides financial assistance and appropriate expertise aimed at promoting **gender equality** into all its development cooperation policies and interventions in developing countries[3]. Finally, the EU promotes the full integration of the **environmental dimension** in the development process and, in particular, the conservation and sustainable management of tropical forests and other forests in developing countries[4].

The European Union currently has an impressive store of **development aid instruments**, spanning the Convention with the ACP countries, special relations with the Overseas Countries and Territories, aid for non-associated countries, the Generalised System of Tariff Preferences, participation in world commodity agreements and aid provided through non-government organisations fighting global problems such as hunger. The **decentralised cooperation approach** places local actors at the focal point of implementation and hence pursues the dual aims of gearing operations to needs and making them viable[5]. The EU participates fully in the International Monetary Fund and World Bank initiative for heavily indebted ACP countries by helping them reduce the net value of their obligations[6]. This variety of forms which development aid takes clearly demonstrates the EU's commitment to an outward-looking approach. In fact, the EU and its Member States provide some 55% of all development assistance to developing countries in the world, whereas the United States provide less than 20%. Moreover, the reform of the common agricultural policy tends to minimise its distorting effects on trade, make it more environment friendly and improve coherence with development policy [see sections 21.2, 21.4.4 and 23.5].

The European Union also has a wide range of **development policy resources**, from industrial and technological cooperation to trade promotion, food aid and financial aid. Financial aid also takes the form of European Investment Bank (EIB) loans and risk capital[7], EIB management of the Investment Facility of the Cotonou Agreement[8], European Development Fund (EDF) subsidies; or grants under other Articles of the Community Budget, concerning in particular food aid. The EDF is funded by a five-year specific contribution of the Member States but is an integral part of the Community Budget [see section 3.4.][9]. The rules on access to Community external assistance instruments govern specifically: access by persons; the hiring of experts; arrangements for the implementation of reciprocity; provisions concerning operations financed through an international organisation; and humanitarian aid[10]. The EU external aid is managed by 78 Commission delegations in the world.

---

[1] Regulation 1905/2006, OJ L 378, 27.12.2006.
[2] Regulation 976/1999, OJ L 120, 08.05.1999 and Regulation 2112/2005, OJ L 344, 27.12.2005.
[3] Regulation 1905/2006, OJ L 378, 27.12.2006.
[4] Regulation 2494/2000, OJ L 288, 15.11.2000 repealed by Regulation 1905/2006, OJ L 378, 27.12.2006.
[5] Regulation 1659/98, OJ L 213, 30.07.1998 and Regulation 625/2004, OJ L 99, 03.04.2004.
[6] Decision 98/453, OJ L 198, 15.07.1998.
[7] Decision 97/256, OJ L 102, 19.04.1997 and Regulation 1085/2006, OJ L 210, 31.07.2006.
[8] Decision 2003/268, OJ L 99, 17.04.2003.
[9] Financial Regulation of the 9th EDF, OJ L 83, 01.04.2003.
[10] Regulation 1905/2006, OJ L 378, 27.12.2006.

Taking account of the objectives agreed within the context of the United Nations and other competent international organisations, the common aid to development policy, must contribute to the general objective of consolidating democracy and the rule of law, the **respect of human rights and fundamental freedoms** in the developing countries [see section 24.4]. In a declaration of 25 May 1993, the Community and its Member States reserved the right to take measures, which might even involve suspending aid if the democratisation process was halted or if serious violations of human rights occurred. In fact, the EU has taken measures such as altering the content of aid programmes, withholding the signatures necessary for the implementation of aid, or even suspending it altogether, while taking care to avoid harming the people of the country concerned. Thus, the Community has withdrawn the Generalised System of Preferences (GSP) entitlement [see section 24.5.] from Myanmar (Burma) and has taken measures against the military regime in place[1]. In implementation of the mandate provided by UN Security Council Resolution 1484 (2003), the European Union is conducting a military operation in the Democratic Republic of Congo to stabilise the security and humanitarian situation in the Ituri area[2]. Restrictive measures, including an arms embargo, are imposed against the Congo[3] and Zimbabwe[4]. Particular attention is given to population policies and programmes in the developing countries, notably the spacing of children and more accessible and better reproductive health care[5].

To accompany the introduction of a new political and administrative structure for assistance and cooperation, the Commission proposes replacing the existing range of financial instruments for the delivery of external assistance with a simpler, more **efficient framework comprising six instruments only**, four of them new[6]. The four new instruments are an instrument for pre-accession assistance, a European neighbourhood and partnership instrument, a development cooperation and economic cooperation instrument, and an instrument for stability. The two existing instruments, for humanitarian aid and for macrofinancial assistance, do not require any changes and will therefore be maintained. The proposals concerning these new instruments and the instruments relating to the environment and nuclear energy form the second 'package' of the financial perspective 2007-13[7].

24.2. EC-ACP Association

In the first years following the entry into force of the EEC Treaty [see section 2.1.], the Community's development aid policy was more or less restricted to the association provided for in the fourth part of the Treaty and **covering the former colonies** of France, Italy, Belgium and the Netherlands. After most of these countries were granted independence, a first Convention was signed in Yaoundé (Cameroon) on July 20, 1963 between the EEC and an association of 17 African countries and Madagascar. The enlargement of the Community in 1973 substantially boosted the ranks of the associated countries, drawing in the former British colonies. This prompted an overhaul of the content of the agreement.

The Convention signed in Lomé (Togo) on February 28, 1975 between the then nine Member States of the EEC and 46 States of **Africa, the Caribbean and the Pacific (ACP)** signalled a fresh start for the common development aid policy. The fourth EEC-ACP Convention, also signed in Lomé on December 15, 1989, firmly cemented cooperation between the EC Member States and 70 ACP States, including the whole of sub-Saharan Africa and, in certain aspects, South Africa.

The fourth Lomé Convention expired on 29 February 2000. Its successor, **the partnership agreement signed at Cotonou** (Benin) on 23 June 2000, although it is still based on the acquis of the four Lomé Conventions, heralds a fundamental change in relations between the ACP States and the Community and its Member States[8]. The term of the new agreement is 20 years. The addition of six Pacific Island States has raised to 77 the list of members of the ACP group of countries.

---

[1] Regulation 552/97, OJ L 85, 27.03.1997 and Common Position2006/318, OJ L 116, 29.04.2006.
[2] Joint action 2003/423, OJ L 143, 11.06.2003 and Decision 2003/432, OJ L 147, 14.06.2003.
[3] Common position 2005/440 and Regulation 889/2005, OJ L 152, 15.06.2005.
[4] Common position 2006/51, OJ L 26, 31.01.2006.
[5] Regulation 1905/2006, OJ L 378, 27.12.2006.
[6] COM (2004) 626, 29 September 2004.
[7] COM (2004) 101, 10 February 2004.
[8] Agreement and Council Decision 2000/483, OJ L 317, 15.12.2000.

The partnership agreement combines substantial **political dialogue between the partners** with innovative forms of economic and commercial cooperation and new development cooperation mechanisms and strategies. Thus the agreement is supported by five interdependent pillars, namely the overall political dimension, encouragement of a participatory approach, a stronger bias towards the aim of reducing poverty, a new framework for economic and trade cooperation and reform of financial cooperation. The objective of good governance has been added to those of respect for human rights, democratic principles and the rule of law as one of the essential elements of the partnership [see details below]. Under Article 11 of the Cotonou Partnership Agreement "the parties shall pursue an active, comprehensive and integrated policy of peace-building and conflict prevention and resolution within the framework of the partnership".

The Cotonou Agreement also includes provisions on cooperation in trade-related areas leading each participating country to negotiate a trade agreement with the Community. The purpose of these agreements is to help developing countries **integrate into the world economy**, step up production and stimulate trade and investment in compliance with World Trade Organisation rules [see section 23.4.]. Where finances are concerned, the various instruments have been regrouped and rationalised so that all resources available under the European Development Fund (EDF) are disbursed via two instruments: a financial package from which subsidies is granted and another from which risk capital and loans is provided to the private sector. Operations must focus on a specific sector (health, transport, etc.) and combine many different aspects of cooperation (economic, environmental, social, etc.) in order to ensure that aid is better targeted [see details below].

The **joint institutions for cooperation** established by the former Lomé Conventions remain in force, namely:

*   **the Council of Ministers**, consisting of members of the Council of the European Union, members of the European Commission and a member of the government of each ACP country, meets once a year to initiate political dialogue, adopt political guidelines and take decisions required for the implementation of the provisions of the Agreement[1];
*   **the Committee of Ambassadors**, made up of the permanent representative of each Member State for the European Union, a Commission representative and a head of mission for each ACP state, assists the Council of Ministers[2];
*   **the Joint Parliamentary Assembly**, made up of an equal number of representatives of Members of the European Parliament and representatives of the ACP States, may adopt resolutions and submit recommendations to the Council of Ministers.

The new system for programming the aid granted by the Community enhances the flexibility of the partnership and entrusts the ACP States with greater responsibility, particularly by establishing a system of **rolling programming** that eliminates the concept of non-programmable aid, i.e. aid programmed unilaterally by the Community. The ACP States now have greater responsibility for determining objectives, strategies and operations and for programme management and selection.

The programming process is centred on results. Financial assistance of a set amount is no longer an automatic right. Grants are allocated on the basis of an assessment of requirements and performances in accordance with criteria negotiated between the ACP countries and the Community. These criteria reflect the partnership's main objectives, such as progress in institutional reform, poverty reduction, etc.

---

[1]   Decision 1/2005 ACP-EC, OJ L 95, 14.04.2005.
[2]   Decision 3/2005 ACP-EC, OJ L 95, 14.04.2005.

The main instrument used for programming grants is the **country support strategy (CSS)**. An CSS is drawn up for each ACP country by the Commission and the country in question. The CSS sets out general guidelines for using the aid and is supplemented by an indicative operational programme containing specific operations and a timetable for their implementation [see details below].

In cases of fluctuation of export revenues, instead of the Stabex and Sysmin instruments of the previous Conventions, the new system of rolling and flexible programming (FLEX system) makes it possible to ensure additional support via the funds allocated within the framework of the CSS and the operational programmes (Annex II to the ACP-EC Partnership Agreement). Additional support in this area is needed because of the ACP States' vulnerability resulting from a high degree of dependence on export revenues in the agricultural or mining sectors in ACP States.

Pillar I of the Cotonou Agreement is a global political dimension, which concerns all of the Agreement's objectives and operations and represents global commitments on the part of the ACP countries in the following domains:

- **political dialogue**;

- **peace-building policies, conflict prevention and resolution** based, in particular, on regional initiatives and aiming, inter alia, to ensure that financial resources are not diverted from development objectives[1];

- **respect for human rights** and democratic principles based on the rule of law and transparent and accountable governance under the responsibility of the country in question;

- **good governance** aiming to prevent and to punish corruption.

Pillar II of the Agreement is the promotion of participatory approaches, including a substantial role for non-State actors in the design and implementation of development strategies and programmes, for example the private sector, economic and social partnerships and non-governmental organisations (NGOs). Further, the participation of these actors depends on certain criteria relating to management and form of organisation.

Pillar III consists in development strategies and priority for poverty reduction. The integrated approach of the partnership stresses three key areas for cooperation, always taking into account the major objective of poverty reduction:

- **economic development** focusing on: investment and private sector development (for example, enhancing export activities); macroeconomic and structural reforms and policies (for example, liberalising trade regimes); sectoral policies (for example, developing the industrial, trade and tourism sectors).

- **social and human development** including: social sectoral policies (for example, improving education, health and nutrition systems, and integrating population issues into strategies); youth issues (for example, protecting the rights of children and youth, particularly girls); cultural development (for example, recognising, preserving and promoting the value of cultural traditions and heritage).

- **regional cooperation and integration** aiming in particular to: accelerate diversification of the economies of ACP States; promote and expand inter and intra-ACP trade and with third countries, which equally benefits the least developed countries (LDC) among the ACP States; implement sectoral reform policies at regional level.

- **thematic and cross-cutting issues** concerning: gender equality; sustainable management of the environment; institutional development and capacity building. The question of integrating sustainable management of the environment covers several subjects, for example tropical forests, water resources, desertification, the use of renewable energy sources, etc.

Pillar IV of Cotonou is the establishment of a framework for economic and trade cooperation, in order to bring it into line with WTO rules and to enable the ACP States to play a full part in international trade, notably through:

- the negotiation of **new trading arrangements** with a view to liberalising trade between the two parties, putting an end to the system of non-reciprocal trade preferences from which the ACP countries currently benefit. Nonetheless, the current system will remain in force for a preparatory period, up to 2008 (the date envisaged for the entry into force of the new arrangements) with a transitional period of at least 12 years. The Community's policy will take account of these countries' social and economic constraints in two ways: one, through social and human development policies (fight against poverty) and, two, through cooperation and enhancing the capacities of ACP States in international bodies.

---

[1] Common Position 2005/304, OJ L 97, 15.04.2005.

- Trade cooperation is not restricted to traditional trading activities; it also affects **other trade-related areas** such as the protection of intellectual property rights, trade and labour standards, etc.

- An improvement in the EC's trade regime for all of the **least developed countries** (39 of which are part of the ACP group) is envisaged. Since 2005, LDC exporters benefit from duty free access for essentially all of their products on the EC market.

Pillar V concerns financial cooperation aiming at the rationalisation of cooperation instruments, especially of the European Development Fund (EDF), the main instrument for Community assistance to the ACP States. All EDF resources will be channelled through two instruments:

- **grants**. These total EUR 11.3 billion under the ninth EDF, EUR 1.3 billion of which is set aside for regional programmes. They are administered jointly by the Commission and the ACP States. Each country should receive a lump sum.

- **risk capital and private sector loans**. This new instrument, allotted EUR 2.2 billion from the ninth EDF, is administered by the European Investment Bank. The Bank may provide loans, equity and quasi-capital assistance. It may also be able to provide guarantees in support of domestic and foreign private investment.

An annual review is provided for in order to adjust the country support strategy (CSS), the operational programme or the resources allocated. Halfway through and at the end of the period of application of the financial protocol, the annual review will also include an assessment of the cooperation strategy, which would either confirm the thrust of the CSS or suggest appropriate adjustments. The volume of resources allocated to the country concerned may be adjusted as a result. Provision is made for local actors to be involved in the annual review in accordance with the principle of decentralisation.

Article 96 of the Agreement lays down the possibility of taking appropriate **measures in cases of violation** by one of the parties of the requirements of essential elements of the Agreement, namely respect for human rights, democratic principles and the rule of law. The Agreement provides for a consultation procedure to resolve the situation by establishing the necessary measures. However, in the absence of an acceptable solution, appropriate measures may be taken, including suspension of the Agreement, although this is the last resort.

24.3. Overseas countries and territories

Article 182 of the EC Treaty associates to the Community the non-European countries and territories which have special relationships with certain Member States. The aim of this association is promotion of the economic and social development of the **Overseas Countries and Territories (OCTs)** and the establishment of close economic relations between them and the Community. In accordance with the principles set out in the Preamble of the Treaty, the association must encourage trade in the interest of the inhabitants of these countries and territories, in a manner leading to the economic, social and cultural development to which they aspire. The regulations relating to the association of OCTs to the Community have evolved in line with the arrangements applicable to the ACP States in the framework of the Lomé Conventions.

The regulations currently in force relating to the association of overseas countries and territories to the EC apply to twenty OCTs **dependent on France, the Netherlands, the United Kingdom and Denmark** (Greenland)[1]. While they come under the wing of Member States, and their nationals are recognised since 1996 as EU citizens, the OCTs do not form part of the Union, but they are associated with it and thus benefit from the EDF and the same types of development cooperation measures as ACP States. Community solidarity towards them is reflected chiefly by the near free access to the Community market for products originating in the OCTs, by the implementation of export stabilisation systems and by financial and technical cooperation drawing on the resources of the EDF and the European investment Bank.

The **fields covered by this financial and technical cooperation** are agricultural and rural development, fisheries, industrial development, the exploitation of mining and energy potential, transport and communications, the development of trade and services, regional cooperation and cultural and social cooperation. Depending on the development

---

[1]   Decision 91/482, OJ L 263, 19.09.1991 and Decision 2001/161, OJ L 58, 28.02.2001.

level and situation of the OCTs, an attempt is also made to establish firm cooperation between them and the ACP States. The partnership arrangements in favour of OCTs include many elements contained in the fourth Lomé Convention and establish a three-way Commission/Member State/OCT partnership. The mid-term review of the partnership arrangements aims to improve the rights of individuals and the status of OCT nationals in the European Union.

24.4. Aid for sustainable development and conflict prevention

The **European Consensus on Development**, adopted by the Council and the Representatives of the Governments of the Member States, the European Parliament and the Commission on 22 November 2005[1] states that the primary and overarching objective of EU development cooperation is the eradication of poverty in the context of sustainable development, including pursuit of the Millennium Development Goals (MDGs). The eight MDGs are to: eradicate extreme poverty and hunger; achieve universal primary education; promote gender equality and empower women; reduce the mortality rate of children; improve maternal health; combat HIV/AIDS, malaria and other diseases; ensure environmental sustainability and develop a global partnership for development. However, the European Community is founded on the values of democracy, the rule of law, respect for human rights and fundamental freedoms and seeks to develop and consolidate commitment to these values in partner countries and regions through dialogue and cooperation. Therefore, the Consensus states also that the EU acknowledges the essential oversight role of democratically elected citizens' representatives and encourages an increased involvement of national assemblies, parliaments and local authorities.

In this context the Community finances measures aimed at supporting cooperation with developing countries, territories and regions included in the list of aid recipients of the Development Assistance Committee of the Organization for Economic Cooperation and Development (OECD/DAC) - referred to as "partner countries and regions" in Annex I. The primary and overarching objective of cooperation under the Regulation establishing a **financing instrument for development cooperation** is the eradication of poverty in partner countries and regions in the context of sustainable development, including pursuit of the **Millennium Development Goals (MDGs)**, as well as the promotion of democracy, good governance and respect for human rights and for the rule of law[2]. Consistently with this objective, cooperation with partner countries and regions should:

- consolidate and support democracy, the rule of law, human rights and fundamental freedoms, good governance, gender equality and related instruments of international law;
- foster the sustainable development - including political, economic, social and environmental aspects - of partner countries and regions, and more particularly the most disadvantaged among them;
- encourage their smooth and gradual integration into the world economy;
- help develop international measures to preserve and improve the quality of the environment and the sustainable management of global natural resources, in order to en-

---

[1] Joint Statement, OJ C 46, 24.02.2006.
[2] Regulation 1905/2006, OJ L 378, 27.12.2006.

sure sustainable development, including addressing climate change and biodiversity loss; and

- strengthen the relationship between the Community and partner countries and regions.

In the implementation of Regulation 1905/2006, a differentiated approach depending on development contexts and needs is pursued so that partner countries or regions are provided with specific, tailor-made cooperation, based on their own needs, strategies, priorities and assets. **Least developed countries** and low income countries are given priority in terms of overall resource allocation in order to achieve the MDGs. However, appropriate attention is given to support the pro-poor development of middle income countries, particularly the lower middle income countries many of which face problems similar to those of low income countries.

In addition to the Millennium Development Goals the EU **Programme for the Prevention of Violent Conflicts**, endorsed by the European Council, underlines the EU's "political commitment to pursue conflict prevention as one of the main objectives of the EU's external relations" and states that Community development cooperation instruments can contribute to this goal and to the development of the EU as a global player. In pursuit of this objective, Regulation 1717/2006, establishing an **Instrument for Stability** allows the Community to undertake development cooperation measures, as well as financial, economic and technical cooperation measures with third countries under the following conditions[1]: in a situation of crisis or emerging crisis, to contribute to stability by providing an effective response to help preserve, establish or re-establish the conditions essential to the proper implementation of the Community's development and cooperation policies; and (b) in the context of stable conditions for the implementation of Community cooperation policies in third countries, to help build capacity both to address specific global and transregional threats having a destabilising effect and to ensure preparedness to address pre- and post-crisis situations. Community assistance under the Instrument for Stability is complementary to that provided for under related Community instruments for external assistance [see also sections 25.6. and 25.8.]. It may be provided only to the extent that an adequate and effective response cannot be provided under those instruments.

Community technical and financial assistance in pursuit of the specific aims of the Instrument for Stability set out in point (a) above may be undertaken in response to **a situation of urgency, crisis or emerging crisis**, a situation posing a threat to democracy, law and order, the protection of human rights and fundamental freedoms, or the security and safety of individuals, or a situation threatening to escalate into armed conflict or severely to destabilise the third country or countries concerned.

Assistance in the context of **stable conditions for cooperation** is granted notably in order to prevent threats to law and order, to the security and safety of individuals, to critical infrastructure and to public health. Community assistance in this context aims at: (a) strengthening the capacity of law enforcement and judicial and civil authorities involved in the fight against terrorism and organised crime, including illicit trafficking of people, drugs, firearms and explosive materials and in the effective control of illegal trade and transit; (b) support for measures to address threats to international transport, energy operations and critical infrastructure, including passenger and freight traffic and energy distribution; and (c) contributing to ensuring an adequate response to sudden major threats to public health, such as epidemics with a potential trans-national impact.

---

[1]   Regulation 1717/2006, OJ L 327, 24.11.2006.

24.5. Generalised System of Preferences

The Community provided the initiative behind the **Generalised System of Preferences (GSP)**, the principle of which was taken on board by the other industrialised countries at the 2nd Session of the United Nations Conference on Trade and Development (UNCTAD) in 1968. The objective of GSP is to assist developing countries' poverty reduction efforts by helping them to generate revenue through international trade and granting them tariff preferences. Although it has traditionally come under Article 133 of the EC Treaty (ex Art. 113) and, therefore, in theory, under the common commercial policy, the GSP is in practice a tool of development. It offers some 130 developing countries tariff reductions or in some cases duty-free access for their manufactured exports and increasingly their agricultural exports as well. Being a tariff instrument, it operates purely at the level of tariffs which is already reduced thanks to GATT. Being an autonomous instrument, its preferences are granted (not negotiated) by the Community and are complementary to the multilateral liberalisation of trade within WTO [see section 23.4.].

The **reform of the GSP** involves simplification of the EU system of trade preferences through a reduction in the number of arrangements for the period 2006 to 2015[1]. It allows a range of 7.200 products duty-free access to the EU, representing an increase of 300 products, principally for the benefit of the agriculture and fisheries sectors. The "Everything but arms" arrangement grants duty- and quota-free access for all imports except arms from least developed countries. The new incentive system (GSP plus) is based on the concept of granting additional preferences to vulnerable developing countries that pursue good governance and sustainable development policies.

24.6. Cooperation at world level

Many developing countries are **heavily dependent on the export of just one or two commodities** and see their earnings rise and fall according to the fluctuations of the world prices of their products. As a consequence, international agreements concluded in the framework of the United Nations Conference on Trade and Development (UNCTAD) attempt to support or stabilise the production of certain commodities. These agreements generally cover three aspects: prices, quantities and mechanisms (production quotas, buffer stocks and so on). The producer countries see these agreements on commodities chiefly as a way of guaranteeing export earnings and ensuring a certain level of income for their producers, whereas importers view them as a way of guaranteeing supply of a given quantity of a product at a price set in advance. The agreements differ from one product to the next, some aiming at better marketing and heightened competitiveness, others involving attempts to intervene in the free play of market mechanisms at world level.

The United Nations **Common Fund for Commodities** supports the operation of agreements on certain commodities, which are regulated by organisations with specific responsibility for them. To this effect, the Fund has two "windows", one contributing to the financing of buffer stocks and national stocks coordinated at international level and managed by international organisations with specific responsibility for certain commodities; the other supporting measures other than storage (for example research and other

---

[1] Regulation 980/2005, OJ L 169, 30.06.2005.

measures seeking to improve productivity and marketing). The Community is a member of the Fund on the same footing as its Member States[1].

The Member States of the Community are importers of most of the commodities covered by **world agreements**. During the seventies, they tended to negotiate the terms of these agreements individually rather than as members of the Community. However, after the fourth UNCTAD Conference in Nairobi in 1976, at which a draft "integrated programme" for commodities was outlined, the Community has taken an active part in negotiating and managing many world agreements, including those on copper and tin[2], jute and jute articles[3], coffee[4], cocoa[5], rubber[6], tropical timber[7], cereals[8], olive oil and olives[9], and sugar[10].

Since 1986, the **United Nations Industrial Development Organisation (UNIDO)** acts, on the one hand, as a forum for the exchange of views on industrial development policies in Third World countries and on cooperation with the more developed countries, and on the other, as the implementer of cooperation programmes revolving around the marketplace and enterprises. The Commission, which represents the Community in UNIDO, shows strong interest in the activities of this organisation in the restructuring of formerly centrally planned economies.

The Community also participates in the work of the **United Nations Food and Agriculture Organisation (FAO)**, whose main tasks are the establishment of some order in international trade in agricultural produce, the replenishment of food stocks following the droughts of recent years and the fight against hunger in the world. In November 1991, the ministerial Conference of the FAO recognised the Community as a member "sui generis", stating its views through the Commission on all matters coming within its sphere of competence, such as forestry or development, and alternately with the Member States. In addition the Community can now accede to any convention or agreement concluded under the aegis of the FAO.

24.7. Fight against hunger and other afflictions

The European Community considers food aid, first and foremost, as a structural instrument of long-term development. Community policy on **food security** has evolved towards supporting broad-based food security strategies at national, regional and global level, limiting the use of food aid to humanitarian situations and food crises and avoiding disruptive effects on local production and markets. It takes into account the specific situation of countries that are structurally fragile and highly dependent on support for food security, in order to avoid a steep reduction of Community assistance to these countries.

The objective of the **thematic programme on food security** of the Regulation establishing a financing instrument for development cooperation is to improve food security in favour of the poorest and most vulnerable people and contribute to achieving the Millennium Development Goals (MDGs) on poverty and hunger [see section 24.4], through a set of actions which ensure overall coherence, complementarity and continuity of Community interventions, including in the area of the transition from relief to development[11]. To achieve this objective the programme includes activities such as:

- contributing to the provision of international public goods, in particular pro-poor demand driven research and technological innovation, as well as capacity development, scientific and technical cooperation and twinning;

---

[1] Agreement and Decision 1999/373, OJ L 182, 14.07.1990.
[2] Decisions 91/178 and 91/179, OJ L 89, 10.04.1991.
[3] Agreement and Decision 91/51, OJ L 29, 04.02.1991.
[4] Agreement and Decision OJ L 2001/877, OJ L 326, 11.12.2001.
[5] Agreement and Decision 2002/970, OJ L 342, 17.12.2002.
[6] Agreement and Decision 96/704, OJ L 324, 13.12.1996.
[7] Agreement and Decision 96/493, OJ L 208, 17.08.1996.
[8] Grain Convention and Decision 96/88, OJ L 21, 27.01.1996 and OJ L 222, 24.08.1999.
[9] Agreement and Decision 2005/800, OJ L 302, 19.11.2005.
[10] Agreement and Decision 92/580, OJ L 379, 23.12.1992 and Extension, OJ C 322, 17.12.2005.
[11] Regulation 1905/2006, OJ L 378, 27.12.2006.

- supporting global, continental and regional programmes which notably: support food security in specific fields such as agriculture, or promote, strengthen and complement national food security and poverty reduction strategies in the short, medium and longer-term;
- addressing food insecurity in exceptional situations of transition and State fragility;
- developing innovative food security policies, strategies and approaches

Another Regulation lays down the objectives of **humanitarian aid** and the procedures governing aid and operations in this context[1]. The Community's humanitarian aid comprises assistance, relief and protection operations to help people in third countries, particularly the most vulnerable among them, and as a priority those in developing countries, victims of natural disasters, man-made crises, such as wars and outbreaks of fighting, or exceptional situations or circumstances comparable to natural or man-made disasters. The kinds of operation covered are specific projects or broader-based plans designed to bring in relief, help with short-term repair and rebuilding work, facilitate the arrival of aid, prevent crises from worsening and help with the repatriation and resettlement of refugees back home. Also included among the eligible operations are disaster-preparedness and activities to protect the victims of conflict.

The framework Regulation gives the **Commission overall control of all the aid mobilisation and delivery operations**. Commission control ends however when the aid is in the hands of the beneficiary country. Furthermore, the successful tenderer is responsible for the aid until its delivery to the location stipulated in the agreement concluded with the beneficiary countries. Finally, the Regulation stipulates that aid is to be monitored by professionals appointed by the Commission to ensure that the operation is correctly followed through. The Community focuses its attention on **food strategies** where food security tops the list of priorities. The European Community participates actively in the Food Aid Convention[2].

The **European Community Office for Humanitarian Aid (ECHO)**, run by the Commission, has the role of enhancing the Community's presence on the ground, of grouping together all its emergency humanitarian actions and improving coordination with the Member States, other donors, NGOs and specialised international agencies. ECHO is wholly responsible for administering humanitarian and emergency food aid, and disaster preparedness. At present, the humanitarian aid of the EU exceeds 1 billion euros a year and its scope has been broadened to cover the violent ethnic conflicts in Africa, the consequences of the collapse of the Soviet Union and the aftermath of the fratricidal wars in former Yugoslavia. In fact, more than 95% of ECHO's activities cover man-made disasters.

The bulk of food aid is allocated by the Commission under the "normal procedure" whereby each allocation of aid is submitted for the prior opinion of the Member States. Community food aid is granted either directly to the governments of beneficiary countries, which distribute the produce free of charge or put it up for sale on the local market, or indirectly through the intermediary of inter-governmental international organisations (UNHCR, WFP, ICRC, LICROSS) or of non-governmental organisations (NGOs), which re-distribute it to refugees and to the most vulnerable categories in the framework of special nutritional programmes. Aid is granted as a priority to low-income countries with a food supply shortfall. Part of food aid is set aside for emergency action. The Community endeavours to give direct financial and institutional support to partners other than the national authorities (local authorities, NGOs, trade and vocational bodies and unions), with the aim of strengthening local management capabilities and initiative.

The three major communicable diseases, namely HIV/AIDS, tuberculosis and malaria cause the deaths of more than five and a half million people each year, their greatest impact being on morbidity and life expectancy in developing countries. Moreover, these diseases wipe out years of development efforts and achieve-

---

[1] Regulation 1257/96, OJ L 163, 02.07.1996.
[2] Convention and Decision 96/88, OJ L 21, 27.01.1996 and OJ L 222, 24.08.1999.

ments and constitute a serious concern in the long run because of their destabilising effects on society. Under the **Programme on aid to fight poverty diseases** (HIV/AIDS, tuberculosis and malaria) in developing countries, the Community provides financial assistance and appropriate expertise to actors in development in order to improve access to health for all and to promote equitable economic growth, within the overall objective of reducing poverty with a view to its eventual eradication[1]. In the allocation of such funding and expertise, priority is given to: (a) the poorest and least developed countries and the most disadvantaged sections of the population within developing countries; and (b) action that complements and reinforces both the policies and capacities of developing countries and the assistance provided through other instruments of development cooperation. The Community contributes to the Global Fund to fight HIV/AIDS, tuberculosis and malaria[2] and participates in a research and development programme aimed at developing new clinical interventions to combat HIV/AIDS, malaria and tuberculosis through a long-term partnership between Europe and developing countries, undertaken by several Member States[3].

In the framework of North-South cooperation, the Community participates in **fighting drug abuse**. Its action focuses mainly on prevention, treatment and rehabilitation and on the provision of alternatives to drug-growing in the developing countries, notably the ACP countries. The cooperation agreements between the Community and the countries of Asia and Latin America also contain clauses on the fight against drugs [see sections 25.6 and 25.8]. The Community is a member of the International Convention against Illicit Traffic in Narcotic Drugs and Psychotropic Substances, concluded in Vienna on December 20, 1988[4], and is a major contributor to the United Nations Fund for Drug Abuse Control. The European Committee to Combat Drugs (ECCD) plays a catalysing and coordinating role in the action of the Member States at international level.

24.8. Appraisal and outlook

The European Union and its member countries are **by far the largest providers of development funds in the world**. Whereas, in the beginning, it was limited only to Associated Countries and Territories, the common development policy now covers almost all the underdeveloped countries of the world. Moreover, the contribution of the EU to the development of countries in Africa, Asia and Latin America is not limited to grants, through the Community budget, and loans through the European Investment Bank. An important part of its development aid takes the form of trade concessions both to ACP and OCT countries, through duty free imports of their products, and to Asian and Latin American countries, through the generalised system of trade preferences [see section 24.5.]. In addition, the Community development aid policy strives - without much success up to now - to support democratic regimes, human rights, women's position and environmental protection in the recipient countries [see section 24.1.].

While much clearly remains to be done, given an international backdrop of economic crisis in the developing countries and the fratricidal conflicts and political instability in many of them, the association agreements of the EU with ACP and OCT countries and its cooperation agreements with Asian and Latin American countries are **a remarkable contribution to solidarity between the North and South** of the planet. Although aid cannot make up for a lack of sound domestic policies or trade outlets, it may be used as a lever for the implementation of economic and political reforms. What is therefore needed is an approach which encourages internal reforms in the developing countries, on the basis of the four main themes expounded in the Treaty on European Union: consolidation and development of democracy, sustainable economic and social development, integration into the world economy and a battle against poverty. The adverse effects of climate change being particularly serious for the least advanced countries, the environmental dimension should be an integral part of the European Union's

---

[1] Regulation 1568/2003, OJ L 224, 06.09.2003.
[2] Decision 36/2002, OJ L 7, 11.01.2002.
[3] Decision 1209/2003, OJ L 169, 08.07.2003.
[4] Decision 90/611, OJ L 326, 24.11.1990.

development policy, the principal objective being to create as many synergies as possible between action to combat poverty and that to tackle climate change.

By improving the arrangements for mobilising Community relief, the **European Community Office for Humanitarian Aid (ECHO)** is meant to provide both an efficient service to needy countries and a higher profile to European humanitarian interventions [see section 24.7.]. It should give, indeed, public opinion tangible evidence of the Community's role as an active contributor in the field of humanitarian aid. EU citizens are entitled to know that they, through the Community budget, make a small contribution to the alleviation of the sufferings of the people of developing countries that the media relate every day.

In the future, the EU should ensure consistency between development cooperation, the common commercial policy and the common foreign and security policy [see section 8.2.], while establishing close relations with the partner countries. Greater coordination of development aid is needed both at the European Union level and worldwide. Internal coordination between the Commission and Member States would enhance the Union's overall effort and increase the effectiveness of this effort. A local EU action plan for coordination and harmonisation should exist in any partner country where two or more EU donors have a cooperation programme. Food security policy should go hand in hand with poverty reduction in the most vulnerable countries and its objectives and instruments should be fully integrated into the Community's overall development policy.

On the global scene, the enlarged Union will become the world's biggest economy. Its ability to influence **global economic governance** will accordingly be greater. As agreed at the Johannesburg World Summit on Sustainable Development in September 2002, the Union must defend a strategy for sustainable development based on the United Nations system and the international financial institutions and reject hegemony or unilateralism. To this end, it should promote the social dimension of globalisation, including bilateral and regional relations, development and external cooperation, trade policy, private initiatives and governance at global level. In view of the role they play in international development, the EU and its Member States should take the lead in revitalising the United Nations and its specialised organisations, the International Monetary Fund (IMF) and the World Bank in order to make them more effective in addressing the causes of hunger and poverty in the world, such as lack of peace, security and stability.

As emphasized by the EU at the Johannesburg World Summit on Sustainable Development (26 August to 4 September 2002), several challenges need to be addressed in relation to the economic, social and financial dimensions of **sustainable development**, such as making globalisation work for all and strengthening governance at international level. On sustainable development in a globalised world, the EU called for a reform of the international financial system to combat abuses of globalisation and for strengthening the role of international financial institutions in order to reduce the risks posed by financial globalisation for the poor countries.

While good governance is indirectly one of the priority areas of development policy, the Community has not yet devised a general framework in this field. To promote **human rights and democratisation** in third countries, the common development policy should entail the signing, ratification and application of basic treaties and agreements on human rights by all third countries wishing to maintain political, economic, commercial or any other type of relations with the European Union. In addition, the Union should suspend any aid to regimes in third countries violating human rights or supporting terrorism. On the other hand, the EU should better define its sustainable development strategy, promoting sustainable patterns of consumption and production, conservation and sustainable management of natural resources. To ensure consistency in the Union's actions in this field it is vital to "communitarise" the common foreign and security policy, thus abolishing the requirement for unanimity concerning political decisions regarding developing countries.

Bibliography on development aid policy

- BARTELS Lorand. "Human rights conditionality in the EU's international agreements", Oxford: Oxford University Press, 2005.
- CLUNIES-ROSS Anthony, LANGMORE John. *Political economcy of additional development finance.* Helsinki: UNU/WIDER, 2006.
- DIAZ-BONILLA E. (et al.). *WTO negotiations and agricultural trade liberalization: the effect of developed countries' policies on developing countries.* Wallingford: CABI Publishing, 2006.
- DIMIER Véronique. "Constructing conditionality: the bureaucratization of EC development aid" in *European Foreign Affairs Review*, v. 11, n. 2, Summer 2006, p. 263-280.
- DOLLAR David, LEVIN Victoria. "The increasing selectivity of foreign aid, 1984-2003" in *World Development*, v. 34, n. 12, December 2006, p. 2034-2046.
- DREHER Axel. "IMF and economic growth : the effects of programs, loans, and compliance with conditionality" in *World Development*, v. 34, n. 5, May 2006, p. 769-788.
- EASTERLY William. *The White Man's burden: why the West's efforts to aid the rest have done so much ill and so little good.* Oxford: Oxford University Press, 2006.
- EUROPEAN COMMISSION. *EU Strategy for Africa: Towards a Euro-African pact to accelerate Africa's development.* Luxembourg: EUR-OP*, 2005.
  - *Migration and Development: Some concrete orientations.* Luxembourg: EUR-OP*, 2005.
  - *Governance in the European consensus on development: towards a harmonised approach within the European Union.* COM/2006/421. Luxembourg: EUR-OP*, 2006.
  - *Mathias and Amadou: teaching manual on the European Union's policy on development cooperation.* Luxembourg: EUR-OP*, 2006.
- EYBEN Rosalind (ed.). *Relationships for aid.* London : Earthscan, 2006.
- KLINGEBIEL Stephan. *New interfaces between security and development: changing concepts and approaches.* Bonn: Deutsches Institut für Entwicklungspolitik, 2006.
- LEFORT Jean-Claude (rapporteur). *Rapport d'information sur la négociation des accords de partenariat économique avec les pays d'Afrique, des Cara[ibes et du Pacifique.* Paris: Assemblée nationale, 2006.
- LOUIS Michel. *European Union strategy for Africa.* Luxembourg: EUR-OP*, 2006.
- *The European consensus on development.* Luxembourg: EUR-OP*, 2006.
- MAVROTAS George, VILLANGER Espen. *Multilateral aid agencies and strategic donor behaviour.* Helsinki: UNU/WIDER, 2006.
- ORGANISATION FOR ECONOMIC COOPERATION AND DEVELOPMENT. *Policy coherence for development: promoting institutional good practice.* Paris: OECD, 2005.
  - *Integrating human rights into development: donor approaches, experiences and challenges.* Paris: OECD, 2006.
- WINPENNY James. *Guaranteeing development?: the impact of financial guarantees.* Paris: OECD, 2005.

The publications of the Office for Official Publications of the European Communities (EUR-OP) exist usually in all official languages of the EU.

Chapter 25

EXTERNAL RELATIONS

Diagram of the chapter

The **external relations of the European Community**, which date back to its first years of existence, should not be confused with the foreign policy of the European Union, introduced by the Treaty of Maastricht, but which comes more under intergovernmental cooperation than the Community procedure. As explained in chapter 8, the common foreign and security policy (CFSP) depends on a special decision-making process [see section 8.2.1.], whereas the external relations of the EC depend on the Community decision-making process [see section 4.3.]. However, the Community's external relations, tied in as they are with the common commercial policy and the Community's development aid policy, give a foretaste of a really common foreign policy and an indication of the scope which it will eventually assume.

The following pages will examine the relations which the European Community as a body has already established with many countries throughout the world. Although **these relations are of economic or commercial origin**, they have on more than one occasion stepped out of this setting into the purely political arena. This is notably the case concerning relations with other European countries. For the student of European integration it is interesting to distinguish the foreign affairs decisions taken under the common foreign and security policy procedure from those taken under the Community external relations procedure. In other words, it is interesting to see just where the European Community's external domain ends and that of the European Union begins. The answer to this question is not straightforward.

25.1. European Free Trade Association and European Economic Area

As stated in chapter 1, the **European Free Trade Association (EFTA)** was set up in 1959 on the initiative of the United Kingdom, which favoured trade liberalisation through intergovernmental cooperation rather than through the multinational integration process aimed at by ECSC and EEC [see sections 1.1.2. and 1.2.]. When the United Kingdom and Denmark switched allegiances from EFTA to the EEC in 1973, the scale of their commercial relations with the other EFTA countries made it necessary to abolish customs barriers between the two groups of countries. As a consequence, free trade agreements were signed in 1972 and 1973 between the Community and the EFTA countries. These agreements abolished customs duties and restrictions on trade in industrial products. Furthermore, the Community agreed to certain compromises on the Common Agricultural Policy, which were matched by reciprocal EFTA concessions in the agricultural field. EEC-EFTA free trade has operated in a satisfactory manner and has brought about sustained growth in trade between the two groups of countries. This trade, by the end of the 1980s, represented 25% of total Community trade and between 40% and 65% of that of the EFTA countries.

In 1989, Jacques Delors, then President of the European Commission, proposed and the European Council agreed to further strengthen the relations between the two European trade blocks. The negotiations were completed in October 1991 between the Community and EFTA as a body on the basic, legal and institutional aspects of such a global agreement. The **Agreement on the European Economic Area (EEA)** was signed in 1992 by the governments of twelve EU countries and six EFTA countries. However, as a result of the negative Swiss referendum on the EEA Treaty, on 6 December 1992, and the accession to the European Union since 1 January 1995 of the former EFTA members Austria, Sweden and Finland, the EEA Agreement associates to the EU **only Norway, Iceland and Liechtenstein**[1]. The new members of the EU have become contracting parties to the EEA Agreement.

The institutional framework of the EEA comprises: the EEA Council, which is made up of members of the Council of the EU and the Commission plus one member for each signatory EFTA government, and which provides political impetus for the implementation of the Agreement and lays down general guidelines; the EEA Joint Committee, comprising representatives of the contracting parties and responsible for the implementation of the Agreement; the EEA Joint Parliamentary Committee; and the EEA Consultative Committee, which provides a forum for representatives of the social partners. The EFTA countries, members of the EEA, participate in the decision-shaping process of the EU in the ambit of the Commission.

The aim of the EEA Agreement is to establish a dynamic and homogeneous integrated economic entity based on common rules and equal conditions of competition. The EFTA States, minus Switzerland, undertook to take on board existing Community legislation concerning the free movement of goods, persons, services and capital, subject to a few exceptions and transitional periods in certain sectors. Apart from the **implementa-**

---

[1] Decisions 93/734 to 93/741, OJ L 346, 31.12.1993, Agreement on the EEA, OJ L 1, 03.01.1994, Decision of EEA Joint Committee 7/94, OJ L 160, 28.06.1994 and Accession of new Member States to the EU, OJ L 1, 01.01.1995.

tion of the "four freedoms" of the common market [see chapter 6], the EEA Agreement also provides for close relations between the Community and the EFTA countries to be reinforced and extended in areas which have an impact on business activity[1], notably social policy, consumer protection, environment, statistics and company law, research and development, information, education, the audiovisual sector, SMEs and tourism. In fact, the EFTA countries (including Switzerland in some respects) participate practically in the common market without participating in the decision making process that governs it, adapting its legislation to their circumstances.

Thus, the EEA countries participate in Community programmes such as EURES (employment) [see section 6.4.2.], Altener and Save (energy) [see sections 19.3.5. and 19.3.1.]. Other agreements cover inland transport, air transport, free movement of persons, agriculture, public procurement [see section 6.3.], mutual recognition of certificates of conformity [see section 6.2.3.], and technological research and development[2] [see section 18.2.6.]. Special arrangements on agriculture, fisheries and transport are provided in bilateral agreements, which accompany the EEA Agreement. This contains provisions designed to iron out economic, social and regional disparities under the cohesion principle. Therefore, the EEA countries contribute to the financing of the Cohesion Fund in favour of Spain, Portugal, Greece and Ireland. Norway and Iceland are associated in the implementation and development of the Schengen *acquis* under the Treaty of Amsterdam [see section 9.2.].

Not being a party to the EEA agreement, **Switzerland** has, nevertheless, negotiated with the EU sectoral agreements on the free movement of persons, air transport, the transport of goods and passengers by rail and by road, scientific and technological cooperation, public procurement, trade in agricultural products, and mutual recognition and conformity assessment[3]. Other sectoral agreements between the EC and Switzerland concern the Schengen *acquis*[4], the Dublin asylum Convention, a free trade agreement on services and an agreement in the audiovisual field. These agreements allow the Community *acquis* to enter Switzerland through the back door. The Swiss case is a good example of a pro-integration political leadership being overruled by a media-led negative public opinion [see sections 9.5. and 9.6.].

25.2. Candidates for accession

Until the end of the 1980s, the part of Europe known as the **"Satellites of the Soviet Union"** was cut off from the rest of the continent by the "Iron Curtain" which closed off frontiers and by the planned economy system, which prevented normal economic relations with market economy countries. Quite apart from the political and ideological problems, trade with planned economy countries was hindered by the fact that their external trade was run by the State and trading relations therefore had to be established between States. When, at the end of 1989, the pace of history suddenly accelerated with the rapid and successive collapse of the Communist regimes in Central and Eastern Europe, the Community rushed to help the people of these countries, working to promote political reform and develop a private sector in their economies. Less than fifteen years after the fall of the Berlin wall, in May 2004, eight of these countries have become **members of the European Community/Union**, but some mechanisms that helped them achieve this status are still in force, in order to prepare the accession of other candidates mentioned in this and the following section. It is interesting to review these mechanisms, which have proved their effectiveness.

This is notably the case concerning the **operation PHARE** (Poland and Hungary: Aid for Economic Restructuring)[5], which was extended in 2000 to Balkan countries[6] and

---

[1] Regulation 2894/94, OJ L 305, 30.11.1994.
[2] COM (1999) 229, 4 May 1999.
[3] Agreements, OJ L 114, 30.04.2002.
[4] Decision 2004/849, OJ L 368, 15.12.2004 and Decision 2004/860, OJ L 370, 17.12.2004.
[5] Regulation 3906/89, OJ L 375, 23.12.1989 and Regulations 1266/1999, 1267/1999, 1268/1999, OJ L 161, 26.06.1999 and Regulation 2257/2004, OJ L 389, 30.12.2004, all repealed by Regulation 1085/2006, OJ L 210, 31.07.2006.
[6] Regulation 2666/2000 repealed by Regulation 1085/2006, OJ L 210, 31.07.2006.

in 2004 to Croatia[1] [see section 25.3.]. Aimed at gearing the programme to preparing the applicant countries for EU membership, the new guidelines are implemented by means of "accession partnerships" drawn up by the Commission [see details below]. They provide the framework for the programming of PHARE funds focusing on two main priorities: institution building and financing investment. Institution building involves assistance to strengthen the applicant countries' democratic institutions and administrations with a view to facilitating adoption of the "*acquis communautaire*" (established Community law and practice) [see section 3.3.] and helping them meet the economic and political conditions for membership. Special attention under this priority is paid to justice and home affairs concerning notably fraud, illegal immigration and organised crime [see section 8.1.2.]. The second priority, the financing of investment, concerns areas where adoption of Community rules requires substantial resources (environment, transport, product quality, working conditions, etc.) and major infrastructure projects connected with the trans-European networks [see section 6.8.].

In parallel with PHARE and in relation with it three **specific but large-scale instruments** were designed for assistance to CEECs and are examined successively below: the European Bank for Reconstruction and Development, the European Training Foundation and the programme of trans-European mobility for university students.

On April 9, 1990 in Paris the text defining the operating provisions for the **European Bank for Reconstruction and Development (EBRD)** was signed[2]. It was inaugurated on April 14, 1991. Today the EBRD uses the tools of investment to help build market economies and democracies in 27 countries from central Europe to central Asia. The EBRD is the largest single investor in the region and mobilises significant foreign direct investment beyond its own financing. It is owned by 60 countries and two intergovernmental institutions, the European Commission and the European Investment Bank (EIB). It invests mainly in private enterprises, usually together with commercial partners. It provides project financing for banks, industries and businesses, both new ventures and investments in existing companies. It also works with publicly owned companies, to support privatisation, restructuring state-owned firms and improvement of municipal services. The Bank uses its close relationship with governments in the region to promote policies that will bolster the business environment. The mandate of the EBRD stipulates that it must only work in countries that are committed to democratic principles. Respect for the environment is part of the strong corporate governance attached to all EBRD investments.

The **European Training Foundation** is constituted in the form of an independent body which is cooperating closely with the European Centre for the Development of Vocational Training (**CEDEFOP**) [see section 13.3.1.]. The Foundation is open to public or private sector participation by non-Community countries and focuses its action on vocational training, on-going training and training in certain specific sectors. Its role is to ensure efficient cooperation in the provision of aid to the countries in question, to help identify their training needs and to define a strategy which can help meet these needs. It acts as a kind of clearing house, matching up information on aid offers and requests and encouraging and helping multilateral assistance.

The **programme of trans-European mobility for university students (TEMPUS)** is cast in the same mould as existing Community exchange programmes, but is adapted to the specific needs of the countries in question [see section 13.4.2.][3]. In addition to

---

[1]   Regulation 2257/2004, OJ L 389, 30.12.2004 and Decisions 2005/40 and 2005/41, OJ L 26, 28.01.2005.
[2]   Agreement and Decision 90/674, OJ L 372, 31.12.1990.
[3]   Decision 1999/311, OJ L 120, 08.05.1999 and Decision 2002/601, OJ L 195, 24.07.2002.

various complementary activities, it makes provision for joint training projects between universities and companies in Eastern European countries and their counterparts in at least two EU States. It also seeks to encourage the mobility of teachers, students and administrative officials. Its priority action fields are management, business administration and language learning.

Although Central and Eastern European countries, finding themselves since the early 1990s in a very difficult transition from centrally planned to free trade and competition economies, could have chosen membership of the EFTA and through it of the EEA [see section 25.1.], they all **applied for membership to the EU**, thus clearly indicating their preference for the multinational integration process rather than for intergovernmental cooperation [see section 1.1.2.]. On their side, the EU Member States responded positively to this application, thus demonstrating that they did not view their successful enterprise as a club of rich countries.

The countries which request accession to the EU should, however, satisfy certain political and economic conditions. According to the **criteria established by the European Council in Copenhagen** in 1993, an applicant country should have: (a) stable institutions guaranteeing democracy, the rule of law, human rights and protection of minorities; (b) a functioning market economy and the capacity to cope with competitive pressure and market forces within the Union; and (c) the ability to take on the obligations of membership, including adherence to the aims of political, economic and monetary union. The EC/EU helps, however the candidate countries to comply with the criteria for their accession. In addition to their participation in various Community programmes and the assistance given through special programmes, notably PHARE, TEMPUS, ISPA and SAPARD [see sections 12.1.2 and 21.5.5.], pre-accession assistance is granted to the countries trying to meet the criteria set at Copenhagen[1]. A Technical Assistance Information Exchange Office (**TAIEX**) allows the associated countries as well as the European neighbourhood policy (ENP) countries [see section 25.4] and Russia to call upon the experience of Commission and Member States officials in drafting, transposing and implementing legislation concerning the internal market and Community programmes[2].

Partnership agreements, containing the principles, priorities, intermediate objectives and conditions of accession, were signed, in 2003, with Bulgaria[3], Romania[4] and Turkey[5]. On 25 April 2005 the Council decided the admission of the Republics of Bulgaria and Romania to the European Union[6]. On 17 and 18 June 2004 the Brussels European Council recommended that accession negotiations should be opened with Croatia. The next Brussels European Council (16-17 December 2004) recommended that accession negotiations should be opened with Turkey.

At its meeting in Thessaloniki, on 19 and 20 June 2003, the European Council reiterated its determination to fully and effectively support the European perspective of the Western Balkan countries, indicating that they would become an integral part of the European Union, once they met the established criteria. In order to improve the efficiency of the Community's assistance to candidate countries, Regulation 1085/2006 established an **Instrument for Pre-Accession Assistance (IPA)**[7] [see section 12.3.4]. All the Western Balkan countries are considered as potential candidate countries; however, a

---

[1]   Regulation 622/98, OJ L 85, 20.03.1998 and Decisions 98/259 to 98/268, OJ L 121, 23.04.1998.
[2]   Decision 2006/62, OJ L 32, 04.02.2006.
[3]   Decision 2003/396, OJ L 145, 12.06.2003.
[4]   Decision 2003/397, OJ L 145, 12.06.2003.
[5]   Decision 2003/398, OJ L 145, 12.06.2003.
[6]   Treaty and Council Decision, OJ L 157, 21.06.2005.
[7]   Regulation 1085/2006, OJ L 210, 31.07.2006.

distinction is made between candidate countries listed in Annex I of the Regulation (Croatia, Turkey and the former Yugoslav Republic of Macedonia) and potential candidate countries, listed in Annex II of the Regulation (Albania, Bosnia, Montenegro and Serbia, including Kosovo). The Community has agreed to assist all these countries in their progressive alignment with the standards and policies of the European Union, including where appropriate the acquis communautaire, with a view to membership.

The European Council of Brussels (16-17 December 2004) agreed that accession negotiations with individual candidate States should be based on **a framework for negotiations**. Each framework, which should be established by the Council on a proposal from the Commission, should address certain essential elements [see details below], while taking into consideration the own merits and specific situations and characteristics of each candidate State.

The **essential elements of each negotiations framework** are the following:
- the substance of the negotiations, which will be conducted in an Intergovernmental Conference (IGC) with the participation of all Member States on the one hand and the candidate State concerned on the other, where decisions require unanimity, will be broken down into a number of chapters, each covering a specific policy area. The Council, acting by unanimity on a proposal from the Commission, will lay down benchmarks for the provisional closure and, where appropriate, for the opening of each chapter; these benchmarks will refer to legislative alignment and a satisfactory track record of implementation of the *acquis* as well as obligations deriving from contractual relations with the European Union;
- long transition periods, derogations, specific arrangements or permanent safeguard clauses, i.e. clauses which are permanently available as a basis for safeguard measures, may be considered, for areas such as freedom of movement of persons, structural policies or agriculture.
- the financial aspects of accession of a candidate State must be allowed for in the applicable financial framework. Hence, accession negotiations yet to be opened with candidates whose accession could have substantial financial consequences can only be concluded after the establishment of the financial framework for the period from 2014 together with possible consequential financial reforms;
- the shared objective of the negotiations is accession. However, these negotiations are an open-ended process, the outcome of which cannot be guaranteed beforehand. If the candidate State is not in a position to assume in full all the obligations of membership, it must be ensured that the candidate State concerned is fully anchored in the European structures through the strongest possible bond;
- in the case of a serious and persistent breach in a candidate State of the principles of liberty, democracy, respect for human rights and fundamental freedoms and the rule of law on which the Union is founded, the Commission will, on its own initiative or at the request of one third of the Member States, recommend the suspension of negotiations and propose the conditions for eventual resumption. The Council will decide by qualified majority on such a recommendation, after having heard the candidate State, on whether to suspend the negotiations and on the conditions for their resumption.

A joint action agreed by the Council on 28 May 1998 established a mechanism for collective evaluation of the incorporation into the applicant countries' legislation and effective implementation of the Community "acquis" in the field of justice and home affairs[1]. On the same day, the Council invited the Commission to take particular account of the rule of law, according to article 49 (TEU), when drawing up reports on the applicant countries preparation efforts.

25.3. Balkan countries

Exceptional trade measures were introduced for **western Balkan countries** and territories (Albania, the Federal Republic of Yugoslavia, the Former Yugoslav Republic of Macedonia, Bosnia and Herzegovina, Croatia and the Kosovo) participating in or linked to the European Union's **stabilisation and association process (SAP)**[2]. After the change of regime in Serbia, the Union has stepped up its assistance to the Balkans by bringing under a single legal basis and a single programme the initiatives covered by the Phare

---

[1]   Joint Action 98/429/JHA, OJ L 191, 07.07.1998.
[2]   Regulation 2007/2000, OJ L 240, 23.09.2000 and Regulation 1946/2005, OJ L 312, 29.11.2005.

and Obnova[1] programmes, clarifying the objectives of Community action and promoting close regional cooperation between recipient countries[2]. The aim of the assistance is the reconstruction and stabilisation of the region, support for democracy and the rule of law, promotion of human and minority rights, and economic development and market economy reforms. The Community's objective is to promote stability, security and prosperity in the western Balkans through the region's progressive integration into the European mainstream. Indeed, the European perspective provides a powerful incentive for political and economic reform in the region and has encouraged reconciliation among its peoples.

The Thessaloniki European Council (19-20 June 2003) reiterated its determination to fully and effectively support the European perspective of the western Balkan countries, which would become an integral part of the EU, once they met the established criteria. The Thessaloniki agenda enhanced the stabilisation and association process with elements from the enlargement process (twinning, allowing participation in selected Community programmes, European partnerships, strengthening of political dialogue and cooperation in the area of common foreign and security policy). In accordance, the Community pre-accession assistance programmes (Phare, ISPA and Sapard) were modified to allow the stabilisation and association process countries to participate in tenders, which were previously limited to the acceding or candidate countries, and therefore move towards EU integration[3].

The Thessaloniki European Council endorsed, in particular, the introduction of the Partnerships as a means of materialising the European perspective of the Western Balkan countries within the framework of the Stabilisation and Association Process. **European partnerships** now cover Albania, Bosnia and Herzegovina, Croatia, the Former Yugoslav Republic of Macedonia and Serbia and Montenegro, including Kosovo[4]. The partnerships provide a framework covering the priorities resulting from the analysis of the partners' different situations, the preparations for further integration into the European Union and the progress made in implementing the stabilisation and association process, including stabilisation agreements. The Council decides by qualified majority the principles, priorities and conditions to be contained in the European partnerships.

To **prepare for the European integration** of the countries concerned in the framework of the stabilisation and association process, the Council set out the principles, priorities and conditions to be contained in the respective partnerships with, respectively, Croatia[5], Turkey[6], Bosnia and Herzegovina[7], the Former Yugoslav Republic of Macedonia[8], Albania[9] and Serbia and Montenegro, including Kosovo[10]. In the light of the priorities set for each country, the Commission expects each partner to prepare an action plan and schedule listing the specific measures which it intends to take. The financial aid allocated under the Community assistance for reconstruction, development and stabilisation (CARDS) programme will be conditional upon progress achieved in the implementation of the Copenhagen political criteria [see section 25.2] and of the specific short- and medium-term priorities laid down in each of the European partnerships. While the EU is ready to provide all support possible, advancement in the process of European

---

[1] Regulation 2454/1999, OJ L 299, 20.11.1999.
[2] Regulation 2666/2000, OJ L 306, 07.12.2000 and Regulation 769/2004, OJ L 123, 27.04.2004, all repealed by Regulation 1085/2006, OJ L 210, 31.07.2006.
[3] Regulation 769/2004, OJ L 123, 27.04.2004.
[4] Regulation 533/2004, OJ L 86, 24.03.2004 and Regulation 269/2006, OJ L 17.02.2006.
[5] Decision 2006/145, OJ L 55, 25.02.2006.
[6] Decision 2006/35, OJ L 22, 26,01,2006.
[7] Decision 2006/55, OJ L 35, 07.02.2006.
[8] Decision 2006/57, OJ L 35, 07.02.2006.
[9] Decision 2006/54, OJ L 35, 07.02.2006.
[10] Decision 2006/56, OJ L 35, 07.02.2006.

integration in the region depends primarily on each country's own commitment and capability to carry out political and economic reform and adhere to the core values and principles of the Union. In any case, all these countries may participate in Community programmes[1] On 25 October 2005, the EU and eight Balkan countries signed the **Energy Community Treaty** in order to create the legal framework for an integrated energy market[2] [see section 19.1.2].

In general, the Balkan countries face a number of **challenges** if they are to sustain a closer relationship with the EU: ensuring the proper functioning of democratic institutions; upholding the rule of law; strengthening their administrative capacity and ability to implement and enforce legislation and reforms; making further efforts to achieve reconciliation in the region; fighting more vigorously organised crime and corruption in the region; improving the business climate and the competitiveness of their industries.

As a consequence of the civil wars between the republics of the **Federal Republic of Yugoslavia** (FRY) and of United Nations Security Council Resolutions, the Community adopted in 1992 and strengthened in 1993 embargo measures against Serbia and Montenegro[3]. The restrictive measures adopted by the EU were lifted following the elections of 24 November 2000 in the Federal Republic of Yugoslavia and the fall of the Milosevic regime. The EU decided to support the democratic regime and to provide macro-financial assistance to the FRY[4]. The Council set out in a declaration, adopted on 29 September 2003, the commitments made respectively by the European Union and **Serbia and Montenegro** to intensify their mutual relations in the political fields in view of a potential accession to the EU. The political dialogue instituted aims mainly at reinforcing democracy in the country and respect for minority rights; promoting regional cooperation and good neighbourly relations; and increasing convergence of the two entities on international issues and the stability of south-eastern Europe. The EU supports the effective implementation of the mandate of the International Criminal Tribunal for the former Yugoslavia (ICTY)[5].

Concerning **Croatia**, the Council has identified the main priority areas in which Croatia has to make progress for eventual further integration into the EU[6]. A protocol to the stabilisation and association agreement between the European Communities and their Member States, of the one part, and the Republic of Croatia, of the other part, takes account of the accession of the ten new Member States to the EU[7]. As part of the pre-accession strategy, Croatia has become a beneficiary country under the Phare, ISPA and Sapard programmes[8]. In September 2004 a European Partnership with Croatia was adopted by the Council and in October 2005, the Member States started negotiations with Croatia on its accession to the European Union. As provided by Regulation 533/2004, European Partnerships are regularly updated. Therefore, a new Accession Partnership with Croatia identifies new priorities for action and provides guidance for financial assistance to the country[9]. These priorities, which relate in particular to Croatia's capacity to meet the criteria defined by the Copenhagen European Council of 1993 and the conditions set for the stabilisation and association process, have been selected on the basis that it is realistic to expect that Croatia can complete them or take them substantially forward over the next few years.

Relations between the Community and **Turkey** have been subject to a number of ups and downs, reflecting the political situation in the latter. The association agreement of 1964[10] has occasionally operated normally and occasionally been put on the back burner. Despite these problems the EC-Turkey Association Council reached agreement in March 1995 on the **completion of the customs union** between the EU and Turkey, an agreement which the Parliament endorsed in December 1995, thereby paving the way for entry into force of the customs union on 1 January 1996[11]. The Helsinki European Council (10-11 December 1999) decided to recognise Turkey as a **candidate country**. At several occasions, however, the European Union reminded Turkey that satisfying the political criteria for accession (democratic stability, the rule of law, respect for human rights and protection of minorities) is a precondition for opening accession negotiations, and that the "Copenhagen criteria" (including the application of the "acquis communautaire") must be met before proceeding with the act of accession itself. Turkey, like other candidate States, has the opportunity to participate in Community programmes and agencies and in meetings between candidate States and the Union in the context of the acces-

---

[1]   Decisions 2005/524, 2005/525, 2005/526, 2005/527, 2005/528, OJ L 192, 22.07.2005.
[2]   Decision 2005/905, OJ L 329, 16.12.2005.
[3]   Regulation 990/93, OJ L 102, 28.04.1993 repealed by Regulation 2382/96, OJ L 328, 18.12.1996.
[4]   Common position 2000/599/CFSP, OJ L 261, 14.10.2000 and decision 2001/549, OJ L 197, 21.07.2001.
[5]   Common Position 2004/694, OJ L 315, 14.10.2004 amended by Common Position 2006/671, OJ L 275, 06.10.2006 and Decision 2005/927, OJ L 337, 22.12.2005.
[6]   Decision 2006/145, OJ L 55, 25.02.2006.
[7]   Protocol and Decision 2005/41, OJ L 26, 28.01.2005.
[8]   Regulation 2257/2004, OJ L 389, 30.12.2004.
[9]   Decision 2006/145, OJ L 55, 25.02.2006.
[10] Agreement OJ L 217, 29.12.1964 and Decision 2005/672, OJ L 254, 30.09.2005.
[11] Decisions, OJ L 35, 13.02.1996.

sion process. In December 2004, the European Council agreed that the EU would start negotiations with Turkey on its accession to the European Union, but stressed that the advancement of the negotiations would be guided by Turkey's progress in preparing for accession, which would be measured, inter alia, against the implementation of the **Accession Partnership**, as regularly revised[1].

An instrument of financial support aims to encourage the economic development of the **Turkish Cypriot community** in the north of Cyprus, with a view to promoting the economic integration of the island and improving contact between the two communities and the European Union[2]. The measures are intended to prepare and facilitate, as appropriate, the full application of the *acquis communautaire* in the areas in which the government of the Republic of Cyprus does not exercise effective control, once a comprehensive solution to the Cyprus problem has been achieved.

A stabilisation and association agreement between the European Communities and their Member States, of the one part, and the **Former Yugoslav Republic of Macedonia (FYROM)**, of the other part, provides a framework to allow the development of close economic and political relations between the EU and FYROM[3]. In order to help normalise the situation in FYROM, the EU has launched a Police Mission (EUPOL), dubbed "Proxima", in the country[4]. European experts monitor and assist the development of a more professional national police service, which can fight organised crime more effectively, ensure border management and restore public confidence. On 22 March 2004, FYROM made a formal application for membership of the EU. The ten new Member States became contracting parties to the stabilisation and association agreements concluded between the European Communities and their Member States, of the one part, and the Former Yugoslav Republic of Macedonia[5] and the Republic of Croatia[6], of the other part.

The EU has established a **monitoring mission** in the Balkans whose main purpose is to supervise political and security developments in the area of responsibility, give particular attention to border monitoring, inter-ethnic issues and returning refugees, provide analytical reports as requested, provide early warning for the Council and help build confidence in the context of the Union's stabilisation policy for the region[7]. A military operation under the European Security and Defence Policy (ESDP) in **Bosnia and Herzegovina** called "Althea" (which took over from the NATO-led operation SFOR) aims to provide deterrence, ensure continued compliance with the general framework agreement for peace in Bosnia and Herzegovina, and contribute to a climate of safety and security in the country[8]. The EU has also a police mission (EUPM) in Bosnia and Herzegovina[9]. It has established a planning team (EUPT Kosovo) regarding a possible EU crisis management operation in the field of the rule of law and possible other areas in Kosovo[10].

25.4. European neighbourhood policy

The Community plays a decisive role in the provision of technical assistance and food aid to the new republics of the Commonwealth of Independent States (CIS). In 1990, it introduced a technical assistance programme in favour of economic reform and recovery in the former Union of Soviet Socialist Republics. From 1996 to 1999, the Community provided assistance to economic reform and recovery in the New Independent States and Mongolia (TACIS programme)[11]. Such assistance generated significant impact on reform and led to partnership and cooperation agreements with 13 states in **Eastern Europe and Central Asia: Armenia, Azerbaijan, Belarus, Georgia, Kazakhstan, Kyrgyzstan, Moldova, Mongolia, Russian Federation, Tajikistan, Turkmenistan, Ukraine and Uzbekistan.**

Under the new **European Neighbourhood Policy**, a set of priorities are defined together by the European Union and the partner countries, to be incorporated in a series of jointly agreed Action Plans, covering a number of key areas for specific action, includ-

---

[1] Decision 2006/35, OJ L 22, 26,01,2006.
[2] Regulation 389/2006, OJ L 65, 07.03.2006.
[3] Agreement and Decision 2004/239, OJ L 84, 20.03.2004.
[4] Joint action 2004/789, OJ L 348, 24.11.2004 and Joint Action 2005/826, OJ L 307, 25.11.2005.
[5] Decision 2005/192, OJ L 63, 10.03.2005.
[6] Decision 2005/205, OJ L 68, 15.03.2005.
[7] Joint action 2000/811/CFSP, OJ L 328, 23.12.2000 and Joint Action 2004/794, OJ L 349, 25.11.2004.
[8] Joint Action 2004/570/CFSP, OJ L 252, 28.07.2004 and Decision 2004/803, OJ L 353, 27.11.2004.
[9] Joint Action 2002/210, OJ L 70, 13.03.2002 and Joint Action 2005/824, OJ L 307, 25.11.2005.
[10] Joint Action 2006/304, OJ L 112, 26.04.2006.
[11] Regulation 1279/96, OJ L 165, 04.07.1996.

ing political dialogue and reform, trade and economic reform, equitable social and economic development, justice and home affairs, energy, transport, information society, environment, research and innovation, the development of civil society and people-to-people contacts. These priorities are consistent with the objectives of the Partnership and Cooperation Agreements and of the Association Agreements. They are also coherent with the objectives and principles of the European Community Development Policy, as outlined in the Joint Statement entitled "**The European Consensus on Development**" [see section 24.4].

In Eastern Europe and the southern Caucasus, the Partnership and Cooperation Agreements provide the basis for contractual relations. Since the European Union and **Russia** have decided to develop their specific strategic partnership through the creation of four common spaces, Community assistance is used to support the development of this partnership and to promote cross-border cooperation at the border between Russia and its European Union neighbours. In the Mediterranean, the **Euro-Mediterranean Partnership** (the Barcelona Process) [see section 25.5] provides a regional framework for cooperation which is complemented by a network of Association Agreements. Hence, the neighbourhood policy for Mediterranean partners takes into account the agreement reached in that context on establishing a free-trade area for goods by 2010 and beginning a process of asymmetric liberalisation.

In order to support the partner countries' commitment to common values and principles and their efforts in the implementation of the action plans, the Community provides assistance to those countries and supports various forms of cooperation among them and between them and the Member States with the aim of developing a **zone of shared stability, security and prosperity** involving a significant degree of economic integration and political cooperation. To this end, the Community created a single policy-driven instrument, the **European Neighbourhood and Partnership Instrument (ENPI)**, which replaced, since 1 January 2007, a number of pre-existing instruments (such as MEDA and in part TACIS), ensuring coherence and simplifying assistance programming and management[1].

Community assistance by the European Neighbourhood and Partnership Instrument should promote enhanced cooperation and **progressive economic integration** between the European Union and the partner countries. Since the European Union is founded on the values of liberty, democracy, respect for human rights and fundamental freedoms and the rule of law, Community assistance seeks to promote commitment to these values in partner countries through dialogue and cooperation inside an area of prosperity and good neighbourhood. The ENPI assists the implementation of partnership and cooperation agreements, association agreements or other existing and future agreements with the following countries and territories (ENP countries): Algeria, Armenia, Azerbaijan, Belarus, Egypt, Georgia, Israel, Jordan, Lebanon, Libya, Moldova, Morocco, the Palestinian Authority, the Russian Federation, Syria, Tunisia and Ukraine. A total of over EUR 11.1 billion under the European Union's 2007-13 financial framework will be provided from the Community budget for implementation of the regulation, of which at least 95% will be allocated to country and multi-country programmes, and up to 5% will be devoted to cross-border cooperation programmes. ENP countries have access to the assistance of the Technical Assistance Information Exchange Office (**TAIEX**)[2] [see section 25.2].

Community assistance under the **European Neighbourhood and Partnership Instrument** is used to support measures such as:

---

[1] Regulation 1638/2006, OJ L 310, 09.11.2006.
[2] Decision 2006/62, OJ L 32, 04.02.2006.

- promoting political dialogue and reform;
- promoting legislative and regulatory approximation towards higher standards;
- promoting the rule of law and good governance;
- promoting sustainable development in all aspects;
- promoting environmental protection;
- supporting policies aimed at poverty reduction, to help achieve the UN Millennium Development Goals;
- supporting policies to promote social development, social inclusion, gender equality and non-discrimination;
- promoting and protecting human rights and fundamental freedoms, including women's rights and children's rights;
- supporting democratisation, inter alia, by enhancing the role of civil society organisations;
- promoting the development of a market economy, including measures to support the private sector and the development of small and medium-sized enterprises.

On the bilateral level, **partnership and cooperation agreements (PCAs)**, laying the foundations for a qualitative change in economic ties based on the market economy and respect for democratic principles have been signed with **Russia**[1] and **Ukraine**[2] as well as with the Independent States of the former Soviet Union: **Armenia**[3]; **Georgia**[4]; **Moldova**[5]; the Republic of **Azerbaijan**[6]; **Kazakhstan**[7]; **Uzbekistan**[8]; and **Kyrgyzstan**[9]. The agreements govern all political, economic and trade relations between the parties and lay the foundations for cooperation in social, human, scientific, technological and cultural matters. Implementation of these agreements, which combine areas of Member State and EU responsibility and have an initial validity of ten years, depends on political and economic developments in each of the countries in question and on the closeness of their relations with the European Union.

An **EU-Russia energy dialogue** was instituted at the bilateral summit in Paris on 30 October 2000. This dialogue provides an opportunity to raise questions of common interest relating to the energy sector, including the introduction of cooperation on energy saving, rationalisation of production and transport infrastructures, European investment possibilities, and relations between producer and consumer countries. At the EU-Russia summit on 29 May 2002, the EU announced its intention of recognising Russia as a market economy and to take the necessary measures in order to allow Russia to benefit rapidly from the associated trade advantages, particularly as regards anti-dumping procedures. It also welcomed the progress made on the project for a **common European economic area**. The EU and Russia recognised the importance of enhancing trade in primary energy, and also addressed issues relating to natural gas, electricity and nuclear power. They undertook to continue and enhance political dialogue and cooperation on crisis management and security. In order to establish a special transit system between Russia and Kaliningrad, which is a Russian enclave within the enlarged European Union, the EU undertook to issue facilitated transit documents (FTDs) and facilitated rail transit documents (FRTDs)[10].

At the St. Petersburg Summit in May 2003, the EU and Russia agreed to reinforce their co-operation by creating in the long term four "**common spaces**" in the framework of the Partnership and Cooperation Agreement: a common economic space; a common space of freedom, security and justice; a space of co-operation in the field of external security; and a space of research and education, including cultural aspects. The Moscow Summit in May 2005 adopted a single package of **road maps** to act as short and medium-term instruments for the creation of the four Common Spaces. They indicate the actions necessary to make the common spaces a reality. They thereby determine the agenda for co-operation between the EU and Russia for the medium-term.

The Community is also heavily involved in the creation and operation of the **International Centre for Science and Technology** which provides employment for certain of the nuclear experts of the ex-USSR, who could otherwise be tempted to emigrate to countries wishing to acquire or build up nuclear weapons capacity [see section 18.2.6.][11].

---

[1]   Agreement and Decision 97/800, OJ L 327, 28.11.1997, Protocol and Decision 2006/456, OJ L 185, 06.07.2006.
[2]   Agreement and Decision 98/149, OJ L 49, 19.02.1998 and Decision 2002/639, OJ L 209, 06.08.2002.
[3]   Agreement and Decision 1999/602, OJ L 239, 09.09.1999, Ptotocol and Decision 2005/252, OJ L 77, 23.03.2005.
[4]   Agreement and Decision 99/515, OJ L 205, 04.08.1999, Protocol and Decision 2007/36, OJ L 17, 24.01.2007.
[5]   Agreement and Decision 98/401, OJ L 181, 24.06.1998.
[6]   Agreement and Decision 99/614, OJ L 246, 17.09.1999.
[7]   Agreement and Decision 1999/490, OJ L 196, 28.07.1999, Protocol and Decision 2007/36, OJ L 17, 24.01.2007.
[8]   Agreement and Decision 1999/593, OJ L 229, 31.08.1999.
[9]   Agreement and Decision 1999/491, OJ L 196, 28.07.1999, Protocol and Decision 2006/712, OJ L 303, 01.11.2006.
[10]   Regulations 693/2003 and 694/2003, OJ L 99, 17.04.2003.
[11]   Regulation 3955/92 and Regulation 3956/92, OJ L 409, 31.12.1992 and Regulation 501/94, OJ L 64, 08.03.1994.

25.5. Mediterranean, Middle East

The countries of the Mediterranean are of considerable economic significance for the European Union, constituting as a group one of its largest trading partners and having close historic and cultural ties with some of its Member States. A prosperous, democratic, stable and secure Mediterranean region, having close economic and political relations with Europe, is in the best interests of the EU. Relations between the Community/Union and the Mediterranean countries have become ever closer since the 1960s, with a new phase of close cooperation beginning in 1995.

An important Euro-Mediterranean ministerial conference took place on 27 and 28 November 1995 in Barcelona between the European Union and its twelve Mediterranean partners (Algeria, Cyprus, Egypt, Israel, Jordan, Lebanon, Malta, Morocco, Syria, Tunisia, Turkey and the Palestinian Authority). At the end of the proceedings, the ministers adopted a Declaration and a work programme instituting a regular political dialogue and enhanced cooperation fostering peace, security, stability and prosperity in the region. The three key components of the **Euro-Mediterranean partnership** based on the Barcelona Declaration are: to establish a common area of peace and stability through a political and security partnership; to create an area of shared prosperity through an economic and financial partnership; to establish a partnership in social, cultural and human affairs, thus developing human resources, promoting understanding between cultures and exchanges between civil societies.

The EU enlargement, on 1st May 2004, has brought two Mediterranean Partners (Cyprus and Malta) into the European Union. Nowadays, the Euro-Mediterranean partnership comprises 37 members, 27 EU Member States and 10 Mediterranean Partners. Libya has an observer status since 1999. The Euro-Mediterranean partners participate in the **European Neighbourhood policy** and benefit from the European Neighbourhood and Partnership Instrument (ENPI), which replaced, since 1 January 2007, the pre-existing financial instrument MEDA [see section 25.4]. A key objective over the next few years will be deeper integration between the partners through liberalisation of trade and services, increased investment and regulatory convergence[1].

The Euro-Mediterranean Partnership comprises a complementary **bilateral dimension**. Indeed, the European Union has bilateral agreements with each country. The most important are the Euro-Mediterranean Association Agreements that the Union negotiates and concludes with Mediterranean countries individually. They reflect the general principles governing the new Euro-Mediterranean relationship, although they each contain characteristics specific to the relations between the EU and each Mediterranean country.

Under the Euro-Mediterranean partnership, Association Agreements have also been concluded or are to be concluded with three **Maghreb countries, Tunisia**[2], **Morocco**[3] **and Algeria**[4] as well as with three **Mashreq countries, Egypt**[5], **Jordan**[6] **and Lebanon**[7]. As indicated above, these Euro-Mediterranean Agreements provide for a regular political dialogue, the step-by-step establishment of a free trade area, provisions on the right of establishment, services, competition rules and free movement of capital, strengthening of economic cooperation on the broadest possible front complemented by social, cultural and financial cooperation.

---

[1] COM (2005) 139, 12 April 2005.
[2] Agreement and Decision 98/238, OJ L 97, 30.03.1998 and Decision 2005/720, OJ L 278, 21.10.2005.
[3] Agreement and Decision 2000/204, OJ L 70, 18.03.2000 and Decision 2005/695, OJ L 266, 11.10.2005.
[4] Agreement and Decision 2005/690, OJ L 265, 10.10.2005.
[5] Agreement and Decision 2004/635, OJ L 304, 30.09.2004 and Decision 2005/702, OJ L 267, 12.10.2005.
[6] Agreement, OJ L 129, 15.05.2002 and Decision 2005/735, OJ L 283, 26.10.2005.
[7] Interim agreement and Decision 2002/761, OJ L 262, 30.09.2002.

The Community has also concluded agreements for the creation of a customs union between it and the principality of **Andorra**[1] and the republic of **San Marino**[2] respectively.

The preferential arrangements for **Israel**, introduced by the 1975 agreement, are operating reasonably well and have resulted in steady growth in trade between the Community and this country. In the framework of the common foreign policy, the EU brought its support to the peace process between Israel and the Palestinian Territories[3]. The new Euro-Mediterranean Agreement establishes an association between the European Communities and their Member States, of the one part, and the State of Israel, of the other part[4]. The aims of the Agreement are: to provide an appropriate framework for political dialogue; to promote the harmonious development of economic relations between the Community and Israel; and to encourage regional cooperation with a view to the consolidation of peaceful coexistence and economic and political stability.

The Community offers the **Palestinian** public administration financial and technical assistance contributing to setting up and improving basic institutions for the development process in the Occupied Territories (the West Bank and the Gaza Strip) and for the implementation of the "roadmap" for peace in the Middle East[5]. A Euro-Mediterranean interim Association Agreement on trade and cooperation has also been concluded between the European Community and the Palestine Liberation Organisation (PLO) for the benefit of the Palestinian Authority[6]. It covers the whole range of economic and commercial relations and sets out the stages leading to full liberalisation of trade between the two sides. A joint action of the Council established a European Union assistance programme to support the Palestinian Authority in its efforts to counter terrorist activities emanating from the territories under its control[7]. An EU police mission for the Palestinian Territories is intended to help establish sustainable and effective policing arrangements managed by the Palestinians[8].

The Laeken European Council (14-15 December 2001) stated that the **position of the EU on the Middle East conflict** was that: the only basis for peace is UN Resolutions 242 and 338; full recognition of Israel's inalienable right to live in peace and security within internationally recognised borders; and the establishment of a viable, independent and democratic Palestinian State and an end to the occupation of Palestinian territories. The Copenhagen European Council (12-13 December 2002) urged the adoption by the Middle East Quartet (USA, EU, UN and Russia) of a joint road map leading to two States, Israel and an independent, viable, sovereign, and democratic Palestine, living side by side in peace and security on the basis of the 1967 borders. While having repeatedly condemned terrorist atrocities against Israelis and recognised Israel's right to protect its citizens against terrorist attacks, the European Union has consistently called on the Israeli government to take action to alleviate the suffering of Palestinians by lifting prohibitions on movement, reversing its settlement policy and reversing the construction of the so-called security fence on Palestinian land. On 11 October 2004, the Council reiterated its view that an Israeli withdrawal from the Gaza Strip and part of the Northern West Bank could represent a significant step towards the implementation of the Roadmap, provided that it was a full and complete withdrawal and implemented in accordance with the five elements laid down by the European Council in March 2004 and that it was not an attempt to replace the Roadmap and the two-State solution it encompassed.

In the Middle East, progress and dialogue are inexorably slow, despite the major efforts of the Community to conduct and expand dialogue with the Arab countries. In September 1981, the EEC's Foreign Affairs Ministers expressed their wish to establish relations with the **Gulf Cooperation Council (GCC)**, then a new body set up by the United Arab Emirates, Saudi Arabia, Bahrain, Oman, Qatar and Kuwait. After exploratory high-level talks lasting several years, a cooperation agreement was finally signed on June 15, 1988 in Luxembourg[9]. This agreement formalises economic and political relations between the two parties and provides for the implementation of all-round cooperation in the sectors traditionally covered by this type of agreement, namely industry, trade promotion, agriculture, science and technology and energy. At the fifteenth Joint Cooperation Council meeting between the European Union and the GCC, on 5 April 2005, the parties said they were committed to concluding negotiations on a free-trade agreement without delay and stressed the need for continued progress, particularly with regard to services, customs duties on industrial products and public procurement.

After the **invasion of Kuwait by Iraq** at the beginning of August 1990, the Community as a body took the decisions required for the imposition of a complete embargo on trade with the two countries. This embargo was lifted as concerns Kuwait after its liberation. Community legislation concerning the embargo on Iraq was adapted to the UN "oil-for-food" Resolution[10]. The Copenhagen European Council (12-13 December 2002)

---

[1] Agreement and Decision 90/680, OJ L 374, 31.12.1990 and Decision 1/99, OJ L 191, 23.07.1999.
[2] Agreement and Decision 2002/245, OJ L 84, 28. 03.2002 and Protocol 2005/663, OJ L 251, 27.09.2005.
[3] Decision 94/276, OJ L 119, 07.05.1994 and Decision 95/205, OJ L 130, 14.06.1995.
[4] Agreement and Decision 2000/384, OJ L 147, 21.06.2000 last amended by 2006/19, OJ L 20, 24.01.2006.
[5] Regulation 1734/94, OJ L 182, 16.07.1994 repealed by Regulation 1638/2006, OJ L310, 09.11.2006.
[6] Agreement and Decision 97/430, OJ L 187, 16.07.1997 and Exchange of Letters, OJ L 2, 05.01.2005.
[7] Joint Action 2000/298, OJ L 97, 19.04.2000.
[8] Joint Action 2005/797, OJ L 300, 17.11.2005.
[9] Agreement and Decision 89/147, OJ L 54, 25.02.1989.
[10] Regulation 2465/96, OJ L 337, 27.12.1996.

stressed its full and unequivocal support for the UN Security Council Resolution 1441 of 8 November 2002 and the disarmament of Iraq's weapons of mass destruction in accordance with the relevant UN Security Council resolutions. In the spring of 2003, however, the EU Member States were split between those which wanted a continuation of the search for weapons of mass destruction in Iraq on the basis of UN resolutions and those which followed the United States policy of immediate overthrow of the Iraqi regime. This division highlighted the weakness of the decision-making procedure of the common foreign and security policy of the EU [see section 8.2.1.]. However, after the occupation of Iraq by allied forces, the EU replaced previous regulations imposing a total embargo on trade with Iraq with specific restrictions relating to petroleum, petroleum products and natural gas from Iraq and to trade in goods forming part of Iraq's cultural heritage[1]. On 29 September 2003, the Council underlined the importance of the restoration of Iraqi sovereignty and the establishment of a fully representative Iraqi Government through democratic elections. The European Union integrated rule of **law mission for Iraq (Eujust Lex)** provides for the training of officials of the Iraqi criminal-justice system (police, judiciary and penitentiary administration) in senior management and criminal investigation[2]. The EU has agreed, on 5 November 2004 and on 21 February 2005, a full assistance programme aiming at the objective of a safe, stable, unified, prosperous and democratic Iraq that upholds human rights, fully exercises its sovereignty and cooperates constructively with its neighbours and with the international community.

In October 2004, the Council stated that **Libya** had proved its willingness to change its policies of the past and its commitment to responsible government. Therefore, the Council agreed to embark on a policy of engagement with Libya with a view to developing relations with it, such as the lifting of restrictive measures[3] and the supply of certain goods and services[4].

25.6. Other Asian countries and Oceania

The **Community Strategy for Asia** is founded on a development partnership and on political dialogue[5]. The priorities of this strategy include notably: backing cooperation schemes aimed at safeguarding peace and security; improving Europe's image in Asia and creating a climate conducive to the development of trade and investment; and improving coordination in the management of development aid so that the region's less prosperous countries experience economic growth and poverty is reduced. Many Asiatic countries benefit from the Community **financing instrument for development cooperation** [see section 24.4.].

The new agreement concluded with **India** is an advanced framework cooperation agreement emphasising economic cooperation and private sector investment, intellectual property rights, technology transfer and diversification of economic and trade relations[6]. Similar **non-preferential agreements, called "third generation"**, comprising three areas of cooperation, namely trade, economic and development cooperation, and making respect for human rights a key condition for the development of dialogue and partnership have been concluded with **Mongolia**[7], **Sri Lanka**[8], **Vietnam**[9] and **Nepal**[10].

Community aid has had a relatively positive impact in the countries belonging to the **Association of South-East Asian Nations (ASEAN)**, which comprises **Brunei, Indonesia, Malaysia, the Philippines, Singapore, Thailand and Vietnam**. The cooperation agreement between the Community and most of these countries dates back to 1980[1].

---

[1] Common Position 2003/495/CFSP amended by Common Position 2004/553, OJ L 246, 20.07.2004 and Regulations 1210/2003, OJ L 169, 08.07.2003 and 1412/2004, OJ L 257, 04.08.2004 last amended by Regulation 785/2006, OJ L 138, 25.05.2006.
[2] Joint Action 2005/190, OJ L 62, 09.03.2005 last amended by Joint Action 2006/708, OJ L 291, 21.10.2006.
[3] Common position 2004/698, OJ L 317, 16.10.2004.
[4] Regulation 1786/2004, OJ L 317, 16.10.2004.
[5] COM (94) 314.
[6] Agreement and Decision 94/578, OJ L 223, 27.08.1994.
[7] Agreement and Decision 92/101, OJ L 41, 18.02.1993.
[8] Agreement and Decision 95/129, OJ L 85, 19.04.1995.
[9] Agreement and Decision 96/351, OJ L 136, 07.06. 1996.
[10] Agreement and Decision 96/354, OJ L 137, 08.06.1996.

1980[1]. It is completed by trade agreements on manioc from Thailand and Indonesia[2] granting better access for their products to the Community market. As a follow-up to its communication on "Europe and Asia: a strategic framework for enhanced partnerships"[3], the Commission proposes revitalising the relations between the EU, ASEAN and the countries of South-East Asia, and identifies the strategic priorities, creating a framework for future bilateral agreements[4].

Relations between the Community and **China**, after the retrogression that followed the events of Tiananmen Square on June 4, 1989, are marking a steady improvement. A 1978 framework trade agreement evolved into the 1985 trade and economic cooperation agreement covering industrial and technical fields[5] and trade in textiles[6]. A 1998 Commission communication on "a comprehensive **partnership with China**"[7] opened the way for a new EU-China relationship embracing four main areas: upgrading the political dialogue; supporting China's transition to an open society based on the rule of law and respect for human rights; integrating China further into the world economy; and raising the profile of the EU in China. On behalf of the Community and its Member States, the Commission negotiated with China a whole series of commitments on the opening up of markets which are of particular importance to the European Union. These commitments were listed in the bilateral agreement signed by the People's Republic of China and the European Community on 19 May 2000, and are set out in the protocol of accession by China to the WTO[8] [see section 23.4.]. The EU's cooperation programme with China has expanded steadily and now focuses on supporting sustainable development to assist the overall reform process in China and the implementation of its WTO commitments[9].

Japan poses problems of a completely different nature for the European Union. Japan has a huge trade surplus with the Community, with its exports to the EU running at three times its imports from it. Japan is at an advantage compared with the other industrialised countries due to such specificities as a limited social security budget, low military expenditure and low aid level to the developing countries. But the success of Japanese policy is chiefly due to certain basic economic factors: strong competitiveness and productivity, rigid organisation of the domestic market, integrated industrial and trade strategy working towards precise and planned objectives. As regards more specifically trade relations with the EU, the determinant factors in the disequilibrium are: the concentration of Japanese exports on a limited number of sectors, high quality, leading-edge products, marketed with highly effective marketing methods supported by a favourable financing system; and, on the other side of the equation, the closing of the Japanese market by various technical and administrative barriers as well as by prevalent Japanese national habits and attitudes. Nevertheless, the Community is becoming an increasingly important trading partner for Japan because of the size of the single European market and the efforts made to develop trade and cooperation.

Closer relations between the Community and Japan culminated in the adoption, on July 18, 1991, of a **joint declaration** similar to those defining the Community's relations with the United States and Canada. It sets out the general principles and objectives of cooperation between the two parties, notably stipulating that access to respective markets

---

[1] Regulation 1440/80, OJ L 144, 10.06.1980 and Decision 1999/295, OJ L 117, 05.05.1999.
[2] Decisions 82/495 and 82/496, OJ L 219, 28.07.1982 and Decision 90/637, OJ L 347, 12.12.1990.
[3] COM (2001) 469.
[4] COM (2003) 399.
[5] Agreement and Regulation 2616/85, OJ L 250, 19.09.1985.
[6] Agreement and Decision 95/155, OJ L 104, 06.05.1995.
[7] COM (1998) 181.
[8] COM (2001) 517 and 518, 19 September 2001.
[9] COM (2000) 552, 8 September 2000.

must be equitable and offer comparable opportunities through the removal of obstacles to trade and investments. It also stipulates the framework for dialogue, with annual summits and other meetings. As regards more especially trade in motor vehicles, the Community and Japan agreed on July 31, 1991 on a solution aiming at gradual liberalisation of the Community market as part of the completion of the single market, while avoiding market distortion caused by exports from Japan [see section 23.5.].

The first joint initiative between the Community and Japan is the consolidation of the **EC-Japan industrial cooperation centre**[1]. Situated in Tokyo, this Centre seeks to contribute to industrial cooperation between the Community and Japan, notably through organising management training programmes for the executives of European companies, supplying information on the Japanese industrial environment and its possibilities, and running programmes for European specialists in alternative energies. In 1993 a method of analysis of trade relations between the European Union and Japan was devised, the Trade Assessment Mechanism (TAM), through which both parties cooperate to reach an objective picture of how European products are faring on the Japanese market. The Commission in cooperation with the Member States is implementing a programme of specific measures and actions to improve access of European Union goods and cross-border services to Japan, in particular through training of executives and businessmen[2].

The rapid industrialisation of the **Republic of Korea** in the second half of the 1980s gave several causes for Community concern: the degree of openness of the Korean market, the abolition of restrictive legislation on foreign investment and equal treatment for foreign and Korean investors; non-discrimination, particularly in the areas of the protection of intellectual property and the problem of diversifying Korean foreign trade; industrial policy and competition problems in the shipbuilding sector. These problems could be better faced in the context of the trade and cooperation agreement that the EU has concluded with the Republic of Korea[3]. This agreement aims to contribute to the development of trade and investment between the European Union and Korea and to encourage cooperation initiatives in a variety of fields, notably justice and home affairs, science and technology and culture.

Australia and **New Zealand** have also been at odds with the European Community since the entry into force of the Common Agricultural Policy and more especially since the entry of the United Kingdom to the Community. The UK had in fact always been the main outlet for the agricultural produce of these two countries and although it tried to protect their interests on its accession, the integration of the United Kingdom into the Community seriously upset its trading relations with Australia and New Zealand. The agricultural problems that had dominated relations until the early 1990s having at last disappeared from the fore-stage following the entry into force of the WTO agreement on agriculture [see section 23.5.], the EU's relations with both Australia and New Zealand are in the process of being strengthened.

The Community and **Australia** in fact have a similar viewpoint on many of the international political problems. On the economic front, both parties are, however, satisfied with their 1982 agreement, relating to transfers of nuclear material from Australia to the European Atomic Energy Community[4] and their cooperation, since 1986, on research, technology and, since 1991, the environment. The completion of the single market, the reform of the Common Agricultural Policy and Australia's new industrial policy are pushing for closer trade links between this country and the Community. Indeed, in 1994, the EU and Australia signed agreements on trade in wine[5], on mutton, lamb and goatmeat[6] as well as on cooperation in science and technology[7].

The trade problems between the Community and **New Zealand** are also in principle settled thanks to arrangements between the two parties concerning the imports of cheese[8] and of mutton, lamb and goatmeat[9]. In addition, an agreement between the EU and New Zealand on sanitary measures applicable to trade in live animals and animal products established simplified certificates, recognising the equivalence of certain commodities and of the parties' certification systems[10].

---

[1] Decision 92/278, OJ L 144, 26.05.1992.
[2] Regulation 382/2001, OJ L 57, 27.02.2001 and Regulation 1900/2005, OJ L 303, 22.11.2005.
[3] Framework agreement and Decision 2001/248, OJ L 90, 30.03.2001.
[4] Agreement, OJ L 281, 04.10.1982.
[5] Agreement and Decision 94/184, OJ L 86, 31.03.1994 last amended by Agreement, OJ L 336, 23.12.2003.
[6] Agreement, OJ L 351, 31.12.1994.
[7] Agreement and Decision 94/457, OJ L 188, 22.07.1994 and Decision 99/510, OJ L 195, 28.07.1999.
[8] Decision 84/561, OJ L 308, 27.11.1984.
[9] Agreement and Decision, OJ L 47, 18.02.1994 and OJ L 191, 12.08.1995.
[10] Agreement and Decision 97/132, OJ L 57, 26.02.1997 and OJ L 333, 10.12.2002.

25.7. North American countries

The European Union is **the biggest trading partner of the United States** and is linked to this country by culture, tradition and cross-investments as well as by common economic and political interests embodied within international organisations such as the Organisation for Economic Cooperation and Development (OECD) and the North Atlantic Treaty Organisation (NATO). The United States were in 2000 the EU's leading investment partner: almost half of the extra-EU investments by Member States went to the United States (EUR 147 out of EUR 304 billion), and almost 80% of investments by non-member countries in the EU came from the United States (EUR 98 out of EUR 125 billion). From the political viewpoint, the United States has always supported European integration. This has not prevented strong economic antagonism between the two richest regions of the planet.

The fall of the Soviet Union and the emergence of the United States as the sole superpower led to the adoption on November 22, 1990 by the United States on the one hand and by the Community and its Member States on the other of a joint **transatlantic declaration**. Considering that their relationship is a vital factor for political stability in a changing world, the two parties confirmed their commitment to continuing and developing cooperation on an equal footing and, for this purpose, they agreed to consult one another on important subjects of common interest and to intensify their dialogue in a formal contact structure. The **transatlantic agenda**, signed in 1995, completed the Transatlantic Declaration and organised the cooperation between the two partners around four pillars: promoting peace, stability, democracy and development throughout the world, responding to global challenges, contributing to the expansion of world trade and closer economic relations, and establishing closer ties between the partners. In addition, an agreement between the Community and the United States established a cooperation programme in the field of higher education and vocational training[1] [see details below].

After the **terrorist attacks** of 11 September 2001 against the United States, the European Council meeting in extraordinary session on 21 September 2001 declared its total support to the American people in the face of the deadly terrorist attacks and its willingness to cooperate with the United States in bringing to justice and punishing the perpetrators, sponsors and accomplices of such barbaric acts [see section 8.2.3.]. On 8 October 2001, the Council declared that the military action taken by the US in self-defence and in conformity with the UN Charter and the UNSCR 1368 was part of a wider multilateral strategy in which the European Union was committed to playing its part, including a comprehensive assault on the organisations and financing structures that underpin terrorism.

However, transatlantic relations are often a **controversial subject** for the EU, since the degree of solidarity with the United States differs considerably from one European country to another. It is, therefore, usually difficult to work out a common reaction to the initiatives of Washington. In general, the vision of the world and of international relations of the USA, which is largely based on national interest and the use of military force, is basically contrasting with the concept of international law that the European nations tend to place above national law. Even the best friends of the USA in Europe are sad to see the new American policy depart from the rules of international law, enacted with the active participation of the USA themselves, on issues such as: the ratification of the Kyoto protocol for the reduction of atmospheric pollution [see section 16.3.4.]; the

---

[1] Agreement and Decision 95/487, OJ L 279, 22.11.1995.

exemption of American citizens from the jurisdiction of the International Criminal Court for war crimes [see section 8.1.2.]; the disrespect of the rules of the World Trade Organisation in general and particularly concerning the huge increase in American farm subsidies (70%) and the protection of American steel products [see details below]; the invasion of Iraq without agreement of the UN Security Council; and, last but not least, the uneven interposition in the conflict between Israelis and Palestinians. On all these subjects the transatlantic declaration of 1990 has not served as a basis of dialogue and cooperation between equal partners. If this situation continues, the European Union will, sooner or later, adopt a foreign policy, which will increasingly diverge from that of the USA.

The Community's relations with **Canada** have originally been based on a cooperation agreement between Euratom and Canada on the peaceful use of atomic energy[1], on a cooperation agreement between the EEC and Canada on commercial and economic cooperation[2] and on a fisheries agreement[3]. The two parties adopted on November 22, 1990 a **joint declaration** based on the preferential relations introduced by the framework cooperation agreement which reinforces the institutional framework for consultations in order to give them a long-term horizon.

Before the ascendancy of the neoconservative policy in the United States, the transatlantic dialogue had given some good results. It had permitted a better **coordination of respective policies** concerning aid to Central and Eastern European countries, Russia and the Independent States, the conflict and the management of peace in former Yugoslavia and the Middle East peace process. In the Uruguay Round, the Blair-House pre-agreement, concluded on 28 November 1992 between the United States and the EU, was a pre-condition for the conclusion of the GATT multilateral trade negotiations. Moreover, a number of trade differences have been settled, notably the ones on trade in large civil aircraft[4] on veterinary matters concerning fresh bovine and porcine meat[5] and on openness in the field of public procurement of the two parties [see section 23.4.][6]. In order to resolve the banana dispute, i.e. the EU helping ACP banana suppliers adapt to the new common market conditions, 100 000 tonnes from the C quota for bananas allocated to the ACP countries were transferred to the B quota open for imports of products originating in all third countries[7].

Nevertheless, several **disputes persist**. Americans have taken action against Community legislation, notably: the hormones Directive[8], preventing meat imports from third countries, like the United States, which do not prohibit the fattening of livestock with hormones. A large number of the complaints lodged by the EU with the dispute-settlement body of the WTO concern the US. Following the US decision to impose extraordinary tariffs of up to 30% on steel imports, the Commission, with the consent of the Parliament and the Council, adopted a regulation instituting safeguard measures on certain iron and steel products[9] and opened a safeguard investigation into those products in order to counter the adverse effects of the US decision on the Community steel market. The Community started on 7 March 2002 a dispute settlement procedure at the WTO calling for consultations to be held pursuant to WTO rules. The EU obtained satisfaction and the safeguard measures were repealed with effect from 8 December 2003[10].

It should be noted that the United States lost 17 trade disputes out of 19 in WTO in 2002, but their legislation has not been changed in any way as a result. Thus, the US anti-dumping act of 1916, which provides for civil and criminal proceedings and penalties against dumping, was found incompatible with the obligations imposed by the World Trade Organisation. Therefore, the EU is protecting its businesses against the effects of the application of this US Act, and actions based thereon or resulting therefrom[11]. The protective measures comprise a prohibition on the recognition and enforcement in the EC of court or administrative decisions based on the 1916 anti-dumping act, and the possibility for EC companies or individuals to counter-sue to recover any outlays, costs, damages, interest and expenses caused by the application of the act in breach of WTO rules.

---

[1]   1959 Agreement, OJ 60, 24.11.1959 and 1995 Agreement OJ L 211, 06.09.1995.
[2]   Agreement and Decisions, OJ L 260, 24.09.1976 and new Agreement, OJ L 346, 22.12.1998.
[3]   Decisions 81/1053 and 81/1054, OJ L 379, 31.12.1981 and Agreement and Regulation 3675/93, OJ L 340, 31.12.1993.
[4]   Agreement and Decision 92/496, OJ L 301, 17.10.1992.
[5]   Agreement and Decision 93/158, OJ L 68, 19.03.1993.
[6]   Agreement and Decision 93/323, OJ L 125, 20.05.1993 and Decision 95/215, OJ L 134, 20.06.1995.
[7]   Regulation 404/93, OJ L 47, 25.02.1993, last amended by Regulation 2013/2006, OJ L 384, 29.12.2006.
[8]   Directive 96/22, OJ L 125, 23.05.1996 and Directive 2003/74, OJ L 262, 14.10.2003.
[9]   Regulation 560/2002, OJ L 85, 28.03.2002 and Regulation 1694/2002, OJ L 261, 28.09.2002.
[10] Regulation 184/2004, OJ L 29, 03.02.2004.
[11] Regulation 2238/2003, OJ L 333, 20.12.2003.

Moreover, the European Union suspended, vis-à-vis the United States, the application of tariff concessions and related obligations concluded under GATT, in accordance with the arbitration decision of 31 August 2004, finding that the Continued Dumping and Subsidy Offset Act (CDSOA) was incompatible with the United States' obligations under the WTO agreements[1].

In contrast, the good cooperation between the EU and **Canada** is manifest in sensible fields such as animal-health regulations and trade in alcoholic beverages[2] as well as in the new fisheries agreement between the EU and Canada, concluded in the framework of the North-West Atlantic Fisheries Organisation (NAFO)[3]. Canada participates in EU civilian and military crisis management operations[4].

25.8. Latin American countries

The Community has been **granting aid to Latin America** as a group of non-associated countries for many years [see section 24.4.]. The Community is aware of its responsibility for development in these countries, home to some of the poorest people in the world. This awareness has been further accentuated since the entry of Spain and Portugal to the Community, two countries which share the same cultural heritage with Latin America. Thus, the Community develops ever closer relations with **regional groupings** in Latin America, i.e. the **Rio Group** (Argentina, Bolivia, Brazil, Chile, Colombia, Costa Rica, Dominican Republic, El Salvador, Ecuador, Guatemala, Honduras, Mexico, Nicaragua, Panama, Paraguay, Peru, Uruguay, Venezuela), the **Central American Integration**, the **Andean Pact** and **Mercosur**.

In 1986 the Community concluded a framework agreement for commercial and economic cooperation and development with the countries of the Central American Economic Integration or **San José Group (Costa Rica, El Salvador, Guatemala, Honduras, Nicaragua) and with Panama**[5]. The cooperation agreement between the Community and the countries of the **Andean Pact or Cartagena Agreement (Bolivia, Colombia, Ecuador, Peru and Venezuela)**, places particular emphasis on the consolidation of the regional integration systems and on the respect of democratic principles and human rights[6]. The main aims of the agreement are: to stimulate, diversify and improve trade; to encourage cooperation between industrialists; and to stimulate scientific and technical cooperation.

The European Union is also providing technical assistance to the common market between the **Mercosur** countries **(Argentina, Brazil, Paraguay and Uruguay)**. In the wake of the Solemn Joint Declaration between the European Union and Mercosur[7], an interregional commercial and economic cooperation framework Agreement between the EU and Mercosur was signed in Madrid on 15 December 1995[8]. Aimed at strengthening existing ties and preparing for eventual association, this Agreement provides: regular, institutionalised political dialogue; trade cooperation leading to trade liberalisation; economic cooperation geared to promoting reciprocal investment; cooperation on regional integration, intended to allow Mercosur to draw upon the experience of the European Union; and wider cooperation in fields of mutual interest, such as culture, information and communication, training on the multinational integration process and on the prevention of drug abuse.

---

[1] Regulation 673/2005, OJ L 110, 30.04.2005 last amended by Regulation 632/2006, OJ L 111, 25.04.2006.
[2] Agreement and Decision 89/189, OJ L 71, 15.03.1989 and Agreement, OJ L 35, 06.02.2004.
[3] Decision 95/586, OJ L 327, 30.12.1995.
[4] Agreement and Decision 2005/851, OJ L 315, 01.12.2005.
[5] Agreement and Regulation 2009/86, OJ L 172, 30.06.1986.
[6] Agreement and Decision 98/278, OJ L 127, 29.04.1998.
[7] Framework Agreement and Decision 96/205, OJ L 69, 19.03.1996.
[8] Agreement and Decision 96/205, OJ L 69, 19.03.1996 and Council Decision 1999/279, OJ L 112, 29.04.1999.

The new opening provided by the Uruguay Round Agreements [see section 23.4.] and the developments in the various integration processes in Latin America are the two vital elements for **intensifying cooperation** between the EU and Latin American countries. In giving its support to the development efforts of the latter (at bilateral level) and to their integration efforts (at multilateral level) the European Union hopes to contribute to the political stability and economic and social development of a region of the world which, despite its current economic and social difficulties, is rich in raw materials and is a vast potential market.

At bilateral level, new economic partnership and political consultation agreements, paving the way for economic and political association, were concluded in the 1990s between the Community and **Argentina**[1], **Paraguay**[2], **Uruguay**[3], **Brazil**[4], **Chile**[5] and **Mexico**[6]. The agreements introduce several innovations and notably a clause referring to respect of democratic principles and of human rights as a prerequisite for any cooperation between the two parties. Efforts have been stepped up in the area of industrial cooperation and a systematic strategy incorporating training activities has been developed in promoting European technologies and investments in SMEs, with the aim of boosting local output and export capacities.

Financial and technical cooperation with the Latin American countries, mentioned in the chapter on development aid, is targeted on the poorest developing countries [see section 24.4.]. The Community's solidarity with the Andean countries which are trying to **combat drug abuse** has been given tangible demonstration with the extension to Colombia, Bolivia, Peru and Ecuador of the generalised tariff preferences applied to certain of the least advanced developing countries[7]. In 1991, these arrangements were extended to Costa Rica, El Salvador, Guatemala, Honduras, Nicaragua and Panama. In addition, the Community has signed with Mexico[8] and Chile[9] agreements of cooperation in preventing the diversion of certain chemical substances to the illicit manufacture of narcotic drugs and psychotropic substances.

25.9. Appraisal and outlook

Whereas at the outset the Community was viewed with indifference, scepticism or even hostility by the rest of the world, it is now **recognised as being a major economic, commercial and, potentially, political power**. In this and in the two preceding chapters we saw that the Community is dealing, negotiating and conversing with many countries large and small throughout the world, which see it as an important group of prosperous, democratic and peaceful countries. Curiously enough, those outside better perceive the common policies of EC/EU countries than those inside it [see sections 10.1. and 10.4.]. In fact, the Union's external policy is made up of a number of common policies, which support one another. It goes beyond the traditional diplomatic and military aspects, which are ostensibly in the ambit of the Union, and stretches to Community areas such as trade and customs affairs, development aid, justice and police matters, environment protection, external relations of agricultural and fisheries policies and external representation of the euro zone. Through its development aid policy, its common commercial policy and its external relations, the European Community has a **strong presence on the world stage**. It notably exerts a strong pressure, through its statements, representations and economic sanctions, on many countries practising serious violations of democratic

---

[1]   Agreement and Decision 90/530, OJ L 295, 26.10.1990.
[2]   Agreement and Decision 92/509, OJ L 313, 30.10.1992.
[3]   Agreement and Decision 92/205, OJ L 94, 08.04.1992.
[4]   Agreement and Decision 95/445, OJ L 262, 01.11.1995.
[5]   Agreement and Decision 2002/979, OJ L 352, 30.12.2002 and Decision 2005/106, OJ L 38, 10.02.2005.
[6]   Agreement and Decision 2000/658, OJ L 276, 28.10.2000 and Protocol, OJ L 66, 12.03.2005.
[7]   Regulation 3211/90, OJ L 308, 08.11.1990.
[8]   Agreement and Decision 97/184, OJ L 77, 19.03.1997.
[9]   Agreement and Decision 98/708, OJ L 336, 11.12.1998.

principles and human rights [see section 24.1.]. It also advocates an effective multilateralism in the framework of an international society based on the rule of law.

However, the fragmentation of initiative, decision and action causes the **inadequacy of the Union's foreign policy**. The European Union cannot exert a political influence commensurate to its economic weight in the world affairs, as long as the external policies of the Community, examined in this part, are not well coordinated or better integrated in the common foreign and security policy of the Union [see section 8.2.]. As we will see in the "European outlook", it is up to its Member States to let the European Union become a world power by accepting to share their political sovereignty in the same way they share their economic and monetary sovereignty [see chapter 7].

The Union has the potential to **play a role as a world power**. To this end, it must propound its democratic values and its integration paradigm, stand up and be counted as the bearer of a shared and sustainable model of development. It must pursue an external policy open to dialogue between civilisations, cultures and religions, and based on cooperation with the countries at its borders and on the resolve to help the economic, political and social development of all the countries in the world. It is significant that after the fall of their communist regimes Central and Eastern European countries ignored the possibility of acceding to the European Economic Area and applied for membership to the EU in order to strengthen their feeble economies and stabilise their fragile democratic systems. By enhancing its power and image in the world arena, the EU could better help other countries in the world, torn by their economic and political differences, imitate its successful formula of multinational integration. In fact, Europe's experience with economic and political unification is being watched with close attention throughout the world and countries in other regions of the globe, notably in Latin America, are trying to imitate it. This could be a valuable contribution of the European Union to world peace and prosperity.

The EU could also contribute in world order and multilateralism by resisting the unilateral tendencies of one superpower and by **reinforcing the role of the United Nations Organisation**. It could help the UN system deliver effective global governance, especially in the fields of sustainable development, poverty reduction, security and peace. It could also enhance its cooperation with the UN in three areas: shaping policy at the UN, cooperation on the ground and EU support to help the UN meet its commitments.

Bibliography on external relations

- ARIKAN Harun. *Turkey and the EU: an awkward candidate for EU membership?* Aldershot; Burlington: Ashgate, 2006.
- BLOCKMANS Steven, LAZOWSKI Adam. *The European Union and its neighbours: a legal appraisal of the EU's policies of stabilisation, partnership and integration.* The Hague: T.M.C. Asser Press, 2006.
- CROCI Osvaldo, VERDUN Amy (eds.). *The Transatlantic divide: foreign and security policies in the Atlantic Alliance from Kosovo to Iraq.* Manchester: Manchester University Press, 2006.
- DAALDER Ivo, GNESOTTO Nicole, GORDON Philip. *Crescent of crisis: U.S.-European strategy for the greater Middle East.* Washington: Brookings Institution Press; Paris: European Union Institute for Security Studies, 2006.
- DODINI <ichael, FANTINI Marco. "The EU neighbourhood policy: implications for economic growth and stability" in *Journal of Common Market Studies*, v. 44, n. 3, September 2006, p. 507-532.
- DREVET Jean-François. "L'Union européenne et ses périphéries" in *Futuribles*, n. 321, juillet-août 2006, p. 67-92.
- DYKMANN Klaas. *Perceptions and politics: the foreign relations of the European Union with Latin America.* Frankfurt am Main: Vervuert; Madrid : Iberoamericana, 2006.
- EUROPEAN COMMISSION. *The European Union, Latin America and the Caribbean: a strategic partnership.* Luxembourg: EUR-OP*, 2006.

- GRANIEN Ronald. "Allies and other strangers: European integration and the American 'Empire by invitation'" in *Orbis*, v. 50, n. 4, Fall 2006, p. 691-707.
- HERMAN Lior. "An action plan or a plan for action?: Israel and the European Neighbourhood Policy" in *Mediterranean politics*, v. 11, n. 3, November 2006, p. 371-394.
- KARP Jeffrey, BOWLER Shaun. "Broadening and deepening or broadening versus deepening: the question of enlargement and Europe's 'hesitant Europeans'" in *European Journal of Political Research*, v. 45, n. 3, May 2006, p. 369-390.
- LARRABEE Stephen. "Danger and opportunity in Eastern Europe" in *Foreign Affairs*, v. 85, n. 6, November-December 2006, p. 117-131.
- LEPESANT Gilles. "La politique européenne de voisinage: une intégration par les normes de l'Ukraine à l'espace européen ?" in *Revue d'études comparatives Est-Ouest*, v. 37, n. 4, décembre 2006, p. 213-242.
- MEN Jing. "Chinese perceptions of the European Union: a review of leading Chinese journals" in *European Law Journal*, v. 12, n. 6, November 2006, p. 788-806.
- PILEGAARD Jess (et al.). "Multidimensional security" in *Studia diplomatica*, v. 59, n. 1, 2006, p. 117-181.
- PROZOROV Sergei. *Understanding conflict between Russia and the EU: the limits of integration.* Basingstoke: Palgrave Macmillan, 2006.
- REHN Oli. *Europe's next frontiers.* Baden-Baden: Nomos; München: Centrum für angewandte Politikforschung, 2006.
- VAHL Marius, GROLIMUND Nina. *Integration without membership: Switzerland's bilateral agreements with the European Union.* Brussels: Centre for European Policy Studies, 2006.
- VAN ROOZENDAAL Gerda. "Regional policy in the Americas: the EU experience as a guide for north-south integration?" in *Intereconomics*, v. 41, n. 3, May-June 2006, p. 159-168.
- ZABOROWSKI Marcin (ed.). *Friends again ?: EU-US relations after the crisis.* Paris: Institute for Security Studies, 2006.

The publications of the Office for Official Publications of the European Communities (EUR-OP) exist usually in all official languages of the EU.

Conclusions

EUROPEAN INTEGRATION AND ITS PERSPECTIVES

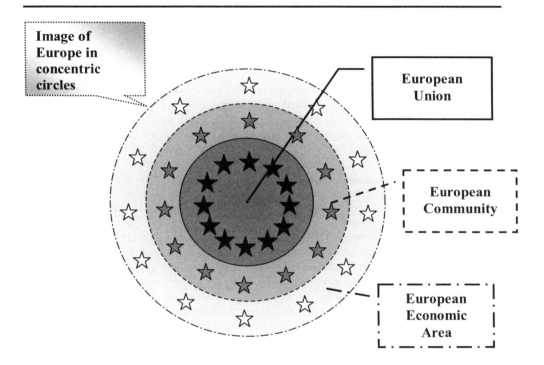

Image of Europe in concentric circles

European Union

European Community

European Economic Area

Europe's history relates in the main the wars for the domination of some nations over the others and the battles of those others for their liberation from their oppressor or oppressors. After centuries of incessant wars, recurring aggressions, revolutions, massacres, human sacrifices, genocides, material destructions, economic disasters, Europe arrived in the middle of the last century at the most devastating war of world history, the economic downfall of all European nations and the world supremacy of a non-European power. Fortunately, however, right after the Second World War, some inspired politicians, like Schuman, Adenauer, De Gasperi and Spaak, realised that the European nations, which had just ruined each other in a nonsensical war for the enlargement of their economic space, were in fact parts of **a single geographic, economic and political entity**, that could guarantee the prosperity of all in a single market.

Realists rather than idealists, those wise political leaders were fully aware of the difficulties of uniting Europe. The famous declaration of Robert Schuman of the 9th May 1950, inspired by Jean Monnet, was clear as to the step by step approach to be followed for European integration. The realisation of a customs union would fulfil the requirements for building a large common market and this would in turn establish the conditions and exert the pressures needed for the attainment of an economic and monetary union. This close economic integration would eventually necessitate a common foreign policy. Thus, political integration would follow the economic one.

Fifty years after the "invitation to union" of Robert Schuman we may say with confidence that the expectations of the fathers of European unification have been largely fulfilled. The European Community/Union has built the three first floors of its edifice – the customs union, the common market and economic and monetary union – and although work is still needed and done daily on them, it has started building the last floor, that of political union. Work at the one wing of this floor, that of home and judicial policy, is advancing satisfactorily. The big question is if and when will work get started on the wing of foreign and security policy.

The work already accomplished qualifies the European model as a **success story**. Multinational integration has established peace in Western Europe, has turned the former enemies into good partners, has secured the equality of all participating nations under common laws, has ensured development opportunities and thus the relative prosperity of all. In short, the European Community/Union has become an island of peace and prosperity in a world that is, unfortunately, still suffering from skilfully cultivated ethnic, racial, religious and other differences, battles for the glory of warmongers, the slaughter and displacement of populations for ethnic and/or economic reasons and, finally, the exploitation of the vast majority of mankind by an unscrupulous minority, equally distributed among various nations.

Unfortunately, despite the fantastic progress of science and technology during the previous century, civilisation has not much advanced in the world. Indeed, if "Civilisation" is taken to mean an advanced system of human values and social development guaranteeing peace, freedom of opinion and welfare for all persons, civilisation is not yet enjoyed by a huge part of mankind. In this sense of civilisation, multinational integration may be considered the **most important socio-political invention since the invention of democracy**, because it spreads and consolidates the values of the latter: the rule of law, the separation of the state from religion, freedom of initiative, equality of nations and individuals, well distributed welfare for all regions and social categories. These capital socio-political discoveries, which go hand in hand (since the concept of integration is inseparable from that of democracy) [see section 1.1.2.], were made on European soil. It is true that Europe also invented colonialism, fascism, anti-semitism and bolshevism and other "isms", but these bad inventions ended in failures and are currently disavowed by the immense majority of Europeans. On the other hand, Europeans have a vital reason to promote the models of democracy, humanism and integration, that they have developed and are still improving, to the nations that are torn apart and starving, exploited by demagogues and plutocrats without scruples carrying all kinds of fanciful banners and propagating myths stirring the hatred of others. The reason is the protection of their own safety and wellbeing against all these false prophets.

In this book we have tried to throw light on all aspects of the phenomenon called multinational integration, which is complicated and difficult to understand even for those who are involved in it. The sad fact is that, because of the complex nature of the integration process and the lack of adequate edification, the citizens of the Member States do not realise that they take part in an experiment that may change for the better not only their own lives but also the course of history. If they did realise the potential of the multinational integration process, they would better accept the hurdles that it has to overcome and they would better appreciate its accomplishments. By presenting all the achievements of the integration process to date, our objective was not advertising **the success story of European integration** in order to embellish its institutions, which are far from perfect, but scrutinising the phenomenon in order to infer certain conclusions concerning its possible evolution and dissemination to other parts of the world. In what follows, we will try to assess the main findings of the study and propose some estimates concerning the advancement of the evolutionary process of multinational integration.

1. Main facts regarding European integration

The course of the multinational integration process in the European Community/Union is determined by **three currents that converge at certain points** and strengthen the main flow: (a) the increasing number of the participants; (b) the continuous raising of their goals through the passage from one integration stage to another; and (c) the constant increase of their activities by the development of common policies. It is worth recapitulating the main findings of our study on these major trends of European integration.

The membership has kept growing together with the tasks assumed by the team. The multinational integration process began in 1951 as a customs union concerning only the coal and steel sectors of six countries on the basis of the ECSC Treaty. In 1958, these same countries extended the operation of the customs union and of the common market to all the sectors of their economies, thanks to the EEC Treaty. In 1973, they were joined by three countries, which had originally preferred intergovernmental cooperation inside a free trade area. In 1992, the builders of the common market had become twelve, had completed the work on that stage of their integration on the basis of the Single European Act and had signed the Treaty of Maastricht leading them to the next stage of their integration [see sections 2.2 and 6.1]. In 1995, the builders of the union were joined by three more states, which had originally believed in the benefits of the free trade area. At the dawn of the 21st century, the fifteen were finalising their economic and monetary union [see section 7.2.3], were progressing in their political union thanks to the Treaty of Amsterdam [see section 8.2] and were opening the door of their enterprise to ten more states [see section 1.2].

Despite the successive enlargements, the multinational integration process in Europe has followed **a steady evolution in stages of ever closer economic convergence** - customs union, common market, economic and monetary union - and is proceeding towards the final stage of political union. The **customs union**, nowadays taken for granted and almost forgotten, formed the solid foundation of the entire European edifice. The problem-free removal of customs barriers to trade filled the apprentices of European construction with the enthusiasm necessary for climbing up the steep and unfamiliar road of integration [see section 5.1.1.]. The stage of the **common market**, completed in 1992, meant the freedom of movement within the single market of goods, persons, services and capital [see chapter 6]. These freedoms revolutionised trade and competition, the working methods and the economic conditions in the Member States of the Community. The reduction of administrative and financial costs of intra-Community trade and the realisation of economies of scale liberated the dynamism and the creativity of European businessmen and gave them a solid foothold from which to sustain international competitiveness [see section 6.2.].

In December 1991 in Maastricht, the Member States decided to initiate the next stage of their integration, viz. **economic and monetary union (EMU)**, implying a single monetary policy, necessary for the management of a single currency, and the convergence of national economic policies, with a view to achieving economic and social cohesion. EMU was based on the common market in goods and services, but itself served the proper functioning of the common market, by eliminating exchange rate variations between Member States' currencies, which hindered the interpenetration of capital markets, disturbed the common agricultural market and prevented the common industrial market from wholly resembling an internal market. This stage of the integration process was completed with the successful circulation of the euro, on 1st January 2002, just ten years after its conception.

At the same time that they designed their monetary integration, in Maastricht, the Member States decided to coordinate their non-economic policies as well, i.e.: justice and home affairs policies, in order to achieve a common area of freedom, security and justice; and their foreign and security policies, so that the economic giant that they were creating through economic integration would have a voice commensurate with its size in the international arena [see section 2.3.and chapter 8]. They have, thus, reached the threshold of **political integration**; but although the new common policies in the political field were given a boost with the Treaty of Amsterdam, foreign and security policy is still detached from the prime objective of the EC/EU: an **"ever closer union among the peoples of Europe"**.

The preceding summary of events and trends demonstrates the **extraordinary success of the multinational integration process** as practised in Europe since the early 1950s. This success was due to the construction method taught by Monnet and Schuman, which is that of a step by step advance after careful evaluation of the previous experience. Brick upon brick, act after act, as taught by the old masters, the European edifice has been built up and is still expanding. Every new measure fits so well into the adjoining provisions that it fills a gap while consolidating the whole structure [see section 3.1.]. In fact, the successful formula of European integration is based on **common policies** built by **common institutions** following the **Community method** [see section 1.1.2.]. These three ingredients of the integration formula, amply brought out in the various chapters of this book, merit some concluding observations.

In the introduction of this book, we made the hypothesis that the fundamental elements of the multinational integration process are **common policies** pursuing common goals and **serving common interests** [see section 1.1.2.]. We supposed that the supreme interests of the citizens of the participating states are the assurance of peace with their neighbours and the increase of their wellbeing. On the basis of the findings brought out in the book, we may assert that the common policies of the European Community/Union serve those interests well. They have transformed the former enemies into partners. War between the members of the Union has become unthinkable and the wellbeing of their citizens has greatly increased through the constant development of their economies and through the abundance of good quality products and services inside the single market. In addition, the common policies attain a great number of secondary common goals. They monitor the free exchange of industrial and agricultural goods between the Member States. They stimulate and support the development of the poorer regions of the Union. They guarantee the rights of the citizens of the Member States to travel, to live and to work wherever they choose within its territory. They facilitate the access of all citizens to the universal banking, insurance, telecommunication and audiovisual services offered in the large European market. They bolster the competitiveness of European industries by imposing uniform rules of competition and by supporting their efforts in research and development. They prepare the future by laying the foundations of the information society and of transport, energy and telecommunications trans-European networks spanning the whole Continent. They try to protect in a uniform way the environment and the consumers of the member countries. Certainly, none of these policies is perfect, but all of them are under the constant scrutiny of the common institutions and they are amended very often, in order to be adapted to the new needs that emerge from internal or external causes.

The **common policies are closely knit together** and support each other. Two horizontal policies - regional and social - pursue the objective of economic and social cohesion [see section 12.1.2.], which is linked to the objective of economic and monetary union. Such a union, implying abandonment of the use of exchange rate adjustment as a means of balance of national economies, would be to the detriment of the poorer Member States, if there was not an efficient **common regional policy** operating capital transfers from the richer to the poorer regions of the EU [see section 12.1.]. In fact, thanks to the common regional policy the standard of living in the Union's poor regions increased considerably and they recovered a great part of their disadvantages. Likewise, inside an economic and monetary union, where governments gradually lose the ability to confront separately the social problems of their peoples, since monetary and many economic decisions are taken in common [see section 13.1.], the process of social integration is pursued through common employment, vocational training and social protection policies. The **common social policy** has already built a "European social model" which guarantees, not only fundamental human rights and the democratic and pluralistic principles, but also the fundamental rights of workers: training adapted to the technical progress, fair pay allowing decent living conditions and social protection covering the hazards of life, illness, unemployment and old age [see chapter 13]. This model is the social bedrock of the European integration process.

Three other **horizontal common policies** - on taxation, competition and environment protection - ensure a level playing field for European businesses. The harmonisation of indirect taxes brought about by the common taxation policy is instrumental for levelling the competition conditions inside the single market of products and services. The common competition policy is not only a necessary instrument for the smooth functioning of the internal market, preventing new compartmentalisation by the agreements of large companies and protectionism by national administrations through national aids, but is also a complement to common sectoral policies - industrial, agricultural, energy, transport - aimed at improving production structures and achieving international competitiveness. The common environment policy is essential, both for even-handed competition between nations respecting both market laws and citizens' welfare and for the sustainable development of the European and world economy.

The large sectors of the European economy - industry, energy, transports and agriculture - are organised gradually at European level by the legislation of the single market and by specific legislation adopted in the context of **sectoral common policies** [see Part V]. In fact, the freedoms of the common market apply to the businesses of those sectors, either directly or through sector-specific adaptations. The sectoral common policies are therefore necessary for the smooth functioning of the customs union, the common market and the economic and monetary union. Both horizontal and sectoral policies, including research and development, strive to boost the international competitiveness of European businesses, while cementing the economic integration of the States of the Union.

The economies of the member states are greatly influenced by common policies. As these economies are gradually opened up to multinational trade and competition, **all economic parameters change**: trade increases enormously within the large internal market, both supply and demand conditions are modified dramatically, state intervention is curbed and new dynamics are set in motion, notably concerning trade and investment opportunities, mergers and joint ventures. The creation and/or extension of multinational companies and the cross investments between them tend to connect the national economies to one another. The common policies build, in fact, a new concept and context of political economy, which has to be reckoned with by politicians, economists and businessmen.

This is not to say that multinational integration has solved all the economic and social problems of the Member States. It cannot do so by itself. **Integration is only an instrument** for building an internal market by consensual methods between formerly antagonistic nations. This large internal market is useful for developing trade and other transactions between the Member States and through them for raising the standards of living of the populations concerned. It is also necessary for providing businesses with conditions of competition similar to those prevailing in other competing large markets, notably the US, Japan, China and India. Upon the internal market was built the European social model, i.e. high standards of social protection for the populations taking part in the integration process. But this social model is more and more threatened by nations practicing social dumping, i.e. providing workers with hardly the means of subsistence and low or no social protection. The internal market and the single currency have placed more than 60% of European agricultural, industrial and commercial transactions outside this wild competition; but for transactions with the rest of the world, Europe must find common answers to the common problem of preserving high social standards, while competing with countries with lower or no such standards at all. In a common market where products from third countries can enter a port in one Member State and therefrom find their way to the markets of all the others, the solution to the common problem can only be found in common economic and commercial policies. This is a major challenge facing European political leaders.

The **rejection of the Constitutional Treaty** by the citizens of two founding members of the European Community/Union, the citizens of France and the Netherlands, on 29 May and 1 June 2005 respectively, has certainly brought a crisis to the functioning of the institutions and to the progress of the integration process. But this crisis is probably temporary. The major reason for this optimistic presumption is that, contrary to what is believed or hoped by eurosceptics, the European Union cannot become a simple free trade area run by a loose intergovernmental cooperation. It has already advanced well into the integration stages of the customs union, the common market and the economic and monetary union. It has already achieved an impressive "acquis communautaire", i.e. common legislation that binds the Member States together. The great majority of the political and economic elite of these States are convinced that the European integration model works and gives better results than a free trade area like the EFTA, which is practically absorbed into the EC/EU. The citizens of these States enjoy the freedoms and the social protection that the European model provides. In their great majority, the citizens of most European countries want European integration to advance to the stage of political union, through the realisation of an effective common foreign and security policy. All these facts show that the majority of Europeans want to move forward, not backward.

Moreover, all common policies function normally and require everyday decisions to be taken by the institutions. Even if decision-making is admittedly difficult in the current institutional and legal context, economic, societal and political needs require that decisions be taken. The very fact that decision-making is difficult in the EU of twenty-seven Member States exerts a pressure on these States to find a solution to the current crisis by amending the Treaty of Nice or, better, by adopting a viable Constitution as suggested below.

2. European perspectives

Common policies, as all other public policies, are there to meet the societal needs which arise in a defined community of nations at a given time. Therefore, not only the objectives which the member states set for each common policy, but the means which they give to the common institutions to attain them and the measures which the latter adopt to implement them change in accordance with the economic, political and social needs which the participant states experience at a certain time. In the case of the EC/EU, the common policies are **in permanent evolution**, demonstrated, for all of them, by the constant amendment of the Community laws (regulations, directives, etc.) that form them, and, for some of them (e.g., agricultural, regional, social and research policies), by the amendment of the Treaty provisions that concern them. Moreover, a common policy tends to spill over onto other common policies, to produce needs, to cause reactions and to nourish their development.

The constant evolution of all common policies, a fact brought out in each new edition of this book, causes the endless evolution of the multinational integration process. In fact, the development of common policies creates ever-stronger economic and political links between the peoples of Europe. Paradoxically, the constant progress of integration in all fields demonstrates both the soundness and the imperfection of the Community model. An organisation and a process that are in a state of permanent evolution can never be perfect. They can only be improved constantly. The "**constant progress syndrome**" is the strong point and the permanent challenge of the European model of integration. It means that the European Union will normally keep developing all the time, trying to reach an integration ideal that it will never attain, since ideals, by definition, cannot be completely achieved.

Although, due to the constant progress syndrome, the common policies examined in this book are all expected to develop in range and improve in efficiency over time, two are practically inexistent: a common information policy and a common foreign and security policy. Both these failures are due to the reluctance of the Member States to entrust the common institutions with large scale tasks in these fields. They both cause the frustration of the citizens of the Union and endanger the very existence of the European integration model.

The absence of a common information policy results in the **information deficit** of the European Union, i.e. a deficiency of reliable information, readily available to the citizens, concerning European affairs and the integration process. Due to the information deficit, most citizens ignore or take for granted the positive and palpable effects of European integration, such as the customs free availability of goods from all over Europe, border free travel and, above all, peace and friendship among their erstwhile bellicose nations. They are unaware of the extent to which they are surrounded by the workings of the Union in their daily and professional lives [see sections 10.1. and 10.4.].

It is strange to see that the Member States, which have developed a great number of common policies in all fields examined in this book, have neglected to set up a common policy for presenting the goals and measures of those policies to their citizens. The neglect of information and/or communication is probably due to a bad habit carried over from the early days of European integration, when the common policies under development were too technical to really interest the citizens. Now, however, the citizens feel that the Union is influencing their lives and regret to be left in the dark by the European institutions and by their own political leaders as to its workings. They show their indignation about this state of affairs in European elections, referendums and opinion polls. The information deficit is, indeed, more responsible for the estrangement of the citizens from the European integration process than the much decried democratic deficit [see sections 9.5. and 10.1.]. It is also worsening even as the integration process is deepening and encompassing an ever-growing number of economic, societal and political sectors.

The information deficit endangers the integration process. If the citizens were led to believe that the disadvantages of integration were greater than its benefits, they might be led to press their political leaders to disengage their country or countries from the integration process or, worse, to halt this process altogether. If we consider the effects of the information deficit on some referenda, in the past (the Danish concerning the Treaty of Maastricht, the Irish concerning the Treaty of Nice and the French and Dutch concerning the Constitutional Treaty), this scenario is not as absurd as it seems at first sight. In a community of people, where a silent majority has no interest in the common affairs and goals, while a determined minority is strongly opposed to its objectives and institutions, there is a strong probability that the minority group would tend to grow over time and to become stronger and ever more convinced of its ideas and ideals. Unopposed by the silent majority, it might thus eventually succeed in reversing the working system that holds the community together. This danger should be taken seriously into consideration by the Heads of State or Government, who in a declaration on the ratification of the Treaty establishing a Constitution for Europe made on 17 June 2005, after the negative referendums in France and the Netherlands, stated that: European integration "…has enabled us to ensure the well-being of citizens, the defence of our values and our interests, and to assume our responsibilities as a leading international player".

Not only all governments but also all major political parties, which are generally pro-integration, should recognize that the information deficit combined with a systematic disinformation on the part of some europhobic media is undermining the common policies that they want to carry through, is debasing the democratic institutions set up and empowered by them to implement those common policies and is halting the progress of European integration. In other words, the political elite should acknowledge that a common information policy, which might have been a luxury as long as the integration process was confined to customs and technical matters, is a necessity now that the process is spreading ever more from the purely economic to the political field. Just as the Union is incorporating ten more Member States, whose citizens are even less informed about the goals, the means and the achievements of the integration process than the citizens of the erstwhile Fifteen, it is high time for the European institutions to forsake the old habits of discretion and neglect of the citizens' opinion. In chapter 10 we called for the inauguration of **a common information and communication policy**, covering all the activities of the European institutions and implemented by a European Press Agency in close cooperation with the governments of the Member States [see section 10.1.3.]. Such a common communication policy, combined with the civic education of young Europeans at school, would bring the citizens closer to the Union and would secure the achievements of all the other common policies.

A paradoxical effect of the information deficit and the absence of civic education on European integration is that, while citizens seem to be indifferent to the European Union, they simultaneously expect ever more important results from it. This is notably the case concerning the **European presence on the world stage**, the second serious flaw of the European edifice. Eurobarometer surveys indicate constantly over a long period of years that two out of three Europeans believe that the European Union should have an effective common foreign policy [see introduction to chapter 10]. Three out of four citizens of the Twenty-five back a really common security and defence policy. These and many more specific findings of the opinion polls indicate that Europeans fail to understand how the economic giant that they have created, the most important power in international trade, now endowed with the strongest currency in the world, cannot make its voice heard in the world arena. They expect the Union to take the lead in monitoring regional conflicts, globalisation, environmental challenges and famines in the world. The tragic inability of the Union to prevent the Balkan wars at its doorstep or to enforce the rules of international law in the resolution of conflicts in the Middle East has greatly reduced the respect of Europeans for their common institutions. Public reasoning is quite simple: as long as the Union cannot act as a mature political giant, it cannot be respected. It is time for the infant giant to grow up.

The citizens' expectations for a powerful Union in the world include the dissemination and defence of the European ideals of peace, welfare, democracy, the rule of law and social protection on the world stage. Europe is open to the world and its citizens understand that they cannot live merrily in a prosperous island surrounded by the misery and envy of other nations. They understand that, for their own peace and security, the Union should contribute more to peace and sustainable development in the world. Europeans know as well that they cannot prevent the new technologies and free enterprise from shrinking the world to the virtual dimensions of a village; but they feel that this, as any village, should have a town hall and that they should have their representatives inside it. In other words, they expect the Union to play **an active role in the globalisation phenomenon** by enhancing the legitimacy and effectiveness of international institutions, notably the United Nations Organisation and its specialised agencies, so that these may impose the law in the fields of peace, durable development, social protection, commerce and competition. We have seen in part VI, that the EU is in the right track in some of these fields; but power sharing between the Community and the Union and between both of them and the Member States diminishes the potential of all in promoting their shared values to the rest of the world.

There is no doubt that the vast majority of European citizens want their integration to step up to the **stage of political union**, including a strong and independent foreign policy and an even stronger and more independent security and defence policy. Why do citizens understand that in an era of integration, globalisation and world predominance of a superpower, national sovereignty in matters of foreign policy and security has no real meaning, while their political leaders do not understand it? Because, for the later, national sovereignty is closely related to their own power, which they do not want to share with their partners, even though this power, in the present geopolitical environment, is waning all the time and only unity can bolster it.

One might suppose that the common foreign and security policy could develop as other common policies have developed in the past. There is, however, a fundamental difference between the common foreign and security policy and the common policies of the Community. Whereas the latter are governed by the Community method of decision-making [see section 4.3.], **the CFSP depends on intergovernmental cooperation**. This means that unanimity is required to make decisions in these fields, that the European Parliament does not participate in the decision-making process, that the Commission is not required to execute the decisions taken by the Council and that the Court of Justice is not competent to settle disputes and enforce the implementation of the decisions taken. Thanks to the intergovernmental method of the CFSP, any Member State may block a common position or common action on an important matter, thus frustrating the will of all the others. Moreover, any Member State may eventually disengage itself from a decision taken, thus thwarting a common action agreed upon. Obviously, the foreign and security policy cannot become "common" as long as it depends on intergovernmental cooperation.

The (now unlikely) coming into force of the **Constitutional Treaty** would slightly improve the decision making procedure of the CFSP, but would not change fundamentally its intergovernmental character. The draft Constitution provides for a Union Minister for Foreign Affairs, who should be Vice-President of the Commission and who should contribute by his proposals to the development of the common foreign policy, which he should carry out as mandated by the Council of Ministers (Art. I-28). The European Union should conduct a common foreign and security policy, based on the development of mutual political solidarity among Member States, the identification of questions of general interest and the achievement of an ever-increasing degree of convergence of Member States' actions (Art. I-40, 1). Before undertaking any action on the international scene or any commitment which could affect the Union's interests, each Member State should consult the others within the European Council or the Council of Ministers. Member States should ensure, through the convergence of their actions, that the Union is able to assert its interests and values on the international scene (Art. I-40, 5). The common security and defence policy should include the progressive framing of a common Union defence policy. This should lead to a common defence, when the European Council, acting unanimously, so decides (Art. I-41,2). Until then, closer cooperation should be established, in the Union framework, as regards mutual defence. Under this cooperation, if one of the Member States participating in such cooperation is the victim of armed aggression on its territory, the other participating States should give it aid and assistance by all the means in their power, military or other, in accordance with Article 51 of the United Nations Charter (Art. I-41, 7).

These provisions seem to be good enough; but, **the unanimity rule still prevails** in the draft Constitution concerning the CFSP. This draft excludes the ordinary legislative procedure in matters of the so-called common foreign and security policy, while it requires it in matters concerning all other common policies of the Union. In fact, European decisions relating to CFSP should be adopted by the European Council and the Council of Ministers unanimously, except when they are implementing decisions of the European Council taken unanimously or if the European Council unanimously decides that the Council of Ministers should act by qualified majority (Art. I-40, 6,7). All this means that, if the Constitutional Treaty was adopted, the CFSP would still be run by intergovernmental procedure and no common action or position could be taken, should one or just a few countries not want it. Hence, the Constitutional Treaty in suspension would do nothing much in order to render the foreign and security policy really common.

Moreover, the unanimity rule prevails for the ratification of the draft Constitution itself and for its possible amendments. The Treaty signed in October 2004 provides in fact that it should enter into force after being ratified by **all the High Contracting Parties** in accordance with their respective constitutional requirements (Art. IV-447). Worse, even the revision of the Constitutional Treaty - necessary for the continuous development of the Union [see section 2.6] - would require ratification by all the Member States. This draft Treaty provides, in fact, that, if two years after the signature of the Treaty amending it, four fifths of the Member States had ratified it and one or more Member States had encountered **difficulties in proceeding with ratification**, the matter should be referred to the European Council (Art. IV-443, 4). The same provision appears as a declaration of the Intergovernmental Conference annexed to the Constitutional Treaty in case of problems encountered in the ratification of this draft Treaty. But, what could the European Council do in this case, which is actual concerning the draft Constitution itself? The probable answer is that the government, which would have encountered difficulties with ratification because of a negative vote of its parliament or of a negative outcome of a referendum, would not be disposed to persuasion inside the European Council, since it would be ensnared in a matter of constitutional order. Hence, both for the ratification of the Constitutional Treaty itself and for that of its future amendments, the problem of one or a few government(s), would become the problem of all, since they would not be able to put into force the Treaty that they would have signed.

This means that, even if and when the Constitutional Treaty were adopted, the CFSP would be run by intergovernmental procedure and could never become a really common policy by an amendment of this Treaty, should one or just a few countries not want it. This stumbling block in the way of a real common foreign and security policy is placed by the politicians negotiating the treaties against the will of their citizens, who in their large majority want such a policy. Whatever eurosceptic circles may say to the contrary, this is **democratic deficit par excellence**, i.e. disregard of the will of the people concerning the political maturity of their union. The democratic way would give the peoples of the European Union the possibility to pronounce themselves as to whether they want to have a real and effective common foreign and security policy or not. Of course, this way is not as easy as it sounds.

To become a really common policy, the CFSP should be integrated into the Community pillar governed by the Community decision-making process or, better still, **the construction of the Union in pillars should be abandoned** and the Union should be considered as a single structure. The European Commission should be involved in the CFSP both at the stage of the initiative for common action and at the stage of execution of the decisions taken by the decision-making authorities. The European Parliament should be involved in decision-making, both by giving its agreement on the common strategies launched by the European Council and by laying down European laws and framework laws with the Council of Ministers. European strategies and European laws and framework laws should be taken by qualified majority, although this could be formed on levels higher than those applying to other common policies, in order to ensure that a vast majority of the Member States, representing a great majority of the population of the Union agrees on a common strategy or a common action in the field of the CFSP. However, it is practically certain that not all the Member States of the actual EU would be willing to confer on the Union the competences necessary for building a genuine common foreign and security policy. Experience to date shows that if the public opinion in some countries is negative on an issue, e.g. the common currency, then, even if they want to, the politicians of those countries cannot follow the common march [see section 7.2.3]. Hence, in a Community/Union of twenty-seven states, it is quite probable that one government, one parliament or a referendum in one country may stop the march of all the others by vetoing the amendment of a treaty (be it named constitutional or otherwise)

The question arises consequently: the Member States whose citizens aspire for a really common foreign and security policy should be **eternally blocked by their partners** who prefer to guard their national prerogatives rather than unite their forces in order to build a superpower able to better serve their common interests? The probable answer is that sooner or later a number of states, under the pressure of their citizens, would like to gain their freedom to proceed at the stage of integration of the political union and to thus establish a truly common foreign and security policy. It is probable that this would be the group of states, which would have a single currency on top of the single market. In fact, the interests of those states would become ever more common and it is natural that sooner rather than later they would feel the need to defend them in common by a genuine common foreign and security policy.

The subsidiary question to the one above is: given the unanimity rule required for the amendment of the Treaty on the European Union, how the Member States of the EU, which would want to advance towards the stage of the political union, could do it, if some of the signatories of this Treaty would oppose the concessions of national sovereignties necessary for taking this step? There are two possible answers to this question. The relatively easier but limited way for building a common foreign and security policy would be by the enhanced cooperation of some Member States, provided for by the actual Treaty of Nice and reinforced by the Constitutional Treaty. The more difficult but sturdier way of proceeding towards the political union of Europe would be by **a Constitution democratically drafted and adopted**, which would engage only the Member States which would have signed and ratified it. Let us consider these two possibilities.

Enhanced cooperation in the field of the common foreign and security policy is facilitated by the Treaty of Nice [see sections 4.3 and 8.1.2.] and even more so by the draft Constitution. The latter provides that authorisation to proceed with enhanced cooperation should be granted by the Council of Ministers as a last resort, when it has been established within the Council of Ministers that the objectives of such cooperation could not be attained within a reasonable period by the Union as a whole, and provided that it would bring together at least one third of the Member States (Art. I-44, 2). Still, authorisation to proceed with enhanced cooperation should be granted by a European decision of the Council acting unanimously (Art. III-419). In plain words, if at least one third of the Member States felt the need to build a real common foreign and security policy among themselves, they would still need the **authorisation of the governments of the rest of their partners** to do so. Only in the unlikely case that they would succeed in obtaining this authorisation, they would surpass the ratification hurdle and would pioneer the way into political integration.

There is no doubt that it would be much better, if all European states agreed to advance towards their political union by waves; but such an agreement could only be sanctioned by a **new European Constitution**, which would go beyond the actual draft Constitutional Treaty in the domain of the CFSP and would allow its ratification by willing states. The experience of the stillborn Constitutional Treaty should lead the debate on a viable European Constitution. The faults committed in the drafting and the handing-over of this Treaty to the people should be avoided. Therefore, the citizens of the Member States should be involved through their representatives in the drafting of the Constitution. This Constitution should satisfy the aspirations of European peoples to see their Union becoming a major actor on the international stage. It should reinforce the institutional framework of the Union so that the latter could function effectively in an increasingly complex internal and external environment. It should be put at ratification in a homogeneous way in all member countries by a referendum organised the same day in all Member States, after adequate explanation of its contents. Last but not least, the Constitution should provide that only willing nations should adopt it and offer an alternative for those that would not want to do so. Let us examine in detail these suggestions.

The drafting of the European Constitution should be entrusted to **a constituent assembly convened for this purpose**. Such an assembly would have the legitimacy necessary to give a vigorous impulse to the European construction. An authority representing all the nations of the EU should, of course, take the initiative to convene the constituent assembly. The European Council could probably not be such an authority. There are two converging reasons, which would prevent it from taking such an initiative. The first is the natural tendency of political leaders to fear a revolution in the good habits of European construction, a revolution which could oblige them to give up portions of their powers in foreign and security policies to supranational institutions. The other reason which would block the European Council from taking this initiative would be the unanimity rule that governs its work and that would hinder the most innovating political leaders to overcome the reluctance of their more conservative colleagues.

Therefore, another European authority should take the initiative of convening a constituent assembly. **This authority could be the European Parliament**. It represents all the peoples of the Union and it is not handicapped by the unanimity rule. It could vote a resolution for the convening of a constituent assembly by the majority of its members, a majority which, if it were important, could be quite impressive. In fact, the European Parliament would have nothing to lose and much to gain from a Constitution which would give it more legislative powers and better control of the European executive power, including in the field of the foreign and security policy. If it took the initiative to call for a constituent assembly, the political leaders of Europe would have much difficulty to oppose it, because the public opinion in all the Member States would certainly be favourable to the idea. The citizens would indeed have what they want, the possibility to express themselves on the future of Europe and on the place of their country in the European construction. By calling for a constituent assembly, the Parliament would thus gain in prestige. Its role could be even more important, if it was called to form the constituent assembly. This assembly could indeed be convened expressly for the task of drafting the European Constitution and be composed by representatives elected for this sole purpose. But it could also be composed by the members of the European Parliament elected by the peoples of the Union with this specific mandate on top of their normal legislative mission.

In any case, before the election of the members of the assembly, a large public debate should take place in all Member States on the initiative of political parties, which would present their candidates for this election. Logically, the two fundamental questions which would dominate this debate would be: (1) if Europe should advance towards the last stage of its integration, the political union, or keep the status quo; and (2) how it should move on to this stage – by waiting for all the partners to decide to advance or by allowing the majority to lead the way? The candidates for the election to the assembly should expose their position on these options as well as on all the big issues of European politics, notably those concerning free competition and social protection, which seem contradictory to citizens, as demonstrated by the French referendum. The majority of the assembly would thus be constituted by europhilic or eurosceptic members independently of their traditional political preferences. Of course, these preferences would also direct the debates in the assembly on many issues, such as the guaranty of human rights in the context of the fight against terrorism, social protection or free competition, which should be regulated by the Constitution.

The constituent assembly would establish working groups, which would draft the provisions on the various chapters of the Constitution, this being structured in a body of fundamental provisions and appendices describing the details. The assembly in plenary session would discuss these partial drafts as well as the amendments suggested both by dissenting members of each editorial group and by other members not participating in the group having written the particular draft. The assembly would thus adopt chapter by chapter by the simple majority of the voters a first draft of the whole Constitution. In its broad lines this new draft could follow that of 2004, since this one was agreed by the governments of all the Member States. It should, however, answer the two fundamental questions which would have dominated the campaign for the election of the members of the constituent assembly: the promotion of the foreign and security policy in a real common policy; and the signature and ratification of the Constitution and of its possible amendments by a majority rather than by all the Member States.

If the majority of the assembly were constituted by eurosceptic members, it could vote for the negative alternatives on these important questions and, thus, bring to a halt the integration process. It is a risk to be taken, in view of a democratic deliberation on fundamental questions for the future of Europe. But, the popular vote could as well carry to the assembly a europhilic majority, an assumption, which taking into account the opinion polls, is most probable. On this assumption, the majority of the assembly would be able to honour the popular mandate which it would have received to reinforce and accelerate the process of integration, in particular by advances in the field of the foreign and security policy. It could in particular replace the intergovernmental cooperation which currently governs it, including the rule of the unanimity in decision-making, by the ordinary integration procedure, which governs the real common policies, i.e. by decision-making with qualified majority and by the implication of all the common institutions in these decisions and their execution. The other fundamental provision which could be registered in the Constitution by a europhilic majority of the constituent assembly would be **the signature and the ratification** of this Constitution and of its possible amendments **by a reinforced majority**, for example the four fifths of the Member States representing four fifths of the population of the Union. This provision would free the European Union from the undemocratic yoke of the unanimity – by virtue of which the stance of only one can thwart the will of all the others - and would allow it to progress without encumbers on the way of an ever increasing integration.

The constituent assembly would adopt the first draft of the Constitution by the simple majority of its members and would submit it to the European Council, the other European institutions and the national parliaments, inviting them to discuss it and to give it, within a reasonable time, their comments, in particular on the provisions of the preliminary draft concerning them. At the end of this period, the assembly would discuss the amendments suggested by the various European and national authorities and would vote the final draft of the Constitution, which it would submit to the European Council. The draft would be adopted by the European Council following the stipulations of the relevant article of the draft Constitution. These conditions would obviously depend on the majority of the assembly, either eurosceptic or europhilic. On the assumption that the draft Constitution would have been written by a europhilic majority of the assembly, the article concerning the signature of the Constitution would allow a reinforced majority of the Heads of State or government to adopt the draft and to subject it to a referendum in all the Member States.

This **referendum should be held the same day in all the countries of the Union** so that the results obtained in a country could not influence the citizens of the other Member States. If they held account of the lessons of the past, the heads of State or government would not invite their citizens to read and to approve the complex legal instrument which would necessarily be the draft Constitution. Instead of subjecting it in its entirety to the approval or the disapproval of the citizens, the governments should offer them a small information paper describing in a non-legal language the new elements contained in the constitutional project compared to the existing Treaties. The governments which would have signed the Constitution should explain to their peoples why they had agreed on the project and ask them **three alternative questions**: (1) if they would approve the plan for the future envisaged by this Constitution; or (2) if they would prefer the status quo based on the existing Treaties; or (3) if they would like to see their country leave the process of European integration. On their side, the governments which would not have signed the project should explain to their peoples the reasons of their reticence and ask them the same three questions

It is obvious that a wide-ranging debate would take place in all the Member States on the initiative of the political parties, the trade-unions and professional organisations and the civil society. Indeed, a debate on the future of a group of nations, which during centuries have played a leading role in the history of humanity, is not held every day. It is natural that this debate would not only hold the attention of the public opinion in these countries, but also in third countries. Considering the interest of the subject, the media would willingly organise the debate and give the floor to all the opinion leaders who would like to speak and to defend their arguments. This debate would thus be very open and very wide-ranging and would be held under similar conditions in all the countries of the Union. Eurosceptic circles would have an excellent occasion to advance their arguments and, if the project of Constitution were accepted by the majority of the peoples, they could not argue any more that European construction is done by technocrats without the knowledge of the citizens.

The scenario described above can have three possible ends: (a) that all the peoples scrutinised by referendum approve the adoption of the Constitution of the Union; (b) that the majority required by the Constitution approves the latter, while certain nations opt for the existing situation; (c) that certain nations express their wish to see their country leave the Union. Each government should follow the preference of its people, if this preference came clearly out of the ballot. If, on the other hand, the attitude of a nation were not clear, the government concerned should organise a new referendum limiting the questions to the two which would have received the greatest number of votes.

If, finally, the referendums were everywhere favourable to the Constitution, this should be ratified without delay by all the governments. It is obvious that in this case there would be no problem and that Europe could follow without encumbers the way towards its political integration. If, on the other hand, the majority required by the Constitution would have opted for it, while certain countries would have chosen the second and others the third possibility, **Europe would be divided into three concentric circles**. The first circle would comprise the countries having adopted the Constitution of the European Union. The second circle would encompass all the countries of the first circle and the countries which would have chosen the status quo, i.e. the countries which would like to continue economic integration with the countries of the EU, but would not wish to take part in the political integration envisaged by the Constitution. The third circle would include both the countries of the first two circles and the countries which would like to remain apart from the political as well as the economic integration process.

In the case that all the peoples of the Union would not have given their assent for the adoption of the Constitution, this one would come into force if it were signed and ratified by the number of Member States provided by it. It would engage these States and them only to carry out a real foreign and security policy. There would thus come into being in Europe **a core of States** pursuing their economic, monetary and political integration with the method of integration prescribed by the Constitution. This would be the first of three concentric circles grouping the European countries - the circle of the European Union.

In this circle, the **common foreign policy** could be closely united with the common commercial policy and with the aid to development policy, so that all three wings of the external action of the Union would work towards common goals by means of the so-called Community method. As is the case with other common policies, the common foreign policy would set the framework for the foreign policies of the Member States by fixing common goals, strategies, guidelines and actions that the Member States would be bound to follow. The qualified majority voting would also be applied to **European security and defence policy (ESDP)** [see section 8.2.3.], thus making it really common and effectual. The European Union can easily build up its power by bringing together the distinct and often overlapping military capabilities of the Member States. The existing military capabilities and military bodies of ESDP would only need to be strengthened and to be completely self-sufficient inside NATO. The reinforcement and independence of ESDP would make third countries take Europe seriously as a world actor.

A truly common foreign and security policy, which would be an attribute of the political union of Europe, would certainly entail new transfers of national sovereignties to the Union [see section 3.2], but would not mean the loss of the political independence of the participating states. These states **would not necessarily form a federation**. In fact, the very concept of the common policy [see section 1.1.2] excludes the concept of the single policy, which is an attribute of a federation of states. It means that a policy is built up and implemented in common by the common institutions and the governments of the Member States. By implementing a great number of common policies, the Member States of the EC/EU perform certain essential tasks of a state, without forming a single state in the traditional sense. The actual draft Constitution clearly declares that the Union shall coordinate the policies by which the Member States aim to achieve common objectives, and shall exercise in the Community basis [i.e. method] the competences they confer on it (Art I-1,1). Under the **principle of conferral**, the Union shall act within the limits of the competences conferred upon it by the Member States. Competences not conferred upon the Union in the Constitution remain with the Member States (Art. I-11, 1) [see section 3.2].

It ensues from this principle, which has been applied since the beginning of the EC/EU, that each member of the group participating in a real CFSP would keep intact its legal personality and sovereignty in all areas not placed under the common competence of the group. It could sign international agreements not conflicting with Community competence. It could keep its diplomatic representations in third countries and in international institutions. The representations of the members of the group would simply have instructions to follow the positions agreed in common, a fact that would enhance the position of the participating states in world affairs [see section 25.9]. In the field of defence as well, each member of the inner group would keep its own army, its armaments and its defence budget. The willing states would only place them under an integrated command, which would be responsible for their coordinated actions. This would not prevent separate actions, compatible with the CFSP, in case of non-agreement by the partners on a common action.

Of course, in order to play a leading role in the global scene, the European Union would need to **adapt and strengthen its institutions**. We have suggested a possible reform of the institutions in section 4.4. The members of the Commission should be proposed by the national parliaments, be elected directly by the citizens of each Member State and be nominated by the European Parliament. The President of the Commission and the Vice-president, responsible for foreign affairs, should be proposed by the simple majority of the heads of State or government (representing at least three fifths of the population of the Union) and nominated by the European Parliament. The European Parliament should invest, control and eventually dismiss a particular Commissioner or the Commission as a body. Its role in the decision-making process should be reinforced thanks not only to the extension of the co-decision procedure to all legislative matters, including the CFSP, but also to its task of coordinating and consolidating the opinions of the national parliaments, the Economic and Social Committee and the Committee of the Regions. These measures would contribute not only to the efficient functioning, but also to the democratic legitimacy of the European institutions. The citizens would feel much closer to a Commission that they would elect themselves directly and would control indirectly through their representatives in the European Parliament. Such governance would have many features of a federal character without being federal, since it would manage common policies and only that part of each common policy, which Member States would have agreed to confer to the competence of the Union.

The separation in three groups of States having more or less close relations between them would mean **a European integration at several speeds**, a situation that has been shunned until now with the result of obliging the whole group of EC/EU to march to the step of the slowest of its members. An EU Constitution, which could but should not be ratified by all the actual Member States, would solve the problem of the conduct of the integration process in a democratic manner, since each country would have the possibility of choosing the rhythm of integration which would suit better its traditions, its interests and its goals. The European States which want to advance in their union could finally do it without being slowed down by the laggards. The latter would voluntarily remain behind the leading group, but could later, if they changed opinion, run to catch up with it. They have done it in the past. They could do it again in the future.

In the second circle, the question of a fundamental charter would arise concerning the relations between the countries which would have adopted the Constitution and the **countries which would have chosen the status quo**, i.e. their participation in the economic integration but not in the political integration of Europe. The Treaty of Nice certainly could not coexist just as it is with the Constitution in order to regulate the relations between the two groups of countries. One of its two constituent parts, the Treaty on the European Union, which provides a timid outline of political integration, would not be of interest to the countries which would have decided by referendum against such integration. On the other hand, this Treaty would not make any sense for the countries of the first circle, since its provisions would be improved on by those of the Constitution, which would aim at a true political integration of the countries which would have adopted it, thanks in particular to the changeover from unanimity to qualified majority for decision-making in the field of the common foreign and security policy. Therefore, the Treaty on the EU should be repealed.

On the other hand, **the Treaty establishing the European Community** - modified so that its clauses, in particular the institutional ones, would not contradict those of the Constitution - could coexist with the latter to manage the relations of the countries which would have chosen integration up to the stage of the common market - and possibly of the economic and monetary union - between them and with the countries which would have adopted the Constitution. A modified Treaty on the European Community could thus be used as the fundamental charter for the countries of the second circle. Undoubtedly, institutional arrangements should be agreed concerning the relations between these two groups of countries of the second circle, inspired by already existing institutional arrangements concerning the monetary affairs. The legislation based both on the Constitution and on the Treaty on the European Community would be adopted by the common institutions and would be binding for all the countries of the second circle. On the contrary, the legislation based only on the Constitution, in particular relating to the common foreign and security policy, would not be binding for the countries of the second circle which would not belong to the EU, but should be applied by them too, if and when they ratified the Constitution. Meanwhile, the decisions taken by the European Union in the field of the common foreign and security policy could be applied by the countries not belonging to the EU on a purely voluntary basis.

For the countries which would choose to leave the process of integration altogether there exists an all set solution concerning the organisation of their relations with the countries of the European Union (first circle) and those of the European Community (second circle). It is offered by the **European Economic Area (EEA)**, whose Treaty signed in 1992 currently binds Norway, Iceland and the Liechtenstein with the twenty-seven States of the EU [see section 25.1]. This Treaty aims to establish a large market based on common rules and equal conditions of competition concerning the freedom of movement of goods, people, services and capital and a reinforcement of the relations between the two groups of country in fields having an impact on the activity of the companies, like consumer protection, the environment, research and technological development, education and tourism. The Treaty on the EEA could thus become the charter of the third circle of the European countries.

EEA membership could serve the objectives of the **countries which prefer a free trade area** governed by an intergovernmental cooperation rather than the process of

European integration, which entails important transfers of national sovereignty. Indeed, certain countries wished, after the Second World War and even after their accession to the EC/EU, to participate in a simple free trade area open to the two coasts of the Atlantic. They reluctantly reached the stage of the European single market, while regretting the transfers of sovereignty and the constraints necessitated by it [see section 1.2]. Their press abounds of misrepresentations of the "meddling and malevolent" bureaucracy of Brussels, which manages this market and which, according to this press, assaults their sacrosanct national sovereignty just for the pleasure of annihilating it. On the other hand, the majority of the other countries of EC/EU wanted and succeeded to reach the stage of the economic and monetary union and, by adopting the Constitution, they would show their will to advance towards their political union. The membership of all in the European Economic Area could satisfy the wishes of the ones and the others. They would have excellent trade relations with countries of the first two circles, but they would not be held by the rigours of the process of integration that the latter would wish to perfect. The relations of the countries participating in this third European concentric circle would indeed be governed by intergovernmental cooperation.

The circle of the EEA, thus reinforced by the countries which would like to leave the process of integration, could be widened one day to include Russia, the Ukraine and other States of the old Soviet Union which would belong to the **large family of nations established many centuries ago on the European continent** and which would have efficient market economies and political and societal institutions and cultural values similar to those of the current members of the EEA. All these countries would develop an effective intergovernmental cooperation from the economic and commercial points of view, a cooperation which would not bind those which would not like it with the European construction. However, the door of the EU would remain open for the European countries of the second and the third circle which would like to sign and ratify its Constitution. By their membership in the European Community or in the European Economic Area these countries could, indeed, obtain a good preparation in the economic matters of integration before plunging into the deep water of political integration. On its side, the European Union, thanks to its solid and adaptable Constitution, could accommodate other European countries, notably the Balkan countries which knock on its door, without fearing its paralysis or, worse, its dissolution.

With non-European countries in its periphery - i.e. Mediterranean countries in Asia and Africa, which have different cultures, traditions and regimes - the European Union should build strong economic and political links through **partnership and/or new neighbourhood agreements** [see section 25.4]. A task of the common foreign and security policy of the Union would be to coordinate the commercial, aid to development and foreign policies of the Member States of the Union so as to create a friendly and therefore secure area around Europe, notably in the Mediterranean and the Middle East.

If and when the European Union would succeed its political as well as its economic integration, it would greatly enhance its position in the world. The links which the EU would have with the other European countries in the two external circles and with other friendly countries in the world, would make of it **a world actor of primary importance**, basing the prestige and security of its members less on the force of weapons and more on the assistance for a sustainable development of friendly countries. Hence, the European Union would not need to match the military power of the United States. The EU is not threatened by any organised state and does not have any hegemonic or policing ambitions in the world. In order to become a world player it does not need to have large armed forces, bases and armaments deployed around the globe. It only needs to have the goodwill of governments and peoples of the rest of the world by fostering sustainable development, democracy, multinational integration and the overall respect of international law. These could be the common goals of the unified "common" foreign, commercial, development and defence policies. In an environment of global anarchic terror, the goodwill of friendly countries could be a stronger bulwark against terrorist attacks than any global defence system.

In a world which aspires to peace, social protection, economic progress and the rule of law, it is very important that a democratic and pluralistic Europe, without hegemonic ambitions, assumes the international role which its history, its culture and its economic power reserve for it. Its successful experiment of peaceful and voluntary integration of nations, which only yesterday were fighting each other, is observed with attention by several nations in the world which suffer from their ethnic, religious and other discords and which are the victims of their dissensions. Carried out, thanks to its Constitution, at its logical continuation, which is the political union, the process of integration could place the old continent **at the vanguard of the march of civilization**, defined as an advanced system of human values, of political freedom, of economic development and of social progress, guaranteeing peace, freedom of thought and the wellbeing of all human beings.

Bibliography on European integration and its perspectives

- ALESINA Alberto, GIAVAZZI Francesco. *The future of Europe: reform or decline*. Cambridge, MA: MIT Press, 2006.
- ARRIOLA Joaquin, VASAPOLLO Luciano. *L'Europe masquée: l'Union européenne à l'heure de la compétition globale*. Paris: Parangon, 2006.
- BAIMBRIDGE Mark, BURKITT Brian, WHYMAN Philip. "Alternative relationships between Britain and the EU: new ways forward?" in *Political Quarterly*, v. 77, n. 3, July-September 2006, p. 402-412.
- BECK Ulrich. *The cosmopolitan vision*. Cambridge: Polity Press, 2006.
- DLUGOSZ Joanna, WITKOWSKI Marcin. *Perspektiven für Europa: eine neue Öffnung? = Perspectives of Europe: The New Opening?* Frankfurt: Peter Lang, 2006.
- DRAETTA Ugo. "After the Constitutional Treaty: the question of a political Europe", *The Federalist*, v. 47, n. 1, 2005, p. 18-30.
- FABBRINI Sergio (ed.)· *Democracy and federalism in the European Union and the United States: exploring post-national governance*. London; New York: Routledge, 2005.
- FORT Bertrand, WEBER Douglas (eds.). *Regional integration in East Asia and Europe: convergence or divergence?* Abingdon: Routledge, in association with the Centre for the Study of Globalisation and Regionalisation, University of Warwick, 2006.
- GILLINGHAM John. *Design for a new Europe*. Cambridge: Cambridge University Press, 2006.
- GINESOTTO Nicole, GREVI Giovani (eds.). *The new global puzzle: what world for the Eu in 2025?* Paris: Institute for Security Studies, 2006.
- GOMES DE ANDRADE, Norberto Nuno. "Enhanced cooperation: the ultimate challenge of managing diversity in Europe. New perspectives on the European integration process", *Intereconomics,* v. 40, n. 4, July/August 2005, p. 201-216.
- HEYWOOD Paul (et al eds.). Developments in European politics. Basingstoke: Palgrave Macmillan, 2006.
- MAGNETTE Paul· *What is the European Union?: nature and prospects*. Basingstoke: Palgrave Macmillan, 2005.
- MOUSSIS Nicolas. "La Constitution est morte! Vive la Constitution: une Constitution rédigée par une assemblée constituante", *Revue du marché commun et de l'Union européenne,* n. 496, mars 2006, p. 151-165.
- NICOLAÏDIS Kalypso, FERRY Jean-Marc. "Après le non français", *Politique étrangère*, v. 70, n. 3, automne 2005, p. 495-522.
- PÖTTERING Hans-Gert. *Our vision of Europe in 2020*. Group of the European People's Party (Christian Democrats) and European Democrats in the European Parliament. Brussels: Éd. Delta, 2006.

- TELÒ Mario. *Europe, a civilian power?: European Union, global governance, world order.* Basingstoke; New York: Palgrave Macmillan, 2006.
- TRECHSEL Alexandre. *Towards a federal Europe?.* Oxon: Routledge, 2006.
- VERHOFSTADT Guy. *The United States of Europe: manifesto for a new Europe.* London: Federal Trust for Education and Research, 2006.
- ZIELONKA Jan. *Europe as empire: the nature of the enlarged European Union.* Oxford: Oxford University Press, 2006.

INDEX AND GLOSSARY